## THE BLUE GUIDES

Austria
Belgium and Luxembourg
China
Cyprus
Czechoslovakia
Denmark
Egypt

FRANCE
France
Paris and Versailles
Burgundy
Normandy
Corsica

GREECE
Greece
Athens and environs
Crete

HOLLAND
Holland
Amsterdam

Hungary

ITALY
Northern Italy
Southern Italy
Florence
Rome and environs
Venice
Tuscany
Umbria
Sicily

Jerusalem
Malta and Gozo

Moscow and Leningrad
Morocco
Portugal

SPAIN
Spain
Barcelona

Switzerland

TURKEY
Turkey: the Aegean and Mediterranean Coasts
Istanbul

UK
England
Ireland
Scotland
Wales
London
Museums and Galleries of London
Oxford and Cambridge
Gardens of England
Literary Britain and Ireland
Victorian Architecture in Britain
Churches and Chapels of Northern Engalnd
Churches and Chapels of Southern England
Channel Islands

USA
New York
Boston and Cambridge

Yugoslavia

*Head of Ramesses II colossus at Memphis*

*BLUE GUIDE*

# Egypt

**Veronica Seton-Williams**
**and Peter Stocks**

*Atlas, street atlas of Cairo, maps,*
*plans and illustrations*

**A & C Black**
London

**WW Norton**
New York

Third edition 1993

Published by A & C Black (Publishers) Limited
35 Bedford Row, London WC1R 4JH



ISBN 0-7136-3590 -8

A CIP catalogue record of this book
is available from the British Library.





Published in the United States of America by
WW Norton & Company, Incorporated
500 Fifth Avenue, New York NY 10110

Published simultaneously in Canada by
Penguin Books Canada Limited
2801 John Street, Markham, Ontario L3R 1B4

ISBN 0-393-30973-8



Please write in with your comments, suggestions and corrections. Writers of the best letters will be awarded a free Blue Guide of their choice.

**Veronica Seton-Williams** was born in 1910 in Melbourne, Australia. She trained as an archaeologist under Sir Mortimer Wheeler at Maiden Castle, and Sir Flinders Petrie in Sinai. After the war, during which she was attached to the Ministry of Information, Middle Eastern Section, Veronica continued her exacvations in Turkey, Cyprus and Syria. In addition to lecturing and teaching, Veronica was appointed lecturer on Swan's Egyptian cruises, a post she held for 25 years. Between 1964–67 she was Field Director of the excavation at Tell el-Fara'in (Buto). Her retirement was spent writing, lecturing and travelling. Veronica Seton-Williams died in May 1992.

**Peter Stocks** was born in Liverpool in 1949. He trained as an artist and was particularly interested in Islamic architecture. He now works in the Oriental and India Office Collections at the British Library. First visiting Egypt in 1969 he began to compile an architectural dossier of the monuments in Cairo and elsewhere in Egypt which was later to become the basis of his section of the Blue Guide. In addition he has assisted and advised in the compilation of catalogues of exhibitions and collections of Middle Eastern interest and has contributed articles to several journals and monographs.

Printed and bound in Great Britain by
William Clowes Limited, Beccles and London

# PREFACE

It is with the deepest sadness that I have had to revise the preface to the third edition of the *Egypt Blue Guide* to record the death of my co-author Veronica Seton-Williams. She died on 29 May 1992 on Jersey in the company of the family of her friend Angela Godfrey.

Our association began in October 1978 when through the good offices of a mutual friend, Carey Miller, I was asked to write the post ancient sections of the Blue Guide—a task that was to take us a total of five years. It was to prove a highly productive relationship since our interests dovetailed very well. Whereas my knowledge of ancient Egypt was hazy at best, Veronica's long experience of lecturing on Swan's Nile cruises and particularly her extended period of excavating at Tell el- Farāʿīn (Buto) gave her a comprehensive knowledge of the country.

To our good fortune Veronica Seton-Williams completed and published in 1988 her autobiography *Road to el-Aguzein* (a village near Buto) where the details of her interesting life are recorded. It is the journal of a 'soil and shovel' archaeologist, one of the last students of Sir William Flinders Petrie. Her great strength lay in her lecturing as her many former students attest and her unique style made her companionship memorable to the thousands of visitors she accompanied on their cruises along the Nile, many of whom returned several times.

The essential points of Veronica Seton-Williams' career have been well covered in her obituaries but for myself it was perhaps her catholic interest that made Veronica such fascinating company, discussing the chemical analysis of rocks from Sīnai one minute and quoting from *Conan the Barbarian*, or Nantucket whaling shanties or giving a precise recipe for her delicious raspberry vinegar the next. Her vivacity was infectious her company never dull, she will be greatly missed by many.

Nearly two centuries of intensive study have not reduced the fascination of the country of Egypt. The ancient religious texts, the 'mysteries' of Egypt, have been revealed as attempts to rationalise the inexplicable, while other more prosaic writing shows the Ancient Egyptians' concern for the mundane, where their fears and hopes are seen to be similar to our own. Scenes in the tombs display aspects of family life familiar to the contemporary visitor. Five thousand years and changes of religion or social order have not diminished the Egyptian appreciation of life.

One hundred years ago a visit to Egypt was the privilege of the leisured people of means but from the 1880s the British presence in Egypt encouraged other visitors, civil servants, military men and entrepreneurs. Since the Second World War there has been a massive increase in the number of people going abroad for holidays, a habit facilitated by improved air transport. These vacations are now taken further afield and Egypt is well prepared to take the influx of visitors. As well as the magnificent monuments there are superb beaches and coasts for relaxation. Scores of companies now organise holidays in Egypt, and facilities are increasing throughout the country.

Since the first (1983) edition Egypt has been experiencing an unparalleled building boom. Whole new towns are rising around Cairo, including scores of new hotels catering for all tastes and pockets. Depsite this the past is not being submerged. Around every corner in Cairo, and the ancient sites throughout the country, there are constant reminders of the significant contribution Egypt has made, and is still making, to the web of history.

Once more I must express the most profound thanks to El-Nabawy El-Setouhy for his constant companionship in Egypt, without his assistance this guide would have been much the poorer. This gratitude extends equally to his wife and daughters for their support. On behalf of Veronica Seton-Williams, acknowledgement must be paid to Angela Godfrey through whose concern, encouragement and friendship Veronica was able to embark on some of her long held ambitions and continue to undertake new travel experiences.

Grateful thanks must be given to the generosity of readers who have taken the trouble to write with suggestions or pointing out inconsistencies and omissions, which I hope have been incorporated in the present edition. It is to be hoped that readers will continue to find the time to voice their criticisms, they are all welcome. Particular thanks are due to Hilary A. Smith.

Regarding the illustrations I wish to thank Imtiaz Karim for permission to use some of his excellent photographs, while formal thanks for permission to use their material must be extended to the Egyptian Museum, the Coptic Museum and the Wizārāt al-Awqāf in Cairo and the Nationalbibliothek in Vienna. The authors are also grateful to the British Museum for allowing them to use the drawing of cartouches.

Peter Stocks
London August 1992

This edition of Blue Guide Egypt was completed at the time of the Cairo earthquake in October 1992. Many of the Islamic buildings described in this guide have been affected. At the time of going to press it was too early to assess the damage caused.

# A Note on Blue Guides

The Blue Guide series began in 1915 when Muirhead Guide-Books Limited published 'Blue Guide London and its Environs'. Finlay and James Muirhead already had extensive experience of guidebook publishing: before the First World War they had been the editors of the English editions of the German Baedekers, and by 1915 they had acquired the copyright of most of the famous 'Red' Handbooks from John Murray.

An agreement made with the French publishing house Hachette et Cie in 1917 led to the translation of Muirhead's London guide, which became the first 'Guide Bleu'—Hachette had previously published the blue-covered 'Guides Joannes'. Subsequently, Hachette's 'Guide Bleu Paris et ses Environs' was adapted and published in London by Muirhead. The collaboration between the two publishing houses continued until 1933.

In 1933 Ernest Benn Limited took over the Blue Guides, appointing Russell Muirhead, Finlay Muirhead's son, editor in 1934. The Muirhead's connection with the Blue Guides ended in 1963 when Stuart Rossiter, who had been working on the Guides since 1954, became house editor, revising and compiling several of the books himself.

The Blue Guides are now published by A & C Black, who acquired Ernest Benn in 1984, so continuing the tradition of guidebook publishing which began in 1826 with 'Black's Economical Tourist of Scotland'. The Blue Guide series continues to grow: there are now 50 titles in print with revised editions appearing regularly and many new Blue Guides in preparation.

# CONTENTS

## II THE NILE VALLEY

**MAPS AND PLANS**

# EXPLANATIONS

TYPE. Main routes are described in large type. Smaller type is used for branch routes and diversions, and for historical and preliminary information, and (generally speaking) for descriptions of minor or specialised importance.

DISTANCES (in front of place names) are given in kilometres between individual points, the total distance of each journey being given at the beginning of each route.

HEIGHTS are given throughout in metres.

ASTERISKS (*) indicate points of excellence, historical importance or of special interest.

DATES. All dates before the Christian era are affixed with the abbreviation BC. Dates of the Christian ere have no affix except where its absence would be a source of confusion.

ABBREVIATIONS. In addition to generally accepted and self- explanatory abbreviations, the following occur in this Guide:

| | |
|---|---|
| AH | After the Hijrah (or Anno Higrae) |
| Ah. | Ahmed |
| b. | Ibn (son of) |
| BM | British Museum (London) |
| bt. | Bint (daughter of) |
| c | circa |
| C | Century |
| CPAM | Committee for the Preservation of Arab Monuments (see also EAO) |
| EAO | Egyptian Antiquities Organisation |
| EAS | Egyptian Antiquities Service (see also EAO) |
| EES | Egyptian Exploration Society |
| EGS | Egyptian Geographical Society |
| EM | Egyptian Museum (Cairo) |
| GIA | German Institute of Archaeology |
| H | Highway |
| IFAO | Institut Français d'Archaeologie |
| £E | Egyptian pounds |
| Muh. | Muhammad (never for the Prophet) |
| MIA | Museum of Islamic Art (Cairo) |
| Met | Metropolitan Museum of Art (New York) |
| Maq. | al-Maqrīzī |
| pl. | plural |
| Sh. | Shaykh |
| Shʿ. | Shāriʿ (street) |
| T.B. | Ibn Taghrībardī. |

# BACKGROUND INFORMATION

## Topographical Introduction

**Geography**. The Arab Republic of Egypt (al-Gumhuriyyah Miṣr al-'Arabiyyah) occupies an area of 1,002,000 sq. km at the extreme NE corner of the continent of Africa and a small area of South-West Asia, between 24° and 36° E and 22° and 31° N. It is bordered on the W by Libya, on the S by the Sudan, on the E by the Red Sea and Israel and on the N by the Mediterranean Sea.

Tectonically, Egypt is on the leading edge of the African Plate, the collision of which with the Eurasian Plate lifted the mountains of the Alpine folds of Southern Europe in the early Tertiary. The African Plate seems at present to be relatively stationary, but the neighbouring Arabian Plate to the E appears to be sheering off to the NE and the Red Sea and the Sinai Peninsula are the products of the stresses between them. The rift between these two plates stretches from the Jordan Valley to the East African Great Rift Valley and even further S, the whole area sharing the movement of the active plate. The recent discovery of hot springs at temperatures of 50–60° C. among the ravines on the Red Sea bottom indicates that the process is continuing.

The physical structure of Egypt is comparatively simple, consisting of the crystalline Pre-Cambrian basement, which makes outcrops particularly in the S, overlain by Jurassic and Cretaceous wind-deposited sandstones, and Tertiary marine limestones and sandstones indicating periodic incursions as the sea level rose and fell; the Nile Valley itself has alluvial strata. Within Egypt four sub-regions can be distinguished:

1. SINAI PENINSULA. A triangular tableland, uptilted towards the Southern apex, consisting of Tertiary sandstone and Pre-Cambrian granite mountains, between 750–1500m high, with occasional much taller peaks—*Gabal Katarīn* (2640m) being the highest. On the SE side (*Gulf of 'Aqabah*) the drop into the sea is steep, but to the SW (*Gulf of Suez*) the mountains approach the sea in a series of steps and a narrow coastal plain is formed. To the N the plateau drops and gives way to a wide coastal plain which extends from Suez into Southern Israel, with shallow dunes and lagoons. Sinai is very arid, receiving an average annual rainfall of 100mm (much less in the S); the mountains are much eroded with wādīs, formed in earlier periods and ranging from shallow to precipitous; these break the whole area into a series of massifs. There is no permanent watercourse, but after the rain the wādīs can fill with surprising speed and whole villages have disappeared as a result. On the N plain there is water at a depth which can be tapped and oasis cultivation practised; further S settlement is more difficult but has great potential. Oil fields and manganese deposits are found in the SW and will doubtless attract larger settlement. There is a population of Bedouin in the peninsula though it is gradually dwindling (see Rte 51).

2. EASTERN DESERT. This lies between the Nile and the Red Sea with the same crystalline basement, much broken and raised, often appearing above the surface in the S, with a covering of Tertiary and Quaternary limestones and sands. The average height of the hills is lower than in Sinai, between 300–750m; the highest peak is *Gabal Shayab* (2185m). This area is also much eroded with many wādīs running E–W. To the W where it borders the Nile Valley it forms a rather ill-defined barrier to the alluvial deposit. Rainfall is even lower than in Sinai, below 100mm

throughout. Again there are no permanent water courses, though water is retained over the harder rock, appearing at the surface as springs. There is little cultivation, due to the aridity, though there are settlements on the Red Sea coast and around the mineral workings, which include petrol, phosphates, manganese and large deposits of iron. There are also Bedouin in this area.

3. WESTERN DESERT. In contrast to the previous regions, here the almost continuous expanse of Pre-Cambrian basement is practically undisturbed. With its covering of narrow later strata, it averages only 200m above sea level, with almost half the area below this and few parts exceeding 300m. There are several large depressions, the edges of which are much eroded, the greatest of which is the huge *Qaṭṭārah Depression* in the N, 120m below sea-level. Some of these depressions are artesian basins forming oases while others are too saline to be utilised. The surface of this area consists of rocky outcrops and stony or sandy wastes, the latter increasing to the SW, culminating in the *Great Sand Sea*, the high isolated plateau of the *Gilf al-Kabīr*, and in the extreme SW, marking the point where the borders of Egypt, Sudan and Libya meet, the *Gabal ʿUwaynāt*. The escarpment formed to the trough of the River Nile is much more precipitous than that on the East Bank, due to lack of erosion.

4. NILE VALLEY. The sources of the Nile are in the lakes of Uganda and Ethiopia which give rise to the White and Blue Niles respectively. The White Nile flows into Sudan passing through the Sudd, previously a lake but now a vast swamp. At Khartoum the two Niles join, N of which the river swings to the W, then S and finally turns N again. It passes over a series of cataracts where it has cut a deep trench through the Nubian sandstone until it enters Lake Nasser which has formed behind the Aswān Dam. Beyond Aswān there are traces of Pliocene marine deposits, showing how far the sea penetrated during that period. The width of the river remains relatively constant at about 1km and the valley at 10km, though the river tends to favour the E valley wall. Just N of Cairo the river divides into two main distributaries, the Rosetta branch to the W and the Damietta (22km longer) to the E. In ancient times there were several other outlets, but five of these have now dried up. The Delta region still contains areas of swamp, but much drainage is being undertaken. The Nile probably developed from several drainage systems in the early Tertiary, the stronger stream gradually capturing the smaller, slower flows.

The periodicity of the flooding of the Nile was of critical importance to the earlier inhabitants of the Lower Nile Valley. Although in the early 19C attempts were made to regulate the flow of the river with barrages and dams, it was not until the completion of the Aswān High Dam in 1970 that this dependence was relieved. The inundation was caused by spring and summer rainfall in the highlands of East Africa and Ethiopia. The minimum level was reached in late May and the beginnings of the flood were seen in late June, with the maximum reached in mid September; if the flood was earlier it produced crop famine. The amount of water also varied but at Aswān at low water an average flow of 45 million cubic metres per second was recorded while high water averaged 642 million cubic metres. 110 million tons of suspended sediment were carried into Egypt, rich in mineral substances; in addition there were 75 million tons of soluble minerals—principally calcium, magnesium, carbonates and sodium chloride. Much of the sediment is now retained in Lake Nasser. So important is this dependence on the Nile that 95 per cent of the population lives in the valley and Delta.

The regulation of the height of the Nile has resulted in an increase in the height of the water-table throughout the valley (including Cairo). This has led to the waterlogging of several important sites and increase in the salinity of the soil.

# Geographical Glossary

ayn: (spring) pl. ʿuyūn
ʿazbah: village
baḥr: sea, river
bīr: well
birkah: lake
buḥayrah: lake
burg: cliff, tower
gabal: mountain, hill
gazīrah: island
ghawr: depression
gilf: gulf
kafr: village
kawm (kom): mound
khalīg: gulf
madīnah: town
mahallah: settlement
manshiyyah: village
marsā: anchorage
mīnā: port
miniyah: village
minshāt: village
mīt: village
muhāfazah: province
nagʿ: village
nahiyyah: town
nahr: river
nazlah: village
qārat: peak
qism: district
rā's: peak, headland
rayyāḥ: canal
sabakhah: salt marsh
tall (tell): mound
tir ʿah: canal
wādī: valley
wāhah: oasis
zāwiyyah: village
North: shamāl
South: ganūb
East: sharq
West: gharb
northern: shamāli or baḥrī (i.e. seaward)
southern: ganūbī or qiblī (i.e. towards Mecca)
eastern: sharqī
western: gharbī
central: wastah

# ANCIENT EGYPT

Egypt owes its very existence to the River Nile. Although the southern boundary of Egypt is just N of Wādī Halfā, the cultivable area throughout history has been the river valley from Aswān, N of the granite barrier known as the First Cataract. Beyond, the river passes through a sandstone deposit that reaches almost as far as Edfū and from which much of the stone used in building the New Kingdom Temples was extracted. To the N of this lie the limestone deposits which comprise the bulk of rock bordering the Nile.

Slightly N of Cairo the river divides and forms the Delta. Although the river now enters the sea through just two channels, in classical times there were more. The ancient Pelusiac, Sebennytic and Canopic branches have dried up, probably because of a slight rise of the land of the eastern Delta, aided by extensive canalisation. Elsewhere the Delta seems to be sinking and this is clearly seen at Alexandria where the subsidence has been about 2.4m in the last 2000 years. In the Pharaonic period the three mouths of the Nile were known as the 'Water of Pre', the 'Water of Ptah' and the 'Water of Amun'.

Within historic times the unification of the Two Lands (i.e. Upper Egypt—the Nile Valley S of Ṣaqqārah—and Lower Egypt—the Delta) remained a problem. The land of Egypt was created by the rich alluvium brought down by the Nile which served to constantly renew its fertility. This was left on the fields by the annual rising of the Nile as a thick black deposit contrasting sharply with the reddish-buff desert areas on either side. The former gave the Ancient Egyptians the name for their country, *Keme* (the Black Land), while the deserts were known as *Deshret* (the Red Lands). Lower Egypt was *To-Mehu* (the Northern Land), while Upper Egypt was *To-Resi* (the Southern Land). The modern name *Egypt*, or similar forms, by which the country is known in most European languages but not in Arabic, comes from the Greek, *Aegiptos*, probably derived from one of the many names of Memphis, *Hwt-ka-Ptah* (House of the Ka of Ptah). Nubia was *To-Sti* (Land of the Nubians) or *To-Kens* (Land of the Bow). The region beyond the Second Cataract (the Belly of Stones) was *Kush* and the Fayyūm was *To-She* (Land of the Pool or Lake). Upper and Lower Egypt were divided into districts, or nomes in Greek, about 22 in Upper Egypt, from Elephantine to Memphis, and 20 in Lower Egypt, the numbers varying from time to time. Lists of these are known from the 3 Dyn. onwards.

The oases of the Western Desert were always regarded as frontier zones and were administered from the Seventh Upper Egyptian Nome, *Sekem*, with its capital at Hiw (Diospolis Parva), near modern Nagʿ Ḥammādī. Except for the oases this area was little used, but the Eastern Desert, lying between the river and the Red Sea, was extensively exploited. It was a mountainous region, full of minerals and rocks which were collected and mined. Sinai was similarly exploited, being rich in copper and turquoise; expeditions were sent there from the 3 Dyn. onwards.

Egyptian civilisation, from the earliest times, was based upon an extremely effective agricultural system. This in turn relied upon irrigation and was dependent for its effectiveness on the annual inundation of the Nile, as rain is scarce through much of Upper Egypt. This system required a strong central organisation, to keep the canals cut and clear and to oversee distribution of seed corn and collection of taxes. The main Egyptian crop throughout recorded history was barley, used to make bread and to brew beer—the Egyptians were heavy drinkers—and to serve as rations for the workers and the army. Emmer wheat was also grown to a certain extent, while flax was grown from an early period for linen. Wheat, known throughout historic times, became common in the Ptolemaic period. The vine was also cultivated from the 1 Dyn. onwards—its hieroglyphic sign is found at Abydos and elsewhere. Dates were cultivated and oil was obtained from the castor oil plant, flax, balanos, sesame seed and the moringa fruit. Cattle were the most important animals and cattle-counts occur from the times of the early dynasties. Asses were domesticated very early and were the main beast of burden until the introduction of the horse under the Hyksos in the 18C BC. Camels were late introductions and do not seem to have been plentiful until Ptolemaic times, but they must have been seen in Egypt at the time of the Assyrian invasions in the first millennium BC and were probably used by the Arab tribes in Sinai.

# Outline of Egyptian History

**The Palaeolithic Period**. The earliest indications of man in the Nile Valley are in the lower sands and gravels of the 30m wādī and river terraces of Upper Egypt and Nubia, dated c 250,000 BC. Primitive hand-axes, flakes and cores were used, similar to those found in Europe in the Lower Palaeolithic. At this time the whole of North Africa was habitable and hunters ranged over a wide area. Towards the end of the period, c 25,000 BC, the climate underwent a drastic change and the grass steppes turned to desert, causing early man to withdraw towards sources of water, either in the oases or in the Nile Valley. This later culture, known as the *Sebilian* from its type-station near ʿAzbat al-Sabīl in the Kom Ombo Basin, was centred in Upper Egypt and Nubia close to the Nile.

By the *Upper Sebilian* period (16,000–10,000 BC), the Nile bed had sunk about 3m below its present level, due to increasing aridity. The kitchen middens of the people of this period contain broken and charred animal bones, freshwater shells and stone pounders and grinders. Other Late Palaeolithic sites have been found on the edge of the Eastern Delta, at Abū Suwayr, Shibīn al-Qanātir near the Ismāʿīliyyah Canal, and at Heliopolis, near Cairo, while Khārgah Oasis, in the Western Desert, has also yielded remains. At Kom Ombo and Qāw human bones were found among those of animals. The fauna included both riverine and desert types, the Cave hyena (*Crocuta hyaena* subsp.), lions (*Felis leo* subsp.), wild horses and asses (*Equus* spp.), hippopotami (*Hippopotamus*), pigs (*Sus*) and short- and long-horned oxen (*Bos* spp.). Many animals then found in the Egyptian area now only occur further S in Africa or have become extinct.

**The Mesolithic Period** (10,000–5000 BC). The population of Egypt at this time comprised a number of different groups of semi-nomadic fishers and hunters who lived in comparative isolation one from another. One of the earliest sites was found in 1871 at Ḥalwān near Cairo and this has marked links with the well-established Natufian culture of Palestine and Syria.

Similar finds have been made near Qūṣ in Upper Egypt. The blade industries missing from the Upper Palaeolithic became common. Other Mesolithic sites are known from Wādī Angabiyyah, called al-ʿUmarı after its finder, and also from the Fayyūm. It is possible that the last survivors of these hunting bands were the men who executed rock-carvings in the cliffs overlooking the Nile Valley, and in the wādī beds leading to the Red Sea, in Nubia and Upper Egypt.

**The Neolithic Period** provides the first positive evidence of the growing of cereal crops. Settlements have been found in the Fayyūm on the edge of the Western Desert, strung out along the side of the lake, from Dimay to Kom Aushim, and also in Middle Egypt. It has not so far been suggested that Egypt was a major source of the cultivation of plants or of the domestication of animals. The most important species of both categories seem to have been introduced from Western Asia. Climatic conditions improved in the 6 millennium BC, and a moist interval probably facilitated agriculture and stock breeding. Fishing was also an important part of these early farmers' economy as harpoons and fish spears have been found. Their huts seem to have been mere primitive windbreaks, of which only the post holes survive along with the ashes of their hearth fires. Weaving was practised—linen and flax have been found, as well as spindle whorls.

Pottery was already in use and most tools and weapons were of flint. Wild game appears to have been abundant and included hippopotami (*Hippopotamus*), elephant (*Loxodonta*), wild pig (*Sus*) and goat (*Capra*). Paradoxically, the earliest settlements in the Fayyūm (Fayyūm A) seem to have been more agriculturally advanced than the later Fayyūm B people who reverted primarily to hunting and fishing, probably for climatic reasons. Settlements in the oases of Sīwah and Khārgah have close affinities with these people. After 5000 BC there was a settlement, at Merimda Banī Salāmah in the Western Delta, ranking as one of the largest prehistoric settlements in Egypt. It occupied an area of some 2 sq. km with a population of about 16,000. A radio-carbon date has given c 4130 BC for the early level, although this method of dating in Egypt has not proved entirely satisfactory. Other settlements have been found at al-ʿUmarī and at al-Maʿadī, now a suburb of Cairo. The latter was defended by a stout palisade, while in the cemeteries bodies were buried in a characteristic contracted position. There are marked cultural links between these people and the early Chalcolithic people of Southern Palestine. Palettes, so typical of later Predynastic settlers, were already in use.

Much work remains to be done on Egyptian prehistory as attention has mainly been focused on the more remunerative historic periods.

**The Predynastic Period** (c 3400–3100 BC). The early phase is disputed and some authorities would place the beginning a little earlier at about 3700 BC, equating the *Badarian* (type site al-Badārī near Asyūṭ), the last culture represented in the Neolithic, with the beginning of *Naqada I* (type-site Naqādah, near Qūs), the early phase of the Predynastic.

Early cultures are normally named after the type-site, where the culture was first found and identified. As a result many modern village names have been given to prehistoric cultures. In Egypt there does not appear to have been an homogenous culture in the country, unlike the al-ʿUbaid in Mesopotamia. This has led to a great proliferation of names for what may be contemporary cultures. The *Tasian* (type site

Deir Tasa in Middle Egypt) has now been equated by some with the *Amratian* (type-site al-ʿAmrah near Nagʿ Hāmmadī), also with *Naqada I* and the *Gerzean* (type-site Girzah, near the Fayyūm) with *Naqada II*. Also a point of contention is *Naqada III*, and most historians would be willing to see *Naqada II* directly precede the Dynastic period. The culture of *Naqada I* seems to have evolved from the *Badarian* and is thus an indigenous growth. The men were small, slim and bearded and were probably related to the contemporary Libyan culture to the NW.

Nothing very much is known about the political organisation of Egypt during the early Predynastic Period, but by the late Predynastic Period two clearly defined confederations start to emerge with political heads which can be defined as kings. In Upper Egypt the capital was at Kom Aḥmar (Neken), the king of which wore a white crown, and in Lower Egypt the capital was at Tell al-Faraʿīn (Buto and Pe), where the king was distinguished by a red crown. This period seems to have been one of continuous conflict, first one side obtaining the ascendency, then the other. According to one version the North was at one time victorious, then defeated, resulting in the Union of the Two Lands. The South thus always claimed ascendency over the North. The scenes of these struggles are shown on a series of slate palettes which must have been dedicated as votive offerings by the victors in the temples. The most famous of these is the Narmer Palette (now in the EM), showing the conquest of the Delta by Narmer.

**The Early Dynastic or Archaic Period** (c 3100–2686 BC). The history of Egypt for the first few dynasties is obscure though a new capital was founded at Memphis, traditionally by the first king, Menes (Hor A-ha) in an area reclaimed from the Nile. The history of the first five dynasties, recorded on the Palermo Stone, is brief and material remains from the

*The Narmer Palette, a late predynastic schist ceremonial palette. On the obverse Narmer is shown wearing the Red Crown, subduing Lower Egypt. On the reverse, wearing the White Crown, he subdues Upper Egypt (EM)*

burnt and looted royal tombs are extremely tantalising. There is uncertainty as to where the earliest rulers were buried as there are two sets of tombs, one at Ṣaqqārah in the N and the other at Abydos far to the S. It is likely that those at Abydos are only cenotaphs, while the former tombs contained real burials.

In Egypt, as opposed to other Middle Eastern countries, there has always been more evidence about death than life. This is mainly because many settlements are now buried under modern towns and have never been excavated, and because the rock-hewn or stone tombs and temples were built to last 'for millions and millions of years' whereas houses and palaces were considered of only ephemeral importance and constructed of mud-brick which readily disintegrated.

It is to Manetho, an Egyptian who wrote in Greek in the 3C BC, that the division of kings into dynastic groupings is due. Little is known of the seven kings of the 1 Dyn. save that they were buried in mastabas (either at Ṣaqqārah or Abydos) and that the remains of their once rich furniture was burnt and destroyed. These tombs were surrounded by subsidiary burials of courtiers and servants who were apparently killed at the time of the king's interrment to accompany him in his journey to the Afterlife. After the 2 Dyn. there are no more of these sacrifices; instead the dead are accompanied by model figures who were supposed to wait upon them by magical means.

About 2890 BC the 1 Dyn. was replaced by the 2 Dyn. The dynasties are connected in the female line in the form of the Great Royal Heiress through whom the crown descended, but for the early period these connections are not very clear. During the 2 Dyn. there was a political upheaval and a struggle for power involving the transfer of religious loyalty of the ruling house from the god Horus to Seth. This change was transitory and, by the end of the dynasty allegiance had been restored to Horus.

**The Old Kingdom** (c 2686–2181 BC) is usually thought to begin with the 3 Dyn. This and the following dynasty can be considered one of the pinnacles of Egyptian history. The 3 Dyn. was a formative period with many innovations, for example the change from building in mud-brick to using stone and the beginning of pyramid construction, with the Step Pyramid at Ṣaqqārah. At this time the basis of the future civilisation of Egypt was established. The most famous ruler of this time was King Netjerykhet Zozer who reigned for 19 years. His chief of works, Imhotep, inaugurated many of the architectural innovations of the reign. Imhotep was later deified and equated with the Greek god of medicine, Asklepios, although there is no evidence that during his lifetime he was connected in any way with medicine. Both Zozer and his predecessor Sanakhte sent expeditions to Sinai, probably in search of copper and turquoise, although in the 1 Dyn. expeditions had already been made as far as the Second Cataract and the southern boundary of Egypt extended from al-Kāb to Elephantine (Aswān).

The monuments of the 4 Dyn. (c 2613–2494 BC) are better known than those of the previous period as this was the age of the pyramid builders when these vast structures were erected at Giza and nearby sites. The pyramid was only part of the complex and was intended to preserve the body of the dead king and to enable him to pass safely to the Afterworld, while the mortuary temple attached to the pyramid was for the worship of the dead king as a divine intercessor. These complexes were surrounded by many mastaba tombs where relatives, nobles and priests were buried. The king had absolute power and the great offices of state were mainly in the hands of the royal family. But towards the end of the Old Kingdom this power gradually became diversified. More is known about the monuments of this period than the personal and national events.

With the 5 Dyn. (c 2494–2345 BC) the centralised power of the crown declined somewhat. The earliest administrative documents from this period were found at Abū Ṣīr where many of the kings were buried. Expeditions to Libya, Nubia and Sinai for trade were more fully recorded. The ideas of kingship were obviously modified during this time and many of the great nobles married into the royal family. The worship of the sun god Reʿ of Heliopolis became important for the first time and, in his honour, successive kings built sun temples at Abū Ghurāb. At the end of the dynasty the Pyramid Texts, a collection of rituals, spells, hymns and myths, make their appearance on the walls of the burial chamber of Unas and continue to be represented throughout the next dynasty.

The practice of decentralisation was carried still further during the 6 Dyn. (c 2345–2181 BC). Much of the power passed into the hands of the great nobles who set up almost independent courts of their own in the various nomes or districts from which they drew their influence. The royal pyramids became smaller and the officials and nobles no longer felt it necessary to be buried in serried ranks surrounding the royal burial place. It was during the reign of Pepi II, who is said to have ruled for 94 years, that the central administration finally collapsed.

A series of bad harvests, low Niles, incursions of foreigners and waning central authority ushered in the little-known period of Egyptian weakness, the 7–10 Dyns, usually known as the *First Intermediate Period* (c 2181–2050 BC). During this time the central administration no longer functioned and there were several parallel local dynasties. Egypt always showed a tendency to fall apart politically if there was not a strong government.

**The Middle Kingdom** (c 2055–1786 BC). The rise of the Middle Kingdom began in a period of civil war. The struggle between the rulers of Thebes and Heracleopolis was finally decided in favour of the former and a series of rulers, called either Inyotef or Menthuhotpe, reunited the land and established the 11 Dyn. (2133–1991 BC). Menthuhotpe II (c 2060) took as his Horus name Sehertowy (He-who-unites-the-Two-Lands), and from this moment the Middle Kingdom begins. The most powerful kings were those of the following 12 Dyn. (1991–1786 BC) who organised Egypt again into a strong centralised state. They ruled from It-Towy, perhaps a suburb of Memphis, originally thought to be a separate town. Expeditions were again sent to Libya, Nubia and Sinai and extended to Syria and Punt.

To ensure continuity of government, the practice of co-regency was introduced, probably necessitated by the murder of the first king of the dynasty, Amenemhat I. The reigning king nominated one of his sons, not necessarily the eldest, to share the throne with him for the last years of his reign. Thus there should be a peaceful transfer of power on the king's death. Steps were taken to limit the power of the nomarchs (the great nobles and governors) who had set up almost independent states within the country. As an initial measure Amenemhat II reorganised the nome boundaries, but it was Senusert III, the greatest king of the dynasty, who finally broke their authority. Though his methods are not clear, after this time they posed no threat to central government.

Gradually, however, the internal strength of the kings declined and a period of weakness and disorganisation, the *Second Intermediate Period* (c 1786–1567 BC), began. This existed during five dynasties, of which two are assigned to outsiders, i.e. Hyksos rulers, until the beginning of the 18 Dyn.

**The New Kingdom** (1567–1085 BC) consisted of the 18–20 Dynasties; it is sometimes known as the *Egyptian Empire*. It began with the expulsion of the Hyksos rulers from the Eastern Delta, where they had their capital Avaris. This was achieved by the native Theban rulers of the 17 Dyn. (1650–1567 BC) who had been governing during the Second Intermediate Period in a subordinate capacity. Not only were the Hyksos defeated in Egypt but they were pursued into Asia and totally destroyed. The 18 Dyn. (1567–1320 BC) produced a number of very able rulers who reasserted Egyptian control over the whole country and in Western Asia to the Euphrates and S into the Sudan, known as Kush, as far as the fourth cataract. Kush was important for its supply of gold, copper and stone, hides and bows, and as a recruiting ground for mercenary troops who formed a sizeable part of the Egyptian army and the internal police force.

Under Makare Hatshepsut (1503 BC), who reigned first as a regent queen and then as a king in her own right, the Egyptian artistic revival began. Her architect, Senenmut, built her a splendid mortuary temple at Thebes and this was followed by a series of temples and tombs built by the reigning kings. Her nephew, Tuthmosis III (1504 BC), was the greatest conqueror that Egypt was to produce. He also organised the expanding Egyptian Empire by bringing young Asiatic princes to be educated at the Egyptian court. On their return home, thoroughly Egyptianised, they governed their states under the control of Egyptian supervisors. It was not until the death of these men that Egypt faced external aggression.

Under Amenhotep III (1417 BC) the Empire reached its zenith, and though he did not conduct any active campaigns he was a great hunter and builder. The country was settled and fairly prosperous so that he was able to devote his attention to building the temple at Luxor and a vast mortuary temple, now destroyed save for the Colossi of Memnon, the two seated statues that stood before it. He issued a series of commemorative scarabs for the principal events of his reign and conducted a number of dynastic marriages with the daughters of the rulers of western Asia.

But there were signs that the vigour of the kings was declining and Amenhotep III's son Amenhotep IV (1379 BC), who took the name Akhenaten, was little interested in the government of the Empire. Probably as a result of a quarrel with the priesthood of Amun, the leading god of Thebes, Akhenaten withdrew to his city Akhetaten, 'The Horizon of the Aten' (modern al-ʿAmārnah). Here he devoted himself to the worship of the Aten, a form of sun god shown as a disk with the rays ending in hands. This was not a new deity, but had been known from the Old Kingdom, although not as a royal god. While Akhenaten and his wife Nefertiti stayed at Akhetaten, the empire declined. An accidental discovery at al-ʿAmārnah has revealed many letters written by the princes of Western Asia to Akhenaten asking him for help in repelling invaders and for the return of the Egyptian garrisons to their cities. Whether Akhenaten ever saw this correspondence is uncertain, but many of the letters apparently remained unanswered. They were written in Akkadian, the contemporary diplomatic language of western Asia, and they provide a vivid picture of the disintegration of the Egyptian Empire.

Towards the end of his reign, Akhenaten took his brother Smenkhkare as co-regent and sent him to Thebes from Akhetaten, but he did not live more than a year or two when they both died from the plague raging at that time in Egypt, leaving Tutankhamun (1361 BC; a son of Amenhotep III) and Queen Tiy to assume the throne. The boy king reigned for about ten years and died just as he was coming to manhood, leaving in his tomb an unsurpassed treasure, found in 1922 practically untouched. The last king of the dynasty, Horemheb, originally a general in command at Memphis, was not of royal blood, although he may have married one of the royal princesses to legitimise his position. He did much to restore Egypt both internally and externally.

The 19 Dyn. (1320–1200 BC) was also not of royal blood; its founders had been generals under the last rulers of the 18 Dyn. Ramesses I, the first King, was already elderly when he came to the throne, and only reigned for two years. His son, Seti I (1318 BC), was in the prime of life. He restored Egypt's position by campaigns in western Asia and by a building programme, of which the best known examples are his temple at Abydos, and his tomb on the West Bank at Thebes. His taste was far superior to anything that the Egyptians had achieved for many years.

His son, Ramesses II (1304 BC), who came to the throne after a co-regency with his father, was also a great builder, but he was too hurried to accomplish really fine work, and his best memorial is probably his temple at Abū Simbel in Nubia. He also carried out further campaigns in Western Asia but here too he was not as successful as his father. There are varying accounts of the Battle of Kadesh, which Ramesses fought against the Hittites, and announced as a great victory. The Hittites, too, claimed success and the battle, in which Ramesses showed considerable bravery but not much judgement, was probably drawn. The Hittite problem was not settled until Ramesses married one of the Hittite princesses and concluded a peace treaty with Hattusilis II of Hatti, 21 years later.

Ramesses was followed by Merneptah (1236 BC), one of his many sons, a man already in middle age. Almost at once he had to face a threat of invasion from Libya but he won a decisive victory in the Western Delta. The rest of the 19 Dyn. is a period of confusion, with incursions from Asia and bad harvests. The last king, Siptah, seems to have been the legitimate heir of Seti II; he died childless and his wife Tawsert assumed the throne as either regent or queen.

Internal stability was not restored before the accession of Sethnakhte in 1200. Thus began the 20 Dyn. (c 1300–1085 BC), the only memorable king of which was the second ruler of the dynasty, Ramesses III (1198), who successfully defended Egypt against attacks from the Libyans and the Peoples of the Sea in his fifth and seventh years. Egypt, by now, was in a poor way. She had lost her Asiatic empire and was thus denied the use of Asian iron; the gold mines of Nubia were exhausted and low Niles and bad harvests upset the internal economy. The later kings of the dynasty, all called Ramesses, are shadowy figures (even their number is disputed), struggling with strikes of the necropolis workers and tomb robberies that they could not prevent. Towards the end the power of the king was shared by the High Priest of Amun, partly because the earlier rulers had given away vast state wealth to the priesthood of Amun, so that the temple became mightier than the state.

**The Late Dynastic Period** (1085–332 BC), sometimes called the *Third Intermediate Period*, was, on the whole, a period of decline, with occasional flashes of energy, as in the 22 Dyn. (945–715 BC). These later rulers controlled Egypt mainly from the Delta where the capital was moved from one city to another, while the High Priest, and later Priestess, of Amun (usually of the royal family) controlled Upper Egypt. Under the 25 Dyn. (c 747–656 BC) Egypt was invaded by the Assyrians and both Thebes and Memphis were sacked. There was slight revival in the 26 or Saite Dyn. (664–525 BC) but more on the artistic than on the political side. Large foreign colonies developed and Egypt, for the first time, opened its borders to the Greeks who settled at Naukratis in the Delta. Many Greek mercenaries joined the Egyptian army. Necho II (610 BC) again ventured into Western Asia but was crushingly defeated by Nebuchadnezzar of Babylon at Carchemish, in 605 BC. Nearly a century later Psamtik III (526 BC), the last king of the dynasty, was defeated by the Persians at Pelusium. Memphis and the whole of Egypt became a Persian satrapy. The 27 Dyn. (525–404 BC) was composed of Persian, not native, rulers and, although there was a brief attempt at rebellion in the 29–30 Dynasties (398–343 BC), Egypt really remained under effective Persian control until the arrival of Alexander in 332 BC.

**The Ptolemies** (332–30 BC). After defeating the Persians, Alexander the Great entered Egypt late in 332 BC and appointed Ptolemy Soter, one of his Macedonian generals, as satrap. One of the most important decisions taken by Alexander was the foundation, on the old site of Rhacotis, of the new capital named, after himself, Alexandria. This became a great Hellenistic city with a good port and the hub of Greek influence in Egypt. It developed as a centre of learning with a museum and library unequalled in the ancient world. Ptolemy governed until the death of Alexander nine years later and, at first, also deputised for Philip Arrhidaeus and Alexander IV. Subsequently he assumed the crown and founded the Ptolemaic dynasty, which ruled Egypt for 300 years until it was conquered by the Romans.

Throughout this period the Ptolemaic navy largely dominated the Mediterranean, exploration was encouraged and voyages were made down the Red Sea, to the Horn of Africa and probably beyond. Often at war with the other Hellenistic states, such as the Seleucids, the Ptolemies also strove to unify the country. One of the ways in which they did this was by restoring and rebuilding earlier Egyptian temples in the Pharaonic style. Some of these, like Dendarah, Philae and Edfū, are still excellently preserved and supply us with information about earlier structures and the rituals carried out within these buildings which would otherwise be unavailable. The Ptolemies also developed the Fayyūm region, reclaiming the land and reorganising the crop rotation.

The greatest point of contact between the Hellenistic settlers in Egypt and the indigenous population was in popular religion and funeral practices. The Greek element adopted the worship of the Egyptian gods, equating them with their Greek pantheon: thus Amun became Zeus and Aphrodite became Hathor. Many of the late temples were, like those of Greece, places of healing, as at Kom Ombo and Dendarah where sanatoria were erected in the grounds of the temples; here pilgrims and the sick would stay.

The Ptolemies were, on the whole, excellent administrators, but the Hellenistic world to which they belonged had no chance against the rising might of Rome. Ptolemy Auletes (80–51 BC), father of Cleopatra, realised this and left Egypt to his children more or less subject to the approval of Rome. It is remarkable that Cleopatra (51–30 BC) was able to keep Egypt at least nominally independent for as long as she did. The defeat of Antony at Actium in 30 BC and Octavian's pursuit of him to Egypt finally put an end to Egypt's position as a sovereign state.

**The Roman period** (30 BC–AD 337). This phase, like the Ptolemaic period, lasted about 300 years and was clearly marked by the impress of a single man, Octavian, the Emperor Augustus. Egypt was incorporated into the Roman Empire as the personal possession of the emperor, governed by an equestrian prefect appointed specially by him, the first, Cornelius Gallus, being assigned to office in 27 BC. Egypt's importance derived from its potential as an imperial granary, supplying Rome with up to five million bushels of grain every year.

The first two centuries of Roman rule were comparatively peaceful. Greek remained the administrative language and the Ptolemaic administration had been so efficient that the Romans had to do little to alter it. The Hellenistic element in Egypt received a fresh accession of strength by the settlement of Roman veterans in the Fayyūm. In the reign of Trajan (AD 98) the Red Sea Canal of Necho was recut, the trade routes to India were reopened and Egypt began a good export trade in glass (manufactured in the Delta), linen, papyrus and jewellery. From the beginning there were invasions from the South, first by the Ethiopians and later by the Blemmyes. In 268 Queen Zenobia of Palmyra invaded Egypt and ruled for a short period before she was dethroned in 273.

At first Alexandria prospered but it was torn by opposition to the Jewish faction and struggles for power among the Christians. After the destruction of Jerusalem, in AD 70, the Jews became very anti-Roman and this led to many disturbances and massacres. By the 3C AD the economic decline of the Roman world caused further misery in Egypt. The coinage was debased, the peasants fled their fields and turned to robbery. The basic causes were over-taxation and lack of security. The Roman emperors did not build as lavishly in Egypt as the Ptolemies had, but nevertheless they did carry out some remarkable works as at Philae (Trajan's kiosk), Dendarah and Esna. They also adopted many of the Egyptian cults which spread out around the empire. That of Isis, for example, had temples at Rome, London and throughout Europe; Serapis was also widely honoured.

Under Diocletian (284), such was the persecution of the Christians in Egypt that the Copts date their era, known as the Martyrs' Calendar, from his accession.

Responsibility for Egypt passed to Constantinople which was too distant and not sufficiently powerful to govern satisfactorily. From the West the North Africans attacked across the desert, from the South the Nubians raided the oases in the reign of Theodosius II (408–450); but of greater consequence and more persistent were the attacks of the Sassanids from Persia in the 5–6C.

# Dynasties and Kings of Ancient Egypt

The form of name following the date is the one used in this book. The brackets indicate the alternatives: [ ] = Egyptian; ( ) = Greek forms.

**Early Dynastic Period** (c 3100–2686 BC). Capital Memphis

*1st Dynasty* (c 3100–2890 BC)
Aha (Menes)
Djer or Uadji
Djet
Den or Udimu
Anedib
Semerkhet
Anedjib
Qaa

*2nd Dynasty* (c 2890–2686 BC)
Hotepsekmemwy
Raneb
Nynetjer
Peribsen
Khasekhem(wy)

*3rd Dynasty* (c 2686–2613 BC)
Sanakhte
Zozer (Djoser)
Sekhemkhet
Khaba
Huni or Hu

**Old Kingdom** (c 2613–2181 BC)

*4th Dynasty* (c 2613–2494 BC)
Sneferu
Khufu (Cheops)
Redjedef
Khafre (Chephren)
Menkaure (Mycerinus)
Shepseskaf

*5th Dynasty* (c 2494–2345 BC)
Userkaf
Sahure
Neferirkare Kakai
Shepseskare Isi
Neferefre
Nyuserre
Menkauhor Akauhor
Djedkare Isesi
Unas

*6th Dynasty* (c 2345–2181 BC)
Teti
Userkare
Meryre Pepi (Phiops) I
Merenre Antyemsaf
Neferekare Pepi (Phiops) II

**First Intermediate Period** (c 2181–2050 BC). Local control only from Memphis and Heracleopolis

*7th Dynasty* (c 2181–2173 BC)

*8th Dynasty* (c 2173–2160 BC)

*9th Dynasty* (c 2160–2130 BC)
Meryibre Khety (Achthoes I)
Nebkaure (Achthoes II)

*10th Dynasty* (c 2130–2040 BC)
Wahkare (Achthoes III)
Merykare

**Middle Kingdom** (c 2050–1786 BC)

*11th Dynasty* (c 2133–1991 BC) Capital Thebes
Tepya Mentuhotpe I
Sehertowy Inyotef I
Wahankh Inyotef II
Nakhtnebtepnefer Inyotef III
Nebhepetre Mentuhotpe II
Sankhkare Mentuhotpe III
Nebtowyre Mentuhotpe IV

*12th Dynasty* (c 1991–1786 BC)
1991–1962 Sehetepibre Amenemhat (Ammenemes) I
1971–1928 Kheperkare Senusert (Sesostris) I
1929–1895 Nubkaure Amenemhat (Ammenemes) II
1897–1878 Khakheperre Senusert (Sesostris) II
1878–1843 Khakaure Senusert (Sesostris) III
1842–1797 Nymare Amenemhat (Ammenemes) III
1798–1790 Makherure Amenemhat (Ammenemes) IV
1789–1786 Sobkkare Sobkneferu, Queen.

**Second Intermediate Period** (c 1786–1567 BC)
*13th Dynasty* (c 1786–1633 BC)
Wuserkare Khendjer
Sekhemre Sewadjtowy Sobkhotpe III
Khasekhemre Neferhotep I
Meryankhre Mentuhotpe

*14th Dynasty* (c 1786–1603 BC) Probably concurrent with 13th Dynasty. Capital Xois.

*15th Dynasty* Great Hyksos (c 1674–1567 BC) Capital Avaris.
Mayebre Sheshi
Meruserre Yakubher
Senuserenre Khyan
Auserre Apopi (Apohis) I
Aqenenre Apopi (Apohis) II

*16th Dynasty* (c 1684–c 1567 BC) Lesser Hyksos. Probably concurrent with 15th Dynasty.

*17th Dynasty* (c 1650–1567 BC) Capital Thebes.
Nubkeperre Inyotef VII
Seqenenre Tao I, the Elder
Seqenenre Tao II, the Brave
Wadjkheperre Kamose

**New Kingdom** (c 1567–1085 BC)

*18th Dynasty* (c 1567–1320 BC)
1570–1546 Nebpehtyre Ahmose (Amosis) I
1546–1526 Djeserkare Amenhotep (Amenophis) I
1525–1512 Akheperkare Tuthmosis [Dhutmose] I
1512–1504 Akheperenre Tuthmosis [Dhutmose] II
1503–1482 Makare Hatshepsut, Queen.
1504–1450 Menkheperre Tuthmosis [Dhutmose] III
1450–1425 Akheprure Amenhotep (Amenophis) II
1425–1417 Menkheprure Tuthmosis [Dhutmose] IV

1417–1379 Nebmare Amenhotep (Amenophis) III
1379–1362 Akhenaten : Neferkheprure Amenhotep (Amenophis) IV
1364–1361 Ankhkheprure Smenkhkare
1361–1352 Nebkheprure Tutankhamun
1352–1348 Kheperkheprure Ay
1348–1320 Djeserkheprure Horemheb

*19th Dynasty* (c 1320–1200 BC)
1320–1318 Menpehtyre Ramesses I
1318–1304 Menmare Seti (Sethos) I
1304–1237 Usermare Ramesses II
1236–1223 Baenre Merneptah
1222–1217 Menmire Amenmesses
1216–1210 Userkheprure Seti (Sethos) II
1210–1204 Akhenre Siptah
1204–1200 Sitre Meritamun Tawsert, Queen.

*20th Dynasty* (c 1200–1085 BC)
1200–1198 Userkhaure Sethnakhte
1198–1166 Usermare Meryamun Ramesses III
1166–1160 Hiqmare Ramesses IV
1160–1156 Usermare Ramesses V
1156–1148 Nebmare Ramesses VI
1148–1141 Usermare Ramesses VII
1147–1140 Usermare Ramesses VIII
1140–1123 Neferkare Ramesses IX
1123–1114 Khepermare Ramesses X
1114–1085 Menmare Ramesses XI

**Late Dynastic Period** (1085–332 BC)

*21st Dynasty* (c 1085–945 BC)
*At Tanis*
Smendes [Hedjkheperre Nesbanebded]
Psusennes [Akhperre Psibkhaemne] I
Userma Amenemope (Amenophthis)
Siamun
Psusennes [Tikheprure Psibkhaemne] II
*At Thebes* (Priest-Kings)
Herihor (time of Ramesses XI)
Paiankh
Pinudjem I
Masaherta
Menkheperre
Pinudjem II

*22nd Dynasty* (c 945–715 BC) Libyan. Capital Bubastis
935–924 Hedjkheperre Sheshonq I
924–889 Osorkon I
889–874 Takelot (Takelothis) I
874–850 Usermare Osorkon II
850 Sheshonq II
850–825 Takelot (Takelothis) II
825–773 Sheshonq III
773–767 Pami
767–730 Sheshonq IV
730–715 Osorkon IV

*23rd Dynasty* (c 818–715 BC) Concurrent with 22nd Dynasty at Tanis
818–793 Petubastis [Pedubast] I
777–749 Osorkon III

*24th Dynasty* (c 730–709 BC) At Sais concurrent with 25th Dynasty
Tefnakhte
Bakenrenef (Bocchoris)

*25th Dynasty* (c 747–656 BC) Nubian. Capital Thebes
747–716 Piankhi (Piye)
716–702 Neferkare Shabaka (Sabacon)
702–690 Djedkaure Shebitku (Sebichos)
690–664 Khunefertemre Taharqa (Torcos)
664–656 Bakare Tanutamun

*26th Dynasty* (664–525 BC) Capital Sais
672–664 Necho [Neko] I
664–610 Wahibre Psamtik (Psammetichus) I
610–595 Necho [Wehemibre Neko] II
595–589 Neferibre Psamtik (Psammetichus) II
589–570 Apries [Haibre Wahibre]
570–526 Ahmose (Amosis) II
526–525 Ankhkaenre Psamtik (Psammetichus) III

*27th Dynasty* (525–404 BC) Persian
525–522 Cambyses (Kanbujiya)
521–486 Darius I (Darayavahush)
486–466 Xerxes (Khshayarsha) II
465–424 Artaxerxes I (Artakhshassa)
424–405 Darius II
405–359 Artaxerxes II

*28th Dynasty* (404–399 BC) Saite. Capital Sais
404–399 Amyrtaeus

*29th Dynasty* (398–378 BC) Capital Mendes
398–393 Nephrites I [Nefaurud]
393 Psammuthis
393–380 Achoris [Khnemmare Hagor]

*30th Dynasty* (380–343 BC)
380–362 Nectanebo [Kheperkare Nekhtnebef] I
362–361 Teos (Djehosetpenanhur)
360–343 Nectanebo [Snedjemibre Nekhtareheb] II

*Second Persian Occupation* (345–332 BC)
345–338 Artaxerxes III Ochus
338–336 Arses (Arsha)
335–332 Darius III Codoman

**Late Period** (332–30 BC)

*Macedonian Kings* (332–304 BC) Capital Alexandria
332–323 Alexander (III) the Great
323–317 Philip Arrhidaeus
317–304 Alexander IV

*The Ptolemies* (323–30 BC) Order and numbers disputed
323–282 Ptolemy I Soter I abd 284, died 282
284–246 Ptolemy II Philadelphus
246–222 Ptolemy III Euergetes I
222–205 Ptolemy IV Philopator
205–180 Ptolemy V Epiphanes
180 Ptolemy VI Eupator
180–145 Ptolemy VII Philometor
145 Ptolemy VIII Neos Philopator
170–116 Ptolemy IX Euergetes II, co-ruler 169–163
116–107 Ptolemy X Soter II, called Lathyros
107–88 Ptolemy XI Alexander I
88–80 Ptolemy X 2nd reign
88 Ptolemy XII Alexander II

| | |
|---|---|
| 88–51 | Ptolemy XIII Neos Dionysos, called Auletes |
| 51–30 | Cleopatra VII Philopator Sister and co-ruler with Ptol. XIV and XV. Mother and co-ruler with Ptol. XVI. |
| 51–47 | Ptolemy XIV—drowned |
| 47–44 | Ptolemy XV—poisoned |
| 44–30 | Ptolemy XVI Theos Philopator Philometor, called Caesarion—executed |

**Roman Province** (30 BC–AD 395)

**Byzantine Province** (395–640)

*Roman Emperors* 30 BC–AD 395.

| | |
|---|---|
| 30 BC–AD 14 | Caesar Octavianus Augustus |
| 14–37 | Tiberius |
| 37–41 | Caligula |
| 41–54 | Claudius |
| 54–68 | Nero |
| 68–69 | Galba, Otho, Vitellius |
| 69–79 | Vespasian |
| 79–81 | Titus |
| 81–96 | Domitian |
| 96–98 | Nerva |
| 98–117 | Trajan |
| 117–38 | Hadrian |
| 138–61 | Antoninus Pius |
| 161–80 | Marcus Aurelius |
| 161–69 | Lucius Verus, co-ruler |
| 180–92 | Commodus |
| 193 | Pertinax |
| 192–211 | Septimius Severus |
| 193–94 | Pescennius Niger (Syria) |
| 198–217 | Caracalla, co-ruler |
| 211–12 | Geta, co-ruler |
| 217–18 | Macrinus |
| 218 | Diadumenianus |
| 218–22 | Elagabalus (Heliogabalus) |
| 222–35 | Alexander Severus |
| 235–38 | Maximinus |
| 238 | Gordianus I, Gordianus II, Balbinus and Pupienus |
| 238–44 | Gordianus III |
| 244–49 | Philippus (the Arabian) |
| 249–51 | Decius |
| 251–53 | Gallus |
| 251–53 | Volusianus, co-ruler |
| 253 | Aemilianus, rival emperor (Egypt) |
| 253–60 | Valerianus |
| 260–68 | Gallienus, co-ruler |
| 268–70 | Claudius II |
| 270 | Quintillus, rival emperor |
| 270–75 | Aurelianus |
| 275–76 | Tacitus |
| 276 | Florianus |
| 276–82 | Probus |
| 282–83 | Carus |
| 283–85 | Carinus |
| 283–84 | Numerianus |
| 284–305 | Diocletian |
| 286–313 | Maximianus |
| 293–306 | Constantius Tetrarchy, 293–305 |
| 293–311 | Galerius |
| 306–37 | Constantine I, the Great |

| | |
|---|---|
| 306–12 | Maxentius |
| 307–24 | Maximinus Daia |
| 308–24 | Licinius |
| 337–40 | Constantine II |
| 337–50 | Constans, co-ruler |
| 337–61 | Constantius II, co-ruler |
| 350–53 | Magnetius, co-ruler |
| 361–63 | Julian, the Apostate |
| 363–64 | Jovian |
| 364–75 | Valentinian I (West) |
| 364–78 | Valens, (East) |
| 375–83 | Gratian, (West) |
| 379–95 | Theodosius, the Great, co-ruler with last |
| 383–92 | Valentinian II, (West) |
| 392–94 | Eugenius |
| 395 | Empire divided |

*Eastern Roman Emperors* 393–641

| | |
|---|---|
| 395–408 | Arcadius |
| 408–50 | Theodosius II |
| 450–57 | Marcianus |
| 457–74 | Leo I, the Great |
| 474 | Leo II |
| 474–91 | Zeno |
| 491–518 | Anastasius |
| 518–27 | Justinius I |
| 527–65 | Justinianus |
| 565–71 | Justinus II |
| 578–582 | Tiberius II |
| 582–602 | Mauricius |
| 602–10 | Phocas |
| 610–41 | Heraclius |

*Third Persian Occupation* (619–29)

*Arab Conquest* 640

# The Names of the King

In pharaonic times the king's titulary was a formula of five names: a birth name and four which were adopted on his accession to the throne.

1. The *Horus name*, also known as the 'Ka name' or 'Banner name', is the earliest to appear on the monuments and takes precedence over the other names. It represents the king as the earthly embodiment of Horus the Elder, the falcon god who early became the dynastic god of Egypt. It is often written within a rectangular frame called a serekh, topped by an image of a falcon. Below the name inside the frame is recessed panelling similar to the facades of the early dynastic tombs or palaces.

2. The *Nebty name* is so called because it is preceded by representations of the two goddesses or ladies, Nekhbet for Upper Egypt and Wadjet for Lower Egypt. The hieroglyphs took the form of the vulture and the cobra, emblems of the goddesses, seated upon baskets:  . This title was probably adopted by Menes when he united the Two Lands and established his capital at Memphis. It is certainly known by the 1 Dyn.

# Names of the Principal Kings of Egypt



1 DYNASTY 2 DYNASTY 3 DYNASTY

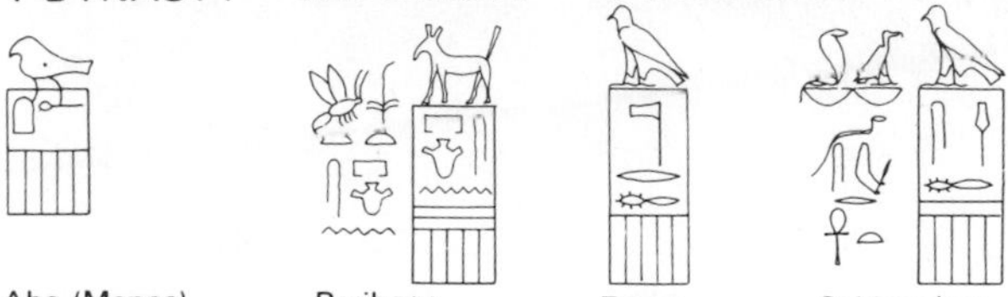

Aha (Menes) Peribsen Zozer Sekhemket

4 DYNASTY

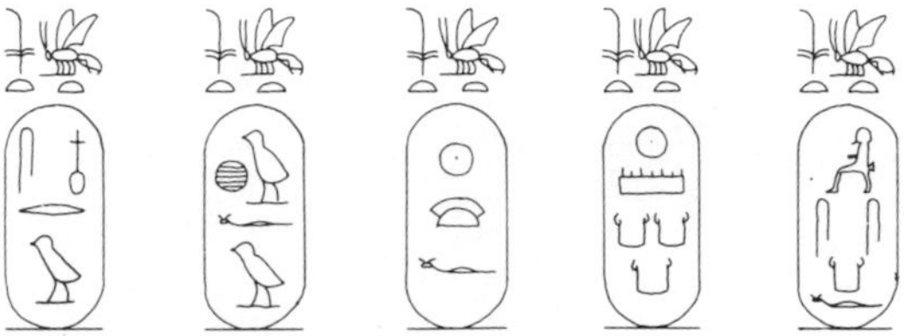

Sneferu Khufu Khafre Mankaure Shepseskaf

5 DYNASTY

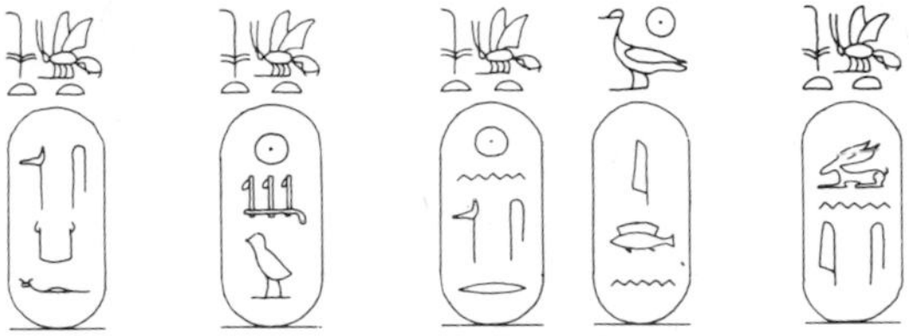

Userkaf Sahure Nyuserre Unas

6 DYNASTY

Teti Pepi I Merenre Pepi II

11 DYNASTY 12 DYNASTY

Mentuhotpe II Amenemhat I Senusert I Amenemhat II

Cartouches reproduced by kind permission of

## 12 DYNASTY

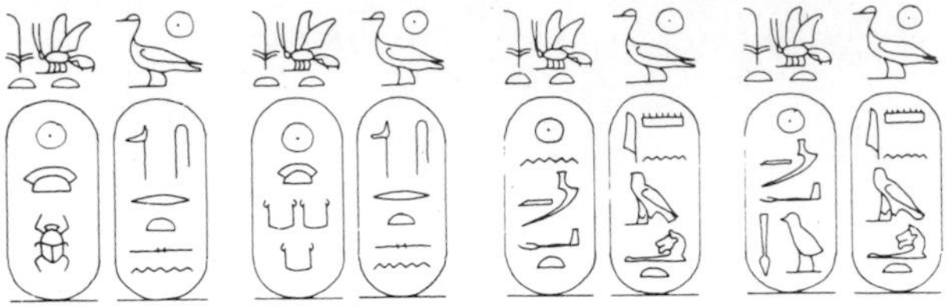

Senusert II | Senusert III | Amenemhat III | Amenemhat IV

## 18 DYNASTY

Ahmose I | Amenhotep I | Tuthmosis I | Tuthmosis II

Hatshepsut | Tuthmosis III | Amenhotep II | Tuthmosis IV

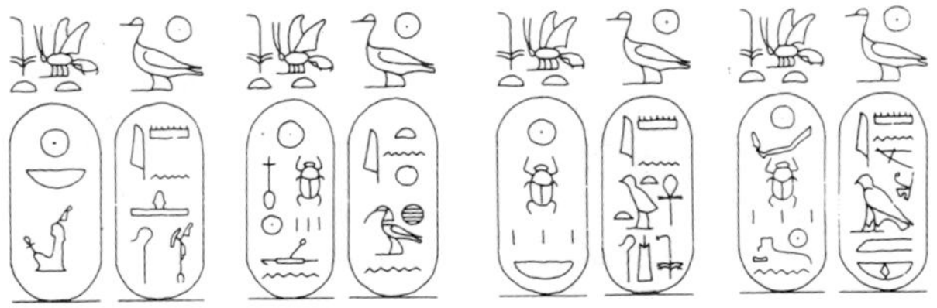

Amenhotep III | Akhenaten | Tutankhamun | Horemheb

## 19 DYNASTY

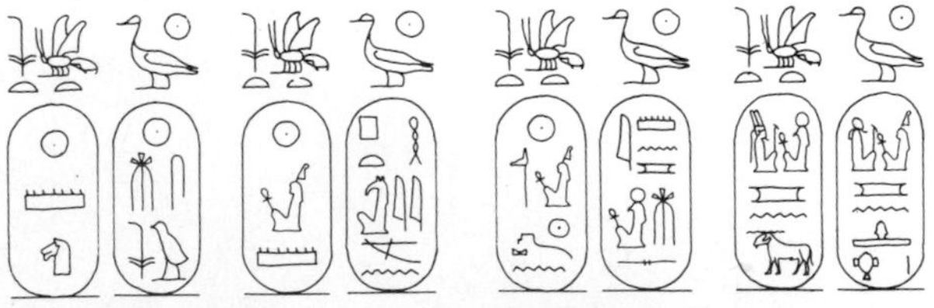

Ramesses I | Seti I | Ramesses II | Merneptah

## 20 DYNASTY

Ramesses III

Ramesses IV

Ramesses IX

## 21 DYNASTY

Nesbanebded

Psusennes I

## 22 DYNASTY

Sheshonq I

Osorkon II

## 25 DYNASTY

Piankhi

Shabaka

Taharqa

## 26 DYNASTY

Psamtik I

Necho II

Psamtik II

Apries

Amosis II

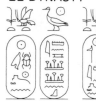

Psamtik III

## 30 DYNASTY

Nectanebo I    Nectanebo II

## MACEDONIAN KINGS

Alexander the Great

## PTOLEMAIC DYNASTY

Ptolemy I    Soter I    Ptolemy II    Philadelphus

Ptolemy V    Epiphanes    Cleopatra VII

## ROMAN EMPERORS

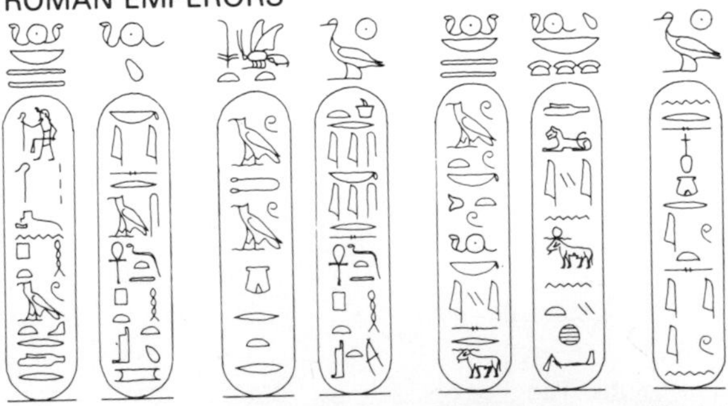

Augustus    Tiberius    Trajan    Diocletian

3. The *Golden Horus name* is an obscure term. It can be taken at its face value, that the king was modelled by the gods as a 'Falcon of Fine Gold'. Alternatively it may mean Horus victorious over Seth. It is shown as the Falcon seated on the sign for gold: , appearing as early as the reign of king Khufu in the 4 Dyn.

4. The *Prenomen* was the name taken by the king when he acceeded to the throne. It was always written in a cartouche (an ornamental tablet of stone or wood intended to be inscribed). The Egyptians showed the cartouche as a double thickness of rope with the ends tied together, , called snw from a verb stem ('to encircle') sni; the idea being that the Egyptian king was ruler of all 'that was encircled by the sun'. It was introduced by a group of signs reading , nesu bit, literally 'He who belongs to the sedge and the bee', that is 'King of Upper and Lower Egypt', these being the symbols for these lands. This name occurs as early as the 1 Dyn. where it is shown on stone vases of King Den (Udimu), the fourth king of the dynasty. This is nearly always compounded with the name of the god Reʿ at the end of the name and seems to have been in general use from the middle of the 11 Dyn. and occasionally earlier.

5. The last name, or *Nomen*, also written inside a cartouche, was the name that the king was given when he was born and equates more or less with a family name, e.g. Amenemhat in the 12 Dyn. or Tuthmosis in the 18 Dyn. This name was introduced by the epithet: 'son of the sun god Reʿ'.

# Ancient Egyptian Religion

It is impossible to appreciate the art and architecture of Ancient Egypt without a knowledge of Egyptian religion. This, however, is a complicated and difficult subject, incompletely understood, and cannot be dealt with in a summary manner. The bulk of Ancient Egyptian literature is religious in nature; much of it consisting of hymns, spells, charms and some very intricate texts, inscribed on the walls of temples and tombs, on stelae, papyri, ostraca, sarcophagi, mummy cases and coffins. It was a processional religion in which minute details were given to the rites and rituals to be carried out daily, the procedures of which are known, but little is comprehended of the thought behind them. Although it was a written religion there was no initial revelation as in Islam or Judaism.

The earliest religious writings are the *Pyramid Texts*, written on the walls of the burial chambers and annexes of the 5 and 6 Dyn. rulers, within the pyramids. In the Middle Kingdom these were transferred from the structures of the tombs onto the coffins, giving them the name *Coffin Texts*. In turn, in the New Kingdom, these are replaced by what are known as the *Books of the Dead*, rolls of papyri buried with the dead man in his coffin, and describing the various ways to get to the Afterworld. Many of these texts, like those in the Pyramids, deal with a period earlier than that in which they were inscribed, as do the long inscriptions on the walls of the Ptolemaic and Roman temples which contain material of a much earlier date.

**The Gods and Myths**. The vast numbers of Egyptian gods portrayed on monuments can be daunting, but many of them are merely different

*Prenomen of Senusert I, from his chapel at Karnak*

aspects of the same god, and in the course of time more and more of the gods became assimilated to a few important ones. In the earliest times there were three important cosmogonies, those of Heliopolis, Hermopolis and Memphis, the most important of which was the Heliopolitan Cycle which eventually became almost universally accepted, parts of the other systems being incorporated within it. Heliopolis was the centre of the various aspects of sun worship. The theory developed by the priests there of the creation of the world was that originally there was nothing but a watery waste or abyss of Chaos known as Nun, personified as a god. From this chaos rose a mound, as an island of sand emerged from the river as the innundation receded. On this mound appeared Atum, the original sun-god always portrayed in human form and later identified with Reʿ. From Atum came the dual deities of the sky, Shu (air) and Tefnut (moisture, clouds and dew). They in turn created Geb (the earth god) and Nut (the sky goddess), who produced Osiris, Isis, Seth and Nephthys. Sometimes included was Horus the Elder (so-called to distinguish him from Horus son of Isis), but if he is excluded, the remainder were known as the Divine Ennead (Nine), and sometimes regarded as a single entity.

Atum

Shu Tefnut

Geb Nut

Osiris Set Isis Nephthys Horus the Elder

Hermopolis Magna, the City of Thoth, capital of the XVth nome of Upper Egypt, independently developed another cycle of creation gods known as the Hermopolitan Ogdoad (company of eight) which consisted of deities grouped in pairs of gods and goddesses; Nun and Nunet, (primordial water), Heh and Hehet (space), Kek and Keket (darkness), and Amun and Amunet (invisibility). Again the watery waste produced a mound on which appeared an egg, and from this came forth the sun-god Reʿ.

The theory developed at Memphis, the text of which is preserved on the Shabaka Stone (now in the BM), in contrast to the other theologies, presents the only Egyptian creation myth which was intellectually conceived, and as such it is extremely attractive to all interested in religious theory. It tells of the creation of the world by thought and the word, long before the Christian theology of the New Testament. Here Ptah becomes the creator-god in his form of Ptah Tatjenen, the earth emerging from chaos at his command.

Of course, other creator gods and myths developed in other districts. Amun transferred from Hermopolis to Thebes also creates the world. Neith as a form of Nut creates the world from the waste of Nun, and creates Reʿ and the opponent of Reʿ. Horus appears as a creator god perched on the primaeval mound as a falcon, and attacked by an enemy, the snake. Khnum creates mankind on the potter's wheel, but Reʿ creates them from the tears of his eyes.

In addition to the great creation legends there were other myth cycles such as the battles between Horus and Seth, and the Death of Osiris. These are complementary and probably date back to predynastic times, being the echoes of battles fought long ago for the possession of Egypt. The story of Osiris the good king who introduced civilisation to Egypt, murdered by his wicked brother Seth, has universal appeal. It continues with the long and weary search of his sister-wife Isis for the body of her husband, finding it only to have it destroyed again by Seth who discovered it while out hunting by moonlight; the goddess has to begin her search again. When Horus the Younger, her son, comes to manhood he struggles with his uncle for the succession to the throne. These conflicts are known as the Contendings of Horus and Seth, a text of which goes back at least as far as the New Kingdom. Some of the struggles involve actual battles between Seth and Horus, both of whom take on a number of different forms, while at other times the struggle moves to the courtroom, where a trial is held before the gods. It is a long drawn-out battle, but in the end the victory is with Horus. Sometimes the fight is about the eye of Reʿ, sometimes Horus is the champion of Reʿ, as on the walls of Edfū. Many of these myths were replayed annually in the form of mystery plays, with the king and priests performing in lieu of the gods.

Many of the gods, like Bes and Tausert, remained only local deities; others, worshipped in towns which became historically important, were elevated into national gods. Amun, for instance, originally associated with Hermopolis, was moved to Thebes, and when this became the capital was associated with Reʿ the sun-god and as Amun-Reʿ became the national god worshipped all over the Egyptian empire. Some of the gods and goddesses had no national shrines; others found a home with one of the other gods.

**Rites.** Various divine cults were maintained in the principal towns of each nome or district and, as with their controlling deities, some of these remained local while others attained national status. All, however, followed a daily ritual which had become fairly standardised by the end of the Old Kingdom. This ritual, based on the Heliopolitan Cycle, was the basis of all religious practices throughout the country. In each of the main temples the king was regarded as the high-priest, but in his absence his place was taken by the usual incumbent. The service was the same whether it was performed by the king or his priestly deputy.

Beginning at dawn with the purification of the priest by water from the sacred lake or well, he was then clothed in special ritual garments, given certain ritual objects and approached the shrine, broke the seals with due care, took the figure of the god out of the naos, washed and reclothed it in fresh linen, lit the fire for the incense offerings, and presented the god with food and drink. All the offerings had to be without blemish. After everything had been purified the attendant withdrew, carefully brushing away his footsteps on the floor of the shrine which was then resealed. At midday further purification rites were performed and natron (native sodas) were sprinkled, and in the evening the doors were again unsealed and another meal and drink proffered after the earlier one had been removed to be consumed by the priests.

The Ancient Egyptians were obsessed with the idea that the world was created out of chaos and an ordered way of life had only been established with immense difficulty. For them the obscure forces of chaos still existed and would overwhelm their world if the correct rites and rituals were not performed daily in the temples. Equilibrium was maintained with a great struggle and only the gods by their ceaseless efforts preserved the existence of the universe.

The temple was the house of the gods; the function of the building and the priestly personnel was to protect the gods from attacks by hostile forces, and to keep them in a state in which they could carry out their cosmic tasks successfully. The temple was built of stone because it was the hardest material known to them. Ceilings were decorated with the goddess Nut and stars and deccans representing the sky. From the floor the columns sprang like the marsh plants and vegetation from which they had once been created, while the walls were decorated with reference to the creation myths, and the endless struggle between good and evil.

The daily rituals carried out in the temple were linked with the ritual to the dead. All offerings were termed the greatest offering of all: 'the Eye of Horus'. Evil forces were strongest at night when the greatest precautions had to be taken. Only the rising of the new sun symbolised the triumph of the sun god Reʿ over the chaos of darkness. The sky itself was insecure and supported on four pillars, therefore a special festival of 'the Raising of the Sky' had to be held annually, as at Esna and elsewhere.

The 'Opening of the Mouth' ceremony animated statues, reliefs of gods, animals and men, as well as restoring life to the dead. It was performed on statues in the 'Rooms of Gold', the sculptors' workshops, and on mummies in 'the Tent of Purification', the embalming tent. Additionally, this ceremony was carried out in the temples, to reanimate the statues of the gods and the images upon the walls after the building of the temple, and annually after its spring clean and redecoration. If this were not done the gods would not be able to receive the offerings made to them, nor act defensively on the people's behalf. The ritual entailed touching the face with a flint instrument, which was forked at one end, and with an adze, a magic rite that must have originated with instruments used in the prehistoric period. In addition, an ox was killed, and the right foreleg, where the physical force was thought to reside, was raised towards the figure to be reanimated.

**Feasts**. In the daily service to the god the public had no part: in fact access to the inner parts of the temple was forbidden to the laity. They were permitted to penetrate to the forecourt and to the corridors surrounding the building, where they could spend the night in those temples devoted to healing. Otherwise the public could only participate in the great festivals.

Each temple had a calendar of feasts and festivities of which a shortened version seems to have been inscribed in the hypostyle hall. The full text, written on parchment or papyrus, would have been kept in the library of the temple archives. In each temple the principal gods were taken in procession several times a month either round the town, or to visit neighbouring temples, usually by river. Some of the feasts only lasted a few days, but the great national ones could extend for 28 or 30 days; many of them were closely connected with agriculture, and the fertility of the fields. One of the chief festivals was the Feast of Opet, held in Thebes during the second month of the Season of the Inundation. At this feast Amun processed by boat from Karnak to the Luxor temple, accompanied by the boats of Mut and Khonsu. Other important festivals were the New Year Feast, the Coming-Forth of Min at harvest time, the Raising of the Sky, the Feast of the Potters Wheel (connected with Khnum), the Feast of Sokar and the Feast of the Valley, both connected with the Necropolis.

As well as feasts and festivals certain temples re-enacted miracle plays every year: for instance the Birth of Horus at Dendarah, the Contendings of Horus with Seth at Edfū, or the Death and Resurrection of Osiris at Abydos. Another was the Coronation Play, which is even earlier. This gave an account of the ritual of the crowning of the king.

An oracular service was also provided, either at the temple or when the travelling statues were being carried through the streets, and petitions were presented. The answers were usually a simple yes or no. The animal cults, such as those of the Apis and Mnevis bulls, also specialised in oracles, as did the special gods of the necropolis such as Amenhotep I and Ahmose Nefertari. They were worshipped by the workers in the necropolis who lived in the workmen's village at Deir al-Madīnah on the West Bank at Thebes.

**Priests.** The priesthood was carefully organised, many positions during the earlier period in the hierarchy being occupied by nobles and officials. But by the New Kingdom it had become a professional body. The ordinary priest, or wb priest, was the lowest order, and the aspirant to high office became successively third prophet, second prophet and first prophet or high priest. Certain priests were reciters while others were concerned with the service for the dead. Women were priestesses of certain goddesses such as Hathor, Isis or Bastet; others were chantresses of Amun, and singers for other male deities. The priests of Sekhmet concerned themselves with medical practices.

**Funerary Beliefs and Practices**. Because of the way that sites have been excavated in Egypt, most material has come from either tombs or temples, which, combined with the classical view that the Egyptian people were the most religious in the ancient world, has encouraged theories that they were obsessed with death and the Afterworld. Actually little work has been done on the major Egyptian cities, but if this were redressed the Egyptians' attitude would doubtless be better understood. It seems rather that they were devoted to life, and could not imagine anything better, and so based their ideas of the Afterworld on that of their own everyday life. However, funerary beliefs are never simple, and in Egypt they cover a particularly long time, during which many ideas changed, or were grafted onto earlier ones.

It is extremely difficult to give an idea of the religious beliefs and funerary practices of all classes of Egyptian society. Originally the best was obviously reserved for the king and the nobles, and it is from their tombs that most information comes. The poorer folk were, like those of the predynastic period, often wrapped in skins, baskets or linen shrouds, and placed in the sand where their bodies survived remarkably well owing to the very dry environment. There is no doubt that the Egyptians' desire to preserve the body came from having observed the state of preservation of some of these early burials, conditions they tried to duplicate when carrying out their own. No definite treatise on mummification exists, but as belief in Osiris grew, and as his powers became diversified (originally only the rulers and ruling classes benefitted from his ministrations), so did the belief in resurrection spread. The Greek authors who were interested in embalming inform us that mummification took about 70 days, but there is one case of an Old Kingdom queen which took about 285 days, perhaps because her tomb-chapel was not ready.

Evidence for the commencement of embalming is uncertain. Already by the 3 Dyn. the body was being dismembered and the limbs wrapped to represent the living body, but by the 4 Dyn. it was certainly taking place, and one of the earliest examples known is that of Hetepheres, mother of Khufu, builder of the Great Pyramid. Although her body was missing from her tomb, the box containing the canopic jars (see below) was present, evidence that she must have been embalmed. Very few mummies have remained from the Old and Middle Kingdoms, but by the New Kingdom the main methods used to preserve the body were understood.

The word mummy comes from the Arabic *mūmmiyā*ʾ (bitumen), the material in which bodies were later soaked in an effort to preserve them, and has really nothing to do with the Egyptians' earlier efforts. The method seems to have been a dry process in which the soft parts of the body like the stomach, intestines and liver, were taken out and placed either in jars or wrapped in bundles; the brain was also usually removed but not the heart. Natron was used to purify and preserve the body, the body cavity was washed out with palm wine, and the body stuffed to preserve its contours.

Various methods were used at different times, those of the 18 and 19 Dyns being most effective, while those of the 21 Dyn. were the most elaborate. After the body had been dried, washed and wrapped, it was covered with an intricate pattern of cross strapping and for protection had various amulets placed upon it. The most important was probably the heart scarab, which contained a short inscription from the Book of the Dead, while among the dozens of others, many intended solely for funerary purposes, the two principal ones were the djed pillar of Osiris and the thet girdle of Isis.

The canopic jars in which the viscera were placed have already been mentioned. The term 'canopic' is a misnomer derived from Canopus, the city where the sailors of Menelaus were said to have died and been buried, and later worshipped as a jar with a human head. The early canopic jars merely had a cap on them and were made of pottery or stone, but in the Middle and New Kingdom they had human heads representing the deceased, which were later replaced by the four sons of Horus—Duamutef (jackal) protecting the stomach, Gebehsenuf (falcon) the intestines, Hapi (baboon) the lungs, and Imsety (human) the liver. Each of these minor deities was under the guardianship of one of the four goddesses of the dead—Neith, Selket, Nephthys and Isis.

The Egyptians also mummified certain animals, for example the Apis and Mnevis bulls, and the ibis and baboon sacred to Thoth. The burials of the Apis bulls are the best known as they are to be seen at Ṣaqqārah in the Serapeum, and their embalming place, complete with huge alabaster tables, was found at Memphis near the Temple of Ptah in 1951. Most of the surviving animal mummies belong to the later periods, but it is obvious that animal worship, particularly the bull cult, is of ancient origin.

**The Afterworld**. As mentioned above, the earliest texts that have survived are the Pyramid Texts written inside the pyramid chambers of the 5–7 Dyn. kings. The first are those of Unas, the last king of the 5 Dyn., buried at Ṣaqqārah. The two main deities of the Pyramid Texts are Reʿ and Osiris, originally only the king benefitting from the spells, hymns, prayers and methods used to get from this world to the Afterlife. With the increase in power of Osiris, this idea of a passage to the Afterworld became available to anyone who knew the right answers, and could perform the correct rituals.

In the Middle Kingdom the texts ceased to be written on the walls of the pyramid chambers and were inscribed on the actual coffins. Though they are virtually the same, the lack of space necessitated shortened versions, these in the main being prayers to Osiris and Anubis and a list of the principal offerings. By the New Kingdom the texts had been transferred to papyri which were buried with the dead in the coffin and were called the Book of the Dead. There was a choice as to which chapters to include with the body, though there were some that were essential for all. Some of the Books were called by other names—'That which is in the Am-Duat', 'The Book of the Gates', 'The Book of the Caverns', 'The Litany of Reʿ' and 'The Book of the Divine Cow'. This religious literature is some of the most difficult of all Egyptian writings to understand. In some cases the texts were placed on the walls of the Royal Tombs, or on the shrines if present, as in the case of Tutankhamun.

The Egyptians had no concept entirely comparable to that expressed by the word 'soul', but they believed that there were a variety of spiritual entities which belonged to each person. There was the *Ba* or *Bai*, represented as a human-headed bird which could move in and out of the tomb at will. The *Ka* was the double, born when a man was born and dying when he died, and represented by two raised arms. It was officially for the man's Ka that all the funerary equipment in a tomb was provided, including the food and drink, and the sepulchre was known as 'the house of the Ka'. In addition to these two aspects was the *Akh*. This was the indestructible entity of the person and represented by a bald ibis in the hieroglyphs, which also meant 'to shine' or 'be bright', so that the dead were often regarded as the shining ones. The texts inform us that 'just as the body belongs to earth so the akh belongs to heaven'. Other elements such as the name of a man, and his shadow, were also important parts of his personality.

In the Pre-dynastic period the Egyptians buried food and objects in the grave with their dead and weapons with the men, ornaments with the women, but in the Old Kingdom they buried models of servants who by magic would be enabled to do the work in the Afterworld. In the Middle Kingdom instead of single models of bakers, brewers, grinders, etc., elaborate models of granaries, ships, kitchens, houses, carpenters' shops and weavers' houses were placed in the tomb, all filled with people doing the necessary tasks. By the New Kingdom they still made model boats, but they were empty, being manned by an invisible crew. In the same way in the Middle Kingdom they began to make *shawabty figures*, models representing the deceased, made of clay or wax and later also of stone or more often of faience. These were inscribed with a part of Chapter VI of the Book of the Dead which would enable the figure to do any work that the dead man would be called upon to do in the Afterworld, such as clearing sand, moving stone from the East to the West Bank, or digging canals.

Originally only one of these figures was placed in the tomb, but later the numbers increased and as many as 400 have been found. Some of the

*The weighing of the heart from the Book of the Dead of the Priest-King Herihor and Queen Nodjmet who are seen before Osiris (21 Dyn.) (Trustees of the British Museum)*

figures carried baskets and hoes, others had whips and acted as overseers. Some of these in the royal tombs were made in the likeness of the deceased, but many others were bulk produced and just inscribed with the name and titles of the deceased. The texts on the walls of the private tombs from the 3 Dyn. onwards listed the basic unit requirements of the dead man as 1000 of bread, 1000 of beer, 1000 of linen, etc., which by magical means were supposed to transform themselves into the actual objects.

## List of the Principal Deities

Starred entries are illustrated.

AKER: earth god, shown with a lion head, guarding the East and West gates of the Afterworld.

AMEN: *see Amun*

AMON: *see Amun*

* AMSET: *see Imsety*

* AMUN: the name means hidden. First found at Hermopolis, he was also the great god of Thebes, known as the city of No-Amun. Always shown as a man with two plumes on his head, and carrying the crook and the flail. At Thebes he was associated with *Amunet*, his female counterpart, and later with *Mut*. The third god in the triad was *Khonsu* or *Khons*, a form of moon god, who was regarded as their son, but in reality was an entirely separate deity. Sacred animals were the ram and goose. In the New Kingdom he was indentified with Reʿ as *Amun-Reʿ*, the sun god as the imperial god of Thebes and personal god of the king.

ANHUR: *see Onuris.*

ANPU: *see Anubis.*

* ANQET (Gk *Anukis*): goddess of the Cataract region, wife or daughter of *Khnum*, represented as a woman with a tall feather headdress. Temple at Seheil Island.

* ANUBIS (*Anpu*): a god of the dead, shown as a jackal, or as a man with the head of a jackal. Closely connected with Middle Egypt and the 12th, 17th and 18th nomes of Upper Egypt. Patron god of embalmers.

APIS: the sacred bull of Memphis, buried in the Serapeum at Ṣaqqārah.

ASAR: *see Osiris*

ATEN: god of the sun-disk worshipped by Akhenaten, although known much earlier. Shown as a rayed disk, the rays terminating in hands (see illustration Rte 32).

* ATUM: creator god of Heliopolis, represented as a man.

* BASTET (*Bast*): cat goddess whose cult centre was at Bubastis in the Delta. Usually regarded as a friendly deity, and the kinder aspect of the sun.

* BES: domestic-god, protector of women in childbirth, also associated with music and dancing, shown as a dwarf.

BUTO: *see Wadjet*

* DUAMUTEF: one of the sons of *Horus*, jackal-headed guardian of the Canopic jar of the stomach.

ERNUTET: *see Renenutet.*

* GEB: earth god, always represented as a man. Symbol, a goose.

* HAPI: one of the sons of *Horus*, baboon-headed guardian of the Canopic jar of the lungs.

HAPY: god of the Nile in innundation. Shown as a hermaphrodite figure with a crest of papyrus on his head, and bearing gifts.

HARAKHTE: a special form of *Horus* connected with Heliopolis. Represented as a falcon.

HARSIESIS: *Horus*, son of *Isis*.

HAROERIS: a form of *Horus*, the elder.

HARPOCRATES (*Hor-pa-khred*): Horus-the-Child, son of *Osiris* and *Isis*. Represented as a naked child.

HATHOR: goddess represented as a cow or as a cow-headed woman, if as a woman wears a horned headdress, and often a disk. Known as the 'Golden One'. Her cult centres were at Denderah, Thebes, Cusae, Gabalayn and Memphis. She was mistakenly equated by the Greeks with Aphrodite.

HEH: god of a million years, depicted kneeling, holding a notched palm branch indicating the years of the king's life. Originated at Antinopolis.

* HEQET: frog goddess, shrine at Antinopolis, assisted at childbirth.

* HORUS: falcon god, and sky god, the living ruler, later connected with *Osiris* and *Isis* as their son, although originally no connection. Worshipped at Behdet and Buto in Delta, and at Hierakonpolis and Edfu in Upper Egypt. See also other forms of *Horus* as *Harakhte, Harsiesis, Haroeris* and *Harpocrates*.

HORUS THE ELDER: one of the primaeval gods of the Heliopolitan Cycle. Represented as a hawk or a hawk-headed man.

IMHOTEP (Gk *Imouthes*): the deified chief of works of King Zozer of the 3 Dyn. Later identified with *Asklepios* and worshipped as god of medicine. Shown as a seated man holding a papyrus.

IMOUTHES: *see Imhotep*

* IMSETY: one of the sons of *Horus*, the human-headed guardian of the Canopic jar of the liver.

* ISIS: wife of *Osiris* and mother of *Horus*. One of the great mother goddesses of Egypt, she is shown as a woman with a throne on her head. Protector of the dead, and guardian of the Canopic jars. Temples at Philae, Denderah, and in the Delta.

KHEPHRI (*Khephra*): the scarab god, represents the rising sun. Shown as a beetle, often within a sun-disk.

* KHNUM: creator god, associated with Elephantine and Esna. Represented as a man with a ram's head, thought to have created man on the potter's wheel.

* KHONSU (Khons): a moon god, represented as a man with a disk on his head or with the head of a falcon. One of the triad of Thebes.

* MAʿAT: goddess of truth, right and order. Shown as a woman with an ostrich feather on her head.

MAFDET: goddess of justice, usually shown in feline form.

MEHIT: lion goddess worshipped at This.

MNEVIS: sacred bull of Heliopolis.

MIN: early god of Coptos, later a desert god associated with Amun and worshipped at Luxor. Represented as an ithyphallic figure, with one hand raised holding the flail, and wearing the plumes of *Amun*.

MONTU (*Munt*, or *Month*): war god of Thebes represented as a falcon, guards the king in battle. Originally connected with Hermonthis (Armant) to the S. of Thebes. Temple to N of main complex at Karnak.

* MUT: wife of *Amun* and second of Triad of Thebes. Represented as a woman, or as a lion or vulture. Temple at Asheru, S of main Karnak temple.

NEBET-HET: *see Nephthys*

* NEFERTUM: third of triad of Memphis, represented as a man with a lotus on head. Associated with perfumes.

NEITH: goddess of Sais, shown as a woman wearing the red crown of Lower Egypt, carrying a shield and crossed arrows. One of the goddesses who protected the dead, and the Canopic jars. She was also a creator goddess.

NEKHBET: tutelary deity of Upper Egypt, the vulture-goddess of Nekheb (El Kab). Shown crowning the king, and represented as a woman wearing the white crown. Otherwise shown as a vulture.

* NEPHTHYS (*Nebet-het*): sister of *Isis* and *Osiris*, married to *Seth*. One of the protector goddesses of the dead, and guardians of the Canopic jars. Her name means 'lady of the house'.

* NUN: the watery abyss of chaos.

* NUT: the sky goddess, wife of *Geb*, shown as a woman or as a cow, spangled with stars.

ONNOPHRIS: *see Unnefer*

ONURIS (*Anhur*): warrior god associated with the cities of This and Sebennytos. Shown as a man wearing high plumes and drawing after him a cord.

* OSIRIS (*Asar*): god of the Afterworld, vegetation, and fertility god. Came

originally from the Delta at Busiris. Became god of Abydos, replacing *Khentamentu*. The king and later all the dead became Osiris when they died and thus through him mankind gained hope of resurrection.

PAKHT: lion-goddess of Middle Egypt worshipped at Speos Artemidoros.

* PTAH: creator-god of Memphis. Represented as man mummified, usually in a shrine, patron god of craftsmen. Has several forms. Equated by Greeks with *Hephaestus*.

PTAH-SOKAR-OSIRIS: a composite god, represented as a mummified king or a naked boy. Incorporates the chief gods of creation, death and the Afterworld.

PTAH-TATJENEN: the creator god personifying the earth emerging from chaos.

* QEBEHSENUF: a son of *Horus*, falcon-headed guardian of the Canopic jar of the intestines.

* REʿ: the sun god of Heliopolis, connected with the king who is regarded as his son. Head of the Ennead of Heliopolis, doubles with *Atum*. Represented as a man often with a falcon's head or if in dead form with a ram's head; has 72 transformations in the Afterworld. Often compounded with other universal Egyptian gods such as *Amun-Reʿ*, *Sobek-Reʿ*.

REʿ-HARAKHTY: (*Horus of the Horizon*): falcon-headed god embodying the attributes of both *Reʿ* and *Horus*.

RENENUTET: goddess of the harvest. Shown as a woman with a snake's head or as a snake.

SARAPIS: foreign god probably from Black Sea region, introduced into Egypt during Ptolemaic period. Shown as a bearded man.

SATET: (Gk *Satis*): female counterpart of *Khnum*, shown as a woman wearing the white crown and horns. Represents the fertility side of the innundation.

*SEKHMET: lion-headed goddess, daughter of *Reʿ*, second of triad at Memphis regarded as wife of *Ptah*. Embodied the cruel powers of the sun. Fought against the enemies of *Reʿ*, and once nearly destroyed mankind.

SELKET: (Gk *Selkis*): scorpion-goddess, guardian of the dead, often shown as a woman with a scorpion on her head.

* SESHAT: goddess of writing. Shown as a woman with a star on her head.

SETH (*Sutekh*): brother of *Osiris* and his murderer. Associated with Delta and Desert. Represented by an unidentified animal.

* SHU: god of air, at Heliopolis.

SOBEK (Gk *Suchos*): crocodile-god, worshipped throughout Egypt, particularly important in the Fayyūm, at Kom Ombo, and Gabalayn.

*SOKAR: god of the dead, associated with Memphis. Usually shown as falcon-headed.

SOPDU: falcon-god associated with Saft el-Hinna in Eastern Delta. Warrior god protector of the Eastern frontier.

SUCHOS: *see Sobek*

SUTEKH: *see Seth*

TATJENEN: *see Ptah*

TAWERET (Gk *Thoeris*): the hippopotamus-goddess, protector of women in childbirth.

* TEFNUT: Goddess of moisture and dew, one of the Heliopolitan ennead.

* THOTH: ibis-headed god of Hermopolis. Scribe and vizier of the gods. Ibis and baboon were sacred to him.

UNNEFER (*Onnophris*): the permanently perfect one, an epithet of Osiris.

WADJET (*Buto*): cobra-goddess of Lower Egypt, site Tell al-Faraʿīn.

WEPWAWET: jackal-headed god of Asyut in Middle Egypt. He was known as the opener of the ways, and was connected with the dead, and *Osiris*.

# EGYPTIAN GODS

**Amun**

Anqet

**Anubis**

Atum

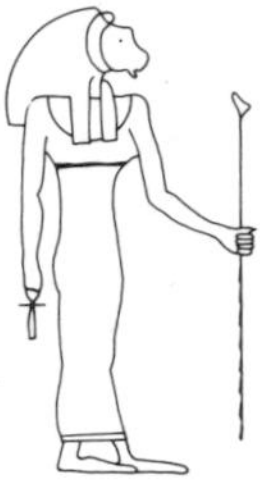

Bastet

Bes

Geb

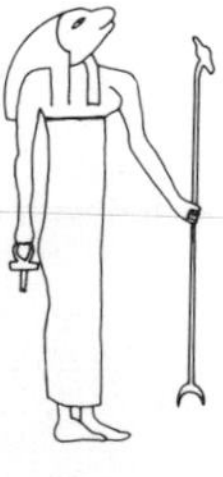

Heqet

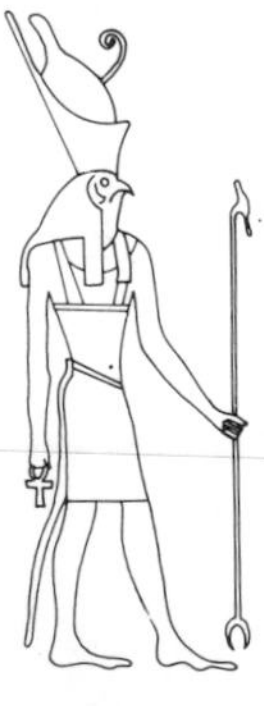

**Horus**

# EGYPTIAN GODS

Children of Horus

**Isis**

Khnum

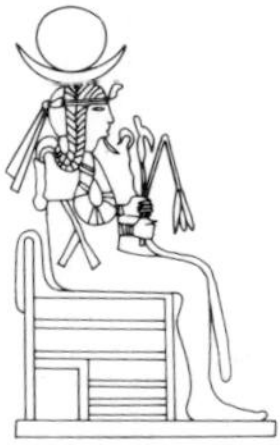

Khonsu

Ma'at

Mut

Nefertum

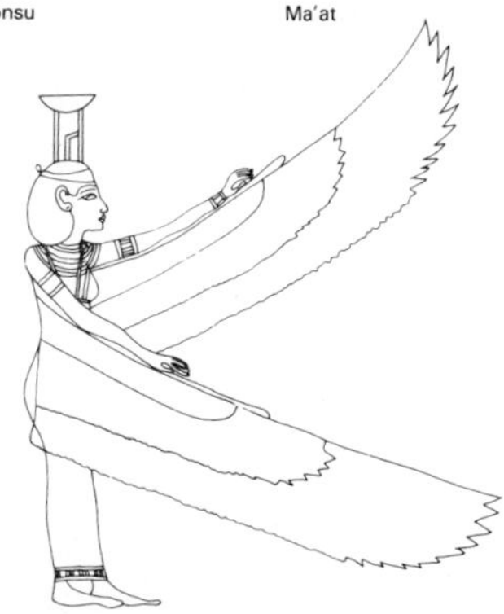

**Nephthys**

# EGYPTIAN GODS

Nun

Nut & Shu

**Osiris**

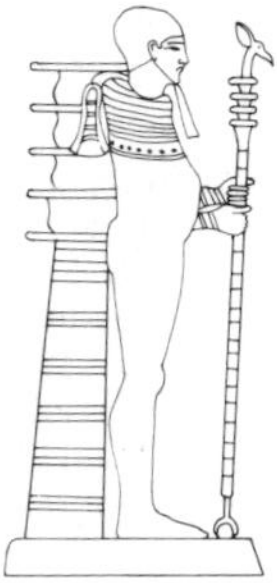

**Ptah**

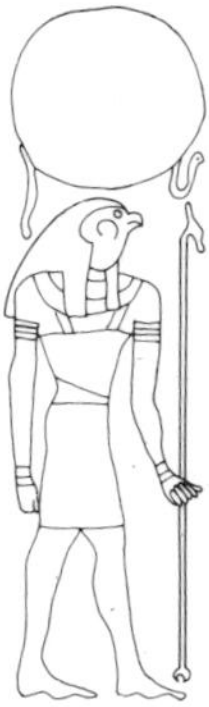

**Re'**

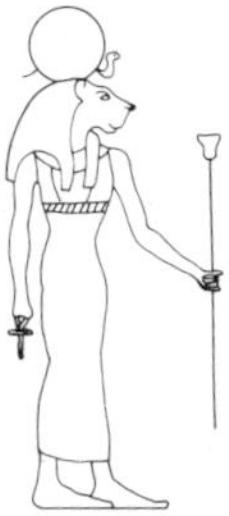

Sekhmet

Shu

Seshat

Sokar

**Thoth**

# Ancient Egyptian Language and Scripts

The Ancient Egyptian language is related not only to the Semitic languages (Arabic, Hebrew, Aramaic, etc.), but also to the group of East African languages of the Hamitic family (Somali, Galla, etc.). The structure of the language is Semitic and it shares, with others in this group, the fact that its word stems consist of triliteral forms. One of the most striking features of Egyptian grammar is its concrete realism and lack of interest in speculative thought. In fact it was difficult to express abstract ideas efficiently in Egyptian. The vocabulary, though rich, was not equally developed in all directions. The key that enabled translators to cope with

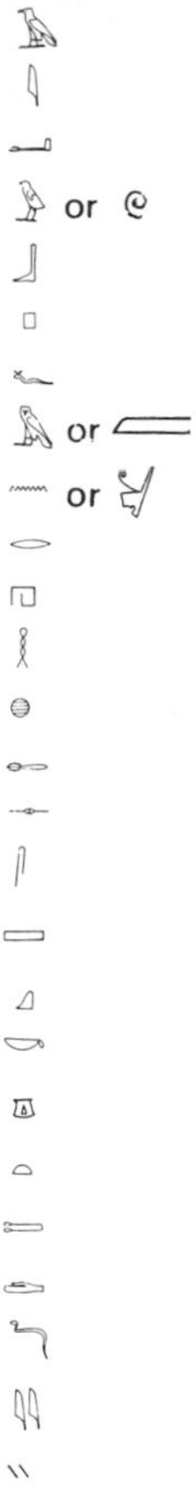

| Hieroglyph | Transliteration | Arabic equivalent |
|---|---|---|
| | a | alif |
| | y | yā |
| | e | ʿayn |
| or | u | wā |
| | b | bā |
| | p | |
| | f | fā |
| or | m | mīm |
| or | n | nūn |
| | r | rā |
| | h | hā |
| | h | ḥā |
| | kh | khā |
| | h (ch) | |
| | s | |
| | s | sīn |
| | sh | shīn |
| | q | qāf |
| | k | kāf |
| | g | gīm |
| | t | tā |
| | th (tsh) | |
| | d | dāl |
| | z (dj) | |
| | y | |
| | ï | |

*The hieroglyphic alphabet, only a fraction of the symbols used in the hieroglyphic system*

Egyptian was the very strict word order and a certain formality that existed throughout the whole period.

The history of the written language is very protracted with differences and developments throughout the period. The main form of writing was a pictorial script known as *Hieroglyphic* (Gk hieros; sacred, and glupho; sculptured), an offshoot of pictorial art. In the beginning hieroglyphs were used for all purposes, on temple walls, stelae, tombs, seals, ivory tablets and potsherds, and were elaborately carved and coloured, but as time went on this writing was confined more or less to monumental purposes, such as official inscriptions on temple walls, although for religious use it was still employed, even on papyrus.

Two classes of signs used in hieroglyphic writing need to be distinguished. These are *ideograms* (sense-signs), which indicate either the actual object that is depicted or something closely related, and *phonograms* (sound-signs), approximating to an alphabet, which therefore meant the pictures did not denote the thing portrayed but indicated something entirely different, perhaps not easily represented pictorially, which happened to have the same sound. For example, the name of Narmer, one of the earliest of the kings, was written on the Narmer Palette by means of the *n'r* (fish) and *mr* (chisel).

In the course of time another script evolved from the hieroglyphic, known as *Hieratic* (Gk hieratikos; priestly), because it was the script used by the priests for their records. It originated in the Old Kingdom and developed from the cursive form of hieroglyphic written with a reed pen. During the Old and Middle Kingdoms it is usually found inscribed on papyrus. Religious texts began to be written in this script about the 21 Dyn.

The last form of cursive script to be developed was the *Demotic* (Gk demotikos; popular). Originally called Enchorial (native), it was first used in the 15 Dyn. and by the Roman period was the normal form of script.

Because of the great length of time for which hieroglyphs were employed for writing, it is necessary to distinguish the following linguistic stages.

*Old Egyptian*: is the language used in the 1–8 Dyns (3100–2160 BC). Mainly official and written in a special orthography, it was used for religious texts and tomb inscriptions, including biographies, funeral formulae and seals.

*Middle Egyptian*: is the classical form of the Egyptian language and forms the basis of all other studies. It was based on the language used in the 11–12 Dyns (c 2133–1786 BC) but later became corrupted with new popular elements. It was retained for monumental and literary purposes right down to the Ptolemaic-Roman period.

*Late Egyptian*: the vernacular of the 18–24 Dyns (1567–715 BC), was used for the official inscriptions from the 19 Dyn. onwards and for literary compositions and business and legal documents; it contains many foreign words. This developed by gradual transformation into Coptic.

*The Rosetta Stone. A copy of a decree passed at Memphis by a general council of Egyptian priests to commemorate the first anniversary of Ptolomy V Epiphanes in 196 BC. It is in two languages Greek and Egyptian (in two scripts hieroglyphic and demotic). It was discovered at Rashid by Napoleon's expedition in 1799 and was the key used by Champollion and Young in their decipherment of the hieroglyphic script (Trustees of the British Museum)*

# Ancient Egyptian Art

## I. Architecture

The early Egyptian builders used the materials closest to hand, mud and reeds, and as the climate was almost rainless the early settlers needed only lean-to shelters to protect them against the wind in winter and the sun in summer. Thus wattle and daub, used even today in parts of Egypt for walls of yards and shelters in fields, was the basis of Egyptian architecture, and this material influenced all later buildings. Another example is the interlaced palm fronds of the lattice which when tied together formed a waving coping to the wall, producing a characteristic shape which, when translated into stone, became the frieze called *kheker*, to be seen in many of the royal and private tomb-chapels. Wood has always been scarce and the larger timber has always had to be imported. None of the very early buildings has survived but there is a contemporary clay model of a Naqada II house showing it to be of lattice and mud, and many representations of 1 Dyn. shrines made of the same material have been found at Abydos. The latter, which seem to have been of a more open latticework pattern, formed the basis for the shrines of Upper and Lower Egypt, the national sanctuaries used throughout the historic period made in many different materials.

Reeds proved too pliant to act satisfactorily as supports for later roofs even when coated with mud, and thus the question of suitable supports arose as soon as sizeable houses were constructed. The front of the porch of the houses needed columns which were made by tying together bundles of papyrus stems. These have a triangular section, and to form a column the Egyptians tied several together, lashing them with cord just below the heads. When these were later copied in stone, an unexpected result was that the architects duplicated everything, including the curve at the top where the original supported the roof: this was the capital. Below this were the lashings in five stylised bands. The base of the pillar bulged, emulating that in the original.

The use of the stone column in Egyptian architecture dates to the 3 Dyn., although some of the early columns were engaged. There are two main types of column, both of early origin. The first type, the square-sectioned pillar, probably derived from the supporting sections left in the limestone quarries, and was later used in temples and tombs. The second type of column derives from vegetable forms, such as tied bundles of papyrus or lotus and palm trunks. These are first found in papyrus form at Zozer's Step Pyramid Enclosure at Ṣaqqārah (Rte 25), though engaged, as the craftsmen had no idea of the tensile strength of limestone. At this site there are also polygonal ribbed and fluted columns, again engaged in pairs. The first step towards turning the square pillar or column into the polygonal must have been the cutting off of the angles of the square pillars as seen at Deir al-Baḥrī in the 11 Dyn. Temple of Menthuhotpe (Rte 36). These, and the 12 Dyn. columns at Beni Hassan (Rte 31) and those of Hatshepsut's temple also at Deir al-Baḥrī, were called 'Proto-Doric' by Champollion. Many of the Egyptian columns do not taper upwards like the Greek, and they are not all fluted, many having flat facets. Probably both Egyptian and Greek polygonal columns developed

## EGYPTIAN COLUMNS

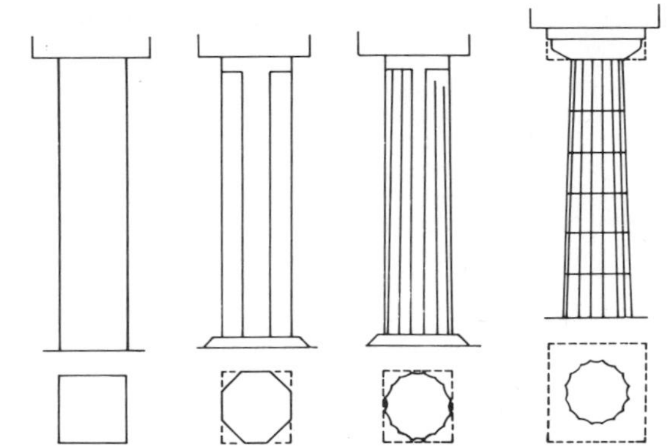

Square-sectioned pillar | Octagonal pillar 11 Dyn. | 16-sided pillar 12-18 Dyns | Greek Doric pillar

independently from the same prototype, the quarry support, but the former are over two thousand years earlier than the latter.

The shaft of the plant column varied with the different form of plant model, which also produced characteristic capitals. The papyrus column had the shaft marked with triangles, where it left the base, and a closed capital with the ridges of the original bundled plant form showing on the ribs; the lotus column had rounded stems and the capital could be either open or closed. The palm column had a plain shaft with a palm leaf capital. These were the classic forms of Egyptian column. In the later Ptolemaic and Roman periods the composite type of column became common; derived from earlier columns but with many added plant forms, they became extremely complicated with as many as 27 different varieties having been noted. The only type remaining practically unchanged was the palm column. Other types of column used for special purposes were those topped with a sistrum capital, or with a representation of the goddess Hathor, or the god Bes. The column was always furnished with either a rounded or square pedestal to the ground, the capitals were always capped with a simple square abacus which joined them to the architrave. Although usually of stone, the columns could be of wood, as at al-ʿAmārnah, and were decorated and painted in bright colours—red, blue, green and yellow. While the smaller earlier columns were made from stone monoliths, they were later sectioned with regularly shaped drums, keyed together, with wood, lead or copper. Many of the joints can be seen today but the key material has been long since stolen.

The Egyptians discovered that they could span spaces up to about 3m with limestone, but wider spans required granite. When they adopted building in sandstone in the New Kingdom, the weight it could bear was unknown and so they tended to make the buildings over-heavy and massive, with a greater danger of collapse than there had been earlier when using limestone and granite. Because of this uncertainty Egyptian architects tended to use a forest of columns to support the roof. In the

## EGYPTIAN COLUMNS

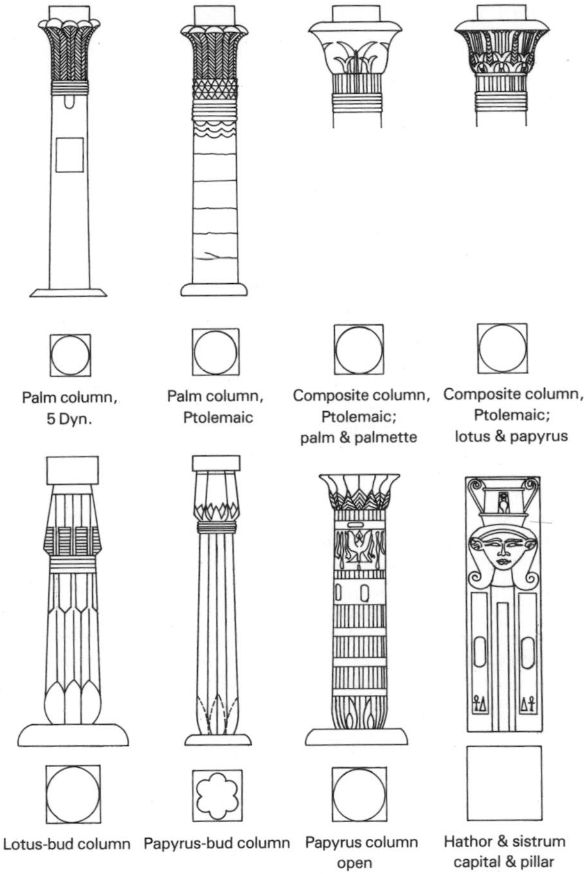
Palm column, 5 Dyn.
Palm column, Ptolemaic
Composite column, Ptolemaic; palm & palmette
Composite column, Ptolemaic; lotus & papyrus
Lotus-bud column
Papyrus-bud column
Papyrus column open
Hathor & sistrum capital & pillar

hypostyle hall at Karnak, for instance, there are 134 columns, the centre aisle being higher to allow for clerestory windows for light and ventilation.

The architectural style of Ancient Egypt arose out of a desire to harmonise with the natural landscape, so that the flat roofed buildings appeared as if they grew out of the background. The arts of sculpture and wall painting developed as adjuncts of the builder's craft. There are two main kinds of architecture in Egypt, domestic and religious.

*Domestic Buildings.* The remains of domestic constructions are limited as the ancient towns lie in many cases beneath modern cities and have not been excavated; or else (where they are away from modern settlements, as in the Delta) they have been largely removed by the sabakkin who take soil from the ancient sites to spread on fields to act as fertilizer. It is possible, however, to reconstruct the appearance of Ancient Egyptian houses, as we have many illustrations in the tombs, particularly of the 18 Dyn. They were built of unbaked mud-brick and must have looked very like the village houses seen today. The better class houses were set in gardens, of which the Egyptians were always very fond, with a pool of water surrounded by sycamore-fig or persea trees. Houses were constructed of mud-brick because of its availability and because the Egyptians were not concerned with their permanency.

This was also true of their palaces which were made of the same material, as in the palaces of Amenhotep III at Malqatta on the West Bank at Thebes and Akhenaten at al-ʿAmarnah (Rte 32). The palaces of the ancient world were more than the habitation of the king, they also encompassed vast storehouses where the goods in kind with which the royal retainers were paid—grain, oil, wine and dried fish—were kept. But though the walls were of mud-brick, rooms were large and decorated with painted walls, and domestic quarters were carefully separated from state apartments.

*Religious Buildings*. From the remotest historic period temples and tombs were built of stone, 'to last forever'. From the earliest times there were two types of temple, the state temple erected to the principal god of the region, and the mortuary temple devoted to the worship of the dead king. In the Old and Middle Kingdom, the latter was attached to the king's pyramid, but in the New Kingdom it became divorced from the tomb, which was at that time cut into rock, and became a copy of the main state temple.

The original mortuary temples, as at Maydūm (Rte 27) and Dahshūr (Rte 26), were very simple structures of one or two rooms, joined to the valley temple by a causeway, but during the 4–6 Dyns they developed an entry court, a main colonnaded court, store rooms, five niches for statues and a sanctuary. No two mortuary temples were exactly alike, but all were stone-built except at Dahshūr, with walls of limestone or granite, columns of granite, and floors of alabaster, with the windows set high in the walls. By the New Kingdom the mortuary temples consisted, like the state temples, of one or more pylons, or ornamental gateways, leading to colonnaded courtyards which in turn led to one or more hypostyled halls followed by vestibules and finally the sanctuary; the inner rooms were surrounded by store rooms or treasuries. The most complete is at Edfu (Rte 37), though the most impressive hypostyle hall is that at Karnak (Rte 36). The Old and Middle Kingdoms used limestone as the main building material along with granite, the New Kingdom sandstone.

The planning of each temple—called *pr-ntr* (house of the god) or *hwt-ntr* (castle of the god)—was divinely guided and was laid out by the king with the aid of the goddess Seshat. The ground was carefully prepared and purified, and a large pit dug covered with fresh sand in which were placed the temple foundations. Scenes of the rituals concerned with the founding of the temple were usually shown in the hypostyle hall. Under the corners and at the doorways were placed foundation deposits consisting of faience and metal bricks, animal and bird offerings and metal tools.

Each temple was constructed so that the floors rose from the front to the sanctuary at the rear: thus each chamber had a ramp or steps at a slightly higher level than the one below. This was so that the sanctuary, theoretically built above one of the primaeval mounds that rose from the original flood, would be at the highest point of the building. To mark the difference between the sacred and the profane areas the sanctuary was isolated as though it was an independent building, a kind of box inside the main structure, with a roof and cavetto cornice distinct from the main roof. In the sanctuary stood the travelling boats of the deities in which they journeyed from temple to temple. Many of the temples had crypts with beautifully carved walls, where much of the best regalia was kept.

All temples must have had chapels on their roofs, but they now only survive in the late temples of Dendarah (Rte 34), Philae (Rte 39) and the Hibis Temple at Khargah (Rte 48) though Denderah was an early foundation whose original building goes back to the Predynastic period. One of these roof chapels was connected with the 'Union with the Disk', when the statues of the gods worshipped were brought up on days such as the New Year Festival, and revitalised by being exposed to the rays of the sun. Other chapels on the roof were connected with the resurrection of Osiris. All temples were surrounded by temenos walls of mud-brick or stone, and within the enclosure lived the priests. There was also a sacred lake or well, and numerous storerooms and there must also have been stabling for the animals. The slaughter court attached to the temple for the killing of the sacrifices was usually entered from the outside.

Sculpture was an integral part of the temples. Statues of the kings were made, often of colossal size to stand inside or in a row at the entry. These were thought to guard the entrance and to act as constant intercessors with the gods, as were sphinxes, usually with a human head on a lion's body (see Giza, Rte 23).

*Tombs.* Originally the tombs were mere graves cut in the soil or in the sand on the desert escarpment. However, as time went on the desire to preserve the body after death led to tombs of one or more chambers being constructed. The early royal tombs at Ṣaqqārah had substructures of mud-brick consisting of several chambers, with the burial chamber at the centre. This was surrounded by store rooms, in which have been found hundreds of stone and pottery vases. They were roofed with timber beams and had a superstructure also consisting of several rooms filled with offerings. Both these and the similar cenotaph-like buildings at Abydos have been burnt, so that it is difficult to see what the full royal collections would have been. These tombs are now called mastabas (Ar. bench) from their similarity to the mud-brick seat found outside most Egyptian peasants' houses. By the 3 Dyn. these mastaba tombs were used also for the burials of nobles and high officials, the superstructure built of stone instead of mud-brick, and the body placed in a chamber at the foot of a shaft leading down from either the courtyard, or from a room containing the false door which usually contained the name and titles of the deceased. Alternatively the upper class citizens could be buried in rock-cut tombs, as they were in the provinces; again the upper chamber, or chambers, served as a chapel, and the body was placed at the foot of a shaft leading down from one of these rooms. The servants and officials of these nobles were later buried in shaft graves cut near to their masters. In the same way the king's officials and members of his family were buried round the king's pyramid. These were known as mastaba fields or pyramid cities, but they were really cities of the dead.

The pyramid was the logical development from the mastaba. The ease with which mastaba tombs were robbed prompted the kings to build larger and heavier structures which the tomb robbers would not be able to enter. This trend had already started by the 2 Dyn. but the first stepped pyramid was not built at Ṣaqqārah until the 3 Dyn.; this was built to Zozer's order by the chief of works Imhotep and was the first building in Egypt to be constructed entirely in stone. In many ways it is unique, with a large enclosure, the walls representing 'the white walls of Memphis' recessed and buttressed like the facade of the earlier mud-brick mastabas. Within the enclosure was a mortuary temple, but no causeway has been found so that there may not have been a valley temple. Beginning with a mastaba, Imhotep built a stepped pyramid with seven stages, standing at one end of the sacred enclosure. The bulk of the enclosure is empty but there are a large number of religious buildings to the east of Zozer's temple and a vast complex of underground passages terminating in a granite chamber which was the king's burial place. It took the Department of Antiquities three years to empty the underground galleries of the large number of stone vases. Many of the galleries and the 'Southern Tomb' are lined with blue faience tiles and the pyramid was laced with Lebanese cedar to strengthen it.

The best known pyramids are those at Giza, but between these and the Ṣaqqārah Step Pyramid stretched a series of monuments, starting with the second unfinished Step Pyramid of Sekhemket, also of the 3 Dyn. (Rte 25). The last pyramid of this dynasty was that of Hu, who built a splendid monument on the edge of the desert at Maydūm (Rte 27). Snefru, first king of the 4 Dyn., built two stone pyramids at Dahshūr, almost as large as those at Giza.

However, nothing can compare with the size and impressiveness of the three pyramids of Khufu, Khafre and Menkhaure, built on the desert edge at Giza. These were built with the aid of ramps, and the size of the stones had greatly increased from the small blocks used at Ṣaqqārah to those weighing several tons.

Although stone continued to be used throughout the 5 and 6 Dyns the great period of pyramid building was over. Attempts had been made in these pyramids to defeat the tomb robbers by the use of portcullises, but without success. Equally unsuccessful was the use of supposedly impenetrable granite for the burial chamber.

The rulers of the 11 Dyn. at Thebes used rock-cut tombs but those of the 12 Dyn. returned to the pyramid. These were built at Lisht (Rte 27), Hawārah (Rte 29), Lāhūn (Rte 29) and Dahshūr (Rte 26) of brick, faced with stone. The outer casing of these has been robbed and the mud-brick core is in many cases very ruined. The tombs of the New Kingdom rulers were cut into the rock and extended sometimes for hundreds of metres into the limestone hillside, as in the Valley of the Kings (Rte 36) at Thebes. These tombs were decorated with scenes from the 'Book of the Dead' or 'That which is in the Am-Duat' or the 'Book of the Gates' and the scenes were entirely concerned with the journey to the Afterworld. The tomb-chapels of the nobles were also painted and decorated but in the 18 Dyn. portrayed scenes of their everyday life. Funeral scenes were also included, but it was not until the 19–20 Dyns that the officials' tombs became almost entirely concerned with the Afterworld. The tombs of the workmen who were engaged on the royal tombs consisted of a small chapel with pyramid roof at the top of a shaft leading to one or more painted chambers.

Pyramids, which went out of fashion for royal burials after the 12 Dyn., were revived by the 25 Dyn. but, as these rulers came from Kush, these tombs were built not in Egypt proper, but in the Sudan at Napata. Very few royal burials after the 20 Dyn. have been discovered, except for a few built tombs at Tanis dating to the 21–22 Dyns (Rte 45). This is because the capital was moved from Thebes to different Delta cities, and most of the royal tombs seem to have been destroyed.

*Fortresses.* The earliest surviving fortress structures appear to be at Abydos and Kom Ahmar (Hierakonpolis). They were built of mud-brick, and have only survived because of the dry Egyptian climate. The finest group of fortresses was in Nubia between the First and Second Cataracts, and in the Second Cataract region. These were built either on promontories overlooking the river, or on islands, and had every kind of defensive device, moats, glacis, round towers with archery slits, drawbridges and ramps leading up to the ramparts for rapid movement. Inside they were laid out in an orderly manner, with roads and two- or three-roomed houses for the soldiers, and a slightly larger one for the commander. There was usually a temple and store rooms, as these forts served a double purpose, protecting the frontiers and as trading posts. Unfortunately with the building of the new High Dam these unique 2 mill. BC structures have been destroyed, as there was no means of moving them.

*Architectural developments.* The Egyptians constructed flat-topped buildings not because they were unaware of the arch but from aesthetic preference. The entrances were usually crowned by a cavetto cornice surmounted by a flat band and this architectural device, so common in Egyptian temples and tombs, was even translated into small objects as many pectorals are of this form. Although the vault and arch were used for house building, they were rarely employed for religious buildings, and this is one of the reasons that so few have survived. The arch was known from the 2 Dyn. and the corbelled vault from the 3 Dyn.; they are found within the pyramids of Hu at Maydūm (Rte 27) and Sneferu at Dahshūr (Rte 26). The Egyptian architects evolved the rounded arch as early as the 3 Dyn. but it was never used where it could be seen externally. It was built of mud-brick, and was a true arch made by setting the voussoirs in their correct place, but the bricks were not shaped to fit, and the gaps between them filled with mud mortar. In stone a kind of false arch was used, as at the temple of Seti I at Abydos (Rte 36), where a flat block of stone was cut into an arch shape. The corbelled arch is not known in ancient brickwork, but appears in stone by the 3 Dyn.

Tombs were built in the desert where the ground was firm, but temples and dwelling houses were built on ground that was annually innundated, causing many problems to the Egyptian builders. The walls were built of moulded sun-dried mud-brick of standard size (different sizes denoting various periods), but not till Roman times did baked bricks occur in large numbers. In building mud-brick walls the surface was usually made with a batter upon one side, so that the base was considerably wider than the top to counteract the movement of the ground. When the Egyptians started building in stone in the 3 Dyn. they copied this form, thus giving the later architecture its characteristic appearance. They also counteracted the effects of ground water by building the walls in sections, without bonding them together, thus enabling them to rise and fall independently, as with the walls at Karnak. Another method was 'pan-bedding', with curved courses of bricks; walls of this type can be seen at Denderah (Rte 34).

## II. Sculpture

Sculpture in the round evolved early in Egypt. The Ancient Egyptians were fortunate in that many of the rocks required for the raw material of their work were indigenous to the country. Thus limestone was available through a large part of the valley, diorite was obtainable in Nubia, while the best form of alabaster came from the Hatnub quarries near al-ʿAmārnah, and red granite came from Aswan. Once sculpture developed from the small statuette to the full-sized figure, it became part of architectural decoration. Statues were not regarded as an end in themselves but only as part of the whole and thus are found only in temples, or tombs serving a religious purpose. They were not meant to be seen close up, or in a good light and usually conform to the rectangular setting of the building for which they were designed. The Colossi of Memnon (Rte 36) were never intended as free-standing figures, but to front the Temple of Amenhotep III, now completely destroyed. Because they were intended as architectural pieces on a scale that matches the landscape they are not dwarfed.

Royal figures sculptured in the round are either solitary, usually walking, or seated with their hand on their knees, or paired with their wives, both seated, standing or kneeling and usually holding some offering. Private statues that come mainly from tombs have certain forms that do not appear in the royal work, like the kneeling or seated scribe, and the family, father, mother and small children. Many of these in the Old Kingdom are of limestone, painted to represent life, or of wood. There must have been many more wooden statues, but few have survived due to destruction by termites, which have also damaged many of those which have lasted.

Colossal statues, although known from the Old Kingdom onwards, do not become common until the New Kingdom, post-1575 BC. Composite statues are also common in the New Kingdom. As well as stone, wood and metal, usually copper, were used for life-size figures, but only fragments of most of this type remain. An exception is the statue of Pepi I, 2332 BC, slightly more than life-size, now in the Cairo Museum. There is a certain amount of controversy as to whether Egyptian sculptures were portraits or not: some certainly were, but the royal ones in the 18 Dyn. were probably somewhat idealised.

## III. Reliefs

Like sculpture, relief was also architectural in inspiration. In the Old Kingdom wall sculpture was usually in bas-relief, where the background is cut away. The figures were then worked up until the right amount of modelling had been achieved and finally painted. Several forms of sunken relief were also used, the outline and model cut as in raised relief but without lowering the background. Thus only the highest parts of the modelled surface are on a level with the background, while the outline can be cut down to any depth, sometimes as much as 2–3cm. This was a much quicker operation than bas-relief and consequently cheaper, and outright sunken relief was used particularly for inscriptions from the Old Kingdom onwards. For instance, by convention the interior decoration of the hypostyle hall was done in bas-relief, the outside walls in sunken relief. Under the New Kingdom nearly all Seti I's work was done in bas-relief, whereas that of his son Ramesses II was done in sunken relief. In the Old Kingdom sunken relief was used for the outer rooms of mastabas and for the inscriptions on the false doors, whereas bas-reliefs was used if possible for the chapel. All were intended to be painted, although this was not always done.

In the Old Kingdom most of the decoration was in relief, little of it merely painting, but in the Middle and New Kingdoms painting greatly increased. It was even quicker and cheaper than sunken relief and was used for ceilings and for depicting the painted mats that decorated tombs from the 1 Dyn. onwards. Painting was never an art in itself, but always subordinate to sculpture and reliefs.

## IV. Painting

Egyptian wall paintings are often described as frescoes but this technique was never used in Egypt and all paintings were executed on a dry surface. The earliest paintings were made on mud-coated plaster, the later ones on gypsum or lime plaster. The colours used were all natural minerals, malachite for the greens, ochres or haematite for reds and yellows, white from gypsum, black from soot, and blue, a royal colour, from pounded lapis, faience or carbonate of copper. Sometimes egg white was used as a bond. Much more work needs to be done analysing the colours and methods used.

In drawing, the first sketch was made in red by the master craftsman, corrections were shown in black, and the Egyptians early became masters of the straight line. Corrections were difficult to hide: they could be cut away or plastered over and painted, but sometimes the plaster has fallen away and the original mistakes exposed: these are clearly seen in several scenes shown on the walls of Madīnat Habu (Rte 36).

Although the Egyptians squared out the walls of the temples and tombs they were about to decorate, they had considerable difficulty in representing the frontal human form. There was little true perspective, although it does occur in isolated instances, as at al-ʿAmarnah in the painting of the two princesses, and in the temple of Seti I at Abydos. Distances were shown by representing the scene in registers, the desert at the top, the main scenes in the middle, and the river at the bottom. The craftsmen drew from memory and human figures were almost invariably represented with the face in profile, very few figures are ever shown full face, but they had much more success with animals and plants. Although the names of many of the Egyptian architects are known, the same is not true for the artist-craftsmen who adorned the temples and tombs.

CANON. A canon of proportion was followed by the Egyptians which varied slightly at different periods. The measurements were never taken to the top of the head, but from the hairline, or where the headdress began: on the upright standing or walking male figure this was the standard. In the Old Kingdom it was 9 units from the head to the foot, calculated as follows: hair to shoulder 1 unit, shoulder to the hem of kilt 5 units, hem of kilt to ground 3 units. In many of the tombs where the paintings are unfinished the squared background can be observed. Thus in the Tomb-Chapel of Ukht-hetep at Meir there are 18 squares from the edge of the hair to the foot.

The Middle Kingdom figures are not so squat as those of the Old Kingdom but in the New Kingdom there is a return to the 9-unit form with an extra half unit for the upper part of the head. At al-ʿAmarnah the proportions are slightly different as the head is much larger than the standard one ninth of the body. In the 26 Dyn. the canon changed from 18 to 21 squares, the head occupying just over two squares and thus being smaller in proportion.

COSTUME. There is considerable variety in the headdresses and kilts of the various periods, so that even without an inscription, usually on the back pillar and the base, it is quite easy to make ascriptions to the correct period. In the Old Kingdom wigs were usually tightly curled close to the head, or parted in the middle and worn shoulder length, while kilts were of a plain and simple design. Women wore plain long skirts with two straps over the shoulders. In the Middle Kingdom the design of the knotting on the wig changed, and although shoulder length hair was still worn the proportions were not the same as the Old Kingdom. In the New Kingdom hair styles became much more elaborate, lotus buds and flowers were often worn in the hair, and the kilts became longer and more closely pleated.

The kings wore a great variety of headdresses. The most usual was the nemes head cloth, a blue and white striped linen covering with lappets. These are even in the Old Kingdom, irregular in the Middle Kingdom, and on seated figures from the latter are unstriped. In the New Kingdom many headdresses were worn, including the blue war helmet or crown (khepresh) and the royal head-cloth (afnet). The main crowns were the white crown (hedet) of Upper Egypt, the red crown (desret) of Lower Egpyt, and the two combined to form the double crown (shemti; Gk pschent). The gods also wore crowns such as the atef crown of Osiris, which consisted of the white crown, two ostrich plumes and a sun disk on top. Towards the end of the period under the Ptolemies the numbers of crowns increased very greatly and the divine and the royal ones became hopelessly mixed up.

## V. Stone Vases

Because stone vases were so much used in Egypt, the drawing of the craftsman making them was the hieroglyphic for workman. Vases occur in large numbers from Predynastic times onwards. Under the 1 Dyn., as well as the softer limestones and alabasters, a large number of very hard stones were used, including porphyry, red breccia, marble, basalt, diorite, granite, syenite and serpentine, and even quartz. Later in the Dynastic period use of some of these very hard stones, such as porphyry, was abandoned and did not come into fashion again until the Roman period. Most of the vases were in simple bold shapes and were made with the bow-drill. In some of the tombs models of vases made of wood, but painted to represent stone, have been found.

## VI. Pottery

Unlike that of Greece, Egyptian pottery never developed into a fine art. The best vases are to be found in the Predynastic period, where the forms are sufficiently distinct to serve as criteria for the change of period, as between Naqada I and Naqada II. In Dynastic Egypt all the pottery tends to be of brown or red fabric with little stylistic variation except for some fine painted pieces in the late 18 Dyn. Even in the Hellenistic period the Egyptians did not move entirely into the main-stream of Greek pottery design. During both the Ptolemaic and Roman periods the bulk of the wares was locally produced, although there were some red-figured imported pots and a vast number of Hellenistic jar stamps, originating from the Greek islands which exported their wines to Egypt; in fact more have come to light here than elsewhere in the Greek world.

# Index of Egyptologists

AMELINEAU (Émile) 1850–1915. French. Clergyman. Professor at École des Hautes Études. Excav Abydos. Main work in Coptic Studies.

BAIKIE (James) 1866–1931. Minister. Writer and lecturer. Wrote *Egyptian Antiquities in the Nile Valley*, 1932.

BELZONI (Giovanni Battista) 1778–1823. Italian. Strong-man and explorer. His extraordinary career took him the length and breadth of Egypt. Made many discoveries including the town of Berenike and Tomb of Seti I at Thebes. Died searching for the source of the Niger.

BIRCH (Samuel) 1813–85. Keeper at the BM. Introduced Champollion system of decipherment into England. Over three hundred written works.

BISSING (Freidrich Wilhelm von) *Frieherr*, 1873–1956. German. Professor at Munich. Excav Abū Ghurāb. Over six hundred written works.

BLACKMAN (Aylward Manley) 1883–1956. Professor at Liverpool. Recorded the temples of Bigeh, Dendur and al-Derr for Arch. Survey of Nubia.

BONOMI (Joseph) 1796–1878. Artist and traveller. Much work for Egyptologists including Lane and Wilkinson. Set up hieroglyphic fount for Birch's dictionary.

BORCHARDT (Lugdwig) 1863–1938. German. Founder and Director of German Inst. of Archaeology. Excav Abū Ghurāb, Abū Ṣīr and al-ʿAmārnah.

BREASTED (James Henry) 1865–1935. American. Professor at Chicago where he set up Oriental Institute. Published many works including *Ancient Records* and *History of Egypt*, 1905.

BRUCE (James) 1730–94. Traveller, discovered Tomb of Ramesses III at Thebes (called Bruce's Tomb).

BRUGSCH (Émile) *Pasha*, 1842–1930. German. Brother of Henrich, next Asst. Curator at the EM (Bulāq). First to enter Royal Cache at Deir al-Baḥarī.

BRUGSCH (Heinrich) 1827–1894. German. Professor at Gottingen, Principal of Khedival School of Egyptology. Excav Ṣaqqārah. Many writings including *Dictionary of Hieroglyphics and Demotic.*

BRUNTON (Guy) 1878–1948. Asst. Keeper at EM. Excav al-Lāhūn and Badārī.

BUDGE (Ernest Alfred Thompson Wallis) 1857–1934. Keeper at the BM. Travelled widely. Many works including translations of Ancient Semitic and Egyptian texts.

BURCKHARDT (John Lewis) 1784–1817. Swiss. Traveller. Journeyed extensively through the Middle East disguised as Sh. Ibrāhīm. Discovered Abū Simbel in 1817.

CALLENDER (Arthur) 18–1931. Engineer. Manager of Egyptian Branch Railways. Assisted Carter in excav of Tomb of Tutankhamun.

CALVERLY (Amice Mary) 1896–1959. Artist. Copied and published the scenes in the Temple of Seti I at Abydos.

CARNARVON *see* HERBERT

CAPART (Jean) 1877–1947. Belgian. Professor at Liège and Director of Musées Royaux du Cinquantaire. Excav al-Kāb. Many books on Egyptian art.

CARTER (Howard) 1874–1939. Field director for Lord Carnarvon. Excav al-ʿAmārnah, Beni Ḥasan and Deir al-Baḥrī. Discovered the Tomb of Tutankhamun in 1922. He worked on clearing the tomb for ten years but due to the death of Carnarvon he never completely published it.

CAVIGLIA (Giovanni Battista) 1770–1845. Genoese/Maltese. Worked for Salt and Vyse. Excav the Sphinx and Pyramids.

ČERNY (Jaroslav) 1898–1970. Czech. Professor at London. Specialised in late Egyptian. Excav Workmen's Village at Deir al-Madīnah. Publications include a *Coptic Etymological Dictionary* and *Ancient Egyptian Religion*.

CHAMPOLLION (Jacques Joseph Figeac) 1778–1867. French. Brother of the next. Archaeologist. Undertook publication of his brother's material after the latter's early death.

CHAMPOLLION (Jean François) 1790–1832. French. Professor at Grenoble. First to decipher hieroglyphic script. Conducted a systematic survey of all the known ancient monuments in Egypt.

CHASSINAT (Émile Gaston) 1868–1948. French. Printer and archaeologist.

Director of IFAO. Excav Meir, Dendera, Asyūṭ and Abū Ruwāsh. Many publications including the Edfu texts.

CLARKE (Somers) 1841–1926. Architect to St Paul's Cathedral. Excav El-Kāb, Kom al-Ahmar and in Nubia. Pubs on Nubian churches and, with Engelbach, *Ancient Egyptian Masonry*.

DARESSY (Georges Émile Jules) 1864–1938. French. Asst Keeper EM. Excav Thebes, and restoration at Luxor. Pubs include works on mummification of humans and animals.

DAVIES (Anna Nina MacPherson) 1881–1965. Wife of next. Artist. Recorded many Theban tomb chapels. Pubs include three vols of the Theban Tomb series and other works on Egyptian art.

DAVIES (Norman de Garis) 1865–1941. Egyptologist. Copied many tombs for the EEF at Sh. Saʿīd, Deir al-Gabrāwī and al-ʿAmārnah. Published many reports of tomb clearance.

DAVIS (Theodore) 1837–1915. American. Businessman. Excav Valley of the Kings, discovered several royal tombs.

DAWSON (Warren Royal) 1888–1968. Broker and historian. Studied Egyptian medicine. Pubs, with G. Elliot Smith, *Egyptian Mummies*, and PHK Gray, *Catalogue of Egyptian Ants* in BM, vol I.

DE BUCK (Adriaan) 1892–1959. Dutch. Professor at Leiden. Main work on the Coffin Texts, 7 vols.

DE MORGAN (Jacques Jean Marie) 1857–1924. French. Engineer and archaeologist. Director of EAS. Excav Dahshūr and Naqādah. Published works on prehistory.

DENON (Dominique Vivant) *Baron*, 1747–1825. French. Antiquarian. Member of Napoleon's Institut d'Egypte. Director-General of Museums and greatly enhanced the French collections.

DE ROUGE (Oliver Charles Camille Emanuel) *Visconte*, 1811–72. French. Conservator at the Louvre and Professor at Grenoble. Founder of philological studies in French.

DRIOTON (Etienne Marie-Felix) 1889–1961. French. Professor at Institut Catholique and Conservator at the Louvre. Publications include *La Religion Egyptienne*, *Egypte Pharonique* and, with Vandier, *Histoire d'Egypte*.

DROVETTI (Bernardino) 1776–1852. Italian. Diplomat and collector. Colonel under Napoleon, French Consul-General. First collection including the Turin Papyrus now in Turin, second collection in Louvre.

EDGAR (Campbell Cowan) 1870–1938 Scots. Classical scholar, Egyptian Antiquities Service 1905–19, Keeper in EM 1919–37. Wrote several vols of Cairo catalogues on classical subjects.

EDWARDS (Amelia Anne Blanford) English author. Visited Egypt and Syria 1873–74. With help of Reginald Stuart Poole and Sir Erasmus Wilson formed the Egypt Exploration Fund (now EES), first secretary of EEF. Left money to University College (Lon) to found first chair in Egyptology and nominated Petrie as first holder. Wrote *One Thousand Miles up the Nile*.

EMERY (Walter Bryan) 1903–1971. Director of Arch. Survey of Nubia, Colonel in Military Intelligence, Diplomatic Service and Professor at London. Spent nearly fifty years in Egypt. Excav at al-ʿAmārnah, Armant, Wadi al-Sabū Ballānah, Qusṭul, Buhen and Ṣaqqārah.

ENGELBACH (Reginald) 1888–1946. Engineer. Chief Keeper at the EM. Excav Heliopolis, al-Lāhūn, Abū Ghurāb. Publications include register of the EM.

ERMAN (Jean Pierre Adolph) 1854–1937. German. Director at Berlin Mus. Reorganised Egyptian philological studies. Published a great amount of work.

FAIRMAN (H. W.) 1907–82. English. Professor of Egyptology at Liverpool University 1949–74. Worked at al-ʿAmārnah. Specialist in Ptolemaic and Roman texts.

FAKHRY (Ahmed) 1905–1973. Egyptian. Professor of Ancient Egyptian History at Cairo University. As director of Desert Research Dept. undertook excavs in the oases. Published *The Pyramids of Egypt* and *The Oases of Egypt* (3 vols).

FIRTH (Cecil Mallaby) 1878–1931. Lawyer. Inspector of Antiquities at Ṣaqqārah. Excav in Nubia and at Ṣaqqārah.

FISHER (Clarence Stanley) 1876–1941. American. Excav at Zāwiyat al-ʿAryān, Girgah, Giza, Denderah, Thebes and Memphis.

FRANKFORT (Henri) 1897–1954. Dutch. Professor at London, Director of Warburg Inst. Excav at al-ʿAmārnah, Abydos and Armant. Pub. many excav reports and archaeological studies.

GARDINER (Alan Henderson) *Sir*, 1879–1963. Egyptologist and epigraphist. Professor at Chicago. Publications include *Egyptian Grammar*, and with Weigall and de Garis Davis several vols in the Theban Private Tombs Series.

GARSTANG (John) 1876–1956. Professor at Liverpool. Excav at Beni Ḥasan, Hierakonpolis, Beit Khalaf and Meroe. Much work in Palestine and Turkey.

GAUTIER (Henri Louis Marie Alexandre) 1877–1950. French. Egyptologist. Inspector-General of the Delta and Secretary-General of the Mission Archaeologie Française (1927–37). Excav at Dra Abū ʾl-Nagaʿ and al-Qattah. Works include the inscriptions at Kalābshah and Wadi al-Sabūʿ, volumes of Catalogue of the EM.

GAYER-ANDERSON (Robert Glanville) *Major, Pasha*, 1881–1945. Administrator and collector. His collection is now in the Fitzwilliam Museum, Cambridge.

GLANVILLE (Stephen Ranulph Kingdon ) 1900–56. Assistant Keeper BM. Professor at Cambridge and London. Excav al-ʿAmārnah. Published articles and books including *The Legacy of Egypt*.

GOLENISCHEFF (Vladimir Samionovitch) 1856–1947. Russian. His collection now in Moscow. Published mainly on Egyptian papyri.

GONEIM (Zakaria) 1911–1959. Egyptian. Chief Inspector at Ṣaqqārah. Excav the Pyramid of Sekhemkhet. Drowned in the Nile.

GRIFFITH (Frances Llewellyn) 1862–1934. Professor at Oxford, founded the Griffith Institute at Oxford. Worked with Petrie. Excav Naukratis, Tell al-Yahūdiyyah. Best epigrapher of generation: published a number of texts.

GUNN (Battiscombe George) 1883–1950. Professor at Oxford. Excav with Engelbach and assisted Gardiner on the Onomastica.

HALL (Henry Reginald Holland) 1873–1930. Keeper at BM. Excav Abydos and Deir al-Baḥrī, other excav in Mesopotamia. Wrote *History of the Ancient Near East*.

HASSAN (Selim) 1886–1961. Egyptian. Professor at Cairo and Director of Dept of Ants. Excav Giza.

HAYES (William Christopher) 1903–63. American. Curator at Met N.Y. Excav Deir al-Baḥarī. Many publications including *The Scepter of Egypt*—a guide to the Met N.Y.

HERBERT (George Edward Stanhope Molyneux) *5th Earl of Carnarvon*, 1866–1923. Collector and amateur archaeologist. Excav on the W Bank at Thebes. Financed the excavations culiminating in the discovery of the Tomb of Tutankhamun.

HINCKS (Edward) *Rev.*, 1792–1866. Irish. Made major discoveries in the translation of both Assyrian and Egyptian languages.

HOLSCHER (Uvo) 1878–1963. German. Architect. Hon. Professor at Chicago. Excav Madinat Habu for Oriental Inst., Chicago. Published many works on the latter excavations.

JEQUIER (Gustave) 1868–1946. Swiss. Many tomb excavations. Published several books on architecture.

JUNKER (Herman) 1877–1962. German. Professor at Berlin, founded Inst. of Egyptian and African Studies at Vienna. Excav Tūrah Nubia and the second pyramid at Giza.

KEES (Herman Alexander Jakob) 1886–1964. German. Professor at Gottingen. Wrote over two hundred and fifty books and articles mainly on Egyptian history and religion.

LACAU (Pierre) 1873–1963. French. Worked on the catalogue of the EM. Director of the EM 1916–36.

LEFEBVRE (Eugene Jean-Baptiste Louis Joseph) 1838–1908. French. Inspector in EAS. Excav in Fayyūm and al-Maʿbdah. Published a number of texts.

LEFEBVRE (Gustave) 1879–1957. French. Director of Miss. Arch. Fr. Worked on the tombs in the Valley of the Kings which he published.

LEGRAIN (George) 1865–1917. French. Chief Inspector at Luxor. Recorded texts between Aswan and Kom Ombo; cleared and restored Karnak.

LEPSIUS (Karl Richard) 1810–84. German. Professor at Berlin, Director of Berlin Mus. Directed 1842 Prussian Expeditions to Egypt. Discovered the Decree of Canopus at Tanis. Pubs, the results of aforementioned expedition in twelve vols.

LORET (Victor) 1859–1946. French. Dir-Gen. of EAS. Worked on texts in Valley of the Kings. Began Dict. of hieroglyphics.

LUCAS (Alfred) 1867–1945. Chemist and restorer. Chemist to EAS. Instrumental in saving many of the objects from the Tomb of Tutankhamun.

LYONS (Henry George) *Sir*, 1864–1944. Officer, engineer and geologist. Director of Science Mus. London. Cleared temple of Buhen and strengthened temples at Philae.

LYTHGOE (Albert Morton) 1868–1934. American. Curator at Met N.Y. Excav Lisht, Thebes and other sites.

MACE (Arthur Cruttenden) 1874–1928. Australian. Assoc. Curator in Met N.Y. Excav Denderah, Hu, Abydos and Lisht. Assisted Carter in clearing Tutankhamun's tomb.

MACKAY (Ernest John Henry) 1880–1943. Archaeologist. Special Officer for Archaeological Survey of India. Photographic survey of the Theban Tombs.

MARIETTE (François Auguste Ferdinand) *Pasha*, 1821–1881. French. Founder of the Egyptian Department of Antiquities. Huge excavation programme at 35 sites in Egypt. Provided the plot for Verdi's *Aida* in 1871.

MASPERO (Gaston Camille Charles) *Sir*, 1846–1916. French. Dir. of EM and arranged and catalogued the collection in 50 vols. First to publish the Pyramid Texts among 1200 books and articles.

MILNE (Joseph Grafton) 1867–1951. Numismatist. Excavated at Thebes. Many articles on Greco-Roman Egyptian coins.

MINUTOLI (Heinrich Carl Menu von) *Baron*, 1772–1846. Prussian diplomat. Excav. at Ṣaqqārah. Large collection now in Louvre and Berlin.

MOND (Robert Ludwig) *Sir*, 1887–1938. Chemist and financier. Supported excavs and restoration at Thebes and also in Turkey and Palestine.

MONTET (Pierre) 1885–1966. French. Professor at Strasbourg. Excav Tanis. Published *Egyptian private lives as illustrated by tomb paintings*.

MORET (Alexandre) 1868–1938. Professor at Coll. de France. Specialised in Egyptian religion and wrote widely on Egyptian history.

MURRAY (Margaret Alice) 1863–1963. Lecturer at University College, London. Excav Abydos and Ṣaqqārah and other Mediterranean sites. Many books on Egyptology and anthropology.

MYRES (Oliver Humphrys) 1903–66. Archaeologist. Excav Mostagedda, Armant, later in Sudan. Publications include work on his excavations.

NAVILLE (Henri Edouard) 1844–1926. Swiss. Excav many sites in the Delta and also at Deir al-Baḥarī. Published many excavation reports and general articles.

NEWBERRY (Percy Edward) 1869–1949. Professor at Liverpool. Recorded at Beni Ḥasan, al-Bersha and at Thebes. Published many articles.

PEET (Thomas Eric) 1882–1934. Classicist. Professor at Liverpool. Excav at Abydos. Interested mainly in philology.

PENDLEBURY (John Devitt Stringfellow) 1904–41. Archaeologist. Excav Armant and al-ʿAmārnah. Shot by Germans in Crete.

PERRING (John Shae) 1813–1869. Engineer. Manager of Public Works for Muḥammad ʿAlī. Assisted Vyse in excav of pyramids at Giza.

PETRIE (Hilda Mary Isabel Flinders) *Lady*, 1871–1956. Wife of next. Hon. Sec. of British School of Archaeology. Excav Abydos and Ṣaqqārah.

PETRIE (William Matthew Flinders) *Sir*, 1853–1942. Edwards Professor at University College, London. Went to Egypt 1880. First to inaugurate systematic method of excav. in Egypt and excavated a vast number of sites. Trained a large body of Egyptologists and found evidence for the previously unknown Prehistoric cultures of Egypt. Published over 100 volumes of excavation reports. The most outstanding British field archaeologist to practise in Egypt.

PETTIGREW (Thomas Joseph) 1791–1865. Surgeon and antiquary. His main interest, mummification.

PIANKOFF (Alexandre) 1897–1966. Russian. Specialised in philology and religion. Proposed a new concept in understanding the texts in the royal tombs and shrines of Tutankhamun.

POOLE (Reginald Stuart) 1832–95. Orientalist. Keeper BM. Many articles on Egyptian subjects.

PORTER (Bertha) 1852–1941. Egyptologist. Compiled in 1927 with Dr Rosalind Moss the *Topographical bibliography of Ancient Egyptian hieroglyphic texts, reliefs and paintings*, which is still continuing.

PRISSE D'AVENNES (Achille Constant Theodore Emile) 1807–79. French. Engineer. Worked for Muḥ. ʿAlī and recorded many sites in Egypt. Discovered the Table of the Kings at Karnak.

QUIBELL (James Edward) 1867–1935. Insp. Gen. of Antiquities, Egypt. Excav Naqādah, Ballas, Hierakonpolis. Published a large number of excavation reports and worked on the catalogue of the EM.

REISNER (George Andrew) 1867–1942. American. Professor at Harvard. Supported by Mrs Hearst excavated at Giza, Zāwiyat al-ʿAryān and in the Sudan. His fully systematic excavations resulted in much of his work remaining unpublished.

ROEDER (Gunther) 1881–1966. German. Curator Berlin Mus. Excav Hermopolis. Specialised in Egyptian religion. Published one volume of Catalogue of EM and many other works.

ROSELLINI (Niccolo Francesco Ippolito Baldessare) 1800–43. Italian. Founder of Egyptology in Italy. Accompanied Champollion to Egypt. Published on Monuments of Egypt and Nubia.

ROWE (Alan) 1891–1968. Australian. Curator Greco-Roman Mus. Alex. Lect. at Manchester. Excav Giza, Alexandria. Published many excavation reports.

SCHAFER (Heinrich) 1868–1957. German. Professor at Berlin. Director of Berlin Mus. Excav Abū Ṣīr, surveyed Philae. Published papers on art and religion.

SCHIAPARELLI (Ernesto) 1856–1928. Italian. Director of Turin Mus. Excav many sites in Egypt, including Tomb of Herkuf, Aswān and Tomb of Kha, Thebes. Published many reports and works on geography and the Book of the Dead.

SCHWEINFURTH (Georg August) 1836–1925. German. Botanist. Founded EGS. Explored Red Sea Coast and Western Desert. His collections form the basis of those in the Agricultural Museum, Cairo. Published many articles on geographical and botanical matters.

SETHE (Kurt Heinrich) 1869–1934. German. Professor at Gottingen and Berlin. Copied and collected a vast number of historical texts.

SHORTER (Alan Wynn) 1905–38. Asst Keeper, BM. Excav al-ʿAmārnah and Armant. Published many articles on religion and funerary practices and popular books on Ancient Egypt.

SMITH (Grafton Elliot) *Sir*, 1871–1937. Australian. Anatomist. Professor at Cairo School of Medicine. Extensive study of mummies. Published one Catalogue of EM on mummies.

SMITH (William Stevenson) 1907–1969. American. Curator, Boston Museum. Excav Giza. Published on history of Giza necropolis and several books on sculpture, painting and architecture.

TURNER (Eric) 1911–83, English. Papyrologist. Professor at University College (Lon).

VYSE (Richard William Howard) 1784–1853. Army Officer. Excav at Giza and with Perring (q.v.) carried out a survey of other pyramids. Published excavation and survey reports.

WAINWRIGHT (Gerald Avery) 1879–1964. Egyptologist. Excav with Petrie and at Abydos and al-Sawāma.

WEIGALL (Arthur Edward Pearse Brome) 1880–1934. Insp. Gen. of Antiquities in Egypt. Excav at the Valley of the Kings, enclosed many Theban monuments and introduced numbering of tomb-chapels at Ṭhebes. Later became a journalist.

WILBOUR (Charles Edwin) 1833–96. American. Businessman and traveller. Discovered the Famine Relief at Seheil Island. Collection of antiquities and books founded the collections at the Brooklyn Museum.

WILKINSON (John Gardner) *Sir*, 1797–1875. Travelled widely in Egypt and excav at Thebes recording many of the tomb paintings. Surveyed the Wadi Natrūn. One of the first to order the Egyptian chronology. Best known works are the *Necropolis at Thebes* and *Customs and Manners of the Ancient Egyptians*, but published many other volumes on architecture, history and hieroglyphics.

WILLIAMS née Ransome (Caroline Louise) 18??–1952. American. Assistant Curator at Met NY. Served with Chicago Expedition to Egypt. Published a number of learned articles.

WINLOCK (Herbert Eustis) 1884–1950. American. Curator at Met NY. Excav in Egypt 1906–32. Published many historical and archaeological papers.

WOOLLEY (Charles Leonard) *Sir*, 1880–1960. Archaeologist. Excav Nubia, Sinai, and al-ʿAmārnah, later in Mesopotamia. Published several popular works on Egypt.

YOUNG (Thomas) 1773–1829. Doctor. Polymath and Professor at the Royal Institution. Pioneer in study of hieroglyphs and discovered the relationship between Ancient Egyptian and Coptic. He also recognised many of the values of the hieroglyphic signs.

# CHRISTIAN EGYPT

## History

Christianity became a sanctioned religion of the province of Egypt, as throughout the rest of the Roman Empire, following the decree of the Emperor Constantine in 312. The ancient Egyptian religion managed to survive for a further two centuries until in 553 the Emperor Justinian, by evicting the priests from their last bastions in the temples of Philae and Sīwah irrevocably closed the door on paganism in Egypt.

The origins of Christianity in Egypt, however, are to be found in the earliest days of the millennium. For the Westerner, for many reasons, the history of early Christianity has tended to emphasise the achievements and personalities of the European Church. While it is true that of the four ancient principal sees, Rome, Alexandria, Antioch and Ephesus (later Constantinople), Rome always occupied the honoured prime position as inheritor of the apostolic succession from St. Peter himself and suffered the most horrendous physical assaults on the believers, nevertheless Alexandria, the second city of the unified church, was much more important in its scholastic dynamism and intellectual vitality. The Egyptian Christians stood foremost among the defenders of the faith against the many challenges, both internal and external, that it had to face. This position they retained virtually unchallenged until the mid 5C when, together with several other Eastern communities, they withdrew from the main body of the church.

*Copt* and *Coptic* in the modern sense are relatively straight-forward terms, applying specifically to the Egyptian Christians and their culture, in contrast to that of the Muslims. Derived from the Arabic *qibṭī* (itself a derivative), it might therefore be considered only applicable since the Arabic conquest of 641. But the historical problem is not quite so simple and consideration of the origin of the terms might help to elucidate the situation.

The Greeks gave the name *Aiguptos* to Egypt and *Aiguptoi* to the inhabitants, both stemming from their rendering of Hut-Ka-Ptah (House of the spirit of Ptah), one of the titles of Memphis, principal cult centre of Ptah and capital of Lower Egypt. These names persisted in Greek and Latin and were eventually bequeathed to Modern European languages in similar form: Egypt, Aegypt, Egitto etc. However, the name the Egyptians gave to their country *Kheme* and to themselves *Niremnkhemi* (People of Kheme) continued in their own language throughout the Greek period, during the Christianising Roman era and long after the Arab Conquest.

Although the Arabs already had their own name for Egypt—Miṣr—they adopted the Greek term for the Christian inhabitants, which by application of Arabic orthography became qibṭī (pl. aqbāt). Since the terms are so specific (although stretching a point) it is perhaps permissable to apply Coptic from the earliest stirrings of Christianity in Egypt, thus emphasising the continuity.

According to Eusebius of Caesarea, writing in the early 4C, St. Mark arrived in Egypt sometime during the fifth decade after the death of

Jesus, founding his community at Baucalis on the coast just outside the E walls of Alexandria. In AD 68 Easter was celebrated at the same time as the festival of Serapis, the celebrants of which suddenly turned on the Christians and dragged St. Mark around the city until he died. His body was buried in the chapel at Baucalis remaining there until 828 when it was stolen by two Venetians and reinterred in the cathedral at Venice. Some relics were returned to Egypt in 1968 by Pope Paul VI.

Early records of Christianity in Egypt are few, the Jews being a much more vocal and obvious community with frequent clashes between them and the Greeks. The monotheistic views of the Jews were well known, and with their seemingly similar attitudes the Christians were probably considered unpatriotic and irreligious eccentrics, but their contempt for the person of the emperor was a perpetual excuse for harassment by the officials. Despite this, throughout the first 200 years, the Christian community grew steadily in numbers with several bishops, the most senior at Alexandria, and a large corps of deacons.

But at the very centre of Christian belief lay a seemingly insoluble problem that was to surface repeatedly, and finally shatter the united body of the church. The pivot of dissention was Jesus himself—his body and his nature. First indications of the conflict were seen in the Docetic theory of the mid-1C which promulgated the illusory human form of the divine Jesus. This idea was integral in the development of Gnosticism a much more widespread syncretic fusion of Christianity and earlier pagan theologies which gained many adherents from the 2C onwards. Gnosis (personal knowledge of God) was reserved for an elite and achieved through complex rituals and incantations. The Deity had created numberless spiritual beings (aeons) who in turn produced the Demiurge responsible for the creation of the immoral temporal world. Jesus as logos of the Deity provided the means by which rejection of this world was possible to the chosen. Although Gnostics considered themselves true believers their teachings were condemned by the church and adherents were found in diminishing numbers until the 5C. There is also evidence in Egypt for small groups of Manichaens, adherents to the religion founded by the Iranian Mani in the mid 3C with an even more convoluted theology. They too did not survive the 5C. Other ideologies to be opposed were the Neo-Platonic theories and Mithraism the secret Cilician cult of the celestial Perseus.

In the late 2C, probably to combat unorthodoxy, the Catechitical College was founded in Alexandria. Existing alongside the ancient Museion but dealing principally in theology and philosophy it was to produce some of the most distinguished early Christian teachers Pantaenus (c 180), Clement of Alexandria (fl. 190), Origen (fl. 215), Heraclas (231) and Dionysius of Alexandria (c 250) providing great stimulus to theological research. Originally independent it became increasingly subject to the authority of the church. Heraclas who became patriarch in 230, was apparently the first to be termed Papa, several centuries before the patriarch of Rome.

The first large scale persecution of Christians was initiated by Septimus Severus (188) who forbade conversions to Christianity or Judaism. However, despite the savagery, at the end of his reign and presumably in response to the need for more covert organisation the number of Egyptian bishops had risen to 20. Under Decius (249) and Valerian (252) Christian persecutions systematically increased, but Gallenius (252), Valerian's son, issued an edict of religious toleration and the churches reopened.

During the following 30 years, the Christians were left in comparative peace due to the chaos in Rome as rival contenders fought for the throne—it was the lull before the storm.

There had always been Christians who wanted to reject the world and pursue a contemplative life, but the first to make a national impact on the Christian community was the patrician St. Anthony, who c 270 sold his estates and retired to the desert. In an attempt to avoid notoriety he retreated ever further into the vastness, but his asceticism inevitably attracted disciples and he finally settled in the barren wastes bordering the Red Sea where a large community of hermits grew around his cell.

On 29 August 284 Diocletian assumed the throne. He began his reign with magnaminity and came to Egypt to defeat a rival. In so doing he reorganised the administration and averted a famine, in gratitude for which a commemorative column (Pompey's Pillar) was raised to him in Alexandria. It soon became apparent that the Christians remained an obstacle to recognition of his absolute divinity. His persecutions began simply enough, at first all soldiers were commanded to sacrifice to the Roman gods but then in 303 churches were closed, Christian literature destroyed, Christian officials dismissed and meetings proscribed. This was but a prologue to an appalling wave of persecution in which Christians were systematically maimed, blinded, tortured and burnt. So horrific was it that the Egyptian Christians chose the day of Diocletian's accession to initiate their era—The Martyrs' Calendar. Diocletian's successor in the east Maximianus Daia (305) continued in the same manner and perhaps scores of thousands of Egyptians were massacred, among them many of the great saints of the Egyptian church.

Constantine was proclaimed emperor in Britain in 306. He had to contend with four rival claimants before he became sole emperor in 323 but during his ascendancy in 312 he issued the Edict of Milan which enforced religious toleration throughout the empire. Although this new freedom was partially offset by his choice, in 330, of Constantinople (and not Alexandria) as his new capital, it did allow the Christians to consolidate and preach freely and the number of converts increased rapidly. However, stability also encouraged the resurgence of the Christological dispute, which was brought to a head in Alexandria.

At this time Alexander was the patriarch of Alexandria but his character pales beside those of the two principal protagonists in the dispute, his own secretary St. Athanasius and, the presbyter of the Church of St. Mark, Arius. Under the influence of his Antiochan masters Arius contended that Jesus was of like essence with God, but begotten and therefore of unequal nature, while Athanasius proposed that God and Jesus were of one and indivisible essence. Support for Arius came from the Greek community while Athanasius, a native Egyptian had the approval of his countrymen. At a local synod in 320 Arius was condemned and exiled, but he refused to be silenced. Constantine attempted to reconcile the disputants, but in the event was forced to convene the first great occumenical Council of Nicea in 325. Although Arius was condemned and exiled his supporters caused a fair amount of trouble over the following years. Athanasius suceeded Alexander as patriarch, but his intransigence made him so unpopular that he was exiled. His position was not improved by the fact that Constantine's son and successor Constantinus II (337) was himself an Arian and he was exiled a further four times, during which period there were even Arian contenders for the pariachate.

The community of hermits which had surrounded St. Anthony encouraged others and settlements were founded throughout the Nile Valley by the 'Desert Fathers', including Amoun at Nitrea (325), St. Makarius the Great at Scetis (Wadi Naṭrūn c 330), Makarius the Alexandrian at Kellia (c 340), and St. Palemon at Fāw. Hermits in these communities would meet once a week to celebrate mass and church festivals. St. Pachomius, one of the disciples of St. Palemon and an ex-soldier, decided that his community could be put to better use and devised rules based on military discipline covering every aspect of life, conduct, food, sleep, travel, and worship. Although very austere, the movement proved extremely popular and by the time of his death (346) there were many such communities throughout Egypt, including some for women.

Celibacy, devotion, labour and education were their principal aims, and the hierarchical structure consisted of an abbot in charge of the monastery, several of which were the responsibility of a superior. Before long the monastic life spread beyond the confines of Egypt into W Asia, Europe and Africa. This was also the age of the Egyptian missionaries who travelled extensively through Asia to India, Africa and Europe, probably even reaching Britain and Ireland. In the mid-4C the Ethiopian nobility became Christians under the influence of two Coptic brothers; the Ethiopian church was to remain a daughter province of the Coptic church until 1948 with metropolitan (abuna) being chosen by the patriarch of Alexandria.

A set-back to the Christians came with the assumption of the Emperor Julian (360) called the Apostate who had been trained for the priesthood but reviled the faith and turned to the worship of the old Roman gods. He not only persecuted the Christians but also followers of the ancient Egyptian religion— fortunately, he reigned for only three years. Arian patriarchs were appointed to the see of Alexandria by the Emperor Valens but after his death Theodosius I the Great in 381 summoned the Council (II) of Constantinople at which Arianism was finally extinguished. Theodosius briefly united the two Roman empires with Christianiy as the official religion but it was irrevocably divided between his sons in 395 with Arcadius receiving the Eastern Empire.

St. Shenute succeeded his uncle as abbot of the White Monastery at Atrib (Suhāg) in 383. He transformed the Pachomian rule with even greater austerity resorting at times even to physical violence against the brothers. He was a great administrator and prolific writer in Sahidic Coptic and his tenure saw a rise in the aggressive promulgation of Christianity. A product of this new attitude was the Patriarch Theophilus (385) who encouraged bands of monks to persecute their previous oppressors. Many pagan temples were attacked and in 389 the Temple of Serapis at Canopus was razed and the pagans were subjected to a great deal of oppression. Finally the Temple of Serapis in Alexandria itself was sacked in 411 and the annexe to the Great Library destroyed.

The successor of Theophilus was St. Cyril the Great (412) whose attitude was even more intracable. He assembled a large corps of dedicated disciples ready to die in his defence and one of their most disgraceful acts was the stoning to death at the Caesareum of the distinguished pagan philosopher and mathematician Hypatia daughter of Theon in 415. Cyril also played the principal part in the second phase of the dispute over the nature of Jesus. His opponent was Nestorius, Patriarch of Constantinople, who rejected the term Theotokos (Mother of God), in reference to the Virgin Mary, preferring the title mother of

Christ, but in so doing once more implied discrepancy in the natures of Jesus. Cyril, supported by Celesius patriarch of Rome, condemned Nestorius and the resulting highly charged débăcle forced the emperors Theodosius II and Valentinian II to convene in 431 the Council (III) of Ephesus. Much acrimony, verbal jostling and the holding of a contra-council by the defendants resulted in the arrest of the leaders of both sides. Cyril eventually triumphed and Nestorius was imprisoned and exiled in Egypt where he died. However, his teachings gave a powerful impetus to the most easterly province known later as the Nestorian Church. Cyril's rigid orthodoxy bolstered by his prodigious literary output made him a paragon to all schools of thought. Despite this, he was directly responsible for the continuing debate which was to resurface after his death, forcing Theodosius to assemble the second Council (IV) of Ephesus in 449 at which the Coptic Patriarch Dioscurus presided. During the proceedings the prime mover Flavian, patriarch of Constantinople, found himself humiliated and deposed. However, he was supported by Pope Leo who called the council a 'highway robbery'. The next emperor, Marcian (450) under the influence of Leo and his wife Pulcheria, sister of the deceased Theodosius, reversed the decision and summoned the Council (V) of Chalcedon in 451 specifically to try Dioscorus who in turn was deposed and exiled. More importantly the council recognised Constantinople as second only to Rome in ecclesiastical matters, a terrible blow to Alexandria and the other provinces. The Egyptians rejected the decisions and withdrew from further debate with the northern church, who contemptuously called them monophysites although they never denied the existence of Christ's two natures but insisted on their mystical unity.

Marcius imposed a patriarch Proterius on the Egyptians who responded by appointing their own, Timothy Aelurus, thus initiating two lines of patriarchal succession. The Greek patriarchs (later termed Melkite, ie royalist) always had few communicants and were never accepted by the Copts. They have existed independently, often with considerable friction, until the present day.

Monophytism, which still had a considerable following in the Eastern Empire, remained a problem for succeeding emperors and in 482 Emperor Zeno announced the Henoticon (act of union) devised by the patriarchs of Alexandria and Constantinople to reconcile both factions, which it signally failed to do. An uneasy truce existed until the assumption of the Emperor Justin I (518) and his son Justinian (527) who were reconciled with Rome. In an attempt to rationalise Christianity the latter actively persecuted the Monophysites, who, however, had a secret ally in his wife Theodora. During this period missionary activities of both factions were active in Nubia, where there were a many conversions.

Justinian appointed Apollonius Melkite patriarch, with prefectural powers, in 541, and punative measures were pursued against the Egyptian clergy. Christianity was ordained as the sole religion of the Empire and the pagan priests were expelled from their last refuges: the Temple of Isis at Philae and the Temple of Amun at Sīwah. Many churches were built throughout the empire, including that at Mount Sinai. Attempting to heal the rift in the Christian communities Justin II in 571 issued the second Henoticon, but it failed as miserably as the first. Heraclius, general of the African armies, deposed the Emperor Phocus in 610 and assumed the throne, but Egypt was lost to the Persians under Khusraw Parwiz in 619. It was finally regained in 627, with the despotic Cyrus imposed as Patriarch/Prefect. Cyrus was to promote the theory of Monethelitism announced in 622, which, while specifically ignoring the nature of Christ, promulgated the unity of his human and divine wills. This also was rejected by the Copts, but in 638 belief became compulsory. Benjamin, the Coptic Patriarch, went into retreat in S Egypt while Cyrus pursued a series of merciless persecutions against the Coptic clergy. It is scarcely surprising that the Muslim invasion of 641 was welcomed by the Copts.

After the Arab conquest the Copts at first filled important roles as translators, scribes and accountants, but, isolated from the main body of the Chirstian community, they exerted little influence. In 706 Arabic was decreed as the State language and this reduced their importance still further. Their subsequent history is entirely subsidiary to that of the Muslims in Egypt, with their fortunes waxing and waning according to the attitude of the ruler, but always declining in number. Today Copts represent about 10 per cent of the population of Egypt.

The title of the Patriarch is Pope of Alexandria and Patriarch of the See of St. Mark. Although he has supreme authority, he does not have the burden of infallibility. He is elected from the monastic community, automatically assuming the bishopric of Alexandria and Cairo. In the mid 11C the seat of the patriarchate was moved from Alexandria to Cairo where it has remained. The hierarchy consists of archbishops (assigned to foreign sees), bishops for each of the sees in Egypt and each of the monasteries, priests, deacons and readers.

The *Greek Orthodox* Patriarch has the same title as the Coptic Patriarch. There are ten metropolitans, three with sees in Egypt, the rest being appointed to other sees in Africa. Two bishops are responsible for the bishoprics of Babylon (Cairo) and Mareotis (Alexandria). There is also an important Arab-speaking Greek Orthodox community.

Probably an even larger community, the *Armenian Orthodox Church* is subject to the Patriarch of Echmiadzin. Head of the church in Egypt is the Metropolitan of Cairo, who is elected by councils in Cairo and Alexandria.

# The Coptic Language and Script

Although attempts had been made in the 2C BC to transliterate the Egyptian language into the Greek script, with little success, it was not until the early 1C AD that a conscious effort was made to express Egyptian in Greek script. This was achieved using the Greek alphabet with the addition of seven characters taken from the late demotic Egyptian for sounds not represented in Greek. This was the origin of the Coptic script which embraced the current Egyptian vernacular, already heavily adulterated with Greek terminology, with perhaps five or more dialects. The most important of these were Bohairic of the Delta and Sahidic from Upper Egypt.

The first examples in Coptic are secular ephemera from the early 2C AD, progressing through glosses to Greek texts, translations from the Greek, and finally Gnostic and Christian works composed entirely in Coptic. Flourishing literatures existed in both dialects. Sahidic, purged of all Greek elements after the Council of Chalcedon, was the more prolific, but since most of the senior hierarchy of the church were northerners, in the mid 11C Bohairic was ordained as the official liturgical language.

*Coptic papyrus codex of Deuteronomy, early 4C (British Library)*

Although now only used in the liturgy, it persisted as a spoken language until the 13C while Sahidic may have survived until the 17C in the South.

## Coptic Art

Defining the difference between Greco-Roman and early Coptic art is very difficult. The capital of Ptolemaic Egypt was Alexandria, famous throughout the Hellenistic world for its learning, and classical buildings and art, little of which has survived. It was to this imported classical art rather than its native precursor that the Copts turned for inspiration. The reason seems to be that all Pharaonic art and architecture was regarded as pagan, and although many of the ancient temples had been turned into monasteries, they wished to detach themselves as much as possible from the ancient tradition.

Probably the finest works of Roman Egypt were the Hawārah mummy paintings. Painted from life in a wax technique, they are the earliest panel portraits to survive. Dating to the first three centuries AD, they represent the Greek population of the Fayyūm, and were hung in the houses of the sitters during life and attached to the coffin and buried with them after death. Others who could not afford paintings had stucco masks painted and attached to the coffins.

Church architecture developed from the domestic buildings first used to avoid detection during the Roman persecutions. It was only after 330 when Christianity became the state religion that churches could officially be built. There should be a transitional type of building between the house-chapel and the basilican church, but this seems missing in Egypt. The earliest churches known from the area seem in all essentials to be of Syrian type and almost certainly were influenced by them in design. The essential framework of the church depended on its liturgical requirements. Nothing that can be related to pre-Christian Egyptian traditions can be said to survive in the ground plan of churches. The difficulty is that there is little uniformity of plan among the early Christian churches. All one can say is that the churches tend to be longitudinal with the main axis E to W and the sanctuary at the E. Two of the earliest churches are to be found in the Sūhāg monasteries of Deir al-Abyaḍ and Deir al-Aḥmar, built traditionally in the 5C. In its simplest form the sanctuary is a single apse, containing one altar, but many of the Coptic churches have three apses in a trefoil arrangement, built under Syrian influence and deriving ultimately from the throne chamber of Byzantine royalty. This arrangement can be seen in the Sūhāg monasteries mentioned above.

The central sanctuary is usually dedicated to the patron saint to whom the church is consecrated and the other two to subsidiary saints. Outbuildings and annexes often change the original plan. A Coptic church usually consists of four distinct sections. At the W end, just inside the entrance, is the narthex. Beyond this is the nave, E of which is the apse, called the haykal (sanctuary). Attached to the sanctuary is the baptistry. The *narthex* is a transverse chamber which crosses the whole width of the church. In the narthex of some of the early churches a hole sunk in the floor was previously used for a service of the Blessing of the Water at the Feast of the Epiphany. Now a portable basin is used for this ceremony.

The *nave* is normally divided into three parts by a double colonnade, the N aisle being reserved for women. Near the E end of the nave is the *ambon* (pulpit) which is usually set against the colonnade of the N aisle. At the E end of the nave is the *choir*, formerly separated from it by a screen, extending over the whole breadth of the church, containing seats for the singers, and lecterns from which the lessons are read. One or more steps leads from the chancel to the *haykal*, which only men may enter, separated from the rest of the church by a solid wooden screen, often beautifully carved and inlaid with ebony, ivory and cedar, in the centre of which is a door covered by a curtain. On either side of the door are two small windows and across the screen is a row of ikons including that of the saint to whom the church is dedicated. In some churches sanctuary lamps hang before the screen, and between them are suspended ostrich eggs.

The N and S sanctuaries are used when the feasts of their particular saints are being celebrated. Behind the main altar is a tribune with seats for the bishop and the officiating clergy. In the niche behind a lamp is kept burning, known as the perpetual lamp. The altar which stands in the middle of the *haykal* is four-sided and made of brick or stone, covered with three layers of cloth, cotton or linen, red silk and white linen overall. Over the altar is a lofty wooden canopy upheld by pillars (rather like the Pharaonic baldachins). On the interior of the dome covering the sanctuary is a painting of Christ as Pantokrator (Lord of the World) surrounded by cherubim and seraphim. In the middle of the altar is the ark, a box with hinged flaps, painted with the Last Supper, the Holy Virgin, an angel and the patron saint, in which the chalice is placed from the beginning of the divine liturgy until the Holy Communion. The *baptistry* is normally situated at the end of the N aisle, though not in the early churches. The font is circular and large enough for complete immersion.

It is sometimes very difficult to date Coptic material: for instance monastic painting, most of which comes from only two sites, Bawit and Ṣaqqārah and which, except for that from the Wadi Natrun and perhaps St Anthony, are all individual paintings, not grouped in schools. Much of the work appears not to have been that of monks but commissioned from itinerant artists.

The greatest collection of Coptic art in Egypt is in the Coptic Museum founded in 1908 and taken over by the government in 1931, situated in Old Cairo in the Fortress of Babylon. The range of subjects displayed can be taken as illustrating the art forms of the Copts. Many of the objects here come from the churches and monasteries, some of which are now completely destroyed, as at Hermopolis. The museum contains many capitals derived in some cases from earlier non-Christian temples; woodcarving, with a splendid 5C panel showing Christ's entry into the Holy City on Palm Sunday; a large number of ikons, some showing strong Byzantine influence, and others typically Coptic. The finest collection is probably that of textiles, which have been preserved by the dry Egyptian air. The motifs are mixed—some are adapted Pharaonic, others Greco-Roman. In the lesser art one notes the riot of decoration without form or reason, because the craftsmen were copying earlier designs which were no longer understood.

With rare exceptions Christian subjects are not found on objects produced in Egypt before the 5C. One of the commonest motifs on textiles are roundels or medallions enclosing floral designs or animals, and these are very frequent in the 5 and 6C. The textiles are in many ways the most interesting of the Coptic arts. They feature designs that were also carried out in wood, stone and ivory. It is not until the late 6C that classical designs die out and Christian motifs alone remain. Most of the textiles are on linen backing, some of the clothing is woollen, as is the tapestry weaving. Cotton is seldom found, and little silk. What is apparent is that Coptic art remained essentially a folk art having something of the same style as modern Egyptian weaving, without the discipline or accuracy of the works of the Pharaonic period, nor the vitality, produced by patronage, of the Muslim art that was to follow.

# ISLAMIC EGYPT

## Al-Islām الاسلام

**Islām**, meaning submission to Allāh (God), Muslims believe to be the only true religion, professed by all the previous Prophets from Adam through Ibrāhīm (Abraham), Nūh (Noah) and Mūsā (Moses) and many others down to ʿIsā (Jesus), finally being revealed through the last Prophet, Muḥammad. All the earlier Prophets received the true revelation and had passed it on to their peoples but, through time and human failing, the messages had become corrupt, in distinction to which the revelations that descended upon Muḥammad were recorded by his followers as they were given and are thus considered the undisputed 'word' of Allāh. Muḥammad was the last of the messengers of Allāh and thus the seal of the prophecy. Shortly after his death, the revelations were collected by one of his successors (khalīfah) ʿUthmān, scrupulously examined by those who had been present when the Prophet gave them and compiled into a book in the form in which they now appear—*The Qurʾān*. Not one word was added or deleted and it is thus the earthly form of the eternal and immutable message that exists in Heaven.

**Muḥammad** was born about AD 570 in Mecca (Makkah), a religious and commercial centre of great importance in W. Arabia. The town occupied by the Quraysh tribe was the centre of a cult of nature gods, images of which were kept in a large square building called the Kaʿbah. He was raised by his uncle, Abū Ṭālib, a merchant, and when he was twenty-five married a widow, Khadījah, fifteen years older than himself. They had four daughters and two sons of whom only Fāṭimah lived to marry and to have children.

Muḥammad habitually retired to a cave on Mount Hirāʾ to contemplate and one night, at the age of forty, during the month of Ramaḍān, he was sitting in prayer when he saw a light and a man standing before him who asked him three times to recite. He replied at first in amazement that he could not, but the third time under duress he repeated what the figure said 'Recite in the name of thy Lord who created, . . .' (Qurʾān 96:1–5) and thus began the first of a series of revelations that were to descend upon him for the rest of his life. In terror he fled home to Khadījah who allayed his fear, believing that it portended a great mission. He later learned that the figure was Jibrīl (Gabriel) and that he had been chosen as a Messenger of Allāh.

Shortly after the first revelations, beside Khadījah, the people closest to Muḥammad accepted Islam; Zayd, his adopted son, ʿAlī, the son of Abū Ṭālib, followed shortly by Abū Bakr, ʿUthmān and other nobles of the tribe, and also some of the poorer people. After three years he had thirty followers and then received the revelation to speak in public. For another six years he spoke the revelations as they came to him, of the glories of nature, the unity of Allāh and the destruction of the idols, of equality and the punishments awaiting disbelief. His rhetoric was so powerful and the message so compelling that the people could not remain unmoved. The Quraysh decided that they must act and turned on the servants and the poor with great ferocity but left the nobles unmolested. In 615 Muḥammad recommended that these people flee to Abyssinia where they were kindly received by the ruler, the Negus.

But still Muḥammad preached to the Quraysh and prayed at the Kaʿbah. He was asked many times to perform miracles but each time his answer was the same, that miracles were Allāh's and that the Qur ʾān was the only miracle. The Quraysh tried in many ways to make him give up his mission, offering him great honours and wealth and when this failed threatened Abū Ṭālib, still a pagan, to persuade Muḥammad to return to their religion. He tried but Muḥammad with great eloquence refused and his uncle was so moved that he promised to stand by him as did the rest of his own tribesmen. At this time one of the greatest of all the tribes, ʿUmar ibn al-Khaṭṭāb, accepted Islam. Previously a violent opponent of Muḥammad, he was to play an important part in the early history of Islam.

The strength of the Muslims alarmed the Quraysh, who forced them by treaty to leave Mecca and dwell in a nearby valley for over two years, at the end of which time the exiles were allowed to return. During the next year, the tenth of Muḥammad's mission, Abū Ṭālib died, still a pagan, followed by Khadījah. Muḥammad called it the 'Year of Sorrow', but throughout this he was sustained by overwhelming belief in his mission. Later that year six men from the N city of Yathrib accepted Islam—an event of great significance.

In the twelfth year of his mission Muḥammad experienced the Miʿrāj (ascension), the journey by night, in which he ascended from al-Quds (Jerusalem) to Heaven. The men from Yathrib returned on two occasions in greater numbers and as the pressure from the Quraysh was growing, in the thirteenth year of the mission, they asked Muḥammad to come to their city. He agreed and advised the faithful to leave secretly. This they did, only the Prophet, ʿAlī and Abū Bakr remaining in Mecca. The Meccans plotted to kill Muḥammad, but on the night that this was planned he escaped with Abū Bakr and, although pursued, they evaded capture by hiding in a cave and eventually reached Yathrib. This journey is called the Hijrah (emigration) of the Prophet. The whole population of Yathrib greeted him and every person wanted the Prophet to live in their quarter, but he allowed his camel to wander and where it stopped he chose to build his house. This town was subsequently known just as Medina (al-Madīnah; The City).

Muḥammad now set about establishing his state, uniting the tribes and creating a defensive force in expectation of a reaction from Mecca. The Meccans harried the caravans of Medina and many small sorties were fought but in the third year after the Hijrah two major battles were fought, at Badr and Uḥud; the first the Muslims won and the latter they lost, but neither was decisive. In the sixth year after the Hijrah Muḥammad wished to visit the Kaʿbah in Mecca, still containing pagan idols but sacred to the Muslims for it had been on this site that Ibrāhīm had built the first shrine to Allāh. At first they were forbidden entry but eventually a ten-year truce was negotiated in which hostilities were ceased and the Muslims were allowed to visit the Kaʿbah in the holy months. At this time the Prophet received a revelation in which he was told that his mission was universal and not merely confined to the Arabs. He sent envoys to the princes of Byzantium, Persia, Ghassan and Egypt, but they all rejected the messages with varying degrees of tact. From Egypt he received a non-commital reply and several rich presents.

After performing their rites and gaining more converts, the Muslims won a victory over the Byzantines in the N, adding a large area to their territory. Shortly after the Quraysh made an attack on one of the allies of the Muslims and so Muḥammad, with an army of ten thousand, marched on Mecca. He entered the city and stopped before the Kaʿbah, taking no retribution, only demanding that the three hundred and sixty idols in the Kaʿbah be destroyed. This was done, Muḥammad exhorted the people to abandon their old ways and at this time many people accepted Islam. The shrines of the neighbouring tribes were peacefully overthrown and though other tribes rose up against the Muslims the latter were successful in all their campaigns. Muḥammad returned to Medina and in this, the ninth year of the Hijrah, representatives of tribes and kingdoms throughout Arabia flocked to make submission to him and ask for guidance. In the next year the Prophet left for the pilgrimage (ḥajj) to Mecca at the head of 120,000 followers, but hinted that he might not be with them in the next year.

During the last ten years of his life Muḥammad had married ten more women, only one of whom had not been married before, ʿĀ'ishah, daughter of Abū Bakr. Each of these marriages he undertook through political or judicial expediency or from sheer humanity. At that time there was no restriction on the number of wives any man could have but a year after he married his last wife, Maymūnah, the revelation came that the number of a man's wives could not exceed four and even this was permitted only with the most rigid conditions. His wives at times gave him a great deal of annoyance but throughout all he treated them with equality.

While arranging a military expedition in 632, Muḥammad fell seriously ill. Although weakening all the time, he was tranquil and was able to lead the prayer until three days before his death. After the last prayer that he attended he entered the house of ʿĀ'ishah and died a few hours later. Abū Bakr announced the death to the dumbfounded Muslims in a speech stressing Muḥammad's mortality and the immortality of Allāh. The Prophet had directed that he should be buried where he died and so he was interred under the floor of his house in Medina.

Muḥammad had named no successor: Abū Bakr was elected the follower (khalīfah) of Muḥammad as leader of the community, but he governed for only two years until his own death. He was followed by ʿUmar, a great organiser who governed for ten years (634–644). It was during this period that Arab forces spread and conquered the whole Persian empire in the East and the Byzantine territories in Syria, Palestine and Egypt in the West. ʿUmār was murdered by a Christian and ʿUthmān was elected next khalīf, governing for twelve years (644–656). He too was murdered by a discontented element among the Muslims and ʿAlī, who had married Muḥammad's daughter Fāṭimah, was the next choice. But the dissention at his election was much greater and there was conflict between his followers and another group led by Muʿāwiyah. Although he governed for five years and moved his capital to Kūfah, he was also assassinated and his rival's faction triumphed. Thus began the rift that was to split Islam into the two great camps of Sunnī and Shiʿah. But, from that time, Islām became the dominant religion from Morocco in the W to Pakistan in the E, later spreading even further into India and South-East Asia.

**The Qur'ān**. The first divine revelation sent down to Muḥammad in the cave on Mount Hirā' in 610 was followed by many others until his death in

632. They were usually conveyed by the angel Jibrīl and could descend to him while awake or asleep, in company or alone. Muḥammad could neither read nor write but his repetition of the revelation was memorised by many of those to whom he gave it. The Arabs, at that time, had a great poetic tradition. Poets were universally honoured and a great meeting was held every four years at which poems could be judged and assessed. This tradition was oral, writing played no part in it. Their memory was phenomenal and if anyone forgot a single word in a poem, a great disgrace, hundreds of other people could give the right one. Thus it was into this great literary, not literate, background that the Qur'ān was revealed. Its form is considered matchless, neither poetry nor prose, but unique. Many who came forward to claim prophecy for themselves were issued with the challenge to produce its like but all failed. After the death of Muḥammad 'Umar decided to collect the whole revelation together and commit it to writing under the guidance of Zayd, the Prophet's secretary. Thus all those who had memorised the Qur'ān were consulted, the various materials on which it had been recorded were compared and it was collated eventually by the third khalīf, ʿUthmān, in 651. No textual variations have been introduced since that time.

Qur'ān is the transliterated form of the word derived from *qara'ā* (to read) and is thus generally rendered 'recitation'. It consists of many *suwār* (chapters: sing. sūrah), 114 in all, each divided into a number of *ayāt* (sections: sing āyah). The suwār vary in length from a few *ayāt* to hundreds and were arranged, under the guidance of the Prophet, with the longest sūrah at the beginning, progressing to the shortest at the end. The first short sūrah, al-Fatḥah (The Opening) does not fit into the sequence. To the heading of each sūrah is attached the place of revelation, Mecca or Medina, and also the number of *ayāt* in it.

The message that was revealed to Muḥammad embodied that which Allāh requires for the guidance of the believer. Covering all aspects of life, it can be divided into five sections: A. Beliefs (Iʿtaqādāt); B. Practical devotions (ʿIbādāt); C. Transactions (Muʿāmalāt); D. Moralities (Ādāb), and E. Punishments (ʿUqūbāt). The first two are outlined below, the last three being matters of law will be dealt with under that heading.

A. **Beliefs** required of a Muslim are six:

**1.** *Allāh* ﷻ. He is unique, having no partners or equals. He is eternal and ubiquitous yet exists in nothing. He is unbegotten and unbegetting and his form is incomprehensible to man. He is omnipotent and the sole creator. He knows all things hidden or manifest. He is the essence of all attributes but not confined by any of them.

**2.** *The Angels of Allāh* (Malā'ikat Allāh) are created of light and endowed with reason; they are his perfect servants. They intercede for men and are also their guardians. They are one of the ways of communication between Allāh and mankind.

**3.** *The Scriptures of Allāh* (Kutub Allāh). From the first to the last there is only one true religion. The Will of Allāh was revealed to many Prophets and many books were sent down, all but the last four—al-Tawrah (the Torah), al-Zubūr (the Psalms), al-Ingīl (the Gospels) and the Qur'ān—have been lost. Any parts of the first three which do not agree with the Qur'ān are to be considered human corruptions, since they were not directly recorded revelations (for example the attribution to Allāh of offspring or of any division in His Being). The Qur'ān is the only tangible 'Word' of Allāh, revealed and written in Arabic and untranslatable.

**4.** *The Messengers of Allāh* (Rusul Allāh). There have been many Prophets, the sequence being sealed with Muḥammad. They delivered the revelation to their respective peoples and warned them of the consequences of disbelief. Of Jesus, the

Qur'ān says that he was the messenger of Allāh sent to rescue the people of Israel. He was virgin-born of Mary, performed miracles and proclaimed the revelation. He was not crucified but was translated to Paradise by Allāh and another was crucified in his place. He had utterly refuted any attribute of divinity.

**5.** *The Day of Resurrection* (al-Yawm al-Ākhir). All the Prophets had passed on the message that after death each individual will exist in eternity and must give an account of his actions; their subsequent state depending on the manner in which they had lived. The date of the Day of Resurrection is unknown to any except Allāh but will be portended by certain signs.

**6.** *Predestination* (al-Qadar). Whatever has been or shall come to pass, whether good or apparently evil, proceeds entirely from the Divine Will and has been irrevocably created after a fixed decree. To question or investigate this point is expressly forbidden.

Two related theological topics should also be mentioned, concerning the Jinn or Afrit and Iblīs. The Jinn, mentioned several times in the Qur'ān, are sentient beings created from fire by Allāh but imperceptible to man. They are subject to the Will of Allāh and his Prophets though their destiny is unknown and only rarely does their path cross that of man. In popular folklore they are depicted as nature spirits at the command of certain savants. Iblīs, or Shaytān, was a Jinn who refused to prostrate himself before the newly created Adam. Upon being humiliated, though granted respite, by Allāh, he swore to corrupt all men: 'I will lie in ambush for thee along thy straight path' (Qur'ān 7:16). Muslim commentators agree that since he was incapable of disobeying Allāh, he too must be an integral, albeit reluctant, part of Allāh's Will regarding the fate of man.

B. **Practical Devotions**. The acts enjoined of Muslims are five, often called the Pillars of Faith: 1. Pronouncing the formula of faith (al-Shahādah); 2. Prayer (al-Ṣalāh); 3. Payment of Alms (al-Zakāh); 4. Fasting in Ramaḍān (al-Ṣawm); 5. Pilgrimage (al-Ḥajj).

**1.** *Pronouncing publicly the formula of faith* as follows, 'I bear witness that there is no god but Allāh and Muḥammad is His Messenger'.

**2.** *Prayer* is performed at five specific times of the day: *ẓuhr* (noon), *ʿasr* (afternoon), *maghrib* (sunset), *ʿishā* (night) and *fajr* (daybreak). For the prayer a Muslim must be in a state of purity, therefore he washes himself in a particular way (*wuḍū'*), including hands, mouth, nasal membranes, face, lower arms, head, ears and feet. It is not necessary to perform this each time, only after some act which has cancelled the purification, for example going to the lavatory or sleeping. For more serious impurities a complete bath (*ghusl*) is necessary. The prayers also have a specified form, and are preferably performed with others. In a mosque the *mu'adhin* pronounces the *adhān* (call to prayer) from the *mi'dhanah* or *manarah* (minaret) or at the side of the mosque. It is this call that is heard echoing through the streets at each of the five periods of the day given above.

The call to prayer runs as follows: 'Allāhu Akbar' (Allāh is greatest) four times; 'Ashhadu an lā ilaha ilā Allāh' (I testify that there is no god but Allāh) twice; 'Ashhadu an Muḥammadan rasūl Allāh' (I testify that Muḥammad is the messenger of Allāh) twice; 'Hayya ʿalā al-ṣalāh' (Come to the prayer) twice; 'Hayya ʿalā al-falāh' (Come to prosperity) twice; 'Allāhu akbar' (Allāh is greatest) twice, 'Lā ilaha ilā Allāh' (There is no god but Allāh). Before the dawn prayer the exhortation, 'Al-ṣalātu khayrun min al-nawm' (Prayer is better than sleep) is called twice, before 'Allāhu akbar'.

The prayer is led by the imām (leader). In fact any adult male can perform this function but it is usually performed by someone particularly well-versed in theology; there is no clergy in Islam. The worshipper faces Mecca, the qiblah (direction) is marked in the mosque by a small niche in the wall, the miḥrāb. Immediately prior to the prayer another call to prayer (iqāmah) is made in the mosque. It is the same as the previous call but with the addition of 'Qad qāmat al-ṣalāh' (The prayer is ready) twice inserted after 'Ḥayya ʿalāʿ falāḥ.'

The prayer begins with the worshippers' intention (al-nīyyah) to perform the prayer. The hands are raised level with the head and the words 'Allāhu akbar' are spoken; the hands are dropped to the sides or clasped on the sternum. After a short prayer, al-Fatḥah (The Opening), the first chapter of the Qur'ān is recited. This is followed by another short portion of the Qur'ān. The worshipper then bends forward with his hands on his knees (*rukū*ʿ). He then stands again and, after a short prayer of praise, kneels down and with his hands before him places his forehead on the ground (*sajdah*) and gives another short prayer of praise. He then sits back on his heels (*jalsah*) and another sajdah completes one rakʿah. After a short prayer he stands again and repeats the whole sequence, but after al-Fatḥah a different section of the Qur'ān is used and at the *jalsah* a short prayer of glorification and the shahạdah are repeated. After this two more rakʿāt are repeated but only al-Fatḥah is recited before the *rukū*ʿ. At the end of the prayer there is a short prayer for the blessings of the Prophet and the shahādah is repeated. Finally the worshipper turns his head to the right and says 'Al-salāmu ʿalaykum wa raḥmat Allāh,' and turns his head to the left and repeats the same.

This completes the enjoined (*fard*) prayer. For the *fajr* prayer only the first two *rak*ʿ*āt* are performed and for the *maghrib* prayer only three. Several other prayers can be performed, based on the practises of the Prophet, before or after the main prayer. On Friday the noon prayer has a special form. It is held in a gathering (jumaʿah) and the first two rakʿāt are replaced by the khuṭbah (sermon) given by the imām (the leader of the prayer, although it can be any adult male Muslin, he is usually one well-versed in theology).

Other special forms of prayer are ṣalat al-musāfir: if a Muslim is travelling he need only perform two raqʿāt at each prayer except at maghrib when the normal three are performed: ṣalāt al-khawf: performed in times of war one rakaʿah is recited by one regiment and then by the other, the sequence is repeated for the second rakʿah: ṣalat al-tarāwih, eight rakʿāt are performed every evening during Ramaḍān after ʿishā prayer. The whole Qur 'ān is repeated during the course of the month.

**3.** *Al-Zakāh* is a payment enjoined on every Muslim of a proportion of his annual income, both money and goods. It is calculated in a very exact proportion. It is paid out to the poor, needy debtors, for the ransom of captives, to travellers, and for those seeking information about Islam and the way of God; that is, the defence of Islam. On gold (general wealth) the amount is 2½%, on goods various dues are required.

**4.** *Fasting in Ramaḍān* (al-Ṣawm) is an injunction, the benefits of which are given in the Qur'ān. 'O you who believe, fasting is prescribed for you so that you may be more able to guard against evil.'(Qur'ān 3:184). The fast begins at dawn after the moon is first seen to mark the beginning of the month of Ramaḍān and continues throughout the month between the hours of dawn and sunset. It must last until the moon of the next month is seen, 29 or 30 days. As the Muslim calendar is based on a lunar month it moves forward through the Christian year, starting about 10 days earlier each year. Nothing must be eaten or drunk or smoked during the hours of fast and sexual contact is also forbidden. The end of the fast is celebrated by the feast and prayer of the ʿĪd al fiṭr.

**5.** *Pilgrimage* (al-Ḥājj). It is enjoined on every Muslim to make the pilgrimage to Mecca at least once during his lifetime, in the month of Dhū 'l-Ḥijjah. The rites are rigid and the main duties are as follows: (i) The wearing of *ihrām*, two seamless cloths that leave the heads of men uncovered; (ii) *Ṭawāf*. Making the circuit round the Kaʿbah seven times; (iii) Saʿy. Running seven times between two small hills near the Kaʿbah; (iv) staying on the plain of Mount ʿArafāt on the 9th of the month. The 10th of the month is the ʿĪd al-Aḍḥā celebrated throughout the Muslim world with sacrifice, prayer and feasting in memory of the Prophet Ibrahim. The pilgrimage has the deepest significance for all Muslims and is considered to be the greatest action that can be taken.

**Law.** The legal system of Islām (Shariʿah) rests on four bases, the Qur'ān, the Sunnah (Actions of the Prophet), Ijmaʿ (unanimous agreement of the Muslim scholars) and Qiyās (reasoned analogy), each with decreasing authority.

Many prohibitions or recommendations are given in the Qur'ān and this is the ultimate authority for all judgment. The second source, the Sunnah, is based on the behaviour, actions or sayings of the Prophet, the collections of which are called al-Ḥadīth (traditions) and were vital to the community who wished to know of Muḥammad's practices for their own guidance. Every person who had contact with the Prophet was continually being asked questions regarding him and eventually his actions and sayings were written down in several large collections as separate from the Qur'ān. The most scrupulous criteria were used in these compilations and each source was subject to vigorous scrutiny. Many thousands were rejected but those which were accepted are all ultimately traceable to the companions or wives of the Prophet.

The implementation of these records rests on the work of four great jurists who in the second century after Muḥammad's death spent their lives interpreting them. These men were Abū Ḥanīfah (d. Baghdad 767); Mālik b. Anas (d. Medina 791) Muḥ. b. Aḥmad al-Shāfiʿī (d. Cairo 819) and Aḥmad b. Ḥanbal (d. Baghdad 885). The work of these men, who were honoured with the title Imām, forms the basis for the four madhāhib (sing. madhhab) or schools of law—Ḥanafī, Shāfiʿī, Mālikī and Ḥanbalī—and all Sunnī Muslims follow one or other of these schools. There is no question that any slight difference between these schools is divisive, they are merely variations in practice. The Shāfiʿī school predominated in N Egypt until the Ottoman conquest in 1517 after which the Ḥanafī's gradually gained in influence. The majority of Southern Egyptians are Mālikī, following the preponderance of this school in N Africa. The Shiʿī adherants had their own traditions.

The last two bases are really self-explanatory and are used when answers cannot be found in the other sources. The arbiters in Qiyās are the qāḍīs, lawyers well versed in the law.

Thus within this framework the concern of the last three sections is as follows:

C. **Transactions** cover marriage, inheritance and commercial dealings. Marriage, a civil contract only, concerns divorce, reconciliation and prohibitions. Inheritance is a complicated matter involving bequests in a specific way. Commercial dealings are concerned with usury, ownership of property and awaqf (religious endowments).

D. **Moralities** concern the behaviour and manner of the believer, covering all aspects of emotion.

E. **Punishment** deals with the justice to be meted to the transgressor of the law, from injuring the human body, property, honour, breaking of the peace, offences against religion or decency and rebellion against the established government. The punishments are precise. It also covers the classification of unlawful acts and prohibited foods.

Although the modern legal system of Egypt is based on the Code Napoleon (itself influenced by Malikī law), the shariʿah is nonetheless the framework within which devout Muslims regulate their lives.

*Waqf* (pl. awqaf) is a religious legal term found in the text which needs to be explained—this is an endowment by an individual of property, the profits from which inalienably and in perpetuity are for specified uses,the upkeep of a certain mosque, school, fountain or provision of food for the poor.

**Sufism**. While the majority of the population are content to live their lives within the tenets of Islam, for some this is not enough; for them the search for knowledge of Allāh has to be actively pursued. Monasticism and isolation from the community are expressly forbidden in Islam so there have evolved within the population groups of men who seek this knowledge and regulate their lives to an Islamic ideal.

These associations of men engaged in spiritual discipline and devotion must have existed since the earliest times but it was not until the early 12C that individuals emerge to be recognised as shaykhs with a following of initiates. These shaykhs claimed to be heirs to a ṭarīqah (way) passed on to them by previous savants in a direct silsilah (chain) from an early master, usually a companion of the Prophet. The groups assumed names derived from that of their shaykh and among the most important in the Western Islamic region were the *Suhrawardiyyah* (Abū Najīb al-Suhrawardī, died Iraq 1168); *Qādiriyyah* (ʿAbd al-Qādir al-Jīlāni, died Iraq 1166); *Rifāʿiyyah* (Aḥmad b. al-Rifāʿī, died Batāih, Iraq, 1182); *Shādhiliyyah* (Abū ʾl-Ḥasan ʿAlī al-Shādhilī, died Ḥumaythrā, Egypt, 1258); *Mawlawiyyah* (Jalāl al-Dīn Rūmī, died Konya, 1273), and a later Ottoman brotherhood, the *Khalawātiyyah* (ʿUmar al-Khalawātī, died Persia, 1397).

Of the cadet branches of the main tarīqahs some of the most important in Egypt were: from the Rifāʿiyyah, the *Badawiyyah* (Aḥ. al-Badawī, died Tantā, 1276), also called Aḥmadiyyah; *Dasūqiyyah* (Ibrāhīm Dasūqī, died Dasūq, 1283), also called Burhaniyyah; and the *Saʿdiyyah* (Saʿd al-Dīn al-Shaybānī, died Jibah, 1385): from the Khalawātī, the *Damirdāshiyyah* (Shams al-Dīn Damirdāsh, died Cairo, 1523), and the *Bakriyyah* (Muṣṭafā al-Bakrī, died Cairo, 1709): and from the Shādhiliyyah, the *Wafāʾiyyah* (Muḥ. b. Aḥ. al-Wafāʾ, died Cairo, 1358). Another group, not considered to be sufīs by the orthodox, was the eccentric *Baktāshiyyah* (Baktāsh al-Khurasānī, died c 1337). Introduced into Egypt with the Ottoman conquest, it was patronised , as in Anatolia, by the troops, particularly the Janissaries. In the reign of Muḥammad ʿAlī, the Shaykh al-Bakrī was made controller of all the sufī brotherhoods in Egypt.

These masters with others directed the devotions of the students with prayers and dhikr (remembrance), which often took the form of chants or complex exercises.

It is supposed that they received the name *sufi* from their garments of wool (ṣūf). Occasionally the most intense students eventually reached such a state of knowledge that they were given permission by the shaykh to found ṭarīqahs of their own. These students returned to their own country or spread throughout the Muslim world, often on the boundaries of Islam or even beyond, and many of them were instrumental in introducing Islam into other areas.

Though the mass of the population remained uninvolved, they regarded the sufis with affection and respect, while they did not interfere with formal devotions or oppose the traditional ʿulamā. Sufism is traditionally credited with being introduced into Egypt by Dhū ʾl-Nūn Miṣrī (died 860), a Nubian, but the movement received its greatest impetus in the 12C under the Ayyūbids who actively encouraged the establishment of the brotherhoods in Syria and Egypt during the great reaction to the Fāṭimids' Shi ʿī doctrines. Hostels (khānqāhs) and mosques (zāwiyahs) were built for them to reside in. They prospered also under the Mamlūks but it was during the Ottoman period that they reached the height of influence. Almost every mosque in Cairo was the headquarters of a brotherhood; this was aided by the fact that many of them received active patronage from the sultans in Istanbul and the bays in Cairo. But in the Arabian Peninsula during the 18C, a movement formed in direct opposition to the practice of the sufis, founded by Muḥammad Ibn ʿAbd al-Wahhāb (died 1765). He preached a fundamentalist doctrine which gathered many adherants and many of the revered tombs of the early Muslims were razed. Although suppressed by Muḥammad ʿAlī, they remained a powerful influence to resurface eventually as the founders of the modern state of Saudi Arabia. In the *Tijānyyah* and the *Sanūsiyyah*, founded in the early 19C, reverence for other shaykhs was minimised.

The strenuous exercises undertaken by some of the sufī groups attracted a great deal of attention from 19C European visitors to Egypt, who completely misunderstood the intent. They were fascinated yet alarmed by the chanting, dancing and exertions of the devotees, unaware that they were under complete control by the shaykh. In 1882 the Khedive Tawfīq, under intense pressure, issued a proclamation banning all these practices.

The *Ikhwān al-Muslimīn* (Muslim Brotherhood), a pan-Islamic movement opposed to the brotherhoods, although also fundamentalist in belief, achieved great influence between the two World Wars. After this set-back, the brotherhoods are experiencing a revival and at many of the mūlids of Egypt their presence is obvious, with their banners and distinctive clothing. Now adherents have to be officially registered as members of an association.

# Islamic Egypt

In the winter of AD 639 ʿAmr ibn al-ʿAṣ, at the head of an Arab army, entered Egypt from Syria. The Arabian Peninsula, Iraq and Syria were safely under Muslim control and the khalīf ʿUmar had turned his armies against the two great hostile empires on his flanks—Persia in the E and Byzantium in the W. ʿAmr entrenched at Pelusium for six months. He advanced in 640, not towards the capital Alexandria but towards a much more strategic goal, the fortress of Babylon about 12km S of the point where the Nile divides to form the Delta. He defeated the Byzantine forces at Heliopolis in July and besieged Babylon. Cyrus, the Patriarch-Governor imposed upon Egypt by the Byzantine Emperor Heraclius, sued for peace, but was accused of treason by the emperor. However, the latter died six months later, and Babylon capitulated in April 641. Alexandria was ʿAmr's next goal and, although a much more difficult objective, by September 642 it was his by treaty. The invaders were welcomed by the Copts who were reconciled to the Arabs as they had rid them of the Greek Melkites and allowed them to reinstate their own Patriarch, Benjamin.

As in other territories conquered by the Arabs, they did not choose the existing capital as their own, but on the orders of the Khalīf ʿUmar built a town beside the fortress Babylon, a loose agglomeration of dwellings called Fusṭāṭ (The Encampment). It was from here that Egypt was administered as an occupied province of the Khalifate, first for the khalīfs in Medina, then the Ummayyads in Damascus and, after a violent transfer of dynasty in 750, the ʿAbbāsids in Baghdad. During this period there were about eighty governors but only two khalīfs ever visited Egypt in person. Marwān II, the last Ummayyad, fled there during the ʿAbbāsid conquest of Damascus but was caught and murdered in 752, while the Khalīf Maʿmūn, son of Hārūn al-Rashīd, went to Egypt in 832 to suppress a revolt in the Delta. During his brief stay in Egypt he tried to force an entry into one of the pyramids.

Egypt provided the lands of the Khalifate with food and considerable revenue, as it had done other empires before. Slowly there was an Arabisation of the native population. Islam, the religion of the occupying army, was gradually accepted by many of the Coptic population and Arabic increased as the popular language. At the same time the invaders were exposed to many modifying influences, not least of which was the four thousand years of civilisation to which the Egyptians were heir. But inevitably, as the strength of the Khalifate declined, rent by dynastic squabbles, the administration of Egypt slowly disintegrated, taxes became intolerable and prices rose. In 868 the Khalīf al-Muʿtazz chose a governor for Egypt and the latter sent his newphew, Aḥmad ibn Ṭūlūn, there to direct his administration for him.

**The Ṭūlūnids** (868–905). Aḥmad ibn Ṭūlūn governed at first from Fusṭāṭ and, over several years, gradually extended his administrative and territorial power. He constructed a new town, al-Qaṭāʿiʾ (The Concessions), to the NE of Fusṭāṭ and built up a great army of slaves. His eventual influence was such that he was able to interfere in a struggle between two contenders for the Khalifate. By the time he died he was in control of much of Syria and independent of Baghdad. He had restored economic stability to Egypt and, although the Khalifate retaliated, the system he instituted outlived him and such was the power of his son and successor, Khumārawayh (884), that he was able to dictate terms to the khalīf delineating his own territory. Although capable he was a spendthrift, the economy decayed and in 896 he was murdered by his slaves. He was succeeded by his two young sons. The first, Jaysh, alienated the troops and was himself murdered after nine months; the second, Hārūn, although managing to govern for nine years, was unable to halt the economic decline and he was also mysteriously murdered in 904. The ʿAbbāsid forces invaded in 905 and, although Hārūn's uncle, Shaybān, tried to rally support, he was captured and sent to Baghdad in chains.

A new governor was chosen by the khalīf and for the next thirty years Egypt was again under direct control of the central government in Baghdad, ruled by a series of military leaders. However, the rule was oppressive and taxation high, the usual signs of ineffectual administration. The Byzantines were again attempting invasion on the N coast and a new power in the W, the Fāṭimids, had made several efforts at conquest. At this point the khalīf al-Rāḍī, looking for a strong self-reliant province of Egypt, appointed Muḥammad ibn Tughj as governor in 935.

**The Ikhshids** (935–969). Muḥammad ibn Tughj repelled a Fāṭimid invasion and set the affairs of Egypt in order. His regime, unlike that of ibn Ṭūlūn, retained a friendly relationship with the ʿAbbāsids and he was awarded the title Ikhshid (an Iranian word meaning ruler) by the khalīf. Included in his territories were Northern and Central Syria and he protected his land with what was probably the largest army in the Islamic world. He was succeeded by his two sons, Ūnūjūr (946) and ʿAlī (961), but the real power was held by their tutor, Kāfūr, a Nubian who, on the death of ʿAlī in 965, was confirmed as ruler by the khalīf. He was capable and extremely talented and, due to his efforts, the country remained at peace. His death in 968, combined with a series of low Niles, famine and the defection of the Wazīr ibn Killis, were the signals for the Fāṭimids to invade. His successor, Aḥmad, the son of ʿAlī, was incapable of repulsing them and fled to Syria.

**The Fāṭimids** (969–1171). The Fāṭimid rulers claimed descent from Fāṭimah, the daughter of Muḥammad, and ʿAlī, the fourth khalīf. The conflict within the Muslim nation subsequent to the election of the latter had split it into two great parties. The supporters of Muʿāwiyyah, who eventually became khalīf, were called Sunnī (Orthodox) and the supporters of ʿAlī Shiʿī (Party [of ʿAlī]). Although the Shiʿī were unable to regain control of the central authority they remained very powerful and evolved a complex esoteric theology based on the reappearance of the 'hidden' seventh Imām Ismāʿil and on interpretation of the 'hidden' meanings in the Qur'ān, principles totally abhorrent to Sunni Muslims. A group of them came from Syria in 909 and settled in North Africa, modern Tunisia and with the support of the Berbers they established themselves and created a new capital, al-Mahdiyyah. But Egypt lay between them and their ultimate goal, Baghdad.

They had made several attacks on Egypt during the early 10C but had been defeated by the Ikhshid army. In 969 Jawhar, commander of the forces of the fourth Fāṭimid khalīf, al-Muʿizz, entered Fusṭāṭ meeting little resistance. He immediately started to build a new city a little to the N of Fusṭāṭ. It was named al-Qāhirah (The Victorious) and consisted of a walled enclosure containing palaces and halls and the great mosque of al-Azhar. When it was finished, al-Muʿizz came with the bodies of his ancestors and dwelt there. The Ṭūlūnids and Ikhshids, although independent of Baghdad, recognised the Khalīf as the leader of the Muslim community and never challenged this office. The aims of the Fāṭimids, on the contrary, were much greater, nothing less than claiming the khalifate for themselves, even assuming the titles and formalities proper to that office.

The first three khalīfs, al-Muʿizz (953), al-ʿAzīz (975) and al-Ḥākim (996), retained full personal control of the government as absolute monarch and imam. The fiscal and administrative systems were revised to great efficiency. The empire was vast, North Africa, Sicily, Syria, the Ḥijāz and Egypt itself as the centre of a vast propaganda machine spreading the cause of the Ismāʿīlī Shiʿī doctrine throughout the Muslim sphere. A great slave army was built up consisting of many races—Berbers, Sudanese, European and Turks—in which the Turks gained dominance over the other groups.

While the first two khalīfs were moderate in their views and great organisers, the third, al-Ḥākim, was mentally disturbed and issued many outrageous laws which greatly offended the population. He disappeared one night while out riding, presumably murdered, and became the object of a cult among a section of the Ismāʿīlīs which eventually gave rise to the religion of the Druzes in Northern Syria. He was followed by two minors, al-Ẓāhir (1021), his nephew, and al-Mustanṣir (1036), the latter's son, neither of whom was fully in control of the government. Al-Ẓāhir was controlled by his aunt, Sitt al-Mulk, who may not have been entirely innocent of complicity in the murder of her brother al-Ḥākim. Al-Mustanṣir, who reigned for almost sixty years, was at first subordinate to the personality of his wazīr and also his mother but eventually managed to become independent.

During these two last reigns, the power of the army commanders grew until they became the controlling force in the empire which, because of these very troubles, gradually dwindled. Inevitably the administration broke down and a series of famines led to chaos. In desperation the khalīf sent for the governor of Acre, Badr al-Jamāli, to come and take control. Badr arrived in secret in 1074 with his Armenian guards and immediately rounded up the army officers and had them executed. He was soon master of Egypt and had all the highest offices, military and civil, invested upon himself, including the wazirate. This post became permanent and he was succeeded by his son and a series of amīrs, some of whom were not Shiʿī but Sunnī, who kept the khalīf in tutelage.

These commanders restored peace, security and prosperity to Egypt and the Fāṭimid khalifate survived for another hundred years. The wazir al-Afḍal, the son of Badr, was powerful enough to choose the successor to Khalīf Mustanṣir, not the elder son, al-Nāzir, but the younger, al-Mustaʿlī. This action destroyed the Fāṭimids' spiritual leadership of the Ismāʿīlī Shiʿīs which passed to Ḥassan-i Sabbāh of the ʿAlamūt in Persia. The modern leaders of this faction are the Agha Khans. This leadership was further eroded when many Ismāʿīlīs refused to recognise as the successor of al-Muṣtaʿlī's son al-Āmir (1101), his cousin al-Ḥāfiz (1131).

The early Fāṭimids produced an able administration resulting in economic stability. Foreign trade expanded in Europe and India, the complex tax system, a great burden on the population, was abolished. Syria remained an important area of supply, providing minerals and timber. By 1079 Northern Syria was controlled by the Saljuk Turks who had invaded from the E, disintegrating into a series of rival states in perpetual feud, with Fāṭimid control confined to the coastal strip. It was at this time that the First Crusade entered Syria from the NW in 1097, aiming to free Jerusalem from Muslim control. The Fāṭimids greeted the Crusaders in a friendly fashion until they attacked Jerusalem in 1098, which had been held by the Fāṭimids for two years; it was captured by the Crusaders in 1099. They established four Christian states on the Syrian seaboard centred on the Kingdom of Jerusalem, though they never established themselves far into the interior.

At first the Muslim states paid scant heed to the new arrivals but one state gradually became all-powerful and was to take the lead in the assault against the Crusaders. The Saljuk Sultan had in his service Zangī, a Turk who was appointed governor of Mosul in 1127. Over the next ten years he extended his control over Northern Syria, capturing Aleppo and threatening Damascus. His success was due to a combination of military strength and the juggling of a series of political treaties with the Christian and Muslim states. He eventually conquered Edessa, the most northerly of the Christian states, in 1145 but died a year later. He was succeeded by his son, Nūr al-Dīn, and, although the arrival of the Second Crusade in 1148 complicated the situation, he extended the territories even further in 1154 by capturing Damascus.

The Kurdish commander of Nūr al-Dīn, Shirkūh was accompanied on his campaigns by Ṣalāḥ al-Dīn, son of his brother Ayyūb. When the crusaders attacked Egypt in 1168, they led an expedition there and were welcomed by the population. After several battles the Christians withdrew. In 1169 Shirkūh became the wazīr of the Fāṭimid khalīf al-ʿĀḍid (who had succeeded in 1160) but died almost immediately. He was replaced by Ṣalāḥ al-Dīn, who by 1170 was virtually independent of Nūr al-Dīn and set about extending his power in Egypt. In 1171, as al-ʿĀḍid, lay dying, Ṣalāḥ al-Dīn instructed an imām to recite the khutbah (Friday sermon) in the name of the ʿAbbāsid khalīf, al-Mustaḍī', thus formally abolishing the Fāṭimid khalifate.

**The Ayyūbids** (1171–1252). Ṣalāḥ al-Dīn, having consolidated his position in Egypt, turned his attention to Syria. After several engagements with the Christians, by 1183 it was his and he was ready to unleash the Jihād (Holy War). He led many successful expeditions culminating in the capture of Jerusalem in 1187. This provoked the Third Crusade, led by Barbarossa accompanied by Richard I of England. Ṣalāḥ al-Dīn died peacefully in Damascus in 1193, his father Ayyūb giving his name to the dynasty that was to follow him and, although his Syrian territories broke up into petty principalities after his death, Egypt remained firm. He had instituted great cultural change within Egypt, which was once more brought into direct contact with the central Muslim lands. The Shiʿī faction was eradicated and madrasahs, schools of orthodox religious teaching, were built. A new social order was introduced and it was a period of growth and prosperity. With expanding relations Egypt became a great centre of Islamic scholarship. Ṣalāḥ al-Dīn also refortified Cairo, building a great citadel and enclosing the city in immense walls.

ʿĀdil I, Ṣalāḥ al-Dīn's brother, became Sultan in 1199 and recovered the Syrian possessions. He was very capable, as was his son and successor, al-Kāmil I (1218). The Christians, realising that Egypt was the key to their advance in the East, initiated the Fifth Crusade specifically with the intention of invading it (the Fourth had ended with the sacking of Constantinople). The Crusaders captured Damietta in 1219 and advanced to Manṣūrah where they entrenched but were driven out in 1221. For the next twenty years there were many battles and treaties with the Crusader states in Palestine. Al-Kāmil was succeeded by al-ʿĀdil II (1238) and subsequently by al-Ṣāliḥ Ayyūb (1240) who built up an immense army of Turkish slaves (mamlūks), mainly Qipchaqs brought from the region to the north of the Black Sea, and installed them in the great River Citadel on Rawḍah Island in the Nile near Cairo from whence they were called Baḥris (baḥr; river).

Another Crusade was launched, led by the French king Louis IX, again aimed at subduing Egypt. Damietta was captured from the sea in June 1249 and by December the Crusaders had seized Manṣūrah. Stalemate was reached and the situation dragged on until April 1250, by which time the Christians were in a sorry state. They decided to retreat and it was no great challenge for the Egyptians to capture the army, including King Louis himself. The latter was kept prisoner in Manṣūrah and only released after the payment of a colossal ransom. At this point occurred one of the most extraordinary episodes in Egyptian history (see Rte 11), suffice it to state here that Ayyūb had died in 1249 and his wife Shajar al-Durr, concealing the fact for some time, ruled in his place while Ayyūb's son, Tūrān Shāh, returned from Syria. Shortly after his arrival he alienated the mamlūks and was murdered in 1250, with his stepmother's approval, by a group of them led by Baybars. Shajar al-Durr was proclaimed sultan but was forced by circumstances to marry the chief mamlūk, Aybak. However, he also gained the enmity of his wife and was murdered in April 1259. Three days later Shajar al-Durr herself was murdered.

**Baḥrī Mamlūks** (1250–1382). The process of choosing the next ruler set the pattern of succession for a long time to come. ʿAlī, the son of Aybak, was chosen as successor, but without power, while the mamlūks chose a leader from among themselves. Qutuz, commander of the mamlūks, was chosen and ʿAlī was retired peacefully. Throughout the previous century waves of Central Asian nomads had swept into Mesopotamia and Syria—Turkomans, Saljuks and, finally, the Mongols, who in the 13C conquered all before them. Persia had fallen and in 1258 they captured Baghdad and massacred the khalīf and all his family. They took Aleppo in January 1260 and three months later entered Damascus; from there making attacks against Gaza and Hebron. The mamlūks, led by Baybars, met the Mongols in Syria at ʿAyn Jalūt (Goliath's Spring) in September and gained a great victory, the first major campaign that the Mongols had lost. The cities in Syria rose up against their conquerors and the Mongols retreated to the N into Anatolia. Although they harried the N borders of Syria for some time after, they were never again to threaten Egypt directly.

**EXAMPLES OF MAMLŪK HERALDIC SYMBOLS**

Cup (sāqī)
Napkin(ustadār)
Penbox(dawādār)
Sword(ṣilaḥdār)

On his return to Egypt Baybars had Qutuz murdered and was elected as Sultan. He set about strengthening his position with a series of military expeditions against the Crusader and Ayyūbid principalities in Syria, the Armenians in Cilicia, the Assassins in SW Asia and, in the S the Nubians. He used diplomacy as well as belligerency and established relations with Christian countries on the N coast of the Mediterranean, even as far W as Aragon. Baybars also legalised his position in another way. An ʿAbbāsid prince, al-Mustanṣir, a relative of the dead khalīf, who had fled during the sack of Baghdad, was rescued from the desert and pronounced khalīf by Baybars in 1261. As well as placing Egypt firmly in the centre of the Sunnī sphere, this also gave him the support of the Sharīf of Mecca and thus control of the Ḥijāz.

In the Mamlūk states slaves were purchased by dealers from countries outside the Muslim territories, usually SW Asia or Europe, given a rudimentary education and brought to the great slave markets in Egypt and Syria. Since the majority of them were Turks, mainly Qipchaqs, Turkish became the language of the Mamlūk state. The slaves were rebought by the great amīrs or the Sulṭan, who had started their own careers in the same way. It was the duty of the new owner to have the mamlūks (owned) instructed in religion and given military training. After several years, when this education was completed, the slaves were formally manumitted at a great ceremony and given a state stipend. They then entered military service, usually in the train of their former masters, to whom they were intensely loyal, since they owed their freedom to them. The most promising were then given official positions in the household, wardrobe, kitchen, stables or treasury, and if they were successful, advanced in rank and were after some years invested as an amīr (commander). The lowest grade was an Amīr of Ten responsible for ten mamlūks, the next grade was an Amīr of Forty, distinguished by having a band which played before his official dwelling. If of exceptional potential, or great nerve, the mamlūk could reach the highest rank of all, the Amīr of One Hundred (mamlūks), commander of one thousand troops, from which group the great state functionaries were drawn. They invariably retained their Turkish birth names, Baybars, Aqsungur etc, but gave Arabic names to their children.

The Sultan had mamlūks of four classes, those purchased by himself, those purchased by his predecessor, those purchased by an amīr and passing on the latter's death into his possession, and those manumitted by an amīr and entering into his service. A small proportion of the Sultan's 2–10,000 mamlūks when they were manumitted were chosen as Khassikiyyah (intimates) who were specially favoured by the Sultan and trusted with the most important palace functions. The most important military officials, Men of the Sword, were the Nā'ib (Viceroy); Atabak (Commander of the Armies), later also called the Amīr al-Kabīr (Grand Amīr); Amīr Ṣilāh (Controller of the Armaments); Hājib (Chamberlain); Amīr Majlis (Controller of the Council Chamber); Amīr Akhūr (Amīr of the Horse, in charge of the Stables); Khazindār (Keeper of the Treasury); Ustadār (Chief Steward); Dawādār (Secretary); Mihmandār (Royal Host), and the two Heads of Guards, of the Mamlūks and of the Amīrs. The Wazīr (Counsellor) was at first a great military official but these duties were gradually assumed by other officials, particularly the ustadār and the rank declined to a civilian post. There were many lesser positions such as Sāqī (Cup-Bearer); Jandār (Wardrobe-Keeper); Jāshnakīr (Taster); Jūkandār (Polo-Stick Keeper), etc. Each of the great amīrs maintained his own household with analagous grades to that of the Sultan. The mamlūks had a complex system of blazon denoting rank which they displayed on their buildings and possessions and it is one of the anomalies of mamlūk life that incumbents often kept these lesser titles with great pride when they had been elevated into the ranks of the great amīrs or even become sultan. Where colours of blazons are mentioned in the text these are taken from other sources, lamps, painted wood etc.

In addition to the mamlūks, who were the elite mounted troops, were the Ḥalqah, the vast army of enlisted free troopers, many of them the sons of previous mamlūks. Although they had their own officers they were controlled by the amīrs.

The civil executive, Men of the Pen, were usually drawn from the Egyptian population and the most powerful of them was the Wazīr, addressed as Sāḥib, but he deferred (see above) to the amīrs in status. The rest were controllers of various financial agencies for the army, privy funds, granaries, etc. A post of great status was the Mu'allim ak-Mi'mariyyah, the chief architect, several of whom are known. The Judiciary, consisting of the representatives of the four schools of law under the authority of the Grand Qāḍī, and the secular officials, the surgeons and physicians, were also Egyptians. Another powerful group waiting to exploit any sign of weakness in the ranks of the amīrs were the eunuchs and the slave girls and in the late 14C, during the unstable reigns of the sons of Sultan al-Nāṣir Muḥammad, they achieved great influence.

The children and wives of the mamlūks, and even amīrs, had no claim to any of their fathers' or husbands' wealth which after their death was distributed among the other amīrs and new intake of mamlūks. Thus within one generation had begun their assimilation into the Egyptian population. Very few of the sons of sultans, although nominated as heirs, had a powerful enough following of mamlūks to maintain their position, which usually fell to the most powerful amīrs, who often seem to have arisen in pairs, with a resultant contest of strength for supremacy.

*A ceremonial scene, probably based on the court of Sultan al-Nāṣir Muḥammad. From the* Maqamat al-Ḥarīrī *(1334) (Nationalbibliothek, Vienna)*

Baybars was followed by his son, Barakah-Khān (1277), who was deposed in favour of his seven-year-old brother Salāmish (1280) but, in the same year, the atabak Qalāwūn assumed the title of Sultan as well as the reality. He founded a dynasty that was to last 100 years, not always through the son, occasionally through a bondsman of the family, but the last sultan of the line, al-Ḥājjī II, was his descendant in the fifth generation. Qalāwūn followed the policies of Baybars, establishing relations as far away as Ceylon and the East African coast. He purchased large numbers of Circassian mamlūks who he housed in the Mountain Citadel and, for this reason, they were called Burgīs (Ar. burg: tower). These mamlūks with other loyalties were continually at loggerheads with the Baḥrī mamlūks from the Island Citadel on Rawḍah which group produced all the early sultans with one exception (Baybars II). Qalāwūn successfully attacked the Mongol and Christian states, the latter being left only with the port of Acre and a small surrounding area. He was followed by his son, Khalīl (1290) who, in 1291 captured Acre and razed the Crusaders' castles. The other Crusader towns capitulated and the Crusaders retreated to Cyprus.

Al-Nāṣir Muḥammad (1294), another of Qalāwūn's sons, became sultan, his reign lasting until 1340 with several short usurpations by Amīrs Kitbughā (1295), Lajīn (1297) and Baybars II al-Jāshankīr (1309). Despite this, his long reign was marked by security and prosperity for Egypt. Political and economic ties were strengthened with European states and treaties made with the Mongol states.

In the 40 years following the death of Sult. al-Nāṣir Muḥammad there was a series of eleven sultans, all his sons or relatives. They were mostly ineffectual, incompetent, or unbalanced, and of the two who did show some ability for government Ismāʿīl (1342) died of grief after the execution of his brothers Aḥmad I and Kujuk, while al-Ḥasan (1345 and 1347) was imprisoned and probably murdered. The power was in the hands of the amīrs who indulged in ferocious internecine conflicts. But external relations during this period were tranquil with trade flourishing and virtually no enemies to threaten the borders.

**Burgī Mamlūks** (1382–1517). In 1382 the sultanate was seized by Barqūq, a Burgī mamlūk from the citadel, and it was the Circassians from this barracks who were to rule Egypt for the next 140 years. Although of different racial origins Turkish remained the all-important unifying language. But another threat appeared from the E. In Persia, Timūr (Tamerlane), an amīr of the Khān, had usurped the Khanate and was harrying lands far from Persia, first to the E, but by 1387 his troops were on the borders of Syria. Timūr was kept at bay by Barqūq, but during the reign of Barqūq's son Farag (1399) he sacked Damascus in 1400. Fortunately Timūr turned E again, but in Egypt the campaign had been paid for by heavy taxes and the stable administration was shattered. This was followed in 1403 by famine and plague. Once again the economy started to deteriorate.

After the death of Farag, the open sultanate was filled for six months by the ʿAbbāsid khalīf, al-Mustaʿīn, who was deposed by Muʿayyad Shaykh (1412). He pushed back the frontiers in Syria, but at further expense to the economy and the imposition of state trade monopolies. After his death in 1421 there were three sultans within a year, a sign of the great struggles that went on among the amīrs for succession, but the next sultan, Barsbay

(1422), was a strong character. His relations with the new power in the N, the Ottomans, were generally friendly, although there was trouble in the NE with the Turkomans. Egyptian influence increased and her sea power was supreme in the Eastern Mediterranean while trade expanded in the Indian Ocean. All this, however, was not enough. State monopolies increased and production dropped, raising the cost of living. These trends continued for the next hundred years, though it was a period of relative peace and cultural vitality.

There were few remarkable sultans during this period but Qāyt-bāy (1468–1498) was an exception. Under him there was a revival, although his building programmes threw a great burden on the economy. But several vital factors were leading towards a crisis. The Portuguese had found their way into the Indian Ocean providing Europe with a direct route to S Asia and the spice trade and, by the time of Sultan Qānṣūḥ al-Gl-Ghawrī (1501), they were powerful enough to penetrate far into the Red Sea. The Ottomans, under Salim I, were engaged in a war with the Ismāʿīl, Safavid Sultan of Persia. Both sides were casting covetous eyes on the territory of Syria. Qānṣūḥ led an army to observe the outcome of the war which the Ottomans won, next turning towards the Mamlūk territories in Syria. Qānṣūḥ was forced into a battle in August 1516, in which he was severely hampered by the defection to the Ottomans of his governor of Aleppo, Khāyrbak. The two armies met at Marj Dabiq but Sultan Qānṣūḥ died of a stroke on the battlefield. On the last day of 922 AH/23 Jan. 1517, Sultan Salim, after some initial resistance, was in Cairo. Tūmān Bay II, who had been made sultan after the death of Qānṣūḥ, offered some opposition but was captured and hanged in Cairo. Khayrbak, the former governor of Aleppo, was made Ottoman governor of Egypt. The last khalīf, Mutuwakkil III, was sent to Istanbul, returning to Cairo some years later as a private citizen. The rule of the mamlūks, it seemed, was finished.

It is one of the anomalies of history that during periods of political turmoil the art of the chronicler flourishes. Egypt was no exception and although it was only one aspect of the great Islamic literary tradition, through these authors the whole history of the Mamlūk period is documented. Four exponents were outstanding and between them provide an unbroken chronicle of the Mamlūk domination from its rise to its fall, if not through direct observation then through intercourse with eyewitnesses and veterans or use of earlier journals.

The earliest was Abū ʾl-ʿAbbās Tāqī al-Dīn Aḥmad **al-Maqrizī** (1364–1442) who had a theological education and became a tutor and administrator. His access to records of an earlier period extend his journal to the rise of the Ayyūbids in 1174. Next was Abū Maḥmud Mụḥ al-ʿAyntabi called **al-ʿ Ayni** (d. 1451) who became an adviser to Sultan Barsbāy to whom he read his journals and translated them into Arabic for him. The upbringing of Abū ʾl-Mahaṣīn Jamāl al-Dīn Yūsuf **ibn Taghrībardī** (1409–70) was very different. He was the son of the atabak Amīr Taghrībardī and was raised in the court circle by his sister who was married to the chief qadi, while his cousin Shīrīn married Sultan Barqūq. Thus he was admitted to the greatest houses in the land and his journals reflect this fact. Lastly Abū ʾl-Barakat Zayn al-Dīn Muḥammad ibn Aḥmad **ibn Iyās** (1448–1524) was also descended from a mamlūk family although of lesser degree and at a greater distance. His humbler training was mainly in administration. The additional importance of his work is that it spans the critical period of the downfall of the Mamlūk state and the first years of the Ottoman occupation.

Another magnificent literary product of the period was Alf Laylah wa Laylah—*The 1001 Nights.* This corpus of stories had been in existence for many centuries and displays diverse origins. At the core are stories from India and Persia translated into

Arabic early in the history of Islam. Grafted on to this is a collection of tales from the golden age of Arabic literature during the ʿAbbāsid Khalifate of Baghdad. To these the Egyptians added from their own great fund of jokes and folktales, some of which had been in existence since ancient times. All these tales and romances, whatever their origin, were decorated with the appurtenances of Mamlūk society and in the 14C were written down much the form in which they are known today.

**Ottoman Period** (1516–1805). The Ottomans were one of the many Central Asian tribes of Turks and Mongols who had moved westward during the course of the previous millennium. They had gradually established themselves by conquest and good fortune as one of the most powerful states in W Asia. Constantinople fell to them in 1453 and; by the end of the 15C they were challenging Persia for control of Mesopotamia. Egypt, as described, was taken by the Ottomans in 1516, her provinces of Syria and Arabia also being absorbed into the empire.

Thus, once more, Egypt became a dependancy of an immense empire, ruled from the N and playing little part in its triumphs and glories. Burdened with a great tax and governed by generally uninterested foreigners more concerned with furthering their careers in Istanbul, it declined as a cultural centre, yet throughout the period retained its importance as a religious fountainhead. It was administered from Istanbul by a series of governors distinguished by the title Pasha, who were trained in the capital as part of the imperial household, their powers severely limited and their terms of office short, thus having little opportunity to found independent dynasties, though this did not stop one or two of them trying.

The importation of slaves from many areas, though mainly from the Caucasus, and their assimilation into the military corps continued unabated during the following centuries and—as under the mamlūks—it was this system which eventually dictated the administration. There were seven active military uchaqs (corps), two of foot, three mounted and two which combined infantry and mounted forces. The organisation of each was similar, commanded by an Āghā (Lord) assisted by the Katkhudā (Lieutenant) in whom generally the power resided. Other ranks included the Ūdahbāshā (Chamberlain), Shurbagī (Steward), Kātib (Secretary) and Yuldash (Private Soldier).

The most powerful corps, though not the most prestigious, were the Janissaries, called in Egypt Mustaḥfiẓān (Guardians), or Inkshāriyyah, the infantry corps responsible for the security of the walls and Citadel of Cairo. They occupied the upper Citadel and acquired control over most of the high revenue agencies, the granary, mint, and awqāf, and provided the principal officers of these. Their āghā was given precedence above those of all the other corps. Another infantry corps, the ʿAzabān (Bachelors), had similar duties but at an inferior level. Their particular responsibility was the protection of the approaches to Cairo, the agricultural areas of Egypt and patrolling the mouths of the Nile. In the late 17C they became extremely powerful and generally had the support of the other corps in opposition to the Mustaḥfiẓān. They occupied the lower levels of the Citadel.

The five others were called the lesser corps. The three mounted corps; the Gonulliyan (Volunteers) later called the Camulyan (Cameleers), Tufankciyan (Riflemen) and the Cerkase (Cirassians), were mainly concerned with providing protection for the provincial governors, delivering official messages and collecting taxes. The two corps which combined infantry and cavalry troops were chiefly for the service of the Pasha and the dīwān. Most prestigious of all the corps was the Mutafarriqah, founded specifically to counterbalance the influence of the two infantry corps. Its income exceeded that of the Mustaḥfiẓān, with control of several high revenue agencies. By the mid-17C, however, the Mustaḥfizān and ʿAzabān were powerful enough to appropriate most of their agencies and they were, in effect, controlled by the Mustaḥfiẓān. The Shawishān, created from mamlūks who declared their loyalty to the Ottomans, were similar to the latter corps but in an inferior position. By the mid 17C they had also declined to a mere appendage to the Mustaḥfiẓān. From the ranks of all these corps were chosen the amīrs, the highest ranking of whom were called Bays and who, with the Pasha and the Qāḍī ʿAskār, the judicial officer sent from Istanbul, comprised the diwān (council) of administration.

Slaves were collected outside Egypt and brought to the slave markets of Cairo and Asyūṭ, where they were purchased by the bays and amīrs and maintained in their households. They were educated and given military instruction and after some years formally freed to obtain posts in one of the corps. In addition to these slaves were the freemen who joined the household for a small salary and who were also trained to the same end as the slaves. A system of transfer and promotion ensured that the most able candidates reached the highest posts and entry into the amirate. There are several important differences from the earlier practice. These slaves took Muslim names, and it became commonplace to bequeath wealth to children.

Although the troops had great influence and by the end of the 16C were capable of deposing a pasha who displeased them, in general the Ottomans were capable of maintaining control of the government and ensuring that the revenues were paid to Istanbul. In the early 17C however, the power of the bays was such that a conflict with the pasha was inevitable. Gradually they appropriated many of the financial agencies which provided the taxes and by the mid-17C the pasha was a mere official figurehead. For twenty-five years (1631–56) Raḍwān Bay, the leader of the bays, was the real power, although he co-operated with the governor. Each bay maintained a large household of retainers who, although they may have been employed in one of the corps or with other merchants, remained loyal to their first master.

Two great factions, of obscure origin, the Dhū ʾl-Faqāriyyah and the Qāsimiyyah, divided the bays. These were allied to similar factions among the artisans and Arab tribes. Raḍwān Bay was the leader of the Faqāriyyah and under his protection they became very powerful until, in 1660, the pasha, at the urging of the Qāsimiyyah, had all the leading Faqārī bays executed or exiled and then in 1662 turned on the Qāsimiyyah and murdered their leader, Aḥmad Bay al-Bushnak. By manipulating their mutual rivalry, the pashas for the next thirty years were able to control the bays.

In 1692 Kujuk Muḥammad, an Udah Basha of the Mustaḥfiẓān supported by the Faqāriyyah, rebelled against the senior officers and had them expelled from the corps and, although he was killed two years later by the officers, the old rivalries were rekindled. The Mustaḥfiẓān became overbearing and resented by the other corps and there were several skirmishes between them. Afranj Aḥmad, another Udah Basha of the Mustaḥfiẓān, and again supported by the Faqāriyyah, in 1711 attacked the other corps led by the ʿAzabān supported by the Qāsimiyyah. The Mustaḥfiẓān were defeated and the Pasha Ibrāhīm who had been their puppet was deposed and replaced by Khalīl Pasha. From this time absolute power resided with the Bays. Ismāʿīl Bay was the leader of the Qāsimiyyah who were all powerful until his death in 1744 when they splintered into several factions. The vacuum thus created was filled by the Qazdughliyyah, a client faction of the Faqāriyyah who, until this time, had possessed little power. Ibrāhīm Bay Katkhudā, the leader of this faction, assumed the title Shaykh al-Balad (Elder of the Town), a post that guaranteed the holder almost royal status. This post and that of the Amīr al-Ḥājj (Commander of the Pilgrimage) were usually held by the two most powerful Bays alternately.

After Ibrāhīm's death in 1754 his subordinate, Raḍwān Bay al-Galfī, succeeded but his assassination was followed by a short period of conflict. In 1757 another of Ibrāhīm's bays, ʿAlī Bay al-Kabīr al-Ghazzāwī (the elder) assumed the post of Shaykh al-Balad but after an attempt on the life of the doyen of the bays, ʿAbd al-Raḥman Katkhudā in 1760 he was deposed and ʿAli Bay (the younger) called Bulut Kapan (Cloud catcher) and also called al-Kabīr was raised in his place. ʿAbd al-Raḥman of the Mustaḥfiẓān, was the most influential man in Egypt, although his own interests lay more in aesthetics than the pursuit of power. Nevertheless in 1765 he was exiled by ʿAlī Bay to the Hijāz as a potential source of reaction. ʿAlī Bay revealed himself as the great avenger of his master and so unpopular did he become that he in turn had to flee to Palestine. However, with the support of one of his amīrs, Muḥammad Bay Abū ʾl-Dhahab, he disposed of the opposition. He was recognised by the sultan as autonomous ruler, but was soon appropriating the tax sent to Istanbul. An attempt was made to invade Syria but he was betrayed by Muḥammad Bay, who negotiated with the sultan and, in 1772, ousted ʿAlī from Egypt. Muḥammad Bay ruled as Shaykh al-Balad for three years but died on a campaign in 1775.

Three protagonists emerged, Ismāʿīl Bay (another former bay of Ibrāhīm Katkhudā), Ibrāhīm Bay and Murād Bay, two of Muḥammad Bay's household. The two latter emerged supreme and alternated the posts of Shaykh al-Balad and Amīr al-Ḥājj between them. In 1786 the Ottoman admiral, Ḥasan Pāshā, occupied the Delta and installed Ismāʿīl Bay as Shaykh al-Balad, which post he held until his death in 1791. Immediately Murād and Ibrāhīm returned from Upper Egypt and resumed their dual rule and were still in power when Bonaparte invaded in 1798.

With the death of Ibn Iyās in 1524 the great chronicle of Egypt was discontinued. In comparison to former times the history of the 16–17C is little known and must be gleaned from official documents or letters. In the 18C however an Egyptian of Somali descent, ʿAbd al-Raḥmān ibn Ḥasan **al-Jabartī** (1753–1825), who obviously had access to some of the Mamlūk journals, decided to contrive his own beginning with the year 1688. He continued this great work until a few years before his death and thus encompassed another crucial episode in the history of Egypt, the French Occupation.

**The French Occupation**. On the pretext of securing the authority of the Ottoman Sultan in Egypt, and incidentally protecting the interests of the European merchants, Napoleon's invasion of Egypt was in reality another campaign designed to control the land route and ultimately the sea route to India, thwarting the British advances in the Indian Ocean. Thus in July 1798 Napoleon's fleet landed near Alexandria. His first act was to issue a proclamation, stressing the equality of all men, to the effect that he had come to rid the Egyptian people of the tyranny of the mamlūks. He also stated that he revered the prophet Muḥammad and the Qurʾān and the French were sincere Muslims. He advanced towards Cairo and was met at Imbabah by a retaliatory force led by the Bays Murād and Ibrāhīm, who were defeated but escaped to the South. Napoleon's retreat was cut off by the British under Nelson who sunk his fleet, commanded by Brueys, at Abū Qīr. This act, and Napoleon's failure to capture Murād Bay, shattered the image of French invincibility and there were several insurrections centred on al-Azhar Mosque which the French bombarded.

The Egyptians were not particularly impressed by the proclamations of the French, who, despite protestations to the contrary, were considered kafir (non-believers). The various scientific devices demonstrated by the French also failed to win the admiration of the Egyptians—a hot-air balloon sent up over the Azbakiyyah Lake was considered by them to be some kind of kite. Napoleon made an attempt at the conquest of Syria but plague and other ailments decimated his troops and the expedition failed. However he did defeat an Ottoman force assisted by the British who attempted an invasion from Abū Qīr in July 1799. Shortly after, Napoleon left Egypt leaving General Kleber as governor. After another two-pronged Ottoman attack the French agreed to leave Egypt in January 1800 but British interference forced the French to entrench. Kleber was assassinated by a Syrian and the governorship was bestowed on Gen. Baron de Menou, who although he had accepted Islam, declared Egypt a French colony. The British under Sir Ralph Abercromby invaded from Abū Qīr in 1801 and occupied Alexandria. Although the French were repulsed Abercromby was killed. Further Ottoman forces were landed, Damietta taken and Cairo attacked. The French were forced to capitulate and in September 1801 they left for Europe.

Napoleon had brought with him from France some of the most eminent professors, which body formed the Institut d'Egypte. An exhaustive survey of Egypt was undertaken by them covering all fields of the sciences and arts. Their findings were compiled into a great work of twenty volumes published in 1809–28 and entitled *Description de l'Egypte.*

Although the technology and scientific expertise that the French displayed had no immediate effects the long-term results were very significant. In a period of three years the Egyptians were confronted with the full impact of Western technology.

**The Muḥammad ʿAlīds**. As soon as the French evacuated Egypt the Ottoman commanders Admiral Ḥusayn and Yūsuf Pasha continued the purge of the Bays. The British brought Muḥammad Bay al-Alfī to Britain to discuss the restoration of power. As the Treasury in Egypt was empty the troops were not paid and the Albanian regiment, under their commander Muḥammad ʿAlī, revolted against the Ottomans. Muḥammad Khusraw Pasha was deposed and his successor Ṭāhir Pasha assassinated. The Albanians became the rallying point for elements discontented with the Ottomans, such as the leaders Ibrāhīm Bay and ʿUthmān Bay al-Bardisi. The bays utterly defeated the Ottoman troops and installed themselves in the Citadel but the return of Muḥammad Bay al-Alfī from England in 1804 provided another leader, splitting the bays for a brief period into two camps with ʿUthmān siding with Muḥammad. The killing of one of ʿUthmān's relatives started a civil war and the Albanians restored control. The latter supported the Ottoman Khurshid Pasha and the two native factions reunited against them and retreated to Upper Egypt.

In May 1805 the population of Cairo urged on by the ʿulamā insisted on the deposition of Khurshid and the investment of Muḥammad ʿAlī as pasha: after hesitating Muḥammad ʿAlī agreed and he was confirmed in the post by the sultan in August. The bays had been ravaging the Delta and Muḥammad ʿAlī invited them to Cairo to discuss their grievances. As they passed the Bāb Zuwaylah his troops fired on them, many were killed while others who sought refuge in the Mosque of Barqūq in the Gamāliyyah were massacred; thus he rid himself of a great deal of the opposition. Muḥammad Bay and ʿUthmān Bay died within six months of each other in 1807 and reduced the opposition further. Although the British made an attempt at invasion in the same year they were blockaded. For the next few years Muḥammad ʿAlī had to acceed to all the demands of the bays. In March 1811, on the eve of the departure of his son Ṭūṣūn to fight the Wahhābīs in Arabia, Muḥammad ʿAlī held a celebration in the Citadel to which 470 mamlūks and their retainers were invited. Lead by Shahīn Bay they descended through the Citadel to re-enter the city. As they approached the main gates the troops opened fire, killing every one. Ibrāhīm Bay and many of the others not at the celebration escaped to the Sudan. They were never again to be a threat to the rulers of Egypt.

*Muḥammad ʿAlī, sketched from the life in May 1811 by Admiral Mitford*

Muḥammad ʿAlī acknowledged the Ottoman sultan as ruler, but was himself in complete control of Egypt. He confiscated the private land of Egypt and incorporated it as his own personal property, he created monopolies of the major products of the country and opened new factories. He planned and built on an immense scale, probably his greatest single work being the construction of the Maḥmūdiyyah Canal between Alexandria and the Nile, during which 20,000 workmen died. A great impetus was given to the economy by the importation of long-staple cotton from the Sudan in 1822 and its subsequent spectacular naturalisation in Egypt under the Frenchman Jumel.

Successful campaigns were fought against the Wahhabīs in Arabia and between 1820–24 Muḥammad ʿAlī reduced the N Sudan and had it incorporated into his personal estate. Public order was restored and he engaged upon a reform of education and medical practice. His navy and army were second to none in Europe and he assisted the sultan in the Greek Wars. The Pashalik was confirmed as the personal property of Muḥammad ʿAlī's family, but he gained the enmity of the sultan who, with the aid of various European powers, greatly reduced his forces and confiscated his Syrian possessions. The barrage at Qanātir over the two branches of the Nile was started in 1847, but in September of the same year his mind gave way and he was set aside for Ibrāhīm who ruled through a regency council until Sept. 1848 when he was confirmed as Wālī. However, he died in the following November and was succeeded by ʿAbbās I his nephew. Muḥammad ʿAlī died in 1849.

ʿAbbās I, son of Ṭūṣūn (1848), followed as Pasha, but he was a recluse. He reversed many of the policies of his grandfather, cancelling the system of commercial monopolies. He was murdered by his servants in 1854 and succeeded by Saʿīd, another son of Muḥ. ʿAlī. He was greatly under the influence of the French and granted to de Lesseps the charter to build the Suez Canal in 1856. But the British were not to be ignored; they were given the concessions for the formation of a telegraph company and the Bank of Egypt. However by borrowing from European bankers Saʿīd incurred the National Debt. He died in 1863 to be succeeded by Ismāʿil, a son of Ibrāhīm. At first he showed a great deal of promise and received from Istanbul virtual recognition of his sovereignty and the title of Khedive (Pers.: Sovereign). Many great schemes for the modernisation of Egypt were undertaken, covering the administrative system, education, communications and transport. However these plans invariably involved further European interference and heavy taxation of the population. In 1869 the Suez Canal was opened, showing great promise, but by 1875 there was no way that Ismāʿīl could raise further funds for his European creditors and he sold a controlling portion of Canal shares to the British. Further involvement led to French and British supervision of the fiscal system and control of transport, ports and the Pasha's holdings of land. A government was set up under Nubar Pasha but collapsed. In 1879 the controlling powers appealed to the sultan who deposed Ismāʿīl naming his eldest son Tawfīq successor.

The final episode of the great Egyptian chronicle was completed by **ʿAlī Pasha Mubārak**(1824–93), for many years Minister of Public Works. His great 18-volume work deals with the most important monuments and people in Egypt.

Several factors had halted the flow of slaves from the Caucasus in the early 19C. The first was the proscription placed on the export of slaves from the area by Ottoman authorities; the European governments disapproved of the principle in general, and Russian territory was expanding into the originating area. Thus by the late 19C the Egyptian army was composed largely of Egyptians, with very close ties to the urban and rural population. An officer called Aḥmad ʿUrābī rose from the ranks and established himself as the head of a faction demanding independence from European and Turkish governors. Although created a pasha and made a member of the cabinet, it was not enough for the population who rioted. The British and French fleets bombarded Alexandria in July 1882 and the former decided to carry the conflict onto Egyptian soil. ʿUrābi was defeated at Tell al-Kabīr and exiled to Ceylon. The prime aim of the British was to re-establish the authority of the Khedive and government, stabilise the economy and then to withdraw, but events were to make this impossible. In 1883 Sir Evelyn Baring—later Lord Cromer—was appointed Consul-general in Egypt. His long tenure in office was to have a great effect on the attitude of the Egyptians towards the British.

The first impediment to withdrawal was the emergence in the Sudan, part of the Khedival dominion, of a leader, Muḥammad Ahmad, who with much popular support, announced himself as the Mahdī, an apocalyptic Muslim leader, heralding an Islamic renaissance. He agitated for the expulsion of foreigners, but his ultimate aim was the unification of all the Islamic lands. Besides being an immediate danger in the Sudan his universal mission also endangered Egypt. The Anglo-Egyptian campaign against him ended with the death of General Gordon at Khartoum in 1885 and the annihilation of the British force. British officials replaced Egyptians in many government positions in Cairo and throughout the country in an attempt to restore the economy, an action resented by the populace. It also necessitated the manipulation of leading government figures by the British, resulting in many reforms in all official departments.

Tawfīq died in 1892 to be succeeded by his son ʿAbbās II. A young idealist with little political experience, he wished to ease British control of the administration. He began by dismissing Muṣṭafā Fahmī, the prime minister, and covertly negotiated with the nationalist factions, under the leadership of Muṣṭafā Kāmil, encouraging an anti-British attitude in the press. However, he underestimated the subtlety of the British who averted friction by forcing through provincial reforms. In 1895, Fahmī was reinstated and for many years the administration worked without serious problem. This relative calm allowed the British between 1896–98 to concentrate their efforts on recovering Sudan from the Mahdiyyah, an action which brought them into direct confrontation with the French, under Maj. J. Marchand, who were attempting to occupy the S Sudan, thus giving them direct access to the Red Sea. The two forces met at Fashoda and after a tense period the superior Anglo-Egyptian contingent under Gen. Kitchener persuaded the French to retreat and abandon their claim. Henceforth, the Sudan was administered jointly by the British and Egyptians with a governor appointed by the Khedive upon the recommendation of the British. Sir Reginald Wingate who succeeded Kitchener as Sirdar was appointed governor-general.

So stable was the situation in Egypt that in 1901 ʿUrābī was allowed to return from Ceylon. In 1903 the British and French, for once in concord, came to an agreement as to their relative areas of influence. France was to confine herself to Morocco, Britain to Egypt as the protecting power. In effect, this meant that Egypt was in full control of its own financial resources. However, the Europeans in Egypt still enjoyed privileges in regard to the land and law, a situation that annoyed the nationalist elements and much criticism was voiced in the press. The injustices of the former Ottoman administration were forgotten and the Turkish sultan was sued by the Egyptians to support their claim. This attitude was inflamed by one of the rare errors of judgment by the British in their support for a gross injustice perpetrated during what has become known as the Danishway Incident.

In June 1906 some British officers were shooting pigeons in the fields near Danishway in the W Delta, despite having been officially warned not to do so. The villagers asked them to go away but were ignored by the officers. An affray broke out, during which several villagers were injured. One of the officers was sent for help but died of heat-stroke, and a farmer who had gone to assist was beaten to death by the soldiers. At the subsequent trial (at which British judges predominated) four villagers were sentenced to death and the others to life imprisonment or flogging. The sentences were approved by Cromer and carried out within sight of the village. Although the imprisoned men were released within two years, the damage had been done: the incident affected adversely even those Egyptians who had supported the British. It became, and remains, a rallying-point for the Egyptian people.

In 1906 after a political argument with the Turks, the NE borders of Sinai were delineated and the peninsula officially agreed to be within Egypt's jurisdiction. Cromer resigned in 1907 to be replaced by Sir Eldon Gorst as agent-general. The much revered Muṣṭafā Kāmil died in 1908, a great blow to the nationalist movement, which, however, continued unabated. The prime minister Fahmī resigned in the same year to be replaced by Butrus Pasha, but the latter was assassinated in 1910 and was followed by Muḥammad Saʿīd. Gorst, who resigned in 1911, was succeeded by Lord Kitchener and, although the Italian invasion of Tripolitania complicated the situation, reorganisation of the administration continued, culminating in the recognition of the legislative assembly in 1913. ʿAbbās did not approve of these developments and Muḥ. Sāʿīd was removed by intrigue and was replaced by Ḥusayn Rushdī.

When war was declared between Britain and Germany, Kitchener was made Secretary of State for War, ʿAbbās was visiting Istanbul, when the British, seizing the opportunity deposed him. Egypt declared for the Allies and when Turkey entered the war on the German side, Egypt was proclaimed a British protectorate and the suzerainty of Turkey terminated. Ḥusayn Kāmil, uncle of ʿAbbās, was elevated with the title of Sultan. Sir Henry McMahon was made High Commissioner to be followed in 1916 by Sir Reginald Wingate. Ḥusayn died in 1917 and Fuʾād, the sixth son of Ismāʿīl, accepted the sultanate.

Opportunities for Egyptians in the administration were increasingly hindered by the number of Britons filling posts and naturally resentment grew. In 1919 after the Great War the promises of self-determination were insistently recalled. Zaghlūl Pasha requested permission to visit London to discuss independence and this was considered so fundamental that the Wafd (delegation) principle became a national focal point. The British were greatly disturbed by this and Zaghlūl Pasha was arrested and deported to Malta. Anti-British disturbances were widespread throughout Egypt, geographically and socially, and Zaghlūl was released. A special commission under Lord Milner was convened to investigate the problem and it made its report in 1920. The delegation lead by Zaghlūl came to London to discuss the implications and, it was hoped, to reach a settlement, but nothing was decided. Negotiations continued but sporadic outbursts of rioting made the administration of ʿAdly Pasha unstable since he did not have Zaghlūl's support. In 1921 Britain declared Egypt an independent sovereign state, though they kept control of defence, communications, the Sudan and protection of foreign residents. Sarwat Pasha was chosen as prime minister and Sultan Fuʿād assumed the title of King. But the continuance of violence against the foreign community prevented the lifting of martial law.

Parliamentary government was established in 1923 under Yaḥyā Pasha. Zaghlūl, although shot by an opponent, visited Britain to discuss the incorporation of the Sudan in the Egyptian state, with the Labour government under Ramsay MacDonald. Again, nothing was agreed. When the Sirdar of the Sudan, Sir Lee Stack, was assassinated in Cairo, Lord Allenby was appointed. Britain demanded full recompence, an apology, and withdrawal of Egyptians from the Sudan. It was also an excuse for Britain to tighten control of the Egyptian administration. Zaghlūl, appalled by this, resigned and his successor was Aḥmad Ziwar. Allenby also resigned the high commission in 1925 and was replaced by Lord Lloyd.

At the next election in May 1926, the Wafdists won an overwhelming victory, Ziwar resigned and a coalition parliament was formed with ʿAdly as prime minister. King Fuʿād visited England in 1927 when a treaty of alliance was concluded. In the same year Zaghlūl died aged 74; he was buried with great ceremony and public grief. The Wafd party rejected the treaty, forcing Sarwat to resign and the new leader of the Wafd, Muṣṭafā Naḥās, was elected premier. He was, however, compromised by two Egyptian newspapers and was dismissed by the king who suspended the constitution, dissolved parliament and resolved to rule by royal decree.

Lord Lorraine was made High Commissioner in 1929 and discussions about the restriction of British involvement were instigated. Although the Wafd won the elections, the friction between the king and Naḥās resurfaced and the latter was dismissed—thus the power of the king greatly increased. A period of instability followed during which three governments were formed. In 1935 a huge meeting in Cairo supporting the Wafdists demonstrated that they still had backing from the masses. In response to their demand the 1923 constitution was restored with ʿAlī Māhir presiding over a caretaker government which lasted until 1936 when Naḥās was returned in a Wafdist landslide.

Fuʿād died in 1936 to be succeeded by his seventeen-year-old son Fārūq. A twenty year withdrawal was negotiated with the British, the High Commission was closed and ambassadors were exchanged. A little later, in 1937, Egypt joined the League of Nations and agreement was reached on the gradual abolition of the mixed courts. A rift soon became apparent between Fārūq and Naḥās, the king showing as scant regard for the prime minister as his father had for Zaghlūl. The king appointed ʿAli Māhir as his political adviser, dismissed Naḥās and appointed Muḥammad Maḥmūd as prime minister. The next two years were a period of instability due to the opposition of the Wafdists and in 1939 Maḥmūd resigned to be replaced by ʿAlī Māhir who formed a strong government with the support of the Ṣaʿād, a splinter group of the Wafd.

With the outbreak of World War II the aggressive attitude of Italy caused the fall of ʿAli Māhir's government and the next led by Ḥusayn Sirrī pursued a neutral attitude, with public sympathy for the Allies, though with much private sympathy for the Axis. This Egyptian neutrality suited the British since at that time they were concerned with directing the war in Europe. (For a more detailed history of the war in Egypt, see the section on al-ʿAlamayn, Rte 49.)

In 1942 an irreconcilable rift developed between the government and King Fārūq. As the Wafd now had the support of the majority of the population, after some persuasion the king appointed Naḥās as prime minister of a Wafd cabinet. British losses in Libya in the summer allowed the Germans under Rommel to force an opening and they reached within 65km of Alexandria. In August Gen. Montgomery was appointed commander of the 8th Army and the great push forward began, culminating in the Battle of al-ʿAlamayn on 23 October. This signalled the decline of the Axis powers in N Africa and within seven months they had been expelled from the area.

Growing Zionist claims in Palestine and the crisis in Lebanon initiated in Oct. 1944 an Arab conference in Alexandria, during which the foundations of the Arab League were laid. Naḥās was dismissed in the same month to be replaced by Aḥmad Māḥir, the brother of ʿAlī. At the subsequent elections the first socialist candidates stood in Egypt. A declaration of war with Germany was announced by Aḥmad in February 1945, immediately after which he was assassinated. Niqrashī Pasha was appointed prime minister. The Wafd demanded the evacuation of the British troops and the uniting of Egypt with the Sudan, the latter in opposition to British plans for the self-government of the Sudan. Popular resentment against the British increased and with the support of the Muslim Brotherhood (a fundamentalist group) the students rioted in Feb. 1946. Ibrāhīm Sidky was again made prime minister and in a fine balancing act suppressed the riots but kept up pressure on the British to leave. Despite this strikes were organised and fighting occurred with British troops. In May Attlee declared the British intention to withdraw troops from Egypt within a certain period but the status of the Sudan still remained a great obstacle. Niqrashī was reappointed prime minister in December and Jan. 1947 saw the evacuation of troops from Alexandria and the Canal area. The Arab League supported Egypt's claim for union with the Sudan and brought it before the United Nations but without result. The British went ahead with plans for the Sudan and by July 1948 an interim measure of self-government was granted.

In the meantime the situation in Palestine had deteriorated. Britain resigned the mandate in May 1948 and Egypt along with other Arab League countries declared their intent to intervene militarily. They did so and by 20 May had captured Beersheba and attacked Tel Aviv from the air. A truce was organised by the UN but fighting broke out again and, because of isolation, Egypt lost the ground she had gained. In Egypt itself the activities of the Muslim Brotherhood increased and on 28 December it was dissolved. Niqrashī was assassinated by one of their supporters within a month, and the leader himself, Ḥasan al-Bannā, was killed on 13 February 1949. Ibrāhīm ʿAbd al-Hādī was made prime minister. The major powers recognised the state of Israel which immediately attacked the Egyptian frontier. With the intervention of Ralph Bunche of the USA, on 19 January 1949 an armistice was signed, under which Egypt was to retain Gaza and Israel Beersheba.

Egypt negotiated a greater share of the profits from the Suez Canal and also more employment for Egyptians in the zone, while the British concession was to run until 1968, after which it would not be renewed. At the same time the privilege courts of the foreigners in Egypt were abolished. In 1950 the Wafd party won the first elections held for ten years, and Naḥās was again prime minister. It was inevitable that the old quarrels with King Fārūq would be renewed. Internal problems prevented improvement of the relationship with Britain and, still in pursuit of unification with the Sudan, the government promulgated the idea of

Fārūq as king of Egypt and the Sudan. Britain, supported by the western powers, rejected this, which led to further clashes with the reinforced British forces in the Canal Zone. The situation deteriorated rapidly and in January 1952 Naḥās was dismissed and the army sent out onto the streets. Although ʿAlī Māhir managed to lead a government for six months, and was followed by ʿAli Ibrāhīm al-Hilālī, the end of the old regime was in sight.

On 23 July a group of officers staged a coup d'état, led by General Mohammed Naguib. Fārūq was made to abdicate and a regency council set up for his young son Fuʿād, while Naguib became prime minister ruling with a Revolutionary Command Council. Fārūq left for exile in Italy on 24 July. The constitution was repealed on 10 December and on 16 January 1953 all political parties were suspended. Naguib assumed supreme control (10 February) and finally on 18 June the royal family was ousted completely and Egypt declared a republic.

**The Egyptian Republic**. The problems confronting the new regime were many but the two greatest obstacles to be negotiated were the status of the Sudan and the Suez Canal. In February 1954, after being accused of dictatorship, Naguib resigned but was restored to power within two days. On 18 April he transferred the premiership to General Abd al-Nasser (one of the dissident officers who staged the coup), but retained the presidency himself. In July 1954 negotiations with the British resulted in an agreement to withdraw all foreign troops within 20 months, although the bases in the Canal Zone were to be kept operational. Accusations of association with the communists and Muslim Brotherhood led to the dismissal of Naguib on 14 November. The relationship with Israel deteriorated severely during 1955.

The last British soldiers left Egypt on 19 June 1956. On 22 June Nasser was elected president and assumed supreme power in a national referendum which also approved a new constitution. For the first time a government concerned for the welfare of the mass of Egyptians was in power. One of the immediate benefits was the redistribution of land among the farmers. One month later Egypt offered to the USA and Great Britain the opportunity to participate in the construction of the new Aswān Dam. The two powers, however, rejected this gesture with the excuse that they considered the project uneconomic. Nasser's reply was almost immediate: he announced the nationalisation of the Suez Canal Company to pay for the work. On 29 October Israel, with the support of Britain and France, launched an attack on Egypt. With foreign soldiers on Egyptian soil the UN on 4 November ordered an immediate cease-fire. Under pressure from the USA the aggressors agreed and all invading forces were withdrawn by 22 December and a UN peace-keeping force installed. This action resulted in the fall of the British prime minister Sir Anthony Eden. The canal had been blocked but was reopened in April 1957.

Egypt and Syria announced a union in January 1958, the resultant state to be known as the United Arab Republic with Nasser as president. Created with the best of motives, it was an unhappy marriage and was dissolved amid recriminations in July 1961. Egypt's involvement in the war in Yemen in 1962 was a great drain on resources without any benefit to Egypt although the medieval regime of the Imam was overthrown. In 1965 the USA terminated economic aid to Egypt and in desperation Nasser turned to the Soviet Union who were pleased to gain a foothold in the Middle East. Israel's only access to their port of Eilat in the E fork of the Red Sea was via the Gulf of ʿAqabah, but in May 1967 Nasser ordered the closing of the Straits of Tiran, thus cutting off Israeli shipping to the port, and shortly after demanded the withdrawal of the UN security forces. Egyptian forces were deployed in Sinai to await the outcome. On 5 June the Israelis moved into the Sinai. At the last moment the strategy approved by Nasser was changed by Abd al-Hakim, the commander of the armed forces, and due to his interference the Israeli air force was able to destroy the grounded planes of the Egyptians. By 8 June Israel occupied the whole of Sinai and had reached the E bank of the Suez Canal where they entrenched. In the evening of 9 June Nasser broadcast his resignation but in a demonstration of approval almost the whole population of Egypt took to the streets asking him to remain in control. The National Assembly also refused to accept his resignation and so he decided to stay on. Abd al-Hakim was dismissed on 11 June and Mahmud Fawzi appointed in his place.

Egypt by now had an arms deal with the Soviet Union and began in earnest to train men in their use. Within six months a defensive line had been established along the W bank of the Suez Canal. From Sept. 1968 sporadic raids were made into the occupied territories and Israel replied with similar incursions into Egypt. Nasser attended the Arab Summit Conference in Morocco on 19 December 1969. He left as vice-president Anwar el-Sadat, a companion since their days at military college. He had founded the Free Officers' Committee of dissident military leaders in 1939 and was a member of the Revolutionary Command Council after the coup. Despite his importance as a confidante of Nasser and as holder of the highest posts in his own right he was comparatively unknown in the West.

Skirmishes between Egypt and Israel continued sporadically in January 1970 and Nasser demanded the delivery of SAM-3 missiles promised by the Soviet Union. However the airforce was still deficient and a decision was taken to approach the USA. The Rogers' Plan for the Israeli withdrawal was formulated. In September 1970 the Arab Summit Conference was held in Cairo. When it broke up Nasser saw the delegates to the aeroplane and returned to his home. The next day, 28 September, he died. He had suffered for a long time with a painful and debilitating diabetic condition. Although he had been the subject of much criticism his death was a great shock to the Arabs, and indeed to the whole world.

Anwar el-Sadat who stayed, with much persuasion, as vice-president was elected president on 15 October 1970. On 15 May 1971 Sadat announced the Second Revolution. The pro-Soviet ministers had been dismissed and the secret control of communications and personnel had ceased. In July 1972 he expelled the Soviet military presence as a threat to the stability of the country. After much planning the Egyptians invaded Israeli-occupied Sinai on 6 October 1973. The campaign was an unprecedented success and revolutionised the tactics of warfare. Most important of all it restored Egyptian hope and broke the myth of the invincible Israeli armament. This success gave Sadat freedom to manoeuvre. Shortly after the restrictions on foreign investment and exchange control were lifted; this 'open-door' policy allowed greater involvement in Egyptian business by Western companies. Following on the victory in Sinai Sadat took the courageous step of negotiating to appear in the Knesset in Israel on 17 November 1977 and give his address personally. This resulted in the Camp David talks on the withdrawal of Israel from the rest of the occupied Sinai and the establishment of a Palestinian state.

On 6 October 1981, while attending a celebration to mark the anniversary of the 1973 Sinai Campaign, Anwar Sadat was assassinated by a group of religious dissidents. Vice-president Husni Mubarak stepped into the breech and was subsequently elected president. He has committed himself to the completion of President Sadat's goals, but has already shown that he has an individual style and thus at present Egypt enjoys a stable relationship with most countries of the world.

# Dynasties and Rulers of Muslim Egypt

(dep. = deposed; ex. = executed; ass. = assassinated; murd. = murdered)

**Governors of Egypt for Rashidūn Khalīfs** 640–658/21–37 AH.

| | |
|---|---|
| 640 | Abū ʿAbd Allāh ʿAmr ibn al-ʿĀṣ: Conqueror and first governor of Egypt. |
| 646–58 | Five other governors. |

**c 30 Governors for Umayyad Khalīfs** 658–750/38–132 AH.

**c 90 Governors for ʿAbbāsid Khalīfs** 750–868/133–254 AH.

**Ṭūlūnids** 868–905/254–92 H.

| | |
|---|---|
| 868–84 | Aḥmad ibn Ṭūlūn: declared independence 166/878 |
| 884–96 | Khumārawayh: son of Aḥ. b. Ṭūlūn, ass. |
| 896 | Jaysh: son of Khumārawayh, dep. and ex. |
| 896–905 | Hārūn: son of Khumārawayh, ass. |
| 905 | Shaybān: son of Aḥ. b. Ṭūlūn, dep. and imprisoned in Baghdad. |

**14 Governors for ʿAbbāsid Khalīfs** 905–35/292–323 AH.

**Ikhshids** 935–69/323–58 AH.

| | |
|---|---|
| 935–46 | Muḥammad ibn Tughj. |
| 946–61 | Unūjūr: son of Muḥ. b. Tughj. |
| 961–66 | ʿAlī: son of Muḥ. b. Tughj. |
| 966–68 | Kāfūr: tutor of sons of Muḥ., regent for ʿAlī. |
| 968–69 | Aḥmad: son of ʿAlī, deposed and fled to Syria. |

**Fāṭimid Khalīfs** 969–1171/358–567 AH.

| | |
|---|---|
| 969–75 | al-Muʿizz, entered Cairo 971. |
| 975–996 | al-ʿAzīz: son of al-Muʿizz. |
| 996–1021 | al-Ḥākim: son of al-ʿAzīz, disappeared, presumed murd. |
| 1021–36 | al-Ẓāhir: son of al-Ḥākim. |
| 1036–94 | al-Mustanṣir: son of al-Ẓāhir. |
| 1094–101 | al-Mustaʿlī: son of al-Mustanṣir. |
| 1101–31 | al-ʿĀmir: son of al-Mustaʿlī, ass. |
| 1131–49 | al-Ḥāfiz: cousin of al-ʿĀmir, at first regent, 1130. |
| 1149–54 | al-Ẓāfir: son of al-Ḥāfiz, ass. |
| 1154–60 | al-Fā'iz: son of al-Ẓāfir. |
| 1160–71 | al-ʿĀḍid: son of al-Fā'iz. |

*All rulers from this point until Ottoman conquest with the title of al-Malik (King)*

**Ayyūbid Sultans** 1169–1250/564–648 AH.

| | |
|---|---|
| 1171–93 | al-Nāṣir Ṣalāḥ al-Dīn Yūsuf (Saladin): Wazīr of al-ʿĀḍid. |
| 1193–98 | al-ʿAzīz: son of Ṣalāḥ al-Dīn. |
| 1198–1200 | al-Manṣūr: son of al-ʿAzīz, dep. |
| 1200–18 | al-ʿĀdil I: brother of Ṣalāḥ al-Dīn. |
| 1218–38 | al-Kāmil: son of al-ʿĀdil I. |
| 1238–40 | al-ʿĀdil II: son of al-Kāmil, dep. and murd. |
| 1240–49 | al-Ṣāliḥ Ayyūb: son of al-Kāmil. |
| 1249–50 | al-Muʿaẓẓam Tūrān Shāh: son of al-Ṣāliḥ Ayyūb, ass. |
| 1250 | al-Ashraf Mūsā: great nephew of al-Ṣāliḥ Ayyūb (jointly with Aybak), dep. |

**Baḥrī Mamlūk Sultans** (Dawlat al-Turk) 1250–1382/648–783 AH.

| | |
|---|---|
| 1250 | Shajar al-Durr: wife of al-Ṣāliḥ Ayyūb, abd. |
| 1250–57 | al-Muʿizz Aybak: mamlūk of al-Ṣāliḥ Ayyūb, ass. |
| 1257–59 | al-Manṣūr ʿAlī I: son of Aybak, dep. |
| 1259–60 | al-Muẓaffar Quṭuz: mamlūk of Ṣāliḥ Ayyūb, ass. |
| 1260–77 | al-Ẓāhir Bāybars (I) al-Bunduqdārī: mamlūk of al-Ṣāliḥ Ayyūb. |
| 1277–80 | al-Saʿīd Baraka Khān: son of Bāybars, dep. |
| 1280 | al-ʿĀdil Salāmish: son of Bāybars, dep. |
| 1280–90 | al-Manṣūr Qalāwūn al-Alfī: mamlūk of al-Ṣāliḥ Ayyūb. |
| 1290–94 | al-Ashraf Khalīl: son of Qalāwūn, ass. |
| 1294–95 | al-Nāṣir Muḥammad I (1st reign): son of Qalāwūn, dep. |
| 1295–97 | al-ʿĀdil Kitbughā: mamlūk of Qalāwūn, abdicated. |
| 1297–99 | al-Manṣūr Lajīn: mamlūk of Qalāwūn, ass. |
| 1299–1309 | al-Nāṣir Muḥammad I (2nd reign): abdicated |
| 1309–10 | al-Muẓaffar Baybars (II) al-Jāshankīr: mamlūk of Qalāwūn, dep. and ex. |
| 1310–40 | al-Nāṣir Muḥammad I (3rd reign). |
| 1340–41 | al-Manṣūr Abū Bakr: son of al-Nāṣir Muḥ., dep. and murd. |
| 1341–42 | al-Ashraf Kūjūk: son of al-Nāṣir Muḥ. dep. and murd. |
| 1342 | al-Nāṣir Aḥmad I: son of al-Nāṣir Muḥ. dep. and ex. |
| 1342 | al-Ṣāliḥ Ismāʿīl: son of al-Nāṣir Muḥ. |
| 1345–46 | al-Kāmil Shaʿbān I: son of al-Nāṣir Muḥ., dep. and ex. |
| 1346–47 | al-Muẓaffar Ḥājjī I: son of al-Nāṣir Muḥ. dep. and ex. |
| 1347–51 | al-Nāṣir al-Ḥasan (1st reign): son of al-Nāṣir Muḥ. dep. |
| 1351–54 | al-Ṣāliḥ Ṣāliḥ: son of al-Nāṣir Muḥ. dep. |
| 1354–61 | al-Ḥasan (2nd reign): dep. and murd. |
| 1361–63 | al-Manṣūr Muḥammad II: son of Ḥājjī I, dep. |
| 1363–76 | al-Ashraf Shaʿbān II: grandson of al-Nāṣir Muḥ., dep. and murd. |
| 1376–82 | al-Manṣūr ʿAlī II: son of Shaʿbān II, dep. |
| 1382 | al-Ṣāliḥ Ḥājjī II (1st reign): son of Shaʿbān II, dep. |

**Burjī Mamlūk Sultans** (Dawlat al-Jarkus) 1382–1517/784–922 AH.

| | |
|---|---|
| 1382–89 | al-Ẓāhir Barqūq (1st reign): mamlūk of Shaʿbān II, dep. |
| 1389–90 | Ḥājjī II (2nd reign: with title al-Muẓaffar): abdicated |
| 1390–99 | Barqūq (2nd reign). |
| 1399–1405 | al-Nāṣir Faraj (1st reign): son of Barqūq, abdicated |
| 1405 | al-Manṣūr ʿAbd al-ʿAzīz: son of Barqūq, dep. and murd. |
| 1405–12 | Faraj (2nd reign): dep. and murd. |
| 1412 | al-ʾĀdil al-Mustaʿīn: ʿAbbāsid Khalīf, dep. |
| 1412–21 | al-Muʾayyad Shaykh: mamlūk of Barqūq. |
| 1421 | al-Muẓaffar Aḥmad II: son of Muʾayyad Shaykh, dep. |
| 1421 | al-Ẓāhir Ṭaṭār: mamlūk of Barqūq. |
| 1421–22 | al-Ṣāliḥ Muḥammad III: son of Ṭaṭār, dep. |
| 1422–37 | al-Ashraf Barsbāy: mamlūk of Barqūq. |
| 1437–38 | al-ʿAzīz Yūsuf: son of Barsbāy, dep. |
| 1438–53 | al-Ẓāhir Jaqmaq: mamlūk of Barsbāy. |
| 1453 | al-Manṣūr ʿUthmān: son of Jaqmaq, dep. |
| 1453–61 | al-Ashraf Ināl: mamlūk of Barqūq. |
| 1461 | al-Muʾayyad Aḥmad III: son of Ināl, abdicated. |
| 1461–67 | al-Ẓāhir Khushqadam: mamlūk of Muʾayyad Shaykh. |
| 1467–68 | al-Ẓāhir Yilbāy: mamlūk of Muʾayyad Shaykh, dep. |
| 1468 | al-Ẓāhir Timurbughā: mamlūk of Jaqmaq, abdicated |
| 1468–96 | al-Ashraf Qāyt-bāy: mamlūk of Jaqmaq. |
| 1496–98 | al-Nāṣir Muḥammad IV: son of Qāyt-bāy, ass. |
| 1498–1500 | al-Ẓāhir Qānṣūḥ I: maternal uncle of Muḥ. IV, dep. and murd. |
| 1500–01 | al-Ashraf Jānbalat: mamlūk of Qāyt-bāy, dep. and murd. |
| 1501 | al-ʿĀdil Tūmān Bāy I: mamlūk of Qāyt-bāy, dep. and ex. |
| 1501–1517 | al-Ashraf Qānṣūḥ II al-Ghawrī: mamlūk of Qāyt-bāy, died on battle-field. |
| 1517 | al-Ashraf Tūmān Bāy II: mamlūk of Qāyt-bāy, dep. and ex. by Selim I. |

**c 110 Pashas for Ottoman Sultans** 1517–1805/922–1220 AH.

**French occupation under Bonaparte** 1798–1801/1213–17 AH.

**Muḥammad ʿAlīds** 1805–1953/1220–1372 AH.

| | |
|---|---|
| 1805–48 | Muḥammad ʿAlī, Pasha. |
| 1848 | Ibrāhīm son of Muḥ. ʿAlī, regent for father. |
| 1848–54 | ʿAbbās I, Pasha: grandson of Muḥ. ʿAlī, murd. |
| 1854–63 | Saʿīd, Pasha: son of Muḥ. ʿAlī. |
| 1863–79 | Ismāʿīl, Pasha: son of Ibrāhīm, Khedive from 1867, dep. by Sultan. |
| 1879–92 | Tawfīq, Khedive: son of Ismāʿīl. |
| 1892–1914 | ʿAbbās II Ḥilmī, Khedive: son of Tawfīq, dep. by British. |
| 1914–17 | Ḥusayn Kāmil, Sultan: son of Ismāʿīl. |
| 1917–36 | Aḥmad Fūʾād I, King from 1922: son of Ismāʿīl. |
| 1936–52 | Fārūq, King: son of Fūʾād I, dep. and exiled by Revolutionary Command Council. |
| 1952–53 | Fūʾād II, King: son of Fārūq, Regency Council, dep. |

**Republic declared March 1953.**

**Presidents of the Republic**

| | |
|---|---|
| 1953–54 | Muhammad Naguib. |
| 1954–1969 | Gamal abd el-Nasser |
| 1969–81 | Anwar el-Sadat, ass. |
| 1981– | Husni Mubarak. |

# The Arabic Language (al-Lughah al-ʾArabīyyah)

**Development**. Arabic belongs to a language group standing between the Southern Semitic group (including Ancient Sabaen, Sokotran, Tigre and Amharic) and the North-West Semitic group (including Hebrew and Aramaic) though probably more closely related to the latter. These are branches of the Semitic language family, a sub-division of the Afro-Asiatic language family, which includes within it Ancient Egyptian and Berber. It is first recorded in Assyrian Chronicles of the 9C BC, its literal form appearing slightly later in a script similar to Dedanite. Later texts in various scripts are found from Mesopotamia to Egypt. The language of the Nabatean Kingdom (100 BC–AD 300) and to a lesser extent the Palmyran (1–3C AD) contained many Arabic elements, though they used the Aramaic alphabet. During the 3–6C AD, while Arabic was developing in the Arabian Peninsular, its current vernaculars in the North assimilated many words from Aramaic, Persian, Greek and Latin, thus extending the vocabulary greatly.

By the 7C, although the language itself was rather uniform amongst the various Arabian tribes and can be termed Classical Arabic, that spoken by the Quraysh is considered by Arab scholars to have been the most pure. After the revelation of the Qurʾān the Arabs had a model text and during the following centuries scholars, with painstaking thoroughness, standardised the language. The literary Arabic used throughout the Middle East today is the product of this process, though the spoken language has developed into various local dialects.

**Egyptian Dialects**. In present-day Egypt the forms used are literary Arabic (*al-ʿarabiyyah al-fuṣḥā*) and the two main vernaculars, *Baḥrī*, spoken in the N, and *Ṣaʿīdī* in the S. Additionally there are several Beduin dialects which have more in common with their congeners throughout the Middle East. *Baḥrī*, of which Cairene is the most influential force, has many peculiarities in pronunciation, making it one of the most distinct dialects of Arabic. It has a long history and was already apparent in late Mamlūk times, several wazīrs being criticised for speaking the language of the street. However, the main impetus to change was the Ottoman occupation and the consequent use of Turkish as the official language. Alexandrian is also a form of *Baḥrī*. *Ṣaʿīdī* does not seem to have undergone such a radical change, but nonetheless still varies considerably from the classical language and is clearly related to the dialects of the Sudan. (For analysis of the language and alphabet see Practical Information: Language, below.)

Other languages spoken in specific areas are Nubian, a Hamitic language related to others found in Sudan, in two dialects Mahas and Kanuzi, and Siwan, a Zenati Berber dialect in the NW oasis.

## The Arabic Script (al-Kitabāt al-ʿArabiyyah)

The Arabic script, written from right to left, like most Semitic scripts, is generally agreed to be essentially derived from the Nabatean script, itself a derivation of Aramaic, and there are examples existing of transitional forms. The introduction of script into Mecca, its first use in the Arabian Peninsular, briefly preceded the revelation of the Qurʾān to Muḥammad. Although the Prophet never learned to read or write the first three khalīfs were adept in both skills. As with the Arabic language, the Qurʾān was central to the development of the script. The first committal of the Qurʾān to writing is described in the history of Islām (see above); this act provided the impetus to read and write among the faithful and to provide the most beautiful vehicle possible to contain the Eternal Message.

There were several variant scripts developed in centres in Arabia but only three main styles, based on angularity, while the rise of the cities in Iraq and the cultural rivalry between them encouraged further development. The script that emerged supreme was *Kūfic*, named after the city of Kūfah. It was an elongated script with short verticals and was used for most of the early Qurʾāns. Throughout the following centuries it evolved into a monumental and elegant but essentially simple script, though often embellished or modified in form. An attempt had been made early in the development of the script to indicate vowels, but it was not successful until a system was adopted from the Christian Syriac scripts which used diacritical points to distinguish between similar letters and placed marks to represent vowels over or below the letters. Calligraphy (*al-Khaṭṭ*) became an important art form and during the 9–13C a canon emerged for the guidance of calligraphers. During the 12C another script, *Naskhī*, which until that time had been a rather ordinary commercial script, benefitting from these new rules, developed into a major script, gradually replacing Kūfic in popularity for both inscriptions and manuscripts. It was a much simpler script, rounder and taller than Kūfic. It has never been bettered for clarity and is the basis of modern printing. Other calligraphic

Kufic

Decorated Kufic

Naskhī

Muḥaqqaq

Thuluth

Nastaʿlīq

Diwānī

styles were also developed, of which the most important were *Thuluth, Muḥaqqaq* and *Rayḥānī*.

The Ottoman Turks after the conquest of Egypt introduced an extremely florid script, *Dīwānī*, from which evolved an even more ornate script, *Dīwānī Jālī*, both used in the main for official inscriptions and documents. Another script which found favour was the Persian oblique script *Nastaʿlīq*. They also used the *Riqāʿ* script, an extremely simplified form which proved particularly easy to write and is the basis of modern Arabic handwriting.

# Islamic Art in Egypt

The expansion of the Arabs as a power in the 7C AD was no gradual rise through ascending cultural levels, but a sudden eruption into the heartlands of two of the greatest civilisations, Persia and Byzantium. The former was conquered completely and of the latter a great portion of territory was claimed—thus, virtually at a stroke, the Arabs were heirs to civilisations stretching back several thousand years. However it has been explained how with the rise of Christianity in Egypt the ancient artistic traditions were studiously avoided, so in turn the Arabs found little in the provincial Byzantine style of Egypt to attract them. Their requirements were very different from those of the static conquered population and few of the religious or aesthetic traditions were adopted.

At first the main influences were from Mesopotamia, which contained the metropolitan centres of Islām but, with increasing independence, from the time of Ibn Ṭūlūn onward local styles emerged. Successive conquests, by the Fāṭimids in the 10C from the W, the Ayyūbids in the 12C from the E, and the Ottomans in the 16C from the N, introduced new fashions and techniques, to be modified in turn by local preference. In addition, despite political frontiers, it was possible to travel widely in the Muslim territories—in fact it was a necessity when going on the ḥajj, which encouraged the wide-scale interchange of ideas. The immense disruptions in the E caused by successive waves of central Asian peoples and in the W by the reconquests of Europeans also contributed greatly to the cultural mix; Egypt as the pivot between the eastern and western territories of Islām received refugees from both. Anomalously, however, some styles remained local and were never adopted throughout. With increasing contact between the dominant Ottoman empire and Europe during the 17–19C western aesthetic traditions were adopted wholesale.

## Architecture

*Domestic architecture.* Prior to the great expansion of the 7C the Arabs had a minimal architectural tradition although familiar with building in stone. After the conquest of Egypt, while the rural population continued to live in the ancient type of mud-brick houses and the inhabitants of Alexandra utilised the buildings already extant, the vast population of Arabs who settled in the area known as Fusṭāṭ had to construct more permanent dwellings for themselves. The earliest houses of which foundations remain are 8–10C and show Mesopatamian influence: an irregular plan of one or more interior courtyards with a large hall leading off and many subsidiary rooms, but none of these has remained intact.

In the 12C another type of building, seemingly introduced from Western Asia, makes its appearance in Egypt. Represented by the Qāʿat al-Dardīr (Rte 6), it has a regular form, the qāʿah (central covered courtyard) which, rising the complete height of the house, was lit by a skylight. From two opposite sides of this lead a līwān, a large open-ended hall. This with slight modifications, i.e. the durqāʿah (a sunken portion in the centre of the qāʿah, often with a fountain), remained the basic element in all large private houses and palaces until the introduction of western architecture in the 19C. From this central feature doors lead to the interior apartments, divided into two sections—the area for men and friends and the ḥarīm for the women—and central courtyard. Some of these houses consisted of several floors and contained living rooms, baths, kitchens, a small prayer hall (*maṣallā*), storerooms and servants' quarters. Two features persisted throughout: the maqʿad (sitting place)—also called takhtābush, overlooking the courtyard—and the uniquely Egyptian feature, the baffled corridor from the main entrance which made several turns before entering the house proper. Sophisticated water systems, including supplies of hot water, were often a feature of these houses. The public façade is often severe, with mashrabiyyah-filled windows resting on giant corbels on the first and higher floors. On the roof was the malqaf (ventilator) with hood pointing N to collect cooling winds. Many of these features can still be seen on existing buildings in Egypt.

*Religious Architecture.* None of the buildings or their appurtanances used by Muslims for prayer is essential for the practice of Islām, they are all additions, albeit ancient, since the time of Muḥammad. The first public place of prayer was just outside Medina, and was probably just a flattened piece of ground. The Prophet lived in a house within a large courtyard in which he used to pray and it was this form that the early mosques were to take: a large walled enclosure with one or more arcades around the inner perimeter, thus leaving a ṣaḥn (open area) in the centre. Alignment was such that the faithful prayed facing SE the direction (qiblah) of Mecca, although the methods of calculation meant that there were eventually several systems in use with slight differences in direction from 117° SE (Mosque of ʿAmr—the qiblah al-saḥābaḥ) to 141° SE (Mosque of Ibn Ṭulūn). The true direction by modern computation from Cairo is 134.5° SE.

During the time of Muḥammad and for some time after, the call to prayer was made from the doorway or roof of the mosque but when the enclosure of the Church of St John in Damascus was used as the mosque after the conquest of that city, the huge towers at the ends of the façade were used. From this time the madhānah or manārah (minaret) became an integral part of mosque architecture and one was added to the Mosque of ʿAmr in 672.

In the centre of the qiblah wall is a small recess called the miḥrāb, in front of which the imām leading the prayer stands. It indicates the direction of Mecca but has no other function. Originally it was probably just a mark on the wall and its present form seems to have been an Umayyad innovation first built in the mosque of Medina in 706 and into the Mosque of ʿAmr in Egypt in 712. Standing to the right of the miḥrāb is the minbar, a stepped rostrum from which the khuṭbah is read during jumaʿ prayer. Muḥammad had a tamarisk wood minbar with three steps. Subsequent khalīfs, in deference to their predecessors, used a lower step until stopped by ʿUthmān. Now the imām stands one step below the top and most minbars have five, seven or nine steps. Its first introduction during the time of Khalīf ʿUthmān was also in the Mosque of ʿAmr.

Although no longer used, the maqṣūrah was once an important element of the great mosques. This was a wood or stone lattice enclosure in front of the miḥrāb in which the sultan or governor, who was also the imām, would lead the prayer. It was introduced by Khalīf Muʿāwiyyah (661–80) after an attempt on his life. It existed for a long time but fell out of use during Ayyubid times. The dikkah (bench) is used by the man who repeats the prayer for those who cannot hear the imām; it usually stands to the side of the mosque and was in use from the 8C onwards. Related to

# SEQUENCE OF MINARETS

Ayyubid.
al-Ṣāliḥ Ayyūb. 1243
Early Baḥrī Mamlūk.
Qalāwun. 1284
Late Baḥrī Mamlūk.
Ḥasan. 1356
Early Burgi Mamlūk.
Qayt-bay. 1473
Late Burgi Mamlūk.
Qānṣūh al-Ghawrī. 1514
Ottoman.
al-Malikah Ṣafiyyah. 1610
19 Cent.
Muḥammad 'Ali. 1848

the last is the kursī al-surah (chair of the chapters) from which the Qur'ān is read and which appeared in Fāṭimid times.

For much of the history of Islām there was a distinction between the jami' (assembly mosque), the great building where the population gathered for the communal prayer on Fridays and festivals, and the smaller local masjid (lit. place of prostration), often of the same form but distinct in size and function.

**Arab conquest to Fāṭimid period** (640–1171). *Mosques*. The Mosque of 'Amr has been much restored and enlarged; nothing remains of its original structure, which was probably of mud and palm logs, and the earliest extant mosque in Cairo is that of Ibn Ṭūlūn, built in 876. This survives almost intact. It continues the tradition of the great enclosure with arcades, the pointed arches of which are raised on piers with engaged columns with tulip capitals. The whole building is executed in baked brick with stucco and wood decoration. Around the building is a ziyādah (extension), an open area in which, to the NW, stands the isolated minaret of spiral type, which though rebuilt in the 14C in stone probably retains the form of the original. This latter, together with the style of the stucco and wood work, demonstrates that the main influence in the design is Iraqi.

Although much enlarged and restored, al-Azhar Mosque (founded 970) preserves the enclosure form but with two important innovations—there is a transept leading to the main miḥrāb; this has a small dome above it, with a smaller dome at each end of the qiblah rīwāq. Antique pillars were used in the arcades although the rest of the building is brick.

Further modifications are found in the Mosque of al-Ḥākim (built 990): a monumental stone porch, a minaret set at either end of the NW façade and stone facing over the whole of the brick façade. Except for the last all these innovations were brought from North Africa by the Fāṭimids. With modifications in the style of decoration this form of mosque persisted until the mid-15C and was the only type in Egypt to possess a dome as part of the mosque proper until the Ottoman conquest. Most of these foundations were royal although several highly placed officials also had them built. Local mosques were also built to this plan but on a much smaller scale, e.g. al-Aqmar Mosque which is also important in being the first building to have its façade built parallel to the road despite its interior alignment to the qiblah, a practice that was to become very common in later periods.

*Tombs* (Ar. sing. qubbah: pl. qibāb). None of the early Muslims had buildings erected over their graves—one of the *hadiths* discourages such vanities. However when Khalīf al-Mustanṣir died in 862 his Greek mother had a canopy built over the grave, a continuation of a Late Antique practice; it presumably escaped interdiction since it did not possess walls. All the early tombs, including those erected by the Fāṭimids in Egypt, are of this type, four piers supporting a dome, usually built of brick. Examples are the Tomb of al-Saba' Banāt (Rte 15) and the tombs at Aswān (Rte 39). At a fairly early stage a miḥrāb was set into one of the piers supporting the dome, but, since this meant that it was assymetrically placed, in later buildings the opening on the qiblah side was filled in and the miḥrāb was placed in the centre. It was then just a small step to close the openings in the other walls, leaving only a small doorway for egress. Thus the elements of tomb architecture, to become so distinctive in the Mamlūk era, were established. The base was usually a cube with a miḥrāb in the qiblah wall. Above this was the zone-of-transition upon which was set the drum of the dome and over all the dome itself. In each side of the zone-of-transition is a window of the same shape as the squinch, while more windows pierce the drum of the dome. The dome was at first merely plastered but in the first part of the 12C the domes were constructed of carved bricks, creating a ribbed effect—a pattern which persisted throughout the era.

There are two basic methods of raising a dome over a square base—the squinch and the pendentive. The former is an arch thrown over each corner of the square, thus producing an octagonal base, from which the dome can easily spring. This element is logically called the zone-of-transition. The pendentive involves starting a dome with the diameter of the diagonal across the square. The point at which each of the four concave inverted triangles so produced meets its two neighbours can be used as the base of the true dome. These solutions had evaded the ancient civilisations of even the Greeks and Romans, which restricted them to small domes over cylindrical bases. The squinch appears first in Persia in the 3C AD, and is the only method used by the Sassanids, while Syria in the 2C seems to have been where the true pendentive was invented, though attempts had been made as far back as the 15C BC by the ancient Egyptians. In religious architecture in Egypt the squinch was used almost exclusively until Ottoman times: the pendentive was confined to military architecture. The squinches used in Egypt in the domes of al-Azhar were first simple but by late Fāṭimid times they had been divided into a series of decorative niches.

A specifically Shiʿī type of tomb was built above the graves of the venerated early relatives of Fāṭimah. This was called the mashhad (place of martyrs), where the visitor was in the spiritual presence of the deceased. A courtyard leads through a triple arched vestibule into the tomb chamber, the main justification for the whole building. The Sunnī reaction after the fall of the Fāṭimids disposed of the majority of these buildings and only a few survive.

**Ayyūbid and Mamlūk periods** (1171–1517). With the ascendancy of Ṣalāḥ al-Dīn (1171) new architectural forms were introduced. One of the first major changes was the introduction from western Asia of the madrasah (college), for Sunnī theological study. These colleges had originated as domestic dwellings with facilities for communal prayer. Thus their form was that of a qāʿah with two side līwāns. To provide for the four judicial schools Sultan al-Kāmil built two identical parallel buildings in 1225, with one school accommodated in each of the līwāns. Little of this now exists but of a similar complex built by one of his successor, al-Ṣāliḥ Ayyūb, one complete half is extant. Included in these complexes were rooms for students, lecture halls, kitchens and ablution facilities. Another type of building with similar origins and design but with different function was the khānqāh, introduced at the same time as the madrasah, but specifically for the sufi brotherhoods.

No mosques have survived from this period but the minarets attached to madrasahs had evolved into two-staged buildings, the lower tier with a square section and an octagonal second tier, the medial balcony supported on a cornice and the whole edifice crowned by a ribbed cap. After the death of Sultan al-Ṣāliḥ Ayyūb his wife Shagar al-Durr in 1243 had her husband's tomb built next to his madrasah. Although this association was posthumous it became an almost universal practice amongst the later

## TYPES OF MOSQUES

(not to scale)

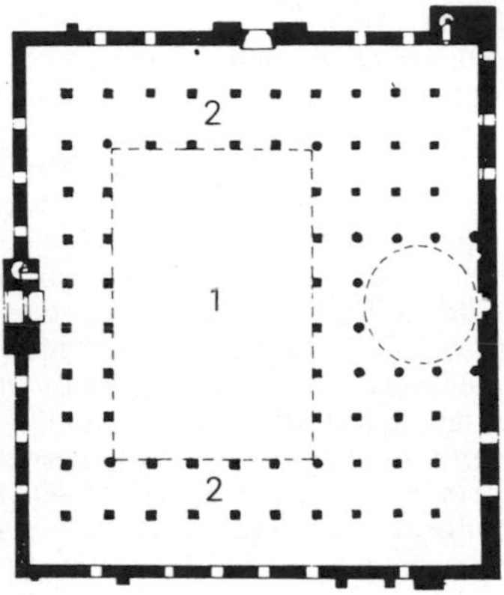
2
1
5
2

**A al-Nāṣir Muḥammad**

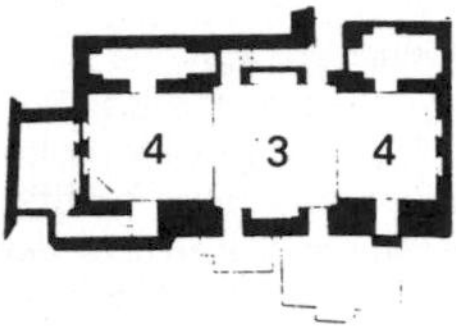
4
3
4

**B Muhibb al-Dīn**

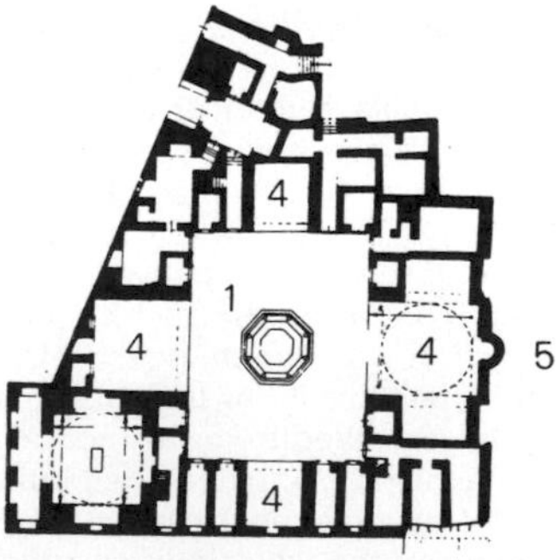
4
1
4
4
5
4

**C Amīr Sarghatmish**

**A Enclosure mosque**
**B Qa^c^ah of a domestic house**
**C Madrasah format**
**D Forecourt mosque**
**E Externally arcaded mosque**

1 ṣaḥn
2 riwāq
3 durqa^c^ah
4 līwān
5 miḥrāb

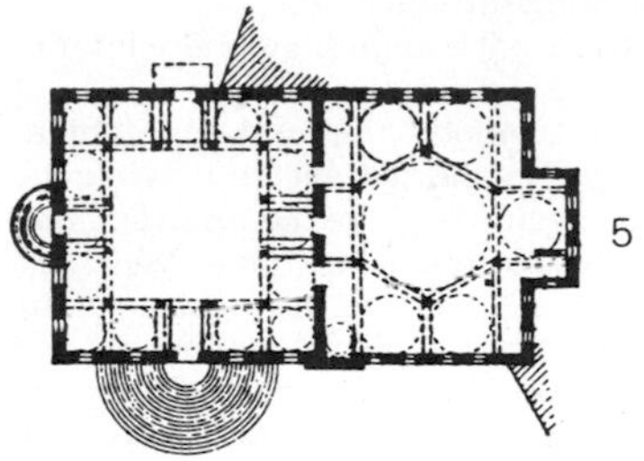
5

**D al-Malikah Ṣafiyyah**

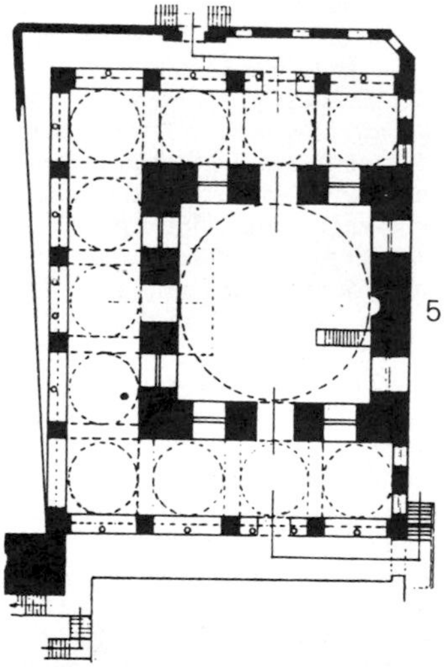
5

**E Muḥammad Bāy Abū l-Dhahab**

sultans and great amīrs to have their tombs built adjoining their greatest mosques during their lifetimes. It is these domes that give the mosques of Egypt their characteristic profile.

During the reign of Sultan Baybārs (1264) the two separate madrasah buildings were combined by the simple expedient of adding two lateral līwāns to the central ṣaḥn, thus forming the cruciform plan that was to become almost universal in Egypt during the following centuries. In several cases each līwān was given to one of the four schools, though this was not general. So attracted were the mamlūks by this format that it was used for all types of religious buildings and virtually supplanted the earlier enclosure form of mosque. In the absence of a foundation inscription it is often difficult to tell whether a building was a mosque, khānqāh or madrasah—a confusion that extended to the architects, for the inscriptions on the outside and the inside sometimes credit the buildings with different functions. One great advantage of this form was that it could be built inside the city without too much disturbance: the façade could conform to the thoroughfare notwithstanding the alignment of the interior to the qiblah.

In Mamlūk times the minaret acquired yet another tier and all combinations can be found of square, octagonal and cylindrical sections. While the buildings were of brick, most of the decoration on the internal and external walls was of stucco, but later, when stone was used, the elaborate carving became an integral part of the fabric. Innovations in the decoration of minarets was often preparatory to similar developments on the dome. Even though the base was of stone the dome was built of brick until the beginning of the 14C when masons acquired the ability to build stone domes. Until the late 14C they were ribbed in the same way as brick domes. Then the masons started to experiment, first manipulating the plain ribbed pattern, and in the late 14C using a continuous horizontal chevron design. Finally, in the early 15C, such complex designs, both geometrical and arabesque, were carved that, with their accompanying minarets, they still stand as paragons of the stone-mason's art. The whole sequence is succinctly illustrated in C. Kessler's delightful book *'The carved masonry domes of medieval Cairo'*. Around the drum of the dome there is almost invariably a band of inscription, while the corners of the zone-of-transition are elaborately decorated with scrolled or geometrical stonework and windows are set in each side. The squinches inside became extremely elaborate with up to nine layers of niches. Minarets followed an evolution parallel to that of domes and a similarly informative source is *The minarets of Cairo* by Doris Berens Abou-Seif.

The cruciform mosque was modified in the early 14C by the roofing over of the ṣaḥn, the court being lit by a central skylight, while later the two lateral līwāns were reduced in size until eventually they were merely recesses, virtually a return to the original form. Another type of mosque appeared in late Mamlūk times. Probably an introduction from Ottoman-held territories, this was a rather unremarkable type with arcades, raised on pillars, parallel to the qiblah wall. Often associated with a religious foundation was the sabīl (fountain) and the kuttāb (school). At first independent units, by early Burgī times (mid 14C) they were integral parts of mosques and madrasahs. The sabīl on the ground floor had grilled openings giving access to the water, while the school which provided elementary religious education, on the first floor, usually had arcaded windows on two sides and a wooden roof. Close to the sabīl there was usually a ḥawḍ (water trough) for animals.

**Ottoman period**. Selim, having subdued Egypt, returned to Istanbul taking with him many of the treasures of Egypt, including the craftsmen of the Mamlūk workshops. There was nobody left to construct buildings in the traditional manner and the preferences of the Ottomans were different from those of the Mamlūks. Although royal patronage was gone and few of the Ottoman governors were interested in building in Cairo, many mosques were built by the powerful bays and merchants. The commonest type, almost synonymous with Ottoman mosque architecture, is the courtyard mosque, in which the building was divided into two parts: a square open courtyard with a peripheral arcade and the covered mosque, also square. A feature of the Ottoman mosques is that the ṣaḥn is covered by a large dome, often with four smaller lateral semi-domes. The minaret was also subject to an abrupt change. The Ottoman type was very severe, a single slightly tapering shaft, often with a medial balcony and a conical cap. Although the basic plan of the mosque had radically changed, the carving on the exterior remained almost unchanged, with bands of torus moulding and muqurnas.

Despite the vast wealth at their disposal, the bays of the Ottoman period were much more modest in their funerary building than the mamlūks. The tabut is more elaborate, but the building is usually no more than a stone, or even wooden, canopy.

**19–20 Centuries**. Much of the architecture of the period follows the traditional pattern, although royal patronage meant a return to the grandiose. Interiors, however, were heavily influenced by western taste, the architects being particularly attracted to the Italianate Rococo style. In the early 20C several experiments were made in mosque architecture. Some were successful, e.g. the Mosque of Abū ʾl-ʿAbbās al-Mursī (Rte 42), others were not. The general trend has been a return to traditional forms built in modern materials.

**Wood and stucco carving**. Although these materials are completely different, the decoration and the use of the two in Egypt is often the same, at least in the early period. The work of the Coptic craftsmen when the Arabs conquered Egypt was in the provincial Byzantine tradition. Natural motifs and Christian symbols were widespread as were less familiar geometrical designs and blind arcading. From the few examples left it can be seen that little progress was made until the Ṭūlūnid period when the designs were derived in great part from the capital of Samarra in Iraq, though with some local development. One of the most important introductions was the technique of bevelled carving. Although the decoration at this time was mainly abstract, in later times motifs such as birds, animals and leaves were reintroduced. Inscriptions, often of monumental size, were also executed in the same technique.

Under the Fāṭimids carving became extremely sophisticated. The bevelled technique was developed and carving at different levels produced a dimensional effect missing from the earlier works. This is apparent even in the minutest carving as well as in monumental pieces. The Fāṭimid affinity with animals has produced the most charming scenes, with hares, gazelles and ducks scampering in a most realistic way through the foliage. Some of the exceptional pieces are in the MIA.

Ayyūbid craftsmen elaborated on Fāṭimid techniques although the period of monumental wood carving was finished. A new technique introduced was the use of small carved polygonal panels in grooved frames which built up into large screens and were fashioned into minbars, ceilings and doors. A related technique was mashrabiyyah, in which small pieces of turned wood were fitted together (without glue) to form a large lattice. It had appeared under the Ṭūlūnids.

During Mamlūk times wood carving was confined mainly to inscriptions, but stucco work, at least during the early period, assumed massive dimensions, a whole wall often being covered with elaborate carving. Mashrabiyyah was also developed (even being copied in marble and bronze), as was the carved panelwork, often inlaid with ebony, other rare woods, mother-of-pearl and ivory.

**Stone carving**. The introduction of stone façades in the Fāṭimid period provided a new medium for architectural decoration. It was not long before these too were being decorated by Egyptian craftsmen (see al-Aqmar Mosque, Rte 5). Soon the façades were elaborated with mouldings and inscriptions; particular attention was given to the entrance. However, the decoration remained rather restrained compared to the lavish interiors. The Mamlūks continued this practice and extended stone carving to screens, miḥrābs and even minbars, producing extremely beautiful patterns with coloured marbles and joggled voussoirs, the jigsaw patterns of the interlocking stone pieces becoming very intricate. One particular elaboration in stone was muqurnas, which, depending from an overhang, gives the appearance of stalactites. So attracted were the Mamlūk architects to this form of decoration that it was introduced at every possible location. It became extremely elaborate and by late Mamlūk times layer upon layer are found under domes, entrance and window arches and along the top of walls.

In one other field the masons were completely unrestrained. This was in the carving on the stone domes above the tombs of the later amīrs and sultans. See the section on religious buildings for the evolution of this technique.

**Ceramics**. The Arab conquest found a flourishing ceramics industry in Egypt, with designs mainly within the Christian canon. During the Ṭūlūnid period pottery acquired originality although no complete example survives. Forms of Fāṭimid pottery are rather stereotyped although the decoration is exquisite and animated. Designs are often of courtly scenes although other more mundane decoration demonstrates that the pottery was used by all classes. *Lustreware* was particularly favoured by the Fāṭimids, most of it painted in sepia on a cream ground, but a few exceptional pieces are on turquoise. *Fayyūmī ware* with polychrome decoration in crude patterns is the Egyptian attempt to reproduce Tang splash wares. Also produced were carved wares of monochrome scrafitto. There was one particular area in which the Fāṭimids produced unique works of art. This was the production of *ḥulūq*, the fretted chokes fitted inside the necks of earthenware jars to restrict the flow of water and thus to facilitate drinking. They were produced in a vast array of patterns from birds and mammals to genre scenes and inscription. The decline in Fāṭimid pottery may have been the result of the burning of the potters' quarter of Fusṭāṭ in 1196.

During the Mamlūk era the predominant type of pottery was the *'enamelled'-ware* carved and decorated with white slip under tinted glazes. It was not particularly well executed and the decoration shows much similarity to contemporary metalwork, some examples even being decorated with blazons. Other types of pottery seem to be copies of Syrian forms or imports. A constant preoccupation of the Egyptian potter, as in many other countries, was to reproduce Chinese celadon ware and in the 14C it was the Mamlūks who succeeded, as they also did with the desirable blue and white ware.

Products of the Ottoman period are usually crude imitations of Istanbul metropolitan ware—tiles, jugs, etc.—although earthenware objects of types still in use were produced throughout Egypt.

**Glass**. Products of Roman Egypt are of exceptional quality and were in demand throughout the empire. So well developed were the techniques that the Muslim craftsmen merely continued the process. One innovation in the early 8C was lustre-painting. Metals were improved and shapes more appealing to the Muslims were introduced. During the Fāṭimid period it was often the case that potters also designed and manufactured glass. The decoration is similar to that found on faience: birds and inscriptions in monochrome lustre on clear vessels. Other types are of gilded, opaque white or turquoise fabric which were probably inspired by imported Sung wares from China. Applied coloured glass threads on plain glass vessels show the persistence of a Roman technique. The popular opaque marbled glass with bands of colour has even older antecedents, being known since ancient times. Similarly, millefiore glass also persisted but was used only for beads, as was Egyptian faience, the brilliant blue frit, very common in Ancient Egypt. Lead glass, often diamond cut, was an obvious but excellent imitation of rock-crystal, although the glass vessels only bore inscriptions. Cameo glass of two layers was also produced and cut, producing very fine works of art.

The cutting of rock-crystal is actually a form of stone-carving, but it is also related to, and provided the impetus for, similar cutting of glass. It was a technique in which the Fāṭimids excelled and the objects produced were in great demand throughout the civilised world. Beakers, bottles and purely decorative or amusing pieces were made; decoration was floral, geometrical or inscription.

As with pottery, the end of the Fāṭimid era saw a decline in glass manufacture. The technique of cut-glass disappeared completely and enamelled decorations replaced lustre painting. Mould-blown domestic glass persisted. Although it is acknowledged that the supreme product of the Mamlūk workshops was enamelled glass, the provenance of much of it is still a mystery. Some of it was doubtless manufactured in the factories of Northern Syria but as most of the examples are found in Egypt and were made for the sultans and great amīrs there must have been a local production centre, although the site has never been positively identified. The decoration on these pieces is of fine arabesque inscription and blazons in gilding and enamels on a clear base. Most frequently found are mosque lamps and their associated ovoids (designed to stop mice getting to the oil), but bottles, plates and other items are known. It was a technique that only lasted about 100 years from the late 13–late 14C, very few pieces being known after 1400. An interesting development in late Ayyūbid times was the setting of glass (some gilded) mosaic into stucco in decorative designs. Stucco windows were also filled with coloured glass in arabesque and calligraphic patterns. This latter practice continuing with the Mamlūks and Ottomans.

**Metalwork**. For the most part the early metalwork of Muslim Egypt continued the Sassanian and Byzantine styles inherited by the Arabs from their neighbours. Techniques naturally improved and during Fāṭimid times bronze casting reached a peak. Many examples are known in the form of aquamaniles, censers and candlesticks or purely decorative objects. Inlay was also practised but only small pieces of jewellery remain, similar in technique to those of Byzantium. The great period of Egyptian metalwork came after the destruction of Mosul, the earlier centre, by the Mongols in the 13C. Many craftsmen fled W and settled in Syria or Egypt. Many Ayyūbid pieces are known—basins, candlesticks, astrolabes, etc. As well as inscriptions they show genre scenes and animals are found among the arabesque inlay.

Under the Mamlūks output increased greatly with other techniques such as plating, piercing and engraving being used in addition to inlay. After the 13C it is possible to distinguish Egyptian products from their Syrian counterparts by the grandeur of the decoration and variety of metals employed—gold, silver, copper and brass, often used with niello. All manner of articles were produced—pen-boxes, swords, ewers, basins, tables and the magnificent doors of palaces and mosques are only a few examples. During the 13–14C the decoration became much more abstract with fewer human figures, although animals persisted for longer. At the beginning of the 15C the quality of the work declined and engraved decoration became predominant. At the same time tinned copper appeared and its ease of production made it a popular medium, even among the amīrs. Doors were often covered with cut and pierced plates of bronze or brass in very elaborate patterns.

**Textiles**. Egypt had long been famous as a weaving centre, in linen, wool and, by the early Christian period, silk. It was a craft little disturbed by the Arab invasions. The motifs were changed, however, as was the market. A special factory was needed for the ruler and his specific needs, the Dār al-Tirāz (House of the Border, the band of inscription around the edge of the fabric). In this field Egypt soon became supreme with many important centres in the Delta and Upper Egypt. Many fabrics were exported to other countries, even to Baghdad, and the influence of Egyptian patterns was very far-reaching. The production of these important commodities continued until the Ottoman invasions, with damask, velvets, silks, block-printed linen and tapestry of great variety. Egypt has recently been recognised as an important production centre for a related craft, that of carpet making, although very few examples have survived.

**Manuscript decoration**. Although the illumination of manuscripts was an ancient art among the Muslims, under the Mamlūks it reached a peak. The strength of the design and the subtle use of colour and gilding combined with superb calligraphy produced magnificent works of art. Decoration was confined to the headings of the surahs of the Qurʾān or chapter headings in lesser works, with medallions and palmettes on the margins. The first pages of the manuscripts usually contained large decorative panels. Although there was an innate distate among western Muslims for reproducing the human form, a certain class of books were illustrated with miniature paintings. These were the books of popular tales, and particularly the *Maqāmāt al-Harīrī*(Assemblies of Hariri) which describes in episodes the confidence tricks of a rascally old man in cities through the Islamic world. Each episode is illustrated by one or more miniatures and the front page with full-length court scenes. The

Mamlūks were very fond of these tales and many very beautiful manuscripts of them were produced in Egypt and Syria. This particular art form declined in the 15C although Qur'āns were still magnificently decorated. The conquest of Selim in 1517 brought a sudden end to these crafts and the Ottoman style was very different.

# Architectural Glossary

Cpt = Coptic, Isl = Islamic.

ABACUS rectangular block on top of column supporting architrave.

ABLAQ (Isl) alternating courses of coloured masonry.

AGORA market or meeting-place.

AMBON (Cpt) large pulpit raised on pillars.

AMBULATORY roofed colonnade around a small temple.

BĀB (Isl) gate or door.

BARK SHRINE Chamber containing boats standing in form of ancient Egyptian shrines.

BASILICA (Cpt) form of church derived from Roman administrative buildings.

BAYT (Isl) house.

BIMĀRISTAN (Isl) hospital, also māristan.

BRECCIA a natural conglomerate stone.

BURG (Isl) tower.

CAVETTO CORNICE concave corbel running around the summits of walls of temple, gates, etc.

CENOBIUM (Cpt) an organised monastic community.

CLERESTORY (Cpt) upper wall of nave, pierced by windows.

COLOSSUS over life-sized figure of king, god, or occasionally private individual which usually stood before or inside a temple.

CORBEL projecting bracket in timber or stone designed to support another structure; also the visible beam of a ceiling.

DĀR (Isl) house or mansion.

ḌARĪḤ (Isl) tomb.

DEIR (Isl) walled monastery (Arabic *dayr*).

DIKKAH (Isl) platform of respondent in mosque.

DUKKĀN (Isl) shop.

DURQĀʿAH (Isl) central section of qaʿah, usually sunken and set with high roof.

FALSE DOOR, a false door in the wall of a tomb, an essential element in ancient Egyptian funerary chapels.

FERETORY (Cpt) shrine containing relics of a saint.

FLUTES grooves down column.

GĀMIʿ (Isl) assembly mosque.

ḤAMMĀM (Isl) bath.

ḤARAMLIK (Isl) private apartments for women.

ḤAWḌ (Isl) water basin.

ḤAWSH (Isl) walled enclosure.

HAYKAL (Cpt) sanctuary of a church.

HYPOSTYLE HALL columned chamber, usually the first, largest and most important room in the temple.

IKONOSTASIS (Cpt) a screen supporting ikons, separating the sanctuary from the nave.

KHĀN (Isl) hostel for merchants.

KHĀNQĀH (Isl) hostel for sufis.

KIOSK small open temple.

KUSHK (Isl) kiosk or pavilion.

KUBRĪ (Isl) bridge.

KURSĪ (Isl) dais for holding the Qurʿān (literally, chair).

KUTTĀB (Isl) elementary school, often attached to a mosque, and situated above the fountain.

LAKAN (Cpt) a basin for washing feet on Maundy Thursday.

LAURA (Cpt) loose association of hermitages.

LĪWĀN (Isl) hall with open side leading from the central court of a mosque or house, also iwān.

MADFAN (Isl) tomb.

MADRASAH (Isl) foundation built specifically as a teaching establishment for theological sciences, and assigned to one or more schools of law.

MALQAF (Isl) wind vent on roof angled towards the northern breeze.

MAMMISI small chapel attached to

a temple as the birthplace of the god, a term invented by Champollion.

MANDĀRAH (Isl) a reception salon.

MANZIL (Isl) dwelling.

MAQʿAD (Isl) sitting area, often with a stone canopy in house courtyard.

MAQBARAH (Isl) tomb.

MAQṢŪRAH (Isl) a reserved area, often around a tomb, and previously around the area reserved for the ruler in the mosque.

MAṢALLĀ (Isl) small prayer room

MASGID (Isl) local mosque.

MASHHAD (Isl) Fāṭimid building over the tomb of a spiritual notable.

MASHRABIYYAH (Isl) decorative screens composed of pieces of turned wood used in casement windows or dividing walls.

MAṢṬABAH (Isl) stone bench, also used in the form mastaba to describe ancient Egyptian oblong tombs.

MIḤRĀB (Isl) niche indicating the direction of Mecca.

MINBAR (Isl) a stepped chair from which the Friday sermon is read.

MUQURNAS (Isl) elongated lower angles of niches decorating porches and corbels. Usually translated as 'slalactites'.

NAOS sanctuary where the divine statues of gods were kept, the innermost usually of wood and the outer of monolithic stone.

NARTHEX (Cpt) transverse vestibule of a church.

NAVE (Cpt) main body of a church, usually flanked by aisles.

OBELISK monolithic tapered shaft. Solar symbols, they stood in pairs before temples.

ORATORY (Cpt) small chapel for private worship.

PAN BEDDING a method of building brick walls in sections to allow independent movement of units without collapsing.

PENDENTIVE a device for raising a dome above a square base (see text).

PERISTYLE HALL an open court with a roofed arcade around the inner walls.

PISHTAK (Isl) Persian decorative feature whereby the pediment of a gate or opening is raised above the level of the roof.

PRONAOS chamber preceeding the sanctuary.

PROPYLON gate standing in front of the pylon.

PYLON massive entrance, consisting of two units joined by a gate, standing in front of a temple.

PYRAMIDION capstone of pyramid or obelisk.

QĀʿAH (Isl) main hall of a domestic building.

QALʿAH (Isl) fortress.

QAṢR (Isl) palace, fortress, or mansion.

QAYSĀRIYYAH (Isl) hostel for merchants.

QIBLAH (Isl) direction of Mecca.

QŪBBAH (Isl) dome, later used for the whole tomb.

REBUS a name represented in cryptic form by symbols.

RIBĀṬ (Isl) originally a fortified frontier post where Muslim scholar-warriors resided.

RIWĀQ (Isl) colonnade running along the inside wall of an open court.

SABĪL (Isl) public drinking fountain.

ṢAḤN (Isl) central court of a mosque.

SALAMLIK (Isl) reception apartments for men.

SOFFIT, the undersurface of an arch or corbel.

SPEOS a rock cut chapel.

SQUINCH a device for raising a dome over a square base (see text).

STELA a block of stone or wood covered with reliefs or paintings.

SŪQ (Isl) market.

TĀBŪT (Isl) coffin, also used for the structure of the grave itself.

TAKHTABŪSH (Isl) salon.

TAKIYYAH (Isl) a building to house a community of sufis.

TEMENOS sacred enclosure.

TRIBUNE (Cpt) raised platform at the end of apse, on which is set the bishop's throne.

TURBAH (Isl) tomb.

WIKĀLAH (Isl) hostel for merchants.

WINDOW OF APPEARANCES, the window in ancient Egyptian palaces and temples where the King showed himself to the people.

ZĀWIYAH (Isl) small establishment built for a sufi shaykh to receive his brotherhood.

# Natural History

Numbers within parentheses refer to the table of hieroglyphics at the end of the section.

In zoological terms the whole of North Africa has much more in common with Europe than with the African Continent of which it is an integral part. There are seven great zoogeographical regions of the world, areas in which the fauna has a certain homogenity although often overlapping at the edges. The present area forms the Southern boundary of the Palaearctic Region which stretches from the Atlantic coast of Europe in the W to the Pacific coast of Russia and Japan in the E. Latitude forms a much more effective barrier to the interchange of faunas than does the Mediterranean Sea. The rest of the continent of Africa below the Sahara is known as the Afrotropical Region and, although certain elements of this fauna are present in Egypt, that of the Palaearctic region dominates. There is also a slight overlap with the fauna of the Oriental Region to the E. Along their common border the two regions are well separated by the arid desert but the Atlantic coast of Morocco and the Nile Valley have always acted as corridors between them and are important flyways for migrating birds. These regional divisions are very ancient, stretching back into the Pliocene and although the borders have been pushed N or S as the world climate fluctuated, the elements in them have remained basically the same. In the past during the warmer Interglacials the proportion of Ethiopian fauna in Egypt was much greater but deterioration in the

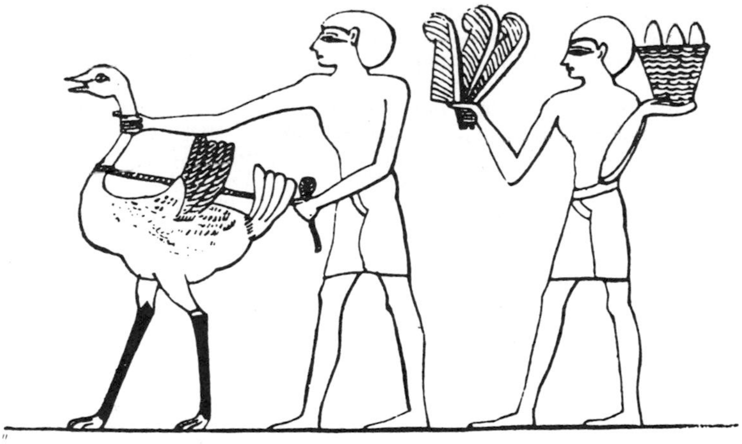

*Scene in a Theban tomb of Egyptians collecting feathers from a pigmy?) ostrich (Wilkinson)*

weather pushed most of them S and the more spectacular species were doomed with the coming of man. In addition to this, Egypt at various times possessed representatives of northern genera or families that never entered the Afrotropical Region—true pigs (*Sus*), deer (*Cervus*), cattle (*Bos*), goats (*Capra*).

Although there would appear to be ecological uniformity in Egypt, in fact most of the major habitats are present, all, however, dominated by that of the pervasive desert, stoney and gravelly to the W and mountainous to the E, with perhaps the most inimical habitat of all found in the far SW, the Great Sand Sea. There are large areas of scrubland and in the Delta extensive marshland, while the oases are a special case and provide valuable stopping places for birds on migration. The Nile Valley itself can perhaps be best understood as a form of parkland, with scattered groves of trees among seasonal crop fields. There is one vital habitat missing in Egypt, forest, and it is very significant that two groups of animals, woodpeckers and squirrels, important indicators of this habitat both in the Palaearctic and Afrotropical Regions, are entirely absent. The life of the river system is mainly Afrotropical since its source is deep within Africa. The two marine environments are very different from each other: the Mediterranean to the N has a modified temperate Atlantic character, while the Red Sea is a finger of the Indian Ocean pushed far to the N of its main confines. Because of its landlocked conformation the Red Sea is almost tropical. Certainly forms indicative of warmer seas are found much further N in this sea than in comparable latitudes on the Atlantic western coast of the continent. Although there is free access via the Suez Canal for species from either sea to pass into the other, very few have made the transition. Another habitat unfamiliar to the European visitor is the mangrove forest, the most northerly in the world, found at the S tip of Sinai.

**MAMMALS**. The mammalian fauna of Egypt has been impoverished but it still has quite an impressive number of species, as to be expected, mostly adapted to desert conditions.

The **Insectivora** are poorly represented with species of only two families, the **Erinaceidae** (hedgehogs) and the **Soricidae** (shrews). Of the former, the two species are the Long-eared hedgehog (*Hemiechinus auritus*), a Palaearctic sp. on the N coast, and the Desert hedgehog (*Paraechinus aethiopica*), an Afrotropical sp. found throughout except for the harshest desert. Both are paler and longer legged than the familiar European sp. and the former has long rabbit-like ears. Of the shrews, the largest has a body length of 100mm. There are no red-toothed spp, but the white-toothed group has representatives of two genera: *Crocidura* (four spp) and *Suncus* (two spp), most of them with very restricted distributions. Two species were known from mummified specimens before they were discovered alive.

The **Chiroptera** (Bats; Ar. sing. waṭwāṭ or khufash: pl. waṭāwīṭ or khafāfīsh) are extremely well represented in Egypt. Doubtless the abundant insect life of the Nile is one of the main reasons for this. The only member of the **Pteropididae** (Fruit-bats), however, is the Egyptian fruit-bat (*Rousettus aegyptica*), which has a wide distribution in the Nile Valley and E of the river, even in Cairo parks, extending into Africa. It has a short tail, large eyes and a foxy face. The remaining species are all crepuscular or nocturnal and belong to various families of the

**Microchiroptera** (Insect-eating bats), with longer tails, small eyes and some form of echo-location system for catching their prey.

The Mouse-tailed bats (**Rhinopomatidae**) (2 spp) have a thread-like tail as long as the head and body of c 6–7cm, large ears and a peculiar upturned snout. They have long legs and are adept at scrabbling about rough walls and rocks in their favoured shelters of caves, wells and old buildings where they live in small colonies, some of which have existed for hundreds if not thousands of years. Sheath-tailed bats (**Emballonuridae**) (2 spp), up to 10cm in body length, also have tails, but enclosed in a sheath. The Egyptian representatives are large swift-flying bats living colonially in caves and large abandoned buildings.

There is only one representative of the small family of Slit-faced bats (**Nycteridae**), the Theban bat (*Nycteris thebaica*), with grooved nostrils, large ears and a tail that ends in a T-joint. Found throughout the Nile Valley and Delta, it lives in small colonies or alone in arid areas, roosting in trees, shallow caves or holes in the ground. It is rather terrestial and its diet includes ground invertebrates such as scorpions and spiders and centipedes. The Leaf-nosed bats (**Rhinolophidae**), with their large pointed ears and complex nose folds, have five spp. in the area, all exclusively insectivorous and highly aerial. Their wings, which are rather rounded and give them a distinctive fluttering flight, are wrapped completely round the body at rest.

The largest and most widespread family, the Typical bats (**Vespertilionidae**), pipistrelles and serotines have few diagnostic features beyond the fact that they are generalised and possess a tail—indeed they give the appearance of 'flying mice'; however, several spp. possess enormous ears. All are mainly insectivorous. The thick-set free-tailed bats (**Molossidae**) (2 spp), often considered to be the most anatomically advanced of the bats are heavy jowled with mastiff-like faces and ears joined above the forehead. Their flight is strong, direct and fast and they are insect-eaters.

The order of **Primates** has lost its two Egyptian members, both of them represented in hieroglyphic signs. The Green monkey (*Cercopithecus a. aethiops*) (1) is now only found in the Sudan S of Khartoum. The Hamadryas baboon (*Papio hamadryas*) (2), sacred to the god Thoth and depicted in many wall paintings and statues, is only found in the mountains of the NE Sudan c 250km S of the Egyptian border. But it must once have been found in the mountains of the Red Sea coast well into Egyptian territory.

Rabbits and hares (**Lagomorpha**; Ar. sing. arnab: pl. arānib) have only one species in Egypt, a subsp. of the wide-ranging brown hare (*Lepus capensis rothschildi*) (3) differing from its familiar European subsp. in being paler. The domestic rabbits (*Oryctolagus cuniculus*) kept in modern Egypt were introduced in the Roman period but find a feral existence difficult in Egypt.

Rodents (**Rodentia**) comprise by far the largest order of mammals. It is an homogenous order but the taxonomy of some groups is disputed. Egypt has about 30 spp., most of them adapted to the desert conditions. The family of voles and hamsters (**Crictidae**) is represented in Egypt by 17 spp. of gerbils and jirds (Ar. sing. jirdh: pl. jirdhā) in which the tail is over half the body length and moderately hairy. They are all more-or-less well adapted to arid areas and tend to be nocturnal, staying in burrows during the day. The genus *Gerbillus* (8 spp) *Gerbillus Dipodillus* has a tufted tail usually much longer than the head and body combined and are divided among spp with naked or hairy soles to their feet. They are found throughout the area. The Egyptian short-tailed gerbil (*Dipodillus kaiseri*), is found only on the NW coast. The Fat-tailed sand rat (*Pachyuromys duprasi*) right on the edge of the Great Sand Sea in the SW, while the equally aptly named Bushy-tailed jird (*Sekeetamys calurus*) is an endemic sp. confined to the Eastern Desert and Sinai. Three members of the mainly Asiatic genus *Meriones* also occur in Egypt. Rather indelicately named, the Fat sand rat (*Psammomys obesus*) is a robust form very variable in colour, closely related to the last genus but not so well adapted to arid regions; it is found in the N and in Sinai.

The mole rats (**Spalacidae**) are superbly adapted for a subterranean life: completely naked, with visible eyes and ears, no tail and immense incisors with which they grind up bulbs and roots encountered in their burrowing. The Egyptian sp. is the Southern blind mole-rat (*Spalax leucodon*), found in N areas.

Typical rats and mice (**Muridae**; Ar. sing. fār: pl. fiʾrān), with their long and thinly haired tails, have seven spp. in Egypt. The Nile grass rat (*Arivicanthis niloticus*) is a large form with a speckled appearance found through the Nile Valley. *Rattus* is mainly an Oriental genus, but two spp. from SE Asia have made an appearance throughout the world as opportunist commensals of humankind: the Black rat (*R. rattus*) and the Brown rat (*R. norvegicus*). The Black rat is very variable with many forms, several of which now co-exist and must have speciated since the original dispersal. In Egypt the form *alexandrinus*, brown above, grey below, tends to associate closely with man, while the form *frugivorus*, brown above and white below, is the dominant form in the fields. Another commensal of man, the House mouse (*Mus musculus*), is also found throughout the Nile Valley and Delta but not in the great numbers found in Europe, presumably because of the widespread and numerous weasels. Spiny mice have the hairs of the back converted to spines; two spp. occur: the Cairo spiny mouse (*Aromys cahirinus*), found throughout the eastern part of the country, and the Golden spiny mouse (*A. russatus*), with its black-soled feet, in the N. An Asian sp., the Short-tailed bandicoot rat (*Nesokia indica*), has a range that includes northern Egypt. Dormice (*Gliridae*) just make an appearance in Egyptian territory with the Garden dormouse (*Eliomys quercinus*), a mainly European sp. which is found in Sinai.

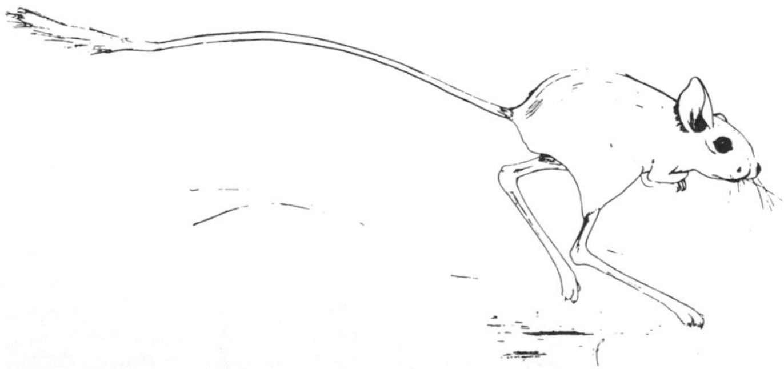

*The Lesser Egyptian jerboa (Jaculus jaculus)*

Another group of rodents beautifully adapted to desert life are the jerboas (**Dipodidae**; Ar. sing. yarbūʿ: pl. yarābiʿ). They usually bound along on their back legs balanced by their long tufted tails, longer than the head and body combined. Like the gerbils, they are nocturnal, spending the hot days in burrows and emerging to forage in the evening, although they tend to be solitary and range further from their burrows. Tremendous jumpers, they can leap almost 2m in a single bound. So impressed were the Eighth Army by these creatures that they called themselves 'Desert Rats', an honorific proudly carried. While the Lesser Egyptian jerboa (*Jaculus jaculus*) is found throughout the region, the Greater Egyptian jerboa (*J. orientalis*) avoids the extremely arid areas and occurs along the N coastal region into Sinai.

Another sp. of a mainly Asian genus, the Four-toed jerboa (*Allactaga tetradactyla*) is also found on the N coast but only E of the Nile. All are large eyed and large eared, with pale sandy fur. Their metabolic rate is very low and they live about twice as long as rats. One more rodent is found, a representative of another unmistakeable family, the Porcupines (**Hystricidae**). Although very large they can be surprisingly secretive and the North African porcupine (*Hystrix cristata*) is found, though rarely, in the S part of the Nile Valley.

As with the birds of prey, the **Carnivora** are well represented in Egypt but the most magnificent sp., the Lion has been lost. The Dogs (**Canidae**) have several members though there is no palaeantological evidence that the Wolf (*Canis lupus*) ever existed in mainland Egypt. Its nearest approach to Africa was and may still be Sinai. All large wild canids are called in Ar. dh'ib: pl. dhi'āb (wolf). Early dogs, presumably introduced from Asia in prehistoric times, were still very wolf-like though already distinct enough to be identified as domestics. The Northern jackal (*C. aureus*), is the largest canid found throughout the country, the Egyptian form being particulary large, though still smaller than the wolf. These lupine dogs and the jackal were revered and sacred to several gods—Anubis, Wepwawet and Duamutef (4, 5, 6). As well as a domestic form of the basengi type (7), other types known from 12 Dyn. wall-paintings include hounds, mastiffs and dwarf forms. Four spp. of fox (*Vulpes*; Ar. sing. thaʿlab: pl. thaʿālib) occur. The Red fox (*V. v. aegyptica*), a paler form of the familiar European sp. but retaining the white tip to its tail, is common in the Delta. In the more arid areas of the N lives the smaller and more lightly-built Sand fox (*V. ruepelli*), an Oriental element in the fauna, also with a white tip to the tail. An African sp., the Pale fox (*V. pallida*), even paler but with a black tip to its tail, intrudes from the S while the smallest and palest of all, but also with a black tipped tail, the Fennec (*V. zerda*), superbly adapted to desert life, inhabits the most arid regions. With its huge ears and large eyes, its senses of hearing and sight are extremely acute, though it is mainly nocturnal, spending the days in deep burrows. It seems to be entirely independent of water, living on a mixed diet of rodents, lizards and insects.

Weasels and martens (**Mustelidae**), have two representatives. The Weasel (Ar. sing. ʿarsah: pl. ʿaras) with its large Egyptian subsp. (*Mustela nivalis subpalmata*) is very common in the Delta and Nile Valley, and even in central Cairo where it can be seen in the early morning and evening running busily about with tail in the air investigating every cranny and nook along the shop fronts. It is probable that the scarcity of house mice and rats is due to these weasels. Found throughout Egypt, the Saharan striped weasel (*Ictonyx libyca*) is quite distinct with a very dark brown pelt striped with white. Strangely there are no otters in the lower Nile despite what seem to be ideal conditions.

The feline carnivores are also well represented. The **Viverridae** have two members occuring here—the Genet (*Genetta genetta*) intrudes from the Sudan in the far SE, and the snake-eating Egyptian mongoose (*Herpestes ichneumon*; Ar. sing. nims: pl. nimsāt), so much the subject of fable and myth in Ancient Egypt, is well-known throughout the Delta and the N Nile Valley. Among the fallaḥīn, it has a reputation for being deaf. Hyaenas (**Hyaenidae**; Ar. sing. ḍubaʿ: pl. ḍabāʿ) are represented by the Striped hyaena (*Hyaena hyaena*) in the NE Delta and Sinai. It is almost wholly a carrion eater while its diminutive relative, the Aard-wolf (*Protoles oristata*), which exists almost entirely on insects, extends to the N border of Sudan and may wander into Egypt. Cats (**Felidae**), always secretive, still have five or six spp. in Egypt. The jungle cat (*Felis chaus*) is found throughout the Delta, Valley and the E side of the country. It is larger than a domestic cat with a short tail and slightly tufted ears. The African wild cat (*F. sylvestris libyca*) is now considered to be of the same species as the European wild cat, although rather different in coat pattern and temperament, but transitional forms occur in the Middle East.

Cats (Ar. sing. qaṭṭ: pl. qaṭāṭ) (8) were probably first domesticated in Egypt. They are found in Predynastic burials, along with other wild animals, at Abydos and al-Badārī, but it is impossible to ascertain whether they are wild or domestic. Apart from an isolated 5 Dyn. tomb-painting at Ṣaqqārah there is no hard evidence of commensality until the Middle Kingdom when an 11 Dyn. inscription from Deir al-Baḥrī mentions a favourite cat of Mentuhotpe II. By the New Kingdom they are shown often as a domestics of man and usually found a place in the household under a chair, assisting in the hunt, or as snake and mouse eaters. The cat was sacred to the goddess Bast and the god Reʿ. Cats were buried in special cemeteries, a practice that culminated in the vast Late Period feline necropolis at Bubastis. The attachment of the Egyptians to their cats was very strong—in 59 BC a Roman politician was hanged for accidentally killing one. The self-colour and unusual conformation of some varieties of cats may be due to hybridisation with the jungle cat. Two other spp. are also found in Egypt. The very rare Sand cat (*F. margarita*) with furred soles, flat head and unmarked coat, except for ringed tail and legs, is found in the dunes of Sinai, and the Caracal (*F. caracal*), a much larger lynx-like sp. with russet coat, tufted ears and short tail, is also found in Sinai and the neighbouring E Delta. The Leopard (*Panthera pardus*; Ar. sing. nimr: pl. namūr) (9) may still have a relict population in the less populated areas of Sinai, but how it has fared during the recent disturbances in the area is difficult to assess. Most impressive of the family, the Lion (*P. leo*; Ar. sing. asad: pl. usūd) (10, 11), is no longer found in Egyptian territory and its range has retreated far to the S though it probably survived well into the Christian era. The lioness was sacred to the goddess Sekhmet and sphinxes were usually represented with the body of a lion. The Cheetah (*Acinonyx jubatus*) almost reaches the S and W borders of Egypt and may wander into the country occasionally.

All the great orders of herbivores have or have had within ancient times representatives in Egypt. The African elephant (*Loxodonta africana*; Ar. sing. fīl: pl. afyāl) (12)was the first to disappear, probably some time before the 1C AD. In Ancient Egypt it was known as abu, giving its name to Elephantine. Despite looking like large rodents the Hyraxes (**Hyracoidea**) are relatives of the elephants and have tiny hooves on their toes. The Syrian rock-hyrax (*Procavia syriaca*) occurs on the rocky outcrops of the Sinai and the Eastern Desert. Another group with common ancestry to the elephants are the Sea cows (**Sirenia**) and the Dugong (*Dugong dugong*) is found reasonably frequently in the coastal waters of the Red Sea. As for the **Perissodactyla**, domestication of the donkey probably occurred in Egypt in Predynastic times, but unfortunately the form of the African wild ass (*Equus asinus nubiana*) that gave rise to the domestic form, with a distinctive dark cross on the shoulders, is now found no closer than the mountains of E coastal Sudan.

Among the **Artiodactyla** many spp. have also suffered at the hands of man. Of the Suiformes the Wild boar (*Sus scrofa*) is now found only in NE Sinai and the Hippopotamus (*Hippopatamus amphibius*) (13), sacred to the goddess Tawert in ancient times, was exterminated fairly recently, the last in the Delta apparently shot c 1815 and one at Aswān killed a year later. From the suborder **Tylopoda**, the one-humped camel (*Camelus dromedarius*; Ar. sing. jamal: pl. jimāl) is the only domestic animal for which no wild form, living or extinct, is known. Its Asian congener, the Bactrian camel (*C. ferus*), still has a wild ancestor in the Gobi Desert, but since *dromedarius* X *ferus* hybrids are only sporadically fertile, it cannot also be the wild form of *dromedarius*. It was probably a native of the Arabian Peninsular and adjacent deserts and was certainly under domestication there by the 1st millennium BC. It can exist on dry food for over 14 days, tolerate a greater depletion of body weight (30 per cent) than most other mammals and it can assimilate a lot of water in a short time. These and many other adaptations ensure that it is superbly tolerant of desert conditions.

Several large spp. are found in the **Bovidae**. It is probable that the Wild ox (*Bos primigenius*) was found in Egypt in the Late Pleistocene but by the early Dynastic period it had probably been assimilated into the domestic population, although kings of the 18 Dyn. hunted some form of large ox in the S. Now critically endangered and confined to the SE Arabian Peninsular, the Arabian oryx (*Oryx leucoryx*) was until recently also found in Sinai. Another sp. also until recently found is the Scimitar oryx (*O. dammah*) (14) which has retreated to the W Sahara. Well known to the Ancient Egyptians, these animals were kept in semi-domesticity. Similarly now confined to the Sahara is the Addax (*Addax nasomaculatus*), an antelope even more highly adapted to desert-life. Some of the Gazelles (*Gazella*; Ar. sing. ghazāl: pl. ghuzlān) (15) are also well adapted to desert life, others less so, and they are highly mobile. Dorcas gazelle (*G. dorcas*) are present in the W Desert to the coast of the Mediterranean while the Yellow mountain gazelle (*G. gazella*), sometimes considered to be a subsp. of the last, is found in Sinai. The Sand gazelle (*G. leptoceros*) is also found throughout the Western Desert while the large Addra gazelle (*G. addra*) is found in the Central Sahara but its wandering may well bring it into Egypt. None of the wild sheep (*Ovis*) penetrated into Africa but two of the goats (*Capra*) managed it: the Nubian ibex (*C. ibex nubiana*) in the hills of SE Egypt and the rather aberrant Barbary sheep (*C. lervia*) in the hills of the Northern Sahara.

**BIRDS** (Ar. sing. ṭā'ir: pl. ṭuyūr).Except for certain insects the most obvious elements of Egyptian fauna are the birds which although varied have also suffered greatly in recent years. This decline has been greatly accelerated since the introduction of mass fertilisation of the land with nitrates and other chemicals. Perhaps the most tragic loss was the Sacred ibis (*Threskiornis aethiopicus*) which managed to survive until the middle of the 19C. It has now joined those other living symbols of ancient Egypt, the crocodile, hippopotamus and hamadryas baboon in being no longer found within the confines of Egypt.

In addition to the resident species there is a massive influx of winter migrants from the N. Many others are spring and autumn passage migrants using the Nile Valley flyway and the oases. Palaearctic species make up the bulk of Egypt's avian population, with incursions by some Afrotropical species and fewer from the Oriental region. Although Egypt has no endemic species, several races of more widespread species are unique to the country. Birds new to the visitor will be encountered throughout, but particularly favoured areas are the Fayyūm with the wintering populations of ducks and waders, Sinai where many species not found in the rest of the country reside, the oases, Red Sea coast, the Delta marshes and Jabal Alba in the far SE where several Afrotropical species intrude into Egypt.

After mammals it was birds which most attracted the Ancient Egyptians and many species are depicted on the walls of their monuments in paintings and reliefs, often distinguishable to the species level and beautifully observed. Perhaps even more ancient is the inclusion of several birds as symbols in the hieroglyphic script. Many of these, however, are harder to identify specifically but are generically unmistakable.

Birds in Egypt, as in the rest of the world, are under threat. Within recent times several important species have been exterminated within the confines of the country. Modern firearms and expeditions of foreigners who come to shoot 'duck' (or anything else with wings and a beak) are decimating the birdlife of Egypt.

The single species of the **Struthionidae**, the Ostrich (*Struthio camelus*; Ar. naʿāmah) (16), once common now only breeds in the far SE although its wandering may well take it further N into Egypt. It provided feathers for fans and other decorations and it is frequently shown on walls and artifacts (e.g. on the fan of Tutankhamun in the EM, where the king is shown hunting and shooting ostriches). They were often farmed and kept in semi-domestication. Of interest is the small form of ostrich depicted in several wall paintings, which maybe the same extinct pygmy sp. known from sub-fossil bones found in Syria and Arabia.

Of the Grebes (**Podicipitidae**) only the Great-crested grebe (*Podiceps cristatus*) and the Little grebe (*P. ruficollis capensis*) breed survive, to be joined in winter by the Black-necked grebe (*P. n. nigricollis*) from Europe. Although none breed in Egypt several members of the **Procellariformes** (Petrels and shearwaters) are regulars in the Red Sea but they are a confusing group and identification needs great care.

The impressive **Pelecaniformes** (Gannets and Cormorants, etc.) have several members breeding in or visiting Egypt. The Red-billed tropic-bird (*Phaethon aethereus indicus*), a striking black-barred, white bird with red bill and long tail streamers breeds on islands in the Gulf of Suez, its closest approach to the Mediterranean. The Brown booby (*Morus leucogaster*) also breeds on islands in the Gulf of Suez and near Hurghādah, while the Masked booby (*M. dactyatra*) and Red-footed booby (*M. sula*) with brown and white morphs are vagrants from the

Indian Ocean. Cormorants are now represented only by migratory populations. The Long-tailed cormorant (*Phalacrocorax africanus*) disappeared from the Delta lakes in about 1875, while the continental race of the Cormorant (*P. carbo sinensis*) and the Mediterranean race of the Shag (*P. aristotelis demarestii*) visit the N of Egypt in winter. One of these species, probably *africanus* was represented in the hieroglyphic script (17). Three species of pelican (Ar. bagaʿ) can be found in Egypt, two as winter visitors in the Delta from Europe, the last as a vagrant from the S. The White pelican (*Pelecanus onocrotalus*) and the Dalmatian pelican (*P. crispus*) are difficult to separate, but the latter has black primaries seen in flight. Much smaller, the Pink-backed pelican (*P. rufescens*) has a browner appearance; it should be looked for on the southern Nile and Red Sea coast. Unidentified Frigate birds (*Fregetta*) have been seen off the coast of Sinai.

Frequenting the water margins, marshes and sea coasts the Herons and Storks (**Ciconiiformes**) have always attracted attention and they provided the Ancient Egyptians with several hieroglyphic signs. The Grey heron (*Ardea cinerea*) is only a winter visitor, while the smaller rusty coloured Purple heron (*A. purpurea*) only appears as a passage migrant. One of them was represented in the hieroglyphic script (18). A much more spectacular species, found mainly in sub-Saharan Africa, is the Goliath heron (*A. goliath*), a small colonies of which breeds around Gabal Alba. Breeding colony of the Little green heron (*Butorides striatus*) are found along the Red Sea.

Of the complex genus *Egretta* the Little egret (*E. g. garzetta*) breeds in some oases and is replaced on the Red Sea coast by the dimorphic Reef heron (*E. gularis schistacea*). The Great White egret (*E. alba*), almost as large as the grey heron, is only a winter visitor. During the last hundred years the Cattle egret (*Bubulcus ibis*) has undergone an incredible expansion in its global range, but it has been one of the most obvious species in the Egyptian fauna for many centuries. Its name in Arabic, *Abū qirdān*, means 'father of ticks' and its association with cattle and general familiarity with man make it an attractive and welcome species. They breed throughout and can be seen in the morning and evening winging their way back to their colonies, even in Cairo. Another small pale species, the Squacco heron (*Ardeola ralloides*), breeds only at Farafrah but migrates in winter. Of the two bitterns found in Egypt the Bittern (*Botaurus stellaris*) is only a passage migrant while the Little bittern (*Ixobrychus m. minutus*) breeds in the Delta.

None of the Storks (**Ciconiidae**) breed in Egypt, but the spectacular flights of the White stork (*Ciconia ciconia*; Ar. *ʿanaz*) down the Red Sea coast and finally across the desert to join the Nile Valley at Qēnā are well recorded. They are a familiar sight in the Egyptian fields in winter as they make their leisurely way south. A much less impressive migration is made by the Black stork (*C. nigra*) and it is more rarely seen. The African painted stork (*Ibis ibis*) (19), with beautiful pink plumage and scarlet face and legs, is now only rarely found in Egypt as a vagrant from the S but it is depicted in ancient paintings where it is associated with the colour red. Close relatives of the storks, the Ibises and Spoonbills (**Plataleidae**) were important to the Ancient Egyptians, all three once-endemic species being adopted as hieroglyphs. The Sacred ibis (*Threskiornis ae. aethiopicus*; Ar. *Abu mangal*; the one with the scythe) (20), dedicated to the moon god Thoth, is no longer found breeding in Egypt but it is occasionally found as a vagrant from the Sudan. A smaller dry-country species, the Bald ibis

(*Geronticus eremita*) (21) is now among the rarest species of bird in the world, although it has been seen recently on the edge of the desert in Egypt. It was connected with the dead. A resident species, the Glossy ibis (*Plegadis falcinellus*) (22), used to breed until recently in the Delta. Only the head of the Spoonbill (*Platalea leucorodia*), which now only breeds on the Red Sea coast, was used in the hieroglyphic script (23). The Flamingo (*Phoenicopterus r. roseus*) was previously known only as a winter visitor but a small breeding colony has recently been discovered in N Sinai.

Although the Nile would seem to be capable of supporting many species of Ducks and Geese (**Anatidae**) in fact only two species breed in Egypt. However, the Delta and the Fayyūm are havens for many overwintering species. By far the commonest species of goose wintering in Egypt is the White-fronted goose (*Anser a. albifrons*) (24) which is depicted on the famous painting from Maydūm. This goose was sacred to the earth god Geb. Its companion on the Maydūm painting is the Red-fronted goose (*Branta ruficollis*), a Siberian bird which now winters no closer than the Black Sea coast. It must once have been a common visitor as it was familiar enough for the artist to distinguish between the immature and adult plumages. Of the Sheldgeese two species are found; the Ruddy shelduck (*Tadorna ferruginea*) a winter visitor, and a breeding resident, the Egyptian goose (*Alopochen aegyptiacus*) less common than formerly, found along all manner of water courses. It is usually seen in pairs and this is reflected in the hieroglyph (25), which also draws attention to its long legs.

Most of the European dabbling ducks of the genus *Anas* winter in Egypt and one, the Garganey (*A. querqedula*), is a passage migrant. Two of them have entered the hieroglyphic alphabet: the Pintail duck (*A. acuta*) in several forms (26, 27, 28), and the Widgeon (*A. penelope*) (29). In addition, a S Mediterranean species, the cryptically coloured Marbled teal (*Marmaronetta angustirostris*), is the only other breeder and is found feeding even on temporary water courses. Several diving ducks (*Netta* and *Aythya*) winter in Egypt but none of the sea ducks are found and of the stiff tails only the White-headed duck (*Oxyura leucocephala*) winters in the Delta.

The diurnal birds of prey (**Falconiformes**) find the environment of Egypt very comfortable since there are many breeding and wintering species, augmented by a number which use the Nile Valley as a flyway. Of the kites, the Black-shouldered kite (*Elanus caeruleus*), almost ubiquitous in the Old World, is a resident throughout Egypt, while the Black kite (*Milvus migrans*) is represented by the breeding subsp. *aegyptius* which is joined by the nominate European form on passage. It can be seen even in central Cairo and nests on some of the more isolated buildings. The Honey-buzzard (*Pernis apivorus*) is a passage migrant while the snake-eating Short-toed eagle (*Ciraetus gallicus*) which breeds now only in Sinai is joined on its autumn journey S by the European populations. It is very owl-like in aspect, its rather large head with a facial disk. Its colour and form correspond closely to the painted hieroglyph (30), usually taken to represent some type of owl. Its habit of feeding almost exclusively on snakes, with which they engage in prolonged struggles, would certainly have been known to the Ancient Egyptians and would have fascinated them, as did the similar habit of the mongoose. It is interesting to speculate whether this was the bird intended in the hieroglyph. Two hawks are found as winter visitors: the Sparrowhawk (*Accipiter nisus*) from Europe and the Levant sparrowhawk (*A. brevipes*) from W Asia.

Each of the harriers (*Circus*) breeding in Europe can be found either as passage migrants or winter visitors floating over the fields and marshes of Egypt. A steppe species, the Long-legged buzzard (*Buteo rufinus*) (31) has a subsp. breeding in Egypt which is joined in winter by a subsp. of the Common buzzard (*B. buteo vulpinus*) from Europe. The great eagles of the genera *Hieraaetus* and *Aquila* all have populations that winter in Egypt. *A. rapax* is represented in two forms: *A. r. belisarius*, a pale subsp. known as the Tawny eagle, and the darker *A. r. orientalis*, called the Steppe eagle. The Booted eagle (*H. pennatus*) and two magnificent spp., the Golden eagle (*A. chrysaetos homeyeri*) and the coal-black Verreaux's eagle (*A. verreauxi*), all probably breed in Sinai.

Almost synonymous with the desert, the vultures are represented in Egypt by six spp. The small white Egyptian vulture (*Neophron percnopterus*) (32; representing the letter A), a very important symbol in Ancient Egypt, is found throughout the country as a summer breeding bird. Two large species are found: the Lappet-faced vulture (*Torgos tracheliotus*) as a casual from the S, and the Cinerous vulture (*Aegypius monachus*) present all year round and which may breed. Most important of all is the Griffon vulture (*Gyps fulvus*) (33), another large species which breeds in the Eastern mountains and in Sinai. Sacred to the goddess Mut, and symbol of Upper Egypt, its head appears next to the uraeus on the circlet of kingship. In the far SE and Sinai the narrow-winged Bearded vulture (*Gypaetus barbatus*) breeds. Probably closer to the vultures than eagles, the African sea-eagle (*Haliaetus vocifer*) has been seen in Sinai. Sole representative of its family, the Osprey (*Pandion haliaetus*) breeds now only along the Red Sea coast.

No less than ten or eleven spp. of the **Falconidae** are found in Egypt, either as residents or migrants. The magnificent Peregrine (*Falco p. peregrinus*) crosses from Europe into sub-Saharan Africa but its close desert relative the Barbary falcon (*F. pelegrinoides*) breeds across North Africa. Two other large spp. are also found: the Lanner (*F. biarmicus tanypterus*) as a breeding resident, and the Saker (*F. c. cherrug*) as a winter visitor from Europe. Medium-sized spp. are the Sooty falcon (*F. concolor*), a breeding resident, and Eleonora's falcon (*F. eleonorae*), on passage along the coast on the way to Madagascar. The Hobby (*F. subbuteo*) and Red-footed falcon (*F. vespertinus*) are only passage migrants but two subspp. of the Merlin (*F. columbarius*) winter in Egypt. Although the Lesser kestrel (*F. naumanni*) is a passage migrant, a subsp. of the Kestrel (*F. tinnunculus*), with male closer to the female in plumage than in the European subsp., is a breeding resident. One of the falcons (34, and many variants) also represented the god Horus, but which sp. was intended has been a matter of contention. The Barbay falcon has been considered but the Kestrel is more likely. Its ability to hover motionless while looking for prey as though sanctifying certain places has always been a source of wonder.

Game-birds (**Phasianidae**) are very poorly represented, only four spp. being found within the confines of Egypt. Subspp. of the Chukar (*Alectoris chukar*) and Barbary partridge (*A. barbara*) breed in Sinai and W Egypt while E of the Nile the Sand partridge (*Ammoperdix hayi*), a desert sp., breeds in three forms. The Quail (*Coturnix c. coturnix*) breeds in N Egypt and Sinai and is also found on passage and as a winter visitor. Many thousands of quail are caught in nets for food. The quail chick was the hieroglyph (35), representing the letter W.

The polymorphic order of **Gruiformes** contains several dissimilar families. Both European cranes are found on passage to the S and appear frequently in wall paintings. All of the rails breeding in Europe are found in Egypt either as breeders or in passage. Of interest are the Purple gallinule (*Porphyrio porphyrio*) which in the green-backed form *madagascariensis* is found throughout most of Africa, and Allen's gallinule (*Porphyrio alleni*) which sometimes strays into Egypt from the S. The Little bustard (*Tetrax tetrax*) is a winter visitor from Europe, but the Houbarah (*Chlamydotis unduluta*) is found in two breeding subspp.: *undulata* with four bands on the tail W of the Nile, and *macqueeni*, with three bands, in the Sinai.

Of the **Charadriiformes** only representatives of the pelagic Gulls and Terns (**Laridii**) and the Waders (**Charadrii**) are found in Egypt. Two members of aberrant families make their closest approach to Europe in Egypt. On the Red Sea coast the Crab-plover (*Dromas ardeola*) is a non-breeding visitor,while the Painted snipe (*Rostratula benghalensis*) is found as a resident in the marshes throughout the country. Among the plovers the breeding spp. are Kittlitz's plover (*Charadrius pecuarius*), an African sp. and the Kentish plover (*C. alexandrinus*) on the N and E coast. The visitors include the Caspian plover (*C. asiaticus*) and the Greater sand plover (*C. leschenaulti*). The breeding species of *Vanellus* is the Spur-winged plover (*V. spinosus*) while migrants are the Sociable plover (*V. gregarius*), White-tailed plover (*V. leucurus*) and the Lapwing (*V. vanellus*), the last occasionally in such large flocks that it was incorporated in the hieroglyphic script (36).

Most of the waders breeding through the N Palaearctic are found in Egypt either as passage migrants or winter visitors. There are also two spp. of Stone-curlews (*Burhinus*, Ar. *Kayrawān*), breeding in Egypt. The Common stone-curlew (*B. oedicnemus*) and the smaller Senegal thick-knee (*B. senegalensis*) are familiar throughout the Nile Valley, often nesting on roof tops even in towns and cities. At night their eerie call can be heard in gardens and parks. Breeding in the NE, the Pratincole (*Glareola pratincola*) is accompanied by the Black-winged pratincole (*G. nordmanni*) in winter. The desert-loving cream-coloured courser (*Cursorius cursor*) is a nomadic resident. Known to the ancients and mentioned by Herodotus for its relationship with the crocodile, the Egyptian plover (*Pluvianus aegyptius*) is now drastically reduced in numbers but it is still occasionally seen at the water's edge or on the outskirts of S villages.

Many spp. of gulls and terns are found outside the breeding season off all Egyptian coasts and along the Nile. Two spp of gull breed in Egypt and six spp of tern. The White-eyed gull (*Larus leucophthalmus*)and Sooty gull (*L. hemprichii*) nest along the Red Sea coast and disperse after breeding. The more unfamiliar spp. of terns breeding along the Red Sea coast are the large Caspian tern (*Sterna Caspia*), Swift tern (*bergii*), Crested tern (*S. bengalensis*), White-whiskered tern (*S. repressa*) and Bridled tern (*S. anaethetus*), while the Little tern (*S. albifrons*) nests on the Mediterranean Seaboard. Additionally the common Noddy is found on the SE coast. The African scissor-bill (*Rhynchops flavirostris*), once common on the upper Nile, is now no longer found but it is still seen in the Sudan and should be watched for.

The **Columbiformes** is composed of two rather disparate families: sandgrouse and pigeons. Sandgrouse are delightful birds, superbly adapted to arid conditions. They are often found in huge flocks and the females are cryptically coloured. To the Arabs they were very important, appearing in early poetry as symbols of yearning love as well as being good in the pot. Egypt has six spp., four breeding and two non-breeding visitors. Some spp. have elongated tail feathers, others are short-tailed—the relationships are complicated. The breeding spp. are the Spotted sandgrouse (*Pterocles senegallus*), found throughout except the Delta; the Chestnut-bellied sandgrouse (*P. exustus*), W of the Nile; Lichtenstein's sandgrouse (*P. lichtensteinii*), in Sinai, and the Coronetted sandgrouse (*P. coronatus*), the most desert-adapted of all, throughout, except for the N coast. Both the visitors are from NW Africa: they are the Pin-tailed sandgrouse (*P. alchata*) and the Black-bellied sandgrouse (*P. orientalis*).

Unlike the last family, the pigeons are ubiquitous and Egypt has five spp. Three pale subspp. of the Rock dove (*Columba livia*), progenitor of the domestic pigeon are found. Doves of the genus *Streptopelia* are represented by four spp. As well as the Turtle dove (*S. turtur*) there is the vivid Palm dove (*S. senegalensis*) with its hysterical call. It is sedentary, found throughout the Nile Valley and it even nests in the middle of cities. In the extreme SE is the African Collared dove (*S. decaocto*) and in the NE its Oriental relative the Asian Collared dove (*S. roseogrisea*).

The Greater spotted cuckoo (*Clamator glandarius*) is a member of the **Cuculiformes** breeding in the E of the country. Of the same family but belonging to another group is the Senegal coucal (*Centropus senegalensis aegyptius*), an endemic subsp. of a bird found much further S. Its undisciplined flight is very distinctive. Sole representative of the **Psittaciformes**, a colony of Rose-ringed parakeets (*Psittacula krameri*) was released at Giza in 1928, and there is still a free-flying population in the district, probably centred on the Zoological Gardens.

Owls (**Strigiformes**) have four resident spp., including the ubiquitous Barn owl (*Tyto alba*), and four winter visitors. The more unusual spp. are Bruce's scops owl (*Otus brucei*), a winter visitor, Hume's tawny owl (*Strix butleri*), resident in the Sinai, and the desert subsp. of the Eagle owl (*Bubo b. ascalaphus*), a breeding species. The other breeding sp. is the Little owl (*Athene noctua*). Among the other visiting spp. are the Long-eared owl (*Asio otus*) and the Short-eared owl (*A. flammeus*). A species of owl was supposedly (see above) used in the hieroglyphic alphabet as the sign for M, the most likely contender being *A. flammeus*, but there are other suggestions.

Elusive and nocturnal, the nightjars (**Caprimulgiformes**) are represented by three spp. The European nightjar (*Caprimulgus europaeus*) is a passage migrant. The two paler breeding summer visitors are the Egyptian nightjar (*C. aegyptius*) and the tiny Nubian nightjar (*C. nubicus*). The aerial masters, swifts (**Apodiformes**) have three summer visitors. These are the Pallid swift (*Apus pallidus*), breeding in the N of the country, the Little swift (*A. affinis*) on passage and the Alpine swift (*A. melba*) which is 25 per cent larger than the familiar swift of Britain. It gives the impression of slow flight but is in fact a very powerful flier.

The majority of the **Coraciiformes** are brightly coloured birds and the familiar Kingfisher (*Alcedo atthis*), in two races, visits Egypt in winter. The resident sp. throughout the Nile Valley is larger and belongs to a different genus. With its striking black and white plumage, the Pied kingfisher (*Ceryle r. rudis*) has the habit of hovering before plunging into the water. It is a familiar bird in the waterside paintings of the Ancient Egyptians. Also beautifully plumaged are the Bee-eaters, with three representatives in Egypt. Despite their attractive appearance they

*Four typical Egyptian birds, two of which have unique subspecies confined to the area. Top left: Blue-cheeked bee eater (*Merops superciliosus*), top right: Egyptian swallow (*Hirundo rustica savignii*), bottom left: Greater spotted cuckoo (*Clamator glandarius*), bottom right: the Senegal coucal (*Centropus senegalensis aegyptius*) (From the* Description de l'Egypte*)*

present rather a problem to bee-keepers, as honey-bees are among their favourite prey. The European bee-eater (*Merops apiaster*) is a passage migrant and the Blue-cheeked bee-eater (*M. superciliosus persicus*) breeds in the N and flies S in winter. Most widespread of all, the Little green bee-eater (*M. orientalis*) is found in Egypt in a unique subsp., *cleopatrae*. It breeds in the N and disperses throughout the country in winter. There are few more charming sights than a flock of these busy little birds at their nest site, or feeding. Both the rollers are visitors, the European roller (*Coracias garrulus*) on passage and the Abyssinian roller (*G. abyssinicus*), with long tail streamers, is a vagrant from the Sudan. Honoured among birds, the Hoopoe (*Upupa epops*; Ar. hudhud) is mentioned in the Qur'ān (27:20–28) as the messenger between the Prophet Sulaymān and the Queen of Sabā'. In Arab folklore he was rewarded for this service with the coronet of feathers that crowns his head. It is still very welcome among farmers and has a confiding nature but it is extremely curious when it is not busy. Such was its familiarity to the Ancient Egyptians that it was represented in the hieroglyphic script (37) and often appears in the iconography. Two subspp. are involved, the European race on passage and the larger, duller sedentary race.

The vast order of songbirds, the **Passeriformes**, forms well over half the bird spp. of Egypt (reflecting its global preponderance). The Larks (**Alaudidae**), despite the meadow habitat of the skylark, are desert birds *par excellence*. All are terrestrial with variegated brown or grey plumages. Thirteen spp. are found within the confines of Egypt, eight of which breed. The less familiar spp. breeding in Egypt include Dupont's lark (*Ammonanes duponti*) in the NW, and its close relation the Bar-tailed desert lark (*A. cincturus*) the large Hoopoe lark (*Alaeman alaudipes*) with butterfly-like black-and-white wings, the suprisingly sparrow-like Black-crowned finch-lark (*Eremopterix nigriceps*) and Temminck's horned-lark (*Eremophila bilopha*).

One of the three breeding species of the Swallow family (**Hirundinidae**) was used as a hieroglyphic (38), but it is difficult to be specific. Two Palaearctic races of the Swallow (*Hirundo rustica*) pass through Egypt but the resident breeder is *savignii*, a most beautiful subsp. with brilliant steel-blue upper parts and wholly pink underparts. Many wagtails and pipits (**Motacillidae**) visit Egypt in winter and form large mixed flocks. No less than five subspp. of the Yellow wagtail (*Motacilla flava*) visit Egypt though in their winter plumage the males are much less distinct than in breeding dress. A small, endemic subsp., *pygmaea*, breeds only in Egypt. In the far S can be found the African pied wagtail (*M. vidua*). Only two spp. of shrike (**Laniidae**) breed in Egypt—the Great grey shrike (*Lanius excubitor*) and in the far SE the Rosy patched shrike (*Rhodophoneus cruentus*)—but other spp. are winter visitors or passage migrants from Europe or SW Asia. Two spp. of Bulbul (**Pycnonotidae**) breed, the Common bulbul (*Pycnonotus barbartus*) found throughout the Nile Valley, and the Yellow vented bulbul (*P. xanthopygius*) in Sinai.

The warblers, thrushes and flycatchers are a vast complex of related species, the first group adapted to creeping through vegetation, the second found mainly on the ground and the last adapted to catching prey in ariel sorties. Few of the Warblers (**Sylviidae**) breed in Egypt, but almost all the European spp. pass through on migration or overwinter. The breeding spp. are the Clamorous reed-warbler (*Acrocephalus stentoreus*) in the N, the Fan-tailed warbler (*Cisticola juncidis*), the Graceful prinia (*Prinia gracilis*), the Scrub warbler (*Scotecerca inquieta*) and the Olivaceous warbler (*Hippolais pallida*). The two other breeding spp. are the Sardinian warbler (*Sylvia melanocephala*) and the Spectacled warbler (*S. conspicillata*), both in the N of the country. These are joined in winter by the Desert warbler (*S. nana*) from Western Asia which, as its name suggests, is an arid country sp. Although the Nile Valley would seem to supply ample insect life the Flycatchers (**Muscicapidae**) do not breed in Egypt, but only visit on passage.

By far the largest family found in Egypt are the thrushes and chats (**Turdidae**), though only three desert genera breed. Among the more unfamiliar visitors are the Blue rock-thrush (*Monticola saxtilis*), and White-throated robin (*Irania gutturalis*). The Rufous bush chat (*Cerotrichas galactotes*) is a dry area resident while the Blackstart (*Cercomelas melanurus*) breeds in the SE. The remaining breeding birds are all wheatears (*Oenanthe*), called in Arabic ablaq (pied) as the plumage of most of them is in bold patterns of black, grey, white and fawn. Breeding throughout are the Desert wheatear (*O. deserti*) and the White-crowned black wheatear (*O. leucopyga*), the Red-rumped wheatear (*O. moesta*) on the N coast and the Mourning wheatear (*O. lugens*) and the Hooded wheatear (*O. monacha*) in the E.

As a family the Babblers (**Timaliidae**) live up to their name, usually being found in large roving bands chattering incessantly. This, together with their unkempt appearance and long tails, gives them rather a rakish appearance. Two spp. are breeding residents: the Fulvous babbler (*Turdoides fulvus*) in the S half of the country and the Arabian babbler (*T. squamiceps*) in the E part of Sinai. Completely unfamiliar to the European visitor are three small members of the **Nectariniidae**, the Pygmy sunbird (*Anthrepetes metallicus*) with beautiful glittering green and yellow plumage and tail streamers, breeding from Cairo southwards; the Orange tufted sunbird (*Nectarinia osea*) in Sinai and in the far SE the Shining sunbird (*N. habessinica*).

Another large complex are the finch-like birds: buntings, sparrows and finches. Again, the breeding spp. are all well-adapted to desert conditions. Of the Buntings (**Emberezidae**) two spp. are passage migrants but only the House bunting (*Emberiza striolata*) breeds. Several of the Finches (**Fringillidae**) are also winter visitors. The two breeding spp. are the pink, red-billed Trumpeter bullfinch (*Rhodopechys githaginea*), throughout, except for the NE, which has a peculiar toy-trumpet call, and the Sinai rose finch (*Carpodacus synoicus*), also pink but brighter, restricted to Sinai. The Sparrows (**Ploceidae**) also have a breeding sp., the familiar House sparrow (*Passer domesticus*). Although the race is smaller and paler here it is also a commensal of man. It was used by the Ancient Egyptians as a hieroglyphic sign (39), the only song bird other than the swallow to be so used. Representing the starlings (**Sturnidae**) is Tristram's grackle (*Onycognathus tristramii*), black with rusty primaries, found in the most desolate areas of Sinai.

Perhaps the most highly evolved and successful of all birds are the Crows (**Corvidae**), and there are several spp. in Egypt. The endemic subsp. of the Carrion crow (*Corvus corone sardonius*) is of the 'hooded' type. A close relative of the raven (*C. corax*), though smaller, is the Brown-necked raven (*C. ruficollis*), a species well adapted to desert and steppe. In S Sinai and the SE is found the strong-billed Fan-tailed raven (*C. rhiphidurus*), adapted to mountainous regions.

**REPTILES**. Tortoises and turtles. (Ar. sing. sulḥafāh: pl. salāḥif). Although highly specialised, the **Chelonia** are the most primitive of living reptiles. Their restricted form obviously has advantages since they have existed virtually unchanged for almost two hundred million years and witnessed the rise and fall of many seemingly more efficient groups. They are characterised by the existence of a hard bony carapace covering the upper body and a similar plastron beneath. In some areas they are still plentiful although Egypt now has only four representatives.

Most familiar are the terrestrial tortoises of the genus *Testudo*, several species of which are kept as pets in European gardens. The Common tortoise (*T. graecae*) is represented in Egypt by a dwarf race *T.g. terrestis*, found throughout the country in arid areas where fleshy leaved plants grow. The yellowish shell has dark markings in the centre of each plate. *T. kleinmanni* is smaller with a paler shell and seems to prefer areas which contain halophytic plants. Now very rare in Lower Egypt, the Nile soft-shelled terrapin (*Triony triunguis*) (40) was once common. The leathery carapace is almost circular and dark brown in the adult, but olive with yellow spots in the juvenile. Although it averages 30cm long it can grow to almost a metre. It is a ferocious predator on fish, amphibians and other small vertebrates, striking with a lightning action; when caught it bites viciously. In Nubia the smaller Nubian soft-shelled terrapin (*Cyclanorbis elegans*) can be found. Around the coasts, particularly in the Red Sea, various species of marine turtle are encountered.

**Crocodiles** (Ar. sing. *timsaḥ* pl. *tamāsīḥ*). Only one sp. of the **Crocodilia** was native to Egypt although it disappeared long ago, the Nile crocodile (*Crocodilus niloticus*) (41). Once it was common throughout the country and along the N coast, W to Tunisia and E to Syria. It was sacred to the god Sobek and kept in small lakes attached to the temples, particularly in the Fayyūm. Despite this familiarity it was still greatly feared and must have been a continual hazard to the river dwellers. To be eaten by a crocodile imparted an almost mystical character to the deceased. Now the Nile crocodile has retreated far to the S in Sudan for, besides the value of its skin, its predatory habits ensured continual pressure from hunters. It can reach a length of 5m, weigh up to 1000 kilograms and probably live up to 50 years.

**Lizards** (Ar. sing. *siḥliyyah*: pl. *saḥālī*). The lizards (**Squamata**) found in Egypt are related, in the main, to African spp. Among the commonest are spp. of the **Gekkonidae** including the House gecko (*Tarentola annularis*; Ar. burs), which enters houses where it chases insects and spiders over the walls and ceiling. This familiarity endeared it to the Ancient Egyptians and it entered the hieroglyphic script (42). Other genera are found in the fields or desert. The **Agamidae** are also fairly common with the Starred agama (*Agama stellio*) inhabiting rocky areas and ruins. Comprising several spp., the Spiny-tailed lizards (*Uromastix*) also inhabit arid areas and have the enlarged scales of the tail arranged in spiny rings.

Most familiar to Europeans are members of the **Lacertidae**, some of which are similar to Northern spp.; others living in the drier areas are less typical. *Acanthodactylus* has fringed toes to enable it to run across the sand. Many spp. of the **Scincidae** are also adapted to desert conditions. The Egyptian skink (*Scincus officinalis*) has a flattened snout with which it digs into the sand. Members of the **Chamaeleonidae** merge into the vegetation in which they find themselves with great facility. The Mediterranean chamaeleon occurs throughout the country.

Most voracious of the lizards are the Monitors (**Varanidae**). Egypt possesses two spp., although both are now rare. They grow to a large size and have granular scales and a long neck and tail. Living in damper areas, the Water monitor (*Varanus niloticus*) can reach a length of 2m and is distinguished by the keeled tail. Its counterpart in the drier areas is the Desert monitor (*V. griseus*) which only reaches about 1.5m and has a tail with a round section.

**Snakes** (Ar. sing. thuʿbān: pl. thaʿābīn). Egypt has 33 species of snake (**Ophidia**), a third of which are venomous—a few highly so. They are not a very obvious part of the fauna in the more populated areas, but are frequently seen in the country districts. Visitors should be particularly careful in turning over stones or when visiting isolated sites.

It is important if bitten to stay as calm as possible—the probability that the bite is not serious is high, but medical assistance *must* be sought. A description of the snake is very useful to the doctor, but to try to kill it is asking for trouble.

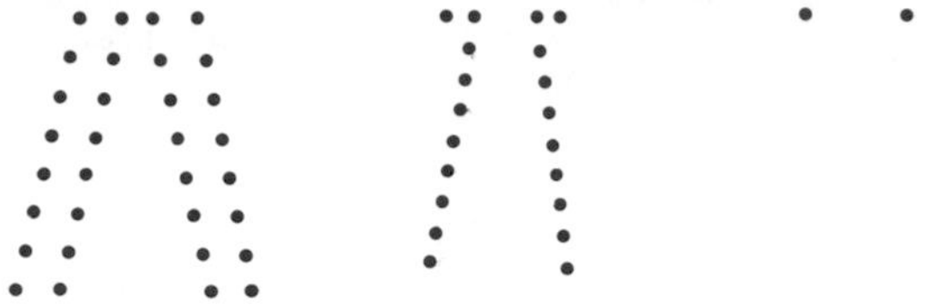

*Non-poisonous* *Cobra* *Viper*

Two very primitive families of snakes each have one representative in Egypt. Worm-like burrowers and little known, their mode of life renders them almost blind and they have tiny eyes under the scales of the head. They are the Egyptian thread snake (*Leptotyphlops cairi*), 20cm long, and the very rare European blind snake (*Typhlops vermicularis*), 26cm long.

Although the world's largest snakes are members of the family *Boidae* the two spp. found in Egypt belong to *Eryx*, a specialised genus of small burrowing snakes which spend much time half-submerged under rough sand or in rodent holes. They are very bad-tempered and bite with a slashing action.

By far the largest family of snakes is the *Colubridae*, a fact reflected in their preponderance among the species of snakes in Egypt. They are generalised snakes with one group capable of delivering venom with specialised teeth at the rear of the mouth, though usually the method of delivery renders them virtually harmless. Similar to the European grass snake in habits, the Diced water-snake (*Natrix tessellatus*), 106cm, is found throughout in suitable wet habitats. The olive-grey colour is relieved by small dark spots in groups of five. Widespread in sub-Saharan Africa, the Wolf snake (*Lycophidium capensis*) has an isolated population in the Fayyūm.

*Coluber* has six spp. in Egypt. The Green flying snake (*C. rodorhachis*), 115cm, olive-green with many stripes, is the most common. It can leap a great distance after its prey: hence the common name. Clifford's snake (*Spalrosophis diadema*), 134cm long, reddish-grey with spots, is common in the Nile Valley. It is found around habitations as well as fields, is very aggressive and bites without provocation. Two rare species of *Contia* are found only in Sinai, both are very small. The Egg-eating snake (*Dasypeltis scaber*), 79cm long, exists almost entirely on eggs. Its mouth is specially adapted to surround the whole egg and it has few teeth. It is fairly common in the Fayyūm, often near chicken farms. In appearance and habits it shows a remarkable similarity to the Carpet viper (see below), even to the scraping of its scales.

The Cat snakes (*Tarbophis*) are the first of the venemous rear-fanged snakes to be considered. Possessing large eyes, they are mainly nocturnal. There are three spp. in Egypt. All are slow movers and unaggressive growing up to 180 cm long. Large and active, well-known in Southern Europe, the Montpelier snake (*Malapolon monpessulana*), 182cm long, is common throughout. It is very powerful, aggressive and unpredictable and is the only one of the group that could prove dangerous. Glossy black scales with four lines render it unmistakable. A close relative, the Molia snake (*M. moilensis*), 103cm long, is a desert species and paler, with a much less aggressive nature. It also has the ability to raise the ribs of its neck to form a hood.

Two *Psammophis* spp. found in Egypt have contrasting environmental needs. The African beauty snake (*P. siblans*), 120cm long, is an attractive snake with several forms, each with thin lines along the length and common in the agricultural areas, often close to houses. Agile and aggressive, it bites easily. Another variable species is Schokar's sand snake (*P. schokari*), 148cm long, confined to the semi-desert, and very quiet in temperament. The nocturnal small Hooded snake (*Macroprotodon cucullatus*), 40cm long, is dark olive with black spots.

The *Elapidae* have fixed teeth in the front of the upper jaw specialised for delivering venom in a chewing bite, which in this case is a powerful neurotoxin affecting the nerves and eventually causing respiratory failure. The proportions are slender with the head smaller relative to the

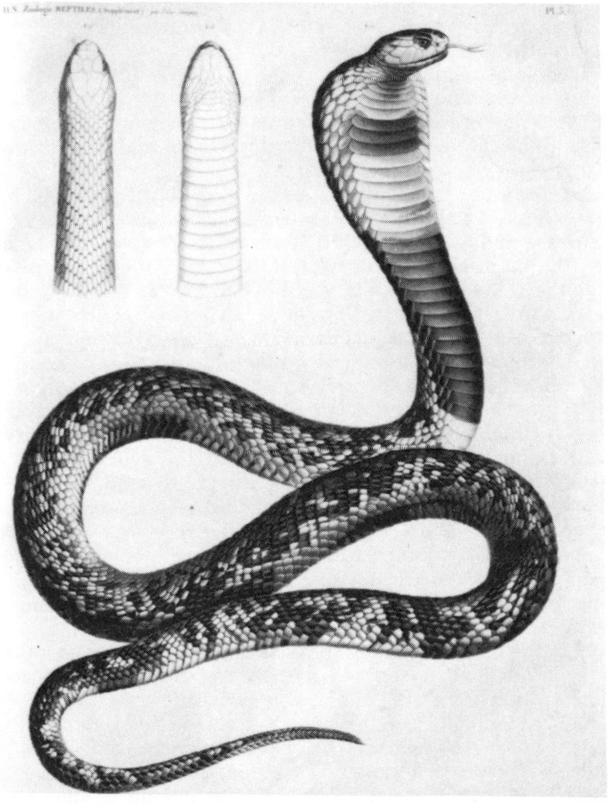

*The Egyptian cobra (*Naja haje*) (From the* Description de l'Egypte*)*

body than in the *Viperidae*, and the scales giving a smooth appearance. Species found in the area can erect the ribs of the neck region, forming a hood. Found throughout the region, the Egyptian cobra (*Naja haje*) (43), around 120cm, but occasionally 200cm long, is very variable in colour, but normally a sandy-olive. It is very catholic in habitat and should be expected anywhere except for the most arid areas. Completely fearless and very active, it has keen eyesight and a well-developed sense of curiosity. It can at times be extremely aggressive. For the Ancient Egyptians it was sacred to the goddess Wadjet and thus symbolised Lower Egypt. Called in later times the uraeus, it appeared in the circlet of kingship beside the vulture of Upper Egypt. It also figured in architecture and friezes of uraei are used from the 4 Dyn. onwards.

Found in S Egypt, the Black-necked cobra (*N. nigricollis*), 200cm long, is even more dangerous because it has an added method of defence. It can project venom from its teeth for up to 3m, aiming with great accuracy usually at the eyes. Affected areas should be washed immediately to prevent permanent damage. The colour is usually darker than N. haje, with a few reddish scales and a dark band on the underside of the hood. Both cobras live in crevices from which they keep watch and they tend to be nocturnal where disturbed. The Night cobra (*Waltersinnesia aegyptica*), 117cm long and black, is a very rare sp. It is mild-natured and slow-moving even when hunting.

The *Viperidae* are also highly venomous. Their poison, delivered in stabbing strokes, is injected through hinged fangs in the upper jaws deep into the victim's tissues. The venom has a haemotoxic effect, destroying red blood corpuscles and causing internal bleeding. They are all thick-set snakes with large heads and dull scales. Most are viviparous.

A rare sp. in Egypt, though several close relatives are common in Europe, the Blunt-nosed viper (*Vipera lebetina*), 150cm long, has been found in the Delta. Confined to the most arid areas are the Sand vipers (*Cerastes*), with two spp. in Egypt. They spend much time hidden beneath the sand with only the eyes showing. Often the only trace of their presence is the trail of Ss left as they travel. They are greyish or yellowish sand in colour with a darker tail and pale underparts. Although their toxicity is great and they will not hesitate to bite if handled or trodden on, they are not normally aggressive. The Horned sand-viper (*C. cerastes*) (44), 72cm long, has small sharp horns above the eyelids. It was greatly venerated, like the cobra, in Ancient Egypt. In modern times it is a favourite with the hawi (itinerant magicians). Much smaller, the Lesser sand-viper (*C. vipera*), 34cm long, is ruddier in colour and lacks horns above the eyes, which, almost in compensation, are set even higher on the head. A very rare species found in Central Sinai is the tiny Fielder's horned-viper (*Pseudocerastes fielderi*), 19.5cm long, also with small horns above the eyes.

Probably the most dangerous snake in Egypt is the Carpet viper (*Echis carinatus*), 72cm long, not only because of the strength of its venom or its aggressive nature but also because it is found closer to houses. It is immediately identifiable by the lighter X on the head, though the body colour is usually sandy reddish or grey with darker and lighter cryptic markings, with paler underparts. Dry agricultural areas are favoured and it is attracted to ruins. The venom is very powerful and in other parts of its range it causes many deaths, pigeons succumbing in 60 seconds. A small one would be quite capable of expeditiously despatching even an ancient Egyptian queen. It can leap from a coil when attacking and will strike indiscriminately at any nearby object. It scrapes its scales together with a characteristic sound to warn enemies off. Found throughout Egypt, it is mainly nocturnal. A rare relative is Burton's carpet viper (*E. coloratus*), 75cm long, without the distinctive mark on the head, found E of the Nile.

An aberrant species of the family is the Burrowing viper (*Atractaspis engudddensis*), 45cm long, a burrowing snake with a small head and eyes and a stubby body. It is very aggressive with poison fangs lying along the side of the mouth which can be used even when the mouth is closed. Very rare, it is found only in Sinai.

**Amphibians**. Frogs and toads (Ar. sing. dufdʿah; pl. dafādaʿ). Despite the ideal conditions of the lower Nile, the area is rather sparsely provided with spp. of amphibia though each one occurs in prodigious numbers. Most apparent are the toads (*Bufo*) of which the commonest is the African toad (*Bufo regularis*). This is a familiar little toad which leaves the canals and ditches in the evenings and wanders around the villages chasing mosquitoes and other insects. It is probably the sp. sacred to the goddess Heket who is therefore a toad rather than a frog goddess. It appeared in the hieroglyphic script (45) and even the tadpole had its own sign (46). The other toad is *Bufo viridis*, a subsp. of the European Green toad. There are also two frogs: a subsp. of the widespread Western bullfrog (*Rana occipitalis*) and the rarer Flower's ridged frog (*Ptychodena floweri*) which is reasonably common in the Delta but is much more aquatic.

**FISH** (Ar. sing. samak; pl. asmāk). The fish (**Pisces**) life of Egypt is particularly rich. Not only are there the two different marine biospheres of temperate and tropical seas, but that of the prodigious freshwater river. Only a short analysis of the major spp. can be attempted here.

THE NILE. In the far S there is a primitive sp. of the **Crossopterygii**. Reaching the Tropic of Cancer, though once found as far N as Asyūṭ, the Nile lungfish (*Protopterus aethiopicus*) spends part of the year, the dry season, hibernating in the dry mud of the river bank. From the **Brachyopterygii**, the Nile bichir (*Polypterus bichir*) is a distinctive elongated fish with a row of small fins along the back. An exclusively African family, the **Mormyridae** has representatives in the Nile. Many are distinguished by long down-curving tubular mouths and the electric organs at the rear of the body which give off weak pulses. *Mormyrops* is a blunt-snouted form as is *Marcusenius isidori* of the Delta region. The Elephant-snout fish (*Mormyrus kanume*) (47) was revered by the Ancient Egyptians in the town of Oxyrhynchus.

One of the predominant orders of the river is the Catfish (**Siluriformes**). Largest is the *Qishr al-Bayad* (*Bagrus bayad*) (48), a popular food fish, which can grow to 1m long and is a voracious predator. *Synodontus schall* reaches 40cm and *Schilbe mystus* 36cm while one of the smallest is *Eulspius niloticus*. The most important economically is the Qarmūt (*Clarius niloticus*) which is found in the main river, canals and creeks, and is fished extensively. Found in slow moving creeks is the Electric catfish (*Malapterus electricus*; Ar. Abū Raʿash—the releaser, a reference to the shock given to fishermen who thereby release the rest of the catch). This fish is capable of giving a severe shock of up to 350 volts, a facility it uses for stunning its prey. It is a great indicator of the salinity of water and disappears at the slightest sign of brackish contamination.

The **Perciformes** are also well represented in the Nile and the largest sp. is found in the **Centropomidae**. This is the Nile perch (*Lates niloticus*)

*The Electric catfish (*Malapterus electricus*) (From the* Description de l'Egypte*)*

which can reach over 2m in length and 80kg in weight. When young it is white with black markings but it turns a dull grey as it matures. It is rapacious and fights fiercely when caught. At Latopolis (near Esna) this fish was revered, mummified and interned in large cemeteries. Males of several spp. of the **Cichlidae** retain their mate's eggs in their mouth until the young hatch. Two spp. of the genus *Sarotherodan*, both called Bulṭī in Arabic, are found, the Palestine cichlid (*S. galilaeus*) in the Delta and the Nile cichlid (*S. niloticus*) (49) throughout. Although mainly marine, some spp. of the **Mugilidae** can live in brackish or even fresh water. An important food fish which does so in Egypt is the Grey mullet (*Mugil cephalus*) (50).

Another mainly marine family is the **Tetrodontiformes**, but several of the puffer-fish live in the larger rivers of the world. The Egyptian representative is the Nile puffer-fish (*Tetraodon lineatus*) (51) and although of little value as a food fish—in fact the livers of the whole family are very poisonous—its habit of expanding when taken from the water fascinated the Ancient Egyptians.

THE MEDITERRANEAN SEA. Of the two marine biospheres, the Mediterranean possesses a fauna similar to that of the adjacent North Atlantic, with the addition of a few endemic spp. It is surprising that since the creation of the Suez Canal and the opening of a sea lane between the Mediterranean and Red Seas very few spp. of fish have made the journey from either sea to establish themselves in the other. Two spp. which have moved from the Red Sea into the Mediterranean are the Blue-speckled parrot-fish (*Leptoscarus vaigiensis*) and the Red grenadier now found along the N coast of Egypt. For the rest of the area the Mediterranean is rich in members of the Wrasse family (**Habridae**), particularly the genus *Centrolobus*, and Gobies (**Gobiidae**).

THE RED SEA. The fauna of the Red Sea is very different, having a totally tropical aspect with corals in fringing reefs, mangroves and representatives of Indo-Pacific groups with probably over 1000 spp of fish. Tropical sharks are much in evidence, with spp. of the swift genus *Carcharhinus*, the Tiger shark (*Galeocerdo cuvier*) and the Red Sea Lemon shark (*Negaprion acutidens*). Also present is the Great white shark (*Carchodon cacharias*). Although there are few records of shark attack in the Red Sea this may be a reflection of the sparse human exploitation of the area to date. Occasional appearances are made by the Whale shark (Rhincodon) and the great Manta rays. Of the bony fish the Moray eels (**Muraenidae**) are found in abundance and have a reputation for viciousness. About six spp. of Barracudas (**Sphyroena**) are present in large shoals.

Among the families, many with brilliant colours, especially well represented are the **Lutanjidae**, particularly *Lutanjus*, the Sea-perches, **Mugilidae**, Mullets and **Serranidae**, Groupers. The **Chaetodontidae**, contain the beautiful coral-fish, of which *Chaetodon* (Butterflyfish) and *Pomacanthus* (Angelfish), are members, both of which among the many spp. present, have several endemic to the Red Sea. Similarly the **Pomacentridae**, with *Abudefduf* (the Sergeant-majors) and *Dascyllus* (the Humbugs), have many brilliant and fascinating spp. The Wrasses (**Labridae**) and Parrot fishes (**Scaridae**) contribute dozens of spp., while the **Zanclidae** provides the charming Moorish idol (*Zanclus cornutus*). Also well represented are the closely related Tangs and Surgeonfish.

Many of the members of the **Scorpaenidae** are well protected by spines connected with poison glands. Some, like the Turkeyfish (*Pteropterus*) or Dragonfish (*Pterois*), have flamboyant colours and feathery fins, the latter genus with two spp.—*P. volitans* and *P. radiata*. Other genera are well camouflaged to blend with the coral detritus, and the supreme example of this is the repulsive and deadly Stonefish (*Synanceia verrucosa*). The spiny dorsal fins are connected to glands which provide a powerful neurotoxin. Great care must be taken with this fish as it can cause great pain or even death. Three closely related families, the Triggerfish and Filefish (**Balistidae**), Porcupine fish (**Diodontidae**) and the Pufferfish (**Tetradontidae**), are also well-represented and are well adapted for life among the coral reefs.

**INVERTEBRATES.** Egypt is too arid to partake of the teeming invertebrate life of tropical Africa. Nonetheless, it has an impressive number of spp., most of which are naturally adapted to desert conditions. Only a minute fraction of this immense fauna is considered here, including those of importance to the Ancient Egyptians or in modern Egypt.

Members of the **Arachnida** (Spiders and Scorpions) were among the first creatures to venture onto dry land, since when they have been continuously successful. Scorpions are found throughout the pantropical zone and are usually nocturnal and solitary. They have a very effective method of defence—a hollow sting in the tail attached to a poison gland. Two types of venom are produced—a mild anaesthetic and a powerful neurotoxin—but very few deaths have been reported recently from Egypt. There are several families, the most important of which in Egypt are the **Buthridae**, pale with slender claws, which are by far the most dangerous, and the **Scorpionidae**, usually darker with larger claws and comparatively harmless. *Buthrus occitans* is also found in Europe but for some reason its venom is much more toxic in N Africa. The venom of the fat-tailed *Androctonus australis* has been known to kill a man in four hours while *Leirurus quinquestriatus* has a more powerful venom, although it is produced in smaller amounts. This is a southern sp. Scorpions were feared in Ancient Egypt and were sacred to the goddess Selket. As a magical prophylactic measure the hieroglyph was modified to exclude the sting (52).

Spiders naturally are plentiful, but with few noticeable spp. Many families are present with the Wolf-spiders (*Lycosa*) particularly prominent. The only potentially dangerous sp. is *Latrodectus schuchi*, a relative of the Black widow, but it is believed to have low toxicity. Wind-spiders (**Solfugae**) are alarming in appearance with a sturdy body supported on eight long powerful legs which take them across the ground at speed. Although non-poisonous they have large jaws which can give a nasty nip and the female will not hesitate to attack animals larger than herself.

The sub-class **Myriapoda** contains the centipedes and millipedes, both of which are represented in Egypt. Millipedes are harmless but some of the centipedes (Ar. umm arbaʿ wa arbaʿīn; mother of forty-four, i.e. legs) can reach up to 15cm and deliver a poisonous bite (53).

Overwhelming in numbers, the **Insecta** make a major contribution to the fauna of Egypt. Prominent along the waterways and lakes are the Dragonflies (**Odonata**), particularly in summer when the many large native spp. are augmented by the migratory *Pantula flavescans* which fly down the Nile from Central Africa. Although harmless, the Cockroaches (**Dictyoptera**) are scavengers and find human habitations particularly conducive. It is this familiarity which probably makes them so objectionable. They all seem to have originated in the Far East and to have travelled W along the sea trade routes. Largest and commonest in Egypt is the dark brown *Periplaneta americana* which is found everywhere in the cities. Two other spp. are smaller and black: *Blatta orientalis* and *Blatella germanica*.

Contained within the **Orthoptera** are the locusts and grasshoppers, among which are some of the most destructive insects known. The Migratory locust (*Schistocerea gregaria*), endemic to an arid area of the Middle East and Southern Asia, used to fly in flocks measuring nearly 50km sq. It depended a great deal on prevailing winds for landfall and so could appear without warning to defoliate great tracts of land. The last appearance in Egypt was in 1924, but modern techniques have ensured that the flocks are dealt with before they reach sizeable proportions. One strange consequence of the disappearance of large flocks of migratory locust was the sudden build up in numbers of the endemic Egyptian locust (*Anacridium aegyptium*) (54) which first appeared in 1928. However, vigilance has ensured that this sp. is also kept within manageable bounds. A surprising genus is *Poeciloceras* which spits a toxic liquid (derived from its food plant *Caltropis*) when disturbed.

The **Paraneuroptera** includes the lice and bugs. Man suffers with the personal attentions of two spp. of lice (*Pediculus*) and two of the bugs (*Cimex*), while many other spp. of bugs are responsible for a great deal of economic damage, e.g. the aphids. The majority are insignificant, but one sp. often seen is the Giant water-bug (*Lethocercus* sp.). This spends much of its life in water, but occasionally emerges to fly to another area. Large and dark brown, it is recognised by the two razor-like front grasping legs. It is best left alone as its piercing beak can give a nasty jab.

Most successful of all insects are the **Coleoptera** (Beetles) with well over a third of a million spp.; it is in fact the largest order within the animal kingdom. They can be found in almost every habitat and are particularly well adapted to desert life. To attempt even a brief review of the families found in Egypt would be impracticable. One however must be mentioned among the many spp. of the **Scarabaeidae**. This is the Sacred scarab (*Scarabeus sacer*), a large black beetle with distinctive habits that attracted the attention of the Ancient Egyptians. Pairs of beetles collect the droppings of herbivores into a ball about the size of an apple and roll it along to a pit where it is buried to provide food for the larvae. The Ancient Egyptians associated this ball with the disk of the sun and the adult beetle emerging from the ground with the resurrection of the dead and the daily rising of the sun. Thus it was personified in the sun god Khephri and appeared in the hieroglyphic script (55). Species to be avoided are the bright Blister beetles (**Meloidae**) which exude poisonous substances, and the massive *Anthia* of the **Carabidae** recognised by their black carapace marked with white, which are highly predatory and can give a nasty bite.

Of the **Lepidoptera** (butterflies and moths) Egypt has few spp. unfamiliar to Europeans. A pair of flamboyant spp. are the poisonous African monarch (*Danaus chrysippus*) and its Nymphalid mimic (*Hypolimnas misippus*). Both are orange with large white markings. Egypt is also particularly rich in Hawkmoths (Sphingidae).

The high mobility of the next two groups ensure that they are the most obvious of all the invertebrate fauna. The **Diptera** (flies) seem to have little to recommend them to mankind. Their sole purpose, it seems, is to be a continual source of annoyance. The large tracts of water, particularly in the Delta, provide a perfect environment for the **Culicidae** (mosquitoes and gnats). Members of the genera *Culex*, *Anopheles* and *Aedes* are present and, particularly in the summer, can make life very uncomfortable for the casual visitor. However, prolonged contact seems to diminish the effect of the bites. Even in the drier areas the visitor is not free for here are found members of the **Psychodidae** (sand flies), particularly *Phlebotomus papatasii*. These minute flies are extremely persistent and cause even greater discomfort but again, protracted contact seems to produce a *modus vivendi*. Most obnoxious of all, the Common house fly (*Musca domestica*) (56) is ubiquitous. During the Old Kingdom it was reputed to have magical powers while in the New Kingdom it became a symbol of valour and golden flies were presented to state heroes.

The **Siphonoptera** (fleas) are represented by the Human flea (*Pulex irritans*).

While many members of the **Hymenoptera** (ants, bees and wasps) are capable of defensive action, they generally keep to themselves unless molested. Their essential value as pollinators of flowers is also appreciated. Most distinctive are the large Carpenter bees (*Xylocarpa*) which are found throughout the country. The Honey bee (*Apis mellifera*) (57) was probably first domesticated in Northern Egypt in Pre-dynastic times and it remained one of the symbols of Lower Egypt throughout. Wall paintings show scenes of bee-keeping, usually in small hives within walled gardens, others show the production of honey.

**PLANTS**. One of the first things to strike visitors to Egypt is the absence of large natural stands of trees. The luxuriant gardens of the Gazīrah in Cairo and other areas show what is possible, and how much of the valley must have appeared in prehistoric times. Now trees in any number are found only in plantations of citruses, date palms and other cultivated trees. Among the shrubs and smaller plants some will be familiar to the visitor from Europe or even America—if not the same species at least a close relative. Other plants will be completely new.

Egypt has a large flora, sited as it is at the juncture of three great botanical regions similar to the zoogeographical areas mentioned above. Additionally, its subtropical climate has permitted the introduction of plants from both the temperate and tropical zones, with varying degrees of success. Although it complicates matters slightly, wild and cultivated species are here considered together as the distinction between the two is sometimes amorphous and many species have achieved a semi-domestic status through their use by man. Over much of the country the vegetation is of desert type, but the rich alluvial soils of the Nile Valley and Delta support a much wider variety of plant life. In fact this is one of the most productive land areas in the world. With temperatures capable of supporting plant growth throughout the year and the added benefit, with the building of the High Dam, of a controlled water supply, production is prodigious. Some crops are in continual production—potatoes, tomatoes, lettuces, with several crops per year—others are seasonal—cabbages and taro—while some have only one crop per year—cotton and rice. Most crops are grown in fields on a rotational basis, but most farmers have small plots where they grow their own preferred vegetables, herbs or fruit, e.g. castor, water-melons, cumin or bananas.

Many cultivated plants have a very long history in Egypt. Some must have originated there while others, introduced from the earliest to recent times, have been remarkably successful. Space permits only a small fraction of the plant spp. to be considered here.

**Fungi, mosses** and **ferns** make an insignificant contribution to the plant life of Egypt. Although many species of toadstool, including the edible mushroom, grow in profusion at certain times of the year, they are regarded with suspicion by the farmers and are pulled up and discarded.

Most of the world's megaflora belongs to the **Spermatophyta** (seed plants) which is divided into two great groups, the **Gymnosperms** (cycads, ginkoes and conifers) and the **Angiosperms** (flowering plants). In Egypt the former can be discounted as most of the species are introduced. By far the most important group is the Angiosperms which itself is divisible into two groups, the **Dicotyledons** (two-seed leaves), including buttercups, willows, potatoes, roses and dandelions, and the **Monocotyledons** (one-seed leaf) which embraces lilies, bananas, grasses, orchids and palms. In most cases only the order is considered but where a family or smaller unit has a particular significance these also are mentioned.

**Dicotyledons**. The **Ranales** is an ancient and cosmopolitan order with many familiar species everywhere. Some of them were important to the Ancient Egyptians. Larkspur (*Delphinium ambigua*), with feathery leaves and pale blue, or more rarely pink or white, flowers was used in Ancient Egypt to garland the dead. They have been found with 3000-year-old mummies still retaining the bright blue pigment. Along the N coast the Turban buttercup (*Ranunculus asiaticus*) with large red, pink, orange or white flowers is one of the commonest among the many spp. of buttercup, while another is the Celery-leaved buttercup (*R. scleratus*) which is found throughout the area in ditches.

Endemic to the Nile are two spp. of water lilies, the lotuses of classical writers. The true Lotus (*Nelumbo nucifera*) was probably introduced from Asia by the Greeks. The wide-petalled White water-lily (*Nymphaea lotus*) is common in canals and ponds in the Delta and the Fayyūm, but of greater importance is the Blue water-lily (*N. caerulea*), which confusingly also has a white form but can be distinguished by the narrower petals. It was the blue form which fascinated the Ancient Egyptians. Now confined to the Delta and oases, it must once have had a much wider distribution as it was one of the symbols of Upper Egypt. It appeared in several forms in the hieroglyphic script: as a bud (58), an open flower (59), the leaf and edible rhizome (60), and as a group in a pool (61). In architecture stylised versions of the bud and flower were the inspiration for two forms of capital.

*The Nile blue water-lily (*Nymphaea caerulea*)*

Although the **Casuarinales** are native to Australasia, one genus of trees has been introduced into Egypt with great success. This is *Casuarina*, the sheeoaks, tall trees with long thin branchlets which give the appearance of pine trees. They are planted as windbreaks and along the sides of roads and as they are quick-growing they provide essential timber when mature. Several spp. are grown, the main ones being *C. equisetifolia* and *C. cunninghami*.

Where date palms are absent, much of the Nile Delta is reminiscent of East Anglia, with tree-lined dykes, ditches and canals. Contributing to this appearance are several spp. of the **Salicales**. The native willow is the Ṣafṣāf (*Salix subserrata*) which grows up to 10m high; the larger *S. tetrasperma* is an early introduction from Asia. Also common is the familiar Weeping willow (*S. babylonica*). Of the related poplars (*Populus*) the endemic sp. *P. euphratica* is now confined to the oases while the Eurasian Black poplar (*P. nigra*) and White poplar (*P. alba*) have been introduced, but have to be propagated by cuttings.

The **Urticales** contain several important groups, one of which, the mulberries (*Morus*), probably originated in East Asia, The Black mulberry (*M. nigra*) is locally grown in the Delta, but the larger White mulberry (*M. alba*), with white, red or purple fruits, is widely cultivated throughout Egypt. Its importance lay in the fact that the leaves provided food for the caterpillars of the silk moth and once the secret of silk production was smuggled from China to Byzantium in the mid-6C Egypt soon became one of the most famous centres of manufacture, a reputation which continued into medieval times.

Three spp. of fig (*Ficus*) are native to Egypt, the fruits of two of which are eaten. The Common fig (*F. carica*) was known in cultivation before

4000 BC in Egypt and was an important source of food in ancient times. Reaching 25m, the Sycamore fig (*F. sycomorus*) has much coarser fruit with crops several times a year. Called *gamayz* by the Egyptians the variety known as falak by the farmers produces very large fruit which are very popular. This tree was a valuable source of timber in Ancient Egypt and the wood was used to make coffins and furniture. The last native sp., the Narrow-leaved fig (*F. palmata*), has small fruit. Decorative spp. introduced mainly from Asia are also grown for timber. Some of them are very large and include the Banyan (*F. benghalensis*), 30m, the Rubber Tree (*F. elastica*), 25m, the Pipal (*F. religiosa*), 20m, and the Weeping fig (*F. benjamina*), 25m, which is common in cities and often cut into topiary shapes. Smaller herbs in the order include Pellitories (*Parietaria*) and Nettles (*Urtica*), among which is the tall and ferocious Roman nettle (*U. pilulifera*).

For the most part the **Polygonales** is an unimpressive order containing Knotweeds (*Polygonum*) and Dock (*Rumex*) which are found throughout the country. Of note is the alien Bride's tears (*Antignon leptopus*) introduced from South America, which is a trailing vine with profuse rose or purple drop-shaped flowers.

Several important families are found in the **Centrospermales**. The **Chenopodaceae** is a family of rather undistinguished halophytic herbs, in which the familiar Goosefoots (*Chenopodium*) are found throughout Egyptian damp areas. Their foetid smell has given rise among Egyptian farmers to several earthy colloquial names. Other herbs include Orache (*Atiplex spp.*), Saltworts (*Salsola spp.*) and seablites, (*Sueada spp.*). The family contains two cultivated spp.: Spinach (*Spinacia oleracea*) which originated in SW Asia, but which has been known in Egypt since ancient times and, Beet (*Beta vulgaris*), a comparatively recent introduction from Europe. Only the red culinary variety is grown.

In the **Caryophyllaceae**, also mainly herbs, the pinks (*Dianthus*) are all rare, but the Campions (*Silene spp*) with pink, red or white flowers are as ubiquitous as they are in Europe. Other familiar genera are Sandwort (*Spergularia spp*), Chickweed (*Stellaria spp*) and Baby's breath (*Gypsophila spp*). From the **Nystaginaceae** two spp. of Bougainvillea have been introduced from South America: *B. glabra* with magenta bracts, and the larger *B. spectabilis* with cerise bracts. The **Amarantheaceae** contains the cultivated Love-lies-bleeding (*Amaranthus caudatus*) which in its wild form with several other relatives is found throughout the Delta.

Adapted to survival in arid areas, the **Aizoaceae** is an interesting family. The Ice plant (*Mesembryanthemum crystallinum*) is covered with hairs that glisten like hoar-frost. With yellow or white flowers, it is common along the North coast along with a relative, *M. nodiflorum*, which has thread-like leaves. Closely related is the New World family **Cactaceae**, only included here for the presence of the Indian fig (*Opuntia ficus-indica*) introduced during the early Ottoman period. The large spiny disks of the plant are found growing in semi-wild state throughout the country and provide a luscious crop of fruits in the summer.

Consisting mainly of herbs, the **Papaverales** contains many familiar spp. Common throughout Egypt is the Corn poppy (*Papaver rhoeas*) along with several spp. of fumitory (*Fumaria*). From the Caper (*Capparis spinosa aegiptica*) the buds are eaten raw or pickled in salt. Two related common herbs are *Cleome arabica* from the Delta and *Gynandropsis pentaphylla*, with white or violet flowers, found throughout.

The **Cruciferae** has provided many essential staple vegetables, herbs or condiments, some of which have been cultivated since the earliest times. They are distinguished by their flower which has four petals arranged in the shape of a cross, which was probably represented in the hieroglyphic script (G2) . The Radish (*Raphanus sativus*), in the large white-rooted form, has been cultivated since ancient times although probably introduced from SW Asia; the small pink form was introduced later from Europe. Many of the genera commonly called mustards are found throughout, though rarely cultivated, and are recognised by their yellow, pink or white flowers and long seed pods. Water-cress (*Nasturtium officinale*) grows throughout Egypt both in beds and wild along the banks of ditches. From the genus *Brassica, B. oleracea* was first probably cultivated in Europe c 3000 BC, and later introduced into the Middle East. It has given rise to several forms, *B.o. botrytis*, Cauliflower and *B.o. capistrata*, Cabbage, among others. A close relative, the Turnip (*B. rapa*) was another ancient introduction from Europe. Several spp. of heavily scented Stock (*Matthiola spp*) are found, of which the commonest is *M. hirida*. In a closely related family is the Moringa tree (*Moringa aptera*). Although now of little economic use the Ancient Egyptians extracted an aromatic oil from the seeds.

The order **Rosales** embraces almost a tenth of all known plants and contains the massive families of the **Rosaceae** (Rose family) and **Leguminosae** (Pea family). The former is of great importance in the temperate regions of the world, but the latter provides vital foodstuffs in almost all climates. Besides the food plants others are of ornamental value. The plants are annual or perennial herbs, shrubs or trees. Some have been cultivated since the earliest times while others have been introduced, a process which is still continuing.

The genus *Acacia* contains pan-tropical dry area trees and among the native spp. is Sant (*A. nilotica*), used for timber since ancient times. Another used particularly for coffins *A. seyal*. Characteristic of the desert areas is *A. tortilis* which, as its Latin name suggests, has contorted branches. Introduced spp. include the Cassie flower (*A. farnesiana*) from South America and Silver wattle (*A. dealbeata*) and Green wattle (*A. decurrens*) from Australia. They all have delightfully scented fluffy yellow flowers in the spring. Two spp. of *Albizia* are found as ornamentals, both with fragrant filamentary flowers: Lebbekh (*A. lebbeck*) from India, with lime green flowers, and Persian labbakh (*A. julbrissin*) from Iran, with pink flowers. The Flamboyant (*Delonix regia*), with brilliant vermilion flowers in the spring, is a native of Madagascar, but was carried by the Arabs throughout East Africa and the Middle East during medieval times. Similarly the Tamarind (*Tamarindus indica*), with yellow flowers followed by pods from which a refreshing drink is made, was introduced from East Africa.

Other ornamental trees include, from Asia, the Orchid tree (*Bauhinia variegata*) with strange round bifurcated leaves, like a camel's foot, and elaborate flowers, and the Sissoo (*Dahlbergia sissoo*) with yellow flowers. From Africa comes *Peltophorum africanum* with panicles of yellow flowers, while South America has contributed *Tipuana tipu*, also with yellow flowers. Three spp. of Coral tree (*Erythrina*) with brilliant scarlet flowers have been introduced: *E. crista-galli* from Brazil, *E. lysistemon* from Africa and *E. indica* from India. Cassia is a large pan-tropical genus and contains several native spp. including the Senna (*C. acutifolia*). Others have been introduced from tropical Africa, Asia and South America. From the pods of the endemic Carob tree (*Ceratonia siliqua*) a sweet drink is made; the pods can also be eaten dry as locust beans. Another native shrub is Camel-thorn (*Alhagi maurorum*) with purple flowers, found growing throughout in scrub and wasteland it exudes sweet sap which dries into brown lumps.

The family also includes herbs or vines, many of them with cultivated forms of prime economic importance as food crops, fodder or soil nitrogenisers. Included amongst the Vetchlings (*Lathyrus*) are the ancestors of the Sweetpea (*L. odoratus*) and the edible Grass pea (*L. sativus*). Two species introduced in ancient times from sub-Saharan Africa are the Cowpea (*Vigna unguiculata*), found throughout both cultivated and as an escape, and the Pigeon pea (*Cajanus cajanus*) which has been found in 12 Dyn. tombs.

Although the genus *Vicia* has eight spp. only the Broad bean (*V. faba*) has been cultivated in several forms. First known in Iron Age Europe it must have reached Egypt at an early date. Two peas, *Pisum sativum* and the drier *P. arvense* have long histories, both probably first cultivated in SW Asia were early introductions into Egypt. Lentil (*Lens esculenta*) is even more ancient, being one of the oldest known cultivated leguminous crops, but its original home is difficult to specify. The Chick pea (*Cicer arietinum*) was known to the Ancient Egyptians, but the wild form is unknown. Also unknown is the place of origin of Horsegram (*Dolichos uniflorus*) although it was definitely in the Old World, but the Hyacinth bean (*Lablab niger*) was probably first cultivated in India. Later introductions include the String bean (*Phaseolus vulgaris*) and the Scarlet runner bean (*P. coccineus*) from South America; both are now essential staples. Also introduced from South America is the Peanut (*Arachis hypogea*) which is now widely grown. The Soya bean (*Glycine mas*) recently introduced from East Asia is easily grown. A native species producing beans which must be soaked before they are eaten is the Egyptian lupin (*Lupinus termis*). The beans are a very popular appetiser and are sold along the streets from little carts; the plant must have been cultivated since very ancient times. Herbs include Liquorice (*Glycyrrhiza glabra*) and Fenugreek (*Trigonella foenum-graecum*), both of which grow throughout. Several spp. of the blue dye plant *Indigofera* are also found.

There are several hundred herbaceous plants in the family, many of which are raised as animal feed. Among the Clovers (*Trifolium*) the classic Egyptian sp. is Birsim (*T. alexandrinum*) which grows to a height of about 60cm and gives between four and six crops per year before producing its pale yellow flowers. Other fodder crops include the Lucernes (*Medicago*), the most important of which is Alfalfa or Lyn's bane (*M. sativa*), and the Bird's-foot trefoils (*Lotus*).

Included among the varied **Geraniales** are some plants which have made a great contribution to civilisation. In the Linaceae, Flax (*Linum usitatissimum*) has been cultivated since prehistoric times. It produced fibre for linen and linseed oil from the seed; vast quantities of it were grown. Until the utilisation of cotton in the 7C it was the principal vegetable fibre used for clothing. Wild flowers of the **Geraniaceae** abound and several spp. of Storksbills (*Erodium*) and Cranesbills (*Geranium*) are common throughout Egypt. The **Zyophyllaceae** are mainly halophytic desert plants and one, *Balanites aegyptica*, the Persea of classical writers, was a favourite garden plant in Ancient Egypt.

From the **Rutaceae** come the citrus fruits (*Citrus*),all of which have a fascinating history although all but one are comparatively late introductions into the Middle East. The oldest known sp. is the Citron (*C. medic*) which has been cultivated in the area since ancient times. The remaining spp. are native to South or East Asia and did not reach the Middle East until medieval times. First to arrive was the Lemon (*C. limun*) in the 10C, followed by another bitter sp., the Seville orange (*C. aurantium*) in the 11C, via Persia. The Lime (*C. aurantiifolia*) and the Shaddock (*C. grandis*) were introduced in the 13C, but the Orange (*C. sinensis*) was not grown until the 15C. Last to arrive were the Tangerine (*C. reticulata*) in the early 19C and recently the Grapefruit (*C. 'paradisi'*), a hybrid between *C. sinensis* and *C. grandis*, from the Caribbean. Also included in the family and widely grown is the herb Rue (*Ruta chalapensis*).

The type genus of the **Euphorbiaceae**, *Euphorbia*, contains variform plants, some are succulents, others small bushes or herbs. Several of the massive African spp. are grown as ornamentals. Well known in Europe at Christmas, in Egypt the Poinsettia (*E. pulcherrima*) is a small bush. Most important of the family is the true Castor oil plant (*Ricinus communis*), known in cultivation since c 4000 BC and a source of oil to the Ancient Egyptians.

The large order **Sapindales** contains few spp. of importance in Egypt. Introduced from India, the Mango (*Mangifera indica*) now grows all over Egypt and there are many varieties. The Christ's thorn jubejube (*Palinurus spinachristi*) is a native of SE Egypt, but it is cultivated throughout and produces small yellowish edible fruits. Of great importance throughout Egyptian history is the Grape (*Vitis vinifera*), cultivated since at least 4000 BC, if not earlier. Many scenes in tombs show various aspects of viticulture including the production of wine.

Several food plants or decorative spp. are found in the **Malvales**. The leaves of Jew's Mallow (*Corchorus oliturus*) are prepared as a glutinous soup to accompany pigeon or rabbit. Several plants of the genus *Hibiscus* are utilised, including Ladies finger or okra (*H. esculenta*), of which the fresh pods are cooked in stews, and in the S Karkadayh (*H. sadbariffa*), where the dried pods are infused into a delicious drink. A plant which transformed agriculture in Egypt is the long staple cotton (*Gossypium barbadense*) which replaced *G. persicum*, the sp. introduced by the Muslims. *G. barbadense* originated in South America but was exported to West Africa in the 17C. From here it spread along the trade routes of the Southern Sahara into the Sudan. It was discovered there by the Frenchman Jumel in 1820, who introduced it into Egypt with remarkable success. In 1850 it was crossed with North American cottons, producing a superior product to either parent and it is the basis of modern Egyptian cottons.

Several ornamental spp. of tree include the weird Indian bombax (*Bombax malabaricum*) and Brazilian bombax (*Chorisia crispiflora*), both of which have swollen trunks and crimson or white flowers followed by enormous seedpods filled with silky fibre.

Of the **Parietales** only the Tamarisks (*Tamarix*) are important. Two spp. are native and widespread: the Nile Tamarisk (*T. nilotica*), a damp area sp., and the more slender Atal tamarisk (*T. aptylla*) found in arid regions. Important spp. found in the **Myrtales** include the Pomegranate (*Punica granatum*), known in Egypt since ancient times, but which probably originated in SW Asia, and the Guava (*Psidium guaraja*), an introduction from South America.

Many spp. of the Australian genus *Eucalyptus* are valuable timber trees and have been introduced into Egypt. Commonest are the Red gum (*E. rostrata*), which can grow to 60m, and the Lemon-scented gum (*E. citriodora*), to 45m.

The **Umbellales** have contributed many herbs and a few vegetables to cultivation. Herbs found in Egypt of undoubted ancient usage are Anise (*Pimpinella anisum*), Fennel (*Faeniculum vulgare*), Parsley (*Petroselinum sativum*), Coriander (*Coriandrum sativum*) and Cumin (*Cuminunum cymlnum*). Vegetables with a similar history include Celery (*Apium graveolens*) and Carrot (*Daucus carota*).

Only decorative spp. are contributed by the **Gentianales** of which the most familiar are the fragrant Jasmines (*Jasminium spp*) which flourish in Egypt. The narrow-leaved Oleander (*Nerium oleander*) has white, pink or red, double or single flowers and is a native sp. found growing throughout Egypt. A close relative, the yellow oleander (*Thevetia peruviana*) has been introduced from South America. Despite their spicy attractive scent all parts of both plants are very poisonous.

From the **Tuberales** the Sweet potato (*Ipomaea batata*) was introduced from the New World sometime in the mid 18C. Many members of the genus are cultivated as decorative creepers with vivid blue, pink or purple trumpet blossoms. Around the S tip of Sinai *Avicennia officinalis* forms a mangrove forest. The **Solanaceae** have provided more staple vegetables, although mainly introduced. An Old World sp. is the Aubergine (*Solanum melongena*) with two forms of fruit, purple and white; it was probably introduced with the Muslim conquest. Species introduced from South America include the Potato (*S. tuberosum*) and the Tomato (*Lycopersicon esculentum*), Sweet pepper (*Capsicum annum*) and the Chilli (*C. frutescens*); all successfully grown on a large scale. Several beautiful trees have been introduced from the related **Bignoniaceae**. Jacaranda (*Jacaranda mimosifolia*) has beautiful mauve flowers and the Yellow elder (*Tecoma stans*) intense yellow flowers, while other spp. include the African tulip tree (*Spathodera nilotica*) and the Sausage tree (*Kigelia pinnata*) with massive seed pods. In a closely related family is Sesame (*Sesamum indica*) which probably originated in Africa and was brought into Egypt c 1300 BC. The seed itself is utilised, and an oil is distilled from it.

Very familiar are the luscious fruits of the members of the **Cucurbitales**. However, the only sp. known to the Ancient Egyptians was the Water melon (*Citrullus lanatus*), introduced from sub-Saharan Africa in remote times. A wild sp. the unpalatable Bitter melon (*C. colocynthus*) which grows throughout in sandy areas, was in Arabic poetry, considered the symbol of hopeless love. Although there are several spp. of wild melon (*Cucumis*) in Africa the Cucumber (*C. sativus*) does not seem to have been cultivated until the 12 Dyn. Another sp., the Melon (*C. melo*) is not apparent until the Roman conquest, after which it was introduced into Europe. The genus *Cucurbita* originated in the New World and both the Marrow/Courgette (*C. pepo*) and the Pumpkins (*C. maxima* and *mixta*) are late introductions. Unknown until Greek times, the Loofah (*Luffa cylindrica*) was probably introduced from Asia. Most peculiar of all, the Bottle gourd (*Lagenaria siceraria*) is the only plant known to have been cultivated in both the Old and New Worlds before the discovery of America. Its remains have been found in Egyptian tombs dated 3500–3300 BC, but in Mexico evidence dates back to 7000–5500 BC. The dried gourds were used as containers, spoons or musical instruments.

Containing upwards of 20,000 spp., the **Compositae** have contributed hundreds of ornamental plants, but comparatively few of food value. Safflower (*Carthamus tinctorius*) provided a source of red or yellow dye and oil to the early Egyptians. Mexico is the original home of the

Sunflower (*Helianthus annuus*) but it has adapted well to Egyptian soil where it is grown for the valuable oil extracted from the seeds and the roasted seeds themselves are very popular. Lettuce (*Latuca sativa*) is one of the oldest cultivated vegetables and probably originated in Egypt. It is known in the long-leaved form from tombs dated 4500 BC and was sacred to the god Min.

**Monocotyledons**. In addition to the spectacular lilies, irises, daffodils and their relatives the **Liliales** also contains the genus Allium. This is an invaluable group and contains the Onion (*A. cepa*) which seems to have originated in SW Asia, but was known in Egypt by the early dynastic period. Garlic (*A. sativum*) seems to have had an even more venerable history of cultivation and was known in Pre-dynastic times, while the Kurat leek (*A. ampeloprasum*) was introduced in historical times. Physically Yams (*Dioscorea spp.*) are very different, being long trailing vines with edible tubers. Certainly of ancient cultivation in Africa, their history is obscure and they probably entered Egypt in post-Roman times. Rushes (*Juncus*) (63) are found along the banks of ditches and canals. They were of importance to the Egyptians: the stems were cut and used as pens from early times. Found in similar areas is a member of the **Pandanales**, the Reed mace (*Typha*).

Only three spp. of the **Palmae** are native to Egypt. Entering cultivation probably in the oases of North Africa the Date palm (*Phoenix dactylifera*) was known in Egypt from the earliest times, but artificial pollenation was only introduced in the 19 Dyn. Dates were of great importance to the many populations throughout the Middle East, not least the Arabs. There are now many varieties, some of which are eaten fresh, unripe or ripe, others are pressed or dried or are turned into drinks. All parts of the tree are used, for weaving, basket-making, ropes or building. The Dūm palm (*Hyphaene thebaica*) is found in the S. This is the only branched palm and has large fan leaves which are used for weaving and thatch while the flesh of the big coarse dry nuts is eaten. Favoured by baboons, who used to live in the multiple crown, the tree was associated with the god Thoth. Until recently the Argum palm (*Medemia argum*) was considered extinct. It appears in Ancient Egyptian wall-painting and also has fan leaves. The violet plum-sized fruit is inedible while on the tree, but sweetens after dropping.

Some magnificent palms have been introduced as ornamentals. Fan palms include the Petticoat palms (*Washingtonia sp.*) from Central America, *Livistona* from SE Asia and the Royal palms (*Roystonea*) from Central and South America. Feather palms include a relative of the date palm, the Canary Island palm (*Phoenix canariensis*), and the Queen palm (*Arecastrum romanzoffianum*) from Brazil.

Among the **Arales** only the Taro (*Colcasia esculenta*), which produces large velvety leaves from an edible corm, is grown in any quantity. Although it originated in SE Asia it was known to the Ancient Egyptians. One plant of importance, for a very different reason however, is found in the **Farinales**. This is the Water hyacinth (*Eichornia crassipes*) with air-filled leaves which float in the water. Although it has a beautiful blue flower and was introduced into many parts of the world from South America as an ornamental, it has become a noxious weed that clogs up ditches and covers vast areas of open stretches of water.

The cultivation of various spp. of the **Graminales** (Cereals) made possible the creation of settled communities which led ultimately to the

*The Dūm palm (*Hyphaene thebaica*) (From the* Description de l'Egypte*)*

rise of great civilisations. The **Cyperaceae** contains one of the characteristic plants of Ancient Egypt, the Papyrus (*Cyperus papyrus*). It was through the discovery that a writing material could be made from this plant and the subsequent proliferation of texts that Egypt became a highly literate society. Considered extinct in Egypt, a subspp. has been discovered recently in the Wādī Natrūn. Papyrus was used until the 10C, well after the Muslim conquest, but was quickly replaced once the practice of papermaking was introduced from the East. In the hieroglyphic system there was a sign for a single stem (64) and another for a clump (65). Papyrus was a symbol for Lower Egypt and in architecture a stylised version was used as a capital first found at the 3 Dyn. complex of Zozer at Ṣaqqārah. Other uses for the plant were ropes and mats while the stalks and rhizomes were used as food. In a related genera the sedges (Carex) are found in ditches and damp areas throughout. This was

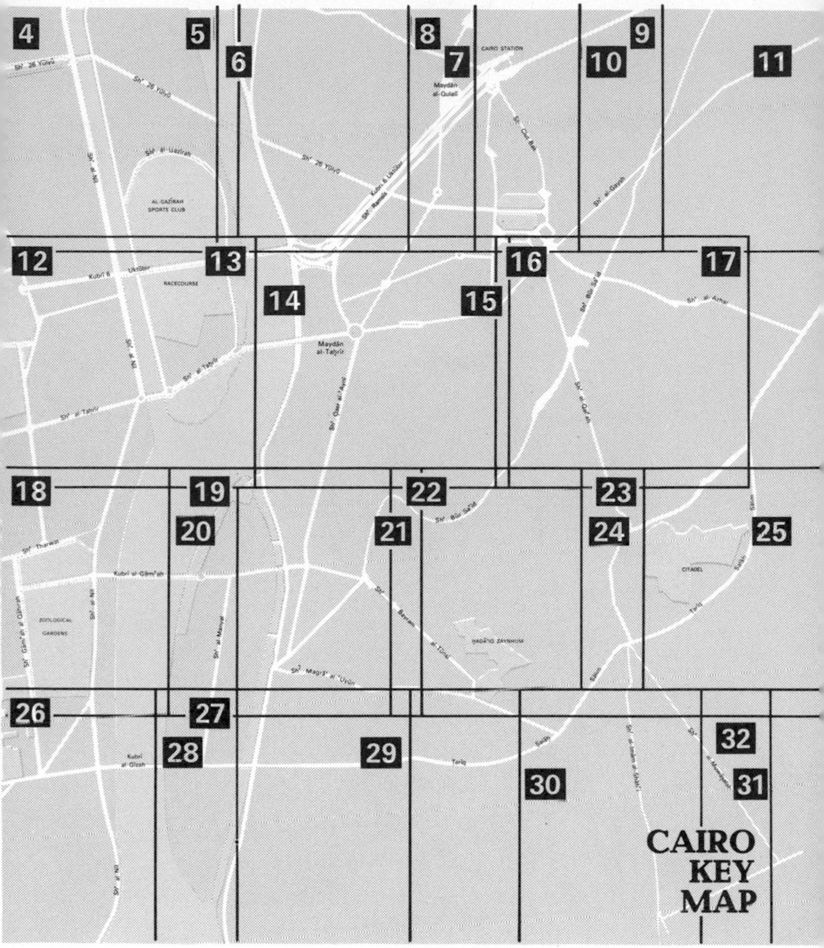
4
5
6
8
7
9
10
11
12
13
14
15
16
17
18
19
20
21
22
23
24
25
26
27
28
29
30
32
31
CAIRO STATION
AL-GAZĪRAH SPORTS CLUB
RACECOURSE
CITADEL
ZOOLOGICAL GARDENS
CAIRO KEY MAP

## Scale for Cairo main atlas

0 50 100 200 300 400 500 metres

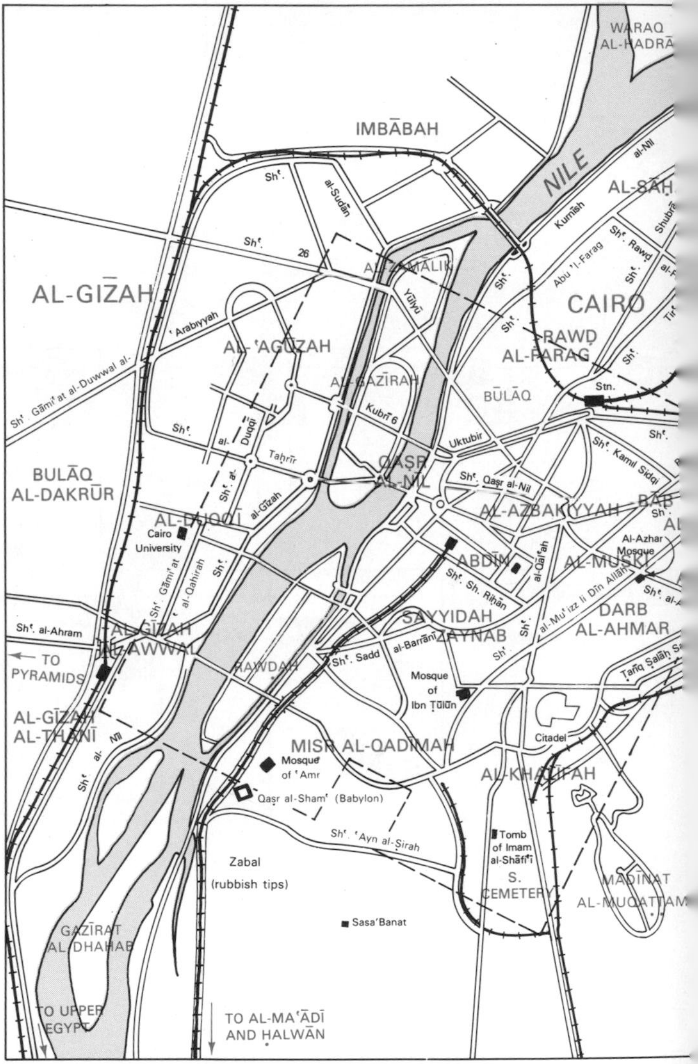
WARAQ
AL-HADRĀ
IMBĀBAH
NILE
al-Nīl
AL-SAḤ
Shubrā
Kurnīsh
Shᶜ.
al-Sudān
Shᶜ.
26
AL-ZAMALIK
Abu 'l-Farag
Shᶜ. Rawḍ
al-F
Shᶜ.
AL-GĪZAH
Yūlyū
Shᶜ.
CAIRO
ᶜArabiyyah
Shᶜ.
RAWḌ
AL-FARAG
AL-ᶜAGŪZAH
Shᶜ.
Shᶜ. Gāmiᶜat al-Duwwal al-
AL-GAZĪRAH
BŪLĀQ
Stn.
Kubrī 6
Shᶜ.
al-
Duqqī
Uktubir
Shᶜ.
Shᶜ. Kāmil Ṣidqī
Taḥrīr
QAṢR
AL-NĪL
BULĀQ
AL-DAKRŪR
Shᶜ. al-
Shᶜ. Qaṣr al-Nīl
AL-AZBAKIYYAH
BĀB
Shᶜ.
al-Gīzah
AL-DUQQĪ
Cairo
University
Al-Azhar
Mosque
ABDĪN
AL-MUSKI
Shᶜ. Gāmiᶜat
al-Qāhirah
Shᶜ.
Shᶜ. Sh. Riḥān
al-Qalᶜah
al-Muᶜizz li Dīn Allāh
Shᶜ. al-
DARB
AL-AHMAR
Shᶜ. al-Ahram
AL-GĪZAH
AL-AWWAL
SAYYIDAH
ZAYNAB
al-Barrānī
Shᶜ.
Shᶜ.
TO
PYRAMIDS
RAWḌAH
Shᶜ. Sadd
Mosque
of
Ibn Ṭūlūn
Ṭarīq Ṣalāḥ
AL-GĪZAH
AL-THĀNĪ
Citadel
Shᶜ. al- Nīl
MIṢR AL-QADĪMAH
Mosque
of ᶜAmr
AL-KHALĪFAH
Qaṣr al-Shamᶜ (Babylon)
Shᶜ. ᶜAyn al-Ṣirah
Tomb
of Imam
al-Shāfiᶜī
Zabal
(rubbish tips)
S.
CEMETERY
MADĪNAT
AL-MUQATTAM
Sasa'Banat
GAZĪRAT
AL-DHAHAB
TO UPPER
EGYPT
TO AL-MAᶜĀDĪ
AND HALWĀN

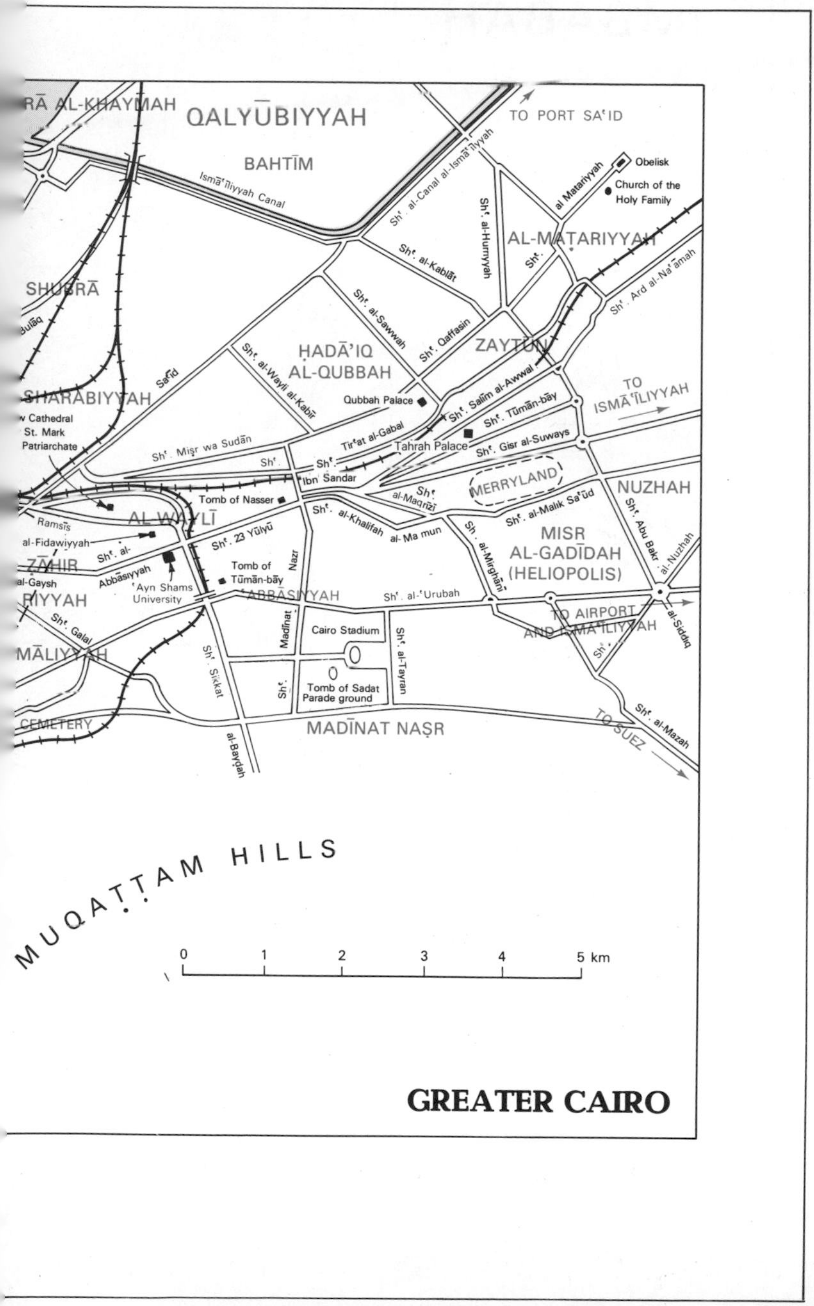
QALYŪBIYYAH
TO PORT SAʿID
BAHTĪM
Ismāʿīliyyah Canal
Shʿ. al-Canal al-Ismāʿīliyyah
Obelisk
Church of the Holy Family
al Matariyyah
Shʿ. al-Hurriyyah
AL-MAṬARIYYAH
Shʿ. al-Kablāt
Shʿ.
Shʿ. Ard al-Naʿamah
SHUBRĀ
Būlāq
Shʿ. al-Sawwah
Shʿ. Qaffasīn
ZAYTŪN
ḤADĀʾIQ AL-QUBBAH
Shʿ. al-Wayli al-Kabīr
Saʿīd
Qubbah Palace
Shʿ. Salīm al-Awwal
TO ISMĀʿĪLIYYAH
SHARABIYYAH
Cathedral St. Mark Patriarchate
Shʿ. Ṭūmān-bāy
Tirʿat al-Gabal
Tahrah Palace
Shʿ. Gisr al-Suways
Shʿ. Miṣr wa Sudān
Shʿ.
Shʿ. Ibn Sandar
MERRYLAND
NUZHAH
Tomb of Nasser
Shʿ. al-Maqrīzī
Shʿ. al-Malik Saʿūd
AL WAYLĪ
Ramsīs
Shʿ. al-Khalifah
al-Ma mun
Shʿ. al-Mirghānī
MISR AL-GADĪDAH (HELIOPOLIS)
Shʿ. Abu Bakr
al-Nuzhah
al-Fidawiyyah
Shʿ. 23 Yūlyū
Shʿ. al-Abbāsiyyah
ẒĀHIR
al-Gaysh
Tomb of Ṭūmān-bāy
Nazr
ʿAyn Shams University
ʿABBĀSIYYAH
Shʿ. al-ʿUrubah
TO AIRPORT AND ISMĀʿĪLIYYAH
al-Siddiq
RIYYAH
Shʿ. Galal
Madīnat
Cairo Stadium
Shʿ. al-Tayran
Shʿ.
MĀLIYYAH
Shʿ. Sikkat
Shʿ.
Tomb of Sadat Parade ground
Shʿ. al-Mazah
CEMETERY
MADĪNAT NAṢR
TO SUEZ
al-Bayḍah
MUQAṬṬAM HILLS
0 1 2 3 4 5 km

GREATER CAIRO

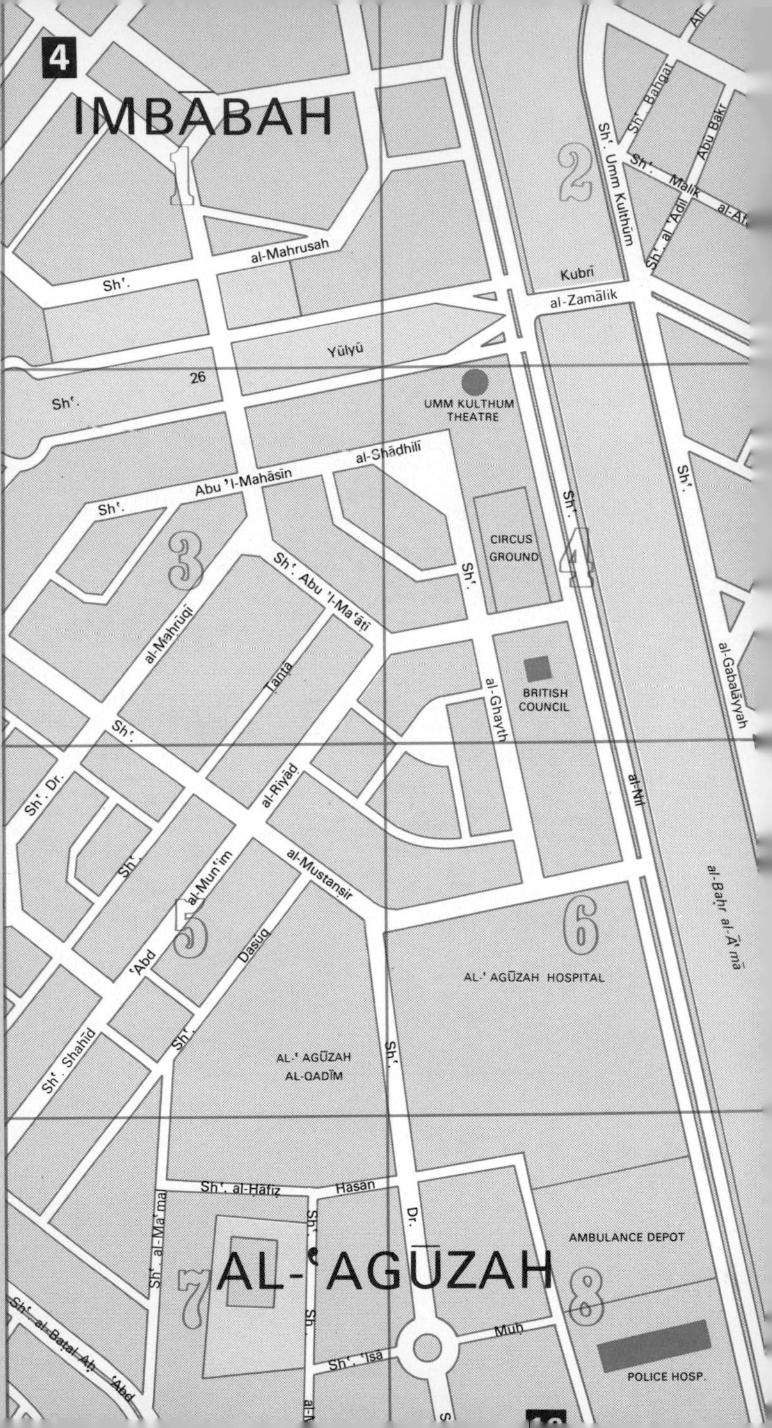
4
IMBABAH
1
2
Sh'. Umm Kulthum
Sh'. Bahgat
Abu Bakr
Sh'. Malik
Sh'. al-'Adil
Kubri
al-Zamalik
Sh'.
al-Mahrusah
Yulyu
26
Sh'.
UMM KULTHUM THEATRE
al-Shadhili
Abu 'l-Mahasin
Sh'.
3
Sh'. Abu 'l-Ma'ati
CIRCUS GROUND
Sh'.
4
al-Mahruqi
Tanta
al-Ghayth
BRITISH COUNCIL
al-Gabalayyah
Sh'.
Sh'. Dr.
al-Riyad
al-Nil
Sh'.
al-Mun'im
al-Mustansir
5
6
'Abd
Dasuq
AL-'AGUZAH HOSPITAL
al-Bahr al-A'ma
Sh'. Shahid
Sh'.
AL-'AGUZAH AL-QADIM
Sh'.
Sh'. al-Hafiz Hasan
Sh'. al-Ma'mal
Dr.
AMBULANCE DEPOT
AL-'AGUZAH
7
8
Sh'. al-Batal Ah
'Abd
Sh'. 'Isa
Muh
POLICE HOSP.

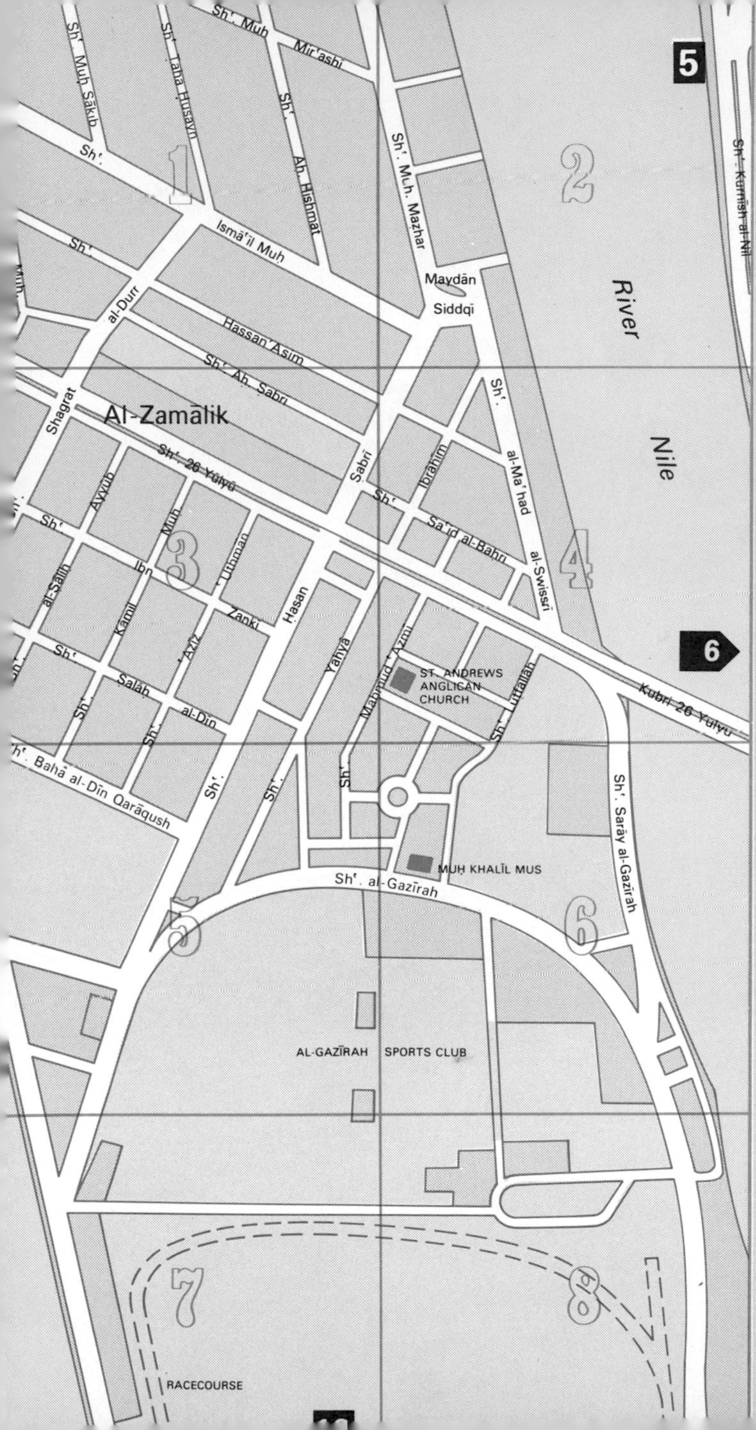
5
Shᶜ. Muḥ Mirᶜashi
Shᶜ. Muḥ Sākib
Shᶜ. Ṭaha Ḥusayn
Shᶜ. Aḥ. Hishmat
Shᶜ. Muḥ. Maẓhar
Shᶜ.
Ismāᶜīl Muḥ
Maydān Siddqī
River Nile
Shᶜ. Kurnīsh al-Nīl
al-Durr
Hassan ᶜAṣim
Shᶜ. Aḥ. Ṣabri
Shagrat
Al-Zamālik
Shᶜ. 26 Yūlyū
Ṣabrī
Ibrāhīm
Shᶜ. al-Maᶜhad al-Swissrī
Shᶜ. Saᶜīd al-Baḥri
Ayyub
Muḥ
ᶜUthmān
Ibn Zanki
Ḥasan
al-Ṣāliḥ
Kāmil
ᶜAzīz
Shᶜ. Ṣalāḥ al-Dīn
Yaḥya
Maḥmūd ᶜAzmi
ST. ANDREWS ANGLICAN CHURCH
Shᶜ. Luṭfallāh
6
Kubri 26 Yūlyū
Shᶜ. Bahā al-Dīn Qarāqush
Shᶜ. Sarāy al-Gazīrah
MUḤ KHALĪL MUS
Shᶜ. al-Gazīrah
AL-GAZĪRAH SPORTS CLUB
RACECOURSE
1
2
3
4
5
6
7
8

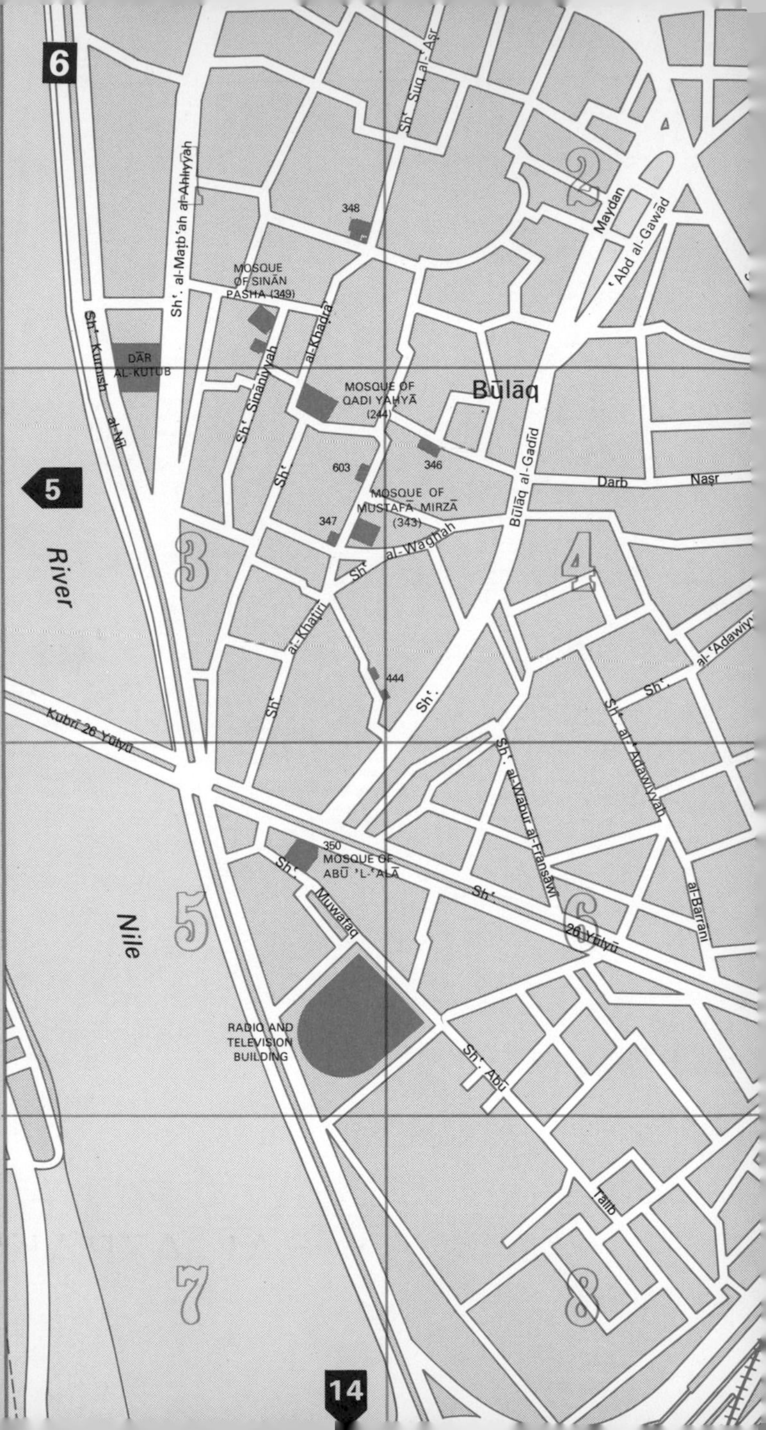

6
Sh'. Suq al-'Asr
Sh'. al-Matb'ah al-Ahliyyah
348
MOSQUE OF SINĀN PASHA (349)
al-Khadrā
Maydan
'Abd al-Gawād
Sh'. Kurnish al-Nil
DĀR AL-KUTUB
Sh'. Sinaniyyah
MOSQUE OF QADI YAHYĀ (244)
Būlāq
5
603
346
Darb
Nasr
MOSQUE OF MUSTAFĀ MIRZĀ (343)
347
Sh'. al-Waghah
Būlāq al-Gadīd
River
3
4
al-Khatiri
Sh'.
al-'Adawiyy
444
Sh'.
Sh'.
Kubri 26 Yūlyū
Sh'. al-'Adawiyyah
Sh'. al-Wabur al-Fransāwi
350
MOSQUE OF ABŪ 'L-'ALĀ
Sh'. Muwafaq
Sh'.
26 Yūlyū
al-Barrani
Nile
5
6
RADIO AND TELEVISION BUILDING
Sh'. Abū
Talib
7
8
14

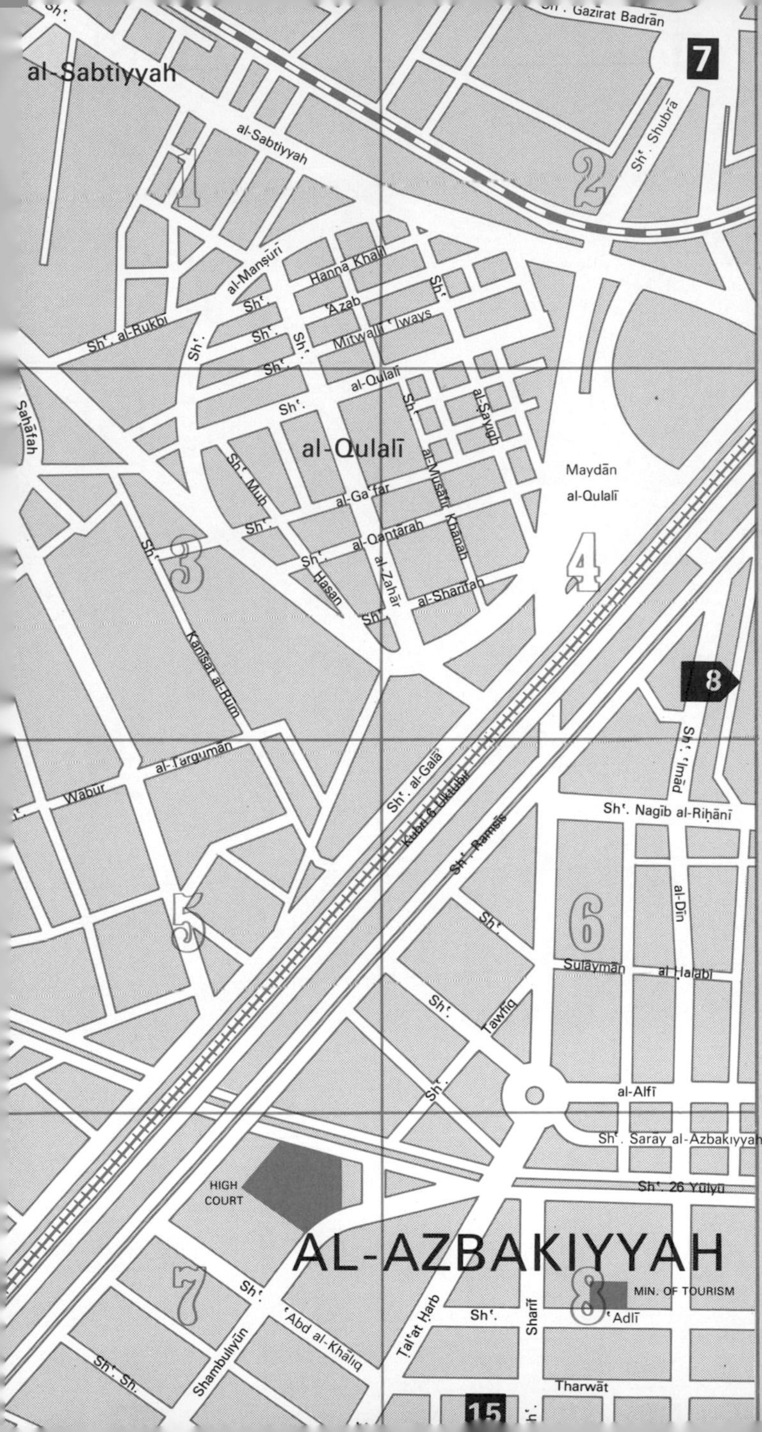
Sh'. Gazirat Badrān
7
al-Sabtiyyah
al-Sabtiyyah
Sh'. Shubrā
Sh'. al-Rukbī
al-Manṣūrī
Hanna Khalīl
'Azab
Mitwallī 'Iways
al-Qulalī
al-Ṣayigh
al-Qulalī
Sahāfah
Sh'. Muh.
al-Ga'far
al-Musāfir Khānah
al-Qantarah
Hasan
al-Zahār
al-Sharifah
Maydān al-Qulalī
8
Kanīsat al-Rūm
al-Targuman
Wabur
Sh'. al-Galā'
Kubrī 6 Uktūbir
Sh'. 'Imād
Sh'. Nagīb al-Riḥānī
Sh'. Ramsīs
al-Dīn
Sulaymān
al Halabī
Sh'. Tawfīq
al-Alfī
Sh'. Saray al-Azbakiyyah
Sh'. 26 Yūlyū
HIGH COURT
AL-AZBAKIYYAH
MIN. OF TOURISM
Sh'. 'Abd al-Khāliq
Ṭal'at Ḥarb
Sh'. Sharīf
'Adlī
Shambuliyūn
Sh'. Sh.
Tharwāt
15

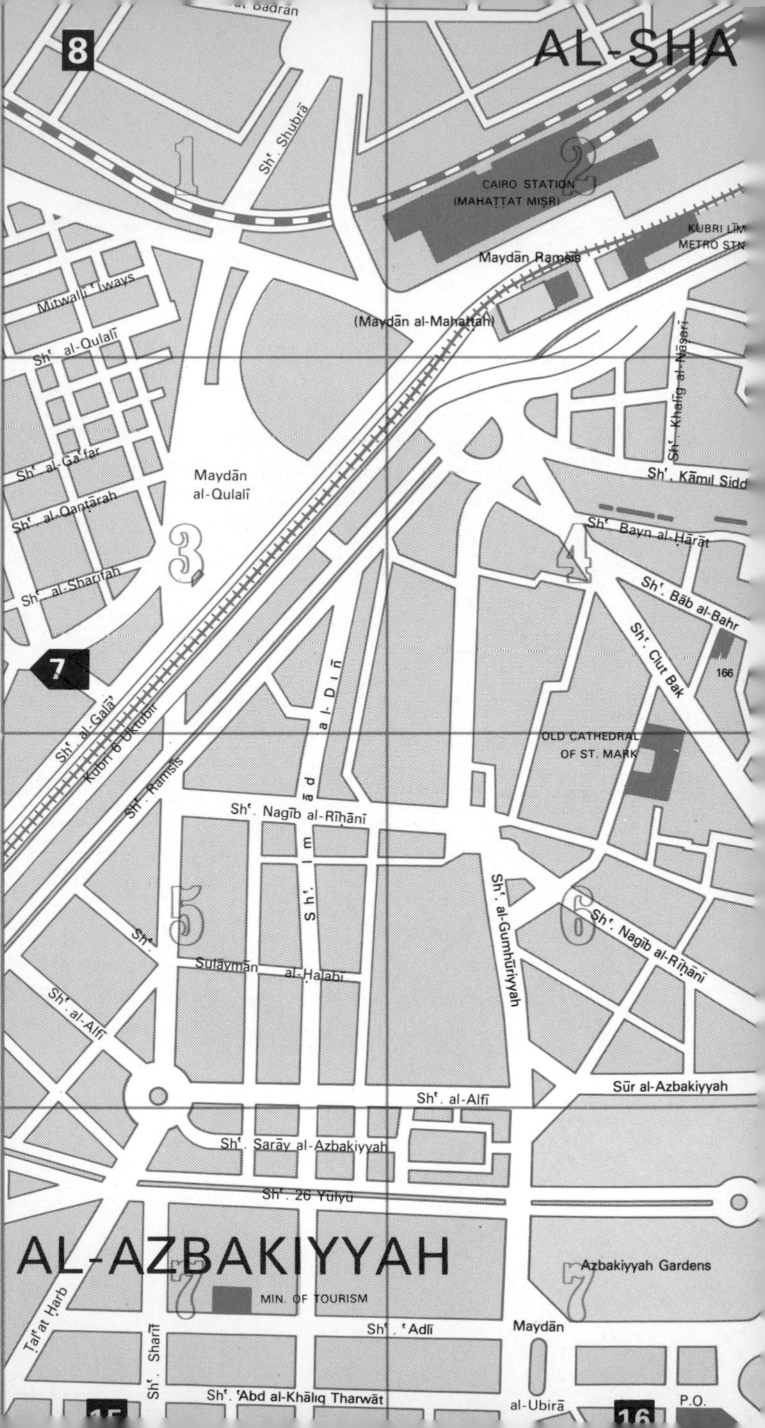
8
AL-SHA
Shubrā
CAIRO STATION
(MAHAṬṬAT MIṢR)
KUBRI LIM
METRO STN
Maydān Ramsīs
(Maydān al-Mahaṭṭah)
Mitwallī ʿIways
Shʿ. al-Qulalī
Shʿ. al-Gaʿfar
Maydān
al-Qulalī
Shʿ. al-Qanṭārah
Shʿ. al-Sharīfah
7
Shʿ. Khalīg al-Nāṣarī
Shʿ. Kāmil Sidd
Shʿ. Bayn al-Ḥārāt
Shʿ. Bāb al-Bahr
Shʿ. Clut Bak
166
OLD CATHEDRAL
OF ST. MARK
Shʿ. al-Galāʾ
Kubri 6 Uktubir
Shʿ. Ramsīs
Shʿ. Imād al-Dīn
Shʿ. Nagīb al-Rīḥānī
Shʿ. al-Gumhūriyyah
Shʿ. Nagīb al-Rīḥānī
Shʿ. Sulaymān al-Ḥalabī
Shʿ. al-Alfī
Sūr al-Azbakiyyah
Shʿ. al-Alfī
Shʿ. Sarāy al-Azbakiyyah
Shʿ. 26 Yūlyū
AL-AZBAKIYYAH
Azbakiyyah Gardens
MIN. OF TOURISM
Ṭalʿat Ḥarb
Shʿ. Sharīf
Shʿ. ʿAdlī
Maydān
al-Ubirā
Shʿ. ʿAbd al-Khāliq Tharwāt
P.O.
16

BIYYAH
9
Sh'. Ramsis
Sh'. al-Qabaysi
Sh'. Hamdi
Sh'. Sabri
Sh'. al-Zahir
Sh'. al-Saba'
Sh'. Qasr al-Lu'lu'ah
Sh'. al-Zahir
Sh'. Habib Shalabi
Sulayman
Sh'. Yusuf
Sh'. al-Gamil
Sh'. al-Gadd
Sh'. Birkat al-Ratli
Sh'. al-Bakriyyah
10
Sh'. al-Dashtuti
Sh'. Bayn al-Harat
Sh'. Faggalah
Harat
Sh'. Sidi Madyan
Suq Zalat
564
82
86
BAB AL-SHA'RIYYAH
600
125
Sh'. Sh. al-'Arussi
Maydan Bab al-Sha'riyyah
Sh'. Amir
Sh'. al-Fuwatiyyah
Sh'. al-Gami' al-Ahmar
AL-AHMAR MOSQUE
364
59
55
58
63
504
Maydan al-Khazindar
Sikkat al
Sh'. al-Ruway'i
Sh'. al-Nubi
Sh'. Bur Sa'id
Sh'. al-Khrunfish
Sh'. al-Bustah
Sh'. al-Gaysh
CHURCH OF THE VIRGIN
Bus stn
Maydan al-'Atabah al-Khadra
16
Harat al-Ya

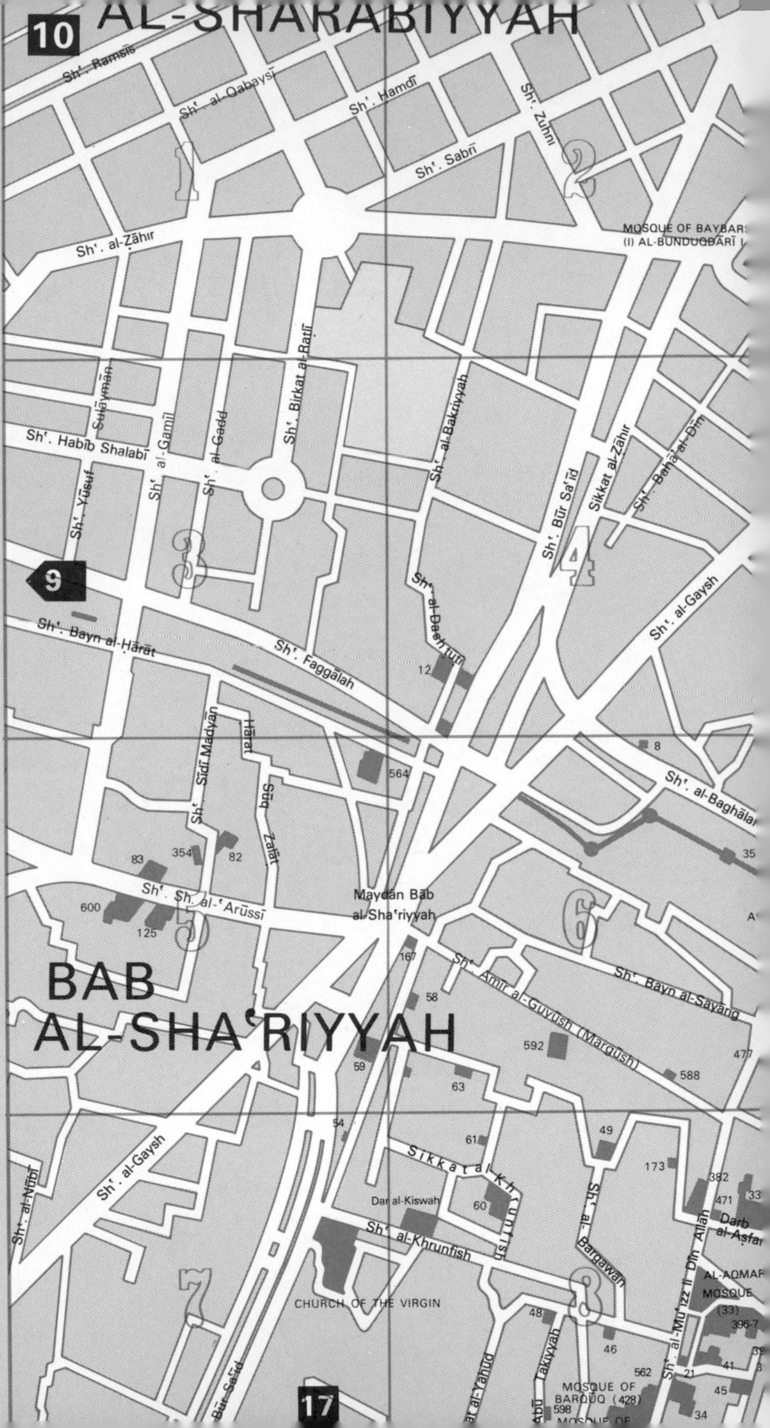
10
AL-SHARABIYYAH
Sh'. Ramsis
Sh'. al-Qabaysi
Sh'. Hamdi
Sh'. Zuhni
Sh'. Sabri
1
2
MOSQUE OF BAYBARS
(I) AL-BUNDUQDARI
Sh'. al-Zahir
Sh'. Birkat al-Ratl
Sulayman
Sh'. Habib Shalabi
Sh'. al-Gamil
Sh'. al-Gadd
Sh'. al-Bakriyyah
Sh'. Yusuf
Sh'. Bur Sa'id
Sikkat al-Zahir
Sh'. Baha' al-Din
3
4
9
Sh'. al-Dashtuti
Sh'. al-Gaysh
Sh'. Bayn al-Harat
Sh'. Faggalah
12
Sh'. Sidi Madyan
Harat
Suq
Zalat
564
8
Sh'. al-Baghalah
83
354
82
35
Maydan Bab
al-Sha'riyyah
Sh'. Sh. al-'Arussi
600
125
5
6
167
Sh'. Amir al-Guyush (Margush)
Sh'. Bayn al-Sayarig
58
BAB
AL-SHA'RIYYAH
592
477
59
63
588
54
61
49
Sikkat al-Khurunfish
173
382
Sh'. al-Nubi
Sh'. al-Gaysh
Dar al-Kiswah
60
Sh'. al-Bargawan
471
Darb
al-Asfar
Sh'. al-Khrunfish
Sh'. al-Mu'izz li Din Allah
AL-AQMAR
MOSQUE
(33)
396-7
7
CHURCH OF THE VIRGIN
8
48
46
41
562
21
45
Bur Sa'id
Takiyyah
al-Yahud
MOSQUE OF
BARQUQ (428)
598
34
17

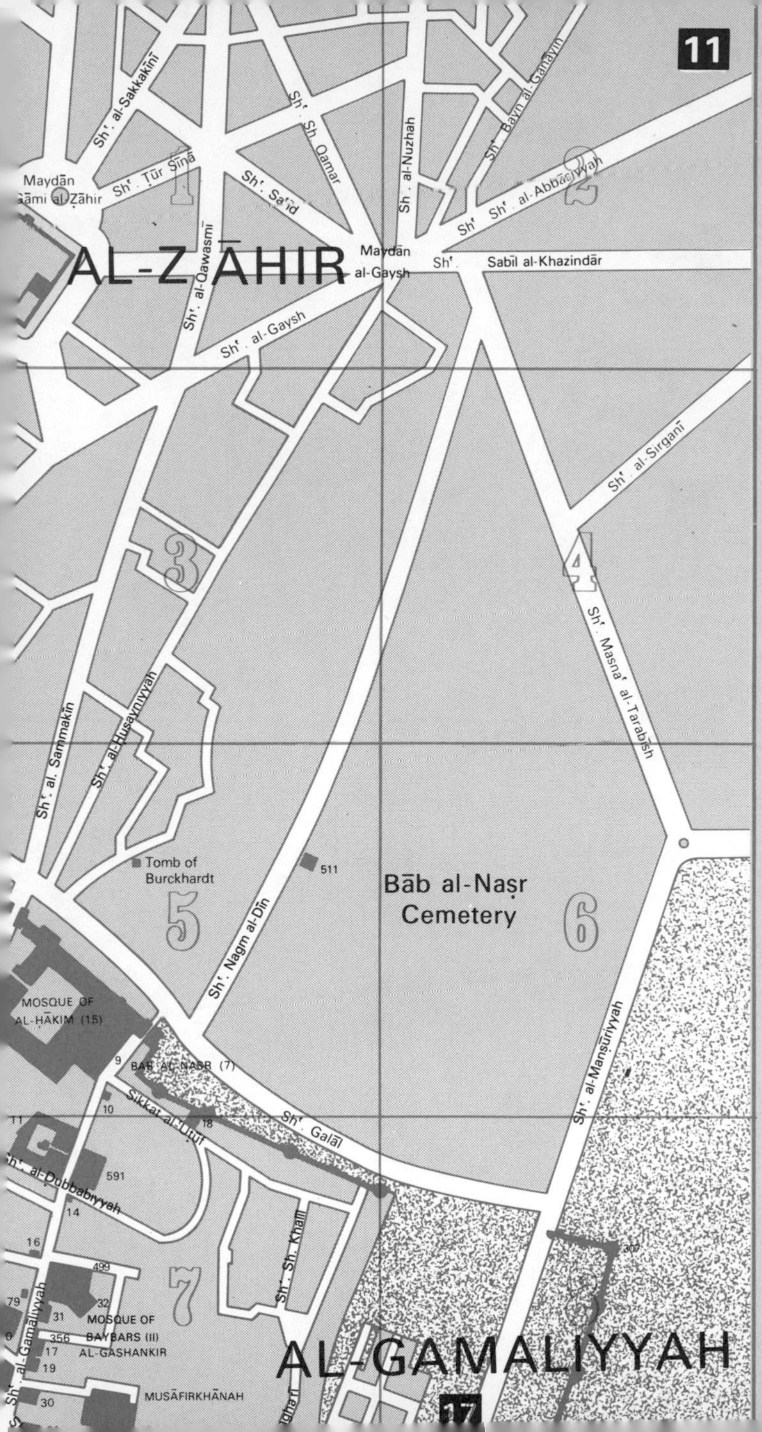
11
AL-ZĀHIR
Maydān
Gāmi al-Zāhir
Shʿ. al-Sakkakīnī
Shʿ. Ṭūr Sīnā
Shʿ. Sh. Qamar
Shʿ. Saʿīd
Shʿ. al-Nuzhah
Shʿ. Bayn al-Ganāyin
Shʿ. al-Abbāsiyyah
Maydān
al-Gaysh
Shʿ. Sabīl al-Khazindār
Shʿ. al-Qawasmī
Shʿ. al-Gaysh
Shʿ. al-Sirganī
Shʿ. Masnaʿ al-Tarabīsh
Shʿ. al. Sammakīn
Shʿ. al-Ḥusayniyyah
Tomb of
Burckhardt
511
Bāb al-Naṣr
Cemetery
Shʿ. Nagm al-Dīn
MOSQUE OF
AL-ḤĀKIM (15)
BĀB AL-NAṢR (7)
Sikkat al-ʿUṭūf
Shʿ. Galāl
Shʿ. al-Manṣūriyyah
Shʿ. al-Dubbabiyyah
Shʿ. Sh. Khalīl
MOSQUE OF
BAYBARS (II)
AL-GASHANKIR
MUSĀFIRKHĀNAH
AL-GAMALIYYAH
Shʿ. al-Gamaliyyah
17
1
2
3
4
5
6
7
8
9
10
11
14
16
17
18
19
30
31
32
79
356
499
591
307

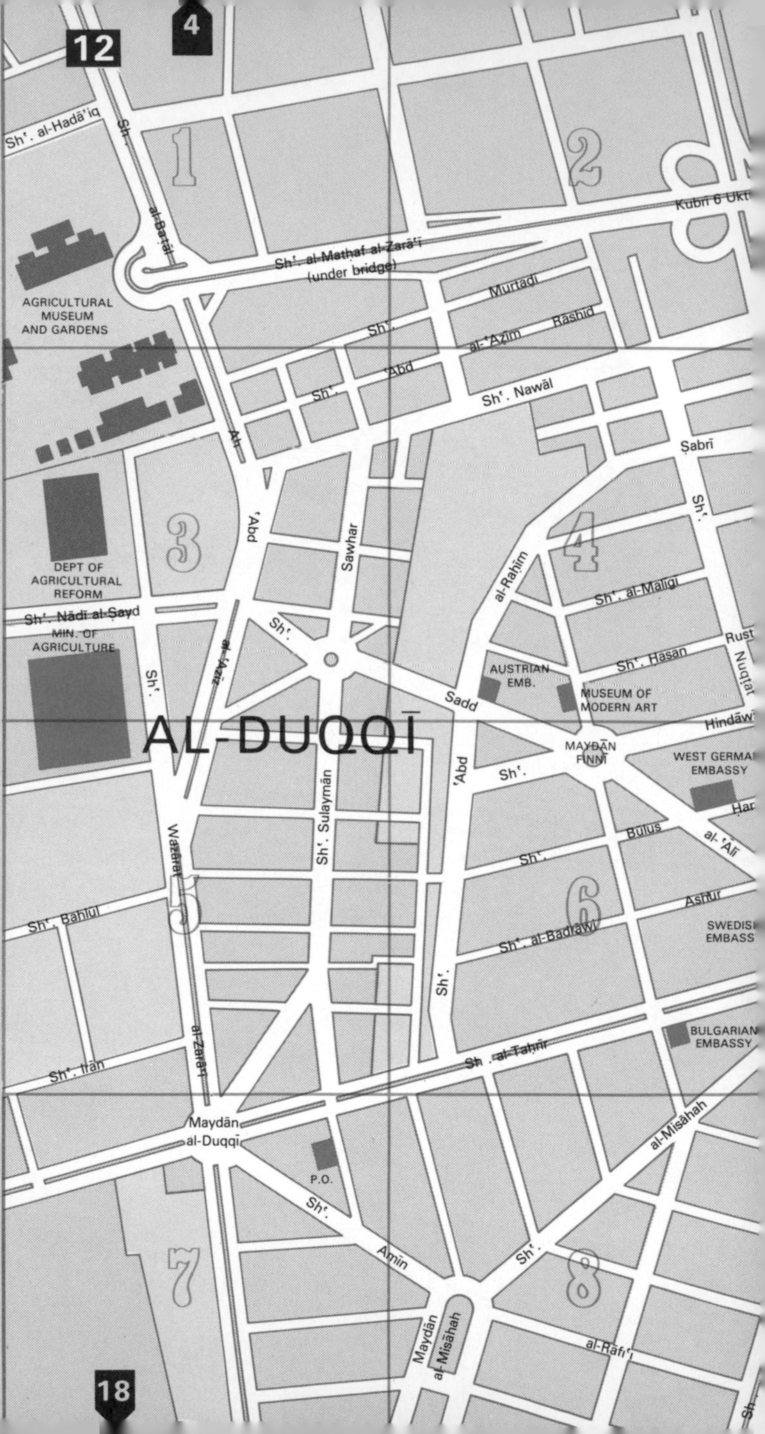
12
4
18
1
2
3
4
5
6
7
8
AL-DUQQĪ
Sh'. al-Hadā'iq
Sh. al-Baṭal
AGRICULTURAL MUSEUM AND GARDENS
Sh'. al-Mathaf al-Zarā'ī (under bridge)
Kubrī 6 Ukt
Murtaḍi
Sh'. 'Abd al-'Aẓim Rāshid
Sh'. Nawāl
Sh'. 'Abd
Aḥ
Ṣabrī
Sh'.
'Abd
Sawhar
DEPT OF AGRICULTURAL REFORM
Sh'. Nādī al-Ṣayd
MIN. OF AGRICULTURE
Sh'.
al-'Azīz
al-Raḥīm
Sh'. al-Maligī
Sh'. Hasan
Rust
Nuqṭat
AUSTRIAN EMB.
MUSEUM OF MODERN ART
Sadd
Hindāwī
'Abd
Sh'.
MAYDĀN FINNĪ
WEST GERMAN EMBASSY
Har
Sh'. Sulaymān
Wazārat
Bulus
Sh'.
al-'Alī
Ashur
SWEDISH EMBASSY
Sh'. Bahlul
Sh'. al-Badrāwī
Sh'.
al-Zarā'ī
BULGARIAN EMBASSY
Sh'. Irān
Sh. al-Taḥrīr
Maydān al-Duqqī
P.O.
al-Misāhah
Sh'. Amīn
Sh'.
Maydān al-Misāhah
al-Rāfi'ī
Sh

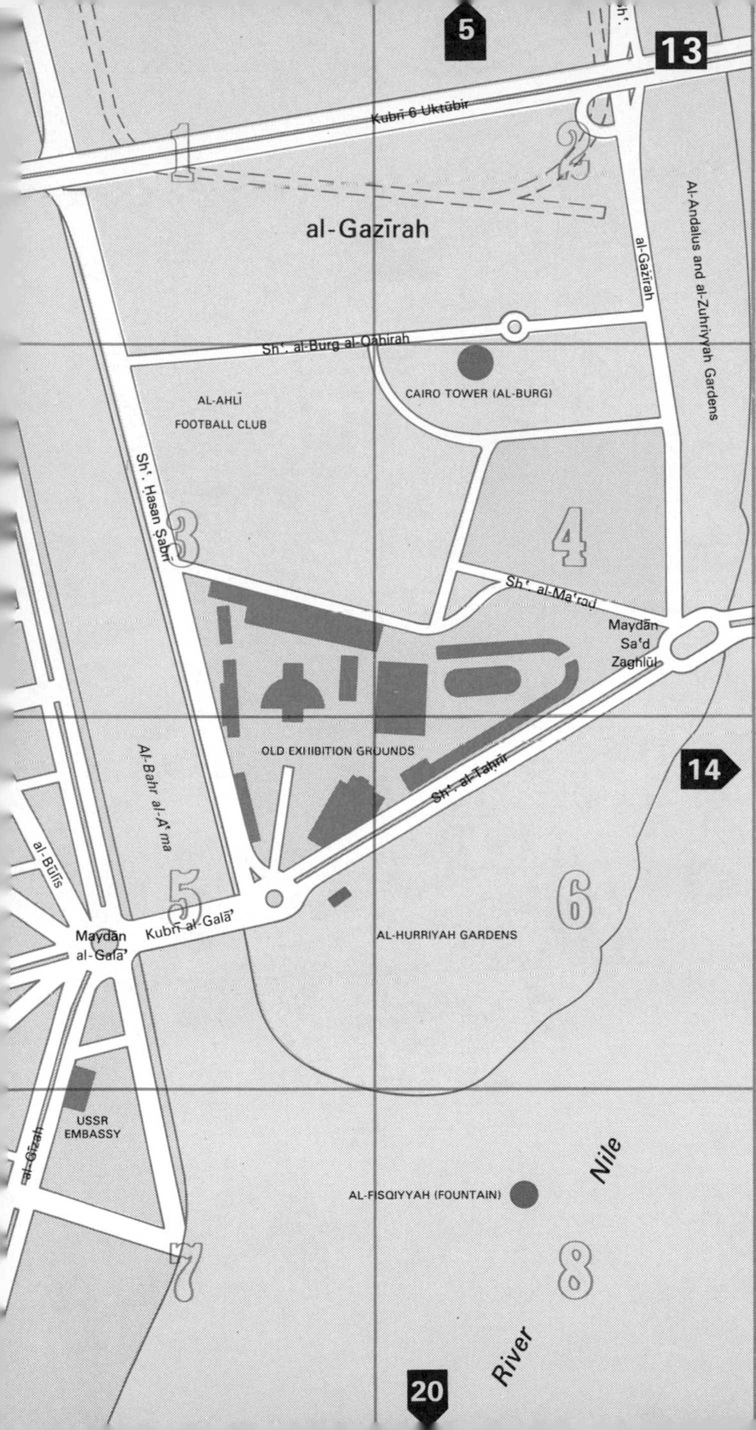
5
13
Kubrī 6 Uktūbir
al-Gazīrah
al-Gazīrah
Al-Andalus and al-Zuhriyyah Gardens
Shʿ. al-Burg al-Qāhirah
CAIRO TOWER (AL-BURG)
AL-AHLĪ
FOOTBALL CLUB
Shʿ. Hasan Ṣabrī
Shʿ. al-Maʿraḍ
Maydān
Saʿd
Zaghlūl
OLD EXHIBITION GROUNDS
14
Shʿ. al-Taḥrīr
Al-Bahr al-Aʿma
al-Būlīs
Maydān
al-Galā'
Kubrī al-Galā'
AL-HURRIYAH GARDENS
USSR
EMBASSY
al-Gīzah
AL-FISQIYYAH (FOUNTAIN)
Nile
River
20

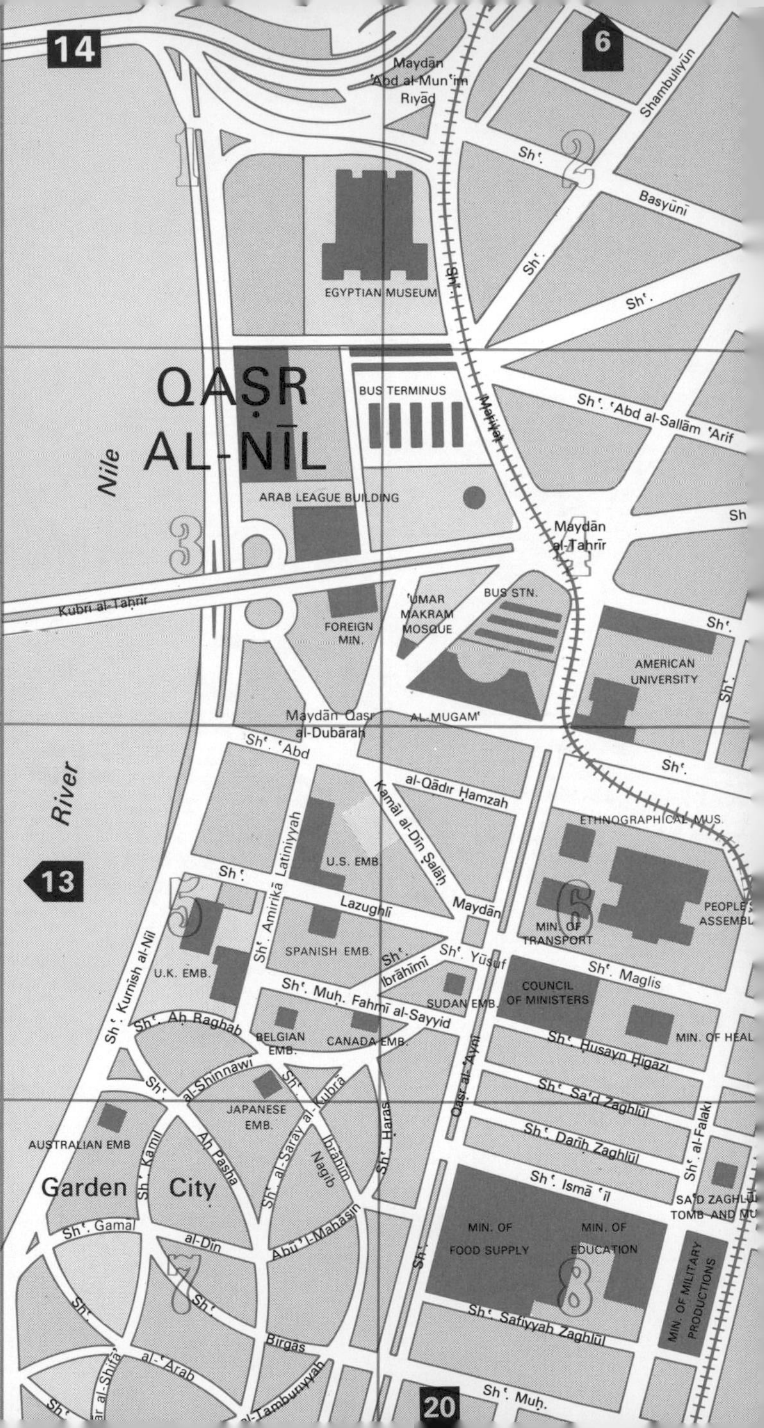
14
6
13
20
Maydān ʻAbd al-Munʻim Riyāḍ
Shambuliyūn
Shʻ.
Basyūnī
EGYPTIAN MUSEUM
QAṢR AL-NĪL
BUS TERMINUS
Shʻ. ʻAbd al-Sallām ʻArif
Nile
River
ARAB LEAGUE BUILDING
Maydān al-Taḥrīr
Kubrī al-Taḥrīr
BUS STN.
ʻUMAR MAKRAM MOSQUE
FOREIGN MIN.
AMERICAN UNIVERSITY
Maydān Qaṣr al-Dubārah
AL-MUGAMʻ
Shʻ. ʻAbd al-Qādir Ḥamzah
Kamāl al-Dīn Ṣalāḥ
ETHNOGRAPHICAL MUS.
Latiniyyah
U.S. EMB.
Shʻ. Lazughlī
Maydān
PEOPLE'S ASSEMBL
MIN. OF TRANSPORT
Shʻ. Amirikā
SPANISH EMB.
Shʻ. Ibrāhīmī
Shʻ. Yūsuf
Shʻ. Maglis
Shʻ. Kurnīsh al-Nīl
U.K. EMB.
Shʻ. Muḥ. Fahmī al-Sayyid
SUDAN EMB.
COUNCIL OF MINISTERS
Shʻ. Aḥ Raghab
BELGIAN EMB.
CANADA EMB.
Shʻ. Ḥusayn Ḥigazi
MIN. OF HEAL
Shʻ. al-Shinnawi
Shʻ. al-Kubrā
Qaṣr al-ʻAynī
Shʻ. Saʻd Zaghlūl
JAPANESE EMB.
Shʻ. Haras
AUSTRALIAN EMB
Shʻ. Kamil
Aḥ Pasha
Shʻ. al-Saray
Ibrahim Nagib
Shʻ. Darīh Zaghlūl
Shʻ. al-Falaki
Garden City
Shʻ. Ismāʻīl
SAʻD ZAGHLŪL TOMB AND MU
Shʻ. Gamal al-Dīn
Abu 'l-Mahasin
MIN. OF FOOD SUPPLY
MIN. OF EDUCATION
MIN. OF MILITARY PRODUCTIONS
Shʻ. Birgas
Shʻ. Ṣafiyyah Zaghlūl
al-Shifā
al-ʻArab
al-Tamburiyyah
Shʻ. Muḥ.

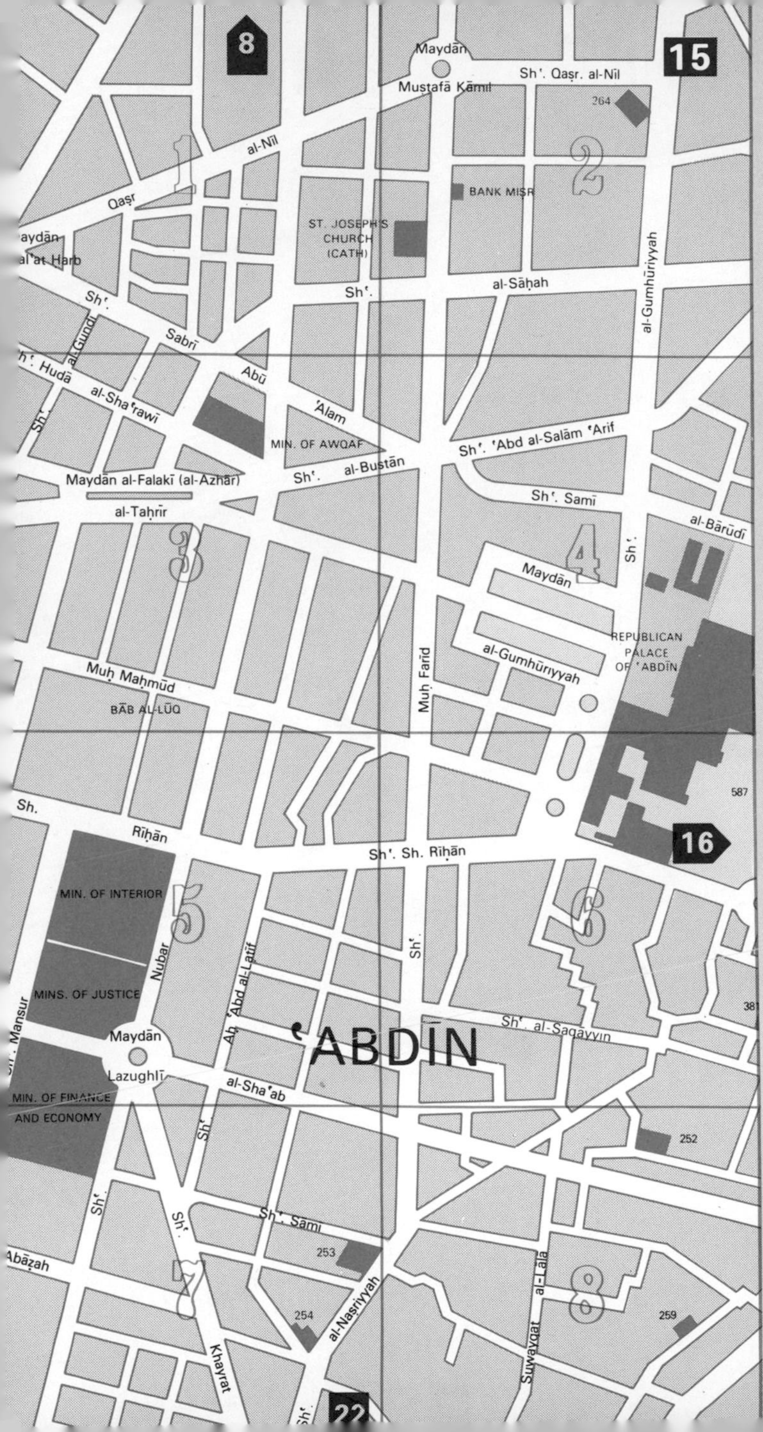

8
15
Maydān
Mustafā Kāmil
Sh'. Qasr. al-Nīl
264
al-Nīl
Qasr
aydān
al'at Harb
BANK MISR
ST. JOSEPH'S
CHURCH
(CATH)
Sh'.
al-Sāhah
al-Gumhūriyyah
Sh'.
Sabrī
al-Gundī
Abū
'Alam
h'. Hudā
al-Sha'rawī
MIN. OF AWQAF
Sh'. 'Abd al-Salām 'Arif
Sh'. al-Bustān
Maydān al-Falakī (al-Azhār)
Sh'. Samī
al-Tahrīr
al-Bārūdī
Sh'.
Maydān
REPUBLICAN
PALACE
OF 'ABDĪN
al-Gumhūriyyah
Muh Farīd
Muh Mahmūd
BĀB AL-LŪQ
587
Sh.
Rīhān
Sh'. Sh. Rīhān
16
MIN. OF INTERIOR
Nubar
Ab 'Abd al-Latīf
Sh'.
MINS. OF JUSTICE
Mansur
Maydān
Lazughlī
'ABDĪN
Sh'. al-Saqāyyin
381
al-Sha'ab
MIN. OF FINANCE
AND ECONOMY
Sh'.
252
Sh'.
Sh'.
Sh'. Sāmi
253
Abāzah
254
al-Nasriyyah
al-Lala
Suwayqat
259
Khayrat
Sh'.
22

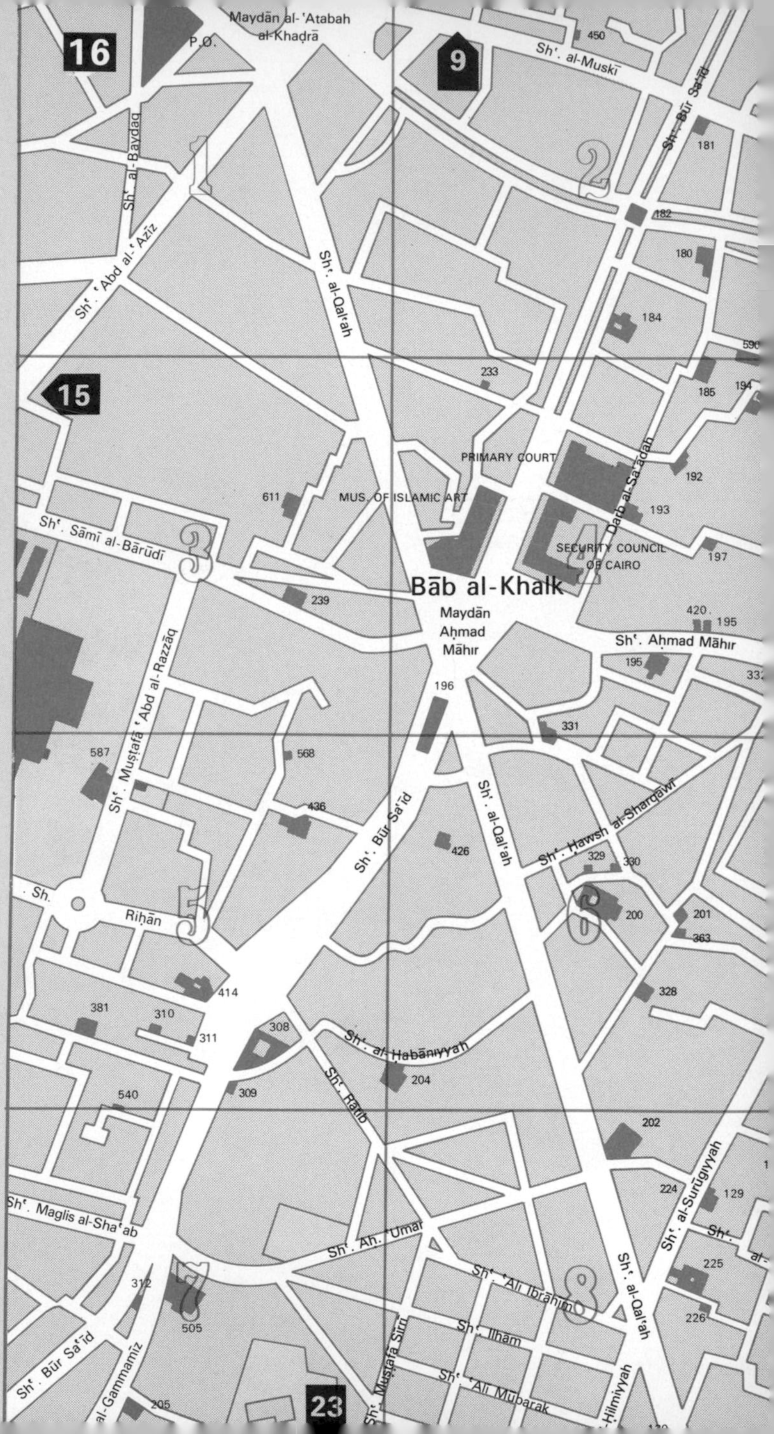
16
9
15
23
Maydān al-'Atabah al-Khaḍrā
P.O.
Sh'. al-Muskī
Sh'. Būr Sa'īd
Sh'. al-Baydaq
Sh'. 'Abd al-'Azīz
Sh'. al-Qal'ah
PRIMARY COURT
MUS. OF ISLAMIC ART
SECURITY COUNCIL OF CAIRO
Darb al-Sa'ādah
Sh'. Sāmī al-Bārūdī
Bāb al-Khalk
Maydān Aḥmad Māhir
Sh'. Aḥmad Māhir
Sh'. Muṣṭafā 'Abd al-Razzāq
Sh'. Hawsh al-Sharqāwī
Sh. Riḥān
Sh'. al-Habāniyyah
Sh'. Rātib
Sh'. Maglis al-Sha'ab
Sh'. Ah. 'Umar
Sh'. 'Alī Ibrāhīm
Sh'. Ilhām
Sh'. 'Alī Mubārak
Sh'. Muṣṭafā Sirrī
Sh'. al-Surūgiyyah
al-Gammamīz
Hilmiyyah
450 181 182 180 184 590 233 185 194 192 611 193 197 239 420 195 196 331 332 587 568 436 426 329 330 200 201 363 328 414 381 310 311 308 204 309 540 202 224 129 225 226 312 505 205

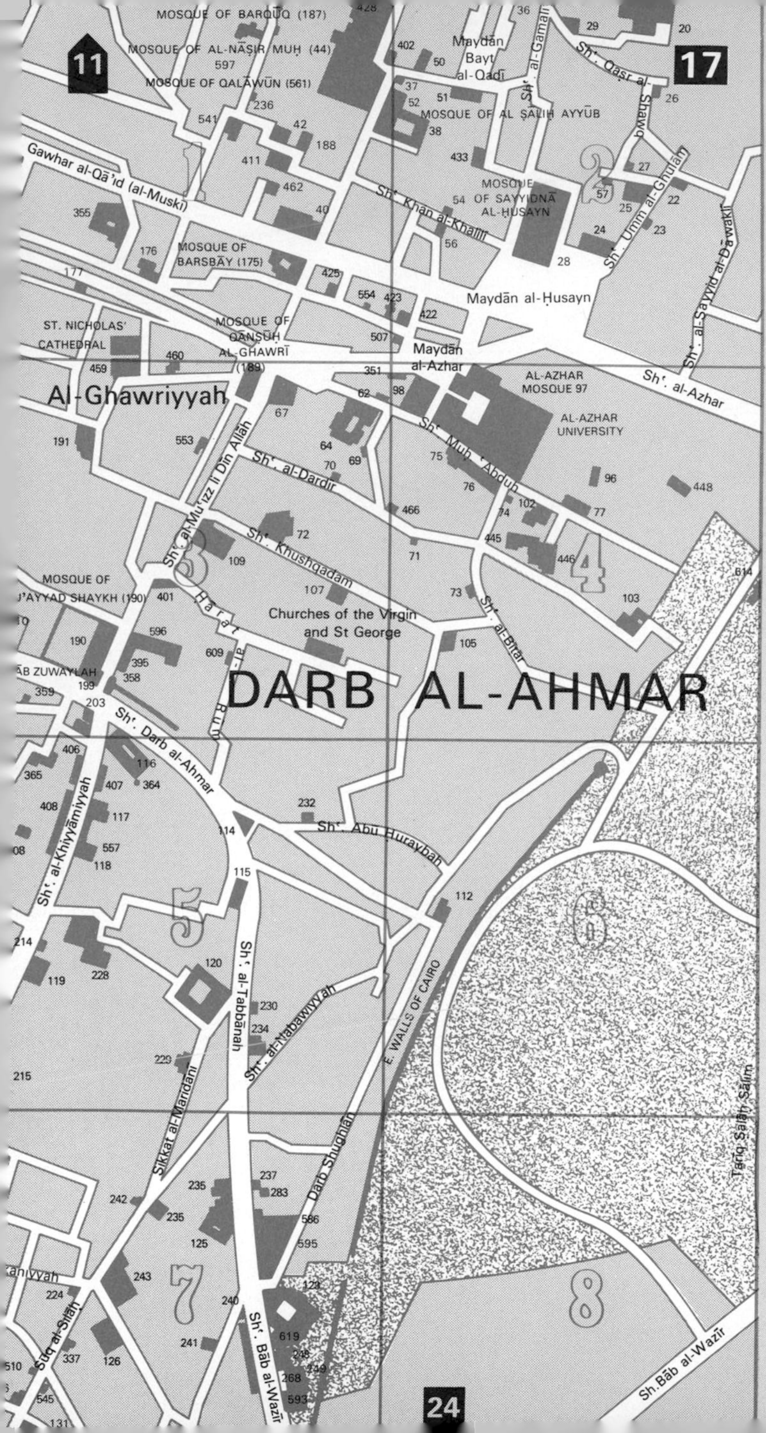
11
17
24
DARB AL-AHMAR
Al-Ghawriyyah
MOSQUE OF BARQŪQ (187)
MOSQUE OF AL-NĀṢIR MUḤ (44)
MOSQUE OF QALĀWŪN (561)
Maydān Bayt al-Qāḍī
Shʿ. al-Gamālī
Shʿ. Qaṣr al-Shawq
MOSQUE OF AL ṢĀLIḤ AYYŪB
Gawhar al-Qāʾid (al-Muski)
Shʿ. Khān al-Khalīlī
MOSQUE OF SAYYIDNĀ AL-ḤUSAYN
Shʿ. Umm al-Ghulām
Shʿ. al-Sayyid al-Dawākhī
MOSQUE OF BARSBĀY (175)
Maydān al-Ḥusayn
ST. NICHOLAS' CATHEDRAL
MOSQUE OF QĀNṢŪH AL-GHAWRĪ (189)
Maydān al-Azhar
AL-AZHAR MOSQUE 97
AL-AZHAR UNIVERSITY
Shʿ. al-Azhar
Shʿ. Muḥ ʿAbduh
Shʿ. al-Dardīr
Shʿ. al-Muʿizz li Dīn Allāh
Shʿ. Khushqadam
MOSQUE OF MUʾAYYAD SHAYKH (190)
Ḥārat al-Rūm
Churches of the Virgin and St George
Shʿ. al-Bīṭār
BĀB ZUWAYLAH
Shʿ. Darb al-Aḥmar
Shʿ. Abū Ḥuraybah
Shʿ. al-Khiyyāmiyyah
Shʿ. al-Tabbānah
Shʿ. al-Nabawiyyah
E. WALLS OF CAIRO
Sikkat al-Māridānī
Darb Shughlān
Ṭarīq Ṣalāḥ Sālim
Sūq al-Silāḥ
Shʿ. Bāb al-Wazīr
Sh. Bāb al-Wazīr

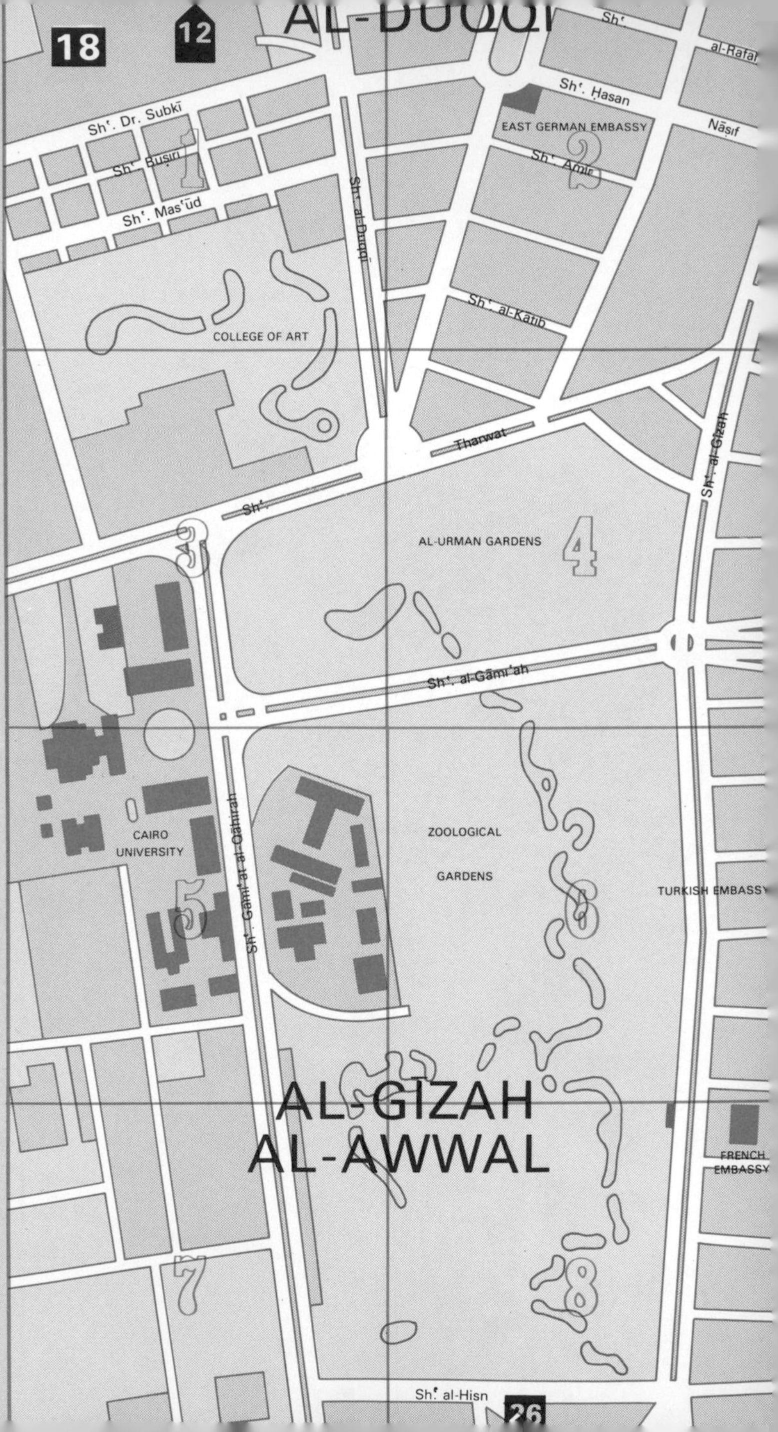
18
12
AL-DUQQI
Shᶜ.
al-Rafai
Shᶜ. Hasan
Nāṣif
EAST GERMAN EMBASSY
Shᶜ. Amir
Shᶜ. Dr. Subkī
Shᶜ. Busiri
Shᶜ. Masᶜūd
Shᶜ. al-Duqqi
Shᶜ. al-Kātib
COLLEGE OF ART
Tharwat
Shᶜ.
Shᶜ. al-Gīzah
AL-URMAN GARDENS
Shᶜ. al-Gāmiᶜah
CAIRO UNIVERSITY
Shᶜ. Gāmiᶜat al-Qāhirah
ZOOLOGICAL GARDENS
TURKISH EMBASSY
AL-GĪZAH AL-AWWAL
FRENCH EMBASSY
Shᶜ. al-Hisn
26
1
2
3
4
5
6
7
8

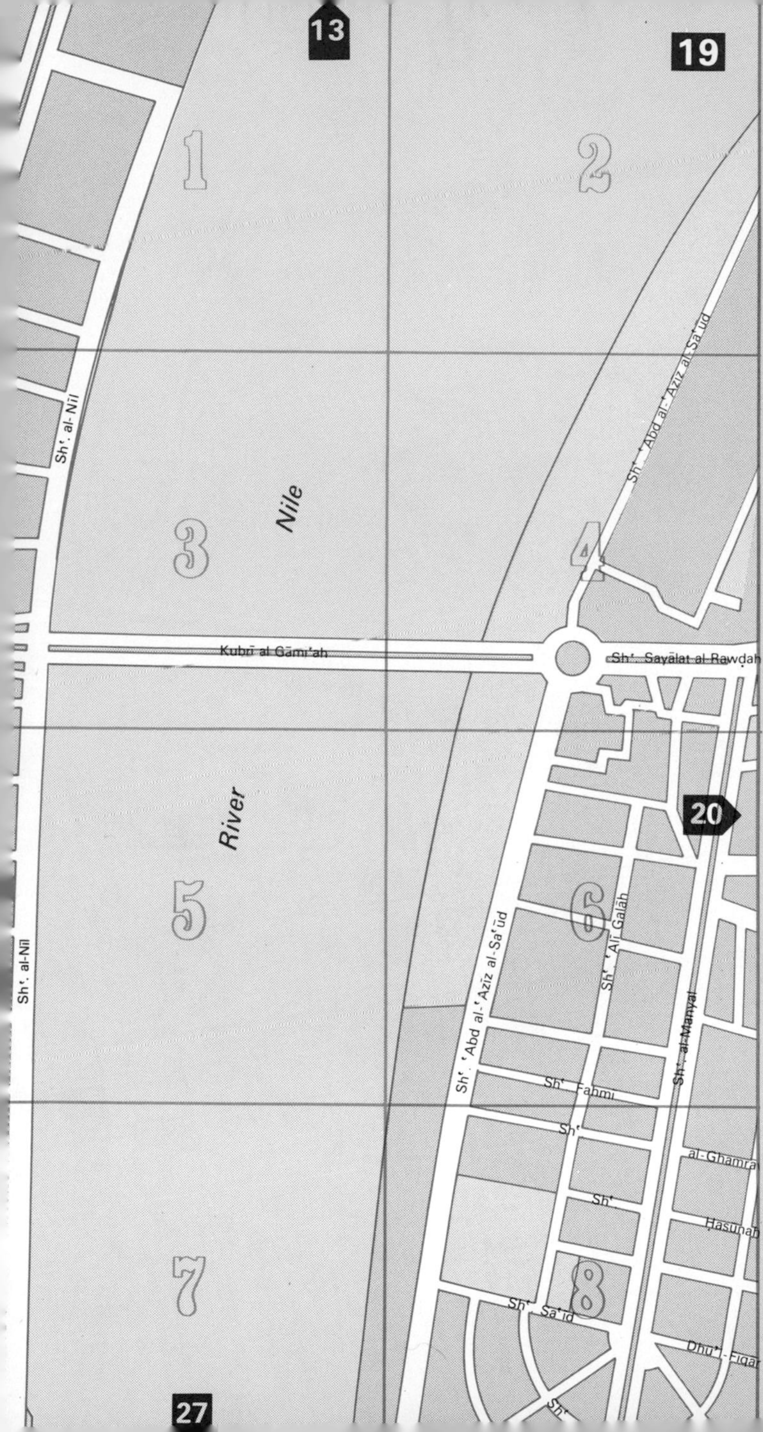
13
19
1
2
3
4
5
6
7
8
20
27
Nile
River
Sh'. al-Nil
Sh'. 'Abd al-'Azīz al-Sa'ūd
Kubrī al Gāmi'ah
Sh'. Sayālat al-Rawdah
Sh'. 'Ali Galāh
Sh'. al-Manyal
Sh'. Fahmi
Sh'.
al-Ghamrā
Hasunah
Sh'. Sa'id
Dhu'l-Fiqar

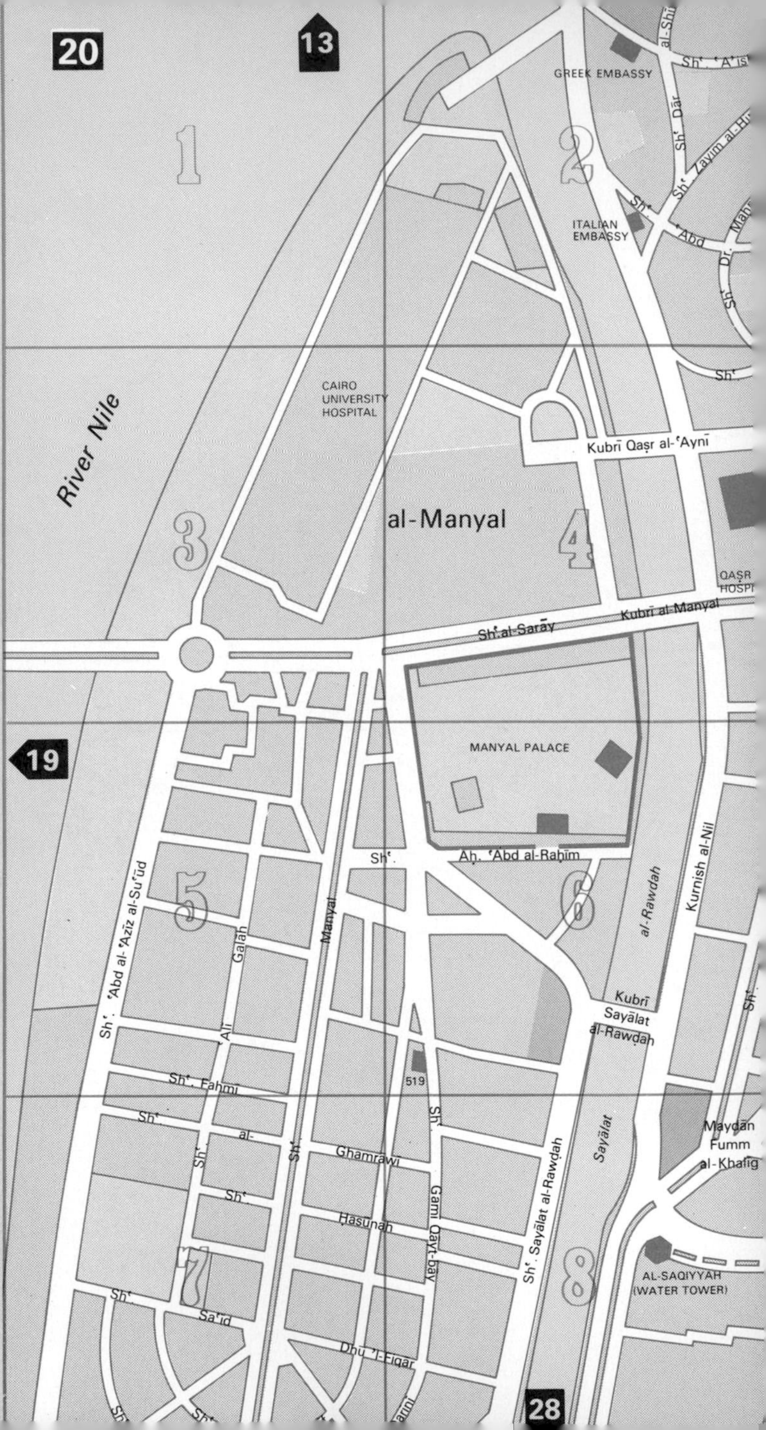
20
13
19
28
River Nile
al-Manyal
GREEK EMBASSY
ITALIAN EMBASSY
CAIRO UNIVERSITY HOSPITAL
Kubrī Qaṣr al-ʿAynī
Kubrī al-Manyal
Shʿ. al-Sarāy
MANYAL PALACE
Shʿ. Ah. ʿAbd al-Rahīm
al-Rawḍah
Kurnish al-Nil
Kubrī Sayālat al-Rawḍah
Sayālat
Shʿ. Sayālat al-Rawḍah
Maydān Fumm al-Khalīg
AL-SAQIYYAH (WATER TOWER)
Shʿ. ʿAbd al-ʿAzīz al-Suʿūd
Galāl
ʿAlī
Manyal
Shʿ. Fahmī
Shʿ. al-Ghamrāwī
Shʿ. Hasūnah
Gamiʿ Qayt-bāy
519
Shʿ. Saʿīd
Dhū ʾl-Fiqār
Shʿ. Dār
Shʿ. Zayim al-Hi
Shʿ. ʿAbd
Dr.
QAṢR HOSPI
1
2
3
4
5
6
7
8

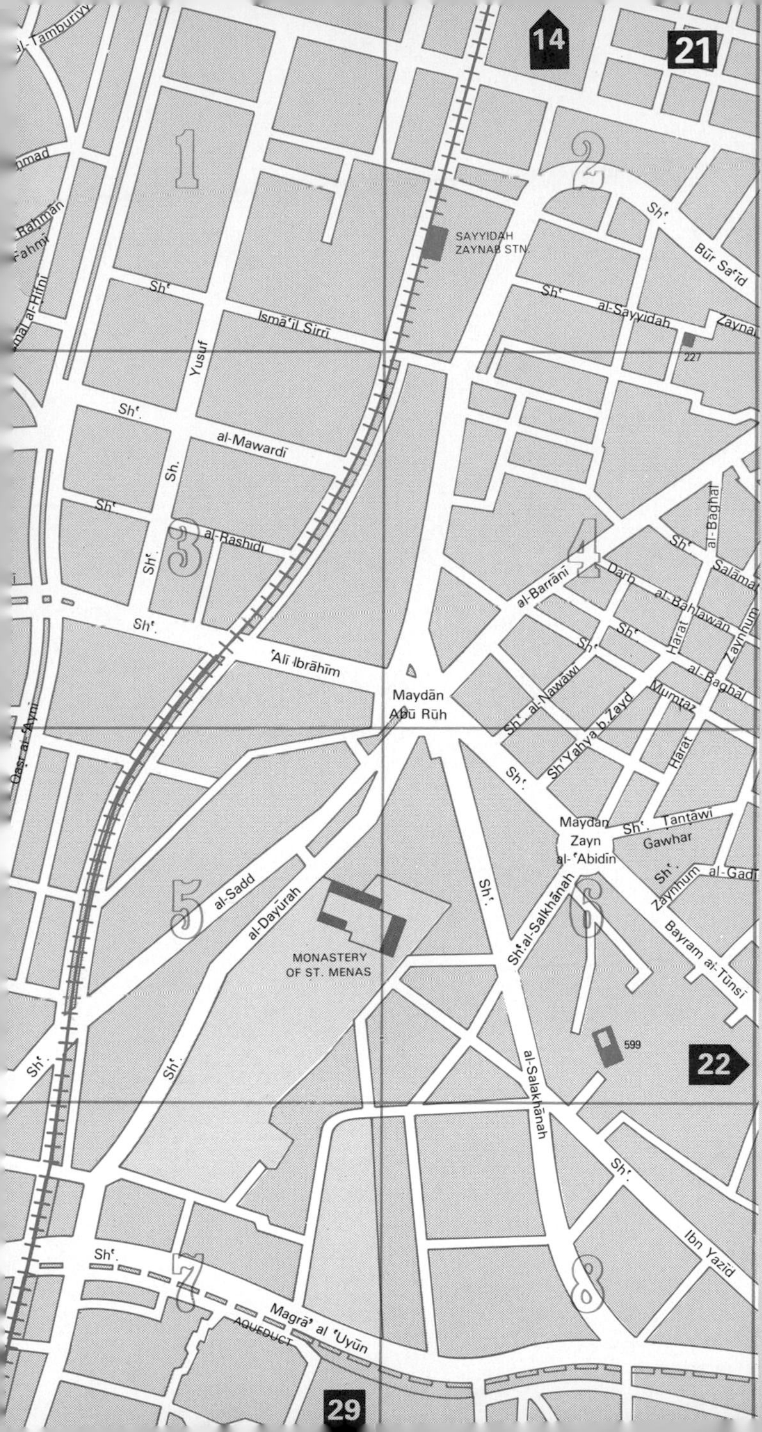
14
21
22
29
1
2
3
4
5
6
7
8
al-Tamburiyy
Rahmān
Fahmī
al-Hifnī
Qasr al-ʿAynī
SAYYIDAH ZAYNAB STN.
Shʿ Būr Saʿīd
Shʿ al-Sayyidah Zaynab
227
Shʿ Ismāʿīl Sirrī
Yusuf
Shʿ. al-Mawardī
Sh.
Shʿ al-Rashidi
Shʿ. ʿAlī Ibrāhīm
Maydān Abū Rūh
Shʿ al-Barrānī
Darb al-Bahlawān
Shʿ Salāmah
al-Baghal
Harat Zaynhum
Shʿ al-Baghal
Shʿ al-Nawawī
Shʿ Yahya b. Zayd
Mumtaz
Harat
Shʿ. Bayram al-Tūnsī
Maydan Zayn al-ʿAbidin
Shʿ. Tantawi Gawhar
Shʿ. Zaynhum al-Gadī
Shʿ al-Sadd
al-Dayūrah
MONASTERY OF ST. MENAS
Shʿ. al-Salkhānah
599
Shʿ.
Shʿ. Ibn Yazīd
Shʿ. Magrāʾ al ʿUyūn
AQUEDUCT

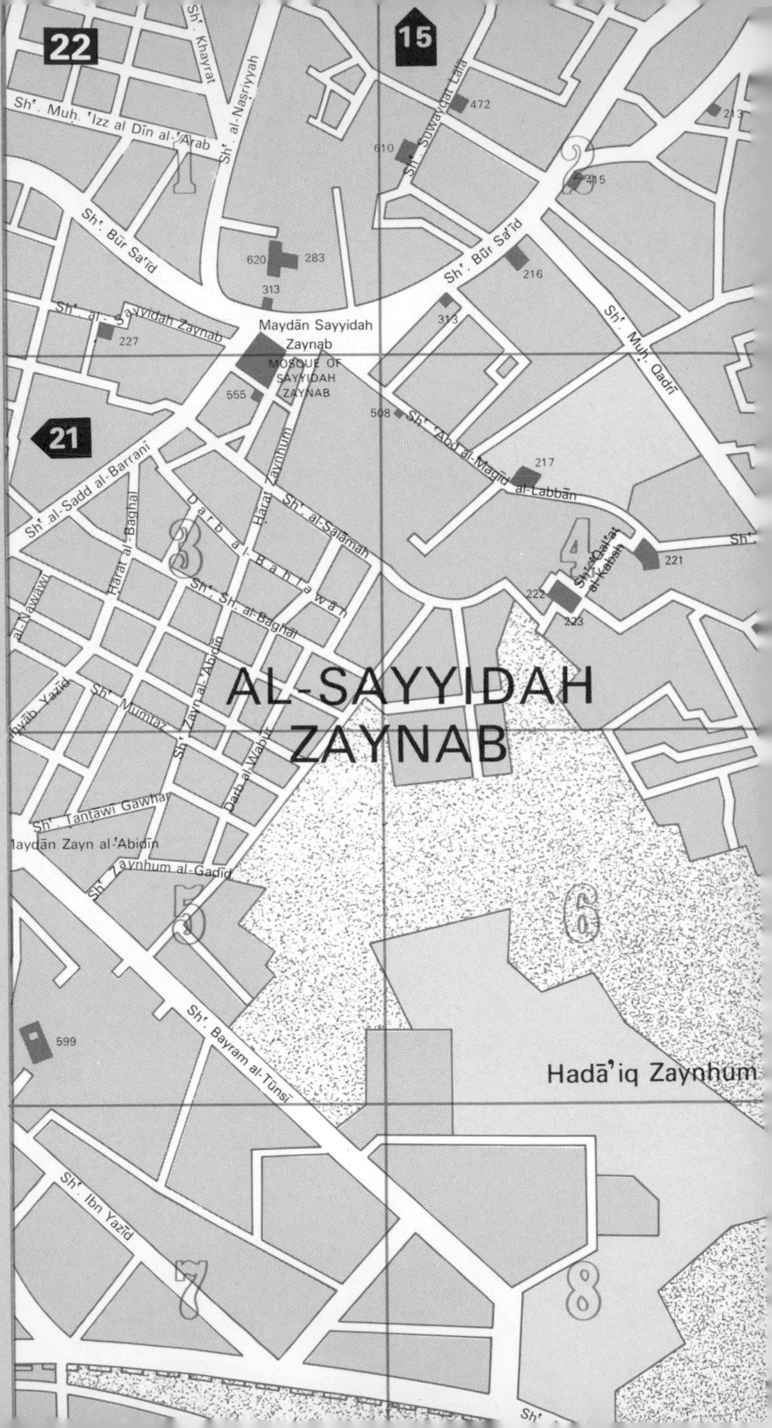
22
15
21
Sh'. Khayrat
Sh'. al-Nasriyyah
Sh'. Muh. 'Izz al Din al-'Arab
Sh'. Suwaydat Lala
472
213
610
415
Sh'. Bur Sa'id
620
283
313
216
Sh'. al-Sayyidah Zaynab
227
Maydan Sayyidah Zaynab
MOSQUE OF SAYYIDAH ZAYNAB
555
508
Sh'. 'Abd al-Magid al-Labban
Sh'. Muh. Qadri
217
Sh'. al-Sadd al-Barrani
Harat al-Baghal
Harat Zaynhum
Sh'. al-Salamah
Darb al-Bahlawan
Sh'. Qal'at al-Kabsh
221
222
223
al-Nawawi
Sh'. Sh. al-Baghal
Sh'. Zayn al-'Abidin
AL-SAYYIDAH ZAYNAB
Sh'. Mumtaz
Darb al-Wabur
Sh'. Tantawi Gawhar
Maydan Zayn al-'Abidin
Sh'. Zaynhum al-Gadid
Sh'. Bayram al-Tunsi
599
Hada'iq Zaynhum
Sh'. Ibn Yazid
Sh'

16
23
24
30
Sh'. al-Qal'ah
Suq al-Silah
Sh'. al-Hilmiyyah
AL-RIFA'I MOSQUE
MOSQUE OF SULTAN HASAN (133)
Maydan Muh 'Ali
Maydan Salah al-Din
SABIL UMM 'ABBAS
Sh'. al-Salibah
Sh'. Shaykhu
Sh'. al-Khalifah
MOSQUE OF AHMAD IBN TULUN (220)
BAYT AL-KIRIDLIYYAH (321, 559)
Sh'. Darb al-Husr
Sh'. Tulun
TOMB AND MUSEUM OF MUSTAFA KAMIL
Maydan Sayyidah 'A'ishah
Sh'. al-Badri
Sh'. Mabarrat Mustafa Kamil
Sh'. Salah al-Din
Sh'. al-Ashraf
Badr al-Din al-Wafa'i
Tariq Salah Salim
Sh'. al-Qadiriyyah
MOSQUE OF SAYYIDAY NAFISAH
ENCLOSURE OF SULTAN BAYBARS
Sh'. al-Sayyidah N
2
3
4
5
6
8
130
131
134
135
136
146
147
148
151
152
153
154
155
156
163
169
171
172
174
207
209
210
211
218
246
247
261
262
263
265
266
267
268
269
270
272
273
274
275
276
279
287
322
324
333
335
378
393
394
405
418
452
461
463
521
548
68

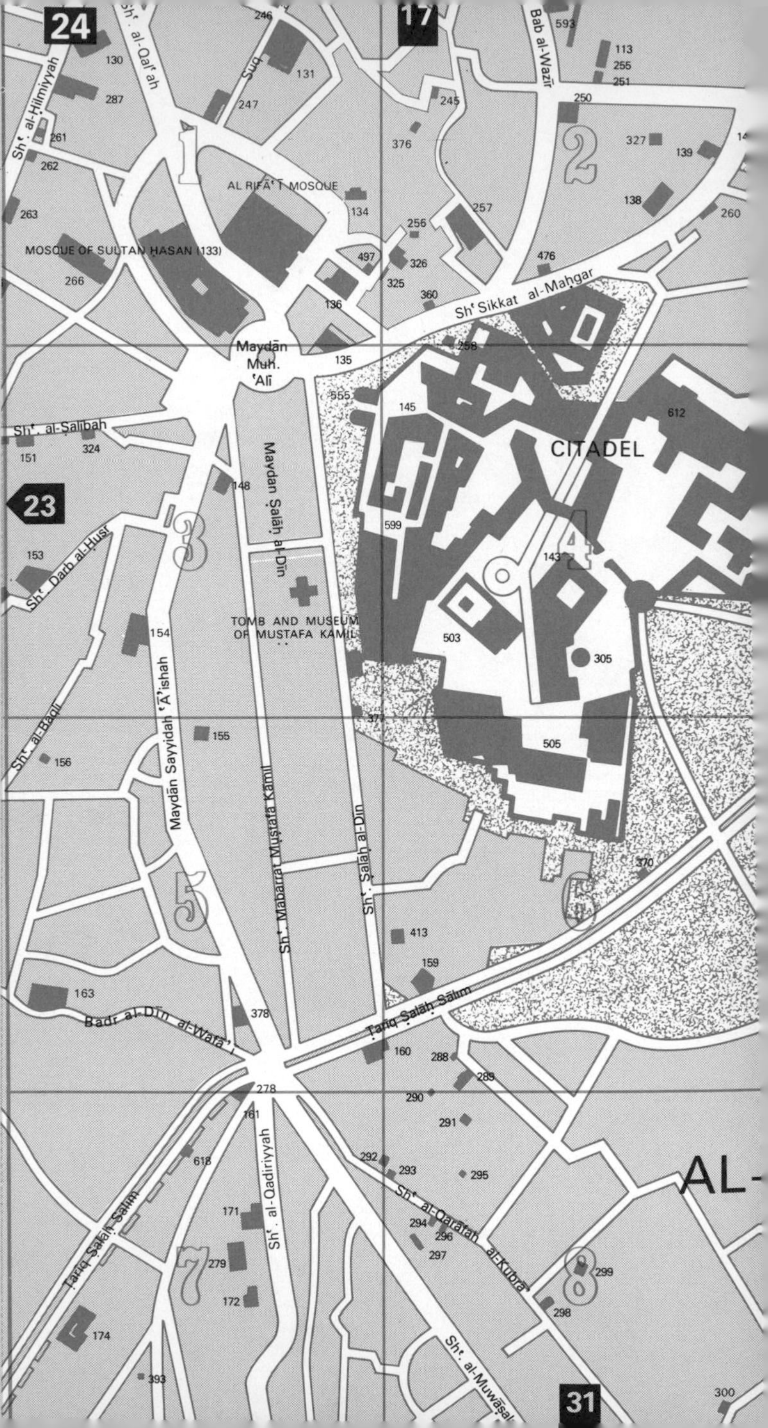
24
17
23
31
Shʿ. al-Qalʿah
Suq
Bab al-Wazir
Shʿ. al-Hilmiyyah
AL RIFAʿI MOSQUE
MOSQUE OF SULTAN HASAN (133)
Shʿ Sikkat al-Mahgar
Maydan Muh. ʿAli
Shʿ. al-Salibah
Maydan Salah al-Din
CITADEL
Shʿ. Darb al-Husr
TOMB AND MUSEUM OF MUSTAFA KAMIL
Maydan Sayyidah ʿAʾishah
Shʿ. al-Baqli
Shʿ. Mabarrat Mustafa Kamil
Shʿ. Salah al-Din
Tariq Salah Salim
Badr al-Din al-Wafaʾi
Shʿ. al-Qadiriyyah
Shʿ. al-Qarafah al-Kubra
Shʿ. al-Muwasal
AL-
1
2
3
4
5
6
7
8
246
593
113
255
251
130
131
287
247
245
250
261
376
327
139
262
134
257
138
263
256
260
266
497
326
476
325
136
360
258
135
555
145
612
151
324
148
599
153
143
503
154
305
377
155
505
156
370
413
159
163
378
160
288
289
278
290
161
291
292
618
293
295
171
294
296
297
279
299
172
298
174
393
300

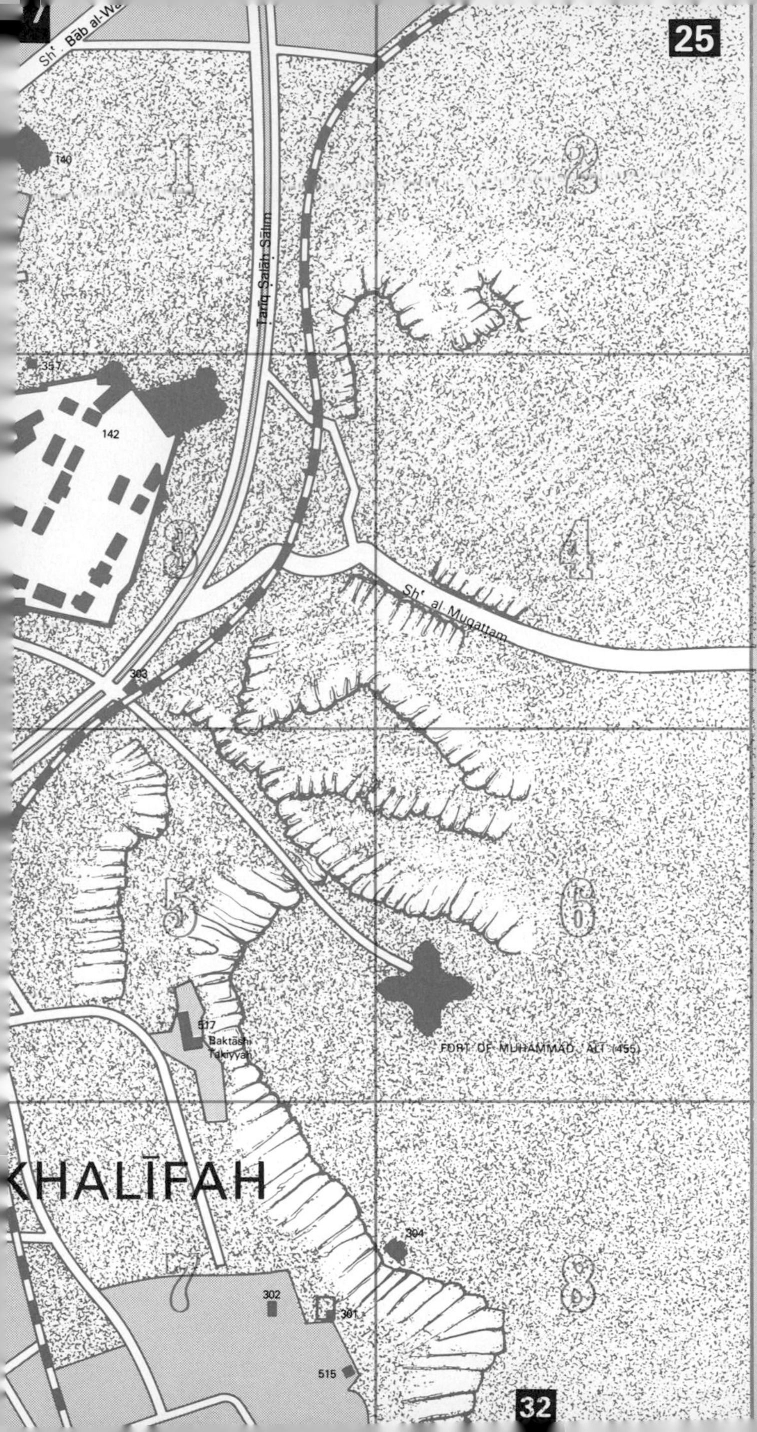

25
Sh' Bāb al-Wa
1
2
3
4
5
6
8
140
357
142
303
Tarīq Salāh Sālim
Sh' al-Muqattam
517
Baktāshi Takiyyah
FORT OF MUHAMMAD 'ALĪ (455)
KHALĪFAH
304
302
301
515
32

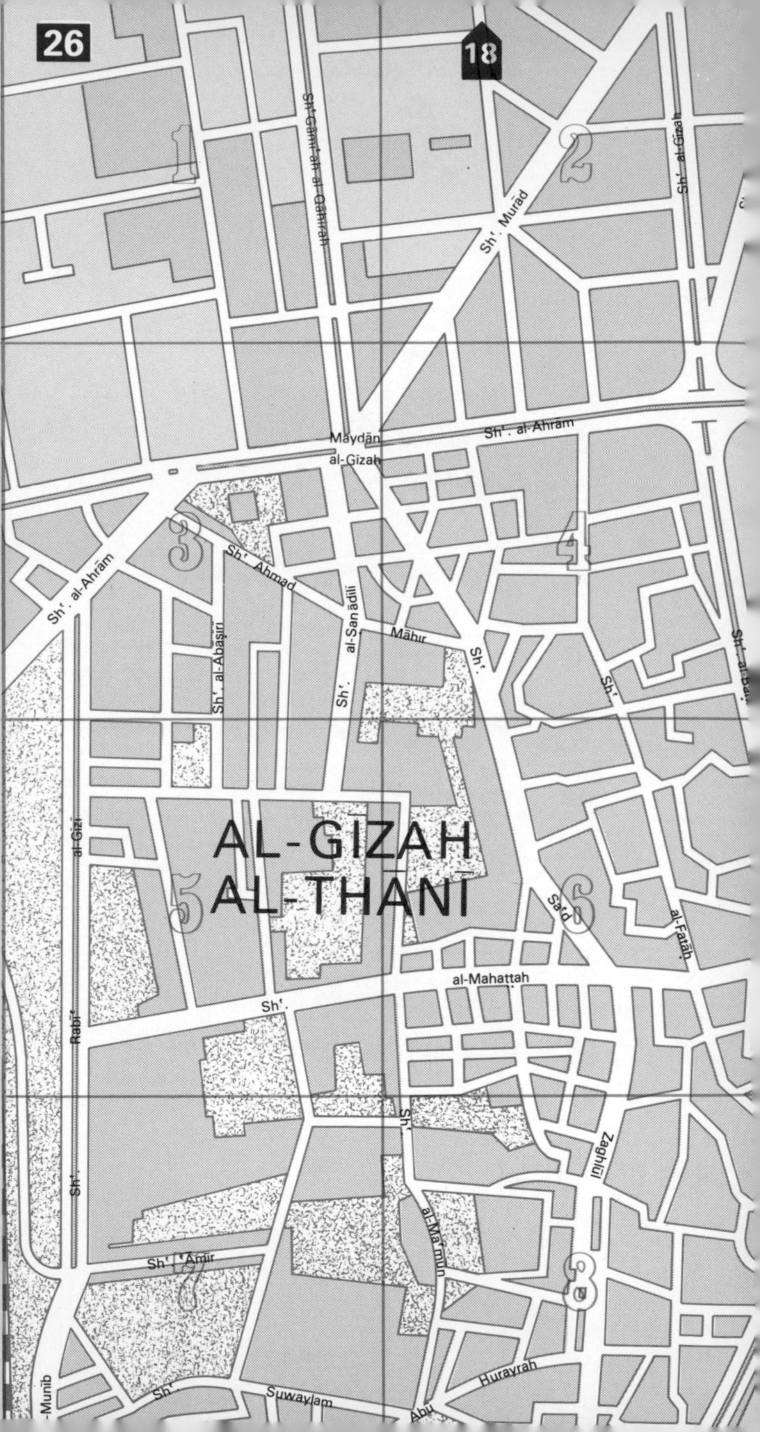
18
Sh'. Gami'ah al-Qahirah
Sh'. Murad
Sh'. al-Gizah
Sh'. al-Ahram
Maydan
al-Gizah
Sh'. al-Ahram
Sh'. Ahmad
Mahir
Sh'. al-Sanadili
Sh'. al-Abasiri
Sh'.
Sh'.
Sh'. al-ba...
AL-GIZAH
AL-THANI
Sa'd
Zaghlul
al-Fatah
al-Mahattah
Sh'.
Rabi'
al-Gizi
Sh'.
Sh'.
al-Ma'mun
Sh'. 'Amir
-Munib
Sh'.
Suwaylam
Abu
Hurayrah
1
2
3
4
5
6
7
8

19
27
28
Sh'
Manyal
Farid Wagdi
Sh'
Sh'
al-Batanuni
Digwi
Sh'
Kubri al-Gizah
Sh'
al-Rawdah
Sh'
al-Malik
al-Muzaffar
Sh'
al-Mamalik
al-Bahriyyah
Sh'
Mukhtar
Sh'
al-Marzuqi
Sh'
Mufid
Sh'
'Abdallah Hatim
al-A'zam
al-Nil
Kurnish
Sh'
79
MUNASTIRLI PALACE
NILOMETER
GAZIRAT AL-DHAHAB

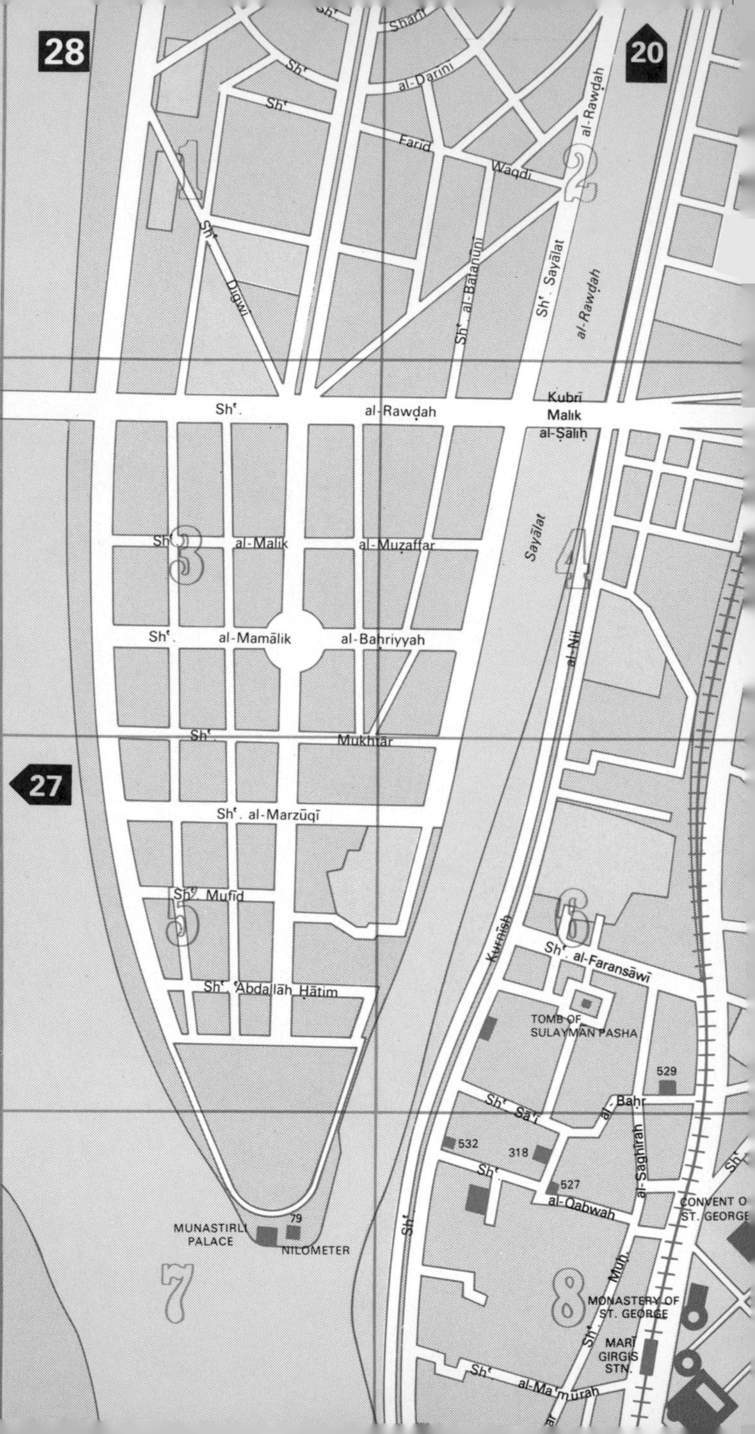
28
20
27
Sharif
Sh'
al-Darini
Farid
Waqdi
al-Rawdah
Digwi
Sh'. al-Batanuni
Sh'. Sayālat
al-Rawdah
Sh'. al-Rawdah
Kubri Malik al-Ṣāliḥ
Sh'. al-Malik al-Muzaffar
Sayālat
Sh'. al-Mamālik al-Bahriyyah
al-Nil
Sh'. Mukhtār
Sh'. al-Marzūqī
Sh'. Mufid
Kurnīsh
Sh'. al-Faransāwī
Sh'. 'Abdallāh Hātim
TOMB OF SULAYMĀN PASHA
529
Sh'. Sā'ī
al-Bahr
532
318
527
al-Saghīrah
Sh'. al-Qabwah
CONVENT OF ST. GEORGE
MUNASTIRLI PALACE
79
NILOMETER
Sh'
Sh'. Muh.
MONASTERY OF ST. GEORGE
MARI GIRGIS STN.
Sh'. al-Ma'murah
1
2
3
4
5
6
7
8

21
29
Abū 'l-Sayfayn
Sh'.
Sh'. Bani Hilāl
al-Madābigh
Sh'. Qāḍī Tāg al-Dīn
Sh'. Sīdī Malik
al-Anwar
al-Imārah
Ṭarīq Ṣalāḥ Sālim
Ḥasan
Abū 'l-Su'ūd
Sīdī
Dār
Sh'. Muḥ. Ṭāhir
al-Raqīq
Sh'. Sīdī Sa'd
Sh'. 'Umar
Sūq
Sh'. Sīdī 'Uqbah
MONASTERY OF ST. MERCURIUS
'Alī Sālim
Gāmi' 'Amr
Girgis
MISR AL-QADĪMAH (old Cairo)
MOSQUE OF 'AMR IBN AL-'ĀS (319)
Gap between here and page 30
Sh'. 'Ayn al-Ṣīrah
Qaṣr al-Sham'
CHURCH OF SITT BARBARA
SITE OF THE CITY OF AL-FUSTĀT
1
2
3
4
5
6
8
8

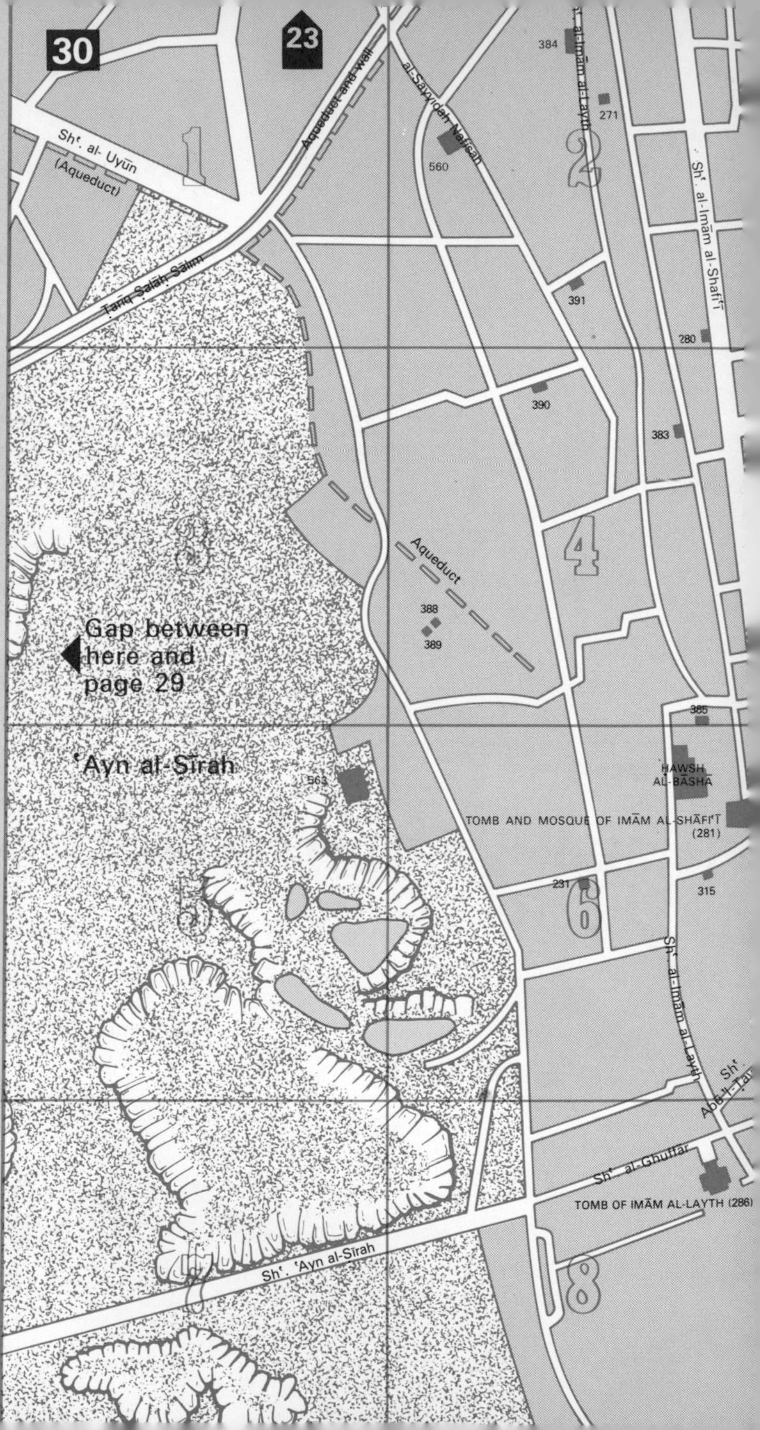
30
23
Shʿ. al- Uyūn
(Aqueduct)
Aqueduct and wall
al-Sayyidah Nafīsah
al-Imām al-Layth
Shʿ. al-Imām al-Shafiʿī
Ṭarīq Ṣalāḥ Sālim
384
271
560
391
280
390
383
Aqueduct
388
389
Gap between here and page 29
ʿAyn al-Ṣīrah
563
385
HAWSH AL-BĀSHĀ
TOMB AND MOSQUE OF IMĀM AL-SHĀFIʿĪ
(281)
231
315
Shʿ. al-Imām al-Layth
Shʿ. al-Ghuffār
TOMB OF IMĀM AL-LAYTH (286)
Shʿ. ʿAyn al-Sīrah
1
2
3
4
5
6
7
8

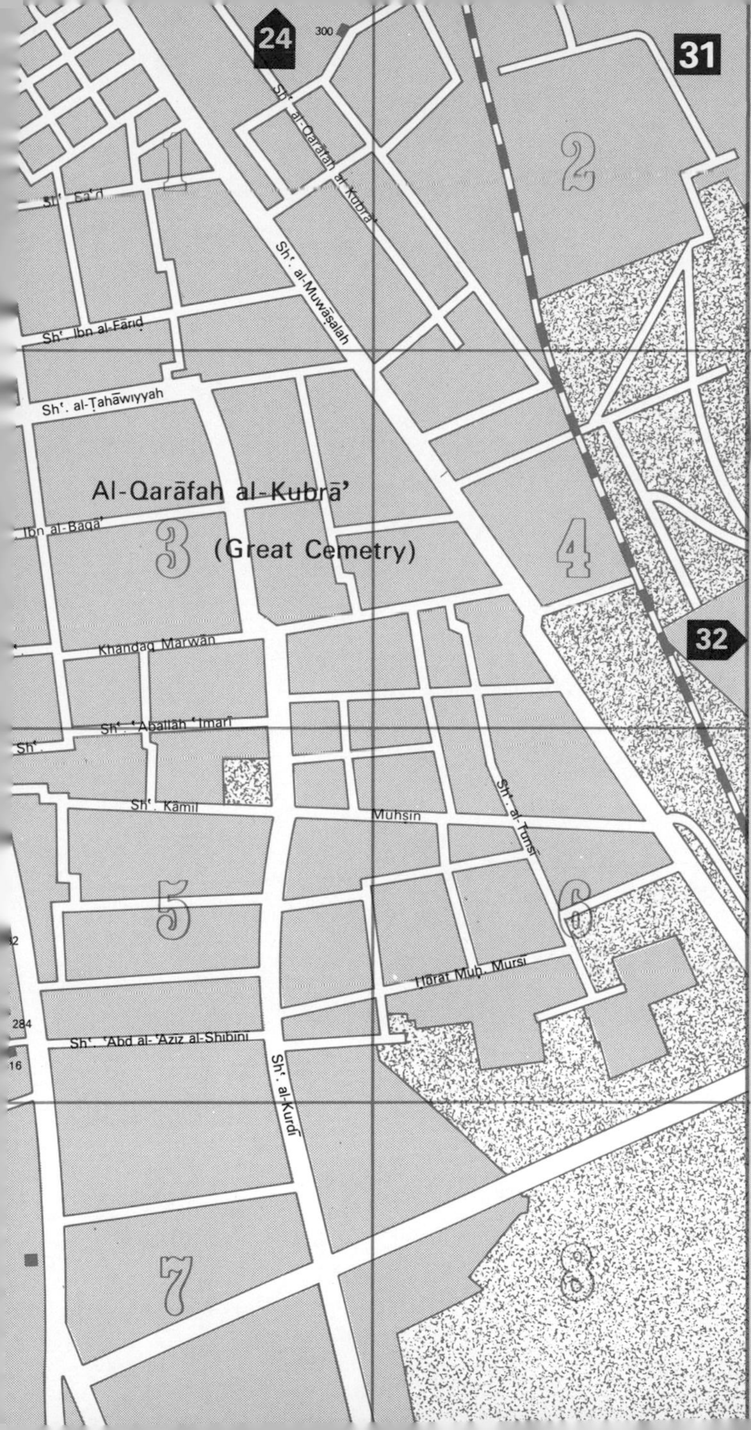
24
300
31
32
Sh'. al-Qarāfah al-Kubrā'
Sh'. Sa'd
Sh'. al-Muwāṣalah
Sh'. Ibn al-Fāriḍ
Sh'. al-Ṭaḥāwiyyah
Al-Qarāfah al-Kubrā'
(Great Cemetery)
Ibn al-Baqā'
Khandaq Marwān
Sh'. 'Aballāh 'Imarī
Sh'.
Sh'. Kāmil
Muḥsin
Sh'. al-Tūnsī
Ḥūrat Muḥ. Mursī
Sh'. 'Abd al-'Azīz al-Shibīnī
Sh'. al-Kurdī
284
1
2
3
4
5
6
7
8

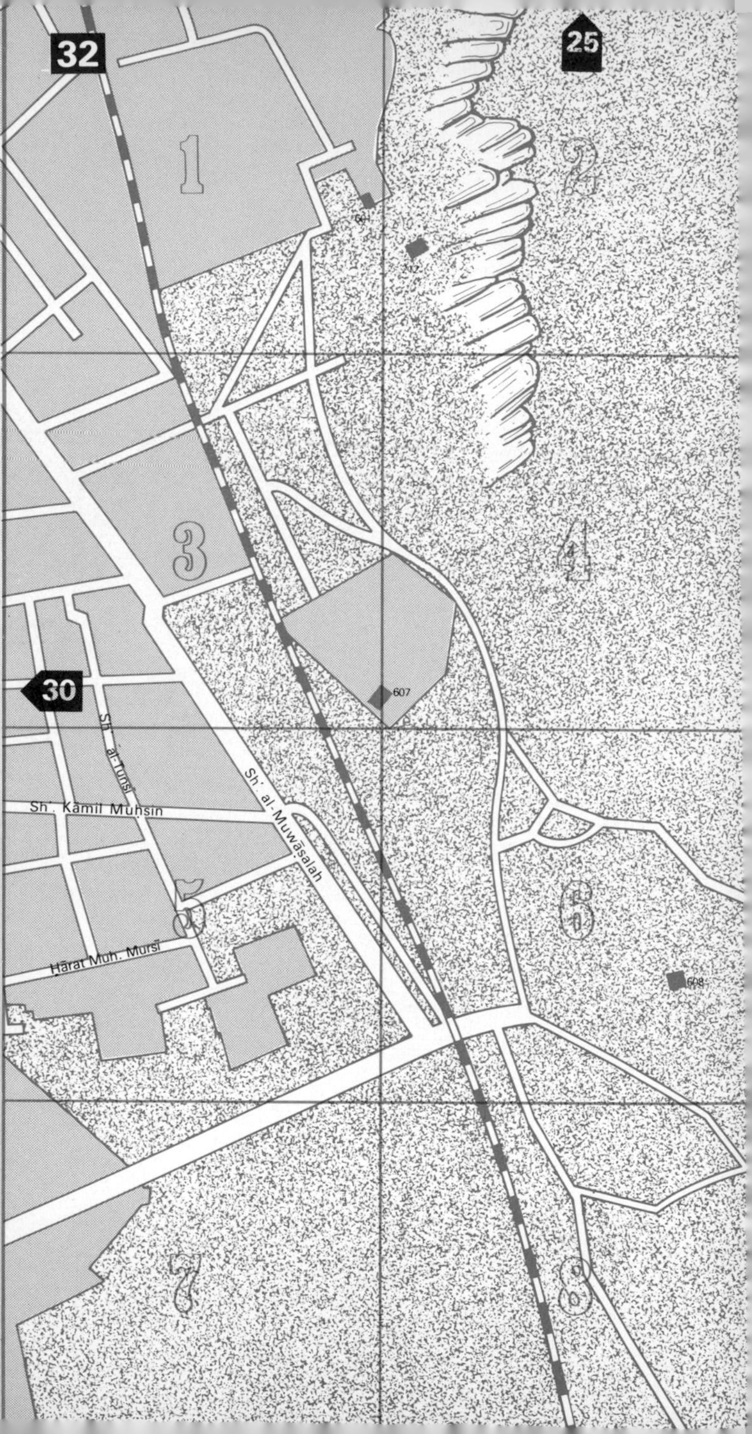

32
25
1
2
212
3
4
607
30
Sh' al-Tunsi
Sh' Kāmil Muḥsin
Sh' al-Muwāṣalah
5
6
608
Ḥārat Muḥ. Mursī
7
8

considered a symbol of Upper Egypt and two hieroglyphs were used: one is the flowering phase (66) and the other the non-flowering phases (67). In a combination with the bee hieroglyph it was used before the king's prenomen.

Several other water-loving plants are found in the **Festuceae** and include the Reeds (*Phragmites australis*) (68) with large flowering tufts, of importance since the stalks replaced the rush as writing instruments in Greco-Roman times. Found in the S is the Giant reed grass (*Arundo donax*), up to 3m high with an even larger plume. From the **Aveneae** Oats (*Avena sativa*) and Rye (*Secale cereale*) were never of importance in the food system of Ancient Egypt but Barley (*Hordeum vulgare*) was one of the earliest cereals to be cultivated, appearing in the Middle East at least 9000 years ago and known in Egypt since prehistoric times. It was used to brew beer and to make a coarse unleavened bread and also as a livestock feed. Of the wheats (*Triticum spp*) (69) Emmer (*T. dicoccum*) was cultivated prior to 7000 BC in SW Asia and was the principal wheat grown in Egypt throughout the dynastic period. Bread wheat (*T. aestivum*) was introduced during the late dynastic period and Durum wheat (*T. durum*) in late Ptolemaic times.

From the **Oryzeae** Rice (*Oryza sativa*) is the single most important food crop in Egypt. Probably first cultivated in Southern Asia c 3000 BC, it had reached Mesopotamia by early Christian times from whence it was exported to Byzantium. Only after the Muslim conquest was it grown in Egypt. The **Maydeae** has contributed Maize (*Zea mays*) which was cultivated in the ancient Americas and did not reach Egypt until the 16C.

The **Andropogoneae** have contributed the Sorghums (*Sorgum spp.*) and Sugar cane (*S. barberi*) which was cultivated in India in prehistoric times. By the 1C AD it had reached Persia and was exported into the Byzantine Empire where it was an expensive commodity. The Arabs also cultivated sugar cane and brought it with them when they colonised Egypt. Besides sugar the plant is an important base of alcohol and spirit.

In the **Scimitales** the most important sp. is the Banana (*Musa acuminata*) which was first cultivated in South Asia and taken to Madagascar in the 5C AD. From there it reached the mainland of Africa and diffused along the coast and had entered the Nile Valley by the mid 12C.

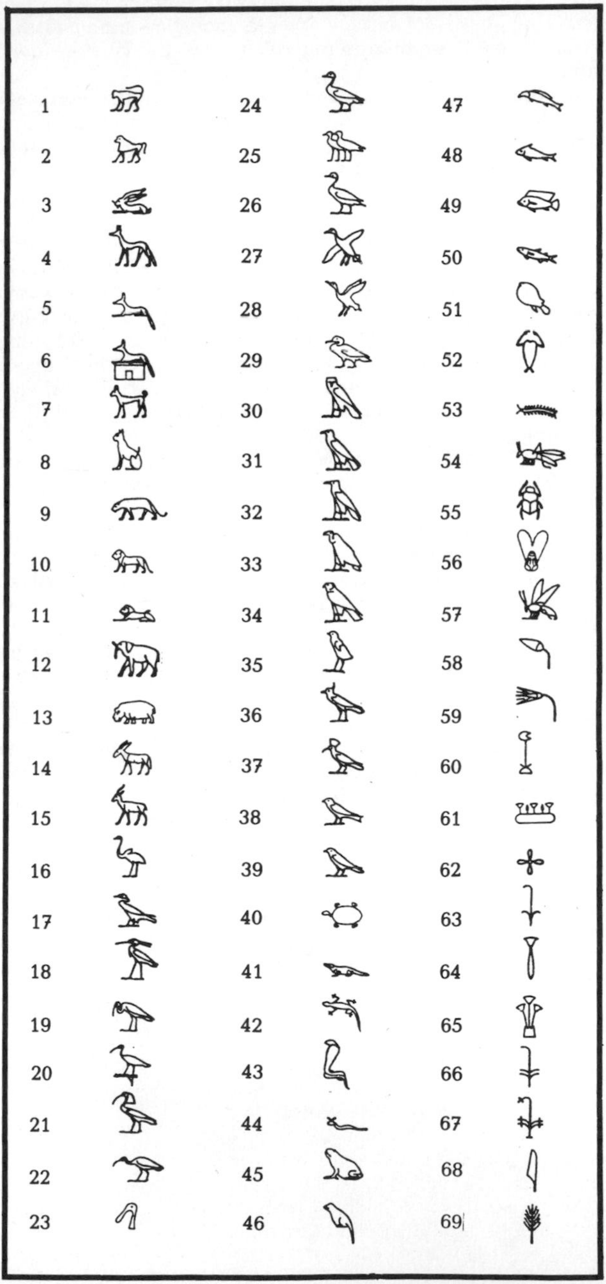
1
2
3
4
5
6
7
8
9
10
11
12
13
14
15
16
17
18
19
20
21
22
23
24
25
26
27
28
29
30
31
32
33
34
35
36
37
38
39
40
41
42
43
44
45
46
47
48
49
50
51
52
53
54
55
56
57
58
59
60
61
62
63
64
65
66
67
68
69

# BIBLIOGRAPHY

Bibliographies of Egypt abound, but tend to be selective. Few scholars have covered the vast range of Egyptian history and therefore indexes tend to concentrate on one particular aspect—Ancient Egypt, the Greek, Coptic or Islamic periods, or on politics, geography or social studies. The following list is intended for the interested visitor and most of the books mentioned contain further bibliographies.

The first traveller to Egypt to write of his experiences was the Greek historian Herodotus who visited the country between 460 and 445 BC. The result of his extensive travels was a nine-volume *History* of which Egypt forms a large section. Although he spoke to people who understood the ancient language his penchant for trivia, gossip and fable reduces the academic value of his work, which yet remains a fascinating document of Egyptian life during the declining years of the ancient culture. There have been many translations of Herodotus' work. Other classical writers to cover Egypt include Strabo (64 BC–AD 22), who has an extensive section on the country in his *Geography*, and Diodorus Siculus who travelled in Egypt during the mid 1–C AD and included these researches in his *Historical Library*.

Many Muslim travellers describe sojourns in Egypt although few have been translated into English. Among those which have are the *Safar Nameh* of the Persian traveller Nāṣir-i Khusraw (died 1061), translated by W.M. Thackston; the *Travels* of Ibn Jubayr (died 1204), translated by R. Broadhurst; ʿAbd al-Laṭīf al-Baghdādī (died 1231), translated by Kamal Hafuth Zand and John and Ivy Videan; and Ibn Baṭṭūṭah (died 1377), translated by H.A.R. Gibb.

Not until post-Renaissance times did European travellers visit Egypt in any number. 18C travellers include Richard Pococke, *A Description of the East and some other countries* (1743); Frederick Ludwig Norden, *Travels in Egypt and Nubia* (1757); and M. Volney (C.F. Chassebeuf), *Travels through Syria and Egypt in the years 1783, 1784 and 1785* (1787). Among the most comprehensive was the journal of Carsten Niebuhr, sole survivor of an ill-fated Danish expedition; it was translated as *Travels through Arabia and other countries in the East* (1792).

After the French occupation Baron Denon, who had accompanied Napoleon, published his journal, illustrated with superb etchings. It was speedily translated into English (with the warning to the reader to remember that it was the work of a Frenchman) as *Voyage in Lower and Upper Egypt* (1802).

During the 19C travels proliferated. One of the earliest accounts is John Lewis Burckhardt's *Travels in Nubia* (1819). His work is particularly interesting in that he travelled in the guise of Sh. Ibrahim and visited many areas usually closed to Europeans. Other early travellers who published their journals include Giovanni Belzoni, Sir R. Legh, J. St. John, J. Carne, A. Kinglake, W.P. Thakeray, Robert Curzon, Prince Puckler-Muskau and R.P. Madden. All these whetted the appetite of the public for the lavish albums produced by the artists who had made their own travels, Pascal Costa, Robert Hay, Prisse d'Avennes and David Roberts, who produced the magnificently illustrated three-volume folio of *Egypt and Nubia* (1846–49). And still the tide increased with publications by W.H. Bartlett, Mrs H. Martineau, R. Burton, W.H. Russell, Sophie Poole,

W.N. Senior and Mark Twain, and dozens more. But it was perhaps Amelia Edwards' *A thousand miles up the Nile* (1877) which most fired the imagination of many Victorian armchair travellers and still makes fascinating reading. Since then visitors' reminiscences have blossomed with archaeologists, soldiers, and politicians contributing to the literature, with varying degrees of success.

The publication of the *Description de l'Egypte* between 1809 and 1822, cataloguing the findings of the French expedition of 1798–1801, displayed the treasure chest of Egypt to European scholars. However it was Champollion's decipherment of the ancient hieroglyphics in 1822 which provided the key for the scientific study of the ancient civilisation.

There are few works that cover the full compass of Egyptian history, but *The History of Egypt from the Earliest Times to the Present Day*, edited by Flinders Petrie and published in six volumes between 1896 and 1901 has sections on ancient history by Petrie himself, the Ptolemaic period by J.P. Mahally, Roman period by J.G. Milne, and Islamic Egypt by S. Lane-Poole.

Introductions to Ancient Egyptian history include: Sir Alan Gardiner, *Egypt of the Pharoahs* (1961), and James Henry Breasted, *A History of Egypt from Earliest Times to the Roman Conquest* (reprinted 1959). *An Introduction to Ancient Egypt* (1979), the guide to the British Museum collections, is also a valuable aid.

The Christian period in Egypt is decidedly understudied, but one book available is *Egypt from Alexander the Great to the Arab Conquest*, by H. Idris Bell (1948). A more recent work *Egypt after the Pharoahs* by Bowman is extremely interesting. A complete history of Muslim Egypt is also badly needed, but the volume by Lane-Poole mentioned above is adequate.

For the later periods Dorothea Russell's *Medieval Cairo and the Monasteries of the Wadi Natrun* (1962) is a fascinating if somewhat romantic account of Fāṭimid and Mamlūk times. This is also an excellent guidebook with the author's love of the city apparent in every paragraph. *The Age of the Crusades* (1986) by P.M. Holt is an indispensible introduction to the history and complicated structure of Mamlūk Egypt, while a more popular work is *Soldiers of Fortune* (1973) by Sir John Bagot Glubb. Holt has also written the most comprehensive and enjoyable history of Egypt during Ottoman times *Egypt and the Fertile Crescent 1516–1922*.

As an erudite exposition of the development of Cairo, Janet Abu Lughod's *Cairo, 1001 Years of the City Victorious* (1971) is the definitive work, while for the structure of 19C Egyptian society Edward William Lane's *An account of the Manners and Customs of the Modern Egyptians*, first published in 1839 and reprinted many times, is a classic literary text in its own right.

Hundreds of superb volumes have been produced on aspects of Ancient Egyptian art and architecture and most excavations eventually produced detailed reports of findings, but for a general introduction *The Art and Architecture of Egypt* by W. Stevenson-Smith, revised by W. Kelly Simpson (1981), is excellent. For a review of the artistic achievements of the Ancient Egyptians throughout the whole country James Baikie's *Egyptian Antiquities in the Nile Valley* (1932) has in many ways never been bettered. For sheer scope and excitingly presented the *Atlas of Ancient Egypt* (1980) by John Baines and Jaromir Malek is superb.

Pyramids are scientifically dealt with by I.E.S. Edwards in *The*

*Pyramids of Egypt* (1947, revised edition 1986), and by Aḥmad Fakhry in *The Pyramids* (1969). Other architecture is well covered in *A History of Egyptian Architecture* (three volumes, 1954–68) by Aḥmad Badawy. An interesting study of the principles governing the ancient art is *The Canon and Proportion in Egyptian Art* by I. Iversen (1975).

Excavation reports were included in the *Annales de Service des Antiquities de l'Egypte* and can also be found in the *Journal of Egyptian Archaeology* of the EES.

Regarding the Christian period, *Coptic Art* by Pierre du Bourguet, translated by Caryll Hay-Shaw (1971) is interesting despite relying heavily on French studies. A wider review is undertaken by Alexander Badawy in *Coptic Art and Archaeology* (1978).

Of those who have made important contributions in the field of Islamic art the indefatiguable K.A.C. Creswell must rank among the foremost. Two works which, although large, are essential reading are: *Early Muslim Architecture* (1933–40), to the end of Ṭūlūnid times, and *Muslim Architecture of Egypt* (1952–60), which covers the period 937–1326. These are seminal works and need to be reprinted in a more convenient format.

An important and fascinating five-volume work by Dr Su'ād Māhir is *Masājid Miṣr wa awliyā'ūhā al-ṣālihūn* (Mosques of Egypt and the virtuous and faithful therein). Besides describing the monuments, biographical details of the deceased are given.

Reports of excavations can be found in the *Annales* and *Bulletin of the Comité de Conservation des Monuments de l'Art Arabe* (1882–1951). A tribute must be paid to the Institut Français d'Archaéologie Orientale, which since the late 19C has produced hundreds of essential archaeological reports, historical texts and travel journals covering all Egyptian periods.

Of the many guides produced during the last century outstanding in scope was Karl Baedaker's *Egypt and the Sudan*, (eight editions between 1878 and 1929). The last edition has been reprinted. *Murray's Handbook of Egypt and the Sudan* is even more venerable, originating in 1847 as an updated version of Sir T. Gardner Wilkinson's *Modern Egypt and Thebes*. This also went through many editions. Most guides of this period have to be read purely for the facts provided, with senses steeled against the insensitive attitudes of the authors towards the Egyptians.

In the Blue Guide quotations from the Qur'ān are taken from *The Message of the Qur'ān* (1980) by Muḥammad Asad, which is a sensitive English interpretation of the Arabic text.

# PRACTICAL INFORMATION

## I Approaches to Egypt

As time is usually the controlling factor in arranging holidays the only practical method of reaching Egypt is by air. It is possible to travel by rail to one of the Mediterranean ports of Marseilles, Genoa, Venice or Athens and take a ship to Alexandria but due to the incompatability of time tables this can take anything between four days and a week. The usual form of visit is with a tour company and although this is an excellent general introduction the visitor will be insulated from the life of the country. The more adventurous can attempt the journey on their own for which they will be well rewarded. Unfortunately the land approach via the Libyan border is forbidden.

**General Information** can be obtained, without charge, from the EGYPTIAN MINISTRY OF TOURISM INFORMATION OFFICE. Very courteous and obliging, they will answer questions though the booking of the hotels, etc. will be left to the intending visitor. There are offices in *London* (168 Piccadilly, W1. Tel [071] 493 5282/3), *Paris* (90 Av. de Champs Elysses), *Frankfurt* (641 Kaiserstrasse 64, Burohaus A), *Rome* (19 Via Bissolati), *Geneva* (11 Rue de Chantepoulet), *Athens* (10 Amerikas St, 6th floor), *Tokyo* (Akasaka 2-Chome Annex, 19-18 2 Chome Minato Ku), *Montreal* (Place Bonaventure, 40 Frontenac), *Stockholm* (9 Strandvagen), *New York* (630 Fifth Ave) and *San Francisco* (323 Geary St, Suite 608). They produce several booklets and maps to assist the visitor. An invaluable book is *A Practical Guide to Cairo* by Deborah Cowley and Aleya Sevour, published by the American University in Cairo Press and kept up-to-date. It is really aimed at businessmen but contains much of use to the general visitor.

There are increasing numbers of **Tour Operators** specialising in Egyptian holidays, most of them offering comprehensive tours.

*Bales Tours*, Bales House, Barrington Road, Dorking, Surrey, RH4 3EJ, deal exclusively in Egyptian travel and offer a variety of tours from the 21-day luxury cruise to a seven-day stay in Cairo; *Swans Hellenic Cruises*, 77 New Oxford Street, London WC1A 1PP, provide similar, comprehensive river cruises (with guest lecturers). London agents include *Club Mediterranee*, 62 South Moulton St., W1, operating from Paris, who also organise cruises, as do *Kuoni Travel*, 33 Maddox Street, W1; *Thomas Cook*, 45 Berkeley Street, W1; *Goldenjoys Holidays*, 51 Dorset Street, London W1H 3FA; *Sunquest*, 43-44 New Bond Street, W1 and *Abercrombie and Kent*, Sloane Square House, Holborn Place, SW1. *Pennworld*, 122 Knightsbridge, SW1, offer a tour for young people (18–38), utilising rail and boat, the necessities provided by a communal fund. *American Express*, 6 Haymarket, SW1. also arrange tours. *Atkins World Travel*, 12 High Street, Lymington, Hants, offers a wide range of tours including one to four centres, and river cruises. Large companies offering Egyptian tours are *Horizon* and *Blue Sky*. But it is always a good rule to make extensive enquiries before finally making a choice.

Specialist tours are arranged to archeological sites by Classic Tours (British Museum), Kent House, 87 Regent Street, London W1R 8LS.

Regular **Air Services** between London and Cairo are maintained by British Airways (daily) and Egypt Air (Misr al-Ṭayrān; daily); both from

Heathrow. Further information can be obtained from *B.A.*, Dorland House, Lower Regent St., London SW1 or any local office; and from *Egypt Air*, London (29–31 Piccadilly, W1. Tel. 071-734 2395/6); Birmingham (Princes Chambers, 6 Corporation St. Tel. 021-643 1249); Manchester (Rm 219, Royal Exchange Building. Tel. 061-834 2552). The day return to Cairo in Concorde is definitely for the dilettante.

In addition Cairo has direct links with most European, Middle Eastern and African capitals and the major N American cities. The offices of Egypt Air are New York (Rm 604, 720 Fifth Ave); Paris (1 bis Rue Auber); Frankfurt a.M. (A.M. Hauptbahnhof 4); Munich (Schwanthalerstrasse 9–11). Cairo is also a vital stopover point for many of the air services from the Far East and Australia. There is an internal service between Cairo, Luxor, Abu Simbel, Hurghadah, Aswan and Sinai run by Egypt Air.

**Passenger boats and car ferries** are run by *Khedival Mail Lines*, Egyptian House, Piccadilly, London W1; *Adriatica Navigazione*, Venice–Piraeus, Alexandria, c/o Sealink, Victoria Station, London SW1 *Danish Seaways*, Ancona–Alexandria, roll-on, roll-off car ferries and passenger boats, 199 Regent Street, London W1. Other ferries operate from Genoa and Cyprus.

**Road routes**. It is possible at present only to enter Egypt from the S, the Sudan, and since renewed contact with Israel to drive from there to Egypt across N Sinai. The road from Libya is closed.

# II Formalities and Currency

**Passports** are necessary for all European and American travellers entering Egypt and must bear a photograph of the holder and be valid for three months subsequent to the visit to Egypt.

All passports must contain a current entry **Visa**, obtained by application from the local A.R.E. Consulate (London, 2 Lowndes St. SW1X, 10.00–12.00 for application). A passport-sized photograph should be provided and a fee. The applicant should be prepared to fill in a form giving details of visit, duration of stay and other relevant information. The process takes 24 hrs and the applicant can collect the passport, 14.00–15.00 hrs, or have it sent to his home. Often these formalities are undertaken by the tour companies. If the visitor has omitted to obtain a visa in his country of origin one can be obtained valid for one month on arrival at Cairo Airport. Renewals can be made at the Ministry of the Interior, Maydān al-Taḥrīr (Rte 1). Visitors staying 7 days or less can do so on a Transit Visa.

**Health Regulations**. A vaccination certificate for yellow fever and cholera is required only if entering Egypt from a country where they are endemic at present.

**Registration**. Visitors, without exception, must register with the Ministry of the Interior at *al-Mūgama*ʿ, Taḥīr Square, within seven days of arrival in Egypt (take your passport to be stamped). Failure to do so will incur a heavy fine. When travelling outside Cairo a visit must be made to the local police station if you intend to stay more than three days in the area. Lost or stolen passports must be reported to the police who will record the details and give a receipt with the file no., after which the details must be reported to the respective consulate.

**Customs**. All visitors must pass through a check by the Customs (*al-Gumruk*) which is just adjacent to the exit and all dutiable goods declared.

**Currency Regulations**. It is forbidden for Egyptian currency to be brought into Egypt or taken out and infringement will incur severe penalties. A form is presented to the visitor before entering Egypt on which **must** be listed **all currency**, travellers' cheques, money orders and negotiable goods including jewellery, cameras, radios, etc. The copy of this form should be kept as an account may be asked for when leaving the country. Currency must be changed by government-accredited agencies, local banks, hotels or the American Express. There is an advantageous tourist rate of exchange which visitors obtain for three months after arrival. Before leaving the country Egyptian money can be exchanged into an international currency.

**Money** (nuqūd or coll. fulūs). The monetary unit is the Egyptian pound (ginīh miṣri) L.E. It is divided into 100 qurūsh (pron. 'urūsh; sing. 'irsh), internationally known as the piastre (pt.). The 'irsh is divided into 10 millīms which are gradually falling out of circulation, but always quoted in financial transactions.

Coins at present in circulation are for values of ½ pt. (5 millīms), 1 pt., 5 pt. (khamsahʿ ūrush or shillin) and 10 pt. Notes are for values of 5, 10, 25, 50 pts; 1, 5, 10, 20, and 100 £E (care should be taken in distinguishing between the two series of notes with the same number: e.g. between 10 pts and 10 £E). There are several issues of notes in circulation, 60 pts may be written £E.0.600 or 60 pt. On display boards the symbol for the pt. is  and for £E  e.g.  250 means £E2.50.

**Banks**. Banking hours, except Friday and for some Saturdays and Public Holidays, are 09.30–12.30 and Sun. 10.30–12.30. The airport and 5-star hotels have a 24-hour banking and money changing service. The major credit cards are taken.

# III Transport

Most visitors confine themselves to guided tours which utilise boat, coach or 'plane in various combinations and thus visit the major sites in the Nile Valley but little else. While it is true that a knowledge of Arabic gives greater mobility, much can be achieved by using the local forms of transport and many less well-known but important sites can be reached.

**Coach Tours** can be arranged by one of the many tourist agencies in Cairo and in addition to the usual tours they can arrange visits to the specific site requested by the visitor. But they do vary a great deal in the quality of transport, accommodation and guide and it is best to visit several offices before making a decision. Below is a selection from over 85 category A agents. *Egyptian Aviation and Travel Service*, 20 Shʿ. Talʿat Ḥarb; *Thomas Cook*, 5 Shʿ. Talʿat Ḥarb; *Eastmar*, 13 Qaṣr al-Nīl; *Miṣr Travel*, 1 Shʿ. Talʿat Ḥarb and *Gulliver's Travel*, 1 Shʿ. ʿAdlī.

**Individual Travel**. Most forms of transport are frequent and regular. The traveller really has to take 'pot-luck' and it is advisable to check with the coach or railway station well before travelling to find out times of departure.

**Air Travel**. Domestic services are maintained by *Egypt Air* from Cairo to Luxor and Aswan several times daily. Other cities or areas, e.g. Sinai, have less frequent services.

**Railways**. A timetable for mainline trains is published every six months, obtainable from main stations. There are three classes of carriage. The 1st and 2nd classes may be air-conditioned. The diesel to Aswan, stopping only at Luxor, has special de-luxe carriages and sleeping cars, all air-conditioned. Students are entitled to reduced tickets with an International Students' card.

Mainline trains run from Cairo to Aswan via Luxor; Alexandria via Ṭanṭā; Suez; Ismāʿīliyyah; Damietta via Manṣūrah; Sallūm via Marsū Mutrūḥ.

**Roads**. The major cities are connected by roads which for the most part are well-metalled. But in other areas certain sections can suddenly become rutted or disintegrate. The secondary roads are often quite good but the tracks leading from them can often take the motorist into trouble with loose sand, mud or gravel. All the roads in Egypt have two great advantages: the ground is for the most part flat and the nature of the terrain makes possible long straight stretches.

A sharp lookout should be kept in rural districts for 'sleeping policemen' (speed bumps) illegally laid across the road by villagers. They can devastate the suspension of a car.

At regular intervals outside Cairo the driver will often encounter a police post (*taftish*) and should be prepared to show documents including passport and licence.

**Petrol Stations and Travel Regulations**. Petrol stations are frequent in the main cities. On the main highways they are placed every 10–20km. On the side roads most of the towns have two or three. However it is always advisable to have a reserve tin of petrol. If travel is undertaken to isolated areas enough petrol must be taken to allow for the return journey. Petrol (binzīn) is much cheaper than in the U.K. but generally of lower octane. It is sold by the litre.

Cars and minibuses (holding up to nine people) can be imported into Egypt for a period of 90 days (renewable). Documents needed are *carnet de passage*, international motor vehicle licence, nationality plates and green international insurance card. Advice should be sought from the AA or RAC. In Egypt membership of the Automobile Touring Club of Egypt, 10 Shʿ. Qaṣr al-Nīl is recommended (Tel. 71243). They will advise on local problems.

**Buses**. Trams and buses serve the capital, run by the government companies *Hayʾit al-Naql al-ʿAm* (Govt Transport Organisation), and *Sharikāt al-Ūtūbīs al-Qāhirah al-Kubrā* (Greater Cairo Autobus Co) from about 05.30 to 01.00 daily. They are frequent but well patronised to the point of bursting and during rush hours it is often a case of entering where a space can be found—speed is essential. The number of the bus and the destination is written in Arabic on the front in the space above the driver. The fare is taken by the conductor (kumsārī) who passes among the passengers. Smoking is forbidden in any of these buses.

LONG DISTANCE BUSES are divided among five companies and each serves a separate area of the country. *Sharq al-Daltā* (Eastern Delta) serves the Canal area, Manṣūrah and Damietta; *Wasiṭ al-Daltā* (Middle Delta) to Kafr al-Shaykh and Manūfiyyah, Ṭanṭā; *Gharb al-Daltā* (Western Delta) to Damanhūr, Alexandria; the NW coast and Sīwah;

*Wagh al-Qiblī* (Southern areas), all areas in the Nile Valley and along the Red Sea Coast, and *Sharikat Ūtūbīs Sīnā'* serving all areas of Sinai. Each has its own terminal and booking office in the N suburbs of Cairo. There are three types of bus: the stopping bus calling at every station; the inter city with fewer stops, and the reserved express or *de luxe*. Standards of comfort are reasonable, the last class with air-conditioning but the others rely on open windows which of course let in the dust. There are now services bypassing Cairo which link the major cities.

LOCAL SERVICES. Each city has its own local service, usually operating from a separate terminal from the long-distance buses, serving the outlying villages which can often be some distance from the main road. They are stopped at the village stops by a raised hand.

**Taxis**, hailed by calling 'tax' and a raised hand, are numerous in the main cities but the drivers are often intractable about the direction in which they wish to travel. However there are ranks outside all the main hotels, monitored by the police. The meter (ʿaddād) is attached to the front of the dashboard (although it is not always in working order) and the rate fixed by the government, this also applies to journeys outside the capital and the charge must be arranged beforehand. There is a government run *Limousine Misr* service operating around the clock. A little more expensive but more certain, it can be contacted by telephone on Cairo 2599813 and the car will be sent to the address requested. It will also provide a service to take the visitor outside Cairo. A word of warning: the taxi drivers are often not so familiar with the alleys and backstreets in Cairo as are their counterparts in London and will often have to be directed. If they do not like the look of the street they will refuse to deliver the passenger to the door.

**Self drive cars**, for which an International Driver's Licence is necessary, can be hired through the hotel or tourist agencies, the tariff depending on the type of car. Typical agencies are: *Avis*, Hilton Hotel and Meridien Hotel; *Dalin Cars*, 52 Shʿ. Qaṣr al-Nīl and *International Cars*, 2 Shʿ. Ṣalāḥ Salim.

*Carriages* (ḥanṭūr: pl. hanātīr) are a delightful way of seeing provincial cities and visiting outlying cities. Their ranks are usually found close to the station and the drivers often know the area better than taxi-drivers; another advantage is that although slower, they can often travel where the taxi cannot.

**Camping facilities** are increasing in Egypt and can be found in all the major towns and coastal resorts.

**Maps**. Sheets for Egypt are available at 1:500,000 in the General World Series (published in Britain by G.S.C.S. ser. no. 1404 in several editions) and Tactical Pilotage Charts TPC H5D, at the same scale, which although very useful are deficient on place names and sites. The series D677, 1:100,000 is no longer available. There is a dearth of good and detailed maps of Egypt, but the best general map is the Freytag and Berndt *Egypt*.

# IV Postal and Other Services

**Postal Information**. Post Offices (*maktab al-barīd*) in Cairo open 08.30–15.00 hrs except Fri. Some of the staff speak English or French, though this should not be taken for granted. Notices are displayed in Arabic and French or English. Letter-boxes are red-painted with a train (inland post), blue with an aeroplane (overseas post) or green with a motor-cycle (internal express). Stamps (*tabʿ*) are available at special counters in the P.O. A registered letter is *khatāb musaggal*. Letters going abroad are sent by air; the service is erratic taking as little as four days, or as long as three weeks. Internal post is reasonable, but again unaccountable hold-ups occur.

*Parcels* require an export licence obtained from the P.O. in Maydān. al-ʿAtabah and the contents must be wrapped in front of an official. Parcels sent to Egypt are not delivered but a notice is sent to the addressee, giving the address of the P.O. where it may be collected. This notice should be taken to the office specified and opened before an official. Duty must be paid and varies, least on books and records, most on clothes and domestic machinery. Gifts are also taxed regardless of use.

**Telephones**. The service operates from separate offices. Calls can be made from private phones, cigarette kiosks or telephone booths in public places and hotels. The user must make sure of the type of coins the machine accepts, brass or alloy, they will not take both. Dial slowly and deliberately. Long distance calls (outside Cairo and the Delta) must be ordered at a Telephone Office and collected in a booth at the office or at any receiver specified, but it can often take some time to contact the other exchange. Overseas calls are also ordered at the Telephone Office and received in the same way. The full name and number of the person being called and the name, number and address of the caller will be needed, and they should be booked well in advance. *Telegrams* in English or French may be sent from the Main Telegram Office in Cairo, with the sender's full name. The Central TT offices at Shʿ. ʿAdlī and Shʿ. al-Alfī, Maydan Gīzah and Heliopolis (Shʿ Uzirīs) are open 24 hrs a day.

# V Hotels and Restaurants

**Hotels** (sing. funduq or lūkāndah: pl. fanādiq or lūkāndāt). There has been an explosion in hotel building in the past few years, the design and subsequent service of which, for better or worse, is of international standard. The building programme will eventually provide hotels at all the tourist sites but at present they exist only in a few of the main cities. But there are hotels of some sort in every city and town, though they may have to be enquired after. The main hotels are usually fully booked and reservations must be made well in advance. The Ministry of Tourism Office will provide a full list, with current rates.

Hotels are listed in six official categories, the terminology of which is rather fluid, running from 5* to Tourist Class. Most of the classified hotels have rooms with a private shower and/or bath and all except a few in the last category have a restaurant. Charges are fixed by the Government and have the force of law. The tariff, plus 10 per cent service charge, 2 per cent Govt tax and 5 per cent Municipal tax per person per day must be prominently displayed in the reception lobby and in each room. Despite official categorisation quality varies greatly and although the large international hotels provide everything the visitor could want, the older hotels often have a much friendlier, almost family, atmosphere, and the service is much more personal. In addition to these tourist hotels there are many others, used by the Egyptians themselves, and for those who can do without the brasserie and bar, they offer a much greater involvement with the Egyptian people. In some hotels visitors should be prepared to provide their own soap and towels and lavatory paper, if it is to be used, in addition to the water provided for the same purpose.

The visitor's passport should be handed to the registration clerk who will take the details and return it.

Only a selection of hotels is listed in this guide. Inclusion is not a recommendation of quality, just as omission is not a condemnation. Hotels are named merely to facilitate the search of the traveller for accommodation.

**Youth Hostels**. The Egyptian Youth Hostels Federation is affiliated to the International Y.H.F. The address is 7 Shʿ. Dr Hamid Saʿīd, Maʿrūf, Cairo, and it should be informed in advance of arrival. There are youth hostels at all the major centres and arrangements can be made to travel to more remote areas.

**Dining out**. Egyptian food can make no claim to be an *haute cuisine* and in the main is simply prepared to bring out the best in the abundant fruits, vegetables, fish and meat available in the country. The simplicity does not imply lack of quality—even the poorest Egyptian demands the best possible, the ingredients are very fresh and some vegetables may well have been in the ground the day before. The many restaurants and cafes in all Egyptian cities, accommodating every pocket and taste, are well patronised by Egyptian families who enjoy eating out, particularly in the speciality restaurants.

**Restaurants** (sing. matʿam: pl. matāʿam). Although large meals are often taken between noon and 2 pm the main meal is more likely to be eaten in the early evening, when the restaurants become very crowded, but most international hotels provide food at western times. Restaurants tend to specialise in certain types of food: fish, kabāb, game, etc. Several hamburger and fried chicken establishments with international names are springing up in the smarter areas but the vast majority of local restaurants still serve the particular delicacies of the area. In the specialist restaurants lemonade can be ordered but tea or coffee (Turkish) should be taken afterwards in an *qahwah* a cafe selling nothing else. Although simple sweets can usually be ordered in a restaurant, confectionery and pastries are best eaten in a shop specialising in these. The method of ordering is to go to the pay-counter, tell them what is wanted, pay for it and take the ticket given to you to the counter where the assistant will provide what you have paid for. Wine and beer are not generally available in most restaurants. The price of food is considerably below that in Britain and the portions are very large, it is usual to order kabāb by the kilo.

Water is always served even with cups of coffee. As a point of interest passers-by may sometimes ask you for this water, never refuse, they would be prepared to do the same for you.

Gumaʿah is the day of the Muslim assembly prayer and most shops are closed.

**Food.** Egyptian dishes are basically a combination of Arab and Turkish, robust and savoury, neither as oily as Greek food nor as heavily spiced as in some countries to the East. The international hotels serve international food in courses but in local establishments most dishes come to the table as they are cooked. The dishes usually first to appear are those that do not need to be cooked: turshī (pickle salad), ḥummus and ṭahīna (chick pea or sesame paste), fūl madammis (broad beans in oil), or various types of soup. The foundation of the meal is usually rice (*rū*), cooked simply, or occasionally pasta (*makarunah*), and the main course meat (*lahm*) or fish (*samak*), which may be baked (*fi 'l-furn*), grilled (*mashwī*), roast (*rustū*), fried (*ma'lī), or boiled (maslū'*).

Other dishes are combinations of meat and pasta or bread. A particularly delicious one is *ru'ā'*, a mixture of Egyptian bread, butter and minced meat cooked like a pie.

Vegetables are rarely served plain, but usually in tomato and onion sauce (*biṣalṣah*). Salads are always served with meals. Fruit usually follows the main dish. Sweets are often taken as a separate meal. They are mainly farinaceous, cornflour, fruit purees or confectionery of which there are many varieties, flaky pastry and nuts or small pastries steeped in syrup. A special diet is called a *rijīm*.

Special kiosks often sell food not prepared in the more conventional restaurants: *raghīf bí laḥm*), hot spiced minced meat in flat bread, or *fitīr*, pancakes with syrup.

The following are among the more usual foods served in restaurants or cafes:

### Appetisers

*ṭurshī*, mixed pickles
*fūl madamis*, broad beans, oil and lemon
*kishk*, yoghurt, onion and butter paste
*ḥummuṣ*, chick pea paste
*ṭa 'miyyah*, falafel, bean rissoles

### Shūrbah, Soups and Stews

*mulūkhiyyah*, Jew's mallow (Corchorus olitorius)
*shūrbat fūl nābit*, braod bean soup
*shūbat 'ads*, lentil soup
*kasarūlah*, casserole
*fattah*, lamb, rice and bread stews, a festival dish

### Samak, fish

*'ishr bayāḍī*, Nile perch
*bulṭī*, Nile circhlid
*'armūṭ*, catfish
*ringah*, herring
*samak mūsā*, flatfish
*būrī*, grey mullet
*murgān*, red mullet
*gambarī*, prawns

### Khudrawāt, Vegetables

*baṭāṭis*, potatoes
*naṭāṭah*, sweet potatoes
*fūl*, broad beans
*faṣūlyā*, haricot beans
*lūbyā*, string beans
*'ads*, lentils
*bisillah*, peas
*kūsah*, marrow
*'arnabiṭ*, cauliflower
*karumb*, cabbage
*gazar*, carrots
*lift*, turnip
*bāmiyah*, ladies' fingers, okra
*durrah*, maize
*firik*, green wheat
*bādingān*, aubergine

## al-Luhūm, Meats

*lahm dānī*, lamb
*lahm batilū*, veal
*lahm kandūz*, beef
*lahm gāmūsī*, buffalo meat
*lahm gamalī*, camel meat
*arnab*, rabbit
*firākh*, chicken
*dīk rūmī*, turkey
*baṭṭ*, duck
*wizzah*, goose
*ḥammām*, pigeons
*dibdah*, liver
*kilāwī*, kidney
*kawari'*, feet
*mūzah*, knuckle
*mukh*, brain
*kirshah*, tripe
*kabāb*, grilled meat
*shāwarmah*, similar to Turkish doner
*kuftah*, rissoles
*nīah*, rissoles
*lahm khinzīr*, pork
*maḥshī*, leaves or vegetables stuffed with meat and rice

## Salāṭah, Salads

*khass*, lettuce
*ṭamāṭim*, tomato
*'ūṭah*, tomato
*baṣal*, onion
*tūm*, garlic
*kurāt*, leek
*khiyyār*, cucumber
*filfil*, sweet pepper
*shaṭṭah*, hot pepper
*bangar*, beetroot
*figl*, radish
*gargīr*, watercress
*ba 'dūnis*, *shabat* } kinds of parsley

## Ḥalāwiyāt, Sweets and Pastries

*khushāf*, fruit compot
*'amr al-dīn*, apricot purée
*mahallabiyyah*, cornflour pudding
*bilaylah*, a milk dish with nuts, raisins and wheat
*ays krīm*, ice cream
*malban*, Turkish delight
*basbūsah*, semolina cake
*baklāwah*, flaky pastry and nuts
*'atayf*, wheat shredded with nuts
*kunāfah*, another variety
*zalābiyah*, pastries dipped in rosewater
*ghuraybah*, short-pastry cakes

## Fawākah, Fruit

*mishmish*, apricot
*kūkh*, peach
*kumitrah*, pear
*tufāh*, apple
*burtu 'āl*, orange
*yūsuf affandī*, tangerine
*līmūn*, lime
*māngah*, mango
*gawāfah*, guava
*mawz*, banana
*farāwlah*, strawberries
*balaḥ*, dates, many kinds
*tamr*, pressed dates
*ʿinab*, grapes, many kinds
*tīn*, figs
*gamīz*, sycamore figs
*tīn shawkī*, prickly pear
*rummān*, pomegranate
*batīkh*, water melon
*shammām*, melon
*kūz al-ʿasal*, musk melon
*tūt*, mulberries

## Sharbāt, Drinks

*mayyah*, water
*tamr hindī*, tamarind
*karkadayyah*, hibiscus
*ʿasīr 'asab*, sugar cane juice
*kharūb*, carob
*yansūn*, anis
*zangabīl*, ginger
*ʿara' sūs*, liquorice
*karāwiyyah*, caraway
*labban*, milk
*shāy*, tea
*'ahwah*, coffee, Turkish
*kākāw*, cocoa
*'irfah*, carella bark

## Miscellaneous

*khal*, vinegar
*zayt*, olive oil
*malḥ*, salt
*khubz*, bread
*ʿaysh*, bread
*bayḍ*, eggs
*murabbā*, jam
*ʿasal*, honey

*'ishdah*, cream
*zibdah*, butter
*gibnah*, cheese
*zubāydi*, yoghurt
*sukkar*, sugar
*naʿnāʿ*, mint
*tirmis*, lupin beans
*lib*, roasted seeds

# VI Language

**The Arabic Alphabet** *(al-Ḥurūf al-Abjadīyyah)*. The Arabic alphabet contains 29 letters, all except seven of which when written can be joined together. The joined letters are modified according to whether they are isolated, initial, medial or final. (See also the section on the Arabic Language, p103.)

CONSONANTS. In the following table the letters are given in all their forms and transliterated into Literary Arabic and the two vernaculars. The initial letter of the English word in brackets is an approximation of the sound of the letter. Those in square brackets are difficult for most European tongues and need to be learned from a speaker of Arabic, although an approximation is given of the letter represented.

VOWELS. All letters except ا , a vowel, are consonants, though و and ي also often perform the function of vowels. Vowels, often omitted in transcription, are indicated thus: َ fathah = a(at), ُ ḍammah = u(up); ِ kasrah = i(it). These are all short vowels but are lengthened or converted into dipthongs when combined with وا or ي .

Doubled letters and other necessities are indicated by other signs, thus: ْ sukun (resting) placed over consonants shows that there is no vowel.

ّ shaddah (strengthening) over a consonant indicates that it is doubled.
~ maddah (lenghthening) written over a ا shows that two alifs occur together.
ال (al) The definite article. In speech the ل of the definite article is modified according to the first letter of the word following:
the letters: ت ث د ذ ر ز س ش ص ض ط ظ ل ي
called sun-letters *(al-ḥurūf al-shamsīyyah)*, assimilate it, before all the others, called moon-letters *(al-ḥurūf al-qamarīyyah)*, it is pronounced as ال ,i.e. al.
ة tā marbutā (tied t) is a letter which may represent two sounds (h or t) according to certain grammatical rules, e.g. wikālah (hostel) but wikālat al-ghawrī.
ء hamzah is found in two forms:
hamzat al-qatʿ (cutting hamzah), a pure glottal stop demanding a vocal break in the word.
hamzat al-waṣl (joining hamzah) assists in the pronunciation of certain combinations of letters by indicating elision, thus ٱ .

Plurals entail a more fundamental change in the form of words than in European languages and, added consonants and supplementary vowels impose patterns too complex to expound here, but some examples are:
sing. رغيف (raghīf): pl. أرغفة (arghafah) = bread/breads
sing. دكان (dukkān): pl. دكاكين (dakākīn) = shop/shops
sing. كتاب (kitāb): pl. كتب (kutub) = book/books

**Transliteration.** There is no completely satisfactory system of conveying the sound of Arabic letters in Western languages. It is a problem that has taxed many scholars for a very long time. There are various local and international systems in use but the most modern and sophisticated of these are really designed to help the academic and

| **Arabic Letter** | | | | | **Transliteration** | | |
|---|---|---|---|---|---|---|---|
| *Isolated* | *Initial* | *Medial* | *Final* | *Name* | *Literary* | *N. Egypt* | *S. Egypt* |
| ا | as isolate | as final | ـا | *alif* | see vowels below | | |
| ب | بـ | ـبـ | ـب | *bāʾ* | b (bat) | *b* | *b* |
| ت | تـ | ـتـ | ـت | *tāʾ* | t (tab) | *t* | *t* |
| ث | ثـ | ـثـ | ـث | *thāʾ* | th (thin) | *t (tab)*<br>*s (set)* | *t*<br>*s* |
| ج | جـ | ـجـ | ـج | *jīm* | j (jam) | *g (get)* | *j* |
| ح | حـ | ـحـ | ـح | *ḥāʾ* | ḥ (aspirated h) | *ḥ* | *ḥ* |
| خ | خـ | ـخـ | ـخ | *khāʾ* | kh | *kh* | *kh* |
| د | as isolate | as final | ـد | *dāl* | d (dot) | *d* | *d* |
| ذ | as isolate | as final | ـذ | *d̲hāl* | d (that) | *d (dot)* | *d* |
| ر | as isolate | as final | ـر | *rāʾ* | r (rot) | *r* | *r* |
| ز | as isolate | as final | ـز | *zāy* | z (zero) | *z* | *z* |
| س | سـ | ـسـ | ـس | *sīn* | s (set) | *s* | *s* |
| ش | شـ | ـشـ | ـش | *shīn* | sh (ship) | *sh* | *sh* |
| ص | صـ | ـصـ | ـص | *ṣad* | ṣ (emphatic s) | *ṣ* | *ṣ* |
| ض | ضـ | ـضـ | ـض | *ḍād* | ḍ (emphatic d) | *ḍ* | *ḍ* |
| ط | طـ | ـطـ | ـط | *ṭāʾ* | ṭ (emphatic t) | *ṭ* | *ṭ* |
| ظ | ظـ | ـظـ | ـظ | *ẓāʾ* | ẓ (emphatic z) | *ẓ* | *ẓ* |
| ع | عـ | ـعـ | ـع | *ʿayn* | (constricted syrinx) | ʿ | ʿ |
| غ | غـ | ـغـ | ـغ | *ghayn* | gh (gargle) | *gh* | *gh* |
| ف | فـ | ـفـ | ـف | *fāʾ* | f (fat) | *f* | *f* |
| ق | قـ | ـقـ | ـق | *qāf* | q (guttural q) | *like hamzah* | *g (get)* |
| ك | كـ | ـكـ | ـك | *kāf* | k (kit) | *k* | *k (kit)* |
| ل | لـ | ـلـ | ـل | *lām* | l (lay) | *l* | *l (lay)* |
| م | مـ | ـمـ | ـم | *mīm* | m (mat) | *m* | *m (mat)* |
| ن | نـ | ـنـ | ـن | *nūn* | n (nut) | *n* | *n (nut)* |
| ه | هـ | ـهـ | ـه | *hāʾ* | h (hat) | *h* | *h (hat)* |
| و | as isolate | as final | ـو | *wāw* | w (wall) | *w* | *w (wall)* |
| ي | يـ | ـيـ | ـي | *yāʾ* | y (yet) | *y* | *y (yet)* |
| ء | carried on ا *or* ي و | | | *hamzah* | ʾ | ʾ | ʾ |

(indicates a break in vocalisation)

the results are often incomprehensible to the lay-reader. Whatever system is used some effort is required on behalf of the visitor, but probably the most useful system is that which bears some resemblance to the reader's own language.

It seems at first glance that several of the letters have similar sounds. This is true but the differences are vital and must be emphasised. The system used here is a slight modification of the old British Museum system and is used to transliterate both the literary and vernacular forms of Arabic in Egypt. To complicate matters, however, the names of towns on signheads and street plates are often the results of primitive 19C English or French systems of transliteration; where these have become well-known they are used and the literary form bracketed. Many of the colloquial vowel sounds vary widely from the classical form and are only approximations in transliteration.

There is a special problem concerning personal names from Tulunid times onwards, many of them Turkish. The Egyptian scribes and stonemasons were often quite ignorant of the correct form of these names in Arabic script, the result being that such names are neither correct nor consistent. There are also several sounds in Turkish that do not appear in Arabic and these were transliterated to the closest similar sound, *ch* for example becoming *j* (this of course becoming g in modern N Egyptian). This must be borne in mind when the visitor is searching for a particular monument and an example is given below:

Chakmak (Turkish) becomes Jaqmaq (Lit. Ar.), Gaqmaq (Mod. Egyptian), but in pronunciation it becomes Ga'ma'.

Numeration. (العـديـة : al-ʿadiyyah). Arabic figures are derived from the Sanskrit system but with the addition of صفر : ṣifr (zero) which was the contribution of the Muslim scientists, revolutionising theoretical mathematics. Unlike letters, Arabic figures are written in their original form from left to right. In the examples given below the pronunciation is in the N. Egyptian colloquial.

| | | | | | | | |
|---|---|---|---|---|---|---|---|
| 1 | ١ | واحد | wāḥid | 18 | ١٨ | ثمانية عشر | tamantāshar |
| 2 | ٢ | أثنين | itnayn | 19 | ١٩ | تسعة عشر | tisaʿtāshar |
| 3 | ٣ | ثلاثة | talātah | 20 | ٢٠ | عشرون | ʿashrīn |
| 4 | ٤ | أربعة | arbaʿah | 21 | ٢١ | واحد وعشرون | wāḥid wa ʿashrīn |
| 5 | ٥ | خمسة | khamsah | 22 | ٢٢ | إثنان وعشرون | itnayn wa ʿashrīn |
| 6 | ٦ | ستة | sittah | 30 | ٣٠ | ثلاثون | talatīn |
| 7 | ٧ | سبعة | sabaʿah | 40 | ٤٠ | اربعون | arbaʿīn |
| 8 | ٨ | ثمانية | tamanyah | 50 | ٥٠ | خمسين | khamsīn |
| 9 | ٩ | تسعة | tissaʿah | 100 | ١٠٠ | مائة | miyyah |
| 10 | ١٠ | عشرة | ʿasharah | 101 | ١٠١ | مائة وواحد | miyyah wa wāḥid |
| 11 | ١١ | إحد عشر | hadāshar | 200 | ٢٠٠ | مائتين | miyyatayn |
| 12 | ١٢ | إثنى عشر | itnāshar | 300 | ٣٠٠ | ثلاثمائة | talātahmiyyah |
| 13 | ١٣ | ثلاثة عشر | talatāshar | 1000 | ١٠٠٠ | ألف | alf |
| 14 | ١٤ | أربعة عشر | arbaʿatāshar | 1001 | ١٠٠١ | ألف وواحد | alf wa wāḥid |
| 15 | ١٥ | خمسة عشر | khamastāshar | 2000 | ٢٠٠٠ | الفين | alfayn |
| 16 | ١٦ | ستة عشر | sittatāshur | 3000 | ٣٠٠٠ | ثلاثة الاف | talātah alāf |
| 17 | ١٧ | سبعة عشر | sabaʿtāshur | | | | |

# VII General Information

**Manners and Customs.** CALENDAR AND TIME. Both the Islamic (Higari) and the Gregorian (Miladiyyah) calendars are in official use, the latter since the period of British Occupation in the 1880s. In addition the Coptic calendar is still valid among the Christians in Egypt and was used by Muslims for annual events until the aforementioned occupation. Egypt is 2 hrs ahead of G.M.T. and therefore one hour ahead of Britain during the period of B.S.T.

The four seasons are الربيع ; al-rabīʿ (spring): الصيف ; al-ṣayf (summer) الخريف ; al-kharīf (autumn) and الشتاء ; al-shitaʾ (winter)

## Months of the year

| Higra (AH) | Miladiyyah (A.D.) | Coptic (M.C.) |
| --- | --- | --- |
| محرم Muḥarram | يناير Yanayār | Tūt (11 Sept Greg. era) |
| صفر Ṣafar | فبراير Fibrāyar | Babāh |
| ربيع الأول Rabī' al-awal | مارس Mārs | Hatur |
| ربيع الثاني Rabī' al-tani | أبريل Abrīl | Kyhak |
| جمادى الأولى Gummādā al-ulā | مايو Mayū | Tūbah |
| جمادى الثانية Gummādā al-taniyyah | يونيو Yūnyū | Amshīr |
| رجب Ragab | يوليو Yūlyū | Baramhāt |
| شعبان Sha'bān | أغسطس Aghustus | Baramūdah |
| رمضان Ramaḍān | سبتمبر Sabtīmbir | Bashans |
| شوال Shawwāl | أكتربر Uktūbar | Baū'mah |
| ذو القعدة Zu'l-qa'da | نوفمبر Nūfimbir | Abīb |
| ذو الحجة Zu'l-higgah | ديسمبر Dīsambir | Misra |
| | | Nasī (supp. monthly) |

## Days of the week

| | | | |
| --- | --- | --- | --- |
| Saturday | السبت ; al-Sabt | Wednesday | الأربعاء ; al-Arb'ā |
| Sunday | الأحد ; al-Aḥad | Thursday | الخميس ; al-Khamīs |
| Monday | الاثنين ; al-Itnayn | Friday | الجمعة ; al-Guma'ah |
| Tuesday | الثلاثاء ; al-Talatā' | | |

Guma'ah is the day of the Muslim congregational prayer and most shops are closed.

The **Higrā year** is composed of 12 lunar months, each being 29 or 30 days long, depending on the appearance of the moon. It is thus 10 days shorter than the Gregorian year and moved forward relative to it by that period per year. Muḥarram is the first month of the Higra year, and Ramaḍān is the month in which Muslims fast. This is taken very seriously by many and it is best to avoid eating, drinking or smoking in public areas during that period. Dhū 'l-Ḥiggah is the month of the Ḥagg, the Pilgrimage to Mecca. The Muslim year corresponding to 1988 is 1408 until 14 Aug. when 1409 starts.

The **Coptic Calendar** is solar, consisting of 12 months each of 30 days and a thirteenth month of 5 days, based on the calendar of Ancient Egypt modified to accord with the Christian view. As the Coptic Church was not in communion with Rome, their calendar was not involved in the Gregorian Reform of 1582 and therefore still follows the Julian System. It dates from the persecution of the Emp. Diocletian in 284 and is called the Martyrs' Calendar.

**Health**. Visitors often experience stomach disorders of various kinds with diarrhoea (*ishāl*) and or vomiting (*istafragh*), usually of short duration but vicious while they last. The afflicted person should stay within easy reach of a toilet, eat nothing and drink only water, the latter necessary since the tissues become dehydrated. The best medicines are anti-spasmodics of which there are excellent proprietary brands on sale in Egypt. Do not accept the local remedy of lime juice in water. Prickly heat is rare in Egypt as humidity is low and perspiration dries immediately, but if afflicted frequent showers, talcum powder and loose clothes are the recommended treatment. Unpleasant seasonal experiences are the mosquitos (namūs) and fleas (barghīt). Although irritating it is best not to scratch the bites.

Colourless iodine is a soothing and detumescent lotion. Animal bites should be attended to immediately by a doctor or hospital. Carnivore bites can be rabid or at very least turn sceptic, as do camel bites. These tend to be lacerations; the wound can be persistent and turn necrotic if not treated right away. Snake (thu'bān) bites and scorpion ('akrab) stings should likewise be attended to with speed—it is very helpful to the doctor to have a description of the type of snake concerned (see p 144). Under no circumstances should any swimming be undertaken in still or slow-flowing water where the host snails of the disease *Bilharzia* are almost bound to occur. If the visitor accidentally falls into such water, a check-up on return from holiday is advised. If planning to spend some time in the countryside a tetanus inoculation is highly advisable as the rich earth is an ideal breeding ground for the bacteria. A course of anti-malaria tablets may also be useful. Although the disease is only of spasmodic occurrence in Egypt, there is a general resurgence throughout the world. Great care should be taken of the feet. Despite taxis and other transport there is still a great deal of walking to be done at the sites. Blisters and abrasions should receive immediate attention.

It is advisable to take out a health insurance policy before leaving the UK.

**Public Holidays**. Official holidays in Egypt follow the two calendars: Islamic festivals the Higrā calendar and thus move forward through the Gregorian calendar each year. These holidays are 1 Muḥarram (Rā's al-Sanā; New Year's Day, July–May 1990s); 12 Rabī'al-Awal (Mūlid al-Nabī; Birthday of the Prophet, September–July 1990s); 1–3 Shawwāl following the end of Ramaḍān; 'Id al-Fitr: April–February 1990s); 10–13 Dhū 'l-Ḥiggah, the month of the Pilgrimage; 'Id al-Aḍḥah, June–April 1990s). The two latter festivals are called by the Turkish names of Ramaḍān Bayrām and Kurbān Bayrām by some Egyptians. The fixed holidays are 1 January, New Year's Day; 22 February, Union Day; 8 March, Syrian National Day; 1 May, Labour Day; 18 June, Evacuation Day (British left Egypt); 23 July, Revolution Day; 1 September, Libyan National Day; 6 October, National Day; 23 October, Suez National Day; 23 December, Victory Day. In addition to these is Sham al-Nassīm (Smelling the Breeze), a spring festival with very ancient roots, probably stretching back to Pharaonic times, falling on the first Monday following Easter. The Coptic festivals recognised only by the Christian community are 7 January, Christmas; 19 January, Epiphany; Easter, not fixed; 21 March, Annunciation, besides many Saints' days.

All the festivals are excuses for marches and celebrations, but the most important is the 'Id al-Aḍḥah. For days prior to 10 Dhū 'l-Ḥiggah the streets are full of sheep, goats, cows and buffaloes waiting to be slaughtered. Visitors are advised to avoid the residential areas of the towns on that day if upset by the sight of blood as the animals are killed, cut up and skinned.

**Shops** are open on weekdays (Saturday–Thursday) 09.30 or 10.00–13.00 or 13.30 and from 16.30 or 17.00–19.30 or 20.00. Most shops are closed on Fridays. Hours in Ramaḍān are usually 09.30–16.30 and again from 20.00–24.00. There are chemists open in the large cities 24 hours a day. Souvenirs are obtainable in the suq (market) of most towns, usually aimed at the tourist market, the best value being the crafts of leatherwork, wood carving, mashrabiyyah work and woven tapestries. Works of art and reproductions can be bought at the Centre for Applied Arts (Rte 12), the artists producing beautiful work in wood, glass, metalwork and fabric. If given enough time objects can be created to order.

*Kiosks* are open for the greater part of the day and sell all manner of sundries.

**Museums and Archaeological Sites**. Admission is charged to a great many of the Pharaonic sites, museums and Islamic sites. The charges vary widely, the better-known sites being the most expensive. The opening hours vary with the season and should be checked under the site concerned. Some are not open on Friday or Sunday, others not in the afternoon. A recent innovation at large sites is to sell tickets for groups of monuments. Make sure that your tickets include the specific monuments you wish to visit. At sites off the beaten track it is often the case that somebody in the neighbourhood (ghafīr; watchman) has the key. It must be remembered that some sites are extremely dangerous and great care must be taken in climbing over ruins. To locate unmarked sites it is often the best policy to find an older local who knows the area well. It is perhaps timely to mention that many of the sites are liberally strewn with pieces of broken masonry, sherds, flints and bones, but the natural inclination to pick them up and keep them as souvenirs should be resisted, since the penalty could be up to four years imprisonment.

Since the recent use of locations in Egypt by several film companies some sites have increased the cost of camera permits considerably. The system however is confusing and no money should be handed over except to a government official in return for a permit.

Monuments are called athār, (pron. asār), Ancient Egyptian: fara'ūniyyah, Islamic: islamiyyah and Christian: qibṭiyyah.

All the Islamic monuments in Cairo are numbered from 1–622, although about 100 have subsequently disappeared or been demolished. They are marked with a small green and white oval enamel panel (see illustration) with the number in Arabic. Some of them, particularly in the Southern Cemetery (Rte 15) for some reason, have suffered the depradations of small boys with stones and have lost all their enamel; however the plaques remain in place to identify them as monuments.

٤٠١

Great care should be taken on entering mosques, especially those still in use. Do not enter while the prayer is in progress, which will usually take about 10 minutes five times a day, but an hour for the major prayer (guma') on Friday. Shoes should be removed or covered with the slippers supplied and clean and respectable clothes worn. The reaction of some of the faithful is unpredictable if these simple precautions are ignored. This also holds while visiting any monument in the more conservative areas in Cairo.

It is advisable, when visiting monuments, both inside and outside Cairo, to wear stout shoes—canvas with thick soles are ideal—as there is often quite a lot of walking and general scrambling about to be done. Sandals are really useless, except for hotel foyers. In Cairo try to avoid visiting monuments at times when children are coming out of school, i.e. between 12.00–14.00. You will be beseiged with well-meaning 'helpers' but the result is general mayhem.

**Equipment**. Sunglasses are recommended as the light is very strong. An electric torch is a necessity for some of the darker sites and for the occasional electrical blackouts. Binoculars are very useful but in the present climate should not be used indiscriminately, ask permission to use them first. The electricity supply in Egypt is 220 volts, and the sockets accept plugs with two round pins.

**Newspapers**. There is one daily English language newspaper, the *Egyptian Gazette*, founded 1880 and its Saturday edn. *The Egyptian Mail*. English newspapers are available, usually two days late, at most of the kiosks in the centre of Cairo.

**Weights and Measures**. The metric system has been adopted by Egypt.

**Season**. The best time of year to visit Egypt if a tour of the sites is to be undertaken is definitely winter, November–May; if for pleasure and sunbathing autumn is the best season. During this period the beaches are not so crowded and there is almost continuous sunshine though the days are rather short. The N coast in spring and early summer can be rough and stormy and the water rather cold at about 15°C. In summer the temp. rises to 25°C. In Cairo temps in winter are 15.8°C and in summer 28°C. Aswan naturally has the highest temperatures—in winter 16.6°C and in summer 33.8°C. Rain is rare in the Nile Valley from Cairo southwards but a much more annoying hazard is the khamasīn (fifty), the dust storm that lasts for what seems like that number of days.

# I CAIRO

**Cairo**, officially al-Qāhirah but popularly and normally referred to as Miṣr (pron. Maṣr), the capital of the Arab Republic of Egypt, is situated at lat. 30°.03′ N and long. 31°.15′ E. The city occupies a triangular plain with the narrowest point to the S on the East Bank of the River Nile where the Muqaṭṭam Hills make their closest approach to the river. The river and the hills form the W and E boundaries respectively. The N limits open onto the extreme N of the Eastern Desert. It is designated as an independent muhāfazah (province) divided into 23 iqsām (districts). Included within Greater Cairo (al-Qāhirah al-Kubrā') on the West Bank of the Nile are several districts of the Province of al-Gīzah and to the N others in the province of Qalyūbiyyah. The total population is now estimated at over 12 million, and including the outlying suburbs occupies c 100 sq. km. The city has two nuclei: the original area of settlement of the Arabs in the SW now called *Miṣr al-Qadīmah* (Old Miṣr), and the later enclosed town of *al-Qāhirah*, the two areas gradually coalescing, while around them new suburbs opened up.

In Cairo the older areas in the main still retain their medieval form, and many of the streets are known from descriptions of them given by early chroniclers. The Ottomans made little contribution to the design of the city but during the 19C it expanded and developed at an unprecedented rate. The newer areas thus have much in common with European cities in general and specific areas with French or English town planning in particular. The architecture, however, is a combination of Ottoman and European elements, commercial building owing more to the latter, especially in the city centre. The suburbs, many of them undergoing extensive rebuilding, are undistinguished with great rectangular blocks of concrete flats. The older areas with their traditional tenements surrounding a central courtyard are very attractive and though they have much in common with those in other Arab cities, nonetheless possess a feeling that is entirely Egyptian.

There are many names for street in Arabic, the most usual being Shāriʿ, abbreviated to Shʿ. Others are Ṭarīq, Darb, Sikkat, ʿAtfat, Zuqāq and Ḥārat, all written in full. Maydān, a square or large area, is also written in full. **Plan references** refer to the 32-page colour section between pp160 and 161, the first figure denoting the page and the second the square. An excellent book of street maps *Cairo A–Z* is published by Palm Press in Egypt. Of necessity it does not contain many of the smaller backstreets.

**Airport** at *Heliopolis*, 15km from Maydān Taḥrīr, for both international and internal flights. Reached by bus Nos 400 from Maydān Taḥrīr or 410 from Maydān al-ʿAtabah.

**Railway Station.** *Maḥaṭṭat Miṣr*, occupying the whole of the NW side of Maydān Ramsīs, is the only mainline station in the city, with separate sections for the Delta and Nile Valley tracks. Most of the major cities can be reached from here, the suburbs of which are served by smaller gauge tracks.

**Hotels.** A selection only is given below, but there are many others scattered throughout the city.

*Maydān Taḥrīr to Maydān Ramsīs.* **Nile Hilton** (Pl14, 3), Maydān Taḥrīr; **Ramesses Hilton** (Pl14, 1), Shʿ. 6 Uktubur; **Semiramis Intercontinental**, (Pl 14, 3) Cornish al Nil; all 5*. **Cleopatra** (Pl14, 4), 2 Shʿ. al-Bustān, 1A, 4*; **Cosmopolitan** (Pl15, 1), Shʿ. Ibn Thaʿlab; **Fontana** (Pl8, 2), Maydān Ramsīs; **Victoria** (Pl8, 6), 66 Shʿ. al-Gumhūriyyah; all 3*. **Everest** (Pl8, 2), Maydān Ramsīs; **Qaṣr al-Nīl** (Pl15, 1), 33, Shʿ.

Qaṣr al-Nīl; **Mena Palace** (Pl8, 6), 5 Shʿ. al-Gumhūriyyah; all 2*. **Garden City House** (Pl8, 6), 23 Shʿ. Kamāl al-Dīn Ṣalāḥ; **Luna Park** (1*). **Cairo Palace** (Pl8, 6), Shʿ. al-Gumhūriyyah; T.

*Maydān Taḥrīr to Ḥadīqat al-Azbakiyyah.* **Atlas** (Pl15, 2), Shʿ. Muḥ. Rushdī; 4*. **Continental Savoy** (Pl8, 8), Maydān Obira; 3*. **National** (Pl15, 1), 30 Shʿ. Ṭalaʿat Ḥarb; **Lotus** (Pl15, 1), 12 Shʿ. Ṭalaʿat Ḥarb; **Tulip** (Pl15, 1), 3 Shʿ. Ṭalaʿat Ḥarb; all 2*. **Minerva** (Pl15, 1), 29 Shʿ. Ṭalaʿat Ḥarb; **Golden Hotel** (Pl15, 1), 13 Shʿ. Ṭalaʿat Ḥarb; **Grisham House** (Pl15, 1), 20 Shʿ. Ṭalaʿat Ḥarb; all 1*. **City** (Pl8, 1), 8 Shʿ. al-Ginaynat Azbak; **Opera** (Pl8, 1), 20 Shʿ. al-Sinbātī; both T.

*Garden City*, **Shepheard's** (Pl14, 5), Cornish al-Nil (overlooking the Nile); **Meridien** (Pl20, 2), Cornish al-Nīl, (on Rawḍah Island with views of the Nile all round); both 5*. **El-Nīl** (Pl14, 5), 16 Shʿ. Aḥ. Raghab; 4*.

*al-Gazīrah to Duqqī.* **Sheraton** (Pl13, 5), Maydān Kubrī al-Galāʾ; 5*. **Cairo Marriot** (Pl13, 4), Shʿ. Sarāy al-Gazīrah; 5* (Khedive Ismāʿīl's palace). **El-Gezira Sheraton** (Pl.13, 6) 5*. **Al-Burg** (Pl13, 4), Shʿ. Sarāy al-Gazīrah; 4*. **Atlas Zamalek**, Shʿ. al-Duwwal al-ʿArabiyyah; 4*. **Sherazade** (Pl4, 6), 182 Shʿ. al-Nīl; **Tonsi** (Pl13, 5), 143 Shʿ. al-Taḥrīr; both 3*. **Balmoral House** (Pl5, 4), 159 Shʿ. 26 Yūlyū; 1*. **Pension Zamalik** (Pl5, 3), 6 Shʿ. Ṣalāḥ al-Dīn; T.

*Maydān al-ʿAtabah to Maydān al-Ḥusayn.* **Khān al-Khalīlī** (Pl16, 1), 7 Shʿ. al-Bustāh; 3*. **al-Ḥusayn** (Pl17, 2), Maydān al-Ḥusayn; 2*. **Central** (Pl16, 1), 7 Shʿ. al-Bustāh; 1*. **Tourist Palace** (Pl0, 0), 21 Shʿ. al-Bidaq; T.

*Shʿ. 26 Yūlyū.* **Carlton** (Pl8, 7), 21 Shʿ. 26 Y; **Horris** (Pl8, 8), 5 Shʿ. 26 Y; **Scarabee** (Pl8, 7), 16 Shʿ. 26 Y; all 3*. **Ambassador** (Pl8, 7), 31 Shʿ. 26 Y; **Grand Hotel** (Pl8, 7), 17 Shʿ. 26 Y; **Omayed** (Pl8, 7), 22 Shʿ. 26 Y; all 2*. **Nasser** (Pl8, 8), 1 Shʿ. 26 Y; **Summer Palace** (Pl8, 8), 3 Shʿ. 26 Y; both T.

**Youth Hostels** (Buyūt al-Shabāb). Shʿ. Abd al-ʿAzīz al-Saʿūd (Rawḍah Island); Shʿ. Ibrahīm, Garden City; Shʿ. Tharwat, Giza. *YMCA*, 72 Shʿ. al-Gumhūriyyah; *YWCA*, 11 Shʿ. ʿImad al-Dīn.

*al-Muquttam.* **Bel Air Cairo Hotel; 4*.**

*Heliopolis.* **Cairo Concorde**, Airport; 5*. **Heliopolis Uruba**, Shʿ. ʿUruʿbaʿ; 5*. **Hyattal-Salam**, Shʿ. Ḥamīd al-Badawī; 5*. **Novotel**, Airport; 4*. **Transit Hotel Egyptair**, Airport; 4*. **Baron Hotel**, Shʿ. ʿUruba; 4*. **Beirut**, Shʿ. Bayrūt; 3*. **Egyptian Riviera Tours**, Shʿ. Muḥ. Yūsuf; 2*.

*Pyramids.* **Mena House Oberoi**, Shʿ. al-Ahrām; 5*. **Siag Pyramids**, Shʿ. Ṣaqqārah; 5*. **Ramadu Renaissance**, Alex. Desert Road; 5*. **Green Pyramids**, Shʿ. al-Ahrām; 3*. **Abu El Hoal**, Shʿ. al-Ahrām; 2*.

**Restaurants.** Omitting those attached to the large hotels some of the more interesting are: *Estoril*, 12 Shʿ. Talaʿat Harb; *Manyal Palace* (Club Mediteranée), Rawdah Island; *Rex*, 33 Shʿ. ʿAbd al-Khalīq Tharwat; *Union*, 28 Shʿ. 26 Yūlyū; these all have western cuisines. *Andrea*, Shʿ. al-Ahrām; *Casino des Pigeons*, Kubrī ʿAbbās; *Kursaal*, 717 Shʿ. al-Alfī.

**Clubs.** All the large hotels have nightclubs, but there are many others throughout the city and along the Shʿ. al-Ahrām. Some have traditional acts, others tend to be discotheques.

**Cafés.** Again there are cafés inside all the large hotels and many others can be found throughout the city. Of particular interest is *Groppi's* with three branches: Maydān Ṭalaʿāt Ḥarb; 2 Shʿ. ʿAbd al-Khalīq Tharwat (the restaurant that has entered the folklore of many servicemen who served in the Middle East), and at Heliopolis.

**Qahwah.** Serving only tea or coffee, these are found at almost every corner and side street, populated mostly by locals playing ṭawlah (backgammon). Shishas (water-pipes) can be hired.

**Post Offices.** (Postal Services) Maydān al-ʿAtabah (Pl16,1), ʿAyn Shams University; (Telegrams and Telephones) Shʿ. al-ʿAdlī, Shʿ. al-Alfī.

**Information Bureaux.** Ministry of Tourism Offices, 5 Shʿ. al-ʿAdlī (Pl7,8); Khān al-Khalīlī (Pl17,2); Maydān Ramsīs (Pl8,2); Pyramids Village, Gīzah; Cairo Airport.

**Travel Agents.** Many in the city centre and at the Airport. A few of the larger are listed here: *American Express*, 15 Sh'. Qaṣr al-Nīl; *Eastmar*, 13 Sh'. Qaṣr al-Nīl; *Egyptian Aviation and Travel Services*, 20 Sh'. Ṭala'āt Ḥarb; *International Wagons-Lits*, c/o Shepheard's Hotel; *Miṣr Tours*, 7 Sh'. Ṭala'āt Ḥarb; *Thomas Cook*, 4 Sh' Champollion. *Zenith Tours*, 19 Sh'. Kamal al-Dīn Ṣalāḥ.

**Shipping Offices.** *Adriatica*, 12 Sh'. Ṭala'āt Ḥarb; *Cairo Shipping Agency*, 7 Sh'. 'Abd al-Khalīq Tharwat; *Egyptian Navigation Co.*, 20 Sh'. Ṭala'āt Ḥarb; *North African Shipping Co.*, 171 Sh'. Muḥ Farīd. To Sudan, *Nile Navigation Co.*. 8 Sh'.Qaṣr al-Nil. Aswan-Wadi Halfa. Mon and Thurs.

**Airline Offices.** *British Airways*, (Pl14,4) 1 Sh'. Bustanīn; *Air France*, (Pl15,1), 2 Maydān Ṭala'āt Ḥarb; *Egypt Air* (Pl0,0), 6 Sh'. 'Adlī; (Pl7,8), Nile Hilton; *Lufthansa* (Pl15,1), 9 Sh'. Ṭala'āt Ḥarb; *PANAM* (Pl15,1), 2 Sh'. Ṭala'āt Ḥarb; *QANTAS* (Pl14,4), 22 Sh'. Qaṣr al-Nīl; *TWA* (Pl14,4), 1 Sh'. Qaṣr al-Nīl.

**Taxicabs** are best obtained outside the large hotels or hailed in the street. Charges: Fares are fixed at a certain price for first km and increased for each additional 100 m. Car hire from *Limousine Miṣr*; *Avis*, 16 Ma'mal al-Sukkar; *Hertz*, 195 Sh'. 26 July.

**Local Railways.** *Kubrī Līmūn*, NE side of Maydān Ramsīs, adjoining mainline station. Metro to Miṣr al-Gadīdah (Heliopolis) via 'Abd al-'Azīz Fahmī, Mirghānī, Maṭariyyah and Nuzhah; Madīnat Naṣr via al-Darāsah and Nuzhah. al-Marg-Ḥalwān Metro, to the N. Services to al-Marg via Dimirdāsh, Zaytūn and 'Ayn Shams; Shibīn al-Qanātir via Abū Za'bal and Khānkah, to the S Ḥalwān via Miṣr al-Qadīmah and Ma'ādī. The line runs underground through central Cairo—Sayyidah Zaynab-Mubarak (Ramsīs) (opened in Sept. 1987).

**City and Suburban Buses.** Between Maydān al-Taḥrīr and al-Azbakiyyah a one-way system operates (except for trams) and the outward routes of buses do not coincide with inward routes. When catching buses take care to check whether the number has a stroke (/) before it. The two types of bus often take different routes.

**Autobuses** (al-Utūbīs). There are 294 routes covering the whole of Greater Cairo (a total of 3500km), with 128 termini. Below is a selection of routes from the main city centres which visitors will find useful, but there are many others.

*From Maydān al-Taḥrīr*. **8** to Pyramids. **/43** to al-Maṭariyyah. **/50** to Miṣr al-Gadīdah (Heliopolis). **66** to Maydān Aḥmad Mahir and al-Azhar. **92** to Gāmi' 'Amr. **140** to Athār al-Nabī. **160** to Sayyidah Zaynab. **210** to Qanāṭir al-Khayriyyah. **400** to Maṭār al-Qahirah (Airport). **900** to Pyramids.

*From Maydān al-'Atabah*. **10** to al-Gīzah. **14** to Mathaf al-Zarā'ī. **17** to Būlāq al-Dakrūr. **43** to al-Maṭariyyah. **50** to Miṣr al-Gadīdah (Heliopolis). **/81** to Imām al-Shafi'ī. **89** to Ḥadā'iq Zaynhum. **/93** to Gāmī 'Amr. **401** to al-Muqaṭṭam. **410** to Maṭār al-Qāhirah (Airport).

*From Maydān al-Ramsīs*. **18** to Imbābah; **30** to Pyramids (al-Ahrām); **174** to al-Qal'ah (Citadel); **412** to al-Ma'ādī; **431** to Ḥalwān.

**Mini-buses** (Mīnī bās), carrying a maximum of 21 passengers, have 61 routes divided among five areas: *North Cairo* (green trim): routes **1–10** to Bigam, and al-Māzāh; *East Cairo* (orange trim): routes **21–34** out to Heliopolis and the Airport; *Central Cairo* (red trim): routes **41–45**; *South Cairo* (fawn trim): routes **51–57** to Basatīn and al-Ma'ādī; *Gīzah* (blue trim): routes **71–85** to Imbābah and the Pyramids. Many of the mini-buses terminate at al-'Atabah, Taḥrīr or Ramsīs Square.

**Trams** (al-Tirāmi) run mainly N–S with 21 routes from al-Māẓah and 'Abbāsiyyah to Imām Shafi'ī and Ḥalwān. In the central city the main termini are at Ramsīs and al-'Atabah Square.

**Water buses** (al-Utūbīs al-Nahrī): eight buses (**1–6**) run from Shubrā' al-Khaymah to al-Ma'ādī serving the central city. They run for six days a week but on public holidays are used for excursions to al-Qanāṭir. Stops at Shubrā al-Khaymah, al-Galā', al-Sāhil, Imbābah, Miṣr al-Qadīmah, Gīzah, al-Markaz, Abū 'l-Fīdā', Gāmi'ah and al-Ma'ādī.

**Long-distance Bus Stations**. *Sharq al-Daltā* (from Maydān al-Qullalī), E Delta. Dumiyāṭ, Port Sa'īd, Ismā'īliyyah and Suez via Banhā, Zagāzīg, Bilbays and al-Manṣūrah. *Wasiṭ al-Daltā* (from Maydān Aḥmad Ḥilmī and Maydān Khazindar, Central Delta, Manūfiyyah, Ṭanṭa, Kfar al-Shaykh and Shibīn al-Kawm. *Gharb al-Dalta* (from Sh'. Aḥmad Ḥilmī), W Delta, Alexandria, 'Alamayn, Marsah Matrūḥ via (Desert route) Wādī Nāṭrūn, (Delta route) Banhā, Damamhūr. *Wagh al-Qiblī* (S areas) (from Sh'. Aḥmad Ḥilmi and Giza), Nile Valley and Red Sea Coast, Fayyūm, Asyūṭ and Luxor. **al-Sīnā'** (from Madīnat Naṣr) to all areas in Sinai, al-'Arīsh in the N and St. Katherine's Monastery in the S.

**Embassies, Legations and Consulates.** *United Kingdom* (and New Zealand), Sh'. Aḥ. Raghab, Garden City (Pl14, 5); *Australia*, 1097 Cornish al-Nīl (Pl14, 7); *Canada*, 6 Sh'. Muḥ. Fahmī al-Sayyid, Garden City (Pl14, 6); *France*, 29 Sh'. Gīzah (Pl13, 7) and (visas) 5 Sh'. al-Faḍl (Pl0, 0); *Germany*, 20 Sh'. Būlus Hannā (Pl13, 5) *USA* 5 Sh'. Amrīka al-Latiniyyah (Pl14, 5); *Sudan*, 1 SH'. Muḥ. Fahmī (Pl14, 6).

**Churches**. ANGLICAN AND EPISCOPALIAN: *All Saint's Cathedral* (See of Jerusalem), Sh'. al-Gazīrah, Zamālik; EVANGELICAL: *St Andrew's United Protestant Church*, 39 Sh'. 26 Yūlyū; CATHOLIC: *Church of the Holy Family*, 55 Sh'. 15 Ma'ādī, *St Joseph's Church* (Franciscan), 2 Sh'. Bank Miṣr, *Chapel of St Charles Borromeo* (German Sisters), 8 Sh'. Muḥ. Maḥmūd, Bāb al-Lūq, *Cordi Jesu Church of the Fathers of Verona* (Combonian Friars), 3 Sh'. 'Abd al-Khalīq Tharwat, *St Joseph's Church of the Fathers of Verona* (Combonian Frs), 4 Sh'. Aḥmad Sabrī, Zamalik, *St Theresa of the Child Jesus* (Carmelite Friars), 163 Sh'. Shubrā; CHRISTIAN SCIENCE SOCIETY: 3 Maydān Muṣṭafā Kāmil.

In addition there are many churches throughout the city catering for the Orthodox Rite and Eastern Catholic Rite with services in Coptic, Arabic, Armenian and Greek.

SYNAGOGUE: Sh' 'Adlī.

**Banks**. Head Offices. *Central Bank of Egypt*, 31 Sh'. Qaṣr al-Nīl; *National Bank of Egypt*, 24 Sh'. Sharīf; *Bank Miṣr*, Sh'. Muḥ. Farīd (also in all large hotels); *Bank of Cairo*, 22 Sh'. 'Adlī; *Bank of Alexandria*, 49 Sh'. Qaṣr al-Nīl. Most international banks have branches in Cairo with exchange facilities.

**Learned Institutions**. *Institute d'Egypte*, 13 Sh'. Sh. Rīhan; *Academy of the Arabic Language*, 15 Sh'. 'Azīz 'Abāzah (Zamālik); *Egyptian Geographical Society*; Min. of Irrigation, Sh'. Qaṣr al-'Ayni; *Egyptian Medical Society*, 42 Sh'. Qaṣr al-'Aynī; *Egyptian Botanical Society*, Tagir Building, 1 Sh'. Uzirīs; *Zoological Society of Egypt*, Zoological Gardens, Gīzah; *Societe Entomologique d'Egypte*, 14 Sh'. Ramsīs; *Academy of Scientific Research and Technology*, 101 Sh'. Qaṣr al-'Aynī, *Agricultural Research Centre*, Min. of Agriculture, Gīzah; *Research Institute for tropical medicine*, 10 Sh'. Qaṣr al-'Aynī; *Institute of Astronomy and Geophysics*, Halwān; *National Information and Documentation Centre*, Sh'. al-Tahrīr (Duqqī); *Dār al-Kutub* (National Library), Sh'. Kurnish (Būlāq); *Institute of Arab Research and Studies*, 1 Sh'. Tulumbat; *Centre of Documentation Studies on Ancient Egypt*, 3 Sh'. al-'Ādil Abū Bakr (Zamālik); *Society for Coptic Archaeology*, 222 Sh'. Ramsīs; *The African Society*, 5 Sh'. Aḥ. Hishat (Zamālik); *Academy of Arts*, Sh'. al-Afghānī, (Giza); *Egyptian Association for Library and Information Science*, Faculty of Arts, Cairo University; *Institut Français d'Archaeologie Orientale*, 37 Sh'. Sh. Rīhān; *Higher Council of Arts and Literature*, 9 Sh'. Hasan Sabrī; *Institute of Arabic Music*, 22 Sh'. Ramsis.

**Clubs**. *Automobile and Touring Club of Egypt*, 10 Sh'. Qaṣr al-Nīl; *Egyptian Cultural Club*, 1 Sh'. Usiris, Tāgir Building, Garden City. See also **Sport.**

**Booksellers.** *American University Bookshop*, 113 Sh'. Qaṣr al-'Aynī; *Lehnert and Landrock*, 44 Sh'. Sharīf Bāshā; *Dār al-Ma'ārif*, 27 Sh'. 'Abd al-Khaliq Tharwat; *Anglo-Egyptian Bookshop*, 165 Sh'. Muḥ-Farid; *al-Shuruq*, 1 Maydan Tal'at Harb. Many others throughout the city, Square, and Maydān al-Ḥusayn.

**Theatres.** *Cairo Opera House*, Hurīyyah Gardens, international ballet, opera and music concerts; *Cairo Puppet Theatre* (puppets from national and visiting troupes), 26 Sh'. 26 Yūlyū; *Cairo University Theatre*, Music and dance by local and visiting groups; *Egyptian National Circus*, 'Abbāsiyyah and 'Agūzah, with many visiting acts; *Umm Kulthum* (formerly Balloon Theatre), Sh'. al-Nīl (Oct–May); *Sayyid*

*Darwish Concert Hall*, Shʿ. Gamāl al-Dīn al-Afghānī; *Sphinx Theatre* (below Pyramids, ballet and concerts in summer); *Zākī Ṭulaymāt Theatre* (prev. Pocket Theatre), Maydān al-ʿAtabah (avant-garde productions); *Sound and Light* at the Pyramids (see Rte 23). In summer there are free folk concerts and dance in the Azbakiyyah Gardens.

**Cinemas.** Many throughout the city. The majority of films are in Arabic, usually with French or English sub-titles. American, Indian, Chinese and Italian films predomiominate the rest with various combinations of English, French and Italian dubbing and sub-titles.

**Public Lavatories** (dawrat miyyāh) are found throughout the city but are inadequately marked. Women are poorly catered for. Men can with care use the facilities of local mosques, but women really have to rely on hotels and rest houses.

**Baths** (sing. ḥammām; pl. ḥammamāt). Unlike toilets there are many of these. The surroundings are rather spartan and the process rigorous, but they perform their function very well.

**Festivals.** Great parade at Madīnat Naṣr on *National Day* (6 October) and other parades held throughout the city on other public holidays. Mulids are held for various shaykhs during the year and are noted in the text.

**Sport.** Temporary membership can be obtained for most of the Sporting Clubs in Cairo, where all sports imaginable can be enjoyed. *Gazirah Sporting Club*, al-Gazīrah; *Heliolido Sporting Club*, Shʿ. Galāl, Heliopolis; *Heliopolis Sporting Club*, Shʿ. Mirghānī, Heliopolis; *Maʿadī Sporting and Yacht Club*, 8 Shʿ. al-Dimashq, Maʿadī; *Nadī Itihād al-Gumhūriyyah*, Shʿ. ʿAbd al-Ḥamīd Badawī, Heliopolis; *Shooting Club*, Shʿ. Nādī al-Sayyid, Duqqī; *Tawfiqiyyah Tennis Club*, Madīnat al-Awqāf, ʿAgūzah; *Cairo Yacht Club*, Shʿ. al-Nīl, Giza; *Turf Club*, 8 Shʿ. ʿAbd al-Kadīr Ḥamzah.

*Bargaining*. Except in food shops and the large 'Prixfixe' shops in the centre the general method of purchase is bargaining, which is a very subtle and protracted process. Except in the general tourist areas it is best not attempted. If it is, a light-hearted approach is preferable.

**History.** The area within 20km of modern Cairo has been settled since the earliest times, as there is evidence of Late Palaeolithic settlements at ʿAyn Shams to the NE and Neolithic settlements at Maʿādī, now a southern suburb. But it was not until the establishment of Memphis, 15km to the S on the West Bank, as the capital of the unified kingdom that the area assumed the importance it has since retained. Memphis was founded, c 3100 BC, doubtless because of the unique significance of the site with its command of both the Nile Valley and the Delta. Another early cult centre 9km to the NE, On, called Heliopolis by the Greeks, also developed into an important city, and a canal cut from the Nile passed close to it. The road between these two cities crossed the river at the southernmost point of Rawḍah Island and on the West Bank was a small settlement. The plain on the East Bank remained unsettled however, a desolate area with several large lakes left by the retreating river which was gradually moving westward at this point. During the late Dynastic period a small fortress settlement called Khery-Aha was built to guard the crossing. This assumed greater importance during the Assyrian or Persian occupation, c 500 BC, when it was named Babylon and fortified.

By the time of the Roman conquest in 30 BC Memphis was second only to Alexandria in population but Heliopolis had dwindled to a ghost city. The emperor, Trajan, appreciating the obvious military importance of the site, had his commander Turbo rebuild the fortress of Babylon and installed one of the three Roman Legions there. Ptolemy the geographer, visiting the area in the 2C, stated that there was a thriving town surrounding the fortress through which ran a canal.

The history of the following centuries is obscure, but with the rise of Christianity and the mass conversions Memphis was abandoned completely while the small settlement of Giza on the West Bank grew into a large town. Babylon was important enough to be the seat of a bishopric, while Tendunyas to the N, the original port of Heliopolis, had also expanded into a sizeable community.

The history of Egypt at this period was tied to that of the Eastern Roman Empire from the assumption of Arcadius as Eastern Emperor in AD 395, and the country was inevitably drawn into the great Christian controversies that rent the 4th and 5Cs. The strength of the Byzantine Empire faltered and in 619 Egypt was occupied by the Persians. It was regained by the Emperor Heraclius in 627, but he managed to retain control for only a few years.

After the Arabs had conquered Egypt in 641, ʿAmr Ibn al-ʿĀṣ was given specific instructions by the Khalīf ʿUmar to create the administrative capital at Babylon, not Alexandria. The area as found by ʿAmr consisted of the deserted triangular plain, at the southern apex of which was the fortress of Babylon; to the NE a small community existed among the remains of Heliopolis (called by the Arabs ʿAyn Shams—Spring of the Sun), and at the NW lay Tendunyas (called by the Arabs al-Maks). ʿAmr settled the Arabs who accompanied him in a great straggling encampment called Fusṭāṭ to the N and E of Babylon which the Arabs called Qaṣr al-Shamʿ either from the wax (shamʿ) signal fires that had been lit on the towers or as a corruption of the Coptic name Khemi (i.e. of Egypt). His first action was the construction of a mosque a little to the NE of the fortress. In 643 the canal to the Red Sea was reopened yet again. The mosque of ʿAmr was the centre and attracted the scattered tribes who each had their own assigned district (khiṭṭah) where they constructed more permanent dwellings.

Egypt was considered an occupied province by the Arabs and as such Fusṭāṭ was the principal city and the seat of the governor. In 750 the last Ummayad khalīf, Marwān II, fled to Egypt and made his final stand there, and during this conflict Fusṭāṭ suffered the first of its great fires. The new dynasty of khalīfs, the ʿAbbāsids, continued the practice of appointing governors but constructed a new enclosed town, al-ʿAskār (The Military Quarter), to the NE of Fusṭāṭ, as the centre of their administration which prospered greatly. Aḥmad Ibn Ṭūlūn, the proxy governor for the ʿAbbāsids, declared himself independent in 868 and to celebrate the fact constructed his own princely city, al-Qaṭaʾīʿ (The Concessions), even further to the NE. In the N of this he built his great mosque in 877. The Northern plain, however, remained undeveloped and this remained the case during the rule of the next dynasty, the Iskhshīds, except that the last influential ruler, Kāfūr, had a large orchard set out by the banks of the canal.

Thus when the Fāṭimids, led by Gawhar al-Siqillī, invaded from North Africa in 969 the whole of the N plain was empty except for the garden of Kāfūr and a few scattered monasteries. Gawhar therefore chose the site for the city of his patron, the Fāṭimid khalīf al-Muʿizz, about 1.5km N of the Fusṭāṭ–ʿAskār–Qaṭaʾīʿ complex, marking it out the day after subjugating the city. When completed the new city contained palaces, pavilions, gardens and al-Azhar mosque, all enclosed with a high brick wall, to house exclusively the khalīf, his family and retainers. Originally called al-Manṣūriyyah, with the arrival of the Khalīf al-Muʿizz in 971 its name was changed to al-Qāhirah (The Vanquishing) as al-Qāhir (Mars) had been in the ascendant when it was started. This name was latinised by Europeans during medieval times and in English became Cairo.

The name Miṣr, the ancient Semitic name for Egypt, used by various SW Asian cultures, and mentioned as such in the Quʾrān, came to be applied to the city of Fusṭāṭ. Exactly how this happened is not clear, but it is unlikely that there was a pre-Arab city called Miṣr at this point. Perhaps the name was given to the city to distinguish it from other towns called Fusṭāṭ of which there were several throughout Arab lands. This city, which soon stretched about 2.5km along the river bank, continued as the mercantile capital of Egypt, even after the building of al-Qāhirah. It struck Muslim travellers with awe—even those who had seen the magnificence of Baghdād. Some of the buildings rose seven or even fourteen storeys. The city of al-Qāhirah also impressed them with its gleaming domes and minarets rising above the walls. The second great conflagration in Fusṭāṭ occurred during the riots precipitated by the khalīf al-Ḥākim in 1020, but it recovered and continued throughout the 11–12C as a city of great prosperity. The enclosure of al-Qāhirah was refortified in stone by the commander Badr al-Gamālī for the khalīf al-Mustanṣir in 1087 and so it remained for the rest of the rule of the Fāṭimids.

Although the Crusader invasions initially disturbed only the Syrian seaboard, by the beginning of the 12C the Christian princes were interesting themselves in the affairs of Egypt, which was experiencing a period of political instability. During incursions by King Amalric I of Jerusalem in 1168 the Egyptian wazīr Shāwar fired Fusṭāṭ so that it could not be occupied by the Crusaders. It burned for 54 days, the worst fire it had suffered and from which it never recovered. The population fled in all directions but mainly towards the great compound of al-Qāhirah where they built temporary homes about the walls. Some parts of Fusṭāṭ escaped, especially those areas near the river, but most of it was razed. When the last Fāṭimid khalīf al-ʿAdid died Ṣalāḥ al-Dīn, his wazīr, assumed complete control, ousting the royal family from the compound of al-Qāhirah and opening it up to the population. From that time it became the commercial centre of the city.

Ṣalāḥ al-Dīn also conceived the complete fortification of the two cities within a single wall from al-Maks to Miṣr al-Qadīmah, controlled from a great citadel built on an outcrop of the Muqaṭṭam Hills. This vast plan incorporated some of the fortifications of Badr al-Gamālī. Construction of the Citadel in the SE provided another nucleus for the city. The centre now consisted largely of the desolate area left by the last fire, which from then on was used as a rubbish dump by the other centres and was only really tackled properly in 1952 when a development scheme was undertaken.

During the period of Mamlūk rule in the 13–15C, while the population of Cairo fluctuated, but generally increased, the city expanded to about five times its original size. The silting of the East Bank accelerated and areas previously only exposed at low water were permanently elevated. The regions of al-Ḥusāniyyah to the N and Bāb al-Lūq on the bank of the Nile were settled and developed. Throughout the period of settlement by the Muslims their cemeteries had been placed outside the city, and as the city grew so did the cemeteries until they almost surrounded the city to the N, E and S. While performing a necessary function they also provided an area for a limited form of settlement.

Sultan al-Nāṣir Muḥammad built a new canal which joined the older one to the N of al-Ḥusāniyyah. A series of plagues and famines in the 14C reduced the population, the remnants of which withdrew towards the nuclei leaving the areas between to decay. Even at its lowest ebb Cairo was still probably greater in extent and population than any city outside S Asia and still abounded in luxury goods. In the 15C more of the E Bank was exposed and Būlāq was developed at the expense of Miṣr al-Qadīmah. The last addition to the medieval city was the Azbakiyyah quarter.

Under the Ottomans Cairo became once more merely a provincial city with public building undertaken only by the local grandees. With the coming of the French in 1798 and the subsequent rise of Muḥammad ʿAlī a new phase was initiated in its development. Muḥammad ʿAlī started a great building programme, both commercial and domestic, sending scientists and architects to glean the latest developments from Europe. By and large this was the policy pursued by the whole dynasty—dams and bridges were built, the banks of the Nile stabilised. The latest inventions—railways, tramways and finally motor cars—all had to be accommodated. New suburbs were developed, various rulers favouring different areas. The last area within the city to be developed was Tawfiqiyyah, a marshy area drained in 1889.

*Southern Cairo from the Citadel, 1849, by J.H. Bartlett (British Library)*

The population Cairo has had to support since World War II has presented a great challenge to the government but since the revolution in 1952 an immense building programme has been undertaken. While the design of some buildings may not be considered beautiful, aesthetics cannot be the prime consideration. Few cities have a greater number of architectural monuments within their confines and the problem of how to preserve them while at the same time providing the prime necessity, homes for the people, is a problem that the Egyptian Government is having to face.

For visitors with very limited time at their disposal, who cannot therefore follow the detailed Rtes in and around Cairo, the list below gives several short intineraries. These cover most of the important monuments; each takes a couple of hours or, at most, a half day.

**1.** North of Khān al-Khalīlī. Within easy reach of this famous market are the large mosque and tomb complexes of Sultans al-Ṣāliḥ Ayyūb, Qalāwūn, al-Nāṣir Muḥammad and Barqūq. The N walls and the Bāb al-Futūḥ (Rte 5).

**2.** Also N of Khān al-Khalīlī but further E is the road to the Bāb al-Naṣr and the N walls. It passes the Musāfirkhānah Palace and the beautiful Madrasah of Sultan Baybars II (Rte 4).

**3.** South of Khān al-Khalīlī, this tour includes al-Azhar Mosque, the dual complex of Sultan al-Ghawrī, and a short walk to the Mosque of Sultan Muʾayyad Shaykh, the S walls and the Bāb Zuwaylah (Rte 6).

**4.** The Mosque of Ibn Ṭūlūn and the Bayt al-Kiridliyyah (Gayer-Anderson) Museum. A short walk to the W to the twin tombs of the Amīrs Salār and Sangar and E to the dual complex of Amīr Shaykhū (Rte 13).

**5.** The Mosque of Sultan Ḥasan and the modern Rifāʿī Mosque (Rte 10) could be combined with a visit to the Citadel and its associated mosques and palaces (Rte 14).

**6.** A visit to Old Cairo (Miṣr al-Qadīmah) would include the Mosque of ʿAmr and the Fortress of Babylon housing the Coptic Museum and several important churches (Rte 16).

**7.** A little further afield are the Tomb of Imām Shāfʿī and the Ḥawsh al-Bāshā in the Southern Cemetery (Rte 15).

**8.** A visit to the Eastern Cemetery could include the Mosque and tomb complexes of Amīr Qurqumas and Sultans Ināl, Farag, Barsbāy and Qāyt-Bāy.

**9.** The Egyptian Museum (Rte 2).

**10.** The Museum of Islamic Art (Rte 7).

**11.** The Agricultural Museum (Rte 22A) and the Zoological Gardens at Gīzah (Rte 22B).

**12.** The pyramids at Gīzah (Rte 23).

**13.** The pyramids and tombs at Ṣaqqārah and the ancient site of Memphis (Rte 25).

Other places to visit could include Heliopolis (Rte 20), the Muqaṭṭam Hills (Rte 14), Ḥalwan (Rte 21) or al-Qantārah al-Khayriyyah and the Barrages (Rte 43A).

# 1 Al-Taḥrīr Square

This Rte (**Cairo Atlas 14, 15**) covers the main tourist area of the city and contains most of the principal hotels. It is used as the central reference point for all subsequent itineraries within Cairo, which in general begin N of this point, and then E and S.

MAYDĀN AL-TAḤRĪR (Liberation Square; 14:3), previously the Maydān Khidiw Ismāʿīl, in the district of **Qaṣr al-Nīl**, is the tourist centre, though not the administrative centre of Cairo. It is a vast open area bounded on the W by the Nile, facing which is the *Hilton Hotel*. To the N lies the *Egyptian Museum* (Rte 2) while the boundary of the E side consists of office buildings, shops and restaurants, on top of which are large advertising signs. The large building to the S is the *Mugāmaʿ* (see below). There is a *Bus Terminus* in front of the Hilton and a large *Bus Station* in front of the Mugāmaʿ. Roads radiate in all directions from the square.

The area was developed by Saʿīd Pasha who had a palace, the Qaṣr al-Nīl, built here in the 1850s. In front of this he constructed a large barracks. In 1866 the

Khedive Isma'īl cut the Ismā'īliyyah Canal, the mouth of which entered the Nile just N of the palace. During the British occupation the barracks were used to house troops. When the British left the camp was razed and the site used for the Hilton Hotel.

Along the E bank of the Nile runs the SH'. AL-KURNĪSH (Corniche), N to Shubrā, S to Ḥalwān. Directly in front is the *Hilton Hotel* with a huge panel of ceramic mosaic of Ancient Egyptian symbols. It was built in the early 1960s, the first of the new generation of international style hotels, and has recently had a large annex built on the E side. The N border of the square is marked by the Egyptian Museum (Rte 2).

From the E side of the Egyptian Museum the Sh'. Ramsīs (see below) leaves the square to the NE, while on the E side of the square beyond a façade of shops and offices three streets radiate from a common point: to the NE the Sh'. Shambulyūn (Champollion), to the E the Sh'. Qaṣr al-Nīl and to the SE the Sh'. al-Bustān. On the S corner of the Sh'. al-Bustān is the office of British Airways, beyond which three more streets leave the square: to the NE the Sh'. Ṭal'at Ḥarb, to the E the Sh'. al-Taḥrīr and to the SE the Sh'. Muḥammad Maḥmūd. Opposite this junction is the central garden of the square. In the centre is a massive monument of granite, marble and sandstone, originally the pedestal of a statue of the Khedive Ismā'il. From the SE corner of the square the Sh'. Qaṣr al-'Aynī runs S. To the W, forming the S side of the square, stands the massive **Mugāma' al-Taḥrīr** (14:4), a concave-fronted building containing an assembly of the public departments of several ministries, Interior, Education, Health, etc., and the Cairo governate. It occupies the site of a palace of Ismā'īl Pasha and was constructed after the revolution. Immediately to the W is the modern *Mosque of 'Umar Makram.*

Opposite the Mugāma' is a wide open garden in the centre of which is a circular pool and fountain. From the SW corner of the square the Sh'. al-Taḥrīr continues to the W. On the S side of the road the Victorian building is the *Wizārat al-Khargiyyah* (Foreign Ministry; 14:3), originally the palace of Prince Kamāl al-Dīn Ḥusayn. The modern building on the N is the *Gāmi'at al-Dūwal al-'Arabiyyah* (Headquarters Assembly Building of the Arab League). The Sh'. al-Taḥrīr goes to the Taḥrīr Bridge, with large guardian lions, which leads to al-Gazīrah (Rte 3E) and Giza on the W Bank (Rte 22).

### North of al-Taḥrīr Square

The area N of al-Taḥrīr Square was until 1912 occupied by the mouth of the Ismā'īliyyah Canal, constructed in 1866, which ran to the NE across Cairo and ultimately to Ismā'īliyyah on the Suez Canal. When this section was filled in the Anglican Cathedral was built here. This in turn was demolished in 1976 as it was on the direct route of the 6 OCTOBER BRIDGE (Kubrī Sittah Uktūbir) which crosses the Corniche and al-Gazīrah to the W Bank (Rte 22). To the NE it runs along the old course of the canal as an elevated motorway to 'Abbāsiyyah (Rte 20). The Corniche continues N, passing to the E the *Dār al-Īdhā'ah wa 'l-tilifiziyūn* (Radio and Television Building; 6:5), housing the main studios, with a semi-circular façade crowned by a tower block and transmitting aerial. Beyond this the Corniche is crossed by the SH'. 26 YŪLYŪ (formerly Sh'. Fū'ād al-Awwal) which crosses to the W Bank on the 26 July Bridge (Kubrī Sittah wa asharīn Yūlyū, formerly Kubrī Abū 'l-'Alā') and to the E runs into Central Cairo and the Azbakiyyah Gardens (see Rte 3B).

Flanking the 6 October Bridge and also running NE are two arterial roads: on the W the SHʻ. AL-GALĀʼ, on the E the SHʻ. RAMSĪS (both to Rameses Sq.). These are also crossed by the Shʻ. 26 Yūlyū, to the N of which lies Būlāq (Rte 17).

E from Shʻ. Ramsīs run the SHʻ. MUḤAMMAD BASSYŪNĪ, the SHʻ. MAʻRŪF (300m) and the SHʻ. ʻABD AL-KHĀLIQ THARWĀT (400m).

On the Shʻ. Ramsīs opposite the N end of Shʻ. Tharwat is the *Entomological Museum* (al-Mathaf al-Intumulujiyyah), founded by King Fūʼād I. It contains examples of the invertebrate life of Egypt with special emphasis on the pests of crops.

## Northeast of al-Taḥrīr Square

Leading from the NE corner of al-Taḥrīr Square, the SHʻ. SHAMBULYŪN (Champollion) runs parallel to the Shʻ. Ramsīs, crossing the Shʻ. Bassyūnī (150m) and Shʻ. Tharwāt (600m). It enters the Shʻ. 26 Yūlyū at the neo-classical *Dār al-Quḍā al-ʻĀlī* (the High Court).

Leaving Taḥrīr Square from the same point is the SHʻ. QAṢR AL-NĪL, which runs further E (through the central business quarter), and enters at 300m Maydān Ṭalʻat Ḥarb, in the centre of which is a statue of the industrialist Ṭalʻat Ḥarb. From this square the Shʻ. Bassyūnī leaves NW; Shʻ. Muḥammad Ṣabrī Abū ʼl-ʻAlam leaves SE and the Shʻ. Ṭalʻat Ḥarb crosses from SW to NE. Continuing further NE Shʻ. Qaṣr al-Nīl passes on the S the massive *al-Bank al-Ahlī al-Miṣrī* (the National Bank of Egypt), formerly the government bank, and crosses the SHʻ. MUḤAMMAD FARĪD (600m) with, at the centre of the crossroads, a statue of the patriot Muṣṭafā Kāmil. Here it turns due E and enters the Shʻ. al-Gumhūriyyah.

The third street to take off from Maydān Taḥrīr is the Shʻ. al-Bustān which runs SE (see below).

From the next junction in the Maydān al-Taḥrīr the SHʻ. ṬALʻAT ḤARB (previously Shʻ. Sulaymān Pasha) also runs NE parallel to the Shʻ. Ramsīs, crossing the Shʻ. al-Bustān and passing on the E the SHʻ. SH. ḤAMZAH, into Maydān Qaṣr al-Nīl and across the Shʻ. Tharwāt (E to Maydān al-Ubirā, see below). The next turning on the E is the SHʻ. AL-ʻADLĪ (to Azbakiyyah Gardens) along which on the N is the *Synagogue*, a huge grey building designed in what can only be called Hollywood biblical style. Further along on the same side of the road is the *Tourist Information Office* of the Ministry of Tourism. Continuing N the Shʻ. Ṭalʻat Ḥarb leads into the Shʻ. 26 Yūlyū, crossing which it continues N as the SHʻ. ʻURABĪ into Shʻ. Ramsīs.

At the same point in Maydān al-Taḥrīr the Shʻ. al-Taḥrīr leads E (see below).

## East of al-Taḥrīr Square

Leaving Maydān al-Taḥrīr from the same point as Shʻ. Shambulyūn and Shʻ. Qaṣr al-Nīl is the SHʻ. AL-BUSTĀN which runs SE into the Maydān al-Falakī (also called Maydān al-Azhār and not to be confused with al-Azhar; see Rte 4), with a tram station. It passes into the area known as Bāb al-Lūq, from one of the old gates which stood here. From the E end of the sq. the SHʻ ḤUDĀ AL-SHAʻRĀWĪ leads NW to the Shʻ Ṭalʻat Ḥarb and on the corner is the *Ministry of Awqāf* built in the early 20C in Neo-Mamluk style. At the SW corner of the square the Shʻ. al-Taḥrīr leads back to Maydān al-Taḥrīr and on the S side are two roads running due S. Easternmost is the SHʻ. AL-FALAKĪ and parallel to it is the wide SHʻ.

MANṢŪR. On the S side of the square is the *Sūq Bāb al-Lūq*, also called the Sūq al-Afrangī, a market which besides selling home-grown vegetables, fruit and meat also specialises in imported fruit for the tourist market and is therefore relatively expensive. Slightly to the E is the *Chamber of Commerce* building (Ghurfah al-Tigāriyyah al-Qāhirah) with the *Gallery of Contemporary Artists* on the ground floor. At the E end of the square are several roads: on the N the Shʿ. Sh. Ḥamzah (N to Shʿ. Ṭalʿat Ḥarb); due N the SHʿ. SHARĪF; due S the SHʿ. NUBĀR, and SE the Shʿ. al-Taḥrīr. The Shʿ. al-Bustān leaves the E end of the square, passing on the N the Shʿ. Muḥammad Ṣabrī Abū ʾl-ʿAlam and Shʿ. Muḥammad Farīd which, running due N, passes on the W the Catholic *Church of St. Joseph* (built 1909) and on the E *al-Bank Miṣr*, built in 1929 (lavish interior in marble, wrought iron and wood and extremely fine coloured marble floor), into Maydān Muṣṭafā Kāmil. The Shʿ. Bustān continues E into the Shʿ. ʿAbd al-ʿAzīz (to Maydān ʿAtabah al-Khuḍrā, see below).

From the same point in Maydān al-Taḥrīr as the Shʿ. Ṭalʿat Ḥarb the SHʿ. AL-TAḤRĪR passes E through the Maydān al-Falakī on to Maydān al-Gumhūriyyah (see Rte 3C).

## Southeast of al-Taḥrīr Square

At the SE corner of Maydān al-Taḥrīr the SHʿ. QAṢR AL-ʿAYNĪ runs almost due S. Just past the square on the E side is the *American University in Cairo*, the main building raised for the Egyptian University (founded 1908, now Cairo University; see Rte 22). Beyond this the road is crossed E to W by the SHʿ. SHAYKH RIḤĀN (E to Shʿ. Būr Saʿid). On the N side is the *Ewart Memorial Hall*, a concert hall attached to the university.

The Shʿ. Qaṣr al-ʿAynī continues S through the central administrative quarter with its many ministries. After 35m (left) is the **Ethnological Museum** (open 09.00–13.00, closed Fridays;) which displays crafts, costume and tools from throughout Egypt. The next road to the E is SHʿ. MAGLIS AL-SHAʿĀB with the *Maglis al-Shaʿāb* (People's Council, i.e. Parliament) building on the N. This road continues E, crossing the Shʿ. al-Falakī, Shʿ. Manṣūr and Shʿ. Nubār, all running N to S. At the last crossroads is a bronze statue of Lazughlī Bay, SE from here the SHʿ. KHAYRAT runs into the Shʿ. al-Naṣiriyyah and the Maydān Sayyidah Zaynab (Rte 12).

After 170m on the E the SHʿ. DARĪḤ ZAGHLŪL leads to the **Bayt al-Ummah** (House of the Nation) the home of Saʿd Zaghlūl (1860–1927) the great nationalist, founder of the Wafd (delegation) party and prime minister 1924. (Hrs. 08.30–17.00, small fee). Contrasting with the elaborate mansions of contemporary notables this building is reminiscent of a rural villa, in keeping with his fallaḥ background. Most of the rooms have remained unchanged since his death and contain many personal effects, photographs, certificates and furniture. Particularly interesting are his study and library.

To the E on the opposite side of the Shʿ. al-Falakī rises the neo-pharaonic **Tomb of Saʿd Zaghlūl**, a massive granite building crowned with a cavetto cornice, built in 1931 by the Egyptian architecht Mustafa Fahmi. A flight of steps leads to the imposing bronze doors flanked by great pillars. Inside rose granite columns surround the tomb which is in the form of an ancient Egyptian naos. Zaghlūl is buried here with his second wife Safiyyah.

*Tomb of Saʿd Zaghlūl*

W of Shʿ. Qaṣr al-ʿAynī lies Garden City (see below) and the road continues S for 1.9km to enter the Corniche at the Fumm al-Khalīg.

**South of al-Taḥrīr Square**

Behind the Mugāmaʿ the SHʿ. AMIRĪKĀ LATINIYYAH leads S past the *US Embassy* on the E and the *British Embassy* on the W into **Garden City** (Gārdan Sītī), bounded on the W by the Nile and on the E by the Shʿ. Qaṣr al-ʿAynī.

This was the site of several great 19C palaces. From N to S these were: Ibrāhīm Pasha's Qaṣr al-Dubbārah (demolished in 1906), the vast Ibrāhimiyyah Palace, and the Qasr al-ʿĀlī, the palace of the Khedive's mother. British planners developed the area and the roads have winding rural routes in the English style, a sharp contrast to the formal French grid-work layout around Azbakiyyah. Many of the mansions built for diplomats and notables are Edwardian in style with large gardens, a number of which were curtailed by the construction of the Corniche. Many of the mansions are still embassies but others have been bought by companies or converted into flats.

The Corniche continues S along the East Bank passing the new *Shepheard's Hotel* and at 1km on the W the bridge to the *Meridian Hotel* on Rawḍah Island. The Corniche itinerary continues in Rte 3D.

# 2 The Egyptian Museum

**Cairo Atlas 14**.

A small road leads from the NW corner of al-Taḥrīr Square to the Corniche, but the whole of the N side of the square is occupied by the ****Egyptian Museum** (al-Mathaf al-Miṣrī; 14:1) surrounded by a garden. Open November–April 09.00–16.00 (Fri closed 11.15–13.50); May–October 08.30–13.00 (Fri closed 11.15); fee, reductions for students. Ticket office at the gate. The garden contains several statues and at the W end is the *Tomb of Auguste Mariette* (1821–81), a sarcophagus surmounted by a statue with the inscription 'L'Egypt Reconnaissante'. At the SE corner of the building is the *Administration Department* and at the SW corner the *Library* (not open to the general public).

*Diorite statue of Khafre from Giza*

Although the Romans were fascinated by Egyptian works of art, many statues and obelisks being transported to Rome or Byzantium, their successors in Egypt, the Muslims, remained unimpressed by archaeological remains. They used the great buildings as stone quarries and reused the pillars and columns in their own constructions. The statues and other works, except for the Sphinx, they ignored. Thus for almost a thousand years the treasures of Egypt, to Europeans, were virtually mythical.

Many objects filtered through to European collections during the 18C but it was not until Napoleon's survey of Egypt at the beginning of the 19C and Champollion's decipherment of the hieroglyphic script that the interest of European academics was drawn in earnest to Ancient Egyptian civilisation. Several collections were made by European diplomats stationed in Egypt but these left the country and formed the basis of the collections in the great museums of Europe's capital cities. Champollion and other concerned people urged the Egyptian authorities to control the export of antiquities and a conservation department was founded in 1834. Although a national collection was formed, it was used as a cache from which to supply visiting dignitaries with presents and in 1855 the whole collection, including the recently-found stelae from Ṣaqqārah, was presented to the Archduke Maximilian of Austria.

August Mariette, upon the recommendation of Napoleon III and de Lesseps, was created director of antiquities in 1858, although without a building to house the collection. He excavated a vast number of sites, storing the objects in a warehouse in Būlāq In 1863 Ismāʿīl Pasha opened a new building in the same area to display the finds. Mariette showed his serious intent when in 1867 the Empress Eugenie requested the cream of the collection and he refused. By the 1890s the Antiquities Service was a department of the Ministry of Public Works. Despite added grants the building in Būlāq proved too small and the whole collection was moved to the Giza Palace on the West Bank of the Nile. An international competition was held in 1895 to design a new building and the winning plan was that of Marcel Durgnon (who died shortly after) with the present neo-classical sandstone building which was inaugurated in 1902 and called the Antiq Khanah or Cairo Museum. This building has in turn become too small to house the collections and a new museum is projected incorporating the most modern features. The first stage of the scheme is a special wing being constructed to house the Tutankhamun treasures. The Department of Antiquities and the Egyptian Museum are now the responsibility of the Ministry of Culture.

Curators of the museum have included Maspero, Lefebvre, Brunton, Engelbach, Mahmud Hamza, Abbas Bayumi, Moharram Kamal, Victor Girgis and Muhammad Hassan. Detailed catalogues of certain sections of the collections under the title *General Catalogue of the Cairo Museum* have been in progress since the early 20C. At present c 100,000 objects are displayed, covering the whole of Ancient Egyptian history from prehistoric times to the Greco-Roman period. The order is roughly chronological with the Tutankhamun treasure displayed almost complete on the first floor. Until recently mummified bodies from the tombs in the Valley of the Kings and other sites were on display but they have been withdrawn and there is a growing feeling that they should all be reinterred.

Inside the museum immediately to the left is the sales area; casts, prints, books and other material can be purchased.

**Ground Floor.** In the body of the museum the objects are arranged in roughly chronological order. On entry turn left into the SOUTH WING (W end).

**Gallery 47.** *S side*. Large sarcophagi including Meres-ʿankh (unfinished), grey granite (6171) and Khufuʿankh, Overseer of the building works of the King, rose granite (44), both from Giza. Nearly all are decorated with the so-called 'palace-façade' and those of some of the priests have leopard skins cut on the lids. *N side*. Three triads showing Menkaure with Hathor and one of the nome deities, slate, Giza, the Valley Temple of the King (149, 158, 180). *W end*. Funeral chamber of painted limestone from the mastaba of Desheri, Ṣaqqārah, 6 Dyn. (48). *Central Cases*. Figures, 4–6 Dyns; reserve heads, Giza, 4 Dyn.; servant figures, baking, grinding, brewing and potting, O.K. (168–73).

**Gallery 46.** *S side*. Sarcophagus of Prince Djedef-khufu (unfinished), red granite, 4 Dyn., Giza (6156). *N side*. Two fragments from mastaba of Itet, Maydūm, 4 Dyn. (70). Door lintel of Sahure, Abū Ṣīr, 5 Dyn.

**Gallery 51.** Fragments from restoration of the Sphinx (door to the Library).

Here are the SW stairs (toilets on first landing).

WEST WING. **Gallery 41.** *S side*. Two sarcophagi, alabaster, Dahshūr,

3 Dyn. (30, 40). Two offering tables with lion head supports, alabaster, Ṣaqqārah, 3 Dyn. (19 A, B).

*State triad of Menkaure, Hathor and the goddess of the Aphroditopolis nome. From the king's valley temple at Giza*

**Gallery 42.** Seated statue of Khafre, diorite, 4 Dyn., Giza (138). Statue of Ka-aper (known as the Shaykh al-Balad), wood, from his tomb, Ṣaqqārah, 5 Dyn. (140). Statue of Menkaure, alabaster, Giza, 4 Dyn. (157).

*Gallery 37*. (closed to public).

**Gallery 31.** Six panels of Hesy-Re, architect and doctor, wood, Ṣaqqārah, 3 Dyn. (88). *E side*. Reliefs, sandstone, Wadi Magārah, Sinai, O.K. (91–4). Inlays, Maydūm, 3 Dyn. (70 A, B).

**Gallery 32.** Old Kingdom Sculpture. *At entry*, Heads of prisoners, Tanis, Ṣaqqārah, Damanhūr, 3 Dyn. *E side*. Dual seated figures of

Rahotep and his wife Nefert, painted limestone, Maydūm, 3 Dyn. (223). Two statues of Ra-nufer, a priest, limestone, no provenance, 5 Dyn. (224–5). Wall painting, the geese of Maydūm, tomb of Itet, 3 Dyn. (136). Statues of King Pepi I and his son, hammered copper over wood, Kom al-Aḥmar, 5 Dyn. (230–3). *N side.* Niche of the dwarf Seneb and his family, limestone, Giza, 5 Dyn. (6010).

**Gallery 26.** Life size statue of King Mentuhotpe, painted sandstone, Deir al-Baḥrī, 11 Dyn. (287). Block statue of Hotep, limestone, Ṣaqqārah, 12 Dyn. (6011). Architrave and columns, sandstone, Madamud, 12 Dyn. (6168).

*Gallery 27* (closed to public).

**Gallery 21.** Statue of Amenemhat III, limestone, Kom Madīnat al-Maʿādī and Ḥawārah, Fayyūm, 12 Dyn. (284, 6259). Colossus of Senusert III, Karnak, 12 Dyn. (10). Statue of Senusert III, granite, Madamūd, 12 Dyn. (6049). Stele of Su-Ubastet, sandstone, quarries in the Western Nubian desert, 12 Dyn. (6216). Five stelae, limestone, Ṣaqqārah, 11 Dyn. (6197).

**Gallery 22.** Burial chamber of Harhotpe containing limestone sarcophagus. Deir al-Baḥrī, 11 Dyn. (300). Twelve statues of Senusert I, limestone, al-Lisht, 12 Dyn. (301). Four canopic jars, Dahshūr, 12 Dyn. (307–10). Stele of Antef and dogs, 11 Dyn. (311).

**Gallery 16.** Mostly Middle Kingdom but material often changed. A statue of two Niles with fish and plants, black granite, Tanis, M.K. (508). Sphinxes, probably of Amenemhat III, but usurped by later kings, black granite, Tanis, 12 Dyn. (507).

*Gallery 17* (closed to public).

**Gallery 11.** New Kingdom statuary. Senenmut, vizier to Queen Hatshepsut, granite statue, Karnak, 18 Dyn. (592). Sphinx of Hatshepsut, limestone, Karnak, 18 Dyn. (6139). Statue of Tuthmosis III, schist, Karnak, 18 Dyn. (400).

**Gallery 12.** 18th Dyn. Statue of Amenhotep III, Karnak (410, relabelled 11620). Block figure of Senmut and Neferure, daughter of Hatshepsut, granite, Karnak (418). Statue of Iset, mother of Tuthmosis III, secondary wife of Tuthmosis II, grey granite, Karnak (424). Chapel of the goddess Hathor who, in the form of a cow, protects Amenhotep II, sandstone, Deir al-Baḥrī (445–6). Relief showing the queen of Punt, Temple of Hatshepsut, Thebes (452). Two figures of the scribe Amenhotpe, son of Hapu, sitting cross-legged; one shows him as a youth, the other in old age (he was later deified); black granite, Karnak (459,461). Khonsu shown with the features of Tutankhamun, granite, Karnak (462). Statue of Amenhotep II and the goddess Mertseger, black granite, al-Qurnah (470). Osiride figures of Hatshepsut, limestone, Deir al-Baḥrī (405, 11627). Stele of Tuthmosis III celebrating victories, black granite, Karnak (420).

NORTH WING. **Gallery 6.** Stele of Tutankhamun, usurped by Horemheb, listing his restorations of the Temple of Montu, red sandstone, Karnak (560). Stele of Amenhotep II recording campaigns in his 7th and 9th regnal years, reused by Prince Sheshonq, quartzite, Memphis, 18 and 22 Dyns.

Here are the NW stairs

**Gallery 7.** Sphinx of Hatshepsut, damaged by Tuthmosis III, painted granite, Deir al-Baḥrī, 18 Dyn. (6152). Kneeling colossus of Hatshepsut, Deir al-Baḥrī, 18 Dyn. (6153, renumbered 11829). Stelae found near Sphinx, limestone, Giza, 18 Dyn. (6304–8).

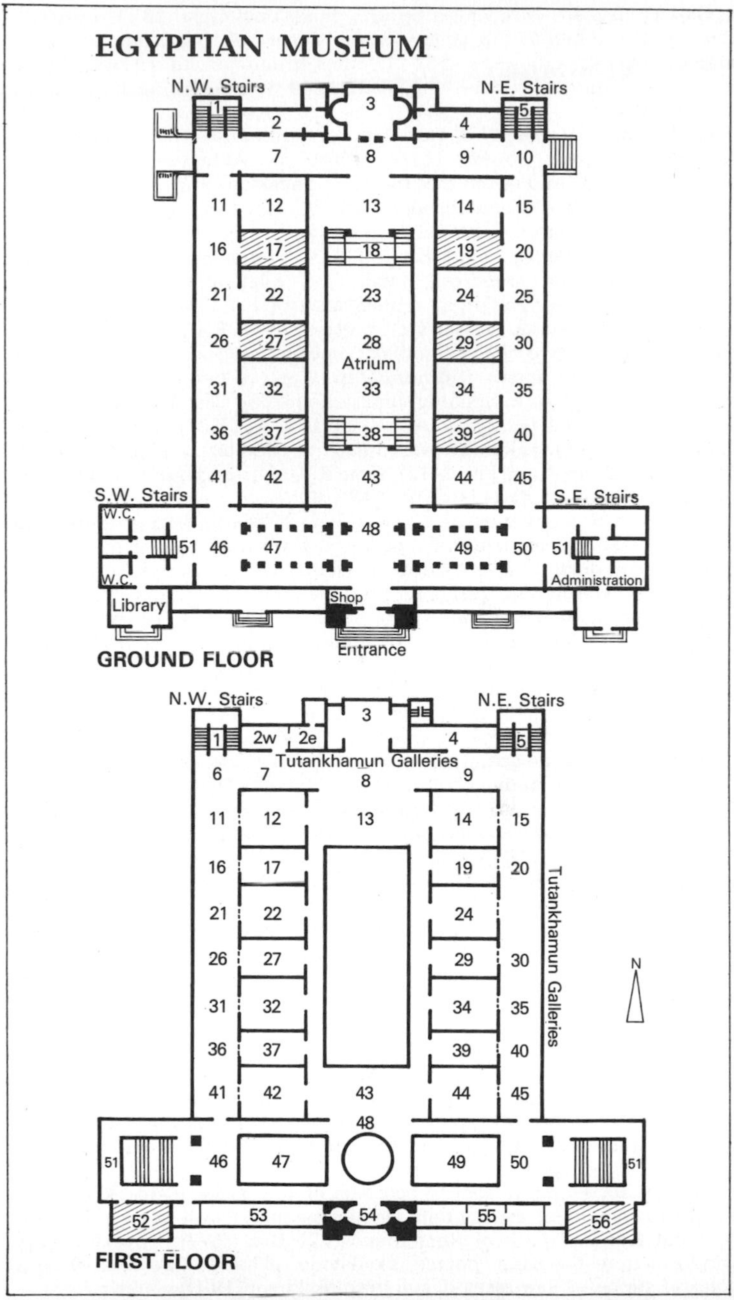
EGYPTIAN MUSEUM
N.W. Stairs
N.E. Stairs
1 2 3 4 5
7 8 9 10
11 12 13 14 15
16 17 18 19 20
21 22 23 24 25
26 27 28 29 30
Atrium
31 32 33 34 35
36 37 38 39 40
41 42 43 44 45
S.W. Stairs
S.E. Stairs
W.C.
51 46 47 48 49 50 51
W.C.
Administration
Library
Shop
Entrance
GROUND FLOOR
N.W. Stairs
N.E. Stairs
3
1 2w 2e 4 5
Tutankhamun Galleries
6 7 8 9
11 12 13 14 15
16 17 19 20
21 22 24
26 27 29 30
31 32 34 35
36 37 39 40
41 42 43 44 45
Tutankhamun Galleries
N
48
51 46 47 49 50 51
52 53 54 55 56
FIRST FLOOR

**Gallery 8.** Stele found near Sphinx, limestone, Giza, 18 Dyn. (6303). Part of stele dated to 5th year of King Merneptah commemorating his victories over the Libyans and Sea Peoples, granite, Delta, 19 Dyn. (6017). Lion's head gargoyle, limestone, S pyramid at al-Lisht, 12 Dyn. (6224, partly restored).

**Gallery 3.** Oval room N of gallery 8, containing the 18 Dyn. collections from al-ʿAmārnah. *Right.* Three colossi of Akhenaten, limestone, Karnak—outside and to the E of the main enclosure (6015–6, 6182). *Left.* Canopic chest of Akhenaten, alabaster, heavily restored (6323). Lid of coffin of Smenkhkare, cartouches destroyed, wood sheathed in inlaid gold, tomb 55—Valley of the Kings (3873). Fragments of a shrine with Queen Tiy's name, wood-gilt, tomb 55—Valley of the Kings (6325). *Centre Case A.* Al-ʿAmārnah tablets inscribed in Akkadian from the Syrian and Palestinian vassal states, clay (1194–7). *Case C.* Altar with royal family adoring the solar disk, limestone, (6056). Base of statue inscribed with the names of Amenhotep III and Akhenaten of a type not used before year 9 of Akhenaten, limestone (6258). *Case F.* Statuettes and reliefs of the royal family, limestone (471, 475, 13234). *Case G.* Three Canopic jars of Smenkhkare with heads of Meretaten, alabaster, tomb 55—Valley of the Kings (3610–12). *Case K.* Unfinished heads and models of princesses, quartzite (474, 476–7, 479, 6057).

**Gallery 9.** Sarcophagus of Khay, standard bearer, black granite, 19 Dyn. (654). Ṣaqqārah Tablet, list of kings down to Ramesses II, Tomb of Teti, 19 Dyn. (660). Colossal statue of Tutankhamun, usurped first by Ay and then by Horemheb, quartzite, Medīnat Habū, 18 Dyn. (6205). Group of Horemheb and the Osiran Triad, limestone, Abydos, 18 Dyn. (6018). Similar but smaller group to last, granite, Abydos, 19 Dyn. (6019). Two columns, pink granite, from Tanis—Temple of Ramesses II, reused, 19 Dyn. (6254). Stele of Ramesses II, limestone, Heliopolis, 19 Dyn. (666).

**Gallery 4.** Numismatic collection. Coins from the Greek to the Mamlūk periods.

**Gallery 10.** Unique group of Horus as a hawk protecting Ramesses II as a rebus of his own name, pink granite, Tanis, 19 Dyn. (6245). Statue of Ramesses III holding sacred standards, pink granite, Armant, 19 Dyn. (664). Fragment of statue probably of Tutankhamun, limestone, Memphis, 18 Dyn. (6183).

Here are the NE stairs.

EAST WING. **Gallery 15.** Two colossal heads of Ramesses II, pink granite, Memphis, 19 Dyn. (671–2). Two sarcophagi of wives of Ramesses II, Henutmire, pink granite, Madīnat Habū, and Bant Anta, granite, provenance unknown, 19 Dyn. (6253–4).

**Gallery 14.** Pedestal of a statue from which emerge the heads of the 'Nine Bows', granite, Madīnat Habū, 20 Dyn. (766). Statue of Seti I, alabaster, Karnak, 19 Dyn. (724). Group of monuments, sandstone, Abū Simbel, 19 Dyn. (728). Block representing the 'Nine Bows', painted sandstone, Memphis—Temple of Ptah, 19 Dyn. (769). Statues of the souls of Pe, with hawk heads, and Neken, with jackal heads, granite, Karnak, 18 Dyn. (6320–1 restored).

**Gallery 20.** Head of seated colossus of Ramesses II, black granite, Luxor, 19 Dyn. (675). Part of door, sandstone inlaid with faience plaques, Madīnat Habū—Palace of Ramesses III, 20 Dyn. (677). Two clerestory windows from the same palace, sandstone, (678–9). Two arms from a colossal statue of Ramesses II, red granite, Luxor, 19 Dyn. (682).

*Gallery 19* (closed to public).

**Gallery 25.** Two statues of Harwa, schist, Karnak, 25 Dyn. (6328–9). *Centre.* Hawk faced lid of sarcophagus of King Harsiesi, pink granite, Madīnat Habū, 22 Dyn. (6251). *Cases D and E.* Statuettes of the 25–27 Dyns.

**Gallery 24.** Naos engraved with deities, granite, Ṣafṭ al-Hinnah, 30 Dyn. (790). Statue of the goddess Taweret, green schist, Karnak, 26 Dyn. (791). Offering table of Psamtik, granite, Ṣaqqārah, 26 Dyn. (854). Statue of Osiris, granite, Ṣaqqārah, 26 Dyn. (855). Statue of Isis with horns and a disk, granite, Ṣaqqārah, Dyn. (856). Goddess Hathor as a cow protecting King Psamtik, granite, Ṣaqqārah, 26 Dyn. (857, compare with similar 18 Dyn. group of Amenhotep II, No. 445–6, Gallery 12). Head of the Counsellor Montuemhat, black granite, Karnak, 25 Dyn. (1184). Head of King Taharqa, black granite, Karnak, 25 Dyn. (1185). Head of King Shabaka, granite, Karnak, 25 Dyn. (6148). Stele copy of a decree of Nectanebo II granting to the Temple of Neith the right to collect a tenth of all imported goods entering the port, black granite, Naukratis, 30 Dyn. (850). Stele of Ptolemy II recording the recovery of divine statues from Persia, granite, Tell al-Maskhūtah.

**Gallery 30.** Statue of Princess Amenartais, divine votrice of Amun, sister of King Shabaka, alabaster with black granite base, Karnak, 25 Dyn. (930). Stele of King Piankhi, grey granite, Gabal Barkal—Sudan, 25 Dyn. (937). Stele of King Tanutamun, granite, Gabal Barkal—Sudan, 25 Dyn. (938).

*Gallery 29* (closed to public).

**Gallery 35.** Objects from pyramids of Nuri and Kuru, Sudan, 7–4C BC (6088). Monuments from Egypt bearing inscriptions in foreign languages, Carian, Palmyran, Aramaic and Babylonian (6089). Proto-Semitic inscriptions from the turquoise mines, sandstone, Serabit al-Khadīm—Sinai (6054).

**Gallery 34.** Graeco-Roman. Relief of the Emperor Antoninus Pius and his family, Roman, (997). Two composite sphinxes, (6037 from Coptos, 6038). Stelae of the Buchis Bulls, limestone, Armant, Ptolemaic-Roman (6159). Two copies of the Decree of Canopus, a trilingual inscription similar to the Rosetta Stone giving rights to the temple by Ptolemy III, (980, 983). Bust of Emperor Maximianus Hercules, red porphyry, Banha, 4C AD (962). Large head of Jupiter-Serapis, marble, Kimān Fāris, 2C AD (1003). *Case B.* Statue of Aphrodite and dolphin, partly restored, Alexandria, 2–3C BC (1010). Stele with shrine inscribed in Greek, the sign board of a Cretan soothsayer, Ṣaqqārah—Serapeum, Ptolemaic (1013). Head of a Galatian prisoner, Rhodes, 3C BC (993). *W wall.* Wall paintings from Tūnah al-Gabal showing Oedipus (6247), Electra before tomb of Agamemnon (6248), Trojan horse (6249).

**Gallery 40.** Objects from Nubia. Meroitic period.

*Gallery 39* (closed to public).

**Galleries 40, 44, 45.** Nubian material, including the material excavated by Emery from the royal tombs at Balanah and Qusṭul.

SOUTH WING (E end). **Gallery 57** Coffin cover, granite, no provenance (308). Column with Byzantine capital.

Here are the SE stairs.

**Gallery 50.** Mummiform sarcophagus of General Pedisamtowi (Potasimto), 26 Dyn. (1270).

**Gallery 49.** Coffin of Petosiris, high-priest of Thoth, Tunah al-Gabal,

4C BC (6036). Altar of Ptolemy III, sandstone, Madamūd (6181). Large statue of Alexander II, limestone, Karnak (1218). Sarcophagus of the sacred ram of Khnum, Elephantine Is., Roman (1301).

CENTRAL HALL AND ATRIUM. **Gallery 43.** Entry. Two large boats, 10m long, wood, Pyramid of Senusert III—Dahshūr, 12 Dyn. (6, 9). Colossus of Senusert III, Karnak, 12 Dyn. (10).

**Gallery 38.** (S stairs to atrium.) Right. Sarcophagus of Ay, granite, broken, Tomb 23, Valley of the Kings, 18 Dyn. (624). Sarcophagus of Princess Nitocris, divine votrice of Amun, red granite, Deir al-Madinah, 26 Dyn. (640).

**Gallery 33.** The Atrium. Seated statue of King Sobek-Kha, pink granite, Tanis, 13 Dyn. (622). Two pyramidia from the unfinished pyramid of an unknown M.K. king, black basalt, S Ṣaqqārah, 13 Dyn. (7173–4). Pyramidion of King Khendjer, basalt, S Ṣaqqārah, 13 Dyn. (6175). Seated statue of King Amenemhat I, red granite, Mendes, 12 Dyn. (6215). Pyramidion of King Amenemhat III, black granite, Dahshūr, 12 Dyn. (626). Seated colossal statue of King Amenemhat I usurped by Merneptah, pink granite, Tanis, 12 Dyn. (625). Sarcophagus and canopic chest of a queen of Senusert II, probably Weret, pink granite, al-Lahūn, 12 Dyn. (6333). Two sacred boats, stone, Memphis, 19 Dyn. (590–1). Outer sarcophagus of King Psusennes I, granite, Tanis, 21 Dyn. (6337). Sarcophagus of King Tuthmosis I, quartzite, Valley of the Kings, 18 Dyn. (619). Sarcophagus of Queen Hatshepsut, quartzite, Valley of the Kings, 18 Dyn. (620). Sarcophagus of Queen Hatshepsut before becoming ruler, quartzite, Valley of the Kings, 18 Dyn. (6024). Bed of Osiris, black granite, Abydos, Saite (?) (621).

**Gallery 28.** Remains of a painted pavement from palace at al-ʿAmarnah, 18 Dyn. (627). Sarcophagus of Ankh-hor, black granite, Samannūd—Delta, Ptolemaic (6142).

**Gallery 23.** Seated figure of Sekhmet, granite, Temple of Mut—Luxor, 18 Dyn. (246). Two statues of vizier Parmessu, black granite, Karnak, 19 Dyn. (578–9). Lintels from temple of Madamūd, Senusert III, limestone, 12 Dyn. and Amenemhat-Sobek, 13 Dyn. (6189–90). Two colossal statues of King Mermesha, one usurped by King Apopi (Hyksos) and the other by Ramesses II, 19 Dyn, granite, Tanis, originally 13 Dyn. (613, 617).

**Gallery 18** (N stairs to atrium) Colossal seated group of King Amenhotep III and Queen Tiy with three of their daughters, found in fragments, limestone, Madīnat Habū, 18 Dyn. (610).

**Gallery 13.** N end. E side. The Israel stele, stele of Amehhotep III usurped by Merneptah with a reference to the crushing of the Israelites, grey granite, from the Mortuary Temple of Amenhotep III at Kom al-Hitan, Thebes, 18–19 Dyns (599). Two sphinxes of Tuthmosis III, pink granite, Festival Hall at Karnak, 18 Dyn. (6144–5). 'Stele of Year 400' of King Set a-pehti-nub, usurped by Ramesses II, granite, Tanis, Hyksos (6204).

**Upper Floor.** On the Upper Floor the arrangement is rather different, with some galleries in rough chronological order and others devoted to specific types of objects. In addition there is a special collection, the *Treasures of Tutankhamun*, which takes up two whole series of galleries in the E and W wings (see below). It is advisable to see the Tutankhamun exhibit in toto either at the start or at the end of a visit rather than in a piecemeal fashion while touring the galleries.

SOUTH WING. From the Ground Floor ascend by the SE staircase to **Gallery 57.** Coffins of the priests of Amun.

**Gallery 56** (closed to the public).

**Gallery 55** covers the geology of Egypt, with aerial photographs and prehistoric flints.

**Gallery 50** contains the funerary shrine of Queen Isimkeb, leather, 21 Dyn. (3848).

**Gallery 49.** Wood and basketry furniture, Giza, 4 Dyn. (6226–7) and foundation deposits of Seti I, 19 Dyn. (6166).

**Gallery 48.** Limestone sarcophagi and wooden coffins of Kawit and Aashit, queens of Mentuhotpe, Deir al-Baḥrī, 11 Dyn. (623, 6033–4). *Case H*: Masterpieces of the Egyptian Museum. Head of Queen Tiy (4257). Statuette of Ptah, gilded (4251). Dancing pygmies, ivory, 12 Dyn. (6128). Hippopotami, blue faience, 12 Dyn. (4221–2). Statuette of Khufu, ivory, Abydos, 4 Dyn. (4244).

**Gallery 54.** Prehistoric. Flints and pottery, near Bani Salamah (Merimde) (6200). Pottery and flints, al-Badārī near Asyūṭ (6059). N side. Wall painting, earliest in Egypt, Hierakonpolis, 1 Dyn.

**Galleries 47 and 46.** Royal coffins of the New Kingdom. Queen Aahotep II, 18 Dyn. (3872). Amenhotep I (3874), Coffin lid of Ramesses II (3877). Coffin lid of Seti I (3881). Tuthmosis IV, Tomb 35 (3882). Kamose, 17 Dyn. (3886). Tuthmosis III (3887). Tuthmosis I (3889). Tuthmosis II (3890). Seqnenre, 17 Dyn. (3893). Coffin of Ahmose I (3894).

**Gallery 53.** Predynastic. Flints with gold handles. Forked lancehead, obsidian, provenance unknown, (6191). Male figure, ivory, al-Mahasna (6201). Mummified animals found in cemeteries (6117–31, 6261).

**Gallery 55.** Prehistoric flint implements (2101–04).

**Gallery 51.** Objects from the tombs of Queen Meritamun and the priests of Amun, Thebes, 11–12 Dyns.

Here are the SW stairs.

Opposite Gallery 46, along the W Wing of the Upper Floor, Galleries 41, 36, 31, 26, 21, 16 and 11 display the museum's collection of coffins.

**Gallery 43.** Early dynastic or Archaic objects, from the Tomb of Hemaka at Ṣaqqārah, 1 Dyn. Wooden sickles with flint teeth, large adzes, arrows, flint knives, alabaster and pottery vessels, (6277). Vase of trefoil form, schist, 2nd Dyn. (6280). Vase intended for lotus flowers, schist, Ṣaqqārah (6279). Reconstruction of a piece of limestone walling set with blue faience tiles from S tomb of the Step Pyramid at Ṣaqqārah, 3 Dyn. (6278). Vase imitating basket work, schist, Ṣaqqārah, 1 Dyn. (6281). Stone vases from the Step Pyramid, 3 Dyn. (6255–6). Vase with cordage marks, alabaster, Abydos, 1 Dyn. (3054).

WEST WING. **Gallery 42.** Material of the 1–2 Dyns from Abydos, Hierakonpolis and Ḥalwān. Stelae erected over brick mastabas of King Peribsen, 2 Dyn. (7); Queen Merneith, 1 Dyn. (3076). Statue of Khasekhem, 2 Dyn. (3056). Ivory statuettes, Hierakonpolis (3057–8). Statue of Khasekhem, schist, Hierakonpolis, 2 Dyn. (3056). Stele of Qa, limestone, Abydos, 1 Dyn. (3066). Tablet with name of Menes, ivory, 1 Dyn. (3051). State palettes including the Narmer palette, representing the unification of Egypt; Narmer is shown twice, as the king of Upper Egypt and as the King of Lower Egypt; schist, Hierakonpolis, just prior to 1 Dyn., c 3100 BC (3055). Slate plaques with royal names, Abydos.

**Gallery 37.** Four Middle Kingdom coffins (3101–4).

**Gallery 32.** Models of Old Kingdom (3139–42, 3123–27).

**Gallery 27.** Models of Soul Houses from Rifeh, M.K. (3270–73). Granary (3274). Goose (3331). Imitation foods (3338–40). Models from Tomb of Meket-Re, Thebes. (3055). Two groups of model soldiers marching four abreast, Nubian bowmen and Egyptian infantrymen with cowhide shields, Asyūṭ, Tomb-Chapel of Meshti, 12 Dyn.

**Gallery 22.** Funerary material. Heart scarabs (3353–59, 3361–62). New Kingdom stelae (3364–65). Statuettes placed on graves (3367). Model coffins with hawk heads, Ptolemaic (3473–75). Hypocephali, disks covered with magical formulae placed under the head of a mummy (3590–91).

**Gallery 17.** Funerary material from 20 Dyn. tomb of Sennedjem, Deir al-Madīnah. Outer coffin and mummy cover (2003). Bed, chair and stools (2004). Square, level and plumb-bob (2005). Door of painted wood (2006a). Funerary figures and other objects (2007). Outer coffin of Khonsu, a relative of Sennedjem, also found in the tomb (2002). Coffin of Sennedjem (2001).

**Gallery 12.** Material from the Royal Tombs, Valley of the Kings, 18 Dyn. Three of the four bricks placed in the wall to protect the tomb, Tuthmosis IV (3731–33). Faience cylinders from tomb of Tuthmosis IV (3734–35). Woven tapestry (3736–38). Wooden head of cow, Amenhotep II (3761). Two uraei representing Mertseger, goddess of the Necropolis, painted wood, Amenhotep II (3764). Two leopards which would have carried statues of the king on their backs, wood covered in resin, Amenhotep II (3766). Statuette of Amenhotep II, covered in resin, (3766). Shroud of Tuthmosis III covered with spells from Book of the Dead (3772). Shawabti box of King Pinujem I, wood, (3782). Inlaid box of Queen Hatshepsut, wood, (3792). Box of Ramesses II, wood and ivory, (3785).

**Gallery 13.** Unrobbed tomb of Yuya and Tuya in the Valley of the Kings, 18 Dyn. Bed with string meshwork, wood and gilded gesso (3613). Osiride grain figures (3614–15). Boxes containing food, wood (3633). Yuya's ceremonial wig (3634). Miniature coffins, wood covered with gold leaf (3635). Amulets of glass, carnelian and stone (3636). Papyrus sandals (3637). Shawabti boxes (3641). Yuya's walking sticks and staves (3648). Boxes painted to imitate ebony and ivory (3649–50). Wig basket (3651). Funerary statuettes, wood, alabaster, bronze (3660). Second mummiform coffin of Yuya (3666). Outer coffin of Yuya (3667). Sarcophagus to hold nesting coffins of Yuya (3668). Inner coffins of Yuya and Tuya (3669 and 3671). Three armchairs inscribed with name of Sit Amun, daughter of Amenhotep III (3672–4). Light chariot, wood and leather (3676). Beds, wood (3679–80). Jars, wood, limestone and alabaster (3686–89). Canopic jars of Yuya and Tuya, alabaster (3690–93). Canopic chests, wood (3694–95).

NORTH WING. Across the Tutankhamun galleries, in the extreme NW corner is **Gallery 6.** Scarabs of all periods including heart and marriage scarabs of Amenhotep III and Queen Tiy; lion hunt and cattle hunt scarabs.

Here are the NW stairs.

**Gallery 2E.** Material from tomb of Queen Hetepheres, wife of King Sneferu, found at Giza, 4 Dyn. Most of the furniture has been reconstructed. Frame of canopy (6199). Vases and dishes, alabaster (6042). Beaker and toilet dishes, gold (6043). Ewer and basin, copper (6044). Tools left by workmen in tomb, copper, (6045). Box containing alabaster jars with named ointments (6046). Canopic jar, alabaster (6047). Head rest, wood overlaid with silver and gold, (6160). Armchair, gilded wood (6161). Bed, gilded wood, (6162). Box containing inlaid silver anklets (6163–64). Sarcophagus, alabaster, (6025).

**Gallery 2W.** Material from the royal burials of Tanis, 21–22 Dyns. Hawk-headed coffin of King Sheshonq, silver, 22 Dyn. (6287). Objects from the tomb of Psusennes I, 21 Dyn. Coffin sarcophagus of red granite (6288–89, 6337). Mask, silver gilt (6290). Collars, gold (6291). Bead from Assyria, lapis, (6292). Armlet with king's name, gold (6293). Four pectorals inscribed with Chapter 30B of Book of the Dead, lapis (6294–95, 8603–42). Ends of a bow, gold (6297). Bracelet inscribed for Osorkon I and Queen Karama, gold, 22 Dyn. (6300). Stele of Amenhotep II reused to cover the funerary chamber of Prince Sheshonq, quartzite (6301). Jewellery belonging to Psusennes II, 22 Dyn. (6291–6).

**Gallery 3.** *The Jewel Room.* This contains 1 Dyn. material from Abydos. Four bracelets of gold, amethyst and turquoise from a queen's arm (4000–03). Amulets of 6 Dyn. from Nagʿ al-Deir (4004). Pendants, sheet gold, 1 Dyn. Nagʿ al-Deir (4005). Head of hawk, gold, 6 Dyn. (4010). Necklaces from al-Bersha, 12 Dyn. (4013–15). Lions, gold, 12 Dyn. (4017–18). Falcon, gold, 12 Dyn. (4020). Objects from the tomb of Queen Aahotope, 18 Dyn. (4030–57), including gold flies which were military decorations, axe of King Amose and dagger. Objects from the tomb of Princess Khnumet, Dahshūr, 12 Dyn. (3898–3991) including two splendid crowns, a usekh collar from the tomb of Princess Itaweret and objects from al-Lahūn, the tomb of Sit Hathor Iniut. Bracelet (3946), circlet (3999); gold pectoral (3998); pectoral with name of Senusert II (3983); lions (3976); pectorals (3970–71); girdle of gold cowries (3950); gold filet from tomb of Princess Merit (3952); amethyst necklaces from same tomb (3951).

EAST WING. **Gallery 14.** Masks, coffins and Roman portraits from the Fayyūm (4260–63 and 4310–20).

**Gallery 19.** Statuettes of deities in metal, stone and pottery. Cippi of Horus (4750); statues of all the main gods and goddesses and their animals (4411–93). Stelae from the Serapeum (4496).

**Gallery 24.** Drawings and trial pieces on fragments of limestone. Plan of a tomb (4371). Sketches of heads of humans and animals.

**Gallery 29.** Papyri, writing materials, writing reeds (2502). Grinders for ink (2503). Palettes (2504). Hieratic papyri (2505 A–C). Documents in Demotic (2506 A–B). Documents in Greek on papyrus and vellum (2507). Aramaic papyri from Elephantine, 6C BC (2508). Ostraca on both pottery and stone (2510–11). Funerary papyri (2512).

**Gallery 34.** Tools, weapons and small objects of various periods, including daggers, lances, axes, weights and measures, games, toys, cosmetics, vases, weaving instruments, sledges (5233, 5330, 5377, 5460).

**Gallery 39.** Graeco-Roman. Vases, figurines, terracottas and bronze vases. (6102–13)

**Gallery 44.** Arts and crafts. Inlays and decorations, mainly New Kingdom, Madīnat Habū (5181 and 5192). Faience inlays from Qantir (5101–6137).

**The Treasures of Tutankhamun.** This collection is exhibited in the E and N wings and includes *galleries 45, 40, 35, 30, 25, 20, 15, 10, 9, 8, 7 and 4.* All of the objects come from his tomb, No. 52 in the Valley of the Kings at Thebes. They are 18 Dyn. in date and are not exhibited in order of discovery. The collection has its own series of registration numbers.

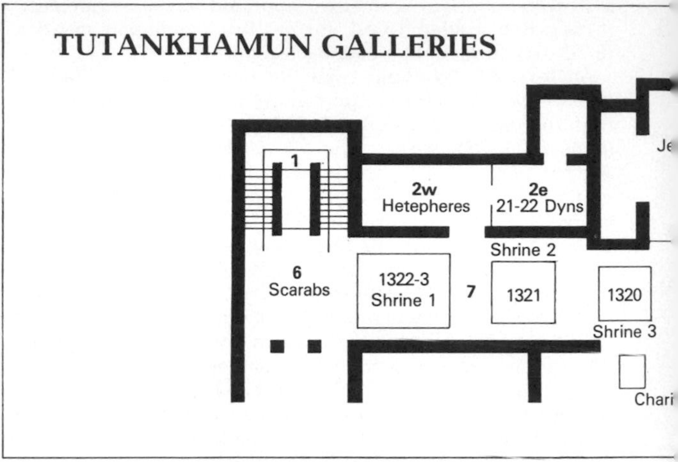
TUTANKHAMUN GALLERIES
1
2w
Hetepheres
2e
21-22 Dyns
Shrine 2
6
Scarabs
1322-3
Shrine 1
7
1321
1320
Shrine 3
Je
Chari

EAST WING. **Gallery 45.** Two life-sized wooden statues of Tutankhamun in ka form, covered in black resin and gesso, gilded headcloth, kilt and sandals. One wears the 'nemes headcloth', the other the 'khat'. Both hold a staff in the left hand and mace in the right (96, 181). Wall cases. Shields, ceremonial, of gilded wood representing the King as a sphinx treading on his enemies, or killing lions. Plain hunting shields covered with leopard skins (753–54, 733). Casket with the King shown hunting and fishing, on the lid the King and Queen are offering flowers, wood inlaid with ivory (1189). Ostrich-feather fan inscribed with King's name, the bent handle ending in a lotus bud (448). Gaming board with stand and playing pieces, ivory (540–42, 566).

**Gallery 40.** Carrying-chest in the form of a naos surmounted by the jackal Anubis. The animal is covered with black resin and has a gold collar. When found it was draped in linen, except for the head, and had a gold leash, wood (447). Model boat rigged for sailing, painted with deck house and steering oars, wood (459).

**Gallery 35.** Cabinet inlaid with ankh and was symbols, and with the King's titulary, set on legs of wood and ivory (738). Five statuettes of the King: with the Red Crown of Lower Egypt on a papyrus boat, gilded wood (407), carried on the head of the goddess Menkarer (408), wearing the White Crown of Upper Egypt (409), wearing the White Crown on the back of a leopard coated with resin (410), with crook and flail (411). The Four Sons of Horus, gilded wood (412–16). Statuettes of the gods placed in the tomb to protect the King, gilded wood: Inhuret-Shu (417); the falcon Sopdu on a perch (418); the falcon Gemhesu on a perch (419); Geb (420); Nephthys (421); Atum (422); Ihy (423); Mamu (424); Isis (425); serpent Neter-ʿankh (427); Sekhmet (428); Horus (429); Sened in mummified form (430); Tata (431); Ptah (432); Tatenen (433); Horus the Great (434). Upright cases on the W side. Shawabti figures of the King, gilded wood, stone, faience (462–69, 472–75, 766–827, 906–08, 1086–1183 and 1351–78). Over 400 of these figures were found in the tomb. Some were placed in black boxes shaped like shrines covered in resin; some carried baskets,

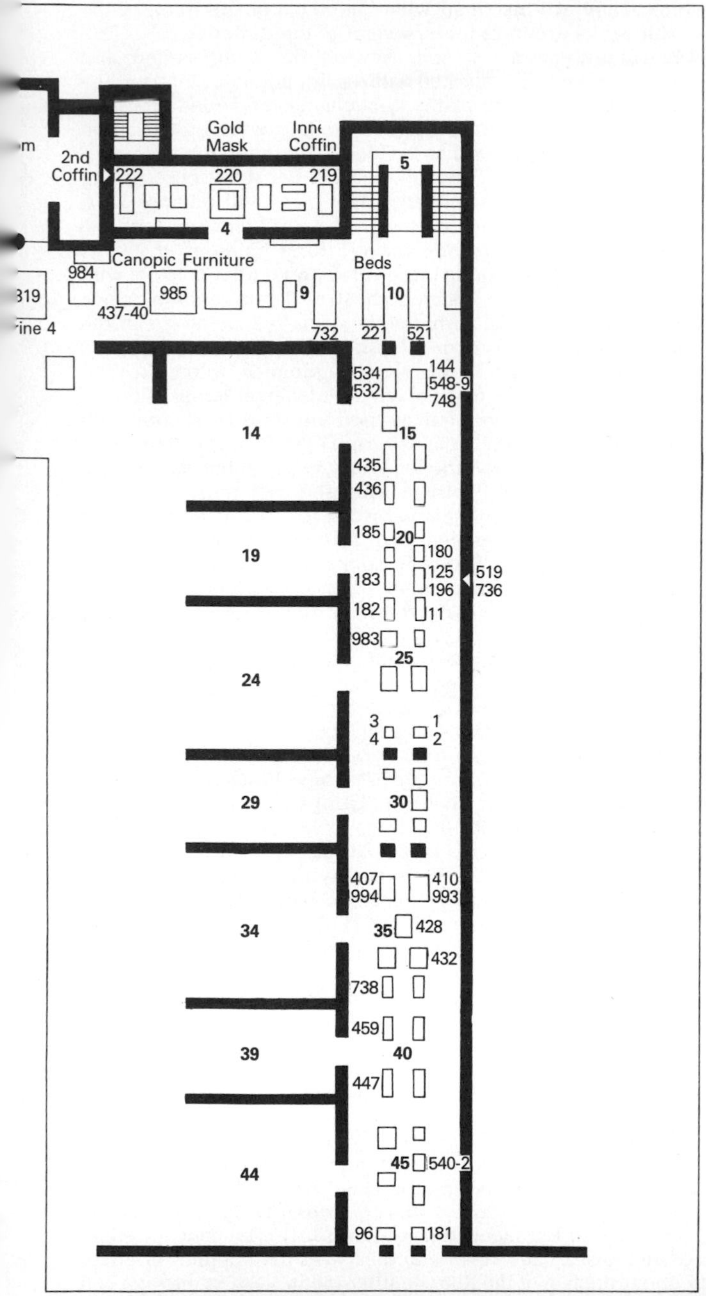
Gold Mask
Inne Coffin
2nd Coffin
222
220
219
5
4
Canopic Furniture
Beds
984
319
437-40
985
9
10
rine 4
732
221
521
534
532
144
548-9
748
14
15
435
436
185
20
180
19
183
125
196
519
736
182
11
983
25
24
3
4
1
2
29
30
407
994
410
993
34
35
428
432
738
459
39
40
447
44
45
540-2
96
181

hoes and whips. They are inscribed with Chapter 6 of the Book of the Dead. These shawabtis are in cases in several of the galleries.

**Gallery 30.** Tutankhamun's throne showing the King seated and Queen offering him a vase. It is marked with earlier and later forms of the King's and Queen's names. The plants symbolising the Union of Upper and Lower Egypt (lily and papyrus) between the legs were broken off in antiquity. Wood covered with gesso and gilded, decorated in polychrome with faience, glass, stones, gold and silver (1). A footstool representing the 'Nine Bows', wood and gesso covered with glass and gilding (2). A chair carved with the god Heh holding notched palm branches, with the ankh sign hanging from his arm, wishing the King 'millions of years'; cedar wood, the disk nails and angle pieces are of gold (3). Footstool with bound prisoners, red wood (4). Painted chest of Tutankhamun which contained clothing and sandals, with unique miniature paintings of the king driving his chariot and destroying Asiatic and Nubian enemies; the ends show the king as a sphinx massacring his enemies, wood, (324).

**Gallery 25.** In this gallery are cases of carved alabaster lamps, some in the shape of a lotus (11), unguent jars painted and decorated, one with hunting scenes, and a reclining lion on the top (183). Folding chair, parts of the sign of the Union between the legs torn away, ebony inlaid with faience, ivory and glass (983). Footstool with tied prisoners. This chair dates from the early part of Tutankhamun's reign before he had discarded the Aten name (982). Two-handled cup inscribed with a name of Tutankhamun, alabaster (229). Throwing sticks (632–40, 612–14, 1060–63). Chair and footstool of Tutankhamun when a child, wood (22–23). Stool, wood and ivory, (24). Vases, some in the al-ʿAmārnah style, earthenware (1499, 1223, 601).

**Gallery 20.** Decorated walking sticks (736, 740–43). Trumpets, copper ornamented with gold (125); silver ornamented with gold (188). Trumpet of Tutankhamun, with wooden block to keep the shape (this trumpet was sounded in 1939 and the lowest note was D), copper mounted with gold (127). Stocks for ceremonial ostrich-feather fans (188, 734). Cartouche of Akhenaten (187) showing King hunting ostriches. Wooden sticks with heads of Nubians and Asiatics (178–80). Lamps and perfume vases, carved and painted alabaster (183–85).

**Gallery 15.** Bed with white string mesh. At foot vertical panel representing the god Bes flanked by two lions, ebony (20). Bed covered with sheet gold, plant decoration on foot panel, wood with white basket work (530). Folding bed, wood with copper hinges (1187). Headrests: turquoise blue glass (531), dark blue faience (532), ivory (533), wooden folding type with god Bes (534). Sacred goose of Amun, wood covered with black resin (194). Model boat on a pedestal with cabin and bow and stern in form of ibex heads, alabaster (535). *W side.* Two symbols of Anubis, carved papyrus stalk supporting skin of animal, gilded and set in vase, wood and alabaster (435–36). Vases with life symbols or sma-tawi, alabaster (548, 748). Unguent vessel in form a ibex, one horn missing, alabaster (144, 545).

NORTH WING. **Gallery 10.** Large couch with mythical animal heads (221). Lion-headed couch probably wrongly inscribed Mehturt (cow goddess), may have been intended as Menhyt (lion goddess) (732). Cow-headed couch, probably Hathor but labelled Isis-Meht (521). The couches are of wood with gilded gesso. *Side cases.* Sandals with the enemies of Egypt represented under the feet of the King, leather (565). Vase in the form of a pomegranate, silver (576). Centre case. Costume jewellery of ʿAmārnah type (944–46).

**Gallery 9.** *Centre*. Canopic containers: (i) frame of the cover, (ii) canopic chest in the form of a shrine set on a sledge surrounded by the guardian goddesses (985), (iii) alabaster canopic chest containing the miniature coffins (984). Between these two is a case containing the four alabaster heads to cap the four compartments of the canopic chest (437–40).

**Gallery 4.** This contains the coffins, mask and jewellery of Tutankhamun. *Centre case*. The gold mask of Tutankhamun. The head is covered by the 'nemes headcloth' with the cobra and vulture emblems on the forehead. The eyes and eyelids are inlaid with lapis lazuli, the broad collar is topped by hawks' heads (220). In the surrounding cases are bracelets worn by the King during life, made of lapis, carnelian and glass (256–57) and pectorals worn by the King in life (227–32). *Side case*. Six sheet gold collars, made only for funerary use, two collars of Nekhbet, the vulture goddess, a collar of Wadjet the cobra goddess, a Horus collar (318–23). *E side*. The sheet gold inner coffin weighs 204kg; it represents the King in Osiride form clasping the crook and the flail, on the lower part the goddesses Isis and Nephthys spread their wings over his legs (219). Originally the coffin was covered with a linen shroud on which were placed wreaths of flowers. In the table cabinets are the four miniature coffins which contained the viscera of the King, gold inlaid with glass and semi-precious stones (452, 1184–86). Two sets of crooks and flails, one for use when the King was a small boy, gilded wood inlaid with glass and carnelian (86, 403–06). A kherep sceptre (536). Dagger, gold (225); dagger, iron (226). *Centre*: to the left of the central case are many pectorals and rings worn by the King in life (342–45, 347–54, 356–60); rings and earrings (363–67); pectorals (369–76); mirror cases (377–78); a papyrus burnisher (379); amulets (384–85, 387–89); pectorals of gold, glass and semi-precious stones (368); writers' palettes (380–82). *Case on the N side*. Diadem decorated with gold rosettes with the vulture and uraeus (317). Perfume box in the form of cartouches of the King surmounted by plumes (223). *W side*. The second coffin, originally intended for Smenkhkare, predecessor of Tutankhamun, whose erased cartouches were filled with the latter's name; the face is heavier and represents an older man: wood with a gold coating, the head and hands are covered with a thicker layer of gold (222). The outer coffin containing the body of Tutankhamun is kept in the tomb at Thebes. *S side*. A flat case containing the gold sheathing found on the mummy and the gold toe and finger stalls (266, 328–31, 336). Gold sandals from the feet of the mummy (327). Trappings of gold found on the mummy (334–36). Gloves (337–40).

Set in the centre of **Galleries 8 and 7** are the four shrines that enclosed the sarcophagus of Tutankhamun. They are of wood covered with gilded gesso, the gold leaf of varying quality. The decoration is of scenes of the Egyptian Afterworld. The doors were shut with ebony bolts, working on silver rings, tied with a cord and sealed. The Fourth (innermost) Shrine is in the shape of the Shrine of Lower Egypt, the Per Nu or House of Flame. On the inside of the doors are figures of Isis and Nephthys with wings outspread protecting the king. On the side and rear walls is the text of Chapter 17 of the Book of the Dead (1319). The Third Shrine is in the form of the Shrine of Upper Egypt (1320) as is the Second Shrine (1321) while the First (outermost) Shrine is in the form of the Heb-sed Hall (1322). A great gilt wooden framework which carried a great pall of linen (now destroyed) between the two outermost shrines (1323).

*Innermost coffin of Tutankhamun. Sheet gold*

*S side*. State and hunting chariots, they were dismantled to take into the tomb. State chariots (97–116, 100–01, 104); hunting chariots (1324–25). Gilded plywood with the bases made from plaited leather thongs, the wheels of bent wood with leather tyres and spokes of glued wood. Chariot harness including spiked disks used to keep the stallions from biting one another (116). Saddles (105–08), gilded falcon finials (111–12); the bits must have been solid gold and are missing. Goads (124, 1698).

# 3 Inner Districts

Rte 3 embraces the areas surrounding the central district of al-Taḥrīr Square. All are within 2km of the square except for the extremities of the islands, both of which can be reached by bus from it.

## A. Ramsīs Square

**Cairo Atlas 8.**

Beyond the Shʿ. 26 Yūlyū, the Shʿ. Ramsīs and the parallel Shʿ. Galā' pass on the W the Shʿ. Shahāfah (NW through Būlāq) and, just beyond, the offices of the newspaper *Al-Ahrām*, on into the area called Bāb al-Ḥadīd and the MAYDĀN RAMSĪS(Ramsīs Square), also called Maydān al-Mahaṭṭah.

This large square is the site of the ancient port of *Tendunyas*, once on the East Bank of the Nile, which served the city of Heliopolis. After the Arab conquest it was called al-Maks (the Customs Point). During the refortification of the city by Ṣalāḥ al-Dīn in the 12C it was the site of the W terminal gate of the N walls, the Bāb al-Ḥadīd (Iron Gate) or Bāb al-Baḥr (River Gate). With the westward retreat of the Nile the port was left high and dry although the gate remained standing until the 19C. It was demolished by Muḥammad ʿAlī in 1847 to make way for the railway station.

Occupying the whole of the NW side of the square is **Cairo Station** (al-Mahaṭṭat Miṣr; 8:2), the main railway station built in 1851 with lines to all stations in the Nile Valley and throughout the Delta and NW coast. At the N end of the building is the **State Railway Museum** (small fee). Hrs 08.30–13.30 ex. Mon. Egypt was one of the first nations outside Europe to adopt the railway, the first tracks being laid between Cairo and Alexandria (1851–56) under the supervision of Robert Stephenson, son of George. Two floors contain a marvellous display for the railway enthusiast with models and plans of bridges, tracks, stations and of course the engines themselves. Most impressive is the mid-19C engine built for Muḥammad Saʿid Pasha lacquered in maroon and gold while on the second floor is the model of the complete train of Khedive Ismaʿil and his harīm with open pavilions and luxurious saloons. The Khedive ʿAbbās II was fascinated by trains and often used to drive them himself. On the NE side of the square is **al-Mahaṭṭah al-Kubrī Līmūn** (opened in 1910), the local railway station, servicing NE Cairo out to Heliopolis. In the centre of the square is an ornamental water tank, at the NE end of which, standing above five water jets, is a rose-granite *Colossus of Ramesses II* with, beside his left leg, Princess Bant Anta. It is 9.7m high and was brought from Memphis in 1955. Beside this is the *Bus Terminal*. The 6 October Bridge crosses the square diagonally from the SW and descends in the NE corner.

Many roads radiate from this square. To the W, reached by a bridge, is the SHʿ. SABTIYYAH (to the Corniche) while slightly to the N, following the S-bound track to the West Bank is the SHʿ. KUBRĪ IMBĀBAH. Leaving from the same point are two other roads: due N the SHʿ. SHŪBRĀ and to the NE the SHʿ. TIRʿAH AL-BŪLĀQIYYAH. From the station the Delta railway line sweeps E and then N with on its W flank the SHʿ. AḤMAḌ ḤILMĪ. Following the local railway line the Shʿ. Ramsīs continues to the NE while from the SE corner of the square running E is the SHʿ. KĀMIL SIDKĪ (to Shʿ. Būr Saʿīd) through the area called al-Faggālah. Also from the SE is the SHʿ. KLUT BAK (Clut Bay to Maydān al-ʿAtabah, see below), from which several roads lead off in turn. First on the N is the BAYN AL-ḤĀRATAY-Nand just beyond the SHʿ. BĀB AL-BAḤR(both to the Shʿ. Būr Saʿīd). Due S the SHʿ. AL-GUMHŪRIYYAH runs to Maydān al-Gumhūriyyah (see below). At the head of the Shʿ. al-Gumhūriyyah on the E side is a large elaborate fountain called the *Sabīl-Kuttab of Zibah Khadījah* (d. 1878) locally called the Sabīl Walīdah built in 1870 by the Italian architect Pantarelli for the last wife of Muḥammad ʿAlī, mother of Muḥammad ʿAlī the Younger. It is now a distribution office for the al-Ahrām newspaper. On the W side of the road stands the recent *Masgid al-Fath*. 20 years in the building it carries the highest minaret in the world (95 m).

## B. Al-Azbakiyyah Garden

**Cairo Atlas 8.**

The **al-Azbakiyyah Garden** (Ḥadīqat al-Azbakiyyah; 8:7) is a large rectangular area, once whole but now bisected E to W by the Shʿ. 26 Yūlyū which terminates here. It gives its name to the whole district.

This area has a fascinating history which begins in the latter part of the 15C. Up to this time it had been a large lake, fed by the Nāṣirī Canal, and surrounded by rich farmlands and orchards. It was chosen in 1470 by Amīr Azbak, atabak of Sultan Qāyt-bāy, as the site for his palace. He had the pool enlarged which encouraged other notables to build houses on the banks and it soon became one of the most prosperous districts of Cairo. During Ottoman times it retained this status, the inhabitants being mainly rich bays and merchants. The most magnificent palace was built on the NW bank by Muḥammad Bāy al-Alfī in the late 18C and it was commandeered by Napoleon during the French occupation as his headquarters. A school of languages was later established in it and in 1849 Samuel Shepheard bought it from the Pasha ʿAbbās I (for two whippets Ben and Bess) and granted permission to open it as an hotel. It was demolished in 1862 and a new *Shepheard's Hotel* built on the same site stood as one of the great hotels of the world until burned in the anti-British riots of 1952. The latest Shepheard's Hotel now stands on the Corniche in Garden City.

By the early 19C, the lake was only flooded during the inundation and was used to grow crops during the rest of the year. Muḥammad ʿAlī had the Nāṣirī Canal filled in and the lake converted into formal gardens. Of such elegance was the area that several of the early pashas would relax in the refreshment pavilions alongside rich Egyptians and promenading foreigners. Much commercial development was undertaken by Ismāʿīl Pasha in the 1870s and Barillet-Deschamps redesigned the garden.

5000 gas lamps in tulip-shaped glasses illuminated the gardens at night. It became the tourist as well as the business centre of Cairo and so it remained until well into the 20C. After the revolution the Shʿ. 26 Yūlyū was pushed through the centre and casinos and cafés were built along the edge, changing the character of the park although many of its large trees are still standing.

Adjacent to the S is the Maydān al-Ubirā (Opera Square), a much smaller square which contained the theatre later called the *Opera House*.

It was built by Ismāʿīl in 1868 for the entertainment of the dignitaries who came to the opening of the Suez Canal in November 1869. The inaugural opera was Verdi's 'Rigoletto'. The same composer was also commissioned to write an opera with an Egyptian theme. 'Aida' was the result, the plot of which was suggested by the Egyptologist Mariette. The Opera House was burnt down in October 1971 and the site now serves as a car park. This was a somewhat poetic demise as the Khedive Ismāʿīl, to facilitate the purchase of the area, had wilfully had the buildings fired, luckily without loss of life.

To the S on the corner of the Shʿ. Qaṣr al-Nīl stands the *Mosque of ʿUthmān Katkhudā* (264; 15:2), built in 1764 but reconstructed by ʿAbbās II.

Along the N side of the square is the *Sūr al-Azbakiyyah*, once known for the second-hand book market. At the W end of the square is a fine equestrian *statue of Ibrāhīm Pasha* by Cordier.

From the SE corner of the square a road leads into the Maydān al-ʿAtabah al-Khudrā (Square of Green Steps; 9:8) containing the *Central Post and Telegram Exchange*. Attached to this is the **Postal Museum**, small fee, tickets from the alley at side. Hrs 09.00–13.00). This again is a delightful exhibition, no single tastefully lit didactic items, but case after case of stamps, dies, letters, models and postal paraphenalia. It displays the history of the postal service from Pharaonic times to the present including the early 19C Suez express to India set up by Thomas Waghorn. In 1858 Anthony Trollope was in Egypt negotiating on behalf of the GPO. At the far end of the gallery is the ornate black lacquer table of the Post Master General and behind this a vast collage of the Sphinx composed entirely of Egyptian stamps produced for the Postal Union Congress held in Cairo in 1934 which led to the establishment of this museum by King Fūʾād. On the S side of the square is the *Central Fire Station* and to the SE the *ʿAtabah Bus and Tram Station*. N from Maydān al-ʿAtabahʾ runs the SHʿ. AL-RUWAYʿĪ. After 300m on the W is the *Mosque al-Ruwayʿī* (55; 9:5). This is a 17C Ottoman mosque with a mid-15C minaret, all that remains of the earlier mosque built for Aḥmad al-Ruwayʿī, Supervisor of Merchants. (His tomb is on the opposite side of the ḤĀRAT AL-RUWAYʿĪ.) The road continues N as the SHʿ. AL-FUWĀṬIYYAH to Shʿ. Sh. al-ʿArūssī (Rte 7).

From the E side of Maydān al-ʿAtabah the SHʿ. AL-GAYSH runs NE to the Shʿ. Būr Saʿīd and on to the Maydān al-Gaysh (Rte 19). Due E is the SHʿ. AL-MUSKĪ (to Maydān al-Azhar, Rte 6) with one of the great street markets of Cairo, attracting vast numbers of Egyptians. Also leaving the square from this point is the SHʿ. AL-AZHAR to the Shʿ. Būr Saʿīd and on to Maydān al-Azhar. Slightly SE is the start of another road, the SHʿ. AL-QALʿAH, which runs SE straight to the Maydān Ṣalāḥ al-Dīn and the Citadel (Rte 14). SW the Shʿ. ʿAbd al-ʿAzīz runs through to Maydān al-Gumhūriyyah (Rte 3C).

## C. Al-Gumhūriyyah Square

**Cairo Atlas 15, 16.**

From the Maydān al-Falakī the Shʿ. al-Taḥrīr continues SE into MAYDĀN AL-GUMHŪRIYYAH (Square of the Republic, previously ʿAbdīn Square; 15:4). On the N is the building of the *Muhāfaẓat al-Qāhirah* (Governate of Cairo) and filling the whole of the E side is the Republican **Palace al-ʿAbidīn**, the state headquarters of the president of the A.R.E. giving its name to the surrounding district of ʿ**Abidīn**.

Originally this was the site, adjoining the ʿAbidīn Mosque (Rte 12), that ʿAbd al-Raḥmān Katkhudā chose for his home. In the mid-18C he built a magnificent palace with a large garden here. This was demolished in 1863 by the Khedive Ismāʿīl who wished to have a presence in the centre of the city and built the palace which remained the official residence of the royal family. A great fire destroyed half of the palace in 1891. Khedive Tawfīq rebuilt it and it was subsequently renovated by ʿAbbās II, Fūʾād and Fārūq. The façade is completely European in style and the interior is decorated in the opulent fashion of the former royal family. After the revolution it was opened to the public but it is now closed. During Ramaḍān a very large tent fills the centre of the square where the people come to hear the greatest reciters read the Qurʾān all day.

Along the N side of the palace enclosure the SHʿ. SĀMĪ AL-BĀRŪDĪ runs E to Maydān Aḥmad Māhir (Rte 7) while along the S side the Shʿ. Shaykh Riḥān runs W to the Corniche near Taḥrīr Sq. and E into Shʿ. Būr Saʿīd (Rte 12). On the E side is the *Mosque al-Fatḥ* (Rte 12). To the N of the square the Shʿ. al-Gumhūriyyah runs due N to Azbakiyyah Garden and on to Maydān Ramsīs.

## D. Fumm al-Khalīg

**Cairo Atlas 20, 28.**

South from Bāb al-Luq the Shʿ. Manṣūr passes Garden City (Rte 1) and Qaṣr al-ʿAyni on the W, the districts of ʿAbidīn (Rte 3C) and Sayyidah Zaynab (Rte 13) on the E. Just E of the road at 1.8km is the Maydān al-Ṭibī. This is crossed by the SHʿ. AL-SADD AL-BARRĀNĪ (NE to Maydān Sayyidah Zaynab and SW to Fumm al-Khalīg; see below). To the SE the SHʿ. BAYRAM AL-TUNSĪ runs to the area of Zaynhum (Rte 11).

On the SE side of the Maydān al-Ṭibī are extensive Christian cemeteries inside which stands the **Monastery of St. Menas** (Deir Abū Mīnā; 21:5), surrounded by a high wall. This complex is first mentioned as being rebuilt in 724; the recent renovation has been underaken by the CPAM. On entering stairs lead down to the *Church of St. Menas*, a basilica with piers separating the nave from the aisles. On the left the anbon is supported on twelve pillars. The central haykal, with the usual screen, contains a bolster with the relics of the brother and sister SS. Behnam and Sarah, martyred by their own father. Relics of St. Menas once kept here were returned to the Shrine of St. Menas (Rte 42E.) in 1962. S of the haykals is the door to a passage leading to the *Church of St. Behnam*. Here are two sanctuaries, the screen to that on the S dated 1775. Stairs give access to the upper floor of St. Menas and the *Church of St. George*. This has a shrine containing relics of the saint and a screen to the N sanctuary dated 1747.

To the SW the Shʿ. al-Sadd al-Barrānī crosses the metro line and enters the Maydān Fumm al-Khalīg on the riverbank. The **Fumm al-Khalīg** (mouth of the canal; 20:8) is the site where the Khalīg al-Miṣrī (Cairo Canal) left the Nile. Although the early history is confused it seems to have been built originally in Ptolemaic times. From here it passed NE through the Delta to join the canal built by Neko (26 Dyn.) along the Wadi Ṭumaylāt and thence to the Red Sea. During the Roman period it was recut, and again after the Muslim conquest by ʿAmr b. al-ʿĀṣ. Sultan Al-Nāṣir Muḥammad (14C) had a new channel cut slightly to the N, and the khedive Ismāʿīl constructed a much larger canal even further N (Rte 18). Thus by the beginning of the 20C this section was no longer used and was filled in; the route it followed through Cairo is now the Shʿ. Būr Saʿīd. (Rtes 7 and 12). During its useful life one of the most important official functions in the calendar was the annual Cutting the Canal ceremony. This took place at the beginning of the inundation season, the exact date decided by the level of river at the Nilometer (Rte 3E). It was attended by the head of state and the most important officials and celebrated throughout the city with festivities and fireworks.

Also from this point an aqueduct crossed Cairo to service the Citadel. The massive hexagonal **Burg al-Saqiyyah** (20:8), an intake tower, can be seen just to the S. This is the last of a series that followed the bank of river as it moved westward and was built by Sultan Qānṣūḥ al-Ghawrī in 1505–08. It measures 38m wide by 25m high, and the masonry is smooth. On the W side is a carved medallion of the sultan. A great cistern which communicated directly with the Nile via a conduit occupies the base of the tower. A ramp wound around the inside serving the oxen which operated the six great water wheels.

The **Aqueduct** (20:8) leaves from the E face; the channel rests on a series of pointed arches with tall piers of rusticated masonry. This runs E for 2155m and then turns NE towards the Citadel and ends at the remains of another water tower. The total length is 3405m. The section built by al-Ghawrī joins a part built by Sultan al-Nāṣir Muḥammad and for the last few hundred metres to the Citadel it runs above the wall built by Ṣalāḥ al-Dīn (Rte 15). The structure was repaired in 1727–28 by ʿAbdī Bak and Napoleon had many of the arches filled and converted it into a wall. In 1810 Muḥammad al-Ṭubāl repaired it for Muḥammad ʿAlī and also built a branch to service the Southern Cemetery which ended just near the Mosque of Imām Shāfiʿī. It remained in use until 1872 when a modern water system was introduced.

Just E of Fumm al-Khalīg the Shʿ. Manṣūr continues S into the old city (Rte 16).

South of Garden City (Rte 1) the Corniche continues along the riverbank passing through the district of **Qaṣr al-ʿAyni**.—500m beyond the Meridian Bridge (Rte 1) is the *Qaṣr al-ʿAyni Bridge* leading to *Cairo University Hospital* on Rawḍah Island. Just beyond this bridge, to the E of the road stands the **Qaṣr al-ʿAyni Hospital**, on the site of a palace built by Muḥ. Bay Abū ʾl-Dhabab. Muḥammad ʿAlī purchased it and transferred his Medical School here from Abū Zaʿbal in the 1830s. Here Dr Antoine

Clot (died 1860), with the title of Bey, trained many of the first generation of Egyptian doctors. One of his most eminent assistants was the brilliant young Theodore Bilharz (died 1862) who revealed the complicated life history of the scourge of Egypt, the Schistosomiasis (Bilharzia) parasite.

The next bridge (150m) is *al-Manyal Bridge* which leads E to Rawḍah Island, as does *al-Ṣayālah Bridge* (475m). Continuing S past the Great Water Tower, at 925m the *Malik al-Ṣāliḥ Bridge* leads to the Shʿ. al-Rawḍah which crosses the island to the West Bank and Giza.

The Corniche continues S into Old Cairo.

## E. The Islands

**Cairo Atlas 5, 13, 20, 28.**

The Kubrī al-Taḥrīr (Rte 1) leads from the East Bank onto the S tip of **al-Gazīrah** (The Island) which stretches N downstream for 3.9km, lying closer to the West Bank. The narrow channel which separates it from the West Bank is al-Baḥr al-Aʿmā (blind river). Three bridges cross from Cairo on the East Bank via the island to Giza on the West Bank.

Unlike Rawḍah, al-Gazīrah is of relatively recent origin, emerging from the river as a series of shifting sandbanks in the 14C. These coalesced into three islands recorded in the map of Cairo produced by the French expedition in the early 19C. By the mid-19C it was a single island and with the building of the first Aswān Dam in 1902 the banks were reinforced and stabilised. In the mid-19C Ismāʿīl Pasha built a palace here which he enlarged to house the distinguished guests who came to the opening of the Suez Canal in 1869. Part of it is now a hotel. During the early 20C much of the land was bought and elegant villas built. Many of these are now occupied by clubs, embassies or international companies.

The Shʿ. al-Taḥrīr crosses the S tip of the island, passing on the S the **Ḥuriyyah Gardens** (13:6). At the W end of the gardens is the **Mukhtār Museum** (open 09.00–13.00, closed Monday; small fee). Displayed are the works of Maḥmūd Mukhtār (1891–1934), an original and distinctive sculptor, whose public works are seen throughout Cairo. N of the road are the **Old Exhibition Grounds** (13:4–6), now replaced by the new site at Madīnat Naṣr (Rte 20). Inside the grounds are several small museums. The **Museum of Egyptian Civilisation** (Matḥaf al-Ḥaḍārah al-Miṣriyyah; open 09.00–17.00; small fee, Friday and Sunday free) shows with models and paintings the achievements of Egypt from prehistoric to modern times. In the *Agricultural Pavilion* is the **Gazīrah Museum** (open 09.00–13.00; small fee, Friday and Sunday free). This is a collection of objects and paintings from Coptic and Islamic times. **Planetarium**: performances daily except Friday at 19.00 and on Thursday at 11.00. Small fee, reduced for students. The new **Opera House** was erected on the site with the assistance of a Japanese company and opened in 1989.

On the W side of the island the *Galāʾ Bridge* crosses the narrow al-Baḥr al-Aʿmā to Giza (Rte 22), but turning N a wide road encircles the island. On the E side of the island it is called the Shʿ. al-Gazīrah and passes on the E the *Andalūs Gardens* and on the W the **National Sporting Club** (al-Nādī al-Ahlī; 13:3), home of the national football club. After 400m on the W a road leads to the *Zahriyyah Gardens* and the **Cairo Tower** (al-Burg al-Qahīrah; 13:4; open 09.00–13.00; fee). This edifice, 187m high, was

*New Cairo Opera House*

built in 1957. It is a cylinder faced with a concrete network which at the top opens in the form of a lotus. On the 14th floor is a revolving restaurant, on the 15th floor a cafeteria and on the 16th floor a viewing platform from which many of the pyramids along the Nile Valley can be seen (particularly recommended after rain). The building is crowned by a television mast.

Passing under the 6 October Bridge, to the E are the *Nile Gardens*, with magnificent specimen palms and other trees, and on the W the *Racecourse* and the vast **Gazīrah Sporting Club** (Nādī al-Gazīrah al-Rayada; 5:5–6). Temporary membership is available.

Here many sports can be enjoyed, including tennis, swimming, squash, golf, football and bridge. These were the grounds of the palace of Ismāʿīl Pasha. When the palace was sold in the 1880s the grounds became the Gezira Sporting Club. During the British Occupation it was a refuge for colonials and officers on their way to or from campaigns throughout the empire. As Major C. Jarvis put it, somewhat cynically, in 'Oriental Spotlight': 'It is on the Gezira polo grounds that the officers of the Cavalry Brigade are tested for military efficiency and fitness for command and on the Gezira tennis courts that examinations are held to decide as to the desirability or otherwise of retaining in the service the British officials of the Government'.

At 150m the Shʿ. al-Gazīrah turns to the W. On the S is the entrance to the Gazīrah Club and on the N the **Muḥammad Khalīl Museum** (open 09.00–13.30, Friday 09.00–11.30; small fee). This is a display of the vast collection of art objects and paintings collected by Muḥ. Maḥmūd Khalīl in the early 20C.

Continuing N along the SHʿ. SARĀY AL-GAZĪRAH, on the W is the *Cairo Marriott Hotel*. This complex is constructed around the original *Palace of Ismāʿīl Pasha*, designed by the German Franz Bey as the ḥarīm for this khedive's three principal wives. It was augmented in 1864 and many of the guests at the opening of the Suez Canal stayed here, principally the Empress Eugenie. The palace was forfeited by Ismāʿīl as part payment of the vast debts he accumulated in the 1870s and turned into the Gezira Palace Hotel after several of the ḥarīm kiosks had been demolished. The present building, the Selamlik, was subsequently bought by the

Lebanese Prince Michael Lutfallah. Acquired by the Egyptian government in 1960, it was reopened as the Omar Khayyam Hotel. In the early 1980s it was carefully renovated and although the lavish, if garish, decoration has been replaced by pastel shades, it remains a magnificent centrepiece to the hotel. Of particular interest are the cast-iron porticoes made in Germany and reassembled on site.

The Shʿ. Sarāy al-Gazīrah crosses the Shʿ. 26 Yūlyū (bridge to the East Bank, see Rte 22A) N into the SHʿ. AL-MAʿHAD AL-SWISSRĪ. All the N end of the island called *Zamālik* is occupied by large villas and apartment buildings, many of which are embassies or company owned, and there is little of interest. From the Shʿ. al-Maʿhad al-Swissrī the SHʿ. MUḤ. MAẒHAR leads to the N tip of the island, along the N shore of which runs the SHʿ. ABŪ 'L-FIDĀ'. This opens at the W into the SHʿ. GABALAYYAH which follows the full length of the W shore. The road runs past Zamālik Bridge which carries the Shʿ. 26 Yūlyū to Giza, the W end of the 26 October Bridge and finally at the S end into the al-Galāʿ Bridge (see above).

To the N of al-Gazīrah opposite (2.6km) Shubrā lies *Gazīrat Warrāq al-Ḥaḍar*. This has no bridges and is purely agricultural.

Between the islands is the *Fisqiyyat al-Nīl*, a fountain from which an immense jet of water plays during festival days.

**Al-Rawḍah Island** (Gazīrat al-Rawḍah—the Garden Island) is c 500m S of al-Gazīrah. It is about 3.2km long and favours the East Bank of the Nile from which it is separated by the narrow Siyālat al-Rawḍah. During early Muslim times, until the emergence of the island to the N, it was confusingly just called al-Gazīrah.

This island with its rock base has remained virtually unchanged since ancient times. The S tip was probably used for the ferry on the route between Heliopolis and Memphis. By Byzantine times there was a fortress which complemented that of Babylon on the mainland and which gave protection to the patriarch Cyrus during the Muslim invasion in 641. During the inundation it was connected to the mainland by a bridge resting on boats, a practice which continued under the Muslims. Shortly after the Muslim invasion the Nilometer at the S end was rebuilt. ʿBadr al-Gamali built a mosque beside it in late Fāṭimid time and this was incorporated within the palace of fortress built in the 1240s by the Ayyūbid sultan al-Ṣāliḥ. The island remained essentially rural until the 1950s although Ibrāhīm Pasha had large gardens laid out in the N half in 1830 and the Manyal Palace was built in the early 20C. The S half belonged to the heirs of Ḥasan Pasha. Since the 1950s there has been a building explosion and it is now an affluent area with high-rent buildings.

From the Corniche (Rte 3D) a bridge leads to the *Meridien Hotel* at the extreme N tip of the island. A wide corniche also surrounds this island. The next bridge S to the island is al-Manyal Bridge and the next is al-Sayālah Bridge, but this completely crosses the island, the W half being al-Gāmiʿah Bridge leading to Gīza and the pyramids (Rte 23). On the S side of the bridge stands the **Manyal Palace** built between 1901–29 as the home of Prince Muḥammad ʿAlī, containing, beside the palace, several pavilions built to house the prince's collection of antiquities and to satisfy his patronage of the revival of traditional Islamic artistic techniques. After the 1952 revolution it was turned into a museum with part of the grounds leased in 1964 to the Club Mediterranée hotel chain. (Ticket office just inside gatehouse.)

Muḥammad ʿAlī (1875–1955) was the son of Khedive Tawfīq and younger brother of Khedive ʿAbbās II Hilmī. Urbane and sophisticated he remained in Cairo after the deposition of ʿAbbās II by the British in 1914 and thereafter concerned himself with the maintenance of his estates, in educational and philanthropic projects and the acquisition of a vast collection of antiques. Heir presumptive to King Fārūq he was president of the Regency Council 1936–37 during this king's minority. He married the Frenchwoman Suzanne Hemon in 1941 but left Egypt with Fārūq in 1952 after the revolution and died in Lausanne. (See Rte 8 for his tomb.)

Surrounding the whole estate (230–300m) is a massive crenellated limestone wall, in the NE corner of which is the *Gatehouse* and entrance. The upper storey contains the decorated *Reception Hall*. From the gatehouse wide paths wind through the gardens filled with semi-tropical trees and shrubs. The right-hand path leads to the *Mosque* built in 1933, a pastiche of Ottoman and N African styles, with lavishly decorated interior. Beyond lies the *Hunting Hall* a later addition of 1963 built to house the hunting trophies of King Fārūq. Besides the heads of many of the world's game animals, including a sad frieze of over a hundred heads of Dorcas gazelles, it contains a large collection of *objects de vertue* and curios fashioned from natural materials.

Returning to the gardens a path leads to the *Palace* with Italianate exterior. Inside all the decoration is in Islamic style, with evocative period fittings. A path leads SE to the *Throne Pavilion*, on the ground floor of which is a reconstruction of the throne room of Muḥ. ʿAlī Pasha. Portraits of the Khedive line the walls, and it is additionally embellished with an elaborately decorated roof. On the upper floor is the *Salon of Ibrāhīm al-Ḥāmī Pasha* in the style of Louis XV transferred from the palace of the prince's maternal grandfather. Beyond this is the *Faience Room* where the walls are covered with highly modelled glazed plants and fruit and the *Panelled Room* executed in timber from the exotic trees in the garden.

Finally in the SW area of the garden the *Museum* is a series of linked pavilions built to display the prince's collection of antiquities and art objects. Case after case is filled with precious stones, gold, silver, jewellery and utensils, fine porcelain, tapestries, manuscripts and paintings. Beyond the palace on the N side of al-Sayalah Bridge is the modern *Ṣalāḥ al-Dīn Mosque*.

South of al-Manyal the SHʿ. AL-MALIK AL-ṢĀLIḤ runs along the E shore of the island. Beyond a small bridge from the East Bank the first road on the W (500m) leads to the **Madrasah of Sultan Qāyt-bāy** (519; 20:6), built in 1481–90 by the court architect Ḥasan al-Ṭūlūnī. It has been heavily restored, particularly during the Ottoman period. The shore road continues S crossing (850m) the *Malik al-Ṣāliḥ Bridge* which crosses the island entirely. At the W end is al-Giza Bridge to the West Bank. Turn right at Shʿ. al-Marzūqī and then left into SHʿ. AL-MANYAL, at the S end of which (800m) beyond the Shʿ. Ḥālim lie the waterworks.

This S part of the island was the site of the *Qalʿat al-Baḥr* (River Fortress) or Qalʿat al-Rawḍah of Sultan al-Ṣāliḥ Ayyūb. Built in 1241, the brick perimeter walls beset by 60 towers measured 3km in circumference and must thus have covered half the island. Within the enclosure were palaces, mosques, stables and barracks for this sultan's immense army of Turkish mamlūks. Al-Ṣāliḥ Ayyūb lived here in preference to the mountain citadel (Rte 14) and the mamlūks installed here were called al-Baḥriyyah (of the river). After the short reign of Ayyūb's son Tūrān-shāh the sultanate was usurped by the mamlūks. Although the first great Mamlūk sultan Baybars left this citadel and resided in the mountain citadel as did all the sultans after him, the Baḥris retained precedence and all the early sultans were drawn from their ranks. Eventually the Burgī mamlūks prevailed and this fortress was abandoned. In the 1820s a gunpowder factory was built on the complex which inevitably blew up in 1830. During the 19C the rest of the remains were destroyed.

A lane leads down the E side of the waterworks to the S tip of the island. Here in a small kiosk with a conical roof stands the **Nilometer** (al-Miqyās; 79; 27:8).

There had probably been a nilometer here since ancient times, but the first Muslim nilometer was emplaced by the governor Usāmah for the khalīf al-Walīd (705–15). This was destroyed by flood waters and was replaced with the present nilometer by Muḥammad al-Hāsib for the khalīf al-Mutuwwakil in 861. Ibn Ṭūlūn seems to have undertaken some reconstruction later in the 9C when part of the foundation inscription was removed. The reading of the height of the water was the traditional right of the al-Raddād family who had guarded the nilometer since pre-Islamic times. The critical height was 16 cubits and once this was reached the signal was given for the ceremony of Cutting the Canal at al-Fumm al-Khalīg on the East Bank (Rte 3D).

The interior of the kiosk is domed and covered with Turkish tiles. Supporting the lantern are eight pillars with classical capitals. The substructure consists of a pit lined with cut-stone. The upper section is 6.2m sq. Steps lead down from the SE corner passing a frieze of beautiful Kufic inscription. That on the N and E wall is original and the rest replacement by Ibn Ṭūlūn. Turning the corner, the steps lead onto a landing on the W wall. At this level on each side is a recess with a pointed arch resting on engaged columns. It is of interest in that this arch is three centuries earlier than the appearance of pointed arches in European Gothic architecture. In the E recess is the uppermost of the three conduits which once connected directly with the Nile. Another flight of steps leads from the landing to a second ledge, with the middle conduit in the E wall. Below this the pit is circular (diameter 4.35m) and further steps lead down to the bottom with the lowest conduit. In the centre, resting on a mill stone, is the octagonal measuring pillar. This is 48cm in diameter and now 11.5m high, 22.5cm having been lost when the pillar was broken. It is marked in 16 gradations of one cubit (54.04cm). At the top of the column is a composite classical capital.

Adjacent to the W is the **Munastirlī Palace** (27:8), built in 1851 for Aḥmad al-Munastirlī, senior advisor to ʿAbbās I Pasha and for a time the headquarters of the Arab League. It has excellent architectural detail, particularly the painted ceilings. This was the site of the *Mosque of the Miqyās* built in 1092 by Badr al-Gamālī and enlarged by Sultan Muʾayyad Shaykh in 1420, but no trace of this has survived. The palace is now the *Centre for Art and Life* (open 09.30–13.30 except Fri. and Sat.), a cultural institute investigating the arts of the Egyptians since ancient times and displaying ancient objects and products of the art students. Students' work can be bought.

Just S (300m) of al-Rawḍah lies the *Gazīrat al-Dhahhab*. There are no bridges to this island which is used for agriculture. Closer to the West Bank lies a smaller island also confined to agricultural use.

# 4 Sayyidnā al-Ḥusayn to Bāb al-Naṣr

Rtes 4, 5 and 6 cover the area of the medieval city of Cairo. At the centre is the Maydān al-Azhar from which each of these routes radiates. Although the distances covered are not great (c 1km in each case) there are a great number of monuments which can be visited and a full day at least is needed if the most is to be made of the itinerary. There are many cafés and restaurants in the area. Bus No. 66 runs from Maydān al-Taḥrīr to the Maydān al-Azhar. Rte 4 (**Cairo Atlas 17, 11**) moves N through the city to the North Walls and into the Northern Cemetery.

Take bus No. 66 from Maydān Taḥrīr and alight at Maydān al-Azhar bus station. The Shʿ. al-Azhar runs from Maydān al-ʿAtabah to Shʿ. Ṣālaḥ Sālim. The whole of this district is called **al-Gamāliyyah**.

This is almost the centre of the enclosure with seven gates that surrounded the original Fāṭimid city of al-Qāhirah built by Gawhar al-Siqillī for the khalīf al-Muʿizz in 969. His mud-brick wall formed a rectangle, the main axis of which ran NE to SW. From al-Azhar Mosque (built here 970–72; Rte 6) the distances to the walls were: NE 700m, SE 300m, SW 400m and NW 700m. The area thus measures 1.1km sq. Contained within it were two great palaces to the E and the W and many other smaller mansions and pavilions. There were numerous gardens and orchards and a magnificent cemetery for the royal family. The enclosure was built for the exclusive use of the khalīf's immense family and their retainers. Except for al-Azhar Mosque most of the buildings have been destroyed, but the alignment of the streets still echoes the original plan.

The city was subsequently enlarged and the walls rebuilt twice, once by the Fāṭimids under Badr al-Gamālī in 1085 and later by Qarāqush for Ṣalaḥ al-Dīn between 1171–76. Nothing remains of the original wall of Gawhar, but of the later work quite a large portion still exists.

Cross into the Maydān Mashhad al-Ḥusayn, passing on the left al-Muskī (Rte 5), and on the right the large modern *Idarat al-Azhar* (al-Azhar Bureau) and a small garden. On the N side of the square stands the **Mosque of Sayyidnā al-Ḥusayn** (28; 17:2), a great assembly mosque on the site of the Fāṭimid Mashhad and tomb of Ḥusayn, one of the sons of the Khalīf ʿAlī and grandson of the Prophet. The present building consists of the 19C mosque with minaret on the W corner, the earlier Ottoman mausoleum of al-Ḥusayn, and, at the S corner of that, a Fāṭimid doorway surmounted by the remains of an Ayyūbid minaret.

This, the principal mosque of Cairo, is attended by the head of state and ministers during the major celebrations. Entry is forbidden to non-Muslims, except by special permission (obtainable from the Wizarāt al-Azhar), it being one of the only two mosques in Cairo to which this rule applies (see also the Mosque of Sayyidah Zaynab, Rte 12).

Al-Ḥusayn was killed at Karbala in 680 by the Bani Umayyah during the disputes over the Khalifate. His head was buried at Askalon, but when that city was threatened by the Crusaders it was brought to Cairo in 1153 by the governor Tamīm. The wazīr Talāʾiʿ b. Ruzzik wished it to be re-buried in the mosque he had built outside the Bāb Zuwaylah specifically for this purpose (Rte 9), but the khalīf al-Faʾīz wanted it interred within the palace grounds and so it was buried in a mashhad built on this site in 1154, occupied then by the Qubbat Daylam. Sultan Ayyūb rebuilt the mashhad in 1237 but it was burnt down in 1248. It was restored by Ḥasan Katkhudā al-Galfī prior to 1712 and subsequently by ʿAbd al-Raḥmān Katkhudā (1761) and the Khedive Ismāʿīl in the 19C.

Ḥasan and Ḥusayn, as the sons of ʿAlī, are paid special reverence by the Shiʿī Muslims and this mosque therefore has particular significance and is a place of pilgrimage for them. The Mūlid of al-Ḥusayn commemorating his birth is one of the most important events in the calendar of religious celebrations and is held for two weeks culminating on the last Tuesday of Rabiʿ II. It is particularly significant for the rural community and the fallaḥīn (farmers) arrive from all over the Delta. This is often their only visit to the capital in the year, each village having its own particular living area in the district. For several days the Maydān al-Ḥusayn and the surrounding area are very crowded with celebrants, booths, side shows and popular entertainers. Many leaders and shaykhs of brotherhoods also stay in the area and are visited by their followers.

During the other major celebrations, Mūlid al-Nabī, ʿId al-Adhā', ʿId al-Fiṭr and Ramaḍān, the area is a very popular meeting place and often crowded throughout the night.

The modern stone building was designed in the 19C by ʿAlī Mubārak at the express wish of ʿAbbās I Pash and Khedive Ismāʿīl. Subsequently modified by Rātīb Pasha it was completed in October 1873, the minaret being finished in 1878. The whole cost £E78,000 of public funds and an undisclosed amount contributed by the khedive himself.

The design of the building is heavily influenced by 19C European Neo-Gothic. It has six doorways, three in the NW façade, one in the NE and one in the SW, all leading directly into the covered ṣaḥn. An entrance in the SE leads to the Library and women's prayer-hall. The cylindrical minaret is set on the W corner, and has a medial balcony. The interior consists of five arcades running the whole length of the building with a decorated ceiling supported by marble columns. The complex miḥrāb constructed in 1886 is in polychrome marble, as is the facing of the dado on the walls which was produced by Ḥāgg ʿAbd Allāh ʿAfīfī and completed in 1964. The recent ebony minbar is considered to be one of the most beautiful in the Middle East, an excellent example of modern craftsmanship.

In the SE wall are four doorways, the first leading to the *Qāʿat al-Zuwwār* (Guest Gallery) where official functions, including marriages, take place, and visitors are received by the director of the mosque. The next two doors lead into the Tomb of Ḥusayn and the fourth door to the left of the miḥrāb leads to the Library on the upper floor. The *Tomb of Ḥusayn* is a square domed chamber, the work of ʿAbd al-Raḥmān Katkhudā (c 1761). The dome is set on the base by semi-domed squinches and is painted and gilded, the decoration being similar to that ordered by ʿAlī Bay al-Kabīr for the Tomb of the Imām Shāfiʿī (Rte 15). The miḥrāb has a coloured marble dado and above it are some verses and the name of the calligrapher Balkhī with the date AH 1187 (AD 1773). A great silver mashrabiyyah screen surrounds the grave of Ḥusayn, a present from the Buhrah Shiʿī Muslims of Bombay in 1960 (see Mosque of al-Ḥākim Rte 5).

The Ayyūbid tābūt of al-Ḥusayn was discovered in 1903, but it was not exposed until 1939 when King Fārūq ordered the repaving of the floor with marble. It turned out to be a superb piece of work, teak covered with small panels of carved inscription in Kufic and Naskhī, and was probably ordered by Sultan Ṣalaḥ al-Dīn at the same time as that for Imām al-Shāfiʿī in 1178 (now in the MIA).

On the right is the *Ḥugrat al-Mukhalafāt* (Room of the Remains), built in 1893 to receive some relics of Muḥammad transferred from the Ribāṭ al-Athār (Rte 16). To the left is a doorway to the prayer-hall for women. Outside at the S end of the SE façade is a small piece of wall c 6m high pierced with a gateway, originally called the *Bāb al-Akhḍar* (Green Gate; 28), and the Bāb al-Ḥasanayn (i.e. Ḥasan and Ḥusayn) until at least the time of Napoleon's occupation. The gate is rectangular (1.9m wide by 2.3m high) and spanned by a heavy beam above which is a recessed panel formed by an arch. The decoration has similarities to that of al-Aqmar Mosque (Rte 5) and probably dates from the mashhad of 1248, though Prof. Creswell felt that some of it was the original work of 1154. Above the gateway is an *Ayyūbid Minaret*, the lower square part with an inscription in the name of a donor Abū ʾl-Qāsim al-Sukkarī dated 1237. Decoration remains only on the SE side and is very fine stucco work in three panels, the middle section in the form of a window with elaborate hood and keel-arched niche. It was probably similar to the minaret of the Madrasah of Sultan Ayyūb (Rte 5), its upper portion with conical cap being the work of ʿAbd al-Raḥmān Katkhudā.

To the right of the SE wall is a modern block of flats erected by the Wizārat al-Awqāf to a traditional plan with apartments above a long façade of shops.

The road along the NW façade of the mosque is the SHʿ. MASHHAD AL-ḤUSAYN, becoming the SHʿ. AL-GAMĀLIYYAH (N to the Bāb al-Naṣr) leading past the *Bayt al-Māl* (Zakāt Treasury) and the *Assay* and *Weights and Measures Office* to rejoin the route at the Mosque of Marzūq al-Aḥmadī (see below). Opposite the Mosque of Ḥusayn is the *Sabīl of Aḥmad Pasha*, a fountain of 1864–65 with an unusual ornate concave front.

Running opposite the mosque is the SHʿ. KHANGAFAH, with, after 50m, the *Wikālah and Sabīl al-Ḥaramayn* (433; 17:2), dated 1856, endowed originally for the poor in Mecca and Medina. It makes no concessions to contemporary European architecture. On the opposite corner is a late *Ottoman Sabīl*.

A slight diversion may be made for 350m up the Shʿ. al-Azhar and down the third street on the left to the *Mosque of Sayyid Muʿadh* (Sidi Maʿaz; 3) which incorporates the Tomb of Sayyid Muʿadh and the Minaret of the Amīr Abū ʿl-Ghaḍanfar Asad. This is a modern mosque built on the site of a Fāṭimid mashhad of 1175. Nothing remains of this building except the minaret; the tomb is late Mamlūk, built in 1462.

The highly venerated Sh. Muʿadh died in 907 and in 1175 Abū ʿl-Ghaḍanfar Asad, an amīr of Khalīf al-Faʿiz, built a mashhad over his tomb. The minaret is important in that it forms a link between the Fāṭimid type in the Mosque of Badr al-Gamālī and the late Ayyūbid form as in the Madrasah of Sultan al-Ṣāliḥ Ayyūb. In late Mamlūk times a madrasah was built over the site and the tomb chamber was reconstructed. This is unusual in being oblong. The windows in the short walls are of three lights and those in the longer walls are of six lights.

E of the Mosque of Sayyidnā al-Ḥusayn is the Maydān al-ʿAdawī. The NE side is taken up by the façade of the modern *Mosque and Tomb of Ḥasan al-ʿAdawī*. Ḥasan al-ʿAdawī al-Ḥamzawi (1806–1886) was head of the Malikī School at al-Azhar, a prolific writer and a courageous and implacable opponent of the Khedive Ismaʿīl. Behind this is the **Madrasah and Tomb of Amīr Ālmalik al-Gūkandār** (24; 17:2), the earliest known example of a cruciform madrasah with a covered ṣaḥn, dated 1319.

Ālmalik built this madrasah, according to Maqrīzī, on the site of the Fāṭimid Qaṣr al-Shawq (Palace of Longing). He intended it as a madrasah for the Shāfiʿī school of law, though the foundation inscription on the doorway describes it as a mosque.

A native of Southern Anatolia, Ālmalik (Orchard) was bought by Sultan Baybars in 1277, passing into the service of Sultan Qalāwūn. He was made an amīr by Sultan al-Nāṣir Muḥammad and created jūkandār (polomaster) in 1319. He served five of the sons of al-Nāṣir Muḥammad and finally became nāʾib (viceroy) of Egypt in 1346, but in the same year he incurred the enmity of Sultan Shaʿbān I and was arrested. Imprisoned in Alexandria he died soon after, over 90 years old.

The façade on the SHʿ. UMM AL-GHULĀM in the NW corner of the Maydān is the SE wall, slightly angled on either side of the centre. It consists of the entrance (closed, see below), two windows, with smaller windows above, set in recesses with stalactite heads, another pair of small rectangular windows over the position of the miḥrāb and a small doorway.

Along the top of the façade is a trefoil cresting. The entrance has a hood of three stalactites surmounted by a fluted semi-dome and a dating inscription. Entry is through the Mosque of Sh. al-ʿAdawī and leads into the SW līwān. To the left is a passage leading to the vestibule with a well decorated ceiling. To the right is the entrance to the *Tomb of Ālmalik*, a bare tunnel-vaulted room (2.5m by 2m), the entrance bay and the opposite archway being framed by fine stucco ornament.

The ṣaḥn (9.8m by 6m) is flanked by the four līwāns, with flat ceilings fronted by pointed arches. Around the walls of the ṣaḥn and līwāns at a height of 2.5m runs a continuous stucco inscription with a huge medallion of stucco ornament at the back of the NW līwān. The miḥrāb has a marble lining and a frame formed by the inscription with carved stucco spandrels. A beading of dark blue faience between spandrels and rectangular frame is a very unusual feature.

40m along the road (right) is the *Sabīl-Kuttāb of Sayyid ʿAlī Amīn b. Hayzʿ* (23), an Ottoman structure of 1646, now the Umm al-Ghulām school. To the left (20m) is the **Mosque and Tomb of Amīr Ṭaqtabāy ibn Bardbak** (25; 17:2) built just prior to 1475, also called Umm al-Ghulām (Mother of the soldier i.e. Ḥusayn).

Son of Amīr Bardbak and Badriyyād, daughter of Sultan Īnal, Ṭaqtabāy was created an amīr of one hundred but fell into disgrace in 1496 under Sultan Qāyt-bāy. The name Umm al-Ghulām arose from an inscription which once surmounted a vault to the S of the entrance stating that in 1254 Amīr Bilbak al-Khazindār erected a mausoleum for Fāṭimah, the mother of Ḥusayn. This slab has now been transferred to the qiblah wall inside the mosque.

The entrance is of the usual trefoil arched type with stalactites but is peculiar in having the webs pierced with a simple arabesque pattern. The tomb is on the N side of the mosque with a foundation inscription on the porch. The three-stage minaret has two octagonal tiers surmounted by a pillared cylindrical section.

Directly N is the Darb al-Qazzazīn down which (15m) is a pair of Ottoman fountains, one on each side of the road. On the right is the *Sabīl al-Bazdār* (Master of the Falcons; 27; 17:2) built in the mid-17C. On the left is the *Sabīl of Ismāʿīl Maghlawī* (57) dated more precisely AD 1657. Both have charming little façades with bands of moulding around the openings.

On the main road, now the SHʿ. AL-QAZZAZĪN (30m), is the **Mosque and Tomb of Amīr Aydamur al-Bahlawān** (22; 17:2), on the corner of a lane. A small mosque built prior to 1346, its minaret is similar to that of the Mosque of Bashtak (Rte 12) being octagonal with a cylindrical section above.

Aydamur, in his youth a wrestler (bahlawān), was governor of Ghaza under Sultan Ismāʿīl in 1344. He came to Cairo in 1345 but, like Ālmalik, fell victim to Sultan Shaʿbān I's wrath and was exiled a year later to Syria where he died and is buried.

The main façade is inside a small courtyard. The entrance is square-headed with pendant stalactites but is not in use; one of the lower windows has been converted into a doorway; above are horseshoe-arched windows. On the left corner is a very attractive little corbel. The tomb is on the left surmounted by a small stone dome, one of the earliest examples, decorated with a rib and fillet design with a band of Naskhī inscription round the drum. The façade is topped by a fleur-de lys cresting.

The road, now the SHʿ. QAṢR AL-SHAWQ, bears left. After 150m the ḤĀRAT QAṢR AL-SHAWQ turns off to the right. On the S is the **Madrasah of Amīr Mughalṭāy al-Gamālī** (26 17:2), built in c 1300 for the Hanafi school. Mughalṭāy (Mongol horse) was a wazīr during the turbulent period at the end of the 13C. All that remains is the exterior wall with a superb band of Naskhī inscription running the whole length and vestiges of stepped cresting along the top. At the E end is the brick tomb with plain dome and stucco window grills. The interior of the tomb, entered through the modern mosque, contains the grave but is otherwise bare. Of the miḥrāb only the brick lining remains. Squinches with multiple niches raise the dome, around the base of which is a fine band of stucco inscription and at the apex a medallion.

Continue down the Shʿ. Qaṣr al-Shawq into the Shʿ. al-Gamāliyyah, here called the ḤABS AL-RAḤBAH. On the corner to the right, next to a pre-1800 *Ottoman House*, is the **Mosque of Marzūq al-Aḥmadī** (29; 11:7), a khānqāh built in 1633. The squat Ottoman minaret has two stages, the balcony resting on a stalactite bracket. It is a covered mosque with a lantern light in the roof and three aisles parallel to the qiblah. The tomb of Marzūq is visible through the square window. The mosque also contains other tombs.

Immediately to the right is the DARB AL-TABLĀWĪ down which (c 40m, bearing round to the left) is the rear entrance to **Musāfirkhānah** (20; 11:7), an Ottoman palace built between 1779–88. The ornate main gate in the parallel Darb al-Maṣmāt is blocked by rubble. It is now used as a gallery for Egyptian artists; their work is displayed on the ground floor and courtyard. (Open 09.00–16.00; small fee.)

Maḥmūd Muḥarram, builder of this palace, was a merchant. From the Fayyūm he increased the family fortune greatly through his brilliant ability and became very rich. His household became the centre of an important social circle. He built this palace and the mosque nearby (see below), connecting them with a takiyyah for sufis. In 1794 he went on the ḥajj, but on his return died of sunstroke.

The palace was subsequently bought by Ibrāhīm Pasha, the Khedive Ismāʿīl being born there in 1829, and it was later used as a lodging house for distinguished state guests. Although similar in many ways to the earlier palaces, a wide mandārah replaces the qāʿah. It has other metropolitan Ottoman features such as the large fireplace and the decoration is certainly to the Turkish taste, one of the first domestic buildings in Cairo to show this.

The entrance leads into a wide corridor (to the courtyard). Just inside to the left is the well and water system of the palace where the original mechanism can be seen. It is reached up a flight of stone steps covered with earth which gave purchase to the donkeys who turned the water wheel. The water was transported to the rest of the house through the small aqueduct.

The great mandārah on the left of the corridor has a marble floor with sunken fountain and a single large raised līwān surrounded by mashrabiyyah screens. All the wooden soffits of the arches and the ceiling are deeply carved and painted and gilded. The doors leading into the court are richly carved with a geometrical pattern. From the courtyard, planted with shrubs and with a central fountain, entrances lead to various parts of the palace. The wooden mashrabiyyah casements of the upper floors rest on intricately carved corbels.

The whole of the S side is taken up with an imposing two-storey takhtabush, the carved roof resting on a huge marble pillar. On the rear wall is a large carved panel. At the W end is the entrance to a smaller well, now blocked. This is the subject of a grisly tradition, that it was used as a private execution chamber by the royal family. After being hanged on the hook above corpses were thrown down the well. The main entrance leads off to the NE under a pillared arcade, but the present door to the upper chambers is in the W corner. The upper rooms of the ḥaramlik and selamlik are all lavishly decorated and gilded, the qaʿah of the ḥarim being particularly elaborate. Attached is a domed bath complex with coloured lights let into the roof. The windows overlooking the court have beautifully carved mashrabiyyah screens with brilliantly coloured glass above. In the floor of the līwān is the usual treasure pit. Returning to the courtyard a small door on the S leads into a utility complex and kitchen, with delicately painted woodwork, cupboards and serving hatches and tiled fireplace.

On the Ḥabs al-Raḥbah (20m) is the **Mosque of Maḥmūd Muḥarram** (30; 11:7), a small covered mosque built in 1792 by Maḥmūd. It has a trefoil arched doorway with engaged columns and inscription and is similar to the mosque of Marzūq al-Aḥmadī, though more richly decorated. The imām was Sh. al-Murtadā al-Zabidī who dwelt here at the request of Maḥmud.

Opposite is the ʿATFAT AL-QAFASĪN (Cage-makers) and (20m on the left) the **Madrasah and Tomb of Khawand Ṭāṭār al Ḥigāziyyah** (36; 10:8), the former built in 1348, the latter in 1360. It has been restored (1980–82) by the GIA and the EAO.

The princess Ṭāṭār was the eldest daughter of Sultan al-Nāṣir Muḥammad. She married the Amīr Baktīmur al-Ḥigāzī. The results of the wealth and influence of her privileged position can be seen in this mosque. The memory of the pious princess who died of the plague in 1360 is preserved and women still affix candles to the window sill of the tomb inside the grill.

The exterior is rather plain with the domed tomb set on the N corner. This is one of the earliest stone domes in Cairo and though plastered it retains the rib-and-fillet pattern of the earlier brick domes; the ribs end in scallops and there is a band of Naskhī inscription around the drum. The octagonal minaret to the W lacks the final stage which fell down several times during construction—there is a tradition that it was never completed. The entrance through a square doorway with an inscription leads into a small porch with a delicately carved and painted ceiling. The strange plan is immediately apparent, for although there is the usual open ṣaḥn, the three līwāns each fronted by a pointed arch are peculiar. The qiblah līwān containing a small miḥrāb in the normal place is shallow, as is the NW līwān flanking the tomb. But the SW līwān is the largest and contains a large and beautiful miḥrāb flanked by marble pillars in the SE wall. That this was the original form of madrasah is apparent by the continuous band of fine stucco inscription that runs round all the walls, but the reason for it is unclear; it may be that the SW līwān was reserved for the princess and her retinue and was probably screened off by mashrabiyyah from the rest of the mosque. Inside the *Tomb* the dome is raised on multiple-niched squinches, with another band of inscription running round the top of the walls. The grave of Ṭāṭār, with a green s cover, lies directly under the dome.

Along the Ḥabs al-Raḥbah on the corner of SHʿ. AL-TUMBAKSHIYYA (to Shʿ. al-Muʿizz li Dīn) is (20m) the cruciform **Madrasah of Gamāl al-Dīn al-Ustadār** (35), built in 1408. It is a beautiful and imposing piece of architecture though dilapidated, with the remains of handsome decoration. It is one of only three cruciform madrasahs built in Cairo for all four schools of law and was one of the magnificent mosques raised by civilian ministers during the early 15C which are spoken of so disparagingly by T.B. It is this mosque that has given its name to the whole district.

Originally from Aleppo and raised in poverty, Gamāl al-Dīn Yūsuf came to Cairo as a tax-collector and befriended the wazīr Ibn al-Ghurāb. His appearance was unprepossessing, and he was blind in one eye, but compensated by his tyrannical method of extortion. He became ustadār and then wazīr to Sultan Farag but his methods aroused such resentment among the great amīrs that in 1409 he was arrested. Under torture he revealed that he had appropriated 1,000,000 dinars, after which he was strangled. T.B. tells us he was not mourned. After his death the inscriptions on his madrasah were defaced by Farag.

The trefoil arched entrance is reached by a flight of steps. The exterior wall in black and white ablaq has a stalactite frieze running just below the top, but there is no cresting. The minaret consists of the lower stage only, the remainder having fallen. The cruciform interior has an inscription running round the open ṣahn and on a lower frieze blue faience columns are inset. The interior walls are topped by fleur-de-lys cresting. The līwāns are fronted by pointed arches. The floor was originally much grander, being composed of sections cut from porphyry columns, but these and the marble facings of the walls were stripped by Salīm after the Ottoman conquest.

Adjoining the Mosque of Gamāl al-Din is the *Wikālah Bazarʿah* (398; 11:7), another 17C Ottoman khān, built by Ḥasan Khatkhudā Abū Shanab. On the E side of the road is a complex of several buildings raised in 1673: a *house* (unclassified), the *Wikālat Dhūʾl-Fiqār* (19), of 1673, one of the largest and most important hostelries in Ottoman Cairo, which dealt primarily in coffee, and the *Sabīl-Kuttāb* of the *Ūdah Bāshā* (17), with wooden roof and tiled releasing arch, both constructed in 1673, though only the façade of the last remains intact. Adjacent is the contemporary **Bawābat al-Ḥārat al-Mabyaḍah (356; Gate of the Dyers' Quarter).**

Although this example is Ottoman (built 1673), street gates were a common feature of the city from Mamlūk times. Very few now exist, having been torn down during the French and British occupations for easy access. At night all these gates were locked, leaving only the main thoroughfares open, and were in the charge of a watchman (ghafīr) who would open them to late caravans and inhabitants. There is a fine example of a medieval gate in the CM.

On the left after 10m is the **Mosque of Saʿīd al-Suʿādāʾ** (480), called al-Ṣalāḥiyyah. Saʿīd, a freed slave of Khalīf al-Mustanṣir, built a palace on this site in the late 11C and it was still standing in 1173 when Ṣalāḥ al-Dīn, who was living close by, chose it for the site of the first khānqāh in Egypt. It became the main centre of sufism in Egypt and was always greatly venerated by the pious. The director was given the honorific Shaykh al-Shuyūkh (Shaykh of Shaykhs), although later this was given to all heads of khānqāhs. It was held in such affection by the population one contemporary poet, quoted by T.B., in comparing it to the gnificent mosques built by the civilian amīrs at the beginning of the C (Gamāl al-Dīn, ʿAbd al-Bāṣit, etc.) wrote that men's hearts were more moved by the battered flagstones of the doorway of this khānqāh than by all the marble and glory of these mosques. In constant use, it was continually being repaired and most of the present structure is 19C.

Immediately to the N is the pre-1739 *Ḥammām al-Gamāliyyah* (unclassified).

On the right is the **Madrasah and Tomb of Amīr Qarāsunqur** (31; 11:7), built in 1300. Only the tomb is intact, the remains of the mosque having been converted into the Gamāliyyah Boys School in the late 19C.

Qarāsunqur (Black Falcon) was a mamlūk of Qalāwūn. When his master became sultan in 1280 he was made a page and then an amīr with the title of jūkandār (polomaster). He subsequently received several provincial governerships and became Nāʾib of Egypt. Although he assisted al-Nāṣir Muḥammad to regain the throne, his criticism of the execution of Baybars II angered the sultan. Qarāsunqur fled to the court of the Ilkhan Abū Saʿīd at Tabriz (Iran), where he was well received. His success in directing the ilkhan's army led to his appointment as governor of Maragha. However, the relationship between Egypt and Persia improved and Qarāsunqur's position became untenable. Realising that he was likely to be handed back to al-Nāṣir Muḥammad he committed suicide in 1328. He built three tombs for himself, one in Aleppo (Syria), this one in Cairo and one in Maragha (Iran), where he is buried.

The façade on the street is the NW wall, with the ribbed brick dome of the tomb at the S end. The present entrance is modern. Five recesses each contain a large lower window with a smaller window above. In the fourth recess the lintel of the large window and the grill of the upper window are more ornate. The walls, 10m high, are crowned with stepped cresting. Raised on a cylindrical drum with 24 windows, the dome is ribbed.

Inside, classrooms occupy the NW līwān. On the rear wall is some geometrical ornament, among the motifs of which, on an undivided field, is a pair of polo-sticks, the blazon of the jūkandār. The *Tomb*, 2m below ground level, is now entered through the playground of the school by a tunnel-vaulted passage though originally entry must have been directly from the ṣaḥn. On the façade over the window of the tomb is a medallion which also depicts polo-sticks. The chamber (6m sq.) has shallow recessed panels in the walls, but only the SE still has the columns which originally flanked them all. The dome is raised on squinches, each of three layers of five niches, the central top niche being pierced as a window. Between are tall windows of three lights. The interior is bare except for the miḥrāb which is very tall and narrow and flanked by slender columns. Around the right-hand column is a bronze band with a short raised inscription and a heart-shaped shield containing polo-sticks. Remains of the original wooden frieze run round the hood which has a wooden lining with the remains of very handsome decoration of gilt and coloured palmettes in gesso, though the right section is defective.

After 20m on the right are the remains of the early 19C *Wikālah of Muḥsin Ramaḍān* (499). Contiguous is the impressive ***Khānqāh and Tomb of Baybars II al-Gāshankīr** (32; 11:7), built between 1306–09 and one of the best-preserved monuments in Cairo.

Probably of Circassian origin, Baybars was bought as a youth by Sultan Qalāwūn. He was later made an amīr and gāshankīr (taster) but did not really begin his rise to influence until the first reign of Qalāwūn's son al-Nāṣir Muḥammad when he was made ustādār (chief steward) in 1294. When al-Nāṣir Muḥammad was deposed he was appointed amīr of a hundred by Sultan Kitbughā in 1295 but was later imprisoned. After Lagīn's assassination in 1299 Baybars was left with only one peer, the Amīr Salār (see Rte 13). Together they reinstated Sultan Muḥammad, now 14, choosing key posts for themselves, Salār as regent and Baybars as atabak. However, they treated the sultan abominably.

In 1309 a ruse enabled the sultan to escape to the fortress of Karak in Syria and he refused to return. Because of his control of the Burgi mamlūks Baybars was elected sultan and managed to reign for a year. But Muḥammad advanced from Syria with the armies of the governors of the provinces. Baybars escaped to Upper Egypt but was promised a Syrian governorship. However on his way to the appointment he was arrested at Suez. He was brought before Muḥammad and, after the sultan reminded him of the deprivations he had received, he was flogged and strangled. His possessions were distributed among his own mamlūks. Muḥammad had the titles of Baybars chiselled out of the walls of the khānqāh and closed the building. Baybars was buried in the cemetery, but some amīrs prevailed upon the sultan who eventually relented and allowed the body to be placed in the great tomb. After a few years the khānqāh was reopened. Only the most eminent theologians were appointed directors of this institution. In 1389 the famous traveller, geographer and philosopher, Ibn Khaldūn was director of the khānqāh while the distinguished polymath al-Suyūṭī during his incumbency in 1498 ended up being thrown into the fountain by the inhabitants during a dispute over pay.

The façade (28m long) consists of the entrance and NW wall of the tomb to the N and the minaret to the S. The portal is crowned with a great semi-circular arch with cushion voussoirs, the doorway being set back in a white marble-lined recess covered by a hood with five layers of stalactites. A square Pharaonic column, with hieroglyphics visible, forms the step. The leaves of the door are plated with geometrical copper sheets, panelled, engraved and pierced with inscription naming Baybars above and below, while the backs are beautifully carved. The projecting façade of the tomb is divided into three recesses, the centre being the largest, with four layers of stalactites at the top and a large brass grill at the bottom.

Along the façade runs a band of carved inscription from the Qur'ān and the name of Baybars, with his royal titles defaced. Stepped cresting crowns the façade and the plain dome, which can be seen from the side-street to the N, has a pointed arch profile. The first tier of the minaret has a square section and is topped by a many-layered stalactite cornice while the second tier is cylindrical and also has a cornice of stalactites. The third stage, also cylindrical, is capped by a ribbed dome, originally covered with green faience tiles, the first example in Egypt of a minaret thus decorated.

INTERIOR. The vestibule has two doors on the left, the first of which leads into an ante-chamber with a wooden ceiling and skylight. It is separated from the tomb by a massive mashrabiyyah screen which contains another inscription naming Baybars. The *Tomb Chamber* is paved with black and white marble and on the walls is a dado of intricate panels, also in black and white marbles. Ventilation cupboards open into a passage within the wall. The grave, directly under the dome, is surrounded by a later screen and contains the remains of Baybars and also a local shaykh, Muḥ. Amīn al-Ḥusaynī who was buried here in 1939.

Above the dado is a band of inscription from the Qur'ān. The impressive miḥrāb is similar in size to that of Sultan Qalāwūn (Rte 5) though not so magnificently decorated. It is in marbles of three colours with an arcade of scallop-headed pillars round the top and a larger arcade below.

The dome (diameter 11.25m) is raised on squinches of four layers of niches, between which are pierced stucco windows set with coloured glass. The interior of the dome is undecorated.

Entrance to the *khānqāh* is via the usual baffled corridor to the ṣaḥn, which measures c 20m by 16.5m with two tunnel-vaulted līwāns. The qiblah līwān is the larger and has an air shaft (malqaf) on either side for ventilation. The miḥrāb is neither so large nor so ornate as that in the tomb. The other two sides of the ṣaḥn are occupied by three storeys of small rooms, the windows of which look into the ṣaḥn. In the centre of each side is a maṣallah (place for prayer) with tall doorways. All the windows and doorways have carved frames and lintels. There was originally accommodation for 400 men.

Immediately adjacent to the N is the *Ḥawsh ʿUṭay* (499) of 1817. Behind that is the *Wikālah of ʿAbbās Agha* (unclassified), built in 1694, another coffee merchants' hostelry.

Opposite is a small shop, behind which is a **Fāṭimid Tomb** (479; 11:7), dated 1133, the only one surviving within the original city of al-Qāhirah. Ask the proprietor for permission and pass through.

On this site and to the W was the Fāṭimid *Dār al-Qubbāb* (Mansion of Domes), the palace of the wazīr, built by al-Afḍal in 1094 and later the residence of Ṣalāḥ al-Dīn; this tomb must have been a late addition to the structure.

It is a small (5m sq.) domed-cube, the exterior walls slightly out of alignment, but the interior nearly square. It is open on three sides suggesting that originally the site was free of obstruction. The qiblah wall is not open and the miḥrāb is about 10° out of true. A kufic inscription from the Qurʾān runs round the four walls. The dome is raised on two layered squinches of three niches covered by one, which alternate with windows of the same shape, an arrangement similar to that found in the tomb of Sayyidah ʿĀtiqah (Rte 11). This building already shows an approach to a problem that was to reach much greater proportions during the ensuing few hundred years, i.e. the qiblah being in alignment at the expense of structural symmetry.

On the left is the Darb al-Aṣfar (Yellow Alley; to Shʿ. al-Muʿizz li Dīn) and on the N corner are the *Sabīl-Kuttāb of Qīṭās Bay* (16) and the remains of the *Wikālat al-Tinah* (unclassified), erected in 1630. On the E side of the road (30m) is the *Zāwiyat ʿAbd al-Karim* (unclassified), pre-1800. A little further N, on the corner of a small lane stands the *Sabīl-Kuttāb of Amīr Muḥammād* (14), of 1605. Further E along the lane is the late 17C *Wikalat al-Shishīnī* (unclassified).

N of the lane on the main street is *Wikālah and Mosque of the Ūdah Bāshā* (591; 11:7), dated 1673. It was also known as the Khān al-Khaysh and frequented by Fayyūmi cloth merchants. Immediately next to it is the 19C *al-Shuhadah Mosque* (unclassified).

The next building of importance on the left corner of the SHʿ. AL-ḌABBABIYAH (to Shʿ. al-Muʿizz li Dīn) is the gate of the **Wikālah of Amīr Qawṣūn** (11), built before his death in 1341. This is the earliest wikālah in Cairo, built a hundred years before that of Sultan Qāyt-bāy (see below). All that remains in original condition is the undated square-headed doorway. In both upper angles of the salient of the doorway is carved the blazon of the sāqī (cupbearer), a post Qawṣūn held early in his career under Sultan al-Nāṣir Muḥammad.

The blazon set in a medallion is not coloured but the colours are found on a mosque lamp made for him, the upper field uncoloured and on a united middle and lower golden field a red cup.

The gate has been moved slightly to the N of its original position, approximately on the line of the North mudbrick wall of Gawhar which extended left and right. Next to it stands the late 17C *Wikālah of Murgān al-ʿArab* (unclassified), once frequented by Palestinian coffee and soap merchants.

From here the road becomes the SHʿ. BĀB AL-NAṢR. 70m further on is the domed-cube **Tomb of Aḥmad al-Qāṣid** (10) dated 1335, in very bad condition, with the interior distempered green. The side entrance is almost as large as the tomb itself and was probably the door of a small later mosque to which the tomb was attached. The base of the tomb has been covered by a later stone wall over which the zone-of-transition and dome can be seen. The octagonal drum has keel arched windows, each frame surrounded by stucco bands of arabesque and around the drum of the dome is a band of nashkī inscription.

The dome is possibly the earliest stone dome in Cairo and its small size is probably due to the tentative grasp the craftsmen had of the necessary technique. The decoration is a simple rib and fillet design as in the earlier brick domes and like them it is covered with plaster. The door has a simple square top, above which is a small relieving arch and a panel of strapwork set in a plain trefoil-arched opening.

Opposite on the left is the **Wikālah of Sultan Qāyt-bāy** (9; 11:5) dated 1480, now converted into flats.

This wikālah was endowed by Qāyt-bāy for the support of the poor in the city of Medina after he had returned from pilgrimage in 1480. In the inscription it is called a khān but in the literary sources a wikālah.

There is an inscription to the right and left of the entrance and above the stone corbels of the first floor is another inscription running the whole length of the building but broken in the centre by the entrance bay.

To the E runs the SIKKAT AL-ʿUṬŪF with, after 100m (right), the *Madrasah of Ibn al-Baqrī* (18), built before 1374 by Shams al-Dīn Shākir called Ibn al-Baqrī, previously a Copt, and the chief administrator of Sultan al-Ḥasan. The whole building is painted in blue and yellow stripes. The portal has a pointed arch in which is set the square-headed doorway. The building has undergone extensive rebuilding, but it has retained its original and very handsome mihrab.

North rise the walls and the massive **Bāb al-Naṣr** (The Gate of Victory; 7; 11:5), the NE limit of the old city of al-Qahirah as realigned by Badr al-Gamālī. This gate, the Bāb al-Futūḥ, (190m to the W), the wall between and 170m of wall beyond that are, with the Bāb Zuwaylah to the SW (Rte 6), all that remains of the stone walls of the city built by Badr al-Gamālī in 1087–92.

The Armenian Badr al-Gamālī was the governor of Acre under the Fāṭimid khalīf Mustanṣir who summoned him in 1074 when the Turkish military commanders and their troops became uncontrollable. Upon arrival he had the malcontents executed and for this he was given the highest civil and military posts, including amīr al-guyushī (commander of the armies) and it is by this title that he is usually known. His first task was to strengthen the defences of al-Qāhirah, the original brick walls of Gawhar having collapsed, and he brought an Armenian architect, John the Monk, and his two brothers to supervise the work. They enlarged the enclosure on all sides, and to the N they brought the Mosque of al-Ḥākim safely within the defences. Working in stone, they added another gate to the existing seven, but only the three mentioned above remain. The tradition that the brothers each built one of the existing gates is almost certainly a fiction.

After the fall of the Fāṭimids when Ṣalāḥ al-Dīn gained control of Egypt, the walls of Badr, though admired, were not considered adequate so he ordered his commander Qarāqush to restore them. The sections E beyond the bend next to the Bāb al-Naṣr, and W beyond the second tower past the Bāb al-Futūḥ are his work. The walls extended to the W as far as al-Maks (modern Maydān Ramsīs) and portions of them are visible along the Sh'. Kāmil Sidqī (Rte 7). The intention was to enclose the whole of al-Qāhirah and Fusṭāṭ within one wall. The magnificent gates were considered to be superlative and were incorporated into the new defences.

The walls and gates of Badr are superb examples of military architecture, the only comparable construction being at Diyarbakar in Turkey. The masonry was never equalled and its supreme quality was acknowledged throughout the Middle East although it was never put to the test of actual siege. The complex is one of the rare examples of pre-Crusader Muslim architecture. Perhaps the most important innovation in Egypt was the use of stone instead of brick but additional details such as the cushion voussoirs and domes on pendentives appear in Egypt for the first time.

This gate replaced the original Bāb al-Naṣr of Gawhar a little to the S and was named the *Bāb al-'Izz* (Gate of Glory) by Badr, but the habit of the people prevailed and it was always known by the name of the earlier gate. As with the other towers of the N walls Napoleon installed his troops here, and named them after his aides-de-camp, the E tower being called Tour Corbin and the W tower Tour Julien.

The portal is flanked by massive three-storeyed flat-fronted towers 21m high, built of dressed stone over a rubble core. There are columns set horizontally for strength, the ends of which are exposed on the outer walls.

A great half-round arch with joggled voussoirs spans the entrance which leads through into the porch. On the right-hand side is the entrance to the interior of the complex (see below). The inner porch is covered by a cross vault at the apex of which is a large carved daisy. On each side wall is a scalloped recess. The immense iron-bound wooden gates are not original but are very similar to those provided for the Bāb al-'Azab at the Citadel by Raḍwān Bay in the 18C. Spanning the portal is a massive joggled beam above which are two releasing arches and surmounting these is Badr's white marble panel containing the Shi'ī shahādah in excellent Kufic script. In front of the gate is another great arch in a square frame with a border. Each spandrel is carved with a decorated stone shield with a sword set obliquely behind. Above runs a corbel that follows the walls of the towers. The towers project 4.5m and on the flanks and front are stone shields. On each two circular carved shields flank a kite shield of the type used by the Normans and Byzantines with whom the Fāṭimids were in direct contact. Above the corbelled frieze are windows.

East of the Bāb al-Naṣr is a 200m section of wall parallel to the SH'. GALĀL, set with three square towers, part of the work of Ṣalāḥ al-Dīn. Only the last tower is accessible. At this point the wall disappears for 200m to reappear to the E next to a *Half-round Tower*. Through a pointed-arched doorway three steps lead down into an inner chamber with a dome raised on squinches. After 55m is the circular **Burg al Ẓafar** (Tower of Triumph; 307; 11:8), the great corner tower of the walls of the city. Unfortunately it has lost its upper section. It is 16m in diameter and flanked by two postern gates. The vault of the staircase in the right section is very richly decorated with carved stone corbelling. Of interest is the dome in the central room which is raised on pendentives, as in other military towers of this sultan. Here the wall turns S. The next section is set with five towers (see below).

Opposite the Bāb al-Naṣr lies the **Bāb al-Naṣr Cemetery**, the NE necropolis, probably once contiguous with the Eastern Cemetery (Rte 8) but now much reduced in area. It contains only two monuments of note, although two others at some distance N, the *Tomb of Sultan Tūmān-bāy* and the *Fidawiyyah* (Rte 19), were originally within it. Running due N is the SHʿ. NAGM AL-DĪN.

After 100m turn left into the cemetery Area 39. Here, inside a small hut, stands the **Tomb of John Lewis Burckhardt** (1784–1817), known locally as Ḥawsh al-Muslimānī. It is a pristine Italian white marble grave with pillars at head and foot, the former surmounted by a carved turban. This is not the original, quite modest tomb which was visited by most important travellers to Cairo in the mid 19C, including Burton. In 1871 Rogers Bey, the British Consul and Josef Hekekeyan took a subscription from the European community in Cairo to erect the present tomb. Burckhardt is named on the headstone as 'Shaykh Ibrāhīm al-Mahdī ibn ʿAbd Allāh Burkhart al-Lawsanī'.

He was born into a rich merchant family of Lausanne but in 1807 came to London. Having acquired many academic friends, he offered his services to the African Association. He travelled to Syria, assuming the disguise of Shaykh Ibrāhīm which he was to keep until his death. He identified and visited the site of Petra and in 1813 he was the first European to see the great temple at Abū Simbel. Further travels took him across the Eastern Desert to Arabia where he stayed at Mecca and Madinah, and across Sinai. His contributions to Oriental studies were the precision and objectivity of his notes; these were published in several volumes after his death.

On the left side of the Shʿ. Nagm al-Dīn (330m) is the **Tomb of Sh. Yūnus** (511; 11:5), dated 1125, related to the Tomb of Sayyidah ʿĀtikah (Rte 11) and other late Fāṭimid tombs but showing several advances. Constructed in plastered brick, for the first time the dome with keel-arch profile rests on an octagonal drum instead of directly on the squinches. Each side of the drum contains an ogival window. The corners of the base are bevelled. The original door in the NW wall having been bricked-up, entry is now through the NE wall. In each wall is a pointed-arch recess. The simple miḥrāb has lost its flanking pillars; a Kufic inscription crossing the wall forms an arch over it. Squinches with three niches covered by one raise the dome. The original occupant of the tomb is unknown but the man for whom the tomb was re-used, Yūnus al-Shaybānī, was one of the most important shaykhs in the Saʿdiyyah brotherhood.

Parallel to the road, now the SHʿ AL-BAGHĀLAH, the wall of Badr al-Gamālī runs W from the Bāb al-Naṣr. The first tower (called by Napoleon *Tour Milhaud*) marks the easternmost wall of the Mosque of al-Ḥākim (Rte 5) inside the enclosure. Beyond this is a second tower and then the Great Salient, above which rises one of the minarets of the same mosque. To the W is the second of the gates set in the N walls of Cairo, the ***Bāb al-Futūḥ** (Gate of Conquests; 6; 11:5), also built in 1087 by Badr al-Gamālī. It likewise replaced an earlier gate placed somewhat to the S, which had been included in the original enclosure wall of Gawhar. The name given to the new gate by Badr was *Bāb al-Iqbāl* (Gate of Prosperity) but once again the populace transferred the name of the old gate to the new. During Napoleonic times this was called the *Tour Lescale*.

Although the construction is similar to the Bāb al-Naṣr, with the structure solid for two-thirds of its height, the form is different. The flanking towers of the gate (23m high from original ground level) have rounded fronts and the bases rest on chamfered rectangular plinths. Each tower is decorated with an arched panel on the front and on the sides. Only the latter are decorated with an inner ring of cushion voussoirs. Above this are three arrow slits in a rectangular panel, surrounded by a continuous moulding which runs around the tower across the gateway and onto the other tower.

The great arch of the gateway is decorated with a carved lattice pattern, inside the lozenges of which are flowers and geometrical motifs. Above are eight decorated brackets which support a stone shelf running between the towers. This supports a shallow arch above which is a large rectangular panel pierced by five round-arched openings. Across the top is a small corbel supported on brackets. The whole structure is crowned with round-headed crenellations. Inside the latticed arch the gate is spanned by a flat massive joggled lintel and under the great arch is an elaborate voussoir with carved keystone.

Behind the doorway a tunnel-vaulted passage leads into the porch. This is covered (unlike the Bāb al-Naṣr) with a shallow dome on pendentives. On each side is a vaulted recess. At the inner end of the porch is a great arch with 27 voussoirs, most of which are joggled. At the summit of the rear face, on a level with the platform on the front, a moulding is carried around the flanks of the gate. Inside each tower is a long vaulted room.

The walls continue to the W of the gate. For c 165m and including a *Rectangular Tower* (Napoleon's *Tour Perrault*) and a *Round-fronted Tower* (*Tour Junot*), this is all Badr al-Gamālī's work. But beyond this at a *Pentagonal Tower* the wall bends SW and is Ṣalāḥ al-Dīn's reconstruction. On the N side of Shʿ. al-Baghālah lies the **Mosque al-Maẓhariyyah** (8; 10:6). This is the site of a madrasah built in 1298, but little remains of the original fabric save for some fine marble carving on either side of the entrance and the magnificent bronze doors covered with geometrical relief.

The visitor can return from here to the Bāb al-Shaʿriyyah to the W (Rte 7) for bus No. 500 to Maydān al-Taḥrīr. Alternatively the next route can be followed back to the Maydān al-Azhar, or Rte 19 to the NE suburbs.

# 5 Bāb al-Futūḥ to Maydān al-Azhar

Rte 5 (1km) returns from the North Walls to the Maydān al-Azhar and includes some of the most important monuments in the city. There are probably more historic sites here than in any comparable area in Cairo. Also included is one of the main tourist centres, the Khān al-Khalīlī. **Cairo Atlas 11, 10, 17**.

Leading SW from the Bāb al-Futūḥ is the SHʿ. AL-MUʿIZZ LI DIN ALLĀH. This, the main highway of Fāṭimid al-Qāhirah, ran the complete length of the city, emerging at the Bāb Zuwaylah, and continuing to Fusṭāt and Miṣr al-Qadīmah. Some of Cairo's most magnificent Islamic monuments are found along this street.

Immediately inside the gate to the left rise the massive walls and minarets of the **Mosque of Khalīf al-Ḥākim** (15; 11:5), built between 990–1013. Founded by the Fāṭimid khalīf al-ʿAzīz, after his death it was completed by his son al-Ḥākim. In 1302 it suffered with many other buildings in the Great Earthquake and was restored the next year by Amīr, later Sultan Baybars al-Gāshankīr who magnificently endowed it as a madrasah. Sultan Ḥasan also had it restored in 1359 and much restoration work has been undertaken by the CPAM. The site of this mosque was outside Gawhar's original brick compound of al-Qāhirah but

## N. WALLS & MOSQUE OF AL-ḤĀKIM

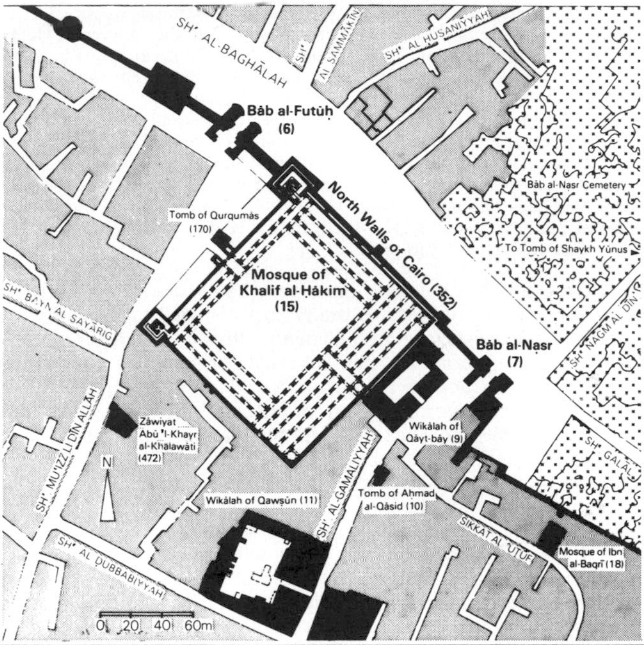
SH' AL-BAGHĀLAH
SH'
AL SAMMĀKĪN
SH' AL HUSANIYYAH
Bāb al-Futūḥ
(6)
North Walls of Cairo (352)
Bāb al-Nasr Cemetery
Tomb of Qurqumās
(170)
To Tomb of Shaykh Yūnus
Mosque of
Khalīf al-Ḥākim
(15)
SH' BAYN AL SAYĀRIG
Bāb al-Naṣr
(7)
SH' NAGM AL DĪN
SH' MU'IZZ LI DĪN ALLAH
Zāwiyat
Abū 'l-Khayr
al-Khalawāti
(472)
N
Wikālah of
Qāyt-bāy (9)
SH' GALĀL
Wikālah of Qawṣūn (11)
SH' AL-GAMALIYYAH
Tomb of Aḥmad
al-Qāsid (10)
SIKKAT AL 'UTUF
Mosque of Ibn
al-Baqrī (18)
SH' AL DUBBABIYYAH
0 20 40 60m

during the later realignment of Badr al-Gamālī it was enclosed within the new stone wall. At present it is used by the Buhrah sect who refurbished it between 1980–81, a process which, while making the mosque functional, has obscured many of the architectural details. This Ismaʿīlī group, based in India, claim direct spiritual descent from the Fāṭimid imams.

Al-ʿAzīz bi-Allāh was the fifth Fāṭimid khalīf, the second in Egypt, and succeeded his father al-Muʿizz in 975. Considered humane and tolerant, encouraging Christians and Jews to participate in the government, he was much more severe against the Sunnī Muslims. His wife was Christian and her brothers, Orestes and Arsenius, were appointed patriarch of Jerusalem and metropolitan of Fusṭāt respectively. He died in 996 as he was about to lead his armies against the Byzantine armies in Northern Syria.

At the age of eleven and a half, al-Ḥākim bi-ʿAmr Allāh, the son of al-ʿAzīz, succeeded to the Fāṭimid Khalifate. Dominated by his tutor and counsellor, the Slav eunuch Barjawān, at the age of 15 he suddenly turned on his protector and had him assassinated as they were walking in the palace gardens. His mercurial nature was soon revealed and his whole reign of 25 years was marked by the enactment and repeal of eccentric laws, executions and general acts of violence, the particular objects of his anger being Christians, Jews, Sunnī Muslims, women and dogs. He had the Church of the Holy Sepulchre in Jerusalem demolished, seized church property, forbade Christian celebrations and executed many Church officials, including one of his uncles. His laws were invoked or cancelled without warning and the rich went in deadly fear of him.

In 1020 rumours began to circulate that he was proclaiming himself a manifestation of Allāh. This provoked riots throughout Fusṭāṭ leading him to perpetrate what was probably his most terrible act, the ordering of his Sudanese troops to ravage and burn the city.

In complete contrast to these public acts, in his personal life he was abstemious, ascetic and charitable, and lavish in distribution of alms. Riding about on a donkey he took to wandering around the city or journeying into the Muqaṭṭam Hills, with only two servants for company. In February 1021 he left his servants to ride on in solitude through the hills. He was not seen again. Among the Druses of Syria he is considered a divine figure.

During late Fāṭimid times the mosque fell into disuse and was used during the Crusades to house prisoners-of-war. They built a chapel inside, which was torn down by Ṣalāḥ al-Dīn who turned it into a stable. During the French Occupation it was used as a storehouse and fortress and gradually fell into disrepair although the qiblah riwāq was partitioned off in the early 19C by ʿUmar Makram and used as a zāwiyah. For many years it was a repository for the Islamic treasures of Cairo, moved to the Museum of Islamic Art in 1896.

This is a large square enclosure mosque with a great porch and several subsidiary entrances, minarets at the N and W corners, riwāqs surrounding the central courtyard, the qiblah riwāq with a central transept, a dome over the miḥrāb and domes at the S and E corners. The ziyādah which once surrounded the mosque has disappeared but its SW porch still exists (see below). The exterior measurement (122m by 115m) is similar in size to the mosque of Ibn Ṭūlūn (Rte 13) and this mosque is also built of brick. It differs in having the outer walls faced with roughly dressed stone. It has several additional features in common with that mosque, but in others it is nearer to the historically much closer al-Azhar mosque: in addition it has features which are innovations or even unique.

The NW façade consists of the outer wall and the massive salients enclosing the minarets and the great porch, the whole being topped by stepped and pierced cresting. The original minarets stood independently of the walls at their respective corners but the great salients were added in 1010 perhaps for added strength. When restoration work was undertaken by the CPAM it was found that the original minaret shafts were still present inside the salients but had been obscured by the rubble infill of Baybars, who built the exposed upper sections with ribbed caps on top of them. This rubble was cleared and the Fāṭimid shafts built of limestone block revealed. The shaft to the N has a round section while that to the W has a square sectioned base with an octagonal upper section. Both of them are decorated with beautiful bands of ornament and Kufic inscription though the styles differ slightly; they can be seen from the interior. The upper sections of Baybars are octagonal and executed in brick and stucco; in each face there is a long keel-arched niche. Each is slightly different and crowned by ribbed cap. In the wall of the W salient is a band of marble inscription but the corresponding one from the N salient has disappeared.

The great porch was an innovation in Egypt and is very similar to that in the Great Mosque at Mahdiyyah, the Fāṭimids' original capital in Tunisia. In stone, it is decorated with crisp bands of interlace, arabesque and Kufic inscriptions. Over the porch is an inscription recording the restoration of Baybars. On each side of the door is a single pointed-arch recess, and there are two in each flank of the porch.

The tall pointed-arched door leads through into the much restored ṣaḥn. There was a riwāq of two aisles against the present NW wall, the riwāqs on the NE and SW walls each had three aisles and the qiblah riwāq had five aisles, the last contains more of the original fabric. The piers of the arches are rectangular with engaged columns at the corners, the original arches are pointed, those with the slight return probably the work of Baybars. There is a transept through the centre of the qiblah rīwāq very similar to that in al-Azhar mosque, as is the dome raised on four squinches, above the miḥrāb. The stucco windows in the drum are probably of Baybars' reconstruction. The piers supporting the dome have great baton pillars with tulip capitals and pedestals. Little remains of the two domes at either end of this riwāq, but the carved wood tie-beams of the arches under the dome are original, and so is much of the carved stucco including the windows in the wall. A stucco Kufic inscription running round the top of the wall and square of the dome is reminiscent of that in the Mosque of Ibn Ṭūlūn where, however, it is in wood. The great miḥrāb niche is now empty but probably once contained a carved wooden lining; the miḥrāb to the S of the original is the work of ʿUmar Makram in 1808 when the zāwiyah was built.

Directly in front of the mosque stood the Tomb of Amīr Qurqumas, but in 1983 this was moved to the Eastern Cemetery (Rte 8). Return to Shʿ. Muʿizz lī Dīn. After 40m, behind a façade of shops, lies the **Zāwiyat Abū ʾl-Khayr al-Kulaybāti** (477; 10:6), which is in fact the SW porch of the ziyādah of the Mosque of al-Ḥākim, built by the Khalīf al-Ẓāhir, his son, in 1021.

Its true significance had long been forgotten, but was recognised by Patricolo in 1919, after which it was restored by the CPAM. A small trefoil entrance between the shops leads down a flight of steps into a square hall. On each side is a keel-arched opening, resting on piers. Above the centre a shallow dome rests on pendentives, though the original was probably a transverse tunnel vault. In the SE arch is a small tunnel-vaulted room of much later date, containing the tomb of Sh. Abū ʾl-Khayr who, during Ottoman times, resided here and received followers of the brotherhood. This room is set obliquely to correct the qiblah.

Passing (left) the Shʿ. Dabbabiyah and (right) the Shʿ. Margūsh (to Maydān Bāb al-Shaʿriyyah, and down which is the late 18C *Sabīl of Huṣayn Shuʿaybī* (588; 10:6), after 140m on the main road is (right) the **Mosque and Sabīl-Kuttāb of Sulaymān Āghā al-Silaḥdār** (382; 10:8), built between 1837–39. Sulaymān was one of the ministers of Muḥ. ʿAlī Pasha, at one time in charge of the city's arsenal. He acquired a lot of property in this area and he was responsible for the construction of other buildings in Cairo including several sabīls. His ruthless character was recorded by E.W. Lane. He also built extensively in the Khān al-Khalīlī, and was still to be seen riding the alleys on his donkey when Bartlett visited the city in 1849. In style the present building is a purely metropolitan Ottoman construction, the façade consisting of the mosque, school, fountain and the gateway of the Ḥārat al-Bargawān. The façade of the first two is of limestone but the sabīl is faced in white marble with cast bronze grills. The whole façade is covered with relief carving, including inscriptions in Diwānī script, and crowned with an overhanging wooden roof. The minaret is set on the NE corner and is an Ottoman cylindrical shaft with median gallery, surmounted by a conical top.

Though Ottoman, the mosque still has to be entered through the usual Cairene baffled corridor from which a flight of steps leads up into the covered court with a central skylight. Against three walls are single-aisled riwāqs with marble columns, obviously reused from other buildings. There is a large qiblah līwān, separated from the court by a door in the SE wall, with the roof supported on two arcades of three arches resting on marble columns. The miḥrāb of white marble is extravagantly carved and gilded in 19C Ottoman Baroque. There is a gallery for women on the NW wall. The rest of the woodwork is elaborately carved.

Behind the Mosque of Sulaymān Āghā is the ḤĀRAT AL-BARGAWĀN with (left) the small *Zāwiyat al-Gulāq* (173). Built in 1466, it is now much ruined. The roof collapsed in 1979 but some fascinating detail remains on the NW side. Follow the road around to the left to the **Madrasah of Qāḍī Abū Bakr ibn Muzhir** (49; 10:8). This elegant building (1479–80) is typical of the period of Qāyt-bāy.

Abū Bakr ibn Muzhir was a powerful civilian minister. Born in 1428, he rose to be private secretary to Sultan Khushqadam and, in 1471, Superintendant of the Chancery of Sultan Qāyt-bāy, a post he held until his death in 1488.

The madrasah is built to a covered cruciform plan and raised above street-level. The two main façades have excellent carved decoration. Above the trefoil entrance rises the elegant minaret with an octagonal first tier. The second, cylindrical, tier is covered with a geometrical honeycomb. Next to the SW façade is a sabīl-kuttāb. A vestibule leads via a corridor into the ṣaḥn. The NW and qiblah līwāns are fronted by three arches supported on pillars, while each of the lateral līwāns has a single arch. Polychrome marble in geometrical designs covers the floor and dado. In the latter bitumen and red paste are set in grooves. Above the fine miḥrāb are windows of stucco fitted with coloured glass. In the central window next to the minbar is a rare example of the name of a craftsman, ʿAbd al-Qādir, the painter. Contemporary with the mosque is the carved wooden minbar which displays the minister's blazon, a shield of three fields with, on the centre field, a pen-box. This is repeated throughout the building. All the wooden ceilings are beautifully decorated and gilded.

A little further down the Shʿ. Muʿizz li Dīn on the right is the *Darb al-Aṣfar*. On the corner is the *House of Muṣṭafā Gaʿfar* (471), the façade of an Ottoman private house of 1713; it belonged to a coffee-merchant. Up the Darb al-Aṣfar (50m) on the left is the **Bayt al-Siḥaymī** (339), a merchant's dwelling, inhabited until 1961. It is actually two houses combined, one of 1648, the other of 1796. It occupies the site of the Ribāṭ al-Baghdādī, founded in 1285 by Khatūn, daughter of Baybars I. It was one of the few khānqāhs for women. The later house was built by ʿAbd al-Hayy al-Tablāwī and in the early part of this century it was inhabited by Muḥ. al-Sihaymī, Shaykh of the Turkish Riwāq at al-Azhar, his wife and sister. The outer façade has a plain wall on the ground floor in which the door is set; the upper floor has overhung mashrabiyyah windows set on large corbels. At the E end of the façade is the tomb of a shaykh. (To gain entry knock on the door.) A baffled corridor leads past the doorkeeper's seat into an oblong court. Varied mashrabiyyah casements look out onto the court and at the opposite end is a takhtabush. There is also a well, flour-mill and various store rooms. The interior contains several salons, women's apartments and kitchens, of which the most attractive is the qāʿah of the ḥarīm. There is a raised dais at each end for the diwans and high cushioned seats in the windows. The walls are covered with 17–18C Damascus tiles and the durqāʿah has a little dome. The house also contains a domed bath and a small maṣallah. Throughout the building are many painted cupboards and several rooms have marble facings.

On the S side of the road is a 19C *Wikālah*.

After 40m on the left of the Shʿ. Muʾizz li Dīn, just past the SHʿ. AL-SANĀNĪN is **al-Aqmar Mosque** (33; 10:8), built by al-Maʾmūn al Baṭ āʾhī, wazīr of the Faṭimid khalif al-Āmir, in 1125. It was restored by the amīr Yalbughā al-Sālimi Dawādār of Sultan Barqūq in 1396. Its name, 'The Moonlit', was derived from the colour of the light grey stone.

This is an open enclosure mosque, but is much smaller than that of al-Ḥākim and rectangular in plan. It has several important architectural features. This site was a little to the N of the Fāṭimid Western Palace and originally occupied by the Coptic Deir al-Haykal (Monastery of the Skeleton).

Al-Maʾmūn al-Baṭāʾihī's family originated in Southern Iraq but his father, came to Cairo and eventually al-Maʾmūn entered the service of the wazīr al-Afḍal in whose subsequent assassination he was implicated. Al-Āmir chose him as the next wazīr in 1121. Believing that he had designs upon the Khalifate al-Āmir had him arrested and imprisoned in 1125. Interred for three years, he was taken out and publicly crucified in 1128.

The street level having risen considerably, the building is now reached down a flight of steps. The façade consists of the NW wall with entrance salient in the centre, above which was set the minaret. The rest of the façade to the S, now obscured by modern buildings, seems to be essentially the reverse of the visible portion although set at a slight angle. It is the first building in Cairo in which the plan is dominated by the line of the street, the interior being set obliquely at 21° to the façade. The decorative units seem rather disparate, but the whole is very impressive.

The entrance is covered by a ribbed and fluted hood with a pointed-arch surrounded by a band of plaiting which also runs round the flanking recesses. In the centre is a large medallion of four concentric rings, the second and innermost of which contain Kufic inscriptions pierced right through the stone, the latter with the names of Muḥammad and ʿAlī, the other two rings containing formal floral motifs and arabesques. The doorway has a flat lintel with joggled voussoirs and above and to the sides bands of Kufic inscription, the former of verses from the Qurʾān across the salient only, but the latter containing the name of al-Maʾmūn runs right across the façade following all the angles.

The door is flanked each side by a square-headed recess containing four layers of stalactites, an elaboration on those in the Mosque of al-Guyūshī which have two tiers and are in brick. Inset in this recess is a niche with a small ribbed semi-dome with an eight-petalled daisy in the centre. Above the recesses is a band of torus moulding which runs across the whole façade, rising to cover the salient and then rising again over the entrance arch to form spandrels in which are set ribbed medallions. Above the moulding are wide shell-headed niches, the flutes of which are crossed by transverse ribs, resting on engaged baton pillars with tulip capitals and bases, those on the right helically fluted. In the centre of this niche is a carved scallop shell, that from the other side having disappeared.

On the left wing of the façade is a large shallow round-headed recess, round which the torus moulding runs, the hood with ribs and flutes, which form two layers of stalactites at the border. In the centre of the hood is a medallion with two rings of Kufic inscription and below the hood is a square-headed niche. Flanking this recess are two lozenge-shaped panels decorated with interlace and above it a circular blank space, now filled with brick, which probably contained another pierced medallion.

*Pierced stone medallion above the gate of the Mosque al-Aqmar. In the centre are the names of Muḥammad and ʿAlī*

On either side of the space are two decorated rectangular panels, that on the left of an arch resting on fluted pillars from which hangs a lamp, but that on the right a simulated cupboard, a very strange design. The lower left-hand corner of the façade is bevelled off and transfers to the square by means of a beautiful cornice, the earliest known, and on the NE wall is another medallion. Across the summit of the whole façade runs a wide band of carved Kufic inscription above which is a cavetto cornice. Of the pierced cresting which crowned the building little remains.

The original minaret was replaced by Amir Yalbughā and the base of the present brick minaret seems to be a remnant of his work. It still carries an elaborate stalactile corbel and the remains of carved stucco. The tunnel-vaulted entrance passage, with a small room to the right and a staircase and larger room to the left inside the angle formed by the façade, leads into the SW riwāq. The ṣaḥn is almost square (9.7m by 10.2m), with single arcaded riwāqs except for that against the qiblah wall which is three arcades deep. They are fronted by keel-arches raised on reused marble pillars with Corinthian capitaḷs, but the corner supports are brick piers. There was a continuous band of stucco Kufic inscription around each arch, only remaining on the NE riwāq, and between each arch was a shallow medallion, now only left on the NE and SE riwāqs. The tie beams are probably modern replacements. Pointed-arched recesses line the walls of the riwāqs, except on the qiblah wall; at the summit of most are stucco grills though the glass in them is probably 19C. Arches at right-angles to the ṣaḥn form the arcades of the riwāqs and support the roof of shallow domes carried on pendentives; these are almost certainly the work of Amīr Yalbughā and very similar to those in the riwāqs of the Madrasah and Tomb of Barqūq in the Eastern Cemetery (Rte 8). At the end of the NE riwāq are two large cupboards, the modern wooden doors containing panels from the Fāṭimid originals. The central recess of the second qiblah arcade contains a skylight and the rear aisle is covered by a flat wooden roof. The miḥrāb has a keel-arch outline, with the marble facing and engaged columns due to the restoration of Yalbughā, for above it is an inscription giving his master Barqūq's name.

On the right is the Sh'. al-Tumbakshiyyah down which (20m) on the S is the *Ma'bad Mūsā* (unclassified) of 1262 and, next to it, are Ottoman hostels: the **Wikālah and Sabīl al-Naqādī** (397; 10:8), built in 1618, and another **Wikālah and Sabīl of 'Abbās Āghā** (396), of which only the portal at the E end is of the original building of 1694. The central island is occupied by a 17C *Ottoman house* (unclassified).

70m further on the right is the SH'. AL-KHURUNFISH (leading to Sh'. Būr Sa'īd).

Down this street on the left (70m) stands the **Mosque of 'Abd al-Laṭīf al-Qarāfī** (46; 10:8), a small mosque built at the end of the 16C, only part of which is left. The tomb of the founder is in the window bay to the left of the miḥrāb. After another 70m the road bears right. On the corner of the SH'. KHĀN ABŪ ṬAQIYYAH is the **Mosque of Muḥibb al-Dīn Abū 'l-Ṭayyib** (48), c 1530, one of the first mosques built after the conquest of Salim I and still completely Mamlūk in conception. It is a small local mosque of cruciform shape with unroofed ṣaḥn, the internal līwāns much reduced and that on the E transformed into an ablution court. The flat-roofed qiblah līwān has wooden braces carved with an inscription.

S along this alley are several Ottoman monuments converted for use as modern workshops. On the left is the *Wikālat Waqf al-Ḥaramayn* (598; 10:8). Further on is the 17–18C *Sabīl-Kuttab al-Kirdānī* (179), once attached to the Khān of Isma'il Abū Ṭaqiyyah, an important hostelry frequented by Armenian precious-metal merchants. On the right stands the *Wikālat al-Muḥammadayn* (597), also 18C, a coffee-merchants' hostelry built by Khwāgā Aḥ. al-Khātib. Further on the alley joins the Ḥārat al-Yahūd (see below).

Sh'. al-Khurunfish continues past the Sikkat al-Khurunfish and the Dār al-Kiswah to (200m) the Sh'. Būr Sa'īd (Rte 7).

Return to the Sh'. al-Mu'izz li Dīn. A few metres S is the **Sabīl-Kuttāb of 'Abd al-Raḥmān Katkhudā** (21; 10:8), built in 1744 on the triangular site where this road meets the S branch of the Sh'. al-Tumbakshiyyah, by one of the most powerful bays. It is a beautiful building, still retaining many Mamlūk features. It was restored by the GIA/EAO in 1980–84. The fountain is no longer used but the room above is still used as a school and community centre. It is on the site of a 13C rab', the remains of which still exist behind. It is composed of two storeys open on three sides, in grey and white stone inlaid, with marble reliefs and tiles and with engaged pillars at the corners. The sabīl windows have bronze grills and are covered with huge double arches with joggled voussoirs. The interior is lined with floral tiles. The kuttāb on the first floor rests on huge decorated corbels; it is surrounded by mashrabbiyyah screens and covered with an overhanging roof. The ceiling is carved and painted, the whole effect being extremely elegant. Behind is a *House*, also built by 'Abd al-Raḥmān.

On the left the DARB AL-QIRMIZ (Crimson Alley) leads after 10m to the entrance (right) of the **Palace of Amīr Bashtak** (34; 10:8), built in 1334–39 and restored by the GIA/EAO in 1982–84).

Immensely wealthy Bashtak, a leading minister of Sultan al-Nāṣir Muḥ, was involved in a long-standing feud with the Amīr Qạwṣūn. After Abū Bakr, al-Nāṣir Muḥ.'s son, succeeded to the sultanate in 1340 Qạwṣūn, then atabak, had Bashtak arrested, executed and his possessions seized. When Bashtak bought this site in 1335 it contained the remains of the Eastern Palace of the Fāṭimids and several dependent mosques and shops. He built his grand palace here, which with five floors, each provided with running water, was renowned throughout Cairo.

If the entrance is locked the warden is usually in the vicinity. In the courtyard on the left is a huge pointed-arched porch with an inscription on either side. On the left-hand side in the shoulder of the arch is Bashtak's blazon, the upper field self coloured, on a white middle field a red napkin, the lower field red (colours from an interior ceiling), indicating that at one time he had probably been ustādār (steward). Inside on the left is a keel-arched doorway. The ceiling is beautifully carved, though neglected. The upper floor is reached through a modern entrance which leads up some steps to a large cruciform qāʿah, with a durqāʿah and four līwāns. The walls are lined with dressed stone, but originally had marble facings, the remains of which can be seen by the large window. A fountain once stood in the centre of the durqāʿah. The major līwāns to the E and W have hexagonally coffered ceilings. Although restored, much of the latter, containing examples of the blazon already described, is original. The two smaller līwāns to the N and S are separated from the qāʿah by an arcade of three horseshoe arches on pillars; they are filled with mashrabiyyah. Above the līwāns runs a gallery with windows overlooking the qāʿah and high in the wall are pierced stucco windows. In the S corner is another small room, also with a coffered wooden ceiling. On the main road the entrance has a very fine flat roofed stalactite arch. At the N end of the palace is the *Mosque al-Figl*; immediately to the S lies the *Wikālat al-Awand* (unclassified), built before 1800 and now the main centre for coppersmiths (nahhasīn).

About 20m further up the road as it turns to the E is the **Tomb of Shaykh Sinān** (41; 10:8), an early Ottoman tomb with two domes built in 1585 and restored by the GIA/EAO in 1976–78. Inside, the main dome on squinches covers the tomb to the SE. A small vaulted chamber contains the miḥrab and the smaller dome. After another 20m stands (right) the **Madrasah of Mithqāl** (45; 10:8), an elegant raised cruciform mosque built in 1361 by Sādiq al-Dīn Mithqāl (sequin) who was the chief eunuch at the courts of Sultans Muḥammad II and Shaʿbān II between 1361–74. He built it near his own house and though small it is very tall. It was restored by the GIA/EAO in 1973–76). To allow access Mithqāl had to raise the mosque above the level of the street and the side-street still passes under it through a tunnel-vaulted passage. In the ablaq façade the windows are set in recesses, as is the door which is reached by a flight of steps. The entrance is covered by a trefoil stalactite-arch with an inscription at 2m. The building is crowned by a trefoil cresting. The interior is panelled and floored with coloured marble and the woodwork is carved and painted. Surrounding the open ṣaḥn, the līwāns have pointed-arch fronts. Those to the SW and NE are unusual in being divided into two storeys by mezzanine floors, each divided into two rooms fronted with mashrabiyyah screens. On the opposite side of the street is an 18C *house* (unclassified).

Return to the Shʿ. al-Muʿizz lī Dīn. Opposite is the **Hammām of Sultan Īnāl** (562), now called the *Ḥammām al-Sulṭān*, all that remains of a huge palace built in 1456 and still in use as a public bath. The superstructure is modern, but the interior is of interest with a great domed steam room and marble reclining slabs. It is on the site of the Palace of Amīr Baysarī, built in 1261.

Adjoining the ḥammām is the small *Mosque of Ḥasan al-Shaʿrāwī Katkhudā*, built in 1752. The doorway was described by Creswell as 'architecturally beneath contempt'; while some may disagree with this, it is certainly not very striking. However, along the corridor, behind the mosque lie the remains of the **Madrasah of Sultan al-Kāmil** (428; 10:8). It was originally a two-līwāned college built purely for the study of ḥadīth (traditions) in 1225. This was the first college for this purpose in Cairo and only the second known (the first had been built by Sultan Nūr al-Dīn in Damascus). For the upkeep of the madrasah the sultan built a huge rabʿ stretching from Shʿ. al-Khurunfish to opposite al-Aqmar Mosque. The madrasah is built on the site of part of the Fāṭimid Western Palace.

Al-Kāmil third of the great Ayyūbid sultans and nephew of Ṣalāḥ al-Dīn was the first sultan to choose the Citadel for his palace, a preference that persisted for the rulers, with one exception, until the last decades of the 19C. His magnanimity was renowned; and he is acknowledged by the Coptic Christians as their most generous sovereign. He received Francis of Assisi in 1219 and politely granted him an audience. During his reign the Crusaders invaded Egyptian soil and occupied Damietta in 1218 but after their defeat in 1221 he allowed them to withdraw peacefully. His relationship with the Christian princes was good and he allowed them access to Jerusalem by treaty with Emperor Frederick II. He died in Damascus in 1238.

All that remains of the madrasah are the NW līwān and the SW side of the SE līwān. The former, in large stone masonry, is nearly square with brick tunnel-vaulted roof and a brick recess, probably a malqaf, with entry to two rooms, now destroyed. Three openings, one either side and one at the back of the recess, are covered by wooden lintels. The SE līwān is c 20m from the former and was about 15cm wider; there are vestiges of students' living rooms. Some stucco work from this building is now in the MIA.

The Shʿ. Muʿizz li Dīn at this point and for about 100m is called *Bayn al-Qaṣrayn* (Between the two Palaces), a name it has retained since it ran between the immense Fāṭimid palaces which lay on either side, the Great Western Palace and the Eastern Palace.

An impressive composite façade now stretches for 185m along the right-hand side of the road comprising three 14C madrasahs. The first of these great buildings is also the latest: the ***Madrasah and Tomb of Sultan Barqūq** (187; 10:8) of cruciform plan, built between 1384–86, the façade consisting of the SE wall, the entrance, dome over the tomb and the minaret.

Barqūq, from the Circassian tribe of Kasa, was brought to Egypt and purchased by the Amīr Yalbughā al-ʿUmārī by whom he was educated and freed in 1363. His master was murdered and Barqūq was implicated and imprisoned. After his release he entered the service of Mangak al-Yūsufī, viceroy of Syria, but was recalled to Cairo by Sultan Shaʿbān II where he was again involved with the amīrs who assassinated the sultan. He was sent to Karak but after ʿAlī became sultan he returned to Cairo and was made an amīr of one hundred and shortly after atabak. He filled all the important military posts with Circassian mamlūks and brought his father Anas and other relatives from his home town to join him. When ʿAlī died in 1382 his brother Ḥāggī II was raised to the throne but there was much disturbance in the city and Barqūq had himself invested, the first Circassian sultan.

The assumption of a Circassian, even though Qipchaq-speaking, inflamed many of the amīrs and in 1389 Barqūq was deposed and exiled to Karak and Ḥāggī II was reinstated. In 1390 Barqūq advanced on Cairo and although defeated at Shayab, while retreating he came upon the tent of Sultan Ḥāggī and the Khalīf al-Mutuwakkil I and Barqūq persuaded the child Ḥāggī to abdicate. They returned to Cairo in triumph and Barqūq was re-elected sultan. Generous and good-humoured, he was a man who craved learning and surrounded himself with clever men. He

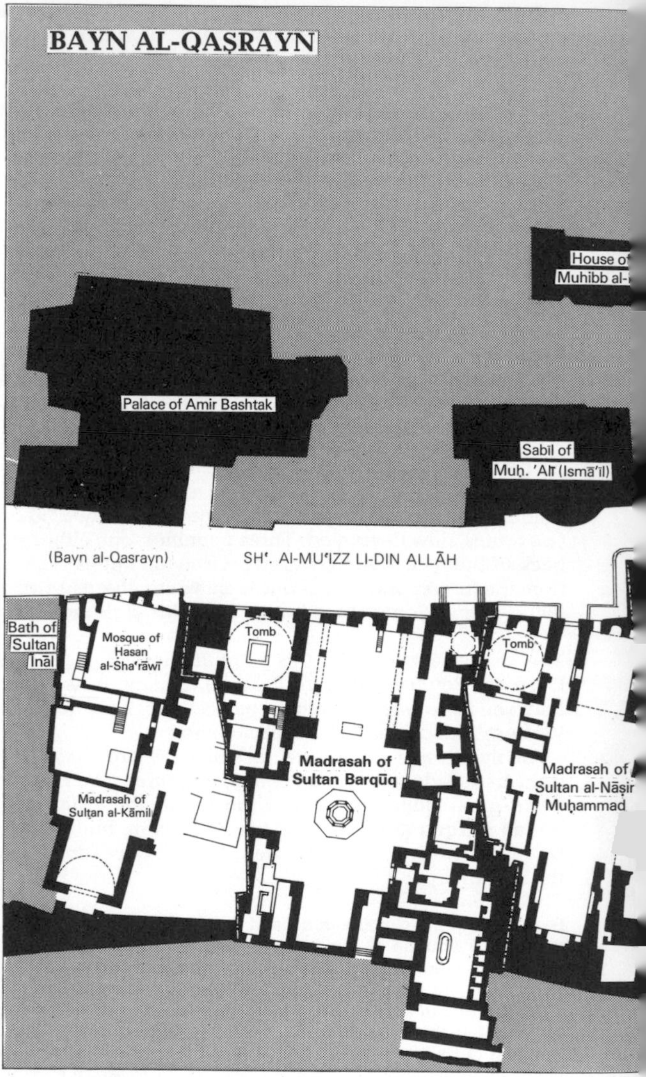
BAYN AL-QAṢRAYN
House of
Muhibb al-
Palace of Amir Bashtak
Sabīl of
Muḥ. 'Alī (Ismā'īl)
(Bayn al-Qasrayn)
SH'. Al-MU'IZZ LI-DIN ALLĀH
Bath of
Sultan
Īnāl
Mosque of
Ḥasan
al-Sha'rāwī
Tomb
Tomb
Madrasah of
Sultan Barqūq
Madrasah of
Sultan al-Nāṣir
Muḥammad
Madrasah of
Sulṭan al-Kāmil

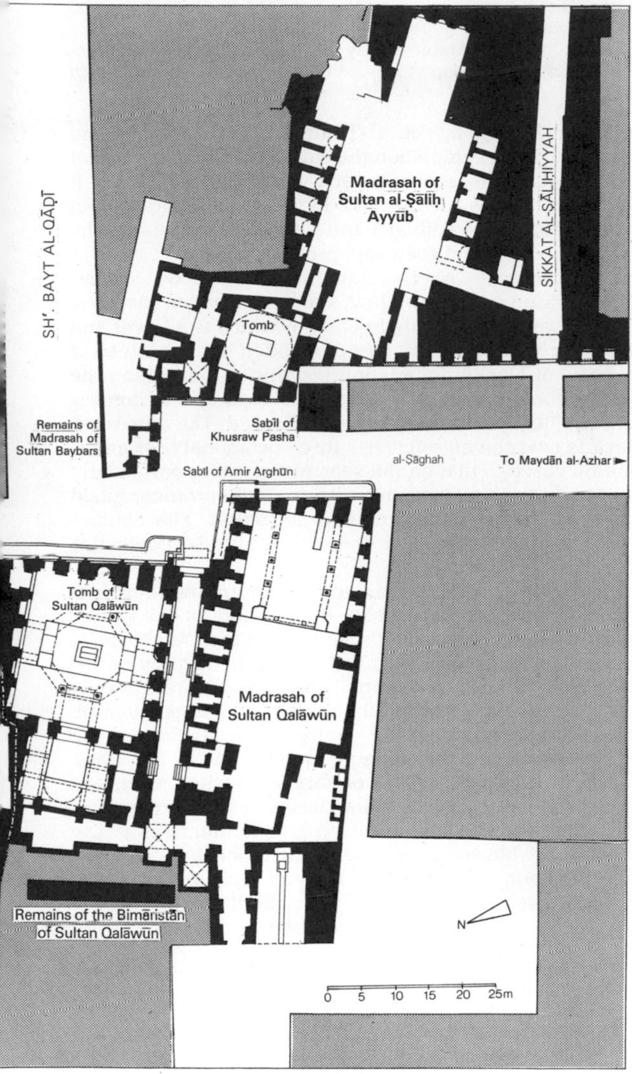
Madrasah of
Sultan al-Ṣāliḥ
Ayyūb
SIKKAT AL-ṢALIḤIYYAH
SH'. BAYT AL-QĀḌĪ
Tomb
Remains of
Madrasah of
Sultan Baybars
Sabīl of
Khusraw Pasha
Sabil of Amir Arghūn
al-Ṣāghah
To Maydān al-Azhar
Tomb of
Sultan Qalāwūn
Madrasah of
Sultan Qalāwūn
Remains of the Bimāristān
of Sultan Qalāwūn
N
0 5 10 15 20 25m

admired piety and often visited shaykhs to discuss theology. He died at the age of 60 in 1399, probably of pneumonia.

His name which means 'plum' in Arabic clearly fascinated people and a compatriot explained that it was a corruption of his Circassian name Malikhuq which meant shepherd.

This mosque was built by Aḥ. b. Aḥ. al-Ṭūlūni, Chief Architect and father-in-law of Barqūq. On its completion the sultan was so pleased that he presented the engineers and labourers each with two gold pieces. It was endowed with lectureships for the four legal schools and Qur'ān reading and discussion, ḥadīth (traditions) and also had facilities for the sūfī brotherhoods. All food, oil and soap was provided free.

The façade of the madrasah, higher than those of the two earlier buildings to the S, is divided into six shallow, stalactite-headed recesses, the two to the N in the wall of the tomb, in each of which is a lower and upper window, the latter with rare examples of wooden lattice instead of pierced stucco. A band of Naskhī foundation inscription runs along the top of the wall and the whole is crowned with foliate cresting. The dome is a replacement built in 1893, the original having collapsed. The minaret at the S end of the façade over the entrance has three octagonal tiers and is covered with beautiful carving, that on the second tier being particularly bold; the whole impression is elegant but robust. The entrance, inlaid with marble, is covered with a trefoil arch and stalactites. The double-leafed doors are bronze-plated with silver inlay, the central medallion is split by the divide.

A corridor leads into the W corner of the open ṣaḥn surrounded by four līwāns fronted by pointed arches. The qiblah līwān, used for the Ḥanafī school of law, has arcades dividing it into three aisles, a feature obviously taken from the earlier madrasah of Sultan Qalāwūn. The slightly horse-shoe arches rest on bulbous capitals supported by reused red granite Pharaonic columns. The ceiling is beautifully carved and painted, though restored. A wooden dikkah occupies the centre of the līwān and the wooden minbar was presented by Sultan Jaqmaq in the 1440s. The *Tomb* lies to the right of the līwān, with a band of carved wooden inscription running round the walls and wooden stalactites at each corner. This ceiling is particularly fine and has been restored to its former beauty. The floors throughout are in marble and have inset circular porphyry sections. The grave in the centre originally held the body of Barqūq, but it was transferred to the madrasah that his son, Farag, built for him in the Eastern Cemetery (Rte 8); it contains other members of the family.

Directly opposite is the **Sabīl of Muḥammad ʿAli Pasha** (402) erected in 1828, in memory of his third son, Ismaʿīl Pasha who commanded the Sudan military expedition. His methods were extremely cruel and he was burned alive, with his officers in 1822. Although the story circulated that this crime had been perpetrated by Mak Nimr of Shendi, there is growing suspicion that it was in fact the result of friction within the Egyptian royal family or the army.

Set back about 2m from the façade of Barqūq's madrasah is the **Madrasah and Tomb of Sultan al-Nāṣir Muḥammad** (44; 10:8) which predates that of Barqūq by about 80 years. It was started by Sultan Kitbughā in 1295, but completed by al-Nāṣir Muḥ. during his second reign in 1304. It is also of cruciform plan, the first for all four schools of law. The interior is now much dilapidated and only traces of the once lavish decoration remain. The 21m-long façade consists of the NE wall of the tomb and the madrasah divided by the entrance, above which rises the minaret. The dome over the tomb fell in 1870 and was not replaced, only the zone-of-transition remains.

In 1294 Sultan Khalīl (see Rte 11), son of Qalāwūn, was assassinated and his nine-year-old brother Muḥammad was elected to the sultanate. The viceroy and regent was the amīr Kitbughā, a Mongol who promptly deposed al-Nāṣir Muḥ. and assumed the sultanate in 1295, appointing the amīr Lagīn as viceroy. Visiting Syria in 1297 Kitbughā had to flee to Damascus. Lagīn was elected Sultan and persuaded al-Nāṣir Muḥ. to travel to Karak for his own good. Though pious and abstemious Lāgin was assassinated in 1299. Al-Nāṣir Muḥ. was recalled from Karak and reassumed the throne but another two powerful amīrs, Baybars al-Gāshankīr (see Rte 4), his atabak and the regent Salār (see Rte 13) dominated the sultan completely. On the pretence of travelling on the ḥajj, al-Nāṣir Muḥ. escaped to Karak in 1309 and Baybars became sultan. Within a year al-Nāṣir Muḥ with the support of the provinical governors was able to lead a great force toward Egypt. Baybars fled but was caught and executed as was later Salar. Al-Nāṣir Muḥ. was restored as sultan and was destined to reign for 30 years.

Though his court was lavish, he was modest in his appetites. He constructed many buildings and public works and was very attentive to his public duties. Small, and lame in one foot, his great passions were his horses and flocks of sheep which he kept in the gardens of the Citadel. He died in 1341 after naming his son Abū Bakr as successor and warning the amīrs of another of his sons, Aḥmad, whom he had exiled to Karak. In all, eight of his sons were destined to rule Egypt in a space of 21 years.

The foundation of Kitbughā reached only to the band of inscription along the wall. He built it on the site of a hammām and the parade ground of the Fāṭimid Great Western Palace.

EXTERIOR. The façade, the S end of which is overhung by the minaret of Qalāwūn's madrasah, has three full-length stalactite-headed recesses, enclosing tall windows with inscriptions on the lintels and decorated relieving arches, the two to the N lighting the tomb, the other the qiblah līwān. A band of Naskhī inscription, originally gilded in an ornamental frame, runs across the façade and above are two more windows, each set over the miḥrābs of the tomb and madrasah respectively. The whole façade is topped by stepped cresting. The minaret is in three tiers, the first a square-sectioned shaft of stuccoed brick on which are set two later octagonal sections, the top of lathe and plaster. The second storey may be a 15C restoration while the cap is Ottoman. The lower storey (which seems Andalusian in form) is covered with superb ornament in very good condition, showing keel-arched panels, bands of Kufic inscription, circular and lozenge-shaped medallions and an arcade of trefoil arches surmounted by a long round-ended panel of Naskhī. The first two tiers are surmounted by an elaborate stalactite cornice, the lower with 16 sides. The door justifies its Gothic appearance as it was brought complete from the Church of St. George in Acre for Sultan Khalīl, after the expulsion of the Crusaders in 1291. Kitbughā saw it in the house of an amīr and wished it to be incorporated in his madrasah. It is in white marble with a pointed arch. The door posts and Arabic inscription are insertions.

INTERIOR. The doorway leads into a passage separating the tomb and madrasah, the wooden ceiling similar to that in Qalāwūn's complex (see below). At the far end are two doors: on the right to the forecourt of the tomb, on the left into the open ṣaḥn of the madrasah. The NW līwān (Shafiʿī School) has a restored arch and roof, the two unequal lateral līwāns SW (Ḥanbalī School) and NE (Ḥanafī School) are without roofs or arches, but remains of the students' rooms can be seen to the left of the latter. The qiblah wall in the SE līwān (Malikī School) is the only area to retain part of the original decoration, with a Kufic inscription running along the top. Two windows in keel-arched frames occupied each side of this līwān. The large miḥrāb, 10m tall, is flanked by two green breccia columns, from Wādī al-Hammamāt, and the hood is decorated with excellent stucco carving. The large frame of the miḥrāb, unfortunately incomplete, is also in stucco with complex design, in the centre of which is the high window in a tesselated frame. This is the last stucco miḥrāb known in Egypt.

*Tomb*. The entrance into the tomb is to the right of the main corridor; the tomb is about 9m sq. A wooden decorative frieze runs around the four walls, the inscription for the most part removed to the MIA, as it was carved on reused Fāṭimid panels. Another wooden band of painted inscription from the Qur'ān runs beneath the squinches, which are of three layers of five niches, and between each a window of three lights. The miḥrāb here is also flanked by two greenish breccia pillars but nothing else remains. The tomb contains the bodies of Sultan Nāṣir Muḥ.'s mother Ashlūn bt. Sukbāy (died 1303), transferred by him from the tomb of Fāṭimah Khātūn (Rte 11) and his eldest son Ānūk (lion cub; died 1340). His own body was interred in his father's mausoleum next door.

The façade of the last and most impressive of the three buildings, the ***Madrasah, Tomb and Bimāristan of Sultan Qalāwūn** (43; 17:1), called al-Manṣūriyyah, projects forward from that of al-Nāṣir Muḥ. by c 9m and extends in two sections divided by the entrance: first the wall of the tomb for 43m, then that of the madrasah, which projects forward another 10m for 24m. The remains of the hospital are situated at the rear of these two and a sabīl is attached to the N end of the façade of the madrasah. The whole magnificent complex was raised in a little over a year (1284–85). It is built on the site of the main body of the Western Palace of the Fāṭimids and recent excavations in the madrasah and the site of the hospital have uncovered the foundations of the earlier structure. The present building suffered slightly in the Great Earthquake of 1302 when the upper part of the minaret fell. It was replaced by Sultan al-Nāṣir Muḥ. in 1303. The hospital was in continual use from its building until late Ottoman times and reconstruction was undertaken by ʿAbd al-Raḥmān Katkhudā (1776), although the service had declined piteously. It was used as a lunatic asylum in the 1800s but in 1910 an Opthalmic Hospital was built on the site, thus giving the site a usage of 700 years.

Qalāwūn was a Qipchaq Turk brought by the amīr Aqsunqur for 1000 (alf) dinars, a great deal of money, and it was never forgotten for he kept the epithet 'alfi' as part of his royal name. He entered the service of Sultan Ṣāliḥ Ayyūb at his citadel on Rawḍah Island and was a barrack companion of Baybars al-Bunduqdārī. Together they incurred the wrath of Sultan Aybak and escaped to Karak where they remained until the deposition of Sultan ʿAlī, the son of Aybak, in 1259.

When Baybars became sultan Qalāwūn's position advanced considerably but upon the succession of Barakah Khān in 1277 he was virtually exiled from Egypt. When it became obvious that he was not going to be allowed back, he advanced on Cairo in 1280. Barakah Khān, deserted by his troops, abdicated and was sent to Karak. Salamish, the seven-year-old second son of Baybars, was elevated and Qalāwūn was created atabak. He gradually eliminated the supporters of Salāmish by exile and trial and after 100 days deposed the child and was elected sultan.

Qalāwūn was a generous man and forgave many of his enemies, destroying incriminating evidence and giving them government positions, but he was very hard on both Christians and Jews and would not have them in official posts. Many campaigns were waged against the Crusader Kingdoms and Qalāwūn died of a fever in 1290, as he was about to launch an expedition against Acre. He was the first sultan to import Circassian mamlūks in large numbers as a counter measure to the Qipchaqs who dominated the armies.

Kalavun is a rare but proper Turkish name meaning 'rich present' or 'great ransome'.

The *façade*, like those of the last two buildings, forms the SE wall of the complex, with the tomb to the N and at the S the madrasah, the entrance in the centre dividing the two sections. The minaret is set at the N end of the façade but the dome over the tomb is a reconstruction. The wall of the mausoleum is divided into a series of pointed-arched recesses, the hoods supported on marble columns with Islamic and Christian capitals used indiscriminately as bases or capitals. In each recess are three windows, the grills in the lower windows of cast iron, while those in the centre are beautifully pierced stucco; the upper windows are of two lights surmounted by an oculus. A band of Naskhī foundation inscription runs above the lower windows. The whole is crowned with stepped cresting covered in foliate decoration.

The entrance, set slightly forward and reached by steps, is covered by a semi-circular arch, the first in Egypt, resting on engaged columns. Inside this is another arch with buff-and-black joggled voussoirs and strapwork spandrels framing a double window and oculus. This window contains a 12C Gothic grill, probably brought from Jerusalem as there is identical work there. The great bronze-plated doors are original, though the base is much restored. Above this is a triple window and oculus.

The façade of the madrasah is similar to that of the mausoleum. At the extreme S of the façade is a bevel-topped buttress which is very Gothic in appearance. At the N end of the façade is the *Sabīl of Amīr Arghūn al-ʿAlāʾī* (561), Chief Jandār (died 1347) under Sultan al-Nāṣir Muḥ., one of whose widows, Umm Ismaʿil, he married. It was added in 1346. This is the earliest remaining example of a public fountain in Cairo. Little remains and the cistern and ducts have disappeared. The NE side is framed by four pointed arches resting on marble columns while on the SE wall is a wooden shelter. A Nashkī inscription runs below the roof. It also contains five panels of faience tiles which would seem to be the work of a Persian artist who left other examples of his work in Cairo at this time.

The minaret, which for the first time is not set over the entrance, rises from the northern corner to a height of 56m has three storeys, the first two in stone of square section and the uppermost cylindrical. In each side of the first storey is a recess flanked by engaged pillars covered by a horseshoe arch in the centre of which is an oculus, the whole resting on a stalactite corbel. The second storey also has a horseshoe-arched recess with cushion voussoirs but without pillars, and the section has a frieze of arches around the top. The third cylindrical storey, a replacement by Sultan al-Nāṣir Muḥ. in 1303 after the original fell in the earthquake of 1302, is in brick decorated with an encircling fretwork arcade. The corbel is a cavetto cornice, an Egyptian device used since earliest Pharaonic times, and the Ottoman cap has a keel-arched profile.

*Madrasah*. The entrance opens into a great corridor, 10m high, with the madrasah to the left and the tomb to the right. The corridor originally lead through to the bimāristan at the rear, but this exit is now closed. It is flanked by tall pointed-arched recesses, in which are set similarly arched windows overlooking the madrasah and tomb. The round-headed recesses are probably 18C work of ʿAbd al-Raḥmān Katkhudā. The

*Madrasah of Qalāwūn. View over al-Naḥḥasin from the minaret of Barqūq*

wooden ceiling rests on a cornice and is decorated with painted fretwork. Entry to the madrasah is through the third recess on the left up two steps.

The steps lead into a vestibule with wooden ceiling opening directly into the ṣaḥn (20.5m by 17m). It will be seen that this madrasah possessed only two līwāns and it was intentionally copied from that of Sultan Ṣāliḥ Ayyūb (see below). In this NE wall are the tunnel-vaulted students' rooms in three storeys; the upper tier, lighted with small rectangular windows, was reached by an internal staircase. The central rooms on the

SW side have been converted into a triple-arched recess, also part of the 18C Ottoman reconditioning. The NW līwān has lost its frontal arch and original ceiling. A doorway on the right leads back into the corridor.

The qiblah līwān to the SE is very unusual and was the model upon which Barqūq based that in his madrasah (see above). It consists of a two-tiered triple-arched front leading into two four-arched arcades running the length of the līwān. The arches are supported on rose granite columns with Corinthian capitals, above which are blocks with elaborate patterns, on which rest square-sectioned piers from which the arches spring. The whole structure is braced by tie-beams, and oculi with stucco grills pierce the area above the arches. Three tiers of windows are set in the walls, the lower pairs set in pointed-arched recesses, the upper are triple windows. The miḥrāb is smaller than that in the tomb. It is flanked by two pillars and decorated with marble and two tiers of blind arcading. The hood and the spandrels have gold mosaic with a design of vines set with mother-of-pearl and above are four lines of inscription. A painted 19C inscription replaces the original wooden carving but the beautiful stucco decoration above the miḥrāb is original. The flat ceiling is not contemporary with the madrasah and the form of the original is disputed. The rather plain wooden minbar was made in 1484 by order of the amīr Azbak b. Tatakh, atabak of Sultan Qāyt-bay, who gave his name to the Azbakiyyah Quarter (Rte 3B).

*Tomb.* The entrance equivalent to that of the madrasah is closed; entry is through a doorway, reached by steps, set in the sixth recess on the right. This leads through a small domed vestibule into a small court surrounded on three sides by single arcaded riwāqs. The arches rest on reused rose granite pillars with Corinthian capitals, braced by tie-beams. The roofs to the NE and SW are each covered by three shallow brick domes resting on pendentives, while the NW is covered by a tunnel vault. The entrance to the tomb in the SE wall is filled with mashrabiyyah and has a two-leafed door. The wall above has some of the most beautiful stucco work in Egypt up to a height of c 18m. There are three round-headed windows in the lower section and above more windows. The whole is topped by a cavetto frieze and cresting.

The tomb chamber has a rectangular plan (21m by 23m). In the centre are four piers and four columns arranged in an octagon, supporting arches which in turn raise a high drum and thence a dome. The reused rose granite pillars have Corinthian capitals, and impost blocks. Eight more arches join the centre unit to the side walls, and the whole structure is braced by tie-beams. The restored ceiling (height 15m), is divided thus into elaborately carved and gilded sections. The corner sections have octagonal coffers, that in the N corner left in its original state. The octagonal drum of the dome has a double window and oculus in each face and the dome (diameter 11.5m) rises to 30m; this is not the original dome which was demolished by ʿAbd al-Raḥmān Katkhudā in the 18C. The replacement was built in concrete by Herz in 1903, using as his model the Tomb of al-Ashraf Khalīl (Rte 11). The original dome was probably in wood; the wooden squinches are still in place. Around the walls are pointed-arched recesses, their windows with bronze or stucco grills, the latter filled with coloured glass. The recesses in the NE wall are cupboards in which some of Qalāwūn's clothes were kept, while that to the N opens into a small room beside the minaret. Double windows with oculi run around the next storey.

Although the floor is only stone the decoration of the walls is very rich, with a dado of marble and mosaic, and the upper walls in fine mosaic, variegated marble and Kufic rectangles. A frieze runs over the engaged columns of the recesses, the lower gilded section with a design of vines with leaves and grapes and the upper with a Naskhī inscription. In addition there is much stucco and painted decoration.

The miḥrāb, 7m high, with a horseshoe plan, is flanked by three pairs of pillars, and the hood has three layers of small arches. The whole is covered with mosaic of marble and mother-of-pearl. Five screens of mashrabiyyah surround the tābūt, and two others divide the mausoleum; they contain an inscription of Sultan al-Nāṣir Muḥ. The tābūt has columned sides supporting a gable top, while the end panels are original woodwork. The grave contains the bodies of Sultan Qalāwūn and his son, Sultan al-Nāṣir Muḥ. who requested burial here rather than in his own mausoleum to the N.

The *Bimāristan* is reached now by an alley along the SW wall of the madrasah. Little remains of the original foundation, much of the site being occupied by the modern Opthalmic Hospital. To the right are the remains of the SE līwān, one side only standing. At the rear is an arched recess containing the remnants of a marble fountain, and a salsabīl. Above is a double window similar to those of the rest of the complex and at the back of the recess is a round arched stucco panel with two windows and four medallions. The doorway from the rest of the complex is probably the work of ʿAbd al-Raḥmān Katkhudā; the beautiful door is now in the Museum of Islamic Art. A strange T-shaped wooden roofed līwān fronted by an arcade of four columns occupies the NE side; the roof has some Fāṭimid decoration. Of the NW līwān only the recess and fountain remain, while the SW līwān has disappeared completely. Behind is the Qāʿah of Amir Aqūsh, governor of Karak and director of the bimāristan in 1320–30. The qāʿah is similar in plan to the Qāʿat al-Dardīr (Rte 6).

During Ottoman times and in the 19C this area was the reknowned Sūq al-Naḥḥasīn (Çoppersmiths' Market), which transferred here from alongside the Mosque of Mu'ayyad Shaykh in the late Mamlūk period.

Opposite the complex of Sultan Qalāwūn the SHʿ. BAYT AL-QĀḌĪ leads N. After 40m (left) house No. 19 is the **Qāʿat Muḥ. Muḥibb al-Dīn al-Muwaqqiʿ** (50; 17:1), the remains of another palace built in 1350, shortly after that of Bashtak. It was restored and used as a residence by ʿUthmān Katkhudā in the 18C and restored again by the CPAM in 1911. The entrance is modern and the visitor should knock. A long passage leads on the left into a huge qāʿah, the durqāʿah in the centre 17m high. Again all the marble facings have disappeared, but the brackets of the archways and other work are 16C. The fountain in the centre is probably ʿUthmān Katkhudā's work, but there is an original salsabīl in the S wall.

Enter the Maydān Bayt al-Qāḍī (House of the Judge). Its name derives from the fact that it was the seat of a court during the last hundred years of Ottoman administration and was known as such in the 'Description de l'Egypt' of the French Expedition. On the SW side is the **Maqʿad of Amīr Māmāy** (51), the remains of yet another Mamlūk palace, but a very late one (1496).

Māmāy b. Khudād started his career as a mamlūk of Sultan Qāyt-bāy. He was manumitted and in 1492 became a second dawādār. In 1495 he was created an amīr of one hundred and sent on several diplomatic missions to Istanbul. He rebelled against Sultan Muḥ. IV in 1496 but lost a battle at Khān Yūnus, was captured and beheaded.

Most of the palace has disappeared; this building stood inside its courtyard. The remaining maqʿad (33m long and 11.2m high) has an arcade of five slightly pointed horseshoe arches. The arches support a very beautiful, though restored, wooden ceiling. The adjoining entrance with its trefoil stalactite head, inscription to right and left of the entrance and flanking engaged columns, closely resembles those of contemporary mosques. The façade is of ablaq and there are several shields with the amīr's blazon (badly eroded): on the upper field a napkin; on the middle field, a cup charged with a pen box placed between a pair of horns, and on the lower field a cup.

On the W side of the square stands the *Bayt al-Qādī* (unclassified). Built before 1800, it is the Ottoman building which served as the seat of justice. Next to it the ḤARAT BAYT AL-QĀDĪ leads by a series of right-angle turns past the *Wikālat Gulshaniyyah* (unclassified), also from before 1800, under the Palace of Bashtak into the Shʿ. Muʾīzz li Dīn.

Return to the Shʿ. Muʾizz li Dīn. On the E side of the road is another complex of three buildings, slightly earlier than those on the W side.

At the NW angle of this complex is a small section of the **Madrasah of Sultan Baybars I al-Bunduqdārī** (37; 17:1), called also *al-Ẓāhiriyyah*. This is all that remains of an immense cruciform madrasah built between 1262–63 on the site of two halls of the Great Eastern Palace of the Fāṭimids. Despite its shape it was not intended for all four schools of law, but for the Shāfiʿī and Ḥanafī school only. The madrasah fell into disuse in later Mamlūk times though most of it was still standing until 1874 when the bulk of it was demolished during the construction of the Shʿ. Bayt al-Qāḍī. In 1882 the minaret fell, killing a number of people. All that is left is a small block of the SW angle (restored in the 1950s by the CPAM), consisting of a room, possibly a sabīl, with two windows in the NW and SW walls. The decoration of the windows is extremely beautiful with joggled lintels and decorated releasing arch in which are two affronted leopards. These animals appear on several of this sultan's buildings and may relate to his Qipchaq name Bay (lord) Bars (leopard) although whether this connection was intended is uncertain. To the E is the side of the SW līwān (miḥrāb a much later addition) and a vaulted room which forms the vestibule to the Tomb of Sultan al-Ṣāliḥ Ayyūb.

To the S is the **Sabil-Kuttāb of Wālī Khusraw Pasha** (52; 17:1), the first such Ottoman foundation in Cairo. Its decoration is still largely Mamlūk.

Khusraw was governor of Egypt between 1534–36. This is the only buidling he erected here, although he was a great patron of architecture and his mosques and kulliyyahs are found throughout Syria and Anatolia.

Behind this and with a façade running for c 90m is the **Madrasah and Tomb of Sultan al-Ṣāliḥ Ayyūb** (38; 17:1–2), called al-Ṣāliḥiyyah, much of the former unfortunately now obscured by modern shops. It took the form of a pair of two līwāned madrasahs, parallel to each other and joined by an elevated passage over the dividing alley-way, now the Ḥārat al-Ṣāliḥiyyah (see below). Each had an associated complex of rooms for students, refectories, etc. This was the first madrasah built for all four schools of law in Egypt and like most later buildings its façade gives no indication of the internal form.

Ayyūb, eldest son of Sultan al-Kāmil, at the age of 15, was exchanged for the Papal Legate, a guarantee for the Crusaders' peaceful evacuation of Damietta. He attempted to usurp his father and as punishment was given a remote command. After his father's death he inherited this outpost while his younger brother ʿAdil II became sultan of Egypt. By alliances with his cousins the Ayyubid princes of Syria ʿAdil was deposed and Ayyūb assumed the sultanate of Egypt in 1240. None too certain of the loyalty of the mamlūks in the Citadel, Ayyūb built his own fortress on the island of Rawḍah and filled it with his own purchased troops, mainly Qipchaq Turks. He began the systematic deposition of his cousins in Syria, and occupied Damascus in 1247. When Louis IX of France invaded Egypt in 1249 Ayyūb led the defence, but he was very ill, probably suffering from tuberculosis and a persistent ulcer in his leg. The Crusaders were besieged in the city of Manṣūrah and Ayyūb died while the campaign was in progress. His death was concealed by his wife Shagar al-Durr, who, with the help of the atabak, performed all the official functions until Ayyūb's son Ṭūrān-shāh could return from Syria.

The façade of the *Madrasah of Sultan al-Ṣāliḥ Ayyūb* (built 1243) consists of the NW wall fronting the two sections of the madrasah and is aligned parallel to the street. In the centre is the entrance which ran between the two sections; above is the minaret. The South Madrasah has disappeared although its undecorated façade with eight windows still stands. However, the façade of the North Madrasah, with nine windows, is elaborately decorated. The windows are set in square-headed recesses, the N three running almost to the top of the wall. The windows are at ground floor level—the first example of this in Egypt. Each has a shallow relieving arch and the top of the window next to the entrance has a ribbed keel-arch. The whole façade has stepped cresting along the cornice. The entrance is elaborately decorated, the doorway with 15 joggled voussoirs and in the centre an eight-lobed disk and shallow relieving arch. Above this is a superb large keel-arched panel with sunburst ribbing and a foundation inscription. Flanking the door are keel-arched recesses, each with another inside. This entrance leads to the Ḥārat al-Ṣāliḥiyyah, see below. The plastered brick minaret, similar to Fāṭimid prototypes, has two stages, the lower with square section, the second stage octagonal. Each side of the lower stage has three keel-arched niches, inside each of which is another, that in the centre being a window. There are also keel-arched niches in each side of the second stage, inside which are niches with multifoil arched openings. At the summit of this section is an elaborate stalactite corbel upon which is set the ribbed cap.

The interior of the madrasah consists of a large ṣaḥn (30m by 20m) with līwāns to the NW and SE, each about 9m wide but that to the SE about 4m longer. The NW līwān, intended for the Malikī school, retains its original pointed-arch vaulting but that over the major līwān to the SE, for the Shāfiʿī school, has fallen. There are three miḥrābs in the SE wall. Along the walls of the ṣaḥn are remains of three storeys of barrel-vaulted students' rooms, six in the NE and two in the SW. That there were riwāqs parallel to these walls is shown by the pillar bases exposed near the NE walls. The entrance to the Ḥārat al-Ṣāliḥiyyah is in the W corner of the ṣaḥn and the entrance to the tomb is in the N corner. The S Madrasah must have been very similar with the NW līwān reserved for the Hanbalī school and the principal SE līwān for the Ḥanafī school.

Abutting the wall of the madrasah to the W and making a salient is the base of the *Tomb of Sultan al-Ṣāliḥ Ayyūb*, built in 1249 (usually locked but the guardian will open it on request). It is of the normal domed cube form and is the first tomb actually attached to the madrasah of the founder, although in this case built by his wife. This was to become general practice among later sultans.

Sultan Ayyūb was buried in his Citadel on Rawḍah Island while his wife, Shagar al-Durr, had this mausoleum constructed. The sultan was reinterred the next year with great ceremony and public grief; all the amīrs came down from the Citadel, including Shagar al-Durr and her second husband Sultan Aybak.

The doorway to the tomb is in the N wall and leads from the ṣaḥn of the madrasah. In the NW wall are three full-length keel-arched recesses each containing a window; there is another in the SW wall where the tomb meets the wall of the madrasah. Stepped cresting similar to that around the madrasah crowns the walls. The octagonal zone-of-transition has a window in each alternate face while the dome has a plain exterior with eight windows in the springing. The interior of the tomb (c 10m sq.) is simple but retains important features. Some fine Ayyūbid carving is to be found on the door, cupboards and the shutters to the windows. More excellent carving can be seen on the tābūt over the grave. It is covered with Kufic inscription and foliate decoration. A band of Nashkī carving in stucco running around the wall contains verses from the Qur'ān. There is a simple marble-lined miḥrāb, which retains in the hood the gilt glass mosaic, used here for the first time in Egypt and favoured by Shagar al-Durr who used it in her own tomb (Rte 11). Two pillars of green breccia flank the miḥrāb, similar to those found in the complex of al-Nāṣir Muḥ. The squinches supporting the dome are also an advance over earlier ones; instead of only two layers of niches, here there are three layers of four over three niches, separated by windows of six lights. The lattice in the SE window is the best preserved; the coloured glass in the lower lights is probably original.

Beneath the minaret the ḤĀRAT AL-ṢĀLIḤIYYAH, which once divided the two halves of the madrasah, terminates at the *Mosque of Badr al-Dīn al-ʿAgamī* (unclassified), built in 1356–57. To the left is an *Ottoman house*.

From the Shʿ. Mu'izz lī Dīn the SHʿ. AL-AṢĪRMĀTIYYAH leads (right) into the **Khān al-Khalīlī** (17:1–2), a large commercial complex of small factories and shops, the principal market for all manner of local crafts, in glass, metal, wood and leather. It is a maze of alleys and dead ends.

This great hostelry was built on the site of the Fāṭimid royal cemetery by Amīr Jarkas al-Khalīlī (died 1388) in 1382, the Amīr Akhur of Sultan Barqūq. He was killed near Damascus fighting the rebellious amīr Yalbughā. It immediately attracted the foreign merchants in Cairo and was several times a rallying area for subversive groups within the city, and constantly raided. Sultan Qānṣūḥ al-Ghawrī reconstructed much of the area in the early 16C. It has remained the principal area for craftsmen in Cairo, although latterly the work had been directed towards the tourist rather than the home market. However, the area is very popular with Egyptians who visit it for special presents or decorations. The workshops of the expert craftsmen are fascinating to visit.

The Shʿ. al-Aṣīrmātiyyah continues, past the Shʿ. al-Qumsangiyyah on the right, into the SHʿ. KHĀN AL-KHALĪLĪ. This roofed street deals with high quality goods, antiques, and jewellery. After 30m is the *Bāb al-Badistān* (53), built in 1511 by Sultan Qānṣūḥ. To the E the SIKKAT AL-BADISTĀN passes on the left the *Wikālat al-Qutn* with a *Façade* (54; 17:2) of Sultan Qānṣūḥ and on the right a *Gate* (56) of the same sultan. The

# KHĀN AL-KHALĪLĪ

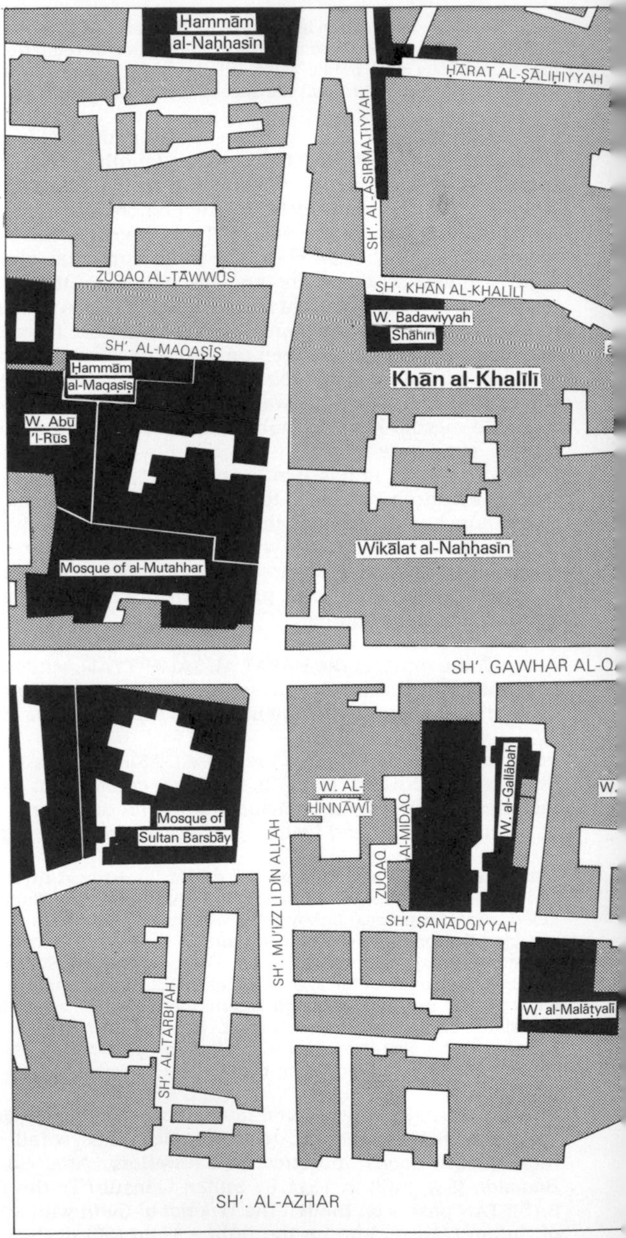
Ḥammām
al-Naḥḥasīn
ḤARAT AL-ṢALIḤIYYAH
SH'. AL-ʿASIRMATIYYAH
ZUQAQ AL-ṬAWWŪS
SH'. KHĀN AL-KHALĪLĪ
W. Badawiyyah
Shāhīn
SH'. AL-MAQAṢIṢ
Ḥammām
al-Maqaṣiṣ
Khān al-Khalīlī
W. Abū
'l-Rūs
Wikālat al-Naḥḥasīn
Mosque of al-Mutahhar
SH'. GAWHAR AL-Q
W. AL-
HINNĀWĪ
W. al-Gallābah
ZUQAQ
AL-MIDAQ
Mosque of
Sultan Barsbāy
SH'. MU'IZZ LI DĪN ALLĀH
SH'. ṢANĀDQIYYAH
SH'. AL-TARBIʿAH
W. al-Malāṭyalī
SH'. AL-AZHAR

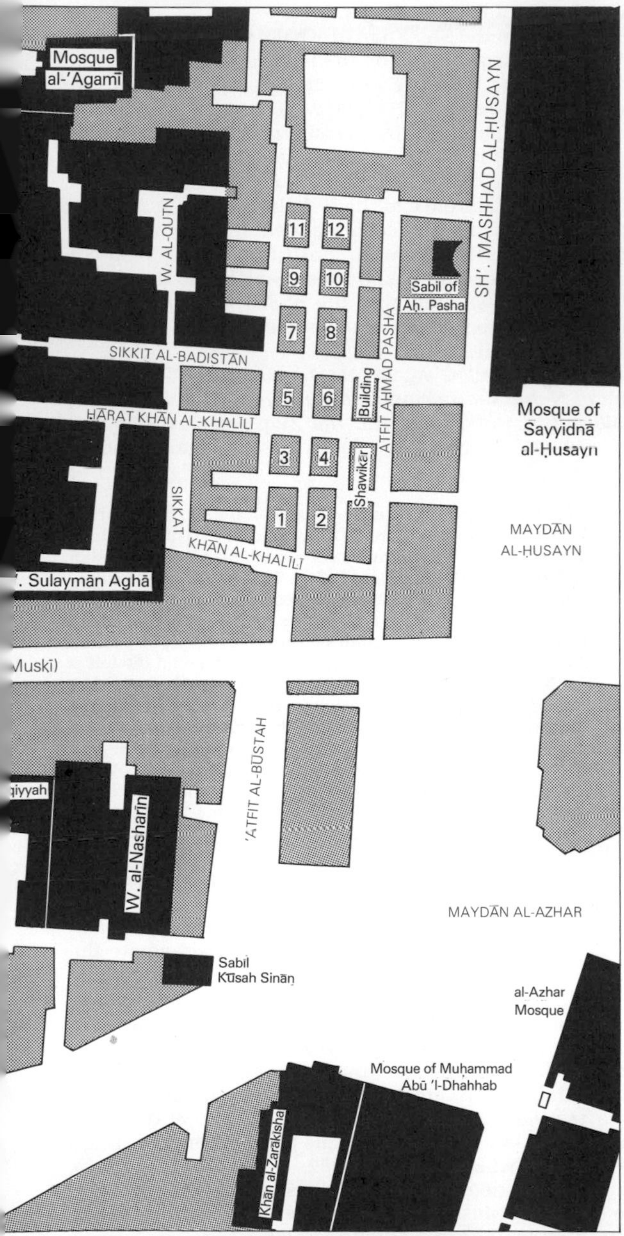
Mosque al-'Agamī
W. AL-QUTN
SH'. MASHHAD AL-ḤUSAYN
11
12
9
10
7
8
5
6
3
4
1
2
Sabil of Aḥ. Pasha
SIKKIT AL-BADISTĀN
ATFIT AḤMAD PASHA
Building
ḤARAT KHĀN AL-KHALĪLĪ
Mosque of Sayyidnā al-Ḥusayn
Shawikār
SIKKAT KHĀN AL-KHALĪLĪ
MAYDĀN AL-ḤUSAYN
. Sulaymān Aghā
Muskī)
'ATFIT AL-BŪSTAH
iyyah
W. al-Nasharin
MAYDĀN AL-AZHAR
Sabil Kūsah Sinān
al-Azhar Mosque
Mosque of Muḥammad Abū 'l-Dhahhab
Khan al-Zarakisha

alley passes through the ʿImārāt al-Shuwīkār (also called Madīnat al-Ḥusayn), apartments built in 1936 on the site of the mid 19C Madrasah of Shawikār, principal wife of Ibrāhīm Pasha.

Beyond the Bāb al-Badistān the Shʿ. Khān al-Khalīlī turns S and passes on the right the *Wikālat al-Maqwah* and on the left the ḤĀRAT KHĀN AL-KHALĪLĪ with the façade of the *Wikālat Sulāymān Aghā al-Silāḥdār* (604) of 1837. This alley cuts across the ʿAṬFAT AḤMAD PASHA in which is *Fishawi's Restaurant*, once patronised by British expatriots and literati. Because of area development it is now much curtailed, but it is still an interesting place to take tea or coffee. The Shʿ. Khān al-Khalīlī continues S, passing on the left another entrance to the Wikālat Sulāymān Aghā: a visit to the workshops inside is highly recommended. It is fascinating to watch the expertise of the craftsmen who construct whole screens of mashrabiyyah, without the use of glue, and brass beaten into shape. On the right are the *al-Dahān Restaurant* and the *al-Sīsī Workshops*, specialising in mosaic-work of wood, ivory and mother-of-pearl. The Shʿ. Khān al-Khalīlī emerges into al-Muskī.

The Shʿ. al-Muʿizz, here called AL-ṢĀGHAH, passes on the W the pre-1800 *Ḥammām al-Nahhasīn (unclassified) and then Al-Bāb al-Thānī al-Ṣāghah, the goldsmiths' workshops, and the Zuqāq al-Ṭawwūs. The next street (20m), the* SHʿ. *AL-MAQĀṢĪṢ*, leads past several Ottoman monuments.

Its appearance is much as it must have been during Turkish times. On the S corner stands the *Wikālat Abū ʿl-Rūss* (unclassified), pre 1718. Beyond that is the façade of an 18C *Ottoman House* (unclassified). Where the street turns N stands the **Wikālah and Sabīl-Kuttāb of Gamāl al-Dīn al-Dhahabī** (411; 17:1). This merchant, probably a gold dealer, had this building erected in 1637; it became a hostel for cloth merchants. His house can also be seen (Rte 6). On the opposite side of the road in the angle where the road turns W again is the **Wikālah of Taghrī-Bardī** (188), built in the 16C by another powerful merchant. A little further down the road on the left is his mosque and tomb. The **Mosque of Taghrī-Bardī** (42; 117:1) retains its Mamlūk exterior. This is a covered madrasah with two līwāns; the tomb chamber is to the left of the miḥrāb. A rare feature is the sunken path leading through the ṣaḥn into the ablution court. Opposite is the pre-1800 *Wikālah of Muḥ. al-Hamsharī* (unclassified). On the corner of the ḤĀRAT AL-YAHŪD is the *Wikālah and Sabīl-Kuttāb of ʿAqush* (236), a very late 18C fountain. Round to the S is the *House of al-Mullā* (541), dated 1654. It was built on the site of a late Mamlūk house. Restored in the 17C, it passed into the family al-Mullā, probably of Persian origin.

The goldsmiths' shops on either side of al-Ṣāghah display many examples of the craftsmens' skills.

Beyond is the ZUQĀQ KŪSAH; on the E side of the road is the *Wikālat al-Naḥḥāsin* (Coppersmiths' Hostel). On the W side of the road where the Shʿ. al-Muʿizz enters the SHʿ. GAWHAR AL-QĀʾID (al-Muskī) stands the *Mosque and Sabīl-Kuttāb of Shaykh Muṭahhar* (40; 117:1), built for the shaykh by ʿAbd al-Raḥmān Katkhudā in 1744. The Shʿ. Gawhar al-Qāʾid runs from E (Shʿ. al-Azhar) to W (Shʿ. Būr Saʿīd) and continues as al-Muskī to the Maydān al-ʿAtabah (Rte 3). Around this crossroads are many shops and kiosks selling scents and spices; wandering around and sampling them is a fascinating experience. A few metres W down al-Muskī on the right a small alley leads to a mosque built well into the reign of Muḥ. ʿAlī Pasha, **al-Gawharī Mosque** (462; 17:1) dated 1845–48, attached to which is the façade of a house of the same date.

On the opposite side of al-Muskī is the **Madrasah and Sabīl of Sultan Barsbāy** (175; 17:1), built in 1423 to a cruciform plan.

Barsbāy (leopard-lord) was only a child when he was brought from the Caucasus. He ultimately entered the service of Shaykh during whose reign he advanced to the rank of amir of one hundred. Sultan Ṭaṭār created him dawādār (secretary), impressed by his loyalty to his previous masters and his avoidance of intrigue and hypocricy. When Ṭaṭār died in 1421 Barsbay was made guardian of ten-year-old Sultan Muḥ. III. It proved impossible to control the senior amīrs and their mamlūks and so in 1422 Barsbay assumed the sultanate himself but treated the deposed Sultan well. The most formidable amīrs, Gānībak and Ṭarābāy, were imprisoned but the former escaped and continued to be a minor embarrassment to the sultan for the rest of his reign.

The Christians from Cyprus had been harrying the North coast of Egypt. Barsbāy therefore had a large armed fleet constructed and invaded the island in 1425 and 1426. King Janus was captured but was treated honourably and was returned to Cyprus in 1427 as the sultan's vassal, on payment of an annual tribute. The intractability of the young mamlūks was increasing and they several times rioted through Cairo, but Barsbāy, perhaps in some part sympathetic to their grievances, took no action, even when they ransacked the house of the atabak Gār Qutlū. Early in 1438 Barsbāy fell ill and he died in June after naming his son Yūsuf heir.

Barsbāy was tall, slender and good-natured; he did not use foul language or drink alcohol or allow his retainers to do so. He abolished the tradition of kissing the ground in front of the sultan and forbade the splitting up of families enslaved after the capture of Cyprus.

The façade, with the entrance to the S and the sabīl beyond, has two stalactite headed recesses, in each of which are set two windows, and above a band of inscription. The summit of the wall has a row of fleur-de-lys cresting. At the N end rises the dome, the octagoal zone-of-transition with scrolled corners and triple round-headed windows covered by three oculi. The drum of the dome contains 12 windows alternating with blind recesses and above a band of inscription, while the dome is carved with a continuous chevron pattern terminated at the base with mullets. The entrance in coloured marbles is capped by stalactites and the wooden door (renovated in 1913) is bound in brass with a beautiful central medallion, above which are two pierced brass knockers. Above the entrance rises the minaret of three tiers; the first with a square section, the second cylindrical, decorated with crisp interlace, and the third of columns supporting the cap.

A corridor leads from the vestibule into the W corner of the open ṣaḥn, which is surrounded by four līwāns, the SE much larger than the others, with the tomb-chamber to the N. The qiblah līwān has a beautiful marble floor and stucco windows, recent reconstructions based on Barsbāy's tomb in the Mamluk cemetery. There are several inscriptions in the līwāns, most foundational, but the continuous band that runs round all the walls is the waqf of the madrasah, giving details of all the properties designated for its upkeep. The original ceiling remains only in the W līwān, the rest is reconstruction, but the wooden minbar inlaid with ivory is original. The tomb-chamber was not used for Barsbāy who was buried in his son's mosque in the Eastern Cemetery (Rte 8). Several members of his family were however buried here including his daughter Fāṭimah (died 1424), brother Yashbak and son Muḥammad (both died 1429).

On the W flank stands the *Wikālat Abū Zayd* (unclassified), built before 1496. Along the S side of the mosque the SHʿ. AL-ḤAMZĀWĪ AL-SAGHĪR leads to the SHʿ. AL-TARBĪʿAH and *ʿAwf*, a large haberdashery store, famous among the fallaḥīn of Egypt. Beyond this the Shʿ. al-Ḥamzāwī leads past the *Khan al-Fisqiyyah* (unclassified; pre-1496) and the contiguous *Khan Saʿid* (unclassified) of 1515. On the N side of the road stands a House of Qāyt-bāy (unclassified; pre-1496).

On the E side of Shʿ. al-Muʿizz is another large commercial complex bisected by the SHʿ. AL-ṢANĀDQIYYAH. This area deals in more practical goods than the Khān al-Khalīlī—food, cloth, stationery and ironmongery. The first alley on the left is the ZUQĀQ AL-MIDĀQ (eponymous site of a celebrated story of the Egyptian novelist Naguib Mahfouz), just E of which is the *Wikālat al-Gallābah* (425; 17:1), a hostelry for slave merchants with a 16C façade.

Its antecedents are much older and this was also the site of a slave market in Mamlūk times. Originally dealing in all types of slaves, in the 19C it dealt only in black slaves from Southern Sudan, Ethiopia and Somalia, white slaves being sold by private contract. Finally, under pressure from Western governments, the whole system was abolished in the 1850s, although it continued clandestinely for much longer.

At the E end of the alley where it leads into the Shʿ. al-Azhar there are two monuments on the left: the *Wikālat al-Ṣanādqiyyah* (423), in the SW corner of which is the *Zāwiyat Gaʿfar al-Sadiq* (unclassified), both of 1688–89, and the *Wikālat al-Nashārīn* (422). On the right of the road is the *Sabīl Kūsah Sinān* (507; 17:2), dated 1814.

The Shʿ. al-Muʿizz runs into the Shʿ. al-Azhar (W to the Maydan al-ʿAtabah; Rte 3) which leads E into the Maydān al-Azhar and up the hill to join the Shʿ. Ṣalāḥ Sālim. On the N side at the top of the hill is the **Ḥadiqāt al-Khālidīn**, public gardens, the venue for circuses and fairs. To the S the Shʿ. al-Muʿizz continues through al-Ghawriyyah into the S part of the old enclosure of Cairo (Rte 6). From the eastern side of the Shʿ. Ṣalāḥ Sālim there is a splendid view across the Eastern Cemetery (Rte 8).

# 6 Maydān al-Azhar to the Bāb Zuwaylah

Rte 6 (1km) lies to the S of the previous itinerary and continues the journey through the Southern section of the medieval city. There are several short diversions and the Rte passes through the S gate of the city and along its southern border. **Cairo Atlas 17**.

At the SE corner of the Maydān al-Azhar stands **al-Gāmiʿ al-Azhar** (97; 17:4), the great mosque university founded by Gawhar al-Siqillī for the Fāṭimid khalīf al-Muʿizz li Dīn Allāh, immediately upon completion of the enclosure wall of al-Qāhirah in 970. The building, whose name means 'radiant', was finished in 972 and the khuṭbah was pronounced from here in June of that year. Originally it must have looked much like the Mosque of al-Ḥākim (Rte 5), though the roof was much lower. It has, however, been much altered, many rulers having wished to contribute in some way to its glorification with endowments if not actual building. In 988 the khalīf al-ʿAzīz, at the suggestion of his wazīr Yaʿqūb ibn Killis, made provision for the lecturers who taught at the mosque and on this simple basis the University of al-Azhar was founded.

Khalīf al-ʿAzīz had the roof of the mosque raised in the 980s and Khalīf al-Ḥākim, although he gave the khuṭbah from his own mosque, presented al-Azhar with a beautiful door (now in the MIA). Khalīfs al-Mustanṣir and al-Ḥāfiẓ also restored the mosque and in 1125 Khalīf al-Āmir presented a wooden miḥrāb (also now in the

MIA). Although it had not been the centre of the Fāṭimid Shiʿi propaganda organisation, Ṣalāḥ al-Dīn forbade the khuṭbah from this mosque. During the reign of the Ayyūbids it was ignored and by the time of Sultan Baybars al-Bunduqdārī it was in a ruinous state. Amīr Aydamur al-Hillī restored the mosque and the khuṭbah was allowed once again, although not without objection from some theologians. It suffered in the great earthquake of 1303 and was repaired by Amīr Salār. In 1309 Amīr Ṭaybārs built his madrasah and tomb beside the NW wall and certain repairs were undertaken by the qāḍī Muḥ. al-Isʿirdī in 1325. Another madrasah-tomb was built beside the NW wall by Amīr Aqbughā in 1334 and yet further restoration was undertaken in 1359 by the gandār Bashīr.

The original minaret was pulled down in 1397 and a new one built, but by 1415 this had started to lean so Amīr Tāj al-Dīn al-Shawbākī had this demolished and rebuilt in stone. Five years later this also tilted and was demolished and rebuilt: Gawhar al-Qunuqbāyī added his madrasah and tomb to the NE c 1435 and in 1446 some work was undertaken by Amīr Sūdūn. Sultan Qāyt-bāy made many alterations. In 1467 he built the huge main gates, and other work was done in 1494–96, when presumably his minaret was erected. Another minaret was built for Sultan Qānṣūḥ al-Ghawrī in 1510.

The Ottomans also undertook much work on the mosque—Muḥ. Pasha in 1596, Ismāʿīl Bay in 1720 and ʿUthmān Katkhudā in the late 18C. But the man responsible for a really massive reconstruction was ʿAbd al-Raḥmān Katkhudā who in 1751–52 rebuilt much of the outer wall, thereby greatly extending the mosque to the SE. He also built his tomb in the S corner. Further work was done for Ibrāhīm Bay in 1810 and during the 19C by ʿAbbās Pasha (1859) and the Khedive Tawfīq (1899–1901).

Since the reign of Baybars this mosque university has remained one of the most influential seats of learning in the Muslim world. During the Ottoman period it was almost the only institution in Egypt teaching theology and the Arabic language, all the others having been converted into sufi institutions. Although methods were rigid the curricula were to form the basis for the present system. At this time the mosque was divided into riwāqs (galleries), each making provision for students from one particular area of Egypt or geographical area outside, but few of these now remain.

The unique status of this mosque has been eroded but its influence and reputation are still great, particularly among the other Muslim communities. It now has a separate faculty for women, the Kulliyat al-Banāt al-Islāmiyyah, and several provincial branches including primary and secondary schools. Annexes were built to the E in the 1930s and '50s and an administration building was added to the N. During the 1960s further buildings were constructed at Madīnat Naṣr. A dormitory town called Madīnat al-Baʿūth (City of Delegations) has been erected to house the foreign students. Al-Azhar has many representatives throughout the Muslim world and maintains Islamic Centres in many other countries.

The traditional method of teaching was for the tutor to sit surrounded by his students at the base of one of the pillars, which were divided among the four judicial schools. The lectures in the morning consisted of tafsīr (exegesis), ḥadīth (traditions) and fiqh (jurisprudence) and at noon the Arabic language. Food was supplied for the students who lived in the mosque or the surrounding area. There were no official examinations, but successful students were given a license to teach the particular subject they had been studying. Study often occupied many years leading to an accumulation of licenses. In the 1870s, after agitation by liberal reformers led by Muḥammad ʿAbduh, changes were introduced and diplomas awarded. In the 20C three stages of education—primary, secondary and higher—were instituted and in 1936 a university syllabus. But in 1961 Law 103 was passed for the fundamental reorganisation of al-Azhar. It was reduced to the status of a university equal to the others in Egypt. New faculties were formed for medicine, agriculture, engineering and commerce, while the Academy of Islamic Research promotes and encourages the work of Muslim scholars throughout the world.

The directorship of the mosque has always been an important post. During Fāṭimid times the director was called al-Mushrif, and under the mamlūks, al-Nāẓir, a theologian of high rank. In Ottoman times this post was given the title of Shaykh al-Azhar and gradually usurped the supreme religious authority from the traditional Shaykh al-Bakrī, Shaykh al-Saʿdāt, Naqīb al-Ashraf and Chief Qāḍī. The incumbent

# AL-AZHAR MOSQUE

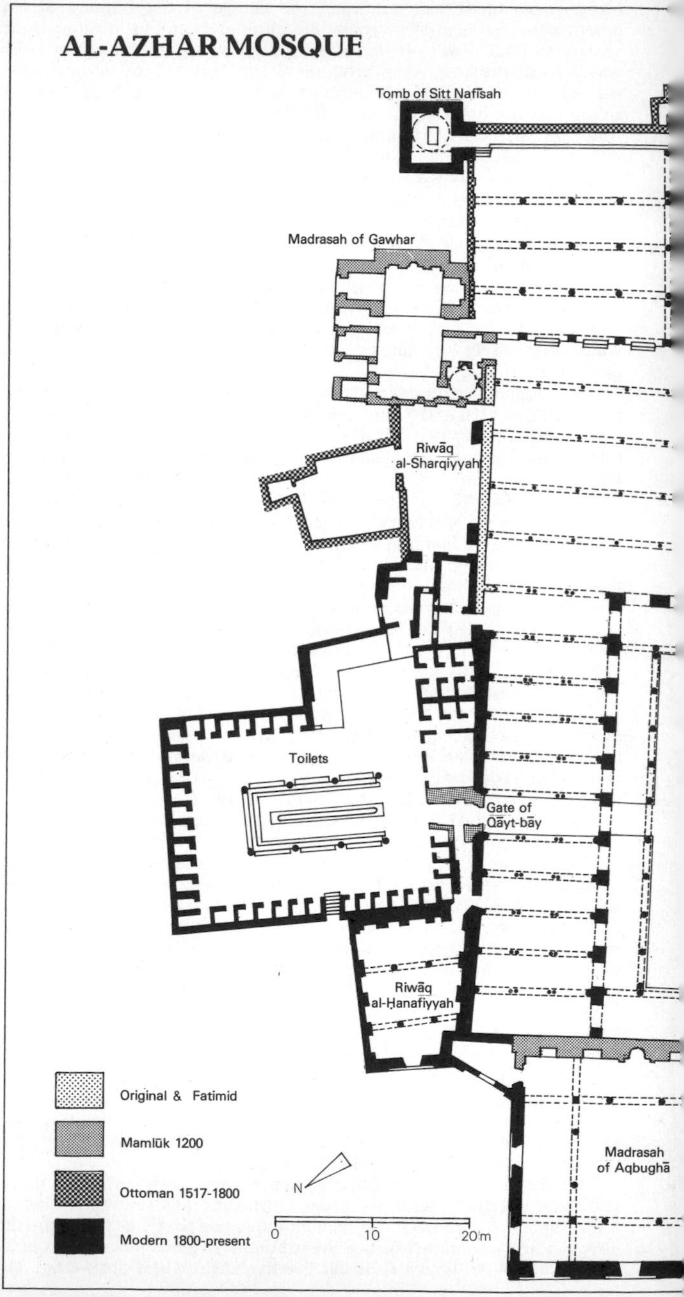
Tomb of Sitt Nafīsah
Madrasah of Gawhar
Riwāq al-Sharqiyyah
Toilets
Gate of Qāyt-bāy
Riwāq al-Ḥanafiyyah
Madrasah of Aqbughā
Original & Fatimid
Mamlūk 1200
Ottoman 1517-1800
Modern 1800-present
N
0
10
20 m

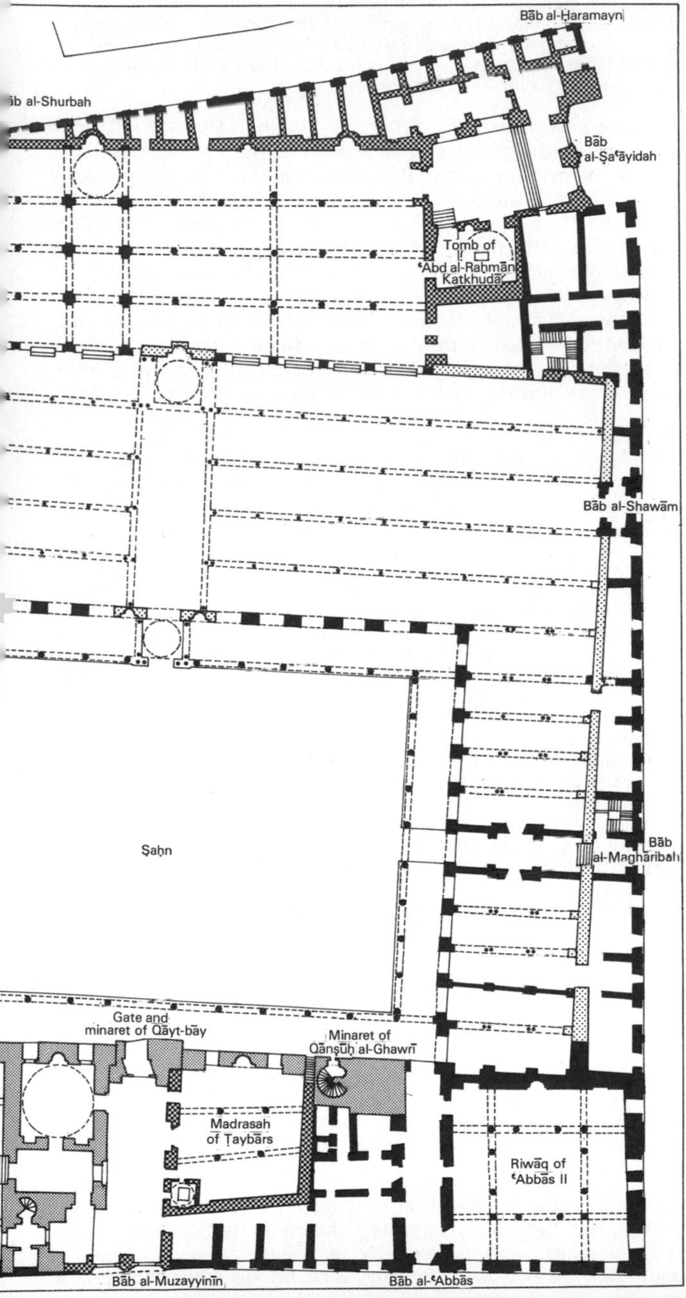
Bāb al-Ḥaramayn
āb al-Shurbah
Bāb
al-Ṣaʿāyidah
Tomb of
ʿAbd al-Raḥmān
Katkhudā
Bāb al-Shawām
Bāb
al-Maghāribah
Ṣaḥn
Gate and
minaret of Qāyt-bāy
Minaret of
Qānṣūh al-Ghawrī
Madrasah
of Ṭaybārs
Riwāq of
ʿAbbās II
Bāb al-Muzayyinīn
Bāb al-ʿAbbās

was appointed by the dīwān for life. So important did this post become that the appointment was often accompanied by much agitation from the various factions within al-Azhar and among the populace. Since 1961 the Shaykh al-Azhar has held the title Shaykh al-Islām, which originally dignified the Grand Mufti in Istanbul, as the supreme religious authority.

The vast enclosure now measures c 100m NE–SW and 115m NW–SE with the main entrance façade, pierced by two doors at the NW. This wall lies c 20m in front of the original line of the mosque and is composite, being mainly the work of the khedive Tawfīq (late 19C) to the N and the khedive ʿAbbās (1892) to the W. At the W end of the latter is the *Bāb al-ʿAbbās*, decorated with gilded calligraphy, while in the centre of the façade is the double *Bāb al-Muzayyinīn* (the Barber's Gate) where the students would have their hair cut before entering the college. This is part of the work of ʿAbd al-Raḥmān Katkhudā and consists of two large, round, elaborately decorated arches resting on composite piers, inside which are set the two entries. A panel of gilded and enamelled decoration runs above the door. This entrance leads into a corridor paved with red-veined marble.

To the SW is the *Madrasah and Tomb of Amīr Ṭaybārs*, built in 1309. Although it was one of the most magnificent madrasahs in Cairo, with gold-plated ceilings, only the qiblah wall remains. The façade was replaced by ʿAbd al-Raḥmān Katkhudā.

This madrasah was built for the Mālikī and Shāfiʿī schools of law and Ṭaybars, atabak of Sultan al-Nāṣir Muḥ., so wished to beautify it for the sake of Allāh that he did not want to see the statements of the cost. It was converted into part of the Library of al-Azhar and contains many of the mosque's most precious manuscripts. The miḥrāb, considered to be one of the most beautiful in Cairo, is set in a white marble frame with black marble decoration, and flanked by porphyry columns with the impost blocks decorated with coloured stones and mother-of-pearl. In the recess a blind arcade of seven stalactite panels covering coloured marble pillars rests on a plain base. Above this is geometrical ornament in coloured marbles, set with blue faience and surrounded by four frames in coloured stone and marble. Over this is another blind arcade on which rests a simple moulding supporting the superb joggled hood of red, black and white marble and blue enamel. Around the arch is a moulding which, for the first time in Egypt, forms a loop above the apex. In the spandrels are fruiting sprays in red, green and yellow glass mosaic inset with mother-of-pearl. In the N corner is the small tomb-chamber.

To the NE of the corridor is the original elegant façade of the larger *Madrasah and Tomb of the Amīr Aqbughā*, built 30 years after that of Ṭaybars in 1333–39.

This amīr was ustadār of Sultan al-Nāṣir Muḥ. Unlike the building of Ṭaybars, this was constructed with forced labour and for this reason it was considered by Maqrīzī to be a gloomy place. It is also now an annexe of the al-Azhar Library. The entrance which is original is particularly attractive, but only the lower 14-sided drum of the tomb is original; the dome is Ottoman. Of the minaret, the lower octagonal-sectioned tier and corbel of the balcony are original; the upper cylindrical upper section was restored in 1945. The entrance leads into a porch, directly ahead is the tomb-chamber and the door to the madrasah to the left. The interior contains a beautiful marble miḥrāb.

The entrance into the ṣaḥn of al-Azhar is through the *Gate of Sultan Qāyt-bāy* (1483), decorated with the magnificence characteristic of the period. Set in a recess and flanked by mastabahs, the flat lintel is elaborately joggled. Above is a releasing arch above which again is a band of dedicatory inscription. At the shoulders of the trefoil stalactite arch which covers the door are small rectangular grills and medallions. Complex crestings run across the top of the wall. To the SW rises Qāytbāy's minaret of three tiers, the lower two with octagonal sections. The lowest tier is decorated with carved keel-arched panels and the second with elaborate plaiting; the cylindrical upper section is plain. Fretted balconies rest on stalactite corbels.

*The main courtyard of al-Azhar Mosque*

In the *ṣaḥn* (48 by 38m) the NW riwāq has only one arcade, the NE and SW riwāqs are four arcades deep while the qiblah riwāq at the SW has seven arcades. These riwāqs front the ṣaḥn with keel-arches resting on marble columns. The whole façade is 4m higher than the true roof which was reconstructed in 1892. Although some of the original work was incorporated in the stucco, most of it is modern. A section of the qiblah façade is raised in front of a transept, an architectural device (called in Persian *pishtak*) copied from the original façade. This is a common and important feature of Persian and Indian mosques where it reaches immense proportions, but it is very rare in Western Islamic buildings.

In the NW riwāq immediately in front of the entrance the arch is raised on two groups of three pillars. To the NE the wall of the Madrasah of Aqbughā containing two windows reaches almost to the N corner, while to the SW runs the similar wall of the Madrasah of Taybars. This is abutted by the great block of masonry supporting the *Minaret of Sultan Qānṣūh al-Ghawrī* (1510), the highest minaret in the mosque. It has three tiers, the lowest octagonal in section, is decorated with keel-arched niches and the second with sixteen facashas a wide band of blue and white tiles. The third tier, however, is unusual, consisting of two rectangular blocks, each pierced with a slot, surmounted by two finials. Further SW is the 19C entrance and running to the W corner are the walls of the *Riwāq ʿAbbās*, the most recent addition to the mosque, built by the khedive ʿAbbās II in 1897. It has three floors and is used for meetings of the Mufti and officials of al-Azhar. Other rooms contain archives and facilities for the students.

The *SW wall*, though now covered with plaster, is part of Gawhar's original construction. In the 4th and 5th bays, however, round-arched niches are the remains of the original windows. This wall contains three doors, enlarged in the 19C. The *Bāb al-Magharibah* (Door of the Moroccans), in the 6th bay, leads into the Shʿ. al-Sh. Muḥ. ʿAbdūh, while a door in the 10th bay leads to the upper floor. The 13th bay contains the remains of some of the original stucco decoration (similar to that in the NE wall; see below) and the 14th bay contains the *Bāb al-Shawām* (Door of the Syrians) which leads into the same street.

The *NE wall* is composite with the first five bays part of the work of Rātib Pasha in 1862. A door in the 4th bay leads into the *Riwāq al-Ḥanafiyyah* built by Rātib at his own expense for the students. The 6th bay contains another *Gate of Sultan Qāyt-bāy* leading to the ablution court. Beyond the next four bays, also probably by Rātib Pasha, is a door leading into some rooms. Between bays 10–14 the wall is Gawhar's original structure containing remains of the early Fāṭimid round-arched windows. Immediately below them are two bands of decoration; the upper with foliate forms, the lower with Kufic inscription. A band of continuous inscription follows the frames of the window, and resting on these frames is a further band of Kufic inscription. A door in the 15th bay leads into the *Riwāq al-Sharqiyyah*, built by Ibrāhīm Bay in 1810 at the request of ʿAbd Allāh al-Sharqāwī, Shaykh of the students from the Eastern Delta, after they had disputed with other students in their original residence, the Madrasah of Ṭaybars.

At the extreme E end of this wall is the entrance to the *Madrasah and Tomb of Gawhar al-Qanuqbayī*, built shortly before Gawhar's death in 1440.

Originally from the Sudan, the eunuch Gawhar (Jewel) was bought by the amīr Qanuq-bāy and on the latter's death entered the service of another Qanuq-bāy, the wife of Sultan Barqūq. His piety, abstemiousness and particularly his mastery of the seven recitations of the Qur'ān earned him a wide reputation. The senior eunuch Gawhar al-Lālā recommended him to Sultan Barsbāy, who made him his treasurer. Despite his great wealth his administration was marked by wisdom, efficiency and beneficence and Sultan Jaqmaq made him chief eunuch. T.B. notes that he died (1440) before Jaqmaq could get his hands on his money.

This charming madrasah, though tiny, resembles in every detail the massive structures built by his contemporaries. It is built to a cruciform plan, with coloured marble floors and upper windows of coloured glass. Cupboards and doors are carved with inscription and foliate motifs decorated with ivory, mother-of-pearl and ebony. The tomb is to the E, covered by one of the smallest domes in Cairo, raised on a squinch of niches. Around the drum are ten windows and the exterior is beautifully carved with interwoven foliate motifs, while a band of crisp carved inscription runs below.

The *Qiblah Riwāq* (85m by 24m) consists of six transverse arcades divided by a raised transept in front of the miḥrāb. This latter feature is known only in two earlier mosques from different parts of the Islamic world, the Great Mosques in Damascus and Qayrawān (Tunisia, c 859). A small dome, part of the work of Khalīf al-Ḥāfiẓ (mid 13C), is raised at the NW end of the transept. It rests on keel-arches, supported by two wall pillars and two groups of three columns, with wooden tie beams. A dome in this position is a North African feature and unknown in Eastern Muslim countries. Four tall, simple squinches alternating with windows of the same shape raise the drumless dome. The interior of this dome is beautifully decorated with stucco carved in varied foliate forms—leaves, stalks, flowers and fruit. The original SE window grill has a lacework of squares set with quatrefoils, with a piece of contemporary yellow or green glass set over each opening—it is thus the earliest stained glass window in Egypt. Around the inside of the dome is one continuous band of inscription in the form of six arches and pillars. This rests on a frieze of trefoils. In the centre of the dome is a six-pointed star. Along the side of the transept the spandrels are carved with foliage. At the NW end the lower panels are modern reconstructions, but the upper panels are original. At the SE end of the transept is another dome, a replacement built by Sultan Qānṣūh al-Ghawrī, supported on two pairs of wall pillars and two sets of three pillars. Most of the SE wall was removed when ʿAbd al-Raḥmān Katkhudā built the additional riwāq to the SE but two sections of the original walls remain; a 7m section containing the main miḥrāb, with salient at the rear, and a 10m section to the SW.

The miḥrāb has a semi-domed hood in a round arched-frame resting on marble columns, with the base of the interior lined with coloured marbles in typical Mamlūk style as is the stucco frame, probably the work of al-Isʿirdī in 1325. The hood and frame were overlaid by a carved wood cover, (now removed to another miḥrāb) which when removed in 1933 revealed the original carved stucco hood and frame of Gawhar. The central motif is a five-lobed palmette and chalice around which twine three five-lobed branches, while lower down each side are further palmettes. The hood is framed by inscription, the upper part curved forward to counteract the fore-shortening. To the SW is the other section of original wall. Here round-arched windows alternate with similar shaped panels, all linked by a continuous band of inscription. Above is a band of foliate ornament. The panels are filled with similar decoration, with the background originally coloured blue. A small section of ʿAbd al-Raḥmān's wall at the extreme S corner contains a subsidiary miḥrāb. At each of the S and E corners of the ṣaḥn there were originally small domes, as in the Mosque of al-Ḥākim (Rte 5), a uniquely Fāṭimid innovation, but these have been removed in subsequent restorations.

The rear of the riwāq opens into a raised *Extension Riwāq* four arcades deep, built by ʿAbd al-Raḥmān Katkhudā in 1751. It is reached from the main mosque by pairs of steps between piers. As this riwāq is set slightly to the E of the original the miḥrāb and transept are not directly behind that in the main mosque. The pillars and piers were restored by the khedive Tawfīq in the late 19C. At the S corner is a complex of buildings raised by ʿAbd al-Raḥmān with another entrance, the *Bāb al-Saʿayidah* (Door of the South Egyptians), similarly double, though even larger than the main entrance to the mosque.

NW is the domed *Tomb of ʿAbd al-Raḥmān Katkhudā*, reached by a flight of steps. SE of the entrance is his minaret, and on the NW side a sabīl.

ʿAbd al-Raḥmān was leader of the Qazdughli faction. Although he joined the Mustaḥfiẓān himself he came into conflict with some of the officers and after a period with the ʿAzabs he rejoined them in a much stronger position and was eventually made katkhudā. Despite great wealth he seems to have had little personal political ambition but used his influence against an old enemy, ʿAlī Bay al-Ghazzawī. While this man was on the pilgrimage in 1759 ʿAbd al-Raḥmān successfully promoted the election of ʿAli Bay al-Kabīr Bulat Kapan as Sh. al-Balad.

ʿAbd al-Raḥmān's charity was legendary but his greatest passion was for building. Not since Mamlūk times had any patron paid so much attention to beautifying the city with elegant buildings. Perhaps his greatest work was the enlargement of al-Azhar mosque to almost double its original size.

Despite ʿAbd al-Raḥmān's support for ʿAlī Bay, in 1764 the Sh. al-Balad, fearing his great influence, had him exiled to Arabia where he lived until 1777 after ʿAli Bay's death. When he returned to Cairo he was very sick. All the greatest bays visited his palace and begged forgiveness. He died ten days later. His last words were 'Live in the mercy of Allāh, reject injustice, do good for this world is transitory. Take heed from my example.'

The SW corner of the mosque is plain except in the extreme S where there is a domed tomb-chamber of uncertain date locally called the '*Tomb of Sitt Nafīsah*', but the person for whom it was built is unknown.

The *SE wall* contains three miḥrābs and two doors; at the S corner is a large miḥrāb which contains the wooden cover removed from the original miḥrāb. A little further to the NE is a very small miḥrāb, next to which is the *Bāb al-Ḥaramayn*, a doorway which is always locked. Next is the main miḥrāb in front of which is a dome which, although Ottoman, is modelled on Mamlūk design. Further NE is the *Bāb al-Shūrbah* (Soup Gate), so called because it was from here that food was dispensed to the students and the poor.

At the SE angle of the door rises the second of ʿAbd al-Raḥmān's minarets, with two polygonal tiers.

On the opposite side of the road to the W is the **Mosque of Muḥammad Bay Abū 'l-Dhahab** (98; 17:4), which also contains his tomb. An Ottoman raised arcaded mosque, it is a modified copy of that of Sinān Pasha at Būlāq (Rte 17) although built 200 years later in 1774.

Muḥammad began his career as a slave of ʿAlī Bay Bulut Kapan in 1761 and after the ceremony in the Citadel at which he was created a bay he scattered gold coins, instead of the usual silver, to the populace and thus the name Abū 'l-Dhahab

(Possessor of Gold). ʿAlī was recognised as Shaykh al-Balad, deposing two govenors in the process, with the Ottomans powerless to intervene. In 1770 Muḥammad captured Damascus, but when Sultan Muṣṭafā III offered him autonomous control of Egypt he withdrew.

By 1772 he was powerful enough to depose ʿAlī Bay who fled to Palestine but was captured during an attempted reoccupation of Egypt and died shortly after. As promised, Muḥ. was allowed to rule Egypt without any interference from the sultan. In 1776 the sultan asked him to send a force against Sh. Ẓāhir, governor of Palestine; he did so but died at Acre.

His externally plain mosque is square in plan. The low undecorated dome is raised on a 16-sided drum from which little turrets rise at each angle. The unique, massive minaret has two square-sectioned tiers and is capped by five squat finials, perhaps in emulation of that of the Mosque of Sultan Qānṣūḥ (see below). To the W are a takiyyah, sabīl and trough. There are two entrances, in the NE and SE façades, each reached by flights of steps. The mosque is surrounded by three riwāqs covered by shallow domes raised on pillars and piers. To the left is the tiled *Tomb of Muḥammad Bay*, a small marble pillar surrounded by a brass screen. Also buried here is his sister ʿAdilah, wife of Ibrāhim Bay al-Alfī. A second screen surrounds the library. The great dome raised on squinches covers the whole interior, once gilded and painted. Below the drum runs inscription from the Qurʾān and a foundation inscription. The polychrome marble miḥrāb is inlaid with mother-of-pearl and there is a subsidiary miḥrāb to the NE. The minbar and dikkah above the main entrance are in wood. A sunken passage leads across the sanctuary to the ablution court.

SW of al-Azhar lies the SHʿ. AL-SHAYKH MUḤ. ʿABDŪH and directly opposite the mosque is the **Wikālah and Sabīl-Kuttāb of Sultan Qāyt-bāy** (75–6; 17:4), the first of the two hostels erected by this sultan in Cairo. Like the other (see Rte 4), this is also called a khān in the foundation inscription and dated 1477. Only the façade remains, but this shows that it must once have been extremely elegant. The lavish decoration consists of carved panels and medallions of foliate designs and inscription. Several of the patterns are repeated on opposite sides of the building, reflecting a desire for symmetry unknown in earlier Mamlūk buildings. The sabīl-kuttāb is attached to the NW corner. To the S runs the SHʿ. MUH. ʿABDUH and on the opposite corner is the **Ḥawd of Qāyt-bāy** (74), a drinking-trough constructed 20 years after the previous two buildings, in 1496, the closing year of his reign. This is also a charming building with some excellent carved medallions.

SE 30m along the Shʿ. Muḥ. ʿAbduh stands the **Madrasah and Tomb of Qāḍī Muḥ. al-ʿAyni** (102; 17:4), built in 1411 and restored by the builder in 1431. Called al-ʿAyni, Abū Muḥ. Badr al-Dīn al-ʿAyntabī came to Cairo where he became a Ḥanafī teacher in the Madrasah of Barqūq. He was popular with three sultans, Barqūq, Shaykh and Barsbāy, sitting with the latter and reading works on religion and history in Arabic and translating the difficult sections into Turkish for the sultan. After the death of Barsbāy he fell out of favour and died in 1451. The exterior is modern. The painted wood ceiling of the vestibule is original and leads into the ṣaḥn where the miḥrāb is unusual in being wholly tiled, as are the flanking pillars, similar to those in the Mosque of Mu°ayyad Shaykh (see below).

Immediately S a lane leads to two merchant's houses. Both of them have interesting detail. First (30m) is the **House of Sitt Wasīlah** (445; 17:4), built in 1664. To the left is the **House of ʿAbd al-Raḥmān al-Harrāwī** (446), built in 1731. Past this lane in the Shʿ. Muḥ. ʿAbdūh is the **House of Zaynab Khātūn** (77), a late Mamlūk house built just before 1468 for Mithqāl al-Sūdūnī, chief sāqī of Sultan Jaqmaq, with Ottoman additions in 1713. This building was restored by Major Dovin with the assistance of the CPAM after World War II. To the N of the latter, inside the grounds of al-Azhar University, stands the **Madrasah al-Ghanāmiyyah** (96), the qāʿah of a small palace built in 1372 by the wazīr Shākir ibn al-Ghannām and subsequently turned into a madrasah by the simple expedient of raising a minaret and installing a miḥrāb. All that remains of the minaret is the lower octagonal section. At the rear of the N līwān is a large marble frame topped by a stalactite-frieze indicating that there was once the salsabil of a fountain here. Above this is a band of foundation inscription. There are two miḥrābs, one set in the E wall of the S līwān and a larger Ottoman one to the N.

Slightly to the NW is the **Mosque and Sabīl of ʿAbd al-Raḥmān Katkhudā** (448; 17:4), another of this great patron's buildings, built in 1754 for Sh. Sīdī Muḥ. al-Ghurayib. At the extreme E end of the Shʿ. Muḥ. ʿAbdūh is (150m) the **Bāb al-Barqiyyah** (the Cable Gate; 614; 17:4), part of Ṣalāḥ al-Dīn's defensive wall of 1171–76.

Turn S at the end of the Shʿ. Muḥ. ʿAbdūh. At the corner of the SHʿ. GAMĀL AL-DĪN AL-AFGHĀNĪ (W to Shʿ. Muʿizz li Dīn) is (150m) the **Zāwiyat Aḥmad ibn Shaʿbān** (103), a small mosque built at the end of the 16C. Follow the Shʿ. Gamāl al-Dīn W until it enters the Shʿ. al-Maqrīzī. A few metres S is the **Sabīl-Kuttāb Abū 'l-Iqbāl** (73), an Ottoman complex built by ʿArifīn Bay in 1713. The Shʿ. Maqrīzī leads again the Shʿ. Muḥ. ʿAbdūh and back into Maydān al-Azhar.

Abutting the Mosque of Abū 'l-Dhahab to the NW, the **Khān al-Zarākishah** (351; 17:4) is an early Ottoman hostel from the beginning of the 16C. 50m S is the **Wikālah of Sultan Qānṣūh al-Ghawrī** (64; 17:3), called al-Nakhlah (the Date-Palm). Originally built as a hostel in 1504, it is one of the best preserved of these commercial buildings in Cairo.

Subsidised by the Ministry of Culture, it now houses a permanent exhibition of folk crafts of the fallaḥīn and Bedouin and from Nubia and the oases. There are also workshops where people are taught the traditional crafts, and facilities for artists to exhibit their works. Open 08.10–14.00 (except Friday). Performances are given by local and visiting folk music and dancing troupes in the courtyard.

Entry is through a huge portal which leads into a large courtyard, surrounded on three sides by single arcaded riwāqs fronted by pointed-arches raised on octagonal piers. These arches are two storeys high, horizontally bisected by a continuous mashrabiyyah balcony. On the ground floor at the rear of the riwāqs are rooms in which merchants stored their goods and animals. On the first floor are rooms for their residence. The upper three floors with windows overlooking the courtyard consisted of a rabʿ (flats), each of three rooms linked by a staircase. In the centre of the courtyard is a large octagonal coloured-marble basin for a fountain.

Follow the Shʿ. al-Azhar W. After 20m it meets the continuation of the Shʿ. Muʿizz li Dīn running S, at this point called AL-GHAWRIYYAH after the next complex. The façade on the corner is the **House waqf of Saʿīd Pasha** (65), actually built by Sultan Qānṣūh al-Ghawrī in 1504. On the opposite corner is a similar façade. Each is attached to the N wall of a magnificent dual complex, the **Tomb and Sabīl-Kuttāb** (67) and **Maqʿad** (66) **of Sultan Qānṣūḥ al-Ghawrī** on the E side of the street, and facing it on the W side the **Mosque of Sultan Qānṣūḥ al-Ghawrī** (189; 17:3). The whole complex, built in 1504–05, is the last great architectural work of the mamlūks prior to the Ottoman conquest. The Ghawriyyah during the Ottoman period was roofed over, covering the Sūq al-Harīr (Silk Market).

The reign of Sultan Qānṣūḥ can be seen as a microcosm of the Mamlūk state and its final downfall. He started his career as a mamlūk of Sultan Qāyt-bāy, but was not manumitted until he was 40 years old. He was made an amīr of ten, held several provincial governorships and eventually in 1501 under Sultan Tūmān-bāy was created grand dawādār. After the deposition of Tūmān-bāy the young mamlūks chose Qānṣūḥ who declined the honour and had to be dragged in tears into the council chamber.

Qānṣūḥ built a beautiful garden on the racecourse at the base of the Citadel, with an orchard and beds of scented flowers. He held his councils in a pavilion there, presenting each amīr personally with a rose. He was attracted to sufis and other pious men; he was also fond of music, read avidly, wrote poetry and was good-natured and loved jokes.

The Portuguese in the 16C were gradually assuming control of the Indian Ocean and in 1509 destroyed the Mamlūk fleet there. The two other great Muslim nations, the Ottoman Turks and the Safavid Persians, were disputing for mastery of Mesopotamia and, as belligerency increased, it became apparent that the Mamlūk state could not stay immobile. In November 1516, under threat from both protagonists, Qānṣūḥ led a force to Syria but found himself inevitably drawn towards war. Salīm, the Ottoman sultan, defeated Shāh Ismāʿīl, and the amīr Khayrbak, governor of Aleppo, defected to him. Although Qānṣūḥ's armies and troops fought bravely the mamlūks were defeated and, as he readied himself for a charge, Qānṣūḥ died of a stroke. His body was never found. Salīm entered Egypt and, after executing the last sultan, Tūmān-bāy II, installed Khayrbak as governor.

This mosque and mausoleum were the last flowering of Mamlūk art and, although traditional in many respects, possess some aspects which had they continued might have evolved into important features. Perhaps the final word should be left to Ibn Iyās, the last of the Mamlūk chroniclers: 'How amazing that al-Ghawrī is not buried at the madrasah on which he had spent 100,000 dinars imagining that he would be interred in a magnificent tomb, but otherwise was destined and he lay stretched out in the wilderness the prey to wolves and leopards.' It was the epitaph of an empire.

Both sections of the complex rest upon a ground floor of shops and the entrances are reached by flights of steps. The *Mosque* to the NW is a cruciform madrasah similar to but larger than that of Sultan Qāyt-bāy in the Eastern Cemetery. The main façade on the street has three recesses containing windows above which runs a band of foundation inscription and verses from the Qurʾān. Across the top of the façade is a complex foliate cresting. The unique minaret which rises at the N corner is very tall, only surpassed by that at the Mosque of Sultan al-Ḥasan (Rte 10). It has four tiers, each with a square section, the galleries resting on stalactite corbels, while at the summit is a five-capped (originally four) finial once covered with green tiles. At the S corner of the mosque is the square *Mint*. A trefoil stalactite hood covers the ablaq entrance, the two leaves of the door being covered with pierced brass plates.

The square vestibule, with polychrome marble floor and carved and gilded wooden ceiling, leads onto a corridor to the roofed ṣaḥn. The līwāns are fronted by pointed horseshoe arches; the qiblah līwān is much larger than the others, larger even, in fact, than the ṣaḥn. The walls have a dado of coloured marble and artificial stone (paste and bitumen), above which is a band of Kufic foundation inscription and verses from the Qurʾān. Another band of inscription runs round the ṣaḥn above the arches and above this is a stalactite cornice. The miḥrāb is in coloured marble, as is the floor, while the wooden minbar is inlaid with geometrical and ivory panels. The dikkah, at the back of the NW līwān, has a panelled balustrade inlaid with ivory and ebony or turned wood. The joisted ceiling is carved and gilded and has a cornice of gilded inscription. At the corners and in the middle of each side are finely carved stalactites.

The *Tomb* to the SE of the street has a beautiful sabīl on its N corner and a façade similar to that of the mosque. It is now a youth centre providing recreational facilities. Two rows of windows are set in recesses; the lower windows have joggled ablaq voussoirs; the upper windows are double round-arched lights surmounted by an oculus. Cresting similar to that of the mosque crowns the walls. The *Sabīl* has three large windows with grills of iron and marble floors. Above is the *Kuttāb* with double arches on three sides and a later wooden roof supported on corbels.

The entrance of the mausoleum leads into a square decorated vestibule and a passage runs into the mausoleum c 12.5m sq. The huge dome, covered with blue tiles, was an innovation in Egypt, presumably emulating the domes of Persia. It proved to be unsafe, probably because of lack of knowledge on the part of the architects, and had to be dismantled during the sultan's lifetime. It was rebuilt twice, and finally fell in 1860 to be replaced by a wooden roof. The dado, floors and miḥrāb are similar to those in the mosque.

The mausoleum contains the bodies of Muḥ, the 13-year-old son of Qānṣūh, and a concubine, both of whom died of the plague, a daughter who died in 1505 and the daughter of Sulṭān Tūmān-bāy II. The body of Tūmān-bāy II, after he was hanged by Selim, was buried in some ground behind the madrasah, but was later transferred here.

In the S corner of the mausoleum is the entrance to the *Maqʿad* and courtyard of the *Khānqāh*, which is fronted by four arches resting on piers. To the N of the vestibule another door leads into a large room with a miḥrāb; the decorated and gilded ceiling is a modern reconstruction.

The street-roofings (550) have been retained in the street to the W of the mosque. Down this street is the *Wikalah al-Sharaybī* (460; 17:2), built by Muḥ. al-Sharaybī (died 1725). It was frequented by Moroccan coffee and cloth merchants.

About 70m down the Shʿ. al-Muʿizz off the E side runs the SHʿ. AL-DARDĪR, 100m down which, on the N, stands the **Sabīl-Kuttāb of Sulaymān Bay al-Kharbūṭlī** (70; 17:3), an early Ottoman complex built in 1637. Opposite, on the S side stands the *Mosque of Aḥ. al-Dardīr*, a great Khalawātī shaykh (1715–86). 75m further on, to the left is a large building from which a baffled corridor leads into the **Qāʿat al-Dardīr** (466; 17:4). (Ask at the mosque for entrance.) This very important monument is the only remaining standing example of a Fāṭimid domestic building, probably a small palace, ascribed to the early 12C. The form shows that by this time the central area of the house had changed from the type found at Fusṭāṭ (Rte 16). This was to remain the design of domestic buildings until the late 18C. The central durqāʿah is sunken as in Mamlūk houses and the tower rises about 13m but must originally have been higher, as the lower sills of windows can be seen at the top. To the E and W are shallow pointed-arched frames inside each of which are two flat wood-lintelled doors leading to small rooms or corridors. Above these doors rise tall, narrow, keel-arched recesses. Between the doors on the E wall is a later carved wooden Kufic inscription, showing that at one time the building was used as a mosque. On the S and N side of the qāʿah are two large līwāns c 11.5m high, each with a frontal arch only slightly narrower than the main qāʿah. They are tunnel-vaulted in brick with semi-domes at their far ends, raised on flat triangular pendentives at each corner of which is a single small keel-arched squinch. In each of the līwāns there are two doors leading to store-rooms, etc. The building is in stone to the springing of the arches, but the upper sections are in brick.

Another 50m along the road, to the N is the *Sabīl-Kuttāb of Khalīl Afandi al-Maqāṭaʿgī* (71; 17:4), built in 1632, so of similar age to that of Sulayman Bay.

On the W side of the Shʿ. al-Muʿizz (30m) the ʿATFAT AL-BĀZARʿAH leads past some more street roofings to the *Sabīl of Muṣṭafā Shurbagī*

*Mustaḥfiẓān* (553; 17:3) of 1683. At the end of the street where it runs into the Shʿ. al-Gudariyyah stands the **Mosque and Tomb of Amīr Baybars al-Khayyāṭ** (191; 17:3), a very late Mamlūk complex finished the year before the Ottoman conquest in 1515. Baybars commanded a section of Sultan Qānṣūḥ II's army and was taken prisoner at Marj Dabiq. Dominating the complex is the tomb at the NE. The rest of the mosque, a covered madrasah, was entirely reconstructed in 1896. The SE wall of the tomb has an oculus over the miḥrāb, and double round-arched windows covered by an oculus in stalactite-headed niches at the corners. The zone-of-transition has geometric angles and in each side are three round-arched windows with triple oculi above. Around the drum are 16 windows while the dome is carved with a continuous chevron pattern, the lowest row terminating with mullets.

100m S down the Shʿ. al-Muʿizz li Dīn the SHʿ. KHUSHQADAM leads E (70m) to the ḤĀRAT KHUSHQADAM and the **House of Gamāl al-Dīn al-Dhahabī** (72; 17:3) of 1637. This merchant's house is another well preserved example from the Ottoman period. Like the others it is beautifully decorated with stone Mamlūk style facias, marble floors and carved wooden ceilings. It has recently been restored, and is the headquarters of the CPAM.

100m to the E stands the small **Mosque of Kāfūr al-Zimām** (107; 17:3), a small gāmiʿ built in 1425.

A eunuch from Anatolia, Kāfūr (Camphor) was first purchased by the amīr Ṣarghatmish and then by the amīr Mankalibughā. When the daughter of the latter married Sultan Barqūq, Kāfūr accompanied her into the royal harīm in the Citadel, of which in 1408 he became supervisor under Sultan Farag. When amir Muʾayyad Shaykh, during his dispute with Sultan Farag demanded entrance to the Citadel, Kāfūr, who was also keeper of the keys, kept him talking while he sent to inform Farag of the imminent danger. When Shaykh became sultan, he appreciated Kāfūr's diligence and retained him. Kāfūr was eventually made khazindār (treasurer) and in his old age became chief eunuch at Medina and died in 1427.

The mosque has a Naskhī inscription running across the N and E façades and a sabīl at the corner. There is no minaret or domed tomb attached to this mosque. Inside it is built to a cruciform plan but with the lateral līwāns greatly reduced, perhaps the first of this type in Cairo.

At the end of the street, on the N side, is the **Mosque and Tomb of Amīr Sūdūn al-Qaṣrawī** (105; 17:4), built just prior to 1468. Sūdūn was freed by Sultan Īnāl and appointed a junior dawādār. He rose to be commander of the Corps of Mamlūks, leading them on a campaign to Aleppo where he was killed in 1468. His complex blazon, which included the pen-box sign of his executive post, is depicted on the wooden ceiling of the mosque. Unfortunately the whole of the superstructure of this mosque has recently been very badly reconstructed in concrete. The tomb, however, is still intact and has a fine plastered brick dome with a rib and fillet pattern.

Returning to the Shʿ. al-Muʿizz, immediately on the corner to the S is the **Gāmiʿ al-Fakahānī** (Mosque of the Fruit-sellers; 109; 17:3), a raised Ottoman forecourt mosque built in 1735 by Aḥmad Katkhudā al-Kharbūṭlī on the site of the Mosque of Khalīf al-Ẓāfir, built 1148, of which now only the magnificent doors, covered with beautiful Fāṭimid carving, remain.

After 20m on the E the SHʿ. AL-SUKKARIYYAH leads to the ḤĀRAT AL-RŪM, 200m down which on the left stands the **Church of the Virgin**. This is a very ancient foundation and was the seat of the Coptic patriarch between 1660–1799. The present building dates to the early 19C. The

Church of the Virgin is unusual in being roofed with a series of 12 domes. Another unusual feature is the South Sanctuary which is dedicated to the Four Bodiless Living Creatures of the Apocalyse. Close by are the Church of St. George, also with a domed roof, and the Convent of St. Theodore.

After a further 40m is the ornate **Sabīl-Kuttāb of Muḥ. ʿAli Pasha** (401; 17:3), raised in 1820 on behalf of Ṭūṣūn, his second son. Aḥ. Ṭūṣūn led the campaigns against the Wahhabis in Arabia and died in 1816. This site is on the S line of the enclosure walls of Gawhar and here stood the original Bāb Zuwaylah. 65m along on the E is the 18C **Ḥammām** (596) **Wikālah** (395) and **Sabīl al-Sukkariyyah** (17:3). The whole vast complex was built in 1796 by the powerful Nafīsah al-Bayḍā (died 1815), widow of Murād Bay. There are several other Ottoman houses in the street behind.

On the W, its twin minarets above the Fāṭimid gate dominating the S part of the street, is the magnificent ***Mosque and Tomb of Sultan Muʾayyad Shaykh** (190; 17:3). This is a large enclosure mosque, the last royal mosque of this ancient design in Cairo, built between 1415–20 on the site of the Kazānat al-Shamāʾil prison which the sultan demolished with great relish. Attached to the mosque is a large bath complex (see below).

## S. WALLS & MOSQUE OF MU'AYYAD SHAYKH

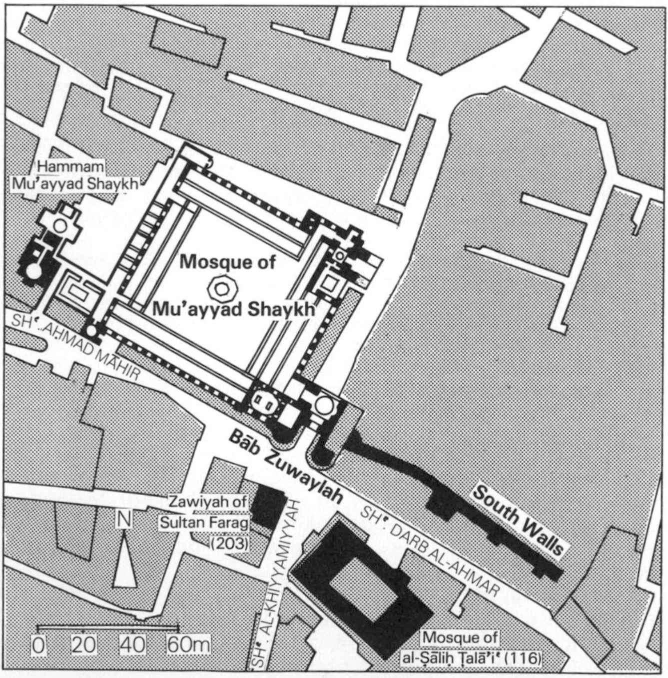
Hammam
Mu'ayyad Shaykh
Mosque of
Mu'ayyad Shaykh
SHᵃ. AHMAD MAHIR
Bāb Zuwaylah
South Walls
Zawiyah of
Sultan Farag
(203)
N
SHᵃ. AL-KHIYYAMIYYAH
SHᵃ. DARB AL-AHMAR
0 20 40 60m
Mosque of
al-Ṣāliḥ Ṭalāʾiʿ (116)

The mosque was still complete in 1829 when Ibrāhīm Pasha made minor restorations. However, by the end of the century it had fallen into great disrepair and was in imminent danger of collapse. The CPAM gutted the inside, except for the qiblah riwāq, rebuilt the other walls and turned the ṣaḥn into a garden.

The 12-year-old Circassian slave Shaykh entered the service of Barqūq who became sultan in 1382. During internment in the Khazānat at Shamā'il prison which occupied this site he made an oath that should he be released he would build a mosque here, a promise fulfilled several years later. He was an amīr of forty when Barqūq died and in the reign of Sultan Farag, Barqūq's son, in 1399, he was made an amīr of one hundred and governor of Tripoli (Syria), during which tenure he was captured by Tīmūr, but later released.

As Farag's reign progressed, his eccentricities became more pronounced but when a council of amīrs agreed on the assassination of the sultan, Shaykh was the only amīr to dissent. With the support of Amīr Nawrūz, Shaykh virtually controlled the empire. The excesses of Farag increased and, Shaykh was goaded to besiege him in Damascus. Farag was murdered a few days later. Meanwhile in Cairo the council of amīrs had deposed Farag and to avert acrimony had elected the khalīf Musta'īn sultan. As soon as Shaykh returned to Cairo he had Musta'īn deposed and was created sultan himself in 1412.

Apart from a revolt of provincial governors engineered by Nawrūz, who was captured and executed, Shaykh's reign was relatively peaceful. Disasters were minimised by Shaykh's personal intervention in the administration of the country, a policy which paid other dividends since the Mamlūk empire reached its greatest extent during his reign. As a result of his drinking, a habit which never left him, although always regretted, he suffered in later years a severe form of arthritis. This apart he was extremely devout and belonged to a sufi brotherhood. He died in 1421 having nominated his year-old son Aḥmad as successor. In the event it was the atabak Ṭaṭār who succeeded to the sultanate.

The façade on the road, raised on a basement of a row of shop cells, is the SE wall with full length stalactite-headed recesses. The lower windows are rectangular while the upper windows are pairs of round-arched lights with an oculus above. Along the top of the wall is trefoil cresting. Resting on the towers of the Fāṭimid gate to the S are the two elegant and identical minarets. Standing on a square base, the first stage is octagonal with keel-arched niches surrounded by simple moulding. The stalactite corbel is very fine as is the pierced balcony. Also octagonal, the second stage is decorated with a continuous horizontal chevron pattern. Another excellent corbel and balcony support the final stage, an eight-pillared pavilion also crowned with a corbel and a finial. During construction the W minaret started to lean and with the sultan's permission it was demolished and rebuilt. Both minarets are signed by the architect Muḥ. b al-Qazzāz and dated 822 AH(1419) and 823 AH(1420).

At the N end of the façade rises the dome over the main tomb-chamber (the tomb to the S is without a dome) with heavy scrolled corners to the zone-of-transition and continuous chevron carving on the dome itself. Below the dome, reached by a flight of steps, is the entrance which, as with this sultan's hospital (Rte 9), rises high above the level of the façade as a pishtak, a Persian architectural device. Around the hood of hanging stalactites is a trefoil arch set within a square frame, the whole carved with arabesques and inscription. On the S inside flank is a panel of square Kufic. The doorway with flat joggled lintel is surrounded by a carved frame in which rest the superb doors. They are of wood covered with bronze and filigree silver with geometrical patterns, the lobes of which are raised and pierced. Originally made for the the Mosque of Sultan Ḥasan (Rte 10), Mu'ayyad Shaykh bought them and had them transferred here.

INTERIOR. Beyond the door is a fine vestibule in which two stalactite cornices support an ornately groined ceiling with an intricate central device. The vestibule leads into the qiblah riwāq. Although there are three arcades of pointed arches, the inner two rows are shorter because of the tomb at the N angle. Most of the columns have classical capitals and were obviously reused from earlier buildings, but in front of the miḥrāb are four octagonal baton pillars. All the arches are supported by wooden tie beams and above and between them are small pointed-arched openings.

The glory of the mosque is the *qiblah wall*, a riot of coloured marble and stucco. On the lower part of the wall are marble panels above which is a frieze of turquoise faience colonettes supporting trefoil arches, running along the length of the wall even inside the miḥrāb. Flanking the beautiful miḥrāb are two porphyry columns with gilded stalactite capitals, while the body is decorated with geometrical mosaic and vertical and diaper panels, all in coloured marbles. In the hood is a continuous

*Enamelled glass lamp made for Amīr Shaykhū, Egypt, c 1350–55 (MIA 328)*

chevron design in black and white marble while surrounding it is an exceptional joggled panel. On the upper part of the wall the marble is in large foliate patterns with turquoise faience insets, and in interlaced circles surrounded by a band of stucco inscription which runs around foliate panels. The ebony minbar is original, inset with mother-of-pearl in a circular pattern. Although the ceiling is reconstructed the original pattern is preserved and is unusual in that it is almost entirely foliate, without a geometrical element. Opposite the miḥrāb is the stone dikkah, the balustrade of which has a monumental inscription. The exterior wall of the riwāq has keel-arched niches between the arches alternating with decorated sunken disks and occasional water spouts. The ṣaḥn is now planted with trees and shrubs but it is known that the other riwāqs each had two arcades.

At either end of the qiblah riwāq are the tombs. To the N is the *Tomb of Sultan Mu'ayyad Shaykh*. The impressive door is surrounded by an ornately carved frame and set with ivory panels. Inside the decoration is sparse; the dome is raised on a squinch with multiple niches. The grave of Mu'ayyad Shaykh is in the centre, the tomb of Ibrāhīm (died 1420), Aḥmad (died 1430) and several infant sons to the W. At the S end of the riwāq the *Tomb of the Women*, containing the graves of some of his wives and daughters, has a similar door.

Directly S is the massive ***Bāb Zuwaylah** (199), locally called the *Bāb Mutwallī*, which once marked the S boundary of the enclosure of the city of al-Qāhirah, slightly S of the original gate of Gawhar. This was built by Badr al-Gamalī in 1092, five years after its two counterparts on the N walls, the Bab al-Futūḥ and the Bāb al-Naṣr (Rte 4). There are excellent views from the roof, reached through the Mosque of Muʿayyad Shaykh.

Its name is derived from one of the Berber tribes, units of the early Fāṭimid army whose barracks were just outside the first gate built by Gawhar. In Mamlūk and Ottoman times it was a place of public execution and the heads of criminals, even if they had not actually been killed here, were exposed above the gate on spikes. The alternative popular name comes from the belief that a mystical figure, the Qutb al-Mutwallī, manifested himself behind the gates.

In construction this gate is similar to the N gates. Pillars have also been used as bonding but one noticeable difference is that the edges of the stone blocks have been left unbevelled.

Two towers, solid for two thirds of their height, are joined by a huge round arch c 4.8m wide; upon this is a platform. Above is another arch forming a portico and the base of a second platform with round-headed crenellations (emplaced by the CPAM). The whole is c 20m high, the ground level having risen about 3m. Between the towers, the passage leads under the arch, with five joggled voussoirs, into a porch covered with a shallow dome raised on pendentives. Flanking the porch were two recesses; that on the E is still intact with the original moulding, but the one to the W was closed during the building of Mu'ayyad Shaykh's mosque and turned into a chamber, a window of which overlooks the porch. Above the iron-bound wooden gates, behind which the Qutb al-Mutwallī was supposed to reside, is the flat lintel. On the exterior is a shallow releasing arch and a frame for an inscription, now empty, and over all a round arch. On each flank of the towers is a decorated niche, while the rounded fronts are decorated on the upper half with a plain moulding with a central pointed-arch decoration. Below are three arrow slits.

*The twin minarets of the Mosque of Sultan Muʿayyad Shaykh*

To the E are c 100m of Badr al-Gamali's *Wall*, now virtually hidden by houses.

Beyond the Bāb Zuwaylah the Shʿ. al-Muʿizz li Dīn Allāh emerges at a crossroads. (It is from this point that Rtes 9 and 10 begin.) To the S it continues past the Mosque of al-Ṣāliḥ Ṭalāʾiʿ eventually to reach the Southern Cemetery. The E section of the road crossing W to E is the Darb al-Ahmar (Rte 9) and the W section SHʿ. AḤMAD MĀHIR along which the route continues. This section of the road was from medieval times known as *Taht al-Rabʿ* (Beneath the Apartments) as a large apartment building ran along the side of the road.

The first lane on the S turning right leads to the small *Tomb of ʿAlī*

*Nagm*, a 17C shaykh. On the main route, immediately W of the wall of the Mosque of Mu'ayyad Shaykh, steps lead up to the *Nādī Darb al-Aḥmar*, the local community club. Inside and to the W stands the **Ḥammām al-Mu'ayyad** (410; 17:3), the bath-house of the mosque (see above). To call it a house is a calumny, it more closely resembles a small palace in its massive yet elegant form. At present it sits in a depression and is often flooded with fetid water. The ground plan is cruciform with a triple window covered by an oculus on each side. Little is left of the dome, but the small stone bricks of which it was made indicate that it was immense and pierced by round-headed windows. Inside there is a very large central ṣaḥn with four similar līwāns, each fronted by a pointed arch. The squinches are commensurate with the size of the dome, each composed of many layers of niches reaching almost to the ground.

On the S side of the street a modern entrance leads down a flight of steps and a corridor to a court in which stands the **Takiyyah and Tomb of Ibrāhīm al-Gulshānī** (332; 16:4).

Gulshānī founded the first Khalawātī zāwiyyah in Egypt. Having been forced to flee from Turkey, he was well received by Sulṭān Qānṣūḥ al-Ghawrī. He retained his popularity after the Ottoman conquests and returned to Istanbul where he triumphantly defended himself against a charge of heresy. He returned to Cairo where he died in 1534.

Although the takiyyah was rebuilt in the early 20C the sandstone tomb containing the body of the shaykh is original (built 1519–24). Later additions to the decorations are the tiles which cover the façade, probably in the 17C. As often in Cairo, there is no logic in their emplacement except round the door where plain green and blue and white flowered tiles alternate.

After 140m on the N side of the street are two adjacent fountains. To the E is the *Sabīl al-Ḥabaysh* (198; 16:4) built in the 18C, and to the W the *Sabīl of Ḥasan Aghā Arzingān* (420) dated precisely 1830. On the S is the **Mosque al-Marā'ah** (Mosque of the Women; 195) also called the *Mosque of Fāṭimah Shaqrā'* on the unfounded tradition that it was built by a daughter of a Mamlūk amīr. It was founded in 1469 but little remains of the original building; the exterior including the minaret is Ottoman, while most of the interior is modern. The original entrance, however, has been retained and is good late Mamlūk work, as is the fine miḥrāb inside. To the S of the road lies the *Stone Mason's Quarter* In scores of workshops the craftsmen can be seen working with local and exotic marbles and stone.

The road continues W into the Maydān Aḥmad Māhir (Rte 7).

# 7 Northern Sh'. Būr Sa'īd

Rte 7 and Rtes 9 to 12 effectively start from the Maydān Aḥmad Māhir, reached from Maydān al-Taḥrīr by bus No. 66. This itinerary follows the Sh'. Būr Sa'īd at it passes through the medieval city. **Cairo Atlas 16, 10.**

From the Maydān Aḥmad Māhir (also called the Bāb al-Khalk) roads radiate in all directions. NW to SE the square is crossed by the Sh'. al-Qal'ah (NW to Maydān al-'Atabah; SE to Maydān Ṣalāḥ al-Dīn, Rte 11). NE to SW runs the SH'. BŪR SA'ĪD (NE is present route, through

ʿAbbāsiyyah and on to Port Saʿīd; SW to Maydān Sayyidah Zaynab, Rte 12). To the W is the Shʿ. Sāmī al-Bārūdī (Rte 12) and to the E the Shʿ. Aḥmad Māhir (Rte 6). The present route follows the N section of the Shʿ. Būr Saʿīd as far as the Bāb al-Shaʿriyyah.

The whole of this road virtually follows the route of the canal which ran between Cairo and Lake Timsāḥ where it joined another that ran through to Suez. Its early history is obscure but the Emperor Trajan had it recut when he enlarged and refortified Babylon. It ran past Heliopolis and Bilbays and joined the canal from Bubastis to Lake Timsah along the Wāḍī Ṭumaylāt. By the time of the Arab invasion it had long fallen into disuse and one of ʿAmr's first acts was to have it recut in 643. It was subsequently cleared several times during the following centuries and Sultan al-Nāṣir Muḥammad built another branch slightly to the N. It left the Nile at the Fūmm al-Khalīg (Mouth of the Canal, Rte 3) and the ceremony of cutting the dyke was held with much festivity at the beginning of the inundation. By the late 19C it was stagnant and fetid, although extremely picturesque, and in 1899 it was decided to fill it in. In 1906 a road was built along the route called the Shʿ. Khalīg al-Miṣrī, changed to Shʿ. Būr Saʿīd in 1958. This is a long and sprawling route with many of the monuments along side streets, the main road now being lined with official buildings, offices and shops.

On the N side of the maydān, with its main façade on the W side of Shʿ. Būr Saʿīd, stands the **Museum of Islamic Art** (Matḥaf al-Fann al-Islāmī; 16:4). Open 09.00–16.00. Friday closed between 11.00–13.30. Fee. The ticket office is at the N end, in front of the garden. Ticket also allows entry to Bayt al-Kiridliyyah (Rte 13).

The first collection of Islamic antiquities was formed around 1880 and housed in the SE riwāq of the Mosque of al-Ḥākim. Later a small museum was built in the courtyard and called the Museum of Arab Art. In 1903 the present building was erected to house the collection and that of the Khedival Library, now the Dār al-Kutub (recently moved to Bulāq; Rte 17). It was inaugurated on 28 December of the same year. Thus was formed the magnificent collection of Islamic art subsequently increased by material from excavations, purchases and donations. The number of objects in the museum now totals almost 75,000. Many specialist catalogues have been published.

The entrance at the N end leads into the vestibule with sales desk to the right. The rooms are numbered from the right.

*Hall 2. Ummayyad Period.* Among the objects in this room note particularly one of the earliest Muslim tombstones dated AH 31 (AD 652). Also the bronze ewer probably the property of the khalīf Marwān II, found where he was killed at Abū Ṣīr near the Fayyūm. The spout is in the form of a crowing cockerel.

*Hall 3. ʿAbbāsid Period.* Stucco panels from Samarra (Iraq) display three styles. Corresponding decoration from Egypt shows the varying influence of these styles. Other objects displayed are pottery and metalwork.

*Hall 4. Fāṭimid Period.* Objects shown here demonstrate the emergence of a national style. Of importance are the frescoes from a Fāṭimid bathhouse. Also to be seen are the wooden panels from the Western Palace carved with genre scenes and animals and birds, still showing traces of colour. Other carvings are on display. The versatility of the craftsmen is also shown by carved rock-crystal, a medium in which the era excelled, pottery with lustre and polychrome decoration, glass and textiles.

*Hall 10 (part). Ayyūbid period.* The highlight of this room is the wooden tabut of Ḥusayn (No. 15025) revealed in the vault of the Mosque of

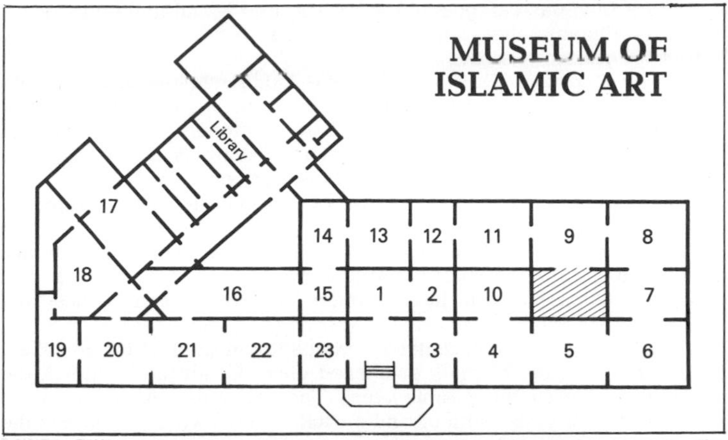
MUSEUM OF
ISLAMIC ART
Library
17
18
14
13
12
11
9
8
16
15
1
2
10
7
19
20
21
22
23
3
4
5
6

Ḥusayn (Rte 4). It dates to c 1178 and is covered with small panels of exquisitely carved inscriptions and foliage.

*Hall 5. Mamlūk Period.* On the right is a huge brass-plated door. Although the decoration appears to be conventional arabesques closer examination reveals tiny animals and birds among the foliage. The splendid craftsmanship of the Mamlūk artisans is well displayed in cases showing enamelled glass, textiles of woven silk, appliqué and printed linen and cotton, metalwork inlaid with silver and gold and polychrome pottery with decoration of exceptional refinement. Notice particularly the mosaic from various mosques including coloured marbles, and faience and mother-of-pearl insets. In this room there is also a 14C mosaic fountain.

*Halls 6–9. Woodwork.* Displaying the extraordinary virtuosity of the Egyptian craftsmen in this medium. Entry to Hall 6 is via the huge doors that the khalīf al-Ḥākim had made for al-Azhar Mosque in 1010. Most of the work displayed here is Fāṭimid. To the right is the wooden miḥrāb from the Mashhad of Sayyidah Ruqayyah (Rte 11). On the left more panels from the Western Palace. *Hall 7* displays minbars, tabuts and sections of mashrabiyyah. *Hall 8.* Ayyūbid and Mamlūk examples. *Hall 9.* Besides woodwork this room contains metalwork ewers, candlesticks and mirrors.

*Hall 10 (part).* In this room is a fine reconstruction, using original elements, of a 17C Ottoman maqʿad. A single marble column, pierced as a fountain, supports a magnificent carved wooden ceiling with three small domes. The water from the fountain falls into a polychrome marble basin.

*Hall 11. Mamlūk metalwork.* At the entrance is the brass-plated door of the Mosque of Salih Talāiʾīʿ made in 1160. Metalwork inlaid with gold and silver includes candlesticks, chandeliers, vases, incense-burners, some with Christian symbols. There is also a case of astronomical instruments including astrolabes.

*Hall 12. Arms and armour,* including swords, daggers, pistols and rifles, some with the names of sultans or amīrs. This must only be a fraction of the glittering armoury of the mamlūks. After the conquest Salim had shiploads sent to Istanbul, and there is a magnificent collection in the Topkapi Saray there.

*Hall 13*. Egyptian ceramics of the Fāṭimid and Mamlūk periods.

*Hall 14*. Ottoman tiles and Islamic ceramics.

*Hall 15*. Islamic ceramics.

*Hall 16*. *Ceramics*. Of interest are the aḥlāq (chokes) from Fāṭimid water jars. They were inserted in the necks of the jars to restrict the flow of water and facilitate drinking. The ḥalq of modern jugs (qullahs) is pierced with simple holes but the Fāṭimid examples are fretted with elegant designs, boats, trees, birds and inscriptions.

*Hall 17*. *Textiles*. A display of textiles in all materials from Egypt and other Muslim countries.

*Hall 19*. *Books*. On show are manuscripts, books and bookbindings, many of them from the library of King Fārūq.

*Hall 20*. *Ottoman art*, including pottery, metalwork and textiles from the 15–19C.

*Hall 21*. *Glass*. This hall contains perhaps the most magnificent collection in the museum, Mamlūk enamelled glass. Of all these objects, the most impressive are the mosque lamps. They are outer containers inside which was set a vessel with oil and a wick. Chains were attached to the handles and suspended from the beams. The great period of lamp production lasted about 100 years from the late 13 to the late 14C. There are lamps here made for Sultan Khalīl (end of 13C), Sultan al-Nāṣir Muḥammad (1st reign 1298), Amīr Salār (c 1308), Amīr Ālmās (1330), Amīr Ālmalik (pre-1340), Amīr Ṭugāytīmūr (c 1344), Amīr Shaykhū (c1355), Sultan Ḥasan (c 1360), Sultan Shaʿbān I (c 1371) and Sultan Barqūq (c 1386). A later group belonging to Sultan Muʾayyad Shaykh (c 1420) and the Amīr Qānī-bāy al-Jarkassī, are much inferior, and the last of the series made for Sultan Qāyt-bāy (c 1490) in Venice is crude and coarse by comparison. Also on display are bottles and cups of incised glass and other special techniques.

*Hall 22*. A superb collection of Persian art, ceramics, metalwork, textiles and manuscripts.

*Hall 23*. Reserved for special exhibitions.

Distributed around the walls of the museum is a selection from the museum's collection of 16–19C Turkish carpets. The stairs to the right of the entrance lead past the library to the second floor.

Opposite on the Shʿ. Būr Saʿīd the large white building is the *Mudirryyat al-Amn al-Qāhirah* (Headquarters of the Cairo Security Council) which controls 35 district stations. To the N is the *Mahkamat Miṣr* (Cairo Primary Court), on the site of the 19C Palace of Manṣūr Yakan Pasha.

On the W side of the Shʿ. Būr Saʿīd the second street past the museum leads N to the **Mosque of Amīr Ḥusayn** (233; 16:4), built in 1319; although much restored it contains some exceptional detail. All that remains of the original are the entrance wall, the qiblah wall and the tomb.

Ḥusayn b. Haydar-bak came from Anatolia with his father and entered the service of Sultan Lāgīn holding appointments in various provinces and was made an amīr of one hundred. His charity and fidelity were renowned and he was much mourned on his death in 1328.

A plain wall with a fluted arch, the ribs terminating in conjoined semicircles, comprises the façade. It is topped by stepped cresting. Above the entrance the minaret (rebuilt 1462) has a conventional octagonal first storey but the second has a ribbed pattern of stone blocks. Steps lead down to the doorway with a joggled lintel and releasing arch and foundation inscription, all enclosed in a carved frame. A vaulted tunnel leads into a bare area with the modern mosque on the right. On the interior qiblah wall is the original superb stucco decoration. It consists of a panel 7m long. Surrounding the miḥrāb is the central panel with a window of three lights above, the main motifs of which are arabesques and blind arcading with medallions in the upper corners. Windows flank the miḥrāb and there are further windows and medallions in the panel. Two round-arched recesses surround the miḥrāb, the hoods resting on small columns. In the spandrels is marble strapwork. Bands of coloured marble line the niche of the miḥrāb, above which is blind arcading. To the left is the bare domed tomb-chamber of the amīr with the dome set on squinches.

Between the police building and the Court is a lane which leads E into the SHʿ. DARB AL-SAʿĀDAH. Directly opposite is the *Mosque of Aqsunqur al-Fariqānī* (193), a typical Ottoman mosque of 1669 with small panels of tiles above the releasing arches of the door and windows. 100m further down the lane, on the S, stands the *Sabīl-Kuttāb of ʿAlī Bāy al-Dumyaṭī* (197), built in 1710. On the Shʿ. Darb al-Saʿādah opposite the NW corner of the Court building is the **Zāwiyah and Tomb of Fayrūz al-Rūmī** (192; 16:4), built in 1426, which although much reconstructed contains the original façade and internal features.

Fayrūz (Turquoise), a Circassian eunuch, served the sultans Muʾayyad Shaykh and Barsbāy. He continued in the service of Sultan Yūsuf, the son of Barsbāy, and, after the deposition of Yūsuf, was made chief eunuch to Sultan Jaqmaq. However, he sacrificed his career by allowing Yūsuf, who was in his charge, to escape from the Citadel. He died in 1427.

It is a very small mosque, typical of those raised by the court eunuchs. On the street is the NW façade with the tomb at the N end. Small recesses with flat stalactite hoods contain the windows and a similar frieze runs along the summit of the tomb. The trefoil-arched doorway has a long inscription above the releasing arch, and square marble panels of Kufic inscription. The first stage of the minaret is octagonal with keel-arched niches flanked by pillars. The second stage is also octagonal but undecorated. Remains of complex cresting can be seen. Shallow ribbing decorates the dome which is probably an Ottoman replacement. There are only two līwāns, each fronted by a pointed horseshoe arch, and the ṣaḥn is covered by a wooden roof. A simple miḥrāb is flanked by two small columns and has an inscription over the hood.

Along the Shʿ. Darb al-Saʿādah a lane on the W leads again to the Shʿ. Būr Sāʿīd, on the N of which is the **Madrasah and Tomb of ʿAbd al-Ghānī** (184; 16:2) built for a civilian amir in 1418 and extensively restored in 1851 by Mumtaz Qādin, concubine of Muḥammad ʿAlī and mother of Ḥusayn Bak.

Fakhr al-Dīn ʿAbd al-Ghānī was born into a ministerial family and advanced by favouritism. Serving Sultans Farag and Muʾayyad Shaykh, he rose to be wazīr. He was dismissed and tortured several times but managed to survive. His methods of tax collecting were harsh and tyrannical. He died in 1418. Ibn Taghrībardī suggested as his epitaph: 'So flawed that if a maid was thus endowed/the only marriage price she'd get would be divorce'.

Of the façade on the street the lower two storeys and the trefoil-arched entrance are original but the third storey of round-arched windows in each recess is an addition. The two-tiered minaret is likewise the work of Mumtaz Qādin whose marble inscription in fine taʿaliq is set above the entrance. The great bronze doors are original. The tomb is also part of the original building.

N of this the SHʿ. AL-MANGALAH leads on the W to the *Sabīl of ʿAbd al-Bāqī* (194; 16:4), dated 1617 and with good decoration. In the ground floor is a trefoil-arched door and marble geometrical panels over the windows while the Kuttāb above has handsome arches over the windows. Immediately to the N on the Shʿ. Darb al-Saʿādah is the **Madrasah of Amīr Asanbughā** (185; 16:4), built in 1370; it is also called the *Mosque al-Būbakrī*. Much was rebuilt in the late 19C, including the sabīl-kuttāb at the S end of the façade. The minaret and qiblah wall are original.

Asanbughā ibn Baktīmūr al-Abūbakrī was an amīr of Sultan Qalāwūn but after the sultan's death spent many years in prison. He was released, however, and rose again to be Governor of Aleppo and Amīr al-Kabīr in 1371. He died, over 70 years old, in 1375.

In the façade are three recesses each containing two sets of windows, the upper pair covered by an oculus. The entrance has a trefoil hood and is flanked by fine coloured marble mosaic panels. The minaret is beautifully decorated with an octagonal first storey, cylindrical second storey, with complex link carving and is crowned by a pavilion with the finial resting on a petal frieze. It rises from a trinagular base, dictated by constriction of space. A wood inscription on the sabīl is flanked by two blazons of the amīr copied from the original ceiling. It shows on a central field of three fields, a sword with two knots.

Down a lane to the N is the **Tomb of Amīr Ṭurunṭāy** (590; 16:2), remnant of a fine Shāfiʿī madrasah built in 1290 and now attached to the modern *Mosque of Faḍl Allāh*.

Ḥusām al-Dīn Ṭurunṭāy was a companion of Qalāwūn and when the latter became sultan he was raised to the amirate. He distinguished himself in battle and uncovered the intended defection of the amīr Sunqur to the Mongols. For this he was made viceroy of Egypt. The son and successor of Qalāwūn, Sultan Khalīl feared him greatly and within three weeks of his father's death in 1290 had Ṭurunṭāy arrested and executed. At first the body was buried in the cemetery but Sultan Kitbughā, another old friend of Ṭurunṭāy, had it reinterred in the tomb.

The mosque is small with only the lowest octagonal tier of the minaret remaining. In the façade are four recesses with windows, the lower lights now below ground level. At the NE of the façade is the Tomb with a plain dome. It is the usual domed-cube, with the modern entry in the NE (the original from the madrasah was in the SW). The interior is undecorated except for painted wooden friezes. Fine stucco decoration remains in the miḥrāb. Squinches with three tiers of five niches raise the dome and above is a series of niches that form the base of the drum. Between each squinch is a window of three lights while around the drum is a series of round-ended panels of inscription separated by medallions. At the apex of the dome is another medallion of inscription. In the centre of the floor is the wooden tabut with painted inscription. The original door in the SW leads into a small walled area; to the SE is a small section of the qiblah līwān of the original mosque with part of the keel-arched miḥrāb visible.

At the end of the lane the Shʿ. Darb al-Saʿādah leads to the Mosque of Sultan Jaqmaq (see below); but return to the Shʿ. Būr Sāʿīd which after 150m is crossed E–W by the SHʿ. AL-AZHAR. On an island at the junction of the two roads is the **Mosque and Tomb of Qāḍī Yaḥyā** (182; 16:2), the first of the mosques built by this powerful civilian minister (see also Rtes 11 and 17). It is a compact mosque built in 1444 and restored by the CPAM between 1884–97. Attached is a Sabīl and a Kuttāb, the latter unusual in being sited not over the sabīl, but over the tomb. In the NW wall is the entrance, decorated with marble foundation inscription and a stalactite arch. To the E rises the minaret of two octagonal stages and a pavilion, the second tier covered with marble marquetry. The entrance leads into a vestibule with a gilded ceiling. The plan is cruciform, the ṣaḥn covered by a wooden roof with a skylight. Slightly pointed horseshoe arches front the līwāns which also have wooden ceilings. All the roofs are excellently carved and gilded with bands of inscriptions from the Qur'ān and stalactite brackets at the corners. The minbar inlaid with ivory and ebony is original, but most of the marble lining of the walls has been stripped. In the NE façade a doorway with a syenite lintel leads to the tomb of *Sh. Farag al-Sitūḥī.*

On the S side of the Shʿ. al-Azhar the first turning is again the Shʿ. Darb al-Saʿādah. On the W side is the **Madrasah of Sultan Gaqmaq** (180; 16:2), built in 1451. Like his other mosque (Rte 13), this is typically small and unassuming and again only the façade has survived.

Brought to Cairo by ʿAlī, the same dealer who sold Īnāl (also later sultan, see Rte 8), Jaqmaq was purchased by Sultan Barsbāy. He also served Sultans Farag and Mu'ayyad Shaykh and under the last reached the post of atabak. In 1438 he retired Shaykh's son Yūsuf and assumed the sultanate. His reign was peaceful but ominous for the rise in power of the royal mamlūks. His confidante Abū 'l-Khayr, a coppersmith, was disgraced and exiled to Anatolia. Jaqmaq was extremely pious, generous and intelligent, encouraging the arts and sciences but discouraging entertainments. He was succeeded briefly by his son ʿUthmān who was deposed by the amīrs in favour of Īnāl.

This very modest mosque is one of the few that does not present a regular façade on the street. The area must have been crowded and the mosque was squeezed between existing buildings. The angled façade has on the E the minaret of only two octagonal tiers with sparse decorations. The second storey, as befits the sultan's asceticism, is only of plastered wood. Likewise the trefoil-arched stalactite entrance is small and without elaborate detail. Of interest in the SE wall is the octagonal window above the miḥrāb instead of the usual oculi.

Running parallel to Shʿ. al-Azhar on the S is the SHʿ. LUBŪDIYYAH. On the S side after 50m is the **Madrasah of Yūsuf al-Gamālī** (178; 17:1), of 1446, for the Malikī School of Law. The doorway has a trefoil arch and black and white joggled marble lintel. Above the releasing arch are two square windows with two square panels of Kufic inscription. The wooden door is heavily carved. Unfortunately the minaret has disappeared. On the N side of the lane (70m) is the **Madrasah of Muqbil al-Rūmī** (177), locally called Mosque al-Dawūdī. Little is left of the original of 1395 save the façade. Muqbil was a eunuch of Sultans Barqūq and Farag. Holding the posts of master of the ḥarīm and chief intendant at the Mosque of the Prophet in Medina, he amassed a vast fortune and died in 1408. This building in addition to being a madrasah was intended as an assembly mosque.

After 50m a road runs to the S, down which on the right stands the **Cathedral of St. Nicholas** (17:1), the seat of the Greek Orthodox Patriarch. It contains several medieval icons. Continuing S the street meets a lane running E–W. A few metres W is the **Mosque of ʿAlī al-ʿArabī** and **House of Muḥammad Maḥrūqī** (459), Chief Merchant of Cairo, both built in 1784.

On the N side of Shʿ. al-Azhar is the 16C *House of ʿAbd al-Wāhid* (355), much ruined, only the E wall retaining some of the original decoration, with large corbels which must have supported the second storey. Slightly to the E is the uninspired *Mosque of Sharaf al-Dīn Nashū'* (176), built in the second quarter of the 14C. This man, originally a Copt, entered the employment of Sultan al-Nāṣir Muḥammad. So powerful did he become that even the great amīrs like Qawṣūn, Bashtak and Yalbughā complained to the sultan. Eventually he and all his relations were arrested and executed (1340). The black and white ablaq entrance has a square hood and the window recesses have six layers of stalactites along the top.

The first mosque past the crossroads (100m) on the NE of the Sh'. Būr Sa'īd is the ruined *Mosque of Murād Pasha* (181; 16:2), built in 1578 by an official who despite the title was not governor. It is a typical early Ottoman mosque with a central path through the ṣaḥn to the ablution court.

Just beyond this mosque the road crosses the SH'. GAWHAR AL-QĀ'ID, better known as AL-MUSKĪ. This is one of the principal shopping streets in Cairo and is thronged all day with stalls, carts and fruitsellers.

Along the W section of al-Muskī (70m) on the N a short lane leads to the **Mosque al-Shawadhliyyah** (450; 16:2), built for the sufi brotherhood by 'Abd al-Raḥmān Katkhudā in 1754.

After 400m on the E the Sh'. al-Khurunfish leads to the Sh'. al-Mu'izz li Dīn Allāh (see Rte 5). At the corner the Ḥārat Zuwaylah encircles the **Church of the Virgin** (10:7), a complex of chapels which may be the most ancient Christian foundation in Cairo. Probably founded in the 4C, it was rebuilt in the 10C (when it must actually have been within the royal enclosure of al-Qāhirah), only to be razed in 1131 during the purges of Khalīf al-Hākim. Shortly after, however, it was rebuilt and from the 14C to 1660 was the seat of the Coptic patriarch. It was closed by Sultan Sulayman in 1559. Most of the extant buildings date from the 18C. The oldest and largest is the *Church of the Virgin* itself, a basilica with narthex and three sanctuaries. It now lies about 4m below ground level. The pillars of the nave have Corinthian capitals and support a massive vaulted ceiling. A dome covers the central haykal which is dedicated to the Virgin. The altar has a canopy. To the left is the haykal of the Angel Gabriel with a wooden screen dated 1778 and a well in the floor. A small side shrine holds a 14C ikon of the Virgin.

At the NW corner is the entrance to the *Church of St. Mercurius*, built in 1774 by Ibrāhīm al-Gawharī. Above the main church is the small *Church of St. George*. Attached is the 19C *Convent of the Virgin* with a library.

80m further along the Sh'. al-Khurunfish on the left stands the *Dār al-Kiswah*, where the curtain for the Ka'bah was made, after Muḥ. 'Alī moved it from the Citadel in the 1820s. Only two embroiderers now remain, making covers for the tombs of shaykhs. The cover for the Ka'bah in Mecca was traditionally supplied by Egypt from early medieval times, a jealously guarded privilege, and it was taken to Mecca with great ceremony with the caravan of pilgrims. Of black silk covered with embroidery of gold and silver wire, it took almost a year to complete. In 1962 during a dispute over fighting in the Yemen, the kiswah was refused by Saudi Arabia and since that time it has been made locally.

Beyond the Dār al-Kiswah the SIKKAT AL-KHURUNFISH leads N (220m) to the **Madrasah of Qāḍī 'Abd al-Bāsiṭ** (60; 10:8), built in 1420, the same year as the great mosque of his master, Sultan Mu'ayyad Shaykh.

In Damascus Zayn al-Dīn 'Abd al-Bāsiṭ joined the household of the viceroy Shaykh and went with him to Cairo. When Shaykh became sultan in 1412 ʿAbd al-Bāsiṭ assumed great power. He was appointed controller of the armies, a post he held for many years. After Muʾayyad Shaykh's death his influence declined and Sultan Barqūq made him ustadār against his will. Under Sultan Jaqmaq, who had long held him in dislike, he was dismissed and retired from public life. Although tall and handsome with a large household and magnificent taste in clothes and horses, he was ignorant, haughty and capricious. He died in 1450.

This madrasah is a very fine example of late Mamlūk architecture, although criticised at the time for flagrancy. The façade is lavishly carved, the minaret being almost identical to those of the Mosque of Sultan Muʾayyad Shaykh. There are entrances in the NE and NW façades, both with trefoil stalactite hoods. It is cruciform in plan with pointed horseshoe arches fronting the axial līwāns. The ṣaḥn is open and the lateral līwāns are reduced in size. All the marble facings of the walls have been stripped but the floor is an excellent example of marble inlay. The woodwork is also of high quality with fine carved and gilded ceilings to the līwāns and the inlaid minbar which is original. In the qiblah līwān is the *Tomb of Sh. Aḥmad al-Subkī* (died 1623), an imām at the mosque.

The *Ribāṭ of Khawand Zaynab* (61), the wife of Sultan Īnāl, which stood further along the road, has now been incorporated in the fabric of a shop and cannot be seen.

Continuing N on Shʿ. Būr Saʿīd, parallel to it on the E runs the SHʿ. BAYN AL-SURAYN (Between the Two Walls), a good example of the persistence of an ancient name. It is a reference to the fact that Badr al-Gamālī built his NW wall of the enclosure of Cairo slightly W of the original wall of Gawhar, which was still standing in parts; thus the people of the area lived in a narrow area lined by the two walls.

The next monument on the E side of the road is the **Mosque and Tomb of al-Shaʿrānī** (59; 10:5), an important and popular sufi shaykh. It is still a venerated and constantly visited mosque.

ʿAbd al-Wahhāb b. Aḥmad al-Shaʿrānī was born in 1493 in Qalyūbiyyah. He came to Cairo and studied under various shaykhs. His literary output was vast, treatises, sermons and admonitory tracts. His admiration of the earlier sufi masters caused him to settle in the area of NE Cairo where they had their tombs, taking a post in the Mosque of al-Ghamrī. He did not hesitate to attack the other brotherhoods for corruption or eccentricity. Many of his tracts show much concern for the plight of the poor and displaced, and he criticised the ʿulamāʾ for their passive response to Ottoman domination. He died as leader of his own brotherhood, the Shaʿrāniyyah, in 1565. His son and successor was ʿAbd al-Raḥmān (died 1603).

The original zāwiyah for al-Shaʿrānī was built during his lifetime by Qāḍī ʿAbd al-Qādir and in addition comprised a great complex of mosque, madrasah, takiyyah and living accommodation for the shaykh and his family. After his death the tomb was built in 1567. Of the complex nothing remains except the tomb. The present is a 19C mosque with the tomb of Sh. al-Shaʿrānī to the left of the qiblah and that of his son on the left side of the ṣaḥn.

Immediately to the N a road leads E and on the S side (100m) is the *Qaʿah and Maqʿad al-Shaʿrānī* (63; 10:6), the remains of a house dated 1725, the rent of which constituted part of the income for the upkeep of the Mosque of al-Shaʿrānī. N of the last road on the E side of the Bayn al-Surayn (60m) is the façade of the mid 15C *Zāwiyat Fāṭimah Umm Khawand* (58). Only the square-headed doorway of this small mosque remains, with an inscription on either side. The builder is unknown although her title 'mother of the lady' bespeaks royal connections. On the E side of the road (30m) is the *Sabīl-Kuttāb of Sulaymān Shawīsh* (167; 10:6), built in 1632, in very fine condition with decoration derived from Mamlūk motifs. There is much woodwork around the kuttāb above the sabīl.

At this point, the Maydān Bāb ak-Shaʿriyyah (which gives its name to the area), the Shʿ. Būr Saʿīd is crossed NE to SW by the SHʿ. AL-GAYSH (NE to Maydān al-Gaysh; SW to Maydān al-ʿAtabah). Running E (to Shʿ. al-Muʿizz li Dīn) is the SHʿ. AMĪR AL-GUYŪSH (shortened to Margūsh). On the S after 180m lies the *Ḥammām al-Malātyah* (592; 10:6), a bathhouse dated 1780 and still in use. Although painted over, the decoration on the façade can still be seen. Immediately inside is the waiting room leading to covered steam, cold-water and massage rooms.

On the N side of the road stood the *Mosque of al-Ghamrī*, one of the most beautiful in Cairo. Muḥ. al-Ghamrī (died 1446) was a Badawiyyah sufi shaykh and, with Madyan, a student of Sh. Aḥ. al-Zāhid (see below). The mosque collapsed early this century.

The remaining monuments of this route are on the W side of the Shʿ. Būr Sāʿid; directly opposite running W is the Shʿ. al-Kharratīn N (to Maydān Ramsīs). The SHʿ. SĪDĪ MADYĀN to the N leads past the *Tomb of ʿAbd al-Laṭīf al-Manāwī* (354) on the W (c 1621) but covered with modern plaster and painted green, to the head of the road and down five steps, to the **Mosque of Sīdī Madyān** (82; 10:5). Built in 1465, only part of it remains standing. The exterior is finely carved with the tomb in the first window beyond the door, and a minaret. It is now used only occasionally.

Madyān b. Aḥ. al-Ashmūnī (died 1458), a Shadhlī sufī, was devoted to his master Aḥ. al-Zāhid (see below), and founded his zāwiyah close to the latter's tomb. After his own death this mosque was built around his tomb.

The interior is in the form of a tiny cruciform madrāsah with stilted arched side līwāns flanked by decorative keel-arched niches. The qiblah līwān has an arcade of three arches.

W of this lane the main street becomes the SHʿ. SH. AL-ʿARUSSĪ and passes the *House of Shaykhs al-ʿArussi and al-ʿIryan* (165), contemporary with the next monument. It is a fine example of late Ottoman building.

Sh. ʿAḥmad b. Muḥ. al-ʿArūsī (1721–93) studied under the leading shaykhs and entered the Khalawātī brotherhood. A great poet and commentator, he became Shaykh al-Azhar in 1778. His son, Muḥammad, and grandson, Muṣṭafa, were also destined to fill this post.

Sh. ʿArūsī's constant companion and father-in-law was Sh. Aḥ. b. Ḥasan al-ʿAryān, an ecstatic visionary. Although totally illiterate, he had a phenomenal memory and could correct the mistakes of readers of classical texts. His characteristic dress was a bulky wollen garment with a red turban, and his usual mount a trotting mule. Many of the great visited him to ask his blessing.

Adjacent is the **Mosque and Tomb of Sh. al-ʿAryan** (600; 10:5), built in 1770 as a suspended mosque over a high basement. It has a very fine façade with five large windows each with a double window above surrounded by heavy carving. The dome of the tomb at the E end of the façade is of simple Ottoman type as is the minaret. Steps at the W end of the façade lead up to a heavy wooden door inside which further steps lead in to the covered ṣaḥn with columns supporting the ceiling. At the shoulders of the miḥrāb are panels of provincial Ottoman tiles. The Tomb of Sh. ʿIryan is to the left of the qiblah wall. Above the grave is an ornately carved canopy. The dome is raised on squinches.

Opposite is the modern *Mosque of Aḥmad al-Ẓāhid* (83); the octagonal base of the minaret remains from the original foundation of 1415. Aḥmad's rebuilt tomb is inside. Aḥmad (died 1417) was one of the leading Shadhilī shaykhs and the first to settle in this area. The mosque was built for him and his followers.

Along the road which becomes SHʿ. BĀB AL-BAHR (600m), down a small lane on the S, is the *Mosque of ʿAlī al-Farrā* (166), another modern mosque with a 16C minaret attached.

N on the Shʿ. Būr Sāʿīd, the next main road to the E is the SHʿ. AL-ṬABLAH, on the S side of which is an 18C bath house, the *Ḥammām al-Ṭanbālī* (564; 10:5). Running W is the SHʿ. AL-FAGGĀLAH with a stretch of Ṣalāḥ al-Dīn's wall (352) along the S side; just to the N is the *Mosque and Tomb of al-Dashtūtī* (12). Although of interest in so far as it was begun in 1506 and not completed until after the Ottoman conquest in 1518, the exterior has been plastered over and painted in red and yellow. The tomb-chamber is now covered with a strange modern dome.

ʿAbd al-Qadir al-Dashtūtī (died 1523) was admired by the most powerful men, including Sultan Qayt-bay. He was equally esteemed after the conquest by Selim in 1517 and the governor Khayr-bāy attended his funeral. His mūlid (26 Ragab) was one of the most important in Cairo with the Sh. al-Bakrī presiding and it was the occasion for the Dawsah (treading) Ceremony when the Sh. of the Saʿdiyyah rode over the prostrate bodies of his followers.

# 8 The Eastern Cemetery

This Rte (3km) is confined to the Eastern Cemetery which runs along the flank of the city. Quite a lot of walking is involved, but the principal monuments are confined to the first 1.5km. The start of the itinerary can be reached from al-Darasah (see below) or by bus No. 500 from Maydān al-Taḥrīr to Maydān al-Barqūq. See map on next page.

From al-Darasah (Rte 6) follow the SHʿ. AL-MANṢŪRIYYAH N (passing on the E a section of the wall of Ṣalāḥ al-Dīn) and the *Burg al-Ẓafar* (Rte 4).

Turn E along the SHʿ GALĀL where to the N is **al-Madīnat al-Buʿūth al-Islāmiyyah** (City of Islamic Delegations), the residences of the single foreign students at al-Azhar. The Shʿ. Galāl then reaches the SHʿ. ṢALĀḤ ṢĀLIM which leads N (700m) to the Maydān al-Barqūq. To the S is the vast QARĀFAT AL-SHARQIYYAH (The Eastern Cemetery), a great necropolis stretching 3.5km to the Citadel. It was popularly called by the occupying Europeans the *City of the Dead* or *Tombs of the Caliphs*, none of whom is buried here.

In fact it is a series of contiguous cemeteries that have coalesced over the centuries: from N to S these are al-Qarāfah al-Ghafīr, al-Qarāfah al-Migāwirīn, al-Qarāfah Qāyt-bāy and, slightly separated, perhaps always so, al-Qarāfah Bāb al-Wazīr. It was much less important as a burial place than the Qarāfat al-Kubrā (the Great Cemetery) to the S until the beginning of the 15C when Sultan Farag built the tomb for his father Barqūq, after which it became the fashionable area for the later sultans and amīrs to erect their own tombs. Most of the tomb buildings and enclosures are 20C, the older Ottoman tombs having been demolished, and are still in use, the

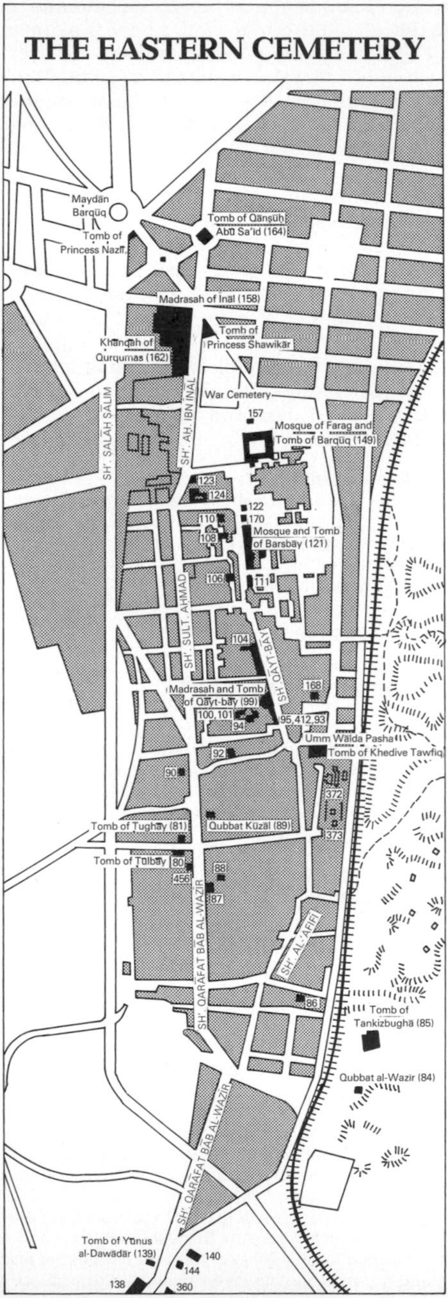
THE EASTERN CEMETERY
Maydān Barqūq
Tomb of Princess Nazlī
Tomb of Qānṣūh Abū Sa'id (164)
Madrasah of Ināl (158)
Tomb of Princess Shawikār
Khānqāh of Qurqumās (162)
War Cemetery
SH'. ṢALĀḤ ṢĀLIM
SH'. AḤ. IBN INĀL
157
Mosque of Farag and Tomb of Barqūq (149)
123
124
122
170
110
108
Mosque and Tomb of Barsbāy (121)
106
111
SH'. SULT. AḤMAD
104
SH'. QĀYT-BĀY
168
Madrasah and Tomb of Qāyt-bāy (99)
100,101
94
95,412,93
Umm Wālda Pasha
Tomb of Khedive Tawfīq
92
90
372
373
Tomb of Tughāy (81)
Qubbat Kūzāl (89)
Tomb of Ṭūlbāy
80
456
88
87
SH'. QARĀFAT BAB AL-WAZĪR
SH'. AL-'AFĪFĪ
86
Tomb of Tankizbughā (85)
Qubbat al-Wazīr (84)
SH'. QARĀFAT BAB AL-WAZĪR
Tomb of Yūnus al-Dawādār (139)
140
144
138
360

bodies being buried in vaults under the floor and cenotaphs erected above. There has always been some homeless peopleliving in the tombs, but with the increase of the population of Cairo this practice has accelerated greatly and now many of the buildings are occupied. To serve this community shops and stalls have sprung up, giving the appearance of a residential suburb. The families of the deceased make regular visits to the tombs, an opportunity for picnics.

At the apex of the Cemetery is the large *Qubbat Nazlī Hānim*. This modern mausoleum contains the tombs of Nazlī (1864–1945), daughter of ʿAbd al-Halīm who was a son of Muḥ.ʿAlī, her daughter Fāṭimah Sharīf (died 1973) and her son Muḥ. Bay Gamīl (died 1920). The mausoleum is set in a gardened enclosure.

The road due SE is the SHʿ. AL-GHAFĪR which leads after 40m to crossroads. In the centre stands the isolated **Tomb of Sultan Qānṣūḥ Abū Saʿīd** (164), built in 1499. This the second and most elaborate of this sultan's tombs (for the first see Rte 9) and is locally called *Qubbat al-Ghafīr* (Tomb of the Watchman).

Qānṣūḥ a Circassian mamluk of Sultan Qāyt-bāy was discovered to be the brother of the sultan's favourite concubine ʿAsal-bāy. He supported Sultan Muḥ. IV, the son of Qāyt-bāy, in 1497 who opposed his father's amirs and was assassinated within two years. Qānṣūḥ was elected sultan but Tūmān-bāy, the dawādār, rose in revolt and beseiged the Citadel in 1500. The sultan escaped disguised as a woman but was caught three weeks later and he was exiled to Alexandria by Janbalat, and executed when Tūmān-bāy became sultan.

This is a typical late Mamlūk tomb built in white and yellow ablaq with windows set in full-length recesses on each side, over each of which are double round-arched windows covered by an oculus. A large round window marks the miḥrāb and above a muqurnas cornice runs around the summit of the wall. Each side of the zone-of-transition with its geometrical corners contains three round-headed windows covered by triple oculi. Ten windows pierce the drum alternating with niches of the same shape; above them runs a good band of inscription. The dome itself is heavily carved with two complex grid-work patterns. The entrance is in the NE wall but the steps have disappeared. Although the interior is much damaged and the lining of the miḥrāb has gone, a good band of inscription runs around the top of the wall. The dome is raised on squinches with multiple niches, seven at the top to one at the base.

The wide SHʿ. AḤMAD IBN ĪNĀL runs SW. After 80m, on the W—passing the Tomb of Ismaʿīl Pasha Sirrī (died 1930) on the corner—are two conjoined mosque and tomb complexes, each with apartment buildings attached. The northernmost and earliest is the **Tomb, Ribāṭ and Madrasah of Sultan Īnāl** (158), the first built while he was still an amīr in 1451, the second a year after his accession in 1454, and the last in 1456.

Although brought to Cairo in c 1397 and manumited by Sultan Farag, Īnāl only became an amīr of one hundred in 1433 under Sultan Barsbāy. Despite this long career he seems never to have learned to read or write, both factors that would seem to mitigate against high government office. ʿUthmān, the son of Sultan Jaqmaq, succeeded to the throne in 1453, but was deposed by the Royal Mamlūks, and Īnāl, now atabak, was elected as a neutral amīr. He was already 72 years old. Īnāl supported the claims of James, illegitimate claimant to the throne of Cyprus against Queen Charlotte in 1460, but died in 1461. His only wife was Zaynab by whom he had two children, Aḥmad and Muḥammad, the former named as heir.

The façade of this complex stretching S to the first minaret comprises the SE wall of the tomb and madrasah. At the corner the exterior of the tomb is typical of the period; the zone-of-transition with simple geometrical corners has triple round-arched windows surmounted by three oculi on each side. Piercing the drum of the dome are 12 round-arched windows above which runs a band of inscription. The dome is decorated with rather conservative horizontal chevrons, but around the base small turquoise faience disks are set into the moulding.

The madrasah has four lower square windows in pairs in full-length stalactite-headed recesses, above each of which is a round-arched window and between each pair an oculus. At the end of this façade the tall door is covered by a trefoil stalactite hood. Above the last is fleur-de-lys cresting which has been lost from the rest of the façade. Next to the door rises the small but beautiful minaret, set on a square-sectioned pedestal with moulding, fretted plaques and bevelled corners. The first section is octagonal, also with moulding and a keel-arched niche in each side. Above, a stalactite corbel supports a balcony and the second cylindrical section with incredible chevron moulding forming pillars, reflecting, but more complex than, that on the dome. Although there is a stalactite corbel the balcony has disappeared and the third section with panels of chevron moulding is crowned by a spear head frieze and finial. The NE façade is the wall and entrance of the ribāṭ.

Inside the main door a vestibule leads into a cruciform madrasah in which the marble floor, dado and the timber roof have been stripped but the miḥrāb still retains its carved stone. At the E corner of the qiblāh līwān is the entrance to the tomb-chamber (now also much despoiled). The four tombs still in place contain the bodies of Sultan Īnāl, his wife Zaynab bint Khassab (died 1479) and their two sons, Aḥmad (later sultan) and Muḥammad. At the rear are the remains of the students' quarters of the ribāṭ. Of particular interest is the well-appointed ablution court; the foundations of the living quarters are to the NW.

Abutting directly onto the SW wall of the last complex are the **Tomb and Khānqāh of Amīr Qurqumas** (162) built between 1506–07 and restored by the Polish–Egyptian group.

Originally a mamlūk of Sulṭān Bāy, by whom he was manumitted, Qurqumas rose to be an amīr of one hundred under Sultan Jaqmaq. Raised to atabak by Sultan Qānṣūḥ al-Ghawrī, who admired his integrity, benevolence and modesty, he died in 1510 at the age of 60 and the whole of Cairo went into mourning. The sultan himself lead the funeral prayer, kissed the corpse and carried the bier some distance towards the tomb. Qurqumas chose this area specifically because of his admiration for Īnāl's complex.

From the first return past the minaret of Īnāl runs the façade of the apartments attached to the khānqāh; the next return contains the entrance and the minaret. Beyond is the façade of the mosque from which the tomb makes a salient before the wall of the khānqāh. The façade of the apartments is low and completely undecorated, but the doorway with its trefoil stalactite hood is impressive and more elaborate than that of Īnāl, and the minaret above is taller. This rises from a square-sectioned base with chamfered corners less elaborate than that of Īnāl, but the first octagonal section is almost a direct copy as is the stalactite corbel. The next stage is of great interest for (as on the minaret of Īnāl) the architect has reused the design on the dome, in this case diapers not chevrons. Above another stalactite corbel rises the top section, an eight-pillared pavilion with a similar cornice.

The rest of the exterior is simple, but rather impressive. At the first corner is a sabīl-kuttāb with large windows below and tall double windows above. Two flat-headed recesses divide the façade of the maṣallah in each of which are two windows at ground level and two pointed-arched windows above; between each pair is an oculus. In the wall of the tomb two full-length recesses contain two pointed-arched windows and an oculus between. In each side of the zone-of-transition with scrolled corners are three round-headed windows covered by triple oculi, all outlined with moulding. Twelve windows pierce the drum, with a band of inscription running above, while the dome has a pattern of diaper fretwork below and horizontal chevrons above. The wall of the khānqāh beyond the last is very simple with five oblong windows.

A baffled corridor leads from the entrance into the unusual maṣallah with a small ṣaḥn with an inscription around the walls and two larger līwāns to NW and SE fronted by pointed arches. On the SW side of the qiblah līwān is the entrance to the large tomb with a huge brick-lined miḥrāb niche, flanked by pillars with tulip capitals. An inscription runs around the wall below the squinch with multiple niches, from seven on the top row to one at the point. To the SW is a small contemporary lavatory with the most beautiful stalactite ceiling. In the courtyard are several tombs and beneath the complex is a warren of narrow tunnels of uncertain purpose.

On the opposite side of the road are two modern tombs in garden enclosures. That to the N is the massive sandstone **Tomb of Princess Shawikār** (knock for admittance). A double door gives access to the tomb chamber inside which the marble floor contains seven graves of the princess's family. In the centre stands the *Tomb of Princess Shawikār* (1876–1947), of monolithic white Italian marble. This remarkable tomb is in the form of a directoire bed with flowered bedspread, flanked by bowls of roses. The elaborate headboard contains the name of Allāh and it is surmounted by a coronet (both originally gold; now replaced with brass replicas). The sculptor was Gabriella Donatelli of Venice.

Shawikār was the grand-daughter of Aḥmad Rifʿat, eldest son of Ibrāhīm Pasha and therefore of the most senior line of the descendants of Muḥ. ʿAlī. She was married in 1895 to Prince Aḥmad Fu'ad (later king) but they were divorced three years later after the death of their son, Ismaʿīl, and the shooting of her husband by her brother, Aḥmād Sayf al-Dīn. She subsequently married in turn four more distinguished men. The site for this tomb was chosen just days before her death.

The three tombs to the left (from the door) are those of *Ismaʿīl* (died 1897), son of Shawikār and Aḥmad Fu'ad; *Hisham Pasha Ḥasanayn*; and *Waḥīd Yusrī* (1907–69), her only son by Sayf Allāh Yusrī, and his wife *Samihah* (1889–1985), daughter of Sultan Ḥusayn Kāmil. The three tombs to the right (from the door) are those of *Luṭfiyyah* (died 1960), Shawikār's daughter by Sayf Allāh Yusrī, and her husband *Ḥamīd al-ʿAbbad* (died 1960); *Dādā Shayistrah* (died 1953), the family nurse, and lastly the tomb planned for *Waḥīd al-Dīn Yusrī.*

The smaller building to the S is the **Tomb of Princess Ruqayyah ʿAbd al-Ḥalīm** (1868–1952). It contains no tābūt, merely having glass lights set in the floor above the grave.

To the SE lies **al-Maqābir al-Shuhadā'** (War Cemetery) for soldiers killed in combat in the recent conflicts. At the SE end is the *Cenotaph for the Enemy* who are thus also honoured. At the W end of the cemetery walls is the small **Tomb of Anas** (157). This, the first important tomb to be built in the Eastern Cemetery, was built originally by the amīr Yūnus al-Dawādār in 1382 for his own interrment; it was given to Anas and Yūnus had another built at the S end of the cemetery (see below).

When Barqūq became atabak he sent for his family from the Caucasus. On arriving, his father Anas scandalised the other amīrs by greeting his son by name without honorifics and was admonished by them. He was so upset that he threatened to return to his village, but was mollified by Barqūq and stayed in Cairo until he died in 1382. He was buried at first in Barqūq's madrasah on Sh'. al-Mu'izz li Dīn, but was later transferred here.

An arcade of seven pointed arches (restored) runs from this qubbah to the magnificent isolated ***Mosque and Khānqāh of Sultan Farag and Tomb of Sultan Barqūq** (149). This mosque took 12 years to build—1398–1411. It is a most remarkable complex including among its buildings two lecture halls and two sabīl-kuttābs.

Sultan Barqūq built his own mausoleum in the madrasah on the Sh'. al-Mu'izz lī Dīn Allāh (Rte 5), but towards the end of his life expressed the desire to be buried in the Northern Cemetery close to several pious shaykhs with whom he associated in his later years. Farag, his son and successor, built this vast complex to honour his father's wish and, when complete, the body of Barqūq was transferred here from his madrasah in the city. Several other members of the family are also buried here, but not Farag, whose unpredictable behaviour led to his assassination during campaigns in Syria.

The exterior of this mosque (c 73m sq.) is rather plain. It may have been so long in construction that impetus was lost and the decoration never completed; none the less it is very impressive. All the façades are divided by a series of occasional narrow full-length niches with square stalactite friezes, in each of which are windows, in the lower storey oblong, in the upper storey with round arches.

The SE façade consists of the qiblah wall, at each end of which are set the huge 31m-high stone domes over the tombs. The men's tomb at the S and the women's at the E are identical, the zone-of-transition with immense scroll corners having three round-arched windows covered by three oculi in each side. Twelve windows pierce the drum alternating with similarly shaped niches; above runs a band of inscription. Carved continuous horizontal chevron pattern decorates the dome, the lowest row terminating in mullets. At the centre of the façade is a much smaller dome covering the miḥrāb; it also has scroll corners and triple windows, but the windows in the drum have keel-arches and the dome has a rib and fillet decoration.

The NE wall is a combination of the tomb and khānqāh, with three storeys of rectangular windows and at the W end the entrance to the ṣaḥn (closed). A broad trefoil arch filled with many-layered stalactites covers the door and in the spandrels large medallions of inscription are surrounded by foliate decoration. On the corner is the first *sabīl-kuttāb*, the fountain below and the school with three round arches resting on pillars above.

The NW main façade contains the other face of the sabīl-kuttāb and six recesses topped with stalactite friezes and pierced by windows. A band of beautiful inscription runs almost the whole length, while above this are remnants of the fleur-de-lys cresting. Two identical *minarets* rise 50m above ground level; the first stage has a square section and medial windows with fretted balconies resting on muqurnas corbels, above which is a band of inscription topped by a stalactite corbel and fretted balcony. The second stage is cylindrical and decorated with chain moulding, another inscription and a muqurnas corbel with fretted balcony. An elegant eight-pillared pavilion with a further balcony and finial completes the whole. At the W end of the façade is the second *sabīl-kuttāb* and set back about 5m is the *entrance* to the complex, similar to that in the NE wall but squatter and with more elaborate spandrels. The SW wall is the least elaborate and similar to the NE, but without an entrance.

INTERIOR. From the vestibule a corridor leads to the NE (notice Ancient Egyptian granite pillar with hieroglyphs visible used as a sill) past residences for the sufis into the *ṣaḥn* measuring 36m by 40m. Above the entrance is a pointed arch with dog-tooth decoration. This strange building with four truncated riwāqs, has a hybrid appearance between that of an enclosure mosque and a cruciform madrasah. The riwāqs to the NE and SW have a single arcade of five arches while those to the NW and SE each have three arcades, the former with five, the latter with seven arches. The arches are all slightly pointed, set on huge piers braced with wooden tie-beams. Each arcade is covered by a series of shallow brick domes circular or oval in plan. An unusual Mamlūk feature, it was only used during the reign of this sultan, although in Ottoman times it was a common device. In the centre of the ṣaḥn are the remains of an octagonal fountain originally covered by a domed pavilion and now surrounded by shrubs.

In the *SE riwāq* is the tall main *miḥrāb*, merely a pointed-arched niche flanked by four rather ugly pilasters, the sumptuous marble facing having long since been stripped. Above is the oculus and above that the small dome resting on squinches with multiple niches, three over two over one. The magnificent stone *minbar* to the S was presented to the mosque by Sultan Qāyt-bāy in 1483. It is deeply carved with geometrical designs inset with floral motifs, even in the muqurnas over the door. On the back panel of the seat is a carving of a lamp surrounded by plant forms. The two smaller miḥrābs have also lost their linings. At either end of this riwāq are the two tomb chambers, each fronted by a great pointed arch.

The *Tomb of Barqūq* lies to the E, the arch half filled with a massive mashrabiyyah screen set with a wooden door. Measuring c 14m sq., the floor has a slightly raised section in the centre. A dado of coloured marble faces the walls; above it is a frieze of decorated niches and a band of inscription. In the centre of the SE wall is the pointed-arched miḥrāb, also adorned with strips of coloured marble flanked by baton pillars, while around the hood is a rich panel of marble marquetry. At a height of 16m runs a frieze of monumental inscription and above this the dome is raised on squinches with ten layers of niches. The whole of the interior of the dome is painted in red, black and white, the niches between the windows with arabesques, above which is a huge band of thuluth script, and bands of chevron and foliate decoration with a great central medallion. Immediately in front of the miḥrāb rests the red and white marble tābūt of Sultan Barqūq with a beautifully carved thuluth inscription. Beside it to the NE stands the Shahīd (literally 'witness'), a cylinder of white marble. In front is the tābūt of Sultan ʿAbd al-ʿAzīz, Barqūq's second son and successor, in white marble with inscription from the Qurʾān. Another marble tomb stands to the N but the person is unknown though obviously important. In the SW corner is a limestone tomb, also of an unknown.

At the S end of the riwāq is the *Tomb of the Women*, essentially of the same plan though the wall decoration is somewhat simpler. The central miḥrāb is unusual in having a horseshoe-sectioned hood though the frame is joggled similarly to that in Barqūq's tomb. Although painted in the same colours the decoration of the dome is quite different from the other tomb; it is even more foliate and the central medallion is full of arabesque. In front of the miḥrāb is the tābūt of Khawand Kharīz, granddaughter of Barqūq (died 1409). In white marble, it has beautiful arabesque carving. To the S lies the white marble tābūt of Khawand Shaqrā' (died 1482), daughter of Sultan Farag, while in the SW corner is a limestone tābūt probably of Khawand Qunuqbāy (died 1432), the wife of Barqūq and mother of ʿAbd al-ʿAzīz. A staircase in the NW corner of the courtyard leads to a complex of students' rooms. There is magnificent view of the whole cemetery from the roof.

W of Barqūq's complex is the **Qubbat ʿAṣfūr** (Sparrows' Tomb; 123) a small but elegant tomb attached to a sabīl. One of the last pre-Ottoman mausoleums, it dates to 1507. The owner is unknown but it is of typical form with stalactite-headed recesses in the walls. Scrolls cover the corner of the zone-of-transition and the tall dome rises on a drum pierced by eight windows. The pattern on the dome is of complex diaper frets.

A small enclosure (124) to the S contains two very interesting tombs. Immediately inside to the left is the **Tomb of Barsbāy al-Bagasī** built in c 1456. Barsbay, who was Amīr Akhūr of Sultan Īnāl, died in 1465 in Damascus. Similar in construction to other late tombs with scrolled corners on the zone-of-transition and chevron-carved dome, it is unusual in the blue faience roundels set in the base of the dome. The second mausoleum, the **Tomb of Amīr Sulaymān**, is unusual on two counts. Built in 1544, well into the period of Ottoman domination, it retains the form of a late Mamlūk tomb; the dome is actually a direct copy of that over the Tomb of Amīr Qanibāy al-Sayfī built in 1503 (Rte 10). There is complex cresting on the cube, geometrical corners to the zone-of-transition. The work however is crass; the craftsmen were either dead or working in Istanbul. An unusual feature is the band of inscription which instead of being carved in stone is a panel of blue and white tiles.

The next monument is the **Qubbat al-Sabaʿ Banāt** (Tomb of the Seven Maidens; 110), a popular name. The builder is unknown, but it can be dated by style to the mid 15C. There are triple lights in the zone-of-transition. Two new features are the frieze of niches at the summit of the walls and the stalactite cornice below the drum of the dome. Close by to the S is the **Qubbat Maʿbad al-Rifāʿī** (108), a rather plain low-domed building probably of the 16C.

SE runs the SHʿ. QĀYT-BĀY and stretching along the E side for c 100m is the **Mosque, Khānqāh and Tomb of Sultan Barsbāy** (121), an impressive elongated complex built in 1432 by the sultan for himself and members of his family and court.

Like his own master, Sultan Barqūq, Barsbāy also built a madrasah and tomb on the Shʿ. al-Muʿizz lī Dīn in Cairo (Rte 5), but similarly later had a much more magnificent complex built in the Eastern Cemetery. The glory of the whole collection of buildings is that it marks the first flowering of the decorated stone dome; the simple ribs and chevrons were abandoned and each of the domes here has an individual geometric pattern and display an evolution in design.

Slightly to the NE but included within the collection of buildings is the isolated **Tomb of Amīr Gānībak al-Ashrafī** (122), built by the sultan for this amīr at the same time as he constructed the mosque.

Gānībak was purchased as a boy by Sultan Barsbāy and remained faithful, even suffering imprisonment with him. When Barsbāy became Sultan, Gānībak was created an amīr of one hundred and dawādār. His generosity gained him a large following and although young he was consulted on law by the great amīrs. During his last illness he was attended by Barsbāy. He was buried in his own madrasah (Rte 10), but was reinterred here by order of the sultan.

The tomb is the usual domed cube, the base containing recesses and the zone-of-transition geometrical corners with two round-headed windows covered by an oculi in each side. Twenty windows pierce the drum and a band of inscription runs above. The dome, the most evolved in the complex, has a beautiful geometrical pattern of frets, with 12-pointed stars as the central feature.

Beside this tomb stands the **Tomb of Amīr Qurqumas** (170), transferred here from outside the Mosque of al-Ḥākim (Rte 5) in 1983. Built in 1511 for an unidentified amīr, it is a simple domed cube with scarcely any decoration.

The façade of Barsbāy's complex running N to S consists of the NW walls of the tomb, the mosque, the entrance and, to the S, the remains of the khānqāh. The most impressive structure is the *tomb*, the recesses in the plain walls containing square stalactite heads and two tiers of windows. Immense scrolls cover the corner of the zone-of-transition and in each side are three round-headed windows and three oculi. Twelve windows pierce the drum with excellent inscription above. A complex carved fretwork covers the outside of the dome, the spaces between filled with eight-petalled flowers. This is the most primitive dome in the complex. Along the plain façade of the *mosque* are several recesses with stalactite heads, in each of which are two windows; while the entrance, covered by a trefoil stalactite hood, is reached by a paired flight of steps and has foundation inscription on each side. A simple three-tiered minaret rises above, a rustic Ottoman replacement, the original having fallen. The walls of the *khānqāh* are much ruined, their only interest being the band of waqf inscription.

The entrance leads into a small porch. To the left of this is the entrance into the small mosque of rather unusual arcaded form with three aisles of pillars. Coloured marble covers the floor and dado, the latter also set with mother-of-pearl, but the miḥrāb has lost its original rich decoration. The beautiful carved wooden minbar was originally made for the now destroyed Mosque of al-Ghamrī in 1451. A band of inscription runs around the upper part of the wall above which is the carved and painted wooden ceiling, some of it original. A doorway in the NE wall leads into the tomb-chamber with floor and walls similar to the mosque, but here the original miḥrāb decoration has been retained with marble marquetry and joggling. The tābūt of Barsbāy rests directly in front of the miḥrāb.

At the rear of the complex are the remains of the enclosure for members of the sultan's family. Here is another tomb of the unusual canopy type, with a large pointed arch piercing each of the four sides. The zone-of-transition has stepped corners with paired windows and an oculus between each. Although there is a band of inscription there are no windows in the drum. As elegant as the other domes here, the motif is also a complex geometrical fretwork culminating in 12-pointed star-shaped openings, although less satisfactory than that on the Tomb of gānībak above.

Just S of this tomb is the much ruined 15C *Takiyyah of Aḥmad Abū Sayf*

(111) while on the W side of the road stands the **Tomb of Khadīgah Umm al-Ashraf** (i.e. Mother of Barsbāy; 106), a traditional but unlikely ascription. Although uninscribed it can be dated by style to c 1430–40, but there are also certain primitive features. The main cube is of brick and the zone-of-transition with stepped corners has a window of three lights in each side, as in early Mamlūk tombs; in the drum are 12 keel-arched windows. The dome is exceptionally powerful but cumbersome. It is ribbed, but the flutes are geometrically entwined creating a very unusual

*Dome of the Madrasah of Sultan Qāyt-bāy showing the magnificent stone carving*

effect. This form was only used once more—in the tomb of Taghrī-Bardi (Rte 13).

To the S (150m) the long façade of the **Rabʿ Qāyt-bāy** (104) stretches along the W side of the street. It is the first of a great complex of buildings surrounding Sultan Qāyt-bāy's tomb. Through the beautiful tall doorway a passage leads to many small rooms. Ibn Iyās gives the completion date as 1474. The road gives on to a square on the W side of which is the **Ḥawḍ Qāyt-bāy** (183), a roofed water-tank, well decorated with shallow recesses and cartouches of the same date as the other structures.

On the S side of the square rises one of the pearls of Islamic architecture, the ***Madrasah and Mausoleum of Sultan Qāyt-bāy** (99), built between 1472–74. This is the focal point of the whole complex. Not particularly large, and asymetrical in plan, its aspect is none the less monumental.

In 1435 Qāyt-bāy was purchased as a boy for 50 dinars by Sultan Barsbāy. His name means 'the restored' or 'returned' and was given to children who had nearly died at birth. After manumission by Sultan Jaqmaq he joined the Khasaqiyyah. Following the death of Jaqmaq in 1437 there was a series of sultans with short reigns and during this period Qāyt-bāy advanced rapidly, being made an amīr of one hundred by Sultan Khushqadam. After the deposition of Sultan Yilbāy, Timurbughā, an old comrade of Qāyt-bāy, was elected sultan in 1467. Qāyt-bāy was created atabak, but within two months the young mamlūks were rioting through the streets. They imprisoned the sultan, but Qāyt-bāy and his forces routed the rebels and released him. It proved too much for Timurbughā and as he and Qāyt-bāy descended from the Citadel the troops proclaimed Qāyt-bāy sultan, to which Timurbughā readily agreed. The companions parted in tears and the former sultan retired with his family to Damietta.

Despite his obvious strength of character Qāyt-bāy's 28-year reign was marked by an increase in the intractability of the young mamlūks. Several times they rioted throughout Cairo, leaving trails of devastation. Once they even sacked the home of the atabak Azbak who had to flee to Mecca. To aggravate this chaos several virulent outbreaks of plague swept through the country. Externally the most important development was the rise of the Ottoman Turks in Anatolia. They gradually extended their power throughout the area, and hostility to the Mamlūk state increased as they tussled over the territory of NW Syria and Albistan. After his death in 1481 the Ottoman Sultan Muḥ. was succeeded by his son Bayazid II but another son, Jem, opposed his brother and fled to Egypt seeking support. This increased the antagonism of the Ottomans and although a peace treaty was signed in 1491 it was only a temporary respite for the Mamlūks.

Qāyt-bāy was a great patron of the arts and his reign marks a peak in both public and private building, distinguished by elegance and fine craftsmanship. In 1496 Qāyt-bāy fell ill; he was 86 years old and obviously dying. He was deposed and his son Muḥammad elected sultan. Qāyt-bāy died the next day.

At the S corner the tomb makes a salient from the main building. There are full-length recesses with stalactite heads in each of which are two windows, the lower with square joggled lintels and the upper with pointed arches. A simple fleur-de-lys cresting runs around the top. The zone-of-transition has shallow scrolled corners, the volutes of which are decorated with chevrons. On each side are triple round-headed windows surmounted by three oculi, flanked by inscribed roundels. All these units are framed by double bands of moulding. Twelve round-headed windows pierce the drum and above a crisp band of inscription rises the dome which is one of the supreme examples of the stone-carver's craft. A basic pattern of angular fretwork is skilfully superimposed over sinuous grooved arabesques, each of these motifs culminating in nine-pointed stars.

In the SE wall of the mosque are three square-headed stalactite recesses, the first two each with two pairs of windows, the lower with bronze grills, the upper with pointed arches and inset with stucco grills. Between each pair is an oculus over the miḥrāb. The last recess is narrower with two oblong windows. At the corner is the sabīl-kuttāb, the large windows below with bronze grills and square, joggled lintels, the kuttāb above with round-headed arches. Trefoil cresting continues around the top of the wall from the tomb. The entrance, which is reached by a flight of steps, runs the complete height of the building and has a trefoil hood with elegant carved decoration in the spandrels and a band of inscription above.

Lying to the right of the entrance, the three-tiered *minaret* is—like the rest of the buildings in the complex—a paragon of decorated masonry. It rises from a square-sectioned chamfered base to the first octagonal storey in each side of which are fluted keel-arched niches, flanked by pillars, all the elements surrounded by double bands of moulding. A complex stalactite bracket supports a stone fretwork balcony and the second cylindrical section decorated with geometrical moulding and topped by a similar bracket and balcony. An eight-pillared pavilion is the final tier, also with bracket and balcony; over all is an ovate finial.

A porch leads into the SE līwān. This is a cruciform madrasah with vestigial side līwāns and a covered ṣaḥn with octagonal roof lantern. The floors and walls are a riot of coloured marbles and black and red bitumen pastes in complex geometrical panels. The architect, not content with fronting the līwāns with pointed horseshoe arches, has them springing from beautiful stalactite brackets. Above is a richly carved, painted and gilded ceiling, with inscription and stalactite border around the top of the walls. Unfortunately the miḥrāb has had its marble lining stripped, probably during the depredations of Salim. The original wooden minbār and the doors of the various cupboards have geometrical decoration, inlaid with ivory. A door in the S corner of the qiblah līwān leads into the tomb, which is decorated with marbles similar to the madrasah. A foundation inscription and verses from the Qur'ān in white marble with red painted background run round the walls, while the dome is raised on a squinch with multiple niches. There is an original wooden Kursī in the tomb. The tomb of Sultan Qāyt-bāy surrounded by a wooden maqṣūrah lies directly in front of the miḥrāb, while in the W corner is another attributed to one of his sisters. A door in the W corner leads to another room with further tombs.

In the late 15C one of the mu'adhins at the Madrasah Muḥ. al-Bināni, whiled away his time by carving inscriptions from the Qur'ān and other religious texts on the inside walls of the minaret. They date from 1480–1505.

To the SW of the Madrasah of Qāyt Bay is the **Mausoleum of Ibn Ghurāb** (94), a traditional, but probable ascription. Sa'd al-Dīn b Ghurāb, a noble and brilliant civil amīr, made his mark early. By the time he was 20 he controlled the privy purse under Sultans Barqūq, 'Abd al-'Azīz and Farag, directing the government in the reign of the latter. He died in 1406 before reaching the age of 30. The style of the building fits in well with this date, and it was left standing in the midst of Qāyt-bāy's complex of which more buildings are found to the W.

Next to this mausoleum is the **Tomb of al-Gulshānī** (100), an uninscribed building built by Qāyt-bāy as his own tomb while he was still amīr, shortly before his elevation to the sultanate in 1468. The disorganised façade of tiles is a much later addition during Ottoman rule, but the dome is original and has a similar pattern to the arabesques on the dome of his final tomb nearby, but lacks the geometrical element. The interior is unremarkable except for the peculiar multiple niched squinches that support the dome; of unequal sizes, the niches are carved with crisp arabesques. Adjoining this tomb are the remains of the palace that Qāyt-bāy had built here in 1474, the only extant section of which is the huge **Maqʿad of Sultan Qāyt-bāy** (101). The façade is as beautifully executed as the rest of his complex; it has five windows with decorated arches and a large band of inscription across the summit in fine sections. Above are the remains of a wooden awning.

Adjoining the madrasah to the S is the façade of the **Tomb of Murād Bay** (95), built about 1474 and therefore an integral part of the complex but subsequently used for the interrment of the grandee, who died of plague in 1801. Further to the S is the **Sabīl of Qāyt-bāy** (412) in the wall of the *Bayt al-Gundī* (House of the Soldier). Now isolated, but once the main entrance in the wall around the whole huge complex, is the adjacent **Bāb Qāyt-bāy** (93), also called Bāb al-Gundī. It has medallions in the spandrels and was built at the same time as the rest.

Down a small lane to the E of the complex lies the **Tomb of Sh. ʿAbd Allāh al-Manūfī** (168). It is undated and generally thought to be the work of Qāyt-bāy but the form of its dome suggests an earlier date. The venerated shaykh died in 1348. The drum of the dome has 20 niches but only four pierce the masonry as windows. Fleur-de-lys in heavy relief and raised carving cover the dome. It was probably built sometime in the early 15C and may even predate the geometrically carved domes of Sultan Barsbāy's complex.

Following the road S, the first turning is a road E which leads after 70m to a small park. Follow the path through a large ornate gateway; directly ahead is the large domed **Qubbat Umm Waldah Bāshā**. It was originally the mausoleum of Bambah Qādin, but it was enlarged in 1881 for the interrment of the Khedive Tawfīq and his family.

Directly inside the door stands the tall white marble *Tomb of Bambah Qādin* (died 1871/2), wife of Ṭūsūn Pasha, mother of ʿAbbās I Pasha, and sister of Fatimah wife, of Ismāʿīl Pasha.

Immediately behind is the *Tomb of Khedive Tawfīq* (1852–92).

Son of a minor concubine (see Rte 15), Muḥ Tawfīq was virtually ignored by his father Ismāʿīl who consistently tried to have him barred from the succession. Unlike his brothers, he was not given the benefit of a foreign education. But circumstances dictated that, as the eldest son, on his father's deposition in 1879 he was elected to the Khedivate. He was a mild and unworldly man and his reign (1879–92) saw the army rebellion under Aḥmad ʿUrabī, defeat by the British at Tell al-Kabīr, and the occupation of Egypt in 1881. He was succeeded by his eldest son, ʿAbbās II.

The tomb is made of ebony inlaid with other woods, ivory and mother-of-pearl. Along the rear wall are a further three tombs. On the right is the white marble *Tomb of Khedive ʿAbbās II* (1874–1944) who succeeded on his father's death (see above).

At first completely dominated by the personality of the British Resident, Evelyn Baring (later Lord Cromer), whom he despised, ʿAbbās had little opportunity to assert his authority. He systematically gained the enmity of the power groups in Egypt and even lost the support of the ʿulama by taking a Hungarian countess as his second wife. His encouragement of nationalist elements and supposed sympathy with the Germans in the First World War infuriated the British who deposed him in 1914 while he was visiting Istanbul. The rest of his life was spent in exile in Europe; he renounced all claim to the throne in 1931. He died in Geneva and his body was returned to Cairo.

In the centre is the *Tomb of Princess Amīnah* (1858–1931), wife of Khedive Tawfīq, mother of ʿAbbās II and Prince Muḥ. ʿAlī. On the left is the *Tomb of Prince Muḥammad ʿAlī* (1875–1955), second son of Tawfīq (Rte 3E). Although he died in Lausanne in 1952 President Sadat gave permission for his reinterment in this tomb.

Against the NE wall are two tombs. Nearest to the rear wall is the wooden *Tomb of the Princes Muḥammad ʿAbd al-Qādir and Muḥammad ʿAbd al-Munʿim*, the two sons of ʿAbbās II. ʿAbd al-Qādir (1902–19) died young; ʿAbd al-Munʿim (1899–1979) was regent for Aḥmad Fūʿad II after the deposition of King Fārūq in 1952. Towards the door is the *Tomb of Princess Fatḥiyyah* (1899–1923), daughter of ʿAbbās II. In the corresponding place on the opposite wall is the family library.

In 1984, because of civic development, the bodies of various members of the royal family were transferred to this mausoleum from the royal vaults of the Mosque of Nabī Danyal in Alexandria. They were placed to either side of the vestibule. On the left side lie the remains of *Muḥammad Saʿīd Pasha* (1822–63), son of Muḥ. ʿAlī and ruler from 1854 to the year of his death. Other members of his family include his mother, *ʿAyn al-Ḥayyat* (died 1849), his wives *Inji* (died 1890) and *Malak Pir* (died 1886), his sons *Maḥmūd* (died 1846) and *Muḥ. Ṭūsūn (1853–76), and the latter's son Muḥ. ʿUmar Ṭūsūn* (1872–1944), the famous historian. On the right-hand side are other children of Muḥ, ʿALī, including *Ḥusayn Bay* (1825–47), *Tawhidah* (1787–1830) who married Muḥarram Bay, and the notorious *Nazlī* (1797–1860) who married Muḥ. Bay al-Daftardār and whose exploits terrified the royal ḥarīms long after her death.

In a small garden to the SW of the mausoleum are the *Tomb of Princess Niʿmat Allāh* (1881–1966) and the *Tomb of Princess Khadīgah* (1874–1951), two daughters of Khedive Tawfīq.

Return along the road and continue W for 150m where, at the corner of a lane running E–W, is the all-brick **Tomb of Amīr Ṭashtīmūr** (92) who was called Ḥummuṣ Akhḍar. The tomb was built in 1334.

During the confused period following the death of Sultan al-Nāṣir Muh. in 1341 many amīrs seized the opportunity to further their position. Qawṣūn, the most powerful, elevated the child Kujuk to the sultanate, but Ṭashtīmūr supported an older brother, Aḥmad, who resided at Karak. In the mêlée that followed Qawṣūn was arrested and executed, and Aḥmad was elected sultan. Ṭashtīmūr was made Nāʾib of Egypt in 1342 but was shortly after arrested by Aḥmad, taken to Karak in chains and executed. His nickname Ḥummuṣ Akhḍar (green chick pea) derives from his youthful fondness for the vegetables.

In the base the entrance has an inscription between two blazons each of which has three fields, the central field containing a cup. This is the insignia of the gāshankīr (taster), a post Ṭashtīmūr held under Sultan Qalāwūn. The plastered brick dome has rib and fillet decoration.

Further W a main thoroughfare, the SHʿ AL-SULṬĀN AḤMAD, runs N–S. On the W side of the road stands the **Qubbat Amīr Azdumur** (90), locally called al-Zumr, the remains of a late 15C complex. In addition to the tomb there is a sabīl and the remnant of a small mosque.

From the next turning to the W it is possible to cross the Ṭarīq Ṣalāḥ Sālim to al-Darrasah and buses (No. 66) returning to Maydān al-Taḥrīr.

Continue S and pass on the E (130m) the **Qubbat Kūzāl** (89) which has the local name of Sīdī Karkar. It was completed in 1403.

At the next junction to the W (60m) are two brick tombs. That to the N is the remains of the **Khānqāh and Tomb of Khawand Ṭughāy** (81), wife of Sultan al-Nāṣir Muḥ., who was also called Umm Ānūk as she was the mother of his eldest son, Ānūk (Rte 5). A Qipchaq and sister of Amīr Agbughā, Ṭughāy was originally a slave but was freed by the sultan. Because of her great beauty and piety she was the sultan's favourite wife, a position which gave her much wealth and power. She outlived her husband and died of the plague in 1348. This building was raised in the same year. Once considered one of the most beautiful buildings in Cairo, little now remains of the complex. The great gateway and wall still retain some excellent stucco work while the dome with its rib and fillet decoration is raised on a drum with a faience inscription, recalling tile decorations on other buildings of this sultan's reign.

Opposite is the **Tomb of Khawand Ṭūlubiyyah** (80) of 1364, wife of Sultan Ḥasan. After Ḥasan's confinement and presumed death at the hands of Amīr Yalbughā al-ʿUmarī she married the latter. She died in 1364; Yalbughā was arrested and executed two years later. This is a much less lavish building; the outer gate with foundation inscription leads into a court in which stands the mausoleum with rib and fillet dome. The stone tābūt inside has an inscription.

The main road becomes the SHʿ. QARĀFAT BĀB AL-WAZĪR and passes through the next section of the cemetery, *al-Qarāfat al-Migāwirīn* (Cemetery of the Students; i.e. of al-Azhār). The next monument to the W (40m) is the **Tomb and Ḥawḍ of Qāḍī Muḥammad Mawāhib** (456), an early Ottoman building of 1685. S of this on the E side of the road (40m) is the **Tomb of Amīr Naṣr Allāh** (88), built c 1441. This civil amīr's nickname, Kuz al-ʿAṣal, meaning 'Pot of Honey', refers to the small sweet musk melon and may have been a reference to his predeliction, appearance or disposition. Although of the usual type the tomb is crudely built with a fleur-de-lys cresting around the summit of the cube, stepped corners to the zone-of-transition and inscription above the windows in the drum. On the dome the continuous horizontal chevron pattern resting on a base of mullets is very coarsely carved. Close by to the S is another small tomb, the **Qubbat al-Amīr Azrumuk** (87), built in 1503–4 by an Amīr of One Hundred of Sulṭān Qānṣūḥ al-Ghawrī. This has complex evolved fleur-de-lys cresting around the cube, while the corners of the zone-of-transition are geometrical with a double round-headed window with an oculus in each side. Several features about the dome are of interest. The pattern is similar to that on the tomb of Sh. ʿAbd Allāh al-Manūfī (No. 168: see above), but lacks the basal motif, and it reverses the raised and sunken areas. In the centre of each element, over the whole dome, is a round or tear-shaped turquoise faience drop.

To the E (c 300m) near the railway line are two monuments of interest. To the N is the much ruined **Tomb of Ṭaybughā al-Ṭawīl** (372), who was an amīr of Sultan Shaʿbān II and later governor of Hamah. He died in 1367 and this building must be slightly earlier than that. Within its walls is the **Tomb of Muḥ. Abū ʾl-Khayr al-Ṣūfī** (373), a theologian, which was built in 1449.

Beyond the Qubbat Azrumuk along the Shʿ. Qarāfat Bāb al-Wazīr (100m) is a crossroads. The road E towards the SHʿ. AFIFI leads to another tomb, **al-Qubbat al-Sādāt al-Shanāhrah** (85), but considered by Creswell to be the Tomb of Amīr Qarāqugā al-Ḥasanī (died 1449). However, it can be dated stylistically about a century earlier, i.e. early 14C and may have been reused for Qarāqugā (who built a mosque; Rte 12). He and his son died of plague on the same day. The summit of the cube has fine stepped cresting, while the octagonal zone-of-transition has stepped corners. No inscription encircles the dome, which is characteristic of the earlier period with rib and fillet carving. As it is unplastered it displays the method of construction.

Beyond the SE borders of the modern cemetery in the empty area on the far side of the railway line and on a low spur of the Muqaṭṭam Hills (300m) are two tombs. The larger building to the N, the remains of the **Khānqāh and Tomb of Amīr Tankizbughā** (85), is important. Little is left of the former, save the walls, but the isolated tomb in the enclosure is intact. The second of this amīr's two tombs, it was built in 1362, four years after his death (the other is in the Southern Cemetery, Rte 15). The two buildings have much in common but also differ greatly in certain features. Although retaining the shape of the domed cube, unlike the earlier tomb, this tomb is in the rare canopy form. The base is undecorated, with a pointed-arched opening in each side, on top of which is a low pedestal upon which is set the octagonal zone-of-transition with a pair of horseshoe-arched windows in each alternate face, all features quite different from that of the other tomb. In the drum of the dome are six keel-arched windows alternating with similar shaped niches, above which runs the band of inscription. The dome is decorated with carved alternating ribs and flutes similar though more elongate than the other tomb; these are the only two domes in Cairo in which this pattern is found. At the far end of the enclosure stands the minaret of only two tiers but the ribbed cap rests on a spear head frange similar to that decorating the other tomb. SW of No. 85 is the **Qubbat al-Wazīr** (Tomb of the Minister; 84), a 14C structure.

To the S down the Shʿ. Qarāfat Bāb al-Wazīr (c 800m) is another group of tombs on the SW edge of the cemetery. The first is the remnant of the **Khānqāh of Niẓām al-Dīn Isḥāq** (140; 25:1), built in 1356. He was the director of the Khānqāh al-Siryāqūs outside Cairo. Just to the W on the road stands the **Sabīl of Amīr Shaykhū** (144; 24:2). It was built in 1354 by the atabak of Sultan Ḥasan who also built the double mosque and madrasah complex at the Shʿ. al-Ṣalībah (Rte 13). This is the earliest free-standing fountain in Cairo and was built around a natural grotto, which probably contained a spring. A large semi-dome is raised above the rectangular base on pendentives. Around the bottom of the dome is a foundation inscription with two carved blazons of the amīr, a cup. In the dome itself are five pointed-arched recesses.

On the W side of the road stands the **Tomb of Amīr Yūnus al-Dawādār** (139; 24:2). Built in the 1380s, this is the second tomb built by this amīr, the first being given to Anas, father of Sultan Barqūq (see above).

Yūnus, a confidant of Sultan Barqūq, was entrusted with the administration of the country, but on his return from Syria, where he had faced a revolt by the amīr Yalbughā, he was captured by the Mirā Arabs and beheaded in 1389.

A small mosque attached to the tomb has almost disappeared. The tomb is distinguished by the unique elongated melon-shaped dome. The octagonal zone-of-transition has windows in each side and supports a tall drum with four trefoil-headed windows and similarly shaped recesses.

*The Tomb of Amīr Yūnus al-Dawādār*

Rich carving covers the area between the windows and includes the amīr's blazon of three fields, on the upper field a penbox, and on the middle and lower fields a cup. The dome has a rib and fillet decoration with each rib springing from a small stalactite bracket. Thus it is similar to other Cairene domes of the period which show this Central Asian feature. Inside the walls are painted with black arabesques.

On the same side of the road to the S (50m) is the **Mosque of Mangak al-Silāḥdār** (138; 24:2), a once extensive complex built in 1349. The door of his palace can still be seen (Rte 9). To the W is the isolated minaret, probably always so. The upper sections are restored.

Mangak al-Yūsufī (died 1375), originally a mamlūk of Sulṭ. Qalāwūn, held many important posts in the stormy times following the death of al-Nāṣir Muḥ. Although spending some time in prison, he finally rose to the posts of Na'ib and Atabak.

Most of the mosque is modern but to the N a long flight of steps leads down into the large arched tomb. The entrance on the road, which is perhaps older, has carbochan mouldings. Directly opposite is the 18C **Sabīl and Basin of ʿAbd al-Raḥmān Katkhudā** (260). The road reaches the top of the hill and runs down towards the Citadel. On the W side is the *Tomb of Ragab al-Shīrāzī* (476), built in 1379, and largely a ruin. The road then becomes the Sikkat al-Maḥgar, passing on the right the Shʿ. Bāb al-Wazīr (Rte 9) and leading into the Maydān Ṣalāḥ al-Dīn (Rte 11).

# 9 Al-Darb al-Aḥmār to the Citadel

Rtes 9 to 12 cover the central areas of the East city. This itinerary (1.2km, with detours totalling several hundred metres) starts at the Bāb Zuwaylah (Rte 6), easily reached from the Maydān Aḥmad Mahīr (Rte 7), and ends at the Citadel. **Cairo Atlas 17, 24**.

The Bāb Zuwaylah is reached from Maydān Aḥmad Mahīr (Rte 7) or Maydān Al-Azhar (Rte 4). Running directly S from the gate is the Shʿ. al-Khiyyāmiyyah (Rte 10), the southern extension of Shʿ. al-Muʿizz li Dīn Allāh, with the Mosque of al-Ṣāliḥ Talā'iʿ on the SE corner (leading to the Maydān Sayyidah Nafīsah). To the E runs the DARB AL-AḤMĀR which gives its name to the whole district.

This road turns SE, passing a 40m-section of the walls of Badr al-Gamalī behind the buildings on the N. At its junction (200m) with SHʿ. ABŪ ḤURAYBAH stands the **Mosque and Tomb of Amīr Qagmās al-Isḥāqī** (114; 17:5), called locally the *Mosque of Abū Ḥuraybah* as it contains the tomb of a 19C shaykh. This is a beautiful late Mamlūk building, although much restored by the CPAM, built in 1480-81.

It demonstrates an extreme and unique solution to the problem, acute by the late 15C, of erecting a large building in a built-up metropolitan area. Although the site is an irregular triangle, the interior is symmetrical with another part of the complex on the N side of the Shʿ. Abū Ḥuraybah reached by a bridge.

The pious and honourable Qagmās, after a distinguished career under Sultan Qāyt Bāy, was created viceroy of Damascus in which city he died peacefully and was buried in 1487. Sh. Abū Ḥuraybah was buried in the tomb-chamber in 1852.

It is a raised mosque resting on a foundation of shops, but this cannot now be fully appreciated as the ground level has risen considerably. Although the exterior is rather plain the proportions are impressive with the tomb in the S angle. At the corner of the building are engaged pillars and the various angles of the tomb are filled with long stalactite-headed recesses, with bronze grilled windows and excellent carving on the lintels. Qagmās's blazon of three fields, in the upper field a napkin, in the middle field a cup between two horns and in the lower field a cup, is engraved on the grills of the sabīl. To the NE above the entrance is the sparsely decorated minaret with three tiers, the lowest octagonal, the second cylindrical and the third composed of a pillared pavilion. Below the minaret is the sabīl-kuttāb. The dome over the tomb, unusually for the period, is completely plain. A trefoil arch covers the doorway which opens onto a porch with two passages leading off to the NE and SE.

The former leads through an original sliding door into the ṣaḥn. This building is a covered madrasah with the lateral līwāns reduced to arched recesses, and the qiblah līwān larger than the ṣaḥn. The līwāns are fronted by pointed horseshoe arches. The decoration is magnificent, though much restored, and typical of the period with an impressive coloured marble floor and geometrical marble and bitumen paste patterned dado and miḥrāb, the latter being inscribed with the name of the decorator, ʿAbd al-Qādir. Fine inscription runs around the summit of the wall above which is the excellent carved and gilded ceiling with stalactite

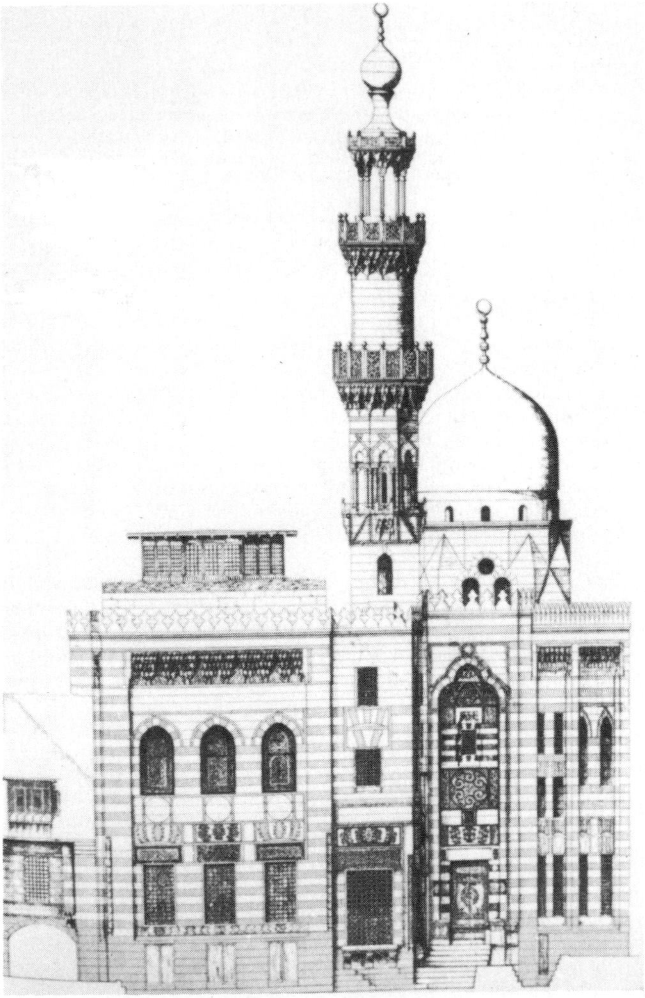

*The Mosque and Tomb of Amīr Qagmās al-Isḥaī*

corners. Also impressive is the contemporary wooden minbār of small wooden panels inlaid with ivory.

From the NE corner of the ṣaḥn a passage leads to the bridge spanning the street (to the ablution court). The SE passage from the porch leads into the tomb-chamber, elegant in proportion but undecorated save for an inscription; it contains only the tomb of Sh. Abū Ḥuraybah. In the sabīl is a fine pavement of blue faience mosaic.

The Shʿ. Abū Ḥuraybah leads E and divides. The NE fork passes (50m) on the W the **Sabīl of Muṣṭafā Musallī Shurbagī** (232; 17:5), built in 1715 by a military official. The fork to the SE leads (250m) to a small square, on the N side of which is the **Mosque and Tomb of Amīr Aṣlam al-Silāḥdār** (112), built in 1344–45.

Created an amīr of one hundred by Sultan al-Nāṣir Muḥ., Aṣlam was the object of a great slander and spent six years in prison but was released and regained his former position. Later he was made governor of Safad in 1341, but gained the enmity of the powerful atabak Qutlubughā who was involved in manipulating the sons of al-Nāṣir Muḥ., Aṣlam was dismissed a year later and died in Cairo in 1346.

There are two façades to this mosque, NW and—the main façade—NE. On the latter much of the decoration has been lost, but there are three full-length recesses each containing two pairs of windows, the upper consisting of two lights with ornate arches covered by an oculus. Bronze grills fill the lower rectangular windows. At the W corner is the minaret, a much later replacement, while the dome of the tomb rises at the S corner. Keel-arched windows pierce the drum, above which runs a rare example, though very dilapidated, of a band of faience marquetry inscription; the dome is ribbed. Along the summit of the wall runs a heavy cinquefoil cresting, perhaps a later replacement.

The entrance in the NE façade is covered by a simple trefoil recess, but the decoration of the doorway itself is very beautiful. Coloured marbles joggle the lintel, while above is a Naskhī inscription and over that a splendid large square of white marble set with coloured marble marquetry in a complex arabesque and star pattern. This entrance, which may have been exclusively for women, leads directly into the NE līwān; to the right is the entrance to the tomb. This mosque is seen to be cruciform, with covered ṣaḥn, perhaps the first of the type. An unusual feature is that each of the lateral līwāns is fronted by an arcade of three pointed arches supported on marble pillars, though the two axial līwāns have the usual great pointed arches. Around the upper wall of the ṣaḥn are sunken stucco medallions, diapers and fluted keel-arched niches, with Kufic inscriptions. In addition a carved wooden inscription runs around the walls. In the qiblah līwān the miḥrāb is a late example of stucco decoration, with the unusual addition of coloured faience insets. The wooden minbar is also a good example, and the pierced stucco window grills are excellent. The ceiling retains some of its rich polychrome pattern. In the tomb the dome is raised on a squinch of three tiers of niches.

The Darb al-Aḥmār now becomes the SHʿ AL-TABBĀNAH. On the W (50m) is the **Mosque and Tomb of Aḥmad al-Mihmandār** (115; 17:5), originally built in 1324, but restored for the Ottoman Sultan Ahmad III in 1732 and at the end of the 19C by the CPAM.

One of the great civilian dignitaries of Sultan al-Nāṣir Muḥ., Aḥmad b. Aqush rose to be Naqīb al-Jaysh (marshall to the army), Mihmandār and finally Amīr al-Ḥajj. He died in 1332.

The main façade is the SE wall of the mosque with the domed tomb at the N corner. Five full-length recesses, each with a different flat stalactite hood, divide the façade vertically, each containing two pairs of windows. Horizontally the façade is divided by a great band of foundation inscription and along the top of the walls is a continuous band of stalactites on which the trefoil cresting rests. The plastered brick dome is tall and somewhat pointed with bold ribs, but the minaret is Ottoman, probably part of the work of Aḥmad III. A richly decorated trefoil-hooded entrance in ablaq masonry and coloured marbles with several small windows opens on to a corridor with a carved wooden ceiling leading into the SW līwān. It can be seen that this is a cruciform mosque with unequal līwāns, the whole of the interior constructed in brick, with the roofed ṣaḥn, lit by a skylight, probably also part of the Ottoman reconstruction. Each of the lateral līwāns is fronted by two arches resting on a central marble pillar and has wooden ceilings, while the NW līwān is tunnel-vaulted with the door way to the right leading to the roof. An arcade of three arches, also supported on marble pillars, separates the qiblah līwān from the ṣaḥn, the central arch being the largest. All the decoration has been lost from the miḥrāb, but the beautifully carved shutters of the flanking windows are well preserved. An inscription on the minbar records the reconstruction of Aḥmad III. To the left is a doorway into the tomb-chamber, inside which the two lower windows are part of the original construction while the upper windows with stucco grills and coloured panes are Ottoman. In the zone-of-transition squinches of three over three niches raise the dome, between which are windows of three lights. A plinth of black and white joggled marble supports the marble grave with an ornamental Naskhī inscription.

Continue down the street on the same side. The next monument (100m) is one of the most ambitious buildings raised by an amīr in the 14C, the **Mosque of Alṭunbughā al-Māridānī** (120; 17:5), a medium-sized but still impressive enclosure mosque. It was built in 1339–40 and extensively restored by the CPAM in 1895–1903. It is now used as an annexe of al-Azhar Mosque.

While still young Alṭunbughā rose to be one of the most powerful amīrs. Soon after his purchase he joined the ranks of the Khāṣṣakiyyah and was quickly promoted to the rank of amīr. He married a daughter of Sultan al-Nāṣir Muḥ., but after the sultan's death was arrested by the amīrs Ṭashtīmūr and Qutlubughā. On the accession of the child Kujuk in 1342 he was released by the amīr Qawṣūn and created governor of Aleppo where he died in 1343, still less than 25 years old. Al-Nāṣir Muḥ. himself took an interest in the building of the mosque and ordered his chief architect Ibn al-Suyūfī to supervise the construction.

The façade is rather plain save for the recesses containing the windows with joggled lintels, a band of inscription from the Qur'ān running along the top of three of the walls, and the impressive stepped cresting around the summit. Over the miḥrāb the dome is plain, part of the modern reconstruction. There are three entrances: in the SW wall, in the NW with fine stalactite hood, and in the NE close to the road. The NE entrance consists of a high pointed vault, on the rear wall of which is the doorway surmounted by a panel of carved stone and joggled marble, and very unusual polychrome faience window grills. Directly to the E of the door is the minaret, the first two tiers octagonal, the lower storey with keel-arched recesses; the third tier, a pillared canopy. This is the first completely octagonal minaret and also the first with bulb crowned canopy. The large indent in the E corner of the mosque may have been intended for the tomb of the founder.

INTERIOR. The qiblah riwāq has four pointed arches, each of the other riwāqs two. The pillars supporting the arches, though fine, are an indiscriminate collection of Roman, Christian and Islamic types. Around the upper walls of the ṣaḥn are circular and diaper-shaped recesses, while those in the spandrels of the arches are keel-arched. Although the cresting around the top of the ṣaḥn is similar to that on the exterior, the section in the centre of each wall is crowned by a peculiar green-glazed inverted cone. In the centre of the ṣaḥn is an octagonal wooden fountain canopy erected during Ottoman times. An immense wooden mashrabiyyah screen divides the qiblah riwāq from the rest of the mosque, a unique feature. Athough much restored this is apparently part of the original design. Along the top is a fine carved Naskhī inscription. The miḥrāb is one of the finest in Cairo, a beautiful example of marble marquetry and joggling inlaid with mother-of-pearl. Above is an extremely fine panel of stucco, carved with unusual tree designs. Also excellent is the carved and inlaid wooden minbar. Eight massive red granite Ancient Egyptian pillars, with gilded Ptolemaic capitals, support the arches under the dome. Pointed and gilded wooden stalactites fill the corners of the zone-of-transition, alternating with carved stucco windows, but the dome (as noted) is reconstructed. A dado of coloured marbles inlaid with mother-of-pearl and Kufic rectangles lines the qiblah wall. The ceiling is painted and gilded, below which runs a carved inscription, painted white on a blue background. In front of the miḥrāb the stone dikkah rests on tall pillars.

From the S corner of the mosque the SHʿ. AL-MĀRIDĀNĪ leads S. On the W side (50m) is the **Tomb of Yūsuf Aghā al-Ḥabashī** (229; 17:5), built by a senior black eunuch beside his house in 1604. On each side of the windows of the tomb are small water troughs for animals, the decoration retaining Mamlūk motifs.

Beyond the Mosque of Alṭunbughā the next monument on the Shʿ. al-Tabbanah (20m E) is the **Sabīl-Kuttāb of Muḥammad Katkhudā al-Mustaḥfiẓān** (230; 17:5), built in 1677. 20m further on is the **Tomb of Yūsuf Abū ʾl-Yūsufayn** (Father of two Yūsufs; 234; 17:5), a popular attribution for a zāwiyah, with a tomb set forward at the N corner, for which inscriptional and documentary evidence is entirely lacking. By style it can be dated to c 1330. It consists of the tomb chamber with ribbed brick dome and remains of a small mosque with only one līwān to the NW; it has suffered much damage. An unusual feature is the oblique entrance from the līwān into the tomb chamber.

Passing the Shʿ. al-Nabawiyyah on the E and the Sūq al-Silāḥ the main road now becomes the SHʿ. BĀB AL-WAZĪR. 150m along on the W is the **House of Aḥmad Katkhudā al-Razzāz** (235; 17:7), an Ottoman complex of 1778 on the site of a rabʿ of Sultan Qāyt-bāy, the doorway of which (dated 1494), with cartouches, still stands. Mashrabiyyah casements overhang the road and the entrance leads to a huge building, probably the remains of the original Mamlūk apartments. The complex is in the process of reconstruction.

Adjacent to, and S of, this is the **Madrasah and Tomb of Sultan Shaʿbān II** (125; 17:7), which since it was built in 1368 by the sultan for his mother, as all the inscriptions verify, is called *Umm al-Sulṭān* (mother of the sultan). Impressed by the beautiful Turbah al-Sultān'yyah in the S cemetery (Rte 14) the architects of this building attempted a similar device of domed tombs flanking the qiblah līwān. However this is much less successful and the form was not repeated.

It is also one of the most extreme examples of a building forced to conform to the constraints of the existing street plan. The axis of the building lying at almost 45° to the main façade.

Ḥusayn, the last surviving son of Sultan al-Nāṣir Muḥ., did not live long enough to ascend the throne after the death of his brother al-Manṣūr Muḥ. (II). In 1363 his son, the ten-year-old Shaʿbān, was invested instead. The most powerful amīr, Yalbughā, tried to depose Shaʿbān, but with the support of the populace and the Royal Mamlūks he survived. Of quiet and pleasant manner, his reign was peaceful, but marred by famines and an impoverished treasury. In 1376 Shaʿbān made arrangements to perform the pilgrimage, but his mamlūks revolted and he was strangled. This mosque was built during the early years of his reign while he was still under the influence of his mother Khawand Barakah, who was to endow the building.

The exterior is divided by full-length recesses with stalactite heads, each containing three windows, the lowest rectangular, those in the centre with pointed arches, and the uppermost double with round arches covered by an oculus. The cresting is of fleur-de-lys type. Above the main façade the first two stages of the minaret are octagonal, the first with keel-arched recesses and engaged pillars, the second with a chevron pattern; the third storey is a modern replacement. The balconies rest on very ornate stalactite corbels.

In the NE façade is the very beautiful entrance with a triangular stalactite canopy, around which is carved a shallow trefoil inscription, the spandrels filled with arabesques. A carved lintel and joggled relieving arch cover the doorway above which is a pair of horseshoe-arched windows and an oculus, the whole surrounded by an inscription in the form of a pointed arch. To the left of the entrance is the sabīl with an exceptionally large and fine wooden grill. The angle between the entrance and the ṣaḥn contains several living chambers. The qiblah façade retreats along a side street and is in fact further curtailed by another alley. Above the tomb chambers the ribbed domes are somewhat small for the height of the façade.

This is a cruciform madrasah with an open ṣaḥn, around which runs a band of Kufic inscription and at the summit fleur-de-lys cresting. In the qiblah līwān the dado and miḥrāb of coloured marbles are not outstanding but the ceiling retains some of the original gilding. The minbar is good but plain and was presented to the mosque by a contemporary amīr called ʿAlī, whose identity is a matter of speculation. It is unlikely to have been Shaʿbān's son ʿAlī, who was briefly sultan after his father's death, as he was much too young. A recess with stalactites flanks each side of the līwān, containing the doorways to the tombs and also a window, each with magnificent carved wood and ivory grills opening on to the tombs, To the N is the *Tomb of the Women* containing the marble inscribed grave of Shaʿbān's sister Khawand Zahrah (died 1368) and to the SW the uninscribed limestone grave of his mother Khawand Barakah (died 1372); Shaʿān was also buried in the same chamber. Decoration is very sparse although with a fine miḥrāb and the dome is raised on four large simple squinches. On the S side of the qiblah līwān is the *Second Tomb*, very similar in construction but smaller.

Opposite this tomb on the E side of the road and set in a small garden are the remains of the **Zāwiyat al-Hunūd** (i.e. of the Indians; 17:7), receiving its name as the residence of Bukharīs of the Qādiriyyah brotherhood in the 19C. Of indeterminate Ottoman date, the remains consist of an arched-fronted līwān in which a semi-domed miḥrāb is set. Behind this rises the **Ayyūbid Minaret** (237) of two stages, built c 1260 during the closing years of the Ayyūbid period. The mosque to which it was attached has disappeared and its name is long forgotten. No foundation or other inscription has been found.

The total height of the minaret is c 20m. It is built of darkened bricks reinforced with palm-trunks; the stucco decoration is in extremely good condition, though darkened with age. It is set on a rectangular sectioned base 3.5m high, inside which is a small room entered by a vaulted tunnel in the E side. The first stage of 6m has a square section, each side decorated with a ribbed keel-arched niche with a keel-arched panel in the centre, the spandrels of which contain ribbed medallions. There are two later windows, one in the W and a smaller one in the N side. The entrance is at the base of the N side but the stair no longer exists. The stages are topped by a balcony, now restored, resting on the original great beams. The second stage (c 9m high) is octagonal with keel-arched panels on each face with decoration in the spandrels. Around the top runs a cornice of stalactites rather more elaborate than that on the minaret of the Madrasah of Sultan Ṣāliḥ Ayyūb. The whole is crowned by a ribbed cap which again differs from that of Ayyūb in being more elongated. These two facts suggest a close relationship to that building, but this minaret is further developed.

The area to the S along this road was much developed during the Ottoman period and many of the monuments for the next few hundred metres date from then. Adjacent to the Ayyūbid Minaret on the E side of the road are the *Sabīl* (238) and *Houses Waqf of Ibrāhīm Aghā Mustaḥfiẓān* (595), the first built in 1639 and the last in 1652.

Ibrāhīm, commander of the janissaries, was a protégé of Raḍwān Bāy and thus of the Faqāriyyah faction. He assisted Ibrāhīm Pasha in the suppression of the Faqāriyyah Bays but was himself exiled to Mecca in 1662. He returned to Cairo and died in 1664. He was responsible for much of the mid 17C building activity in this area.

At the corner of the building is the DARB AL-SHAGHLĀN. Up this, behind the last complex, is the *Tomb of Ibrāhīm Khalīfah Gindiyān* (586) which must have been standing when the houses were built as it is dated 1593. On the W side of the Shʿ. Bāb al-Wazīr on the corner of the DARB AL-QAZZAZĪN is the *Tomb and Sabīl of ʿUmar Aghā* (240), built in 1652. Along the W of the Darb al-Qazzazīn is the *Zāwiyat Muḥammad Ḍirghām* (241), a 16C mosque.

Also in the Shʿ. Bāb al-Wazīr, stretching down the W side, is the *House of Bagwārah* (240), while on the E side lies the **Mosque of the Amīr Aqsunqur** (123; 17:7), also called the *Mosque of Ibrāhīm Aghā* or alternatively by Europeans the *Blue Mosque*. Raised originally by Aqsunqur in 1346–47 and used for the interment of the child sultan Kujuk in 1345, it had fallen into ruin and was extensively remodelled by Ibrāhīm Aghā in 1652 when it received the wall of blue tiles from which it receives its popular name. Like the Mosque of al-Māridānī, this was built by the Chief Architect, Ibn al-Sufuyī.

Aqsunqur (White Falcon) was a mamlūk of Sultan al-Nāṣir Muḥ. and when he became an amīr he married one of the sultān's daughters. After the death of al-Nāṣir Muḥ. he advanced to reach the rank of viceroy of Egypt under Sultan Ismāʿīl. He was assassinated during the political intrigues of Sultan Ḥājjī I in 1347.

Designed as an enclosure mosque, the exterior has been little changed. The façade on the street is the NW wall at the N end of which the tomb, covered with a ribbed dome, makes a salient. In the wall is a fine round window with joggled voussoirs. At the S end rises the simple but elegant minaret with two (originally four) cylindrical sections, the second with ribs, and an octagonal third tier with a cap supported on pillars. In the centre is the entrance with a great round arch springing from graceful brackets and inside (left) the *Tomb of Sultan Kujuk* is part of the original structure.

Kujuk (Puppy) was raised to the throne in 1341 at the age of six by the rapacious amīr Qawṣūn, replacing his deposed eldest brother Abū Bakr. He reigned for a few months only until the arrest and execution of Qawṣūn by his arch-enemy the amīr Yalbughā. Aḥmad, another older brother, was invested as sultan and Kujuk was returned to the ḥarīm, where he lived until 1345 when he died, probably by strangulation, on the order of another brother, Sultan Shaʿbān I.

To the E of Kujuk's tomb is a small building containing the *Tomb of the Amīr Aqsunqur*, while the *Tomb of Ibrāhīm Aghā* is to the right, a flat-topped building, the interior covered with faience and marble panels. The single arches of the NW, SW and NE riwāqs were originally raised on massive piers with cross vaulting but for the most part these were replaced by Ibrāhīm with pillars and the vaults by a wooden roof. Of the two arcades in the SE riwāq the outer now also rests on pillars but the inner still retains the octagonal piers and vaulting. In the centre of the ṣaḥn is an octagonal fountain built for the amīr Ṭughān in 1412. In the qiblah riwāq is a fine miḥrāb with a double-pointed arched frame supported on baton pillars; the decoration consists of nice joggling and marble marquetry, with two blind arcades of trefoil arches supported on double pillars. Above is the dome raised on a tall octagonal drum which rests on simple squinches, between each of which is a double window. To the right is the really magnificent marble minbar, one of the earliest of the type, with coloured marble inlay on the sides, a stalactite lintel over the door and a canopy with complex arches. Each of the doors is beautifully inlaid. Another radical change wrought by Ibrāhīm Aghā was the facing of the whole of the qiblah wall with tiles of provincial Ottoman type probably made in Damascus. The tiles display floral patterns, in shades of blue, green and turquoise, some of them in large panpanels of lamps flanked by cypresses. Although charming and unusual in Cairo, in comparison with metropolitan Ottoman types they are distinctly inferior besides being somewhat delicate for the strong lines of a Mamlūk mosque.

Immediately adjacent to the S is another *House Waqf of Ibrāhīm Aghā* (619; 17:7), of similar date to the last, and further S the irregular but impressive façade of the **Mosque, Tomb and Sabīl-Kuttāb of Amīr Khayrbak** (248). The tomb was built while he was an amīr in 1502 but the mosque and sabīl were erected after the Ottoman conquest during his term as first Turkish walī of Egypt. It is important because it spans the transitional period between the Mamlūk and Ottoman eras.

Born in Samsun on the Black Sea, Khayrbak, with his brother Gānbalāṭ, was bought as a youth by Sultan Qāyt Bāy. Sultan Qānṣūh al-Ghawrī invested him with the governorship of Aleppo in 1504, a post he still held in the dramatic year of 1516 when Sultan Salīm advanced against the Mamlūk Empire. Khayrbak however had already made his choice and, although he welcomed Sultan Qānṣūḥ and his defending army and was commander of the left wing of the Mamlūk army at the decisive battle of Marj Dabiq, he defected at the critical moment to Sultan Salīm. After the conquest Khayrbak was created governor of Egypt, for which he had to suffer the punning title of Khayn (traitor) bak from the sultan. His treachery was complete: he dressed in Ottoman style and spoke only in the Ottoman dialect. His period of office was disastrous for the Egyptians. He was cruel and harsh and Ibn Iyas stated that the happiest moment the people knew during his tenure was his death in 1522.

The façade on the road consists of the NW wall of the Sabīl-Kuttāb to the first return, the entrance and facia of the mosque, and at the next salient the tomb. In common with the rest of the later section the *Sabīl* is solidly

*The Mosque and Tomb of Amīr Khayrbak*

built with engaged pillars at the corners and grills set in the masonry on three sides, each opening onto a trough with joggled lintels and double bands of moulding. Above is the *Kuttāb* with wooden casements. The entrance has a conventional but debased trefoil hood with stalactites in the side lobes, but departs from convention in having a pointed arch over the doorway surrounded by dogtooth moulding; in the spandrels are marble marquetry panels. A wide recess flanked by two small recesses, all with stalactites, fills the façade of the *Mosque*, in which are windows, the lower rectangular, the upper with pointed arches. Above the angle of the tomb rises the minaret, unusual in springing from a vaulted room on the second storey rather than the usual solid block of masonry. Only two stages remain; the first octagonal with keel-arched niches in each side, and above the complex stalactite corbel the second, cylindrical and quite plain.

In contrast to the later sections, the *Tomb* is refined in construction. It is a typical late tomb with two sets of windows, the upper paired with round arches and covered by an oculus. Triple windows with three oculi pierce the zone-of-transition, the corners of which are geometrical. The drum has narrow windows and above is the marvellous carved dome, with two interlaced patterns, a plain knotted ogee imposed over riotous grooved arabesque; the overall effect is extremely beautiful. From the SE wall a large round arch connects the building to the palace (see below).

INTERIOR. To the left of the porch is the entry to the sabīl, but a passage leads into a yard to the right of which is the entry to the Mosque. Inside are two lateral līwāns each fronted by a round arch. The ṣaḥn, however, is unique in Cairo, the roof being formed of an enormous cross vault in the centre of which is an octagonal skylight. All the masonry is executed in ablaq red and yellow stonework. In the centre of the coloured marble wall the miḥrāb has a pointed arch set in a similar frame; to its right is the good wooden minbar. It would seem that the plan of the interior was changed after the external walls were built since the stonework of the vaults obscures part of the two window frames on the qiblah wall. A stone dikkah fills the small recess opposite the miḥrāb. In the SW līwān are two doorways, the smaller leading to the vaulted room beneath the minaret; the door to the S is much larger, similar to the main entrance except that it has a flat lintel, and leads into the tomb chamber, which like the exterior is of traditional Mamlūk type and well decorated. In the S corner stands the tomb of Ganbalat, Khayrbak's brother who was interred here in 1502, and Khayrbak himself 20 years later.

As mentioned above, the tomb is externally attached by a great round arch to the **Palace of Alīn Āq** (249; 17:7), an amīr of Sultan Khalīl. The only part of this structure, built originally in 1293, to remain untouched is the great square-headed portal at the S end. The great qāʿah at the rear was reconstructed by Khayrbak who used it as his residence, and it subsequently received much redecoration during Ottoman times. To the W on the roadway is the large *Drinking-trough of Ibrāhīm Aghā* (593) built in 1659. The road then begins to rise and further to the S on the E (100m) is the **Madrasah and Tomb of Amīr Aytmish al-Bagāsī** (250; 24:2). Built in 1383–84, it is much ruined but the tomb is interesting.

Aytmish was an amīr of Barqūq who because of his courage and loyalty reached the highest rank of atabak in 1398. After the death of Barqūq he was made, with the amīr Taghrībardī, regent for Farag, but was forced to allow the young sultan to rule alone. He rebelled and escaped to Damascus where he was captured and executed in 1400.

Above the cubic base with fleur-de-lys cresting, the zone-of-transition has stepped corners and rhomboidal windows in each side. Above the drum, with keel-arched windows alternating with similar niches, rises the dome. It is an example of the period when the stone-masons, completely at home with the ribbing technique, were beginning to experiment; in this case the ribs rise conventionally enough but above a quarter of the way up bend obliquely to the right and continue in a curve to the apex.

A lane leads beside the N wall of the madrasah into the W section of the **Qarāfat Bāb al-Wazīr,** the cemetery immediately to the SW of the Eastern Cemetery (Rte 8). To the N (60m) is the **Tomb of Amīr Azdumūr** (113; 24:2), one of the last monuments of the Mamlūk era. Built at the beginning of the 16C for one of the chief dawādārs of Sultan Qānṣūḥ al-Ghawrī who died in 1507 and also built a mosque (Rte 15), the present building is much ruined and only the minaret is original. Just S of it is the **Tomb, Sabīl-Kuttāb and Door of Amīr Ṭarābāy al-Sharīfī** (255) who was chief of the Corps of Mamlūks. This is the remains of a madrasah complex built in 1503. The tomb is a magnificent example of late Mamlūk workmanship, with stalactite-headed recesses in the cube, complex cresting and triple windows covered by three oculi flanked by cartouches, all the elements surrounded by double bands of moulding. Large scrolls cover the corners of the zone-of-transition, but only six windows pierce the drum, and the band below the dome is of arabesque only, while the dome has a simple but very well carved and constructed continuous chevron pattern. Notice that the upper domed unit has tilted slightly and now sits at an angle on the cubic base.

Adjacent to this tomb is the **Trough of Amīr Aytmish al Bagāsī** (251; 24:2), built in 1383, the same year as his mosque.

To the SE (60m) on an elevation stands the **Tomb of Ṣandāl al-Mangakī** (327), built at the end of the 14C for the pious and respected Greek eunuch, treasurer of Sultan Barqūq, who died in 1397. It is a simple stone structure of typical form, with pointed-arched recesses with windows in each side of the base. The zone-of-transition has simple scrolled corners and a double window with an oculus in each side, while the drum is pierced by eight windows and supports a plain dome.

Opposite the Mosque of Aytmish a road leads NW and then S into a small square. On the SE side (100m) stands the **Ribāṭ and Tomb of Aḥmad ibn Sulaymān al-Rifaʿī** (245; 24:2) built in 1291. The original building is in stone with the brick tomb inserted in the E corner. All of the NW wall (the main façade) and the SW wall are restorations of the CPAM.

Aḥmad b. Sulaymān was a descendant of the Rifaʿī family from S Iraq and was shaykh of the brotherhood in Egypt. This ribāṭ was built for him and he died here in 1292.

Inside, a row of three oval pillars forms an arcade in front of the miḥrāb while a pillar against the NW wall shows that there must originally have been another such row. The main miḥrāb has a ribbed hood inside a keel-arched frame with Naskhī inscription. Surrounding it is a stucco frame with foliate spandrels and inscription in round-ended panels. To the S is another miḥrāb which must have been similar to that in the tomb (see below). There are two entrances to the tomb chamber, that on the SW now with a wooden grill. Around the walls of the tomb is a painted inscription on wood. Squinches of two tiers of niches raise the drum which has keel-arched niches and four windows, one of which retains its original foliate stucco grill. The whole of the interior of the dome is thickly covered with carved stucco, this mosque and that of Zayn al-Dīn Yūsuf (Rte 15) being the only two buildings in Cairo to retain this feature. The miḥrāb has a keel-arched hood framed with carved foliate stucco and inscription. This is conventional enough, but incorporated in the decoration are small glass panels painted with green, brown and black patterns, a technique unknown in any other Muslim building. In the centre of the chamber is the wooden tābūt of Aḥmad carved with an inscription and inlaid with ivory (the first use of this technique in Cairo).

Along the SW side of the square is the *Sabīl of Amīr Khalīl* (376) of 1761.

150m along the E side of the Shʿ. Bāb al-Wazīr is the SIKKAT AL-KAWMĪ, down which the impressive rectangular mass of the **Bimāristān of Sultan Muʾayyad Shaykh** (257; 24:2) rises in isolation.

Shaykh built this hospital between 1418–20, the second of these great public works erected in Cairo. He chose an area previously occupied by the Madrasah of Sultan Shaʿbān so patients could benefit from the elevation and the cooling breezes blowing from the N. A prayer hall was added in 1421. Unlike the hospital built by Sultan Qalāwūn, this one did not remain in continuous use and was probably turned into dwellings. In the early 18C the Gāmiʿ al-Sukkarī was built against its façade. The latter was removed in the early 20C, and the imposing façade reached by a large flight of double steps was exposed.

The first element that strikes the eye is the towering portal, one of the largest and most impressive in Cairo. It is built in Persian style with a pishtak rising above the height of the façade, a feature also found in this sultan's mosque (Rte 6). A pointed arch covers a stalactite canopy in the centre of which is a half dome. Below this is a double window in a keeled-arch recess, flanked by panels of geometrical carving. Although the doorway and lintel are plain, on each flank of the portal on the main façade, below a keeled-arch recess, is a very large panel of rectangular Kufic inscription in white marble and dark blue faience. The whole façade is divided into panels by a huge linked S frieze and on each side of the entrance is a pointed arch window in a square recess. In the interior the roof has fallen but the walls still stand and the essential features of the building with its cruciform plan can be distinguished. To the left inside the doorway is a very finely carved pillar and behind the porch is a fine triple window, each light having a round arch.

The Shʿ. Bāb al-Wazīr enters the SIKKAT AL-MAḤGAR below the NW walls of the Citadel and the route descends down the hill. On the left is the **Tomb of Sulṭan Qānṣūḥ I Abū Saʿīd** (360; 24:2). Although he reigned only for one year in 1499, he managed to have two tombs built for himself, one in the Eastern Cemetery (Rte 8) and this monument. This is much the smaller; inferior in design and construction, it was presumably the first one built. Several primitive features—the geometrical windows with three lights in the zone-of-transition, the keel-arched windows in the drum and the plain dome—all point to an earlier date, and it may well be that it was constructed while he was still an amīr.

Opposite is the Zāwiyat Ḥasan al-Rūmī (Rte 14) and at the foot of the hill to the N the free-standing **al-Maḥmūdiyyah Mosque** (135; 24:3). This was built in 1567 for Maḥmūd al-Maqtūl, Ottoman governor of Cairo between 1566–68. His harsh administration resulted in his assassination by gunshot. The façades are divided into a series of stalactite-headed recesses containing windows on two levels. In the NE and SW walls are the doorways and against the SE wall a tomb chamber, with a plain dome and many windows around the drum. Against the S corner rises the ribbed and carved cylindrical minaret; the three tiers, with the two balconies supported on stalactite corbels, are surmounted by a cone. The alignment of the elements of the building is exactly the same as in the nearby Mosque of Sultan Ḥasan and indeed throughout the building the decorative motifs are Mamlūk. A sunken path leads across the interior to the ablution court. Four great antique granite pillars support arches which raise the lantern. All the ceilings are of painted and gilded wood below which runs a carved foundation inscription. The windows are of coloured glass set in pierced stucco, while the minbār is of wood. To the left of the stone miḥrāb is the entrance to the tomb chamber.

The road descends further, past the Mosque of Sultan Ḥasan (Rte 10) to the N and the Bāb al-ʿAzab of the Citadel, to the Maydān Ṣalāḥ al-Dīn (Rte 13).

# 10 Shʿ. al-Khiyyāmiyyah to the Citadel

This itinerary starts from the same point as Rte 9 and takes alternative roads to the Citadel. **Cairo Atlas 17, 16, 24**.

Immediately opposite the Bāb Zuwaylah (Rte 6) is the SHʿ. AL-KHIYYĀMIYYAH (Street of Tentmakers), taking its name from the men who sew the beautiful applique panels that are then made up into the large marquees. It has been a centre of this craft since the 17C. Sections of the work can be purchased. This road is really an extension of the Shʿ. Muʿizz li Dīn Allāh from the enclosure of Cairo running S towards the Old City. As with other long streets in Cairo its name changes several times along its course. From Fāṭimid times, the area just outside the Bāb Zuwaylah was used for executions, either by beheading or hanging.

On the W corner of the street is the **Zāwiyah and Sabīl of Sultan Farag** (203; 17:3), called al-Duhayshah, built for the sultan by Yūsuf al-Ustadār c 1408. Although minute it reproduces in detail the architectural features of the larger mosques in stone and coloured marbles. The fountain from the interior is now in the MIA.

During the 17C this area was developed by the powerful grandee Raḍwān Bay, leader of the Faqiriyyah faction, and was called the Qasbat Raḍwān. He built many structures here including a small mosque, a sūq, apartment houses and a palace for himself. Raḍwān's great influence brought him into direct conflict with the Ottoman viceroys, although he held the post of Amīr al-Ḥājj for over 25 years. After an attempt by Muḥāummad Pasha to have him sent to Abyssinia in 1638 Raḍwān went to Istanbul to plead with Sultan Murād IV. However, he was held in confinement, but on the accession of Sultan Ibrāhīm in 1640 released. His opposition to the viceroys did not cease and with the support of his colleague ʿAlī Bay he retained his supremacy. He died in 1656. Directly behind the zāwiyah is one of the apartment buildings erected by Raḍwān and down the small lane to the W is the *Zāwiyat Raḍwān Bay* (365; 17:5), his mosque of 1650.

Set on the E corner of the street is the magnificent **Mosque of Wazīr**

**al-Ṣāliḥ Ṭalā'ī'** (116; 17:5), built in 1160. It has several innovations, some of which became permanent features in later buildings, others remained unique. Although essentially still in the form in which it was built, it was badly repaired in the early 20C and features were added with little reference to the true structure. The ground plan covers an area of c 60m by 20m and the construction is brick with a stone facing to the outer walls. This is a suspended mosque, the first built in Egypt and a practice that was to be followed often in succeeding centuries. The basement consists of a series of small vaulted shops, once at ground level, upon which the body of the mosque rests. Besides providing income for the upkeep of the mosque it also ensured that the precincts would be kept clear of surrounding buildings and markets.

In 1154 the assassination of the Fāṭimid khalīf al-Ẓāfir resulted in bloody riots in Cairo. During the chaos the women of the palace in desperation cut off their hair and sent it to the most powerful amīr in the country the Armenian-born Ṭalā'i' ibn Ruzzīk, governor of Ashmunayn. He entered Cairo at the head of a great army and Al-Fā'iz was proclaimed khalīf. Ṭalā'ī', with the title al-Ṣāliḥ, restored order and disposed of the recalcitrant amīrs and officers. Al-Fā'iz died in 1160 and another child, al-'Ādid, was raised to the khalifate. Soon after al-Ṣāliḥ Ṭalā'ī' was poisoned by an aunt of the khalīf but survived long enough to see her executed in front of him. He had two dying regrets: that he had not conquered Jerusalem, and that he had built the present mosque on this site, which being just outside the walls could be used by an enemy as a fortress. In character al-Ṣāliḥ Ṭalā'ī' was cultured and refined, a poet and patron of the arts, and extremely generous and approachable.

The mosque suffered badly in the great earthquake of 1303 and the original minaret set over the main entrance fell. The amīr charged with the reconstruction was Baktīmūr al-Gukandār. Further restoration was undertaken by a merchant, al-'Aynī, in 1440 and the amīr Yashbak min Mahdī in 1477. By the end of the 19C the ground level had risen considerably, the shops below had fallen into disuse and the complex was hemmed in by buildings. In 1923 the Mamlūk minaret also fell, which prompted the CPAM to undertake a complete restoration of the mosque. At present al-Azhar maintains a junior school on the premises.

The NW façade, containing the main entrance, has a salient at each end formed by rooms projecting from the mosque. These are joined in front of the entrance by an arched screen, which thereby forms a large portico with an arcade of keel-arches raised on antique columns with Corinthian capitals. This unique feature with North African precedents was never repeated in Cairo. Between the columns are sections of mashrabiyyah copied from those which formed the original maqṣūrah. The remains of the bridge leading to the entrance were found which allowed people to visit the shops without detouring around the steps. The bridge has been reconstructed, but the bifurcated section is a modern device to save space. Windows in the corner salients are set in fluted keel-arched recesses, with a medallion in the centre of the hood. The practice of setting windows in recesses was to become universal in the buildings of Cairo. In the spandrels of the arches are decorated medallions, and bands of inscription cross the recesses. The chamfered corner of the wall is converted to a right-angle about half-way up by means of a fine corbel. Little remains of the carved cornice and the undercut stepped and decorated cresting has also disappeared (sections can be seen in the interior).

In the NE façade is a medial portal set in a small salient. Shops occupied only the N end of this façade and the windows are also set in recesses with keel-arched hoods. The SW wall is for the most part reconstructed, while the rear wall is pierced only by windows. In the façade containing the main entrance are five recesses with decorated keel-arched hoods. In the central recess is the entrance. The ceiling of this portico contains sections of the original while the fine double bronze-plated doors are copies of the originals (now in the MIA).

A tunnel-vaulted passage leads into the NW riwāq. The ṣaḥn (23.5m by 18m) is surrounded on the other three sides by riwāqs, the lateral riwāqs with one arcade, the qiblah riwāq with three arcades. Creswell proved conclusively that the present NW riwāq was a modern innovation and did not exist in the original. The lateral riwāqs present six keel-arches raised on pillars on the ṣaḥn, and the qiblah riwāq five arches. Above each arch is a fluted medallion and between each a keel-arched panel resting on small columns. In the qiblah riwāq the impost blocks and tie-beams are original but the ceiling is modern. A band of stucco Kufic inscription runs around the arches, as in the al-Aqmar mosque, and rectangular openings with grills surmount the apex, while in the spandrels are fluted medallions. The only decoration left in the miḥrāb is a fragment of coloured mosaic in the left shoulder flanking octagonal pillars and the wooden lining of the hood with indistinct painted design. The superb minibar, the fourth oldest in Egypt, was presented by Amīr Baktīmūr in 1300, prior to the great earthquake. It is of wood in geometrical panels with mashrabiyyah bannister and pointed arched canopy surmounted by a finial. Directly behind it is a malqaf (wind vent), the first appearance of this device in a mosque in Cairo, surrounded by a decorated border. Seven pointed arch windows pierce the rear wall, each surrounded by the original carved frames of decorated Kufic and palmettes. The central window is set in a decorated panel. In the S corner a blind frame contains an original Naskhī inscription, one of the first appearances of this script in monumental form in Egypt. Against the SE corner is the Ottoman *House of ʿAbd al-Ḥamīd Waʿdī* (364; 17:5) of 1606.

Beyond the Mosque of Talāʾīʿ the *façades* (406, 407) on each side of the road are mid-17C Ottoman and were constructed by Raḍwān Bay. Incorporated within them are earlier structures. The street has retained its roofing which preserves much of the original appearance. Along each side of the road are small shops used by craftsmen. On the E (100m) is the **Madrasah and Tomb of Maḥmūd al-Kurdī** (117; 17:5), a small building of 1375 with a decorated façade.

Maḥmūd (died 1396) was a poor student who rose to be ustadār of Sultan Barqūq. He took on to his staff the indigent Sāʿad al-Dīn b. Ghurāb (see Rte 12) who undermined his authority. Barqūq had Maḥmūd arrested and his goods seized.

The zone-of-transition of the dome has stepped corners and the drum has eight windows. Of great interest is the dome as this is the first stone dome to depart from the rib and fillet decoration. It has a continuous horizontal chevron pattern which was to become very common and supercede completely the earlier pattern. The brick minaret is cylindrical, plain except for vertical ribs on the central section and stalactites which support the balconies.

On the W side of the road a small lane leads to the *Maqʿad Raḍwān Bay* (208), the remnant of the grandee's palace built (like the other buildings in the area) c 1650.

At the end of the façade of the qasbah on the W side (80m) are the 17C

*Sabīl al-Wafa'iyyah* (557) and the **Madrasah and Tomb of of Īnāl al-Yūsufī** (118; 17:5), built in 1392.

A courageous man, Īnāl was raised to the amirate by Sultan Shaʿbān II and became viceroy of Syria. He supported the rebellion of Yalbughā and after the restoration of Barqūq in 1390 he was made atabak, a post he retained until he died.

Like Mahmūd al-Kurdī's mosque, this is a small and charming building. The two tombs are related in that Inal's has the last ribbed dome in Cairo, albeit of a modified type. The ribs divide and entwine at the base and alternate with flutes.

Beyond the covered qasbah the road becomes the SHʿ. AL-MAGHARBILĪN (Street of Sievers) and after 70m on the E side the Shʿ. Māridānī passes the remains of a **Pavilion of Sultan Qāyt-bāy** (228; 17:5) built in 1485. An arched porch at the angle on the S side of the lane leads into a court. At the S end is a very fine façade with a large maqʿad of three colonnades with a small portal at the SE corner. Why the sultan should have built this small palace here is unknown. It may have been for a retreat from the bustle of the Citadel.

Just beyond the lane (50m) is the façade of the *Zāwiyat ʿAbd al-Raḥmān Katkhudā* (214), a small mosque. It was raised in 1723, the first building constructed by this great patron who for the next 30 years was to adorn Cairo with his structures. It has excellent detail around the windows and arched entrance. Above the latter is a small balcony resting on a stalactite corbel which in the absence of a minaret was used for the call to prayer. S is the **Mosque and Tomb of Amīr Ganī-bak al-Ashrafī** (119; 17:5) of 1426. This man was an amīr of Sultan Barsbāy and such was the sultan's regard for him that he transferred the body to a tomb within his own complex in the Eastern Cemetery (Rte 8). Although of cruciform type it is specifically described as a mosque in the inscription. The dome above the tomb has a stepped zone-of-transition and a horizontal chevron pattern. The two-tiered minaret is devoid of ornament.

Just S of this the road changes its name again to SHʿ. AL-SURŪGIYYAH (Street of Saddlers) and on the E side of the road (100m) is the *Tomb of the Awlād al-Asyād* (215) of the 14C. Further S (70m) on the same side a small lane leads to the *Tomb al-Qimārī* (128; 17:7), built c 1329. Beyond this lane on the W side (75m) is the magnificent *Gate of the Mosque of Qawṣūn* (224), all that remains of the mosque built in 1329 (noted in Rte 11). Locally it is called the Bāb al-Mahkamah (Gate of the Law-court). In the left shoulder of the portal is a sundial signed by Aḥmad al-Ḥarīrī in 1383.

Directly opposite stands the **Madrasah and Tomb of Amīr Gānim al-Bahlawān** (129; 16:8), the brother of Amīr Yashbak (Rte 11). It was raised in 1478 and the tomb was added in 1510. On the street is the NW façade with the tomb at the N end. The building was very well restored by Herz and the CPAM in 1896. The minaret is exceptionally rich. On the chamfered pedestal are stalactite brackets, while the octagonal first tier has keel-arched niches, the hoods supported on pillars. Above the pierced stone balcony resting on a stalactite corbel is the cylindrical second tier with deep arabesque carving. The final tier is in the form of a pavilion. At the S end of the façade is the entrance. The interior has a strange T-shaped plan and three arcades parallel to the qiblah wall. This arrangement was to appear quite frequently in Ottoman mosques, but is unique in Mamlūk architecture. A sunken path leads through the ṣaḥn to the ablution court. Above is a wooden ceiling with a central lantern.

Also on the E side of the road (50m) is the **Takiyyah and Madrasah of Sulaymān Pasha** (225; 16:8), built in 1543 by the khādim Sulaymān, governor of Cairo (1524–34) and wazir of Sultan Sulaymān II, the Magnificent. Steps lead through a gateway decorated with Mamlūk motifs into the raised court which is surrounded by an arcade, the arches raised on antique columns. The roof of the arcade is composed of shallow domes. At the rear of the arcade are small rooms for sufis and against the SE wall is a small mosque. This plan was repeated for the Takiyyah of Sultan Maḥmūd (Rte 12) 200 years later.

MOSQUE OF SULTAN ḤASAN

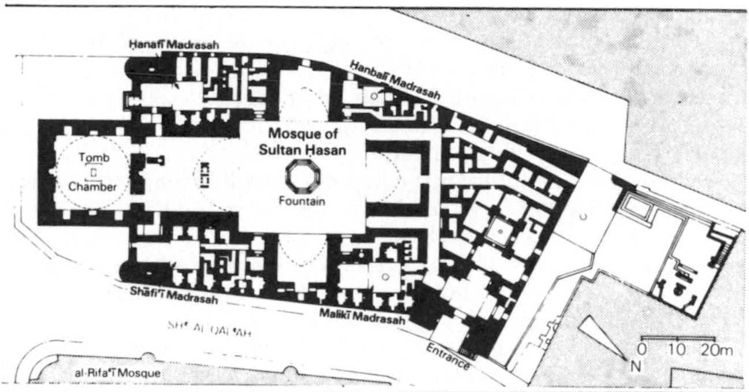
Ḥanafī Madrasah
Ḥanbalī Madrasah
Mosque of Sultan Ḥasan
Tomb Chamber
Fountain
Shāfiʿī Madrasah
Mālikī Madrasah
Entrance
al-Rifaʿī Mosque
0 10 20m
N

Just beyond is a crossroads. The Shʿ. al-Ḥilmiyyah (Rte 11) continues SW while the Shʿ. al-Qalʿah runs NW (to Maydān Aḥmad Māhir, Rte 7) and SE. Turn S along the latter and walk up the hill where the road passes between two colossal mosques, the sheer walls of stone giving the appearance of a man-made gorge, a fact commented upon by many visitors. On the W side of the road (400m) is the magnificent ***Madrasah and Tomb of Sultan Ḥasan** (133; 24:1), built between 1356–60. Its size was unprecedented (it is one of the largest mosques in the world).

Sultan al-Nāṣir Muḥammad had many sons who were eligible to reign at his death in 1340. He also bequeathed to Egypt his sons-in-law and other amīrs, all waiting to manipulate the succession for their own gain. Within a period of seven years five sons had succeeded and been disposed of by the amīrs, some of the most powerful of whom had fallen with their protégés.

At a meeting of the amīrs in 1347 Ḥasan was the unanimous choice as successor. He was at this time 12 years old, with red hair and freckles and gradually began to show signs of independence. He dismissed several prominent amīrs and to prevent his own dismissal the amīr Ṭāz confined Ḥasan to the harīm in 1351, raising the younger al-Ṣāliḥ to the throne. However the amīr Shaykhū waited until Ṭaz was away hunting in 1354 when he seized al-Ṣāliḥ, who in turn was sent to the harīm, and reinvested Ḥasan. The sultan, now 18, had spent his confinement in valuable study and with Shaykhū as his principal amīr concerned himself fully in the affairs of state. In 1357 Shaykhū was assassinated in the divan. His successor Ṣarghatmish rose to great power but was arrested and executed within ten months.

Ḥasan started to fill the official posts with civilian amīrs raised by himself, presumably in an effort to break the power of the military amīrs. In 1361, before he had time to put his intention fully into effect, the amīr Yalbughā al-ʿUmarī the Atabak rose in revolt. Ḥasan escaped from the Citadel and hid in the city but he was discovered and imprisoned by Yalbughā. He was never seen again but was probably murdered. He was succeeded by his nephew al-Ḥājjī II. Yalbughā married Ṭulubiyyah, wife of Ḥasan, but after further interference in the succession he was assassinated by his own mamlūks in 1365.

*The Madrasah of Sultan Ḥasan*

Why Ḥasan chose to build on such a scale (the measurements are at least twice those of normal mosques) is another imponderable. The building is in the form of a cruciform mosque with tomb, but it also contains separate madrasahs for each of the four schools, each with rooms for students. Ḥasan gave the order for its construction under the supervision of Amīr Muḥ. b. al-Muḥsinī in 1356 and work continued ceaselessly for four years. It was almost complete when Ḥasan disappeared after which it was finished by one of his functionaries, Bashīr al-Gandār. Craftsmanship throughout the building is of the highest quality. Two palaces belonging to the amīrs Yalbughā al-Yaḥyāwī and Tanbughā al-Māridānī occupied the site. The material is stone; internal details are in brick faced with stone. Four immense minarets were planned, one at each of the S corners and two above the great portal, but only three were built. That over the entrance, the W minaret, fell in 1361, shortly before Ḥasan's disappearance, killing over 300 people. The E minaret fell in 1659 and its collapse must have shaken the whole structure for the dome fell the following year. Ḥasan Aghā at the behest of Ibrāhīm Pasha undertook the reconstruction of both in 1671. The monumental character of the mosque made it almost a fortress and it was used as such several times during the conflicts of the amīrs, the roof providing an excellent site for the emplacement of catapults and cannon for the bombardment of the Citadel. To forestall its use against him Sultan Barqūq destroyed the steps and sealed the entrance, while Sultan Mu'ayyad Shaykh purchased the magnificent doors in 1416 and incorporated them in his own mosque (Rte 6). In 1422 it was reopened by Sultan Barsbāy.

On the Sh'. al-Qal'ah is the NE façade, stretching 76m from the entrance which, as with so many Mamlūk buildings, is rather severe (see below). The sheer walls (36m high) have narrow stalactite-headed recesses, each with four pairs of windows set vertically. At the summit of the walls is a massive cornice of five layers of stalactite which projects 1.5m. Above this was fleur-de-lys cresting but this was removed during Ottoman times, to relieve the weight, and it only remains around the tomb. At the S end of the façade is a semi-circular bastion which once supported the E minaret; the present much smaller Ottoman replacement consists of two undecorated octagonal tiers. In the centre of the SE face the tomb chamber (24m sq.) rises the full height of the main façade, each side has two recesses with rounded stalactite hoods, containing two pairs of large windows, the upper window of double lights with an oculus. Between each recess is a large medallion with a central oculus surrounded by carved decoration. Original cresting can be seen along the summit of the wall. Above, the dome is set on a high multifaced drum. It has a relatively shallow profile and is supported by eight pairs of semi-round buttresses. This is the Ottoman restoration, but the original was probably similar to that over the tomb of Imām Shāfi'ī (Rte 15), a timber frame covered with lead sheeting, with a stucco or faience facing.

Above the W corner is the remaining original minaret, the highest and most massive in Cairo (81.6m). Although sparsely decorated its sheer size is impressive with two octagonal storeys surmounted by a pavilion, each with a stalactite cornice. The SW façade is similar in decoration to the NE although incomplete. The odd angle at which this portal is set was quite deliberate, so that it could seen and admired from the royal palace in the Citadel.

Set at a slight angle at the N end of the NE façade is the massive portal. On the corners of the slight salient are full-length, helically carved, engaged columns. Flanking the entrance two screen walls contain a series of carved rectangular panels, that in the centre with geometrical decoration. Between the panels and the entrance are full-length bands of foliate carvings with huge carved medallions at the base. Next to these are square pillars with chevron capitals (perhaps removed from a Christian building), that on the right with little carved insets of buildings. In the thickness of the portal are decorative panels below which on each side are two recesses, flanked by small columns, with stalactite semi-domes. Over these are panels of decorated Kufic inscription in green and white (Sūrat al-Fatḥ v.1). Above is a further series of similar panels containing the shahādah and the names of the first four khalīfs. Over all is the immense stone hood, of conical section, filled with many layers of stalactites and surmounted by a ribbed semi-dome. The doorway itself is rather simple and modern wooden doors have replaced the superb doors which Muʿayyad Shaykh removed to his own mosque, Rte 6. An inscription running across the bay contains a fine Naskhī inscription from the Qur'ān (Sūrat al-Nūr vv.36–7).

INTERIOR. The vestibule (8.5m sq.) is covered by a large dome raised on pendentives and in each side, other than the entrance, are līwāns. On the flanks of the W līwān are keel-arched recesses and on the rear wall a panel of marble marquetry of superb quality. A door at the rear of the N līwān leads on to a balcony but that in the S līwān leads to the right up some steps. A corridor which bends to the left leads into the N corner of the ṣaḥn (34.6m by 32m). Again the scale of the building is apparent. Each of the līwāns is roofed with a brick-pointed tunnel-vault with a stone arch. Around the summit of the walls is the original cresting. Windows in the side walls open on to rooms for students and below these, flanking the NW and SE līwāns, are doorways with flat stalactite arches decorated with joggled voussoirs giving access to the four madrasahs which fill the angles of the cruciform plan. The madrasahs are placed thus: at the S corner Shāfiʿī, W corner Ḥanafī, N corner Ḥanbalī and E corner Malikī. Each consists of a central open ṣaḥn with a tunnel-vaulted līwān opening to the SE, that of the Malikī school being the largest, surrounded by the students' rooms. (On request to the guardian it is possible to ascend to the roof of the complex.)

The marble floor of the central ṣaḥn is a later addition, a poor substitute for the original, presumably removed by Salīm I. In the centre is the *Fawārah* (fountain) consisting of an octagonal wooden canopy on octagonal marble baton pillars, and surmounted by a bulbous stucco-covered wooden dome resting on an octagonal drum. The emplacement of the fountain is original (it used to be filled with sherbet on festival days) but the superstructure is enigmatic. Although the band of Naskhī inscription around the dome, beside a Qur'anic verse, gives the date 1364–65 (several years after the completion of the building) no other dome in Cairo has this peculiar profile and the drum and windows, set with coloured glass seem rather too coarse for the period. Perhaps this is an Ottoman replacement, which included the original inscription (or a copy of it).

Little ornament is retained in the NW or lateral līwāns but the principal *SE līwān* has retained much of the original work. Running around the walls of this līwān below the springing of the vault is a superb monumental stucco inscription in elongated Kufic on a field of arabesques (c 1.5m high) containing Sūrat al-Fatḥ (vv.1–5) which tells of the mercy of Allāh and the paradise awaiting the true believer. This is the only known architectural use of this script which was more generally used for the headings in illuminated manuscripts. It has the rare distinction of being signed. The facing on the lower part of the side walls is a replacement; the original probably reached up to the inscription. In the qiblah walls are two windows in recesses and an oculus above the miḥrāb. The marble panelling on this wall is set in carved wood frames held in place with wooden cleats. The pointed-arched *miḥrāb* is fine and covered with marble marquetry, arcades in the recess and chevrons in the hood. Double columns support the frame with complex joggled voussoirs. On the rectangular outer frame is a band of Naskhī inscription. The marble minbar has a large stalactite cornice above the entry. The doors are wood covered with bronze. Flanking the miḥrāb are windows with bronze grills. At the front of the līwān is the marble dikkah raised on eight pillars and three piers, the outer pair with polychrome columns attached. Around the platform is a marble balustrade. Hanging from the roof of the līwān are the chains that once held the beautiful enamelled glass lamps (some of which are now in the MIA).

TOMB. At either end of the qiblah wall doorways lead into the tomb chamber. The door on the right retains its original bronze facing with gold and silver inlay. The tomb chamber is set directly in front of the qiblah wall, an innovation since up to this time the tomb had occupied a position in one of the angles to the right or left of the qiblah.

The tomb chamber (21m sq.) has walls faced in a similar fashion to the qiblah wall, marble surrounded by carved bands of wood. In the centre of the NW wall is a large marble marquetry panel. Above the dado, running around all the walls, is a huge carved wooden frieze (2m wide) of Naskhī inscription, blue letters on a gold background. Above this, held out from the wall on brackets, is a frame for the suspension of lamps, richly carved and gilded. The miḥrāb is only slightly smaller than that in the mosque and the decoration is similar except that in one of the blind arcades the columns are of blue faience, not marble. At the corners of the walls are the lower parts of the wooden squinches of eight layers of stalactites—carved, painted and gilded—that supported the original roof. The whole of the N corner of the tomb has been restored to its original condition. In the centre of the floor is the unimpressive grave, with tābūt of coloured marble surrounded by a small wooden screen. Whether Ḥasan was interred here is not known but some of his descendants were, including his sons al-Shihāb Aḥmad (died 1386) and Ismāʿīl (died 1396).

Directly opposite, on the E side of the Shʿ. al-Qalʿah stands the **Mosque al-Rifāʿī** (24:1), its walls rising to the same height as those of Sultan Ḥasan's madrasah.

In the 19C this site was occupied by the Zāwiyat al-Rifāʿī, which contained the tombs of Sh. ʿAlī Abū Shibbak al-Rifāʿī and Sh. ʿAbd Allāh al-Anṣarī. It was purchased together with the surrounding buildings by the Princess Dowager Khushyar, mother of the khedive Ismāʿīl, in 1869. She wished to build a mosque incorporating tombs for the two shaykhs and herself and descendants. The mosque was designed by Ḥusayn Pasha Fahmi, Minister of Awqaf, and supervised by the chief eunuch, Khalīl Aghā. Princess Khushyar died in 1885 and was buried in the incomplete building, as was Ismāʿīl in 1894. In 1905 the khedive ʿAbbās II ordered that the mosque be completed under the supervision of Herz Pasha, chief architect to the CPAM, and the Italian architect Silvagni. It was finished in 1911.

Although immense, there is little innovation in the design of the mosque, all the decoration being derived from Mamlūk sources. The principal (NW) façade, admittedly impressive, faces a garden and contains the main entrance (formerly reserved for the royal family). It is regular, with the entrance reached by a high flight of steps. On the Shʿ. al-Qalʿah, the SW façade contains two entrances flanked by semi-round bastions from which rise the two neo-Mamlūk minarets. It is a covered mosque, the wooden roof with central lantern being raised on four massive piers with pointed arches. The workmanship is of high quality, if a little gaudy, and one of the most interesting aspects is the chance to see marbles in pristine condition, giving some indication of the original appearance of the weathered stone in the older mosques. Great marble tābūts surrounded by mashrabiyyah screens cover the tombs of Sh. ʿAlī and Sh. ʿAbd Allāh.

Behind the tomb of Sayyid ʿAlī lies another tomb chamber (not open to the public at present) which contains the tombs of *King Aḥ. Fū'ād I* (1868–1936); his mother *Firyāl*, a wife of Khedive Ismā'īl (died 1912); *King Fārūq* (1920–65), son of Aḥ. Fū'ād, his body transferred from the Ḥawsh al-Bāshā in 1975, and *Fawqiyyah* (1897–1974), daughter of Aḥ. Fū'ād and Princess Shawikār. Also buried here is *Muḥ. Reza Pahlavi* (1919–80), the last shah of Iran who died in Cairo.

Leave by the rear entrance into a vast arcade with four pavilions which contain further tombs of the former royal family. The first chamber to the left contains the *Tomb of Princess Khushyār* (died 1885), wife of Ibrāhīm Pasha and mother of the Khedive Ismā'īl; she was responsible for the foundation of this great mosque. Beside her tomb is the *Tomb of Khedive Ismā'īl* (1830–95). He reigned from 1863 to 1879 when he was deposed and exiled to Italy and then Turkey where he died. The second pavilion contains the tombs of Ismā'īl's wives: *Jasham Āffat* (died 1907), the third wife; *Jānanyār* (died 1912), the second wife; and *Shuhrat* (died 1895), his principal wife. Inside the third pavilion is the *Tomb of Sultan Ḥusayn Kāmil* (1853–1917), son of Khedive Ismā'īl, who succeeded upon the deposition of his nephew 'Abbas II in 1914. Beyond is the *Tomb of Princess Malak* (1869–1950), his second wife.

In the pavilion to the right of the exit are the tombs of the children of the Khedive Ismā'īl. Left of the door lies *'Alī Jamīl* (died 1893), and to the right of the door lies *Ibrāhīm Ḥilmī* (1860–1927), favourite son of Ismā'īl and Jānanyār and the one he really wished to succeed him. In the centre is the *Tomb of Tawhīdah* (1850–89) daughter of Shuhrat and close to the wall is the *Tomb of Zaynab* (1856–76), full sister of Ibraḥim Ḥilmī.

Just beyond these two mosques the Sh'. al-Qal'ah emerges into the Maydān Ṣalāḥ al-Dīn (Rte 13).

Turn along the SE wall of the Mosque al-Rifā'ī. Built on the extremity of the outcrop containing the Citadel is the **Madrasah and Tomb of Amīr Qānī-bāy al-Sayfī** (136; 24:1), a very late Mamlūk structure of 1503. He also built another mosque (Rte 12).

Qānī-bāy, who has the names Qarā (Black) and al-Rammah (Lancer) was originally a mamlūk of Sultan Qāyt-bāy. He was made an amīr of one hundred and rose to be amīr akhūr al-kabīr (grand master of the horse). His successful career continued after the conquest of Egypt by Selim.

Despite the elevation of the mosque the entrance has to be reached by a long flight of steps. The main façade is the SW wall; it is divided into a series of stalactite-headed recesses each with two pairs of windows. Against the SE wall stands the tomb, the zone-of-transition with geometrical corners and in each side triple windows with oculi above. Above the sixteen-sided cornice there are sixteen windows in the drum and excellent inscription. Rich carving covers the dome, a ground of grooved arabesque outlined and balanced by a plain lobed ogee. At the W end of the façade is the entrance covered by a plain trefoil arch. Above this is a three-tiered minaret, of typical later Mamlūk type. Each of the stages has a square section, the first two topped by a stalactite corbel. The third stage consists of two separate units each capped with a finial. Beyond the entrance is the sabīl, connected to the mosque by an arch (both are restorations).

The interior is of conventional cruciform plan with the līwāns fronted by pointed horseshoe arches. However, the ceilings of the līwāns, instead of being roofed with wood, show various types of vaulting. Above the SE līwān is a shallow dome on pendentives while the NW līwān has a cross-vault; the small transverse līwāns are barrel-vaulted. The inscription around the dome of the SE līwān still contains traces of gilding. Most of the marble facing of the walls has been stripped but the minbar is original. At the S end of the qiblah līwān is the entrance to the *Tomb*. In the tomb chamber the dome is raised on squinches with multiple niches below which runs the foundation inscription.

Behind the mosque to the NW is the 18C *House of ʿAlī Afandī Labīb* (497; 24:1). A little to the N on the opposite side of the road stands the 14C **Gate of the Darb al-Labbanah** (Alley of the Milkmaid; 325). This is one of the few remaining gates of the Mamlūk city. It consists of a carved stone porch with a pointed arch surrounded by heavy moulding.

Return to the Maydan Muḥ. ʿAlī. High on the W is the **Mosque of Gawhar al-Lālā** (134; 24:1).

Gawhar al-Julbānī was a Sudani eunuch who passed from Amīr Bahādur into the service of Sultan Barsbāy. He was tutor (lālā) to the princes and after the death of Khushqudam al-Rūmī in 1435 he was made chief eunuch. When Jaqmaq became sultan Gawhar incurred his displeasure; in 1438 he was dismissed and his money was seized. He died the next year.

This mosque, built in 1430, has been extensively restored. The dome over the tomb is a rustic Ottoman replacement and the fabric of the minaret was badly restored probably at the same time. It was restored by the CPAM in 1895–98. Most of the façade is original. A large recess with a flat stalactite hood contains two pairs of windows and an oculus. At the S corner an angled wall contains another pair of windows. The entrance porch with a flat stalactite hood covers a doorway with carved releasing arch and a window in a recess.

Opposite the N corner of al-Rifaʿī Mosque the SŪQ AL-SILĀḤ runs NE. At the corner on the W side stands the **Gate of Amīr Mangak al-Silāḥdār** (247; 24:1), all that remains of a palace built in 1346–47 by the same amīr who built the mosque near the Citadel (Rte 14). The gate consists of a massive stone cube, with two open sides. Steps lead down from the round-arched entrance on the road to a similar arch in the back wall, which is built at a lower level. The ground inside is now at a uniform level due to the accumulation of debris. A shallow dome resting on pendentives forms the roof, around the base of which is a band of inscription. Dividing the inscription is the amīr's blazon, a shield of three fields, in the central field a sword.

120m further, on the E side, is the **Madrasah of Amīr Ālgāy al-Yūsufī** (131; 17:7), built in 1373.

Ālgāy (Compatriot) was one of the mamlūks who made their mark during the mid 14C—the confused period of the reign of the sons of al-Nāṣir Muḥammad. He attained the position of an amīr of one hundred and the posts of amīr jandār and amīr silāḥ. He married Barakah Khātūn, widow of Ḥusayn, last of the sons of al-Nāṣīr Muḥammad and mother of Sultan Shaʿbān II. After her death in 1373 he disputed with the royal mamlūks over the immense property of this powerful woman. He was defeated in the same year and drowned in the Nile, although whether by accident or design is unknown.

This mosque is very elegant as the NW façade on the road testifies. Four full-length recesses divide the façade. Two have flat stalactite hoods and each contains three sets of windows in three tiers. The two other recesses are narrow and have fluted keel-arched hoods, and three windows. On the S corner is set the dome of the tomb. The zone-of-transition with stepped corners and triple windows with three oculi above is conventional enough, but the dome itself is unique. Although it is ribbed the masons, with complete mastery of this particular technique, experimented further. They have deflected the ribs at a 45° angle to the right and then swung them back to the left over the shoulder of the dome. This particular display of

*The Madrasah and Tomb of Amīr Ālgāy al-Yūsufī*

virtuosity was never repeated. To the N is the minaret with its octagonal first storey set with keel-arch recesses alternating with windows. A fine stalactite corbel supports the second plain cylindrical storey, but the third storey in the form of a pavilion is a reconstruction. At the N corner of the mosque are the remains of a sabīl, above which a solitary baton pillar supports the remnant of a stone canopy of a maqʿad. Above the entrance is a trefoil stalactite hood.

The interior is of cruciform plan, with an open ṣaḥn. In the SE and NW līwāns are the remains of fine gilded ceilings but the marble facings of the walls have been stripped. The minbar, although damaged, is contemporary with the mosque.

Directly opposite is the *Sabīl of Muṣṭafā Sinān* (246; 17:7), built in 1630; beyond this on the E side of the road (50m) is the *House of Muṣṭafā Sinān* (545; 17:7), probably built at the same time. On the W side of the road is the *Tomb of Sh. Saʿūd* (510; 17:7), a very early Ottoman building of 1534.

50m N on the E side is the exceptionally fine **Sabīl-Kuttāb of Ruqayyah Dūdū** (337; 17:7), built in 1761. This lady, whose nickname means parakeet, of the family of Shāhīn Bay was obviously very rich. The semi-circular fountain on the ground floor is very elaborately carved. Flanked by engaged pillars, three magnificent bronze grills gave access to the water. Above the wooden awning is the Kuttāb, also in wood with fine carving. This too has a wooden canopy, but with complex indentations, instead of the usual semicircular form.

40m further N, to the W is *Ḥammām Bashtak* (224; 17:7), of which only the entrance, fronting a modern bathhouse for women, has survived. Built c 1340, it consists of a fluted keel-arch surrounded by coloured marble mosaic and the blazon of this amīr (see also his palace, Rte 5). Along the lane running E. is the *Mosque of Alṭī Barmaq* (126), his name meaning 'six fingers'. Although built in 1711. it continues the tradition of Mamlūk decoration. The interior has an unusual basilican form. Around the miḥrāb is a facing of provincial Ottoman tiles.

E on the Sūq al-Silāḥ, just N of the last lane, is the site of the Mosque of Sudun min Zadah (127), a Mamlūk construction demolished in the 1970s. On the W side stands the *Sabīl-Kuttāb of Ḥasan Aghā Kukliyān* (243) of 1694. 90m further N, on the W is the *Madrasah of Amīr Quṭlūbughā al-Dhahabī* (242; 17:7), virtually in ruins. There is evidence of much rebuilding on to the original structure of 1347, both in Mamlūk and Ottoman times. Quṭlūbughā (Fortunate Bull) assisted the amīr Yalbughā in the deposition of Sultan Ḥasan in 1361 but managed to survive the transition to Burgī Mamlūk domination and died in 1406. On the E side of the road is the *House of Aḥmad Katkhudā al-Razzāz* (235; 17:7), the Ottoman entrance to the Mamlūk house mentioned above (Rte 9). Just beyond, the Sūq al-Silāḥ joins the Shʿ. al-Tabbānah (Rte 9).

# 11 Maydān Aḥmad Māḥir to the Maydān Sayyidah Nafīsah

This itinerary (2.4km) covers quite a distance and it might be best to attempt it in two stages. In this case termination at the Shʿ. Salībah (1.3km) is suggested. **Cairo Atlas 16, 23**.

The S section of the Shʿ. al-Qalʿah leaves the Maydān Aḥmad Māḥir to the SE. Along the first turning to the E is the derelict **Sabīl-Kuttāb of Ibrāhīm Bay al-Kabīr** (331; 16:4), built in 1753 by this powerful grandee. It is in the elaborate metropolitan style, with bow front and bronze grills. Within in the complex he incorporated the Tomb of Sh. Mubārak Zayn al-ʿAbidīn.

250m further, on the same side a small lane leads to the **Mosque of al-Malikah Ṣafiyyah**(200; 16:4). Although built in 1610 by ʿUthmān Aghā, it was subsequently claimed by Ṣafiyyah, grandmother of Sultan Aḥmad I.

The beautiful Ṣafiyyah, an Albanian, was the favourite of the Ottoman Sultan Murad III, which priviledged position did not protect her from the wrath of his Venetian mother the Velide Sultan, Nur Banu. But she survived and after the death of Nur Banu in 1583, of which she may not have been entirely innocent, she came into her own reaching the height of her power as Velide Sultan, when her son Muhammad III became sultan in 1595 after executing his brothers. She retained her authority until his death in 1603, but his son the 14 year old Ahmad I was very different and after refusing to dispose of his brothers he confined Safīyyah to the ḥarīm until her death in 1618.

ʿUthmān, chief black eunuch of Ṣafiyyah, had been released and went to Cairo where he built this mosque, providing several villages and houses for its upkeep. He died shortly after and Ṣafiyyah made representations to the chief qāḍī that ʿUthmān had still been her slave when he built the mosque and that it was therefore her property. The court agreed and thus credit for the mosque was transferred. Ṣafiyyah's agent was ʿAbd al-Raḥmān, ʿUthman's successor. As a reward he was made guardian of the mosque. Originally the mosque was surrounded by a garden entered by gates (see below). Ṣafiyyah provided 90 pieces of silver per day to pay for a Hanafi jurist, two imams, four muadhins, readers, lamplighters, cleaners, gardeners, waterers and a handyman.

The garden has long since disappeared, but the mosque is in exceptionally good condition. It is a forecourt mosque raised on a high windowless base with pairs of windows in the upper section. Access is by a high flight of semi-circular steps on the SW. In the centre of the same side is set the minaret of conventional Ottoman type with vertical ribbing and a stalactite corbel supporting a medial balcony. At the top of the stairs a wide trefoil arch surrounds the doorway with arched lintel. This leads into the small open forecourt. Each riwāq consists of three arches supported on columns and roofed with a series of small shallow domes, raised on pendentives, the central dome in each being oval. In the E corner is a more conventional Cairene dome covering a small room reached from inside the mosque. The exterior of the main dome is undecorated. The decoration on the SE wall is Mamlūk and a fine stalactite door leads to the interior.

The inside walls are of red and yellow ablaq. The centre is covered by the brick dome raised, uniquely, on six pointed arches supported by six granite columns, with classical capitals, in a hexagonal formation. On the NE and SW sides two smaller domes flank the central dome, and a similar sized dome covers the extension on the SE that contains the miḥrāb. In addition there is a small dome in each of the W and N corners. All the domes are raised on pendentives that accommodate themselves to the shape of the springing. Above the doors is a marble dikkah with wooden balustrade and around the base of the dome a gallery rests on wooden beams. Pierced stucco windows in the dome are set with coloured glass and there are also small circular openings in the dome. The white marble miḥrāb is decorated with other marbles in red, black and yellow. To the left is a panel of marble surrounded with an S-border. To the right is a lovely minbar of white marble, including even the doors. The open carved design on the sides is a copy of the wooden trellis in Barqūq's mausoleum (Rte 8). A mashrabiyyah screen leads to the domed room on the N corner that was probably reserved for women.

From a small lane to the NE of the mosque an alley leads to the *Gate of the Mosque* (330; 16:6) which is the only entrance to the garden remaining. In decoration it is entirely Mamlūk. Against the NE corner of the mosque is the *Sabīl-Kuttāb of Muḥammad Muṣṭafā al-Muḥasibgī* (329) dated 1716.

To the S, on the corner of SH'. AL-DAWIDIYYAH (80m), is the anomalous **Mosque al-Burdaynī** (201: 16:6). Although dated to the late 17C it is entirely Mamlūk in form and decoration inside and out. The founder was Karīm al-Dīn al-Burdaynī. The minaret, the earliest part of the structure, was built in 1629, also in Mamlūk style. This must have existed before the mosque was built in 1694. It is a compact mosque with stalactite-headed recesses each with two pairs of windows, below rectangular, above a pair of round-headed lights with an oculus. The minaret has two tiers, the lower octagonal with keel-arched niches surrounded by elaborate moulding, the second cylindrical carved with a reticulate pattern. The interior is in exceptional condition. Almost all the surfaces are covered with marbles of many colours in elaborate geometrical panels.

With its carved and gilded ceilings and beautiful miḥrāb it is difficult to believe that this mosque was built well into the Ottoman period. Where the particular craftsmen responsible for the various techniques came from is unknown for no work of similar competence had been produced in Egypt for almost 200 years and likewise there were no successors.

Immediately S of the Sh'. al-Dawidiyyah is the *Sabīl of Ibrāhīm Shurbagī Mustaḥfiẓān* (363; 16:6), built in 1694 by a janissary officer. Just beyond, returning to the main route, stands the *Sabīl-Kuttāb of Shāhīn Aghā Aḥmad* (328), built a little earlier in 1673.

On the W side of the Sh'. al-Qal'ah is the SIKKAT AL-ḤABBĀNIYYAH.

The large mosque on the E side of Sh'. al-Qal'ah (200m) is the *Mosque of Amir Qawṣun* (202; 16:8). It is almost entirely reconstructed and only a small part of the qiblah wall retains some of the original fabric. However the fine gate of the complex still stands to the E (see Rte 10).

After 200m there is a crossroads from which the Sh'. al-Qal'ah continues S to the Citadel (Rte 14). To the NE is the Sh'. al-Surugiyyah (to the Bāb Zuwaylah) and to the SW the SH'. AL-ḤILMIYYAH down which the route turns. The first mosque on the E side of the road (100m) is the **Mosque of Amīr Ālmās** (130; 23:2), built by a powerful amīr of Sultan al-Nāṣir Muḥammad. Ālmās (Diamond) rose to be ustadār and finally Viceroy of Egypt but was arrested and executed in 1333. This is a modified enclosure mosque with a stark exterior. At the NW angle is the tomb chamber with plain dome and to the right of the main entrance the minaret restored in Ottoman times. Along the top of the wall is an inscription from the Qur'ān and above a trefoil cresting. In the N wall is the fine entrance, with flat stalactite arch flanked by large octagonal baton pillars. On each side in the thickness is a stalactite panel. Above the complex joggled lintel and relieving arch is a double window filled with a rare carved wooden grill in place of the usual stucco.

Inside, the constricted space has necessitated a truncated form. It was only possible to construct the SW riwāq in the complete form, all the others are deficient. There are two arcades against each wall, except for the NW which has one, all with baton pillars supporting arches, those in front of the miḥrāb being more massive. All the riwāqs have wooden roofs. Remains of stucco ornament face the open ṣaḥn. The miḥrāb is decorated with coloured marbles flanked by fine columns, but little remains of the carved marble surround.

50m beyond is the *Rab' Tughug* (289; 23:2), a small section of a 15C apartment building, and on the N corner of the SH'. AL-MUẒAFFAR (100m) is the small **Tomb of Amīr Sangar al-Muẓaffar** (261). Built in 1325, it is now isolated, but was once attached to a mosque which appears in several 19C drawings. The restrained decoration has engaged columns on the outer corners. Recesses in each side contain windows and an entrance at the N end. An octagonal zone-of-transition supports the drum with eight windows and a band of inscription. The ribbed stone dome is one of the earliest in Cairo. On the S corner of the road is the *Sabīl Yūsuf Bay* (282; 23:2), a late Ottoman fountain of 1772.

On the W side of the road (60m) is the *Sabīl-Kuttāb and Rab' al-Qizlār* (265; 23:1), a complex erected by a black eunuch, the aghāsī qizlar (lord of the girls, i.e. the concubines). Many of the senior black eunuchs, after retiring from the Sultan's ḥarīm in Istanbul, chose to settle in Cairo. Opposite is the **Tomb of Amīr Sunqur al-Sa'dī** (263; 23:2), locally called the *Tomb of Ḥasan Ṣadaqah*, attached to which is a Mawlawiyyah takiyyah.

Built in 1315 by Sunqur al-Sa'dī, chief of the royal mamlūks of Sultan al-Nāṣir Muḥammad, it was intended as a madrasah for women. The tomb of the founder and several shaykhs is all that has survived. During late Ottoman times the Mawlawiyyah takiyyah (see below) was built on the site of the madrasah.

On the street is the façade of the NW wall of the complex in which is set the main entrance with minaret to the left and the walls of the tomb and the NW līwān. The entrance has a trefoil arch with fine layers of stalactites and elaborately joggled lintel to the doorway; above is a fine panel of carved stucco. The minaret is of early Mamlūk type—a square-sectioned base with keel-arched niches. Above the wooden balcony rise the octagonal second section, also with keel-arched niches, and an elaborate cornice of two tiers of stalactites supporting the ribbed cap with keel-arched profile. Unusually the finial is not crescent but in the form of a Mawlawiyyah Sufi hat. In the façade are two recesses with flat stalactite hoods containing windows. Above the lower windows of the tomb is another with two lights and an oculus (probably an addition). The zone-of-transition of the tomb is elaborately decorated with stucco. Borders of foliate tracery divide it into sections, set with round and oval panels. In the centre a window of three lights is surrounded by a pointed horseshoe frame resting on tulip baton columns. The frames and shoulders are filled with elaborate arabesques and inscriptions, motifs which are repeated in the window grills. Eight windows alternating with panels are set in the drum, and are also intricately decorated. A band of Naskhī inscription runs below the undecorated shallow brick dome.

From the entrance a narrow corridor leads to the rear of the tomb, with the entrance to the chamber on the right. Inside it measures c 8m sq. In the SW wall is the entrance to the NW līwān of the former madrasah. The lower walls are undecorated as is the wide shallow miḥrāb, but around the upper walls are two stucco inscriptions, the lower rising over the miḥrāb and window. This inscription is dated in figures 721 AH (AD 1321), a feature unique prior to the Ottoman conquest. Between the squinches of three tiers of fine niches are windows with three lights and, set in a beautiful stucco border in the drum, eight windows alternating with blind panels. There are four tābūts in the chamber. In front of the miḥrāb the largest is the *Tomb of Amīr Sunqur*, inscribed with his titles. To the S is the *Tomb of Shaykh Ḥasan Ṣadaqah* who died in 1315.

Fronting the NW līwān is the original arch, beyond which is the *Mawlawiyyah Takiyyah* built on the site of the ṣaḥn of the earlier madrasah.

The Mawlawiyyah Brotherhood were followers of Jalāl al-Dīn Rūmī (1207–73) who lived under royal patronage in Konya (Turkey). The Mawlawiyyah initiates in voluminous white skirts and tall hats are perhaps the most familiar of the sufi brotherhoods to the Westerner. It was disbanded in Turkey in 1926, and in Egypt just before World War II.

The building is being restored by the Italian Cultural Institute in Cairo with the help of the CPAM. Although mid 19C in date its condition renders it very unusual in the Middle East, most of the other buildings of this brotherhood being in great disrepair. It consists of a great domed hall called the Samaʿ-khānah (Listening House) with a central circular floor surrounded by a gallery on the ground floor, and another above. In the upper gallery sections, with the original mashrabiyyah, are screened off for women and the musicians. In the shoulders of the arches are medallions with the names of former mawlawīs. Contemporary paintings of genre scenes surround the base of the dome above which are painted foliate inscriptions. At the apex of the dome in gold on a blue ground is the foundation date 1274 AH (AD 1857). On the SE side is a small miḥrāb; opposite this are the gates of the shaykh above which is the inscription 'Ya hadrat mawlanā' (O our blessed lord, i.e. Rūmī).

Off the E side of the road runs the SHʿ. QARQŪL AL-MANSHIYYAH (to

Maydān Ṣalāḥ al-Dīn). At the second turning on the right (100m) stands the **Palace of Yashbak min Mahdī** (266; 23:2), also known as the *Ḥawsh Bardaq*, the most complete Mamlūk palace remaining. It was probably second in size only to the sultan's palace in the Citadel. It was built by the amīr Sangar al-Shugā'ī for the court of Sultan al-Nāṣr Muḥ. by the architect Muḥ. b. Aḥ. al-Shāmī. Later it was reconstructed by the amīr Yashbak whose tomb can be seen (Rte 19).

The ruins cover a large area. In the exterior NE façade is a magnificent salient portal standing about 15m high with a stalactite hood. At the back of the entrance recess is the doorway, above which is a stalactite frame. This is probably all part of the original work of Sangar. But on each side of the releasing arch are medallions of Sultan Muḥammad, son of Qāyt-bāy, and the inscription along the flanks is of Yashbak's reconstruction. The doorway leads into an immense room with a wide dome, and on the upper floor is a large qā'ah.

On the E side of Sh'. Ḥilmiyyah the ḤĀRAT NŪR AL-ẒALĀM leads W into the SH'. MUḤ. SHĀKIR. The first building on the left (110m) is the *Madrasah of Bashīr Aghā al-Gamdār* (269; 23:1), built in 1359 by an important civil royal functionary.

Also on the left (100m) a lane leads to the 17C *Wikālah al-Tūtungī* (548; 23:3) and beside it the fountain known as the *Sabīl-Kuttāb 'Abbās Aghā* (335), built in 1677 by 'Alī Katkhudā 'Azabān. Following the road on the W is the *Mosque of Amīr Mughalbāy Ṭāz* (207). All that is left of the original structure of 1466 is the façade and the minaret, although only two storeys of the minaret remain the second has a particularly fine floriate carving.

The lane returns N to the Sh'. Muḥ Shakir; 100m along, on the N where it meets the SIKKAT AL-FĪL is the **Mosque of 'Alī Pasha Ṭāhir** (210; 23:1) and his brother 'Abdīn Bey, relations of Muḥ. 'Alī. Although built in 1809 it has an archaic façade and almost all the decoration derives from the Mamlūk tradition. The façade consists of the tomb, the entrance and a sabīl-kuttāb above which rises the minaret. Above the entrance rises a high frame crowned with unusual triangular cresting and covered with ornate carving. Each side of the entrance are highly decorated panels and windows, those to the left overlooking the tomb, to the right the sabīl. The zone-of-transition of the tomb has scrolled corners and the large dome has shallow ribs. The minaret is wholly Mamlūk with an octagonal first storey and cylindrical second and third storeys decorated with keel-arched niches and moulding. Inside, the floor is in coloured marble and six marble columns support the painted ceiling with a central lantern. Coloured glass fills the stucco window grills.

Directly S of the Sh'. al-Qaraqūl is a fine complex dominated by the **Palace of Amīr Ṭāz** (267; 23:2), the remnant of a very fine building of 1352. Ṭāz b. Qutghāj (died 1362) was a mamlūk of Sultan al-Naṣīr Muḥ. The most impressive features are the stalactite entrance and the lower part of the massive qā'ah and maq'ad that lies behind. Conjoined to the N corner of the palace is a modern mosque in which is incorporated the **Tomb of Amīr Aydakīn al-Bunduqdārī** (146; 23:2) and that of his adaughter, all that remains of a khānqāh built in 1284. It has the local name of *Zāwiyat al-Abbar* (i.e. of the wells). All that can be seen on the street is the NW wall of the amīr's tomb which once stood at the W corner of the khānqāh, now flanked by modern houses.

Aydakīn, bought by the amīr Aqsunqur, passed into the service of Sultan al-Ṣāliḥ Ayyūb and was made a bowman (bunduqdār). One of his own mamlūks was Baybārs who later became sultan. This was the period of Aydakin's greatest posts. Under Sultan Barakah Khān he suffered deprivation, but commanded the left wing of the Mamlūk army. He died in 1285.

The original doorway of the tomb has been converted into a window but along the top of the wall is an inscription, important in that it contains the first blazon known in Egypt, the gold affronted bows of the bunduqdar on a red undivided field (colours taken from painted inscription). Above stepped cresting rises the dome decorated with ribs. A doorway between the tomb and the house leads into a corridor (to the zāwiyah); the left wall is the SW wall of the tomb. The present door is half-way down. The interior (c 6m sq.) has plain stone walls with a keel-arched miḥrāb which retains the fine stucco decoration in the hood. Access to the khānqāh was through the NE wall (now bricked up). In the centre is the wooden tābūt of Aydakīn with Naskhī inscription. Squinches with two layers of three niches raise the dome and between are windows of three lights. Around the drum are 16 windows with a fine Naskhī inscription in round-ended panels with medallions between, while at the apex of the dome is another medallion surrounded by inscription.

Enter the modern zāwiyah and cross to the door in the left-hand wall. Pass around the side wall to the *Tomb of the daughter of Aydakīn*. It is smaller than the other but also in stone, the brick dome with a narrower profile, on which some of the original decoration is retained. The stucco window grilles are also original with double rows of palmettes and Kufic inscription. The interior (5m sq.) is plain, the miḥrāb having lost its decoration. More complex squinches raise the dome with three tiers of five niches, the first of this type. Although the windows now have three lights, originally they had six, the lower three having been filled in. A band of Naskhī inscription runs below the 24 windows in the drum. Above are two other bands of inscription, one in Kufic, the other in Naskhī characters.

The S corner of the palace is occupied by the *Sabīl-Kuttāb of ʿAlī Aghā* (268), built in 1677 with Mamlūk decoration by an Aghā Dār al-Saʿādah, the chief black eunuch.

Continuing S (120m), cross the Shʿ. Ṣalibah (E to Maydān Ṣalāḥ al-Dīn; W to Maydān Sayyidah Zaynab; Rte 12) with the Sabīl Umm ʿAbbās to the right. The first monument on the E (50m) is the **Tomb of Gawhar al-Nāṣiri** (270; 23:3), built in 1315 by the chief eunuch of Sultān al-Nāṣir Muḥammad. It differs from all other known tombs and is a rectangular building (10m by 8m) divided into four approximately equal areas. On the street is the NW wall of the domed tomb and the open entrance porch. Parts of the NE and SW walls are also visible. In the tomb the window is set in a stalactite-headed recess with another small rectangular window above. The dome was pierced, probably during Ottoman times, with four lights set with greenish glass. The NE wall contains two windows, while the SW façade is plain and supports the wooden roof of the porch. Around the top of the wall is a frieze and over that a foundation inscription and stepped cresting. Steps lead down to the porch at the W corner, at the back of which is the elegant face of the S room. On the left a stalactite portal leads into the undecorated tomb chamber at the N corner. Squinches with three tiers of niches raise the dome and in place of the usual miḥrāb is a doorway into the E room which is in the form of a small masallā, bare except for the miḥrāb and cupboards. It has been proposed that this small room is due to Gawhar's reservations about having a miḥrāb in the tomb chamber. In the SW a door leads into the S room.

South and on the W side of the road (70m) is the dilapidated *Mosque of Aḥmad Bay Kūhyah* (521) which, although ascribed to an Ottoman official, was founded in 1310 by an unknown amīr. On the E side of the road stands the *Zāwiyah, Wikālah and Sabīl of Muṣṭafā Bay Ṭabaṭabāy* (272), a large complex of 1637. Beyond this (70m) is a crossroads; to the W runs the SHʿ. ṬŪLŪN (past the Mosque of Ibn Ṭūlūn, Rte 13) and to the E the SHʿ. DARB AL-HUṢR leads to two monuments.

First (200m) on the N is the *Sabīl of Aḥmad Kathkhudā* (405; 23:4), who was secretary of the ʿAzabān corps. His sabīl was built in 1701. Just beyond stands the **Madrasah of Khushqadam al-Aḥmadī** (153), of interest in that it is the great qāʿah of a domestic palace, built c 1370, converted into a mosque a hundred years later.

The palace was built by Ṭashtīmūr al-ʿAlāʾī, who served the last descendants of Sultan al-Nāṣir Muḥammad. He was the first amīr to bear the title grand dawadār and later became Viceroy of Egypt and then Syria. Under Sultan Ḥājjī II he was created atabak but after the assumption of Barqūq in 1382 he was dismissed and imprisoned in Damietta and Jerusalem where he died in 1384. Khushqadam, who converted the palace, was a eunuch who rose through the ranks of the pages to become warden of the princesses and wazīr under Sultan Qāyt-bay. He too fell into disgrace and was exiled to Suakin (Sudan) where he died in 1489.

The minaret on the NE corner is obviously part of Khushqadam's conversion and is a good example of late Mamlūk work. From it a modern wall runs to the mosque. On the entrance is a foundation inscription of Ṭashtīmūr and in the corridor leading from it another with the blazon of the amīr. On the ceiling are several painted blazons including that of Khushqadam. In the qāʿah a block of masonry has been hollowed out as a miḥrāb. The blazon of Ṭashtīmūr consists of crimson upper and lower fields and on a golden middle field a black pen-box; that of Khushqadam is more complex—on a red upper field a white napkin, on a white middle field between two red horns with white openings, a black cup, and on a black lower field a white cup. The other blazon of a pen-box on a white napkin is probably that of Amīr Shihāb al-Dīn Muʾayyad who owned the palace c 1460.

Back on the main route, now the SHʿ. AL-KHALĪFAH, on the W (100m) stands the *Tomb of Muḥammad al-Anwār* (68; 23:5), an Ottoman construction of 1780 over the grave of a Fāṭimid shaykh who died in 1020.

The next turning (80m) on the W, adjacent to the modern *Mosque of al-Sayyidah Sakīnah*, leads after 250m to the *Mosque al-Baqlī* (156); only the minaret remains of the original mosque built around the tomb of Shʿ. ʿAlī al-Baqlī (died 1297). The square base is similar to that of Fātimah Khatūn (Rte 11) and the octagonal pillared second storey is also similar to that which once crowned the former minaret.

The following area is geographically included within the confines of the Southern Cemetery, although it is much more residential than the rest of Rte 15. The first monument of note on the E side of the road (80m) is the **Tomb of Shagar al-Durr** (169; 23:5), raised in 1250.

The history and achievements of Shagar al-Durr (Spray of Pearls) are remarkable in that she rose to be sultan in her own right, the only female sultan in the history of Islam. She was a slave of Khalīf al-Mustaʿṣim at Baghdad who presented her to Sultan al-Ṣāliḥ Ayyūb to whom she bore a son, Khalīl, who died in infancy. During the siege of Manṣūrah in 1249 al-Ṣāliḥ Ayyūb died, but Shagar al-Durr concealed the fact and with the help of the chief eunuch forged the sultan's signature on documents. Although King Louis IX was captured Tūrān Shāh, Ṣāliḥ Ayyūb's son and successor angered the amīrs and they assassinated him at Fariskur. So admired was the leadership of Shagar al-Durr that she was proclaimed sultan in Cairo, the first of the Mamlūk line. However the reaction of the orthodox was immediate. The khalīf, her original owner, was appalled and he wrote from Baghdad to the effect that if there were no man capable of leading the country he would send one himself. His message ended thus: 'Do you not know that the Prophet said, "Woe unto nations governed by a woman"'. To stem criticism in late 1250 Shagar al-Durr married the atabak Aybak. The Ayyūbid rulers in Syria rose against Aybak to reinstate their line but were defeated, and another expedient Mūsā, the six-year-old great-grandson of al-Kāmil, was invested as joint ruler. In 1257 Shagar al-Durr learning that Aybak intended to marry the daughter of the sultan of Mosul, she arranged for several amīrs to strangle Aybak. The mamlūks rioted and Aybak's faction was victorious, proclaiming his son ʿAlī sultan. Shagar al-Durr was arrested and confined in the Red Tower in the Citadel (see Rte 14). Shortly after, dressed only in a shift and trousers her body was thrown out of the tower. It was retrieved some days later and interred in her mausoleum.

Measuring c 9m sq and 14m to the apex of the dome, the whole fabric is brick covered with stucco. It is closely related to the Tomb of the ʿAbbāsid Khalifs (see Rte 12). The decoration on the NE wall has disappeared through being in contact with a 19C mosque (now demolished) and that on the NW has suffered since it was inside the mosque. Against the SE wall is a salient on which two keel-arched recesses contain similarly shaped panels with geometrically ornamented medallions or lozenges at the spandrels. In the SW wall is the main entrance above which is a scalloped keel-arch frame flanked by similarly arched panels, the spandrels with medallions or lozenges. A small section at the N corner is all that remains of a porch that must have covered the entrance. The zone-of-transition has only one step, above which is the dome with keel-arched profile.

Inside, the walls are decorated with oblong stucco panels; below them runs a wooden frieze of Kufic inscription from the Qurʾān probably removed from a Fāṭimid tomb and later covered with a stucco Naskhī inscription. Over the stucco panels is another wooden frieze painted with a later inscription, containing the name of Shagar al-Durr in a form reserved for sultans. The miḥrāb is very fine. It has a mosaic band of lozenges on a gold background while the central motif is a branching tree in green, black and red with fruit in mother-of-pearl (perhaps a reference to her name). This is the first extant use of gold mosaic in Egypt. The squinches have two tiers of three niches, the central lower niches containing the seal of David. Between the squinches are windows of three lights. A wooden tābūt over the grave is modern but sections of the original have been incorporated in it. It contains the body of one of the ʿAbbāsid Khalīfs, either al-Mutuwakkil I (died 1406) or the last Khalīf, Mutuwakkil III (died 1538), most probably the former. Among the inscription from the Qurʾān on the tābūt is the verse: 'Oh you who stand beside my grave, show not surprise at my condition,/Yesterday I was as you, tomorrow, you will be like me.' Shagar al-Durr was also buried here but whether in the central grave or under the doorway in the NE wall where there used to be another tābūt is not known. The burial must have been hurried and it is probable that the inscriptions were defaced at the same time.

In an enclosure on the W side of the road are three Fāṭimid monuments built over the graves of three descendants of Khalīf ʾAlī who emigrated to Egypt. At the N are the conjoined **Tomb of Muhammad al-Gaʿfarī** and **Tomb of Sayyidah ʿĀtikah** (333; 23:5), both built about the same time, the first c 1110 and the second a little later. They are both brick-built domed cubes covered with stucco. The more northerly of the tombs is that of al-Gaʿfarī with stepped zone-of-transition and trefoil window on each side. Much of the dome is reconstruction but a small piece of the original seems to indicate that it was always plain. The present entrance is in the NE side, the original entrance being closed when Sayyidah ʿĀtikah's tomb was built to the S. This is very similar to al-Gaʿfarī's tomb but the dome is ribbed, the first example in Cairo. Inside, al-Gaʿfarī's tomb retains only fragments of decoration. Squinches of two layers of niches, one over three, raise the dome. In the NW door the palm-trunk lintel of the original door can be seen. The interior of the tomb of Sayyidah ʿĀtikah is similar but much more of the stucco has survived. A band of Kufic inscription runs below the decorated frame with a similar one around the recess. In the spandrels are fluted bosses, the rest being filled with palmettes.

To the S is the **Mashhad of Sayyidah Ruqayyah** (273; 23:5), built in 1133 over the grave of Ruqayyah, daughter of Khalīf ʿAlī (not by Fāṭimah, but another wife) who came to Egypt with Sayyidah Zaynab, her step-sister.

During the Fāṭimid domination the descendants of ʿAlī and Fāṭimah had particular significance to the Shiʿī rulers and all the graves of the family received a lot of attention. These tombs are still held in great reverence by many local people. Only the tomb chamber now remains of a once larger complex. The courtyard in front of the tomb must have been the ṣaḥn flanked by riwāqs. At some time the tomb had been filled with rubbish and walled up, but in 1916 the CPAM opened it up and cleared it. Thus the decoration is in very good condition.

A three-arched opening, each keel-arch resting on two columns, fronts the building, above which rises the octagonal drum, in each face of which are two ogival windows. A fine ribbed dome covers the tomb chamber. Flanking the entrance are two fluted keel-arched recesses with medallions in the centre of the hood. The interior has a large central chamber flanked by two līwāns half as wide. Frames, reflecting the shape of the arches resting on columns at the entrance to the līwāns, surround the doorway and the miḥrāb. The squinches of the dome are similar to those in the tombs last visited but the innovation in the zone-of-transition is that the windows (although walled up) possess a Y-shaped frame, thus converting them into windows of three lights. Of the original stucco decoration only a section below the NE window remains. A painted foundation inscription runs around the drum and the 24 flutes of the dome are painted alternately blue, green, yellow and red.

The main miḥrāb is a most imposing piece of work. In the keel-arched hood flutes radiate from a medallion with the name of ʿAlī in the centre and Muḥammad repeated around the circumference. Bosses in the spandrels are now bare but must once have been spirally fluted (as in the līwāns). At the top is a cavetto cornice of Kufic inscription and above this a frieze of complex interlace, the whole surrounded by the strange frame. The later marble panelling has disappeared except for a narrow band of coloured marbles in triangular shapes. Each of the side līwāns has a smaller miḥrāb with a fluted hood and bosses with spiral flutes in the spandrels. A magnificent moveable wooden miḥrāb built between 1155–60 was found here (now in the MIA). An Ottoman screen surrounds the beautiful tābūt which is covered with inscription and arabesque and was presented by the widow of Khalīf al-Āmir in 1139.

On the E side of the road a lane leads (200m) to the 15C *Mosque and*

*Sabil of Badr al-Dīn al-Wanāʾī* (163; 23:6); only the façade and minaret are original.

The W side of the road is flanked by a great bank which marks the periphery of the Great Kharābah (Ruin Field) that once stretched between this area and Fusṭāṭ. It was the central area of S Cairo. Called Tallūl Zaynhum and formerly an area of desolation, it has now been transformed into a residential area with houses and parks. On the E side of the road are two tombs each once part of a large madrasah complex, architecturally related to the Madrasah of Qalāwūn (Rte 5). The first, with a distinctly northern Mediterranean aspect, is the **Tomb of Fāṭimah Khatūn** (274; 23:5).

This is a late ascription as it was built in 1284 by the amīr Sangar al-Shugaʿī to the order of Sultan Qalāwūn for the burial of Princess Umm ʿAli (died 1284), mother of his eldest son. ʿAlī, who died in 1288, was buried here, as was his full sister Ghaziyyah, who died the same year, wife of Sultan Barakah Khān. Another of Qalāwūn's wives, Ashlūn (died 1303), mother of Sultan al-Nāṣir Muḥammad, was also interred here until her son transferred her body to his own tomb in the Bayn al-Qaṣrayn. Finally Sultan Ṣāliḥ, a son of al-Nāṣir Muḥammad, was buried here in 1359.

The complex consists of a minaret, the entrance and, at an angle, the tomb chamber. Immediately striking the eye is the massive stone minaret, a square-sectioned pillar 6m sq. and 21m high. Around the top is an ogee moulding and on the N side a medial window with a solid semicircular arch. In each side of the upper section is a pointed arch divided into two horseshoe-arched windows covered by an oculus. Until the 19C there was a tall brick pillared octagonal storey with a round cap. A room at the top of the minaret is roofed with a dome on pendentives. Left of the minaret is the high pointed-arched portal which is flanked by a wall which has a return and then forms a right-angle at an antechamber in front of the tomb; in this wall are recesses with windows. Behind is the huge brick tomb c 14m sq. The dome has fallen but was probably similar to that of the next monument (see below). It was once covered with stucco. In each side of the base is a single round-arched frame enclosing two horseshoe-arched windows covered by an oculus, the first occurrence of the form in Egypt. Only on the NE side has any of the decoration survived. An octagonal drum above contains a keel-arched window in each face, set in a round-arched recess supported on baton columns.

At the back of the entrance a doorway leads into an open space. On the right is a narrow hall, once tunnel-vaulted, which leads on the SE into the antechamber which must once have had a flat wooden roof. Two keel-arched recesses flank the entrance in the NW wall. In the tomb chamber each wall has two round-arched salients, the pillars of the outer one forming the support for the octagonal drum. Unique squinches consisting of two layers of niches covered by a large recess raise the drum. All decoration has disappeared from the interior.

Directly S is the **Tomb of Sultan Khalīl** (275), built about five years later in 1288, probably by the same architect, for another son of Sultan Qalāwūn.

After the death of Qalāwūn in 1290 Khalīl, was the natural heir and inaugurated his reign by executing his father's atabak and friend the amīr Ṭuruntāy. He continued his father's campaign against the Crusader presence in Syria and in May 1291 Acre fell to him. The other occupied cities soon capitulated and the Crusaders finally retreated to Cyprus. In similar fashion Khalīl attacked the Mongol-held cities and the Mongols too were expelled in 1292.

Khalīl was very energetic and highly educated and never signed a document without reading it thoroughly, often profferring amendments. Despite this and his personal charm his preference for his own mamlūks angered the older amīrs. He was also conceited, disrespectful and neglected his religious duties, perhaps the greatest crime of all to the amīrs. After being publicly insulted by Khalīl, Baydarah the atabak and several other amīrs, including Lāgīn, decided to kill him. They surprised him as he was out hunting and hacked him to death. His body lay unattended until collected by a local official and buried in this tomb.

Only the tomb chamber (c 14m sq.) remains. It is also a massive domed cube. There are the remains of a similar antechamber but only the NE wall is standing. High in the centre of each wall is a pointed-arch window, two of which retain inscription in a cavetto moulding. Stepped cresting surmounts the wall. The zone-of-transition has stepped corners and on alternate sides of the octagonal drum are triple windows surmounted by an oculus and surrounded by an arched recess. Above the step is a smaller window. The tomb has a strange profile and eight buttresses alternating with windows of hyperbolic shape (it was copied for the modern restoration of the dome of the Tomb of Qalāwūn, Rte 5). A plain door in the NW wall flanked by two recesses leads into the tomb. There are also entrances in the NE and SW walls. Most of the interior decoration has disappeared as has the tābūt. The squinches have three layers of five niches, with a window piercing the central top niche. Around the drum runs a band of excellent inscription from the Qur'ān, in panels separated by medallions. Above are 24 oculi with stucco grills, eight of which are open as windows, some still containing the original blue, green and yellow glass.

The road finally leads into the Maydān al-Sayyidah Nafīsah. On the E side is the *Sabīl of Sultan Muṣṭafā III*, a fine royal Ottoman foundation of 1756, and to the left the *Gate of 'Alī Pasha Ḥākim* (394; 23:7) which leads to the modern **Mosque of Sayyidah Nafīsah**, the last of a series of mosques built on this site around the tomb of Nafīsah bint Ḥasan.

The great-granddaughter of Ḥasan, son of Khalīf 'Alī, she was born in Mecca and raised in Medina. She came to Cairo in 809 and dwelt in a house on this site. As well as being a ḥāfiẓāt al-Qur'ān (knowing the Qur'ān by heart), she was a commentator and extremely pious. Her constant companion was the Imām Shāfi'ī (Rte 15) who had accompanied her to Egypt. It is said that she dug her own grave before she died in 824. Shortly after 'Ubayd Allāh Sarī, the governor, built a tomb over her grave and the Fāṭimid Khalīf al-Mustanṣir turned it into a mashhad in 1089; this was repaired by Khalīf al-Ḥāfiẓ in 1138. Sultan Baybars also built in the precinct (see Tomb of the 'Abbāsid Khalīfs, below) and a new mosque was raised by Sultan al-Nāṣir Muḥammad. Much reconstruction was undertaken by 'Abd al-Raḥmān Katkhudā (of course) in 1760. In 1892 most of the mosque was burnt in a great fire and the khedive 'Abbās II ordered a complete rebuilding between 1893–97; this is the building which still stands.

The building is completely modern in the neo-Mamlūk style with the portal in the centre of the façade, above which rises the two-tiered minaret. Although the decoration inside is good modern work, there is little out of the ordinary apart from the superb miḥrāb. In the E corner is the tomb surrounded by a brass grille.

Along the N side of the mosque is a passage; on the right side can be seen remains of the earlier mosque. Further along on the left on the W corner of a house in an enclosure stands the *Tomb of Muwafī al-Dayn*

(394; 23:7), a small 11C Fāṭimid brick building with keel-arched squinches and inside a very fine tābūt inscribed on the ends and sides. The man's strange name means 'repayment of a debt'.

Pass the house and turn right and right again into a small court. On the S side of this is a stone keel-arched doorway in a recess. Unusual cresting tops the wall on either side. A porch leads into a huge brick enclosure, the **Ḥawsh of Sultan Baybars**, c 45m sq., the walls 5.5m high and 1m thick. It is interrupted at the W corner by the Tomb of Sayyidah Nafīsah. This enclosure and doorway were probably constructed by the Sultan c 1266 when his son was interred in the Tomb of the Khalīfs. Against the S wall are seven keel-arched miḥrābs, the largest in the centre. This may have been an early attempt at mosque building by Baybars, abandoned later in the same year in favour of the site in the deserted area N of the enclosure of al-Qāhirah (Rte 19). The S wall is aligned with those of the original Tomb of Sayyidah Nafīsah and the Tomb of the Khalifs.

Inside the enclosure the oldest and largest tomb, standing slightly to the NW against the wall of the Mosque of Sayyidah Nafīsah, is the **Tomb of the ʿAbbāsid Khalīfs** (276; 23:7), dated to the mid 13C. The earliest burial inside is that of an ambassador of the khalīf from Baghdad, dated 1242 (before the transfer of the khalifate to Cairo).

Whether the tomb was built for him is, however, open to question. It has the appearance of a royal tomb and the only sultan of the period whose tomb is not known is Tūrūnshah. After assassination the body of Tūrūnshah was recovered by the Kalif's ambassador and it may well be that he was buried here.

When Abū Nadlah, the khalīf's ambassador, died in Cairo in 1242 he was interred in the tomb. In 1258 the mongol Hulagu invaded Iraq, sacked Baghdad and murdered the khalīf al-Mustaʿsim and his family, thus seemingly ending a dynasty that had held the khalifate for over 500 years. A year after Baybars I assumed the sultanate in Egypt in 1260, Aḥmad, son of the khalīf al-Ẓāhir (1225–26), and other of the khalīf's relatives were found living with the bedouin in the N Arabian desert. Baybars had him proclaimed khalīf as al-Mustanṣir and provided him with forces to attempt the retaking of Baghdad. However he was defeated and killed and another relative Abū ʾl-ʿAbbās was raised to the khalifate as al-Ḥākim. Thus the khalifate continued to function in Cairo. Although the prestige gained by Egypt was considerable, the status of the khalīf was drastically changed—'No longer Commander of the Faithful but Commander of the Wind' as a contemporary amīr said.

During the next 250 years they remained mere figureheads living in a palace in the Citadel and wielding little power. Whenever they tried to interfere in state affairs they were speedily replaced by a relative. Only one, al-Mustaʿīn, managed to reign for six months in his own right, during the confused period following the death of Sultan Farag in 1412. But with the arrival of the powerful amīr Shaykh he was quickly set aside. Following the defeat of Sultan Qānṣūḥ al-Ghawrī by the Ottoman Sultan Selim in 1517, the khalīf al-Mutuwakkil III was taken to Istanbul and divested of his office. After being involved in a property scandal, he returned to Cairo where he lived happily as a private citizen, and is perhaps buried in the Tomb of Shagar al-Durr. Many members of the khalifal family are buried here, a practice that only ceased within recent times, but only two khalīfs are acknowledged in the inscriptions. Baybars I also interred two of his sons here.

The building is c 9.5m sq., similar to the tomb of Shagar al-Durr. Each of the sides except the SE has three recesses with decorated keel-arched hoods and in the centre of these three sides is a keel-arched doorway (that in the SW bricked up and in the NE converted into a window). In the NW wall the recesses are hollowed out, while in the SE wall a salient replaces the central recess. Above the keel-arches are fluted disks and geometrically decorated lozenges. The zone-of-transition has stepped corners and in each face a three-lighted window, while the plain dome has a keel-arched profile.

The interior has exceptionally fine detail with superb stucco work and painted decoration. A painted Naskhī inscription runs around the wall, above which a keel-arched panel occupies the centre of each wall, those on the SE and NW wall recessed. All the hoods are scalloped—in the centre of the recessed ones are medallions while the other two have another keel-arched panel. Decorated Kufic inscription surrounds the panels. Squinches of three over three niches raise the dome, decorated in gold, red, green and black. Stucco grills fill the windows fitted with painted glass, the two lower lights in the SW being original. Around the base of the dome is a gilded inscription of attenuated and tortuous Kufic characters. Above this the interior of the dome is covered with a unique decoration of gilded medallions on an ultramarine and crimson ground set in rows of 16 around the dome.

There are eight tābūts in the tomb with the largest, No. 1, on the SW side (the rest numbered counterclockwise from this). No. 1 is an inscribed tābūt on a marble base. The inscription names Abū Nadlah with the date 640 AH, (i.e. AD 1242). Seventeen other epitaphs include two khalīfs, al-Wathiq I (died 1341) and al-Muʿtaḍid I (died 1362), and sons, daughters and brothers of the ʿAbbāsid family. In front of the miḥrāb Tābūt 2 contains the body of Khawand Qamar (died 1423). Tābūts 3 and 4 in the E corner lack names or dates. Tābūt 5 against the NE wall contains Anas-bāy (died 1266), a son of Baybars I. Tābūt 6, to the W of the door, is uninscribed, but on the E side of the door in Tābūt 7 lies ʿUmar (died 1269), another son of Baybars. Tābūt 8 has no epitaph.

From the SE angle of the Maydān Sayyidah Nafīsah the SHʿ. AL-SAYYIDAH NAFĪSAH leads to the S Cemetery (Rte 15) while from the S the SHʿ. NO. 1 runs for a short distance directly S.

# 12 Southern Shʿ. Būr Saʿīd

Rte 12 (1.6km) is the southern counterpart of Rte 7 and follows the course of the old canal. The final section where the canal entered the river is covered in Rte 3D. **Cairo Atlas 16, 22, 21**.

This route follows, for the most part, the S section of the Shʿ. Būr Said, which was created in 1906 after the Khalīg al-Miṣrī (Egyptian Canal) had been filled in. This had existed since it was dug at the behest of Sultan al-Nāṣir Muḥ. Therefore all the monuments along the route must have been built specifically on the banks of the canal.

From the Maydān Aḥmad Māhir several main roads radiate; to the E the SHʿ. SĀMĪ AL-BĀRŪDĪ; crossing from NW to SE the Shʿ. al-Qalʿah (Rte 11); crossing from NE to SW the Shʿ. Būr Saʿīd (below and Rte 7) and to the E the Shʿ. Aḥmad Māhir (Rte 6).

On the N side of the Shʿ. al-Bārūdī (150m) is the *Mosque of Amīr Sultan Shāh* (239; 16:3). Although founded shortly before 1496, there is little left of the original structure built by this amīr with two grandiose names except the octagonal columns and the façade of the E līwān. The exterior is crude and the minaret clumsy. Turn N up the lane on the W flank of the mosque where on the W (70m) stands the *Mosque of Gawhar al-Muʿaynī* (611), a very late Ottoman building raised in 1814. Leading S off the Sh'. Sāmī al-Bārūdī and running along the rear wall of the 'Ābidīn Palace (Rte 3C) is the SH'. MUṢṬAFĀ 'ABD AL-RAZZĀQ. On the W half-way down (inside the grounds of the 'Ābidīn Palace and reached from the street by a flight of wide steps) is the **Mosque of 'Abdīn Bak**, also called al-Fatḥ (587; 16:5). Not much remains of the original built in 1728 by 'Ābidīn Bak, commander of the Sultan's Bodyguard, as the whole was restored by King Fū'ād in 1920. The façade including the Turkish minaret is of finely carved white marble. Inside, a large dome is raised on four columns and arches, flanked by four smaller domes. Much of the interior is painted and gilded in the ornate taste of the Egyptian royal family. Another entrance leads into the gardens of the palace (entry forbidden).

Dominating the S end of the Maydān Aḥmad Māḥir in the centre of the Sh'. Būr Sā'īd stands the **Mosque of Yūsuf Aghā al-Ḥīn** (196; 16:4), an Ottoman mosque built in 1635. The façade is simple but strong in line. On the N corner is an elegant sabīl-kuttāb with a large arch of coloured tiles with marble joggling and fine woodwork surrounding the kuttāb. The minaret is a typical tapered shaft with two tiers. In the SE wall is the trefoil-arched entrance. This is a covered cruciform mosque with sunken path through the main mosque to the ablution court.

50m S on the same road, down the first lane to the W is the *House of Ḥusayn Katkhudā Shanān* (568; 16:5), a very late Turkish house of 1802. On the E side of the road, 100m further down, another lane leads to the *Mosque of 'Alī al-'Amrī* (426; 16:6), painted in bright yellow and red stripes. The mosque is modern but the three-tiered minaret on the S façade is a complete anomaly. It is massive, much too large for the mosque, and is of Mamlūk type, with no record in the literature, although stylistically it can be assigned to c 1500. The stalactites are extended with decorative drops, an eary Ottomam devise. Almost opposite on the main road is an alley down which (S) is the *Mosque, Tomb and Sabīl of Shaykh Ramaḍān* (436; 16:5), built in 1762 for the shaykh by the tireless 'Abd al-Raḥmān Katkhudā. There is little left of the original structure. It is in the form of a small zāwiyah with a domed tomb at the N corner and heavy trefoil cresting.

On the E the Sikkit Rātib Bāshā (running to the Sh'. al-Qal'ah) leads (20m) to a short street with the **Mosque of Qāḍī Yaḥyā** (204), the last of the three mosques he built in Cairo. Like the mosque in Būlāq, it is a small enclosure mosque and the exterior is similar in decoration. Inside the lateral riwāqs are reduced in size and the arcades are raised on pillars with classical capitals often used as bases. Above the miḥrāb is a small dome. After some distance on the W side of the road a lane leads to *al-Khalawātī Mosque* (414), a late Ottoman building of 1759. Down the next lane on the W (215m) are two monuments, the first the *Sabīl of Kulsūn* (311), a 17C fountain, and a little further down the *Tomb of Sīdī Ibrāhīm al-Anṣarī* (310). Attached to a modern mosque and named after a shaykh who was buried there in the 19C, the tomb is in fact much older. A foundation inscription gives the date 1370, but the name of the owner has been lost. It is constructed of stone with a brick dome and excellent, very well-preserved, carving.

Almost opposite the last lane on the Sh'. Būr Sa'īd, its façade stretching down the street, is the **Takiyyah and Sabīl-Kuttāb of Sultan Maḥmūd II** (308; 16:5), similar in plan to that of the earlier takiyyah of Sulāymān Pasha (Rte 10).

The eunuch Bashīr (see below) had it built at the behest of the Ottoman sultan in 1750 beside his own sabīl. It was used by the Mawlawiyyah sufis until 1956 when the building was closed. Al-Azhar University reopened it for the teaching of the sunnah and it is now the Cairo headquarters of the ʿAshīrah al-Muḥammadiyyah, a pan-Islamic organisation.

In the centre of the façade is the arched opening with tiles in the shoulder. At the S end of the wall is the ornate semicircular *Sabīl-Kuttāb* of carved white marble with marble grills (bricked up); above the sabīl is a canopy above which is the Kuttāb with a lobed canopy overall. From the main entrance steps lead up into a shady central courtyard with an arcade of five arches on each side. In the centre is a small raised garden filled with trees and a domed central pavilion. At each corner of the arcade are shallow brick domes which must originally have continued along each arcade, but they now have flat wooden roofs. Along each wall are rooms once used by the sufis; on the SE wall is a delightful small maṣallā with a good painted and inscribed ceiling. In the W corner is the entrance to the interior of the sabīl, now used as a lecture theatre. It consists of two rooms with marble floors. The interior room, on the site of the original fountain, has an incredible array of various provincial Turkish tiles in panels. On the wooden ceiling is a carved star pattern.

Opposite, on the corner of the small lane, is the **Sabīl-Kuttāb of Bashīr Aghā** (309; 16:5), who was responsible for erecting the takiyyah for Sultan Maḥmūd. This building makes a fine contrast, being his own simpler and earlier effort built in 1718, relying much more heavily on Mamlūk decoration. Bashir was a black eunuch and Aghā Dār al-Saʿadah (Lord of the House of Joy, i.e. master of the harīm). Whereas the lines of Sultan Maḥmūd's sabīl were curved, here they are angular, with a fine stalactite entrance and a carved ropework frame around the windows and medallions.

On the opposite side of the road a small lane leads W. On the N (150m) is the *Mosque and Sabīl of Gānbalāṭ* (381; 16:5), a very late Ottoman mosque built in 1797 just prior to the French occupation. Also on the W side of the Shʿ. Būr Saʿīd, the next lane (150m) leads to the *House of ʿAlī Katkhudā* (540; 16:5), called al-Rabʿmayyah (Water Apartments, i.e. near the canal), built in 1776.

On the same side of Shʿ. Būr Saʿīd, the next turning, the SHʿ. KHALĪL ṬĪNNAH, leads (250m) to a small maydān and a much more important monument, the **Mosque of Ḥadaq Sitt Miskah** (Lady Musk) (252; 15:6), a small enclosure mosque built in 1339 but in disrepair.

Ḥadaq was a slave of Sultan al-Nāṣir Muḥ. holding a high and respected position at court as the wet-nurse to the royal children and instructress of the princesses. She obviously accumulated great wealth and her splendid entourage was seen on the ḥajj at Mecca in 1328 by the great Arab traveller Ibn Baṭṭutah.

In the SW façade on the street are full-length stalactite-headed recesses each containing a double window separated by a baluster pillar and surmounted by an oculus. The entrance in this side also has a square stalactite hood. A continuous band of inscription continues on to the NW façade which contains the main entrance in a full-length stalactite recess. To the NE is an anomalous squat cylindrical minaret with medial balcony, almost certainly a 19C replacement. In the interior each riwāq has three pointed arches raised on massive piers, the N corner containing a tomb. The miḥrāb has a pointed-arched hood and the rare remains of beautiful gold mosaic.

This lane leads into the SUWAYQAT AL-SABAʿĪN which runs S into the SHʿ. AL-NAṢRIYYAH down which on the W (300m) are two monuments. The first is the *Mosque of Arghūn Shāh al-Ismāʿīlī* (253; 15:7) of which only the façade and minaret remain of the original fabric of 1347. To the S is the **Madrasah of Amīr Qānī-Bāy Qarā al-Rammāḥ** (254), a late Mamlūk foundation built by the same amīr who raised a mosque near the Citadel (Rte 10). This is a later building dated 1506, but it is similar externally, even down to the square-sectioned minaret with dual finials. The interior is cruciform with reduced lateral līwāns.

On the Shʿ. Būr Sāʿīd, just S of the lane the road divides. The Shʿ. Būr Sāʿīd runs SW, the SHʿ. AL-GAMMĀMĪZ SE, to rejoin after 500m. There are several monuments in each section. About halfway down the Shʿ. Būr Sāʿīd to the W is the *Mosque of Yūsuf al-Shurbagī* (259; 15:8), an Ottoman mosque built in 1763.

To the W (250m) is the parallel SHʿ. AL-HANAFĪ; S are two mosques. On the E side of the road lies the *Mosque of Dāwūd Pasha* (472; 22:2), an unusual very early Ottoman building raised in 1548. Dāwūd was governor from 1538 until his death in 1549. He was an enlightened man who encouraged learning, providing many of the mosques in Egypt with books. The exterior is conventional enough but the entrance is in the form of a large porch with steps which seems more like the interior hall of a domestic house and has no precedent in Egypt. The rectangular interior is spanned by a huge arch, a practice used occasionally in Mamlūk mosques. On the W side of the road is *al-Kurdī Mosque* (610), also Ottoman but built nearly 200 years later in 1732.

Down the Shʿ. al-Gammāmīz on the left stands the the **Mosque of Amīr Bashtak** (205; 16:7), all that remains of the E half of a mosque-khanqah complex built in 1336. The mosque was extensively restored in 1860 by the Dowager Princess Ulfat Qādin, widow of Ibrāhīm Pasha and mother of his third son, Muṣṭafā Faḍl.

The façade on the road is all part of the restoration and all that is visible of the original fabric is the octagonal first story of the minaret; the two upper cylindrical stories seem to be part of the restoration of Ulfāt Qādin, although with reworking of the original stone, when the unique ogee arched grooves on the second storey were added. Inside, the modern entrance leads into a large vestibule, on the far side of which is the impressive original entrance salient with a flat stalactite arch similar to that of his palace (see Rte 5), all that remains of Bashtak's mosque. The mosque itself has parallel rows of arches and in the SW wall steps which lead up into the tomb of Muṣṭafā Faḍl Pasha, at present used as a storeroom. Inside are four carved and guilded marble late Ottoman tombs. The most grandiose is the *Tomb of Muṣṭafā Faḍl Pasha* (1830–75). The others are those of his sons, *Muḥammad ʿAlī* (1857–1915), *Aḥmad Rushdī* (1858–79), and *Ibrāhīm* (1861–1907).

Muṣṭafā Faḍl spent most of his career in Istanbul and was heir to his half-brother, the Khedive Ismāʿīl, to whom he sold his estates and claim to the throne for £2 million. Soon afterwards Ismāʿīl gained the Sultan's sanction for the succession of his own descendants. Muṣṭafā held several high ministerial posts in the Ottoman administration but was exiled to Paris in 1866 where he became involved in the 'New Ottoman' movement. He returned to Turkey and again joined the administration but overtly supported the opposition and never really gave up his claim to the Egyptian throne.

On the opposite side of the street is the site of the long-destroyed

Khanqah of Bashtak. The site is now occupied by the *Sabīl-Kuttāb of Ulfat Qādin*, wife of Ibrāhīm Pasha, erected in 1863.—To the S (and also much ruined) is the *Tomb of Saʿd al-Dīn ibn Ghurāb* (312) of 1400–06, only the Tomb remaining of this once-magnificent khānqāh. It was a domed cube but the dome has fallen. In each side are the usual flat-headed stalactite recesses, the upper window in each has a small horseshoe arch covered by an oculus. The entrance has a trefoil stalactite arch with good panels of faience and coloured marble above the lintel.

On the E side (150m) at the corner of the ḤĀRAT AL-SĀDĀT is the **Mosque of Qarāqugā al-Ḥasanī** (206; 22:1), a small but charming mosque built in 1441. What immediately strikes the eye is the detached minaret standing isolated on the N side of the ḥārat, reached from the main mosque by a bridge. It has an octagonal first tier, with fluted-keeled arch niches on each side and a stalactite cornice supporting the balcony, and a cylindrical second tier with heavy chain moulding decoration. The interior has a cruciform plan with reduced side līwāns and open ṣaḥn. Each of the transverse līwāns and the qiblah līwān are fronted by slightly pointed horseshoe arches springing from stalactite brackets, while the NW līwān is unusual in having a surround of a carved wooden screen. The ceilings retain remains of fine painting and gilding but the marble facings of the walls and miḥrāb have gone.

On the same side (120m S) is the 16C *Sabīl of Yūsuf al-Kurdī* (213). It has a symmetrical façade and a trefoil entrance arch, flanked by stalactite recesses. Along the lane immediately to the S (250m) is the **Manzil al-Sādāt al-Wafāʿiyyah** (463; 23:1). Now surrounded by 19C building, it is a beautiful example of an Ottoman mansion of two periods—1659 and 1754—with excellent architectural detail, mashrabiyyah woodwork and carved stone.

Descended from the family of the Khalif ʿAlī and the Idrisid Dynasty of Tunis, the Wafāʿiyyah family were founders of a Shadhilī sufi brotherhood in the mid 14C. They were extremely powerful during Ottoman times and in the mid 18C the Shaykh of the brotherhood, Sayyid Muḥ. Abū'l-Hadi (died 1762), became the first native Egyptian Naqīb al-Ashraf (Marshal of Notables i.e. the descendents of the Prophet), a post which alternated between this and the al-Bakrī family but which was finally kept by the latter until 1952. The Shaykh al-Sādāt Wafāʿiyyah was responsible for the Mulīd of Sayyidnā Ḥusayn and held the waqf of the mosque. (See Rte 15 for their mosque and tombs.)

At the SW corner of the façade is a *Sabīl*, beside which is the entrance. Among the various rooms, the most magnificent is the *Great Qaʿah*, lined with Ottoman tiles and surmounted by a complex carved ceiling. On the first floor, the *Harīm*, with an elaborately domed and carved roof, was a particular favourite with 19C artists such as Frank Dillon, who was in Egypt several times between the 1850s and '80s.

At the corner (180m) where the Shʿ. al-Gammāmiz and Shʿ. Būr Saʿīd join and enter the Maydān Sayyidah Zaynab stands the *Mosque and Tomb of Dhū 'l-Fiqār Bay* (415; 22:2), built in 1680 by a grandee. The minaret is conventional and divides the façade; the interior has two arcades of arches parallel to the qiblah. In the qiblah wall are five panels of tiles.

To the S (100m) stands the **Mosque, Tomb and Sabīl of Amīr Timrāz al-Aḥmadī** (216; 22:2), built in 1472. This is one of the few monuments in Cairo built by a lesser amīr. Timrāz (died 1482) was a second Amīr Akhūr, and therefore only an amīr of forty, under Sultan Qāyt-bāy and rose no higher. The façade is divided into two sections by the entrance which is a trefoil-arched bay with pendentives supporting the lobes and good joggling over the lintels. Above this rises a fine Mamlūk minaret. To the N is the *Tomb* with stalactite recesses in the base and a tall plain dome set on a high octagonal drum. At the S end of the building is the *Sabīl*. The interior is not very interesting but the minbar is part of the original furnishing provided by Timrāz. Inside the tomb chamber are two tombs, that of Timrāz and another of Muḥammad Shamsī. Below the ceiling of the sabīl is an inscription divided by two blazons of Timrāz—on the upper field a napkin, on each of the middle and lower fields a cup.

Pass the *Sabīl of Sitt Ṣāliḥah* (313) of 1741 and enter the Maydān Sayyidah Zaynab where the S side is dominated by the **Mosque of Sayyidah Zaynab** (22:3), a modern mosque on the site of an ancient mashḥad.

Zaynab was the daughter of Fāṭimah, daughter of the Prophet, and the khalīf ʿAlī and the sister of Ḥasan and Ḥusayn. She was born in 6 AH, (AD 628) and named by the Prophet. After the death of her brother Ḥusayn at Karbala she was arrested and sent to Damascus but the khalīf Muʿāwiyyah released her. She settled in Medina but had to leave because her family connections kept her at the centre of the controversy about the succession. She travelled to Cairo where she settled in Fusṭāṭ and died there the next year, 680. Her mūlid starts on the 13 Ragab and reaches a climax on the 27 Ragab. Like the celebration of Ḥusayn it is very important for the rural community who come to Cairo from all over the Delta. The site, because of the antecedents of Zaynab, is visited by many Shiʿī Muslims from outside Egypt. This is the second mosque in Cairo forbidden to non-Muslims (see also Sayyidnā al-Ḥusayn, Rte 4).

There had been a mashhad here over the tomb of Sayyidah Zaynab since Fāṭimid times but precise details are known only from 1549 when it was rebuilt by ʿAlī Pasha. It was subsequently rebuilt by ʿAbd al-Raḥmān Katkhudā in the mid 18C and repaired by ʿUthmān Bay al-Murādī in 1798 but left incomplete because of the French occupation. Muḥ. ʿAlī continued the work as did ʿAbbās I, and it was finally finished under Sāʿīd Pasha in 1859. The khedive Tawfīq ordered the total rebuilding and thus the present mosque was completed in 1884. King Fārūq had the annexe built on the S in 1942.

The exterior is neo-Mamlūk in decoration with the dome over the tomb at the N corner and grills overlooking the street. Inside, the roof is supported on seven arcades, with rich marble facing the walls and miḥrāb, the work (as in many other modern mosques) by Ḥāgg ʿAbdallāh ʿAfifī. In the NW corner is a small enclosure containing the tombs of Sh. al-ʿAtrīs and Sh. al-ʿAydarūs.

Sh. ʿAbd al-Raḥmān al-ʿAydarūs (1723–78) came from a rich family. After joining the Wafaʾiyyah sufi brotherhood he travelled extensively in Arabia and Syria, and then went to Istanbul where he was given a magnificent reception. Further travel took him to India where he stayed for ten years. He died in his home in Cairo. Sh. ʿAtrīs was a 13C sufi and companion of Ibrāhīm Dasūq.

The *Tomb of Sayyidah Zaynab* in the N angle is surrounded by a magnificent silver maqsurah provided by the Buhrah Brotherhood of India.

The ḤĀRAT MUNG on the N side of the maydān leads to two conjoined houses, the 19C **House Waqf Sayyidah Zaynab** (620; 22:1) and the **House of Ibrāhīm Katkhudā al-Sinnārī** (283) built in 1794.

Ibrāhīm Katkhudā al-Sinnārī (died 1801/2), from Dunqula in the Sudan, began his career as a bawwāb (doorman) in al-Manṣūrah. His knowledge of occult arts brought him a large clientèle among the bays and he grew very rich, acquiring large estates. He became an intimate of Murād Bay and maintained a large slave household of mamlūks and girls.

During the French Occupation many of Napoleon's scholars were housed here, the ḥārat being named after one of them, Gaspard Monge (1748–1818).

It is now the Maʿhad al-Funūn al-Tashkiliyyah (Institute for Applied Arts) for research into Egyptian art techniques throughout the ages from ancient times. Students' work is exhibited and certain pieces can be bought. Work can be made to order (faience, glass, fabrics, wood and metalwork). Other workshops conserve and reconstruct material for mosques and other ancient buildings. (Open 09.00–14.00 except Friday.) The houses themselves are very interesting with two courtyards and a well-preserved complex of rooms, in particular the hammam and mashrabiyyah casements.

On the N side of the square is the **Sabīl-Kuttāb of Sultan Muṣṭafā III** (314; 22:1), built in 1759 and similar to other late Ottoman royal fountains in the city. On the W side of the maydān the SHʿ. AL-SAYYIDAH ZAYNAB leads to the **Mosque of Tanam al-Ruṣāṣ** (227), called locally Tamīm al-Ruṣāfī, built in 1463 for a junior amīr, like that of Timrāz al-Aḥmadī (Rte 12), nearby.

Tanam was only an Amīr of Forty under Sultan Khushqadam, but he was a barrack-comrade of the immensely powerful Amīr Gānī-bak. In 1463 Tanam was innocently caught up in the murder of that amīr (see Rte 15). Although unarmed, he fought the killers valiantly, but was himself murdered. Several Royal Mamlūks were punished for the crime.

The mosque has a good Mamlūk exterior, the façade on the street being the NE wall. Above, the minaret has an octagonal first tier, and a cylindrical second tier with continuous chevron carving. The upper tier is an eight-columned pavilion. Elaborate stalactite corbels support the balconies. Two stone benched flank the high porch which has a trefoil stalactite hood. Inside, the saḥn has two arcades of fine arches parallel to the qiblah wall. The interior decoration has been stripped except for two excellent carved baton pillars on either side of the miḥrāb.

# 13 Maydān al-Sayyidah Zaynab to Maydān Ṣalāḥ al-Dīn

Routes 13 to 16 encompass the southern city and include two important centres—the most ancient city, Babylon, and the last medieval area, the Citadel. Rte 13 (1.3km), in contrast to all the other routes, which run N to S or vice versa, travels from W to E. This reflects the importance of the street as the main transverse thoroughfare across the medieval city. It probably began as the main street of the city of al-Qataʾīʿ built by Ibn Ṭūlūn to the NE of al-Fusṭāṭ and the ʿAbbāsid city of al-ʿAskar. This city lay on the southern shore of a large lake, the Birkat al-Fil, which dried up during Ottoman times.

Like many other in Cairo, this road changes its name several times along its length. The oldest name seems to be Shʿ. al-Ṣālibah (Cross Street, since it ran laterally across the city). Bus No. 431 goes from Maydān al-Taḥrīr to Maydān Sayyidah Zaynab. **Cairo Atlas 22, 23.**

From the Maydān al-Sayyidah Zaynab the SHʿ. AL-SHAYKH ʿABD AL-MAGĪD AL-LABBĀN leads SE On the right (100m) is the **Sabīl of Ibrāhīm**

**Bay al-Munastirlī** (508; 22:4), built in 1714. 140m further (left) is the façade of the **Mosque of Sultan Gaqmaq** (217) of 1449. Like his madrasah (Rte 7) the mosque is modest in size with excellent workmanship but very simple. Only the plain octagonal first storey of the minaret has survived. Opposite to the E is the Ottoman *Sabīl of Yūsuf Bay* (319) of 1639.

70m further on a road leads off to the S, winding tortuously up a steep hill called QALʿAT AL-KABSH (Citadel of the Ram). On the summit, now standing alone but once part of á very large complex, is the **Madrasah of Sultan Qāyt-bay** (223; 22:4), built in 1475 on a site previously used by Sultan al-Ṣāliḥ Ayyūb. If anything it is even more heavily decorated than his mosque in the Eastern Cemetery (Rte 8) though rather more dilapidated. The minaret also lacks the elegance of the other, the first stage being much shorter than is normal and the first balcony resting on an unusual cavetto bracket. Two entrances lead into the cruciform interior, with reduced lateral līwāns and covered ṣaḥn. The miḥrāb, minbar and ceiling are all very fine and there

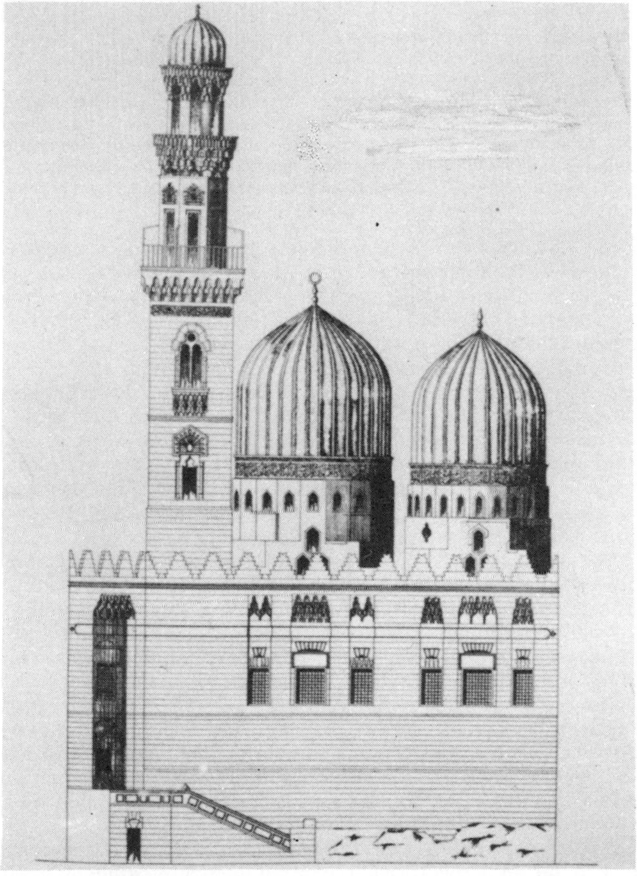

*The Madrasah and Tombs of Amīrs Salār and Sangar*

is a balcony in the NW līwān. Close to the S entrance is the **Drinking-trough of Qāyt-bay** (222) with a fine panel of inscriptions.

Back on the main route the road shortly turns due E. To the S, raised on a commanding eminence of rock, is the beautiful **Madrasah and Tombs of Amīrs Salār and Sangar** (221; 22:4), with twin domes dominating the façade. It was once a huge complex but only the tombs and part of the attached khānqah now stand. It was built in 1303 on the site of the barracks of Ibn Ṭūlūn's city, beside a palace of Sangar, now destroyed.

Salār, an Oirot Mongol, was captured during the wars against the Saljuks. He quickly found promotion in the ranks of the amīrs and formed a friendship with Sangar al-Gawlī who had come from Asia Minor. Sangar pursued a conventional career and generally steered clear of the political arena while Salār involved himself in the intrigues of the court, associating with the amīr Baybārs (Rte 4) and in the tribulations of the young Sultan al-Nāṣir Muḥ. When Sultan al-Nāṣir Muḥ escaped to Karak, Salār refused the sultanate and Baybārs ascended the throne, with Salār as viceroy. After the reinstatement of al-Nāṣir Muḥ. as sultan in 1309 and the execution of Baybārs, Salār was made governor of Shawbak. In the following year al-Nāṣir Muḥ. suspected Salār of being involved in a plot against him and persuaded the amīr to return to Cairo, where he was arrested, thrown into prison and died the same year. Sangar had him interred in the larger and more ornate of the mausoleums. He continued his own career as governor of Gaza and, after a period in prison between 1320–28, as governor of Ḥāma, he died peacefully in 1344, 34 years after his companion, and was interred in the second mausoleum. They had the mosque built during the second reign of Sultan al-Nāṣir Muḥ. while Salār and Baybārs controlled the country.

The façade of the mosque is plain but very impressive containing only the six windows of the tomb in square-headed stalactite niches, the central window in each tomb being twice as wide as the flanking windows. Undercut stepped cresting runs the entire length of the façade. The two brick domes, although part of the same structure, are rather different in design. That to the E over the tomb of Salār is larger and has a low stepped zone of transition with three rhomboidal windows between. A high 20-sided drum with keel-arched windows in each facet and a fine band of inscription supports the ribbed brick dome. The W dome, over the tomb of Sangar, is slightly smaller and more conventional in design, the stepped corners are larger in proportion and the 24 sided drum lower, though each facet also contains a keel-arched window and the dome is similar to Salār's. At the E end of the façade an angled wall has a full-length flat stalactite arch containing the entrance. The minaret rises to a height of 45m above the road level. The tall first storey in stone has a square section; in each side are two windows resting on stalactite sills, double lights with round arches with an oculus over, and on the SE side with a horseshoe arch. A continuous band of inscription runs under the stalactite corbel which supports the next brick octagonal storey, this with full length openings in each side and a fluted keel-arched recess above each under a very ornate cornice. The final tier is also octagonal with a fine ribbed cap. It has a much more slender outline than earlier minarets, a precedent that was to set the fashion. A flight of steps leads up the face of the ledge to the entrance set in a full-length recess topped by a flat stalactite arch. In the porch a door on the left leads to a flight of steps to the higher level. At the top are the remains of a dome and opposite an entrance to the vaulted corridor containing the tombs, while on the left is the entry to the remains of the madrasah and further steps to the roof.

On the right of the former corridor are the carved entrances and windows of the tombs. The *Tomb of Salār* is about 7m sq. with a very fine marble miḥrāb and a wooden frieze running around the four walls. Squinches of four over three over three niches raise the undecorated dome, while around the drum the windows have geometrical stucco grills except in the central lunar window which is foliate. Some of the windows contain a very unusual design, the shape of a mosque-lamp in the stucco filled with blue glass. The tomb of the amīr is in the centre of the room. Two entrances lead into the *Tomb of Sangar al-Gawlī* which is smaller, measuring 6.5m sq., and less ornately decorated. In the miḥrāb is a ribbed hood on a row of stalactites. The dome, also plain, is raised on squinches of four over five niches.

At the end of the corridor is the *Tomb of an Unknown Amīr*, entered through a door with a charming corbel. Only 4.5m sq., it has two oblong windows. Squinches with two tiers of three niches and a drum with eight windows raise the first stone dome known in Egypt, in this case a plain hemisphere. The amīr buried here was killed in 1348.

On the SW side of the corridor are four unequal pointed arches supported on large pillars, the first empty, the other three filled with pairs of elaborately carved and pierced *stone screens*, unique in Egypt. Each screen is different but all show superb craftsmanship. In the first are palmette motifs; the second has a similar pattern but larger, while the third is based on vines with leaves and grapes. On the other side of the screens is a small cemetery surrounded by houses.

Crossing the small landing at the top of the stairs from the lower level, a doorway leads into a wide hall, now roofed but originally open. It is extremely difficult to reconstruct the original form of this area as it is not aligned to the qiblah. In the W and S walls are small rooms for the students with grills over the doors, and above are a stucco inscription and medallions. To the E is a large higher līwān with a much later miḥrāb on the S wall.

In the small cemetery on the outside wall of the W ṣaḥn are the remains of one of the original stucco miḥrābs of the complex, but of the hall of which it was part nothing can be seen, except for stucco inscription and medallions on the adjoining wall. Opposite the entrance to the wide hall is a corridor leading to the *Upper Gateway* which has a stalactite portal with ribbed semi-dome.

From this bend the road becomes the SHʿ AL-KHUḌAYRĪ. At 140m the SHʿ. MUḤAMMAD QADRI leaves to the NW, just beyond which (30m) is the **Mosque of Sulaymān al-Khuḍayrī** (552; 23:3). Built in 1767 for a Khalawātī brotherhood, it contains good panels of Ottoman provincial tiles. On the S side of the road lies the **Madrasah and Tomb of Amīr Ṣarghatmish** (218; 23:2) built in 1356.

Probably of Mongol origin, Ṣarghatmish was purchased by Sultan al-Nāṣir Muḥ. in 1337 and rose through the ranks of the amīrs until in 1364 he was one of the amīrs who supported Shaykhū in the re-election of Sultan Ḥasan. After the assassination of Shaykhū he followed him as Amīr al-Kabīr but his crass attempts to make Ḥasan conform to his will led to his arrest in 1358, banishment to Alexandria and execution. His body was later transferred to this mosque.

Although in need of repair the mosque has several points of interest. The façade in the street is the NW wall. The minaret at the N end consists of two undecorated octagonal tiers crowned by an eight-columned pavilion. To the S of this is the tall arched entrance, the frame rising slightly above the height of the façade. A series of half-height recesses divides the wall, each containing two pairs of windows. The upper windows are large with round arches filled with stucco lattice, the lower windows rectangular with bronze grilles. Above is a stepped cresting. The *Tomb* makes a salient at the W end, the brick dome of which is very unusual. It rises directly from a high circular drum with large windows and the remains of a fine inscription, above which a stalactite frieze makes a slight overhang from which the plain dome takes off. This creates a strange profile for an Egyptian dome. The interior reveals a cruciform plan, the open ṣaḥn, surrounded by students' rooms, having stepped cresting and a marble floor with an angular pattern and octagonal fountain in the centre. Big pointed arches front the līwāns of which the qiblah līwān is the largest. Little is left of the facing of the walls but the dome over the miḥrāb is unique among cruciform mosques in Egypt. Unfortunately the dome itself is an uncomfortable reconstruction in concrete (originally it was probably similar to that over the tomb), but the excellent multiple-niched squinches are original. In the miḥrāb of 1700 are well-carved marble panels naming the founder. A door in the NW līwān leads to the *Tomb Chamber* with a marble tomb inscribed with Naskhī. Although the dome has many-niched squinches they differ from those above the miḥrāb.

This mosque abuts the NW wall of the façade of the massive **Mosque of Aḥmad Ibn Ṭūlūn** (220; 23:3). Built between 876–79, it is the largest mosque in Cairo and the earliest retaining its original fabric. To enter turn up the street on the right.

Son of a Turkish commander Aḥmad (born 835) received his military and theological training in Samarra and Tarsus. His unusual intelligence and courage attracted the attention of the khalīf and in 868 he was made proxy for his step-father Bākbāk's governorship of Egypt. As a countermeasure against the revolt of other provinces Aḥmad built up a large slave army of men from Central Asia, Sudan and Asia Minor. At this time the khalīf al-Muʿtamid divided the administration of the empire between his son Jaʿfar, who received the Western provinces, and his brother al-Muwaffaq, the more powerful of the two, who received the Eastern provinces. Revolts and internal discord preoccupied al-Muwaffaq and Aḥmad seized the opportunity to declare his independence. An abortive attempt to remove him encouraged Aḥmad to occupy Syria, which he did despite a revolt by his son ʿAbbās in Egypt. After several more attempts to dislodge Aḥmad by propaganda and force it became apparent to al-Muwaffaq that Aḥmad's position would have to be formally recognised. For the first time since the Roman occupation the wealth of the country was retained and Egypt prospered. Aḥmad died in 884 to be succeeded by his son Khumārawayh.

To accommodate the immense army, the administration and other followers, and also to enhance his own claim to independence, Aḥmad decided in 870 to construct a new city to the NE of al-ʿAskar, which itself was just NE of Fusṭāṭ. He chose an area where the first foothills of the Muqaṭṭam range rise from the plain, bordered to the E by the hills that now contain the Citadel and on the W by the Qalʿat al-Kabsh (see above). This city, called al-Qaṭāʾīʿ (the Concessions), contained a huge arena, a palace, the great mosque and countless dwellings and markets. It was served by an aqueduct that had an intake tower at al-Basatīn to the S (Rte 15). Of this marvellous city only the mosque and part of the aqueduct and intake tower remain.

The site chosen for the mosque was an outcrop of rock called Gabal Yashkur. Some time previously the architect of the intake tower of the aqueduct, a Jacobite Christian from Syria, had been imprisoned, but when he heard that Aḥmad wished to build a mosque without robbing churches of their columns he wrote to tell him that he could do this. Brick piers had recently appeared in the mosques in Iraq but were an innovation in Egypt and when the drawings were shown to Aḥmad he was well pleased. The plan of the mosque, although showing certain similarities to those

# MOSQUE OF AḤMAD IBN ṬŪLŪN

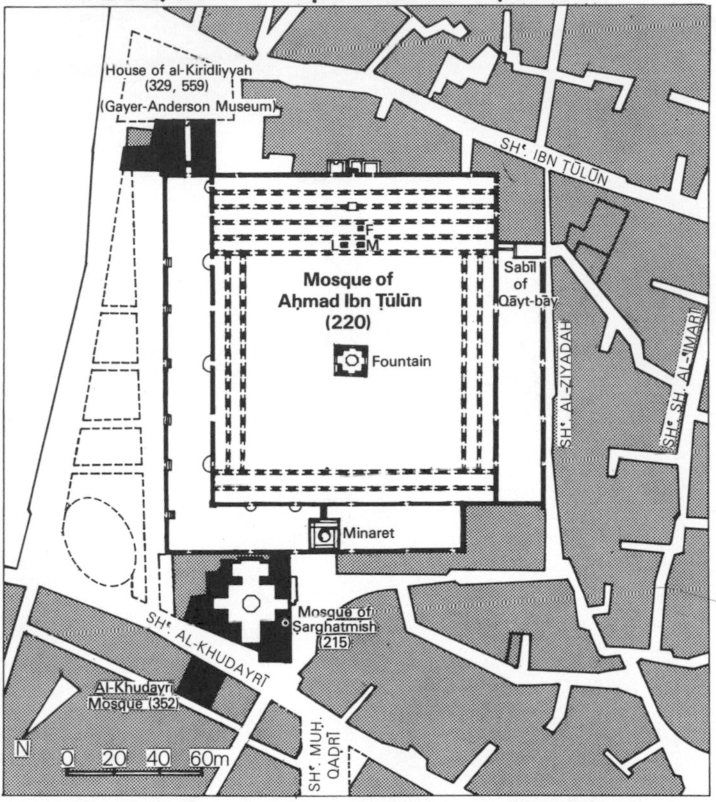
House of al-Kiridliyyah
(329, 559)
(Gayer-Anderson Museum)
SH'. IBN ṬŪLŪN
F
L
M
Mosque of
Aḥmad Ibn Ṭūlūn
(220)
Fountain
Sabīl
of
Qāyt-bāy
SH'. AL-ZIYADAH
SH'. SH. AL-'IMARI
Minaret
Mosque of
Ṣarghatmish
(215)
SH'. AL-KHUDAYRĪ
Al-Khudayrī
Mosque (352)
SH'. MUḤ. QADRĪ
N
0 20 40 60m

previously constructed in Iraq, seems to have taken much of its inspiration from the Mosque of ʿAmir as it appeared in the 9C.

A small fire in the mosque necessitated repairs by the Khalīf al-ʿAzīz in 995 while further restoration was undertaken by Badr al-Gamālī in 1077 and his son al-Afḍal in 1094. By the mid 13C the mosque was surrounded by desolation, the main commercial activity having moved N to al-Qāhirah. In 1294 the amīr Lāgīn, who had been implicated in the assassination of Sultan Khalīl, sought refuge here. The mosque was lit at night by a single lamp and he swore that if his circumstances changed he would restore the mosque to its former glory. His circumstances did indeed change and in 1297 after the deposition of Sultan Kitbughā he was elected sultan. True to his oath he ordered the amīr ʿAlam al-Din Sangar to undertake the work, spending 20,000 dinars on the project. This restoration included the fountain in the centre of the ṣaḥn, the minaret, a miḥrāb, and the dome above, a minbar and many of the window lattices. Strangely his architect chose in several cases to reconstruct in the ancient style and not to use the current Mamlūk forms; whether under direct instruction from Lāgīn or personal whim is not known. Sultan Qāyt-bāy built a sabīl in the SW ziyādah in the 15C. During Ottoman times the mosque received little attention, although in 1684 Bilāl Aghā renewed some of the woodwork. By the end of the 18C it was a woollen factory and in the mid 19C a hospice for the disabled. When the first arcade of the qiblah rīwāq fell in 1882 it was decided by

*The ṣaḥn and minaret of the Mosque of Ibn Ṭūlūn*

the newly-formed CPAM that the building should be restored. In 1918 King Fū'ād I allotted £E40,000 for work on the mosque. Much work has been undertaken since then and it now has much of its original appearance although without its pristine gleaming white walls and gilded decoration and inscriptions.

The whole building as constructed for Aḥmad consists of small red bricks covered with fine plaster in which the decoration has been carved. Much of the original wooden decoration has been retained. The only stone parts are those added by later sultans.

The façade on the street is the wall of the *NE Ziyādah* (extension); at 8m it is lower than the mosque proper. This wall is plain except for a frieze of squares with central circles. Along the top of the wall runs the unique open work cresting, 2m high; it has no known precedent. Ziyādahs (open precincts) were intended to separate the mosque from the secular areas of the town as the avenues of several markets ended at the doors of the precinct. Several mosques in Egypt possessed such precincts but this is the only one in which they are retained. It surrounds the mosque on three sides—NE, NW and SW—and the area covered makes the ground plan of the mosque an almost perfect square, 161.5m by 162.25m. Instead of a ziyādah, the SE wall was abutted by the Dār al-Imarah (House of government; now destroyed), with its own entrance into the mosque. Here Aḥmad would stay and bathe before leading the Friday prayer.

There are six plain doorways in the wall of the NE ziyādah, as in the SW, but seven in the NW. The interior of the ziyādah, 19m wide, is some height above ground level, and on the opposite side is the wall of the mosque proper. Similar to the wall of the ziyādah, it is higher (13m), and has a row of windows along the whole length of the wall, c 7m above the floor of the ziyādah. The pointed arches rest on squat pillars and between each is a small multiple-lobed niche. The frieze along the summit of the wall and the cresting are similar to those on the ziyādah wall. Doors corresponding to those in the ziyādah pierce the wall of the mosque higher than ground level; there are two more at the SE corner. There are also seven in the SW ziyādah and five in the NW, all originally reached by semicircular flights of steps, several of which have been restored. The lintels are composed of palm-trunks, boxed with wood and above a releasing arch. Two of the large doors at each end of the qiblah riwāq retain their original carving.

The mosque proper measures 140.3m SE–NW and 122.2m NE–SW with a central ṣaḥn 92m sq., surrounded by riwāqs of two arcades on the NE, SW and NW sides and five arcades in the qiblah riwāq. There are a total of 13 arches in each row of the first two riwāqs and 17 in each of the last two. Each riwāq presents 13 arches around the ṣaḥn. The piers of the arches are oblong with engaged brick columns at each corner c 4m high, those in the qiblah riwāq being a half-metre higher; wooden plates are inserted into the piers as strengtheners. All the arches are pointed, with a slight return giving an ogival outline. The capitals of the columns are derived from late antique Corinthian forms with the addition of vine-leaf motifs. Around the arches of the ṣaḥn runs a continuous band of carved foliate decoration and between each arch is a pointed-arch opening, the decorated frame resting on small pillars. Flanking these openings are sunken eight-lobed disks. Above runs a frieze of carved daisy medallions, but the cresting has disappeared.

All the soffits of the arches were originally decorated with carved stucco but only a few in the SW riwāq have survived, with geometrical framework and cursive insets. The inner arcades are ornamented in a similar fashion although the decoration around the arches is in a style that derives from Samarra while the frieze above is of an entirely different type to that in the ṣaḥn. There are no disks flanking the openings. Below the roof a continuous Kufic inscription from the Qur'ān carved in sycamore fig wood circles the mosque several times; in total it is over 2km long. Some of the most outstanding features of the mosque are the window grilles though only a few at the E end of the qiblah riwāq, composed of circles and part circles, are original. The remainder are the work of Sultan Lāgīn.

In the centre of the ṣaḥn is the *Fawwarah* (20m high), built for Sultan Lāgīn by the court architect Ibn al-Rūmiyyah to replace the wooden one built by Khalīf al-ʿAzīz in the 980s; this had in turn replaced the original decorative fountain. In design it reiterates one of the favoured Mamlūk forms, the domed cube. The stone base measures 14m by 12.7m and has a pointed-arched opening in each side; in the NE wall is a staircase. The zone-of-transition has stepped corners with a window in the uppermost step and a large window of three lights on each side. Above, the dome is plain without a drum, eight windows piercing the base. The interior walls are plain; the dome is raised on a squinch of three tiers of five niches. Above this a continuous stalactite frieze runs around the base of the dome and above that a band of Naskhī inscription from the Qur'ān dealing with ablution. A medallion at the apex of the dome also contains an inscription from the Qur'ān. In the centre of the floor is an octagonal stone basin.

In 1882 the first arcade of the *Qiblah Riwāq* fell and restoration work immediately started on the mosque. On each of the two central piers of the second arcade is a flat carved stucco miḥrāb. That on the right is the *Miḥrāb of the Wazīr al-Afḍāl* (M), son of Badr al-Gamālī, added in 1004. It is 3m high and surrounded by a wide band of decorated Kufic inscription. Below the upper border are three horizontal panels, the small first panel is inscription, the next ornament and the third panel more inscription. Filling the shoulders of the arch is geometrical decoration with a round space for a conical boss on each side. The pointed arch is composed of two lines of inscription raised on two small columns, and the tympanum is filled with palmettes and floral decoration. In the body of the miḥrāb are the remains of a monumental Kufic inscription (a cast of this miḥrāb taken in 1903 is on display in the MIA and shows much more detail than can now be seen). This has no precedent among the Fāṭimid miḥrābs in Cairo, and Creswell has given convincing evidence of its relationship to contemporary Persian miḥrābs, although why this should be remains a mystery. On the arch in the left-hand side is a very similar *Miḥrāb* (L), added by Sultan Lāgīn, an example of his archaic reconstruction.

On the right-hand central pier of the third arcade from the ṣaḥn is a *Foundation Inscription* (F), a rectangular slab of marble 97cm by 1.6m, in Kufic characters. It contains the Ayat al-Kursī (Throne Verse) from the Qur'ān, and the date 265 AH (AD 879). The two central piers of the fourth arcade from the ṣaḥn flanking the dikkah also each contain a miḥrāb, probably 10C. In the SE wall are four entrances, two flanking the miḥrāb that led originally directly from the Dār al-Imarah into the mosque. The *Main Miḥrāb* consists of a double pointed-arched recess flanked by a pair of marble columns with basket-work capitals. The interior is decorated in Mamlūk style with strips of polychrome marble above which is a band of Naskhī inscription in black mosaic on a gold background containing the *shahādah*. In the spandrels are two large bosses and round the whole is a frame of carved stucco. To the left beneath the ninth window from the NE wall is a further flat stucco mihrab with Naskhī and Kufic inscription known as the *Miḥrāb of Sayyidah Nafīsah*, probably 13C. Above the main miḥrāb is a wooden dome, raised on a squinch of three over three niches. While the dome is undoubtedly Mamlūk, the miḥrāb with its windows of coloured panes shows Ottoman influence and was probably contributed by Bilāl Aghā. The *Minbar* is one of the earliest and finest in Egypt, made for Sultan Lāgīn in 1296 and consisting of heavily carved panels and a richly decorated stalactite canopy. There are only two older minbars, both Fāṭimid, the first in St. Katherine's Monastery, Sinai, and the second in Qūṣ.

Directly behind the mosque the wall of the *NW Ziyādah* rises about 1.1m; in the ziyādah, although not centrally placed, stands the *Minaret*, 40m high. Of unique form and constructed of limestone, it is connected to the roof of the mosque by a bridge supported on two large horseshoe arches. Evidence shows that this was part of the restoration of Sultan Lāgīn in 1296 although built, at least in part, to the original spiral design similar to that at Samarra. The first storey has a square section. 21.3m high, it is decorated on each face with a pair of blind horseshoe-arched niches. A massive cylinder, 8.5m high, with a staircase circling the outside provides the second storey, while the third and fourth storeys are octagonal and more conventional in design, crowned with a ribbed dome. At the S end of the SW Ziyadah stands the *Sabīl of Sultan Qayt-Bāy*.

At the E corner of the mosque on the SHʿ. ṬŪLŪN stands the **Bayt al-Kiridliyyah** (House of the Cretans; 321; 23:3), also called the *Gayer-Anderson Museum* (Hrs. 09.00–15.00. Fri closed 11.00–13.30. Fee but tickets to Mus. of Islamic Art includes entrance to this monument). It is set at the S end of the NE ziyādah of the Mosque of Ibn Ṭūlūn with its own entrance into the mosque precinct. There are two houses on either side of a small alley, the ʿAtfat al-Gamiʿ, that on the W built in 1540 and that on the E in 1631, joined by a bridge at the second storey.

For 100 years prior to 1934, the houses had been the home of the family al-Kiriʿdlī, originally from Crete, and the last owner, Sh. Sulāymān, sold it to the government. Major Robert Gayer-Anderson (1881–1945), a distinguished doctor and member of the Egyptian Civil Service, who had long expressed the desire to restore one of the buildings in Cairo, was given guardianship of the buildings, attended often by Sh. Sulāymān himself. He proceeded to scour old buildings and palaces for Ottoman furniture and fittings, and by the time he returned to England because of ill-health in 1942 he had completely restored and refurnished the building throughout. Both houses are constructed of sandstone and the decoration in both, as in most other Ottoman buildings, relies heavily on Mamlūk themes.

The *East House*, built originally for Muḥ. Ibn Galmān, was in later times used as the ḥaramlik. On the SW corner is the *Sabīl* with bronze grilles. A baffled corridor leads to the central courtyard with a fountain in the centre. An arched recess holds the Bīr al-Waṭāwīṭ (Well of the Bats), about which many fables were told in the neighbourhood; in fact the whole house was a source of fantastic tales for the local story-tellers. Rooms on the ground floor were used as kitchens, store-rooms and servants' quarters. Stairs in the W side lead into a high taqtabush overlooking the courtyard fronted by two arches. A decorated ceiling contains a foundation inscription. On the E side of the court a door leads up more stairs into the Ḥarīm, the finest room in the house. The many built-in cupboards and other woodwork are finely decorated and the windows are filled with mashrabiyyah. Also surrounded by mashrabiyyah screens is a roof-garden. On this storey where the two houses join is a series of rooms given over to the fruits of Gayer-Anderson's tireless collecting—the Library, Byzantine Room, Picture Gallery, Queen Anne Room, Persian Room, Damascus Room and Turkish Room, also called the Muḥammad ʿAlī Room with a contemporary portrait of the Pasha himself.

Crossing the atfit into the *West House*, which was the Salamlik, another corridor leads to a small court which gives on to the great Qāʿah, taking up two floors of the house. In the centre of the ornate marble floor is a mosaic fountain. There are two great līwāns at either end of the qāʿah and galleries on each side fronted with mashrabiyyah screens, behind which the women could watch the activity below. A room was added later to the roof and this has been decorated in 17C style from a demolished house in Damascus. All the walls and the ceiling are covered in lacquer and gilding with intricate patterns including a fine calligraphic poem which includes the date 1103 AH (AD 1691). On the N corner of the E building is the *Tomb of Sīdī Ḥārūn*, claimed as a descendant of al-Ḥusayn.

On the opposite side of the main route the ḤĀRAT AZBAK leads to the N; after several metres on the W, occupying a corner site, is the **Madrasah of Amīr Azbak al-Yūsufī** (211; 23:3), built in 1494. It is without a dome as there is no proper tomb chamber.

A mamlūk of Sultan Jaqmaq, Azbak became governor of ʿAynṭab in 1471 and after a period of disgrace rose again to be Amīr Maglis and Counsellor of State. He died in 1499.

The main tall trefoil entrance is in the SW wall. N of that is the minaret with octagonal lower storey with keel-arched niches and deeply carved cylindrical second storey; the uppermost pavilion is a reconstruction. The upper windows have double lights covered by an oculus while the lower windows have finely carved lintels. On the N side is the *Sabīl-Kuttāb* with a separate entrance on each side of which is the amīr's blazon; in the upper field a napkin between horns, in the middle field a cup between horns and in the lower field a cup between two napkins, the upper and lower fields sunk and the middle field raised. At the N end of the façade is a *Drinking-trough*. The interior is built to a cruciform plan with covered ṣaḥn and skylight, and an intricate polychrome marble floor. Each of the līwāns is fronted by a pointed arch and, although the marble facing has been stripped, the walls of the ṣaḥn and the voussoirs are covered with fine but uninspired carving. Above the undecorated miḥrāb is another excellent panel of carving. The NE līwān has been converted into a tomb chamber separated from the rest of the mosque by a wooden maqsūrah. Buried inside are Azbak, his wife Bunukh (died 1494) and her son Farag (died 1483) by a previous marriage to the amīr Tamīm. All the woodwork, including the ceilings, minbār and kursī, is contemporary.

Along the small lane to the E is the Ottoman **Sabīl of Aḥmad Afandī Salīm** (461; 23:3) of 1699.

The next section of the main route retains its original name of the SHʿ. ṢALĪBAH. After 80m on the S are the remains of the **Palace of Sultan Qānṣūḥ al-Ghawrī** (322), consisting of a section of wall with inscriptional cartouches and six massive corbels, which once supported the upper floors. At the N end is the original portal. On the N side of the road (60m) stands the **Madrasah and Tomb of Amīr Taghrībardī** (209; 23:3), built in 1440 and locally called Saghri Wardi.

Although originally a mamlūk of Sultan Farag, Taghrībardi al-Buklumushī, noted for his belligerent wit, rose to become grand dawādār under Sultan Jaqmaq. He was assassinated by his own discontented mamlūks in 1442.

*The Madrasah and Tomb of Amīr Taghrībardī al-Buklumushī*

The façade on the street is the SW wall of the mosque, at the W end of which is a trefoil-arched entrance with pishtak rising above the level of the roof. To the left is a *Sabīl-Kuttāb*; the former has almost disappeared but the kuttāb above retains a fine wooden arched canopy. Above this rises the minaret with square-sectioned base and corbel supporting the second geometrically carved cylindrical tier; the third storey is an ugly Ottoman replacement, the original having fallen. On the rest of the façade full-length recesses contain two tiers of windows while a trefoil cresting runs along the summit of the walls. At the SE corner, resting on an octagonal base, is the dome, very similar to that above the Tomb of Khadīgah (Rte 8), being heavily carved with geometrically entwined ribs, and doubtless executed by the same architects. However, it is a pattern unsuited to the subtle curve of the dome and was not repeated.

Inside the entrance is a vestibule, on the right leading to the *Tomb Chamber* in which the amīr is buried, the dome raised on squinches with two tiers of niches. On the left a baffled corridor leads into the cruciform interior, with the ṣaḥn now open although originally roofed, and the two lateral līwāns only slightly reduced in size. The qiblah līwān is the largest and all have the remains of fine ceilings, while the contemporary minbar is good work.

Continuing E the road passes on the N (70m) the *Sabīl Umm ʿAbbās*, a 19C fountain and library built in 1867 for the dowager Princess Bambah Qādin, widow of Ṭūsūn and mother of ʿAbbās I. It is a riot of highly carved marble with bronze grilles and gilded inscriptions on blue or red backgrounds. The road crosses the Shʿ. Ruqbiyyah (Rte 11, NE to the Citadel, S to Maydān Sayyidah Nafīsah) where it becomes the SHʿ. SHAYKHŪN. This road is flanked on either side by the marvellous dual **Complex of Amīr Shaykhū**. Although there is five years difference between the building of the two parts of the monument, the façades, in ablaq masonry, have been built as an integrated whole with the twin minarets dominating the street. It is interesting to note that while the façades on the road are similar the interiors are used in entirely different ways.

Originally a mamlūk of Sultan al-Nāṣir Muḥ., Shaykhū became one of the leading amīrs during the first reign of the former's son Ḥasan. When Ḥasan was deposed in 1351 by the amīr Ṭāz and his younger brother Ṣāliḥ elevated in his place, Shaykhū bided his time. While Ṭāz was away hunting in 1354 Shaykhū with the agreement of the other amīrs had Ṣāliḥ returned to the ḥarīm and Ḥasan reinstated. Although there was a great struggle when Ṭāz returned to Cairo the two amīrs were finally reconciled. Shaykhū was made Amīr al-Kabīr, the first time the title was used. In 1357, while officiating in the diwān, Shaykhū was assassinated by the discontented Royal Mamlūks. Without this powerful strut Ḥasan was at the mercy of the other amīrs and in 1361 was seized by the amīr Yalbughā and deposed.

On the N side of the road is the **Mosque of Amīr Shaykhū** (147; 23:3), the earlier of the pair, built in 1349. It has a fine façade with joggled lintels to the lower windows and iron grills. At the W end of the façade is the stalactite-arched entrance above which rises the minaret of two octagonal tiers and cylindrical top surmounted by carved finial, perhaps emulating lotus buds and further evidence of Mongol influence. The lower balcony rests on moulded corbels the second on a double corbel. In the vestible are primitive black glass mirrors. To the E is the *Tomb Chamber* which only contains the tomb of an unrecorded shaykh. At the N the vestibule opens onto the cruciform madrasah with open ṣaḥn and much reduced lateral līwāns, perhaps the first such in Egypt. In the centre of the ṣaḥn is an octagonal fountain, probably a later addition. Each of the axial līwāns has two arcades supported on classical pillars. Steps lead up to the qiblah līwān, in the central arch of which is the unusual dikkah with carved marble insets. Much of the fine original work is preserved in the miḥrāb.

With a 17C *Drinking-trough* (323) at the E end, the façade of the **Khānqah and Tomb of Amīr Shaykhū** (152) is in essentials the same as the mosque, but built in 1355 and repaired in 1685 by the aghā Bilāl. It is a warren of small rooms for sufis surrounding a central ṣaḥn. Three storeys of windows with pointed arches overlook the courtyard. In all 700 sufis resided here in a total of 150 rooms. Here as in the mosque classical pillars support the arches. To the left of the qiblah riwāq in the NE corner is the *Tomb Chamber*, inside which is the Tomb of Sh. Akmāl al-Dīn (died 1378), the first director of the Khānqah, and beyond is the Tomb of Shaykhū himself.

Further E on the S side of the road lies the *House and Sabīl of ʿAbd Allāh* (452; 23:4); 60m further is the **Mosque of Amīr Qānībay al-Muḥammadī** (151), built in 1413. This has no foundation inscription and the association with this amīr relies on literary evidence. There is little of the original fabric of this mosque probably built for the brilliant Qānībay who rose to be viceroy of Damascus before he was 40, but rebelled against Sultan Shaykh and was executed in 1415. The minaret has two octagonal stories and the dome is covered with chevron moulding. Also on the S (50m) stands the **Sabīl-Kuttāb of Sultan Qāyt-bāy** (324; 23:4), built in 1479, a free-standing structure, the first fountain and school built as such. Although the upper storey is much reconstructed, the lower part is still very interesting with exceptional marble facing to the interior in the NW corner. Beyond, the road runs into the W side of the small Maydān Muhammad ʿAlī, which is at the N end of the immense Maydān Ṣalāḥ al-Dīn.

The MAYDĀN ṢALĀḤ AL-DĪN is a rectangular site (700m long) below the Citadel. This was once the vast Qarāmaydān (Meeting Place), the sporting arena of the mamlūks where they held their horse races, polo matches and tournaments. At the N end is the Maydān Muḥammad ʿAlī, previously al-Rumaylah (sandy area), the ceremonial parade ground. Here all the processions into the city started and it was here that the mamlūks and amīrs received their stipends, presents and honours. The area is now occupied by gardens flanked by wide roads.

On the W road there is only one monument, which lies directly against the Citadel wall. This is the **Mosque of Qarā Muḥammad ʿAlī Pasha** (377;24:5); only the minaret remains of the building of 1701. Muḥammad was governor of Egypt in 1699–1704. This mosque was a large complex built for poor Turks of the Khalawātī Brotherhood and contained a kitchen, school and bath. The massive minaret consists of two circular tiers.

In the middle of the central garden stands the domed **Tomb of Muṣṭafā Kāmil** (24:3) which incorporates the **Muṣṭafā Kāmil Museum** (Hrs 09.00–15.00. Fri 0900–1300; fee). Just inside the entrance is the tomb chamber, the beautiful tābūt above the grave is executed in highly polished, light-coloured marbles. Surrounding the chamber are rooms which contain the personal belongings of the nationalist politician Muṣṭafā Kāmil (1874–1908), correspondence, photographs, clothing, and his library. Murals of the Danishway incident (at the trial after the affair he was leading council for the defence) cover some of the walls.

From the N end of the maydān, at the junction with the Shʿ. Ṣalībah, the SHʿ. AL-FATḤ runs in a curve to re-emerge at the S end of the maydān. Immediately on the left is the *Mosque of Sultan Qānṣūḥ al-Ghawrī* (148). Little is left of the original building of 1504 except the qiblah wall which contains two inscriptions. After 250m on the W side stands the **Mosque of Amīr Qānī-bāy al-Jarkassī** (154; 24:5), a small enclosure mosque originally built in 1413 but much reconstructed.

Qānī-bāy was one of the leading amīrs of Sultan Jaqmaq under whom he became Grand Amīr Akhūr. He disputed the succession of Sultan Īnāl and in 1453 was imprisoned at Alexandria. In 1461 he was released by Sultan Khushqadam but died in Damietta the same year.

The external walls are plain; above the NW corner rises the original minaret. It rests on a square base and consists of a single cylindrical tier with a curved chevron decoration. In the NE wall the entrance with simple trefoil hood is probably reconstructed. Inside, each wall has a single wooden-roofed riwaq with pointed arches raised on pillars. The entire facing of the walls and miḥrāb has been stripped.

On the E side of the road stands the small **Zāwiyah of Qarā Muṣṭafā Pasha** (155; 24:5). This was built in 1625 by a governor who was in office in 1622 and 1623–25. It is a well-preserved and charming early Ottoman building with moulding around the trefoil entrance.

400m further the road emerges at the S end of the Maydān Ṣalāḥ al-Dīn where the Shʿ. Ṣalāḥ Sālim crosses from E to W. To the E and S stretches the vast Southern Cemetery (Rtes 14, 15). At this southern point of the square in the Maydān Sayyidah ʿĀʾishah stands the **Mosque of Sayyidah ʿĀʾishah** (378). Although this building has had a chequered history there is nothing left of the various stages prior to the modern reconstruction.

ʿAʾīshah, a descendant of al-Ḥusayn, came to Egypt in 762 and died in the same year. Ṣalāḥ al-Dīn was responsible for transforming the tomb into a large mosque and actually modified the alignment of his city walls to accommodate the building. Much work was also undertaken by ʿAbd al-Rahmān Katkhuda in the 18C.

# 14 The Citadel

Route 14 is confined to the Citadel and the area immediately to the S. Although the distance covered is not great there is a great deal of walking to be done inside and if a journey outside the walls is included it can add up to several km.

Bus No. 82 goes from Maydān al-Taḥrīr to the Citadel. **Cairo Atlas 24, 25, and see map on pp 364–65.**

*View across Cairo from the Muqaṭṭam Hills past the Mashhad al-Guyushī and the Mosque of Muḥammad ʿAlī*

The SHʿ ṢALĀḤ SĀLIM runs W of the E Cemetery (Rte 8) and turns S to run E of the Citadel, passing on the E the Shʿ al-Muqaṭṭam (see below). Beyond this to the W is the main entrance to the Citadel. The surrounds have been landscaped into a park with several cafés and there is parking for cars and coaches.

The **Citadel of the Mountain** (al-Qalʿah al-Gabal or al-Burg; 24:4) commands the cities of Cairo and Fusṭāṭ from the only piece of high ground between the River Nile and the Muqaṭṭam Hills, but its obvious significance as a defensive position was not realised until Ṣalāḥ al-Dīn included it in his grand design for the fortification of the city.

The hill, composed of early Tertiary limestone, is a wedge-shaped spur of the Muqattam Hills which rise to the E to a height of 200m, while the maximum height of the hill is 75m. The E face has been quarried, leaving the hill isolated from the main rock mass, but a portion of the S area has been built up artificially. It stands 1.5km SE of the southernmost point of the enclosure of al-Qāhirah and 2.5km NE of Fusṭāṭ. Once the walls were completed the only route past the city was the pass between the Citadel and the Muqaṭṭam Hills.

During the British occupation the Citadel was used as a military base and hospital and continued so after the 1952 revolution. Recently with a reorganisation of military sites it was decided to develop the Citadel into a cultural tourist attraction, with a series of excavations; clearance of redundant structures; conservation of historical monuments and the erection of new lecture centres and cafés.

**History**. There may have been a Roman garrison sited on the hill, but apart from this the area remained uninhabited until after the Arab conquest. In 810 Ḥātim, an ʿAbbāsid governor, built a pavilion, the Qubbat al-Hawā (Dome of the Winds) there. This was popular with all the rulers until the deposition of the Ṭūlūnids when it was destroyed. Gradually the area was incorporated in the great cemetery surrounding the city and several mosques were built on the heights, remaining thus until the rise of Ṣalāḥ al-Dīn in the 12C. It is known that he contemplated the fortification of the city while still an amīr of Shirkūh and started to rebuild some of the N walls as early as 1167. But it was not until he gained supreme control of Egypt as sultan in 1171 that he could put his ideas into practice. The plan involved nothing less than the complete enclosure of al-Qāhirah and Fusṭāṭ within one wall commanded by the Citadel. His assistants in this project were his brother al-ʿAdil and his atabak the amīr Qarakūsh—a conjunction of three brilliant minds with the work force of an almost unlimited number of captured Crusader soldiers.

Ṣalāḥ al-Dīn Yūsuf, born in Takrit on the Tigris c 1137, was of Hadhbānī Kurdish descent. His father Ayyūb and uncle Shirkūh were amīrs of the Zangid rulers of Syria. Ayyūb became governor of Baʿālbak and Shirkūh an army commander. Little is known of Ṣalāḥ al-Dīn's early life except that his main pursuits were theological study and sport. The parlous state of Egypt in the mid 12C was aggravated by the conflict of the two wazirs of Khalif al-ʿAdid, Shāwar and Dirghām. In 1163 they allied themselves to the Zangid ruler Nūr al-Dīn and King Amalric of Jerusalem respectively. Nūr al-Dīn sent an expedition under Shirkūh, accompanied by a reluctant Ṣalāḥ al-Dīn, to Egypt to forestall a Crusader invasion. The outcome was indecisive and during the next five years there were several more confrontations on Egyptian soil. During the final battle, from which Shirkūh emerged victorious, Shāwar set fire to Fusṭāṭ. Dirghām was assassinated, and so the protagonists were Shirkūh and Shāwar. Shāwar attempted to have Shirkūh poisoned, but the plot was discovered by Ṣalāḥ al-Dīn and he was executed on the orders of Khalīf al-ʿAdid. Shirkūh was made wazir, but when he died two months later at a banquet the wazirate was bestowed upon Ṣalāḥ al-Dīn. Within months he was in complete control of the country, the young Fāṭimid Khalīf retaining only nominal authority. In 1171 al-ʿAdid fell gravely ill and on 10 September Ṣalāḥ al-Dīn ordered that the khutbah at the Friday prayer should include the name of the Sunnī ʿAbbāsid khalif al-Mustaḍī of Baghdad. Al-ʿAdid died two days after this momentous act which extinguished the Shiʿī Fāṭimid khalifate.

Ṣalāḥ al-Dīn was now master of Egypt, though he still deferred to Nūr al-Dīn. He dispossessed the Fāṭimids from their palaces in the enclosure of al-Qāhirah and distributed their vast treasure between Nūr al-Dīn and his own amīrs and officials. He brought his father, brothers and other relatives from Syria to form the basis of his administration. Although there were several minor revolts by the followers of the Fāṭimids, they found no popular support as the majority of the population had remained Sunnī. To promote the Sunnī canon Ṣalāḥ al-Dīn encouraged the

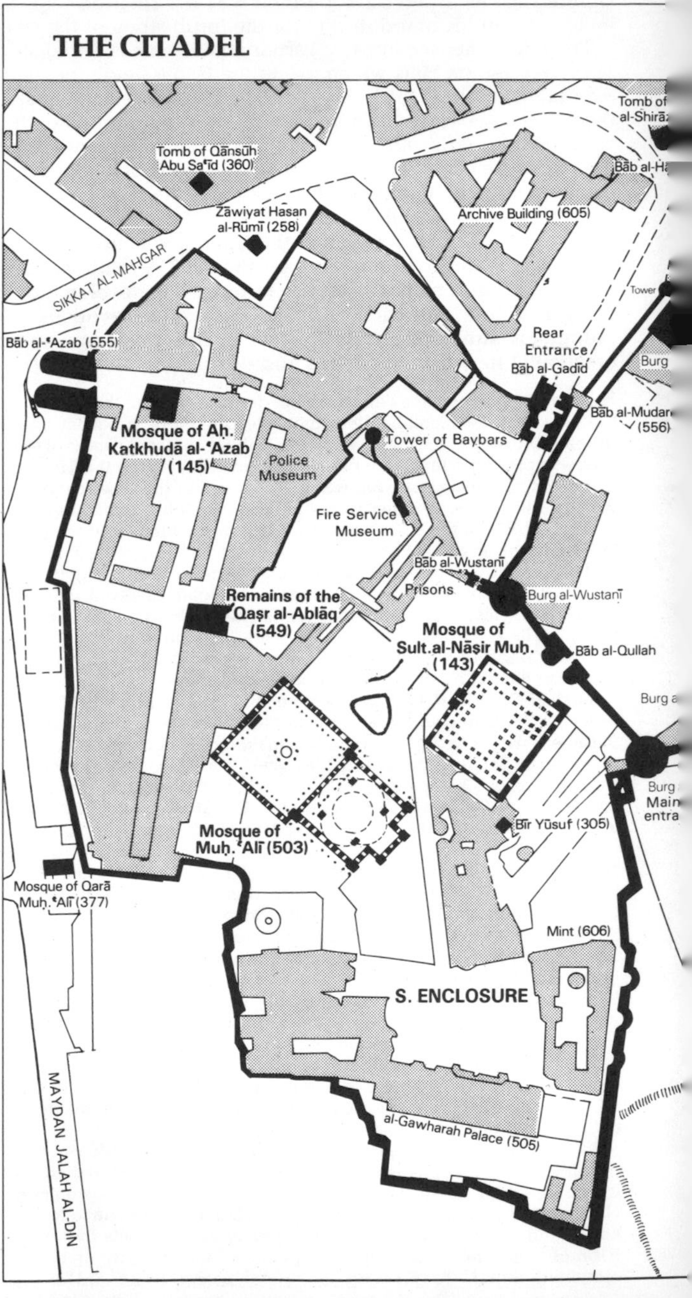
THE CITADEL
Tomb of Qānsūh Abu Sa'īd (360)
Zāwiyat Hasan al-Rūmī (258)
SIKKAT AL-MAHGAR
Archive Building (605)
Bāb al-'Azab (555)
Mosque of Aḥ. Katkhudā al-'Azab (145)
Police Museum
Tower of Baybars
Rear Entrance Bāb al-Gadīd
Bāb al-Mudar (556)
Fire Service Museum
Bāb al-Wustanī
Prisons
Burg al-Wustanī
Remains of the Qaṣr al-Ablāq (549)
Mosque of Sult. al-Nāṣir Muḥ. (143)
Bāb al-Qullah
Mosque of Muḥ. 'Alī (503)
Bīr Yūsuf (305)
Mosque of Qarā Muḥ. 'Alī (377)
Mint (606)
S. ENCLOSURE
al-Gawharah Palace (505)
MAYDAN JALAH AL-DIN
Tower
Burg
Tomb of al-Shirā
Bāb al-Ha
Burg a
Burg
Main entra

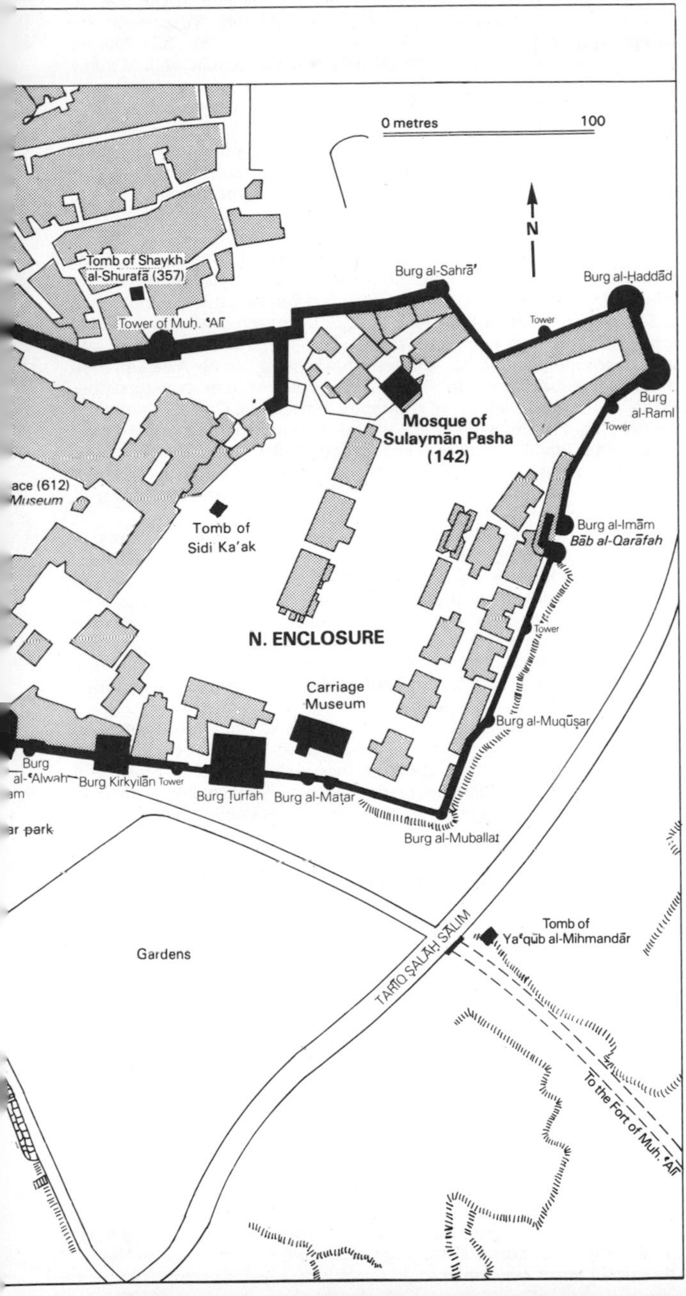
0 metres
100
N
Tomb of Shaykh al-Shurafā (357)
Tower of Muḥ. ʿAlī
Burg al-Sahrā'
Burg al-Ḥaddād
Tower
Burg al-Raml
Tower
Mosque of Sulaymān Pasha (142)
ace (612)
Museum
Tomb of Sidi Ka'ak
Burg al-Imām
Bāb al-Qarāfah
Tower
N. ENCLOSURE
Carriage Museum
Burg al-Muqūṣar
Burg al-ʿAlwah
Burg Kirkyilān
Tower
Burg Ṭurfah
Burg al-Maṭar
Burg al-Muballaṭ
ar park
Gardens
TARĪQ ṢALĀḤ SĀLIM
Tomb of Yaʿqūb al-Mihmandār
To the Fort of Muḥ. ʿAlī

establishment of madrasahs and khāngāhs throughout Egypt. Nūr al-Dīn died in 1174 leaving his empire to his son Ismāʿīl, an 11-year-old boy. To prevent the Crusader states appropriating the territory Ṣalāḥ al-Dīn deposed the child. During the next two years, supported by his brothers al-ʿAdil and Tūrānshāh, he had many military victories in Syria and Arabia culminating in the brilliant victory of the Horns of Harmah against the Zangids, his former masters. Thus when he returned to Egypt he controlled the whole of Syria and Arabia. He stayed in Egypt reorganising the administration and supervising the military constructions and, although the Citadel was complete, he still dwelt in the Dār al-Qubbab in al-Qāhirah. (Rte 5).

In 1182 with the fortifications virtually complete he left Egypt, never to return. This was the period of his great victories. Jerusalem fell to him in 1187 and by 1189 the only major cities retained by the Crusaders were Antioch, Tyre and Tripoli. Europe, alarmed by the fall of Jerusalem, launched the Third Crusade. Ṣalāḥ al-Dīn's relationship with King Richard of England is well documented, though the two never met. ʿAkkah (Acre) was regained by the Crusaders but Jerusalem remained in Muslim hands. Ṣalāḥ al-Dīn died in February 1193 in Damascus, his only personal wealth 47 copper dirhams and one gold piece. The empire was divided into principalities and distributed among his relatives; his second son al-ʿAzīz and then his grandson al-Manṣūr succeeded to the throne of Egypt, but both were incompetent and in 1200 al-ʿAdil seized control. He continued work in the Citadel, modifying some of the original plan. He also lived in al-Qāhirah and installed his son al-Kāmil as Na'ib (Viceroy) in the Citadel. When al-Kāmil became sultan in 1218 he stayed in the Citadel and built his palace there. From this time it became the official residence of the rulers, all of whom dwelt there except for Sultan Ayyūb who built his own Citadel on Rawḍah Island (Rte 3).

The Citadel as constructed by Ṣalāḥ al-Dīn consisted of two great enclosures, to the NE the military area, and to the SW the residential area, conjoined along their shortest walls. The walls, built of limestone quarried from the outcrop, had an internal gallery and were beset every 100m or so by half-round towers and pierced by several interior gates. Along the summit of the walls are large round-headed crenellations. In addition there was a lower enclosure containing a park, gardens and animal stalls. Many of the later sultans modified the interior of the Citadel: the SW enclosure was greatly expanded, but the NE has retained much of its original wall.

Although the Citadel was never put to the test by enemies from outside, it came under attack from rival factions among the mamlūks many times. It could not be reached by fire from the Muqaṭṭam Hills, but after the construction of the Mosque of Sultan al-Ḥasan the roof of this mosque made an ideal surface from which to bombard the Citadel, a fact that various Mamlūk commanders and Bonaparte were quick to grasp.

On the W side of the Maydān Muḥammad ʿAlī, the **Bāb al-ʿAzab** (555; 24:3), the entrance flanked by two massive half-round fronted towers, is all that remains of Raḍwān Katkhudā al-Galfī's rebuilding of the walls of the Southern Enclosure in 1754. The model was obviously the Bāb al-Futūḥ in the N walls (Rte 4). The great wooden brass-bound and rivetted doors are contemporary with the building.

The gate leads into the S enclosure and the road leading down to it between high buildings was the site of Muh. ʿAlī's bloody triumph over the Bays. By 1811, although acknowledged Pasha of Egypt by the Ottoman sultan, Muḥ. ʿAlī was not without rivals. The powerful Bays still held him in scant regard and had the support of large sections of the populace. On the eve of his son Ṭūṣūn's military expedition against the Wahhābīs in Arabia Muḥammad ʿAlī held a great banquet. The most prominent Bays were invited and after feasting magnificently left on horseback to re-enter the city. As they descended they passed between these buildings from which Muḥ. ʿAlī's guards shot them down. The gates being closed, there was no escape. All were killed except, according to tradition, Ḥasan Bay who galloped back up the ramp and leapt with his horse off the ramparts, surviving to escape to Nubia. Thus Muḥ. ʿAlī crushed much resistance.

Just inside the entrance opposite the gate is the **Mosque of Aḥmad Katkhudā al-ʿAzab** (145; 24:4), the mosque for the ʿAzabān corps, just as that of Sulaymān Pāshā in the N Enclosure was for the Mustaḥfiẓān (see p 370). Built in 1697, it is a typical early Ottoman mosque with cylindrical minaret. It probably occupies the site of the Masgid al-Iṣtabl (the Stable Mosque) which stood just outside the walls of the stables of the original Citadel.

Aḥmad Bay was a man of great influence. Under the patronage of the Bay Ismāʿīl Iwadh he rose to be premier Ūdah Bāshā, Katkhudā of the ʿAzabs and finally Admiral (Amīr al-Bahrayn: Lord of the Two Seas, i.e. Mediterranean and Red Sea). This aroused much resentment among the older officers of the corps. After Ismāʿīl died he gained the enmity of Ibrāhīm Katkhudā and was exiled to Abū Qīr. Ibrāhīm was assassinated in 1724 and Aḥmad was called out of retirement by Sultan Aḥmad III to organise an expedition against Shah Tahmasp of Persia. His expedition left, but he died in Istanbul in 1727 before they returned.

The interior contains the remains of a small *zāwiyah* built by Sultan Muʾayyad Shaykh in the 1420s. Although little is left of it, there are obvious decorative features in common with his other works (Rtes 6, 9).

From this point it is possible to proceed directly into the Citadel (see below) or traverse outside the walls.

*THE WALLS.* S for 550m, SE for 150m and finally N for 275m, the whole of the wall of the **South Enclosure** consists of almost unbroken curtain wall built and realigned in the late 18–early 19C. There are three insubstantial towers in the E wall. However, from the angle where the wall of the **North Enclosure** turns W and for the remainder of the circuit, most of the walls and towers are original.

At the angle of the wall there is a small enclosure constructed by the governor Yakan Pasha in 1785 to protect a gateway he had driven through the walls of the S Enclosure (now the main access to the Citadel, with space for cars and coaches to park). From here a track leads SE, crosses the Tariq Ṣalāḥ Sālim and joins the causeway to the Fort of Muḥ. ʿAlī (see p 376). In the angle rises the *Muqaṭṭam Tower* from which the wall of the N Enclosure takes off to the W. This wall is of smooth masonry pierced by arrow slits. The first tower (150m) is the square *Burg al-Ṣuffah* (Tower of Alignment), built astride the walls of Ṣalāḥ al-Dīn by his brother al-ʿAdil; the interior has a cruciform chamber, but the upper storey and battlements have disappeared.

The next tower (10m), the *Burg al-ʿAlwah* (the View Tower), is half-round and part of the original work. It also has a cruciform chamber inside, but has the original upper storey preserved. A massive glacis built by Muḥ. ʿAlī strengthens the next two sections of curtain wall which are separated (30m) by another square tower, the *Burg Kirkyilān* (Tower of Forty Serpents), also the work of al-ʿAdil. Some of the crenellations here are original and there is a later machicoulis at each end, operated from the catwalk. Another stretch of curtain wall (30m) with a half-round *tower* (unnamed) leads to the largest tower of all (15m) the *Burg al-Ṭurfah* (Masterpiece Tower) almost 30m sq., built by al-ʿAdil. Internally it consists of two unconnected sections. The parapet is modern but must originally have been like those of the Burg Kirkyilān. More of Muḥ. ʿAlī's reconstruction is apparent in the stretch of wall (25m) which ends with the double towers of the *Burg al-Maṭar* (Tower of the Flight Platform). This was originally a gateway with a baffled entrance, but it was blocked up in the late 15C by Sultan Ganbalāt. During Ottoman times it probably housed the carrier pigeons used for communications.

Halfway along the next stretch of curtain wall the base rock rises above ground level and at (50m) the *Burg al-Muballat* (Paved Tower) reaches 9m high. This is the corner tower and the wall turns N.

Directly S of this tower (c 30m), on the S side of the Shʿ. Ṣalāḥ Sālim, is the twin-domed **Tomb of Yaʿqūb Shāh al-Mihmandār** (303; 25:3), built in 1495–96. One of the domes covers a cistern, while the other may have been intended to be a tomb: a unique combination. A foundation inscription runs across the middle of the façade in which the obscure Yaʿqūb lauds Sultan Qāyt-bāy and celebrates the defeat of the Ottomans at the Battle of Adana (1486). Dr J.M. Rogers, discussing the inscription, has suggested that the eccentric Arabic may indicate that the amīr composed it himself.

A strange solid tower which abuts the cliff a little way along seems to be late Ottoman and may cover a subterranean exit from the Citadel. A long stretch of curtain wall (c 170m), running along the top of the cliff, is beset by two half-round towers, the first (55m) called the *Burg al-Muqūṣar*, the second (50m) unnamed. The next great tower (40m), the *Burg al-Imām*, is double and was originally another exit from the Citadel, the *Bāb al-Qarāfah* (Cemetery Gate). It consists of a huge baffled entrance. The core of the towers is the work of Ṣalāḥ al-Dīn, but they were subsequently enlarged with the rusticated masonry of al-ʿAdil. Sultan Ganbalāṭ had it filled in with rubble in the late 15C—like the Burg al-Maṭar,—as a measure against any attack by the Ottomans. It was cleared by the CPAM, encouraged by Creswell in 1923, when its true function was revealed. During Ottoman times it was probably the residence of the imām of the Sīdī Sāriyyah Mosque, when it presumably received its present name.

There follows another long stretch of curtain wall, broken only by one half-round tower, which terminates in two great round towers joined by a short piece of curtain wall. The first tower (65m) is the *Burg al-Raml* (Sand Tower) and the second (30m) which is slightly larger, the *Burg al-Ḥaddād* (Tower of the Blacksmith). Both have the rusticated masonry of al-ʿAdil surrounding the cores of the original towers.

The wall now turns W; beside the last tower is another postern gate, now walled up, and (35m) a half-round tower (unnamed). Beyond (35m), the wall turns NW 40m to the *Burg al-Sahrā* (Desert Tower), also half-round and reinforced internally by a large square tower of al-ʿAdil which covers up another postern gate. The wall turns W again at 80m and from this point to the next tower (60m) has been reinforced with rusticated masonry, also probably in late Mamlūk times by Sultan Ganbalāṭ. The next round tower is part of Muḥ. ʿAlī's realignment of the wall, though the original wall of Ṣalāḥ al-Dīn runs for some 40m S from this point inside the N Enclosure. Muḥ. ʿAlī's wall is very thick and runs unbroken except for a half-round tower to the NW point of the Enclosure (120m). To the N of this last tower (c 20m) is the **Tomb of Sh. al-Shurafā** (359; 25:3), a simple domed cube built c 1496.

In the interior of the NW corner of the Enclosure is another of al-ʿAdil's great square towers, which may well be the Burg al-ʿAḥmar (Red Tower) where Shagar al-Durr was imprisoned and murdered after having had her husband Sultan Aybak assassinated. Just below this point the wall turns to join the route into the Citadel from the Bāb al-ʿAzab.

The route into the Citadel from the Bāb al-ʿAzab ascends NE up the Sikkat al-Maḥgar with al-Maḥmūdiyyah Mosque (Rte 9) on the left. Where the wall retreats from the road (60m) is the **Zāwiyat Ḥasan al-Rūmī** (258; 24:4), built in 1522, shortly after the Ottoman conquest. The name is a popular ascription as the builder is not known. It is a very small mosque and in all probability was only meant for a shaykh and his followers. Opposite is the *Tomb of Sultan Qānṣūḥ I* (see Rte 9).

The road ascends past the **Dār al-Maḥafūẓāt** (605), the Archives Building, the great mass of it constructed in 1828 during Muḥ. ʿAlī's work on the Citadel, but the double-bowed entrance is an addition of the late 19C on the site of the old Menagerie. The road climbs and curves to the right; at the bend called the *Bāb al-Haṭṭābah* the Shʿ. Qarāfat Bāb al-Wazīr branches off (to the N Cemetery). Still ascending the road turns S and reaches the NW corner of the N Enclosure of the Citadel. Here it joins the route around the walls.

The original main entrance was on this side of the Citadel through the Bāb al-Mudarrag, and Ottoman times vies the Bāb al-Jadīd. This is still a pedestrian entrance but to provide facilities for coach and car parking a new entrance has been made off the Shʿ Ṣalāḥ Sālim on the E side. There is an entrance fee which includes admission to all the buildings within the Citadel.

The massive wall of Muḥ. ʿAlī runs S to the point where it meets *Bāb al-Gadīd* (New Gate). Passing through this a passage to the left leads to the original gate of the Citadel, the **Bāb al-Mudarrag** (Gate of the Steps). High on the wall of the Citadel are three inscriptions referring to works done by Sultans Gaqmaq, Qāyt-bāy and Tūmān bāy I in the 15C. Above the doorway is a square Ottoman tower, but the entrance is original. This is set in a shallow recess with a round arch in a moulded square frame, with blank medallions in each corner. Over the arch of the inner doorway is a marble foundation inscription in Naskhī, one of the earliest examples of this script in Cairo; it gives details of the construction by the amīr Qarāqūsh under the order of Ṣalāḥ al-Dīn with the assistance of his brother al-ʿAdil in 579 AH (AD 1183). Only one half of the iron door remains and the entrance leads into a vestibule covered with a shallow dome raised on pendentives. The centre of the dome is decorated with a spiral relief, and the name of Sultan al-Nāṣir Mūḥ. in white lettering on red. It was discovered that this inscription had been written and painted over three times, corresponding with this Sultan's elevations and subsequent depositions. There are recesses, flanked by baton pillars, for arrow slits and the tunnel-vaulted corridor leads into the interior of the N Enclosure, the exit framed by the arch of the corridor with joggled voussoirs within a rectangular frame. It is somewhat overwhelming to reflect that most of the great public figures, from Ṣāḥ al-Dīn until Muḥammad ʿAlī must have passed through this doorway.

Inside the Bab al-Gadīd the wall of the N Enclosure to the right was reconstructed by Muḥ. ʿAlī over the core of Ṣalāḥ al-Dīn's. The road leads up through the *Bāb al-Wusṭānī* (Middle Gate) into the S Enclosure. Immediately on the left is the *Burg al-Wusṭānī* (diameter 21m) and the immensely thick wall connecting the two enclosures, at the SE end of which is the larger *Burg al-Muqaṭṭam*, 24m in diameter and 25m high. The masonry of this tower is unique in the Citadel, the interior vaults being in brick, not used anywhere else. There is a domed chamber inside and a stairway leading to the summit, which is crowned by a heavy cornice. The gateway to the N Enclosure in the centre of the wall is flanked by two massive polygonal towers. The whole of this work is 16–17C Ottoman, but the actual gateway, the *Bāb al-Qullah* (Waterpot Gate), was built by Muḥ. ʿAlī.

The **Northern Enclosure** measures 560m E–W and 320m N–S, and in contrast to the Southern Enclosure its alignment has changed very little, except in the NW corner, since it was built by Ṣalāḥ al-Dīn. It was designed as the military and civic area of the Citadel and contained a great circular keep. During Mamlūk times it contained the palaces of the viceroy and wazīr, Diwān al-Inshā (Sultan's Secretariat), the Army Bureau and the barracks of the Mamlūk Corps. Sultan Qalāwūn imported a great many Circassian mamlūks and housed them here, from which they received the name Burgīs (burg: tower), and this became the traditional area for those soldiers. The Qipchaq Turkish mamlūks were housed on the Citadel in Rawḍah Island and were called Baḥrīs (baḥr: river); the conflicts between the two groups were several times to bring Egypt to the verge of ruin. During the early period the Baḥrīs controlled the sultanate but in the late 14C the Burgīs prevailed and all subsequent sultans were elected from their ranks. The Mustaḥfiẓān (Janissaries), as the most powerful military group, occupied this area during Ottoman times.

Directly opposite the Middle Gate in the N Enclosure is the **Qaṣr al-Ḥaram** (612; 24:4), the Ḥarīm Palace. Built in 1827, it is an example of the extent to which European taste was pursued by Muḥ. ʿAlī. During the British Occupation it was turned into a military hospital and in 1937 part of it was set aside as the **Military Museum** (open 09.00–14.00 except Mon.; small fee). The decorated wall and ceilings have been restored. The exhibits are designed to show the art of warfare in Egypt from the earliest times to the campaigns of October 1973. The instruments of war, such as swords, firearms and cannon, are amply displayed and there is also a section devoted to costume. In the courtyard are tanks and other military equipment captured in the October 1973 war.

Follow the SE wall of the Ḥarām Palace, cross over the small square to the right, past the small *Tomb of Sh. Kahki*, and continue to the NE (150m) to the **Mosque of Sulaymān Pāshā** (142; 25:3), also called Sīdī Sāriyyah. Built in 1528, it is an Ottoman forecourt mosque, the first of the type to be built in Egypt, only 11 years after the conquest of Salim I. However, the sparse stone decoration is still largely Mamlūk in inspiration.

The khadīm Sulaymān, a white eunuch of the court of Sultan Sulaymān the Magnificent, was governor of Egypt between 1524–34 and 1536–38, his term being interrupted by the appointment of Khusraw. When he finally returned to Istanbul he was made grand wazir. He built this mosque for the Mustaḥfiẓān and it was the last of a series that had occupied the site since Fāṭimid times, over the tomb of Sayyid Sāriyyah, a shaykh whose origins are forgotten.

Entry to the enclosure is through a gateway reached by a flight of steps, originally the orchard and garden which the Ottomans were in the habit of planting round their mosques. The exterior is rather plain with no indication of the lavishness of the interior. The minaret, set on a square-sectioned chamfered base, is an Ottoman polygonal shaft, with two galleries each supported on tiers of stalactites and capped by a green-tiled cone. The entrance to the right of the minaret has a stalactite hood and leads into the courtyard of the mosque, paved with polychrome marbles in geometrical patterns and surrounded by single-arcaded raised riwāqs. The arcades are composed of piers supporting pointed arches, and the roof is covered with shallow domes resting on pendentives. In the NW corner is a *Tomb*, also with a shallow dome, in which are several Ottoman graves, probably of officers of the Mustaḥfiẓān around the larger *Tomb of Sh Sāriyyah*. The plain dome of the mosque is visible above the SE riwāq, which contains the rectangular entrance set slightly off centre.

To the S is the **Coach Museum** (decorated with carved horses heads) with a large collection of coaches used by the royal family and ministers.

Inside, the walls have a dado of coloured marble panels. The *miḥrāb*, set in the curved wall supporting a half-dome, is also polychrome marble. The *minbar* is of plain white marble with pierced panels in the side. The whole interior is covered by a shallow dome, with three flanking half-domes, all raised on pendentives and strengthened by cross-beams, while above the door is a carved wooden gallery. The upper parts of the walls, the interior of the domes and all the woodwork are richly decorated with painted foliate and geometrical motifs and inscriptions, all the work being original and the effect overwhelming. At the rear of Mosque is the small *Madrasah*.

The **Southern Enclosure** is slightly smaller than the Northern Enclosure, measuring 270m E–W and 510m N–S. It originally covered only half this area, but the walls have been rebuilt and realigned several times and now include much of the stables area of the lower levels.

This was the area of the royal residence and the first palace was built here by Sultan al-Kāmil. Sultan al-Nāṣir Mūh. demolished it in the 14C and replaced it with his towering Qaṣr al-Ablaq (Striped Palace). This second palace consisted of a series of huge interconnected courts and terraces, including the throne room and other rooms for the sultan's personal use. Within the complex were the residences of his wives, the Great Pillared Hall for the first wife (khwand al-kubrā': great lady), the Ramaḍān Hall, the Muẓaffariyyah Hall and the Suspended Hall for the second, third and fourth wives respectively, while the Baysariyyah Hall was reserved for the concubines. A huge porticoed court, the Palace of Justice, on the site of Muh. ʿAlī's Mosque, was the ceremonial dīwan where the sultan sat for official public audiences and dispensed judgment. In addition, this enclosure contained the barracks of the Corps of Zimāmiyyah (Eunuchs) and of the Royal Mamlūks, the Treasury, Mint and the Silver Hall where state prisoners were kept until their trial. There were also kitchens, orchards and gardens, set with fountains and aviaries.

During Ottoman times this area remained as the residence of the Pāshā though many of the buildings were demolished or had collapsed. The lower area, however, was used to house the ʿAzab Corps, and there was much friction between them and the Mustaḥfiẓan who occupied the upper N Enclosure. Each of these corps were in charge of half of the armaments and were not averse to using them on each other.

Opposite the Bāb al-Qullah is the NE wall of the **Mosque of Sultan al-Nāṣir Muḥammad** (143; 24:4), an enclosure mosque founded in 1318, but enlarged by the same sultan in 1335. The exterior walls are plain and higher in proportion to length than those of the earlier enclosure mosques of Ibn Ṭūlūn, al-Ḥākim, Baybars, etc. A row of pointed-arched windows originally filled with stucco grilles runs round the upper part of the wall. The walls are crowned with undercut stepped cresting. There are two entrances, in the NE and NW walls, with tall pointed-arched stalactite hoods. There are also two minarets, one at the E corner and the other to the right of the door in the NW wall. Stylistically they have no parallel anywhere in Egypt and were probably built by a Persian artisan brought back from Tabriz and the court of the Mongol sultan Abū Saʿid. That on the NW consists of three stone cylindrical tiers, the lower two incised with large chevron patterns, the lower perpendicular, the second horizontal; the upper tier is grooved. The two balconies, resting on great corbels, are carved and pierced marble and the whole is crowned by a strange ribbed melon-like cap, originally covered with green faience tiles, many of which are still in place. To the E the plain cylindrical tiers are surmounted by a similar melon cup but set on four pillars.

INTERIOR. The central ṣaḥn is surrounded by riwāqs, those to the SW, NW and NE two arcades deep and the principal riwāq against the qiblah wall four arcades deep, with a dome covering three arcades over the miḥrāb. The decoration is rather austere for the period, but enhances the beauty. The marble columns and capitals are all reused and represent various architectural styles. The columns support half-round arches with pierced openings on which rests the richly decorated wooden ceiling of octagonal panels covered with geometrical designs, restored by the CPAM. The original marble floor and facings of the walls were removed by Salim I and taken to Istanbul, but the whole mosque was refaced by the CPAM for King Fārūq. The dome over the miḥrāb is supported on ten great red granite Ancient Egyptian columns brought from al-Ashmūnayn and used for the second building of the mosque. Above the square base the dome was raised on wooden squinches and around the base runs a wooden foundation frieze in the name of al-Nāṣir Muḥ. with the date 735 (AD 1335). The dome fell in 1468, killing the guardian and his son, and was rebuilt by Sultan Qāyt-bāy, but this also fell sometime during the Ottoman period and the present one was erected by the CPAM in 1935.

A word of warning: descent into the next monument is not without a certain danger, as, for natural reasons, mains illumination cannot be taken to the bottom of the well. It is therefore advisable to take a torch or even a candle and care should be taken at the bottom as there is no barrier between the end of the ramp and the cistern.

To the S across a piece of open ground lies the **Bīr Yūsuf** (Joseph's Well; 305; 24:4) also called the *Bīr al-Ḥalazūn* (Spiral Well). The Yūsuf referred to is Ṣalāḥ al-Dīn and not the Prophet Joseph. It was excavated by the amīr Qaraqūsh during the original construction of the Citadel in the 1170s, his workforce, prisoners-of-war taken during the campaigns against the Crusaders in Syria. The Andalusian traveller Ibn Jubayr states that he saw an incalculable number of them engaged on the work. The entrance is covered by a tower and leads down to the shaft itself. It is an awesome piece of work, the shaft (c 10m sq.) being cut 87m perpendicularly through the limestone down to the water-table where the water seeps into the base through natural channels. Another shaft is cut at an angle and spirals round the central well, with shallow rough-cut steps intended to take the traffic to the water level. At each turn in the steps two windows are cut through into the central shaft. Originally there were two wooden platforms, one at the bottom and one half-way up for the oxen-operated machines that raised water into the Citadel. The steps were covered with earth (many still are) and are of such a pitch that oxen or donkeys could walk down to the cistern. When the Khedival family moved out of the Citadel in the 19C into palaces scattered around Cairo, their water was supplied daily from this well.

Across the square W of the entrance to the Mosque of al-Nāṣir Muḥammad, an arch leads into the old *Citadel Prison* opened to the public in 1987. Immediately inside to the right are some original *Cells* each of which contains models dressed as prisoners from various epochs of Egyptian history. Beyond is a café and next to it the *Fire Service Gallery* with examples of fire-fighting equipment including old horse-drawn fire carts. Beside this is the **Police Museum** a fascinating collection for the student of crime.

As well as displays of uniforms, arms and other paraphenalia of the Egyptian Police Force, it has interesting didactic exhibits of police and criminal methods including examples of specific crimes. In the 'Rogues Gallery' are histories and mementoes of well-known felons including the highly successful six-fingered pick-pocket and the appalling sisters Sakinah and Rdyyā who in the 1920s headed a gang that lured young women to meetings called *zars* and murdered them for the sake of their jewellery. They were finally apprehended and executed, and have entered Egyptian folklore, recently being the subject of a popular long-running play.

At the extreme NE corner of the enclosure is the recently excavated cylindrical base of the medieval *'Tower of Baybars'* associated with the sultan since it has a lively procession of leopards or lions sculptured aroung the base. Some of which still show signs of stucco and red paint.

Occupying the S end of the enclosure are foundations and cellars the sad remains of the **Qasr al-Ablaq** (549) the magnificent Striped Palace of

Sultan al-Nāsir Muḥammad. Near the wall lie several massive red granite columns (reused from Pharaonic buildings)–8m high, some of them inscribed at the summit with the sultan's titles.

It was built between 1313–15 as the residence of the sultan in the Citadel. Consisting of several courts with access to the other palaces, it was constructed in alternate courses of yellow and black stone and the walls of the interior were a blaze of marble, gold and mother-of-pearl mosaic, the woodwork magnificently carved and painted and the windows set with brilliant coloured glass. The floors executed in imported marbles were also one of the wonders of the age. The great qāʿah built by the architect Muḥ. b. al-Kuwayz stood for a long time after the rest of the palace fell in ruins in Ottoman times and was the place where the kiswah, covering the Kaʿbah in Mecca, was embroidered. Muḥ ʿAlī finally transferred his work to a factory in the Shʿ. Khurunfish (Rte 7) and the hall, called the Hall of Joseph by the French, was used as a powder magazine. In 1824 the magazine exploded leaving only a few columns standing, and Muḥ. ʿAlī ordered the area to be cleared for his projected mosque. Much of the rubble from the palace was used to build up the ground.

To the S of the entrance to the Police Museum are the *Toilets*.

*The destroyed Qaṣr al-Abaq, the Palace of Sultan al-Nāṣir Muḥammad in the Citadel, from the* Description de l'Egypte

Return to the Bāb al-Qullah. To the N are the steps up to the plateau on which stands the **Mosque of Muḥammad ʿAlī Pāshā** (503; 24:4), also called the Alabaster Mosque. It was built between 1830–48, although not completed until the reign of Saʿīd Pāshā in 1857.

Its form is that of an Ottoman forecourt mosque with no debt to the Mamlūk style that had persisted for so long in Egypt. The architect was Yusuf Bushnak from Istanbul and the model was the Yeni Mosque in that city. The ground on which the mosque was constructed was built up with debris from many of the earlier buildings of the Citadel. Before it was completed ʿAbbas I had the alabaster stripped from the upper walls to line his own palaces and replaced it with wooden panels painted to resemble marble. In 1899 it showed signs of cracking and repairs were undertaken. As these were inadequate, restoration was ordered by King Fūʾād I in 1931 and was finally being completed under King Fārūq in 1939.

The main material is limestone but the lower storey of the mosque and forecourt is faced to a height of 11.5m with alabaster which has unfortunately deteriorated and turned grey. The external façades are rather severe and angular, those of the mosque rising four storeys to the level where the lead-covered shallow domes rise in billows to a height of 52m. At the E and S corners are small domed turrets while at the W and N corners are the slender octagonal minarets with two balconies and conical caps which rise to 82m. The miḥrāb salient on the SE wall is three storeys high and is covered with a semi-dome. Rising to the second storey are the arcades on the NE and SW sides, supported on columns and covered with domes, with an entrance on each side. There are also entrances on each of the three sides of the forecourt; the usual entry is through that on the NE side.

The forecourt measures 50m sq. and is surrounded by single arched riwāqs raised on pillars and roofed with small domes. Opposite is the doorway in the SW wall. At the far end in the centre of the NW riwāq is a pavilion, above which is the elaborate French clock presented to Muḥ. ʿAlī by Emperor Louis Philippe in 1845. (The Pāshā reciprocated with the obelisk now in the Place de la Concorde in Paris.) In the centre of the forecourt is an octagonal ablution fountain covered by a large lead-domed canopy, resting on eight pillars, the awning carved with extravagant ornament. The entrance to the mosque is in the NW façade.

The interior (41m sq.) gives an incredible sense of space, with the central dome resting on four large arches, supported by massive piers. Surrounding the dome are four half-domes and covering the corners are four smaller domes, while the miḥrāb is covered by a half-dome at a lower level. The domes are painted and covered with medallions and other motifs in relief while at their bases are galleries with bronze balustrades. Alabaster panels face the walls and pillars to c 11m and above are panels of baroque painted decoration. Above the entrance is the Grand Gallery supported on marble pillars with a bronze balustrade. Beneath it to the right of the entrance is the three-tiered *Tomb of Muḥammad ʿAlī*, of white marble carved with floral motifs and painted and gilded inscription. His body was transferred here from the Ḥawsh al-Bāshā in 1857. The bronze grill was provided by ʿAbbās I Pāshā.

Muḥammad ʿAlī was born in the port of Kavalla (in modern Macedonia, Greece) in 1770, the son of Ibrāhīm, a tobacco merchant. One of 11 children, he was raised by Ḥasan Shurbajī, the local governor, and joined the police force, as well as being involved in the family business. He married Amīnah, a girl from a nearby village, who was to be his only contracted wife, and they had three sons and two daughters. The area had many settled Albanian inhabitants with whom Muḥammad ʿAlī was intimately involved in the course of his business; he was therefore made second in command of the local Albanian contingent sent to Egypt in 1801 in the Ottoman counter-offensive to the French occupation. By subtle manipulation of the various factions within the Ottoman forces and the Egyptian elites he quickly became commander of the Albanian regiments and in 1805, with the removal of the Ottoman walī, he was elected to that post by the Egyptian ʿulamā.

His post confirmed by the sultan, he slowly and surely elimated or neutralised the groups which had once supported him. After the massacre of the mamlūks in 1811 he was virtually unassailable and turned his attention to foreign involvements, using his sons and close relatives to command his forces. Initial successes in Arabia (1811–18) and the Sudan (1812–20) encouraged him to participate in the Greek campaign (1821–27), but his plans were frustrated by European interference.

He later had much greater success in Syria and Anatolia (1830–40), his forces, under his son Ibrāhīm utterly defeating the Prussian-trained forces of the sultan, whose capitulation he was about to receive when the Western powers again intervened. In return for withdrawal, Muḥammad ʿAlī demanded acknowledgement of the hereditary right of his family to the governorship of Egypt—it was granted.

In Egypt he attracted European scholars and scientists to introduce modern education, medical care and industrial techniques. He sent students to France and Britain to qualify in various professions and he reformed the army under European officers. A printing press was introduced in 1822 and the economy was realigned. Probably the greatest of his works was the building of the Maḥmūdiyyah Canal to Alexandria, not achieved without great loss of life. From several concubines he had a further score of children, though only six sons lived to produce descendents.

In 1848 Muḥammad ʿAlī's health broke and he declined rapidly. Ibrāhīm was made Pasha but died after two months. ʿAbbās I succeeded to the Viceroyalty and Muḥammad ʿAlī died in 1849. ʿAbbās did not bother to attend the funeral.

Against the E Pier is the kursī and on the W wall the dikkah supported on alabaster columns, also with a bronze balustrade. In the E corner is a subsidiary miḥrāb, but the main miḥrāb is in a salient, to the right of which is a marble minbār provided by King Fārūq. The immense original minbār is to the right near the S pier, made of wood and gilded; but its position is unfavourable, hence the new one presented by Fārūq. Great chandeliers depend from the domes.

S of the Mosque of Muḥ. ʿAlī is the **Qaṣr al-Gawharah** (505), the Jewel Palace, built in 1814, and the first of the two palaces Muḥ. ʿAlī constructed in the Citadel.

Like its counterpart in the N Enclosure its architecture is unremarkable, being heavily influenced by the severe early 19C French style. However, the interior contains many painted walls and ceilings. When the khedives moved their residence to the ʿĀbdīn Palace in the city, it was opened to the public and after the Revolution turned into a museum. In 1972, during a theft attempt, the NW wing was gutted by fire. Much of the personal property of the former royal family is displayed, furniture including the Golden Lion throne of Mohammed ʿAlī, objects d'art, mementos and portraits.

To the E of the palace is the **Mint** (606) built in 1812. The avenue to the N leads to the *Eastern Entrance*, with car and coach parking facilities.

From the Sh. ʿSālim the SHʿ. AL-MUQAṬṬAM leads E past a military post and winds around the foothills of the Muqaṭṭam range. Whole hillsides have been quarried since ancient times and there are many large caves in the rock-face. It was used by the British as an arms depot and much of the area is still under military occupation. On the way to the summit there are awe-inspiring sights, not least of which is the sheer 200m drop of the cliff below the television mast. After 2km on the W a small road leads 500m to the cliff edge on which is perched the **Mashhad al-Guyushī** (304; 25:7), unfortunately at present within the military area.

Although seemingly of normal mashhad form, this mosque built by Badr al-Gamālī (d 1094) in 1085 presents several anomalies. The tomb chamber against the NE wall was never used for the founder, who was buried in the N Cemetery, although his tomb is unknown. The siting of the mashhad in what was a desolate location is difficult to justify, as is the massive construction. However in an erudite analysis of the building Farid Shafeʿi has suggested that the building in fact was an integral part of Badr's fortification of Cairo (Rtes 4 and 5), although presenting the innocent exterior of a small mosque. From the roof it is possible to see the whole of the city of Cairo and Giza and the surrounding area and from the minaret visual contact could be made with the towers of the Bāb Zuwaylah. This does not lessen the piety of the man who raised it; he merely killed two birds with one stone.

The exterior (c 18m by 15m) is quite plain and is constructed of small stone slabs to the level of the roof above which it is brick. At the SE end is a dome on an octagonal drum, while the tomb chamber is against the NE wall. Dominating the NW end is the minaret, the earliest complete example in Cairo. The lower tier has a square section and around the top of this is a simple stalactite corbel, the first appearance of this device in Egypt. Above this is another square tier, each side with a round-arched doorway, which supports an octagonal drum, with a round-arched window in each facet. The brick dome is almost hemispherical with a small peak. Two smaller turrets, which must have served as sentry-boxes for the guards on the roof, flank the minaret.

At the base of the minaret is the entrance—just over 1m wide, another factor encouraging the military theory. A tunnel-vaulted porch leads through a vestibule flanked by two small rooms. In the S room is the stairway to the minaret. The vestibule opens into the open ṣaḥn with two tunnel-vaulted rooms either side, that to the N containing the entrance to the tomb chamber roofed with a shallow dome. Around the walls of the ṣaḥn is an unusual cresting. Fronting the SE side of the ṣaḥn is a fine triple arch, the central span being the widest, with pointed arches raised on double pillars. Behind this are three cross vaults and in front of the qiblah wall are another three pointed arches raised on piers. The stucco panel surrounding the pointed arched miḥrāb is superb with a decorative border and bands of Kufic inscription. At the spandrels are arabesques, variously patterned palmettes and at the summit the inscription is curved to counter foreshortening. Around the top of the walls is a very fine decorated Kufic inscription; the painted plaster on the walls and squinches is dated 1731. Simple squinches raise the octagonal drum with eight windows and at the apex of the dome is the original stucco inscription with the names of Muḥammad and ʿAlī.

About 800m further up the mountain the Shʿ. al-Muqaṭṭam reaches **Madīnat al-Muqaṭṭam** (Muqaṭṭam City), a recently developed town built on the plateau. (Bus No. 401 from ʿAtabah Sq.) It consists of wide avenues and streets flanked by villas, apartment buildings, restaurants and expensive casinos. Surrounding the complex and circling the edge of the plateau is the Muqaṭṭam Corniche with spectacular views of Cairo and the surrounding area across to the Pyramids at Giza.

Beyond the road to Madīnat al-Muqaṭṭam the Shʿ. Ṣalāḥ Sālim bisects the *Causeway* from the Citadel to the elevated **Fort of Muḥammad ʿAlī** (455; 25:6), an isolated fortress built in 1810 in case the pasha had to beat a hasty retreat from the Citadel. At present it is occupied by the military.

From the entrance to the Citadel the Shʿ. Ṣalāḥ Sālim turns W crossing the S end of the Maydān Ṣalāḥ al-Dīn passes through S Cairo (N of Mīṣr al-Qadīmah) and crosses the R Nile at Rawdah Island onto the W bank.

To the S of the Citadel past the S end of the Maydān Ṣalāḥ al-Dīn are a number of tombs within the confines of the S Cemetery (Rte 15).

Where the Shʿ. Ṣalāḥ Sālim crosses the maydān, a little way up the hill and to the N is the *Tomb of Sh. ʿAbd Allāh* (413; 24:6), a small plastered building of the 16C. It is devoid of external decoration and painted in red and yellow stripes. Sh. ʿAbd Allāh was the ghafir (watchman) of the area and renowned for his piety. There is a mūlid in his honour on the 27 Shaʿbān. Directly facing the main road to the S is the **Mosque of Sultan Qānṣūḥ al-Ghawrī** (159), one of the lesser works of this sultan. Little remains from the original except for the minaret and part of the entrance. A Naskhī foundation inscription gives the date of 1509. The minaret is set on the E corner and has only two tiers, the first with an octagonal section and the second cylindrical. Stalactite corbels support balcony and finial and there are small turquoise faience disks in the decoration of the base.

On the opposite side of the road to the S is the **Mosque of Sh. Nūr al-Dīn al-Qarāfī** (160; 24:6), built in 1575 as a madrasah and tomb for the shaykh by the governor Massīḥ Pāshā.

This shaykh had a large following among the Ottoman troops. The khadim Massīḥ was a white eunuch and Ottoman governor of Egypt (1574–86).

The exterior of the mosque is almost completely Mamlūk in design but the polygonal two-tiered minaret is typically Ottoman, as is the interior which, although now ruined, indicates that it was a covered mosque with three arcades parallel to the qiblah.

Pass along the E wall of the mosque in the cemetery. 70m SE are the remains of a large and beautiful, though uncompleted twin-domed complex, the **Turbah al-Ṣultāniyyah** (289), which should be associated with the Northern Minaret (see below). Its date is a matter of dispute but on present evidence the mid 14C seems likely.

Not the least of the mysteries concerning this building is that it is not known for whom it was built and, unfortunately, the foundation inscription which must have been intended to fill the groove running the whole length of the NE façade was never inserted. It may be associated with the mother of Sultan Hasan.

The remnants comprise a vaulted qiblah līwān, flanked to the S and E by twin-domed tomb chambers (the dome of the latter rebuilt). The minaret to the N is also thought to belong to this complex, but the intervening mosque was demolished in the 19C and the area used for later burials.

The bases of the chambers are undecorated and each dome, without a zone-of-transition, is raised on a very tall drum, pierced by 12 windows, round the top of which is a band of inscription from the Qur'ān. The space between the windows on the E dome is covered with foliate carving. The domes themselves are unique: slightly pointed with a small return and thus superficially similar to the brick Timurid domes of Persia, though differing in construction and built of stone. They have a rib and fillet pattern, each unit of which springs from a small stalactite bracket, a feature known in only one other dome in Cairo, the equally strange tomb of Yūnus al-Dawādār (Rte 8) of similar date.

Entry is through the NE wall of the S tomb which has a bare interior; its plain dome is raised on stalactite squinches, unique in having the niches set directly above each other and not alternately. The E tomb is similar but the squinches, although more conventional, are also unique in Egypt. The līwān has a repaired stone tunnel-vault, below which runs a band of inscription from the Qur'ān. The miḥrāb also displays peculiarities for the period. It is in stone, in contrast to the conventional marble, with a pointed-arched hood decorated with stalactites, while the spandrels contain carved decoration. The two tombs inside the līwān are modern.

The *Northern Minaret* (c 30m NW; 24:6) is in red and white stone, and has three tiers set on a square-sectioned base, with carved decoration on the chamfer. All the tiers are octagonal, with the balconies resting on stalactite brackets. There are windows in each alternate face of the lower tier and all faces of the top-most tier. The cap has fallen.

A little to the S of the Sulṭāniyyah is a complex with similar remains, the main building having disappeared leaving only the **Tomb of Amīr Qawṣūn** (291; 24:8) and the **Minaret of Qawṣūn** (290). The area of the original khānqāh has been usurped by later tombs. This is the last of Qawṣūn's several buildings in Cairo, and was completed in 1335, six years before his death.

The form of this building can be reconstructed as it appears on the map of Cairo prepared by the French Expedition in 1800 where its plan is that of an enclosure mosque with single arcade riwāqs around the inner walls. It probably also had two domed tombs flanking the qīblā riwāq.

Qawṣūn, a Mongol merchant, came to Cairo in 1320 in the train of Princess Tulbiyyah who was to be married to Sultan al-Nāṣir Muḥ. After persuading Sultan al-Nāṣir Muḥ. to purchase him for the unprecedented sum of 8000 dinars he joined the khassakiyyah (royal pages) and, despite the opposition of the other amīrs, was created an amīr of one hundred. He married a daughter of al-Nāṣir Muḥ. who in turn married one of his sisters. After the death of al-Nāṣir Muḥ. in 1340, his son Abū Bakr, was elevated and, Qawṣūn was made atabak. He arrested his long-standing rival, the amīr Bashtak, and had him executed. In 1341 he deposed Abū Bakr, exiled and then murdered him and raised another son, the seven-year-old Kujuk. But in 1342 Aḥmad, the eldest son of al-Nāṣir Muḥ., marched on Cairo, and Qawṣūn, deserted by the other amīrs, was arrested, sent to Alexandria and strangled.

The tomb has a square-headed entrance in the SW wall, decorated with stucco panels and inscription, while a band of inscription runs round the upper part of the walls. Broken walls at the E corner indicate that this tomb was at the S corner of the khānqāh. The zone-of-transition is stepped, the low drum has a band of inscription and the dome a rib and fillet design. The *Tomb of Qawṣūn* is to the right of the simple miḥrāb. The dome is raised on a squinch with multiple niches, the central upper niche in each forming a window. Between each squinch is a window of six lights.

About 50m NW stands the *Minaret* of three tiers, the base with a square section, the second tier octagonal and the upper tier cylindrical. In the base is a balcony covered by a roof supported on three arches, and in the square section a window on each side with balconies supported on stalactite corbels. On each face of the second section are blind keel-arches and the top is pierced by six scroll-linteled windows. The whole is capped by a keel-arched ribbed dome in stone, one of the first in Cairo and the model that the masons took for the larger stone domes over tombs. Below the cap is a spear-head fringe. A section of the khānqāh wall is still attached to the base of the minaret, capped by fleur-de-lys cresting.

At the NW corner lies the modest *Tomb of Jalāl al-Dīn al-Suyūti* with battered ribbed dome. This extraordinary polymath (1445–1505) whose interests ranged from theology to advising the love-lorn, wrote a vast number of books, and was consulted by many scholars and amirs, but his idiosyncrasies also caused friction with several sultans.

Bear SW for about 100m, among the maze of later tombs, to the **Tomb of ʿAlī Badr al-Qarāfī** (292; 24:8), built in 1305. The base is c 10m sq. There are windows in each wall except the SE, two in recesses covered by stalactite hoods, that in the NW wall with a moulded frame. Also in this wall is the door, above which is a round arch with cushion voussoirs. The stepped zone-of-transition has windows of three lights set in a horseshoe arch on engaged columns; traces of stucco decoration can be seen. The brick dome has a rib and fillet decoration. Little decoration remains inside the tomb chamber, the panelling having been removed, but there are traces of a wooden frieze high on the wall. The dome is raised on squinches of three tiers of five niches, the central niche pierced by a window. Around the drum are four stucco cartouches of Naskhī inscription separated by medallions. The hood of the miḥrāb has ribs resting on stalactites; all the other decoration has disappeared.

Just to the S is the massive **Southern Minaret** (293; 24:8), another isolated remnant of a much larger complex of about 1340. This minaret has three tiers, the first octagonal and the two upper stories round. Since the third storey is unpierced it has been suggested that there was a fourth in the form of a pavilion.

Continue SE for 70m to reach the SHʿ. AL-QARĀFAH AL-KUBRĀʾ, running SE the whole length of the cemetery, and to the right of it the *Tomb of Muṣṭafā Aghā Gāliq* (295) built in 1667—an open stone canopy. The pyramidal cover is supported on four pointed arches raised on thick piers with a trefoil cresting running around the summit. Drawings by Puisse d'Avennes in the mid 19C show that there was a small ribāt and enclosure attached.

Directly SW stand a pair of abutting domed cube tombs of great interest since they span the period of Mamlūk domination with 219 years between their building. The earlier building to the S is the **Tomb al-Sawābī** (296; 24:8), built in 1285 and repaired at the end of the 14C. The person for whom the tomb was built is unknown. The base measures 7.5m sq. and the structure rises to a height of 15m, with the wall exposed to the base. The NE and SE walls of dressed stone are unchanged, but that on the NW of small blocks, now containing the wooden door, was probably in contact with another building and is later work. In the NW wall (which adjoins that of the next tomb) is the original door set in a stalactite recess, and there is another door in the SE wall. The trefoil cresting around the top of the wall is part of the later repair. The upper part of the tomb is in plaster-covered brick with a stepped zone-of-transition and the drum with 16 sides has remnants of stucco cartouches of inscription separated by medallions and windows in the alternate faces; the dome has a rib and fillet decoration. The present entrance in the SW wall leads into the base interior, the miḥrāb much changed from its original condition. The squinches of the dome have two tiers of three niches and above them runs a frieze of 16 niches corresponding to the external faces of the drum. The interior of the dome is undecorated, save for a stucco medallion at the apex.

Immediately NW is the larger **Tomb of Sūdūn Amīr Maglīs** (294; 24:8), built in 1504 entirely in stone.

Sūdūn al-ʿAgami was a mamlūk of Sultan Qāyt-bāy. Rising to the post of amīr maglīs (amīr of the council chamber) in 1502, he was finally created atabak by Sultan Qānṣūḥ al-Ghawrī. His courage and horsemanship were renowned; he was killed on horseback as he led the first charge against the Ottoman Sultan Salim at Marj Dabiq in 1517.

The base of the tomb is c 12m sq. The windows are set in narrow stalactite-headed recesses, between each of which is a large round window. There are rectangular lower windows (filled in) and upper round-headed windows in pairs covered by an oculus. Across each side runs a band of inscription and at each corner of the cube is an engaged column topped by stalactites. Complex cresting runs around the top of the walls. The zone-of-transition has great scroll corners and between each one triple round-headed lights covered by three oculi, flanked by large carved medallions. In the drum of the dome are 12 round-headed windows and above them runs another band of shallowly carved Naskhī inscription. The dome is carved with a horizontal chevron pattern, the lowest row terminating with lozenges. In the SW wall is the entrance covered by a trefoil-arched hood and reached by a flight of steps.

Behind these tombs to the W (20m) lies the **Līwān Rihān** (297), the remaining SW wall and riwāq of the courtyard of an early Ottoman mosque built in 1534 which probably incorporated the two previous tombs. It consists only of an arcade of four pointed arches raised on large piers and roofed by shallow domes. On the rear wall, corresponding to the front arches, are pointed-arched recesses.

South along the Shʿ. al-Qarāfah al-Kubrā' (170m) on the E stands an anonymous tomb called the **Tomb to the North** (i.e. of the Tomb of Tankizbughā) (299; 24:8). This is another domed-cube probably built in the second quarter of the 14C during the first experiments in the construction of stone domes. It was almost certainly intended for an amīr. The base is undecorated except for a band of inscription running around the upper part of the walls. In the centre of each side of the stepped zone-of-transition is a pair of round-headed windows covered by an oculus. Around the drum is a band of Naskhī inscription and the dome itself has a rib and fillet design. Inside the stucco decoration around the miḥrāb is unusual, but in very bad condition, and the dome is plain except for a stucco medallion in the apex.

Slightly to the SW is the **Tomb of Amīr Tankizbughā** (298; 24:8), the first tomb built by this amīr in c 1359 (the second larger tomb is in the Eastern Cemetery; Rte 8).

Little is known of Tankizbughā al-Māridānī who was an amīr of Sultan Ḥasan. Although he rose to be an amīr of one hundred and amīr maglīs, he refused the viceroyalty of Syria, which considering the feuding amongst the other powerful amīrs at that time was probably wise. He died in 1360.

The base of this tomb is plain with windows set in flat-headed stalactite recesses. There is no cresting and the zone-of-transition is a low rectangle set on the lower cube with pairs of round-headed windows in the centre of each face. Above this rises a great decagon topped by a stalactite frieze. Pointing outwards from the top is a spear-head fringe, unique in tomb construction, though previously seen on minarets (e.g. Qawṣūn's, see above). Eight keel-arched windows alternating with niches of the same shape pierce the drum of the dome. The dome has a rather steep profile and is sculptured alternately in ribs and flutes. The interior is undecorated, with the dome raised on single-arched squinches, which experienced a short-lived revival at this time.

250m S along the Shʿ. al-Qarāfah to the E stands the **Tomb of ʿAbd Allāh al-Manūfī** (300; 28:4), the remains of a tomb-mosque built at the end of the 13C. It consists of a large tunnel-vaulted qiblah līwān flanked by the tomb to the SW. The whole building is in brick, quite plain, but the huge dome of the tomb is surmounted by a strange cupola. The interior of the līwān is also undecorated with only the frame of the keel-arch miḥrāb remaining, the stucco ornamentation having disappeared. To the left is a large pointed-arch portal leading into the tomb and on each wall is a recess of a similar shape. A huge squinch of three layers of stalactites, three over two over one, raises the dome, and in each side of the zone-of-transition is a single window. On the opposite side of the līwān is another doorway, now bricked up.

To the E the quarry railway line runs S. E of this the land rises to the base of the Muqaṭṭam escarpment. Several monuments lie in this area, although access to them is somewhat stony.

The first and northernmost of them (at present occupied by the army) is actually in the base of the cliffs themselves, almost directly beneath the Fort of Muḥ. ʿAlī. The complex surrounds the **Kahf al-Sudān** (Cave of the Blacks; 519), a Fāṭimid Mashhad of unknown purpose, built in 1013. More recently it was the site of the **Baktāshī Takiyyah**, principal base of the Brotherhood in Egypt.

The Baktāshīs were an extremely unorthodox dervish brotherhood, unrelated to any sufi group, with its origins in the wilds of central Anatolia. Although named after Ḥajji Baktāshī, a 14C mystic, it did not become prominent until the 16C with patronage from the Janissaries in Turkey. By 1570 they had three takīyyahs in Egypt. The dogma was a syncretic amalgam of Sunnī, Shiʿah (veneration of the Khalif ʿAlī and the 12 imāms), and even Christian (celibacy of initiates) practices. The massacre of the Janissaries in Turkey in 1826 ended their activities and, labelled heretics, they were proscribed throughout the empire.

They were allowed to reform in 1839 and in Egypt the Khedive Ismāʿīl transferred them from the Qaṣr al-ʿAynī to the present site in the 1860s. Their membership had always been drawn predominantly from the European Ottoman territories and for the last few decades they were almost exclusively Albanian. With the revolution of 1952 all takiyyahs in Egypt were closed. The Baktāshīs were moved to al-Maʿādī where their last shaykh, Aḥ. Sirrī Bābāh, died in 1965.

Steps lead up through a gateway into a large open court surrounded by the rock-cut cells of the initiates. A vast cave contains the graves of the Baktāshīs and at the far end, surrounded by a grille, stands the *Tomb of Sayyid ʿAbd Allāh al-Maghāwrī.* To the N of the court stands the *Shaykh's House* and to the S the large *Kitchen.* Beyond the house is a terrace with magnificent views across Cairo. At the far end of the terrace, inside a smaller cave stands the **Tomb of Prince Kamāl al-Dīn** (1874–1932), eldest son of Sultan Ḥusayn Kāmil.

On his father's death in 1919 he renounced the succession, preferring to continue the pursuits of archaeology and art collecting. His most important discovery was Gabal ʿUwaynāt in the extreme SW desert of Egypt, with traces of prehistoric settlements and rock drawings. He often visited this takiyyah for the solitude of the area.

S of the last monument (800m) stands the *Tomb and Sabīl of Sulaymān Aghā al-Ḥanafī* (302; 25:7) of 1792. 50m to the E is a building called *Qubbat Ikhwāt Yūsuf* (301; 25:7), the remains of an early 12C complex. The significance of the name, which means tomb of the brothers of Joseph, is unknown.

Follow the line of hills S for 100m to reach the remnants of a Fāṭimid mashhad, the *Mosque of Luʿluʿ* (515;). Unfortunately the rock base has decayed and only the qiblah wall of the building, containing an interesting triple miḥrāb, stands.

150m further S, inside a modern mosque is the **Tomb of ʿUmar ibn al-Fāriḍ** (601; 31:1), one of the most famous sufi poets. The small domed tomb was built over the grave of the shaykh in 1460 by Amīr Barqūq al-Nāṣirī, viceroy of Damascus.

ʿUmar ibn al-Fāriḍ (1182–1235) was the son of a jurist and devoted his life to sufi ideals. His poems of the intoxication of divine knowledge ('Purity without water and sense without air, and light without fire and spirit without body') had a great influence on later sufis.

Outside, the small dome has a continuous chevron pattern, while inside it is raised over the base on simple squinches.

On the S side of the courtyard of the mosque stands the *Tomb of Princess Gamīlah Fāḍilah* (1869–96), one of the daughters of the Khedive Ismaʿīl. She was particularly devoted to the writings of the shaykh and had her tomb built here: unfortunately she died in Istanbul.

A lane leads along the E side of the mosque and winds up the Muquṭṭam hills for 100m to the **Mosque and Tomb of Shāhīn al-Khalawātī** (212; 31:2). Built in 1538 but now in ruins, it is dramatically perched on a spur of the hills. An Azeri Turk, Shāhīn was admitted to the Khasakiyyah mamlūks of Sultan Qāyt-bāy, but he retired to study sufism in Tabriz (Iran). When he returned he was patronised by the great amīrs. However, his unorthodox methods alienated his pupils, many of whom defected to Damirdāsh al-Muḥammadi. The tomb was stripped of its tiles and marble decoration in 1917.

# 15 The Southern Cemetery

Rte 15 follows the main road through the Southern Cemetery (2.1km) with several lengthy detours. It is a continuation of Rte 14. **Cairo Atlas 24, 25, 30, 31, 32. And see map on p 383.**

Stretching S 2.3km from the southernmost point of the Maydān Ṣalāḥ al-Dīn is the vast necropolis called **al-Qarafah al-Kubrā'**, the Great Cemetery, also called the *Southern Cemetery* and by Europeans *The Tombs of the Mamlukes*, although in fact none of the sultans are buried here. Also within the Southern Cemetery are two areas included in other itineraries—that immediately S of the Citadel (Rte 14) and the area from the Tomb of Shagar al-Durr to the Maydān Sayyidah Nafīsah (Rte 11).

Since the earliest settlement of the city of Fusṭaṭ in the mid 7C the area has been important as the cemetery serving the city. As the active centre of the city moved N with the building of successive suburbs, so the area of the cemetery was enlarged. Thus it contains some of the earliest Muslim tombs known in Egypt. The Fāṭimid Khalīfs chose to be buried within their own palace enclosure and the early Mamlūk sultans in tombs attached to theological foundations inside the city. Thus the importance of the Southern Cemetery declined though the presence of the Tomb of the Imān Shāfiʿī ensured that it would always be a place of reverence. After the Ottoman conquest in the early 16C, perhaps because of its association with many of the pious early settlers, it was the favoured area for the burial of the great bays and officials. After the death of Muḥ. ʿAlī many members of the royal family chose to be buried in a royal enclosure close to the Tomb of the Imān Shāfiʿī. As in the Eastern Cemetery there has always been a population who live in and around the tombs, which has increased because of housing pressures. Here also services are being provided for the inhabitants.

Crossing the S end of the Maydān Ṣalāḥ al-Dīn, close to the Mosque of Sayyidah 'Aʿishah (Rte 13), is the wide arterial Shʿ. Ṣalāḥ Sālim on a flyover. In the SW corner of the square leading S is the SHʿ. AL-QAḌIRIYYAH. At the S side of the road (50m) stands the **Bāb Qāyt-bāy** (278; 24:7), the former main gate of the cemetery. At present it is a pile of dismantled stones and will presumably be re-erected. It bore two medallions in the name of Sultan Qāyt-bāy. Adjacent to the S is the **Tomb of Amīr Tīmūr-bāy al-Ḥusaynī** (161), a small, conventional Mamlūk tomb in which the dome has fallen. There are no dedicatory inscriptions, and the ascription is literary. This amīr was promoted in the fatal year 1516.

Running SW from the rear wall of the tomb is a further section of the **Wall of Ṣalaḥ al-Dīn** (78) with one of the original gateways, the **Bāb al-Qarāfah** (618), 50m S of the Bāb Qāyt-Bāy. The wall runs SW to meet the **Aqueduct of Sultan al-Nāṣir Muḥ.** (78) coming from the W.

Continue down the Shʿ. al-Qādiriyyah. On the W side is the **Tomb of Amīr Gānī-bak, Nā'ib Giddah** (171; 24:7), built in 1465 but in very bad

# THE SOUTHERN CEMETERY

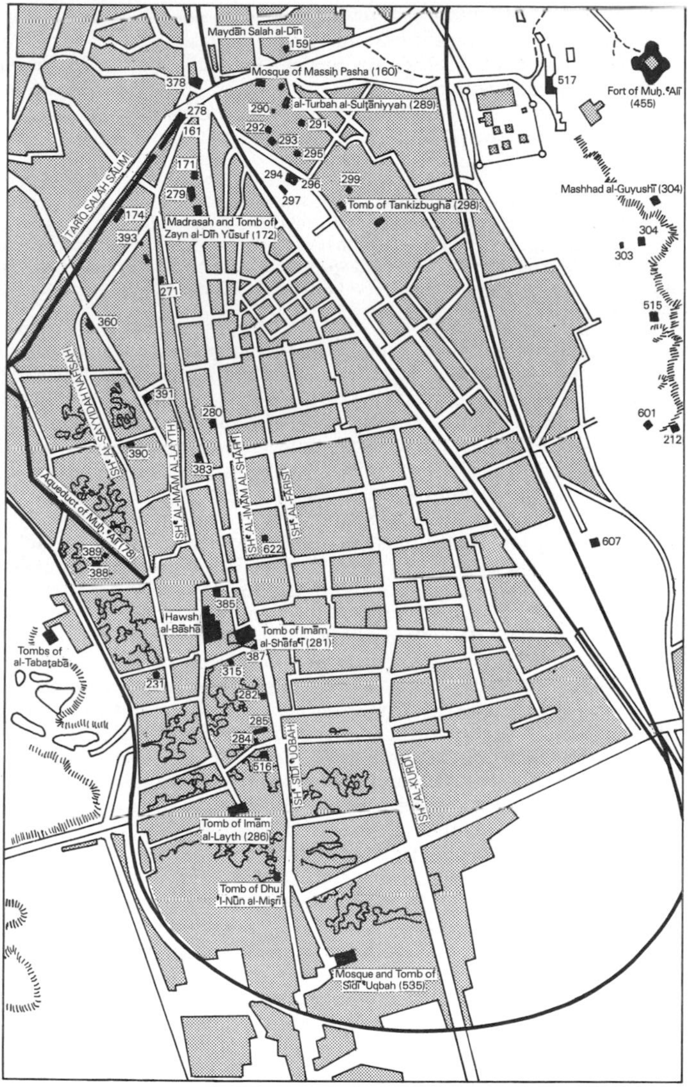
Maydān Salah al-Dīn
159
Mosque of Massīḥ Pasha (160)
378
517
Fort of Muḥ. ʿAlī (455)
278
161
290
al-Turbah al-Sulṭāniyyah (289)
292
291
293
295
TARIQ SALĀH SĀLIM
171
294
296
299
279
297
Tomb of Tankizbughā (298)
Mashhad al-Guyushī (304)
174
Madrasah and Tomb of Zayn al-Dīn Yūsuf (172)
393
304
303
271
515
360
SHʿ AL-SAYYIDAH NAFĪSAH
391
601
212
280
390
SHʿ AL-IMĀM AL-LAYTH
SHʿ AL-IMĀM AL-SHAFIʿI
383
SHʿ AL-FARISĪ
Aqueduct of Muḥ. ʿAlī (78)
607
622
389
388
385
Hawsh al-Bāshā
Tomb of Imām al-Shāfaʿī (281)
Tombs of al-Tabaṭabā
387
315
231
282
285
284
SHʿ SIDĪ ʿUQBAH
516
SHʿ AL-KURDĪ
Tomb of Imām al-Layth (286)
Tomb of Dhu ʾl-Nūn al-Miṣrī
Mosque and Tomb of Sidī ʿUqbah (535)

disrepair. Only the entrance remains standing of this once considerable tomb complex.

Gānī-bak, the grand dawādār, an honourable man and at one time governor of Jeddah (Arabia), was a contender with Khushqadam for the sultanate. The latter was elected in 1461 and Gānī-bak retired gracefully. He was murdered by the Royal mamlūks in 1463, and the tomb was therefore raised after his death presumably by Sultan Khushqudam in reparation of the way his mamlūks had dealt with his rival and friend.

An oblong portal surrounds the trefoil-arched entrance, the upper lobe of which, supported on pendentives, has stalactite decoration. A joggled lintel covers the doorway and on each side is a foundation inscription.

Immediately to the S, set slightly back from the road, is the so-called **Tomb of Muṣṭafā Pasha** (279; 24:7), in fact the *Ribāṭ of the Amīr Azdumur al-Ṣāliḥī*, built c 1270.

That it was a study centre for sufis is confirmed by the layout of the building and also two burials that occured here almost immediately after it was built. The first was that of Sh. Abū 'l-Farag, director of the Madrasah of Sultan Kāmil (Rte 5), in 1273, and the second in 1297 of Sh. Yūsuf al-ʿAdawī (grandfather of the builder of the next monument) who traced his descent to the Quraysh Tribe and was the leader of a sufi brotherhood.

The form of the building is unique in Egypt and several of the decorative features are innovations while others are introductions from Syria. This building has a strange alignment—N–S—which has caused some problems regarding the miḥrāb. The façade is of stone but the internal walls, vaults and arches are in brick. Originally measuring 26m by 19m, the whole of the W side has fallen and is partially replaced by a modern wall. The entrance at the E end of the N wall is a rectangular frame with an unusual pattern enclosing a round arch with ornamental voussoirs, a Syrian feature. A vestibule leads into the large ṣaḥn, c 11.5m sq. Behind the N wall, instead of a līwān there is a long room with a transverse vaulted roof while along the E wall are five tunnel-vaulted living rooms with the remains of a second storey of the same. It may be presumed that the W wall consisted of further rooms. To the S is the great līwān, also with tunnel-vault. The miḥrāb is set at an angle to compensate for the alignment of the building. Above is a triple-lighted window flanked by excellent carved stucco with fine inscriptions in Kufic and Naskhī. E of the līwān is a room occupying the SE corner of the building. A large triple miḥrāb covers the whole of the S wall, the niche again set at an angle. The whole wall has delicate and complex stucco carving. Of particular interest are the bands of Naskhī inscription in panels separated by medallions, the first time that this feature appears in Cairo, but which was to become almost universal on later buildings.

30m S is the **Madrasah and Tomb of Sayyid Zayn al-Dīn Yūsuf** (172; 24:7), locally called Sīdī Ulay, a corruption of Uday, one of the shaykh's names. It stands in a paved depression due to a rise in the road surface. The building was raised in 1298 and restored in 1325 and latterly by the CPAM in 1915. Immediately in front of the building is an isolated portal with flat stalactite arch, all that remains of a zawiyah built in 1335. Built 40 years after the main structure, it makes an interesting contrast to the earlier entrance.

Zayn al-Dīn Yūsuf, grandson of the shaykh buried in the last monument, traced his ancestry to the Umayad khalīf Mu'awiyyah. An extremely picus man, his family were traditionally leaders of a sufi brotherhood and he was chief qāḍī under Sultan Qalāwūn. He died in 1297, the year before the madrasah was completed. Latterly the building was held in trust for the CPAM. In 1907 the intendant, attempting to rid himself of the burden of supervision, set fire to the tomb. The carved wooden frieze was destroyed, as was the original finely carved tābūt, but fortunately the stucco work survived.

The NE façade, facing the street, is decorated, as is the SW façade. There are four recesses in the former, the outer two with trefoil arches, the inner pair with flat stalactite arches; each recess contains a rectangular window with carved lintels. In the SE façade are fine niches, each of the outer pairs with fluted keel-arches and that in the centre with a pointed arch and medallion. The lintels and spandrels of the windows are finely carved, the former with inscription. There is no minaret but the tall dome of the tomb in the S corner has a sextuple window in the zone-of-transition and a high drum with carved panels in the lower part and 20 keel-arched windows above, over which is a band of inscription. The plastered brick dome has a rib and fillet decoration.

Inside the entrance a porch contains two doorways: that to the left with a keel-arch leads into the NW līwān of the cruciform interior. Each līwān is a different size though all are covered with tunnel-vaults. Flanking the NE līwān are small rooms while at the back of the SW līwān is a fine stucco window. The arch of the qiblah līwān is supported on columns with tulip capitals; on the left of this līwān is a small room, and on the right the entrance to the tomb chamber. A band of very fine carved foliate Naskhī inscription of surah Yā Sīn from the Qur'ān runs at a height of 2.5m around all the walls, forming a frame for the miḥrāb which is finely carved with a later coloured-marble interior.

In the Tomb Chamber, c 5m sq., the dome is raised on squinches of three over three over four niches. Two layers of marble face the lower walls, which before the fire were crowned by a carved wooden inscription. The stucco work in the zone-of-transition, including the squinches, is exceptional and the elegant stucco window lattices were once filled with coloured glass. The flutes of the dome are also carved, terminating at the apex in a large rosette with geometrical ornament and inscription from the Qur'ān.

South of this point the road divides, the main road continuing S as the SH'. AL-IMĀM AL-SHĀFI'Ī, passing the Tomb of 'Abdallāh al-Dakrūrī and the Tomb of al-Maznī (see below) to arrive at the Tomb of the Imam Shāfi'ī. Running SW, but after a little distance turning directly S to run parallel to this road, is the SH'. AL-IMĀM AL-LAYTH (pron. Lays), to the W of which most of the monuments lie.

The majority of the monuments described here are of minor importance being mainly Ottoman, and some of them are difficult to locate. Directly to the W (200m), against the Wall of Ṣalāḥ al-Dīn, is the remnant of the *Mosque of Amīr Azdumur* (174; 24:7) which, although built comparatively late in 1495–1502, is very much ruined, only the minaret surviving of the complex which included a madrasah tomb and palace. The minaret has a square-sectioned base on which rests the octagonal first stage with keel-arched recesses. Above, a simple stalactite corbel supports the next undecorated cylindrical stage which has a trefoil cornice. The final stage is also cylindrical with full-length keel-arched recesses and a spear-head cornice. On the way back to Sh'. al-Imām al-Layth (70m) is a small enclosure in a maze of modern graves containing the *Tomb of Amnah Qādin* (393), a small carved marble tābūt, built in 1756 for a wife of one of the bays. Before reaching the main road, 70m S of this tomb, on the SH'. AL-IQDĀM is a large platform supporting a stone canopy raised on columns, containing the **Tomb of Raḍwān Bay** (384; 30:1) and several others of his following. Elaborately carved, it was raised in 1686 for Raḍwān who was the most powerful bay in Cairo, leader of the Faqāriyyah faction and first Shaykh al-Balad. S on the Sh'. al-Imām al-Layth (70m) is the **Tomb of 'Uthmān Bay al-Qazdughlī** (271), built in 1766 for another leading bay. Down the Sh' al-Imām al-Layth and some distance SW (170m) is the **Tomb al-Sādāt al-Malikiyyah** (560), of early 14C date though in great disrepair. Little remains of the 14C fabric, but the base of the octagonal minaret can be seen above the entrance.

Further S (150m) and also some distance W is the 16C *Tomb of Amīr Burham* (391) and following the road 100m to the SW the *Ḥawsh of ʿUthman Bay Abū Sayf al-Sinnārī* (390; 30:3), built in 1763.

Return to the Shʿ. al-Imām al-Layth where to the E on the Shʿ. al-Imām Shāfiʿī (150m) is the **Tomb of ʿAbd Allāh al-Dakrūrī** (280; 30:1), built for a pastry-cook from the Bāb al-Lūq who had a great reputation for piety. He died in 1466 and was interred in this tomb. A little to the S, W of the Shʿ. al-Imām al-Layth (100m) is the **Tomb of Abū Gaʿfar al-Ṭaḥāwī** (383; 30:3), built in 1753. 170m to the S and 75m E of the Shʿ. al-Imām al-Shāfiʿī is the 17C **Tomb of al-Maznī** (622; 30:4). 400m W of the road beyond the *Aqueduct of Muḥammad ʿAlī*, lies the **Tomb of Muṣṭafā Bay Shāhīn** (389; 30:3), built in 1753, and next to it to the N the **Tomb of Ruqayyah Dūdū** (388), built in 1757 for one of his female relations. She was the woman who built the beautiful sabīl-kuttāb on the Sūq al-Ṣilāḥ (Rte 10).

The Shʿ. al-Imām al-Shāfiʿī terminates (250m) in a small square on the W side of which stands one of the most important monuments in Cairo, the ***Tomb of the Imām Shāfiʿī** (281; 30:5).

Abū ʿAbd Allāh Muḥammad b. Idrīs al-Shāfiʿī (founder of the Shāfiʿī School of Law) was born in Gaza in 767. Although his descent was traced to the Quraysh he was brought up by his widowed mother in poverty. He spent much time with the bedouin learning grammar and poetry. In 787 he went to Medina to study under Mālik b. Anas (founder of the Māliki School of Law) and stayed until Mālik's death in 796. He visited Egypt in 804 but returned to Baghdad to teach. Among his pupils was Aḥmad b. Hanbal (founder of the Hanabalī School of Law). In 815 he went to Egypt with Sayyidah Nafīsah to settle and died in Fusṭāṭ in 820.

He was buried in the vaults of the family of ʿAbd al-Ḥakam which occupied the present site. Although greatly venerated by the native populace the tomb was neglected during the Fāṭimid period as the work of Imām al-Shāfiʿī was of little interest to the rulers, who had their own Shiʿī schools of law. When, however, Ṣalāḥ al-Dīn assumed control of Egypt he chose this site to build the first of his madrasahs to support Sunnī orthodoxy. He built the Shāfiʿī madrasah in 1180, incorporating in it a beautiful tomb chamber for the imām. One of his wives, Princess Shamsah, was buried here as was their son Sultan al-ʿAzīz (died 1198). Sultan al-Kāmil, after the death of his mother in 1211, rebuilt the tomb chamber and had her buried here. A tomb was prepared here for him too but he died in 1238 in Damascus. In 1482 Sultan Qāyt-bāy ordered the restoration of the complex, including the tomb, by his chief architect, Ibn al-Zamīm, and work was also done by Sultan Qānṣūḥ al-Ghawrī in the early 16C. By the mid 18C the madrasah was in ruins and ʿAbd al-Raḥmān Katkhudā built a mosque on the site and decorated the tomb. Further decoration was applied by ʿAlī Bay al-Kabīr in 1772. In turn the Ottoman mosque decayed and in 1891 the khedive Tawfīq erected the present mosque.

Thus at present the monument consists of 19C mosque and to the SW the Ayyūbid Tomb of Imām al-Shāfiʿī, the whole complex entered through an ornate gateway contemporary with the mosque.

The base of the Tomb is c 20m sq. At 6.5m is a moulding above which in each face is a pointed-arched window, flanked each side by two niches. Above these is a frieze of geometrical ornament which runs beneath a balcony of brick and stucco trellis-work supported on brick piers decorated with calligraphic and foliate ornament. The second storey is inset about 1m, leaving a broadwalk behind the trellis. Recesses decorate the walls with fluted keel-arches raised on small columns, and ornamented disks or lozenges alternate between the shoulders of the arches. The central niche in each wall corresponds to the top section of two rhomboidal windows piercing the wall beneath. The corners of this storey are chamfered to accommodate keel-arched doors with fine stucco work on the flanks and shoulders. Steps lead directly up to the outer base of the dome. Excellent undercut stepped and pierced cresting surmounts this storey.

Although the extreme thickness of the walls could easily support a brick or stone dome, the present dome of wooden beams covered with lead sheets is an anomaly. The lead sheeting was supplied by ʿAlī Bay al-Kabīr in 1772 but underneath are the remains of an earlier covering of green faience tiles. The interior support for the dome suggests that it must have been reconstructed in the late 15C by Sultan Qāyt-bay and covered with green tiles by him or Sultan Qānṣūḥ al-Ghawrī. In the early Ottoman period when the tiles started to decay the dome was covered with lead sheets which were renewed by ʿAlī Bay. Around the base are 16 windows and the apex is crowned with a bronze boat finial, which in former times was filled with seeds and water for birds.

INTERIOR. The entrance is in the NE wall and makes a corridor through the thick walls, at each end of which are double doors. Those at the exterior end are silver-plated and modern, but the inner doors are original with excellent Ayyūbid carving and Naskhī inscription naming the Imām al-Shāfiʿī. A pavement of faience mosaic forming a star pattern covers the floor, probably contributed by ʿAbd al-Raḥmān Katkhudā, as was the carved and painted ceiling. Measuring c 15m sq., the chamber has a geometrical patterned marble dado and at this height is pierced by two windows. That in the NE wall with a pointed arch is a later addition, but in the NW wall is another that may have been the original entrance to the chamber. It has a coffered ceiling with octagonal inserts, the first in Egypt. On the frame and lintels of the windows are decorative carvings and inscriptions. There are three miḥrāb recesses in the SE wall, probably originally decorated in stucco as a triple miḥrāb. The present Mamlūk decoration is contemporary with the dado. For some reason the chamber is considerably out of alignment to the qiblah and a supplementary miḥrāb has been inserted in the SE corner. The great frieze of carved Kufic inscription is original. From this project eight beams supporting an octagonal framework, also finely carved, for the suspension of lamps—the only original example extant in Egypt. High on each side are the pointed-arched windows with reconstructed stucco grilles based on the originals. Elaborate wooden squinches with three tiers of three over seven over five niches support the dome, the work of Sultan Qāyt-bay. The whole of the upper section of the chamber including the squinches and dome were decorated with excellent painting and inscription by Ṣāliḥ Afandī for ʿAlī Bay al-Kabīr.

Within the precinct are four tombs. Northernmost of the group is the *Tomb of Imām al-Shāfiʿī*. The tābūt of 1178 made by ʿUbayd b. Maʿalī is one of the finest pieces of carved woodwork in Egypt and is similar to the tābūt of al-Ḥusayn in the MIA. In teak, it consists of carved and inscribed panels within a framework of batons. Along the gable is a Naskhī inscription (the rest are in Kufic). Surrounding the tomb is a fine maqṣūrah, provided in 1911 by the khedive ʿAbbās II, inscribed by Yūsuf Aḥmad and painted by an Italian artist, Prinzivalli. To the SW stands the marble *Shāhid* (tombstone; lit. witness) also with a Naskhī inscription. Abutting the last to the S is the uninscribed *Tomb of Muḥ. ʿAbd al-Ḥakam*, a member of the family in whose vault the Imām al-Shāfiʿī was buried. Close to the SW wall is the *Tomb of Princess ʿAdiliyyah* (died 1211), mother of Sultan al-Kāmil. This also has a fine carved wooden tābūt with Kufic and Naskhī inscriptions. Towards the S corner in front of the miḥrāb is the *Uninscribed Tomb*, perhaps originally intended for Sultan al-Kāmil who died in Damascus, with a maqṣūrah that originally surrounded the tomb of Imām al-Shāfiʿī. Of the tombs of Princess Shamsah and Sultan al-ʿAzīz nothing can now be seen.

At the rear of the building is the **Mosque and Tomb al-Bakriyyah**, of little architectural importance, but interesting as it is the burial place of the Shaykhs al-Bakrī. The al-Bakrī family is descended from Abū Bakr, the first khalīf. They migrated to Egypt perhaps as early as the 8C but rose to prominence during Ottoman times after Muṣṭafā al-Bakrī (died 1709) founded a Khalawātī brotherhood. The head of the family was the Shaykh al-Mashayikh, leader of all the sufi brotherhoods in Egypt and there was great rivalry with the family of Sādāt al-Wafāʿiyyah for the post of Naqīb al-Ashraf (marshall of notables). The Shaykh al-Bakriyyah was responsible for organising the Māwlid al-Nabī celebrations, among many other important functions.

100m N of the Tomb of Imām al-Shāfiʿī a road leads to the E. A small alley leads off (75m) to the S to the **Tomb of ʿAlī Bāy al-Kabīr and Ismāʿīl Bay al-Kabīr** (385; 30:5), two marble tābūts, the first erected in 1773, the second in 1791, beneath a decaying wooden canopy.

ʿAlī Bay al-Kabīr generally known by the Turkish title Bulut Kapan (cloud catcher) was originally a mamlūk of Ibrāhīm Katkhudā (died 1754), leader of the Qazdughliyyah faction. After Ibrāhīm's death the doyen of the faction, ʿAbd al-Raḥmān Katkhudā during the absence of another ʿAlī Bāy (also known as al-Kabīr) made ʿAlī Bay Shaykh al-Balad. He collected an immense household of mamlūks and by 1763 was head of the faction having exiled ʿAbd al-Raḥmān. He deposed two Ottoman walīs, began to mint his own coins and led campaigns in Arabia and Syria. During the latter his senior bay, Muḥ. Abū ʾl-Dhahab, rebelled and turned the army against his master. ʿAlī fled from Cairo to Syria where he raised a large army but was defeated, imprisoned and probably poisoned in Egypt.

Ismāʿīl, a mamlūk of ʿAlī Bay, was a contender for the leadership of the bays after the death of Muḥ. Bay Abū ʾl-Dhahab. The two other contenders were Murād Bay and Ibrāhīm Bay. Surviving assassination attempts and campaigns against him he was Shaykh al-Balad from 1786. After managing to govern for five years he succumbed to the terrible ravages of the plague in 1791.

To the N runs the Shʿ. Sayyidah Nafīsah, up which on the right (100m) stands the **Hawsh al-Daramalī**, with tombs of a notable 19C family. The oldest tombs are those of *Muḥ. Faḍl Pasha* (died 1870/1) and *Muḥ. Afandī Rustum (died 1877/8). Five other members of the family are also buried here.*

From the Tomb of ʿAlī Bay, turn S into (75m) the SHʿ. ḤAWSH AL-BĀSHĀ. After 50m, on the E are the sandstone domes of the **Ḥawsh al-Bāshā**, the mausoleum of the family of Muḥammad ʿAlī Pasha.

A columned portico leads to the main complex, on the left of which an open court contains the *Stone-canopied Tomb* of a First Secretary of Muḥ. ʿAlī. On the far side of the court under a domed arcade lie the *Tombs of Khadīgah al-Khāzindar and her sisters*. All the tombs in this complex are constructed in an extravagant Ottoman style, with two or three tiers, in ornately carved marble, brightly painted and gilded.

At the end of the portico opposite the entrance, a separate chamber contains the *Tomb of Shafaq Nūr* (died 1883), the largest monument in the complex. It is a huge marble edifice, gilded and painted, with formal plaits surmounting the front pillar. A minor concubine of the Khedive Ismāʿīl, she did, however, bear his eldest son, Tawfīq, during whose reign she bore the title Walidah Pasha. On the left side of the portico is a door. Immediately inside this, on the right, and surrounded by a massive bronze maqṣūrah, stands the *Tomb of Aḥmad Ṭūsūn Pasha* (1793–1816), second son of Muḥ. ʿAlī and father of ʿAbbās I. He led the campaigns against the Wahhabis in Arabia but died of cholera in Egypt. His was the first royal tomb on this site, originally used for the multiple graves of the mamlūk leaders massacred in the Citadel by Muḥ. ʿAlī in 1811. These lie directly behind this tomb: the largest is that of *Murād Bīk*, on the right. To the left of Tūṣūn's tomb stands the *Tomb of Mahūsh Qādin* (died 1889), principal wife of ʿAbbās I and mother of Ibrāhīm al-Ḥāmī.

Opposite is a group of tombs of the family of Ismāʿīl Pasha. Nearest the entrance is the *Tomb of Ismāʿīl Pasha* (1795–1822), third son of Muḥ. ʿAlī, who commanded the campaigns in the Sudan with great cruelty. He was burnt to death at Shendī, supposedly by the Mak Nimr, but evidence seems to be growing that he was the victim of familial or military revenge. Behind lie the tombs of his children. The first two are those of *Malak Ṭūsūn* (died 1825/6) and *Khalīl* (died 1902/3). Beyond them are those of *Ruqayyah* (died 1823/4) and *Fāṭimah* (died 1834/5). On the far side is the *Tomb of Aminah* (died 1823/4), wife of Muḥ. ʿAlī, in front of which is a space probably occupied by his own tomb before its transfer to the Citadel in 1857.

Inside the main pavilion the tombs are roughly in five rows running N to S. They contain the graves of further descendants both of Muḥ. ʿAlī and of his brothers and sisters, generally distinguished by the family name Yakan (nephew).

In the row furthest to the right against the rear wall are six tombs. From nearest to furthest these are of: *Fāṭimah* (died 1851/2), daughter of Ibrāhīm Pasha; *Amīnah* (died 1864/5); *Zaynab*, wife of Dawūd Pasha; unknown; *Ismāʿīl* (died 1872), son of Ibrāhīm al-Ḥāmī; and *Shams* (died 1891), wife of Aḥmad Rifʿat Pasha. In the same order, the tombs in the second row are those of: *ʿAbbas I Ḥilmī Pasha* (1813–54), son of Aḥ. Ṭūsūn and ruler after the death of Ibrāhīm in 1848. He was murdered in his palace at Banhā; *Ibrāhīm al-Ḥamī* (1836–60), his son, drowned in the Bosphorus; *Tawḥidaḥ* (died 1881), sister of Bambah Qādin; and *Aḥmad Rifʿat Pasha* (1825–58), eldest son of Ibrāhīm Pasha and heir apparent, who was killed in a railway accident at Kafr al-Zayyāt, a journey which his brother Ismāʿīl fortuitously missed.

The first tomb in the short third row is that of *Muṣṭafā* (died 1836), another son of ʿAbbas I. The other two are the tombs of Ruqayyah and Firdaws Yakan. In the fourth row to the left of the entrance all eight tombs are of the Yakans. Against the outer wall in the fifth row the first eight tombs are also of the Yakans, while the ninth is that of *Shams al-Safar* (died 1846), a concubine of Muḥ ʿAlī and mother of two daughters who died young. Last stands the magnificent *Tomb of Ibrāhīm Pasha* (1779–1848), eldest son of Muḥ. ʿAlī and his successor.

Born in Nusretli near Kavalla (Macedonia), Ibrāhīm later joined his father in Egypt. In 1805 he stayed in Istanbul as surety for his father's debts; on his return he held several important civil posts but gained great reknown for his campaigns in Arabia and Sudan. However, his greatest victories were in Greece and Syria. During his invasion of Turkey he would have achieved the capitulation of the Sultan were it not for the influence of the European powers. When his father became senile, Ibrāhīm headed the regency council and he was confirmed as pasha in September 1848. He died of pneumonia in November of that year.

Muḥammad ʿAlī was buried here in 1849 but his remains were transferred to his own mosque in the Citadel in 1857. King Fārūq was also buried here in 1965 but reburied in the Rifāʿī Mosque in 1975.

Directly W across the railway line, 500m beyond the Tomb of Imam al-Shāfiʿī, lie the remains of the only Ikhshid monument in Egypt, the **Mashhad of the Family Ṭabāṭabā** (563; 32:5), built in the mid 10C.

Ibrāhīm (died 786), a descendant of ʿAlī, lived in Medina and received the nickname Ṭabāṭabā because he had a speech impediment and pronounced the letter qāf as ṭāb. His sons came to Egypt and had a great reputation for sanctity. His grandson Aḥmad, a poet, was a confidant and adviser to Ibn Ṭūlūn and Aḥmad's son ʿAbd Allāh (died 959) was a friend of the Ikhshidi ruler Kāfūr. The whole family were known for their honesty, piety and generosity. The building was constructed shortly after the death of another of Aḥmad's sons, al-Sharīf, in 943.

There is now little to see. A walled enclosure, containing the remains of the bases of cruciform and T-shaped brick piers and a miḥrāb, outlines a building of c 18m sq. The cross-pieces of the piers show the remains of engaged columns and it is evident that this was not an enclosed tomb but uniquely of canopy-form with nine domes. In the E corner of the enclosure is a covered well and on the SE wall a building erected in the mid 19C to contain the bodies reburied from the Ṭabāṭabā vault.

Directly S of the Tomb of Imām al-Shāfiʿī runs the SHʿ. SĪDĪ ʿUQBAH. On the corner of the next lane to the W is the **Tomb and Sabīl-Kuttāb of Raḍwān Bay al-Razzāz** (387; 30:5), built in 1754 for yet another powerful Ottoman official. Further down the same lane (75m) is the half-buried **Tomb of Muḥ. al-Ḥaṣawātī** (315) built in the mid 12C. It is a domed canopy tomb with keel-arched opening on three sides (two walled-up). Each side of the zone-of-transition contains a keel-arched window flanked by similar shaped recesses. The drumless dome is undecorated. The interior is plain with the dome raised on four simple tall squinches. There is a fine miḥrāb only a little smaller than that in the Mashhad of Sayyidah Ruqayyah (Rte 11). After a further 150m on the S is the **Sabīl al-Aḥmar** (231) a 17C fountain.

Returning to the Shʿ. Sīdī ʿUqbah and continuing S, all of the monuments are on the W side of the road. The first (after 130m) is the **Tomb of Amīr Abū Manṣūr Ismāʿīl** (282; 30:6), locally called the *Qubbat al-Sādāt al-Thāʿlab*. It consists of two isolated elements which were probably part of the same building of 1216. The stone *Entrance* has a flat arch and a very beautiful carved frame decorated with Kufic inscription and foliate and geometrical ornament. Below the lintel is a fine foliate Naskhī inscription. Inside is the remnant of a brick-built vestibule. A little further down the street is the *Vaulted līwān*, the oldest known in Egypt, built of excellent brickwork. Flanking the līwān are two side-rooms with arrow-slit windows. In the SE wall is the miḥrāb, 5.3m high, with a scalloped semi-dome at the back of which is a keel-arched panel. Above is a window of six lights. In the centre of the līwān is a grave with a foundation panel that was originally set in the entrance. This is not the original tomb of the amīr (remains of the original wooden tābūt are in the MIA and the Victoria and Albert Museum, London) and the exact function of the building is not known, but it may have been a madrasah to which his tomb was attached. The body was probably removed to the līwān after the collapse of the tomb.

There follows a series of 12C tombs of a single 9C family, descendants of the Khalīf ʿAlī through his son Ḥusayn. 75m S of the Tomb of Amīr Abū Manṣūr lies the **Mashhad of Yaḥyā al-Shabīhī** (285; 30:6). He received his nickname al-Shabīhī (similarity) from his supposed resemblance to the Prophet. This is a large building of c 1150 with most of the E half occupied by a tomb. It is the most complete of the group and typical of them all. The ribbed dome has a stepped zone-of-transition. Entry is from the W into an ambulatory around the *Tombs*. On the left is a keel-arched entrance to the chamber. Similar arches raised on double-pillars pierce the SE and NE walls. The drum is raised on simple squinches and the ribs of the dome taper to a central medallion of inscription. Beneath the dome are five brick-built tombs. That to the S is of Yaḥyā b. Qāsim (died 877) and next to it is that of his brother ʿAbd Allāh (died 875). On the opposite side is the grave of their mother.

The side corridors have wooden roofs but the qiblah corridor has a vault at either end and a central smooth dome. In this wall are three keel-arched miḥrābs with fluted hoods, that in the centre being larger. At the NE is an annexe entered through an arcade with three keel arches. In the W corner is a chamber containing the tomb of Ismāʿīl ʿĀṣim, an official of Muḥammad ʿAlī.

W of this complex stands a small recent room. Against the back wall is a miḥrāb, probably the remains of a tomb built in the 10C, just prior to the Fāṭimid invasion.

Immediately to the S is a small lane, the SHʿ. SĪDĪ SHABĪHĪ, and on the N stands the **Tomb of Qāsim Abū Ṭayyib** (284; 30:6), which seems originally to have had the same form as the last mashhad, i.e. a tomb with an ambulatory around the sides. Only the base of the 12C building remains, the upper part being 14C. At the SE side is a wall with the three miḥrābs. Qāsim Abū Ṭayyib was the father of Yaḥyā al-Shabīhī.

Opposite is the modern **Tomb of Sayyidah Kulthūm** (516; 30:6). She was the sister of Yaḥyā al-Shabīhī, renowned for her piety, and died in 912. All that remains of the original tomb of 1122 (probably of the same mashhad form as the foregoing tombs) is the superb round-arched miḥrāb. The hood is decorated with alternating ridges and flutes, which emerge from a central rosette. In the shaft is an elegant star trellis decoration inscribed with the name of ʿAlī.

S along the Sh.ʿSīdī ʿUqbah (100m) the next turning to the W is the SHʿ. AL-GHUFFĀRĪ down which (150m) on the S stands the **Mosque and Tomb of Imām al-Layth** (286; 30:7). This is an Ottoman building of 1786 surrounding a much older complex. Just within the portal is the *Gate of Sultan Qānṣūḥ al-Ghawrī.*

Al-Layth b. Saʿd was born at Farmā (Pelusium) in 712 into a very wealthy family, immigrants to Egypt from Isfahan (Persia). He spent his youth studying the Qurʾān and religious law in which he became extremely knowledgeable. As he grew older his piety and generosity displayed themselves in many ways. He gave much of his wealth away as charity, feeding the needy with meat and sweetmeats while contenting himself with bread and olives. Many scholars corresponded with him, including the great Imām al-Malik. His reputation spread and even the khalīf Ḥārūn al-Rashid asked him to arbitrate in a dispute he was having with a wife. He died in 791 and was buried here. Later the Imām Shāfiʿī visited his grave and said that the only regret he had was not having met Imām al-Layth, whom he considered even more knowledgeable than his own teacher, Imām al-Malik. Al-Bukharī, the traditionist, spoke of him as among the greatest of Muslims.

Imām al-Layth originally had a simple grave within an enclosure but in 1244 Sultan al-Ṣāliḥ Ayyūb built a magnificent tomb over the grave. This was replaced in 1408 by Sultan Farag who also built a mosque. The lady Raḥbā bint Ibrāhīm reconditioned the building in 1428. Further work was done by the sultans Qāyt-bay and Qānṣūḥ al-Ghawrī who provided the beautiful door (now in the tomb of Imām al-Shāfiʿī). Much work was undertaken by Mūsā Shurbajī Mustaḥfizān in 1725. Finally in 1833 Ismāʿil Bay reconstructed almost the whole building to its present form. The Tomb-chamber is in the SW corner of the rectangular mosque. As well as Imām al-Layth, his father Saʿd ʿAbd al-Raḥīm, his brother Shuʿayb and his step-brother Muḥ. b. Ḥārūn are buried here. After 250m the Shʿ. al-Ghuffarī crosses the railway line and joins the Shʿ. ʿAyn al-Ṣīrah (for the Tombs of Sabaʿ Bañat, see below).

Return E into the Shʿ. Sīdī ʿUqbah. To the E (175m) is the **Tomb of Dhū ʾl-Nūn Miṣrī** (316; 30:8), in a small covered enclosure. The only indication is a narrow original tomb stone with an angular Arabic inscription.

Dhū ʾl-Nūn (died 860), a Nubian, was a famous mystic and a central figure in the introduction of sufism into Egypt. Beyond this where the street terminates (300m) is the southernmost monument in the cemetery, the **Mosque and Tomb of Sīdī ʿUqbah** (535). Built in 1652 by Muḥammad Abū Nūr it is, like other mosques in the area, based around a much earlier foundation.

ʿUqbah ibn ʿĀmir (died 677) was a companion (ṣahābah) of the Prophet. Originally a servant, he went with Muḥammad to Medina and was one of those who helped to gather together the Qurʾān for the khalīf ʿUthmān. He came to Egypt and was made governor in 664.

ʿUqbah is the only companion of the Prophet whose tomb is known in this cemetery. In yellow sandstone, the elegant façade is dominated by the minaret which is set upon a square base with a decorated frieze. The shaft has 16 sides and a medial balcony. Behind is the dome which is Mamlūk in inspiration. Around the drum are eight windows which alternate with niches; the dome is decorated with elegant double ribs. To the right of the minaret a small door leads into a small cemetery which contains much fallen masonry, presumably from the original building. Above this door is a sundial. The entrance to the mosque is set in a single trefoil arch.

Inside, the mosque has two arcaded wings, with the wooden roof painted, carved and gilded. To the right is the tomb chamber with a wooden tābūt, dated 1655, surrounded by a maqṣūrah. To the S is the second wing. The fact that the miḥrāb is inserted in the corner of the building suggests that this mosque has been curtailed, perhaps part of it collapsed.

To the E parallel to the Shʿ. Sīdī ʿUqbah the SHʿ. AL-KURDĪ runs the whole length of the S Cemetery and then continues S (See below).

1.4km to the E of the Mosque of Imān al-Shāfiʿī, beyond the railway line and just outside the confines of the cemetery stands the **Zāwiyah af Qādī al-Fādil Shātbī** (607, 32:4) built in 1802. To the SE (500m) lies the **Mosque of al-Sādāt al-Wafāʾiyyah** (608, 32:6), built by Sultan ʿAbd al-Ḥamīd in 1777 around the tombs of Shams al-Dīn Muḥ. al-Wafāʾ (died 1361) and his son ʿAlī (died c 1400), founders of the Wafāʾiyyah Sufī Brotherhood (see p 346 for their house and history). This is a typical Ottoman mosque, the flat roof supported on large arches tied with wooden cross-beams. The coffered ceiling is richly painted and the walls are faced with decorated marbles. Inside, a large wooden maqṣūrah lies the *Tomb of Muḥ. and ʿAlī al-Wafāʾ* and their descendants.

At its W end the Shʿ. al-Ghuffārī (see above) runs into the SHʿ. AYN AL-ṢĪRAH which then turns to the SW. Beyond it on the N side lie the alkaline pools of *ʿAyn al-Ṣīrah* (which give their name to the area) while to the S much of the area has been used as the main rubbish tip (zibal) of Cairo. The only way that the next monument can easily be reached is across this dump, since access from the S is barred by a housing development. 1km along the Shʿ Ayn al-Ṣīrah cut across the tip (500m) to the **Sabaʿ Banāt** (seven sisters, unnumbered) the remains of six tombs aligned SW–NE built in 1010. Four of the tombs have much of the structure left, though all domes have collapsed while the two northernmost consist only of foundations. Despite extensive excavation no trace remains of the seventh tomb.

According to al-Maqrizi (via Creswell) these are the tombs of seven members of the family of Wazīr Abūʾl-Qāsim al-Maghrabī who were executed by Khalif al-Hākim after the wazir fled to Makkah. Local tradition gives the popular name of the monument, that is that these are the tombs of the seven daughters of Badr al-Gamālī whose mashhad dominates the heights of Muqaṭṭam to the E.

These buildings are important in that they are the first covered tombs in Egypt of which there are any remains. It was a vanity that was to culminate in the vast and elaborate tombs of the Mamluk sultans and amirs. They also display the first tentative building in stone.

All the tombs are similar differing only in size and minor details, c 6.4m sq, cubic bases are built of small limestone blocks, each side with a keel-arch opening. The zone of transition and the octagonal drum are built of brick, as must have been the domes. The whole was stuccoed overall. In each face of these units there is a window. Inside simple squiches form the zone of transition, and there is the remains of stucco on the walls. The second tomb which is slightly larger has two mihrabs in the pillars. Originally each stood in its own brick enclosure with an entrance in the NW wall. They are all obviously related to the tombs in the Fāṭimid cemetary at Aswan.

Following the Shʿ al-Kurdī S (see above) it crosses the railway line (200m) and continues due S passing through the area of Basātīn (the orchards) which as its name suggests was once a lush agricultural region abounding in groves of fruit trees and date palms, and was the southernmost region of the original city of ʿAmr b. al-ʿĀṣ. At 1.5km turn W through the new housing development (you may have to ask as there are no signposts) for the (500m) *Bīr Umm al-Sulṭān* and the **Aqueduct of Ahmad Ibn Ṭūlūn** (unnumbered) reported to have been built c 870 by the same Syrian Christian who was later to build Ibn Ṭūlūn's mosque.

This great building stood on the N shore of the Birkat al-Ḥabash (Lake of the Abyssinians) and carried water 4½km N to the Ibn Ṭūlūn's city of at Qatāʿī (Rte 13). Now reduced to a sump, the well which fed it was once much more extensive and the ancient banks can be seen among the reeds and rubbish on the E side of the structure. With the drying up of the Birkat al-Ḥabash the whole area became desiccated and only revived in the present century.

The water tower (c 6m high) is a substantial brick built rectangular structure with the intake channel on the E side covered by a large round arch. Stout piers with pointed arches raise the roof which once supported the raising mechanism. Although restored in the late 19C the S façade still shows several original niches, similar to the windows in Ibn Ṭūlūn's mosque. From the W side the aqueduct takes off almost due N and about 500m of it are still traceable. It is supported on piers and round arches built of brick with the interior spaces filled with rubble.

# 16 The Old City

Rte 16 is centred on the ancient fortress of Babylon, with its Christian churches and the associated Mosque of ʿAmr b. al-ʿĀṣ. There are, however, several other important sites close by that should not be missed. The total distance involved is c 1.5km. **Cairo Atlas 28, 29, and see map on p 396.**

**Bus No. 431 goes from the Maydān al-Taḥrīr to Maydān Masgid** ʿAmr b. al-ʿĀṣ.

S beyond Shʿ. Sadd al-Barrānī the Shʿ. Manṣūr cuts through the aqueduct (Rte 30) and after 50m crosses over the Shʿ. al-Rawḍah into **Miṣr al-Qadīmah** (the Old City), roughly defined as the area surrounding the Fortress of Babylon and the longest settled area in the city. Immediately on the E bounded by SHʿ. ABŪ 'L-SAYFAYN is a group of Christian cemeteries. At the S end stands the **Monastery of St. Mercurius** (Dayr al-Maqāryūs or D. Abū ʿl-Sayfayn; 28:3–5), surrounded by a high wall. Contained within the complex are three churches and a convent. A single entrance gives access into the enclosure (the original iron-bound door is now in the Coptic Museum).

The **Church of St. Mercurius** was first mentioned in the late 10C when it was used as a store for sugar cane. Later, in 1080 after it had been restored, the canons of the

Coptic rite were formalised here at the request of Badr al-Gamālī, the commander of the Fāṭimid khalīf al-Mustanṣir. After being rebuilt it was burnt in 1168, during the great fire of Fusṭāṭ, but rebuilt again within ten years.

Like most of the churches of Old Cairo it is of basilican type. Piers separate the nave from the side aisles and there is a fine ambon with mother-of-pearl inlay, set on marble pillars. The S haykal is dedicated to the Archangel Raphael, the N haykal to the Virgin, while the central haykal, with canopy over the altar and tribune behind, is dedicated to St. Mercurius. All have fine wooden screens. On the walls, covering all the available space, are ikons, seemingly representing the whole corpus of Coptic saints. Some of them date to the 16C. From the N aisle a stairway leads down to the *Crypt of St. Barsūm al-ʿAryān* (the Naked) who dwelt here for 20 years and died in 1317. Beside the door to the crypt is a doorway into a court in which (left) is a *Small Church* with three haykals dedicated to St. James the Sawn-asunder, St. George and the Archangel Gabriel. On the right is the *Baptistery*, while steps lead up to the *Upper Church* with five disused chapels.

Adjacent is the **Church of St. Shenute** (Shanudah) where the 46th patriarch Khayl was elected in 743. After a brief term as a mosque under Khalīf al-Ḥākim in the early 11C it was restored to the Christians and rebuilt in the early 14C by the patriarch Benjamin II.

In this church the aisles are separated from the nave by marble pillars. The ambon is also of fine workmanship but supported on eight wooden columns. The haykal screens are all inlaid with ivory. The screen to the central sanctuary dedicated to St. Shenute is modern, but that fronting the now disused N sanctuary is much older. The S sanctuary is dedicated to the Archangel Michael. Near the entrance are steps leading to the *Upper Church* with three disused sanctuaries and a baptistery.

Inside the main enclosure, the first turning on the left leads to the **Church of the Virgin** (al-ʿAdhrā) which is also called *al-Damshiriyyah* after a Coptic notable who restored the church in the 18C. It seems that this church was founded in the 7C, destroyed in the 8C and rebuilt soon after. It has a simple plan of a narthex, nave and two side aisles, each separated by three pillars and high wagon-vaulted roof. The modern ambon rests on two pillars.

Beyond this is the **Convent of St. Mercurius**, still inhabited by nuns.

An isolated monument stands some distance to the E. Cross the railway line and follow the SHʿ. IBN YAZĪD for 300m. There on the left is the **Mosque of Zayn al-ʿĀbidīn** (599; 21:6), a 19C building on the site of a Fāṭimid mashad over the tomb of Zayn. Zayn was the son of Ḥusayn; he carried on his father's campaign against the Bani Ummayah. He was killed in 741. His burial-place in unknown but there was a tradition that his body was sent secretly to Cairo and interred there.

The Fāṭimid fabric has disappeared except to the right of the qiblah riwāq. The tomb chamber was built in the 15C and the iron maqṣūrah was replaced in 1863. The rest of the building is a reconstruction of 1805 by ʿUthman Aghā Mustaḥfiẓān.

Running SE is the SHʿ. ʿAMR IBN AL-ʿĀṢ which leads into the Maydān ʿAmr ibn al-ʿĀṣ. The SHʿ. SĪDĪ ḤASAN AL-ANWĀR leaves to the N and on the SE side of the square (300m) is the **Mosque of ʿAmr ibn al-ʿĀṣ** (319; 29:5). Founded in the winter of 641–42 immediately following the conquest of Egypt, it was the first mosque on the continent of Africa. Nothing remains of the original structure which has been overlain by later rebuilding but its exact location is known (see below). The present aspect of a large enclosure mosque (116m by 108m) is the result of thirteen centuries of alteration and reconstruction it is currently the object of further restoration including a completely new portal.

ʿAmr ibn al-ʿĀṣ was born c 570 into the tribe of Quraysh at Mecca. Little is known of his early life but he seems to have been neutral in the early stages of the aggression of the Quraysh towards Muḥammad and the other Muslims. Similarly, after the flight of the Muslims to Medina in 622, he played little part in the battles of the Meccans against them. He accepted Islam just before the Muslims finally conquered Mecca in 630. His subsequent successful career is well known. In 632 he was sent to

Oman by Muḥammad where the brother kings Jayfar and ʿAbbād accepted Islam. Muḥammad died while ʿAmr was on this mission. The next year he led the army of the first khalīf Abū Bakr and conquered Palestine, where he was given an estate. As commander of the Arab army he conquered Egypt for the second khalīf ʿUmar in 640–42. He was by this time 60 years old. ʿUthmān, the third khalīf, recalled him from Egypt and he retired to Palestine where he remained until ʿUthmān's assassination in 656. Upon the accession of ʿAlī to the khalifate there was much dissension among the Muslims. Muʿāwiyyah, a kinsman of ʿUthmān and governor of Syria, led the largest rival group. It was to this faction that ʿAmr allied himself. He commanded Muʿāwiyyah's army at the indecisive battle of Ṣiffīn and then in 658 re-entered Egypt and easily defeated the governor who was a supporter of ʿAlī. At a court of arbitration between the two contenders. ʿAlī and Muʿāwiyyah, ʿAmr succeeded in having both their claims invalidated. ʿAlī was murdered at Kufa in 661 leaving Muʿāwiyyah unopposed in Damascus where he was elected khalīf, thus establishing the dynasty of Umayyads. ʿAmr remained in Egypt as governor until his death, aged over 90, in 663. He was buried in the desert close by, but his tomb has not been found.

ʿAmr's mosque measured about 30m along the qiblah wall, by 17m wide, with two doors in each side except the qiblah wall. The walls were probably of mud-brick while the mud and palm thatch roof was supported by beams resting on palm-trunk columns. There was no central court and the floor was unpaved. It must also have served as a council chamber and meeting place. In 673, ten years after the death of ʿAmr, the populace complained that it was too small and Maslamah, the governor, had it enlarged to the NE and NW, inserting in the process a central court and erecting four minarets, one at each corner. The walls were plastered and rush matting spread on the floor. During the next century or so it was reconstructed several times, usually being enlarged in the process. In 698 it was reconditioned by ʿAbd al-ʿAzīz ibn Marwan, the governor; in 710 by Qurrah ibn Sharīk; in 750 by Ṣalāḥ ibn ʿAlī and in 791 by Mūsā ibn ʿAlī. By this time it had reached exactly half its present size, but in 827 ʿAbd Allāh ibn ʿAlī added a similar sized extension to the S, thus producing the present dimensions. This was by no means the end of the reconstruction and rebuilding.

Khalif al-Ḥākim acquired the mosque for 100,000 dinars in 1012–13 and added two extra riwaqs around the ṣaḥn bringing them up to the present number. Much attention was also lavished on it by the later Fāṭimids. Although Ṣalāḥ al-Dīn totally restored the mosque during later Ayyūbid times it fell into neglect. Once Sultan Baybars was established in the mid 13C he had the whole of the NW wall rebuilt. Like the other great mosques it suffered in the great earthquake of 1303 and the amīr Salār was responsible for the subsequent restoration. Burhan al-Dīn, the chief of Cairo merchants, had the whole of the qiblah wall torn down and rebuilt in 1401–02. By the 18C it had decayed and the grandee Murād Bay undertook very extensive restoration. More work was done on the mosque by Muḥammad ʿAlī, the first of several 19C restorations. The piecemeal enlargements and reconstructions recorded above have resulted in the plan of the mosque being somewhat out of square. In the 1980s extensive work restored the interior to the state of the building of 827. This mosque has always been close to the heart of the populace. In 1980 a single anonymous donor gave money for lighting, air conditioning and carpeting throughout the mosque.

On the long stretch of the *NW wall* the central section between the two outer entrances is the work of the amīr Salār, but the portal is part of the recent restoration. The W entrance was built by Murād Bay and includes the minaret to the right of the door, with lower octagonal and upper cylindrical stages. Windows in this wall have been reconstructed to the original plan, but the crenellations are conjectural. The *SW wall* is also hybrid. A small section at the W corner is of 827, beyond which is more of Salār's work. The central section was built in 1845 but at the S end is a further part of the 827 work including some windows. Above the S corner is the second of Murād Bay's minarets. The 827 fabric continues along the

*SE wall* for almost half its length but terminates just before the miḥrāb salient. Beyond this the wall is of an indeterminate period. The tomb at the E corner is the work of Murād but beyond this on the *NE wall* is a short section of 827 fabric. The rest of this wall is also of indeterminate age.

Enter through the new *Portico*. The doorway in the Mamlūk wall is the work of Murad, but to the right is a *Miḥrāb* built by Salār with the remains of very fine stucco decoration. The doorway leads into the *NW riwāq*, now being reconstructed into its original form of seven transverse arcades. Murād Bay's reconstruction left only one riwāq along this wall. Both of the side riwāqs are also being reconstructed. It is known that while the *SW riwāq* had perpendicular arcades, strangely those on the *NE riwāq* were transverse. In the centre of the ṣaḥn the *fountain* is modern, although the first one in the mosque was built by Khal. al-ʿAziz in 989.

Rounded arches resting on piers alternating with two pillars front the *qiblah riwāq*. During the reconstruction of Murād the original transverse arcades were rebuilt in perpendicular form. The original mosque of ʿAmr ibn al-ʿĀṣ occupied a rectangular area at the N end of this riwāq. It is known that the present northernmost miḥrāb is in a direct line with, but 15m in front of, the miḥrāb of ʿAmr's mosque. The main miḥrāb is plain.

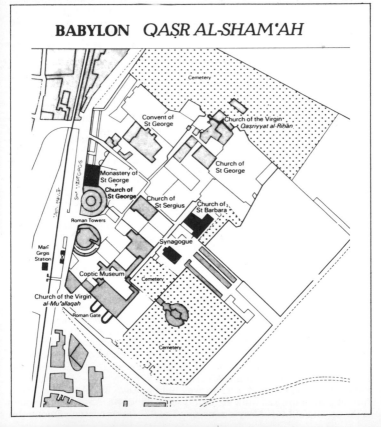

**BABYLON** *QAṢR AL-SHAMʿAH*

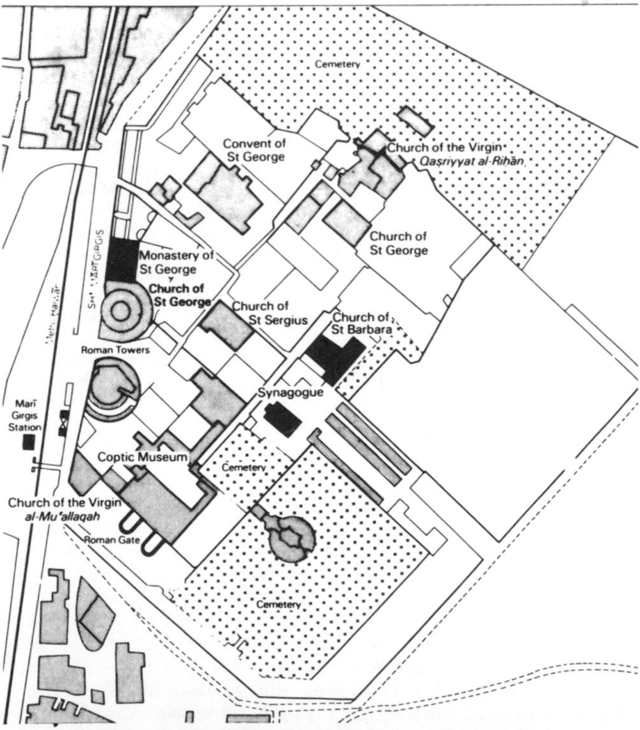
Cemetery
Convent of St George
Church of the Virgin
Qaṣriyyat al-Rihān
Church of St George
Monastery of St George
Church of St George
Church of St Sergius
Church of St Barbara
Roman Towers
Synagogue
Marī Girgis Station
Coptic Museum
Cemetery
Church of the Virgin al-Muʿallaqah
Roman Gate
Cemetery

At the S end of this riwāq are five pillars from which the transverse arcades of 827 sprung. In the N corner under a dome and surrounded by a bronze screen is the *Tomb of ʿAbd Allāh*, the first son of ʿAmr. He was born when his father was 13 years old. He became a Muslim before his father and was noted for his courage and honesty. As a close companion of Muḥammad he transmitted many traditions. He became the governor of Egypt in 683 after his father, but lived only for another year, dying in 684 aged 72.

From the Maydān ʿAmr ibn al-ʿĀṣ the SHʿ. MĀRĪ GIRGIS runs SW. (Several monuments, described at the end of this Rte, lie to the W of the railway line.) After 300m it passes E of further Christian cemeteries, to the N end of the site of the **Roman fortress of Babylon** (28:8), later called Qaṣr al-Shamʿ (Fortress of the Beacon). After the Arab conquest the defensive function of this fortress became obsolete and it was occupied largely by the Copts who built several churches and monasteries within the precinct, several of which still exist.

Much of the early history of this site is obscure. Originally it was probably a settlement where the ferry serving the road from Memphis to Heliopolis crossed the Nile. Being safely within the confines of Egyptian territory there was little need for fortifications. During either the Assyrian or Persian occupations a fortress was erected here, since their hold on the territory was purely that of military superiority. By Roman times this fortress was known as Babylon of Egypt, although whether this was the original name is uncertain. One of the Roman legions was installed here and Trajan had the whole complex rebuilt. When the Arabs invaded, Cyril the Byzantine patriarch and governor, held out for some time within the fortress but finally capitulated. At this time the Nile still ran directly beneath the W wall of the fortress, and the Arab town built by the followers of ʿAmr straggled to the NE. In the mid 19C much of the original structure was still standing, but the British, despite condemnation by expatriate residents, demolished a large part of it during extensive alterations. Only parts of the towers and gates have survived.

The N part of the wall is also original and in this section a lane leads to the SE. At the end this turns S and on the left (80m) is the Coptic **Convent of St. George** (Deir Mārī Girgis; 28:8), still inhabited by nuns. A small gate leads into a court, from which steps lead down to the 10C section. Cells can be seen in the walls (some sealed) while a door on the S gives on to a *Shrine* with a well and relics of St. George.

Beyond the convent an alley leads from the lane (50m) to the **Church of St. George**. The first church was built here by Athanasius the Scribe in 681, but it was destroyed by fire in the mid 19C. All that remains of the earlier structure is the *Hall of Nuptials*.

At the N end of the lane (30m) stands the **Church of the Virgin** (al-ʿAdhrā), also called *Qaṣriyyat al-Riḥān* (Pot of Basil). Little is known of the early history of this church but Arsenius, Greek patriarch and uncle of the khalīf al-Ḥākim, gave it to the Greek community. At some time it must have passed back to the Copts, to whom it now belongs. The whole structure was rebuilt in the 18C. It has a square plan and the main objects of interest are a series of ikons painted by John the Armenian, dated 1778. The haykal screens are inlaid with ivory; that to the S dedicated to St. Sarapamon is dated 1775, that to the N dedicated to St. Michael is dated 1778.

SW the lane leads into the southern complex of buildings, but return by the same route and turn S along the W wall (150m) to the twin **Roman Towers**. The one to the N is almost completely rebuilt, while the S tower

*Oil-press in the tower of the Roman Fort*

has the W half demolished and various layers of construction can be seen in the hollow cylindrical structure. The foundation layers consist of large well-cut blocks of stone and are pierced with several doors. Above this is irregular aggregate masonry with bands of smaller rectangular blocks at regular intervals. One pillar remains of those that once supported the ground floor. Just beyond the N tower is the Greek Orthodox **Monastery of St. George** (Mari Girgis; 28:8) with the church built on the actual tower. This is the seat of the Greek patriarch of Alexandria.

This Greek foundation originated at Memphis and probably moved here when that city was abandoned after the foundation of Fusṭāṭ. It is first mentioned in the 10C when it was briefly administered by the Copts. As the fortunes of the Greek church waxed and waned it passed several times between them and the Copts, but it has been a Greek Orthodox church since the late 15C. From the 16C it also contained a convent, hospital and an old people's refuge. In 1904 the complex was destroyed by fire although the ikons and relics were saved. A new church was rebuilt in 1909. The mūlid of Mari Girgis (called the Panegyris) is held on 23 April and is one of the largest Christian celebrations in Cairo.

The present modern *Church of St. George*, set on top of the N tower, is circular in plan. On the second landing of the stairs is a relief of St. George. Beneath the church are chapels to various saints and a small *Museum* containing ikons, liturgical objects and vestments. N of the church is the *Monastery* which contains the *Hall of Saints*, divided into sections dedicated to various saints.

Behind the N tower are several lanes. Turn SE down some steps and follow the lane, turn right and at the first corner (50m) is the **Church of St. Sergius** (Abū Sargah; 29:7). It is built on one of the sites by tradition visited by the Holy Family during their flight into Egypt and may be one of the most ancient foundations in the fortress.

From 859 the Coptic patriarch was elected in this church and continued to be so until the 12C. After being pillaged in the same century it was rebuilt by Hanna al-Abāh. The connection with the Holy Family attracted the attention of Europeans, and there are records of their visits to the shrine from the 14C onwards. This church is dedicated to St. Pachon (Bucchus).

Basilican in plan, the nave is separated from the aisles by 12 columns with Corinthian capitals. On the only red granite column are the remains of life-sized paintings. The central sanctuary has a 13C screen, the upper section inset with panels of ebony and ivory. Behind the altar, with domed canopy, the walls show traces of early paintings of the two patron saints and the Virgin. The S sanctuary is disused but the altar in the N sanctuary also has a domed canopy. To the W of this is the *Baptistery*. From the S sanctuary steps lead down to the subterranean *Sanctuary of the Holy Family*, where they traditionally halted on their journey.

Turn right from this church and then left (50m) to arrive at the **Church of St. Barbara** (Sitt Bārbārah; 29:7). Entry is from the NW (the ancient door from here is now in the Coptic Museum).

The first church built here in 684 by Athanasius the Scribe was dedicated only to SS. Cyrus and John, the unmercenary physicians. Later the relics of St. Barbara were brought here and an annexe built. Barbara, who lived in the 3C, was the daughter of a pagan merchant of Nicomedia. She was converted to Christianity by the Egyptian Origen and with her companion Juliana she attempted to convert others. They were both tortured by the Roman governor and executed.

Beyond the narthex five columns divide the nave from each of the aisles. The central sanctuary has a 13C wooden screen with carved ivory panels of religious scenes and inscriptions. Along the summit are ikons, dated 1745, of Jesus, Mary, two archangels, and apostles. The altar is covered by a large canopy supported on marble columns, behind which is the tribune. The W sanctuary is now a shrine to St. Barbara and contains her relics. Adjacent is the *Church of SS. Cyrus and John*, the original patron saints. Almost square in plan, the E sacristry is dedicated to St. George and the W to SS. Cyrus and John. Beside the sanctuaries lies the Baptistery.

S of the southernmost Roman tower an entrance leads into a court. On the W side is the **Coptic Museum** (Mathaf al-Qibti; 28:8) (open Nov–April 09.00–16.00, Friday closed 11.00–13.00; May–Oct 08.30–13.00, Friday closed from 11.15).

This was the last major museum to be founded in Cairo. By the beginning of the 20C both the Egyptian Museum and the Museum of Arab Art (MIA) were well established. Therefore, at the urging of Marcus Simaika, a group of Coptic notables under the patronage of Sultan Ḥusayn Kāmil formed a committee to establish a museum to display specifically Christian works of art. Land belonging to the Coptic Church was provided within the ancient fortress and by 1908 the building was complete. Many treasures were collected from ancient churches and houses and several private collections were presented to the museum. In 1931 the museum passed into state control and relevant material was transferred from the EM and the MIA. It has subsequently been enlarged. Rooms 18–30 are closed at present.

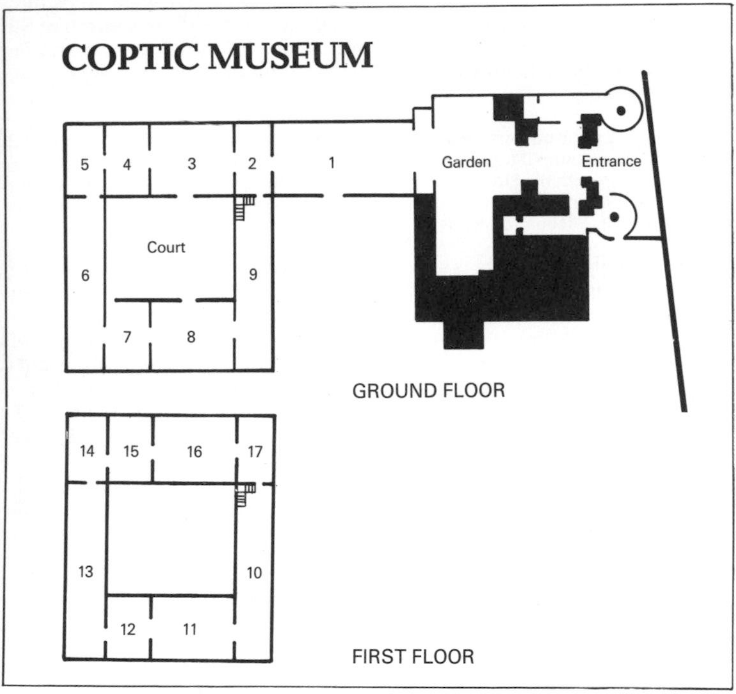
COPTIC MUSEUM
5
4
3
2
1
Garden
Entrance
Court
6
9
7
8
GROUND FLOOR
14
15
16
17
13
10
12
11
FIRST FLOOR

LOWER FLOOR. *Room 1*: Pre-Christian sculpture to the 5C AD, mainly from Ihnas (near Bani Suwayf). A door leads into the *Courtyard* (WC) which displays Classical and Antique pillars and capitals. A passage leads to the basement of the *Roman Gate* (often flooded) with store rooms containing stables, a mill, bakery and wine-press. *Room 2*: 5C sculpture. *Room 3*: Sculpture and other objects from Bawit (near Asyūṭ) excavated by Maspero in 1913. Among the more impressive objects are 5–6C wall-paintings of Christ in Glory, the Virgin and 12 apostles and two Coptic saints. Also a fine display of marble jar stands. *Rooms 4–5*: Sculpture, including corbels and capitals. *Rooms 6–7*: Material from the Monastery of St. Jeremiah (Ṣaqqārah) including capitals and stucco work and an excellent stone ambon. *Room 8*: Funerary stelae from Upper Egypt. *Room 9*: 11C wall-painting of Adam and Eve before and after the Fall, from Umm al-Birgat (al-Fayyūm).

*Apse painting from Bawīṭ, 7C. The Ascension of Christ and the Virgin with the infant Jesus and apostles*

UPPER FLOOR. *Room 10*: Coptic, Nubian and Arab MSS including the Gnostic Nagʿ Hammādī Codices (see Rte 34). *Rooms 11–12*: Coptic and Ethiopian textiles. *Room 13*: Ikons, ivories and beads. *Room 14*: Woodwork, including painted coffin portraits from the Fayyūm. There is also a massive gate from one of the quarters of Cairo. *Rooms 15–16*: Metalwork, including jewellery. *Room 17*: Recent acquisitions, including material obtained during excavations in Nubia during the 1950s and '60s.

S of the museum a flight of steps leads up to the **Church of the Virgin** (28:8), called al-Muʿallaqah (the Suspended) as it rests on top of the two bastions of the Roman Gate.

This building was probably founded in the late 7C, although it is first mentioned in the mid 9C when the upper section was demolished by order of the governor of

*A Nile God, 3–4C AD*

Egypt. It was rebuilt in 977 and in the 11C was involved in an argument with the Church of St. Sergius as to which was the premier church of Babylon. Several of the patriarchs were subsequently consecreated here. During the reign of al-Ḥākim it was turned into a mosque but after his death it was restored to the Christians. Much restoration was done in the late 19C.

At the top of the long steps is the late 19C portico, above which the residences of the clergy are surmounted by two modern towers. Inside there is an open court which leads into the narthex in the form of a second portico. The wagon-vaulted central nave is separated from the aisles by 16 pillars, one of black basalt. Along the centre of the nave are a further three pillars against the southernmost of which is the 13C marble ambon decorated with scallop and cross patterns. The central haykal is dedicated to the Virgin and has a fine 13C carved ebony screen inlaid with ivory. Along the summit are ikons of the Virgin and various saints. Behind the altar is the stepped tribune. The S haykal, dedicated to St. George, has a similar screen and 17 ikons by John the Armenian (dated 1771) depicting the martyrdom of St. George. Ikons by the same artist crown the haykal of the N sanctuary dedicated to St. John the Baptist. To the E lies the *Little Church*, built inside a bastion of the gate. The roof is supported by a massive pier. This is part of the original 4C church. On the SE side a 13C screen divides the church. The section nearer the door is the *Sanctuary of Takla Haymanot*, the patron saint of Ethiopia, while the farther section is the *Baptistery*. On the E wall are the remains of excellent wall-paintings probably of the 7–8C.

Just inside the SE wall of the fortress stands the **Synagogue** (29:7). Originally this was the *Church of St. Michael the Archangel*, but after being closed by the khalīf al-Ḥākim it was purchased by the Jewish community. Much of it was rebuilt in the late 19C, although the basic fabric is original. During the rebuilding a hoard of several hundred Hebrew manuscripts and fragments (11–14C AD) was uncovered. These are known as the Geniza documents, and provide a unique source for the history of the period from the early 11–16C (many are now in the BL and Cambridge).

From the S point of the Fortress of Babylon the SHʻ. ʻAYN AL-ṢĪRAH runs E. 500m to the N of this road lie the remains of the town of **Fusṭāṭ** (29:8), the meagre foundations giving little indication of the teeming city that once stood here. Its appearance is that of a rubbish tip which is hardly surprising since for the last nine centuries it has been one. After the fire of 1168, started deliberately by Shawar to stop Amalric, King of Jerusalem, occupying it, the city was devastated and never recovered. Usable material was extracted and the area became a waste land, used for the dumping of Cairo's rubbish. A minute section of the area has been excavated since 1912, first by Ali Baghat and lately by the American University in Cairo under the directorship of G. Scanlon. The walls of some buildings have survived to a height of 2m, others have been reconstructed. A system of unpaved roads has been uncovered, and extensive and sophisticated sewage, drainage and water supply ducts. Basically, although the external walls of the houses are asymmetrical, the internal plans are regular with rooms surrounding one or two courts with fountains and flower beds. The material used was baked brick, with stone for the floors and doorways. These buildings date from the Ṭūlūnid and Fāṭimid periods; of the earliest structures very little has been found. Some of the most interesting finds are the remains of workshops of ceramic, glass and metal workers.

**West of Shʻ. Manṣūr.**

About half-way down the Shʻ. Mārī Girgis a road runs to the W. It crosses the metro line and directly ahead another road leads to the SHʻ. MUḤAMMAD AL-SAGHĪR which runs S. Follow this and take the first lane W. Here, inside a low enclosure, stands the **Qubbat al-Faransāwī** (tomb of the Frenchman), an unclassified but very important monument. It is, actually, the Tomb of Sulaymān Pasha al-Faransawī, a beautiful structure of brick and cast iron built in the mid 19C. The use of cast iron on this scale is unique in Egypt and is obviously due to the latest European advances in the use of the material; in fact it was probably constructed in Europe and transported to Cairo. The plastered brick octagonal base is surrounded by an ornate cast-iron verandah decorated with scrolls and flowers. Above, the cupola is also in cast iron, each section with rosettes and sprays of flowers. In its original state it was probably painted and gilded. There are door in alternate walls of the base. Inside, the marble tābūt is in a very bad state (at present it is used as a paint store).

Sulaymām Pasha (1788–1860) was born Joseph Seves in Lyon into a family of cloth merchants. He joined the army and participated in Napoleon's campaigns in Europe, briefly being held captive in Austria. In 1819, after the collapse of the Republic, he came to Egypt where Muḥ. ʿAlī was looking for European instructors for his new army. Joseph did well but, after a rebellion by Muslim soldiers against their European teachers, he accepted Islām and took the name Sulaymān. He accompanied Ibrāhīm in the Greek and Syrian campaigns and was made a pasha. During the reign of ʿAbbās I he was ignored, but he had a brief period of respite after the succession of Saʿīd.

NW is the domed brick-and-plaster tomb of his Greek wife, Maryam (died 1895), mother of his four children.

*The cast-iron Tomb of Sulaymān Pasha*

The whole of the area to the S now occupied by houses and shops was once the palace of Sulaymān. To the W on the Corniche stands the *Masgid al-Faransāwī*, built by Sulaymān in the mid 19C and reconstructed by Muḥ. Talʿat al-Faransāwī, a descendant, in 1952. Only the provincial Ottoman minaret remains from the original mosque.

Further S on the Shʿ. Muḥammad al-Saghīr on the E is the **Mosque of Muḥammad al-Saghīr** (529; 28:6); only the façade and minaret of 1426 remain of the original fabric. 150m further S the SHʿ. AL-QABWAH leads off to the W. After 100m on the S is the *House of Shiḥātah Aḥmad* (527; 28:8), built in 1786, although all that remains is the fine decoration and the doorway, carved medallions and ropework moulding. Immediately opposite is the SHʿ. SUWAYDĪ with, on its W side, the **Mosque al-Suwayadī** (318; 28:8).

This mosque was begun c 1420 by Badr al-Dīn al-Suwaydī. He intended it as a madrasah and left 4800 dinars for his son Wagh al-Dīn to complete it. This he did, but he was requested by Sultan Barsbāy to convert it into a mosque. In 1441 Fatḥ al-Dīn, Wagh's son, obtained a decision from the qadi to reconvert it into a madrasah, but within a month Barsbāy ordered it to be turned into a mosque once more. The reason for this acrimonious quarrel is not known but it certainly lasted a long time and involved three generations of one family.

Although the façade is original the minaret is Ottoman. The trefoil stalactite hood of the entrance is set in a square frame. Around the doorway is fine yellow and black ablaq joggling.

W along the Shʿ. al-Qabwah on the riverbank (100m) are the remains of the *Madrasah al-Kharūbiyyah* (28:8), built in 1349. S along the Corniche on the E (300m) stands the *Mosque of ʿAbdīn Bak* (524), built in 1660 for the tomb of Sīdī Rūwaysh.

Return E to the Shʿ. Muḥammad al-Saghīr which at this point joins the SHʿ.ATHĀR AL-NABĪ, also running S. After 500m on the W a small close leads to the **Ribāṭ al-Athār** (Hospice of the Relics; 320). The setting is charming and it is surrounded by trees and bushes.

Although the present building is Ottoman, dated 1666, it was founded in the early 14C by the wazī Muḥammad ibn Fakr al-Dīn and his son for the poor. As its name suggests it contained mementos of the prophet. It received much attention from the rulers and in 1809 an annex was built by Maḥmūd Bazakhān. The relics were transferred to the Mosque of Ḥusayn (Rte 4) in 1888 with great ceremony.

It consists of a large hall with bronze grilles in the windows. At the N corner is the minaret, of provincial Ottoman type. Inside, the woodwork is painted while the walls have panels of 17C tiles. The miḥrāb and minbar are excellent examples of Ottoman work.

Nearby is the **Geological Museum** (al-Maṭhaf al-Jiyulūjiyyah), moved from Taḥrīr Square because of the excavations for the new metro line. It contains excellent examples of Egyptian rocks and minerals, with didactic displays on oil exploration. There is a complete series of invertebrate trace fossils, while among the more imposing vertebrate fossils are those from the late Eocene-Oligocene strata of Qaṣr al-Ṣāghah and Gabal Qaṭrānī in the Fayyūm. These include the early elephantids Moeritherium, Palaeomastodon and Phiomia, the bizarre horned Arsinotherium, as well as important early primates. From the Miocene deposits of the Muquṭṭam Hills there are early sea-cows and whales.

# 17 Būlāq

Route 17 (600m) logically follows on from Rte 1A. However it covers the last area of the medieval city to be developed and this is best understood in relation to the preceeding itineraries. **Cairo Atlas 6**.

N of the Broadcasting Building, the Corniche crosses the SHʿ. 26 YŪLYŪ (running SE to Shʿ. Ramsīs; NW crossing Kubrī 26 Yūlyū to al-Gazīrah and the West Bank, Būlāq al-Dakrūr). The area to the N of the Shʿ. 26 Yūlyū on the East Bank is called **Būlāq** (Map 6).

Until the 12C the area was on the bed of the Nile but the westward movement of the river caused the formation of a large sandbank in the early 13C which was exposed at low water. By the late 13C the sandbank had become a permanent island which by the early 14C was habitable. The arm of the Nile separating it from the E bank silted up, becoming a marsh with a causeway to the island. A port was developed which during later Mamlūk times became the principal port of Cairo, while that at Fusṭāṭ declined. During Ottoman times the marsh was dyked and the dry ground incorporated into the habitable zone of Cairo. By the time of Muḥammad ʿAlī it was a populous area and he chose it for his industrialisation programme. Many workshops and factories were built, including the printing press established here in 1822. During the 19C thousands of important texts were printed here and these early Būlāq editions of books are still considered to be among the best in Middle Eastern book production. It is still to a large extent an industrial area.

Just E of the junction with the Corniche on the S side of Shʿ. 26 Yūlyū stands the **Mosque and Tomb of Abū ʾl-ʿAlāʾ** (340; 6:5), a shaykh who is now, for reasons unknown, dignified with the title sultan.

The mosque was built c 1485 by Ibn al-Qanīsh for Shaykh Ḥusayn Abū ʿAlī (of which the modern name is a corruption) who died in 1495 and was buried in the tomb. Much of the cruciform building collapsed in the late 19C and it was reconstructed in a different form in 1914; thus it is now an arcaded mosque. Only the main façade, minaret and tomb remain of the original fabric.

Dominating the W end of the façade is the minaret (dismantled and rebuilt) above the entrance. It carries the most extensive inscription in Cairo. The first stage is octagonal with carved moulding, the second stage cylindrical and the third stage a pavilion. Behind is the tall plain dome of the tomb raised on a high drum. The entrance has a trefoil arch and to the left are two full-length recesses each containing a pair of windows. At the E end of the façade is a *sabīl-kuttāb*.

Opposite, running N, is the SHʿ. BŪLĀQ AL-GADĪD (to Maydān ʿAbd al-Gawād). Take this road and then (50m) the first on the left, which runs NW. On the left (50m) is the *Mill of Sitt Rabiyyah* (444; 6:3), the interesting façade of an 18C commercial building. Cross the SHʿ. AL-KHAṬĪRĪ where the road turns due N; after 175m on the E is the **Mosque of Muṣṭafā Shūrbagī Mirzā** (343), a fine and very well preserved mosque built in 1698. The exterior is typical of the period with Mamlūk decoration, but a tall Ottoman minaret. The interior is in the form of a small covered enclosure mosque with marble columns supporting a wooden roof with central lantern. The sunken floor of the central area is a magnificent example of coloured marble inlay. Around the wall is a fine dado and on the SE and NE walls a large and heterogeneous collection of Ottoman provincial tiles.

On the opposite side of the road is the fountain built by the same official, the *Sabīl al-Mirzā* (347), and (40m) one of his commercial establishments, the *Mill al-Mirzā* (603). Beyond the road turns W. To the E is the *Mosque of al-ʿAmrānī* (346; 6:4 ), a modern building, but with a 13C minaret. The base is octagonal with keel-arched niches and windows with small stalactite balconies on alternate sides. Above a stalactite corbel the second cylindrical stage has sharp vertical ribs. The third stage is also cylindrical.

W along the road at the N end of SHʿ. AL-KHUḌRĀʾ (250m) stands the **Mosque of Qāḍī Zayn al-Dīn Yaḥyā** (344; 6:3), a very fine building. This, the second of the three mosques built by this powerful civilian minister, dates to 1448.

Zayn al-Dīn Yaḥyā was of Armenian descent and rose to be ustadār of Sultan Jaqmaq. During this reign he built three mosques and a zāwiyah (now destroyed), a display of the vast wealth he accumulated. One of the amīrs who suffered particular persecution in his pursuit of taxes was Qāyt-bay and the two had many violent arguments. When Qāyt-bāy became sultan in 1469 he lost no time in having Yaḥyā, by now an old man, imprisoned in the Citadel. He was flogged in the presence of the sultan until he fainted, a punishment repeated for several days. During one of these sessions he died, but Qāyt-bāy refused to believe it until he had seen the corpse and kicked it to make sure.

Like his other mosque (Rte 11) this is an enclosure mosque. The exterior is plain with entrances in the NW and SW walls, the latter with a trefoil hood and a pishtak rising above the level of the roof. Above this doorway rises the much decayed minaret with solid octagonal first storey crowned by a cavetto conice with diaper pattern. Remains of trefoil cresting can be seen around the wall. The interior has two arcades against each wall except the SE which has three. On each side three arches front the open ṣaḥn. In each riwāq the arches which support the wooden roof are raised on marble pillars with varied capitals. In the qiblah riwāq little is left of the decoration in the miḥrāb save for the inscription and complex decoration in the hood. Over the miḥrāb is an oculus with carved moulding. The small dome above is fashioned completely in wood including the stalactite supports. There are 16 windows in the drum. A fine minbar and kursī are part of the original furniture supplied by the founder. In the NE wall is a door leading to the ablution court.

Opposite the NW wall of the mosque a road runs W into the SH'. AL-GĀMĪ 'AL-SINĀNIYYAH. Follow this and the subsequent turn to the N (100m) to the fine **Mosque of Sinān Pasha** (349; 6:1). Although small it is one of the few Ottoman mosques in Cairo that owes nothing to the Mamlūk tradition, being almost completely within the Istanbul architectural canon.

The basic form of the mosque is a square base with a shallow dome and an exterior flanked on three sides by a colonnade. Built in 1571, it made little impact on the architects of Cairo and remained unique until copied, except for the minaret, by Muḥammad Bay Abū 'l-Dhahhab 200 years later in 1774 (see Rte 6). Sinān was an Albanian raised in the imperial Ottoman court who entered the service of Sulaymān Qanūnī. He was an exceptional soldier and led the forces that captured the Yemen for the Ottomans. He followed the assassinated Maḥmūd Pasha (Rte 10) as governor of Cairo in 1568 and held the post again in 1571. He subsequently became wazīr five times in Istanbul. There are many of his buildings in Turkey and W Asia.

Against each side except the SE is an arcade with pointed arches supported on baton pillars alternating with stone piers. Outside under the trefoil cresting and above the pillars are medallions carved with rosettes. Shallow brick domes form the roofs of the arcades. On the S corner is set the squat minaret of typical Ottoman form with perpendicular ribbing and single balcony resting on an elaborate stalactite corbel. In the centre of each arcade is an entrance with two pillars, the main door being in the NW. Externally the high drum is octagonal, with a buttress at each corner and a pair of pointed-arched windows in each face. The base of the plain dome has 16 smaller buttresses alternating with elaborate ogival windows. In each side of the mosque are two oblong windows with bronze grills flanking a tall doorway.

The NW door leads beneath a wooden dikkah into the single-chambered hall. The miḥrāb is executed in coloured marble and is the only detail that would not look out of place in a Mamlūk mosque—even the minbar is crowned by the typical Ottoman cone. Wide pointed arched squinches raise the drum of the dome with a single elaborate niche. It is similar to those used in the Qubbat al-Fidawiyyah (Rte 19). Internally the drum has 16 sides, each one with a window of nine lights, a central large oculus surrounded by eight smaller ones. Immediately above, supported on a stalactite cornice, a gallery runs around the brick interior of the dome at the level of the ogival windows which are filled with brilliantly coloured glass.

Within the precincts of the mosque immediately to the SW are the remains of *Takiyyat al-Rifāʿiyyah* (442), built in 1744 for the sūfī brotherhood. In front of the Mosque of Sinān Pasha a road leads E into the Shʿ. al-Khuḍra. After 50m, at the corner of the SHʿ. SUQ AL-ʿAṢR, is the *Mosque al-ʿAlaya* (348; 6:1) of which only the brick and stucco minaret is of any age. It was probably built for a descendent of the Seljuks, who died in Cairo in 1507.

From the Shʿ. 26 Yulyu the Corniche continues N. At 150m the SHʿ. AL-MATBʿAH AL-AHLIYYAH leaves slighty to the W. Between the two lies the new **Dār al-Kutub** (Place of Books), the National Library (6:1–3) and headquarters of the *General Egyptian Book Organisation* (the State Publishing Office). This building is on the site of the Printing Press established by Muḥ. ʿAlī in 1822.

(Facilities for students. Open 09.00–18.00; closed Friday. Small fee.) The national collection was founded in 1870 by the Khedive Ismāʿīl, through the efforts of ʿAlī Mubārak Pasha, as the Kutubkhānah Khidiwiyyah. Originally located in the Shʿ. al-Gamamīz, the German Spitta Bay was the first librarian. It later shared the same building as the Museum of Islamic Art in Maydan Aḥ. Māhir, but was transferred here in 1979. Collections held by various mosques and palaces were gathered together. There are now nearly four million volumes including both manuscripts and printed books. The more important items are displayed in the Exhibition Hall. A copy of each book printed in Egypt is deposited in the library.

Some of the fascinating MSS displayed include early legal documents on papyrus in both Coptic and Arabic. Perhaps the most charming are the Fāṭimid drawings on paper (10–11C) which display the same vivacity as other art forms produced under this dynasty. The library possesses a magnificent series of Qurʾāns with the lavishly decorated products of royal Mamlūk studios holding pride of place.

# 18 North-West Suburbs

Rtes 18–21 cover the outer suburbs of Cairo, continuing from the main roads followed in the inner city itineraries. The distances covered are much greater.

Rte 18 leads directly from Rtes 1A and 17 out as far as the Ismāʿīliyyah Canal (5km) and into the province of Qalyubiyyah. **See Greater Cairo map.**

North of Būlāq (Rte 17) across Shʿ. Kubrī al-Imbābah, which follows the main-line railway on to the W Bank, lies the district of **Shubrā**. This large well-populated area has little of historical interest. It is called Shubrā al-Balad to distinguish it from Shubrā al-Khaymah to the N. It is mainly geared to industry, with many small workshops scattered throughout the residential area.

As with Būlāq, this area started as a large island, which appeared above the Nile in the 12C and was called Gazīrat al-Fīl (Island of the Elephant), traditionally from a ship of that name that foundered on the shoals. Because of its distance from the medieval city it was not exploited and by the 14C the westward movement of the bed of the Nile had left it incorporated with the land of the E Bank. It was used for orchards and plantations with several small villages. So it remained until 1808 when Muḥammad ʿAlī Pasha built his first palace here. By 1820 there were several factories, mainly for fabrics, and later in the century colleges for agriculture and veterinary science were built. In 1912 the S mouth of the Ismāʿīliyyah Canal was filled in and the bed of the canal which ran through the centre of Shubrā was used for the construction of the main road, the Shʿ. Tirʿah al-Būlāqiyyah. Once built, the road was soon lined with palaces and villas. The vast area was split up in the 1950s into several smaller districts. Since then it has been the preferred residential area for the Copts of Cairo.

The E boundary is the SHʿ. AL-ḤILMIYYAH which runs parallel to the Cairo–Alexandria railway line from Ramsīs Sq. Also starting from the W side of Ramsīs Sq., the SHʿ. AL-TIRʿAH AL-BŪLĀQIYYAH runs NE through Shubrā to the Shʿ. Al-Ḥilmiyyah. Leaving from the same point of Ramsīs Sq., the SHʿ. SHUBRĀ runs NW, crossing at 1.75km the Shʿ.Rawḍ al-Farag. At 5km it passes over the Al-Ismaʿiliyyah Canal, the N boundary of the district. Midway along the Shʿ. al-Tirʿah al-Būlāqiyyah to the W, the SHʿ. RAWḌ AL-FARAG bisects the district E to W and runs into the W boundary, the SHʿ. ABŪ ʾL-FARAG. N of the Ismāʿīliyyah Canal is the district of **Shubrā al-Khaymah**, in the province of Qalyūbiyyah, although still within Greater Cairo.

N of the Ismaʿiliyyah Canal (1½km) a high yellow wall to the left surrounds the *Faculty of Agriculture* of ʿAyn Shams University standing in the grounds of the former **Shubrā Palace** of Muhammad ʿAlī, his favourite residence. (Entrance from the Shʿ. Shubrā to the E.) The palace itself is destroyed, but still standing is the famous *Fountain Kiosk* described by so many 19C travellers in Egypt. Steps lead up to the main entrance opening into the entrance porch. Arcades with extravagant ogee roofs overlook the square pool with salients in the centre of each side which extend over the water. The ceilings are painted with arcadian scenes in the Italian manner. In the centre of the pool is a marble island raised on crouching lions while at each end are ornate fountains.

W of the Shʿ. Abū ʾl-Farag, between Shubrā and the Nile, is the district of **Rawḍ al-Farag.** This is one of the districts created from the partition of Shubrā, and is the main port of Cairo. N of Rawḍ al-Farag is another recent district, **al-Sāḥil,** which is mainly residential.

The area to the E of Shʿ. al-Shubrā, N of Ramsīs Sq., is the district of **al-Sharābiyyah,** bounded on the E by the Shʿ. Būr Saʿīd. This district is important because the major oil companies have their petrol depots here. There is little to attract the visitor.

# 19 Northern Suburbs

Rte 19 continues N from Rtes 4 and 7 (10km) to the northern limits of Cairo. **See Greater Cairo map.**

From Bāb al-Shāʿriyyah (Rte 7) the Shʿ. Būr Saʿīd runs NE through the district of **al-Ẓāhir** (pron. al-Dahir), another small but densely populated area. After 750m the SHʿ. AL-ẒĀHIR crosses W to E. The E branch leads into the Maydān al-Ẓāhir. Filling the centre of the square is the massive **Mosque of Sultan Baybars I al-Bunduqdārī** (1; 11:1), one of whose titles gave the district its name. Built between 1266–69 as a great enclosure mosque, it has suffered greatly and much of the interior has been turned into a public garden.

During the French occupation it was used as a barracks and named Fort Schulkowski in honour of one of Napoleon's generals. Subsequently it was used as a soap factory and then as a bakehouse and finally closed by Ismā'īl Pasha. He used the pillars for the reconstruction of al-Azhar mosque and his palace at Qaṣr al-'Aynī. Under the British it was an army store and a slaughter-house but King Fu'ād had these removed and gardens laid out. The outer walls survive and the qiblah riwāq has been retained as a smaller mosque.

This site N of the enclosure of Cairo was used by Sultan Baybars as a polo ground. He decided to use it for the present foundation and supervised the precise details of the plan himself. The wazīr Bahā' was the overseer of the project and Amīr Sangār al-Surūrī, governor of Cairo, supervised the labour force. Building material was collected throughout Egypt. After his capture of Jaffa in Palestine, Baybars had many of the Crusaders' buildings demolished, participating in the work himself, and had the marble and wood returned to Egypt for the mosque. He was extremely pleased with the finished building but specified that he was not to be buried in the mosque saying, 'I have given it up completely to Allāh'.

Baybars was a Qipchaq Turk sold in Damascus to the amīr Aydakin. Although he had been returned by a previous owner because of a defect in one of his eyes, he eventually entered the service of Sultan al-Ṣāliḥ Ayyūb, distinguishing himself in the campaign at Manṣūrah against the Crusade led by Louis IX.

Under Sultan Qutuz he led the guard which halted the inexorable advance of the Mongols at 'Ayn Jalūt. After the assassination of Qutuz, Baybars was unanimously elected sultan. He proved himself an extremely capable ruler, and reorganised the administration, stabilised the economy and undertook many public works. In foreign relations he concluded treaties with many countries including Byzantium. But it was his military conquests that set him among the greatest rulers of Egypt. He transformed the navy and regained control of the seaboards. With his magnificent army he disposed of the remaining Ayyūbid principalities in Syria and harried the Christian cities—Safad, Caeserea, Jaffa and Antioch were razed. At Acre he was attacked by Edward, Prince of Cornwall (later King Edward I) but a treaty was signed and hostilities ceased. Although Hulagu captured the Assassins' stronghold at Alamut it was Baybars who finally destroyed the lesser citadels of this extremist sect in Syria. Expeditions were also launched into Nubia, Iraq and Cyrenaica.

In 1258 the Mongols sacked Baghdad and murdered the khalīf al-Musta'ṣim and all his relations but Baybars established a scion of the Khalīfal house in Cairo (see Rte 11). The status that this conferred on Egypt was incalculable and was used as a political weapon on many occasions.

In character Baybars was modest and pious. The drinking of alcohol was forbidden and the immoral houses were closed by him. In 1268 he went on the pilgrimage in secret, mingling with the other pilgrims incognito. In 1277 during one of his expeditions to Damascus he fell ill after drinking a cup of kumiss (mare's milk) and died a few days later. He was only 50 years old and had named his son Baraka Khan successor. His popularity was not extinguished with his death; his exploits entered the realms of epic folklore and, much augmented, are known as the *Sīrat Baybars*.

This great mosque measures 106m by 103m. At the four corners are unusual salients and buttresses against the NE and SW walls. In the NW wall is a monumental gateway, and there are subsidiary entrances in its NE and SW walls. The minaret, the base of which existed over the main gate until the early 19C, was probably similar to that at the Madrasah of Sultan al-Ṣāliḥ Ayyūb (Rte 5). The walls are faced externally with dressed stone and internally with smaller blocks. The main gateway is very impressive with a large arch with cushion voussoirs. The decoration consists of keel-arched and scallop-headed recesses and panels and includes inscriptions and carved strapwork. Inside the porch is a shallow dome set on pendentives and at the far end a foundation inscription. Above are five large windows with stucco grilles. This gate was ordered specifically by Baybars with the instruction that it should be identical to that at his madrasah inside the city (Rte 5).

The entrance, now in the SE wall, leads into the small mosque formed from the qiblah riwāq. Originally the NE and SW riwāqs each had three colonnades, the NW riwāq two colonnades, and the qiblah riwāq six. Each was divided by a transept. The arches rested on brick piers and only those forming the maqṣurah before the miḥrāb had engaged columns. All the inner arcades were of columns. Above the maqṣūrah was a large dome, which fell long ago, but was also specified by Baybars to be exactly the same size as that covering the tomb of Imām al-Shāfiʿī. This instruction was carried out to within centimetres. Around the top of the wall and over the windows runs a band of kufic inscription, bordered with a band of decoration. The wooden roof is a replacement. The model for the mosque was doubtless that of al-Ḥākim (Rte 5), differing in the extra arcade to the riwāqs, transepts from the subsidiary doors, and the wooden dome over the maqṣūrah.

From the Maydān al-Ẓāhir the Shʿ. Sakākīnī runs NE and after 350m enters a small circus. In the centre is the **Museum of Hygiene** (small fee). The building was the House of Habīb Sakākīnī Pasha, built in 1897, and is an unbelievable architectural confection covered with statues in niches and roccoco decoration.

Leaving the Maydān al-Ẓāhir to the E is the Shʿ. al-ʿAbbāsiyyah running to the Maydān al-Gaysh. N of al-Ẓāhir the Shʿ. Būr Saʿīd crosses over the main railway line and Shʿ. Ramsīs on the Ghamrah Bridge (750m) and, passing through the district of **al-Waylī**, after 3km enters the district of **Hadāʾiq al-Qubbah**. The SHʿ. AL-WAYLĪ AL-KABĪR leaves to the E. 2km further N it meets the Ismāʿīliyyah Canal from the W and runs N beside it with al-Maṭariyyah to the E. A road leaves to the E (2km) to the obelisk (see below). Beyond this it leaves Greater Cairo (Rte 19) and crosses the Delta to Port Saʿīd.

From Ramsīs Sq. the SHʿ. RAMSĪS runs NE into the Ghamrah area of the district of al-Wayli. At 2.1km it passes under the Ghamrah Bridge; after 900m on the W stands the **Coptic Cathedral of St. Mark** (al-Karāzah al-Marqusiyyah). This building, raised in the 1970s, replaced the old seat of the patriarchate in Azbakiyyah. Architecturally it is unique. Relics of the body of St. Mark were returned to Egypt from Venice by Pope Paul VI on 2 June 1968 and interred with much ceremony beneath the main altar. Adjacent to the N is the **Church of SS. Peter and Paul** (al-Buṭrusiyyah), built in 1911 by the prominent Coptic family of Buṭrus Ghālī.

To the NE stands the immense domed *Tomb of Aḥmad Maḥir and Muḥ. Fahmī al-Nuqrashī*. Both were prime ministers and both were assassinated; the first in 1945, the second in 1949.

After 1km the Shʿ. al-Damirdāsh leads due N to the **Mosque and Tomb of Damirdāsh al-Muḥammadī**. This is a very interesting 16C building which contains the original cells into which the sufis would retreat 40 days before the Mūlid of Damirdāsh (14 Shaʿban). This retreat (khalwah) was one of the principles of the brotherhood and from it they received

*The Coptic cathedral of St. Mark*

their name. This practice was greatly criticised by the orthodox shaykhs. The tomb is on the N side of the minbar, surrounded by a maqṣūrah.

Damirdāsh, like Shahīn, was a Mamlūk of Qayt-bay and he also studied under the Khalawātī shaykh Rawshānī at Tabriz. He returned to Cairo c 1500 and founded his own brotherhood. He was reknowned for the orchard he kept for the benefit of the poor at this site. He died in 1523. During Ottoman times the Damirdāshiyyah was an extremely powerful brotherhood.

Beyond this the Shʿ. Ramsīs turns sharply SE to run through the Maydān al-ʿAbbāsiyyah (350m) and on to the Maydān al-Sikkah al-Bayḍah (900m).

At the Bāb al-Shaʿriyyah (Rte 7) the SHʿ. AL-GAYSH (from Maydan al-ʿAtabah, Rte 3B) crosses the Shʿ. Būr Saʿīd and runs further NE through al-Ẓāhir to the Maydān al-Gaysh (1.35km). Here it meets the SHʿ. AL-ʿABBĀSIYYAH and continues NE through the ʿAbbāsiyyah area of the district of al-Waylī. After 1.1km it enters the Maydān ʿAbduh Pasha, from which the SHʿ. AL-SARAYĀT leaves also NE past the Engineering College of ʿAyn Shams University. The Shʿ. al-ʿAbbāsiyyah turns slightly N, and at 500m passes on the W **al-Qubbah al-Fidāwiyyah** (5). This is the late and unique Mamlūk tomb, built in 1479–81, of Amīr Yashbak min Mahdī. It must once have been within the confines of the N Cemetery (Rte 4).

Sold by the dealer al-Mahdī, Yashbak entered the service of Sultan Jaqmaq. After his manumission he established himself in several minor posts including shikardār (master of the hunt) during the reign of Sultan Khushqadam. His morality attracted the attention of Sultan Qāyt-bāy under whom he rose to be one of the foremost amīrs, holding the posts of dawādār, ustadār and wazīr simultaneously. He commanded the armies that defeated the White Sheep Turkmans of E Anatolia in 1472 and brought Suwar, Amīr of Albistan, and his court to Cairo in chains where they were executed. In 1479 he accompanied Qāyt-bāy on the pilgrimage and was made viceroy of Egypt. He again campaigned against Shah Yaʿqūb of Anatolia in 1480, but was captured and executed. His tomb was completed by Qāyt-bāy and the interior was considered to be one of the marvels of the age. It was the object of visits by the populace well into the Ottoman period and influenced the decoration of many buildings during that period. It was restored by the CPAM in the late 19C. Yashbak also built the huge palace inside the city (Rte 10).

Although the building is basically a domed cube it is unique in that the dome has no zone-of-transition and the exterior therefore appears rather out of proportion. The stone base and brick dome are undecorated except for the entrance and foliated parapet. Originally the ground floor consisted of open arches leading to the burial area, but they have been filled in and the tombs are reached from the interior. On the SW side modern marble steps lead up to the entrance, which has a stalactite hood and is flanked with inscriptions from the Qurʾān.

Unfortunately the interior has lost its magnificent facing of coloured marbles, but it retains the painted stucco which covers the drum and the dome. Raising the dome are unusual two-hooded squinches lined with stalactites. This system is so similar to that in the much earlier Seljuk Great Mosque in Isfahan (Iran) that it is almost certain the architect had some knowledge of it. On the N side steps lead down into the vaulted tomb chambers.

750km N the Shʿ. al-ʿAbbāsiyyah enters the Maydān al-ʿAbbāsiyyah, where it meets the Shʿ. Ramsīs coming from the NW. At the SE corner of the square the SHʿ. FAKHRĪ ʿABD AL-NŪR leads to the head office of the **Egyptian Antiquities Organisation** (Hayʾit al-Athār al-Miṣriyyah), where all applications to the organisation for excavations, expeditions and special visits are processed. NE of the square the road continues as the SHʿ. TALATAH WA ʿASHRĪN YŪLYŪ (23 July, previously Shʿ. al-Kalīfah al-Maʾmūn). Immediately to the left is the ʿ**Ayn Shams University**, founded in 1950. This is the Zaʿfaran Palace, originally built by Khedive Ismaʿīl for his mother Khushyar, reputedly in 40 days. When the Egyptian University (now Cairo University) was founded in 1908 this was one of the buildings in which it was housed. Beyond is the district of Hadaʾiq al-Qubbah. 1.3km along the Shʿ. Talatah wa ʿashrīn Yūlyū on the N side of the road stands the **Tomb and Mosque of Gamal ʿAbd al-Nasser**. This flat-topped building is completely contemporary in style; the minaret at the N corner has a strange canopy reminiscent of an Indian Temple. Behind the mosque is the *Tomb of ʿAbd al-Nasser*, the former president (died September 1969), with a vaulted ceiling. The grave has a white marble tābūt with carved and gilded lettering, made by Ḥājj ʿAbd Allāh ʿAfifi.

Beyond the mausoleum the road (as the Shʿ. Khalīfah al-Maʿmūn) turns E into Miṣr al-Gadidah (see Rte 20). Turn W (1.5km) into the Shʿ. Miṣr wa Sudān, cross the Shʿ. Tirʿat al-Gabal and turn N into the SHʿ. AL-QAFFASĪN (750m). This runs along the W wall of the *Qubbah Palace* built by Ismāʿīl Pasha. It is now a presidential residence used for conferences. Surrounding it is a vast garden enclosure. The palace is in the district of al-Zaytūn (Rte 20) while to the W of the road is the district of **al-Ḥadā'iq al-Qubbah.** After 1.75km the road crosses the SHʿ. AL-SAWWAḤ (from Shʿ. Būr Saʿīd), entering the district of **al-Maṭariyyah**, and after 1.2km the SHʿ. KĀBLĀT. Beyond the SHʿ. AL-ḤURRIYYAH (30m) it becomes the SHʿ. AL-MAṬARĀWĪ and runs into the Maydān al-Misallah (Obelisk Square). In the centre stands an obelisk which, with **Tell Hiṣn** to the NW, marks the site of the northern *On*, called *Heliopolis* by the Greeks, a very important cult centre in Ancient Egypt and capital of the 13th nome of Lower Egypt. (Modern Heliopolis is a new suburb some distance to the E, see Rte 20.) It was a large city, the walls enclosing over 5sq. km.

Atum, the creator and sun god, was the original deity of the city. An elaborate cosmogony was developed around him, which became the accepted creation theory throughout Egypt. He was later assimilated into, and usurped by, Reʿ, the universal sun god. Kept in the city was the Mnervis bull which was considered to be a manifestation of the god and deified. During the Ptolemaic period the equation of Reʿ with the Greek sun god Helios gave the city its classical name. Heliopolis remained essentially a religious and intellectual centre and was probably always strategically dependent on Memphis. During the later period it attracted many leading thinkers, perhaps the greatest of whom was Plato. However, the decline of the city after the building of Alexandria, was rapid and in 24 BC, according to Strabo, it was virtually desolate. Although the Arabs camped here in 640 before their assault on Babylon little development took place until the present century. When the chronicler ʿAbd al-Latīf al-Baghdādī visited the site in the 1190s he mentioned that this was still recognisable as an ancient town, though the wall was demolished. Many statues were still standing, one 15m high.

Virtually all that is left of the ancient city is this **Obelisk of Senusert I** (12 Dyn.), one of a pair that stood in front of the Temple of Reʿ Harakhty which had been built by Amenemhat I, Senusert's father. They were raised to celebrate the king's Heb-sed (Jubilee Festival). The pink granite obelisk stands 22m high. On each side is an identical text containing Senusert's name and titles and ending with the exhortation, life may be given to him for ever and ever. Although both obelisks were on site when al-Baghdādī visited it, he found that one had already fallen and broken in two, but the standing one retained its coppercap. It must have disappeared soon after that. Two obelisks erected here by Tuthmosis III (18 Dyn.) were removed to Alexandria during Roman times. One of these was presented to the British Government (Cleopatra's Needle on the Embankment, London), the other to the USA (now in Central Park, New York). Petrie found a third obelisk of the same king buried here (now in the EM). Recently an excavation by Cairo University found the entrance to a Temple of Ramases III including some columns and the statue of a lion.

To the S along the Shʿ. al-Qaffasīn lies the **Church of the Holy Family**, which commemorates their visit to the area during the Flight into Egypt. Although there seems to have been a church here since early Christian times all vestiges of it have disappeared and the first of which evidence exists was built in 1504. The present church was built in 1904. Nearby is a small compound which contains the **Virgin's Tree**, a sycamore fig, associated with Mary, mother of Jesus, who is said to have rested here. The original tree died in the 17C and a new one was planted in 1672. This in turn fell in 1906, but a shoot was saved, resulting in the present tree. Watering the enclosure is a well, fed by a spring known as the Holy Well. This spring, close to the ancient temple, fed a sacred pool at which it was said Reʿ had washed his face when he first rose on the world. From this arose the Arabic name of the area, ʿAyn Shams (Spring of the sun), probably a direct translation from the Greek.

# 20 North-East Suburbs

Rte 20 leads on from Rte 8 through the most recently developed areas of Cairo as far as the airport (12km). It is covered by bus No. 400 from Maydān al-Taḥrīr. **see Greater Cairo map**.

From the Mausoleum of ʿAbd al-Nasser (Rte 19) the SHʿ. IBN SANDAR continues NE while the SHʿ.AL-KHALIFAH AL-MAʾMŪN runs to the S. At a large junction (700m) two roads, the SHʿ. SALĪM AL-AWWAL and the SHʿ. TŪMĀN-BĀY lead off to the N and run through the district of **al-Zaytūn** (the Olives) which lies to the W. (150m along the latter road stands the pink brick *Tahrah Palace*.) This largely residential district received its name from the large olive groves once situated here. The Shʿ. Ibn Sandar becomes the SHʿ. GISR AL-SUWAYS. On the E side of the road lies the district of **Miṣr al-Gadīdah** (New Cairo), a modern suburb.

Heliopolis, a model city founded in 1906, is not actually on the site of ancient Heliopolis (which lies 4km E at al-Maṭariyyah. Rte 19). When the scheme was proposed there were fears that the new development would destroy ancient remains, but in fact none were found and the only evidence of previous occupation was provided by some predynastic remains discovered in 1950 during the conversion of the racecourse.

*House of Baron Empain*

The whole scheme was the brainchild of Edouard Empain (later Baron; 1852–1929), a Belgian banker and entrepreneur. Under the umbrella of the Cairo Electric Railway and Heliopolis Oases Company he envisioned the creation of a self-contained garden city. He gained the patronage of the most influential members of the Turkish, British and other foreign communities and work started in 1905, although the decree was not signed until the following year. The planned town was surrounded by wide peripheral avenues connected by streets in a grid pattern. The population was split into several class quarters, the elite (ie Europeans and Turks) occupying palaces and villas in the choicest areas, the professionals (Greeks, Italians and Armenians) in smaller maisonettes in the intermediate zones, and the manual workers (ie Egyptians, tastefully termed indigenes) in apartment blocks in a special area.

The most important architects to design buildings here were Ernest Jaspar and Alexander Marcel, both Belgians who, besides designing mundane residences, were responsible for some of the more spectacular flights of fancy.

The scheme was a success as a European enclave: in 1916 out of a total population of 7000 there were 2100 Catholics, 470 Protestants; Muslims (1400) were also outnumbered by Greeks and Copts (1900), and almost matched by Jews (1150). After the First World War the British moved in in numbers and the proportions became more representative of their presence in Egypt. The area of *Roxy* is named after a cinema that stood here, the first such on the continent of Africa. Another attraction was the funfair Luna Park.

The *Basilica*, built in 1913, was designed by Alexander Marcel. It is supposed to be a quarter-sized copy of the Aya Sophia in Istanbul, but it is not too succesful. In the crypt are the tombs of Baron Edouard Empain, his wife and his son.

The vast *Heliopolis Palace Hotel* was the contribution of Ernest Jaspar, now a governmental palace.

To the E of the Shʿ. Gisr al-Suways (1.2km) is *Merryland*, a vast club and garden complex with a restaurant and open air cafés set around a large lake. Beyond this the road crosses the Shʿ. Abū Bakr al-Siddīq and continues out into the desert.

Follow the Shʿ. al-Khalifah al-Maʾmūn SE 1.2km into the SHʿ. AL-MIRGHĀNĪ which passes N (150m) of the *Heliopolis Sporting Club* (Nādī Hiliyūbūlīs al-Rayadā). To the N is the SHʿ. AL-AHRĀM (which crosses the district from SW to NE) while the Shʿ. al-Mirghānī crosses the Shʿ. al-ʿUrūbah and continues around the S area of the district (with Madīnat Naṣr to the SW). It terminates at the SHʿ. AL-NUZHAH (1.6km). Turn N up this street. At 1.2km is a crossroads with the Shʿ. al-ʿUrūbah and the Shʿ. Abū Bakr al-Siddīq. To the N is the district of **al-Nuzhah**, the easternmost district of Cairo and mainly residential.

Beyond the Maydān al-Barqūq (Rte 8) the Tarīq Ṣalāḥ Sālim runs NE into the Maydān al-Sikkah al-Bayḍah. From this square the Sikkat al-Bayḍah leads E into the district of **Madīnat Naṣr**.

This is a new suburb built in the 1960s and '70s. Much of it is residential and there are many small industries. Several government departments have their headquarters here. The vast housing projects are coalescing to the S with those of the Madīnat al-Muqaṭṭam.

On the right of Al-Sikkah al-Bayḍah (700m) a wide road leads to the Cairo Stadium and, after another 1km, the very wide SHʿ. AL-NAṢR runs through the city from N to S. This follows the vast *al-Ard al-ʿArḍ* (Parade Ground), about 3km long. Here all the military marches and exercises are held. In the centre stands the pyramidal *al-Naṣr al-Tadhkārī* (Victory Memorial). On 6 October 1981 President Anwar Sadat was assassinated here while attending the anniversary celebrations of the 1973 war with

Israel. He was buried temporarily beneath the Victory Memorial. The Shʿ. al-Naṣr terminates at the SHʿ. AL-TAYRĀN which runs W into the Shʿ. al-ʿUrūbah.

N of the Maydān al-Sikkah al-Bayḍah the Shʿ. Ṣalāḥ Sālim runs N between the districts of Madīnat Naṣr to the E and Miṣr al-Gadīdah to the W. Immediately to the NW, is the *ʿAbbāsiyyah Army Camp.*

Standing in the centre of the parade ground is the **Tomb of Sultan Tūmān-bāy I** (2). It is not possible to visit it at present and photography is forbidden. It was built in 1501 as a much larger complex including a madrasah, and was once probably included in the N Cemetery (Rte 4).

Tūmān-bāy was a mamluk of Sultan Qāyt-bāy and was responsible for the assassination of his son Muḥammad IV. By manipulation he deposed the next two sultans Qānṣūḥ I and Janbalāt, and with the assistance of the governor of Damascus Qasrawh declared himself sultan in 1501. Qānṣūḥ and Ganbalāṭ were strangled on his orders and he similarly despatched Qasrawh after a banquet with the words 'Grand Amīr I fear you'. After a reign of just a few months his own mamlūks revolted because of his treatment of them. He escaped from the Citadel one night but was caught and executed. He was succeeded by Qānṣūḥ al-Ghawrī.

This building is in exceptionally fine condition. It has the usual domed cube form with the windows set in stalactite recesses. In the SW wall the door has a fine joggled lintel. The zone-of-transition has two layered geometrically angled corners, between which are triple round-arched windows, each with three oculi above. The dome is beautifully carved with a regular foliate and ogee pattern, the two motifs being harmoniously combined. It is related to the domes of Amīr Khayrbak (Rte 9) and Amīr Qānī-bāy al-Ṣayfī (Rte 10) and was probably produced by the same master mason. Sadly, they mark the last phase of this unique art form.

Opposite the army camp is the *ʿAbbāsiyyah Psychiatric Hospital* and to the S the new grounds of the **Cairo International Fair** (Sūq al-Qāhirah al-Dawliyyah). At 1.8km a wide road leads into Madīnat Naṣr, to the *Cairo Stadium* (Istād al-Qāhirah), the venue for international sporting events and displays. To the W the road runs into the Shʿ. Mirghānī (1.2km), beyond which it becomes the SHʿ. AL-ʿURŪBAH and passes through S Heliopolis. On the S is the *House of Baron Edouard Empain*, in the form of an Indian temple, actually incorporating some monumental architectural material from India and designed by Alexander Marcel. Empain was responsible for the initial development of Heliopolis in the early 1900s (see above). The Shʿ. al-ʿUrūbah continues through Heliopolis to the Maydān Abū Bakr al-Siddīq (2km) where it is crossed N to S by the Shʿ. al-Nuzhah and NW to SE by the Shʿ. Abū Bakr al-Siddīq and after 5km reaches **Cairo International Airport**.

# 21 Southern Suburbs

This itinerary is a continuation of Rte 16 along the shore of the Nile. It is followed by bus No. 431 from Maydān al-Taḥrīr and the metro from Bāb al-Lūq. **See Greater Cairo map**.

S of Miṣr al-Qadīmah (Rte 16) the Corniche continues along the river bank. On the E at 4km is the *al-Maʿādī Military Hospital*, the largest medical centre in the Middle East, which treats most of the serious cases among military personnel. Beyond this the road runs into (1km) the town of **al-Maʿādī**. Although the area has palaeolithic settlements, it was not developed as a town until recent times. It is a leafy suburb and was very popular with the British; many of the houses were designed by British architects. Just to the S on the H54 is (3km) **al-Ṭurah** within the foothills of the Muqaṭṭam Hills where the limestone quarries have been in continuous use since prehistoric times. **Al-Maʿsarah**, 4km further S, has more quarries. At the **Wadi Ḥawf** (3km) is the site of *al-ʿUmarī* with a prehistoric cemetery. The H54 continues S but the road following the railway turns SE and runs (4km) into the centre of **Ḥalwān**, a spa town in the al-Ṣaff region of Giza Province. (*Hotels*: Happy Day Chalets, 2*; El-Omara, 16 Shʿ. Duktur Safwat; Evergreen, 26 Shʿ. Zaki, 1*.)

The town stands on a plateau above the Nile valley, and the area has been inhabited since prehistoric times. It is probable that the thermal springs were visited by the Ancient Egyptians, Greeks and Romans, but it remained relatively undeveloped until after the Muslim Conquest. For a few years it was the capital of Egypt. After ʿAbd al-ʿAzīz, son of Khalīf Marwān I and governor of Egypt (684–703), had been cured of a disease here, he decided to settle in the area and named it Ḥalwān after a town in his native Iraq. His successors, however, returned the seat of government to Cairo. During the mid 19C with the revival of interest in spas Ismāʿīl Pasha developed the town and many villas and houses were built, supplementing the recent post-revolution building boom.

There are several places of interest in the town. At the E end of the road where the railway terminates, the SHʿ. MUḤAMMAD MUṢṬAFĀ MARĀGHĪ, is the *Japanese Garden* (Hadīqat al-Yābūniyyah). This beautiful garden, surrounding a large lake, and dotted with figures of Buddha, pagodas and Japanese bridges, is a rather strange amalgam.

To the NE just outside the town, is *Ḥalwān Observatory*, built in 1903 (open Wed. pm). Other attractions include the *Ḥalwān Museum*, (small fee) which was originally a palace built by King Farūq and now exhibits local finds. The *Wax Museum* (Matḥaf al-Shamaʿ) displays episodes in Egyptian history using life-sized models. At the S end of the town is the *Sporting Club*, while at the NE near the railway is *ʿAyn Ḥalwān*, the large treatment centre where many ailments are tackled with the sulphurated waters. It was built in the 1890s and renovated in 1955. These springs have a high sulphur content (27mg%) and the centre is open all year, 08.30–12.00.

3km N are the *Mineral Springs*, another health centre, but with saline waters.

SE (10km) lies the **Wadi Garāwī**, with the remains of an *Old Kingdom Dam*, which was used by the ancient quarry men.

From the junction to Ḥalwān the H54 continues S through al-Ṭabbīn (bridge to the W Bank and Dahshūr).

# 22 Al-Gīzah

This itinerary can conveniently divided into northern and southern sections. The latter leads W to Rte 23 and S to Rte 24 and the subsequent itineraries.

The al-Galāʾ Bridge (Rte 3E) leads on to the W Bank and the District of **Giza** (al-Gīzah) in Giza Province. Just beyond the bridge is the Maydān

Kubrī al-Galā' from which the Shʿ. al-Taḥrīr continues to the W. Running N and S along the river bank is the SHʿ. AL-NĪL.

The town of al-Gīzah was officially founded in the 4C BC. It had probably been a small community since the earliest times, at the place where the route between Heliopolis and Memphis crossed the Nile at the upstream point of the Island of Rawḍah. With the growth of Christianity Memphis declined in importance and became subordinate to Giza which benefited from its proximity to the fortress of Babylon. After the Muslim Conquest Memphis was completely abandoned but Giza was refortified by ʿAmr and he settled the two Arab tribes of Hamḍān and Ḥimyar there. In later times several great mosques were built in Giza but nothing now remains of them. Gradually the area stagnated, as it was subject to flooding during the inundation of the Nile. Thus it remained a small town, surrounded by agricultural and fishing villages, as part of the Waqf al-Hutiyyah until the 19C. The Francophile ruler Ismāʿīl Pāshā built himself a palace there with the gardens laid out by Barillet-Deschamps; this was used between 1889–1902 as the Egyptian Museum until the completion of the new building in the Maydan Qaṣr al-Nīl (Maydān al-Taḥrīr) in 1902. The gardens were turned into the Zoological and Botanical Gardens (see below).

In 1869 the Suez Canal was opened with great ceremony by Ismāʿīl and the guest of honour, among other European princes and statesmen, was Empress Eugénie of France. A massive redecoration scheme was undertaken in Cairo and to facilitate the travel of these guests to the Pyramids the Shʿ. al-Ahram (Road of the Pyramids) was constructed. With the effective incorporation of Egypt within the British sphere of influence there was much building undertaken in Giza and between the wars many beautiful villas were constructed in the town and along the Shʿ. al-Ahram, though in 1945 the area opposite Zamālik was still under cultivation. Since then there has been a boom in utility building—houses, office buildings and embassies, with areas for engineers, teachers and other professions. Many of the larger mansions have now been converted into dubious night clubs and bars, and urban buildings now completely line the route to the pyramids (Rte 23).

## A. Northern Giza

**See Cairo Atlas 12, 4.**

N of the Maydān Kubrī al-Galā' lies the district of **al-Duqqī** (pron. Du'ī), a modern high-rent residential area. N along the Shʿ. al-Nīl, with the island of Al-Gazīrah to the E, the third road on the W, the SHʿ. AL-HINDĀWĪ, leads to the Maydān al-Sadd al-ʿĀlī. N of this, in the SHʿ. ISMĀʿĪL ABŪ 'L-FUTŪḤ, is the **Museum of Modern Art** (open 09.00–15.30, Fri. 09.00–11.30; small fee). This museum concentrates on paintings and sculpture by contemporary Egyptian artists.

To the NW the Shʿ. al-Sadd al-ʿĀlī runs into the SHʿ. WIZĀRAT AL-ZARĀʿĪ opposite the *Ministry of Agriculture* building, to the N of which is the *al-Islāḥ al-Zarāʿī*, the department dealing with agricultural reform and the reapportioning of land.

Adjacent to the N is the **Agricultural Museum** (al-Mathaf al-Zarāʿī; 12:1; open in summer 09.00–14.30; in winter 09.00–16.00; Fri. throughout closed 11.30–13.00; small fee). Set in a beautiful garden of specimen trees, the museum consists of three separate buildings. Immediately to the left of the gateway is the *Historical Museum* with displays of agriculture in Pharaonic times. Left wing: examples of cultivated plants and foods found at town sites and in tombs, some of the loaves, dates, dūm nuts etc. remarkably well preserved. Right wing: fish, bird and mammal remains, also with the emphasis on food or domestic species. It includes skeletons of the Apis Bulls, found at Ṣaqqārah.

To the N is the *Cotton and Agricultural Museum*. Here the emphasis is on modern agriculture, particularly cotton, and a visit is a necessity for anyone interested in the history and production of this vital crop.

Ground floor. To the left of the entrance is Gallery 1, cotton commerce, from carding to manufacture. Model of a cotton factory and samples of hundreds of varieties of cotton fibres. Gallery 2, world cotton production, with types of cotton and machinery. Gallery 3, a miniature collection of beautifully made ploughs of the world. Gallery 4, cotton agronomy, demonstrating the life cycle of the plant and pests and diseases. Gallery 5, the cotton plant. Gallery 6, large relief map of Egypt showing agricultural areas. Gallery 7, rice production. Gallery 8, maize and sorghum. Gallery 9, bread and bread production. Gallery 10, cereals including samples of grains, flour machinery and storage techniques.

Upper floor. At the top of the stairs Gallery 1 displays seed cleaning and testing. To the left is Gallery 2, horticulture and commerce. Gallery 3, fruit. Galleries 4–4A, timber production. Gallery 5, fruit production. Gallery 6, vegetables. Gallery 7, tobacco. Gallery 8, industrial alcohol production. Gallery 9, sugar cane. Gallery 10, leguminous vegetables. Gallery 11, oil plants. Gallery 12, fibre plants.

On the W side of the gardens is the large *Administration Building* and to the N the *Natural History and Ethnological Museum*.

The entrance displays agricultural production in Egypt. Ground floor. Left-hand gallery, the arts and crafts of Nubia. Central gallery, Egyptian rural industries and activities. Products displayed include pottery, glass, weaving, embroidery, jewellery, costumes and musical instruments. Life-sized scenes show a weaver, potter, glassmaker, a market, a village teahouse and in the centre a marriage procession. At the rear of the gallery is a didactic display of the Irrigation of the Nile Valley which includes marvellous original models of the barrages of the Nile and the old Aswan Dam. These are all carved in sycamore fig with details in brass.

Stairs to the left of the entrance lead to the Upper floor. On the N side, the first gallery is devoted to domestic hens and turkeys, the second to egg production. The third gallery, ducks, geese, pigeons and rabbits. The fourth, sheep, goats, and wool production. The fifth, marine fisheries. The sixth, insect pests. The seventh, insects generally. The rear of the upper floor shows examples of mammalian skeletons and on the S side the ninth and tenth galleries demonstrate diseases of cattle, and milk production. The eleventh gallery deals only with camels, the twelfth with cattle and buffaloes, the thirteenth with donkeys and mules, the fourteenth with horses. All of the galleries contain beautifully made models of domesticated animals. In the fifteenth gallery are examples of horse furniture and above the entrance the sixteenth gallery has a genetic exhibition. The central area contains taxidermic specimens of the fauna of Egypt.

A large section of the E end of the garden has been taken for the terminal of the SHʿ. AL-MAṬḤAF AL-ZARĀʿĪ which runs E to meet the 6 October Bridge. To the NW lies the area of *Madīnat al-Muhandissīn* (Engineers' City), a very modern development with sections devoted to various professions, teachers, doctors, lawyers, etc.

Continuing N on the Shʿ. al-Nīl into the district of **al-ʿAgūzah**, the road runs past the ʿAgūzah Hospital on the W to the Shʿ. 26 Yūlyū (from the E Bank on al-Zamālik Bridge) which leads W across the railway line into the district of **Būlāq al-Dakrūr** to join a road N of Abū Rawāsh. W along the Shʿ. 26 Yulyu the SHʿ. GĀMIʿAT AL-DUWWAL AL-ʿARABIYYAH runs SW through al-Muhandisīn, just N of which is the Zamālik Sports Club, the second of Cairo's football clubs.

N of the Shʿ. 26 Yūlyū lies **Imbābah**, a separate region in Giza province, where the Bays were defeated by Napoleon in the Battle of the Pyramids in 1798. The Sh'. al-Nīl passes the Imbābah Bridge (from the E Bank, Rte 43), which carries the mainline railway. N (300m) to the Maydān al-Kitkāt. From here the SH' SUDĀN leaves to the NW. Follow this for 1km where it turns SW flanking the railway line. Cross the line onto the SH' AL-MATĀR which follows a branch line in a curve to the N. At 2km cross the al-Zumur Canal and continue W to the **Suq al-Gimāl** (Camel Market). Small fee, Fri–Mondays, sunrise–11.00. The camel dealers are tough characters and have their own terminology on the finer points of the camel trade. Some of the camels have been brought from as far away as Sudan and in earlier times Somalia and the Sāhil. Beyond Maydān al-Kitkāt the Sh' al-Nīl continues on to al-Qanātir (Rte 17).

## B. Southern Giza

**Cairo Atlas 12, 18, 26.**

From the Maydān Kubrī al-Galā' the Sh'. al-Taḥrīr continues SW to the pyramids (Rte 23), while the SH'. AL-MISĀHAH runs further to the S. Directly S runs the SH'. AL-GĪZAH, dominated on the E side by the Sheraton Hotel. The first large building to the W is the USSR Embassy past which is the SH'. 'ASSAM AL-DĀLĪ leading to the Sh'. al-Nīl and the river.

On the river itself is the *Cairo Yacht Club*, with moorings for private and club boats, the latter rented by the hour by members and guests. Up-river about 100m is the *Papyrus Institute* (open 08.00–15.00), located on three house-boats. Founded by Dr Hassan Ragab, it is surrounded by a plantation of living papyrus. Examples and souvenirs can be obtained.

Passing through a residential area lined with shops, the road has several other streets leading from it. After 800m turn slightly to the E. On the W side the SH'. AL-SARWAT leads to the *Youth Hostel* (900m) on the right past the ICL building. Immediately S are the *Urman Botanical Gardens*, the smaller section of the garden of Ismā'īl's palace, with many beautiful specimen trees and in the centre a café on an island reached by a half-moon bridge, in summer surrounded by tall flowering lotuses. The main entrance is in the Sh'. al-Sarwat. At the S end of the gardens is the SH'. AL-GAMI'AH (a wide road with central islands at the head of which is a large modern statue) leading to *Cairo University*, the dome of which can be seen in the distance. Founded in 1908 as the free Egyptian University in the Za'faran Palace building (Rte 19) and adopted as the State University of Fu'ad I in 1925, it was moved to Giza and in 1953 became Cairo University. It is one of the great research centres of the world with eleven faculties and higher institutes. The clock in the central quadrangle is renowned throughout Egypt as the chime sounds the hours on Egyptian radio.

On the S side of this road extending along the Sh'. al-Gīzah are the **Gīzah Zoological Gardens** (al-Ḥadīqat al-Hayawānat al-Gīzah; 18:6. Open daily, summer 09.00–17.00, winter 09.00–15.00; small fee).

Covering 52 acres, it is the greater part of the former gardens of Ismā'īl Pasha, laid out by Barrillet-Deschamps, the French landscaper, whose work Ismā'īl had seen in Paris. It was founded as a zoo in 1891 and reorganised with the foundation of the

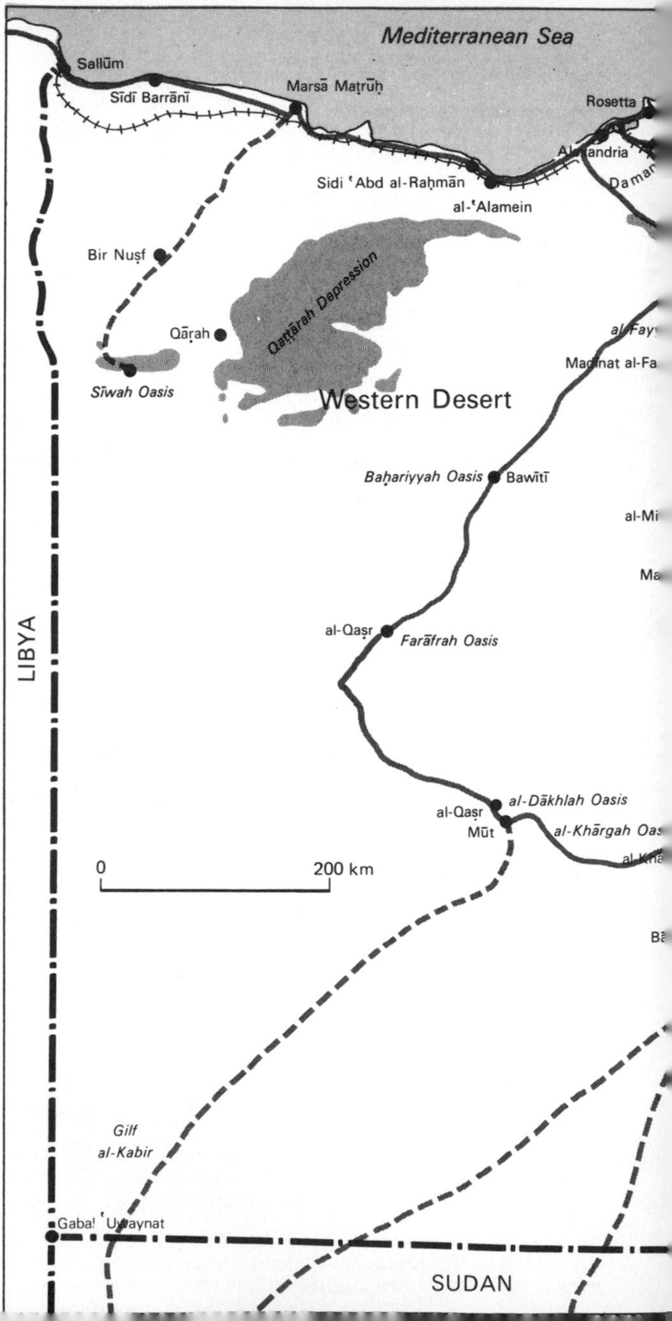
Mediterranean Sea
Sallūm
Sīdī Barrānī
Marsā Maṭrūḥ
Rosetta
Sidi ʿAbd al-Raḥmān
al-ʿAlamein
Bir Nuṣf
Qattārah Depression
Qārah
Sīwah Oasis
Madinat al-Fa
Western Desert
Baḥariyyah Oasis
Bawītī
al-Mi
Ma
LIBYA
al-Qaṣr
Farāfrah Oasis
al-Dākhlah Oasis
al-Qaṣr
Mūt
0
200 km
Gilf
al-Kabir
Gabal ʿUwaynat
SUDAN

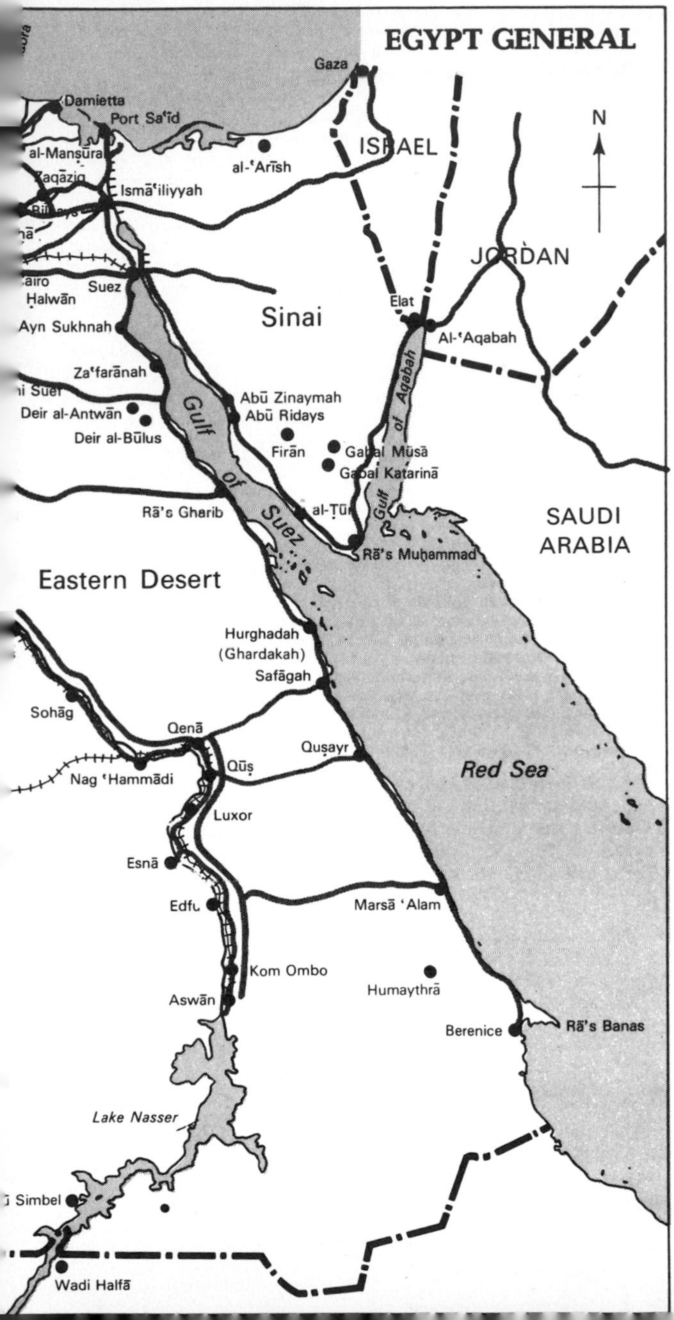
EGYPT GENERAL
N
Gaza
Damietta
Port Sa'id
al-Manṣurah
Zaqaziq
Ismā'iliyyah
al-'Arish
ISRAEL
JORDAN
Suez
Halwān
Sinai
Elat
Al-'Aqabah
Ayn Sukhnah
Za'farānah
Abū Zinaymah
Abū Ridays
Deir al-Antwān
Deir al-Būlus
Gulf of Suez
Gulf of Aqabah
Firān
Gabal Mūsā
Gabal Katarinā
Rā's Gharib
al-Ṭūr
Rā's Muḥammad
SAUDI ARABIA
Eastern Desert
Hurghadah
(Ghardakah)
Safāgah
Sohāg
Qenā
Quṣayr
Qūṣ
Nag 'Hammādi
Red Sea
Luxor
Esnā
Edfu
Marsā 'Alam
Kom Ombo
Humaythrā
Aswān
Berenice
Rā's Banas
Lake Nasser
Simbel
Wadi Halfā

Egyptian Zoological Society by Stanley Smyth Flower. The setting is beautiful, full of flowering trees and palms. Many of the pathways retain their original polychrome mosaic pebble pavements and in the centre is a very strange grotto constructed of contorted shapes. There are several cafés, and the restaurant is on an island. On Fridays and public holidays, especially Sham al-Nassīm, the zoo is very popular and becomes extremely crowded with huge picnic parties on the lawns.

This zoo specialises in animals of the Nile Valley of which it has a good collection, though representatives of other areas are also kept. There are 400 species altogether, and the zoo has a very good breeding record. Particularly noteworthy is the breeding colony of rare Nile lechwe (*Kobus megaceros*) from the Sudan, rarely seen in European collections. The hippopotamus enclosure contains a huge lake and the inmates seem to be fed constantly. Other interesting animals include the grotesque and lethargic Shoe-billed storks (*Balaeniceps rex*) and several species of gazelles. There is a free-flying colony of African ring-necked parakeets (*Psittacula krameri*).

S of the Zoo the SHʿ. MURĀD leaves to the SW and after 550m turns into the SHʿ. AL-AHRĀM (Road of the Pyramids, E to al-Gīzah Bridge and Old Cairo), a fine dual-carriageway which runs 8km SW to the site of the pyramids (Rte 23). To the S, following the mainline railway, runs the Ṭarīq Aswān H2, the start of the main road to Upper Egypt (Rte 24, etc.).

# II THE NILE VALLEY

## 23 The Pyramids of Giza

Rtes 23–27 (total distance 80km) are contiguous and between them cover the vast necropolis of the ancient city of Memphis. All are within an hour's drive from Cairo. As with all sites, the time needed varies with the aims of the visitor, but as the distances between monuments are considerable it is really only practicable to visit two sites in one day. Ṣaqqārah, however, needs a whole day. Only Giza and Ṣaqqārah have rest-houses and therefore the visitor is advised to take food and drink to the other sites. Some of the sites may be under military occupation (check with a travel agent) and special permission is needed to visit these.

Rte 23 (18km) includes the most famous monuments of Egypt, the pyramids at Giza and the Sphinx. They are only a short distance from Cairo and can be reached by local buses (Nos 8, 9 and 900) from Taḥrīr Square.

From S Giza the Shʿ. al-Ahrām passes under a railway bridge (*Giza Station* 25m to the left, mainline to Southern Egypt) and runs due W. 1km further, to the S, is the SHʿ. GAMĀL AL-DĪN AL-AFGHĀNĪ with the *Sayyid Darwish Concert Hall*, which has been enlarged and served as the Opera House since that in the al-Azbakiyyah Garden burnt down in 1972. Performances are given by the Arabic Music Troupe, Cairo Symphony Orchestra and visiting foreign and local dance and music groups. At 4km the *Madīnat al-Fanān* (City of Artists) lies S of the road. The gate and the island in the centre of the road are marked by giant contemporary limestone statues. It is a higher institute dealing with fine and applied arts, music and dance.

*The pyramids at Giza seen from the desert to the SW*

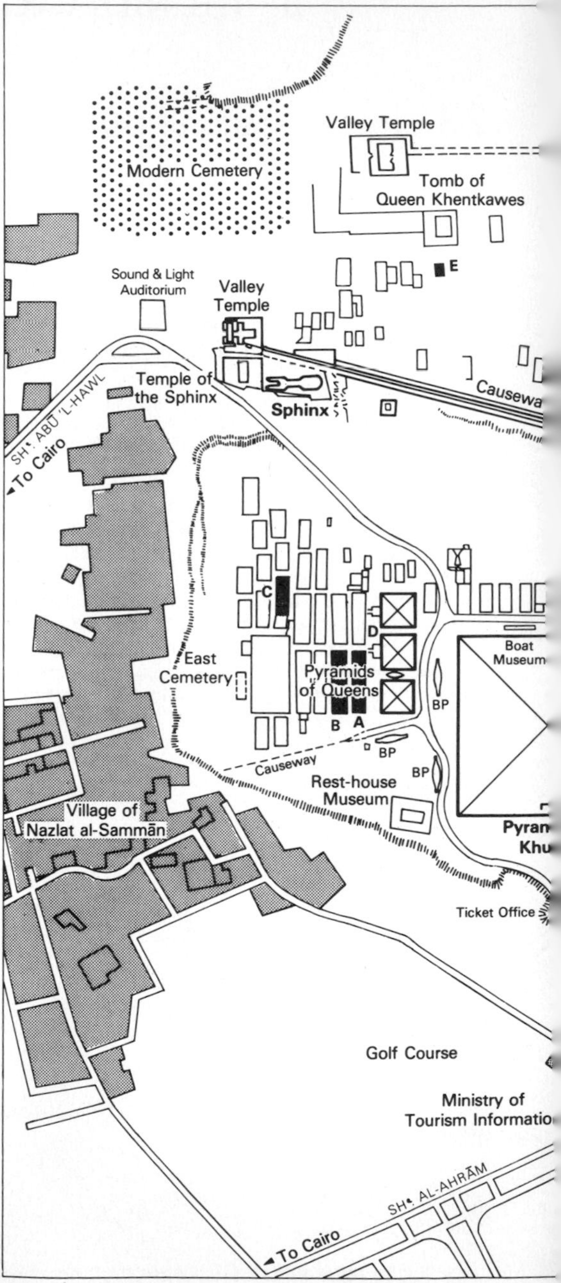
Valley Temple
Modern Cemetery
Tomb of Queen Khentkawes
E
Sound & Light Auditorium
Valley Temple
Temple of the Sphinx
Sphinx
Causewa
SH. ABŪ 'L-HAWL
To Cairo
C
D
Boat Museum
East Cemetery
Pyramids of Queens
BP
B
A
BP
Causeway
BP
Rest-house Museum
Village of Nazlat al-Sammān
Pyran
Khu
Ticket Office
Golf Course
Ministry of Tourism Informatio
SH. AL-AHRĀM
To Cairo

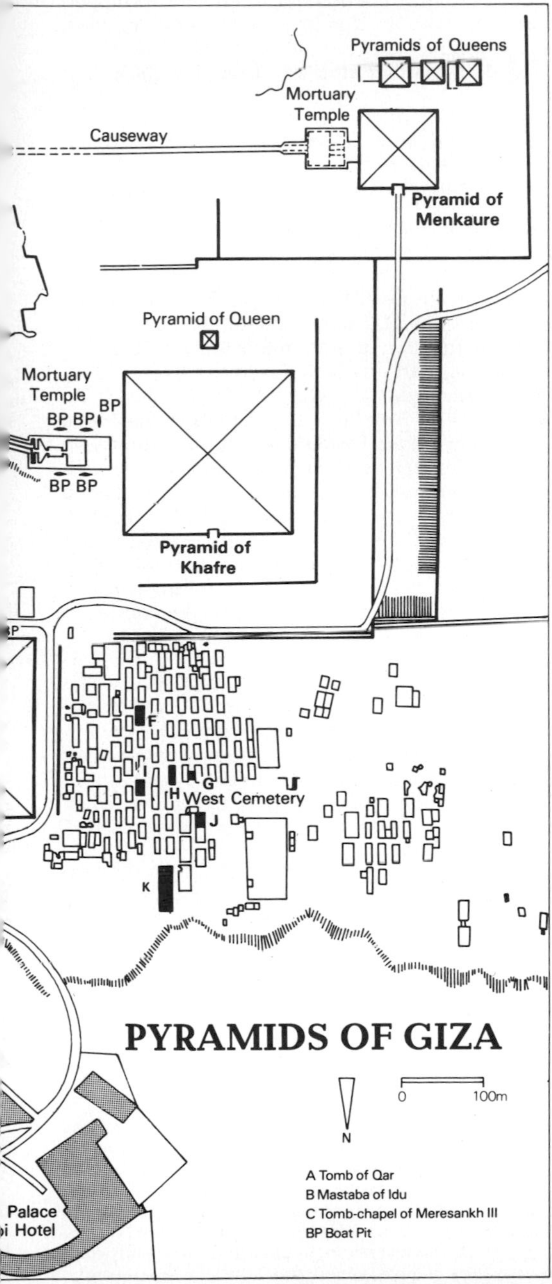
Pyramids of Queens
Mortuary Temple
Causeway
Pyramid of Menkaure
Pyramid of Queen
Mortuary Temple
BP BP BP
BP BP
Pyramid of Khafre
BP
F
I
G
H
West Cemetery
J
K
PYRAMIDS OF GIZA
N
0
100m
A Tomb of Qar
B Mastaba of Idu
C Tomb-chapel of Meresankh III
BP Boat Pit
Palace
i Hotel

Large areas on either side of the road are being opened and developed as residential estates, while the road itself is lined with clubs, casinos, bars and three film studios. At 8km a road crosses the Sh'. al-Ahrām (N to the Delta, S to Ṣaqqārah) as does another after a further 2km (N to Abū Ruwāsh, S to Ṣaqqārah).

This road leads N to the village of **Kirdāssah** (15km). Here are two workshops specialising in weaving tapestries, other materials and dresses. S of the Sh'. al-Ahrām lies the village of **al-Ḥarrāniyyah** (6km) with the renowned tapestry workshops developed around the natural talents of the inhabitants by the architect Ramsīs Wissā Wāssif and since his death managed by his wife. The tapestries from this village have found their way into many art collections.

At 2km a main road branches off to the NW This is the H11, the desert road to Alexandria (Rte 41). SW is the H22 to al-Fayyūm (Rte 29) and al-Baḥriyyah Oasis (Rte 48). At the junction of these roads lies the village of **Nazlat al-Sammān**, the residential part of which lies to the S.

The village is dominated by the pyramids which tower overhead. On the right is the *Mena House Oberoi Hotel* (5*) incorporating the *Mena House Hotel*; to the left of the road are the *Post Office, Tourist Information Office* and the *Tourist Police Office* (tel. 850251). The area is dotted with traders and kiosks selling souvenirs and refreshments. At weekends and public holidays it becomes extremely crowded and should be avoided. Many vendors offer camel and horse rides (stables also in the village) and this can be a very pleasant way to see the area. However, it is essential to ensure that your bargain with the dealer includes the return journey; unprepared visitors may find themselves with a couple of kilometres to walk back across the dunes.

The ***Pyramids** stand on the limestone plateau which here rises about 50m above the flood plain. Two roads climb to the summit, one from the Mena House and one from the village. The former ascends the escarpment. Tickets for admission to the *monuments* can be bought at the kiosk on the left of this road, although access to the *site* is free. The site is very popular with Egyptians, especially on Fridays and public holidays, when it becomes very crowded. A visit in the early morning is recommended.

Except for the very energetic, a visit to the interior of only one of the pyramids is recommended. The Great Pyramid is structurally the more interesting, but the second is less tiring. Because accidents were frequent, climbing the pyramids is forbidden except with special permission.

These pyramids were constructed between c 2589 and 2530 BC by three of the rulers of the 4 Dyn., Khufu (Cheops), Khafre (Chephren) and Menkaure (Mycerinus), of whom very little is known, though their monuments have survived virtually intact.

Each of these structures is a complex of buildings, rather than just a pyramid. The site was prepared by removing the thick layers of sand and gravel, then levelling the rock, smoothing the uneven surface and constructing a limestone platform, which extended beyond the projected pyramid on all sides. Finally, round this was built an enclosure wall. The pyramid was orientated to the cardinal points. The core was built of the local limestone, but faced with finer limestone from quarries at Ṭurah (S of al-Ma'adī on the West Bank) and red granite from the Aswān quarries.

Each pyramid had to the E a small mortuary temple built against the structure and, at a greater distance, a valley temple joined the latter by a causeway.

## SECTIONS THROUGH THE PYRAMIDS AT GIZA

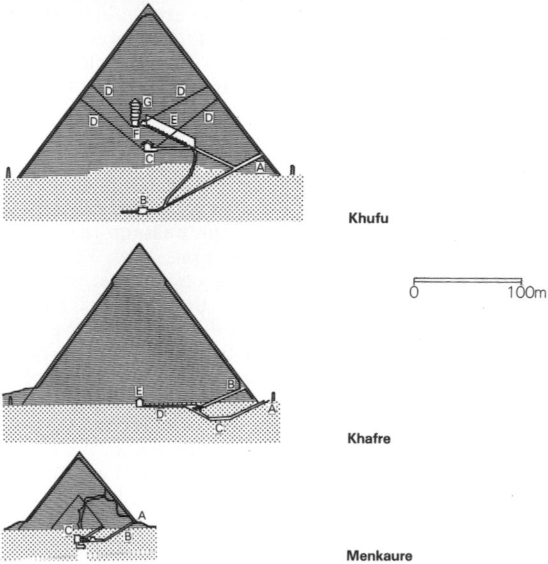
D
D
G
D
E
D
F
C
A
B
Khufu
0
100m
E
B
D
A
C
Khafre
A
C
B
Menkaure

This served during the construction of the pyramid as a slipway to bring the casing stones up to the pyramid and, when the building was finished, as a ceremonial route between the two temples. In addition each had subsidiary pyramids; to the E in the case of Khufu, to the S in those of Khafre and Menkaure. These are thought to have been the burial places of the principal queens. Each of the pyramids was given a name. Around all the pyramids were mastaba fields where the relations and nobles were buried close to the kings' tombs. Many attempts have been made to prove that the pyramids were not burial places, but there is no evidence to support this.

**The Great Pyramid** (called 'Khufu is one belonging to the horizon') now stands 137m high but was originally 140m (indicated by a survey point erected on the summit). Each side once measured 230m (440 cubits), but due to the loss of casing blocks they are now only 227m. The angle of the sides was 51°50′. A visit to the interior takes about one hour.

Khufu (the Horus Medjedu) seems to have been an absolute ruler with complete control over the administration which was largely in the hands of his immediate family. Beneath the structure is a knoll of uncertain size. This makes an exact calculation impossible, but an estimate has indicated that at least 2,300,000 stone blocks averaging 2.5 tons were used, although some were much larger—up to 15 tons. Herodotus (Book II, 124) estimated that 100,000 men were required to build the pyramid, but some American engineers have suggested that this large work force would have been unmanageable and that no more than 4000 could be employed at any one time. This smaller number includes the quarry men at Aswan, as well as the boatmen and the men dragging the blocks into position by means of ramps. The whole project was the work of skilled craftsmen, not untrained slaves, as has been so often suggested, and would have been undertaken during the months of the inundation.

There are three chambers within the pyramid, two inside the built section and one underlying the structure; these are thought to mark changes in the plan of the whole building. The Burial Chamber (B) was originally the unfinished chamber cut in the natural rock, reached after a descent of about 120m, but now inaccessible as the excavators Perring and Vyse filled the descending passage with immovable blocks. The original entry (A) to the pyramid was in the centre of the N face in the thirteenth course of masonry, and about 20m from ground level, but this is also now locked.

The present *Entry*, forced by the Khalīf Ma'mūn in the 9C when he visited Egypt, is cut in the sixth course of masonry, below and to the W of the original. After descending 36m the passage reaches the junction of the original ascending and descending passages. The ascending passage (36m long and about 1m high) leads to a horizontal passage 35m long and 1.75m high which leads in turn to the chamber called the *Queen's Chamber* (C) (incorrectly; there is no evidence that the queens were ever buried within the pyramid during the Old Kingdom period). It is built entirely of limestone and measures 5.2m by 5.7m. The roof, c 6.13m high, is pointed, but the pavement of the chamber seems never to have been laid. On the E side of the chamber is a large recess, the purpose of which is uncertain. On the N and S walls are two rectangular openings made in 1872 by a British engineer for the purpose of locating the ventilation shafts (D) from the room. This, with the unpaved floor, is evidence that the chamber was never finished (some Egyptologists think that these were not ventilation shafts, but had some religious significance).

After the construction of this second burial chamber the builders seem to have changed their plans again; the main structure was further enlarged and a third burial place constructed at a higher level. To reach this visitors pass through the *Grand Gallery* (E), the most impressive part of the construction of the pyramid, over 47m long, and 8.5m high in the centre with a corbelled roof similar to those in the internal chambers of the pyramids of Maydūm and Dahshūr. On each side are rectangular holes, perhaps for holding beams to retain the plug holes intended to block the gallery. The whole is built of fine-grained Muqaṭṭam limestone, so well cut that it is almost impossible to insert anything in the joints.

The Gallery ends in a *Horizontal Passage* or antechamber 8.4m long, lined with granite, slotted for the insertion of portcullises of the same material. The portcullis plugs were very little narrower than the passage and must have been difficult to manoeuvre into position. Beyond is the main burial chamber usually called the *King's Chamber* (F), also lined with highly polished red granite slabs, measuring 5.2m by 10.8m and 5.8m high. It contains two ventilation shafts set in the N and S walls about 1m above pavement level; these were also located by Perring and Vyse in their pyramid survey. The lidless sarcophagus of red Aswan granite stands at the W end of the room, finely polished but uninscribed. It is 2.24m long, 0.96m wide and 1.03m high; the lid had vanished before the first scientific examination of the pyramid was made. Above this room are the *five relieving chambers* (G) designed to take the weight of the upper part of the pyramid, and prevent it crushing the burial chamber; the first was found by Davidson in 1765, and the other four were recorded by Perring and Vyse in 1837. They can only be reached by ladder, from a passage cut in the upper part of the Grand Gallery, where Perring and

Vyse found an inscription bearing the name of Khufu, the builder of the pyramid.

**Khufu's Mortuary Temple** stands to the E of the main structure and is closely associated with it. Unfortunately little remains but the foundations and part of the basalt pavement, but it is quite unlike the other mortuary temples at Giza, or those at Maydūm and Dahshūr. The entry led into a colonnaded court, orientated N to S; the roof of the portico was supported by granite pillars of which little remains. The W side of the temple has been entirely destroyed. Ricke has suggested that there were five statue niches, but there is no certain evidence for this number.

This temple was joined to the Valley Temple by a *Causeway* still largely intact in the middle of the last century, though now only a few blocks remain. The **Valley Temple** situated under the modern village of Nazlat al-Sammān has been located by the OEA but it is not at present possible for the public to visit it.

In 1938 Selim Hassan found some blocks of the causeway decorated with reliefs, but at the time they were not thought to be contemporary, in spite of the fact that Herodotus said that it had been decorated with sculptures. Not until similar sculptured blocks had been found at Dahshūr in Snefru's Valley Temple was it recognised that temples and causeways were decorated before the time of Khufu.

To the N and S of this building are two boat-shaped pits cut in the rock, lying slightly outside the E enclosure wall of the pyramid. They were empty when found, as was a third on the N side of the causeway near the temple. However, in 1954 a fourth *boat-pit* was found to the S of the enclosure wall, containing a partly dismantled boat of cedar, 43m long. Inscriptions on the roof of the boat-pit suggest it was completed by Redjedef. This boat has been reconstructed and it is now housed in a specially air-conditioned *Solar Boat Museum* (additional fee). Judging by an analysis of the mud, it seems that the boat had been used on the Nile. A further pit containing another boat has been identified but not opened.

These boat-pits, usually found empty, are known from the time of the 1 Dyn. royal mastabas, but the exact function of the boats has not been determined. Some may have been used for the funeral procession, others perhaps were intended for the king in the afterworld when he voyaged with Re'.

On the S side of the causeway is a row of three smaller **Subsidiary Pyramids** which probably belonged to Khufu's queens. To the E of each of these is a small mortuary chapel. The *North Pyramid* also has a boat-pit and probably belonged to his principal wife and full sister Meritites. The *Middle Pyramid* has no name, though the queen's titles were found in the mortuary chapel. She was probably the mother of Redjedef, the third king of the dynasty who was buried at Abū Ruwāsh. The *South Pyramid* was the burial place of Hensutsen, another of Khufu's queens and the mother of Khufu-Kaf who is buried nearby; she may also have been the mother of Khafre. In the 21 Dyn. the *Chapel* of this pyramid was enlarged and used as a temple for Isis, Mistress of the Pyramid, by which time the name of its original owner was long forgotten.

It used to be possible to ascend the pyramid (20–30 minutes) from the NE corner but, due to the large number of accidents, this has been forbidden to tourists. From the top there is a splendid view of the desert and the cultivation.

The **Pyramid of Khafre** (called 'Great is Khafre'), preserving a considerable part of the limestone casing near the top, has the most complete complex of them all. The height of this structure is 136.40m (originally about 145.15m) and the base was 214.80m sq. although the outer casing here has almost entirely disappeared. The angle of the side was 53°8′, slightly steeper than that of Khufu. This pyramid seems larger than the Great Pyramid but it is actually slightly smaller, the illusion being caused by its position, higher on the limestone plateau. A visit to the interior takes about half an hour if the pyramid is entered through the lower passage. It was first entered in recent times by Belzoni in March 1818.

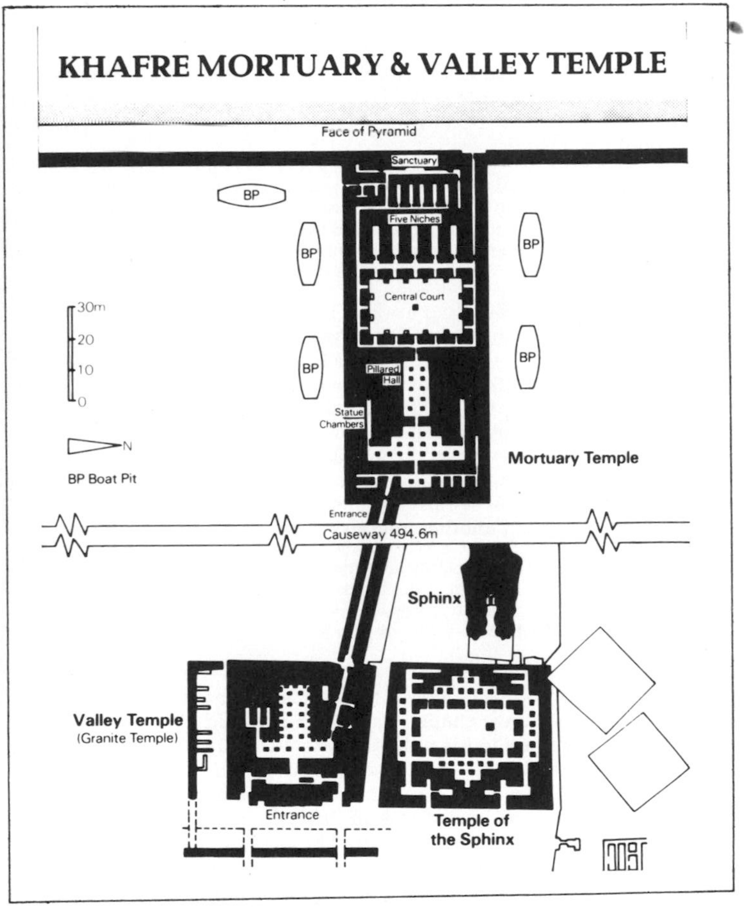
KHAFRE MORTUARY & VALLEY TEMPLE
Face of Pyramid
Sanctuary
BP
Five Niches
BP
BP
Central Court
30m
20
10
0
BP
BP
Pillared Hall
Statue Chambers
N
Mortuary Temple
BP Boat Pit
Entrance
Causeway 494.6m
Sphinx
Valley Temple
(Granite Temple)
Entrance
Temple of the Sphinx

The two entrances on the N side belong to different stages in the construction of the building; the *Lower Entry* (A) now in use is 2.6m from the base of the pyramid, the *Upper Entry* (B) is 11.35m above the base. The original rock-hewn *Burial Chamber* (C) was 10.42 by 3.14m with a roof only 2.6m high, pointed but never finished and not centred beneath the apex of the pyramid. Later the upper passage was constructed and the *Second Burial Chamber* (E) made part of the built pyramid, again not centred but slightly to the N. Measuring 4.97m by 14.13m, with a roof of pointed limestone blocks, it is entered through a granite-lined *passage-way* (D) 60m long, and partly rock-cut. At the W end of the burial chamber is the uninscribed red granite sarcophagus, empty when found by Belzoni, who has celebrated his discovery by writing his name in lamp-black in the chamber. The sarcophagus is 2.62m long, 1.06m wide and 0.96m high. Set into the room's granite pavement, it is still in its original position with the lid nearby. Against the S wall of the room is a square cavity in the pavement, which may have marked the position of the canopic chest, now missing.

On the E side of the pyramid is the **Mortuary Temple** measuring 110m by 45m. It is much larger than that of Khufu, but unfortunately over the centuries it has served as a quarry for local building and has lost much of its outer granite casing. It was excavated by Von Sieglin in 1910 and is unlike the mortuary temples that preceded it, being much more complex. The core of the walls is of limestone, cased with granite, some of the blocks unusually large (between 100 and 400 tons), and the floors of alabaster. It is entered from the causeway to the E by a narrow door, leading to two rooms on the S and a vestibule on the N, the roof originally supported by two pillars, long since robbed, and beyond that, on the N, a series of store rooms and the remains of a stairway leading to the roof. The main passage leads to a large hall, the roof of which was held up by 14 square pillars. At the N and S sides of this hall are two long narrow chambers intended for statues. This first hall leads to a long and narrow second hall, also with 14 square pillars, and on into the great court of the temple surrounded by a colonnade supported on heavy rectangular pillars, against each of which was a large statue of the king. On the W side of this court were the five niches (which became an invariable feature of later mortuary temples) and S of this a corridor leads to five small storerooms lying directly behind the niches. At the W end of the temple is a long narrow shrine in the centre of which was a large granite stele. A passage on the N side connects the central court with the pyramid court.

Flanking the mortuary temple are what appear to be *six boat-pits*, two pairs lying parallel to the N and S walls of the temple. No boats or wood were found in these pits which contained only pottery and statue fragments.

At the centre of the S side of the pyramid is a *Small Pyramid*, originally some 20.1m sq. Most of the superstructure has been quarried away and practically nothing is now to be seen except the entry passage. W of the pyramid, outside the main enclosure wall, were many rectangular rooms (26.75m by 2.90m) thought to have been the barracks block of the workers employed on the structure.

It used to be possible to walk from the Mortuary Temple down the *Causeway* (550m), the walls of which have disappeared except near the **Valley Temple**, sometimes called the *Granite Temple*. It was discovered in 1852 by Mariette and partly cleared by him in 1860 and again in 1869. (A wall now prevents access to the Valley Temple from the Causeway.) This is the most complete of all the buildings in the complex, standing up to roof height. The core is limestone lined with red granite, finely polished and closely jointed, and giving the temple its alternative name. The temple faces E and opens on to a quay fronting a canal (never excavated). It is 45m sq. with the 13m high walls still standing. There are two entrances on the E side, each with an inscription giving the royal titles of which only part remain. The entrances lead into a narrow antechamber and then into a T-shaped room where, in front of the pillars, 23 diorite statues of the king stood. Broken fragments of these were found in a pit in the antechamber but one was complete and is now in the EM. (138.) Enough of the walls remain for the slit windows at their tops to be still visible. Three side chambers on the S side of the main hall may have served as store rooms, and a further chamber leads off the passage which was in line with the causeway leading to the mortuary temple. Probably flanking each of the outer doors was a pair of sphinxes.

To the N of the causeway just where it leaves the temple is the figure of **The Sphinx** (Ar. Abū 'l-hawl; the wonderful, or terrible, one), the mythical animal with the body of a lion and head of a man, partly fashioned out of a natural knoll and partly built-up.

This figure has been cleared by various people starting with the French engineers of Napoleon's expedition. In 1816 Captain Caviglia excavated the Sphinx, starting on the N. He noted the double casing on the body and paws and the remains of red pigment with which one side had been painted, but he had great difficulty clearing the shifting sand from the front, where he found the stele of Tuthmosis IV. By the 18 Dyn. the small 4 Dyn. temple in front of the Sphinx was totally covered and had been forgotten while later, in the Roman period, a stairway and ramp were built over the whole thing. Mariette failed to clear it when dealing with the valley temple in the 1860s and the work was carried on by Maspero who again had neither the time nor the money to finish it. This activity led to many stories of hidden entrances, treasures and trapdoors, all without foundation. Nothing more was done until 1925 when Baraize was entrusted with the task of clearing away the sand which had again covered the Sphinx and he built large coffer-like walls (demolished by Selim Hassan in 1936–37), cleared the whole area and repaired the various holes that his predecessors had made in the monument. It is now more or less complete except that the beard and part of the ureaus and nose are missing.

The Sphinx dates to the period of Khafre (4 Dyn.). Although it has his face, it does not represent him but rather a guardian deity of the necropolis, a god known variously as Hwron or Rwty. During the Middle Kingdom it was, with other sphinxes, known as *seshep-ankh* (the living statue) and by the New Kingdom it was associated with the sun god and regarded as a version of Hor-em-akhet or Hor-akhty (Horus of the Horizon), an appropriate name as the whole cemetery was called Akhet Khufu or the Horizon of Khufu. During the Ptolemaic period the Sphinx must have been freed from sand as a poem was found scratched, in Greek, on its toes; in part it reads:

> Our ornaments are festive clothes,
> Not the arms of War,
> Our hands hold not the scimitar,
> But the fraternal cup of the banquet;
> And all night long while the sacrifices are burning
> We sing songs to Harmakis (Hor-em-Akhet)
> And our heads are decorated with garlands.
> (from Selim Hassan, *The Sphinx and its Secrets*)

The Sphinx, being made of soft stone, has suffered considerably from erosion. Blocks of limestone used for restoration, probably in the Ptolemaic period, may be seen on its paws, tail and flanks. It is now suffering great damage from the rising water-table and parts of it have become detached. In front of it is the granite stele placed there on the orders of Tuthmosis IV (1423–1417 BC).

He rested in the shade of the Sphinx one day while hunting in the Valley of the Gazelles and because he had a dream which promised him the throne if he cleared it of sand, did so. This stele was not the only one discovered in the area. It was apparently a standard practice to erect a stele worshipping the Sphinx and the other gods of the locality and it seems to a certain extent to have been a place of pilgrimage, particularly frequented in the 18 Dyn. The earliest of these stelae was one of Prince Amen-mes, a son of Tuthmosis I (c 1525–1512 BC). However, the most interesting is a series of stelae which may have been erected by the brothers of Tuthmosis IV, of whom he may have had to dispose before the prophecy of the Sphinx could be fulfilled. Amenhotep II is known to have built a temple here, and erected a large stele. The 19 Dyn. kings continued to erect monuments here, including Ramesses II.

Beyond the paws is the *Temple of the Sphinx*, a solid structure of limestone faced with granite, also of the 4 Dyn. In the façade are two entrances leading to a colonnaded court. The pillars must each have been fronted by a statue probably also of Khafre, and there was a large offering table in the middle of the Courtyard.

*The Sphinx, with the Pyramid of Khafre in the background*

The third pyramid to the S is the **Pyramid of Menkaure** (called 'Menkaure is divine'). It is the smallest of the group and was built between 2533 and 2505 BC, although finished by Menkaure's son Shepseskaf. The lower 16 courses were cased in granite, but the rest was never completed. The main pyramid is built on the edge of the sloping plateau and originally stood 66.5m high and 108m sq. at the base. The angle of the sides is 51°. The *Entry* (A) is in the N face about 4m above the surface of the limestone platform; the descending passage (B) with a slope of 26°2′ is 31m long, faced with granite blocks. It leads, after passing through a panelled vestibule (the original burial chamber) and a horizontal passage with three portcullises, into the underground *Burial Chamber* (D). This is lower than the earlier chamber (C) and is cut entirely in the rock, but lined with granite.

Here Colonel Vyse found a panelled basalt sarcophagus which was lost at sea off the

Spanish coast when the ship carrying it to England sank during a storm. He also found some bones, and the fragments of a wooden coffin inscribed with the name of Menkaure, at first thought to be his original coffin dating to the 4 Dyn. However, the type of inscription suggests that it was a 26 Dyn. replacement (now in the BM).

S of the pyramid stand three **Subsidiary Pyramids**, none of which has been completed; each with a small mortuary chapel on the E, finished in mud-bricks, probably the work of Shepseskaf. The largest of these, the *East Pyramid*, cased in granite blocks, was probably intended for Queen Khamerernebty II, Menkaure's principal wife. It is 44.3m sq. by 28.27m high. The *Mortuary Chapel* is relatively large—21m by 25m. The *Central Pyramid* was used and the burial chamber contained a granite sarcophagus with an inner coffin which contained the bones of a young woman, probably another of Menkaure's wives. The *West Pyramid* was perhaps never used. The **Mortuary Temple** of Menkaure's pyramid is on its E side. It is well preserved; the walls of local limestone, intended to be lined with granite, were finished off instead in mud brick with a thin limestone facing. A long entrance corridor leads from the causeway to the central court, on the W side of which are six square red granite pillars and in the centre a basin and drains. Behind the W side is a long narrow room, and, on the N side, reached by a narrow passage, are five small rooms but, to the S, the temple never seems to have been finished. At the W end is a small sanctuary set right against the pyramid, paved with red granite with traces of an offering table before a false door.

This temple is linked to the Valley Temple by a *Causeway* (660m) passing the curious Tomb of Queen Khentkawes on the left (see below). The **Valley Temple** now buried under sand, though originally cleared by George Reisner, lies very close to the Muslim cemetery of the village of Nazlat al-Samman and is partly covered by the modern graves.

It was built of mud brick, with only the thresholds and paving in stone. The E entrance opened into a small vestibule, with storerooms on either side, four in all. A door in the back of the vestibule leads into the main courtyard which had a mud-brick wall decorated with niches, a mud-brick pavement and a limestone basin and drain. A gangway led to a hall, with the roof supported by six pillars behind which was the sanctuary, with six chambers on one side and five on the other. In the S room were found the complete and fragmentary triads in alabaster and slate representing Menkaure, Hathor and the gods of the various nomes (now in the EM and the Boston Museum). The causeway was paved with limestone blocks covered with mud brick, as were the walls. It was roofed with palm logs and joined the enclosure wall, although Reisner found no direct connection with the main part of the temple.

S of the pyramids is the **Tomb of Queen Khentkawes**, shaped like a giant sarcophagus, excavated by Selim Hassan in 1931–32. It is built on a limestone outcrop into which the *Mortuary Temple* is also cut.

Queen Khentkawes seems to have been the bridging figure between the 4 and 5 Dyns and may have been the wife of Shepseskaf. She appears to have been the mother of at least two kings, judging from her titles, and to have reigned at a time when the male line was almost extinct. Her husband may not have been royal, perhaps a priest of the sun god, and she is probably the inspiration for a story found in the Westcar Papyrus about the throne leaving the direct family of Khufu.

The entry to the substructure is to the W from the second room of the temple. The rock foundations are almost square, measuring 45.5m each way, and 10m high. The superstructure is much smaller—27.5m by 21m and 7.5m high. The outer walls were recessed like the palace façade and later they were lined with fine limestone blocks, but these have now fallen away leaving the skeleton of the structure exposed. It was enclosed by a mud-brick wall, and has at least one rock-cut boat-pit in the SE corner.

Surrounding the pyramids are many mastabas and some entirely rock-cut tombs, usually associated with the king whose pyramid they surround (most are inaccessible to general visitors). One of those which may be seen near the pyramid of Khufu is the **Tomb of Meres-'ankh III** (G. 7530), wife of Khafre, which lies under that of her mother Hetep-heres II (daughter of Khufu and wife of King Redjedef), and dates to the end of the 4 Dyn. It consists of a small ruined interior chapel and inscribed niche. Under the chapel is a large subterranean rock-cut tomb-chapel of three rooms. The doorway has her name and titles and probably dates to the time of Shepseskaf. It is interesting in that it gives the time taken to prepare the mummy after death. Inside scenes show sculptors and metal smiths at work and on the left the deceased is shown with a lotus flower. There are three registers of offering bearers, officials and funerary priests. The false door, almost opposite the main entry, shows the deceased at table and on the pillar in the centre is the offering text, Meres-'ankh in a papyrus boat with her mother Hetep-heres pulling the papyrus. Other registers show mat-making, birds in cages, men bringing birds and cattle and boatmen fighting; usual scenes in Old Kingdom tombs.

**THREE TOMBS AT GIZA**

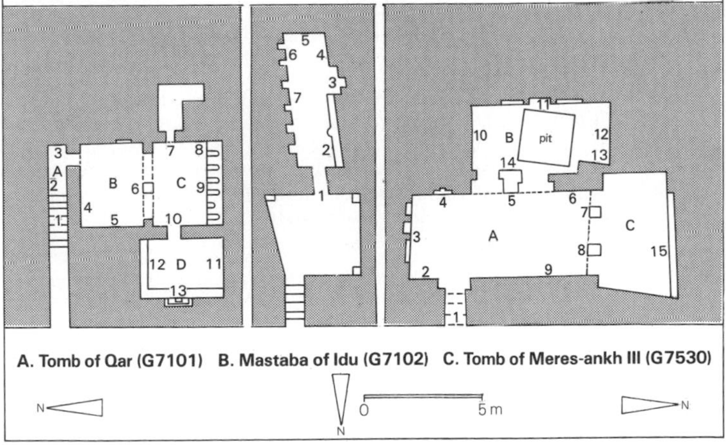
pit
0
5 m
N

**A. Tomb of Qar (G7101) B. Mastaba of Idu (G7102) C. Tomb of Meres-ankh III (G7530)**

(1) Titles on lintel. (2) Occupations: scribes, sculptors, goldsmiths, carpenters. (3) Deceased with officials. (4) False door. (5) Offering texts on lintel. (6) Mother, Hetepheres II with children. (7) On pillars, deceased with two young sons. (8–9) Father, Kawab and mother in boat; agricultural scenes. (10) Offering lists. (11) False door flanked by rock-cut statues of deceased and mother and stelae. (12) Deceased with musicians and wine-making scenes. (13) Agricultural occupations. (14) Deceased with accounts. (15) Niche with ten rock-cut statues: from left, three of daughters, four of deceased, three of mother.

Other tombs recently opened are **Prince Sbt Neferma'et** (G 7060) King's son, Hereditary Prince, Vizier of Khafre, Overseer of Netcheb, his mother was Nefetkau

(4 Dyn). It is a stone built mastaba. (1) Four registers of men bringing offerings before deceased and wife. (2) Deceased seated before offerings with dog under chair. (3) Deceased with wife (name lost). (4) False door, deceased with son Sneferukha'ef (see next tomb).

**Prince Sneferukha'ef** (G 7070) Treasurer of the King of Lower Egypt, son of Neferma'et and grandson of Khufu (4 Dyn). Another limestone mastaba. (1) Lintel with offering texts and geneology. Deceased and sons. (2) False door, shaft. (the uninscribed sarcophagus is in the EM 34936).

**Khufukha'ef** (7130–40) Vizier and Chief Justice, son of Khufu and Q. Hensutsen, his wife is Nefertkau (4 Dyn). It is a twin mastaba at the W end of the S row and consists of two rooms and alcove burial chamber, partly lined, somewhat altered by Ptolemaic cutting. Statue in EM. 46. (1) Offering texts, large figure of Anubis. (2) Deceased preceded by mother Hensutsen, three registers of scribes, officials and Ka servants. (3) Deceased with sons, following are two more sons and scribes. (4) Names and titles, wife and two sons, list of offerings, animals and food. (5) Deceased seated with daughter, offerings, linen and clothing. (6) Deceased at table with offering lists and priests. (7) Four registers of estates and live animals. (8) False door with entrance to Ptolemaic burial cut through. Five registers of offerings, deceased at table.

Just S of the causeway of Khufu's pyramid is another easily-visited tomb, the **Tomb of Meryre'nufer, called Qar** (G. 7101), overseer of the pyramid towns of Khufu and Menkaure. This dates to the beginning of the 6 Dyn. and is a stone-built mastaba. His wife was Gefi, a priestess of Hathor. The mastaba consists of a staircase passage, a court room and an offering chamber. Some of the reliefs from here are now in the Boston Museum.

(1) Deceased at table. (2) Hunting with son, Idu. (3) At table. (4) Funerary rites. (5) Deceased at table with wife, Gefi. (6) Architrave, titles of deceased. (7) Sister of deceased. (8) Deceased carried by attendants. (9) Five statues of Qar and one of his son, Idu. (10) Offering texts with deceased as priest. (11) Offering list. (12) Deceased and wife at table. (13) False door.

Slightly to the E and also dated to the early 6 Dyn. is the stone-built **Mastaba of Idu** (G. 7102), son of Qar. Idu was inspector of the priests of Khufu and Khafre and overseer of scribes. The doorway leading from the court has biographical details on the jambs. The narrow chapel contains a bust of Idu with a list of the sacred oils and offering bearers, butchers, dancers and a scene of hunting in the marshes.

(1) Biographical text, deceased with son, Qar, funeral scenes. (2) Deceased with wife, Meritotes. (3) False door. (4) Offerings. (5) Deceased and register of entertainments and occupations. (6) Men in boats, animals. (7) Niche with four statues of Idu and one of Qar (his son).

**Senezemib** (G. 2370) good name Inti, Vizier, Overseer of all the works of the King (Dyn 5 1st year of Unas). His son also called Senezemib, but called Mehi was likewise vizier. This is a large chapel with a forecourt, four rooms and an E–W orientated offering room, and is entered by a sloping passage.

(1) Text of son Senezemib called Mehi. (2–3) Text of funeral (damaged) and transport of sarcophagus across river. (4–5) Deceased fowling and fishing. (6–7) Text (damaged) cattle crossing river; letter from Isesi. (9–10) Deceased and son. (11–16) Boatmen fighting, funerary procession, marsh scene and cattle, various industries. (17–18) Tribute of estates. (19–22) Bringing offerings, animals, birds, agriculture, vineyards. (23–24) Tribute of estates. (26) Stelae, deceased wife and son, Granite sarcophagus with name and two blocks with family and priests.

Between the Sphinx and the Pyramid of Khufu is the **Tomb of Pakap** (LG.

84), good name Wehebre-emakhet, overseer of scribes at the king's meal, of the 26 Dyn. It is also called 'Campbell's tomb', as it was discovered by Colonel Vyse in 1837 and named by him after the British consul-general in Egypt. The superstructure has been destroyed but there is a line of text round the substructure. The shaft, just over 16m deep, leads to a vaulted burial chamber which contained two sarcophagi (the inner one of basalt is now in the BM). In the subsidiary chambers are other burials of the 26 and 27 Dyns.

**Debhen** (LG 90) Overlord of Nekheb, Secretary of the toilet house, Master of Largesse in the Mansion of Life (5 Dyn, time of Menkaure).

(1) Entry lintel with offering text, drum with name and titles of Debhen, deceased with son, attendants and a dog. (2) Niche with thirteen rock cut statues (all destroyed); text describing tomb as a gift of K. Menkaure. (3) Deceased seated with monkey under the chair, five registers of offerings, dancers, singers, flautists, harpists and a female dwarf. (4) Names and titles of deceased. (5) Funerary priests performing rites, offering of birds and animals including a hyaena, statues drawn on sledges. (6) False door with names and titles. (7) Titles (partly damaged). (8) Marsh scene with hippopotamus hunt and fish.

**Seshemnufer** (G 4940) First under the King in the palace of Redjedef, Prophet of K. Qaa of the 1 Dyn. (4 Dyn). This is a mastaba cased with white limestone, fully decorated, but damaged. The serdab complex is built S of the mastaba.

(1) Four registers, procession of estates, list of offerings, bearers, list of Ka-priests. (2) Deceased seated with two Ka-servants. (3–4) Deceased and family between two false doors.

The **Tomb of Hetepheres I** cannot be visited, but the material (now in the EM) from here is so important that a word must be said about the circumstances of its discovery.

In 1925 the photographer of the Boston Museum Expedition, under the direction of George Reisner, was working near the N end of the row of small pyramids attached to that of Khufu when his tripod sank. Investigation showed a shaft, but no superstructure. The shaft had been carefully filled with limestone blocks and was about 30m deep. The small burial chamber (5m by 2.5m) was packed with a sarcophagus and canopic jar, both of alabaster, the frame for a canopy, a bed, chair, carrying chair and a mass of pottery, stone vases, silver bracelets, toilet objects such as razors and perfume vases, but there was no body. The arrangement of the objects was the reverse of that usually found in unplundered graves with the sarcophagus put in last.

It is possible, though not certain, that this was a reburial of Hetepheres, mother of Khufu, builder of the great pyramid and wife of Snefru. She had obviously died during the reign of Khufu as the inscriptions call her 'Mother of the King' and the tomb had clay sealings bearing the impressions of his funerary officials. One theory accounting for her reburial is that she was originally interred at Dahshūr near her husband's pyramid, but this tomb being robbed soon after, she was reburied for greater security near her son's pyramid. This presupposes that the body was destroyed during the tomb robbery and that Khufu's officials were afraid to tell him of this destruction. No tomb that can be attributed to her has been found at Dahshūr though this area has not been completely investigated.

# 24 Zāwiyat al-ʿAryān, Abū Ghurāb and Abū Ṣīr

South of Giza, this Rte (total distance approx. 26.5km) includes three sites lying in the desert at an average 12km to the W of the main valley road, the H2. There is consequently a good deal of driving over agricultural roads, and much walking over soft sand.

**Cairo**.—21km **Zāwiyat al-ʿAryān**.—3.5km **Abū Ghurāb**.—2km **Abū Ṣīr**.

The SHʿ. RABIʿ AL-GĪZĪ, the road to Upper Egypt, leads S from the Shʿ. al-Ahrām (Rte 23) and swings E through *Giza al-Thānī* to the riverbank. From here it continues S with the railway line to the W for 7km, passing the area of al-Munīb where it reaches a police control point and leaves the metropolitan area. Beyond (as the motorway, H2) it runs S. At 2.5km take the road to the W, passing the village of (2km) *Abū 'l-Numrus* and crossing the cultivation to (4km) *Shubrāmant*. The route crosses Baḥr al-Libaynī, a road running from N to S (from Shʿ. al-Ahrām to Ṣaqqārah) and several smaller canals to reach (3km) a lake at the edge of the cultivation and another N–S road. Take the N branch to (2.5km) the area of **Zāwiyat al-ʿAryān**.

This field contains two pyramids probably of the 3 Dyn. though their ownership is disputed. Each of these pyramids is covered in sand and difficult to make much of. The more northerly of the two is known as the **Unfinished Pyramid**, begun by king Neferke (Re) Nebka and called 'Nebka is a star'. The lavish use of granite in this structure has suggested to some that the pyramid might be rather later in date, belonging to the 4 Dyn. and the little-known ruler Baufre who succeeded Khafre. After the substructure was built and the enclosure wall had been planned the whole thing seems to have been abandoned and the surrounding ground is covered with granite and limestone chippings and unfinished limestone blocks.

1.5km SE is the **Layer Pyramid**, built of small stone blocks, which may well have been intended to be a step pyramid. Its method of construction points to a 3 Dyn. date. This was excavated unsatisfactorily by Barsanti, the architect of the Antiquities Department. Beside this pyramid in a 3 Dyn. tomb were found eight stone bowls inscribed with the name of Khaba which appears to be the Horus name of the fourth king of the 3 Dyn. This personal name is unknown, and little else is known about him.

Follow the road S along the edge of the cultivation to (3.5km) the site of **Abū Ghurāb**. The way leads past rose gardens; after c 70m of sand are two sun-temples. That to the N is the **Sun-Temple of Nyuserre**, at first erroneously thought to be the base of a pyramid and called the Pyramid of Riga. It records the renewing of the king's life in the Heb Sed. It was excavated in 1898–1901 by Borchardt and Schaefer, and is now partly covered by drifting sand. The base of the large *Solar Obelisk* is still in position, although the obelisk has long since vanished; this base is the main feature of the site, and from its top a fine view of the surrounding desert can be obtained. The base is at the W end of a large court, 100m by 75m, in the centre of which is a large altar. To the right are ten alabaster basins used in the sacrifices, and beyond these are store rooms. The entry to the ramp up the base is through a small *Chapel*, now much ruined (reliefs in the EM), flanked with two uninscribed granite stelae. N of the obelisk base is a small *Slaughterhouse* set within the perimeter wall and on the E a small *Chapel* marks the entry to the *Causeway* leading to the

*Valley Temple*. This has two entrances, though both are heavily sanded over. To the S is the mud-brick emplacement for a large solar boat. The scenes in the temple were of particular interest as they showed the king as a griffin trampling upon his enemies.

SE is the very ruined **Sun-Temple of Userkaf** which does not repay a visit.

2km further S lies the field of **Abū Sīr**, taking its name from the village to the S. Cross a bridge over a small canal, turn right and then left, following a garden wall to the edge of the desert. 60m on is the causeway of the **Pyramid Complex of Sahure**, the most complete of the four complexes at this site. It was originally excavated between 1902–08 by a German expedition led by Borchardt. The *Causeway*, c 235m long, is still clearly defined and leads to a *Valley Temple* with two entries opening off a landing-stage leading to a canal. The portico of the E entry has eight columns, the S entry has four. The temple measures 40m by 30m and is now much ruined and partly filled with sand. It had a hall supported on granite palm columns with walls decorated with carved reliefs (now in the Berlin Museum).

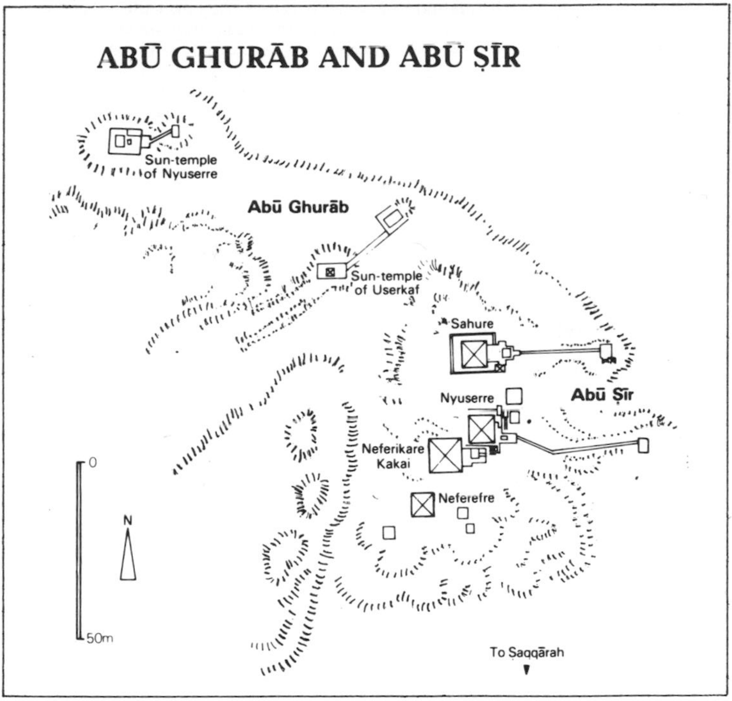
ABŪ GHURĀB AND ABŪ ṢĪR
Sun-temple
of Nyuserre
Abū Ghurāb
Sun-temple
of Userkaf
Sahure
Nyuserre
Abū Ṣīr
Neferikare
Kakai
Neferefre
0
50m
N
To Ṣaqqārah

At the upper end of the causeway is the *Mortuary Temple*, entered through a corridor whose walls still stand to a height of 3m. This leads to a court originally enclosed in a colonnade of 16 palm columns in red granite inscribed with the name of Sahure. The black basalt pavement is still largely *in situ*, but the walls of limestone with coloured reliefs are now in the EM and the Berlin Museum. Some of the scenes represent the king smiting his enemies, later to become a standard Egyptian theme, but here depicted for the first time. Surrounding the colonnaded court is a wide corridor, also paved with basalt, and once decorated with limestone reliefs including one of the king making offerings to the cat goddess Bastet. This goddess, in the New Kingdom, appears to have been confused with the lion-headed goddess Sekhmet, the wife of Ptah, god of Memphis, at which time the corridor seems to have been roofed in, and transformed into a sanctuary for one of her local forms, Sekhmet of Sahure. This ensured that this part of the temple survived in a rather better state than the rest.

W of the court and beyond the corridor are several rooms and stores. Behind the court nearer to the pyramid were five niches for statues and more storerooms, on two levels, with stairs still visible. S of the niches were 17 further storerooms. Both these magazines were reached from square recesses upheld by red granite papyrus form columns. Behind the niches are five cult chambers, and the sanctuary, with an alabaster altar, and at the W end a granite false door.

The temple originally had an elaborate drainage system, the rain water from the roof being carried away by lion-headed gargoyles, and falling into open channels cut in the pavement. Inside the temple were five copper-lined basins, with lead plugs (one in the sanctuary itself), and copper pipes were used to carry off the liquids used in the various ceremonies from the basins. These connected with an underground drainage system, also of copper pipes going under the temple paving and causeway, to an outlet at the S.

The *Pyramid of Sàhure* (called 'The soul of Sahure gleams') has been much damaged, but originally stood some 48m high, with a base 78m sq. and an angle of about 50°36′. The core is of local limestone filled with sand and rubble, cased with fine white limestone, most of which has been robbed. There were apparently six layers decreasing in size from the centre one (model of the building and its complex on the first floor of the EM). The entrance is at ground level at the N face, not quite central (now inaccessible). The passage lined with black granite leads to an antechamber some 8m long and closed by a granite portcullis at the S end. Beyond is a 25m-long corridor lined with white limestone leading to the burial chamber.

SE is the *Mastaba of Ptahshepses*, Sahure's chief of works, discovered by de Morgan in 1893 and re-worked by the Czechoslovak Institute of Archaeology. It consists of an entry, a colonnaded court with 20 square pillars, a pillared portico leading to a hall with statue niches, a side room with pictures of the family, and also some much later graffiti of year 50 of Ramesses II. (Permission to visit required from Dept of Antiquities.)

The next complex to the S is the **Pyramid Complex of Nyuserre**, the fourth king after Sahure. He built his pyramid between those of Sahure and Nefirkare, and seems to have usurped the Valley Temple and causeway of the latter. To do this he diverted the upper part of the *Causeway*, giving it a sharp turn to the NW so that it enters his *Mortuary Temple* at the SE corner of the enclosure wall. The temple has an unusual L-shape with the outer and inner parts of the building set on two different axes. This may have been due to existing buildings or tombs, or to the land surface. The causeway leads into a wide corridor, with storerooms on each side, which opens into a colonnaded court with 16 red granite papyriform columns, and a black basalt floor. The W doorway in the centre of the wall leads to the part of the temple on a different angle. There are two corridors, five niches, and storerooms with the inner rooms again reached from a square room supported by a single column, beyond which lie an antechamber, sanctuary and other rooms. A *Subsidiary Pyramid* is situated at the SE corner of the pyramid, surrounded by its own enclosure wall. The base is 15m sq. and it is now some 11m high.

The *Pyramid of Nyuserre*, (called 'The places of Nyuserre are enduring') was originally 52m high on a base 80m sq. The core is again of local limestone mixed with sand and rubble, and it too was faced with finer limestone; it is a layer pyramid with five inner facings. The entrance is on the N side (now inaccessible) and leads to a passage, a vestibule and a long passage finally closed before the burial chamber by three portcullises and an antechamber.

The **Pyramid Complex of Neferikare Kakai** who succeeded Sahure is just to the S of that of Nyuserre. It seems that he had intended his pyramid buildings to be larger versions of those of Sahure; however, his short reign did not give him time to complete his building, which was modified and completed in mud brick by his successor. The *Valley Temple*, also with two entrances, is now completely wrecked, but was built of granite, basalt and limestone blocks. The *Causeway* is unusual in that it has a dado of black basalt, some of which has remained in place. The upper part of the causeway was diverted by his successor to serve his own temple. The *Mortuary Temple* consists of the usual corridor leading to a colonnaded court, but with the columns of wood on a limestone base, probably because of the king's early death. The inner section of the temple again has five niches, storerooms, and sanctuary.

The *Pyramid of Neferikare* (called 'Neferikare has become a soul'), is the largest of the group, originally being 70m high and 106m sq., with an angle of 53°. Although made of local limestone cased with finer limestone, the lower course was cased in red granite. The entrance is on the N face (now inaccessible).

To the SW is the **Pyramid Complex of Neferefre** who succeeded Shepseskare. This king apparently had a short reign, of uncertain length. He could not finish his pyramid and it was never completed for him. The *Pyramid of Neferefre* (called 'The Souls of Neferefre are divine') consists of a low mound of limestone 60m sq. going up some courses of masonry. The burial chamber was never finished, nor were the internal passages lined with better quality stone. The causeway and temples never seem to have been built. The core as it stands is of local stone, so that there was no necessity to make a causeway to carry the better limestone blocks.

Recently discovered at this site and at present being excavated by a Czechoslovakian team is a *Pyramid of Queen Khentkawes I* with associated temples.

The agricultural road continues along the edge of the cultivation to the southern sites.

# 25 Memphis and Ṣaqqārah

Continuing S from Rte 24, the sites on this route (total distance approx. 18.5km) also lie W of the road. Memphis is surrounded by cultivation but Ṣaqqārah lies further W on the edge of the desert. There is a lot of walking involved in visiting these sites.

**Abū Sīr**.—16.5km **Mīt Rahīnah** (for **Memphis**).—2km **Ṣaqqārah**.

The H2 runs S along the riverbank passing (2km) *Manyal Shīhah* and continuing through cultivation to (7.5km) **al-Hawamdiyyah** with a large sugar-processing plant. After a further 4km the road reaches *al-Badrashayn* from which another road leads W. It crosses the ruin fields of the ancient city of Memphis to (3km) **Mīt Rahīnah**.

Surrounding the village are the remains of the town of **Memphis**, founded by Mena or Menes, traditionally the first king of the 1 Dyn., on land reclaimed from the Nile in about 3100 BC. Memphis or Menufer became the capital of the country during the Old Kingdom and probably during the 12 Dyn. When the capital was moved to Thebes during the New Kingdom Memphis remained an important provincial city, as indeed it did even after the foundation of Alexandria as the capital by Alexander. It was finally deserted during the early Muslim era. Today little remains

*The alabaster sphinx, 18 or 19 Dyn., at Memphis*

of the garden city of Memphis grouped round the vast temple of its patron god Ptah, protector of craftsmen. A small *Museum* on the left of the road shelters a colossal limestone *Figure of Ramesses II*, of excellent workmanship, depicting the king when young, discovered by Caviglia and Sloane in 1820. It lies on its back and must have been originally about 12.8m high, the feet and the back much eroded by water. Given to the British Museum by Muḥ. ʿAlī, it was raised to its present position by the Royal Engineers in 1888. Various other *granite statues* of the king were found when clearing a space to build a cafeteria opposite and these lie in the enclosure beside the museum. The high water table has hindered excavation here.

The uninscribed *Alabaster Sphinx* inside the enclosure weighs 80 tons and was excavated by Petrie in 1912. It is either 18 or 19 Dyn., probably of Amenhotep II, but it has also been greatly damaged by water. Other stone objects and sarcophagi can also be seen. The *Temple of Ptah* before which these colossal figures stood was excavated by Petrie before World War I and now lies half covered with water beside the village of Mīt Rahīnah. Beyond the village Petrie found the Saite *Palace of Apries*, very much ruined but with the plan still visible, unrewarding except for the archaeologist. Just to the N of the road the Department of Antiquities discovered in 1951 the *Embalming Place of the Apis Bulls*, contained within a mud-brick wall, with immense alabaster embalming slabs, decorated with lions.

At Miqyas on the E side of the site the EES survey discovered the *Roman Port*, with quay and nilometer.

**PYRAMID AND MORTUARY TEMPLE OF UNAS**

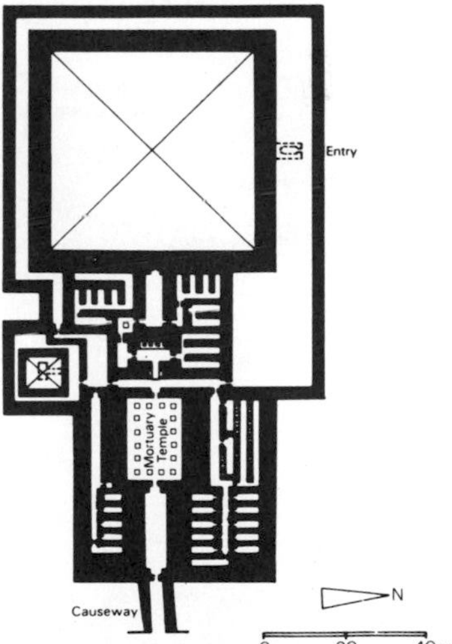
Entry
Mortuary Temple
Causeway
N
0
20
40m

W of Mīt Rahīnah the road crosses the Baḥr al-Libaynī and the road running N to S (from Shʿ. al-Ahrām). Turn N. After 2km another road leads W to the N–S road on the edge of the cultivation. It terminates here on the E edge of the vast cemetery of **Ṣaqqārah**.

The site lies on a plateau at the edge of the Libyan desert directly W of the ancient city of Memphis. It is part of the necropolis of that city which extends along the edge of the Nile Valley for some 80km, from Abū Ruwāsh to Maydūm. The Ṣaqqārah field is some 7km long and at its greatest width 1500m, dominated by the Step Pyramid of Zozer. The road continues past Mīt Rahīnah and leads to the escarpment opposite the Valley Temple of Unas and the *Ticket Office*. Tickets are sold separately for different areas of the site. Ṣaqqārah may be conveniently divided into northern and southern sections and it is the former section that is usually visited by tourists; the southern area requires special permission from the Dept of Antiquities.

Past the ticket office the road climbs the limestone escarpment past rock-cut tombs (excavated by the University of Pisa) and forks, left to the Step Pyramid, right to Mereruka. The **Pyramid Complex of Unas** is reached from the car park with the Step Pyramid to the right. The *Causeway*, about 600m long, runs between the Pyramid and Mortuary

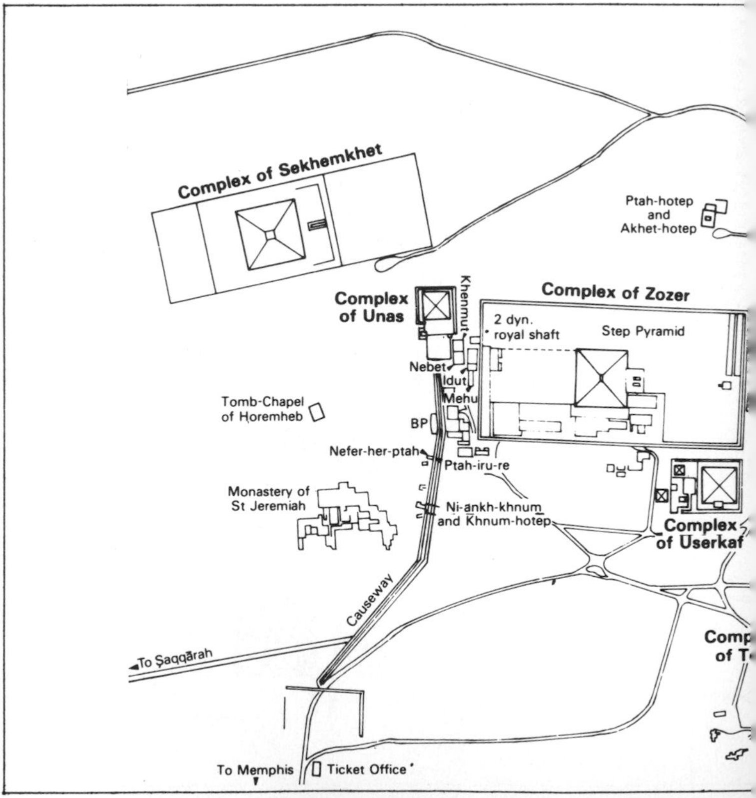
Complex of Sekhemkhet
Ptah-hotep and Akhet-hotep
Complex of Unas
Khenmut
Complex of Zozer
2 dyn. royal shaft
Step Pyramid
Nebet
Idut
Mehu
Tomb-Chapel of Horemheb
BP
Nefer-her-ptah
Ptah-iru-re
Monastery of St Jeremiah
Ni-ankh-khnum and Khnum-hotep
Complex of Userkaf
Causeway
To Ṣaqqārah
To Memphis
Ticket Office

Temple in the W and the Valley Temple in the E, with several turns to avoid uneven ground. It was built of limestone slabs to enable the blocks facing the pyramid to be hauled up with the least difficulty and was afterwards decorated with carved scenes of offerings, hunting, animals, famine, the transport of granite columns, market scenes, goldsmiths and ships. Many of these decorated slabs were found lying haphazardly around the causeway. A small section of the wall and roof, decorated with yellow stars on a blue background, has been reconstructed to show its original condition. To the SW (proceeding towards the Mortuary Temple) are two large *Boat pits* cut in the limestone, for the funerary boats of Unas; originally there must have been more of them. The *Mortuary Temple*, with a general plan like that of Sahure at Abū Ṣīr, has been very much ruined. It is entered through a granite gateway, inscribed with Unas' names and titles by his successor Teti, who finished the temple for him after his death. The floors are of alabaster, the walls of limestone, and the palm-shaped columns are of granite. On the S face of the pyramid is an inscription recording that Khaʿemwaset, son of Ramesses II, when high priest of Memphis restored the Pyramid of Unas as it had fallen into decay and re-inscribed his name. It was excavated twice, once partially by Barsanti in 1900–01 and again rather more carefully by C.M. Frith in

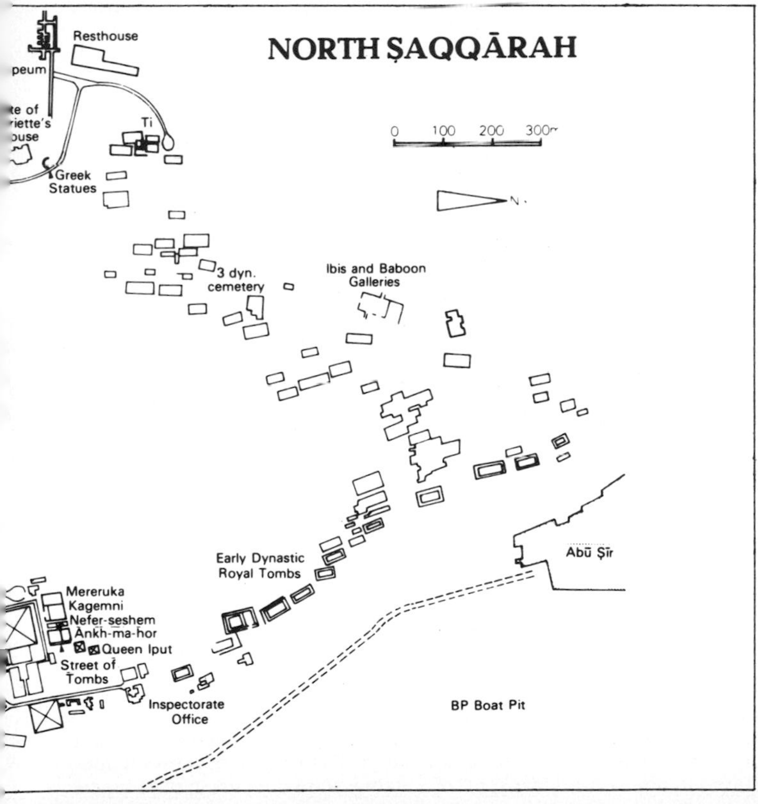
NORTH ṢAQQĀRAH
Resthouse
peum
te of
riette's
ouse
Ti
Greek
Statues
0 100 200 300m
N
3 dyn.
cemetery
Ibis and Baboon
Galleries
Early Dynastic
Royal Tombs
Abū Ṣīr
Mereruka
Kagemni
Nefer-seshem
Ankh-ma-hor
Queen Iput
Street of
Tombs
Inspectorate
Office
BP Boat Pit

1929. The narrow entry vestibule leads into a colonnaded court with 16 columns of granite and quartzitic sandstone, several transverse chambers and a series of niches for statues.

The base of the *Pyramid of Unas*, called 'Beautiful are the places of Unas', 44m sq., is of local limestone, cased with finer Ṭurah stone, some of which is still in position. The entry is at ground level on the N side, almost in the centre of the face of the building, and was originally shut with a limestone plug. A sloping passage descends 14.35m to a vestibule, with three portcullises, slabs of granite. These block the horizontal passage which is 18m long and leads to an antechamber, off which to the E are three recesses probably for statues. This antechamber probably acted as a turning chamber for the black granite sarcophagus, which is still in position in the burial chamber to the W. The walls of the burial chamber of alabaster and limestone are inscribed and painted blue, with part of the Pyramid texts, the first use of these on a pyramid.

This pyramid was opened at the expense of Thomas Cook and Son by Gaston Maspero when he was director of antiquities as a tourist attraction. It remains one of the most interesting and easiest of the pyramids to enter.

The plan of the *Valley Temple* has never been entirely recovered because it lies partly under the modern approach road which would have to be re-routed before further work could be carried out. Enough has been done to show that it too was decorated with palmiform granite columns. When clearing the temple a splendid schist sarcophagus was found containing the body of Ptah-shepses, perhaps a son of Unas, though how it came to be placed in this temple is unknown. The most interesting thing found on the body was a gold and bead belt (now in the EM).

Immediately SW of the complex of Unas is the **Pyramid Complex of Horus Sekhemket**, discovered in 1950 by Dr Zakaria Goneim of the Dept of Antiquities. This consists of an unfinished step pyramid and panelled enclosure wall similar to that of Zozer's complex and probably also built by Imhotep. The Horus Sekhemkhet was apparently Zozer's successor although nothing is known of him beyond his monuments. This pyramid was never completed and the splendid alabaster sarcophagus found in the burial chamber seems not to have been used. The *South Tomb* contained a wooden sarcophagus with the body of a two-year-old child. This complex is not usually open to the public without special permission from the Dept of Antiquities.

The Pyramid of Unas is surrounded by mastabas of the relations and officials of the king. S of the Pyramid of Unas is the **Persian Shaft** (access down a spiral stair) containing the tombs of three officials of the Persian period. These are *Psamtik*, chief physician (found complete with gold mask and jewellery which is now in EM), *Zannehib*, commander of the king's ships, and *Paydees*. The *Tombs of Queen Khenut and Queen Nebet* are built just to the N of the Funerary Temple. The former is largely ruined, but the ground plan of the latter is almost complete, and there is a delightful scene with Nebet seated smelling a lotus. Close to the Step Pyramid enclosure is the ruined brick *Mastaba of Haishtef*, a priest of the Pyramid of Unas, and to the E is the *Tomb of Idut* (also called Seshseshat), a princess of the 5 Dyn. probably a daughter of Unas who usurped this tomb-chapel of a 5 Dyn. vizier called Ihuy. It is a large mastaba consisting of ten rooms, of which five are undecorated. The first room shows fishing and farming, the second transport of a statue, Muu dancers at the funeral, the pilgrimage to Sais, while Idut is shown in a papyrus boat. The chapel has the usual false door and offering scenes.

Adjacent to the E is the small but interesting *Mastaba of Mehu* (special permission needed from the Dept of Antiquities), found as late as 1940. It is 6 Dyn. when Mehu, son of Idut, was vizier under the early kings. It is brightly but rather crudely coloured. There are pictures of Mehu at the entrance, and on the W side a is chapel to an unknown individual called Mery-re-ankh. Hetep-ka, Mehu's son, is also shown.

Beside the N wall of the Pyramid of Unas and extending partly under its monuments the department excavators found at the beginning of the century a *Shaft and Storeroom* belonging to either the Horus Hotep-Sekhemawy or the Horus Raneb, one of the earliest kings of the 2 Dyn. This was the first time that tombs dating from this early period had been found at Ṣaqqārah and it was the prelude to the discoveries by the late Professor Emery of 1 Dyn. tombs (see below).

In clearing the causeway of the Pyramid of Unas towards the valley temple a number of mastabas were recovered including the *Mastaba of Ptah-iru-ke*, chief of the roads of the slaughterhouse, with rather crude colouring; a *Tomb of Akhti-hotep* with some wooden statues (now in the EM) and the *Mastaba of Nefer-Her-Ptah* which must have pre-dated the causeway which covers part of the entrance. This tomb belongs also to the 5 Dyn., but before the reign of Unas, and it was never finished. It has agricultural scenes of all kinds, including the vintage and the gathering of papyrus, while birds in cages have given this tomb-chapel the name of 'the Tomb of the Birds'. There are also some rock-cut tombs further down the causeway including those of *Ni-Ankh-Khnum* and *Khnum-Hotep*, 5 Dyn. priests of Re' in the Sun Temple of Nyuserre. These tombs also predate the causeway, as their entrances were largely blocked by this construction. Of the others one of the most interesting is the *Tomb of Nefer* where the body was recovered well-preserved.

S of the Causeway are several monuments which need to be mentioned. The recently rediscovered 18 Dyn. **Tomb-Chapel of Horemheb** was built before he became king; many of its very fine carved blocks are in museums all round the world. The other building to the S of the Tomb-Chapel of Nefer is the Coptic **Monastery of St. Jeremiah**, founded c 470, rebuilt several times and finally destroyed in 960 by the Muslims. It was cleared by Quibell before World War I. The main buildings were of mud-brick and the church had excellent stone columns and capitals. There were also some interesting religious paintings and Coptic inscriptions. (Many objects from here are now in the CM and the Louvre.)

Also discovered by the EES and Leiden Museum (in 1983) was the *Tomb of Tia*, sister of Ramesses II, and her husband, also named Tia, very unusual in being crowned with a small pyramid. In 1986 they refound the *Tomb of Maya*, treasurer to Tutankhamun, already known to be in the vicinity from the German discovery in the mid 19C.

The ***Step Pyramid Complex of Zozer** is undoubtedly the most splendid monument at Ṣaqqārah and it is unique in Egyptian architecture. This remarkable building—the work of Imhotep, the chief of works of Zozer, second king of the 3 Dyn. who reigned c 2667–2648 BC—was the first large construction in stone. The enclosure wall, also of stone, has only one entry and is decorated with recessed and panelled buttresses representing either the palace façade or the White Walls of Memphis.

It was not realised at first that Zozer was the king for whom this was built, as the building describes him under his Horus name of Netjerykhet. It was not until the

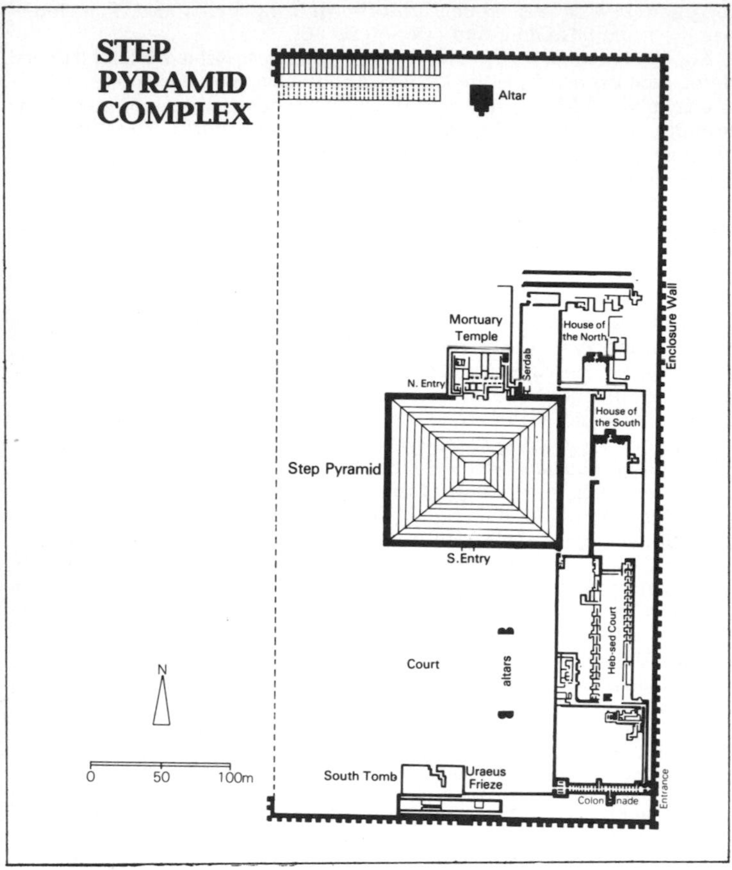
STEP PYRAMID COMPLEX
Altar
Mortuary Temple
House of the North
Serdab
Enclosure Wall
N. Entry
House of the South
Step Pyramid
S.Entry
Heb-sed Court
Court
altars
N
0
50
100m
South Tomb
Uraeus Frieze
Colonnade
Entrance

discovery of the Famine Stele at Seheil Island by C.E. Wilbur in 1888 that it was recognised that the two were one and the same.

It can be entered either by the single entry in the NE corner into the Heb Sed complex, or over the top of the enclosure wall at the S, passing the frieze of uraei and the Southern Tomb (see below) and proceeding directly to the pyramid and the mortuary temple, returning via the Heb-Sed buildings. It is more convenient to follow the second route.

The earliest account of this pyramid is that of the Prussian Consul-General von Minutoli who penetrated the subterranean galleries in 1821. He found part of a mummy and some inscriptions which he sent to Europe and which were lost at sea off the coast of Spain. The next man to examine the site was Colonel Howard Vyse who with his assistant J.S. Perring surveyed the pyramids here and at Giza and Dahshūr. Perring's work was remarkably accurate, and it is his survey which gives a first account of the subterranean galleries of this pyramid, and the rooms lined with blue faience tiles bearing the name of the Horus Netjerykhet. The work of Vyse was followed by that of the German Karl Lepsius who, after doing a further survey, removed part of the tiled walls to Berlin. It was not until after World War I that the

*The Pyramid of Zozer*

Dept of Antiquities began excavations around the pyramid. C.M. Firth, who was in charge of the work from 1920 until his death in 1931, found a large number of galleries packed with funeral vases of various stones such as alabaster, diorite, granite, schist and breccia, weighing over 90 tons in total, which took the department three years to remove. In 1927 M. Lauer joined Firth as his architect and he has been largely responsible for the work of restoration on the pyramid and its complex.

The buildings are constructed in fine white limestone, the first extensive use of stone in Ancient Egypt, while many of the architectural elements employed in this building also appear here for the first time. None of the stone blocks used by Imhotep was very large, as he was experimenting with the tensile strength of stone. However, the effect of the whole is extremely satisfactory, with delicate carving and pleasing lines. Although there was a mortuary temple, no causeway, or valley temple associated with the Step Pyramid has so far been discovered.

The whole complex is surrounded by a great limestone *Wall* measuring 545m from N to S and 277m from E to W. Of the walls 14 gates 13 are false, there being only one true entrance, at the S corner of the E side. The wall originally stood 10.4m high (20 cubits) and it is buttressed to represent the palace walls. After entering the single enclosure entrance through a series of engaged reeded columns the main court is reached. Here there are two B-shaped altars round which the king was said to run in the Heb-Sed ceremonies. The *Step Pyramid* began as a mastaba 63m sq. and 8m high. The core was of local limestone faced with finer Ṭurah material. Later Imhotep added 3m to this on all sides, and later 9m on the E making it a rectangle. He then added four mastabas, one above the other, to form the stepped pyramid. It finally measured 140m E to W and 118m N to S and was 60m high. This superstructure overlaid a 7m-sq. shaft sunk in the rock to a depth of 28m, at the base of which was an oblong burial chamber built of granite blocks, entered through a hole sealed with a granite plug weighing 3.5 tons. Surrounding the burial chamber, four underground passages and galleries were cut to contain the burial equipment. Some of these galleries were never finished, others were covered with blue faience tiles. Zozer's family was buried near his tomb in a series of shafts of which 11 were cut 32m deep. Tomb robbers had entered them all but in one was found the mummy of a child in an alabaster coffin, and the foot of another mummy, said to be of Old Kingdom date, found in the main burial chamber was probably all that was left of Zozer.

These galleries can only be entered with special permission from the Dept of Antiquities and they should not be attempted by those suffering from either vertigo or claustrophobia as the passages are narrow and dusty and often entail climbing up or down vertical ladders. The journey takes several hours and there is no lighting. If entered from the S there is a passage to the main shaft supported by 26 Dyn. columns, indicating that the pyramid had already begun to collapse in ancient times.

To the N of the pyramid is the *Mortuary Temple*, and beside it to the E is the *Serdab*, a small doorless room facing onto the casing with a seated statue of Zozer (a replica, the original has been removed to the EM). The outer wall of the Mortuary Temple is well preserved to a height of about 2m, but the interior is very much ruined. It is from here that the entry to the underground chambers is made.

Returning from the Mortuary Temple, on the N side of the pyramid is the *House of the North* with a façade of engaged fluted columns, while inside there is a cruciform sanctuary with three niches, and within a shallow recess in the wall of the court three engaged papyriform columns, the earliest so far known. Proceeding S, the *House of the South* is reached, only part of which remains; originally it stood some 12m high with four fluted and engaged columns in the façade. The chapel has been largely rebuilt by Lauer, and inside there are graffiti of the 18–19 Dyns extolling the beauties of the temple and mentioning the name of Zozer as its builder. The *Heb Sed Court* has been entirely rebuilt; the buildings are dummies and cannot be entered.

They are being reconstructed largely as a result of the scenes portrayed on the jar sealings, and ivory labels found in the 1 Dyn. tombs at Abydos, but the work is not yet finished. All that was left when Lauer started were the bases of the walls of the chapels and pavilions; he began in 1964 with an arched roof chapel with slender fluted columns. This was finished by 1968 and is joined by a curious curved wall to the main enclosure. A series of further dummy chapels are now being restored. The Heb Sed (or Festival of the Tail) was a feast carried out traditionally after 30 years of the king's reign. In fact it often took place more frequently; sometimes the king having waited 30 years to carry out his first Sed Festival then repeated them at more frequent intervals. It was an occasion when the officials and deities from all over Egypt came to wherever the king was and renewed their allegiance. All the ceremonies had to be carried out twice, once as King of the South and once as King of the North. In the Heb Sed pavilion, the king is seen seated back to back with his image each wearing the appropriate crowns and robes of the Two Lands.

Enter the Step Pyramid enclosure from the E. To the S is the *Southern Tomb*, the exact purpose of which is still uncertain. It may have served as an alternative tomb analogous to those of the 1 Dyn. kings at Abydos. However, this seems unlikely as it is known that Zozer had as a second tomb a mud-brick mastaba at Bayt Khallaf. Another suggestion is that it may have housed his viscera, as it is certainly connected with Osiris in some way, being decorated with djḍ-pillars. The tomb is also decorated with blue faience tiles. Nearby to the E is the earliest known *Uraeus Frieze*, another motif that was to become extremely popular later.

Just to the E of the NE corner of the Complex of Zozer is the **Pyramid Complex of**

**Userkaf**, the first king of the 5 Dyn. (c 2494 BC), identified in 1928 by C.M. Firth. The whole area is extensively ruined as it was used as a quarry in Saite times. The *Pyramid of Userkaf* (called Pure are the places of Userkaf) is built of local limestone, faced with finer Turah material. It has been robbed, probably in antiquity. The site is unusual in that there is only a *Small Chapel* on the E while the main *Mortuary Temple* is on the S. The excavator thought this was due to lack of space, but Riche and Fakhry have suggested that it was due to the growth of sun worship in the 5 Dyn. The complex was surrounded by a temenos wall, and was approached by a basalt-paved *Causeway*, originally with a portico supported by red granite columns. From this temple comes a granite head of Userkaf three times life size, now in the EM. The *Queen's Pyramid* is on the S and a *Subsidiary Pyramid* is on the W side of the temple. If a whole day is being spent at Ṣaqqārah this complex should be visited after that of Zozer; if time is limited it should be omitted.

NW of the Complex of Zozer is the **Mastaba of Ptah-hotep II and Akhet-hotep**, found by Mariette and cleared and recorded by N. de Garis Davies in 1898. It is easily reached on foot from the *Tented Rest House* situated near the site of Mariette's old house. Ptah-hotep was inspector of the prophets of the pyramids of Isesi, and Menkhauhor, and of the priests of the pyramid of Nyuserre, and therefore 5 Dyn. Akhet-hotep, overseer of the pyramid-town of Zadkare, seems to have been Ptah-hotep's father, but their relationship is uncertain. The entry and first hall are devoted to Akhet-hotep. The first corridor (A) shows his titles, but the upper register is damaged. In the section devoted to Ptah-hotep (B) there is a good scene of a desert hunt, with saluki-type dogs hunting ibex and oryx. There are vintage scenes and games which include a jumping game still practised in Egypt and also shown in the Mastaba of Mereruka (see below).

## MASTABA OF AKHET-HOTEP AND PTAH-HOTEP II

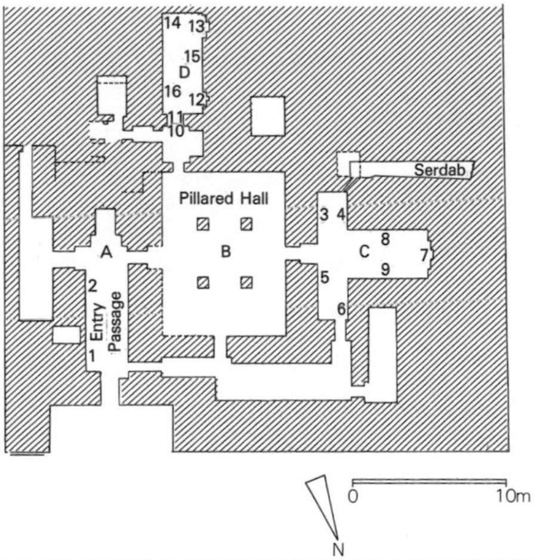
14 13
15
D
16 12
11
10
Serdab
Pillared Hall
3 4
8
C
7
9
A
B
5
6
2
Entry Passage
1
0
10m
N

(1–2) Corridor, offering scenes, wine jars, calves, boats and harvest scenes. (3–4) Akhet-hotep watching people bringing papyrus, boatmen, cattle. (5–6) Offerings of antelope, and products of the marshes. (7) False door. (8–9) Offerings. (10–11) Men with animals and offerings belonging to Ptah-hotep. (12–13) False doors with (14) list of estates. (15–16) Jewellers, musicians, officials and offering bearers.

NW is the **Serapeum**, the burial place of the Apis bulls, also called the House of Osarapis by the Ancient Egyptians. (The term 'Serapeum' properly refers only to the temple above ground.) The visitor usually sees only the underground rock-cut chambers. The Avenue of Sphinxes leading to this complex from the E was discovered by Mariette in 1850. He found that the sphinxes led to a dromos containing Greek statues of animals connected with the rites of Dionysius—peacocks, leopards and mythological creatures—and also a semicircle of Greek philosophers and poets that stands before a Temple of Nectanebo II (largely ruined).

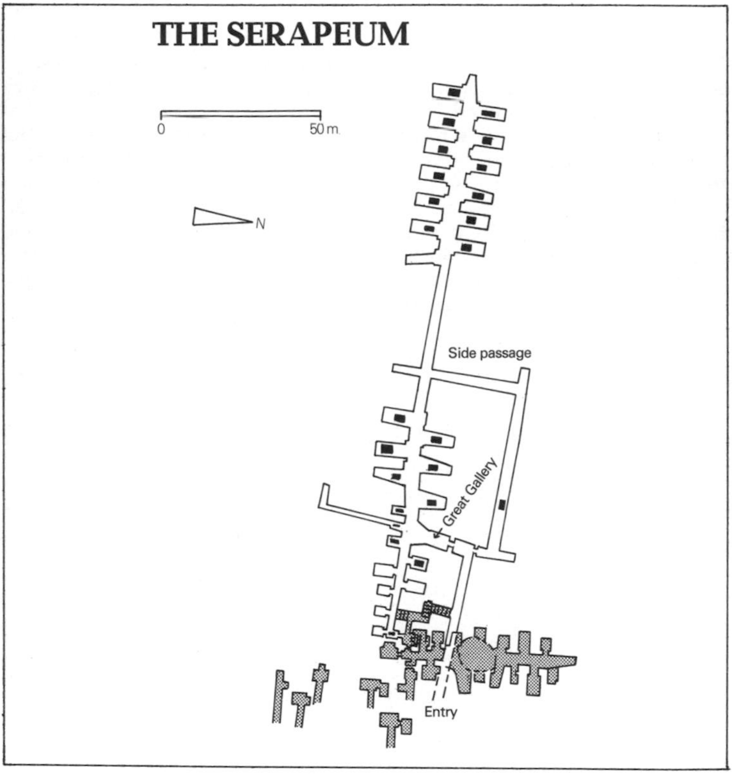
THE SERAPEUM
0
50 m
N
Side passage
Great Gallery
Entry

The cult of Serapis was introduced into Egypt from Europe by Ptolemy I with the intention of providing a god capable of being worshipped by both Greeks and Egyptians. Apis bulls were considered sacred from very early times in Egypt, as a representation of the soul of Ptah, and they also had close connections with Osiris as deliverers of oracles. In addition other gods such as Anubis, one of the gods associated with embalming, were worshipped here.

The actual burial place of the bulls was discovered after a long search in 1851 by Mariette from the Temple of Nectanebo II situated above it. There are several galleries dating from Amenhotep IV–Ramesses II; from the 19 Dyn. until Psamtik I (26 Dyn.) and from then to the Ptolemaic era. At the entry is a series of niches which once contained official and private stelae (now in the Louvre) recording many pilgrims who visited the sanctuary. There are 24 bull sarcophagi in the accessible galleries made of granite, basalt or limestone, mostly uninscribed. They are very large, 3.4m high and 5m long. The only listed ones are those of Amasis (26 Dyn.), Cambyses (27 Dyn.) and Khababash (30 Dyn.), the last native king of Egypt. Mariette found most of them robbed, only a few containing even the bones of the sacred bulls. It would appear that the bulls had been eaten to obtain merit, certainly under Khaʿemwaset, high-priest of Ptah at Memphis, son of Ramesses II, who was buried amidst them. One sarcophagus was intact and the jewellery from here is now in the Louvre.

Further NW, to the N of the site Mariette's House, is the 5 Dyn. **Mastaba of Ti**, overseer of the sun temples of Neferikare and Nyuserre, also discovered by Mariette. It consists of four rooms, a columned court with a shaft leading to the burial chamber (2), a long corridor (4), a small narrow room off this (3), and a rectangular pillared hall (5), off which opens a serdab (6), or closed corridor containing statues of the deceased (a replica, original in EM). It has some of the finest 5 Dyn. sculptured blocks so far found. The entry is through a columned portico with Ti carved on each side with his names and titles (1). Reliefs in the courtyard show some fine bird scenes (pigeons, cranes, storks) while in the inner chamber are offering scenes, hunting in the marshes, craftsmen at work and offering-bearers from Ti's estate. This mastaba is noted for its scenes of agricultural life.

It is generally advisable after visiting the Step Pyramid Enclosure to proceed directly to the **Mastaba of Mereruka** (good name Mera), situated

## MASTABA OF TI

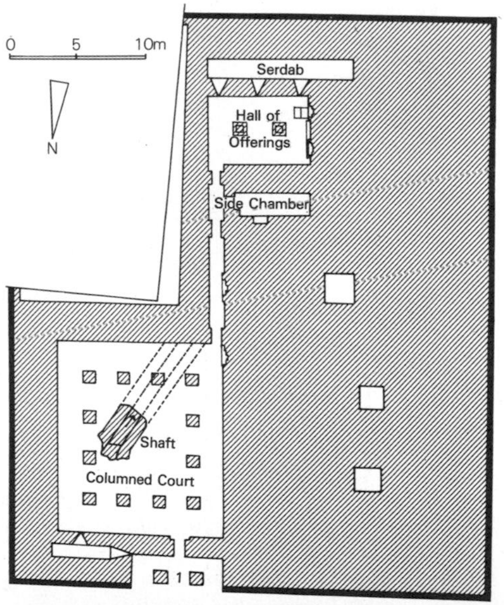
0
5
10m
N
Serdab
Hall of Offerings
Side Chamber
Shaft
Columned Court
1

just beside the Pyramid of Teti. The largest mastaba in Ṣaqqārah, containing 32 rooms, this is a family tomb; Mereruka's wife and son Meri-Teti are buried in chambers beneath. Mereruka was the vizier of Teti, whose daughter Har-watet-khet, good name Seshseshet, he married. He held a vast number of titles, including priest of the Pyramid of Teti, and his burial place was close to that of the king. When excavated the bodies of Mereruka and his wife were in their tombs; both were middle-aged. In the entry passage of the mastaba Mereruka is shown with titles (1–2) painting a picture of the seasons (4), while on the E wall he is depicted playing zenet, a sort of draughts (3). The best way to visit this mastaba is to turn right, see the first three rooms (Section A) with scenes of hunting, goldsmiths and furniture making (5–9). Turn into the large hall with four pillars, go on through room XI, passing Mereruka's false door and burial shaft (special permission must be obtained to visit the burial chamber), to the chapel with six pillars, Room XIII, where there is a fine statue of Mereruka. On the left of this are scenes of the Egyptians domesticating animals such as gazelles, goats, hyenas, etc (10) and boat-building (11–15). The rooms off this chapel to the N (Section C) are devoted to Meri-Teti and have not been finished. Har-watet-khet's group of rooms situated to the left of the door (Section B), containing a serdab and a false door over the burial shaft, should be visited last.

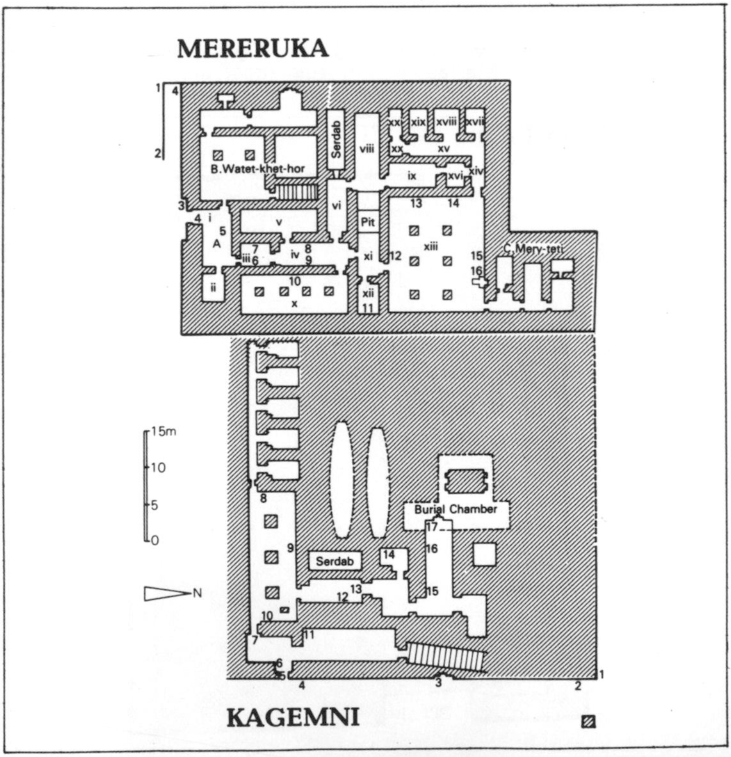
MERERUKA
B.Watet-khet-hor
Serdab
Pit
A
C.Mery-teti
15m
10
5
0
N
Burial Chamber
Serdab
KAGEMNI

To the E and abutting is the **Mastaba of Kagemni**, also a vizier of the 6 Dyn. The decoration on the walls of this small mastaba is of better quality than that of Mereruka. The scenes show Kagemni with titles (1–2) being carried in a carrying chair, fine scenes of cattle and birds including hunting and netting, and an aviary containing geese and ducks. There is also a notable scene of the feeding of a piglet.

Behind this are further mastabas in what is known as the **'Street of the Tombs'**. The best-known of these is probably that of **Ankh-ma-hor** (good name Sheshi), vizier and overseer of the Great House in the 6 Dyn. It is also known as the *Doctor's Tomb* because of the scenes of circumcision and medical treatment; it also has scenes of daily life. It consists of six rooms, No. 5 being the serdab. On each side of the door are (1–2) seated and standing pictures of Ankh-ma-hor wearing the official clothes of a vizier. (3) Winnowing and cattle in the water. (5) Scribes recording baking activities. (4) W wall, upper scenes destroyed, water scenes with crocodiles and hippopotami. (6) Market scenes on both sides. (7) Sculptors and metalsmiths. (8) Offering bearers. (9) The entry and room itself are decorated with offering scenes to the dead man, showing gazelles, oryx and geese. (10) Offering scenes and a false door in the serdab, representations of funerary furniture. (11–12) Room VI only partly decorated, entry, surgical scenes of circumcision, and operation on the right hand, and large toes and a pregnant woman. (13–14) The funeral procession. In the same street are other mastabas of 6 Dyn. officials of Teti, *Nefer-Seshem-Ptah*, *Nefer-Seshem-Re*' and *Nikau-Isesi*, usurped by *Sheshem-Nefer*, vizier to Teti. These are sometimes open for visiting, but at other times they are locked.

## MASTABA OF ANKH-MA-HOR

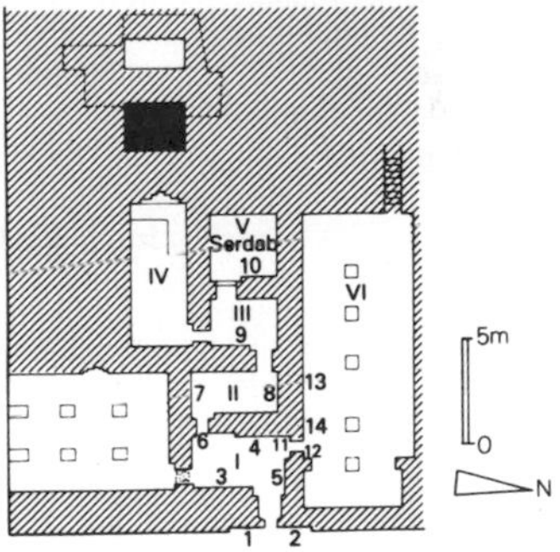
V
Serdab
10
IV
VI
III
9
7
II
8
13
14
6
4
11
12
I
3
5
1
2
5m
0
N

The **Pyramid Complex of Teti**, first king of the 6 Dyn., has a commanding position overlooking the valley on the edge of the plateau. It was excavated in 1881. The *Pyramid of Teti*, called 'The Place of Teti son of Re' is enduring forever', is much ruined. It is built of local limestone; its facing of better-quality stone, has been robbed though a few of the outer blocks are still in position. It is now some 65m sq. and stands 20m high. The entrance is at ground level in the centre of the N face. The door was blocked by a small offering chapel whose false door overlies the entry. The sloping passage is 15m long and leads to a vestibule, a short horizontal passage blocked by portcullises, and a turning chamber, on the E side of which is a recess probably for a statue of the king. The burial chamber still contains the basalt sarcophagus of the king. The wooden inner sarchophagus is in the EM. The ceilings are painted blue and covered with five-pointed stars, and the walls are decorated with sections of the pyramid texts. Unfortunately the walls have been very badly damaged and some of the blocks have been removed. There is a large *Mortuary Temple* with five niches and a small sanctuary set against the face of the pyramid; it appears to have been destroyed during the Second Intermediate Period, as Teti's cult was still flourishing during the Middle Kingdom. The Causeway has vanished and the Valley Temple, if it existed, has not been located. To the N are two small pyramids of Teti's queens but both are covered by sand.

The *Pyramid of Queen Iput* appears to have been completed by her son Pepi. This was excavated by the Dept of Antiquities under Loret in 1897–99 and later by Quibell in 1907–08. It measures just some 15.5m sq. by 4.5m high. The burial chamber at the bottom of a deep shaft contained a limestone sarcophagus, with its lid still in position, although it had been robbed. The queen's skeleton was inside a cedar coffin and the thieves may have been disturbed as they overlooked some fragments of the queen's jewellery. These were parts of a necklace and one bracelet. Her small *Mortuary Temple* is ruined, but there are the remains of a large false door of limestone with her name and titles and an offering table of red granite. The *Pyramid of Queen Kawit* has been largely destroyed.

In 1984 the French Mission discovered an 18 Dyn. *Funerary Complex* reused in the 22 Dyn. A large number of cat mummies were recovered. Examination proved that many of them were young animals, while others were wild, not domesticated.

On the ridge of the escarpment, beyond the Teti complex, running N from the Dept of Antiquities Offices, the late Professor Emery discovered the *1 Dyn. Royal Tombs*. These tombs consist of a vast pit burial chamber and a mud-brick superstructure with many store rooms. They are now difficult to identify as they are half filled with blown sand and are of interest only to archaeologists. There are some 12 of these early mastabas decorated with the palace façade, but they have not all been satisfactorily identified. Some, though not all, duplicate other tombs at Abydos which are probably only cenotaphs of the early kings. To the N lies the village of Abū Ṣīr (Rte 24).

S of the ticket office is the village of (2km) **Ṣaqqārah**, with further monuments known as **South Ṣaqqārah**. Visits to this area require special permits from the Dept of Antiquities. The village is a rambling collection of houses set amid the palm groves about 15 minutes' walk from the monuments. It can be reached from the agricultural road which extends S from the ticket office at Ṣaqqārah. Donkeys may be hired at the rest house in N Ṣaqqārah and the journey to the southern monuments takes about half an hour. However, the village has to be visited to obtain the keys for the Pyramid of Pepi II and the Mastabat al-Farāʿūn.

Due W of the village is the **Pyramid Complex of Pepi I**, unfortunately extremely ruined and still being excavated by a French team. It appears as little more than a heap of debris about 70m sq. and 12m high. From one of the pyramid's titles the name 'Memphis' was given by classical authors to the whole area and the city.

The whole of the centre of the *Pyramid*, including the immense limestone corbels of the tomb chamber, has collapsed. The black basalt sarcophagus was smashed in antiquity, but a rose granite canopic chest containing alabaster jars was found (now in EM). The pyramid texts are of exceptional quality, those in the corridor being smaller than those in the tomb chamber and filled with green pigment. When clearing NE of the pyramid numerous builders marks were uncovered giving the date of construction. Some of the blocks were incribed with the name of Q. Sesehot the mother of Teti, which had been reused.

A survey was carried out by the French Misson of the plateau of Pepi I. Soundings revealed a mastaba of Meryre Ankh, a pyramid priest of Pepi I. Also discovered was a limestone pyramid of one of Pepi's queens in an excellent state of preservation.

To the SW is the **Pyramid Complex of Merenreʿ**, brother and successor of Pepi I. The *Pyramid* was never finished and it was vandalised by tomb robbers. Inside was a black basalt sarcophagus (though the mummy seems to have been that of a later king). The entrance was in the N face. Of the *Mortuary Temple* only the base can be seen on the E side. A series of beautiful limestone figures of prisoners of the North and South was found in 1968–69. They probably lined the processional way from the Valley Temple to the Mortuary Temple.

Both of these monuments have recently been excavated by the CNRS and EAO.

The **Pyramid Complex of Djedkare Isesi** lies 400m to the SE of the Complex of Pepi I on the edge of the plateau.

It was identified comparatively recently by an Egyptian Egyptologist, Abdel Salam Hussein. It had been investigated in the last century, but the interior was uninscribed and could not be identified. Not until 1946 was Hussein, excavating the Mortuary Temple, able to identify the owner as Djedkare Isesi, penultimate king of the 5 Dyn.

The *Pyramid of Djedkare Isesi* (called 'Isesi is beautiful'), partly sanded over, still stands c 25m high, a similar size to that of Pepi II. It had been robbed and the entry passage on the N side is still not passable. The interior plan seems similar to that of Unas. A small vestibule leads first to a horizontal passage, an antechamber and the burial chamber. The horizontal passage has three granite portcullises, all raised. The blocks lining the antechamber and the burial chamber have been removed, but the pitched roof built of huge limestone slabs is still in position. The basalt sarcophagus originally set at the W end has been shattered. Some fragments of a mummified body of a middle-aged man were found, probably an indication that Isesi had been buried here.

The *Mortuary Temple* has been almost completely robbed, having been destroyed in the 17 Dyn. and later used as a burial ground during the 18 Dyn. However, it must originally have been beautifully decorated, as the excavations revealed many good reliefs, as well as interesting architectural fragments of the temple such as statues of foreign prisoners, lions, bulls and sphinxes. In spite of the devastation it seems that the plan was similar to other 5 Dyn. mortuary temples.

Excavating in 1952–53, Ahmed Fakhry found the *Queen's Pyramid* and, attached to it, a *Mortuary Temple* rather larger than had hitherto been found. It was again severely damaged, but was decorated with a fine selection of reliefs. The *Causeway* leading from the main pyramid to the *Valley Temple* can be clearly seen but the temple itself has not been excavated.

700m SW of the Complex of Pepi I is the curious structure called locally

**Mastabat al-Farā'ūn** (Seat of Pharaoh), the monument of King Shepseskaf of the 4 Dyn. It is constructed of huge blocks of limestone, in the same sarcophagus shape as that of Queen Khentkawes at Giza (Rte 23). Nearby, M. Jéquier, the Swiss excavator, found a Middle Kingdom relief re-establishing the worship and cult of King Shepseskaf; there seems little doubt that this was connected with the present building. The outer casing has been destroyed but Jéquier found enough to show that it had been covered with a fine layer of Turah limestone blocks, over a lower layer of granite blocks, ending as a vast sarcophagus with an arched top. The interior of the monument has been thoroughly investigated, first by Lepsius in 1843, then by Mariette in 1858, and finally by Jéquier in 1924. The entrance to the substructure in the centre of the N side leads to a long descending passage opening into a horizontal corridor, opening off which is an ante-chamber, with the burial room on the right, and several storerooms on the left. The stone is well dressed but the structure was never finished, and Jéquier's opinion is that it was not used for a burial. Only fragments of a sarcophagus were found. Where Shepseskaf was finally buried is uncertain.

Attached to it on the E face was a *Mortuary Temple*; of which only the inner shrine, built of dressed blocks again with a granite base, remains in position. The walls of the temple have been destroyed but there are still visible channels in the pavement leading to a rectangular basin. The king must have died before the temple was finished, as it has been completed in mud brick rather than stone. A *Causeway* which can be traced for 760m leads to a so-far undiscovered Valley Temple that must lie under the modern village of South Ṣaqqārah. The Causeway is 1.6m wide and roughly plastered; it was roofed but undecorated. In the Mortuary Temple were found fragments of a statue whose name finished with an f, which may have belonged to Shepseskaf.

Immediately W of the Mastabat al-Farā'ūn is the **Pyramid Complex of Pepi II** of the 6 Dyn. Pepi II is the king credited with the longest known reign, some 94 years. The complex consists of a pyramid, three subsidiary pyramids, a complex mortuary temple, causeway and valley temple. It was excavated in 1926–36 by Jéquier on behalf of the Dept of Antiquities. It is the most complete of all the 6 Dyn. royal monuments found at Ṣaqqārah, even though it was extensively robbed in the Middle Ages by people hunting for the well-dressed limestone blocks. The *Valley Temple* lies on the edge of the cultivation, facing E, and is entered by two ramps situated on the N and S ends of a large platform, which probably acted as a landing stage. The platform seems to have been bordered by thick masonry walls with the main entry in the E facade, slightly off-centre. The roof was supported on rectangular pillars rather like those of the 4 Dyn. and unlike the palm columns normally found in 5 and 6 Dyn. structures at Ṣaqqārah and elsewhere. The Valley Temple was decorated with limestone blocks carved in a delicate but conventional style similar to those in Sahure's temple at Abū Ṣīr. The *Causeway* is partly destroyed but can be easily followed by the embankments still showing. To the N is the small *Pyramid of King Nakare-Aba* which is probably of the 8 Dyn. There are at least two granite doorways in the upper part of the causeway, with the door jambs bearing the king's names. One had a vestibule and a small porters' shelter, probably for the guardians of the area. The whole causeway is over 500m long.

The *Mortuary Temple of Pepi II* is for the most part fairly clear. It is entered through a destroyed entry and a small passage, leading in turn to a second passage, opening onto a vestibule, some 38m long. The walls have been decorated with reliefs, many of which have been replaced, showing hunting and triumph scenes. This vestibule leads to a central court which was surrounded by a colonnade of 18 quartzite pillars. Only their bases remain, although one has been re-erected. They seem to have been decorated with reliefs of the king clasped by a deity. The walls of the court were apparently plain but fragments found on the ground suggest that some of the surrounding chambers were decorated. The sanctuary is reached through a narrow antechamber; it is decorated with sacrificial scenes. Although the temple was small, the work on the reliefs was carefully carried out. A *Temenos Wall* surrounds the pyramid complex. Close to the SE face of the pyramid is a small *Subsidiary Pyramid* built of limestone blocks. In addition to the usual temenos wall surrounding the pyramid complex, there was a high thick *Girdle Wall* set against the pyramid itself. It has been suggested that this was added later to preserve the stability of the pyramid after an earthquake.

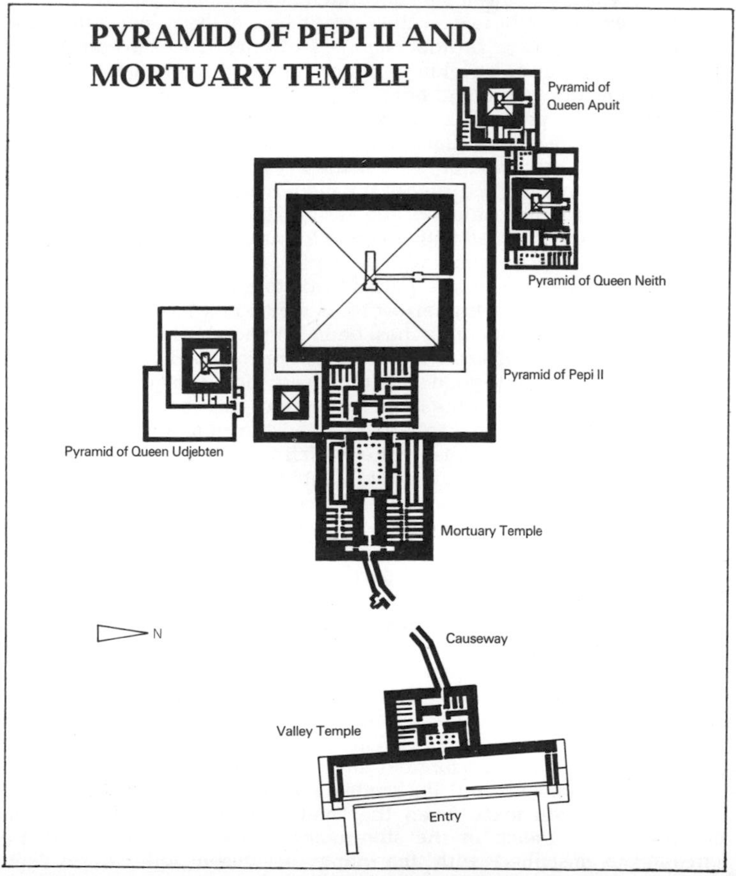
PYRAMID OF PEPI II AND
MORTUARY TEMPLE
Pyramid of
Queen Apuit
Pyramid of Queen Neith
Pyramid of Pepi II
Pyramid of Queen Udjebten
Mortuary Temple
N
Causeway
Valley Temple
Entry

The *Pyramid of Pepi II* (called 'Pepi is established and alive'), built of coarse limestone blocks, originally stood 52m high and 76m sq. with an angle of about 53°. Some of the better quality casing stone is still in position on the W side. The entrance is at ground level on the N side, where there are a few traces of the small *Offering Chapel* that once stood here, now largely removed, probably during the building of the girdle wall, and the stone re-used. Internally the pyramid is like that of Pepi I. The passage, some 16m long, descends into the natural rock and all the passages and chambers of the burial section are rock-cut. About mid-way down the passage is the fitting for a granite portcullis, the stone of which has been removed. The passage leads to a vestibule decorated on the ceiling with stars and on the walls with sections of the Pyramid Texts. During the excavation alabaster jars and a gold implement of uncertain use were found here. Beyond the vestibule is a 38m-long passage, with three portcullises. This passage ends in an antechamber. The gabled roof of this room is decorated with stars and the walls with Pyramid Texts. From the W edge of the antechamber a short passage leads to the burial chamber, which also has a star-decorated ceiling and Pyramid Texts on the walls, except for those near the sarcophagus at the W end of the room which have a 'palace façade' style decoration. The sarcophagus of polished black granite is still in position. The lid, though not the box that held the canopics, was found here.

Attached to the pyramid complex of Pepi II are the pyramids of three of his queens, interesting in that they also contain sections of the Pyramid Texts. The best preserved of these is the *Pyramid of Queen Neith*, lying directly opposite the NW corner of the main pyramid. It is about 21m sq., but now only 4m high, much of the casing stone is still in position. It is enclosed in a temenos wall with an entry through a narrow passage in the E corner of the S wall. The vestibule walls were covered with reliefs. A colonnaded court with square pillars leads to a cult chamber and three niches. There is also a long narrow room which may have served for the serdab statue. The sanctuary has been damaged and the false door removed; before it was an offering table. This pyramid also has a small *Subsidiary Pyramid*, in a good state of preservation. The queen's pyramid is entered in the centre of the N face (the entry was concealed by a false door). The passage, at an angle of 25°, leads down to a vestibule at the end of which was a portcullis, part of which was still in position. Beyond this is an antechamber leading straight into the burial chamber; both the antechamber and burial chamber are decorated, the ceilings with stars, the walls with Pyramid Texts. The wall behind the granite sarcophagus is decorated to represent the palace façade. There is also a granite canopic chest. The inscriptions and wall decorations are very much cruder than those in the temple, or in Pepi's pyramid.

To the W lies the small *Pyramid of Queen Apuit*. The entry to this complex is far better preserved than that of Neith, with door jambs and lintels of red granite. The plan of the complex is similar to that of Neith differing only where the topography restricted the builders. No fragments of reliefs were found in this temple and the store rooms were in the reverse position to those of Neith. The whole pyramid is in a poor state of preservation, the burial chamber largely destroyed, the granite sarcophagus in fragments and the walls damaged although they too were once covered with texts. Even the small *Satellite Pyramid* has been destroyed. In a trench in the storerooms was found a black granite sarcophagus inscribed with the name of Queen Ankhnes-en-Pepi, another of Pepi's wives, who was apparently the mother of a king called Neferkare of the 7 Dyn. The sarcophagus had a re-used lid of basalt with the original names and titles erased. Nearby was a broken stele of limestone with the queen's names and titles.

On the S side of Pepi's pyramid is the *Pyramid of Queen Udjebten*, also badly damaged. The Mortuary Chapel has suffered most, being virtually razed, but although the outer walls of the pyramid have been robbed, the walls of the burial chamber are still virtually intact and contain many texts.

The whole of Pepi's complex is surrounded by *Tombs of Nobles and Officials*. These were also examined by Jéquier who found that they consist of a burial chamber reached by a shaft orientated from N to S and entered usually from the N side. The shafts vary in depth from 2–12m; in the better tombs they are lined and roofed with limestone slabs. Some are decorated in relief, some only painted. The inscriptions contain prayers to Osiris and lists of offerings.

A group of three pyramids lies 1.6km SE of the Mastabat al-Faraʿun, of which only one, that to the N, has so far been identified. This is the **Pyramid Complex of Userkare Khendjer** of the 13 Dyn., enclosed within two temenos walls, the outer of mud-brick, the inner of white limestone. The *Pyramid of Userkare Khendjer* excavated by Jéquier in 1929 follows the general Middle Kingdom plan of a mud-brick core and a limestone facing; originally it must have been about 35m high. An inscription left by one of the architects of Ramesses II indicates that the 19 Dyn. was responsible for removing the casing stone though why this should be so when his son was restoring monuments at North Ṣaqqārah is remarkable. The entry is on the W side but the interior is not accessible. To the E is the *Mortuary Temple* while on the N side is a small *Offering Chapel*, where a small black granite pyramidion, inscribed on all sides, was found (now in EM). At the NE of the complex is a *small pyramid* belonging to one of his queens. About 25m sq., it appears to have been unused.

To the S are the pyramids of Dahshūr (Rte 26).

# 26 Dahshūr

Although the most northerly monuments on this route can be reached from Rte 25, the total distance via the H2 is approx. 12km with another drive across cultivation to the desert site. Again a tour of the site involves a good deal of walking over sand.

**Al-Badrashayn**.—10km **Minshat Dashūr**.—2km **Dashūr**.

Continuing S from al-Badrashayn (Rte 25) the H2 passes (4km) *al-Marāzīq*, beyond which (4km) a road crosses E to W (E across a bridge to the East Bank; Rte 28). Turning W, it crosses the Libayni Canal and (2km) the N–S road and continues to the village of **Minshat Dahshūr**. The road goes on NW across the desert to the Giza–Fayyūm road but just beyond the edge of the cultivation (2km) lies the pyramid field of **Dahshūr**. Opposite the Pyramid of Amenemhat III a dirt track leads into the desert, passing the modern cemetery.

It is possible to take a donkey or a sand-cart from Ṣaqqārah. The site is easily seen on a clear day from the wall of Zozer's pyramid. The 3km site contains pyramids of the 4 and 12 Dyns, the earliest and most imposing of which are the two massive stone pyramids of Sneferu, founder of the 4 Dyn., the pyramid at the N being conventional, but that to the S is of unusual shape.

Although both pyramids were visited in the 17C and later, it was not until Perring's investigation in 1839 that any proper account of them was given. Towards the end of the 19C Dahshūr was examined by de Morgan who excavated the pyramids of Amenemhat II and Senusert III near the edge of the cultivation. Not until 1945 were further extensive works undertaken when the Antiquities Service created a new department for pyramid studies under the direction of Abdel Salam Hussein. The death of Hussein in 1949 put a temporary end to this work, but it was recommenced under Ahmed Fakhry in 1951. He cleared the interior of the Bent Pyramid and found a valley temple. This was a remarkable find as the area had been extensively robbed for the medieval buildings of Cairo. Excavations have restarted near the Pyramid of Amenemhat III where further royal tombs have been found.

At the N of the field, on the edge of the escarpment, is the 12 Dyn. **Pyramid Complex of Senusert III**. It was investigated both by Perring and

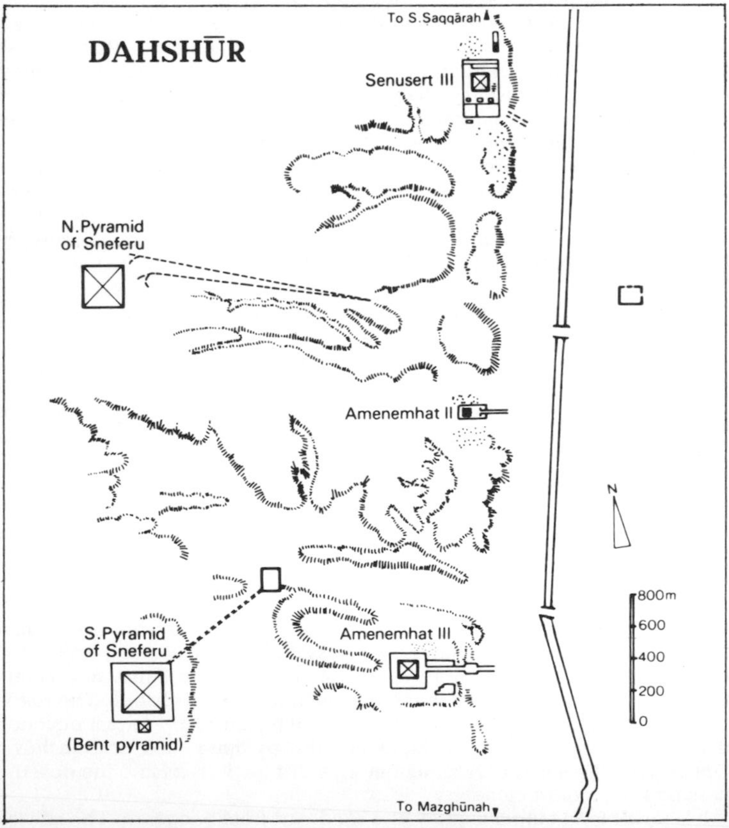
DAHSHŪR
To S.Saqqārah
Senusert III
N.Pyramid of Sneferu
Amenemhat II
N
800m
600
400
200
0
S.Pyramid of Sneferu
(Bent pyramid)
Amenemhat III
To Mazghūnah

Vyse in 1839 and de Morgan in 1894. Both found inscriptions of the king in the ruined *Mortuary Temple*. The *Valley Temple*, which has never been cleared, is joined to this by a *Causeway*. The *Pyramid of Senusert III* is built of mud brick, cased with limestone blocks bonded together by cramps, some of which may still be seen, but the pyramid is now greatly ruined. It is entered through a pit on the W side (the interior is inaccessible), the N entry having apparently been abandoned for reasons of security. The burial chamber as described by de Morgan was lined with red granite and at the W side stood a panelled red granite sarcophagus. A gallery from the NE side of the pyramid leads to the *Royal Tombs* of several members of the king's family.

Here de Morgan found the jewellery of the princesses of the dynasty (now in the Jewel Room of the EM), material of the highest quality. S of the surrounding wall three perfect cedar boats some 10m long were found, and fragments of another five vessels. With them was a large sledge used for their transport. (Two of these boats are in the EM, the third is in the Chicago Natural History Museum.) It seems almost certain that Senusert III was buried in this pyramid surrounded by his family and officials.

To the SW is the **North Pyramid Complex of Sneferu**. Recently not accessible, the *North Pyramid of Sneferu*, called 'Sneferu gleams', is built of local limestone, cased with finer Ṭurah material, but much of which has been lost. In size it resembles the pyramids at Gīzah being 220m sq., 99m high, with an angle of 43°40′; in fact it considerably exceeds the Pyramid of Khafre in volume, thus being the second most massive pyramid. The entry is in the middle of the N face, c 28m above ground level (interior inaccessible) and leads to a passage descending at an angle, 60m long. This leads to three chambers with corbelled roofs similar in style to those of the S Pyramid (see below). No trace of a royal burial was found here either when investigated in the last century by Perring and Vyse, or more recently by Fakhry.

The Valley Temple and Mortuary Temple have not been found. If Sneferu was buried in either of these structures it is far more likely to have been in the southern one. Work on this pyramid has been hampered by fallen blocks.

The **Pyramid Complex of Amenemhat II**, called 'Amenemhat is strong'. Lying to the SE, also on the edge of the escarpment, is the earliest 12 Dyn. complex on the site. The Valley Temple of this pyramid has never been discovered, but must have existed as a *Causeway* over 800m long extending from the edge of the cultivation to the pyramid. The *Mortuary Temple* is very much ruined but contained sufficient slabs inscribed with the name of Amenemhat to identify the monument. The *Pyramid of Amenemhat II* was excavated by de Morgan (1894–95). He found it ruined but was able to penetrate the interior. It is so damaged that even the overall dimensions are slightly uncertain. It is built of brick divided into compartments filled with sand, and must originally have been faced with limestone, but this has been robbed long since. The entry is in the N face (now inaccessible), from which a long sloping gallery protected by two portcullises leads to the burial chamber. The sandstone sarcophagus is still in place on the W side of the burial chamber. Amenemhat was probably buried here, as to the W of the pyramid are the *Tombs* of the queen and four of his princesses.

SE of Amenemhat's pyramid is a mass of limestone blocks with a *Causeway* running towards the cultivation; this has never been investigated and almost certainly represents the remains of another *Pyramid*.

Directly S is the **Pyramid Complex of Amenemhat III**, close to the cultivation and the village of Minshat Dahshūr. It was joined to an undiscovered valley temple, which must be situated near the cultivation, by a *Causeway* c 600m long and c 18.5m wide, originally paved with limestone slabs. E of the pyramid is the *Mortuary Temple*, now almost entirely destroyed, and nearby are a number of mud-brick structures probably used to house the temple officials. The mud-brick *Pyramid of Amenemhat III*, (called 'Amenemhat is beautiful'), was originally about 100m sq. and cased in limestone which has been systematically robbed, as has much of the brick core, though Perring was able to calculate that the angle was 57°20′. A grey granite pyramidon bearing Amenemhat's name was found here (now in the EM). The entry to the pyramid is off-centre on the E side (now inaccessible) and the burial chamber contains a red granite sarcophagus. But it is certain that the king was not buried here, but at his second pyramid at Ḥawārah (Rte 29) and that this served as a cenotaph. Recent work by the German Archaeological Institute in Cairo has found a well and the foundation depsoits of the pyramid, with foundation bricks, two bulls' skulls, and a great deal of pottery. Also within the complex lie the *Tomb of Awibreʿ Hor* and a small *Pyramid of Ameny ʿAamu*, two 13 Dyn. kings.

Due W lies the **South Pyramid Complex of Sneferu** from which rises the immense bulk of the *South Pyramid of Sneferu*, also known as the 'Bent Pyramid' or 'Rhomboidal Pyramid'. It is probable that this was where King Sneferu was buried. This structure measures 188.6m sq. and is 101.15m high. The angle of the slope is 54°31′ to a height of 49.07m, and then changes to 43°21′; this change of slope gives the pyramid its popular names. It is constructed of local limestone, cased with fine white Ṭurah limestone laid in sloping courses, the blocks being tilted from the outside to the inside, which makes them very difficult to remove. In construction it is similar to the 3 Dyn. pyramids.

No satisfactory explanation for the change of angle has been forthcoming. One theory has it that if the original angle had been maintained the great weight of the masonry would have crushed the interior structures—they are certainly cracked, and have been repaired anciently by plastering. Others suggest that the pyramid needed to be finished in a hurry, and that by changing the angle this was accomplished. Yet another proposal is that the casing would have slipped, but this is impossible because of the method of construction. A recent theory is that the collapse of the Maydum pyramid while this one was building caused the change of plan.

The entry to the pyramid is on the N face at 11.8m. On either side are sockets for a flap door. A descending passage 79.53m long but only 1.1m high ends in a horizontal corridor with a corbelled roof 12.6m high. To reach the lower chamber a ladder has to be climbed to a point on the wall 6.25m above the floor. The lower chamber is also corbelled and on the S wall are the entries to two passages. One is vertical and leads to no known passage or room. The other, higher in the wall, c 12.6m with damaged ceiling, slopes upwards to a horizontal passage leading to the upper chamber lying beyond a portcullis. A remarkable feature of this room are the cedar beams which must have been imported from the Lebanon. From the horizontal passage a further corridor slopes up to the W face of the pyramid, where it emerges 33.32m from the base. Climbing about inside this pyramid, which is unlit, gives a very good idea of the conditions that the early pyramid investigators encountered, even though the modern visitor is helped by the ladders left by Fakhry.

At the E of the pyramid is a small *Mortuary Temple* consisting of a little shrine, open to the E and W, under which was a large limestone slab surmounted by an alabaster offering table. The shrine is flanked by two large stelae and surrounded by a mud-brick wall. Alterations were made to the temple both in the Middle Kingdom and the Ptolemaic period, when the worship of Sneferu was revived, and the excavators found a bowl of charcoal still on the alabaster offering table waiting for the incense to be added.

A *Subsidiary Pyramid* lies to the S of the main structure. It was cleared (1946–47) by Hussein and found empty; no trace of any burial was dicovered, only some pottery. It was too small to have contained the material of Sneferu's Queen Hetepheres found at Gīza (Rte 23) and so far her original burial place remains undiscovered. The *Valley Temple* of the pyramid lies to the E of the building about half way to the cultivation. It is a simple rectangular building (47.16m by 26.20m) surrounded by a thick brick temenos wall. It contains an interesting collection of sculptured friezes representing the royal estates of Upper and Lower Egypt as well as two large limestone stelae adorned with the names and representations of the king. Additionally there must have been larger-than-life statues of the king, but only fragments of these remain, and the whole temple is gradually sanding up.

The road runs S along the Libaynī Canal for a further 4km where a track leads W to the pyramids of **Mazghūnah**. These two pyramids are almost completely destroyed and all that can be seen are low mounds of stones. They appear to be 12 or more probably 13 Dyn.

To the S the road runs into (2km) the village of *Dahshūr*.

# 27 Al-Lisht, Maydūm and Banī Suwayf

In this continuation of Rte 26 the distances covered are much greater—approx. 80km. The two major sites again lie in the desert to the W of the valley road.

**Minshat Dahshūr**.—18km **al-ʿAyāt**.—5km *al-Matāniyyah*.—3km **al-Lisht**.—32km **Maydūm**.—2km **Ishmant**.—20km **Banī Suwayf** (—12km **Ihnasiyyah al-Madīnah**).

From the road to Minshat Dahshūr (Rte 26) the H2 passes (5km) the village of *Mazghūnah* and continues to (13km) **al-ʿAyāṭ**, capital town of the district in the province of Giza. 5km beyond lies **al-Matāniyyah** from which a road leads W across the Libayni Canal to (3km) **al-Lisht**.

It is possible to drive on to the plateau and park to the S of the pyramids although buses cannot get through the narrow roads of the village.

There are two pyramid complexes in this section of the field, those of the first two kings of the 12 Dyn. That to the N is the **Pyramid Complex of Amenemhat I**, the founder of the dynasty. It is called 'Amenemhat is high and beautiful'. The larger of the two monuments it was excavated in part by the Metropolitan Museum. The pyramid and its associated buildings are situated in a commanding position, on two levels; burials of the royal

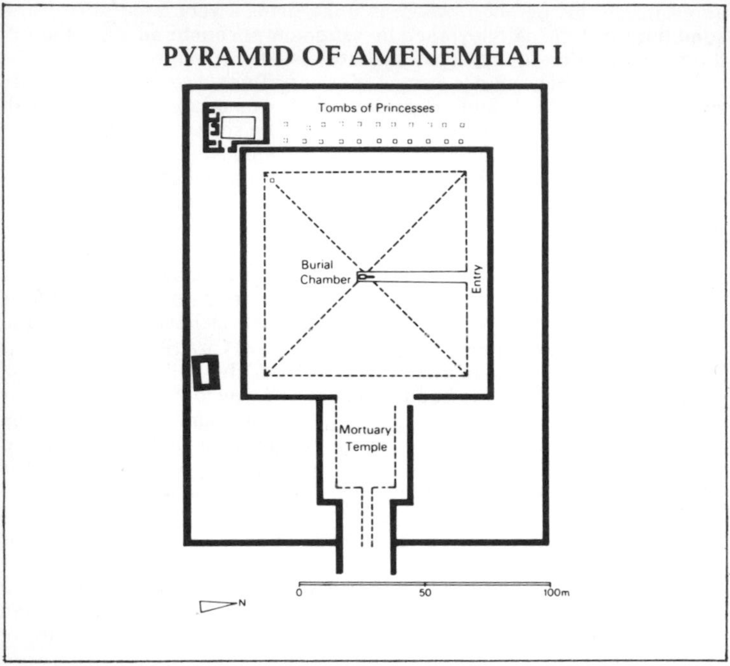
PYRAMID OF AMENEMHAT I
Tombs of Princesses
Burial Chamber
Entry
Mortuary Temple
0
50
100m
N

family and officials were also included in the complex. The Valley Temple which must have existed, as there is a *Causeway* leading to it, has not been found. The pyramid and buildings are surrounded by a temenos wall, and the *Mortuary Temple*, very ruined, is situated on the E side. This temple was decorated with reliefs, and had a ceiling spangled with stars, blocks of which are still lying about the site. Much of the stone used in the construction came from Giza and Ṣaqqārah and was Old Kingdom in date. At present the *Pyramid of Amenemhat I*, called 'The places of Sehetipebre (the prenomen of Amenemhat) are shining', stands about 20m high, but originally it was some 38m higher, and 84m sq. The entry is on the N side where a passage slopes down to an upper room, below which is the burial chamber (now under water).

The **Pyramid Complex of Senusert I**, son of Amenemhat I, is S of that of his father; it is slightly more difficult of access. It was named 'The one who is associated with the places of Senusert'. No valley temple has been found but the presence of a *Causeway*, constructed of fine white limestone blocks decorated with coloured reliefs, suggests that there was one. The Pyramid is surrounded by two *enclosure walls*. The outer wall, of mud brick, enclosed the *Nine Lesser Pyramids* of the royal family, each built of local limestone blocks, with its own Mortuary Temple, and within its own enclosure. The inner wall enclosed the mortuary temple and originally stood some 5m high, decorated with relief panels (most of which have been removed); the bases of a few on the S and W sides remain in situ.

The *Mortuary Temple* is similar in plan to those of the late Old Kingdom, and it had a granite offering table (many of the reliefs from here

## PYRAMID OF SENUSERT I

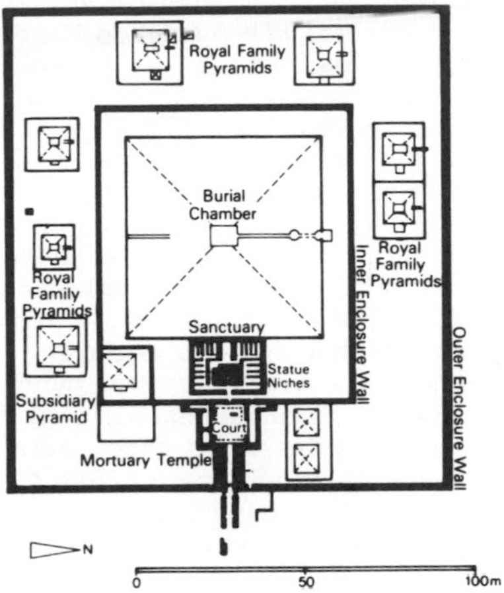
Royal Family Pyramids
Burial Chamber
Royal Family Pyramids
Inner Enclosure Wall
Royal Family Pyramids
Sanctuary
Outer Enclosure Wall
Statue Niches
Subsidiary Pyramid
Court
Mortuary Temple
N
0
50
100m

are now in the EM). In a small cache just N of the temple were found ten seated and painted life-sized statues of Senusert I, also now in the EM. S of the pyramid is a small *Subsidiary Pyramid*, within its own enclosure wall, and still retaining some of its limestone casing blocks. The *Pyramid of Senusert I*, called 'Senusert surveys the Two Lands' in the foundation deposits but 'Protected are the places of Senusert' in other sources, originally stood 61m high with a base 105m sq. and an angle of 49°. It has a core with walls separating the fill into a number of irregular chambers. The chambers were then filled with rubble and sand, and faced with good limestone. In the centre of the N face of the pyramid is a small *Offering Chapel* covering the entry to the pyramid which is now blocked. The burial chamber is below water level. The descending passage was lined with red granite.

About 200m E of the outer wall of the complex is one of the most interesting monuments at Lisht, the **Tomb of Senusert Ankh**, the high-priest of Ptah at Memphis and royal builder. It is usually locked and arrangements should be made before leaving Cairo to have the caretaker in attendance. The mastaba has now been destroyed, but entry to the burial chamber may be made through a shaft 11m deep. The burial chamber (5.4m by 2.6m) is decorated with painted reliefs of great interest in that some of the Old Kingdom Pyramid Texts are reproduced. The ceiling is decorated with stars and the sarcophagus to the S seems to have been made of blocks of stone set in a cavity in the floor.

The agricultural track leads S to Maydūm.

S of al-Matāniyyah the H2 continues to (7km) *Kafr ʿAmmār*. Just to the S is the site of *Ṭarkhān*, excavated by Petrie (1912–13). It contained the remains of a 23–25 Dyn. temple and large cemeteries ranging from Proto-dynastic to Roman, including those of the High-Priests of Khnum in the 21st nome.

Beyond Kafr ʿAmmār is (5km) *al-Qaṭūrī*, immediately beyond which, at **al-Girzah**, a road leaves W to the Fayyūm, crossing the mouth of the Libaynī Canal where it leaves the Nile. To the S it runs through (7km) *Ifwah* and at 5km a road turns off NW to (5km) **Maydūm**, NW of which lies the pyramid. (Obtain tickets from the Site Office.)

The **Pyramid Complex of Maydūm** in its impressive desert setting, like all the others in the vast field, stands on the edge of the escarpment overlooking the cultivation. The pyramid dominates the landscape for many miles and is the most complete early complex. It was once thought to be the work of Sneferu but though it is likely that he finished the structure, it was probably founded by and for his father Huni, last king of the 3 Dyn. The *Pyramid of Maydūm* resembles a vast stepped tower, but it is in reality a structure with a nucleus mastaba and eight added layers of masonry, finally filled-in to form the first true pyramid. Originally it was 144m sq. and 92m high with an angle of 51°53′. It stands on a prepared platform which runs under the casing stones. Recent work by the EAO suggests that the outer casing collapsed before the pyramid was completed. Several bodies have been found under the debris. The *Entry* (A) is on the N face of the structure, some 30m from the ground. A wooden ladder now provides access (until recently visitors had to hang by their hands from the ledge above and drop into the entry guided by the guard).

The interior is similar to Dahshūr; a long *sloping passage* (B) of 57m descends into the natural rock below the superstructure, to a short *horizontal passage* (C), once closed off by a wooden door, and then a vertical shaft leading up to the limestone lined *Burial Chamber* (D) in the body of the pyramid, with its base at rock level and a splendid corbelled roof like that of Sneferu's Southern Pyramid. Petrie found a wooden coffin here which he thought had belonged to Sneferu.

To the S are the remains of a small *Subsidiary Pyramid* found by Petrie with immense labour, and to the E a small *Mortuary Temple* enclosed within a wall. On the roof are two stelae, now uninscribed but probably with the inscription removed by wind-blown sand. On the inside walls of the temple are New Kingdom graffiti which led to the pyramid being

*Maydūm. The core of the pyramid surrounded by the debris of the superstructure*

attributed to Sneferu, before it was discovered that he already had two others at Dahshūr. A walled roofless *Causeway* paved with limestone led to a *Valley Temple* at the edge of the cultivation. (This has never been cleared because during the earlier excavation the water table was too high. It would now present no obstacle.)

The *Mastaba* (No. 17) beside the pyramid (torch required) contained the defleshed body of a man in a sarcophagus larger than that now to be seen in the Great Pyramid at Giza. A narrow passage from the S entrance (c 1m high) leads to a ladder and a drop of 10m to a lower chamber with the sarcophagus.

Among the 3 Dyn. finds from Maydūm now in the EM were some fine reliefs (including the Maydūm geese) and the splendid statues of Rahotep and Nofert in painted limestone which came from a group of mastabas further N.

Return to the H2 which continues S into the province of Banī Suwayf, passing through (5km) *al-Maymūm* and (12km) *Ishmant*. From here a road leads W to the village of **Abū Ṣīr al-Malāq** (10km). Here in 750 the last Ummayad khalīf, Marwān II, having fled from Baghdad, fought his final battle against the usurping ʿAbbāsid forces. He was killed and buried beside the local mosque.

The next village S is (12km) *Būsh* and the H2 continues to (8km) **Banī Suwayf**, capital of the province and noted for its cotton-spinning and carpets. Just beyond Banī Suwayf a road leads SW to **Ihnāsiyyah al-Madīnah** (12km), site of the ancient city of *Henen-nesut*, later *Herakleopolis Magna*. The rubbish mounds cover about 300 feddans. Harishef (Arsaphes), a local ram-headed god, was the deity honoured here. It was settled from the 1 Dyn. but only rose to importance in the First Intermediate Period (9–10 Dyns). Its rulers controlled large areas of Northern Egypt and in the very early 11 Dyn. probably governed the whole country but they were eclipsed by the powerful Theban princes.

The *Temple of Harishef*, situated on a salt-encrusted lake, was built by Ramesses II. It was first excavated by Naville (1892–93) and Petrie (1904) and more recently by a Spanish team. A granite triad of Ramesses II between Ptah and Harishef was found (now in the EM).

SW lies Gabal al-Sidmant (15km), site of the *Necropolis of Herakleopolis*. Petrie excavated here in 1920–21. It extends over a large area and contains tombs of the Old Kingdom and 9–10 Dyns revealing earlier occupation of the site than has so far been discovered at Herakleopolis.

# 28 Ḥalwān to al-Bayaḍ al-Naṣārah

This route (approx. 90km) connects Ḥalwān, the southernmost district of Greater Cairo, with the itineraries of the Nile Valley. The road runs for only three-quarters of the route and there is only one site of any importance.

The H54 leaves the main Cairo–Ḥalwān road (Rte 21) just before it enters (2km) Ḥalwān and continues S along the East Bank of the Nile. At 2km the **Wadi Garāwī** leaves to the E. Here there are remains of an Old Kingdom quarry with a stone-cutters' settlement and the well-preserved dam which must have supplied them with water.

At 6km is **al-Tabbīn** with a bridge to the West Bank at Dahshūr (Rte 26). The road continues S, passing (4km) *al-Minyā*, (11km) *al-Qubbābāt* and (7km) *Aṭfīḥ*. It terminates at (12km) **al-Barumbul** and **al-Bayaḍ al-Nasarah** (opposite al-Wāsṭā on the West Bank). S of this point there is no road until al-Hibā (Rte 30) although a projected highway along the East Bank to Asyūṭ should be completed soon (1988).

# 29 The Fayyūm

The Fayyūm is described in four itineraries centred on the main town, **Madīnat al-Fayyūm**. If the distant sites are to be visited an extended stay in the area is necessary although a tour through Madīnat al-Fayyūm and back on the H2 can easily be accomplished in one day from Cairo.

The H22 branches N from the Sh'. al-Ahrām at Nazlat al-Saman (Rte 23; with the desert road to Alexandria breaking off to the NW) and turns SE. A road to Baḥriyyah Oasis (Rte 48) branches off at 1km. The road crosses the desert with fine views of the pyramids to the E. At 15km a road branches off E (to a bridge over the Nile and al-Tabbīn; Rte 28). The H22 reaches (5km) the first cultivated area, *Kom Aushim* (see below) and (14km) **Madīnat al-Fayyūm** (and continues through the Fayyūm to emerge at Banī Suwayf).

The province of al-Fayyūm is the largest and westernmost of the several oases scattered across the Western Desert. It differs from all the others in being fed directly by an offshoot of the Nile which leaves the main river at Manqabād just N of Asyūṭ. The depression, surrounded by low mountains, is roughly triangular, c 100km NE to SW and c 90km across the S base. Only the area at the N apex is cultivable, about one-third of the total area. This is watered by extensive canalisation of the river, the Baḥr Yūsuf, which enters the depression through a break in the surrounding hills at al-Lāhūn in the SE. These canals finally drain into the Birkat Qārūn, a large lake, about 40km long and only 8km across at its widest point and about 45m below sea level, which lies NW of the cultivated region. The chief town and administrative capital, Madīnat al-Fayyūm, is roughly in the centre of the cultivated area and roads radiate in all directions to the many other towns and villages throughout the region. The average temperature in January is 14.9°C and in July 29.5°C. Annual rainfall is 18.7mm.

**Geology**. The geological history of the Fayyūm has been studied in some detail as the measures of the Gabal Qaṭrānī and Qaṣr Qārūn 20km to the NW of Birkat al-Qārūn produce a whole sequence of Early Tertiary strata from the late Eocene to late Oligocene. These show the development of the area from purely marine through brackish marshland to high forest and savannah. The lowest late Eocene strata are marine deposits with abundant remains of sharks and early whales but the latest Eocene shows a brackish coastal marshland with whales and sea-cows among the marine types, and giant tortoises and crocodilians representing the land forms. Of particular note are fossils of *Gigantophis*, a 12m python, and, most important of all, *Moeritherium*, the elongated primitive elephantid, whose dynasty was to produce such gigantic forms in later geological ages. The early Oligocene deposits show that the Fayyūm was well inland and covered with lush tropical forest. The relations of *Moeritherium* were *Palaeomastodon* and *Phioma*, much larger with longer tusks and closer to modern forms. Other relatives of the elephants were very common. Now represented by small rabbit-sized animals, the hyraxes produced giant forms—*Megalohyrax* was as large as a pony. Yet another relative was *Arsinotherium*, 2m at the shoulder and armed with immense bone horns projecting forward from the nose, and possessing a battery of grinding teeth. Among smaller mammals were little tarsier-like primates. By the middle Oligocene the forest had given way to savannah, the most important fossil found being *Propliopithecus*, an early ape, which showed several hominid traits. The late Oligocene beds indicate a return of the lush forests and the associated fauna. Elephantids were even more advanced and another simian was present, *Aegyptopithecus*, which as a forest animal had more in common with the modern gorilla. The whole sequence is terminated abruptly by a basaltic lava flow signalling the end of the Oligocene and presumably the local extinction of the fauna. Fossils of all these forms can be seen in the Geological Museum in Cairo.

**History**. There is evidence of settlement in the Fayyūm from Neolithic times onwards but its isolation and difficulty of access prevented exploitation. Two of the early cultures, called Fayyūm A and B, are dated to 4500 BC. They were discovered after World War I in the terrace overlooking Lake Qārūn. It was not until dynastic times under Amenemhat I of the 12 Dyn. that the region called Ta-she (Land of the Lake) was developed and the marshes drained. This was primarily achieved by the installation of a regulator at al-Lāhūn—the first of a series that has continued until the present day. This development was accelerated under Amenemhat III, who showed great interest in the area and had his pyramid built at Ḥawārah. At this time it was known as the Twentieth Nome. Thus it continued throughout the period until the reign of Ptolemy II Philadelphus when it was developed further. It was called the Arsinoite Nome and renowned for its rich and varied crops and the wildfowl and fish from Mer-Wer (The Great Lake, Lake Moeris) which then covered perhaps twice its present area. Much information is available for this period since Apollonius, the treasurer of Ptolemy, had estates here and introduced new methods of cultivation, drainage and rotation of crops among other improvements. During the 3C BC a large settlement of Jews resided in the area. Under the Romans the agricultural policy of the Ptolemies was abandoned and the whole area was used exclusively for the cultivation of grain for the Roman market; this continued during the domination of the Byzantine Empire.

The Fayyūm was one of the early centres of Christianity, its isolation providing a certain amount of protection from persecution. It was called by the Copts *Phiom* (Sea), of which the modern name is an Arabisation. With the Arab conquest, although a large proportion of the population of the Fayyūm accepted Islām and there was a large influx of Muslim beduin who settled in the area, it remained a great centre of Christianity. In the 13C Abū Ṣalīḥ records that there had been 35 monasteries in the area. In Muslim folklore it was the prophet Yūsuf (Joseph) who developed the area for the ruler Faraʿūn during his captivity in Egypt. In a punning folktale the name of the region is derived from this association: when Faraʿun saw the achievements of Yūsuf, the digging of the Baḥr Yūsuf and the canals, he said in wonder, 'This is the work of a thousand days' (alf yawm). During the early part of the period the exclusive production of corn was abandoned and the main crops were rice and flax, but with the canalisation of the Delta region its importance declined. In the mid 13C Sultan Baybars installed a regulator at al-Lāhūn, which, though restored, is still in service. A modern regulator was built early in the 20C. However the region was too valuable to be ignored and was included in the reorganisation of the country undertaken by Muḥ. ʿAlī Pāshā at the beginning of the 19C. The province is now one of the most productive areas in Egypt, staple crops being cotton, vegetables, fruit and flowers; some types grown here grow nowhere else in Egypt. Among the diagnostic features of the Fayyūm are the sawāqih al-hadīr (roaring water-wheels), powered entirely by the force of the water flow and producing a perpetual drone, and the pigeon houses (burg al-hammām) of a form not found elsewhere in Egypt.

Although a visit to the Fayyūm is usually confined to one day and includes the pyramids of Ḥawārah and al-Lāhūn, it is well worth extending the tour to include the ancient 12 Dyn., Ptolemaic and Roman towns surrounding the oasis.

The Fayyūm is now heavily cultivated and within the last 80 years many sites, originally in the desert, have become surrounded by cultivation. After 2000 years of recession the water level of Lake Qarun is again rising, probably because of the stability of the level of the Nile since the construction of the High Dam at Aswān. This has caused the submergence of many fields and houses and the lakeside road has had to be raised considerably and rebuilt.

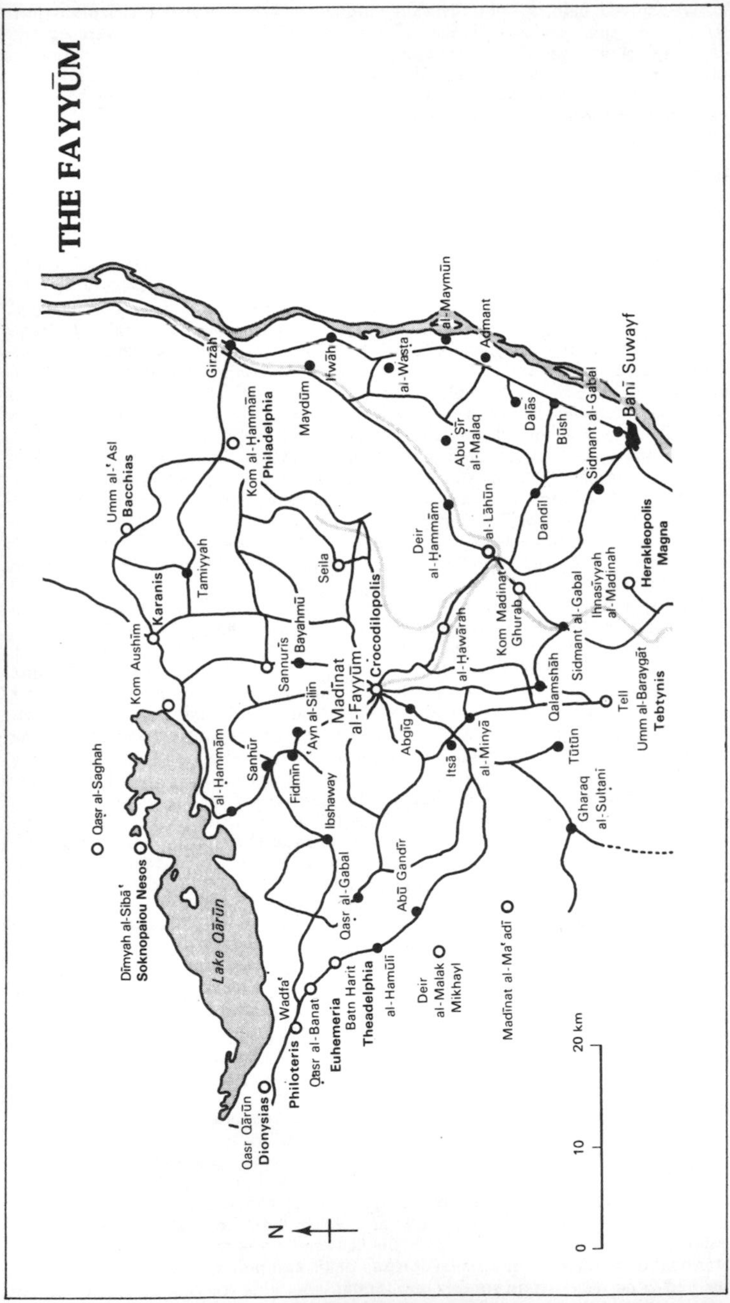
THE FAYYŪM
Girzāh
Iṭwāh
Maydūm
al-Maymūn
al-Wasṭa
Admant
Dalās
Būsh
Sidmant al-Gabal
Banī Suwayf
Abu Ṣīr
al-Malaq
Kom al-Ḥammām
Philadelphia
Umm al-ʻAsl
Bacchias
Tamiyyah
Karanis
Kom Aushīm
Seila
Bayahmū
Sannurīs
Deir
al-Ḥammām
al-Lāhūn
Dandīl
Herakleopolis
Magna
Ihnasīyyah
al-Madīnah
Kom Madīnat
Ghurab
Sidmant al-Gabal
Crocodilopolis
Madīnat
al-Fayyūm
al-Ḥawārah
Qalamshāh
Tell
Umm al-Baraygāt
Tebtynis
ʻAyn al-Silīn
Sanhūr
al-Ḥammām
Fidmīn
Abgīg
Itsā
al-Minyā
Tūtūn
Gharaq
al-Sulṭanī
Ibshaway
Qaṣr al-Saghah
Dīmyah al-Sibāʻ
Soknopaiou Nesos
Lake Qārūn
Qaṣr al-Gabal
Abū Gandīr
Madīnat al-Maʻadī
Deir
al-Malak
Mikhayl
al-Hamūlī
Batn Harit
Theadelphia
Qaṣr al-Banat
Euhemeria
Wadfaʻ
Philoteris
Qasr Qārūn
Dionysias
N
0
10
20 km

There are no good maps of the Fayyūm and therefore it is really necessary to contact a guide for the area to be visited in Madīnat al-Fayyūm. Because of the slow-going on the tracks, mainly along the edges of canals, plenty of time must be allowed for the visit.

**Madīnat al-Fayyūm** is capital of the province and it was also capital of the nome in ancient times (as *Crocodilopolis*). It is basically an agricultural centre with all the varied produce of the province for sale. While there is little of architectural interest it is nonetheless extremely attractive. The Baḥr Yūsuf, crossed by many bridges, flows through the city centre in a conduit and the streets are lined with produce-sellers. At the centre is the *Railway Station* and the two bus-stations, *Mahaṭṭat Miṣr* (buses to Cairo) and *Mahaṭṭat al-Ḥawatim* (local buses to all parts of the Fayyūm). Between these two stations in the SHʿ. AL-GUMHURIYYAH is the central square where travel companies drop visitors. To the left (facing the river) is the *Casino al-Madīnah*. In the garden in front are working models of Fayyūmī water-wheels.

Following the fast flow of the river on the E bank the fifth bridge, at the Bāb al-Maṭāfī (Bāb al-Wadaʿ) is Kubrī Qāyt-bāy (Bridge of Qāyt-bāy). On the W side of the river is the **Mosque of Khawand Aṣal-Bay**, built in 1499 (usually referred to as the Mosque of Qāyt-bāy).

Aṣal-Bay was the favourite concubine of Sultan Qāyt-bāy, mother of Muḥ. IV and sister of Sultan Qānṣūḥ I. After the death of Qāyt-bāy she married Sultan Jānbalāt and it was during this period that the mosque was built. However, with the assumption of Sultan Tūmānbay I, who had married Qāyt-bāy's legitimate wife Fāṭimah, in 1501 Aṣal-Bay was publicly insulted by him and disgraced.

Little is left of the original structure which was a cruciform assembly mosque. The building of the mosque was supervised by Sh. ʿAbd al-Qādir al-Dushtūti (died 1518, and buried in Cairo; see Rte 7). The greater part of it fell into the Baḥr Yūsuf in 1892, although it was already much ruined. The remains were taken in hand by the CPAM and incorporated in a new building. Of the entrance the portion below the trefoil arch is original; it has the usual mastabahs and tirāẓ foundation inscription, where ʿAsal-bay is named as Khawand Walīdat (Lady Mother) al-Malik al-Nāṣir Muḥammad, and medallions above. Inside, the area to the right is the remaining portion of the qiblah līwan. The white marble pillars are probably from the original mosque, but are now used in arcades to support a wooden roof. The miḥrāb has a round arch with hood supported by two helically-fluted slate columns and a band of tirāẓ inscription runs round the cornice covered by a stalactite frieze. To the left of the miḥrāb is a marble panel from the original mosque set in the modern plaster. The superb gilded teak minbar was given to the mosque by the foundress. The sides are geometrical panels inset with ivory (some dyed green) and mother-of-pearl; on each side are dedicatory inscriptions to the princess.

Following the road upwards, it curves to the left. After 100m, on the right stands the *Mosque and Tomb of Sh. ʿAlī al-Rūbī* (died 1390/1), the most important sufi shaykh in the Fayyūm. His mūlid is held in mid-Shaʿbān. Little is left of the original structure. On the opposite site of the Bahr Yūsuf is the **Mosque of the Amīr Sulaymān**, called locally Sīdī Muḥammad, built in 1559 known locally as al-Muʿallagah. Sulaymān was the inspector of the district. Built partly in brick in the local style, this mosque retains a typical late Mamlūk entrance porch.

From the W end of the Shʿ. al-Gumhuriyyah, the SHʿ. KIMĀN FĀRIS leads N to the area of **Kimān Fāris**. This is the site of the ancient city of

*Arsinoe* or *Crocodilopolis*. At the beginning of this century it covered an area of 300 feddans but the growth of the modern town has reduced it to just 10 feddans. During the Ptolemaic period it was capital of the Arsinoite nome but it was obviously founded much earlier as there are remains from the Middle Kingdom. Sadly, it now consists merely of a series of low mounds beside the railway line, covered with rank reeds and grazed by sheep. Many fine objects from here are now in the EM and other museums, including a number of papyri. Today only ardent archaeologists will find it worth visiting.

## A. North-West Fayyūm

**Madīnat al-Fayyūm**.—14km **Sannūris**.(—26km **Shakshūk**.)—8km **Kom Awshīm**.—23km **Qaṣr al-Ṣāghah**.

The H22 (Cairo road) leaves Madīnat al-Fayyūm due N and runs through (7km) **Byahmu** (Bīhmū). In a field are the masonry bases of two colossi of Amenemhat III (8m high; statues destroyed). When the lake covered a larger area the statues must have stood in it. (7km) **Sannūris**. From here the H48 runs NE (see below) and 10km further N the H50 leads across the cultivation to *Lake Qarūn* and along the S shore to **Shakshūk** (16km). A boat can be taken across the lake, passing on the way the *Gazīrat al-Qarn* (Island of the Horn) to **al-Kanisah** on the N bank. A track leads 2.5km W to the ruins of *Soknopaiou Nesos* (Island of Soknopaious), now 65m above water level.

This site was examined by Grenfell and Hunt in 1920–21 and by Prof. Zuker and the University of Michigan in 1931. A paved processional way leads up steps from the old lake shore 410m to the city gate, then between two ruined pylons to the *Temple*, its high brick walls still standing. The Michigan team also uncovered several houses and dated the remains from Ptolemaic (Ptolemy II Philadelphus) to Roman (Septimius Severus). It appears to have been abandoned before the Christian period as there are no relevant remains. N lies Qaṣr al-Ṣāghah (see below).

N of the H50 the H22 continues N to (8km) **Kom Aushīm** where the road leaves the oasis. Much of the cultivated area has been reclaimed from the desert by the Ministry of Agriculture. This is the site of ancient *Karanis*, marked by a large oval mound investigated by the University of Michigan in the 1920s. E of the road is a small but excellent *Museum* containing material recovered from Karanis and other sites around the Fayyūm. Arrangements should be made here to visit the sites of Soknopaiou Nesos and Qaṣr al-Ṣāghah. The curator can provide a guide, but arrangements should be made the day before a visit. W of the road is a small lake, *Birkat Kom Awshīm*.

There are two temples. The *N Temple*, probably dedicated to a local form of the crocodile god Suchos and Isis, seems to have been in use from the 1C BC to the 3C AD, at which time economic depression coincided with the rapid expansion of Christianity. However, remains of an earlier structure have been found beneath the foundations. This temple was cleared in 1925. In limestone, it has two pylons and consists of three rooms. In an outer court several cult objects were found, including a headless female deity, a hawk-headed crocodile and a limestone altar with a bearded god on each side. This court leads into an inner court and a sanctuary with a large stone altar. An inner room approached from the W was probably used for oracular purposes. The stone built *S Temple* (cleared in 1929) is very similar, even to the hidden chamber, although it was built in the late 1C or early 2C AD. It was dedicated to two local crocodile gods, Pnepheros and Petesouchus. There are some inscriptions of the reigns of Nero, Claudius and Vespasiun. Around the temples are remains of the *Town* with a well preserved *Bath house*, which appears to have been deserted by the mid 5C. 1.5km N, cut into a low rocky mound, is the *Necropolis*.

A track leads from Kom Aushīm across the desert to (23km) **Qaṣr al-Ṣāghah** at the foot of a limestone cliff. The site was discovered by Schweinfurth in 1884 and contains a small *Temple*. It is built of large, irregularly cut blocks of stone. It was never completed and consists of a narrow forecourt off which are seven statue niches. Beneath is a crypt. Originally considered to be Old Kingdom, investigations by the German Archaeological Institute in Cairo showed it to be late 12–early 13 Dyn. A stairway leads to the terrace. Remains of a *Workmen's Town* and some military buildings were also found. The cemetery included some pan graves. N are the cliffs of Qaṣr al-Ṣāghah while the higher Gabal Qaṭrānī range is to the SE. The measures of both these outcrops have provided a magnificent sequence of fossils.

Further W into the desert, and needing the services of a guide as there is no road, lies the **Deir Abū Līfah**.

It is entered through a door in the rockly ledge which borders the *Gabal Abū Līfah*. There is a series of cells cut into the rock, many walled-up, joined by a passage. One contains a well. The monastery was inhabited from the 7–9C and is said to have been founded by St. Panoukhius, a founder of Egyptian monasticism. It was used as a place of refuge during attack by desert tribes.

A road branches off the H22 just N of Madīnat al-Fayyūm and runs NW. Passing through *Minshāt ʿAbd Allāh* (2km) and *Banī Ṣāliḥ* (5km), it reaches (4km) **ʿAyn al-Siliyīn**, a pleasure park created around natural mineral springs. It is a pleasant spot with a swimming pool and café, but can be very crowded at weekends and holidays. Beyond this the road turns W to run through *Fidmīn* (2km) and then bears NW again to *Sanhūr*(5km) and on to *al-Ḥammām* on the bank of the Birkat Qārūn (7km).

# B. North-East Fayyūm

**Madīnat al-Fayyūm**.—14km **Sannūris**.—12km **Ṭāmiyyah**.—12km *Kom al-Hamman*.—12km **Girzah**.

Madīnat al-Fayyūm to Sannūris, see above. From Sannūris the H48 runs due E through the fields to (12km) **Ṭāmmiyah**. To the N an agricultural road leads across a canal to **Umm al-ʿAsl** (5km) with two mounds marking the ancient site of *Bacchias*.

In the area c 1500 sq.m. the southern mound has been virtually destroyed and is now under the cultivation while the northern mound, set in the desert, has been much damaged by the sabbakhin. It lies on the edge of the ancient road from Memphis to Arsinoe. The main feature is the large mud-brick *Temple* oriented NE–SW in the S quarter of the town, dedicated to Sokanobkonneus, a local crocodile god. Hogarth investigated the temple in 1900 when the pavement was still visible. This has now been removed and it can be seen that the Ptolemaic building was raised over an earlier structure. Like most of the Fayyūm temples, it consists of two courts and a sanctuary with subsidiary rooms. The temple was founded in the 3C BC; Ptolemaic pottery and papyri were found here, which seems to indicate that it declined from about AD 250 and was abandoned in the mid-4C. Surrounding the temple is the contemporary town, with the roads of mud built houses centred on the temple.

E of Ṭāmiyyah the H48 crosses the Wardān Canal and passes (12km) **Kom al-Hammām**. This is the site of *Philadelphia* but the remains are rapidly being removed for nitrate.

It was a prominent town founded under Ptolemy II Philadelphus and is notable for the discovery of the prodigious *Archives of Zenon*, estate manager of Apollonius, treasurer of Ptolemy II Philadelphus. These papyri provided much valuable information on Ptolemaic administration in the Fayyūm, as well as more general information on social life. One of the most delightful is a letter from Zenon's brother, Epharmostos, which begins: 'The letter you wrote to Menon about Kallikon's money has been eaten by mice...' (now in BM). All that is visible today are the baths and mounds covered with debris extending over c 1 sq. km.

Continuing E the H48 joins (12km) the H2, the main Nile Valley road, at **Girzah** (Rte 27).

A road leaves Madīnat al-Fayyūm due E (S of the railway line to al-Wastā). Follow this for 15km where the village of *Seila* (Sīlah) lies to the N. Continue until a track turns N (5km). It follows a canal and after 5km arrives at a gravelly ridge on which stands the **Pyramid of Seila**. (It is not visible from a great distance as it is set in a cleft.) This is a small incomplete pyramid standing 16 courses high. The blocks are irregular, some being laid lengthways, others sideways. Only a gaping hole shows where the burial chamber should be, but there is no visible internal structure. There is no evidence of a mortuary temple. Excavations in 1987 revealed a stele with the name of Sneferu, first king of the 4 Dyn. The road runs N into *Kom al-Hammām* on the H48 (see above).

## C. South-West Fayyūm

Most of the important sites in this area are on the edge of the desert and are accesible only after long journeys on agricultural tracks by canals.

**Madīnat al-Fayyūm**.—15km **al-Minya** (—5km **Tuṭūn**).—10km **Gabal Madīnat Maʿādī**.—10km *al-Ḥamūlī*.—9km **Baṭn Ihrīt**.—3km **Qaṣr al-Banāt**.—10km **Qaṣr Qārūn**.

A road runs due S from Madīnat al-Fayyūm passing through *Abgīg*, *Iṭsā* and (15km) **al-Minyā**. Here a road continues S while another leads NW to Qaṣr Qārūn (see below). Take the track to the S. At 1.5km it divides. The SW fork runs to *al-Gharaq al-Sulṭāni* (8km) but the SE fork leads to **Tuṭūn** (5km). Due S of Tuṭūn is **Umm al-Braygāt** (4.5km), location of the ancient city of *Beten*, Gk *Tebtynis*.

It seems to have been an ancient site refounded by Ptolemy I. It has been excavated by an Italian mission. The complex is similar to that at al-Madīnat Maʿādī (see below) with an even longer stone paved way (c 200m) flanked at intervals by lions, sphinxes and altars. There is a kiosk with eight columns. Additionally there are a number of mud-brick buildings which may have served as lodgings for the priests. Fronting the *Temple* is a vestibule with Ptolemaic reliefs including one of Sobek. Although the mud-brick enclosure wall is virtually complete, the temple has been almost entirely destroyed. A small square tank in the courtyard is thought to have been for the sacred crocodile attached to the temple. There were unidentified brick buildings within the precinct. An extensive crocodile cemetery was attached to the town. The crocodiles were wrapped in reused papyri, including many literary pieces.

The NW track from al-Minyā crosses a canal and runs into the desert where it peters out. (10km) **Mādinat Maʿādī** is a low ridge covered with gravel and sand. On the S side is the site of the ancient town of *Dja*, Gk *Narmouthis*. Transport should be left at the near side of the ridge (take care not to park in soft sand).

The *Temple* is situated in the desert and partly filled with sand. It was excavated by the University of Milan. A limestone paved processional way, now also largely sanded-up, extends S for more than 150m. Its beginning is marked by two crouching lions facing one another. S of these are two sphinxes in front of limestone basins. Between the right-hand lion and sphinx is a limestone altar dedicated to Renenutet, the harvest goddess, of the 1C AD. The paved way leads through a kiosk with eight columns and ample space through the centre for a procession to pass. Continuing S, there are various partly buried sphinxes. The temple dates from the 12 Dyn. with Ptolemaic additions. It consists of five units of which the outer three are late and the inner two—of darker sandstone and superior construction—date to the original foundation.

Entry is through the ruined portico into a transverse vestibule with four engaged columns. The pilasters have been removed (to the Greco-Roman Museum, Alexandria) and replaced with replicas. They are decorated with dedicatory inscriptions and hymns, one of which mentions Amenemhat III. In the second vestibule is a limestone altar, set slightly right of the doorway, while the third vestibule contains two palm columns. Beyond is the 12 Dyn. section, a small hall with two papyrus-bud columns leading to the sanctuary. Here are three chapels resembling statue niches. In the central niche, the largest, was a statue of Renenutet flanked by Amenemhat III and IV. The other niches contained statues of Sobek and Amenemhat III to both of whom the temple was dedicated. At the rear of the temple on one of the side walls is a well-delineated carving of Sobek as a man with a crocodile's head. At the sides and rear are many subsidiary and storage chambers. The University of Pisa excavating here in 1984 discovered *Five Churches*, NW of the temple site, dating to the 5th and 6Cs. They have recently uncovered a *Coptic Basilica* with seven naves, an unusual form for an Egyptian church, dating to 4–5C.

S of the track at 10km is *al-Ḥāmūlī*. 1km SW across two canals is the *Deir al Malāk Mikhayl* (Monastery of the Angel Michael). The ruins have made a slight mound 3m high, covered with potsherds. Here a fine collection of manuscripts (now in the Pierpont Morgan Library, New York) was found in 1910 by Egyptians digging for sabakh. The manuscripts date to between AD 823 and 914, judging from the colophons.

Continue W along the same track for 9km. To the S lies **Baṭn Ihrīt**, site of ancient *Theadelphia*.

At the beginning of the century the mound stood 3–4m high but nothing remains except the ancient mounds, left after the soil had been removed for use as fertilizer by the local farmers. Many papyri were found here, often set in niches in the walls of the ancient houses. Eighty years ago these houses still stood up to roof level. They were made of mud-brick with matting ceilings. The *Temple*, dedicated to another crocodile god, lay to the W on the outskirts of the town; it was smaller than that at Euhemeria (see below).

NW along the track, the next site lies to the N at 3km and is difficult to reach. This is **Qaṣr al-Banāt**, site of *Euhemeria*.

Originally built on a series of low mounds extending over c 1 sq. km, the area is now very much reduced. The houses, of unbaked brick, have been systematically robbed. The *Temple*, also brick, was situated to the NW; little now remains of it. It was dedicated to a form of Sobek, associated with Isis and Horus. The site has yielded a vast quantity of papyri of Ptolemaic and Roman date, belonging mainly to the 1 and 2C AD. By the 4C it was starting to decay and was abandoned.

Passing *Wadfa*ʿ (S of the track at 6km), site of the town of *Philoteris*, the track terminates at (4km) **Qaṣr Qārūn**, at the S end of Lake Qārūn. Here is the site of *Dionysias*. The most noticeable feature is the large stone Ptolemaic *Temple* dedicated to Sobek-Reʿ. The building is rectangular (30m by 20m) but riven by an earthquake. A limestone stele found during the clearing of the temple in 1948 showed Sobek inside the solar disk with rays, flanked by Ma'at and a lion god (now in the EM). The building consists of a ruined portico which gives access to three successive vestibules. The *sanctuary* is a narrow room, with three statue niches at the rear. Off the vestibules and the sacred corridor running partly round the sanctuary are subsidiary chambers for cult objects, vestments and jewellery. There are several secret chambers in the thickness of the walls; some may have had an oracular purpose. On each side of the sanctuary are stairways to the roof, and a room above the sanctuary which may have served as a 'Chapel of the Disk', similar to the chapel at Dendārah where the statues received the rays of the sun to revivify them on New Year's Day.

The town seems to have been laid out on a grid plan. From the temple an extensive causeway leads to a kiosk similar to those at Madīnat Maʿādī and Umm al-Braygāt. The latest building seems to have been a large mud-brick Byzantine *Fortress* lying some 200m NW of the temple. It is not easily visible as the remains are filled with sand, and the yellow walls stand only about 1m high. It is, however, the footings of a very substantial building (83m by 70m) with walls 3.8m thick. Inside the fortress was a basilican structure with Corinthian and other stone capitals reused from the earlier buildings of Dionysias. The fortress seems to be 4C and there are no records after about AD 395 when it may have fallen into disuse.

Very few other buildings on the site seem to have been excavated. Near some houses to the S are the baths, while another thermal establishment lies between the temple and the fort. Another causeway, S of the existing one, with a kiosk-like structure at one end, suggests another temple, but orientated in the reverse direction.

## D. South-East Fayyūm

**Madīnat al-Fayyūm**.—6km **al-ʿAzab**.—3km **Ḥawārat al-Maqtaʿ**.—9km **al-Lāhūn** (—6km **Deir al-Hamam**).—15km **Banī Suwayf**.

Leave Madīnat al-Fayyūm SE on the H22. The first village of importance is (6km) **al-ʿAzab**; the *Deir al-ʿAdhrā* (Monastery of the Virgin) to the N can be recognised by its domes. It was founded probably by Bishop Butrus (Peter) of the Fayyūm in the 12C or the patriarch Cyril III in the 13C, but it has been unoccupied since the 18C. The old *Church of al-ʿAdhrā* is in the SE of the courtyard; inside are three haykals, to the Virgin (centre), St. Anthony (N) and St. Michael (S). To the W is the new *Church of Abū 'l-Sayfayn* (St. Mercurius), containing the tomb of Anba Abram, a popular Coptic saint. The annual mūlid of the Virgin is held here from 15–22 August, and attracts a large number of pilgrims.

Turning S and driving parallel to the *Baḥr al-Gharaq* to the bridge and then E through the desert, the **Deir al-Malāk Ghubrayal** (Monastery of the Angel Gabriel) can be seen on the skyline (4km). It is one of the earliest monasteries in the Fayyūm having been built in the 7th or 8C. Enclosed within a wall, the court is reached through a gate by the lodgings of the priest and his family. The church is ancient and reuses earlier material including Corinthian columns from some earlier temple. There are connections with Jacob who is said to have rested here. It is mentioned by Abu Ṣāliḥ (13C) and al-Maqrīzī (15C), but it has not been used as a monastery since the 17C. There is an annual mūlid here, on the feast of St. Gabriel, 22 Kihak (18 December).

The next site of importance is at (3km) **Ḥawārah** (Ḥawārah al-Maqtaʿ). Turn NE across the Baḥr Yūsuf and then (3km) NW beside the *Baḥr Saylāh* across a bridge. On the West Bank lies the **Pyramid Complex of Amenemhat III**. There does not appear to have been a causeway or valley temple attached to this pyramid. Of the *Pyramid of Amenemhat III* only the mud-brick core with brick filling between stone walls remains; the limestone casing has long since disappeared. It was originally 58m high and 100m sq. with a slope of 48°45′; there is still a splendid view of the Fayyūm from the top of the pyramid. The entry is to the S (now inaccessible) and was intended to mislead the tomb robbers, with false burial shafts. The quartzite sarcophagus had a curved lid and a panel design at the foot, but the tomb had been robbed and the body destroyed and burnt. It was excavated with great difficulty by Petrie who found the chamber half full of water. Fragments of vases with the name of Amenemhat III upon them were recovered. Apparently it was not finished at his death and was completed for him by his daughter Sobek-Nefru who came to the throne as the last ruler of the 12 Dyn. after the depletion of the male line. This site was famous for its *Mortuary Temple*, known in Classical times as the Labyrinth, said to have been carved from a single rock. It was still in existence when Herodotus visited Egypt; he saw it and thought that it far surpassed the pyramids as a building. Now little remains of the vast structure, said to have contained over 3000 rooms, except piles of debris and a vast quantity of chipped stone fragments.

It was near here in a cemetery in the desert to the N that Petrie found the Fayyūm portraits, painted in wax encaustic on flat boards and dating to the Roman period. Painted during life and attached to the coffins after death, they are among the earliest portraits known (now in the EM and BM and elsewhere).

The road continues SE and reaches (9km) **al-Lāhūn**, a small village. Here the Baḥr Yūsuf enters the Fayyūm; to the N of the modern regulator is the **Qantarah of Sultan Baybars**. It is merely the last of a series of regulators built here from the time of Amenemhat III in the 18C BC. Baybars' work, built in the 1260s, is an immense bridge of masonry blocks pierced by three parallel tunnels, above the S end of which are three sluice gates. The upstream (S) section was reinforced by Muḥ. ʿAli Pāshā in 1825 but the N section is original. The three arches are pointed and between each one is a pyramidal buttress. The water rushes through the tunnels and after falling a few metres forms a large lake on the N. At present the structure is occupied by the army and photography is forbidden.

The H22 swings S but another road turns N and after 3km reaches the **Pyramid Complex of Senusert II**, also of the 12 Dyn. The *Valley Temple*, 1.6km to the E, is very ruined. On the edge of the cultivation c 2km NE are the remains of an extensive mud-brick town, *Kahūn*, probably built to house the temple officials although Petrie, who excavated it, thought it was for the workmen. Against the E face of the pyramid the *Mortuary*

*Temple*, now also much destroyed, probably in the 19 Dyn., is of red granite and decorated with inscriptions and carvings. The *Pyramid of Senusert II* stands on a natural outcrop of rock and is built of mud brick, originally with a stone casing which was extensively robbed in antiquity. The entrance is on the S side (now inaccessible) to confuse the tomb-robbers; the burial chamber is lined with red granite slabs and contained a red granite sarcophagus. To the NE is a *Subsidiary Pyramid*. Around both pyramids is a mud-brick wall. Within the entry were several *Tombs* belonging to members of the royal family. In one of these Petrie and Brunton found jewellery belonging to Sit Hathor Iniut, one of the royal princesses (part in the EM and part in the Metropolitan Museum). This is some of the finest jewellery discovered in Egypt.

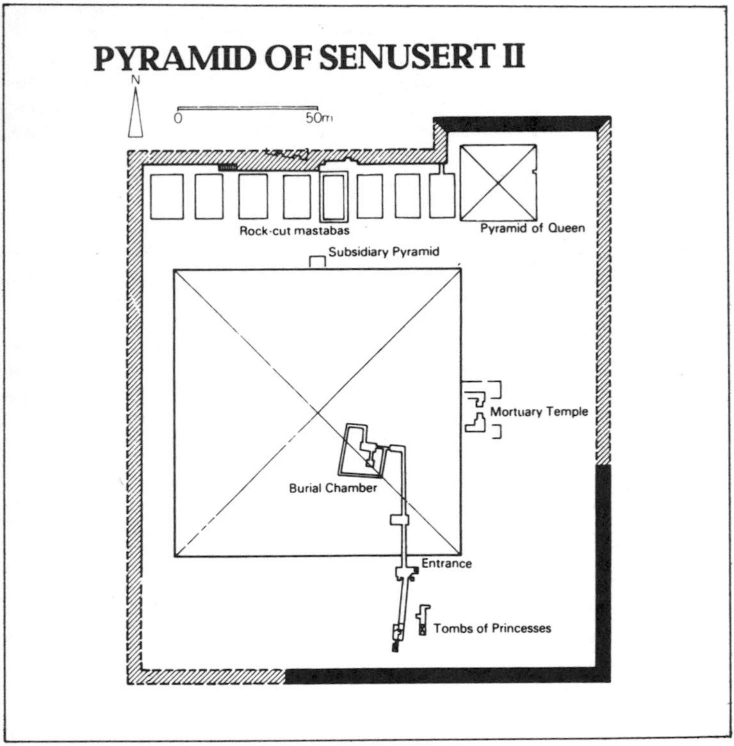
PYRAMID OF SENUSERT II
N
0
50m
Rock-cut mastabas
Pyramid of Queen
Subsidiary Pyramid
Mortuary Temple
Burial Chamber
Entrance
Tombs of Princesses

About 6km NE of al-Lāhūn along a track is the village of *al-Ḥammām* and just to the W is the **Deir al-Ḥammam**, the most picturesque of all the monasteries in the Fayyūm. It was originally founded in the 6th or 8C but the present building is the second on this spot. Surrounding the site is an extensive field of debris and it must at one time have covered a much wider area. Excavation was undertaken by Mackay; many pieces of Coptic papyri were found. At one time the complex was surrounded by a triple wall. The *Church of the Virgin* is inside the courtyard and has two haykals remaining, to the Virgin (centre) and St. George (S). Although not used as a monastery, there is a married monk in residence.

The road divides at al-Lāhūn. The H22 runs S but another road runs SW and after

10km reaches **Sidmant al-Gabal** where a boat can be taken down the Baḥr Yūsuf to *Deir al-Marī Girgis* (Monastery of St. George), the most recent foundation in the area, the church and cells being built in 1914. There was a monastery of St. George in Sidmant in the 13C but by the 15C it had been abandoned. This resettlement was started by two monks, Abunā Buqtur al-Antūnī and Abunā Mitias Antūnī, in the early years of the 20C. Their relics are in a feretory in the NW corner of the nave. Thousands of pilgrims come to the annual mulid held a week before the Feast of the Ascension.

NW of Sidmant al-Gabal is the *Necropolis of Heracleopolis*. But the present route continues SE crossing the Baḥr Yūsuf to **Ihnāsiyyā al-Madīnah** (9km) and the site of *Heracleopolis Magna* (Rte 27). Turn NW to the H22 (12km) and W for Banī Suwayf (10km) or E to return to Madīnat al-Fayyūm.

From al-Lāhūn the H22 runs S and then E, reaching (8km) **Dandīl** (2km further the road to Būsh branches off to the NE) and reaches Banī Suwayf (5km) and the H2.

## Monastery of St. Samuel

At the extreme southern end of the Fayyūm depression lies the **Deir Anba Ṣamwā'īl**, one of the most isolated of the Coptic foundations (guide required). It is necessary to use animal or heavy-duty transport to reach it as there is only a track from the S and no road at all from the N. To reach the monastery from the Fayyūm follow the track S of *al-Gharaq al-Sulṭānī* (see above). The track peters out and the monastery is 32km to the SW on the N slope of the *Wadī al-Mawāliḥ* (Valley of Salts). The alternative route is from the S at *Maghāghah* on the H2 (Rte 30). Travel W to (8km) *al-ʿIdwah* and cross the Baḥr Yūsuf on the car ferry, continue W to *al-Qāyyāt* and meet the track going N at (15km) *al-Shinrā*. Turn to the W. The track gradually turns NW approaching the al-Gabal al-Qalāmun and enters the Wadi al-Mawāliḥ from the S. After 30km it reaches the **Monastery of St. Samuel**, built beside two springs, ʿAyn al-Samar and ʿAyn al-Burdī.

The monastery has a long history. It was probably founded in the 4th or 5C and it is still occupied. It was destroyed in the 9C during the Patriarchate of Anbā Shanudah (Shenute) but was restored soon after. By the 12C it was flourishing with 130 monks and was considered to be one of the most important monastic establishments in the country. However by the 15C it had begun to decline and was abandoned in the 16C. It was resettled in 1898 by Abunā Isḥāq al-Baramisī and ten monks from the Wadi al-Naṭrūn.

The mountain of al-Qalāmun was a retreat of ascetics from the 3C onwards. St. Samuel, after whom the monastery is named, was born in either 597 or 598 at Tkello and became a monk in Scetis at an early age, as a disciple of Agathon. In the persecution arising from the Melkite efforts to make the Coptic Church conform, St. Samuel took refuge in the Qalāmun monastery. He was taken prisoner by the Berbers and beaten by the emissaries of Cyrus, Patriarch of Alexandria for not conforming to Monethelite principles. After performing various miracles he was set free by the Berbers and finally returned to Qalāmun where he died in peace. Before the monastery was built the monks lived in natural caves, the largest and most important of these being the *Cave of St. Samuel*, 4–5km E of the monastery, on the Gabal al-Qalāmun. It is situated at a height of some 150m and about 15m below the summit, facing W and extending about 30m into the rock. It has a cistern which is filled by the rare rains. Traditionally St. Samuel is said to have passed the last years of his life here, only visiting the monastery at intervals.

The earlier monastery must have been considerably larger, and the remains extend over some 12 feddans, enclosed by a thick wall. The overall measurements of the monastery are 60m by 50m with walls standing 5–7m high; the gate is at the N end of the E wall. The well is outside the monastery walls and is slightly salty; another well used for irrigation and washing is within the walls. The present monastery has three churches. The *Catacomb Church*, a subterranean sanctuary probably dating to the 7C, is dedicated to St. Samuel. It is situated under the watch tower, and also served once as living quarters. The new *Church of St. Samuel* was built in 1905 on the top storey of the qaṣr. Two feretories on the NW side of the church contain the relics of SS. Samuel and Justus. The new *Church of the Virgin* with nine domes was recently built by monks, some of whom had been civil engineers.

# 30 Banī Suwayf to al-Minyā

Continuing S from Rtes 27 and 28, this route (total distance approx. 130km) includes both banks of the Nile. The main road and the major sites are on the West Bank. The East Bank, with several minor sites, has to be reached by ferry until a new road is completed.

**Banī Suwayf**.—10km *Bibā*.—14km **al-Fashn** (for **al-Ḥībah**).—52km **Banī Mazār**. (—14km *Ṣandafā* for **al-Bahnasā**).—25km **Samalūṭ**.—29km **al-Minyā**.

From Banī Suwayf the H2 continues S, passing (2km) **Tizmant** (ferry to East Bank) and (8km) *Bibā*.

A road leads W to *Ṣafṭ Rāshīn* (11km) and the H53. On the W bank of the Baḥr Yūsuf is **Dishāshah** (10km) with an Old Kingdom necropolis in the hills to the W, excavated by Petrie. S on the H53 is **Ṣamusṭā** (10km) with a track across the desert to Deir Ṣamwā'īl (Rte 29).

The H2 enters the province of al-Minyā and runs on to (14km) **al-Fashn**, with a ferry to the East Bank for **al-Ḥībah**, site of ancient *Ankyronpolis*. Beyond (21km) *al-Maghāghah* the H2 reaches (13km) *Abū Girg* and continues to (18km) **Banī Mazār**.

From here a road runs NW crossing the H53 at 9km to *Ṣandafā* (5km). Opposite, on the W bank of the Baḥr Yūsuf, lies **al-Bahnasā**, site of ancient *Oxyrhynchus* (Ancient Egyptian *Per Medjet*), capital of the 19th nome of Upper Egypt where the Elephant-snout fish (*Mormyrus kannume*) was revered. The vast rubbish tips of the Greek period have yielded great quantities of valuable papyri, often of previously unknown or defective texts. A track leads to *al-Baḥriyyah Oases* (Rte 47).

At Banī Mazār a ferry crosses to the East Bank and the road across the Eastern Desert to *Rā's Ghārib* on the Red Sea Coast (Rte 50).

The next towns on the H2 are (11km) *Maṭāy* and (14km) **Samalūṭ**, with another track to the *al-Baḥriyyah Oases*. At 4km there is a turning (E) to **al-Bayahū** (1km) for boats to the East Bank.

The boat must be hired specially as there is no regular ferry (if there is little wind the crossing can take up to 2 hours). Under a high range of hills, the *Gabal al-Ṭayr* (Mountain of the Birds), stands the **Deir al-ʿAdhrā** (Monastery of the Virgin), also called *Deir al-Bakarah* (Monastery of the Pulley), reached by a rock-hewn flight of 166 steps through a fissure in the rocks.

It stands 130m above the river and was originally reached by rope and pulley. The monastery is enclosed within plain walls 27m high. This is another monastery traditionally founded by the empress Helena; in support of this a tablet set in the W wall of the church gives the date 328; it is certainly of considerable antiquity.

The church is built in an ancient quarry with the addition of plastered masonry. A narrow door gives on to a flight of steps leading to a wide side aisle separated from the nave by thick octagonal columns surmounted by heavy square capitals, rather like those in Ancient Egyptian temples, which support a clerestory. The roof is flat, constructed of palm-trunks covered with reeds and earth. The raised choir and haykal are cut into the rock and at the other end of the nave the narthex is probably the most ancient part of the church. Inhabited until the late 19C, the monastery had a large library and was visited by many travellers. Today it is used only at the Feast of the Assumption of the Virgin (22 August) when thousands of pilgrims visit the church from Minyā, Asyūṭ and even Cairo.

To the S lies Ṭihnā al-Gabal (see below).

Next on the H2 is (25km) **al-Minyā**, popularly called *al-Minyā al-Fulī* (after Sh. Aḥ. al-Fulī) to distinguish it from other towns with the same name throughout Egypt. This is one of the most important cities in the Nile Valley and has been chief city of the province and district of the same name since 1833 when the former was created, replacing Mallawī.

Mainline railway station; long-distance and local bus stations in town centre.

**Hotels**. *Nefertiti* (2*), 8 Shʿ. al-Nīl; *Lotus*, (2*), Shʿ. Būr Saʿīd; *Savoy* (2*), Shʿ. al-Mahaṭṭah; *Ibn Kassif* (2*), behind station; *Seti Hotel* (3*).

This is a pleasant city, with a university, overlooking the Nile. There is a large Coptic community and a cathedral. It is a good centre from which to visit al-Ashmunayn, al-ʿAmarnah, Banī Ḥasan and Zāwiyat al-Amwāt.

W of al-Minyā is **al-Tallah** and the airport (for internal flights).

From al-Minyā a boat can be taken S to the East Bank for **al-Sawādah** (4km).

Here a donkey and guide can be taken to **Deir Abā Hūr** (1km), a site with a Christian church of great antiquity and beauty. At the foot of the sheer cliffs close to the village and great cemetery is the *Church of St. Hor* (torch necessary). It is entirely rock-cut and subterranean, entered down a narrow stepped tunnel. Hor, the son of a blacksmith, went to Pelusium in the late 3C and confessed his Christianity. After being tortured he converted the governor and his family. The next governor executed his predecessor and sent Hor back to Antinoe for execution. His mulid is 12 Abib (6 July) when many pilgrims come from Minyā, camping in the cemetery. The nave surmounted by a dome is separated from the side aisles by four pillars. Fine ivory work can be seen in the wooden haykal screen in front of the two sanctuaries dedicated to St. Hor (N) and the Virgin (S). In the former is an ikon of St. Hor (1838) while above is reputed to be the tomb of the patron saint. There is a well in the NW corner.

Above this church is the *Upper Church of St. Damyana*. The haykal has a wooden screen and although there were originally three altars only that in the centre dedicated to the patroness is now in use. There are 19C ikons of the apostles, angels and Jesus. It is possible to climb from the outside onto the top of the church. Next to the dome is a fine 5C marble frieze serving as a threshold. In the cemetery is the *Tomb of Guy Weldon Baker*, son of Baker Pasha VC, who died of cholera on 27 July 1896, aged 25, while serving as an officer in the khedive's Coast Guards. His tomb was erected by Bishay Effendi Antunios of Minyā.

4km S of Sawādah is **Zāwiyat al-Amwāt** (or Zāwiyat al-Mayitīn; Place of the Dead, a reference to the ancient cemetery), the site of an ancient necropolis. The necropolis is grouped around an unidentified structure, said to be an unfinished 3 Dyn. *Step Pyramid*, but examination in 1912 proved inconclusive. There are 19 **Tombs of the nobles of Hebenu**, capital of the Oryx Nome, six of which are Old Kingdom. The area has been used as a quarry, destroying many of the tombs, and those left are not well preserved. Only two of the tombs are enclosed and the site scarcely repays a visit. One of the best preserved is the 18 Dyn. *Tomb of Nefer Sekeru*, 'Great Steward and Royal Scribe'. The East Bank road also leads N to (10km) **Ṭihnā al-Gabal**, site of ancient *Akoris*. A Japanese team has recently excavated a *Temple of Nero*, including the sacred way.

A boat can also be taken from *al-Minyā* to the East Bank for *Banī Ḥasan* (see below).

# 31 Al-Minyā to Mallawī

Running due S from the end of Rte 30, this route (total distance without the major detours approx. 47km) also suffers from lack of a permanent track on the East Bank, which here contains several major sites, reached by ferry.

**Al-Minyā**.—17km *Abyūhā*.—(3km) **al-Madīnat al-Fikriyyah** (for **Banī Ḥasan al-Shurrūq**).—11km **al-Maḥras**.—4km junction for **al-Ashmunayn** (1.5km), **Hermopolis** (12km) and the **Tombs of al-Bersha**.—12km **Mallawī**.

From al-Minyā the H2 runs S to (17km) *Abyūhā* and (3km) **al-Madīnat al-Fikriyyah**. E lies *Abū Qūrqās* where a ferry for the East Bank and **Banī Hasan al-Shurrūq** can be obtained.

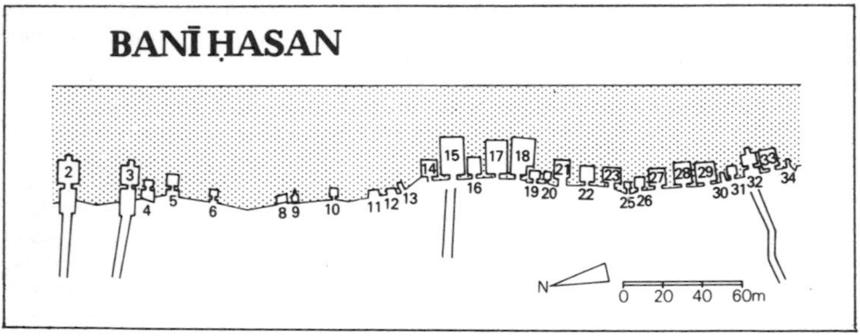
BANĪ ḤASAN
N
0 20 40 60m

Arrangements have to be made in advance for a boat from al-Minyā (half-day excursion) or from the river steamer (2½–3 hour excursion). The landing place which used to be to the S has been moved to the N and now emerges close to the resthouse. Tractors are no longer used but there are still donkeys to be hired. The ascent to the site is a climb of about 80m.

The name of the area is derived from the Banī Ḥasan Arabs who settled here in the 18C. In ancient times this was the *Necropolis of the Governors of the Oryx Nome*, chosen because of the narrow band of good quality limestone running along the cliff face.

There are 39 tomb-chapels; all of Middle Kingdom date. Only 12 are decorated and many are unfinished. The tombs of the nomarchs are all on one level. In front of them are the shaft graves of their officials and servants. They are chapels rather than tombs as the burials are in shafts in the rock-cut chambers. These tombs fall into three types. First and most numerous are those of the 11 Dyn. with uncolumned single rooms and a false door on the inner wall. The second type has delicately painted lotus bud columns (many of which have been cut away) quite unnecessarily supporting the roof. The third type (12 Dyn.) consists of an ante-chamber with two columns in antis and an inner room with burial shafts in the floor. In front of the ante-chamber are the remains of causeways, lined with flint boulders, leading down the side of the hill. The main group of tombs is decorated with paintings of great interest in that prayers are written to Osiris and Anubis and other deities are mentioned but no gods or goddesses are depicted. Many of the scenes are partly obscured by dirt and a film of dust; some are being cleaned by the Dept of Antiquities.

The first tomb-chapel of interest is 11 Dyn., that of **Kheti** (No. 17), governor of the Oryx Nome, son of Bakht III, with the chapel divided by lotus columns. Scenes on the walls depict hunting and offering bearers, fighting and wrestling, and a stele.

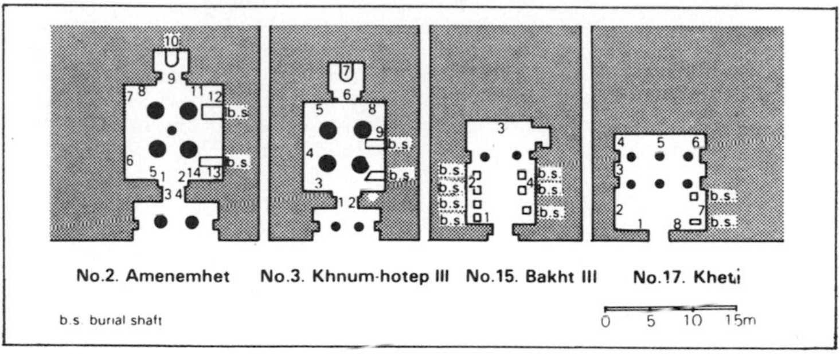
No.2. Amenemhet
No.3. Khnum-hotep III
No.15. Bakht III
No.17. Kheti
b.s. burial shaft
0 5 10 15m

(1) Harpooning fish and netting birds in papyrus swamp. (2) Hunting, linen workers, weavers, offering bearers. (3) Hunting in desert. (4) Offerings. (5) Wrestling, attack on fort, offerings. (6) Vintage and bird trapping. (7) Statue of Kheti in shrine, dancers. (8) Offerings.

**Bakht III** (No. 15), 11 Dyn. governor of the Oryx nome, a rectangular tomb-chapel with two columns and seven tomb shafts.

(1) Hunting in the marshes and gathering papyrus. (2) Hunting in the desert, Bakht and wife watching weavers and acrobats, counting cattle, arts and crafts; this decoration is interesting in that it depicts mythological animals among those of the desert. (3) Wrestling, and attack on fortress, soldiers and dancing. (4) In a shrine, offerings and an altar before Bakht. (5) Bakht watching funeral procession, offerings, potters and metal workers. (6) Offerings, desert scenes and goats, flax harvest, granaries and boats.

Other 11 Dyn. tomb-chapels worth visiting are those of *Bakht I* (No. 29), nomarch; *Remushanta* (No. 21), nomarch, and *Nuternakht* (No. 23), governor of the Eastern Province, with some Coptic inscriptions.

Two 12 Dyn. tombs are the best preserved. Both are entered through an ante-chamber, now largely gone, with two proto-Doric columns cut in the limestone. **Khnumhotep** (No. 3), of the time of Amenemhat II, is the finest (still being cleaned so only parts of the scenes are clearly seen). Besides that of governor, Khnumhotep held many titles including Prince of Menhat Khufu (birthplace of Khufu, within the Oryx nome). This chapel is famous for its finely drawn animal and bird scenes, and the Amu and their donkeys.

(1–2) Biographical text. (3) Harvest, ploughing, voyage to Abydos. (4) Hunting in desert. (5) Khnum-hotep and wife fishing and fowling in papyrus swamp. (6) Shrine. (7) Statue of deceased. (8) Harpooning fish. (9) Priests with wife, offering bearers and sons. (10) Dyers, carpenters, boat building. (11) Above door: acrobats and men dragging statue in shrine.

**Amenemhat**, called Ameni (No. 2) (time of Senusert I), nomarch and commander-in-chief of the Oryx nome. This again is a rectangular chapel with four columns and two burial shafts. It is entered through a columned doorway portico in antis.

On each side of the door are (1–2) the names and titles of Amenemhat; (3–4) biographical text giving the date of the burial (year 43) of Senusert I, and an account of the expeditions that Amenemhat made to Kush and his address to visitors to the tomb chapel: 'O you who love life and hate death, say: Thousands of bread and beer, thousands of cattle and wild fowl for the ka of the hereditary prince ... the Great Chief of the Oryx Nome ... Ameni justified' (a term for the dead). (5) 7th Register: knife-makers, leather-workers, carpenters, goldsmiths. (6–7) 6th Register: hunting, funeral procession, offerings. (8) 1st–3rd Registers: wrestlers. 4th Register: attack on fortress. 5th Register: voyage to Abydos. (9) Shrine. (10) Statues (destroyed) of Amenemhat between wife and mother. (11) 1st–3rd Registers: wrestlers, 4th–5th Registers: fighting. 6th Register: voyage to Abydos. (12) Offerings. (13) Attendants and harpers. (14) Painted false door.

1.5km SE of Banī Ḥasan is a wadi running in from the river with (550m) the **Speos Artemidos** (Grotto of Artemis), popularly called *Iṣṭabl ʿAntar* (Stable of ʿAntar, a warrior-poet of the pre-Islamic Arabs, the subject of many folk-tales). This rock-cut temple, dedicated to the lion goddess Pakht, dates from the 18 Dyn., largely the work of Hatshepsut and Tuthmosis III. The main inscription gives an account of the work performed by Hatshepsut to restore damage caused by the Hyksos. However, the queen's cartouches were hammered out under Seti I, who inserted his own name and titles. A road leads from *Banī Ḥasan* to the S passing **al-Shaykh Timay** (3km) and on to *al-Shaykh ʿIbādah* (see below).

Beyond *al-Fikriyyah* on the H2 are (5km) *Itlīdim* and (6km) **al-Maḥraṣ**.

The highway continues to *Mallawī* (see p 494), but at 4km there is a junction leading to the W and **al-Ashmūnayn** (1.5km), in ancient times site of *Khmunu*, capital city of Unu or Wnu, the Hare Nome. In Ptolemaic times it was called *Hermopolis Magna* but the Coptic name, *Shumun*, was derived from the ancient name and is perpetuated in the modern Arabic.

Khmunu was the city of the moon god Thoth, and therefore also known as Pr Thoth (House of Thoth). Thoth was the vizier of the gods and in his lunar aspect the reckoner of time, thus leading the Greeks to equate him with Hermes Trismegistos (the thrice great) and to rename the city Hermopolis-Magna (to distinguish it from Hermopolis Parva at Tell Baqliyyah in the Eastern Delta). Another ancient epithet of the city was Sesnou—City of the Eight—referring to the primaeval gods of the Hermopolitan ogdoad, male and female principals of chaos, Nun and Nunet, Hu and Huket, Kuk and Kuket, and Amun and Amunet. In common with many others in Egypt this was a dual city, one secular, the other sacred, the first perhaps with the same name as the nome while Khmunu was the sacred city. As far back as the Old Kingdom the High Priest held the title Governor of the Two Places. The city extended to both sides of the river, the quay to the SE lying just N of the modern landing stage at Rayramūn and the early necropolises on the East Bank at al-Sh. Saʿīd and al-Barshā, but in the Ptolemaic period Tūnah al-Gabal on the West Bank was used. After the Arab conquest it continued as the chief town of the district. It was renowned during the Middle Ages for its good earth and the production of carpets but in the mid 18C it was superseded as chief town by Mallawī and subsequently by al-Minyā. The first examination of the site was by Napoleon's scholars. In the 20C it has been studied by the Germans under Roeder between 1929–32, and presently by the British Museum.

Little of the ancient city can be distinguished except for large mounds of rubble, mud-brick and potsherds; much of it must lie under the modern town. The German excavations to the N of the town revealed the foundations of a Middle and New Kingdom *Temple of Thoth*, very despoiled as the site was used for building materials from Ptolemaic to Muslim times. A large enclosure wall, partly buried, partly free-standing, was found. It contained an area of c 637sq. m and in front of what must have been the main gate stand two stone baboons (much weathered); there were originally six. A second enclosure must have stood to the S surrounding the now-destroyed Temple of Ramesses II, but the modern town has encroached over it. At the N of the site a later *Temple of Thoth*, erected by Philip Arrhidaeus, was discovered by the French but was destroyed in 1822; only the bases of the columns remain.

The N wall of the sacred enclosure of the Temple of Thoth has been discovered, and probably the Dromos of Hermes mentioned in the Greek papyri of Hermopolis. This was the principal axis of the city during the Ptolemaic city until the 3C AD. An earlier Temple of Thoth has also been discovered, destroyed to make way for the Ptolemaic building.

In the centre of the city stands the *Kom al-Kanīsah* (Mound of the Church), originally, but mistakenly, thought to be the site of the agora (market place). Excavations by the Dept of Antiquities and Alexandria University revealed the remains of a basilica, built with material from an earlier temple dedicated to Ptolemy III, Euergetes I and his wife Berenice, by Greek soldiers settled in Hermopolis. There must have been four structures, all built of limestone from quarries near Tūnah al-Gabal, within the enclosure wall of this temple, the main Doric Temple, an Ionic building with a fine doorway and a large Corinthian building of which some of the capitals survive. Thus this site shared with Naucratis (Rte 45) buildings of Greek religious form rather than Egyptian or hybrid type.

In the *Basilica* many columns survive in their original position but the walls have disappeared, the stone being used in the local lime kilns. On constructional evidence the church would seem to date from the 5C, being similar in some respects to the churches of Abū Mīnā (Rte 42), Suhāg (Rte 33) and Dendārah (Rte 35). It is certainly large enough to have served as the cathedral of the town. The dedication of the church is uncertain, but it is known that several churches in al-Ashmūnayn were dedicated to the Virgin and this may have been one of them. It is entered through either of the two main doors in the N and W walls; a triumphal arch leads into the nave (with a span of 13.8m), separated from the side aisles by monolithic red granite columns which are linked to a similar transverse arcade passing across the E end in front of the trefoil apse. The remains of the small pillars which raised the altar table can be seen at the E end of the nave.

To the W in the desert is **Tūnah al-Gabal** (6km) and 6km to the SW is the late **Necropolis of Hermopolis**. Just before the site to the N is the rock-cut *Stela of Akhenaten* (A) (c 10 minute walk through soft sand), one of the boundary markers that this king set around the city of Akhetaten on both sides of the river. Here Akhenaten is depicted with Nefertiti and two of the princesses before the sun-disk and an offering table. It is dated

Year 6 of the king's reign. Stela B lies several kilometres S of the wadi. On the right of the entrance to the **Necropolis** is a government rest-house.

A team from Cairo University under Sami Gabra has examined this site which is centred on a Temple of Thoth and a complex of animal hypogea. There are whole streets containing in total 60 brick funerary houses and nine limestone tomb-chapels dating from Ramesside to Roman times. In addition there are inns and lodging places for the many pilgrims who visited the temple and animal necropolis. The scenes on the walls are a mixture of Egyptian and Greek themes, the latter including the epic of Oedipus, Pluto abducting Persephone, the Trojan Horse and tragic and comic masks, while more orthodox Egyptian motifs are the Last Judgement, various deities and a black skeletal figure representing the soul. One house is dedicated to Dionysiac rituals, revetted in simulated marble, similar to the House of Menander at Pompeii. The scenes in some of the buildings are executed by Alexandrine artists. Owners of some houses cannot be identified; others are known to have belonged to families from Alexandria or elsewhere, but of great interest is the cosmopolitan nature of the people buried here—indeed after the Persian invasions and throughout the Ptolemaic and Roman periods the population of Egypt must have been an amalgam of peoples.

Most important of the monuments is the free-standing *Tomb-Chapel of Petosiris* (Pedosiri), High Priest of Thoth, dated to c 300 BC, erected for his father Seshu and elder brother Zed-Thoth-ef-Ankh. Its form is that of a rectangular late Egyptian temple, 6m by 7m. In front of the entrance is a limestone horned altar. The burial chambers are 8m below ground level, and three generations of high priests were buried here. On the walls the paintings show a strong Greek influence in the form of clothing, the type of sacrifice and the use of perspective. Many generations of pilgrims must have used this tomb as it is covered with graffiti, often over the scenes on the walls. Some of these people seem to have been slaves, worshippers of Mithras, perhaps descendants of Persian slaves who settled here.

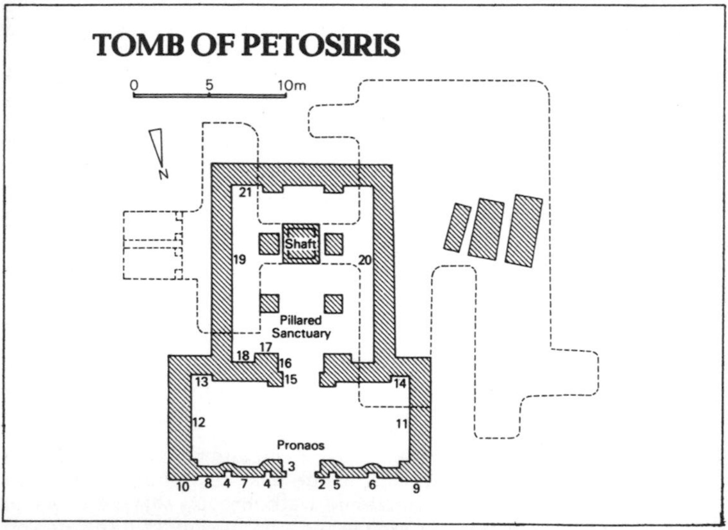
TOMB OF PETOSIRIS
0
5
10m
N
21
Shaft
19
20
Pillared Sanctuary
17
18
16
15
13
14
12
11
Pronaos
3
10 8 4 7 4 1
2 5 6 9

(1–2) Texts of the life of Petosiris. (3) The speech of Petosiris. (4–6) Titles of Petosiris. (7–8) Petosiris offers to Thoth and (9) to Sokar-Osiris and (10) Osiris and Isis. (11–12)

Cattle, the vintage, harvest and winnowing. (13–16) Bibliographical texts of Petosiris, Zed-thoth-ankh and Sheshu. (17) Hymn to Osiris. (18) Sheshu and wife before Nut in a tree. (19) Mummy of Sheshu with grandson Zeho making offerings, text of the 'Opening of the Mouth'. (20) Zed-thoth-ankh adores Osiris and is taken to him. (21) Sheshu before genii. On the columns are the titles of Shesu and Zed-thoth-ankh.

To the SE is the small funerary *Chapel of Ptoemais*, slightly raised and entered by six steps. The entry is to the S reversing the usual practice and in front of it is a horned altar. Stylistically the decoration is transitional between Egyptian and Greco-Roman with a frieze of uraei, and solar disk and false windows. To the left is a small white two-storeyed structure, the *Tomb-Chapel of Isadora*, of the time of Antoninus Pius (AD 138–61). Isadora was drowned in the Nile, a death which resulted in the establishment of a cult. The lower storey was used for prayers and has three niches and imitation marble decoration. On the first floor is the mummy chamber, a lion bedstead, unfortunately damaged when the tomb was robbed. There is also a series of plaster funerary masks. To the W stands a *stone structure* in the form of a step pyramid c 3m high, the monument of a merchant, a servant of Thoth. E of Petosiris's tomb-chapel is the monument of one of his relatives, the *Tomb-Chapel of Petekaken*, royal scribe of accounts of P-mek in the Hermopolitan Nome, prophet of the Living Cat in the Temple of Pakht. His father Dhuty is also buried here.

The temple of Thoth, called the *Temple of the Superior Spirits* (much destroyed), was attached to the subterranean gallery tombs of the sacred animals and birds. There is also the site of a park where the sacred ibis were kept and balustrades mark the limits of the pilgrims' route. The birds were generally poorly mummified; they were either wrapped in linen or placed in a box or jar deposited on shelves or in niches, or just piled up in side galleries leading off the main passage. There must have been many thousands of them in each of the galleries but they were not buried with any objects.

N of the temple (c 800m) is *Gallery A*, primarily consecrated to the cult of the ibis but other birds such as falcons and flamingoes were also buried here. At the entrance was a limestone funerary chapel (destroyed). It is reached by 75 rock-cut steps leading into an ante-chamber. *Gallery B*, entered by 80 steps, partly built and partly rock-cut, leading to an ante-chamber, is the largest of the underground chambers with three corridors from which galleries radiate in all directions, their shape conditioned by the nature of the rock. If the ancient excavators came upon friable rock they used it to cut communication passages, not side galleries or locculi. One of the corridors is 240m long and leads into *Gallery C*, which seems to be the oldest so far discovered. Although the Chapel is dedicated to Alexander the Great and his wife Roxane, the gallery itself dates to the 19 Dyn. and the reconstruction of the chapel is probably the last of many. This gallery was reserved for the sacred baboons of Thoth and in some cases the bodies of the high priests who had elected to be buried amid their sacred charges. At the entry was the Archive Bureau, four rooms opening consecutively which in spite of the depredations of robbers still contained some important papyri arranged in an orderly manner in carefully sealed jars. The jars contained, among many others, a judicial papyrus concerning the administration of the priests of Thoth and seven letters in Aramaean on their way by courier from Elephantine to Memphis during the Persian period. Also in this gallery were many figures of priests in wood, stone or bronze. (Objects from here are now in the museum at Mallawī.)

From the junction below **al-Maḥras** on the H2 a road also runs E along the bank of the Nile, circling past **al-Rawḍah** (8km) and **al-Rayramūn** (4km) to Mallawī (see below). Just above al-Rawḍah a ferry can be taken to the East Bank for the village of **al-Shaykh ʿIbādah**, E of which lies the large site of the ruined town of *Antinopolis*, or Antinoe, founded in 130 AD by Emperor Hadrian in memory of his favourite, Antinous. The latter accompanied Hadrian on his tour of the empire but drowned near this site during the visit to Egypt. It was said that Antinous had sacrificed his life to thwart a prophecy that had predicted a calamity for the emperor. He was deified, temples were built and statues, coins and gems of him were distributed throughout the empire. To the NE of the village below the cliffs are the remains of an *ancient monastery* surrounded by three ruined churches (wall paintings, Coptic graffiti and architectural detail).

Walk 2km E to the ruined **Church of al-ʿAdhrā** (excavated and partly restored in 1934), shut with an iron door (keys with Antiquities Guard who lives in Sh. ʿIbādah). This was not the first church on the site as the walls of a much larger church can be distinguished. There are still some interesting wall paintings (partly damaged) and the Virgin can be traced on the S wall. At the far end of the site the remains of a *Ramesside Temple* can be seen.

Further S (also reached by boat from al-Bayāḍiyyah below al-Rayramūn) lies the village of **Deir Abū Ḥinnis** (Monastery of St. John) and the *Church of Abū Hinnis* (St. John the Short) consisting of narthex, nave, sanctuaries and baptistery (keys with priest who lives next to the church). It is another church traditionally founded by St. Helena though there is no proof of this. St. John the Short was a native of Tese near Oxyrynchus during the 4C. He founded a community of hermits at Scetis.

This church is of interest as it represents the transition from the basilican form to that roofed with domes, the crude supporting piers make the building rather dark. The nave is divided into three bays covered by domes and many columns with acanthus capitals taken from a neighbouring ancient temple. There are two haykals, dedicated to the Virgin and St. John the Short. Among the paintings of interest are a 17C ikon of the Virgin and 18 and 19C ikons of St. John the Short and a copy of Raphael's Madonna di San Sisto.

SE of the village, past several cemeteries, is (3km) the *Cave Church of Abū Ḥinnis* (key with priest in Deir Abū Ḥinnis), built into three caves. An impressive entrance approached down a flight of steps leads into a very large narthex. There is a particularly rich collection of 6–7C wall paintings (unfortunately defaced) representing scenes from the life of Christ, including the Massacre of the Innocents, the Visitation, the Flight into Egypt, the Wedding Feast at Cana and the Resurrection of Lazarus. In addition there are many Coptic graffiti. Work has recently been done here by the University of Helsinki and two pharaonic stele were discovered.

S of Deir Abū Ḥinnis lies (4km) **Deir al-Bersha** (Dayr al-Barshā) and an ancient monastery, the *Deir Anbā Bishuy*, now ruined, with remains of well, saqiyyah and mill. However, the church, consisting of two buildings in the NE of the enclosure, is well preserved (key with Coptic priest in village). This monastery was traditionally founded by St. Bishoi and in the 6–7C had a population of a thousand monks, half of whom lived in the surrounding rock-cut tombs. The church was regularly in use until recently but is now only used for special occasions.

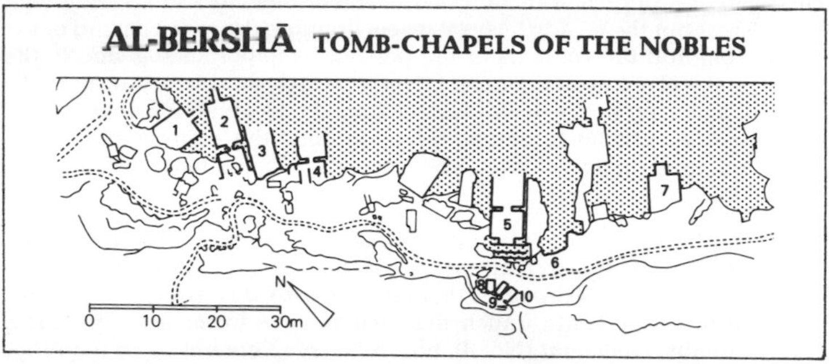
AL-BERSHĀ TOMB-CHAPELS OF THE NOBLES
1
2
3
4
5
6
7
8
9
10
N
0
10
20
30m

The lower church, called the *Church of Anbā Bishuy*, has three haykals dedicated to the patron saint (centre) and the Virgin and St. George to the sides. Ikons cover the haykal screen, which is unusually constructed of baked brick and seems to be ancient. At the SW corner is a bakery and in the NW the baptistery while to the S are the tombs of two priests. At the N end is the stairway to the *Upper Church*, certainly of greater antiquity. There are two haykals with a screen dated 1866 and the five domes, perhaps dating to the 13C, are finely decorated with geometrical motifs including stars and crosses.

N of the village (half an hour by donkey followed by a steep climb up the hillside) are the **Tomb-Chapels of al-Bersha**, which can be seen from the causeway leading up to the terrace, clearly marked by large boulders. The main group of tombs (Nos 1–10) are 12 Dyn. in date. The whole area has been riven with earthquakes and later extensively quarried. From NW to SE the tomb-chapels are those of *Dhutinakht VI* (No. 1), nomarch and vizier, destroyed by an earthquake, next to which is that of *Dhutihotep II* (No. 2), governor of the Hare Nome during the reigns of Senusert II and III, the most important of the group. This tomb was

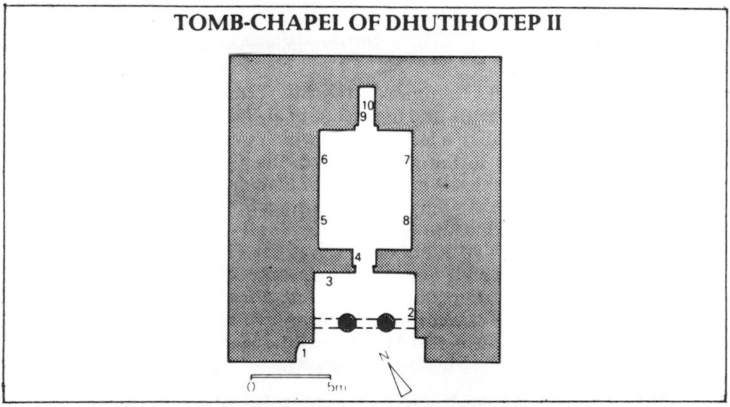
TOMB-CHAPEL OF DHUTIHOTEP II
10
9
6
7
5
8
4
3
2
1
N
0
5m

(1) Texts destroyed. (2) Hunting. (3) Hunting. (4) Texts damaged. (5–6) Transport of colossus. (7–8) Agricultural scenes, bread-making. (9–10) Funerary scenes.

discovered in 1817 by two English naval officers, Irby and Mangles, having been overlooked by the Napoleonic survey. The tomb originally consisted of a portico, a rectangular chamber beyond and a shrine with burial shaft but the façade has collapsed, bringing down the ceiling of the outer room and the columns of the portico. Its importance is due to the scene on the NW side of the inner chamber which shows the transport of a colossal alabaster figure of Dhutihotep from the Hat Nub (SE of al-ʿAmarnah) quarries. Owing to damage done in 1890 the scene is difficult to make out and many of the other paintings have been deliberately damaged.

*Sep* (No. 3), destroyed; *Neheri* (No. 4), destroyed, except the back wall; *Ahanakht* (No. 5), nomarch and vizier, is complete but the entry and some of the paintings are destroyed; *Dhutinakht* (No. 6), destroyed; *Neheri* (No. 7), great priest of Thoth, much destruction. At a lower level are three smaller tombs, *Ahanakht* (No. 8), nomarch, complete but some paintings destroyed; *Khnum-nakht* (No. 9) and *Ahanakht* (No. 10).

Below the last group are some Old Kingdom remains. To the W are further important Middle Kingdom tombs, all of 12 Dyn. officials (numbered according to Kamal): *Sitipi and Ankh* (No. 17); *Sepi I* (No. 15); *Sepi II and Sepi III* (No. 14) (outer coffin of Sepi III in the EM, No. 28083); *Neferi* (No. 13); *Neheri* (No. 11); *Sit-Hez-hotep* (No. 20), and another of the same name on top of a mountain NE of this group. Nearly all the funerary remains were excavated by Kamal and are in the EM.

Beyond al-Rayramūn (2km) the H2 runs on to **Mallawī**, chief town of the district in the province of al-Minyā. In early Ottoman times this town usurped the position of al-Ashmūnayn as chief town of the area but in 1824 it was itself replaced by al-Minya. It has a railway station, long-distance and local bus stations. The *Museum* has local finds, the most important of which are from the site of al-Ashmūnayn. They incude statues, sarcophagi, bronzes, pottery and mummified ibises and baboons. It is often shut so arrangements must be made with the Tourist Office in al-Minyā for the keys to be available. Of interest are the local beehives made from pottery drain pipes similar to those depicted in Saite tombs at Thebes.

From Mallawī visits may be made to *al-Sh. ʿIbādah, al-Ashmūnayn, Tūnah al-Gabal* and *al-Bersha* (see above); *al-Sh. Sa ʿīd, al ʿAmārnah* and *Mīr* (see below).

# 32 Mallawī to Asyūṭ

With no permanent track on the East Bank, this route (total distance approx. 91km) runs down the West Bank. The important sites on the East Bank are reached by ferry, and there are rewarding diversions on the West Bank.

**Mallawī**.—4km *al-Maʿṣarah* (for **al-Shaykh Saʿīd** and, 10km S by boat, **al-ʿAmārnah**).—10km **Deir Mawās**.—12km **Ṣanabū**.—10km **al-Qūṣiyyah**.—43km **Manqabād**.—12km **Asyūṭ**.

Below Mallawī the H2 continues S, reaching (4km) **al-Maʿṣarah** and the ferry for the East Bank. Directly opposite is Deir al-Quṣayr with ancient quarries and a stele of Ramesses III. Just S of the last is the village of

**al-Shaykh Saʿid**, its name derived from the tomb of a local shaykh which overlooks the river; he also gives his name to the ridge behind, the *Gabal Shaykh Saʿīd*, which terminates at the S in the Wadi Zubaydah (named after the tomb of another local shaykh) which runs from the al-ʿAmārnah plain. In the hills overlooking the river are the **Tomb-Chapels of Shaykh Saʿid**, an important Old Kingdom Necropolis. The chapels, some of which have unfortunately been quarried, show up clearly in the rock face which rises a further 100m above them. A track over a steep spur leads up to the chapels which are on two levels joined by a stoney track. They can be reached by tractor up the wadi from al-Till or by crossing the river from Mallawī.

First reached are *two small chapels* (un-numbered) and then the major group of 90 tombs, six of which are the most important (the numbers originally given to the tombs by Davies are indicated by D). *Serfka* (No. 1; originally called Urana C, D24), prophet of Khufu and Userkaf, has a recessed door, with the top almost destroyed, the architrave with the hotep di nesu (offering text). The tomb consists of two chambers with a tomb shaft in the inner room and remains of statues of Serfka and wife in a recess on the E wall. The painted scenes show offerings, musicians, taxes being received, dancers and fishing. *Werini* (No. 2; D25), son of Serfka and overseer of the New Towns, originally seems to have had two chambers but the rock wall between was destroyed when the tomb was used as a retreat by Coptic ascetics. The paintings were plastered over, thus helping preservation, though others were deliberately destroyed. *Meru* called Bebi (No. 3; D20), Ruler of the House of Pepi and Chancellor of Lower Egypt, was originally quite an elaborate tomb-chapel with four rooms and two tomb shafts, but the façade has fallen away. The path now passes under the cliff face in front of several damaged tombs, of which only a few show traces of decoration. At *No. 11* is a rock ledge round which the path deviates and on this is *Teti-Ankh* called Imhotep (No. 6; D15), restored in the 12 Dyn. Also on this ledge are two smaller burial places. The path descends, covered with loose stones almost obscuring *Mehu* (No. 5; D15) which is cut in the stone above, reached by rough steps up an almost vertical face. This tomb was also occupied by his wife Henet. Next are two small tomb-chapels. Along the upper range are *Tomb-Chapels Nos 40–89*, crowded and mainly uninscribed, with shattered façades. *Tomb-Chapels Nos 26–34* are all uninscribed but *No. 37* is interesting because of its proportions and *No. 39* was turned into an early Coptic chapel. The later inhabitants of these tombs seem to have been Copts in nearly all cases, but with at least two periods of occupation. Outside some of the tombs are traces of mud walls. Some had been made into quite comfortable dwellings, others had been used as a later burial place. The date of occupation was probably 4C AD.

By following a track leading beside Tomb No. 34, the *Southern Group of Tomb-Chapels* is reached (Nos 90–93). They are not worth visiting. Downhill are a further nine tomb-chapels, all uninscribed. To the SE over the hill beyond a dried watercourse is another *small cemetery*, also probably Old Kingdom in date.

S of al-Shaykh Saʿīd lies the site known as **al-ʿAmārnah** (10km), called erroneously Tell al-ʿAmārnah. The whole area takes its name from a local tribe, the Banī ʿAmrān. It can be reached by ferry from *al-Maʿṣarah* or from the steamer which berths at the N of the site. Four villages lie along the rather infertile plain between the river and the hills; from N to S these are **al-Till** (the village mentioned above; the ferry docks to the N of this

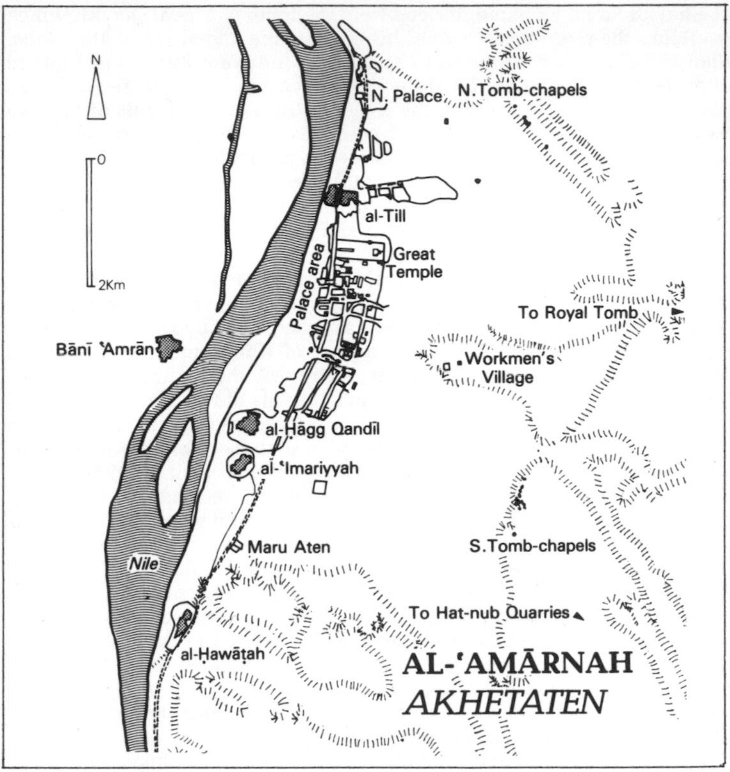
N
0
2Km
N. Palace
N.Tomb-chapels
al-Till
Great
Temple
Palace area
To Royal Tomb
Bānī ʿAmrān
Workmen's
Village
al-Ḥāgg Qandīl
al-ʿImariyyah
Maru Aten
S.Tomb-chapels
Nile
To Hat-nub Quarries
al-Ḥawāṭah
AL-ʿAMĀRNAH
AKHETATEN

village, opposite the hospital), (3.5km) **al-Ḥāgg Qandīl**, (0.5km) **al-ʿImariyyah al-Sharqiyyah** and (3km) **al-Ḥawaṭah**. This rather unattractive site is prone to flooding during the infrequent rain storms as the rainwater builds up into a shallow lake behind the hills and bursts out suddenly, inundating the plain. In the mid-1960s a flood completely washed away the village of al-Till except for the only concrete building—the police station.

The site can be approached from either al-Till or al-Ḥāgg Qandīl, usually the former, where steamers and the car-ferries from the road junction for Mallawī berth. Tractor-wagon or donkeys are necessary if anything other than the main city site is to be visited. To see the remains of the town and the N tombs a good half day is required. To the E of the village of al-Till is a resthouse where refreshments can be obtained.

The fame of the site derives from the fact that here Akhenaten decided to build his short-lived capital Akhetaten. This was a mistake as it lay within the bounds of Hermopolis, city of the moon god Thoth, and one of the largest provincial cities in Ancient Egypt. The site of Akhetaten stretches for some 5–6km along the river about 1km inland from the river's edge and the whole complex of scattered buildings is joined by a road, the Sikkat al-Sulṭān (Road of the Sultan) cut by a modern drainage canal. To the E in the hills is a necropolis with two groups of tombs to the N and S.

In years 4 and 6 of his reign Akhenaten, who had changed his name from

Amenhotep (IV), issued proclamations announcing the foundation of Akhetaten 'as a new residence for the Aten', at the same time making an oath never to leave the city even after his death. He set up a series of stelae marking the boundaries of the new city, the W one across the river near Tūnah al-Gabal, the S ones ran just S of the route to the Hat Nub stone quarries. The chief architect of the new city was Hatiay, but the man who probably had most to do with the construction was Nanakhtef, 'the Overseer of the Bricklayers of Akhetaten'. The city is a blend of structures, the residential quarters mixed with temples and state buildings. All the buildings, houses, palaces and even temples were constructed of mud-brick with stone or wood only used for columns and doorsills, the impression being that the whole complex was constructed in a hurry. The city was only inhabited for about eleven years between 1373 BC and Akhenaten's death in 1362 when it was abandoned and the whole court returned to Thebes.

From the landing place to the NE it is possible to visit the *North Palace*, very much ruined but with column bases still in position. The **Northern Tomb-Chapels** are c 5km E; at the end of the walk, tractor or donkey ride

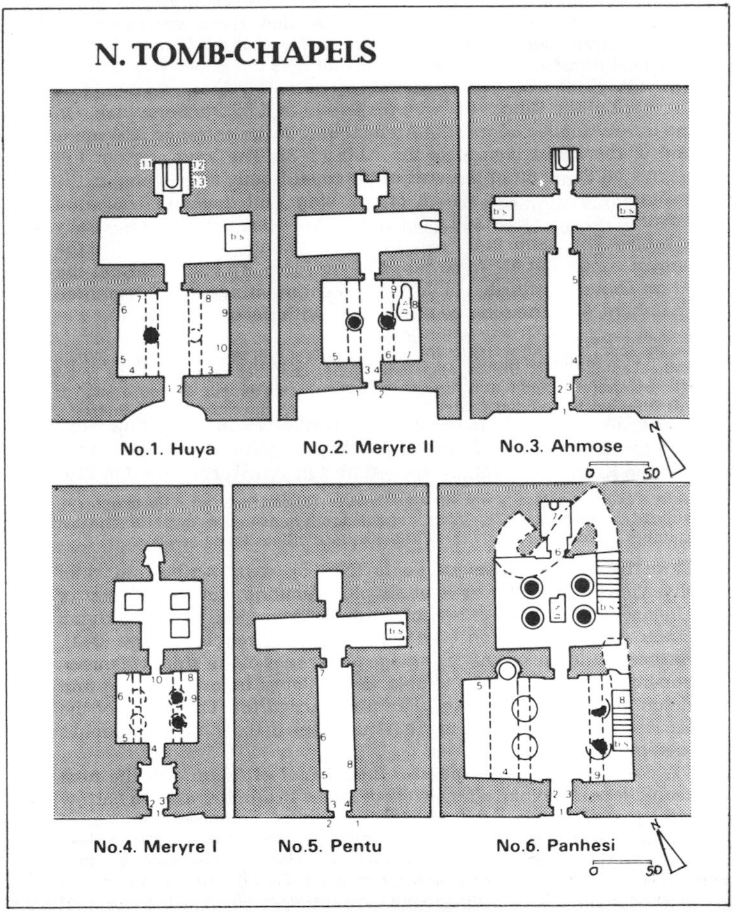
N. TOMB-CHAPELS
No.1. Huya
No.2. Meryre II
No.3. Ahmose
No.4. Meryre I
No.5. Pentu
No.6. Panhesi
N
0 50

there is a steep climb (70m) to the necropolis which is cut in the limestone escarpment. The limestone boulders scattered about are covered in iron oxides. None of the notables of Thebes seems to have accompanied Akhenaten to Akhetaten and all the men honoured seem to have been raised to their positions by the king, except for Ay, who had a tomb prepared for him in the S group. The decorations in all the tomb-chapels are notable for the fact that they give more space to Akhenaten's activities than those of the owners. Northernmost is that of *Huya* (No. 1), Superintendent of the Harem and Steward of Queen Tiy, one of the few tomb-chapels that were actually used. It is possible that Huya died during Tiy's visit to Akhetaten in year 122 of Akhenaten's reign. It consists of a pillared chamber, and an inner chamber with burial shaft and a shrine.

On the door jamb is the Hymn to the Aten (1–2). To the right of the first chamber the king and queen with two daughters at a table with Queen Tiy and one of her daughters (3), to the left king and queen and Queen Tiy drinking wine. On the left wall the royal family receives tribute from Syria and Kush (5–6). To the right and left of the entrance to the inner chamber Huya is rewarded (7) and wears decorations (8) while on the right wall Akhenaten and Queen Tiy visit the temple (9–10). In the shrine funeral furniture (11–12) and the funeral rites are shown (13). The statue of Huya is badly damaged.

The next tomb-chapel is that of *Meryre II* (No. 2), Royal Scribe, Overseer of the two Treasuries and Overseer of the Harem of the Great Royal Wife Nefertiti. This tomb is of interest in that it must have been constructed late in Akhenaten's reign or under his successor, as his cartouches have been replaced by those of Smenkhkare and Nefertiti's by those of her daughter Merytaten.

In the entry is the Hymn to the Aten (1–2) (largely destroyed), and Meryre is shown adoring the Aten (3–4) in the entrance passage. To the left of the first chamber Nefertiti offers Akhenaten a drink (5) and the upper register to the right shows Meryre rewarded by Akhenaten (6). Further inside are scenes of tribute (7–8) and another scene of Meryre rewarded by Semenkhkare (9).

There is quite a distance to the next tomb-chapels in this group which are beyond the next valley. The first is *Ahmose* (No. 3), Fan Bearer on the right of the King, very well preserved and of cruciform plan. On the lintel Ahmose adores the Aten (1) and in the entrance passage is one of the finest Hymns to the Aten (2–3). The long corridor has scenes on the right of the visit of the royal family to the temple, the military escort and a sketch of the king and queen in a chariot (incomplete) (4–5). In the lower register are scenes of the royal family at tables. The statue in the niche is much damaged. Next is one of the largest chapels at al-ʿAmārnah, *Meryre I* (No. 4), High Priest of the Aten. Though unfinished, it has important paintings. There are three chambers, only the pillared central one with decoration.

On the lintel the king worships the Aten (1). In the entrance passage are hymns to the Aten (2–3) and the entrance to first inner chamber depicts his wife Tenro (4). This chamber had four columns of which only two remain. The decoration in this latter hall is moulded plaster. To the left Meryre is invested as High Priest (5). On the NW wall are scenes of the royal family and escort leaving the palace for the temple (6), very important as they show the elevation of these two buildings. It was due to this and wall paintings in other tombs that the ancient appearance of some of the buildings of al-ʿAmārnah could be reconstructed. On the other walls are the royal family worshipping the Aten (8) and the king at the temple (9), while at the entrance to the interior chapel are hymns to the Aten (10). The last chamber is unfinished, only three of the square pillars have been cut.

Close by is the chapel of *Pentu* (No. 5), royal scribe and chief physician to the king. It is of simple cruciform shape, like that of Ahmose. At the entrance Pentu adores the Aten (1–2) while the Hymn to the Aten is found on both sides of the entrance passage (3–4). Further inside the entrance passage are scenes of the king and queen worshipping at the Aten temple (5–6), Pentu before the king and queen at the temple (7) and Pentu rewarded (8). The statue of the deceased which had been in the statue niche in the inner chamber has been removed.

A considerable gap separates the chapel of Pentu and the next tomb-chapel (reached after a walk of about 15 minutes along a narrow path), that of *Panehesi* (No. 6), chief servant of the Aten. Consisting of two chambers with four columns in each and two tomb shafts, it was never completed and the inner chamber was undecorated. During early Christian times it was converted into a Coptic church and the false door at the rear of the inner hall was changed into a baptistery.

On the lintel the royal family worship the Aten (1) and on the thickness of the entrance is the Hymn and scenes of Aten worship (2–3). In the first chamber Panehesi rewarded by the king (4), the royal family visit the temple of the Aten (5). In the second chamber on the right (10), the king drives from the palace (8) and the royal family worship the Aten (9). In the shrine (6) there is a scene of Panehesi's family at table (11) but his statue has been cut away.

To the S of al-Till (20-minute walk, 10 minutes by tractor) lie the remains of the central city, the northernmost building of which is the **Great Temple** set on an E–W axis enclosed within a vast temenos wall straddling which on the N is the *Hall of Foreign Tribute*. The temple contains the sanctuary, *Pr Hai* (House of Jubilation) and the *Gem Aten* (Aten has been found). The main entry to the temple lies in the middle of the W wall where there is a thin brick pylon. There are a number of pits containing Nile mud which must have contained trees planted in the enclosure. The inner and outer courts were filled with offering tables set around the altar. A theory that only vegetable offerings were made is disproved by the discovery of a *Butcher's Yard* outside the NW corner of the sanctuary, complete with tethering blocks for the animals. An *Avenue of Sphinxes* lying to the E leads to the *Sanctuary* which must have been built before year 9 of Akhenaten's reign as the early form of the Aten was used in the inscriptions. It is thought to have been deliberately destroyed by Horemheb. S of the main temenos walls are the main storehouses and magazines.

The '*House of the Rejoicing of the Aten*' lying to the S is divided into two parts: to the W of the road is the *Pr Aten* (House of the Aten), the Great State Palace, linked to the *Private Quarters* to the E by a brick bridge, traces of which can still be seen. The remains of the *Great State Palace* extend c 700m along the W side of the Sikkat al-Sulṭān and most probably originally occupied all the area between the river and the road but only about half the district has survived. When excavated by the EES in 1934–37 it was found to have been deliberately destroyed. Until the last few years there was little local encroachment on the area but now water seepage from the cultivation has rotted the plaster and destroyed much of the foundations on the riverward side. The palace was surrounded by a strong mud-brick wall and the original nucleus was added to during the

*Akhenaten, Nefertiti, and a princess worshipping the Aten. From a balustrade of the Palace (EM)*

reign of Smenkhkare. To the W of the road is the *Sunken garden* marked by column bases and fragments of painted pavements. S of this are the two harems. Constructed partly of stone, they have been more extensively robbed than the brick buildings. The *North Harem* is represented in the Tomb-Chapel of Ay (see below) and the *South Harem* abuts the remains of the road bridge. S of these are magazines and the vast columned hall added by Smenkhkare called the *Coronation Hall.* E of this complex is the Records Office where the cuneiform correspondence from Western Asian princes was found.

Another temple, the *Hat Aten* (Palace of the Aten), lies S of the Private Quarters, on the E of the road. The outer walls, heavily buttressed on all sides except the W, measure 400m by 100m. The entry is in the W wall between massive pylons, each with a low plinth and slots for flagstaffs. There seems to have been a double-leafed door and the stone sockets are still in position. From the main gate a whitewashed ramp leads to the first court. Offering tables of white-washed brick stood on either side and between them an altar and several bases may have supported statues. None of this is now easily visible as much has been sanded over.

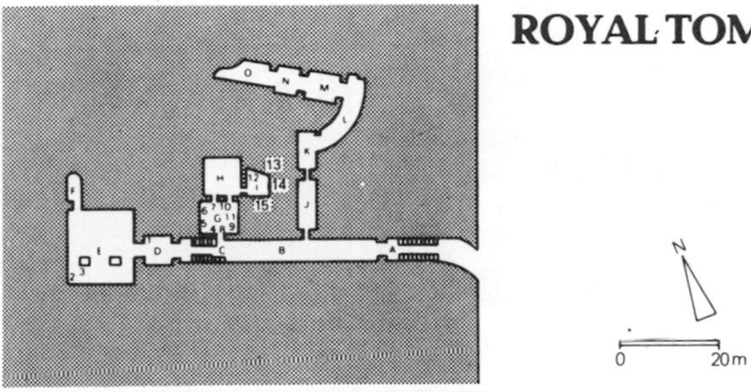
ROYAL TOMB
O
N
M
L
K
J
H
13
14
15
G
F
E
D
C
B
A
N
0
20m

Little can be discerned among the remains of the houses of the southern end of the town but in the *House of Dhutmosi*, master-sculptor, Burchardt found the famous bust of Queen Nefertiti (now in the Berlin Staatliche Museen). Further S, still just N of al-Ḥawaṭah, stands the *Maru Aten*, another temple.

E of the central complex lies the **Workmen's Village**, a collection of mud-brick huts similar to those at Deir al-Madīnah, though in the main much sanded up. They are now being re-examined.

To the E of the Workmen's Village lies the *Wadi Abū Ḥaṣā al-Bạhri* down which (5.5km) is the **Royal Tomb** (not accessible to visitors), the first 18 Dyn. royal tomb to run straight to the burial chamber (A–F) instead of curving to one side. However even this is not orthodox as there is a branch corridor to the right (G) as well as another complex of chambers on the same side further inside (H–K). It was certainly used for one of the princesses, Meketaten, second eldest daughter of Akhenaten and Nefertiti; scenes of her funeral are shown. But it may have been intended as a family sepulchre as fragments of a red granite sarcophagus inscribed with the name of Queen Tiy, the king's mother, were found near the tomb. It is possible that Nefertiti was buried here, but whether Akhenaten was also interred is more difficult to establish. It was cleared by Barsanti and the Dept of Antiquities, and later by the EES.

Shallow steps lead to the corridor (A) (25 fragments of ushabti figures of Akhenaten were found here, now in the EM), with the side passage off to the right. Then follow two corridors (B, C), the latter with another complex leading to the right, and a small square hall (D). The wall is undecorated until just before it reaches the square-pillared tomb-chamber (E) at the end. On the right on the door jamb is a woman, perhaps Princess Meketaten (1) and at the base of the wall are remains of a defaced text. On the W wall of the burial chamber is a burial scene and mourners (2) and on the innermost pillar part of the text 'royal acquaintance pure of hands' (3). Off corridor C are three rooms (H–K). On the NW wall of room H are registers of foreigners (4), soldiers (7) and the king and queen worshipping at the temple (5–6). On the W wall is the scene of the royal family mourning (8) and worshipping the Aten in the temple (9–10), the latter with a lower register of gazelles, ostriches, etc.

and soldiers (11). Fragments of a red granite sarcophagus thought to be that of Princess Meretaten were found in the corner of the room by Barsanti (now in Berlin Museum).

In the small room to the right is a famous scene with two princesses mourning beside a bier carrying Meketaten (14–15). There are also other mourning scenes, offerings and the king and queen (the scene of the princess on the bier has been destroyed) (12–13).

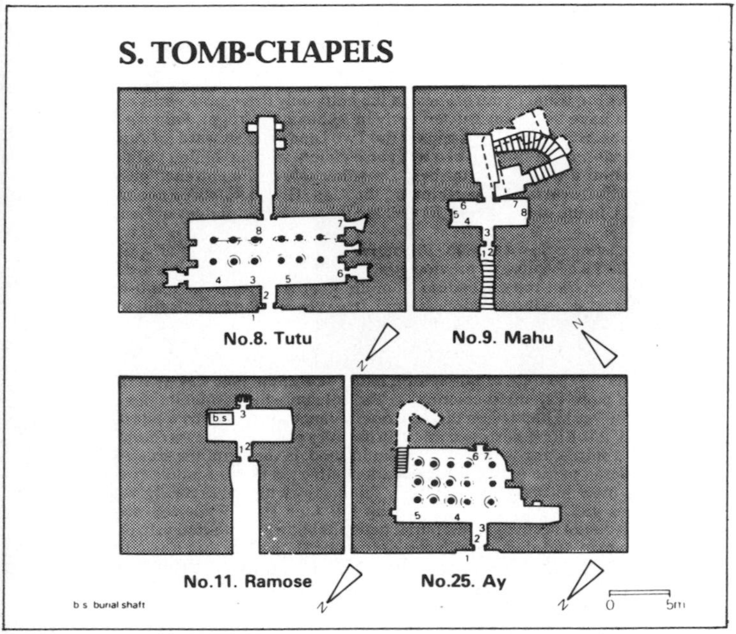
S. TOMB-CHAPELS
No.8. Tutu
No.9. Mahu
No.11. Ramose
No.25. Ay
b s burial shaft
0 5m

S of the wadi containing the Royal Tomb (2km, half an hour's drive by tractor from al-Till) are the **Southern Tomb-Chapels** (Nos 7–25) scattered over seven low hills in two groups, 7–15 and 16–25. There is no steep climb up the escarpment as there is with the Northern group. These tombs are seldom visited and special permission must be obtained along with a man to dig away the sand which blocks most of the doorways. The most interesting are those of Tutu, Mahu, Ipy, Ramose, Any, and Ay.

First is *Tutu* (No. 8) Chamberlain of Egypt, which though unfinished is unusual in combining the appearance of a rock-cut tomb with that of a free-standing mastaba, an effect achieved by hollowing out a free-standing rock, the floor cut to a lower level reached by a shallow sunken alley. It consists of two chambers, an outer pillared hall (unfinished) with three statue niches nearly completed in the SW wall, and an inner corridor running into the rock. On the door jambs the deceased kneels worshipping the Aten (1–2, damaged). In the entrance passage the royal family worship the Aten (3); Tutu kneels, and a Hymn to the Aten (4), largely destroyed. In the chamber Tutu before the king and queen (destroyed) seated in a door of the palace; Tutu with officials outside palace (8); Tutu rewarded from the Window of Appearances (9–11); Tutu adores Aten cartouches (12–13) and royal family and deceased worship the Aten (14–15).

*Mahu* (No. 9), Commandant of the Police, is a roughly cut irregular cruciform chapel with two burial shafts from the inner room. It is fairly small and has a long undecorated entry passage. Unfortunately this tomb has recently been badly damaged by tomb robbers. At the entrance is the Burial Petition (1–2, damaged) and in the passage the royal family with Merytaten worship the Aten (3), and Mahu with Hymn to the Aten (4). Inside the chamber Mahu rewarded by the king (5, partly destroyed); on a stela, the king and queen before altar with deceased; Mahu and troops before the temple (7–8); king and queen in chariot leave to inspect the defences (9–10), (the two last being of great interest) and on a stela the king and queen before an altar.

In the same group is *Ipy* (No. 10), Royal Scribe and Steward. It is unfinished and shows the usual hymn scenes. In the entry only three princesses are shown so it must have been constructed early in Akhenaten's reign. *Ramose* (No. 11), royal scribe, commander of troops of the Two Lands and steward (of Amenhotep III) is cruciform and consists of a tranverse gallery with an infilled burial shaft in the E corner; it was never finished. On either side of the entrance passage are scenes of the royal family worshipping the Aten (1); and Ramose kneeling with a prayer (2). In the niche on the SE wall are the remains of statues of Ramose and his wife (3).

Some distance S is *Any* (No. 23), scribe of the king, overseer of works of the Lord of the Two Lands and previously steward to Amenhotep II; it is indicated by one of the chariot routes leading from the river. This, and the tomb-chapel of Huya (No. 1) were the only tombs used. It was excavated by Barsanti in 1891. It was constructed late in the occupation of Akhetaten and differs from all the other chapels in the S group, being more like one of the N chapels. It is unique in other ways, being reached by a long flight of steps leading to an external (unfinished) portico taking the form of porches on either side of the doorway as if they were ends of a more extended colonnade. The column which supports the corniced architrave was to have been the only one, balanced probably by a pilaster in the rock wall. It is a long narrow tomb with an entry passage and two chambers, the hall and a shrine, the walls and floor unfinished. In the vestibule six stelae were found offered to the deceased as a mark of affection by his brother, friends and servants (now in the EM). The entry lintel shows the royal family with three princesses and attendants worshipping the Aten (1–2) while the door jamb, unusually, is not occupied with burial petitions but with a salutation to the regnal power human and divine, with the deceased (3), the fact that it is a late tomb indicated by the form of the Aten cartouche. Although the paintings are unfinished the bands of red and green and blue give a finished appearance to the hall. The walls are covered with a yellow wash reminiscent of some of the Theban tombs and the pictures are surrounded by a red and blue border. Inside the door is a short Hymn to the Aten with Any carrying a bouquet and staff (4). He must have been an old man as his stewardship to Amenhotep II was 50 years before this. A shaft in the floor of the corridor leads to the fairly large burial chamber and lies mainly under the shrine. It has two small recesses in the rear wall to hold lights and a further shaft underneath. Above the entry to the shrine is a coloured cornice. The doorway is decorated with ink which has faded. A seated statue of Any (badly preserved), on a dais reached by steps, almost fills the shrine. The walls are decorated with drawings of Any seated and attended by his servant Meryre and his unnamed wife who outlived him and was responsible for cutting the tomb (5). These last drawings are in red paint corrected by another hand also in red paint.

Almost at the edge of the slope is *Ay* (No. 25), Divine Father, which would have been, had it been completed, the finest of the tomb-chapels at al-ʿAmārnah. Ay was brother of Queen Tiy (wife of Amenhotep III) and thus uncle of Akhenaten, holding the posts of Fan Bearer on the Right of the King and Overseer of the all the horses of His Majesty. He succeeded Tutankhamun on the throne. The chapel consists of a transverse hall, incompletely cut (giving a good idea of how the Egyptian masons worked). The 12 columns on the left on entering are more-or-less complete, but of those corresponding on the right only the centre row was finished. There is a small statue niche at the back. The decoration is mainly in the entrance and on the front wall.

On the lintel is a scene of the royal family worshipping the Aten (defaced) (1) and Ay and his wife Teye kneeling (2). Teye, called a Royal Ornament, was the nurse of Nefertiti. In the entrance passage on the left are the king and queen followed by three princesses, Nefertiti's sister Mutnodjme (called Mutbenret in some earlier publications) and two female dwarfs (3–4). To the right is a Hymn to the Aten with Ay and Teye kneeling (5), one of the finest reliefs from Amarnah. In the hall on entering to the left are scenes in the upper register of Ay rewarded by the king and queen and three princesses all standing on the palace balcony (6–8) and a garlanded Ay escorted by friends (9). Above the door is an unfinished scene of the palace (10). In the inner door which may have been intended as an entry to an inner room rather than a statue niche are pictures of Ay and Teye kneeling adoring the Aten (11–12).

The other chapels in this group are *Nekhtpaaten* (No. 12), chancellor and vizier, *Neferk-Khepau Her Sekheper* (No. 13), mayor of Akhetaten; *May* (No. 14), Fan-Bearer on the Right of the King; *Suti* (No. 15), standard bearer; *Unknown* (No. 18); *Sutau* (No. 19), overseer of the Treasury; *Unknown* (No. 20); *Unknown* (No. 22); *Pa-aten-emhab* (No. 24), royal scribe.

Just N of the royal wadi is *Stela U* (year 6), cut high in the rock. It shows the king, queen and two princesses before the Aten. Most of the other stelae, particularly those in the S, have been totally destroyed.

To the SE are the alabaster quarries of **Hatnub** (12km), used throughout the dynastic period and famed for their high quality stone. The site is difficult to get to and requires special transport as it is some 12km from al-Till. On the way up the wadi are remains of workmen's huts (recently examined by the EES) and pottery of all periods. Unfortunately many of the inscriptions in the quarries have recently been defaced or removed.

Beyond al-Maʿṣarah the H2 passes (10km) **Deir Mawās** and (10km) **Dayrūṭ** into the province of Asyūṭ. W lies (13km) *Dashlūṭ*, to the SW of which is **Bāwiṭ** (3km) and W of this, 1km into the desert, the **Deir Anbā Abulū** (Monastery of St. Apollo), founded in the 5–6C and inhabited until the 11C. There is little now to be seen at the site, formerly consisting of several buildings, save for a series of mounds covered with potsherds.

Some important objects from here are in collections around the world. The most famous is the early wall-painting of Christ enthroned with the Virgin and Apostles, now in the CM.

The H2 continues to al-Qūṣiyyah (see below) but S of Dayrūṭ a road leads W from the H2 to (12km) **Ṣanabū**.

A road (SW) leads to **Meir** (Mayr; 13km). SW into the desert are the **Rock Tombs of Meir** (6km), the necropolis of the governors of the 14th nome of Upper Egypt, the capital of which was *Cusae*, called during the Greek period or more anciently Qis (see below).

The site is more easily reached from al-Minyā or Asyūṭ where a taxi can be taken to *Deir al-Muḥarraq* (see below) and a jeep obtained for the journey to the site. Turning off the Meir road onto a dirt track signposted to Meir (easily negotiable by car) which leads to the Resthouse near the escarpment. A path has been built up to the tombs.

Having arrived at the site there is quite a steep climb over sand to the tomb-chapels which are of Old and Middle Kingdom date. Early Christians used the tombs as cells and there is much graffiti. The hills are also honeycombed with the shafts of the servants of the Nomarchs. (Owing to the irregular formation of the ridge containing the tombs they have been divided into groups A–E, making for a duplication of numbers.)

The most northerly is Group A, of which the first tomb is that of *Nisankh-Pepi-Kem* (A1), chancellor of the King of Lower Egypt (reign of Pepi I). It consists of a large pillared room leading to a smaller undecorated one; on the W wall is an unfinished false door. Next is *Pepi-ankh*, good name Heni-kem (A2), overseer of the duck-pond (Pepi II), consisting of five rooms, one of which is undecorated. The reliefs are stylistically excellent and there are some interesting funeral scenes drawn in ink. *Ukh-hotep* (A3), nomarch and superintendent of prophets, is later (Senusert I–Amenemhat II), consisting only of one small room with a statue recess. Last in this group is *Hepi-Kem* (A4) (Pepi II–Merenre II), overseer of Upper Egypt.

To the S is Group B of related men; the first tomb-chapel is that of *Senbi* (B1) nomarch (Amenemhat I), a single chamber (with broken roof) with splendid naturalistic paintings. *Ukh-hotep* (B2) (Senusert I), nomarch and chancellor of the king of Lower Egypt, son of Senbi, is similar to B1. *Senbi II* (B3) (Senusert I–Amenemhat II), overseer of prophets, is unfinished. *Ukh-hotep* (B4), nomarch and son of Ukh-hotep (A3) (Amenemhat II), consists of two rooms. It has been much damaged but contains some of the finest reliefs in the necropolis, some executed in plaster and delicately painted.

Further S along a small sand track (15 mins walk) is Group C, consisting of *Ukh-hotep* (C1), nomarch and overseer of prophets (Senusert II), a single chamber with paintings along two walls, naturalistic but with strange paintings of women in men's kilts; and close by *Kha Kheperre*, good name Iy (C2), nomarch (12 Dyn.). Group D has two 6 Dyn. tomb-chapels, *Pepi* (D1) and *Pepi-ankh* (D2), with several decorated chambers. Group E are all Old Kingdom but cannot be attributed to any one ruler except that of *Pepi-ankh* (E3), probably of the time of Pepi II.

From *Meir* the road continues S, passing **Rizqat Deir al-Muḥarraq** (11km) which receives its name from the **Deir al-Muḥarraq** (the Burnt Monastery), also called the Monastery of the Virgin, on a site traditionally visited by the Holy Family during the Flight into Egypt.

When they stayed at Qusquam (al-Qūṣiyyah) they sheltered during times of danger in a small cave on the spot where the monastery was later built. This is not a remote desert community like many others and is the largest and richest Coptic foundation in Egypt. Its history is obscure. Its situation and present discipline suggest a Pachomian origin. A theological seminary was founded in 1905 and it has between 70–80 monks in residence. Between 21–28 June c 50,000 pilgrims attend the Feast of the Consecration of the Church of the Virgin.

Standing to the E of a large cemetery, it is a walled complex, the outer wall trapezoidal in plan (c 275m by 133m) with inner and outer courts. The inner court contains both modern and ancient buildings, the latter to the W. The *Church of al-ʿAdhrā* (the Virgin) is on the site of the Holy Cave. Claims have been made that this is the earliest church in Egypt. The floor level is c 1m below the courtyard and the haykal, over the traditional site of the cave, has a carved screen from the Upper Church of SS. Peter and Paul demolished in the 19C, while the altar bears the date 747. The destroyed upper church was replaced by the largest building in the complex, the *Church of St. George*, built in 1888 in neo-Byzantine style. Close by is the *Keep*, entered by a drawbridge on the first floor from a small ancient tower. On the second storey is the small mid-16C *Church of the Archangel Michael*. From here there is a good view of the surrounding area. The modern buildings, including the Pachomian Citadel, are in an elegant and sophisticated style.

From Deir al-Muḥarraq the road leads NE to **al-Qūṣiyyah** (8km).

Beyond Ṣanabū the H2 runs on to (10km) **al-Qūṣiyyah**, site of ancient *Qis*, in the Greek period called *Cusae* and later, in Coptic, *Qusquam*. The next village is (15km) *Banī Rāfi'* and this is followed by the towns of (10km) *Manfalūṭ* and (18km) *Manqabād*. A road leaves NW, passing the *Airport* (internal flights only), to al-Khārgah Oases (Rte 48), café and petrol (last before al-Khārgah). Past this the H2 reaches (12km) **ASYŪṬ**, the largest and most important city in Upper Egypt and chief city of the province of Asyūṭ. It is a pleasant place, with tree-lined avenues and open spaces. But it is not geared to the tourist industry and facilities are therefore extremely limited.

*Airport*, 10km NW (see above).

*Railway Station* in Sh'. al-Mahatah. *Bus Station* for national and local buses.

**Hotels**. *Asyūṭ, Savoy, Windsor*, all 1*, in town centre. Food may be obtained at the *Asyūṭ Sporting Club* beside the bridge or at the *YMCA* in the town centre.

In ancient times this was the site of the city of *Zawty* (Greek Lykopolis; Coptic Siout), capital of the 13th nome of Upper Egypt whose principal god was the jackal Wepwawet. Its importance resided in the fact that it was the terminus of the long caravan route from al-Khārgah Oases and ultimately the Sudan. It was one of the early centres of Christianity and retained status as the chief town of the province after the Muslim conquest. Little is subsequently heard of the city, though it remained prosperous. Its vital status as an economic centre probably gave it a degree of protection. Among its more important industries were weaving in wool, cotton and linen and a distinctive red and black pottery. It rose to prominence at the end of the 18C when it was a centre from which dissident bays attacked their rivals in the N. There has always been a large Christian community in Asyūṭ and this is testified by the number of churches. Plotinus (AD 205–70), the lugubrious neo-Platonist, was born here.

Nothing remains of the ancient town within the modern city limits except for the tombs of the nobles (see below). In the centre of the city is the Suq, part of which is the *Ḥammām al-Qadīm* (the old bath). It seems to be of great age and probably dates from the earliest Muslim occupation. The central dome is raised on ancient granite columns reused from an earlier building. In the centre is a fine white marble fountain. To the N of the town centre the *Ibrāhīmiyyah Canal* leaves to the NW, providing water for a considerable tract of land in Middle Egypt. Across the Nile at this point is the *Asyūṭ Barrage*, constructed between 1898–1903 by John Aird & Co. to the design of Sir W. Willcox. It carries a wide road. There are 111 sluices, with steamer and turning locks. Water is supplied to the Ibrāhīmiyyah Canal.

1.5km W of the city lies the recent cemetery with many domed tombs while the hills behind, which rise to 240m, hold the rock-cut *Tombs of the Nobles* (now inaccessible). They are 9, 10 and 12 Dyn. and Ramesside tombs, some of which were reused by Christians during the 6–7C. St. John of Lykopolis (died 394) was a teacher here of such reputation that Emperor Theodosius sent one of his eunuchs to consult with him. Also above the cemetery stands the recent *Tomb of Sh. Abū Tūg*.

From Asyūṭ a track leads due S along the edge of the cultivation. On the W side are several Ancient and Christian sites. The first at 2km (1km W of the road) is *Deir al-'Izām* with the remains of a basilican church. On the bank (8km) lies the *Deir Durunkah* and in the hills are an ancient Christian cave village and the *Church of the Virgin* (the new church was built in 1955). A large mūlid commemorating the flight of the Holy Family to Egypt is celebrated between 7–22 August.

Another 2km S (800m W of the road) are Rock Tombs reused by Coptic monks, beyond which (8km) is **Deir Rifeh** (Rīfah), a series of Ancient Egyptian tombs (now inaccessible), many reused to form the basis of a monastic village. Attached to this community is the rock-cut *Church of the Virgin* and the small brick *Church of St. Theodore* (Anbā Tadrụs), probably of the 13C. 2km beyond is *Deir Zāwiyah* with a fortified and decorated Coptic village, now secular but which once contained a monastery. A small wadi (4km) contains the *Deir al-Balāyzah*, the remnant of a 7–10C monastery and associated buildings. Continue along the track to Wadi Sargah (see below).

From Asyūṭ a road crosses the barrage to the East Bank where it joins the H57 which runs from N to S.

To the N the H57 passes W of the village of **Bānī Mūrr** (2km), home of the family of Gamal ʿAbd al-Nasser (born in Alexandria). The village has a small museum. The H57 continues to the town of (3km) **Abnūb**, to the E of which is the village of **Bānī Rīzah**. From Abnūb several sites can be visited but they will need the services of a knowledgeable resident.

A track leads along the base of the hills N, passing **Buqṭur Shū** (5km) with the *Church* of a local martyr, St. Victor of Shu. After 2km, at the base of the Gabal Ṭawīlah, is the village of **Deir al-Gabrāwī** with a *Church* dedicated to St. Victor of Antioch. At the summit of the rock-face are the *Tomb-Chapels of the Nomarchs* of the 12th nome of Upper Egypt (now heavily quarried), some dating to the 6 Dyn. although others are much later. Several were reused as Christian hermitages. The H57 continues S along the East Bank (Rte 33).

# 33 Asyūṭ to Sūhāg

## A. West Bank

(Total distance approx. 97km.) **Asyūṭ**.—4km **Shuṭb**.—24km **Ṣidfā**.—2km **al-Dawīr**.—8km **al-Birbā**.—8km *al Ghanāyim*.—7km *Tell al-Zawakī*.—12km **Ṭulīhāt**.—30km **Awlad Nusayr**.—2km **Suhāg**.

The H2 leaves Asyūṭ SE following the riverbank. At 4km it passes **Shuṭb**, ancient *Shashotep, Greek Hypselis*, capital of the 11th nome of Upper Egypt with *Temple of Khnum* and *Church of St Mercurius*, and continues to (12km) *Abū Tīg* and (12km) **Ṣidfā**. From here a road follows the riverbank (see below) but the H2 swings inland to (2km) **al-Dawīr**.

Due E across the cultivation a road runs past **Kom Isfaḥt** (2km), ancient *Apollonospolis*, and **Deir al-Ganādlah** (2km). 2km beyond the village into the desert is the *Monastery of the Virgin*. Inside the enclosure to the W of the 19C *Church of the Apostles* stands the ancient *Church of the Virgin*. Just S of the monastery a valley breaks the cliff face, here c 200m high. This is the **Wadi Sarga**, site of an ancient Coptic community during the 6C. It was excavated by R.G. Campbell-Thompson (1913–14). The mouth of the valley had been walled with a high brick rampart; many dwellings were uncovered as well as several rock churches, some with fine paintings. It had been an industrial community and many pots and artifacts were found. This community was founded by St. Thomas and prospered from c 550–600. It then declined and was abandoned in the 8C.

From al-Dawīr the H2 turns S again to (8km) *al-Birbā* and the province of Suhāg. It turns W again to (8km) *al-Ghanāyim* where it finally turns S. It then runs through the small villages of (6km) *Umm Dūmah* and (1km) *Tell al-Zawakī*. Just to the E is **Ṭifah**, site of ancient *Aphrodito*. At (12km)

**Ṭulīhāt** a road leads E to Ṭahṭā but S on the H2 the next villages are (10km) *Gihaynah* and (20km) **Awlad Nusayr**, E of which lies the *Deir al-Ahmar* (best visited from Sūhāg; see below). 2km **Sūhāg**.

Leaving Ṣidfā, a road continues along the bank of the Nile, passing through *Ṭimā, Ṭahṭā* and *al-Marāghah*, before reaching **Sūhāg** (53km).

Sūhāg is a small agricultural town and chief town in the district. A bridge crosses the Nile to the East Bank and the town of Akhmīm (see below). From Sūhāg a small road leads due W to fortress-like **Deir al-Abyaḍ** (White Monastery) or *Deir Anbā Shanudah* (Monastery of St. Shenute), its massive white limestone walls, relieved only by two rows of blind windows, giving the building its name. It is surrounded by foundations of a much larger community.

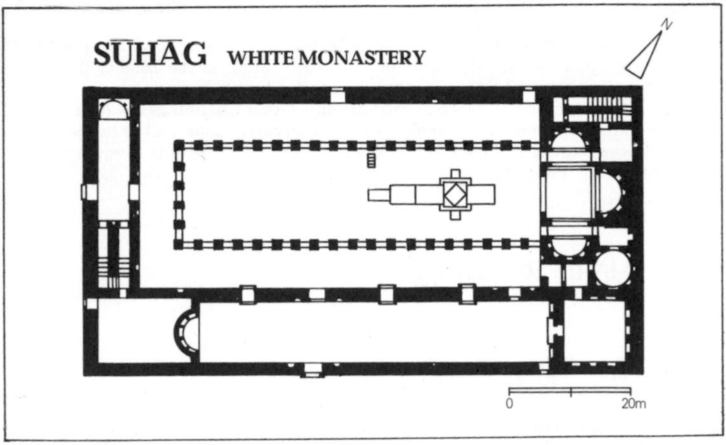
SŪHĀG WHITE MONASTERY
N
0
20m

Shenute was the nephew of St. Bigoul, who formulated a rule for monks similar to that of Pachomius. After his uncle's death (385) Shenute became head of the community and was present at the Council of Ephesus (431,) where he denounced Nestorius, and the Council of Chalcedon (451). He was a great friend of St. Bishoi. As far as religious observance was concerned he was a martinet, occasionally resorting to physical restraint. He founded this monastery in 440 and died c 446. In the 11C many monks here seem to have been Armenian; they included Bahram, the former wazir of the khalīf al-Ḥākim. Although attacked during the battle between the Fāṭimid wazir Shawār and Shirkuh in 1168 the monastery survived. Restoration was undertaken in the 13C, in the 19C, by Muḥammad ʿAlī Pasha, and again in 1907.

Entry is from the SW from where it will be seen that the *Church of St. Shenute* occupies most of the enclosure. Retaining most of the original structure, it is built of burnt brick and measures 75m by 35m. The basilican plan comprises a narthex, a nave and two side aisles and a triple apse. On the SE side running the whole length of the building is another section divided into two halls of unknown use, perhaps a refectory. The narthex has niches along the walls and at the NW end a semi-circular apse. At the SE end crumbling stairs lead to the roof (fine view of the Nile Valley). In the central part of the church 19 columns (taken from nearby Athribis) separate the central nave from each aisle. Halfway along on the left the ambon (pulpit) is carved from a granite monolith. At the NE end beyond the modern haykal screen is the triple apse, each lobe with a semi-dome. Two layers of pillars with decorated capitals and niches embellish the walls. The NE sanctuary, its dome decorated with the Dormition of the Virgin, is dedicated to St. George, while the central sanctuary, with the Pantocrator painted in the dome, is dedicated to St. Shenute. The sanctuary to the SE depicts the Resurrection and is dedicated to the Virgin. To the S is the well covered by a 19C dome.

N of the Deir al-Abyaḍ, situated in a village is the smaller **Deir al-Aḥmar** (Red Monastery) or *Deir Anba Bishoy* (Monastery of St. Bishoi) which, like the Deir al-Abyaḍ, shows evidence of much more extensive building. In this case the material used to construct the enclosure is baked brick and this also gives the building its name.

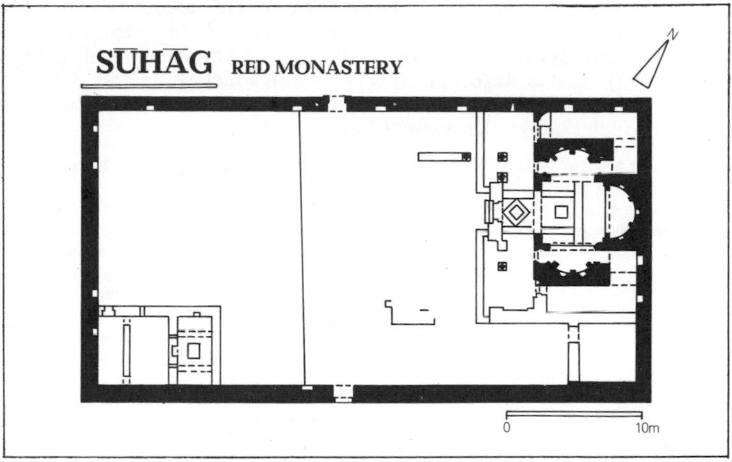
SŪHĀG RED MONASTERY
N
0
10m

The history of the foundation is obscure. It was built by Besa, a disciple of Shenute, and hence presumably dedicated to St. Bishoi. It almost certainly dates from the same period. The earliest inscription on the walls is that of Mercurius, a monk who entered the monastery in 1301. In 1798 it was sacked during the conflicts of the bays in Upper Egypt.

Entry to the enclosure is from the SW. In the S corner is the *Church of the Virgin*, not part of the original foundation but none the less ancient. Other buildings occupy what must have been the central nave and aisles of the original *Church of St. Bishoi*. At the N corner of the enclosure is all that remains of the church, the triple apse of similar plan to that of St. Shenute, even to the remains of the two long rooms against the SE wall. The walls of the apses are decorated in similar style with two layers of columns, which although fewer have more elaborate decoration, and wall recesses. In similar fashion, the semi-domes of the apses have fine paintings although they are very grimy.

## B. East Bank

(Total distance approx. 100km.) **Asyūṭ**.—**Marāwnat**.—7km **al-Badārī**.—14km **al-Hammāmiyyah**.—2km **al-ʿItmāniyyah**.—46km **al-Salāmūnī**.—2km **Akhmīm** (bridge to **Sūhāg**).

From the E end of the bridge at Asyūṭ the H57 runs S and passes *al-Waṣṭā, al-Biṣra, al-Ghārīb* and (29km) **Marāwnat** where a track leads E to *Deir Tāsā*, once considered a type-site of one of the earliest Egyptian predynastic cultures (c 4500 BC) but no longer recognised. There is little to see. The road then passes (7km) **al-Badārī**. 6km E in the foothills lies the important type-site of another predynastic culture (*Badarian*) but again there is little to see.

Continue S. The H57 runs through (14km) **al-Hammāmiyyah** with two 4 Dyn. rock tomb-chapels beyond the cultivation. The next village is (2km) **al-ʿItmāniyyah**, on the NE outskirts of which is the site of Ancient Egyptian *Tjebu* (Gk *Antaeopolis*). The village which stood here, Qaw al-Kabīr, was washed away by the river in 1821 along with a Ptolemaic temple which marked the ancient town.

Still extant are the 12 Dyn. *funerary complexes of the nomarchs* of the 10th nome of Upper Egypt, partly built and partly rock-cut. The tombs are terraced, with pillared porticoes, a sloping causeway and courtyard leading to the rock-cut tomb chambers. In some respects they are similar to the later mortuary temples of Mentuhotpe at Deir al-Baḥrī. The best preserved tombs are those of Wahka I, Wahka II and Ibu. There are also some later chapels. The site was excavated by Schiapereli (1904–05), Steindorf (1913–14) and later by Petrie. According to the Greeks during Herakles' African journeys this was the site of his combat with Antaeus, son of the primaeval Earth goddess Gaia, mother of the Titans. Antaeus' immense strength was renewed every time he touched the ground. Herakles vanquished him by holding him in the air and crushing him.

Still following the Nile S, the H57 passes *al-Khazindāriyyah, al-Kitkātah* to reach (46km) **al-Salāmūnī** with an 18 Dyn. rock-chapel dedicated to Min.

Close to the town is the *Deir al-Malak* (Monastery of the Archangel Michael) which may date to the 13C. To the NE of the village the Wādī Bīr al-ʿAyn also runs NE. Follow it for 9km to the *Deir al-Gabal al-Sabaʿ*. This, unusually, is the remains of a laura (free association of monks). The church stands in the valley but the hermitages are high on the cliff walls.

Just beyond al-Salāmūnī a road leads W from the H57 to (2km) **Akhmīm** with a bridge across the Nile to *Sūhāg*. This is the site of the ancient city of *Ipu* (Gk *Khemmis*) which, since it was dedicated to the worship of Min, equated by the Greeks with Pan, was also called *Panopolis*. It was the capital of the 9th nome of Upper Egypt but little is left of the ancient city beyond the remains of an 18 Dyn. rock-cut temple and two Ptolemaic temples, one (dedicated to Min) W of the town, and the cemeteries are virtually unexcavated. However, recent excavations by the EAO have uncovered a temple of Ramesses II with a colossal statue of Queen Bant Anta and two statues of Ramesses II.

# 34 Sūhāg to Qēnā

The good road continues on the East Bank although in this Rte the major sites are to the W of the main road on the West Bank.

## A. West Bank

(Total distance without detours approx. 147km.) **Sūhāg**.—2km **Rawafi'al-Quṣayr**.—36km **Birbā**.—15km **al-Ballyana** (—10km SE **Abydos**).—23km **Abū Ṭisht**.—18km **Nag'Ḥammādi**.—3km **Hiw**.—47km **Dendārah**.—3km **al-Tarāmsah** (bridge to **Qēnā**).

The H2 leaves Suhāg S, passing (2km) **Rawafi'al-Quṣayr** where another road goes E to follow the riverbank (see below). W a track leads to **Winnīnah** (2km), Ancient Egyptian *Hat Repyt*, Gk *Athribis*, with remains of a *Temple of Repyt* (a lion goddess) built by Ptolemy XVI Caesarion and another Ptolemaic temple beside several late tombs. Continuing past several small villages, the H2 reaches (36km) **Birbā**, a contender for the site of the ancient city of *This* or *Thinis*, capital of the earliest dynastic kings.

W from Birbā a secondary road leads to **Bayt Khallāf** (8km). Here, on the edge of the desert, are five massive 3 Dyn. brick mastabas. They were probably built for officials of the district of This and had clay sealings of several kings, including Zozer.

Beyond Rawāfi'al-Quṣayr a road running along the riverbank goes past *Balaṣfūrah* and (18km) **al-Manshāh**, site of the ancient city of *Ptolemais Herminou*, and on to **Girgā** (20km), the other possible site of *This* (see Birbā, above). Beyond Girgā the road rejoins the H2.

S of Birbā the H2 passes (7km) *Minshāt Bardīs* to reach (8km) **al-Ballyana**, with railway, bus stations and car-ferry to the East Bank. This was the Coptic *Tabourame* and noted during Muslim times for its date groves and agricultural produce.

SE the R69 runs to **al-'Arābā al-Madfūnah** (10km) and the site of **Abydos**.

The site can be reached on a day trip from Luxor (including Dendārah) or by taxi or car from Ballyana. The journey by taxi takes c 30–40 minutes. The road follows the canal through a fertile strip of country growing mainly sugar cane and grain. If a personal visit is undertaken arrangements should be made to spend the night at the *Aluminium Hotel* at Nag'Ḥammādī (see below).

Al-'Arābā al-Madfūnah is a large village, part of which is built around the central monuments of Abydos. There is a small rest house on the right at the arrival point where refreshments may be taken.

Abydos lies in the centre of predynastic Egypt. Al-'Amrah (8km SE) was the typesite of the culture (Amratian) now called Naqada I while Naqādah itself lies further S, as does Hiw (Diospolis Parva). It is one of the most impressive sites in Egypt; nowhere else does the cultivation come so close to the Libyan hills which at this point rise to 243m. These hills form a kind of bay nowhere more than 4km from the cultivation. Along the edge of this bay for 1.5km stand the cemeteries and temples, while within the circle of the hills in the desert are the cenotaphs of the 1 Dyn. kings.

Abydos seems to have been primarily a funerary site: its original name was Abedju. It was situated in the 8th nome of Upper Egypt and may have been the

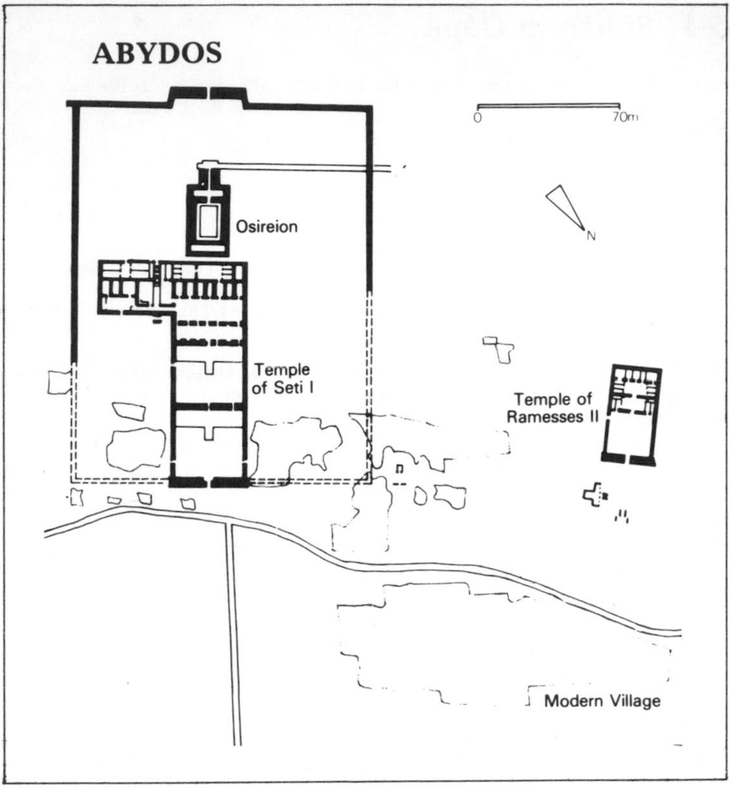
ABYDOS
0
70m
N
Osireion
Temple of Seti I
Temple of Ramesses II
Modern Village

cemetery of the earliest capital This or Thinis, which, however, has never been satisfactorily located although al-Birbā (W of Girgā) or Nagʿal-Mashayakh (Lepidontopolis, SE of Girgā) have been suggested as probable sites. It was used as a necropolis from prehistoric times, and the entrance to the Underworld was thought to lie in a gap in the hills to the W.

When Petrie found and identified the great mastabas at the beginning of the century they were thought to be the burial places of the kings of the first two Dyns. However, the discovery of even larger duplicate tombs at Ṣaqqārah has suggested that these are merely cenotaphs. In the historic period the Tomb of Horus Djer, one of the earliest 1 Dyn. kings, was thought to be the burial place of Osiris because some of his emblems were found there and it became an important place of pilgrimage. If the Ancient Egyptian could not visit it in his lifetime, he was meant to make the voyage to Abydos after his death. Scenes portraying this are shown in many of the New Kingdom tomb-chapels at Thebes.

The original god at Abydos was a member of the dog family, shown lying recumbent on a standard coloured black. He was known as Khent-Amenty, 'the One at the head of the West', a name indicating that he was a god of the dead. His temple (found by Petrie) was situated at the point where the road to the early mastabas leaves the cultivated land, and is one of the earliest religious structures at Abydos. Later he became associated with Osiris, as Osiris-Khentamenty. From the Old Kingdom onwards Osiris is called Lord of Abydos, although he originally came from Busiris in the Delta. According to some legends his head was buried here, others say his whole body. Osiris was associated here with two other canids, Wepwawet, 'the

Opener of the Ways', the messenger and champion of the kings, shown on the royal standards carried before them, originating from Asyut; and Anubis, overseer of the mysteries of embalming, another jackal-headed deity originally from Cynopolis in Middle Egypt.

After the 2 Dyn. the court moved to Memphis, and the reputation of Abydos as a holy place and a place of pilgrimage increased. So important did it become in the Old Kingdom that the kings granted special privileges to the temples, and freed them from taxes. Pepi I married two daughters of nobles from this area, increasing its prestige even further. Under the Theban kings of the Middle Kingdom Abydos again became an important place of pilgrimage, and grew rich on the pilgrim trade.

Mariette excavated or rather plundered the Middle Kingdom cemeteries and many of the Middle Kingdom stelae now in museums throughout the world come from here. These commemorative stelae give a great deal of information about the festivals that existed, mainly to do with the dead. The chief of these was the great Osiris Festival of the month of Khoiak, the fourth month of the Inundation season. At this time the Mystery plays connected with the legend of the life and death of Osiris were performed in his temple. Another of the great festivals was carried out in the month of Thoth and was called 'the Great Going Forth'; this celebrated the search for, the discovery of and the mourning for Osiris.

The whole area is scattered with cemeteries and tombs and at the NW end of the site stand two forts or residences. One of these is a very battered mud-brick structure called *Shūmat al-Zibīb* (Raisin store), with walls that were originally c 13m high, covered with white plaster, like the white walls of Memphis, enclosing an area 120m by 27m. The interior seems to have been full of small dwellings. This is said to date to the 2 Dyn., but some Egyptologists contest that it is as old as this. Another such structure, the so-called *Middle Fort*, lies closeby to the NW near the *Temple of Khentamenty*. Immediately to the NE, close to the village of *al-Khirbah*, is the *Temple of Osiris* called Kom al-Sulṭān (Mound of the Sultan), and its enclosure (almost totally destroyed).

SE of the central area are the mastabas of the 1 and 2 Dyn. kings. The tomb thought to be that of Osiris was in fact that of the Horus Djer, one of the earliest of 1 Dyn. kings. It has given its name to the area *Umm*

*The façade of the Temple of Seti I*

*al-Qaʿāb* (pron. gaʿāb), Mother of Pots, from the large number of votive vessels left at the spot by the ancient pilgrims. The mud-brick mastabas of the early kings were surrounded by secondary burials belonging to members of their court, servants and animals. The kings' cenotaphs were marked by the fine stone-cut stelae, a feature not found at Ṣaqqārah. This part of the site requires more time than can be spent on the average visit from the river or Luxor.

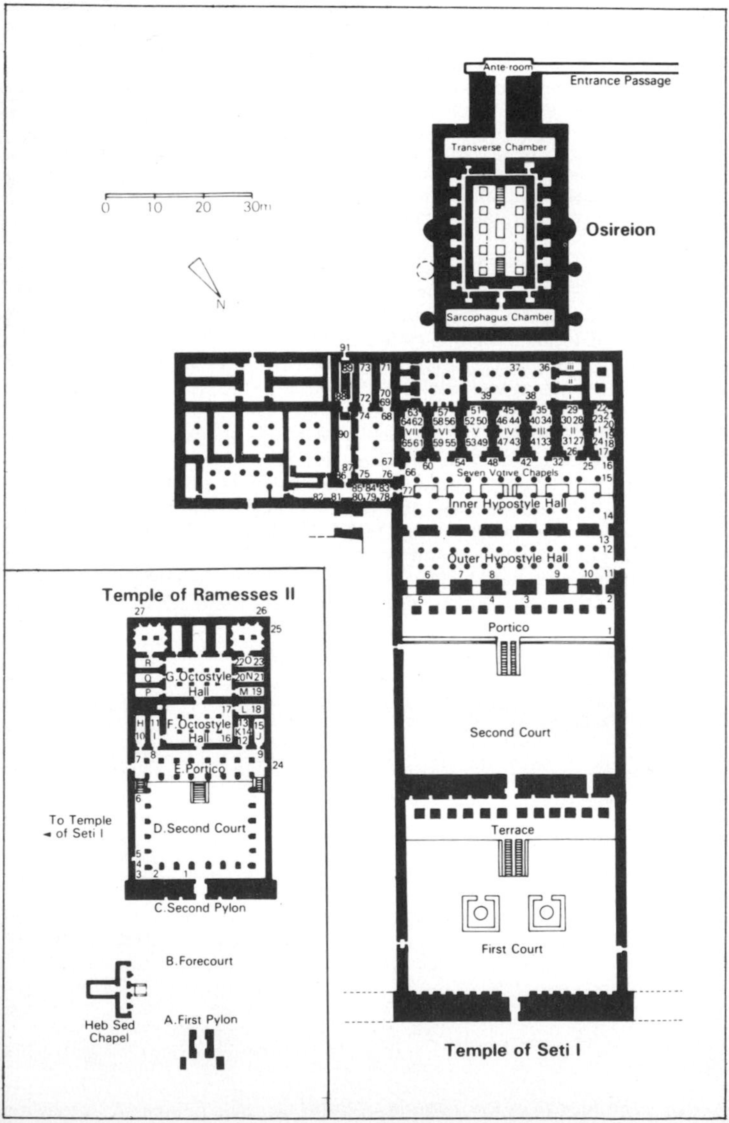

Ante-room
Entrance Passage
Transverse Chamber
Osireion
Sarcophagus Chamber
0 10 20 30m
N
Seven Votive Chapels
Inner Hypostyle Hall
Outer Hypostyle Hall
Portico
Second Court
Terrace
First Court
Temple of Seti I
Temple of Ramesses II
G.Octostyle Hall
F.Octostyle Hall
E.Portico
D.Second Court
C.Second Pylon
B.Forecourt
A.First Pylon
Heb Sed Chapel
To Temple of Seti I

About 1.5km E, near the village of al-ʿArābā *al-Madfūnah* itself, are three well preserved temples built by three consecutive 19 Dyn. kings: a small Temple of Ramesses I, the great Temple of Seti I and the Temple of Ramesses II, his son.

The small *Temple of Ramesses I* (inaccessible), now in the village itself, was built by Seti I for his father. About 50m SE is the **Great Temple of Seti I**, called 'The House of Millions of Years of King Menmare joyful in the heart of Abydos', a very unusual structure. Seti died before the temple was completed and it was finished by his son Ramesses II and endowed from the gold mines at Wādī al-ʿAbādī.

At Abydos two daily rituals were carried out: first the daily ritual for the gods, especially Osiris, and secondly the ritual for the Royal Ancestors, performed in the Chapels of Seti, the Memphis Triad, and in the Hall of the Ancestors. The Seti temple is unusual, being L-shaped instead of rectangular, and having seven chapels. Whether the shape was due to the water table, or the presence of the Osirieon behind is uncertain, but probably the latter. This was not strictly speaking a mortuary temple, as this needed to be placed near to and in association with the burial place of the dead king, and Seti already had one in Thebes on the West Bank at Qurnah.

The first two *Courtyards* (A–B) are the work of Ramesses II, who is seen greeted by the gods on the colonnade fronting the temple. The second court is at a higher level up a ramp to a portico (C) fronted by square columns. (1) Ramesses kills Asiatics before Amun-Re. (2) Ramesses worships Osiris. (3) Ramesses II before Isis and Horus. (4–5) A large dedicatory inscription, to complete it Ramesses had to fill in certain of the exits planned by his father.

Beyond is the First *Hypostyle Hall* (D), again at a slightly higher level. This is wide and shallow with 12 rows of papyrus-columns, 7.5m high, arranged in pairs to make seven aisles, begun by Seti I and completed by Ramesses II. The walls are of sandstone except for that to the N which is faced with limestone. Seven doors separate this hall from the next but the names on the lintels of the doors have been defaced by Ramesses II.

(6) King drags boat of Sokar. (7) The king kneels on the emblems of Upper and Lower Egypt. (8) The king offers to Amun. (9) Preparation of the temple building with the king and the goddess Seshat measuring the structure. (10) The king offering the completed temple to Horus. (11) The king takes a bird to Horus. (12) The king kneels before Thoth who writes his name.

The *Second Hypostyle Hall* (E) is similar but deeper and the columns are arranged differently. The ground slopes upwards to reach a broad terrace. There has been a certain amount of subsidence in the centre of the hall, where it runs over the old canal leading to the Osireion, which must have been built prior to the building of the present temple, and may account for its curious L-shape. The E and W walls are of sandstone, the N and S of limestone. This hall was actually the last part of the temple to have been decorated by Seti, and even here the paintings were not finished when he died. At the base of the W, N and S walls are depicted the nomes of Egypt, now thought to be fertility figures.

(13) Dedicatory texts of Seti usurped by Ramesses. (14) The king before Horus. (15) The Osiris Emblem. (16) The king receives the emblems of sovereignty followed by Hathor.

Leading off from the rear walls are *Seven Chapels* dedicated to various deities, a very unusual feature. The gods thus honoured are (from SE to NW) the Triad of Osiris, Isis and Horus, the Triad of Amun, Mut and Khonsu, Reʿ-Harakhte, Ptah and the deified Seti I. Between each door is a niche with the king making offerings to the various deities of the chapels. Each chapel is built in emulation of an early hut shrine with curved roof cut from a single block of stone and all end in false doors except the Osiris Chapel. In all the six chapels dedicated to the gods of Memphis and Thebes the scenes are related to the daily service, decorated with the king's titles and show the gods in their boats, the *Chapel of Amun* also with the boats of Mut and Khonsu. Thus it would seem that boats were central to the ritual at Abydos. In the *Horus Chapel* are seven scenes of the kingship ritual and the king offering to the god. The king is shown making further offerings in the *Isis Chapel*. He offers incense and ointment to the goddess who in turn presents him with the insignia of royalty. In the *Seti Chapel*, however, the duties are reversed. Here gods offer to the deified king and Horus performs the htp-di-nesu for the dead king, who is led by him and Isis into the presence of Osiris. These three chapels would seem to represent the scenes of the installation of the king first as Horus, Lord of the Living, then as Osiris, Lord of the Dead, and thus appear to have a dual purpose.

The *Osiris Chapel*, with the titulary of Seti on either side of the door and the king portrayed on each side wall, is a passage leading to the *First Osiris Hall*. Here the scenes (reading from left to right) depict Seti engaged in a series of offerings, a libation, wine, bread and Maʿat to Horus, wine and incense to Osiris and nmst vases to a minor deity, here represented as a black bull; he then offers bread to Osiris, incense to Anubis, flowers to Geb and Nut and opens the shrines of Hapy, Nephthys and Min. On the SW/W wall are scenes of raising the djd pillars before the gods of Thinis. The upper register is largely destroyed. On the W wall are three entrances to *Chapels to Seti, Isis and Horus*, while on the SE wall is the entrance to the *Second Osiris Hall* with most scenes except the lowest destroyed. In these two halls the Mysteries of Osiris were performed.

*Chapel of Horus* (I). On the lintel (17) double scenes of the king and divinities. (18) The kingship ritual, the king embraced by Horus. (19) The king before Horus unbolting shrine and offering incense. (20) The king sweeping the sanctuary before Horus the Elder (destroyed). (21) The king clothes Horus. (22) False door. (23) The king receives life from Horus. (24) The king offers collar to Horus. (25) The king receives sceptres from Horus and life from Isis.

*Chapel of Isis* (II). (26) Dedication text. (27) The king offers incense to Isis. (28) The king cleans the sanctuary. (29) False door, the king offers wine. (30) Four scenes of the king offering Isis insignia, ointment and crowns. (31) The king offers Isis pectoral and linen (damaged). (32) The king followed by Isis censes Osiris, is embraced by Wepawet and receives life from Horus.

*Chapel of Osiris and Osiris Halls* (III). (34) Three scenes showing the king sweeping the sanctuary before Osiris, anointing the god, and before Osiris and Isis. (35) Over the lintel, the king is conducted by Wepwawet and Horus and kneels to Osiris and Isis. (36–37) Raising the djed pillar. (38) The king offers bread to Wepwawet and incense to Horus. (39) The king offers wine to Heqet, Maʿat to Horus and ointment to Merhy. (40) The king before Isis and Osiris (partly destroyed). (41) The king offers natron to Osiris and Thoth.

*Chapel of Amun-Reʿ* (IV). (42) The king receives his insignia from Amun and life from Khonsu. (43) Further acts in the daily ritual, the king stands before the shrine and breaks the seals. (44) The king offers incense and libations before the bark of the Theban Triad. (45) False door, and the king offers wine to Amun-Reʿ. (46) The king offers ointment, insignia and emblems to Amun. (47) The king offers a pectoral and cloth also to Amun.

*Chapel of Reʿ-Harakhte* (V). (48) The king kneels before Reʿand receives his insignia from Amun. (49) The king opens the shrine and offers incense before Reʿ-Harakhte. (50) The king offers incense and libations before the god's bark. (51) False door and the king offers wine to Reʿ-Harakhte. (52) The king offers ointment and emblems to Reʿ-Harakhte. (53) The king offers collars to Amun.

*Chapel of Ptah* (VI). (54) The king's name inscribed and he receives life from Hathor. (55) The king before Ptah. (56) The king offers before the bark of the god. (57) False door (damaged). (58) The king offers ointment and cloth to Ptah. (59) The king offers collar and cloth to Ptah.

*Chapel of deified Seti I* (VII). (60) The king offers flowers to Ptah and Sekhmet and is embraced by Nefertum. (61) The king united with his ancestors and is followed by Thoth and the Souls of Nekhen. (62) The dead king is shown with Inmutef and a list of offerings before him and his ka. (63) False door and the king and his ka and the royal titles. (64) Thoth offering before the king. (65) Horus-Inmutef, the goddesses of Upper and Lower Egypt and the king crowned by Horus.

In the S corner of the Second Hypostyle Hall are two entrances to further halls. Beside it to the N is the door to the *Hall of Nefertum and Ptah-Sokari.* A little to the SW is the entrance to the *Hall of Ancestors* (also called the Hall of Lists), containing the names of 76 previous kings, arranged in two rows, and a list of gods. In the list the names of the rulers of the First Intermediate Period through to the mid-11 Dyn. are omitted as are those of the 13–14 Dyns and some of the late 18 Dyn. such as Akhenaten, the sequence ending with Ramesses II. On the W side of the hall a passage called the *Corridor of the Bulls* leads to the Osireion. It originally had a vaulted ceiling and was partly finished by Seti. On the N wall is a scene of Ramesses II and Prince Amun-hir-Khopshef in the act of lassooing a bull in the presence of Wepwawet. On the S wall Ramesses drives four dappled calves towards Khonsu and Seti I is shown as a dead deified king. This is the representation of an Osirian rite frequently shown in temples, as at that of Sahure at Abū Ṣīr and at those at Deir al-Baḥrī, Karnak and Edfū.

The ceremony of the calves was probably originally a harvest act, when cattle or sheep were driven over the threshing floor. Another scene on the S wall shows the king catching birds in a clap-net and presenting them to Amun-Reʿ. This, like so many other representations in the temple, had a magical significance. The upper scenes in the stairway passage show the foundation of the temple.

To the W of the Hall of the Ancestors is the six-pillared *Hall of Barks*, on the bench round which the sacred boats used in the temple processions were probably stored. It is now used for storage and is not generally open to the public. At the far end of the gallery a stair leads to the roof where the priests could carry out their astronomical observations. On the walls the sacred boats are depicted but the decoration was never finished, in some cases only the outlines have been drawn. Later the room was used as an oracle where the god Bes could be consulted. The decoration was more-or-less completed by Ramesses, who is shown wearing various crowns and making offerings.

To the SE of the Hall of the Ancestors is the *Butchers' Hall*, a rectangular court bounded on three sides by a colonnade. On the W are doorways to various rooms. The main hall was built as a slaughter house, and scenes indicating this are shown on the N wall. This was a necessary adjunct to all temple premises, but had to be kept apart from the main temple and sacred areas.

The workmanship of the reliefs is not of a very high quality. Scenes of butchering the animals and censing the offerings are shown on the N and W walls. A ritual for killing animals was known from the 6 Dyn. onwards, and the scenes of the lassooing, slaughtering, and cutting up of the wild animal into pieces were probably part of it.

In the passsage are the following scenes: (66) the king running with a bull and an oar (partly destroyed). (67) The king receives life from Sokar. (68) Titles of Sokar and offering to him in 43 lines. (69) The king running with an oar and hap to Sokar and Mert. (70) Upper register, the king kneels before a list of 52 Memphite gods. Lower register, the resurrection of Osiris. (71) The king before Osiris, Anubis and Nekhbet. (72) The king kneels before Sokar. (73) The king presents a list of offerings before Min in his shrine, the king kneels before a lion-headed Nefertum. (74–75) Four niches and six Osiride gods. (76) The king censes the Sokar boat.

On the lintel (77) the king and Ramesses II shown with offerings before Osiris-Onnophris and Isis. (78–80) Offerings are made to many deities, Prince Ramesses offers a libation and Seti censes the gods. (81–82) Seti presents offerings to Amun-Reʿand ReʿHarakhte. (83) Seti and Prince Ramesses before Sokar and Sekhmet. The list of previous kings starts just before the Corridor of the Bull (84–85) with Prince Ramesses with a papyrus roll containing their names, and Seti censing the list. (88–89) The god Thoth with a speech and Ramesses, now king, offering to the deified Seti, goddesses and the Ennead (partly destroyed).

To the W directly behind the Temple of Seti I lies the **Osireion**, sometimes called the Cenotaph of Seti I, sited considerably lower than the other temple, in fact at water level.

It was constructed on a mound surrounded by a lake and there was a plantation of trees thought to be connected with the original mound which arose from the watery waste of Nun. The building is partly of hard quartzitic sandstone and partly of granite. Although this structure has Seti's name inscribed upon it, there is some doubt as to whether he originally built it. The construction does not resemble other work of the 19 Dyn. who were not known to build in granite and it looks Old Kingdom rather than New Kingdom in the style of stone cutting. Margaret Murray first cleared this structure working under Petrie in the early years of this century, and later excavations were carried out in 1930 by Henri Frankfort. It is a difficult site to work, being in a deep hollow, but the Department of Antiquities proposes to carry out further investigations in the area.

The main building is reached by a *Long Passage* (100m) erected by Merenptah, and decorated with extracts from the Book of the Am-Duat, the Book of the Gates, the Book of the Caverns and other portions of the Books of the Dead. The passage is partly roofed with a brick vault, and the wall paintings are in poor condition. The arrangement of the scenes is similar to those in the Royal Tombs in the Valley of the Kings at Thebes. The *Main Hall* is a large room supported by massive square granite pillars, probably originally roofed but now open to the sky. Although now permanently under water since the rise of the water table, it was originally dry except during the inundation. This hall was thought to simulate the tomb of Osiris with a place for the sarcophagus and canopic chest. At the E end is a *Transverse Hall* (27m by 25m) with an arched roof of sandstone. This contains scenes with Nut, a list of the deccans and constellations.

About 300m NW of the Temple of Seti I (10-minute walk over soft sand), between the remains of some late mud-brick buildings, with the Dept of Antiquities house on the NE, is the **Temple of Ramesses II**, erected in year 6 of his reign. The roof and upper parts of the walls are missing but enough remains to give a good idea of the building. Cleared by Mariette, it seems to have been almost intact when Napoleon's scholars first examined it, since when it has suffered badly. However, the limestone walls retain much of their bright colouring and the standard of work, probably by men trained under Seti, is higher than the average Ramesses II relief.

The first pylon (A) and the first court (B) have been destroyed and the temple is now entered through the *Second Pylon* (C), the top of which is destroyed. A square *Court* (D) is surrounded by square pillars with Osiride figures of Ramesses. The walls show offering scenes, animals being led in procession for the sacrifice, prisoners and texts of Ramesses IV.

(1–2) Attendants with bulls, gazelles and oryx. (3) Offerings, including bull and calf. (4) The king's titles. (5–6) Offerings.

Steps lead up to a portico (E) from which open successively two *Octostyle Halls* (F, G). The bases of the pillars are decorated with figures of rekhyet birds (some with human heads), and the bases of the walls with Niles, nome goddesses and priests raising a shrine to the king. In the first chamber (I) on the left of the first Octostyle Hall the second Tablet of Abydos was found (now in the BM). It is a further list of Egyptian rulers. The *Chapels* to the right of the second Octostyle Hall are dedicated (left to right) to Osiris (M), Min (N), and Onuris (O) and the cycle of the gods. To the left are rooms for linen (P) and offerings (Q, R). On the outside of the N and W walls are scenes from the Battle of Kadesh, and the Poem of Pentaur.

(7) African captives. (8) Figures representing Geblain and Tod (sites in Upper Egypt). (9) Asiatic captives (to balance the African captives). (10) The bark of Seti. (11) Place where the Tablet of Abydos was found. (12) Dedication text of the temple. (13–14) A goddess and king with a small Mert in boat drawn by Souls of Neken and Pe. (15) Inmutef and Thoth offering to the deified king. (16–17) Priests carry shrine to the king. (18) The king offers to the god. (19) The king offers Ma'at to Osiris. (20–21) The king censes the divine standards and the Min emblem. (22–23) The king running with hes vases.

3km N of this temple are the remains of the Coptic *Monastery of Anba Mūsā*, while some distance SE on a fold of the hills are some monuments of Senusert III (12 Dyn.) and Amosis (18 Dyn.), much destroyed, dangerous and inaccessible.

Running S the H2 arrives at (23km) **Abū Ṭisht** in the province of Qēnā. 3km further a road turns off to the NE to the *Nagʿ Hammādi Barrage* (3km) and SW to *Farshūṭ* (4km) but the H2 continues to (15km) **Nagʿ Ḥammādi** (55km downstream from Qēnā), a small town where the H2 and the railway cross the Nile to the East Bank. (*Hotel*: Aluminium Hotel, 3km S of Nagʿ Hammādi.)

Despite its small size it has been the chief town of the district in Qēnā Province since 1846 when the administration was moved from Farshūt. It is a very important agricultural centre with a large sugar factory S of the town (extensive garden on the riverbank). The barrage carrying the road was constructed by John Jackson Ltd in 1928–30, the last of the main Nile barrages to be built, replacing a road bridge of 1895. It has 100 sluices, steamer and turning locks and irrigates 622,800 feddans of land in the province of Qēnā. S of the barrage is a rail bridge.

The H53 leaves the town S and runs along the West Bank of the river to (3km) **Hiw**, site of the ancient city of *Kennet*, later called in Greek *Diospolis Parva*. Mounds of ruins cover a wide area to the W—broken walls, collapsed buildings and piles of pot-sherds. The area has been greatly disturbed and despoiled by the sabakhin. On the river edge until recently were the remains of the ancient quay but this has disappeared. A mud-brick Roman fortress was situated on the edges of the desert. In the surrounding cliffs are the remains of some Old Kingdom tombs, while nearby in the desert are *ancient cemeteries* dating from prehistoric times to the 18 Dyn.—most have been deliberately robbed or cleared long since.

About 1.5km S of the village lies the *Deir Mārī Minā al-Ajaybī*. Overlooking the Nile is the domed tomb of Sh. Salīm, who died in 1891. Tracks lead S to Danfīq and Luxor.

Following the river E, passing (13km) **al-Waqf** to the N, the next town of any size is (34km) **Dendārah** (Ar. Dandārah), set where the Nile takes a great sweep to the W. It possesses a berth for steamers (70km downstream from Luxor) and can also be reached by taxi or ḥantūr from Qīnā (4km) or on a day trip from Luxor (60km). It takes its name from the ancient site, 1.5km S (15-minute walk). Its ancient name of *Iunet* was corrupted in Greek to *Tentyra* and thence into Arabic. The area has been settled since prehistoric times and remains have been found on the East Bank at Guzariyyah. There are *Archaic Period burials* to the S of the main site and remains of other periods are present though very scanty.

Iunet was the capital of the 6th nome of Upper Egypt but of the settlement little is now evident. The goddess worshipped here was Hathor (i.e. Hat-hor, dwelling place of Horus), the Venerable Lady of Dendarah. She is also a sky goddess, a variant of Nut. Closely associated with Re, she is said to be his daughter in one of her many aspects, she is also a tree fertility deity and in some aspects a Goddess of the West and thus a form of the Goddess of the Dead. At Dendārah she is closely associated with Isis, and often identified with her. In Ptolemaic times she was assimilated to Aphrodite, but, in reality, had little to connect her with the Greek goddess of love. The two young gods associated with her, Iḫy and the young Horus, are each represented in anthropomorphic form, as young boys with the side lock of youth.

During the Old Kingdom it was an important provincial centre and its proximity to the route to the Red Sea from Qenā enhanced its significance. It retained its importance throughout dynastic times and into the Roman period but with the coming of Christianity it declined though a church was built on the temple site. Early in Muslim times it was made the capital of a district and became quite prosperous, depending for its wealth on the extensive date plantations for which it was renowned. In popular Arab folklore the temple was guarded by a two-horned, lion-headed jinn (possibly connected with the representations of Hathor) and it was the site of the Tree of ʿAbbās which closed its leaves when threatened and opened them when reprieved.

The visit itself takes a minimum of two and a half to three hours as the temple is well preserved and there is much to see. There is a small resthouse to the right just before the temple, where drinks can be obtained. Torches are required for the interior, the vaults, crypts and the stairways leading to the roof. Entrance fee.

The main temple was built on a stone platform overlying a sand foundation some 5.7m deep and orientated to the river which, because of the great sweep to the W, results in it being set N to S, not E to W. It is placed inside a mud-brick enclosure wall. Recently a mud-brick structure, predating the present one, and an offering table of Mentuhotpe II have been found. Beside the main temple within the sacred enclosure walls there is an ornamental Roman gate, two mammisi, a Coptic church, sacred lake, sanatorium and a small temple to Isis. Although certain uninscribed pieces may date to the Middle or New Kingdom the earliest structure on the site at present is the Mammisi of Nectanebo.

The **Temple of Hathor** is one of the best preserved in Egypt, although it

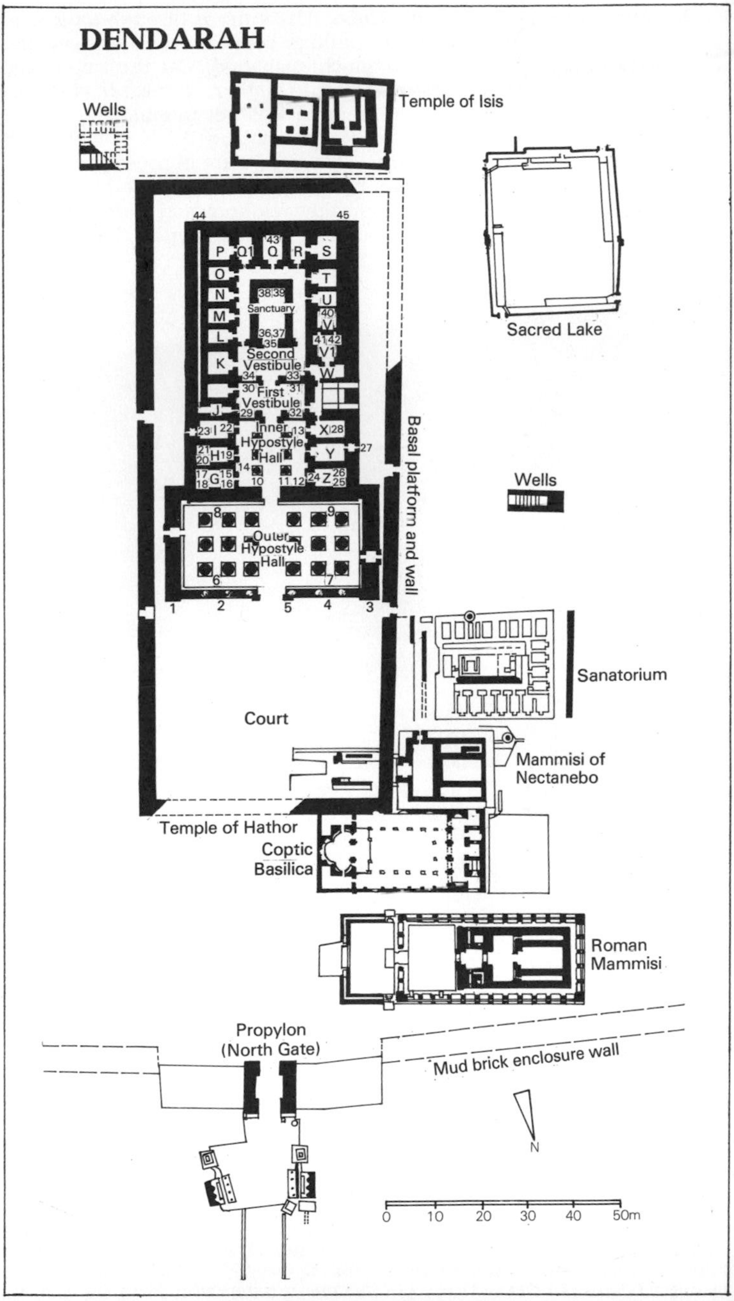
DENDARAH
Wells
Temple of Isis
Sacred Lake
Sanctuary
Second Vestibule
First Vestibule
Inner Hypostyle Hall
Outer Hypostyle Hall
Basal platform and wall
Wells
Court
Sanatorium
Mammisi of Nectanebo
Temple of Hathor
Coptic Basilica
Roman Mammisi
Propylon (North Gate)
Mud brick enclosure wall
N
0 10 20 30 40 50m

has been greatly damaged by the Copts. The entry is through a passage flanked by Roman columns with Corinthian capitals. The *Gateway*, the work of Domitian and Trajan, is much damaged. On the outer face Domitian is shown offering wine and birds to Hathor, Horus, Ma'at, Horus the Elder, and Iḫy. Apparently the temple was not intended to have a pylon, and the entry is through the *Pro-pylon*. The *Walls* of mud-brick surrounding the temple enclosure are in a good state of preservation and show an excellent example of pan-bedding, the technique of building walls in short sections not keyed into the neighbouring portion. It was practised by the Egyptians when building, as here, upon the alluvium which rose and fell with the annual flood of the Nile.

*Dendārah. The façade of the Temple of Hathor showing the Hathor-headed capitals*

The Temple of Hathor consists of a transverse Hypostyle Hall supported by 24 columns, the inner Hypostyle Hall supported by six columns, a short ramp to the First Vestibule or Hall of Offerings, a second ramp to the Inner Vestibule or Hall of the Cycle of the Gods, the passage between the profane world and the Divine Sanctuary. Round the sanctuary are a series of small rooms and chapels, used for storing linen, perfumes, treasure and the temple furniture.

The temple, dedicated to Hathor and to Horus the Elder, was traditionally founded by 'the Followers of Horus'. A text in one of the crypts mentions a building dating from the time of Pepi I of the 6 Dyn. and a temple is known to have been here at the time of Thuthmosis III of the 18 Dyn., but the present building is late Ptolemaic and Roman in date, constructed between 125 BC and AD 60. It is impossible to date much of the decoration with certainty as the cartouches are blank, although three of the underground crypts contain the name of Ptolemy XII Auletes (80–54 BC). The temple seems to have been partly built by a priest of Hathor called Pennut and his son Ptolemy of whom a statue was found by Daressy (now in the EM). The title Hathor Lady of Dendārah dates back at least to the 6 Dyn. and is found among the titles of the priests of that period buried in the Necropolis. The rites at Dendārah are closely linked with those of Horus the Bhedite of Edfū. Once a year the goddess undertook a voyage to visit Edfū, and another to the nearby site of Khadit, also sacred to Horus.

A court (A) leads to the *Hypostyle Hall* (B) built in year 21 of Tiberius Caesar by the prefect Aulus Evillus Flaccus with the aid of the inhabitants of the district and the town. The 24 columns of the hall are capped by Hathor-headed capitals with her symbol over her head. The ceiling represents the goddess Nut in the form of an elongated woman, swallowing and then ejecting the sun. Much of the ancient colour still remains to lighten this section.

(1) Tiberius offers wine to Horus and Hathor. (2) Claudius offers to Hathor and Iḥy. (3) Tiberius before the Gods. (4) The king as sphinx before Hathor and Horus. (5) The king before Gods. (6) Intercolumna walls, dedication scenes (partly destroyed). (7) Dedication scenes by Nero: leaves palace with standards. (8) The king before Gods. Top register shows Augustus. (9) Texts of Claudius and Augustus.

This hall with its forest of columns leads to the Second Hall (C), also called the Hall of Appearances, the roof of which is supported by six columns. Here Hathor could appear in joy, the gods jubilant at her approach, and where she was surrounded by the various gods and goddesses of her court before she issued from the temple. Scenes on the walls show the foundation of the temple, its layout, the necessary offerings, and finally its consecration.

The most interesting of the surrounding rooms is the *Laboratory* (G), first on the left, where the perfumes and essences were prepared. Next door to this the *Harvest Room* (H), flanked on the left by a room for offerings (Y), with another on the other side; on the right a room for *Libations*, and the *Treasury* (Z), where the necklaces, pectorals, collars and statuettes of precious metal, as well as the chests of raw minerals from which they were manufactured, were kept. Here, under the floor, can be seen remains of an earlier temple. Two of the rooms acted as passages through which the wet and the dry offerings were brought into the temple and the second room on the left seems to have been the place where the statues were reanimated by being joined to their bas.

(10) Offerings and oblations to various gods. (11) Offerings and oblations to various gods. (12–13) Foundation ceremonies (cartouches blank). (14) Foundation ceremonies (cartouches blank). (15–16) The king offers ointment to Hathor. (17–18) The king offers incense and ointment to Hathor and gods. (19) Calendar texts. (20–21) The king offers bouquets, papyrus and Ma'at to Hathor, Horus and Iḥy. (22) Calendar texts. (23) Augustus makes offerings to Hathor. (24) The king offers casket of jewels to Hathor. (25–26) The king offers necklace and pectoral to Hathor. (27) Texts of instructions to the priests. (28) Offering symbolising long life and Ma'at to the Gods. (29) The king offers libations and incense to Hathor. (30) The king offers wine to Hathor. (31) The king offers bouquets, offering lists to Isis and Hathor, Below the Nile Gods and Field Goddesses. (32) The king before five lion-headed gods with knives.

Each of the large inner chambers of the temple was reached over a raised sill, each pavement higher than the previous one, culminating in the sanctuary as the highest point, as over the primaeval mound. The *First Vestibule* (D) was also the Hall of Offerings, and it must be imagined not empty as it is today but cluttered with every kind of altar and offering table, full of fruit, flowers, drinks and perfumes all changed regularly several times a day. Once the savour had been absorbed by the goddess the food and drink were divided among the priests. One of the most important feasts of Dendārah was the Festival of Drunkeness that took place on the 20th day of Thoth, when the chief priest danced and sang before Hathor, while making an offering of a menu-vase. The *South corridor* shows the objects sacred to Hathor, the menat-collar, a clepsydresta, several sistra, an object representing an egg flanked by the three plants of the South and the North, a pot of milk, a jar of wine, a crown and a pylon.

The next room or *Second Vestibule* (E) was also called the Hall of the Ennead or the Hall of the Gods, and occupies the area between the general part of the temple and the sacred portions. It was also the place where the gods could gather to protect their mistress. (33) Four registers: The king offers calves to Osiris and crowns to Horus. (34) The king offers shrines to Horus the Elder, sceptres to Horus, wine to Hathor and Iḫy. The door opens directly from here into the *Sanctuary* (F), Great-Seat or the 'Sanctuary of the Golden One' (a reference to one of the aspects of Hathor), which was to all intents a separate structure roofed independently with a cavetto cornice, and entered by a sloping ramp. The reliefs on the inside of the chamber show that there was a stone naos and a wooden shrine enclosing the boats of Hathor and Horus, each ornamented with the head of their respective deity. At Dendārah only six of the ritual acts were shown, the others being known from Abydos and elsewhere.

The Sanctuary is surrounded by a corridor off which open a number of *chapels*. The first on the left seems to be that of the Nome or District (L), but its use is not entirely clear. The next one, called the Seat of Repose (M), seems to be associated with Isis, sometimes translated as 'The Day and Night of the Child in its Cradle'. The next chamber is sacred to Sokar (N), the God of the Dead of Memphis, followed by that of the Sacred Serpent (O). The S part of the corridor has three chapels opening off it, the centre one (Q) is called Pr Ur, the Shrine of Upper Egypt, 'The Great House'. It is flanked on the right by 'The House of Flame', the Shrine of Lower Egypt (R). On the left was the Chapel of the Sistrum (P). Under these rooms were the *crypts*, 32 in all, 11 of which were decorated (many cannot now be visited); some have been extensively damaged. In these were stored the more precious temple relics. It must have been extremely difficult to get the larger statues set on travelling poles and carried by six or more priests out of the crypts. It was in the S crypt, opening on the House of Flame, that the most precious objects seem to have been kept. Although the objects kept here have long since disappeared, they are clearly represented on the walls, with their names and the materials from which they were made. In the third crypt on the W side the temple archives were kept.

The rooms on the right are (from the S) respectively the Throne Room or Chapel of Reʿ(S), the Jewel Room (T), the Room of Purification (U), the Birth Chapel, the Silver Room (V) and The New Year Chapel (V1), which really consists of three rooms with a short stair leading up from an open court. This court is very small, only 4.50m by 5m and must have been extremely crowded at the New Year Festival.

Here were offered all kinds of fruits, flowers, meat, incense, live animals, perfumes and precious oils. The object of the ritual carried out here was to perpetuate and renew the cosmic order, which might otherwise fall again into the chaos from which it had emerged. It is for this reason that stress is here laid upon the duties of the eight Hermopolitan gods and goddesses, who with Thoth aided in the creation of the world.

The upper chapel shows on the ceiling the body of Nut the sky goddess, stretched over the Earth, and the birth of the sun.

(35) New Year texts. (36–37) Offerings of beer, incense, libations, victims and musical instruments. (38–39) Scenes in the interior of the sanctuary show the king making offerings, bread, collars, vases, mirrors, pectorals, ointment and natron. Also censes the barks of Hathor and Horus. (40–42) The king offers natron to Hathor and Iḥy, purifies the Gods, and offers cloth to gods including Tayt (Goddess of Weaving). Roof scene shows Nut as a woman with Hathor emblem in plaque. Entry sphinxes and text of New Year offerings hymns to Nut, hymn to Reʿ, offerings in court include papyrus and boats, gold and silver, lapis lazuli and turquoise. (43) The king offers to Hathor a mirror, figure of Ma'at, building texts at base of walls. (44) Cleopatra VII and her son Ptolemy XVI (Caesarion).

*The roof and its chapels*: From the First Vestibule the ascending stairway to the roof, which was followed at the time of the New Year Procession, is on the W. It winds round several bends above the New Year Chapel, and passes on the right a small room (The House of Gold). Reliefs show the order of the procession, with the standards at the head, opening the way, beginning with Ophois of the South, a jackal perched on its standard, Thoth in the form of an Ibis, and the standard of Itdi (composed of hieroglyphs in a rebus of its name), and then the king followed by priests.

Facing the top of the stairs is the *Chapel of the Union with the Disk*, a small light kiosk set in the SW angle of the roof, protected from the observation of the profane by a high wall. It is impossible to date as none of the cartouches has been filled in. Well designed and elegant, it is complete except for two columns (replaced by the Dept of Antiquities in 1924). There are 12 columns with Hathor-headed capitals and a shallow screen wall. There is no roof, but it probably had a light wooden cover, removed to expose the statues to be revivified to the full rays of the sun. There were chapels at other temples as at Edfū, but they have disappeared.

Other important elements of roof decoration were the twin *Chapels of Osiris*, one open on the W near to the W stair, the other on the E. Both were arranged in the same way, consisting of an open court, a covered court, and a completely enclosed room, dark except for a small slit in the roof. These chapels had nothing to do with the worship of Hathor but were concerned with the resurrection of Osiris which took place in the month of Khoik. The first court shows the procession of the priests representing the different Egyptian districts before Osiris in that month. The first enclosed room had on the ceiling a unique zodiac, removed in 1820 by the French collector Saulnier and his agent Lelorrain (the original is in the Louvre, Paris). It has been replaced by a cast. The rest of the ceiling is taken up with two large figures of the sky goddess Nut bent over the Earth, with the boat of the sun shown at different hours of the night. The inscriptions on the walls give instructions for making moulds of the gods at various cities. The inner room represented the tomb of the god, who was shown on the walls at various stages in his resurrection. The outside of the temple is extensively decorated and the fine lion-headed gargoyles for removing water from the various temple roofs are particularly noteworthy. The rear wall shows reliefs of Cleopatra and her son Caesarion.

Behind the main temple lies a small structure, the **Temple of Isis**, sometimes regarded as her mammisi. This consists of a court, a small hypostyle hall of four columns leading to a second four-columned hall.

There was a stairway leading to an independent edifice, set at right-angles to the other building, consisting of a Hall of Offerings and two lateral chapels, and a central sanctuary. This part of the temple has been savagely destroyed, indicating the fear in which the worship of Isis was held by the early Christians. The scenes on the walls must have represented the birth of Isis and an inscription in the E chapel points to the tendency towards unification in the later forms of Egyptian religion. Here Isis was worshipped under many names as a universal Egyptian goddess.

There are in addition two mammisi in the courtyard; the earlier is the **Mammisi of Nectanebo** of the 30 Dyn. Rebuilt several times, it consists of a court surrounded by a low wall with entry through a palmiform screen wall. The floor was originally of several coloured stones such as basalt, and alabaster. The *Hall*, now covered, was originally open. The *Sanctuary* is decorated with scenes that link the Birth House to the birth scenes at Deir al-Baḥarī and Luxor, which is emphasised by the fact that Amun and his Ennead are represented here. The carvings have a certain charm and are a good deal clearer than the earlier ones at Thebes. They represent the birth of Iḫy but, though Hathor is the mother, Amun not Horus is the father. The scene begins on the far W in the first register with Amun, his Ennead, Atum and Montu. In the second register Amun gives life to Hathor, and announces that the young god Iḫy is to be born, two of the Hemsut spirits holding the divinities by the feet; Khnum assists and at Amun's request models the child upon the potter's wheel; Khnum and Thoth lead Hathor to the birth place; Amun receives his child and recognises him, and Thoth promises him a long life and many jubilees. At the E end of the wall the child is nourished by the divine cows, Hesat and Sekhat-Hor, givers of the divine milk, represented as women with cows' heads; the god-child is then enthroned before the Ennead of Karnak. On the E side Khnum and Heqet introduce Nectanebo in the form of their lieutenant upon Earth, while behind the group Anubis rolls a full moon, a symbol that the child's future is assured. There is no trace of paint on these figures, and they were probably covered by a thin sheet of gold held in position by gum or gesso, further indicated by the name given to it in the Edfu Calendar—the Hall of Electrum.

Mention must be made of the ceremonies carried out in the Mammisi of Nectanebo in the month of Pachons starting on day 11, the Mystery of the Birth of the Divine Child, the Son of Amun and Hathor. These mystery plays probably took place all over Egypt in the Birth Houses but they may have been celebrated on various days. Here the play consisted of 13 scenes and two intermissions, and represented the scenes shown on the walls of the sanctuary. In form it was a mixture of Greek drama and the medieval mystery play. When it was successfully carried out it ensured that the fertility of the land as well as the royal house was safe for another year, but like all religious ceremonies in Egypt it had to be re-enacted annually to ensure this protection.

During Roman times the rites carried out at the mammisi changed somewhat and this led to the erection of another building under the early Roman Emperors. The plan of the **Roman Mammisi**, built some 400 years later, is somewhat different from that of Nectanebo. It is the work of Trajan but originally the cartouches were misidentified for those of the earlier Augustus. It is in essence like the construction at Edfu, with a gallery of columns encircling the central structure. This enabled the sacred procession of the religious drama to come out of the building and circle it without being exposed to the profane gaze. The building consisted of a podium with a court, surrounded by a low wall with the entry guarded by two sphinxes, all of which was destroyed by the Christians when they built their basilica. The interior of the temple had evolved considerably since the time of Nectanebo. The size of the *Hall of Offerings* had been much reduced, two corridors serve as the ambulatory, and in the *N corridor* a stair is shown going to the roof. Here a procession is shown ascending them, so that certain rituals were carried out on the roof. Against the *S corridor* is a narrow chapel, and beside it two crypts, today half destroyed. They are shut by applying pressure on part of the reliefs. To the N and S of the sanctuary were *two long rooms* where the apparatus connected with the mysteries was kept. The *Sanctuary* was of considerable size, 5.35m by 8.50m, but it was undecorated. The tabernacle would have been kept against the W Wall and there would have been a statue of the mother and child in the wooden shrine inside the stone naos. Hathor and the child Ihy were again represented and although in the main the scenes are similar to those in the Mammisi of Nectanebo, there are variations. The figures portrayed on raised stands represent statues rather than the actual gods and in addition to Khnum modelling the child, Ptah now fashions him in stone and the gods endow the child with all the powers inherent in them. However the wall decoration was never finished.

Dendārah was one of the healing temples to which pilgrims and sick people came to be cured and the foundations of a brick building which must have served as a **Sanatorium** have been found, situated between the temple proper and the Mammisi of Nectanebo. Its purpose has only been recognised recently and it was not cleared and planned until 1968. It consists of an enclosure wall, largely destroyed, enclosing a limestone threshold and a passage leading to an interior court, with a burnt-brick structure leading off. There were traces of a chute for running water and 11 rooms intended to house the pilgrims.

One of the blocks of stone found near the doorway seems to have been part of one of the magical statues over which water was poured and which are now to be found in many of the museums of the world. The patient either drank or bathed in the water and there was a bath where the sacred water, having been impregnated with magic, could be used by the patients. Around the bath were chambers where the sick could be induced into a cataleptic sleep (described in papyri now in London and Leyden), after which they were wakened by Hathor or Horus, 'The Good Doctor', and plied with herbal remedies, certain herbs which could be used for medicinal purposes and which even today grow round the temple.

The **Christian Basilica**, probably dates to the 5C and is one of the earliest Coptic buildings in Egypt still extant, related by its decoration and basilical hall and trefoil apse to the two monasteries at Sūhāg. The roof has disappeared, and further excavation and clearing needs to be undertaken before the definitive plan can be produced. It has two lateral doors, one to the N and the other to the S, enabling easy access to the narthex which has apses decorated with shells. Three doors open towards the W, the central one leading to a chapel and baptistry. The building is constructed out of the earlier temple stones. The **Sacred Lake** to the N is almost complete, lined with stone and reached by a stone stairway.

After (3km) **al-Tarāmsah** a bridge crosses the Nile to **Qenā** (see below).

## B. East Bank

(Total distance approx. 144km.) **Akhmīm.**—35km **Awlad Yaḥyā Baḥrī.**—30km **al-Balābīsh.**—19km bridge to **Nagʿ Ḥammādī.**—25km **Fāw Qiblī—35km Qenā**.

The H57 from Akmīm (bridge from Sūhāg) passes (35km) **Awlad Yaḥyā Baḥarī** and (30km) **al-Balābīsh** before reaching (7km) the *Nagʿ Ḥammādī Barrage* (see above). 12km further is the bridge to the West Bank town of *Nagʿ Ḥammādī* where the road joins the H2 and turns NE continuing parallel with the railway line on the riverward side.

At 8km a track leads 3.5km S to the villages of *al-Qaṣr* and *al-Ṣayyād* (ancient Chenoboskia) where stand the scant remains of the ancient *Monastery of St. Palamon*. On the N side of the H2 a similar track leads 3.5km to the village of *Ḥamrah Dūm*. In the hills behind rises the Gabal al-Ṭārif (350m) with near the summit c 150 caves many of which were used as tombs. Most important is the 6 Dyn. *Tomb of Thauti*, while others range up to the 1C AD and many were occupied by Christian hermits. Sometime in the late 4C a jar containing gnostic manuscripts was concealed in one of those caves which must have collapsed and fallen to the valley floor. The jar was discovered by two brothers from al-Qaṣr in 1945. The subsequent dramatic history of the manuscripts reads like a detective novel but they were all, except one, recovered and are now known as the *Nagʿ Ḥammādī Codices* repose in the Coptic Museum in Cairo. Written in Coptic they are all translations from Greek gnostic works and consist of 12 leather-bound papyrus books (one was burned). The contents are 52 tracts of which 42 are unique and unknown. They have all been published by the International Committee for the Nagʿ Ḥammādī Codices and translations in English, French and German are in progress.

A further 10km N of the H2 stands **Fāw al-Qiblī** (Gk Pabaw; Coptic Baphou). Here St. Pachomius (c 290–346) founded the first monastic rule and built his monastery. Remains of an immense *Basilica* have been excavated by an international team from 1975. The building measures 75 x 37m and was probably built in the 5C and restored and extended in the 7C. It was totally destroyed in the 11C. Evidence was found of earlier buildings, a 4C church, possibly that of St. Pachomius himself and beneath that foundations of 4C and 3C buildings. Remains of even 1C AD occupation of the site have been found. 5km beyond Fāw on the riverward side of the railway line lies **Dishnā**.

30km **Qenā** (Ar. Qīnā) is the chief city of the district and province. It has bus and railway stations and docking for steamers.

**Hotels**. *Lotus* (2*), opposite station; *New Palace*, Maydān al-Mahaṭṭah.

This is the site of the ancient city of *Shabit*, later under the Greeks becoming *Kainopolis*. The Romans honoured another emperor and called it *Maximianopolis* but the Copts derived the name *Kournah* from the Greek. During the early Muslim period it remained a dependency of Qūṣ and in Ottoman times it was included in the vast Wilayat Girza until 1826 when the latter was divided. In 1883 it was created a province and the district was formed in 1890. It is now a very large town.

Qenā's most important monument is the *Tomb of Sh. Abd al-Raḥīm al-Qināʾī* (died 1196) and the annual mūlid (14 Shaʿ bān) is an important event, attended by the provincial officials.

To the NE the H77 runs to *Būr Safāgah* (161km) on the Red Sea Coast (Rte 50).

# 35 Qenā to Luxor

The main road (the H2) crosses on to the East Bank at Qenā and this side of the river therefore takes precedence on this Rte.

## A. East Bank

(Total distance approx. 58km.) **Qenā**.—23km **Qifṭ**.—10km **Qūṣ**.—5km **Shanhūr**.—7km *Khuzām*.—13km **Luxor**.

3km from Qenā the H2 passes *al-Gabalāw* and continues to (20km) **Qifṭ**, a small town situated at the closest point to the Red Sea attained by the Nile.

The modern name of the town is derived from the Gk *Koptos* and ultimately from the Ancient Egyptian *Kebt*. It was occupied from early historic times, though there are prehistoric cemeteries in the Bīr Umm Fawakhir hills to the E. The town probably developed due to its proximity to the breccia quarries and the gold mines of the Wādī Hammamat (c 75km E) which were worked from the first two Dyns onwards. The extension of this route leads to the Red Sea and thence to the Land of Punt, increasing the importance of the town. It retained its position throughout the Old and Middle Kingdoms and it is known that Senusert III (12 Dyn.) worked the quarries and probably fortified the town. During the New Kingdom it declined in importance although Tuthmosis III rebuilt the temple, and indications are that the mines were not working to full capacity. Prosperity was not regained until Ptolemaic times when it was the capital of the Fifth Nome of Upper Egypt and under the Romans it was one of the terminals of the routes to the porphyry quarries at Gabal Dukhān and white granite quarries at Umm Atqal (Mt Claudius). Min, god of the desert, was the local deity. During excavations in 1893–94 Petrie found three colossal archaic figures (now in the Ashmolean Museum, Oxford) in the temple dedicated to Min.

The town was a major centre for early Christian converts who during the persecutions of the Emperor Diocletian in AD 292 felt powerful enough to rebel, with dire consequences—the Emperor razed the town. It gradually recovered a great deal of its former prosperity and during Muslim times it was a great agricultural and industrial centre, specialising in sugar and soap which it supplied to the rest of Egypt and even exported. Its houses were renowned for their domes, to build which a merchant had to own over 10,000 dinars, according to the geographer Idrisi. With the rise of the city of Qūṣ to the S in the 10C as an important mercantile centre Qifṭ declined in importance and trade was diverted. It was assumed that this town with its large Christian population gave its name to the Egyptian Christian Copts but it has been mentioned specifically in Arabic sources that the Arabs called them Qibṭī (Aigiptoi) to distinguish them from their own people.

Just S of Qift a road leaves the H2 to the SE running to the Red Sea at Qusayr, through the Wādī Ḥammāmāt. This road has been used since ancient times as it is not only the shortest route across the E desert from the Nile to the Red Sea, but also led to the breccia quarries and gold mines. Along it passed the foreign imports of successive empires and during Muslim times it was an important route for the pilgrims to Mecca.

At (45km) *Laghaytah* the road turns NE to run between high cliffs to (17km) *Qasṛ al-Banāt* with the remains of a Roman watering station and another at (70km) *Bīr al-Ḥammāmāt*. After 18km at *Wadi Ḥammāmāt* below Gabal Abu Kuwah are the major stone quarries and on the S side of the valley, the greatest concentration of ancient inscriptions. The earliest date from the 1 and 2 Dyns although there are also prehistoric rock paintings. Recently the IFAU have been recording and photographing all the inscriptions, including the only known inscription of Ahmose first king of the 18 Dyn.

After another 5km lies *Bīr Umm Fawākhīr* the only settlement in the valley (refreshments). Here to the N of the road are numerous remains of the stone huts of the Roman gold miners. Also on the N side is a black basalt *shrine* decidated to Amun covered in Greek inscriptions. A sounding behind the naos revealed pottery dating from the prehistoric period, with above shards of the New Kingdom.

Beyond the road continues NE, with the remains of Roman watch towers on the heights and hostels beside the road, for 92km to the town of Quṣayr (Rte 50) on the Red Sea coast.

From Qifṭ a road follows the river to arrive at (10km) **Qūṣ**. In medieval Islamic Egypt Qūṣ was second only to Cairo in size and importance.

It is an ancient site called *Geza* and in Gk *Apollinopolis Parva*, and in the 3C, *Diocletianopolis*. For the Copts the town was *Kus Berbir* from which the modern name is derived. During the early Islamic period Qifṭ to the N was still the major city in the area but during the 9–10C it declined and Qūṣ was its successor, the Nile terminal for the goods coming and going from the great port of Qūṣayr on the Red Sea. Now only the remains of a Ptolemaic temple can be seen.

During late Fāṭimid and Mamlūk times the importance of the post of governor was reflected in the fact that the city had its own mint and, like Alexandria, it was a place of exile for deposed sulṭans and khalīfs. As a mercantile centre its importance was such that it had almost a monopoly of eastern trade as its orchards, vegetable fields and gardens were renowned. However it had a reputation for 'bad airs' and many scorpions. With the discovery of alternative sea-routes by the Europeans in the 15–16C its importance declined greatly and under the Ottomans much of its territory was appropriated to another area. It became just another town in the Wilayat Girgā.

At the centre of the town in the Shʿ. Abū ʾl-ʿ Abbās is the **al-ʿ Amrī Mosque**, a Fāṭimid building founded in 1083 during the reign of Khalīf al-Mustanṣir but much restored during Mamlūk times under Sulṭan Khalīl and later by the Amīr Muḥ. Kāshif and Muḥ. Bay Khawāgī in the 1810s. It preserves its ancient form as an open enclosure mosque but has had several extensions. The façade and minaret are modern but a section of the original Fāṭimid wall remains to the E and SE running across the qiblah riwāq. The latter contains the original round-arched miḥrāb, the hood and the surround decorated with the most magnificent stucco work added in Mamlūk times. Inside the miḥrāb are arches with ogee heads set with arabesque and geometrical patterns. Around the frame is a beautiful inscription; the whole frame is a riot of arabesque and thuluth inscription. At the N end of this wall are the remains of a maqsurah, which, with the door, is set with ebony hexagons and roundels. The Kursi for the Qurʾān, inlaid with ebony, ivory and mother-of-pearl, is also Mamlūk work. The magnificent minbār beside the recent miḥrāb is one of the earliest in Egypt and was made for the wazir al-Ṣalīḥ al-Talāʾiʿ, who was governor here, in 1155. It is in teak, heavily carved with geometrical patterns and Kufic inscription. By the N wall is the tomb of Sh. Muḥ. b. Jah-Jah.

At the SE exterior corner leading to the toilets is the remnant of a very early *Ayyūbid tomb* in brick which preserves the earliest example of the pierced dome. It was built for Mubarak b. Maqlid in 1172. Only the zone-of-transition, drum and dome are original, the cubic base having been replaced, though retaining the shape of the original. The height to the zone-of-transition is almost 5m. The NW side is completely open, while the SW wall against the side of the mosque has two round-headed windows. The NE wall is the only solid part of the base; the SE wall has a pointed-arched door where the miḥrāb used to be. Above this door are three panels, the lateral ones round-arched with crimped edges and six-pointed star niche, the central one with a trefoil-hood, similar to the window above, inset with a peculiar fix-lobed niche. The octagonal zone-of-transition is similar to those of late Fāṭimid mausoleums, with squinches formed of one niche over three, with a similar shaped window between each; a trefoil window pierces each of the spandrels of the niches. The 16-sided drum is pierced by eight pointed-arched windows, which alternate with similarly shaped blind niches. The dome reverts to eight lobes each pierced with a six-pointed star, above which are three tear-shaped openings. On the exterior the zone-of-transition is not stepped, but has small semi-domes covering the squinches, and the drum is supported by eight concave buttresses.

The H2 passes (5km) **Shanhūr**, an ancient site with its modern name an arabisation of the Coptic; (7km) *Khuzām* and to the E (7km) **Nagʿ al-Madāmūd**, easily reached in an afternoon excursion from Luxor (Rte 36). This is an ancient site, actually a suburb of Thebes, called *Madu*, marking the N boundary. The tutelary deity was Montu, the god of war. Under the Copts its name was *Madamout* from which the present Arabic name was derived. In this village lies the **Temple of Montu** in his aspect as a falcon.

There had been a temple here since the Old Kingdom and during the New Kingdom it was a place of great importance (some excellent reliefs from here can be seen in the EM and the Louvre) but the extant remains are largely Ptolemaic and Roman. The French think that this was a site which contained a sacred mound set with growing trees, similar to the Osircion at Abydos. Excavations were undertaken by the French Oriental Institute between 1925–33 (after which they moved to Nagʿ al-Tūd, S of Luxor), but soundings continued to be made between 1932–39 in an attempt to establish a sequence of building levels and to increase knowledge about the earlier temples.

The temple is situated inside a mud-brick *enclosure wall*, entered through an *avenue of sphinxes* leading from a quayside. The wall was built by Tiberius, as was the monumental sandstone *Gateway*. The façade is interesting because here, as at the small temple at Madinat Habu, an experiment was taking place with the use of colonnaded kiosks (A). The gate leads to a *Court* (B) with a colonnade on three sides built by Antoninus Pius. The inner end is marked by a *Portico* (C), only five columns remaining, which appears to be the work of Ptolemy IX Euergetes II. This leads to a small *Hypostyle Hall* (D) with four columns, in front of two *Vestibules* (E–F)—the outer one for offerings, the inner the hall of the gods. Beyond this is the *Sanctuary* (G), with the naos for the sacred boats, and around it nine *subsidiary rooms* intended for the temple furniture, incense, offerings and the treasury. The passage round the sanctuary led to two colonnaded courts; the *North Court* (H) built by Ptolemy VII Philometor, and the *South Court* (I).

Behind and at right-angles to this temple is a further **Smaller Temple** (J), which seems to have been dedicated to the sacred bull of Montu. The outside may have been built by Trajan and Domitian and there are reliefs showing Trajan adoring the bull. The whole is built over the earlier 12 and 18 Dyn. temples and contains much re-used material.

The H2 continues S for another 8km where a road leaves W to (5km) **Luxor**.

**MADĀMŪD TEMPLE OF MONTU**

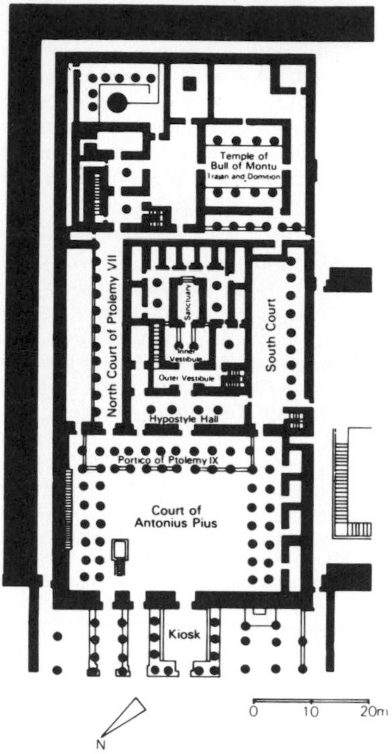
Temple of
Bull of Montu
Trajan and Domitian
North Court of Ptolemy VII
Sanctuary
Inner Vestibule
Outer Vestibule
Hypostyle Hall
South Court
Portico of Ptolemy IX
Court of
Antonius Pius
Kiosk
0 10 20m
N

# B. West Bank

(Total distance approx. 49km.) **al-Tarāmsah**.—13km **al-Ballāṣ**.—3km **Ṭūkh**.—8km **Naqādah**.—10km **al-Qiblī al-Qamūlā**.—15km *al-Qurnah* (for **Thebes**).

From al-Tarāmsah the H53 passes through (13km) **al-Ballāṣ**, an ancient site called in Coptic *Balous*, and (3km) **Ṭūkh**.

To the S are the remains of *Ombos*, an ancient site whose name derives ultimately from the Ancient Egyptian *Nubty* (Golden, from the local gold mines). The town's history stretches back to prehistoric times; the cemeteries lie to N and S of the area. The town god was Seth and the temple built for him in early times was restored by Ramesses II and again in the 22 Dyn. It was built in limestone, but little can now be distinguished among the piles of debris and there is not much to attract the casual visitor. The population of Ombos seems to have had a long-standing feud with the people of Dendārah and there is a description of a fight between them in Roman times.

The next village of importance is (8km) **Naqādah**, with a large Christian population.

It is notable for its prehistoric and Early Dynastic remains excavated by de Morgan (1897) and Petrie (1894–95). The most important is a mastaba (excavated by de Morgan) of King Hor-aha and Queen Neith-hotep. This village is the typesite for two predynastic cultures. On the edges of the desert are the ruins of four Coptic monasteries.

The road continues S to (2km) *Danfīq* and (8km) **al-Qiblī al-Qamūlā** (W of which is the **Deir Malak Mikhā'il**), and on to (15km) **al-Qurnah** (for **Thebes**).

# 36 Luxor

Until the beginning of the 19C **LUXOR** (Ar. *al-Uqsur*; the Palaces) was a small undistinguished provincial village in the province of Qēnā. Its fame for Muslims derived from the grave of Abū 'l-Hajjāj, a 12C shaykh, whose tomb was and is still the object of reverence (see below). Although the name given to the area by the Muslims acknowledged their appreciation of the number of ancient buildings, most of the monuments on the East Bank were buried and those exposed were neglected or used as habitations. Those on the West Bank, save the Colossi of Memnon, were almost totally unknown. Several of the early European explorers mentioned the area but it was not until the survey of Napoleon's expedition that the importance of the site became apparent. Even so, many discoveries remained to be made and an almost continual programme of excavation has revealed, and continues to reveal, remains of the greatest importance. The new-found fame of the site attracted an increasing number of visitors during the early 19C; when Thomas Cook inaugurated his tourist route the number rose dramatically and hotels were built to house them. In 1896 it was made the chief town of the district which increased its importance and in 1985 it was given the status of a province. It is now the most important tourist site in Upper Egypt and the present aspect is that of a modern town with hospitals, shops, government offices, bus and rail stations and an airport.

**Airport** 6km E of town centre, direct route along the Sh'. al-Maṭār. It accommodates internal flights from Cairo, Alexandria and Aswān.

**Railway Station**, inland in the E of the town in the Maydān al-Mahaṭṭah. Roads lead W to the river. There is a regular mainline service from and to Cairo and the N towns and to Aswān and the S towns.

**Hotels**. *East Bank*, Sh'. Nahr al-Nīl (Corniche): Winter Palace (5*); Akhenaton Hotel Village (4*); Etap International-Wagon Lits (4*); Savoy (4*). *In town*: Luxor, Sh'. Ma' bad Karnak (3*); Families, Sh'. Ma' bad Karnak (2*); Phillip
, Sh'. Ma'bad Karnak (1*); Hotel Dina, Sh'. Ma'bad Karnak (1*); Nile Belladona (1*); Horus Hotel. Sh'. Ma'bad Karnak: New Karnak, Maydān al-Maḥaṭṭah.

*West Bank* (all basic in services provided): Habou Hotel, near entrance to Temple of Madīnat Habū; Mersam Hotel, opposite offices of OEA at Colossi.

**Youth Hostel**, 16 Sh'. al-Manshiyyah.

**Restaurant**. *Marhaba*, above the Tourist Arcade.

**Information Bureaux**. Min. of Tourism offices, Tourist Market (near Winter Palace Hotel), Luxor 6615.

**Travel Agents**. All the major companies in Egypt have representatives in Luxor. They are all in the block of shops near the Winter Palace Hotel. Tours can be arranged to sites within a wide area.

**Airline Offices**. The Egypt Air offices are in the Winter Palace Hotel.

**Buses** are available to the nearer towns; for longer journeys there are intercity services. The only practical method of local transport is by ḥantūr (horse carriage).

**Bicycles and donkeys**. There are several businesses in Shʿ. al-Mahaṭṭah hiring bicycles in Luxor and they provide an excellent way to see the sights of the area. For the more adventurous donkeys can also be hired.

**Ferries**. The most regular and reliable service is the local ferry from the bank in front of Luxor Temple to the commercial jetty on the West Bank. Bicycles extra.

**Taxis** are available from commercial and tourist jetties on the West Bank. Bicycles may be carried on roof. Hanturs abound in Luxor.

**Tickets Offices**. Tickets for the temples on the East Bank can be obtained at the individual sites. Tickets for those on the West Bank can also be obtained at the office where the ferry docks.

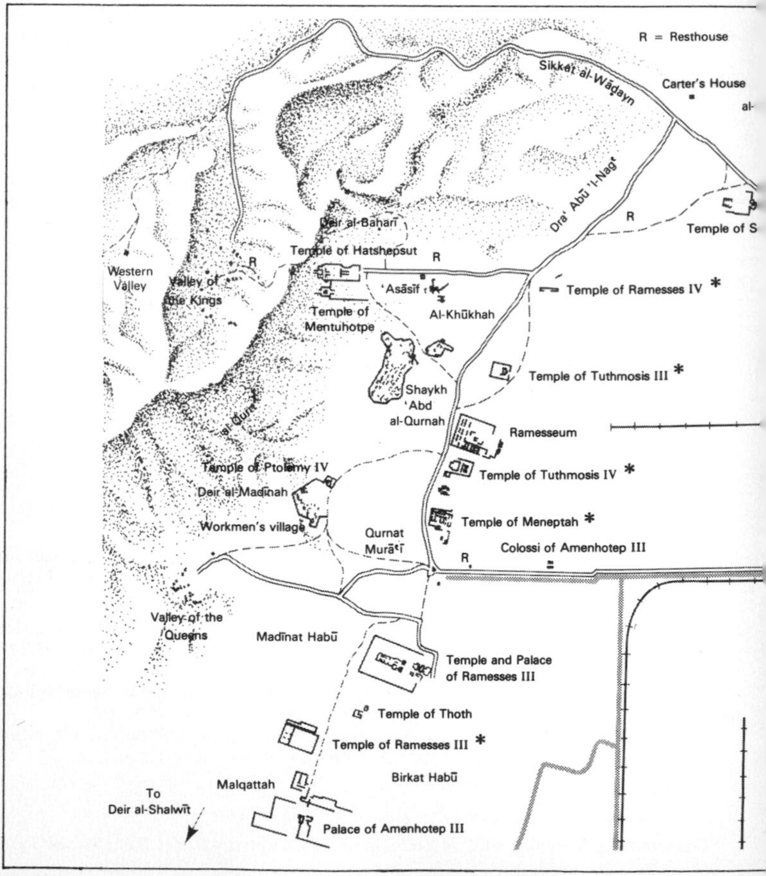
R = Resthouse
Sikkat al-Wādayn
Carter's House
Dra' Abū 'l-Nagā
Temple of S
Deir al-Baharī
Temple of Hatshepsut
R
Western Valley
Valley of the Kings
'Asāsīf
Al-Khūkhah
Temple of Mentuhotpe
Temple of Ramesses IV *
Temple of Tuthmosis III *
Shaykh 'Abd al-Qurnah
Ramesseum
Temple of Ptolemy IV
Deir al-Madīnah
Temple of Tuthmosis IV *
Workmen's village
Temple of Meneptah *
Qurnat Murāʿī
Colossi of Amenhotep III
Valley of the Queens
Madīnat Habū
Temple and Palace of Ramesses III
Temple of Thoth
Temple of Ramesses III *
Malqattah
Birkat Habū
To Deir al-Shalwīt
Palace of Amenhotep III

**Pronunciation**. It should be remembered that the people in this area, unlike those in Cairo, pronounce the letter qāf like the g in get (e.g. sūq is pronounced sūg, Qurnah is Gurnah) and the letter jīm retains its original sound as in jam (e.g. Luxor, jabal; Cairo, gabal). For consistency all names are written in the Northern Egyptian colloquial form, but when pronounced the local conventions should be used.

**History**. The history of Thebes, the city of Amun, really remains to be written. It consists of two entirely different entities, the East Bank, site of the city and main state temples, and the West Bank with its mortuary temples and tombs. To the Ancient Egyptians this was Waset or No-Amun (City of Amun), the former the name of the nome as well as its capital city. Hermonthis (Armant) to the S had originally been the capital but the status was transferred to Thebes by the 11 Dyn. kings. The city was also known as the Southern On or Anu, thus balancing the Northern Anu (Heliopolis).

Thebes was the capital of the Egyptian Empire (17–20 Dyns), but had been settled from a very early period; many worked flints have been found in the western hills, and there was a small settlement here in Old Kingdom times. It did not, however, become important until the early rulers of the 11 Dyn. established their capital here. Whereas Memphis is dominated by its tombs, Thebes is dominated by its temples on

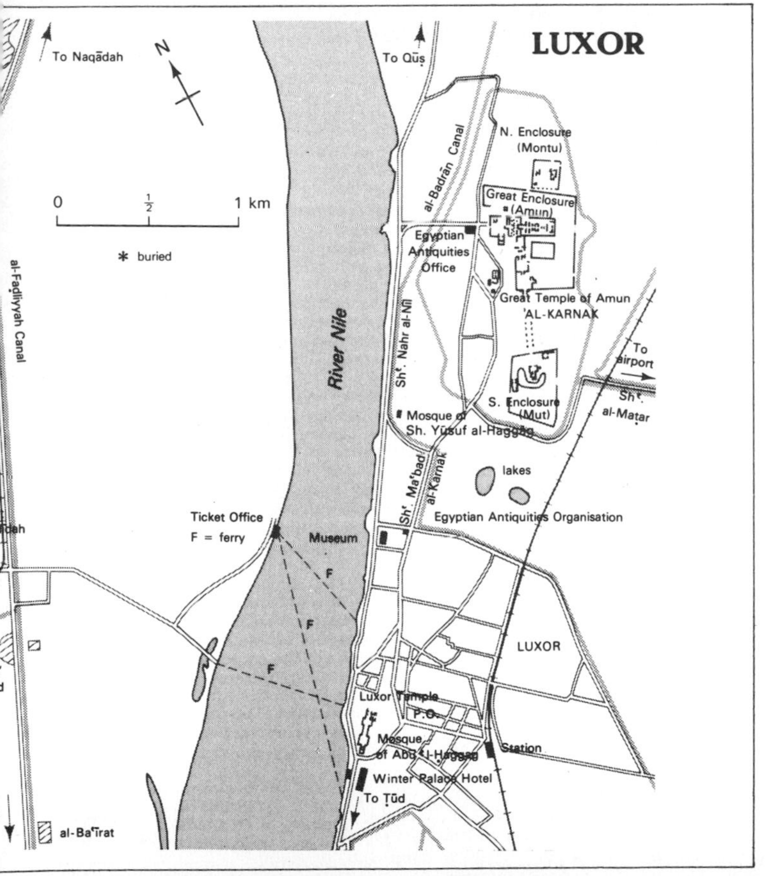
LUXOR
To Naqādah
N
To Qūs
0
½
1 km
* buried
al-Fadliyyah Canal
al-Badrān Canal
N. Enclosure
(Montu)
Great Enclosure
(Amun)
Egyptian
Antiquities
Office
Great Temple of Amun
ʿAL-KARNAK
To
airport
Shʿ.
al-Matar
River Nile
Shʿ. Nahr al-Nīl
S. Enclosure
(Mut)
Mosque of
Sh. Yūsuf al-Haggāg
lakes
Shʿ. Maʿbad
al-Karnak
Egyptian Antiquities Organisation
Ticket Office
F = ferry
Museum
F
F
F
LUXOR
Luxor Temple
P.O.
Mosque
of Abū'l-Haggāg
Station
Winter Palace Hotel
To Tūd
al-Baʿīrat

both banks. The earliest ruler yet known to have built here is Nebhepetre Mentuhotep II who erected a temple in a fold of the western hills at Deir al-Baḥarī, and whose nobles were buried in the surrounding hills overlooking al-ʿAsāsīf. The 12 Dyn. rulers moved their capital to It-Tawy to the N near Memphis but Thebes remained the seat of the princes who rose to supremacy at the end of the 17 Dyn. It was to be the capital of Egypt throughout the Empire for some 500 years, except for the short reign of Akhenaten, until the death of the last Ramesside king in 1085 BC. Although thereafter the capital was either Memphis or one of the Delta cities, Thebes remained an important provincial city, and the centre of administration for Southern Egypt. During the Empire the wealth of the known world poured into Thebes and much of it went to adorn the temples of Amun-Reʿ, king of the gods, and even when Thebes was no longer the chief city, Amun remained the chief Egyptian god until very late in the country's history. To Homer it was 'hundred-gated Thebes', but to the Egyptians it was 'The City', the prototype of all cities.

Waset is the pattern of every city,
Both the flood and the earth were in her from the beginning of time,
The sands came to delimit her soil,
To create her ground upon the mound when the earth came into being.
Then mankind came into being within her;
To found every city in her true name
Since all are called 'city' after the example of Waset.

Under the 25 Dyn. kings Thebes fell before the Assyrians and was sacked twice, in 671 and 663 BC. This was the first time that one of the great Egyptian cities had been taken by an aggressor and the shock reverbrated throughout Western Asia.

In later Egyptian history the power of Thebes steadily declined. The political capital moved N, and although she remained the administrative centre of the S, imperial glory had departed. Even so, Thebes proved difficult to rule. Before the sack of the city, she rebelled against the 22 Dyn. rulers, and again under the Ptolemies and Romans; Ptolemy V had to restore order severely. But the Ptolemies built widely here, not only facing part of Pylon 2 at Karnak but building the gate in front of the temple and some works in the centre of the complex, as well as erecting temples on the West Bank.

The name Thebes was given to the city by the Greeks but the reason for this is obscure. What connection or similarity it had to their own city of Thebes is not known. Later it was also called Diospolis Magna (City of the God). During early Christian times it was an important centre and several shrines were turned into churches, but the general trend was one of decline, although it was never completely deserted as was the N capital of Memphis. After the Muslim conquest the district was called al-Ṭībah and the name al-Uqsur was applied to the town. Perhaps the greatest factor contributing to the preservation of the monuments was that there was no large city in the vicinity and the buildings were thus spared being used merely as a quarry. The ground level, as in towns throughout Egypt, has risen considerably during the period of occupation and any remains of secular palaces or dwellings are probably forever covered by the modern town.

**Itineraries**. Unfortunately it is impossible to produce chronological itineraries to the vast number of monuments available and so the area has been divided into several units each of which has a geographical or architectural integrity. They can be tackled *in toto* over a period of days or as individual units. The major division is between the monuments on the East or West Banks which are then subdivided into smaller itineraries, those on the West Bank progress from the most northerly to those in the S.

East Bank: 1) Luxor Temple; 2) Karnak Temple.

West Bank: 1) Temple of Seti I and the Valley of the Kings; 2) Deir al-Baḥrī ʿAsāsīf and al-Khūkkah; 3) Shaykh ʿAbd al-Qurnah and the Ramesseum; 4) Qurnat Murāʿī, Deir al-Madinah and the Valley of the Queens; 5) the Colossi, Madīnat Habū and the monuments to the south.

# A. East Bank

Just N of the Ministry of Tourism offices, facing the river is the ***Temple of Luxor**, temple of the Southern Apt or Opet. Here Amun-Min, the fertility aspect of Amun, was worshipped with Mut and Khonsu, who formed the Triad of Thebes. The temple runs parallel to the river and is therefore aligned N–S, not E–W. Additionally, the pylon and first court are slightly angled to the axis of the main temple, presumably to include an earlier shrine to the Theban Triad. An earlier 12 Dyn. temple stood towards the S end of the site and some limestone blocks from the earlier edifice have been recovered under that of the 18 Dyn.

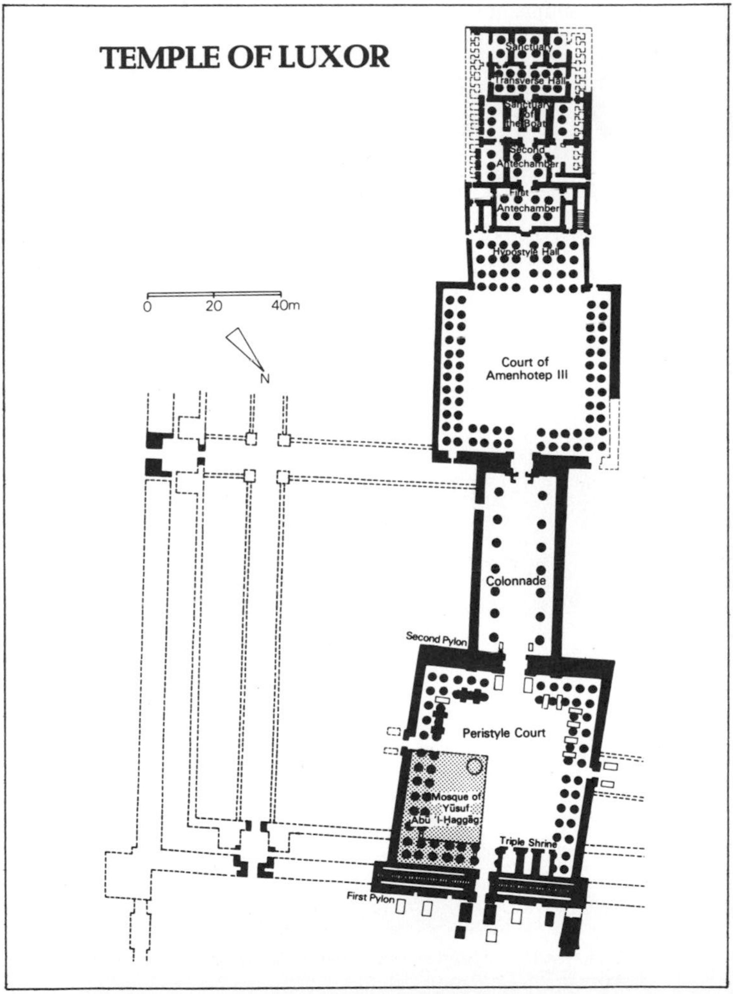
TEMPLE OF LUXOR
0
20
40m
N
Sanctuary
Transverse Hall
Sanctuary of the Boat
Second Antechamber
First Antechamber
Hypostyle Hall
Court of Amenhotep III
Colonnade
Second Pylon
Peristyle Court
Mosque of Yūsuf Abu 'l-Haggāg
Triple Shrine
First Pylon

As this is a much smaller and more compact unit than the Karnak temple and much easier to understand, it is advisable to visit it first. Unfortunately the temple has been much damaged by flooding; salt encrustation shows clearly on the walls up to the point where it was filled with debris which Maspero began to clear in 1883.

Entering the temple from the N, before the main body of the temple runs the 30 Dyn. *Avenue of Sphinxes*, revealed by recent excavations of the OEA, extending towards Karnak. These sphinxes, with human heads, bear dedications of Nectanebo I. The way was paved with sandstone slabs and has been excavated as far as the al-Magashgish mosque which has precluded further northward clearance. To the E are the remains of a small 25 Dyn. *Chapel of Taharqa* dedicated to Hathor, which excavations show had been removed except for the foundations, some 5m thick. Of the Chapel of Serapis built by Hadrian no trace remains. In its heyday the Luxor Temple would have been enclosed behind tall temenos walls. Around the whole complex are the remains of a Roman brick town.

Standing in front of the pylon were two obelisks and six colossal figures

*The Avenue of Sphinxes and the first pylon of the Temple of Luxor*

of Ramesses II, two seated and four standing. The two red granite obelisks were presented by Muh. ʿAlī Pasha to France in 1819 and the one on the W, 22.8m high, was removed (now in the Place de la Concorde in Paris), but fortunately the *E obelisk*, 25m high, is still in place. *Two seated figures* flank the entrance but of the standing figures the two to the E were also given to France (now in the Louvre) and only one of the two on the W remains in place. The *Pylon of Ramesses II* (originally 24m high and 65m wide) has part of the top course missing. The outer face shows scenes of the Battle of Kadesh, the battle in the upper register and the camp with chariots below. On the lower part is the battle record and the poem of Ramesses. In the entrance passage of the pylon are carvings of Shabaka (25 Dyn.) showing the king before Amun and Amunet. On the inner E face of the pylon is a continuation of the record of the Battle of Kadesh; on the W side is a dedication inscription. The temple's lower courses are heavily salt-encrusted.

Beyond the pylon is the large *Peristyle Court*, also built by Ramesses II. This embraces (on the r) a small earlier *Triple Shrine* or way station built by Tuthmosis III which must originally have stood in the clear space before the temple. Unlike the pylon and surrounding columns, it is of granite and the work is of a greater delicacy. The three shrines are dedicated to Amun (centre), Mut (W) and Khonsu (E). In the Amun shrine Tuthmosis is shown running towards Amun and there are additional cartouches of Merneptah. Both the shrines of Mut and Khonsu show the sacred boats. Around the court is a double row of 74 papyrus-bud columns (not of the finest quality) showing Ramesses before different deities. These arcades used to be roofed. On the E wall are scenes of the king offering to Min, and being received by Montu; most of the texts are of Ramesses II but Pinudjem and his family also appear. On the W side of the S wall is a picture of the pylon in all its glory with flags flying. Also on the last two walls are the family of Ramesses II, 17 of his sons, and by the E gate the queen and royal children. This court contains a large number of statues of Ramesses II, several usurped. Some others belong to the early stage in his reign when they were made as idealised portraits of the young king.

The left-hand gallery has not been excavated and the columns are still buried up to the capitals, the height of the debris prior to Mariette's clearance. The reason for this is that the space is occupied by the **Mosque of Abū 'l-Haggāg**. Most of the mosque, including the minaret, is 19C, but the N minaret is much older. It is one of a series erected through Southern Egypt by Badr al-Gamālī to mark his victories over the Nubians in 1077. It is interesting as a provincial contrast to the minaret of Badr's own mosque in Cairo (Rte 14).

Yūsuf Abū 'l-Haggāg, a descendant of the khalīf ʿAlī, was born in Baghdad c 1150. By the age of 40, his beloved wife and parents had died, so he moved with his sons to Mecca (c 1185). He was advised to seek quietitude in Egypt and arrived at Luxor c 1193. His piety gained him a wide reputation; Sulṭan al-ʿAzīz invited him to Cairo and offered him an official post. He did not stay in Cairo long but travelled to Alexandria which at this time was a meeting place for the foremost sufi masters from the western lands of Islam. He became a student of al-Jazūlī and returned to Luxor where he maintained a zāwiyah on top of the Temple of Luxor. He died in 1243 over 90 years old and was buried in a tomb in the same mosque. Many of his descendants still live in the area.

He is considered one of the greatest shaykhs of Southern Egypt and his mūlid, held on the 14 Shaʿbān, is visited by thousands of people from all over the country.

The ceremony involves a procession in which a large boat is paraded around the town. Parallels have been drawn between this ceremony and those in ancient times in which one of the gods was taken from their own temple to that of another in a boat. At Karnak this was the Feast of Opet. However, although appurtenances may be the same the basis is very different. In Islamic symbolism the boat is often considered as a vehicle for spiritual knowledge and thus the procession may well focus the attention of the populace upon the search for this.

The mud-brick minaret stands on a stone lintel of the ancient temple. It has a base 4.5m square which tapers slightly. Wooden beams strengthen the sides and at the top of this section there are small buttresses at the corners. Above this is a tapering cylindrical shaft surmounted by a small dome surrounded by crenellations. Although the ancient mosque is cracked and the Dept of Antiquities has built a new mosque just outside the walls to the west, this building is greatly venerated and the worshippers refuse to move.

Between the columns on the S side are several standing *statues of Ramesses II* (some damaged).

Leading S is a passage flanked on both sides by two *seated statues of Ramesses II*. Those on the N side are inscribed with the name of Ramesses but bear the features of Tutankhamun representing Amun and Mut. Next is a *Colonnade* built by Amenhotep but usurped by Horemheb, consisting of 14 large open-papyrus capital columns arranged to make a tall processional avenue. Perhaps it was originally intended by Amenhotep as the first step towards the construction of a hypostyle hall, or as a processional way leading to a pylon. It is walled in a long rectangular court decorated by Tutankhamun and Horemheb with scenes of the feast of Opet in the NW corner continuing round to the NE corner. First is the representation of the gate of the Karnak temple with the procession issuing from it, consisting of the portable sacred boats, carried by priests, a troop of soldiers with standards and musical instruments, one

*Luxor. The Court of Amenhotep III*

of the sacred boats towed by a rowing vessel, a group of Nubians with music, and two royal chariots led by grooms. The presentation of food and drink by Tutankhamun to Amun and Mut follows, with piled offering tables before their shrines. The reliefs are of the high quality and delicate outline of the best 18 Dyn. work.

The colonnade leads into the *Court of Amenhotep* III (52m by 46m), which, like the Court of Ramesses, is a peristyle court surrounded on three sides by double rows of columns with papyrus-bud capitals. This court is the glory of the Temple of Luxor and is an example of the best 18 Dyn. work. The columns are well proportioned and in a good state of preservation except at the N end. Originally the colonnade was covered, which would have provided the court with charming chiaroscuro, but the roofing blocks have gone. The account given in the king's building inscriptions, referring to the rebuilding of the earlier 12 Dyn. temple in the S part of the building, affords some idea of its original splendour.

'He made it as a monument for his father Amun-Reʿ king of the gods, erecting for him the temple anew, of fine white sandstone, made very high and wide, adorned with electrum throughout, a place of rest for Amun ...'.

In 1988 a collection of statues was found under the floor of this court. They will eventually be exhibited in the Luxor Museum.

The *Hypostyle Hall*, sometimes called the Vestibule, leads off the last court to the S and consists of 32 bud columns grouped in four rows of eight. In front of the central columns are fragments of an architrave with the cartouches of the 13 Dyn. king Sobekhotep III which must have come from the earlier temple. Ramesses IV and VI have usurped the columns by inscribing their cartouches. On the E wall Amenhotep is shown bringing offerings before Amun and Amunet, and killing a gazelle before the god. To the S open four long rooms, three of which are chapels; those on each side of the central doorway to Khonsu and one on the E to Mut. Against the doors of these are dedicatory inscriptions of Ramesses II indicating that he had repaired the temple. The other room on the W has stairs leading to the roof. On the side of the hall is a *Roman altar* dedicated to the Emperor Constantine (AD 324–37).

The hypostyle hall opens S into the *First Antechamber* which originally had eight columns, but these were removed when the chamber was turned into a Christian Church in the 4C. On the S wall where the entry to the sanctuary should have been, an apsidal recess flanked by two granite columns was built, and the reliefs of Amenhotep III were covered with a thick coat of whitewash and fine Christian paintings (now almost completely destroyed). Amenhotep can still be seen on the S wall kneeling before Amun-Reʿ and a lion-headed goddess. On the N wall there are scenes of a procession with priests and musicians including the king (defaced) going to worship Amun. When the temple was converted to a church dismantled sections like screen walls and column drums were placed under the pavement; these confirm that Shabaka in the 25 Dyn. built a colonnade in front of the temple.

Beyond is the smaller *Second Antechamber* with four columns. On the walls the king is shown driving sacred calves to be killed before the god, offering incense, chests, sistra and sceptres to Amun-Reʿ. This was the offering chapel which stood in front of the next room, the *Sanctuary of the Sacred Boat*. Originally another antechamber with four columns, it was converted to a sanctuary by Alexander the Great who built the chapel opening N and S in the centre of the chamber. This sanctuary probably replaced an earlier wooden shrine which, in turn, may have replaced a stone one. Alexander's dedication indicated it was more of a replacement than an original: 'He made it as a monument for his father Amun-Reʿ, in white stone, with doors of acacia inlaid with gold, as it was in the time of Amenhotep III'. It is decorated with scenes of Alexander before Amun, Mut and Khonsu, and he is shown presenting a feather crown and vases to Amun. The king is also shown making offerings to the sacred boat of Amun.

To the E a passage leads out into a side room, with three columns and much-damaged reliefs, from which in turn a door leads to the *Birth Room*. This is of great interest because here Amenhotep claims divinity as the son of Amun-Reʿ, one of the main reasons for his extensive rebuilding work at this temple.

In common with other such scenes it is rather confusing. Starting at the bottom from right to left Amun-Reʿ, Hathor and Tuthmosis IV's wife, Queen Mutemwia, are embracing. Amun, disguised as Tuthmosis IV, is led by Thoth into the queen's chamber. Then Amun and the queen are seated together on the symbol for heaven supported by the goddesses Selket and Neith. Amun reveals his divinity, holds 'the breath of life' to the queen's nostrils and instructs that the forthcoming child be called Amenhotep. He instructs Khnum to model Amenhotep and his double (ka) on the potter's wheel after which Hathor gives life to one of the figures. In the 2nd register (left to right) the queen is taken to the birthroom by Khnum and Hathor, then the goddesses who preside over the birth present the child to Amun. Next, children are shown suckled by cows and goddesses and the last scene shows Amenhotep as a fully grown man, purified and blessed by the gods.

The last *Transverse Hall*, with 12 bud columns, is sometimes called another antechamber but must have originally been intended as a hypostyle hall. Sadly the scenes, of excellent workmanship, are very damaged. At the entrance to the sanctuary to the S there is a scene of the king in front of a tree before Amun-Reʿ and the king followed by the goddesses of the South and North, Nekhbet and Wadjet. The *Sanctuary* is a small square room with four columns. Here the god represented is Amun-Min. On each side there are two small two-columned rooms. The back SW corner of the temple is severly damaged, as is part of the E wall.

To avoid returning the length of the temple it is possible to leave by the E gate.

The outside walls on the W are covered with further inscriptions and designs representing the Battle of Kadesh. Beginning on the N end in the upper register they show the attack on the city of Dapur (in Syria), and the king attacking the enemy with his chariots. The lower register shows the king attacking a fortress in Naharayn.

To the NE along the Shʿ. Nahr al-Nīl (1km) on the corner of the Shʿ. Tuḥtmus stands the **Luxor Museum of Ancient Art** (open 17.00–20.00; fee), set in a small garden with several statues, the nucleus of a projected open-air display.

Constructed to the plans of Dr Mahmud El-Hakim, it was opened in 1975 and is the newest museum in Egypt. Although it is fortunate in having an up-to-date catalogue it cannot attempt to display more than a small fraction of the material from the storehouses of the OEA. There is a large ground floor gallery and an upper gallery. Objects on display range from the prehistoric to the Mamlūk periods. None is intended for permanent display and some are still unnumbered.

The main part of the collections consists of statues from the Karnak cache, some material from the tomb of Tutankhamun (returned from Cairo), many decorated sandstone blocks from the temples of Akhenaten at Karnak, and several statues of Sobek, including a splendid seated figure of the god accompanied by Amenhotep III. A fine collection of Christian and Muslim antiquities found during the recent excavations in the vicinity of the Luxor temple is also shown.

Continue NE on the riverbank past the *Mosque of Yūsuf Abū 'l-Haggāg*. At 1.5km the Shʿ. al-Karnak leads SW 500m to the extensive site of **AL-KARNAK**.

The religious centre of al-Karnak is an extremely complex series of structures divided between three areas dedicated principally to the Theban Triad, Amun-Reʿ, Mut and Khonsu, but there are also other temples within the precincts.

The whole area was known as Iput-Isut, 'the most esteemed of Places'. To the N, with its own enclosure wall, is the Temple of Montu the war god, 'Lord of Thebes'. Also inside its own enclosure and connected to the main temple with an avenue of sphinxes, the Temple of Mut the consort of Amun lies some distance to the S. Beside the Great Temple of Amun, the central enclosure (550m by 520m) contains a temple of Khonsu-Neferhotep, the third member of the Triad of Thebes, just within enclosure wall at the SW. There is also a Temple of Ramesses III, a small way-station of Seti II, and numerous other structures. Even Akhenaten built here; the site of his temple has recently been discovered just outside the main temples beyond the E wall. There is a Temple to Ptah and Sekhmet on the N side of the area; a Festival Hall of Tuthmosis III to the E of the original buildings; a small Temple of Amenhotep II between Pylons 9 and 10 and Chapel of Tuthmosis III between Pylons 7 and 8, as well as temples to Osiris and Apet. Although the main axis of the Great Temple is from W to E, it also has a N–S extension. A large number of blocks of earlier temples, chapels and other structures have been recovered from the ruins and from within the pylons, including a chapel of Senusert I, an alabaster chapel of Amenhotep I and the talatat (stone blocks) of Akhenaten's destroyed temples.

## Central Enclosure

The original temple lay further to the E of the present building and may even have dated to the Old Kingdom. Some 12 Dyn. columns of Senusert I were still standing when Wilkinson examined the site in the early 19C between the sanctuaries and the Festival Hall of Tuthmosis III. Now all that can be seen are the granite sills of the early doorways and remains of an alabaster pedestal of Senusert I.

Karnak consists in essence of the same elements as are usually found in a state temple: a pylon, colonnaded court, hypostyle hall, vestibule, shrine and storerooms, but the fundamental plan has been overlaid by extra pylons, added courtyards and colonnades and even subsidiary shrines, the whole time the temple moving further W, presumably following the retreating bank of the Nile. Structures were added by each king who came to the throne so that this extended building period has ensured that the unity present in the mortuary temples built at a single time for a single purpose is missing.

To follow the chronological order of the **Great Temple of Amun** would necessitate beginning at the E. However, today, to make sense of the temple it is necessary to enter at the W end. First is an *Avenue of*

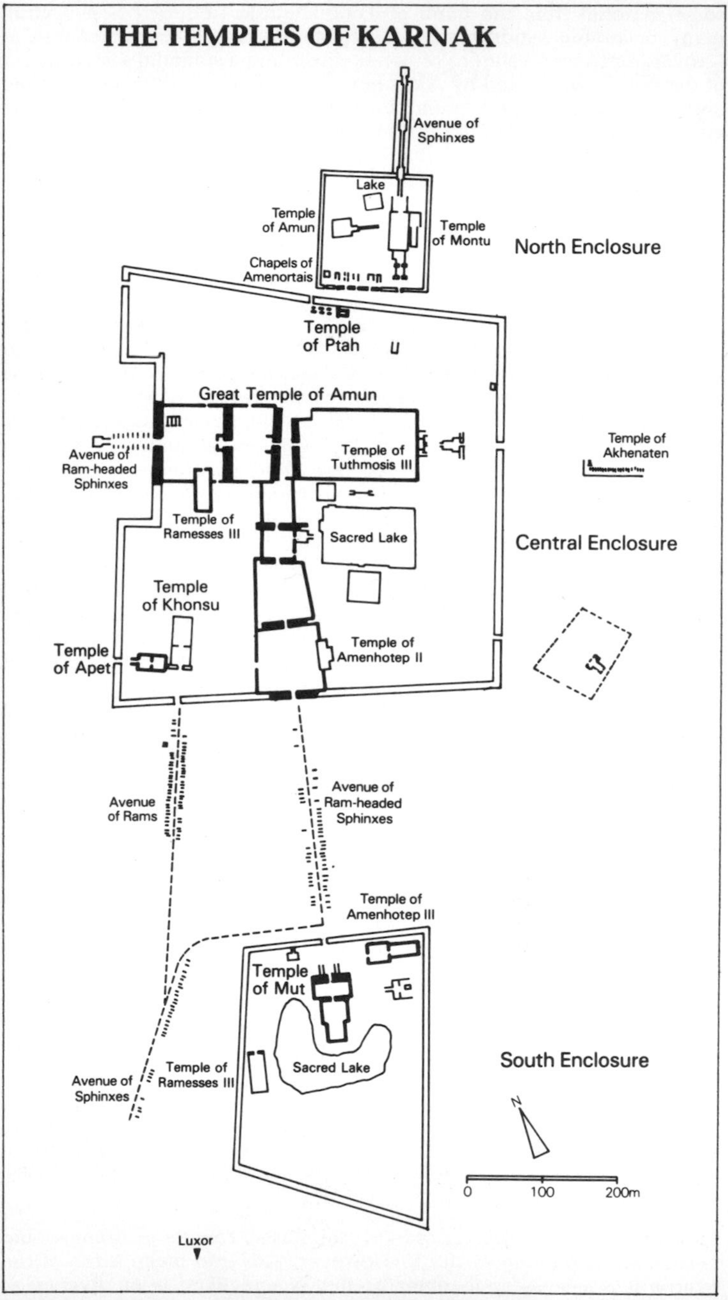
THE TEMPLES OF KARNAK
Avenue of Sphinxes
Lake
Temple of Amun
Temple of Montu
North Enclosure
Chapels of Amenortais
Temple of Ptah
Great Temple of Amun
Avenue of Ram-headed Sphinxes
Temple of Tuthmosis III
Temple of Akhenaten
Temple of Ramesses III
Sacred Lake
Central Enclosure
Temple of Khonsu
Temple of Apet
Temple of Amenhotep II
Avenue of Rams
Avenue of Ram-headed Sphinxes
Temple of Amenhotep III
Temple of Mut
Sacred Lake
South Enclosure
Temple of Ramesses III
Avenue of Sphinxes
N
0
100
200m
Luxor

*Ram-headed Sphinxes*, probably erected by Amenhotep III or Horemheb but later usurped first by Ramesses II and again by Pinudjem. This leads to the incomplete *First Pylon* (130m wide).

Recent work by the Centre Franco-Egyptien, created in 1967 to coordinate the work at Karnak and preserve the art and architecture of the site, has established that there are several Ptolemaic and Roman levels in front of the pylon. It has been revealed that there are slipways for raising the sacred barks from the canal in front of the temple and a garden planted in front of the sphinxes watered by channels. The exact date of the slipways has not yet been established, but they must be later than the 22 Dyn. as some of the blocks used in their construction bear cartouches of Sheshonq.

The *First Forecourt* (103m by 84m) seems originally to have been planned by the 22 Dyn. rulers, though never completed. On the left on entry is the small *Shrine of Seti II*, really a way-station of the sacred barks with chapels to Amun, Mut and Khonsu. It was cleared by Legrain in 1912, previously only the top courses being visible. The structure is of quartzite sandstone and originally stood in isolation in front of the temple. The façade shows Seti making offerings to different deities and above is a frieze of cartouches and crowned uraei alternating with red and white crowns. Surmounting this is the winged disk of Horus with the inscription 'He of Bhdt, Lord of the Sky, Great God bright of plumage'. Interior scenes show the barks of the gods. The walls are unnecessarily thick, with the hieroglyphics and inscriptions poorly executed. The Set animal used for the king's name has in many cases been erased. The foundations of the building are of stone from the quarries of the Gabal Ahmar near Cairo. Excavations done for the building of the first pylon close by caused the collapse of the W wall of this structure, damaging the shrine of Mut, but it was subsequently replaced.

In the centre of the court are *ten columns of Taharqa*, part of a kiosk some 26.5m high, of which only one is standing. On the S side of the courtyard is the Temple of Ramesses III (see below), beside which is the *Bubastite Portal* of the 22 Dyn. whose kings originally planned the whole courtyard. It has scenes of Sheshonq's victories over the Palestinians while to the N of the gate are scenes celebrating Prince Osorkon's work as High Priest of Amun. The *Second Pylon*, called 'Illuminating Thebes' (a copy of the third pylon, see below), and the vestibule were built by Horemheb. To the left is a colossal standing *statue of Ramesses II* (15m) with his daughter Benta anta in front of his legs. It was usurped by Pinudjem in the 21 Dyn. The interior was filled with blocks from a temple of Akhenaten. The small *Temple of Ramesses III* on the S side of the courtyard is dedicated to Amun in the two forms in which he appears most frequently, 'Amun-Reʿ, king of the gods and Lord of Karnak' and 'Amun-Reʿ-Kamutef, he who is before his harim'. It is not certain when it was built but it must have been between years 11–22 of the king's reign. When it was built it stood isolated in front of the pylon.

The name of the temple was 'The House of Ramesses Ruler of Heliopolis in the House of Amun'. The dedication to Amun reads in part: 'I made for you ... in your city of Waset, in front of your forecourt to the Lord of the Gods, being the temple of Ramesses in the Estate of Amun, to remain as long as the heavens bear the sun. I built it sheathed it with sandstone, bringing great doors of fine gold; and I filled its treasuries with offerings that my hands had brought'. It is known as the N Building of Ramesses III, as he built several others at Karnak. It was cleared of debris by Legrain in 1896–97 and published by Henri Chevier in 1933. Like the other temples

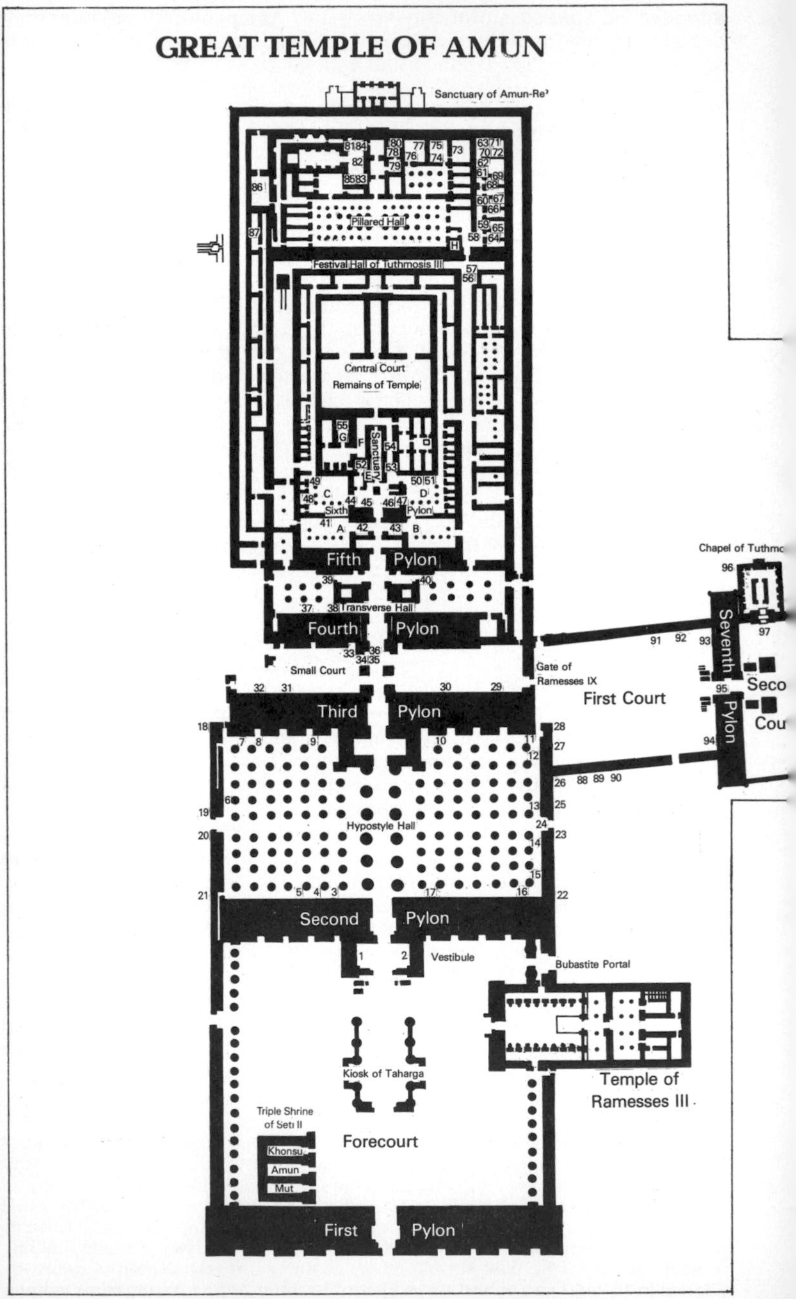
GREAT TEMPLE OF AMUN
Sanctuary of Amun-Re'
Pillared Hall
Festival Hall of Tuthmosis III
Central Court
Remains of Temple
Sanctuary
Sixth
Pylon
Fifth
Pylon
Transverse Hall
Fourth
Pylon
Small Court
Third
Pylon
Gate of
Ramesses IX
First Court
Chapel of Tuthmo
Seventh
Pylon
Seco
Cou
Hypostyle Hall
Second
Pylon
Vestibule
Bubastite Portal
Temple of
Ramesses III
Kiosk of Taharga
Triple Shrine
of Seti II
Khonsu
Amun
Mut
Forecourt
First
Pylon

it shows signs of damage by flood water and salt erosion and has been extensively restored.

It consists like other state temples of a pylon (10m wide), flanked each side by a colossus of the king, a court, decorated square pillars with Osiride figures of the king, leading to a portico with four columns, a hypostyle hall, and a series of sanctuaries dedicated to the Triad of Thebes. The deeply incised relief work of the figures and inscriptions in this temple still shows traces of colour, but the workmanship is inferior to that of Madinat Habu built by the same king. Many of the hieroglyphs are blurred by the use of plaster which has run. Some of the reliefs have been altered, sometimes more than once; others have been copied from earlier ones in the main Amun temple.

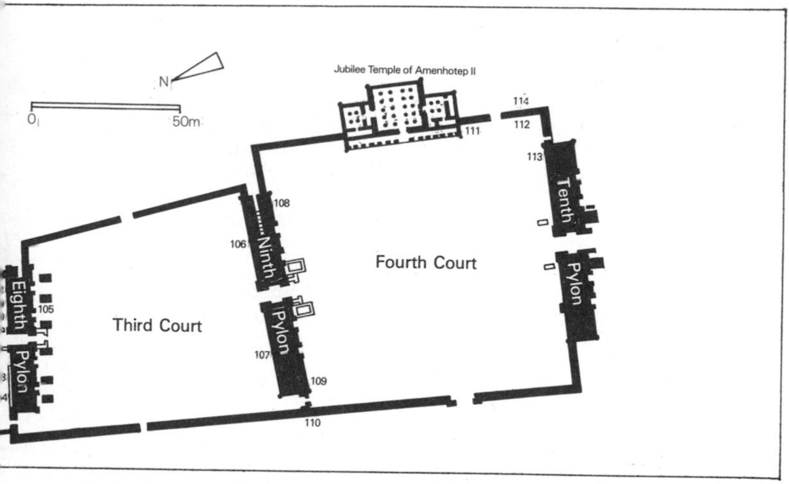
N
0
50m
Jubilee Temple of Amenhotep II
114
112
111
113
Tenth
Pylon
108
106
Ninth
Pylon
107
109
110
Fourth Court
Third Court
Eighth
Pylon
105

In the second pylon the *Vestibule of Horemheb*, finished by Ramesses II and cased by Ptolemies III and IX, leads into the immense *Hypostyle Hall* (102m by 53m). Erected by Seti I with additional decoration by Ramesses II, it is called 'the Temple of Seti is glorious in the domain of Amun'. In total the area covered is 6000sq. m (large enough to contain both St. Peter's Church in Rome and St. Paul's Cathedral in London).

The hall contains 134 columns, the 12 flanking the processional way higher (23m) to accommodate clerestory windows, some of the sandstone grids of which are still in position. Sandstone slabs which roofed the hall have been dislodged by earthquakes. The remaining 122 columns have papyrus-bud capitals and are set each side in nine rows of seven columns each. Thus they provide a forest of columns intentionally representing, it seems, a papyrus marsh, a return to the original venue of the early temples. It has been suggested by Nims that the centre colonnade was originally intended to have formed a separate long narrow hall as shown in certain tomb paintings (cf. the Tomb-Chapel of Neferhotep).

There is quite a lot of colour still left on the upper part of the columns and on the roof slabs still in position. The N side of the hall was decorated by Seti I in delicate raised relief, and the S side by Ramesses II, whose artists abandoned the raised style for the less time-consuming sunk relief.

The columns have been inscribed by several kings, starting at the top with the vertical cartouches of Seti I and at the base by Ramesses II. Ramesses IV and VI also inscribed them, the order being the same in each case. The central part of the column is taken up with offering scenes, the king before the deities of the temple, and those of Egypt in general.

Amun-Reʿ appears most frequently, and among his epithets are 'Lord of Thebes', 'Lord of the Two Lands', 'Master of the Thrones of the Two Lands'. He is accompanied by his consort Mut, shown wearing either the white crown or the vulture head-dress of the queens. She is called 'Lady of Ishru', or 'Lady of the Two Lands'. Amunet, his older consort, called 'the Lady of the South', is also represented wearing either a white crown or a crown and sun disk. Khonsu-Neferhotep, third member of the triad, is also shown. He appears as a young man wearing the side lock of youth and with a disk and crescent on his head.

On the inside wall of the second pylon Seti is shown followed by Khonsu and led by Hathor to Amun-Reʿ. Further N on the same wall are shown Ramesses I before eight divinities; Seti I kneeling before Seth and Nephthys, and Ramesses I before Horus and Hathor, Sobek and Wadjet. In a lower register Seti I is shown with four bulls before Amun and Hathor; the king is also shown before Amun-Reʿ-Kamutef, with Nubians climbing poles. On the S side of the N wall are some very delicate scenes of Thoth writing Seti's name on the sacred ished tree, while the king kneels before him. On the far side of the door the king receives a sceptre, and offers vases to Amun-Reʿ.

On the front of the third pylon there are a further 37 scenes of Seti before the gods receiving serpent sceptres from Mut, pouring libations on an altar, and making offerings in which Ramesses II joins him. The scenes outside on the N wall show Seti's Syrian and Palestinian campaigns, including the capture of the city of Yenoam, the king driving in his chariot, offering prisoners to Amun-Reʿ, and returning from his

*Luxor: Festival Hall of Tuthomosis III*

campaigns across the canal that marks the border of Egypt. The N Gate of the Hall leads to the small Temple of Ptah (see below).

The S side of the Hypostyle Hall was largely decorated by Ramesses II. On the E face of the third pylon the king is shown before Amun-Reʿ and on the lintels over the S Gate he is shown running to Amun-Reʿ and Mut, and again to Amun-Reʿ and Khonsu. Just E of the door the king is shown in a boat with a goose on the prow before Amun-Reʿ. Other scenes show the divine barks carried by priests in procession, and the king adoring the Theban Triad. On the outside of the S wall of the hall are scenes from the battle of Kadesh and his Palestinian and Syrian wars. At the E end prisoners are shown before the Triad of Thebes, while scenes throughout show the capture of Palestinian cities (much damaged), Ramesses II attacking a fortress, and the king binding captives. Beside the gate the king is slaying captives taken in the war.

(1–2) Ptolemy V and divinities. (3–4) Seti I led by Hathor to Amun and Mut. (5) Ramesses I before eight divinities. (6–7) Thoth writing the king's name on sacred tree; Seti I kneeling; sacred boats carried in procession. (8–9) 37 scenes of Seti I. (10–11) Seti I offering to gods. (12–13) Scenes of Ramesses II, crowned by Horus and Thoth, presented to Amun; running with vase to Amun, Horus and Thoth binding the Southland and the Northland beneath the king. (14–15) Ramesses before Amun-Reʿ with sacred boat; the king running to Amun. (16–17) Boat of Amun being towed, blocks of Amenhotep III and Ay built into pylon. (18–19) Campaigns of Seti I in Asia, Syria and Palestine including submission of Lebanese rulers, capture of Yenoam; the king binding prisoners, march through Palestine, presentation of prisoners before Theban Triad, return to Egypt across a canal. (20–21) The king before Amun and Isis, capture of Kadesh, campaigns against Libyans and Hittites. (22–23) Campaigns of Ramesses II, capture of Palestinian cities, the king attacking fortresses and binding captives, the king charging in chariot. (24) Door of Ramesses II, description and name. (25–26) The king fighting against a fort, charging enemy chariots. (27–28) The king and princes lead prisoners before Amun.

The *Third Pylon* was built by Amenhotep III. In the foundations were found several dismembered earlier shrines, some complete. They included a limestone *Chapel of Senusert I*. This was a way station where the boats of the gods could be rested during processions. Beautifully carved, this small chapel has square pillars and a stand on which the boats were laid. An alabaster *Chapel of Amenhotep I* is not of such high quality (both re-erected in an enclosure N of the forecourt called the Open Air Museum. Special permission required for visiting), parts of a quartzite shrine of Hatshepsut (one block in Luxor Museum) and sections of alabaster shrines of Amenhotep II and Tuthmosis IV. On the E face is a long text of Amenhotep, listing tribute while scenes show the sacred boats of the gods.

From the hypostyle hall two other temples can be visited. NE against the enclosure wall is the Temple of Ptah (see below) and in the S corner of the enclosure the Temple of Khonsu (see below).

Between the third and fourth pylons is a *small court* that originally contained four obelisks, but only one is now standing. The two bases nearest the pylon held obelisks of Tuthmosis III and the blocks are scattered around the court. Beyond these are the bases of the two obelisks of Tuthmosis I, of which the southernmost is still standing (23m high, 143 tons), embellished with later cartouches of Ramesses IV and VI. The blocks of the other obelisk are lying on the ground. They were erected by the architect Inneni and would have stood at the entry of the temple as completed by Tuthmosis I. When Amenhotep added the third pylon it boxed the obelisks in the narrow court. At the S end of the court is the *Gateway of Ramesses IX* to the court and pylons on the N–S axis (see below). To the S lies the Sacred Lake (see below).

*Third Pylon*. (29–30) Remains of 71 columns of text of Amenhotep III. (31–32) Sacred boats and text of Ramesses II, Amenhotep III offering. *Fourth Pylon*. (33) Text of Seti II restoring pylon. (34) Restoration text of Tuthmosis IV. (35) Restoration text of Shabaka. (36) Tuthmosis IV before Amun, text of Shabaka.

Although the *Fourth Pylon* was constructed by Tuthmosis I, of sandstone faced with limestone, the restoration texts on the outer face are of Tuthmosis IV, Seti II, Shabaka and Ptolemy VIII. It stands in front of a narrow *Transverse Hall* built by Tuthmosis I or III, now with 14 papyrus columns although probably originally with 16. Hatshepsut had two obelisks erected, one each side of the passageway; only the N one is still standing (27.5m high, 320 tons). The blocks of the S obelisks are lying in the court with the pyramidion cap removed near to the lake (see below). These two obelisks are depicted in transport from Elephantine to Thebes on the lower terrace at Deir al-Baḥrī (see below). Including the quarrying and river transport the process took seven months. They are dedicated to Amun, Presider over Karnak and Lord of Thebes. Another inscription quashes any insolent enquiry from the future as to their purpose thus: 'O ye people who shall see this monument in after years and who shall speak of that which I have made, beware lest you say 'I know not why it was done', I did it because I wished to make them as a gift for my father Amun, and to gild them with electrum'. Tuthmosis III's disapproval of Hatshepsut here took the form of encasing the obelisks as far as the ceiling of the hall. To a great extent this preserved the lower parts, but the upper sections were defaced by Akhenaten.

(37) Colonnade of Tuthmosis I, Osiride pillars on W side. (38) Upper register, figure of Tuthmosis III and list of foreign countries. (39) Jambs, dedication text of Tuthmosis III. (40) Remains of a Chapel of Amenhotep II; the king and file of Asiatic prisoners.

Forming the E wall of the transverse hall is the limestone *Fifth Pylon* with the name 'Amun great of prestige', also attributed to Tuthmosis I. On the W face are pictures of the king with Asiatic prisoners. On the same side are the remains of a small Chapel of Amenhotep II. Beyond the pylon is a *Smaller Transverse Hall* attributed to Tuthmosis III, divided by an enclosure, the two sections known as the *North and South Pillared Courts*. The 20 columns are somewhat smaller than those in the previous halls.

Beyond is the sandstone *Sixth Pylon* of Tuthmosis III, called 'Amun secure of prestige'. Although much damaged, it contains interesting historical texts including a geographical list of the king's conquests. On the W face is a list of peoples conquered at the battle of Megiddo.

(41) Dedication text of Tuthmosis III after Battle of Megiddo. (42) Names of people conquered at Megiddo. (43) Names of peoples of the South.

The area beyond the pylon is rather confused, but as after the pylon there is a vestibule flanked by two courts. In the centre of the *Vestibule* are two granite pillars showing Tuthmosis III embraced by Amun, the N with the symbols of Lower Egypt, the S with those of Upper Egypt. On the N side are two *colossi of Amun and Amunet* with the likeness of Tutankhamun. Against the W wall is a *seated statue of Amenhotep II*. Beginning on the N side and continuing around the walls are the annals of Tuthmosis III.

The two flanking courts have the remains of columns indicating their original colonnaded aspect. In the *N court* a large number of fragmentary statues were found, some of the Middle Kingdom (now in the BM). N and S are several chapels, now ruined, built by Amenhotep I, usurped by Tuthmosis III.

Directly beyond the vestibule is the *Granite Sanctuary of Philip Arrhidaeus*, the passage around which continues the texts of Tuthmosis III from the vestibule. The king is shown offering to Amun-Reʿ and accounts are given of the years 23 and 25 of his reign. The exterior of the rose-granite sanctuary has scenes of Philip before Amun-Reʿ, standards and the king offering and running before Amun. Three registers show the king with deities and boats. The long narrow interior consists of two rooms. In the E room are texts giving an account of the building by Philip. It replaced an earlier structure, probably of Tuthmosis III.

(44) Tuthmosis III (years 28–29) and statistical table. (45–46) Annals of Tuthmosis III. (47) Dedication text of Tuthmosis III,

On the N side a dark granite doorway opens on a series of rooms built by Hatshepsut but altered considerably by Tuthmosis III with her cartouches replaced by his. The *Room of Hatshepsut* (extra fee for opening this room) was walled up by Tuthmosis III which protected the decoration, and the colours have remained very bright. Hatshepsut is seen purified by Thoth and Horus. S of the sanctuary is another complex of rooms (from the steps in the northernmost of which a good photograph of the boats may be obtained). E of this complex lie the scattered alabaster and limestone blocks, the remains of the original 12 Dyn. temple which stood here, built by Senusert I.

(48) Dedication text of Tuthmosis III. (49) Tuthmosis III running towards Hathor with Ihy. (50) False door, dedication text of Tuthmosis III. (51) Tuthmosis dedicates treasure to Amun.

(52) Section of Tuthmosis' annals, year 23. (53) 11 Scenes of Philip with divinities and boats. (54) The king before Amun-Reʿ. (55) Hatshepsut purified by Horus and Thoth.

On the E side of this ruined area stands the *Festival Hall of Tuthmosis III*, unlike any other Egyptian building. Like so much 18 Dyn. work it was erected transversely across the axis of the temple. Called 'Men-Khepheru-Reʿ, blessed through his monuments', it is 44m long and 17m wide. There is a central nave and at a lower level two side aisles. It was later used as a Christian church. Entry is from the SW through a vestibule into the *Pillared Hall* where the strange plan becomes apparent. The centre columns are of a unique form and are considered to represent the tent-poles used in the campaign tent of Tuthmosis. They are higher than the square pillars in the side aisles and allowed for the use of clerestory windows. In the small room in the SW corner of the hall were found the stele known as the Karnak Table of Kings (now in the Louvre, No. 13481). On the N side are the remains of two uninscribed statues and a kneeling figure of Sety II. Behind these are several narrow rooms dedicated to the Triad of Thebes. To the SE is a *series of rooms* usurped by the Ptolemies, with one decorated by Alexander the Great. Just N of these is the *'Botanical Room'* with reliefs of alien flora and fauna said to have been brought back by Tuthmosis from his foreign campaigns in Asia. Beyond the NE wall of the hall is a room usurped by Ramesses IV. He is seen on the walls while on the floor is an altar of Ramesses III.

Dedication texts and titles of the king on the architrave pillars: the king wearing white, red and double crowns before Amun and Horus. (56–57) Dedication texts. (58) List of Syrian cities. (59) Three registers of seated divinities. (60) Two registers of heb-sed. (61) Top register, the king and Inmutef, Seth and Horus teaching the king to shoot. (62–63) The king offering malachite, incense etc. to Amun-Reʿ. (64–65) Speeches of Amun and Amunet. (66–67) The king running with vases followed by Horus of Edfu and running with oar and rudder. (68–69) The king dedicating treasure to Amun. (70) Dedication text. (71) The king with Atum and Montu. (72) The king between Seth and Nephthys.

(73) The king in carrying chair with hawk-headed souls of Pe. (74–75) The king offers incense and collar to Amun. (76) The king before Sobek-Reʿ. (77) The king receives palm branches from Seth (destroyed). (78) Portrait head of Alexander before Amun. (79) Alexander before eight divinities. (80) Alexander with ka before Amun. (81–82) Plants and animals. (83–84) Plants and animals. (85) Birds.

(86) Ramesses III usurping texts of Tuthmosis III. (87) Tuthmosis III, two of scenes of building the temple.

A *girdle wall* built by Tuthmosis III surrounds the area and beyond the E wall is the *Eastern Sanctuary of Amun-Reʿ*, built by Hatshepsut. Cut from a single block of alabaster, it is flanked by two lateral rooms and entered by a vestibule. On either side are the pedestals of two obelisks raised by Hatshepsut, of which nothing else remains.

Many small temples and shrines lie to the N of the great temple (see below) and it is better to visit them from this point before continuing with the N–S axis of the Great Temple.

On the S side of the small court between the third and fourth pylons (see above) is the entry to the transverse complex of the Great Temple. It is entered through the doorway constructed by Ramesses IX which leads into the *First Court* built by Tuthmosis III. This court is interesting in spite of its ruined state, as a cache containing thousands of royal and private statues was found here in 1902–09. The W wall was decorated by Ramesses II, the most important text being the Hittite Treaty of year 21. On the E wall is a long inscription of Merneptah, some 80 lines, listing his victories. S of this is a copy of the *'Israel Stele'* (original, from the destroyed temple of Merneptah on West Bank, now in the EM), which is the only Egyptian text to mention Israel. In front of the pylon at the S end of the court stand several statues, *four colossi of Tuthmosis III* and to the W *three smaller figures*, two 13 Dyn. kings and Amenhotep II at the end. Against the pylon face is a stele of Horemheb. Remains of several buildings were found in the court, the earliest dating to Senusert I, and a complex of Amenhotep I.

(88) Four registers, battle of Ramesses II with Syrians. (89) Hittite treaty of year 21 of Ramesses II. (90) Ramesses storming Ascalon. (91) Victories of Merneptah. (92) Israel Stele of Merneptah. (93) Southern peoples. (94) Northern peoples. (95) Text of Tuthmosis III.

The *Seventh Pylon* (much ruined), built by Tuthmosis III, is decorated with the usual victory scenes with the names of conquered districts and the king killing the enemies before Amun. The doorway of granite is capped with an alabaster lintel. Immediately inside the Second Court are two *Colossi*, to the W Ramesses III and to the E Tuthmosis III (upper sections destroyed). Beyond is the base of an obelisk of Tuthmosis III; that corresponding on the W was removed by the Byzantines and still stands in Istanbul. Off this court to the E opens a small granite *Chapel of Tuthmosis III* (very ruined). The interior texts mention the king's jubilee and there is an alabaster shrine with a dedication text. (Tuthmosis's statue and sphinx from here are in the EM). On the external E wall of the court are scenes of Ramesses IX. The *Eighth Pylon* was raised by Hatshepsut but the cartouches have been altered. The name of Amun was erased by Akhenaten and replaced by Seti I who added his own cartouches. Seti and Tuthmosis are seen on the reliefs instead of Hatshepsut. The clear traces of burning on this pylon probably derive from one of the sieges that destroyed Thebes. The doorway shows Tuthmosis II (originally Hatshepsut) and Tuthmosis III. To the E of the last two courts is the sacred lake (see below).

*Karnak: Seti I offering to Amun and Mut, Hypostyle Hall*

(96) Ramesses IX and his texts. (97) Dedication text of Tuthmosis. (98) Ramesses IX before the gods. (99) Seti I before Amun followed by 15 divinities. (100) Upper register, boat of Amun and Tuthmosis I. (101–102) Door jambs originally Hatshepsut, changed to Tuthmosis II and III. (103) Boat of Amun-Reʿ carried by priests. (104) Ramesses III crowned by Atum and Reʿ.

In the *Third court* (closed at present) the S wall of the pylon shows Amenhotep II killing prisoners. Several *colossi* in various states of disrepair stand in front of the pylon; one to the E and four to the W. The two flanking the doorway are Tuthmosis II, the second to the W is Amenhotep I (most complete) and the third is Amenhotep II. All were restored by Tuthmosis III. There is little of interest in the rest of the courtyard. Horemheb built the *Ninth Pylon* (much ruined) and its interest lies in the fact that he reused many of the talatat (stone blocks) from the five early temples of Akhenaten, deliberately destroyed by Horemheb. Several low stores on the edge of the court have been filled with blocks from here.

(105) Amenhotep II smiting enemies before Amun. (106) Horemheb; cartouches of Ramesses IV. (107) Horemheb before sacred boat.

Immediately inside the *Fourth Court* are the bases of two colossi of

Ramesses II. Straddling the E wall of the court is the much-ruined *Jubilee Temple of Amenhotep II*, entered through a pillared portico extending the whole length of the building. Beyond this is the 20-pillared hall with a small square-pillared hall leading off each side, that to the N with a small vestibule. The low reliefs here are of particularly fine workmanship. On the outer walls, probably constructed by Horemheb, are blocks of Tutankhamun and Amenhotep III. The walls of the court have reliefs of Horemheb with on the W wall the Battle of Kadesh. In front of the next pylon flanking the entrance are two headless colossi of Horemheb usurped by Ramesses II. On the face of the *Tenth Pylon* are scenes of the victorious king and against the W side the Horemheb Stele giving an account of his reforms. A granite gateway leads through the pylon which was also constructed by Horemheb. Incorporated within it are more talatat of Akhenaten. In the thickness Horemheb is seen before the gods, including Amun-Reʿ. Directly outside the pylon, which was the S face of the temple, are the remains of two colossi; that on the W of Amenhotep III and that on the E Amenhotep II.

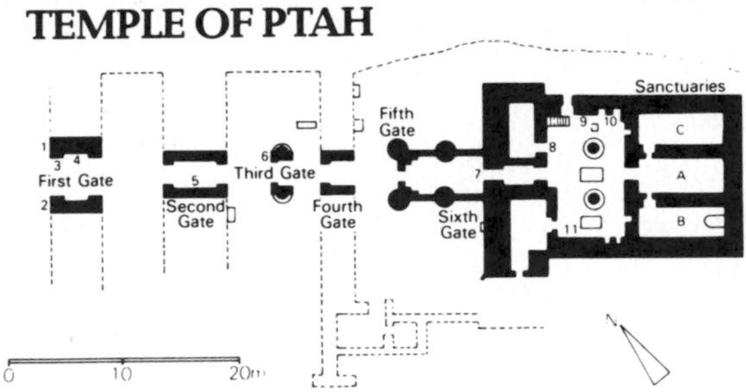
TEMPLE OF PTAH
Sanctuaries
Fifth Gate
First Gate
Third Gate
Second Gate
Fourth Gate
Sixth Gate
1
2
3
4
5
6
7
8
9
10
11
C
A
B
0
10
20m

(108) Marriage stele of Ramesses II. (109) Stele of Ramesses II with the king killing prisoners, battle of Kadesh. (110) Counting hands and soldiers. (111) Horemheb with rulers of Punt. (112) Horemheb with captives offers to Amun. (113) Horemheb killing northern prisoners. (114) Horemheb killing southern prisoners.

From the S face of this pylon an *Avenue of Sphinxes* with rams' heads, erected by Horemheb, leads southwards to the Luxor temple.

Reached from the Hypostyle Hall of the main temple and situated against the N wall of the great enclosure in a picturesque setting of palm trees is the small **Temple of Ptah**. It well repays a visit even at the expense of an extra donation to the guardian. This is an attractive little building of two main periods, 18 Dyn. and Ptolemaic. It was built by Tuthmosis III on the site of an earlier mud-brick building.

The foundation inscription of Tuthmosis dedicates it thus: 'I made it as a monument to my father Ptah, the Beautiful of Face, Lord of Life of the Two Lands, presiding over the Great Seat, erecting for him the House of Ptah anew of white sandstone, doors of new cedar of the best of the terraces. It is more beautiful than it was before, when His Majesty found it built of mud-brick with wooden columns. My majesty commands that there be built a temple of Ptah, South of his Wall, in Thebes, where he [may rest] on the day of 'Bringing in the God' and at all his feasts during the year, when he proceeds to the treasury of the South'. Tuthmosis also re-equipped the temple with everything requisite for the god's services and rites. He inlaid his throne with electrum, and all the vessels used in the temple were of gold, silver and of 'every fine and costly stone'. The clothing was of fine white linen, and ointments and unguents were provided. On Tuthmosis' return from his first campaign he endowed the temple richly with oxen, geese, bread, incense, wine and fruit.

Entry is from the W through a series of six gates. *Gate 1* is the work of three Ptolemies—Ptolemy VII, Philometer I; Ptolemy XI, Alexander I and Ptolemy XIII, Neos Dionysos. The outer face shows Ptolemy VII with a scribe's tablet in front of Ptah and Ma'at and before Khonsu and Mut. At the base with the Nile fertility gods is Ptolemy XIII. *Gate 2* was built by Shabaka (26 Dyn). The upper scene at the entry shows the king with wine before Amun-Reᶜ, Mut, Ptah, Hathor and Ament. The inner face is very damaged. *Gate 3*, built by Ptolemy XIII Neos Dionysos. *Gate 4*, built by Shabaka and Tiberius. Just to the N of this gate are five stelae including those of Horemheb and Seti I. The stele of Tuthmosis III from here has been removed to the EM. *Gate 5*, built by Ptolemy III Euergetes I. *Gate 6*, probably built by Tuthmosis III and restored later by Ramesses III (20 Dyn.), *Ptolemy* III Euergetes I and Ptolemy IV Philopator. The outer face has the original restoration texts of Tuthmosis III above the scenes on the jambs.

This gate leads into a small *Vestibule*. At the E side are two columns of Tuthmosis III, but there are strong traces of Ptolemaic restoration work. Above the door Ptolemy IV offers a sphinx to Ptah. The Tuthmoside dedication text is on the N side just by the N door. Horemheb also restored the temple and his inscription (only partly legible) is on the S side of the vestibule. In this court are three offering tables, the central one of which is of Tuthmosis III and that to the S is of Amenemhet I, presumably reused from the earlier mud-brick sanctuary. Beyond the vestibule are *Three Sanctuaries*, one for each of the triad of Memphis. The central sanctuary is for Ptah (A), with that of Sekhmet to the right (B) and Nefertum to the left (C). Reliefs in Ptah's chapel show Tuthmosis offering to Amun and Ptah and in the middle of the room is a headless statue of Ptah. In the S chapel is a very effective though broken statue of Sekhmet in lion form. There are many local stories about this figure.

(1) Ptolemy VII with scribal tablet before Ptah and Ma'at. (2) Ptolemy before Khonsu and Mut. (3) Ptolemy XIII before gods, including Nefertum. (4) Cartouches of Ptolemy XI. (5) The king with wine before Amun. (6) Cartouches of Ptolemy. (7) Restoration texts of Tuthmosis III. (8) Ptolemy IV offers image of Ma'at to the Theban Triad. (9) Dedication text of Tuthmosis III. (10) Tuthmosis III followed by ka figure. (11) Text of year 1 of Horemheb.

Just W of the temple a gate in the great enclosure wall leads to the N enclosure and the Temple of Montu (see below).

On the S side of the main temple, reached either from the Hypostyle Hall or the Gateway of Ramesses IX, is the **Sacred Lake**. It is 200m by 117m and fed by underground channels from the Nile and so follows the fluctuation in height of the river. Recently extensive repairs have been made to the fabric. A series of priests' houses were discovered on the E side during the construction of the seating for the Sound and Light programme. Steps lead down to the lake surface and at the S is a station where the sacred geese could enter. Attached to the lake is a *Nilometer*. In ancient times the lake was used for certain ceremonies and the sacred boats would sail on it. Memories of this lingered until the 19C with local tales of golden boats with music playing seen on the lake.

From the S side of the Hypostyle Hall a path leads through the dismantled blocks of the main temple to the SW corner of the enclosure where the **Temple of Khonsu** stands. It is 125m long and typical in construction. Most of it is the work of Ramesses III and IV, with additions by later kings. However, it was probably founded earlier as blocks of Amenhotep III have been excavated.

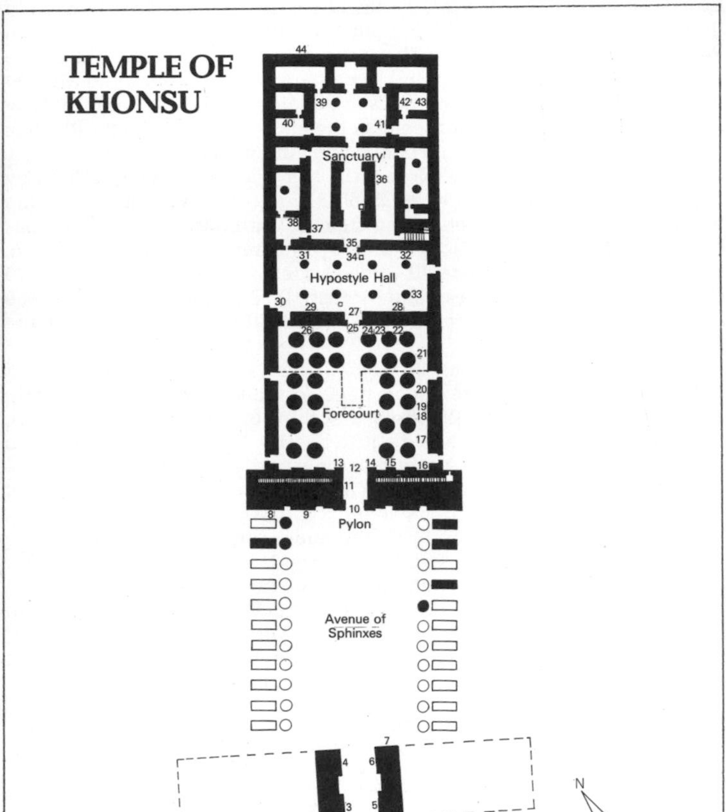
TEMPLE OF KHONSU
Sanctuary
Hypostyle Hall
Forecourt
Pylon
Avenue of Sphinxes
Propylon
N
0
10
20
30m

At the S the *Propylon* was erected by Ptolemy III. Beyond this there was a double row of columns with rectangular pillars behind the sphinxes. Most of these have disappeared. The arcade joined the propylon to the *Pylon* which is almost complete. It is 17.2m high and 31.9m wide with four vertical grooves for flagstaffs. On the outer face are inscriptions of Pinudjem I (21 Dyn.) making offerings to Amun, Mut and Khonsu. At the entry Alexander is seen offering to Mut and Khonsu while the ceiling has a cartouche of Ptolemy II Philadelphus.

(1–2) Ptolemy adoring divinities. (3) The king with cows before Min. (4) Ptolemy offering to gods of the elements, and to Osiris, Isis and Khonsu. (5) The king killing enemies before Osiris and Isis. (6) The king before his parents makes offerings. (7) Base, dedication text. (8) Pinudjem pouring libation before Amun-Reʿ and Khonsu. (9) Above, the king offers collar and pectoral to Amun-Reʿ and Mut. Below, Queen Makere and Hentawi with sistra, (10) Architrave, Alexander before Amun and Khonsu.

On each side of the *Forecourt*, except the S, is a double row of columns. This is the work of Herihor (26 Dyn.) and on the E wall is a relief of the pylon of the temple with a text of this king. Other scenes show him before various deities. To the N the papyrus-bud columns are on a low platform and depict Herihor offering libations and flowers to Amun and Khonsu.

(11) Pinudjem offers flowers and ointment to Amun-Reʿand the Theban Triad. (12) Architrave, Ptolemy II before the gods. (13) Pinudjem before Khonsu. (14) The king before Khonsu and Montu and dedication text. (15) Text of Herihor. (16) Herihor before gods. (17) Third register, scene showing temple pylon. (18) Herihor and two goddesses between Seth and Horus. (19) Herihor followed by Hathor before Theban Triad and Queen Ahmose Nefertari. (20) Herihor receives sceptres from Hathor. (21) Herihor before Amun-Reʿand Khonsu. (22) Herihor before Amun and Inmutef. (23) Stele of Herihor. (24) Nectenebo II before Khonsu. (25) Architrave, cartouches of Nectanebo II. (26) Text of Pinudjem.

At the entry to the next hall are cartouches of Nectanebo II (30 Dyn.) but the architrave has texts of Herihor. The *Hypostyle Hall* extends across the width of the building and is divided by eight papyrus columns with dedication texts of Ramesses XI on the capitals. The columns at the sides are of bud form but those in the centre are open and also higher, thus forming a kind of nave. Most of the reliefs in this chamber are of the time of Ramesses XI and show Herihor before and after his accession. On the W side is a dedication text of Herihor. In the SE corner is a Ramesside altar.

(27) Architrave, titles of Herihor. (28) Ramesses presenting his name to Amun and Mut. (29) Ramesses purified by Thoth and Horus. (30) Architrave, cartouches of Thuthmosis III usurped by Ramesses XI. (31) Ramesses before the gods. (32) Sacred boats. (33) Columns with texts of Herihor and offerings to the gods, Ramesside altar. (34) Architrave, Moon adored by divinities and Ptolemy X.

The next doorway also has an inscription of Nectanebo II. Beyond is the *Sanctuary*, where a statue of Khonsu was found beneath the floor (now in the EM). The red-granite shrine was made for Amenhotep II but was usurped by Ramesses IV. In the corridor are scenes of the king before the

**TEMPLE OF APET**

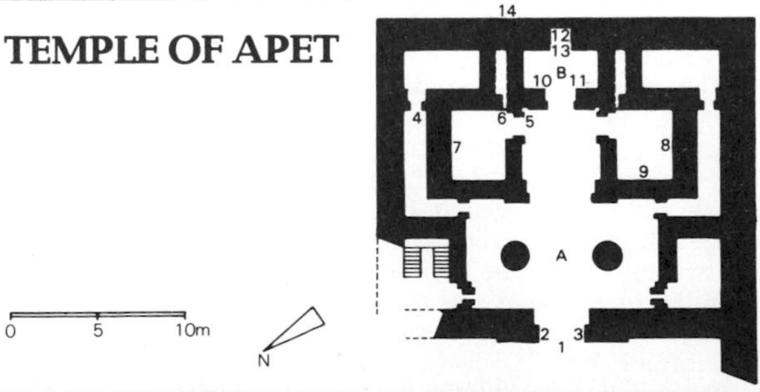
14
12
13
10
B
11
4
6
5
7
8
9
A
2
1
3
0
5
10m
N

Triad of Thebes. W of the Sanctuary are three side chambers and to the E another side chamber and the stairs to the roof (excellent view of Karnak). To the N is a room with four columns; although the doorway was provided by Ptolemy II, the rest is the work of Augustus Caesar. There is an interesting contrast in this room between the decoration of the later Ramesside period and that of the Roman period. W are three rooms of Ramesses III and IV. In the rooms to the E much of the original colour is retained and one contains cartouches of Ramesses IV.

(35) Renewal text of Ptolemy VIII. (36) Ptolemy before Thoth. (37) Above door, Ramesses IV between Horus and Seth. (38) Ramesses IV before divinities. (39) Augustus before Amun and Ptah with image of Ma'at. (40) Ramesses III before Amun and Mut. (41) Queen Tentapi with sistra before Khonsu. (42) Ramesses IV before lion-headed and ox-headed gods. (43) The other three walls show Ramesses III before divinities. (44) Cartouches of Nectanebo II.

Adjacent to the SE is the small, square **Temple of Apet**, the goddess traditionally said to be the mother of Osiris. It was constructed by Ptolemy II with additions by later Ptolemies and into the Roman period. It was never completed.

Entry is from the E through two ruined forecourts into a two-columned *Portico*, which although it has windows is very dim. At the entry to the *Sanctuary* are texts of Ptolemy II and Cleopatra II and III. On the E wall are scenes of Ptolemy before divinities and a niche where he is shown with Apet. Beneath the sanctuary is a crypt dedicated to Osiris. Surrounding the sanctuary are nine dark chambers. The exterior was decorated by Augustus Caesar with dedications and offering scenes on the N and W walls.

(1) Doorway, Ptolemy Auletes texts and cartouches. (2–3) Dedication text. (4) Ptolemy VII before Osiris. (5) Above cornice, procession of deities. (6) Ptolemy before gods. (7) Osiris on couch. (8) Ptolemy with child Horus. (9) Ptolemy and Cleopatra II before goddesses. (10) Text of Ptolemy and Cleopatra II. (11) Text of Ptolemy and Cleopatra III. (12) Ptolemy before Apet. (13) Ptolemy and Apet standard. (14) Kneeling goddess with food.

The University of Toronto has uncovered the NE corner of the Temple of Gem-pa-Aten erected by Akhenaten. It is in a poor state of preservation with a gutted foundation trench. It contained relatively few talatat (block) fragments. Some fragmentary sandstone and quartzite colossal statues of Akhenaten and Nefertiti were recovered.

## Northern Enclosure

Leaving the great Central Enclosure by the gate in the N wall near the Temple of Ptah (see above) almost immediately the visitor arrives at the wall of the **N Enclosure**. This is smaller (150m sq.) and contains several temples and chapels, the largest of which is the Temple of Montu. A visit here takes more time than the usual half-day afforded to Karnak.

The **Temple of Montu**, the war god, for an unknown reason is orientated N to S so that the visitor arrives at its rear. It is best to walk around to the front. It was built by Amenhotep III (18 Dyn.) whose cartouches appear in various rooms, but was restored by Ramesses IV (20 Dyn.) and his cartouche can be seen at the entrance to the hypostyle hall. Uncovered in the foundations was the Stele of Tutankhamun (now in the EM) recording his restoration of the temples of Thebes. It had been usurped by Horemheb.

The temple consists of a *Forecourt*, with 20 columns and screen walls and the bases of two obelisks of Amenhotep III. Beyond this the *Hypostyle Hall* is more of a columned chamber with a double row of columns on the S side, in which a portico leads into the columned vestibule. Off this is a series of subsidiary chambers. The *Sanctuary* to the S is a long narrow room. In the NE area of the enclosure are remains of the *Sacred Lake*.

To the W is the **Temple of Amun**, a small, square building raised by Nectanebo II (30 Dyn.). Against the SW wall of the enclosure are six small chapels, each with its own gate through the wall. The southernmost four are ruined but the other two are more complete. The second from the end is the **Chapel of Queen Amenortais** (daughter of King Kashta, 25 Dyn.) where a statue of the queen was found (now in the EM). She also constructed the gates for the chapels in the wall. Northernmost is the **Chapel of Nitocris** (i.e. Shepenwept III, daughter of Psamtik I, 26 Dyn.).

Outside the enclosure to the NW are several ruined temples including *two Temples of Osiris*, one 18 Dyn. reconstructed by Taharqa (25 Dyn.) and the other 26 Dyn. Beyond the village to the E is another *Chapel of Nitocris* (26 Dyn.) and at a greater distance to the W are *two Ptolemaic temples*, one dedicated to Thoth.

## Southern Enclosure

S of the central Great Enclosure along an *Avenue of Sphinxes* (350m) lies the **Southern Enclosure**, surrounded by a mud-brick wall (350m by 250m). This contains another group of temples and a large lake. The main entry at the end of the avenue is in the S wall. It is the work of Ptolemies II and VII as is also the *Propylon* to the main building in the enclosure, the **Temple of Mut**. This temple, orientated N to S, is very ruined. It was partly cleared by the Misses Benson and Gourley in 1895–96 and recently reinvestigated by Brooklyn Museum. Amenhotep III founded the temple on the site of an earlier one which was probably Middle Kingdom. Earlier 18 Dyn. material was also found including statues of Senenmut, Hatshepsut's architect. It was restored by Ramesses II and III. An avenue of sphinxes joined the propylon to the Pylon built by Seti I, probably the remains of the original avenue. The pylon also has a bas-relief of Bes and Ptolemaic texts including a hymn to Mut.

In the *Forecourt* are two statues of Sekhmet, that on the W wall with an inscription of Pinudjem. Beyond this is a colonnaded *Court*, a smaller Hypostyle Hall and an early shrine. N of the temple overlaying the great wall is a small shrine probably erected when the main temple was falling into ruins. From here steps lead down to the **Sacred Lake**. This has an unusual horseshoe shape and extends from the rear of the temple and along the flanks.

(1–4) Cartouches of Ptolemy II and seven nomes of Upper Egypt and six nomes of Lower Egypt, Ptolemy VII. (5) Bas-relief of Bes. (6–7) Ptolemaic texts including hymn to Mut. (8) Inscriptions of Mentemhet.

At the NE corner of the enclosure is the smaller **Temple of Amenhotep III**, orientated W to E. It was restored by Ramesses II. Entry is through a *Court*, once with a colonnade. On the N side are circumcision scenes. There were 16 columns and a portico leading to a small *Hypostyle Hall* with two groups of eight columns and a central aisle. Beyond is a *Vestibule*, with four transverse columns, where a short flight of steps leads into the *Second Vestibule* or Hall of Offerings. This also has four

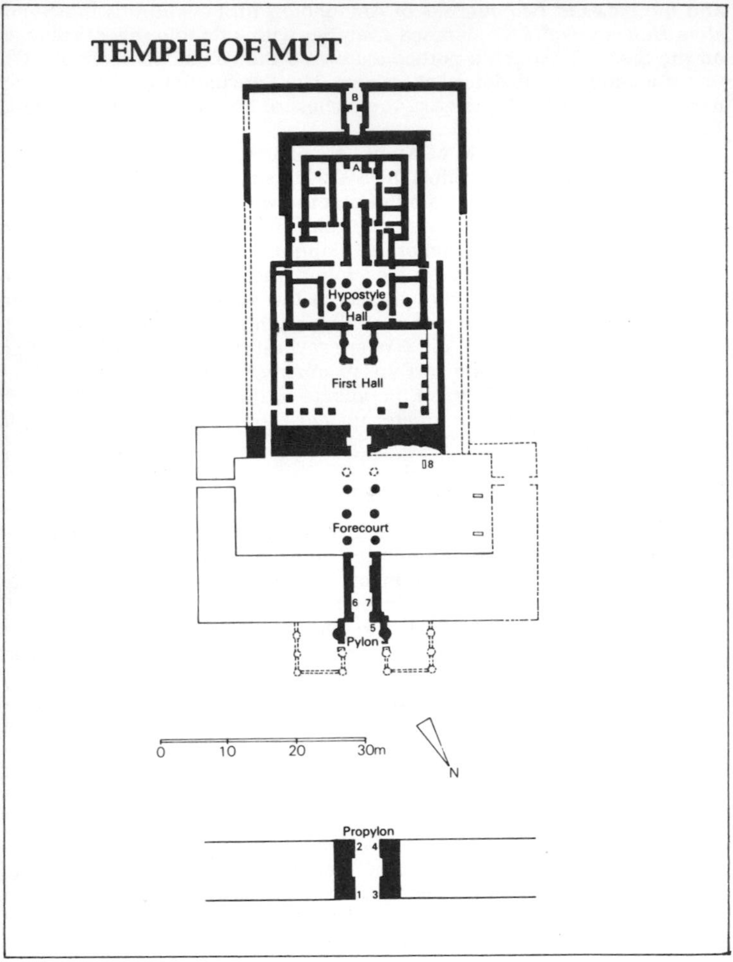
TEMPLE OF MUT
B
A
Hypostyle Hall
First Hall
8
Forecourt
6 7
5
Pylon
0 10 20 30m
N
Propylon
2 4
1 3

columns but forming a square. Chapels lead off each side. The *Sanctuary* containing the altar does not open off the W as is usual but from the NE chapel. Only the bases of many of the walls remain. Thus only the feet of the figures can be seen but enough is visible to indicate that this was one of the temples built by Amenhotep III to demonstrate, with Amun as his father, his divine birth.

W of the Temple of Mut is the southern **Temple of Ramesses III**. Its full title is 'Temple of Ramesses, Ruler in Heliopolis, on whom be Life, Health and Strength, Possessed of Joy in Karnak'. Much of the building has been despoiled and the stone removed. The thick *Pylon* was once flanked by two statues of Ramesses III, but only that on the W remains. Beyond this is a peristyle *First Court* with rectangular pillars originally faced with statues of Ramesses as in his temple at Karnak. A ramp leads to a transverse columned *Vestibule* which opens into a small *Hypostyle Hall* with four columns. Side chambers surround this hall; the two to the E are chapels. Behind is a narrow transverse *Hall of Offerings*. At either end are side chambers and to the S the *Sanctuary of Amun*. On each side of the sanctuary is a chapel, for the other two members of the Theban Triad. Along the exterior W wall are scenes of the wars of Ramesses against the Libyans and Sea Peoples.

# B. West Bank

From the quay on the Gazīrat Saʿd, the road runs SW to join the road from the old ferry. It turns NW, crossing the narrow W branch of the river on to the West Bank and then over the al-Faḍliyyah Canal just S of **Qurnat al-Gadīd**. Here is a crossroads, the NW road running past the Colossi to the Valley of the Queens (see below). The SW road leads past al-Baʿirah (2km) to Armant (Rte 37). Take the NE road running along the W bank of the canal with the sugar company railway to the W.

At 2.25km a road branches off to the W (to the N the H57 runs near **al-Tarif**, with inaccessible rock-cut tombs of 11 Dyn. kings, and on to al-Qibli al-Qamūlā; Rte 35).

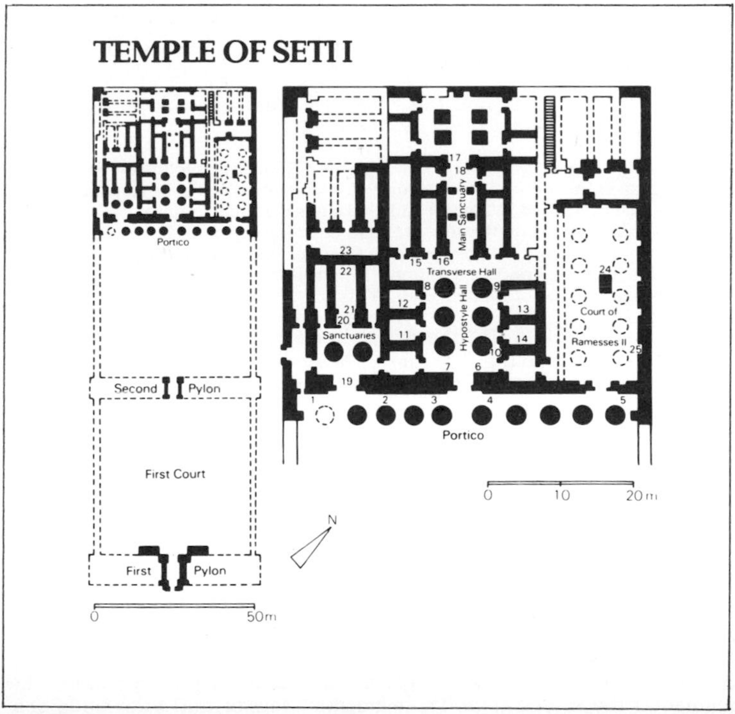
TEMPLE OF SETI I
Portico
Second Pylon
First Court
First Pylon
0
50m
Main Sanctuary
Transverse Hall
Hypostyle Hall
Sanctuaries
Court of Ramesses II
Portico
1
2
3
4
5
6
7
8
9
10
11
12
13
14
15
16
17
18
19
20
21
22
23
24
25
0
10
20m
N

## TEMPLE OF SETI I

Take the W road. Just before it divides (300m) to the S is the **Temple of Seti I**, the northernmost of a 4km series of mortuary temples that stand near the foothills of the Theban hills on the edge of the cultivation.

It is dedicated to Amun-United-with-Eternity, Ramesses I, who reigned for two years and had no time to build himself a temple, Seti I, after whom it is clearly named, and Ramesses II, who finished it. Thus it was called 'the temple of the spirit of Menmare Seti (I) in the House of Amun on the West of Thebes'. This temple must have been an imposing structure and even in its ruined state it is very impressive. Built of white sandstone from al-Gabalayn, to the S, it consisted of two courtyards each fronted by pylons, a portico, a six-columned hypostyle hall off which are six chapels. Behind the hall was the Sanctuary, now much ruined, where the bark of Amun stood. The temple has been investigated recently by the German Archaeological Institute of Cairo, which has cleared the foundations of the pylons and found the bases for the sandstone Sphinx Avenue which remained *in situ* until the middle of the last century. The base of the first sphinx has foreign countries represented by the Nine Bows on its base.

On the *First Pylon* are the cartouches of both Seti I and Ramesses II. Entry used to be via this pylon but is now by the side into the *First Courtyard* which rises gently through the ruined *Second Pylon* and *Second Courtyard* to the *Portico*, with ten columns (that to the SW destroyed). The central part of the temple is dedicated to Seti I and the S section to Ramesses I. Three doors pierce the wall.

(1) The central door has the Horus names of Seti I and Ramesses II. (2) Centre section, Seti and Ramesses II are seen before the bark of Amun. (2–3) Base, Nile gods and a dedication of Ramesses II. (4) Stele of Siptah. (5) Niles and a text.

The central door leads into the *Hypostyle Hall*, with six bud columns, flanked on each side by three small chapels.

(6) Ramesses II before divinities in two registers. (7) Ramesses followed by Mut and Khonsu receives the heb-sed from Amun-Re'. (8) Ramesses as a child suckled by Mut. (9) Seti as a child suckled by Hathor. (10) Seti offers his name to Amun-Re' of Luxor.

In the second chapel on the left: (11) Seti before the gods of the Ennead. In the third chapel: (12) Thoth before the sacred boat of Seti in a shrine. (13) The king offers to the Theban Triad in a shrine. (14) Purification scenes before Thoth and Horus. Dedicatory text of Ramesses III.

Beyond the Hypostyle Hall there is a *Transverse Hall* at a slightly higher level and this leads to the *Sanctuary*. The stone base for the boat of Amun still stands in the centre of the narrow chamber.

(17) The sacred boat of Amun. (18) The king offers to the boat of Amun.

Beyond this is a series of much ruined rooms.

The SW door of the portico leads to a *Two-Columned Vestibule* with dedication texts and a deified Ramesses I (19). Off this to the W open three *Sanctuaries*.

(20–21) Dedication texts of Seti I. (22) False door with a double scene of the deified Ramesses I. To reach the ruined rooms behind the Sanctuary return to the Vestibule and take the door to the S. On the wall just behind the Sanctuary and slightly north of the false door (23) Ramesses running with an oar before Amun-Re'.

Behind this section of the temple there is a small pool, probably the remnant of the *Sacred Lake*. There are also traces of mud-brick buildings, priests' houses and store-rooms, between the temple and the ruined temenos wall.

From the N end of the portico a door leads to the roofless *Columned Court* of Ramesses II. This court originally contained ten columns (destroyed). The hall is decorated with inferior incised relief. All this part of the temple was decorated by Ramesses II, probably because Seti never finished his work on the building. In the centre is a rectangular altar of Ramesses II (broken, 24) while on the right of the court (25) Ramesses is shown before Ahmose-Nefertari, a deified 18 Dyn. queen, protector of necropolis workers.

To the S lie the sites of two destroyed temples; the small Temple of Nebwenenef and the Temple of Amenhotep I and Queen Ahmose-Nefertari.

## VALLEY OF THE KINGS

The road to the NW is the SIKKAT AL-WADAYN (Track of the Two Valleys). It passes on the SW a track to the S monuments (see below) and to the N *Howard Carter's House* on the bluff immediately above. The NW road curves through a valley leading after 3.75km to the ***Valley of the Kings** (Ar. Bibān al-Mulūk; Tombs of the Kings, or Wādī al-Mulūk; as English, a local name bestowed by inspired guesswork rather than of direct knowledge of the function of the area. Open 08.00–18.00. but negotiable and special times can be arranged. Resthouse with refreshments inside valley. Fee). It consists of two main sections, the E valley where most of the tombs (not all accessible) are located and the W valley with only two royal and two other tombs (special permission required). If an early visit is wanted, prior arrangements should be made (at agency in Luxor) so that the tombs can be opened and illuminated. Although most are lit by electricity (e.l.), this occasionally fails and for this reason, and to see others that are not lit, it is advisable to take a torch. Those that can be visited are so large and contain so much material that it is not practicable to see more than four or five at one time; it is better where possible to make two or more visits. It is best to visit the site as early in the day as possible. After 11.00 large groups start to arrive.

A new Resthouse has been designed for the Valley of the Kings, meanwhile the facilities of the old one have been upgraded. A new road will be constructed to the valley.

The Tomb of Tutankhamun has been closed indefinitely for restoration. At the moment the only tombs that can be visited are those of Seti I, Seti II and Ramesses VI, and this last will soon be closed for further protection.

The valley is a deep, much-riven cleft in the limestone hills with sheer walls and with many side valleys, dominated by the Gabal al-Qurn (Hill of the Horn) to the SW, in ancient times sacred to a local goddess Mertseger—she who loves silence. The first king to have his tomb cut here was Tuthmosis I after which the necropolis continued in use throughout the 18–20 Dyns. It contains 62 tombs, not all royal, certain high officials were also buried here. Some of the tombs are uninscribed, others were never completed.

There are two types of tombs. The first, used in the early 18 Dyn. (Tuthmosis I–Amenhotep III), consists of a series of descending galleries entered by steps leading to a rock-sunk pit or well, with the dual purpose of taking off rain water and confusing tomb robbers. Beyond is an offering chamber with square columns where the king is depicted offering to the gods. Leading from this at an angle to the entry axis is the rectangular burial chamber, often with rounded corners. In the tomb of Amenhotep III's son Akhenaten cut at al-ʿAmārnah the galleries and tomb chamber were on the same axis and it was in this form that the late 18–20 Dyn. tombs were cut

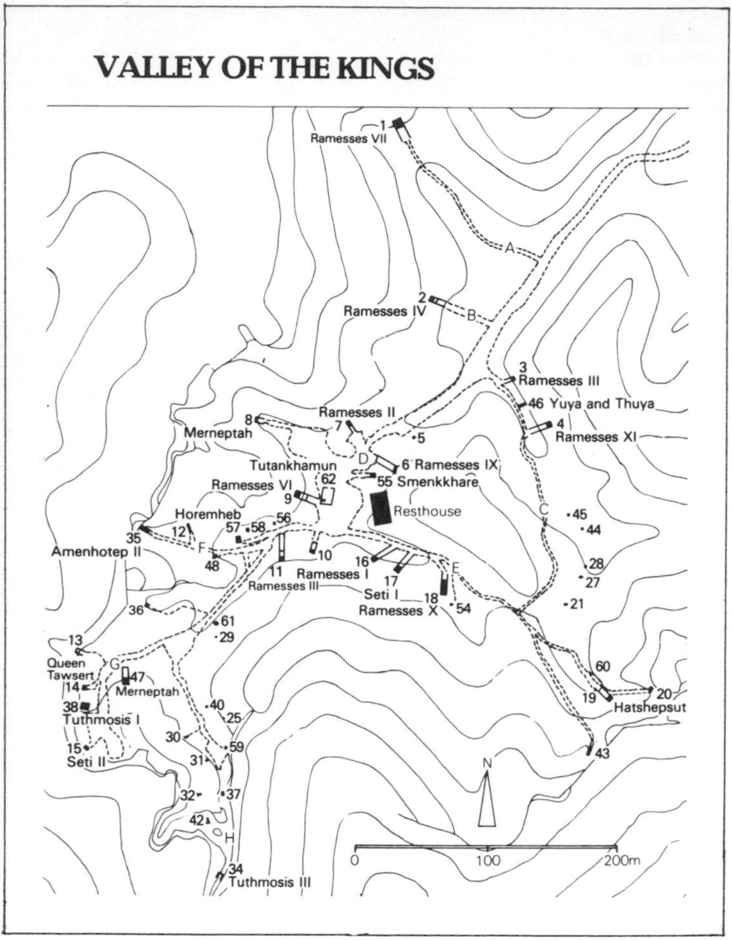

VALLEY OF THE KINGS
1 Ramesses VII
A
2 Ramesses IV
B
3 Ramesses III
46 Yuya and Thuya
4 Ramesses XI
8 Merneptah
7 Ramesses II
5
D
6 Ramesses IX
Tutankhamun
62
55 Smenkkhare
Ramesses VI
9
Resthouse
C
45
44
Horemheb
12
57
58
56
35 Amenhotep II
F
48
10
11 Ramesses III
16 Ramesses I
17 Seti I
18 Ramesses X
E
54
28
27
21
36
61
29
13 Queen Tawsert
G
14
47 Merneptah
38 Tuthmosis I
15 Seti II
40
25
30
59
31
32
37
42
H
34 Tuthmosis III
60
19
20 Hatshepsut
43
N
0
100
200m


in the Valley of the Kings. An exception is the tomb of Tutankhamun, but this had not originally been intended as a royal burial place.

The decoration of the various tombs differs considerably. In the earlier tombs of the 18 Dyn. it is on a soft grey or light yellow background, as though intended to represent papyrus. The scenes in these tombs are confined to parts of the Book of the Am-Duat and the Litany of Reʿ. In the later tombs of the 19–20 Dyns they are on a darker orange background and have parts of a greater number of the Books of the Dead including the Book of the Gates, the Book of the Caverns, the Ritual of the Opening of the Mouth, parts of the Litany of Reʿ, parts of the Book of the Divine Cow and the Book of Day and Night.

Because of the national disorders at the end of the New Kingdom the bodies of the kings were removed from their tombs and placed together in several caches. The first was discovered in 1881 by Emile Brugsch, as the result of an investigation into the activities of tomb robbers, in Tomb 320 in the Deir al-Baḥarī cemetery (see below). Among other mummies it contained the remains of Tuthmosis III, Seti I and Ramesses II and III. Another cache was discovered in 1898 by Loret in the Tomb of

Amenhotep II (35) in this valley. Beside Amenhotep II himself this cache included the mummies of Tuthmosis IV, Amenhotep III, Merneptah-Siptah and Ramesses IV, V and VI. The speed with which the re-wrapped bodies had been originally transferred in the 21 Dyn. resulted in many of them being placed in the wrong coffins. They were removed to the newly opened EM at Būlāq but in the damper atmosphere of the capital many of them started to decompose and had to be hurriedly unwrapped. Some could not be restored and were reburied, the remainder are in the EM (no longer on view) although there is a growing opinion that they should be reinterred.

Greek and Coptic graffiti testify that a number of tombs have been open since ancient times but the first to mention the valley in modern times was the traveller Richard Pococke who visited the site in 1737. Bruce discovered the Tomb of Ramesses III (11) in 1769 and Napoleon's expedition discovered several more. They were followed by Belzoni between 1815–20. After this the area was visited by many 19C Egyptologists and the number of known tombs increased to 62 in November 1922 with the discovery of the Tomb of Tutankhamun by Howard Carter and Lord Carnarvon. The numbering of the tombs was first tackled by Wilkinson in the mid-19C and in general follows the order of discovery.

Just before the main complex down a small valley (A) to the W lies the **Tomb of Ramesses VII**. Although decorated (much damaged), it is small and seldom visited. Over the outer lintel are the king's names with a disk and scarab (1). In the Corridor (A) are scenes from the Book of the Gates with the king shown as Osiris purified by Inmutef (2). The Burial Chamber (B), containing the granite cartouche-shaped sarcophagus (5), has scenes from the Book of Aker (3), divinities with captives (4), and an astronomical ceiling, with Nut, constellations and a calendar of feasts. The Inner Chamber (C) is guarded by uraei and a winged disk and has offering scenes.

Down the next valley to the W (B) is the **Tomb of Ramesses IV** (2). Robbed in antiquity, the body of Ramesses was found in the cache in the tomb of Amenhotep II. This is the only one of the royal graves of which the original plan is preserved, (now in the Turin Museum). It must have been open for centuries as there are Ptolemaic and Coptic inscriptions on the walls. It is entered by steps leading to three Corridors, A and B with sections of the Book of the Litany of Reʿ (1–4). C has sections of the first two divisions of the Book of Caverns (5–6). The Hall (D) is decorated with parts of the Book of the Dead (7), and the Negative Confession (8). In the square Burial Chamber (E) is the Book of the Gates. Divisions 1 and 2 are on the left wall (9) and divisions 3 and 4 on the right wall (10). There is an astronomical ceiling with Shu supporting Nut. The granite sarcophagus (11) has texts and magical scenes while on the lid is the king protected by Isis and Nephthys. Rooms S and H beyond show the Book of Caverns (12–13) and mummified figures of the king. Foundation deposits found by Carter included faience plaques and tools.

On the E side of the valley is a transverse gully (C), on the N side of which is the first **Tomb of Ramesses III** (3), left undecorated, and abandoned probably because of the poor quality of the rock. He had another tomb cut (11) and was buried there. Next to it is the **Tomb of Yuya and his wife Thuya** (46). The title of Yuya was Divine Father and of his wife Chief of the Harim of Amun. They were the parents of Queen Tiye, wife of Amenhotep III. It was found by Davis and although undecorated it was interesting for the collection of funerary furniture it contained (now in EM). Beside this is the **Tomb of Ramesses XI** (4), unfinished and undecorated save for some figures outlined in red near the entrance.—60m along the valley some distance up the N face of the cliff is

# ROYAL TOMBS

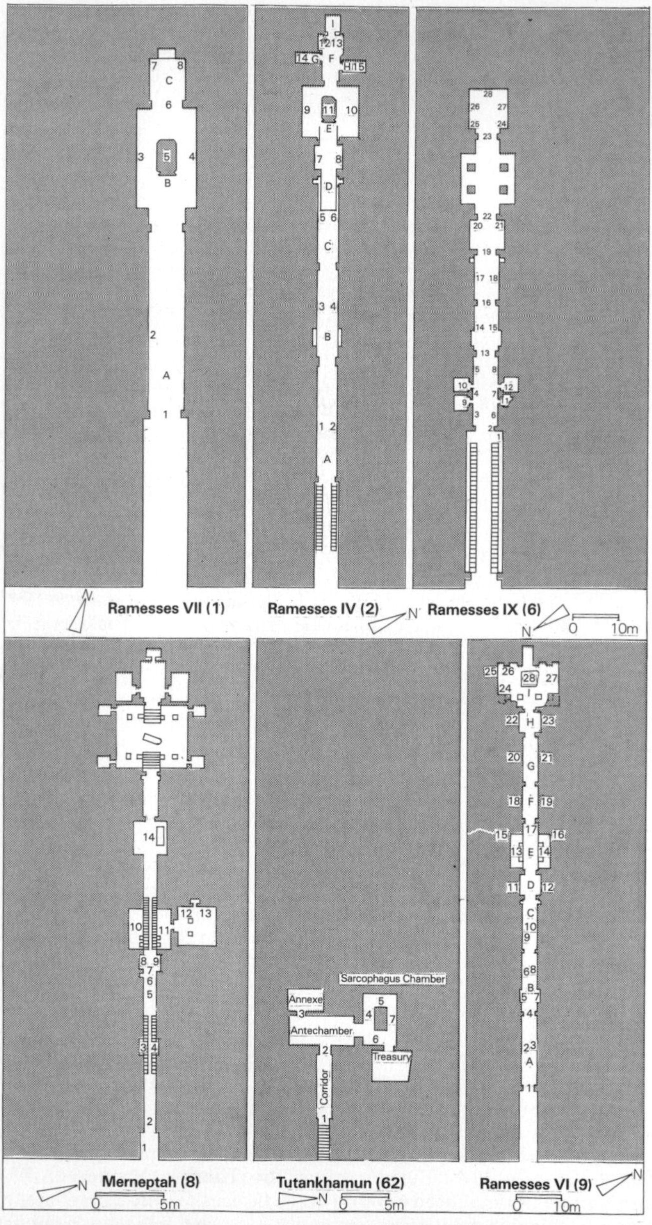

Ramesses VII (1)
Ramesses IV (2)
Ramesses IX (6)
0 10m
Merneptah (8)
0 5m
Tutankhamun (62)
0 5m
Sarcophagus Chamber
Annexe
Antechamber
Treasury
Corridor
Ramesses VI (9)
0 10m
N

the *Tomb of Userhat* (45), an 18 Dyn. official. It was reused for Merekhons, another official, of the 22 Dyn. As the gully curves around to the S there are *four tombs* (44, 28, 27 and 21), all uninscribed. The gully leads into the next transverse valley (see below).

In the main valley (D) there is a walk of c 200m S. On the E side is an uninscribed and *undecorated tomb* (5) also attributed to Ramesses II. Just S is the *Barrier* and **Ticket kiosk**, beyond which lie most of the tombs.

Immediately beyond the barrier to the E is the **Tomb of Ramesses IX** (6) (e.l.), a typical late Ramesside tomb with long, straight corridor. Three corridors (A–C) contain scenes of the king before the gods (1–4). Corridor B also has part of the Book of the Caverns (2nd to 24th divisions) (5) and an astronomical ceiling. Corridor C in addition has the Book of the Am-Duat (2nd division), in three registers, above kneeling captives (6). Beyond are three square halls (D–F), including the Offering Hall (E) with four square pillars. The Burial Chamber (F) is decorated with scenes from the Book of the Caverns, (7–8), goddesses (9–10) and the king in a boat with some gods (11). On the ceiling is a double scene of the Book of the Night, with Nut and the divine boat drawn by jackals. There is no sarcophagus.

Adjacent to the S is the **Tomb of Smenkhkare** (55), although undecorated, the subject of much controversy. It was cleared by Davis in 1907 and the coffin found here had been made for Akhenaten by Queen Nefertiti. Parts of a shrine made for Queen Tiye, wife of Amenhotep III, were found in the passage-way. It was probably used by Tutankhamun to inter his predecessor.

On the W side of the valley, opposite Ramesses IX, is the **Tomb of Ramesses II** (7) (not accessible). It is a very long tomb; although decorated it is badly preserved. The conformation is similar to the early 18 Dyn. tombs with the end chambers at an angle to the entrance corridors. Robbed during the 20 Dyn., the body was moved to the tomb of Amenhotep I but finally ended up in the royal cache in Deir al-Baḥrī.

To the S and set right back against the cliff face is the **Tomb of Merneptah** (8) (e.l.). The tomb is some 80m long and consists of five corridors, two halls, several side chambers and annexes off the burial chamber. This tomb has been much damaged. Sections of the texts have been cut away, as has one of the pillars in the ante-room to the burial chamber. Corridor A shows the Litany of Reʿ (2) and the king before Reʿ-Harakhte (1), Corridor B sections of the Book of the Gates (3–4) and Corridor C sections of the Book of the Am-Duat (5). Hall D, the lintel with the king's names and the thickness with part of the Book of the Am-Duat (7), on the left Osiris and two of the sons of Horus (8); on the right the king as Inmutef (9). Hall E has hymns to Osiris and the third division of the Book of the Gates (11). The Side Chamber (F) off this shows Osiris, Isis, Nephthys and the four sons of Horus (12–13). This tomb is interesting as it shows Seth in the solar boat with Horus. A stairway from Hall E leads to Hall H with the outer lid of the granite sarcophagus decorated with a section of the Book of the Gates (initial section, divisions 1, 7 and 8) and the Book of the Am Duat (5 divisions) (14). Down another short flight of steps is the Burial Chamber (J) which contains the inner red granite sarcophagus lid decorated with the first division of the Book of the Gates (the remains of an alabaster sarcophagus from here are now in the BM).

In the centre of the valley opposite the resthouse is the **Tomb of Tutankhamun** (62) (e.l.). Discovered by Howard Carter in 1922, the story has been told many times, but it is not often realised that the tomb took

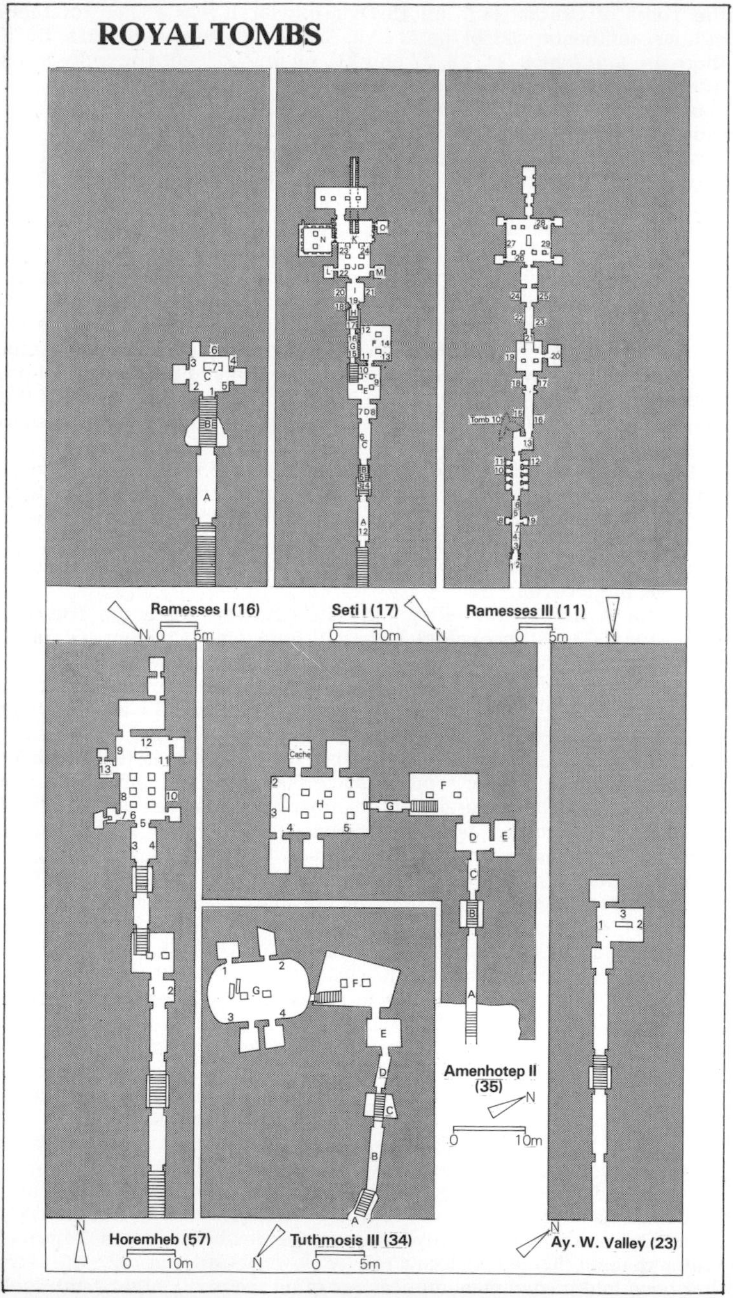
ROYAL TOMBS
Ramesses I (16)
N 0 5m
Seti I (17)
0 10m N
Ramesses III (11)
0 5m N
Tomb 10
Cache
Amenhotep II
(35)
N
0 10m
Horemheb (57)
0 10m
Tuthmosis III (34)
N 0 5m
N
Ay. W. Valley (23)

almost ten years to clear of the unprecedented treasures. Never intended as a royal tomb, the door was sealed twice, above with the seal of the necropolis, a jackal with nine captives, and below with Tutankhamun's device. It had been robbed twice. It consists of a short entrance corridor and four rooms, but only the Burial Chamber is decorated. On the S wall Hathor gives life to the king (1), who is followed by Anubis and Isis. The W wall has a scene from the Book of the Am-Duat (first division), showing the boat with the Khephri beetle, and three registers with four baboons of Thoth in each (2). On the E wall is the funeral procession with nine friends and three officials dragging the sarcophagus on a sledge (3). The N wall has three scenes: King Ay performing the Opening of the Mouth Ceremony before a mummified figure of the king, Ay in front of Nut and Tutankhamun embraced by Osiris (4). In the Burial Chamber is the quartzite sarcophagus (5) and the granite lid. Lying within is the outermost of the three coffins, which contains the body of Tutankhamun *in situ*. Most of the material objects found in the tomb are now in the EM except for some objects in the Luxor Museum.

Above No. 62 is the **Tomb of Ramesses VI** (9) (e.l.), usurped from Ramesses V, one of the longest tombs in the valley and well decorated.

It is one of the few that have been adequately published, and has proved vital to the understanding of the Egyptian conception of the Afterworld, containing some sections of books not otherwise available. The thesis portrayed is of birth, life and death as a continuous process. In death the soul becomes strong enough to be reborn. The long series of six corridors is broken only by the Hall of Offerings.

On the outer lintel is a disk containing a ram-headed Reʿ and a scarab (1). Corridor A has scenes from the Book of Gates (initial scene and 1st and 2nd divisions) (2–3). There is an astronomical ceiling. Corridor B below a lintel with the winged disk has Ramesses' names on the door jambs (4). There are four sections of the Book of the Gates (5–6), on the left the Hall of Osiris, on the right the Book of Caverns (2nd and 3rd divisions) (7–8). Corridor C has the Book of Gates (6th and 7th divisions) (9) as well as part of the Book of Caverns (3rd and 5th divisions) (10). There is an astronomical ceiling with the Book of Day and Night. Hall D with the Book of Gates (8th and 9th divisions) (11), Book of Caverns (5th division) (12). The astronomical ceiling is carried on from the previous corridor.

The Offering Hall (E) on the left has the Book of Gates (10th–12th divisions) (13) and on the right is the Book of Caverns (7th division) (14). There is also a double scene of Ramesses VI offering and making libations before Osiris (15–16). On the pillars Ramesses is offering to Khonsu, Amun-Reʿ, Mertseger, Ptah-Sokar, Ptah and Reʿ-Harakhte. On the left of the descent to the next corridor are Nekhbet and Neith shown as serpents and the Book of Am-Duat (1st division). On the right are Mertseger and Selket also as serpents and the Book of Am-Duat (6th division) (17). Corridor F has the Book of Am-Duat (introductory section and parts of 6th–8th divisions) (18–19). On the ceiling are parts of the Books of Reʿand the Book of Day and Night. Corridor G has more of the Book of Am-Duat; on the left the 4th and 5th divisions (20) and on the right the 8th–11th divisions (21). The ceiling has a cryptographic text. In Hall H Ramesses VI is shown before the gods (22–23), while the ceiling depicts the resurrection of Osiris, cryptographic texts and parts of the Book of Day and Night. The *Burial Chamber* has four pillars. On the left Ramesses VI is seen kneeling at each end (24–25). On the far wall is the Book of Aker (26). The right wall shows a mummy in a mound, and part of the Book of Aker (27).

On the ceiling are astronomical scenes in which the goddess Nut is accompanied by the hours. In the middle of the room is a large unfinished granite sarcophagus which has been broken (28).

Opposite is the second Eastern gully (E) down which on the S, approached by a double row of steps, is the **Tomb of Ramesses I** (16) (e.l.), small but well-decorated. Consisting of a burial chamber (C) with three annexes, it was never finished, the king reigning for only a short time. On each side of the entry is the goddess Ma'at (1). Inside the king is shown offering to Anubis, Horus and Nefertum (2–3). On the right is the Book of Gates (2nd division) (4–5), while behind the sarcophagus the king kneels before the souls of Pe and Neken (6). The granite sarcophagus is decorated in yellow with a figure of the winged Isis on the end (7). A wooden figure of the king was found here (now in BM, 854). Immediately W of this tomb is the track over the hills to Deir al-Baḥrī.

Next to the E is the **Tomb of Seti I** (17), the finest and one of the longest in the valley, discovered by Belzoni in October 1817. Due to the increase in visitors it has suffered recently from lack of ventilation and is not always open. It consists of five corridors, some of which are descending steps, leading over two pits and through four rooms, excluding the burial chamber, from which another corridor leads for a considerable distance. The decoration is in bas-relief and beautifully coloured although parts of it were unfinished. It must have been open at an earlier period as there are some Greek graffiti.

Corridor A depicts the king before Reʿ-Harakhte and a disk containing the ram-headed Reʿ and the Khephri beetle (1). Also shown are the 75 transformations of Reʿ from his Litany (2). The ceiling is adorned with flying vultures. Corridor B is a stairway with Isis and Nephthys (unfinished) on each side and again the Litany of Reʿ (3–4). On the entry to Corridor C is a kneeling figure of winged Ma'at (5), and beyond is the journey of the sun through the Afterworld, the Am-Duat (5th division) (6). Hall D has scenes of the king before the gods (7–8). Crossing over a pit, Hall E has four pillars with the king making offerings before the gods of the Afterworld. On the right side of the hall is the Book of Gates (5th division) (9) and on the far side the king presented by Horus to Osiris (10). Opening off Hall E is Hall F, containing part of the Book of Am-Duat (9th–11th divisions) but unfinished (11–14). On the two pillars the king offers to Nefertum, Reʿ-Harakhte, Ma'at, Atum, Osiris, Hathhor and Ptah-Sokar. The descent continues from Hall E, crossing another pit. Corridor G has part of the Ceremony of the Opening of the Mouth (15). Corridor H has a winged disk over the lintel (16) and on the walls the seated king before a table of offerings (17). There is an Offering List and the Litany of the Eye of Horus (18). Corridor I is also entered under a winged disk with the king's names on the sides (19). Beyond, the king is embraced by the gods and receives life from them (20–21). Hall J is decorated with the Books of the Gates (1st, 2nd and 4th divisions) (22–24). This is really an ante-room to the Burial Chamber and has six pillars on which the king is shown making offerings to the gods of the Afterworld. Hall K is the **Burial Chamber** with an astronomical ceiling. (The alabaster sarcophagus, decorated with the Book of Gates, is now in Sir John Soane's Museum, London). The side rooms (L–O) are inscribed with the Book of Gates, the Book of the Divine Cow and the Book of Am-Duat.

Beyond, also on the S side, is the **Tomb of Ramesses X** (18), previously thought to be Ramesses XI. It used to house the electric generator for the valley. Although inscribed, the work is rather inferior. Above the entry is the disk with the ram-headed Reʿ and Khephera. Just above is *Tomb 54*, uninscribed and unidentified. Here Theodore Davis found a cache from the tomb of Tutankhamun, material from the funeral feast and embalment (now in the Metropolitan Museum, New York).

Further up the side valley the track divides, the left branch leading to the **Tomb of Prince Montu-hir-Khopshef** (19), son of Ramesses IX. It is unfinished and has two corridors showing scenes of the prince adoring the gods. There are some hieratic graffiti. Nearby to the N is uninscribed *Tomb 60* but at the E end of the gully is the **Tomb of Queen Hatshepsut** (20), one of the longest tombs in the valley (214m) although none of the corridors is straight, but bend round almost in a half circle from the entrance to the tomb-chamber. The tomb is not decorated but some limestone slabs found in the tomb inscribed in red with the Book of Am-Duat must have been intended to line the chamber. It was cleared by Carter working for Theodore Davis in 1903. Hatshepsut's quartzite sarcophagus, as well as that of her father Tuthmosis I, which she transferred from his own tomb to rest with her, are now in the EM. The body of Tuthmosis I turned up in the royal cache but the body of Hatshepsut was never found.

The right branch of the track leads up to the **Tomb of Tuthmosis IV** (43). Typically early 18 Dyn. in shape, it is similar to that of his father, Amenhotep II, but much smaller. It was robbed in antiquity and Horemheb ordered his superintendent of works, Maya, to restore it, whose hieratic instructions are seen inscribed on the wall in ink. There are two consecutive corridors joined by steps which lead to the well; this is followed by another passage at a right-angle and the tomb-chamber. The walls show the king before the gods. In the *Tomb-Chamber* is the red granite sarcophagus. The body was found in the cache in the tomb of Amenhotep II.

At the N end of the main valley is the (usually inaccessible) **Tomb of Amenemesses** (10) who reigned for a short time after Merneptah. It is a straight tomb with three corridors and a small square hall, leading to a large four-pillared hall. The scenes in the tomb seem to have been deliberately erased. At the level of the four-pillared hall the tomb has been broken into by the adjacent tomb No. 11. To the W is the **Tomb of Ramesses III** (11) (e.l.), also called the *Harpers' Tomb*, after the most famous scene, or *Bruce's Tomb* after one of the early discoverers. It is one of the most interesting tombs with certain unusual features, but is inaccessible beyond the burial chamber as the roof has collapsed. It was started for Sethnakhte but was abandoned when it met tomb No. 10. Ramesses III, his son, moved the axis to the right and continued into the rockface. No attempt seems to have been made to hide the entrance, which is decorated with four Hathor-headed pilasters (1–2). The tomb was entered by a flight of steps with an inclined plane between, to facilitate the sliding of the sarcophagus into the tomb. The lintel has the disk with the ram-headed Reʿ adored by Isis and Nephthys (3). On the thickness are the king's names. There are three corridors (A,B,E), decorated with the Litany of Reʿ (4–9), and two chambers on each side, those on the left showing provisions being brought and cooked (8) and on the right the Litany of Reʿ and the voyage to Abydos (9). Room 4 on the left depicts the bull and seven sacred cows (10) and Room I has the harpers' figures (11). The rooms on the right show the fields of Yaru and funeral furniture (12). In the last room (J) is Osiris in twelve forms. Hall N is where this tomb broke through to that of Amenmesse. The king is shown on the walls making offerings to the gods including Atum, Ptah, Ptah-Sokar, Isis, Osiris and Anubis (13). The corridor (O) leading from here has the Book of Am-Duat (5th division) (15) and shows the king smiting his enemies (16). This leads into a small square hall (P) where on the right of the door a cow-headed Hathor is shown (17). On the left wall are the sons of Horus and to the right Osiris with his emblems (18). In the four-pillared hall (Q) the king offers to Ptah, Reʿ-Harakhte, Khephri, Atum and Nefertum on the pillars. On the base of the left wall are representations of the enemies of Egypt, the Nine Bows (19). Above is the Book of Gates (4th and 5th divisions). The side room opposite is damaged and the walls are much blackened, but it has the Book of Gates (6th section) (20), showing the king in the presence of Osiris. Beyond this point the tomb is unlit. Above the entrance to the descending corridor (S) is a double scene of the king before Osiris (21), while the wall shows Nekhbet and Wadjet (22–23). (Halls T and K are inaccessible at present.) Hall T has the king's names and divinities in their shrines (24–25). The *Burial Chamber* has eight pillars, and depicts part of the Book of Gates, the Book of Aker and the king is seen offering to Atum, Thoth, Reʿ-Harakhte, Horus, Anubis, Geb, Reʿ, Ptah-Sokar and Onuris (26–29). In the side room (K) are Osiris and other divinities. (The sarcophagus of red granite with scenes from the Book of Am-Duat is in the Louvre and the lid showing the king and goddesses is in the Fitzwilliam Museum, Cambridge.)

On the opposite side of the valley are two tombs which although uninscribed proved of some interest when excavated. The first, *Tomb 56*, was called the 'Golden Tomb' by Davis who discovered it. Several jars of faience and alabaster inscribed with the name of Seti II and Ramesses II were found lying above the floor. They contained a diadem, earrings, bracelets, rings and plaques; a cache apparently deposited after the tomb was cut perhaps from the burial of Q Tausert (now in the EM). Just W of this is *Tomb 58* (uninscribed).

Slightly E of this is the **Tomb of Horemheb** (57) (e.l.), long and straight but unfinished. The descent is steep, through undecorated corridors to the well beside the first Hall (E). This is the first decorated section and shows the king introduced to a series of gods. On the left is Hathor of the West, Isis, Osiris and Horus the Elder (F) and on the right Hathor, Anubis, Osiris and Horus the Elder. In the antechamber (A) before the burial chamber these gods and goddesses are repeated (3–4). At the *Burial Chamber* (J) Ma'at guards the entry. On the left side is the Book of the Gates (1st–4th divisions) (6–9), with the 7th–5th divisions and the Hall of Osiris (10–11) behind the red granite sarcophagus. In a side room (I) Osiris is shown before the djed pillar.

To the W in the first gully (F), on the S flank is the uninscribed *Tomb 53* and beside it the *Tomb of Amenemopet* (48), governor of the town and vizier at the time of Amenhotep II. It is undecorated and when cleared by Davis was found to have been robbed, with the body unwrapped. Fragments of the coffin were scattered about and the owner's name was recovered from the shabti figures. On the same side of the valley are *Tombs 49–52*, all uninscribed; in No. 50 were found some animal burials. Opposite on the N slope is *Tomb 12*, also uninscribed.

At the head of this side valley is the **Tomb of Amenhotep II** (35) (e.l.)

which, although unfinished, is one of the deepest tombs in the valley with over 90 steps inside. The type of outline drawing and the delicate quality of the colouring are similar to those in Tomb 34 (see below). When the tomb was discovered in 1898 and cleared by Loret, the body of the king was still in the sarcophagus. In one of the inner chambers were found nine other royal mummies removed from their original tombs, including Tuthmosis IV, Merneptah-Siptah, Seti II, Sethnakhte, Ramesses III and IV and Queen Tiye, wife of Amenhotep III. The body of Amenhotep II was left in the tomb after it was cleared but a further tomb robbery prompted the authorities to transfer it to the EM with the others. Only the inner part of the tomb is decorated. A corridor leads over a pit somewhat deeper than that of Tuthmosis III to a two-pillared hall where the direction of the tomb turns 90°. This is the first decorated area, on the S and W walls. After another short corridor is the *Burial Chamber*. The ceiling is painted blue and decorated with yellow stars. In the slightly sunken burial area at the far end of the room is the quartzite sarcophagus. On the walls of the Burial Chamber (N) is an abbreviated form of the Book of Am-Duat (1st–12th divisions) (1–5) and the pillars show the king receiving life from Osiris, Anubis and Hathor. The cache of royal bodies was found in the second chamber on the right. The coffins from here and other finds including wooden statues of Amenhotep II, complete and broken wooden leopards and magical bricks are now in the EM.

To the S is another shallow valley which leads to the *Tomb of Mahirper* (36), standard bearer during the time of Hatshepsut. It was opened in 1899 by Loret and contained a wooden sarcophagus, three wooden coffins and a canopic box with alabaster jars and a fine copy of the Book of the Dead (all now in the EM). On the opposite side of the main valley are two uninscribed tombs, *Tomb 61* and *Tomb 29*.

Beyond this the valley divides, the longer arm leading S, the shorter arm SW. Down the S arm (H) for a distance of c 80m the first series are unindentified *Tombs 40, 26* (E side); *30* (N side); *59* (E side); *31, 32* (W side) and *37* (E side). After 100m on the E side is *Tomb 42*; unfinished and uninscribed, it has been attributed to Tuthmosis II or Meritre Hatshepsut (wife of Tuthmosis III). Inside is an uninscribed quartzite sarcophagus. On the E side of the valley, *Tomb 33* is uninscribed, but as the valley rises steeply after 30m is the **Tomb of Tuthmosis III** (34) (e.l.), requiring a steep climb up a wooden staircase. It is entered down a steep passage and a flight of steps. Three corridors lead over a shallow pit and two halls, all undecorated. At the ante-chamber the axis turns 90° to the left. This chamber has two pillars and on the walls are lists of divinities. Steps lead into the rounded *Tomb-Chamber*, the last tomb to retain this form, also with two pillars. On the walls is the Book of Am-Duat (1st–12th divisions) (1–4) with an abridged version on the pillars, with the king's mother Isis shown in a boat, and his wives on the first pillar. The red granite sarcophagus and lid are still in position. Four annexes lead off this chamber where some funeral furniture was found (now in the EM). The body of this king was found in the Deir al-Baḥrī cache. Other finds in the tomb were a wooden statue of the king, faience plaques and wands, and alabaster vases including one inscribed with the name of his wife Merytre-Hatshepsut. Beyond this at the end of the valley is the uninscribed *Tomb 39*.

In the SW valley (9) the first tomb, high on the E side, is the **Tomb of Merneptah-Siptah** (47), a long, straight Ramesside tomb. It was excavated by Ayrton for Davis in 1905. A double shallow flight of steps with ramp leads to the plaster-coated doorway decorated with the king's titles and above ram-headed Reʿ and a scarab in a disk between Isis and Nephthys (1). The first three corridors are decorated, the first (A) with a ceiling of vultures, the second (B) has the Litany of Reʿ (2) and the Book of the Dead (Chapter 151), and the four sons of Horus; three further corridors lead through a square ante-chamber into the *Burial Chamber* (L) with four pillars. The red granite sarcophagus is still in place. The body of Merneptah-Siptah was included in the cache in the tomb of Amenhotep II; his cartouches had been erased and later restored.

On the W side of this valley is the *Tomb of Bay* (13), a chancellor of Merneptah-Siptah. It is filled with stores and inaccessible. Also on the W side is the **Tomb of Queen Tawsert and Sethnakht** (14), originally built for the wife of Merneptah-Siptah (after his death marrying Seti II). The tomb was subsequently usurped by Sethnakht who used Corridor B, Hall E and the Burial Chamber, J, after his own tomb (*No. 11*) broke through the wall of its neighbour. This tomb is not usually accessible although it is decorated throughout. It consists of several corridors leading to an eight-chambered hall which was originally intended as the tomb-chamber of Tausert. These show scenes from the Book of the Dead (Hall F), the Ceremony of the Opening of the Mouth and the Book of the Gates (Corridor F), usurped by Sethnakhte. Other walls depict the Book of Caverns (Hall J). On the eight pillars in the *Tomb-Chamber* (X) Sethnakht is shown offering to the gods. His broken granite sarcophagus is in position.

Further up this valley is the first royal tomb to have been cut in these hills, the **Tomb of Tuthmosis I** (38). It is intentionally inconspicuous. A rough flight of steps leads into an irregular corridor, a square ante-chamber and the oval *Burial Chamber*. Only the last is decorated—with the Book of Am-Duat (12th division). Remains of the shattered quartzite sarcophagus of the king (now in the EM) lead to the supposition that Hatshepsut's discovery that her father's tomb had been robbed led her to construct a second sarcophagus for him and have him reinterred in her own tomb.

At the head of the valley the **Tomb of Seti II** (15) was unfinished. This is a straight Ramesside tomb and during Carter's excavation of Tutankhamun's tomb it was used as a storage and restoration area. Three corridors (A–C) lead to an ante-chamber (D) and the four-pillared burial chamber (E). The cartouches in the entry have been erased and recut. All the corridors and chambers are decorated with good low-cut relief.

In the W valley the northernmost tomb is the **Tomb of Amenhotep III** (22), a typical early 18 Dyn. construction consisting of three corridors (A), a chamber where the axis of the tomb turns 90° to the left; another corridor to the four-pillared offering chamber where the axis changes 90° to the right leading directly into the *Burial Chamber*. The walls have scenes from the Book of Am-Duat (2nd and 3rd divisions). Inside is the broken red granite sarcophagus lid. The coffin lid was usurped by Seti I (now in the EM). S of this is the **Tomb of Ay** (23), interesting in that it displays a blend of royal and nobles' decoration. Long and straight, it consists of four corridors (A–D) and a hall leading to the *Burial Chamber*, which is decorated with the Book of Am-Duat. However, on one wall Ay is seen in a boat spearing fish and birds like a traditional noble. The red granite sarcophagus was found intact but broken later (now in the EM). Tombs 24–5 are uninscribed.

Returning from the Valley of the Kings by the same route, below Carter's house the SW road runs along the base of the hills for several km. From this road the rest of the monuments can be reached. E of the road (500m) is the *O.H.A. Resthouse*, opposite a mosque, and to the W the **Draʿ Abū 'l-Nagaʿ Cemetery**. This is the first of a series of contiguous cemeteries that lie scattered throughout the whole monument field along the lower slopes of the Theban Hills and generally called the *Tomb-Chapels of the Nobles* (see Sh.ʿ Abd al-Qurnah, below). None of the 114 tomb-chapels in this section is accessible. W of the cemetery is the ruined monastery of *Deir al-Bakhit*.

## DEIR AL-BAḤRĪ, ʿASĀSĪF AND AL-KHŪKHAH

Beyond the Resthouse (500m) is the area known as **Deir al-Baḥrī** (Ar. Dayr al-Baḥrī; Northern Monastery), named after a Coptic complex that stood in one of the monuments. To the S of the road are three destroyed temples. The easternmost is the *Temple of Ramesses IV*, while to the W is a *mid-Ramesside Temple*. Between them is the *Valley Temple of Hatshepsut*, excavated by Carter prior to his discovery of the Tomb of Tutankhamun. From here the causeway, aligned exactly on Karnak and lined with sphinxes, extended NW for 1km to the ***Mortuary Temple of Hatshepsut**, set in a fold of the Theban Hills with the cliffs as a splendid backdrop. Designed and built by Hatshepsut's steward and architect Senenmut, it rises in a series of terraces to the sanctuary. It was known as Djer-Djeseru and she dedicated it to her father Tuthmosis I, Amun-United-with-Eternity, and herself, at a place probably already sacred to Hathor in her aspect of Goddess of the West.

*The Mortuary Temple of Hatshepsut*

This temple is one of the most remarkable structures in Egypt. It is said to have been inspired by the tomb-chapels of some of the Middle Kingdom nobles at Qaw al-Kabīr (Middle Egypt), but whatever the antecedents the result is very striking. Recently the walls built by Senenmut to hold back the friable rock have been uncovered and augmented. Long after the temple was abandoned it was used as a Coptic monastery, the Deir al-Baḥrī, the name of which is now used for the whole area. First examined by Napoleon's savants, it was partly cleared by Wilkinson, but it was Lepsius who realised the connection between this site and Hatshepsut's work at Karnak. Mariette worked here spasmodically from 1853–66, but it was not fully cleared until the work of the EES between 1906–09. Makare Hatshepsut reigned in 1503–1452 BC. The temple was the work of her mature years, taking eight years to build between her 8th and 16th regnal years. Her tomb as reigning king (she had had one built earlier, Valley of the Kings No. 20), was constructed so that the tomb-chamber lay directly beneath the sanctuary of this temple, presumably so that services in the temple would have been dedicated to her memory. However, it is not known for certain that Hatshepsut was buried here.

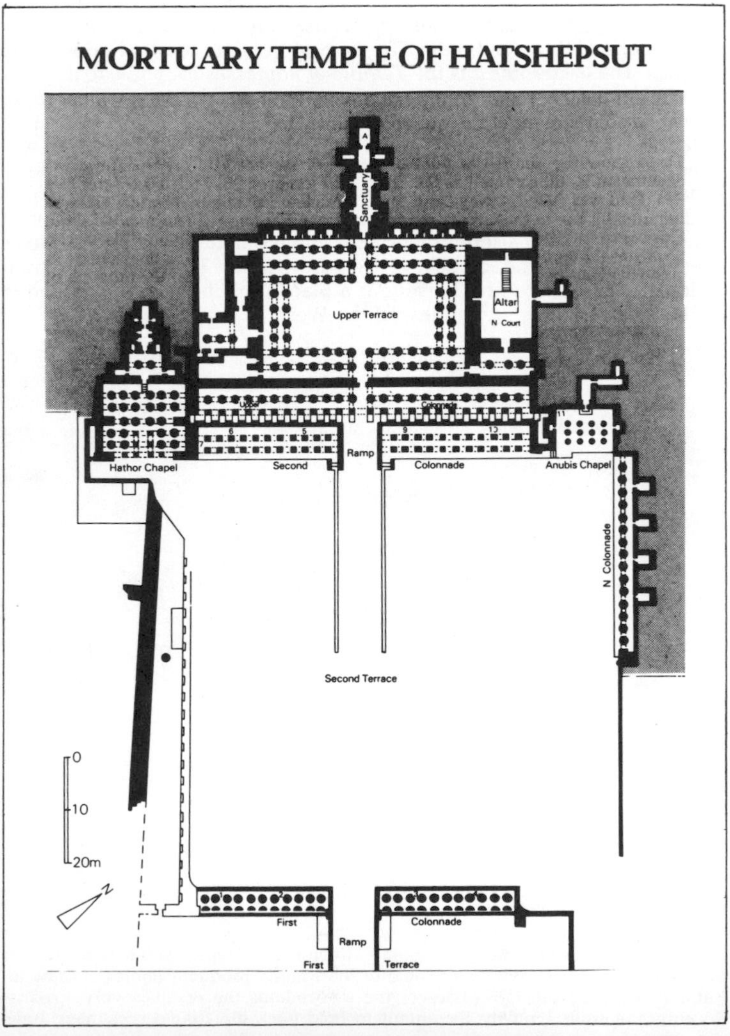
MORTUARY TEMPLE OF HATSHEPSUT
A
Sanctuary
Upper Terrace
Altar
N Court
Upper
Colonnade
Ramp
Second
Colonnade
Hathor Chapel
Anubis Chapel
N Colonnade
Second Terrace
0
10
20m
N
First
Colonnade
Ramp
First
Terrace

The temple rises in three imposing terraces; the lower two would have been full of trees. The stumps of some are still visible. Enter the *First Terrace* and proceed to the southern end of the *First Colonnade* (largely restored). Here are (1–2) scenes of boat-building and the transportation of Hatshepsut's two obelisks for the temple at Karnak (a task performed in seven months). On the N side of the colonnade (3) Hatshepsut offers four calves to Amun-Reʿ, and also (4) royal statues.

The *Second Terrace* is reached by a ramp, but originally had stairs. On the S side of the *Second Colonnade* are (5) texts to Amun-Reʿ (Queen defaced) and (6) the famous Punt reliefs. On the S wall is a replaced fragment of the queen of Punt (7).

These show the journey to Punt in search of incense and myrrh. The exact destination is still disputed as the same products grow on each side of the Red Sea. Punt was called 'God's Land' by the Ancient Egyptians. The incense was required for use in the temple services. Many other objects, like monkeys and hides as well as timber, were also brought back from this expedition. This was by no means the earliest of the Egyptian expeditions to this region as they had been going to Punt since the Old Kingdom, trading Egyptian goods for the products of Punt.

To the S is the *Hathor Chapel*, probably situated on the site of the original shrine of the area. The court leading to this has columns where Hathor with a woman's face and cow's ears is shown with her sistrum; on the walls she is depicted as a cow. However, the area was much defaced by Tuthmosis III who erased Hatshepsut's name in many places. Akhenaten in turn erased the name of Amun. The temple was later restored, first by Horemheb and then by Ramesses II who had the name of Amun reinserted. In the third room on the left is a picture of Senenmut. On the N side of the *Second Colonnade* is (9–10) the birth scene, showing the conception and birth of Hatshepsut. She claimed that her father was really Amun, who approached her mother Ahmose in the guise of Tuthmosis I. A similar claim was later made by Amenhotep III both at the Luxor Temple and at that of Mut. Beyond the colonnade further to the N is the *Anubis Chapel*. Anubis, although extremely important in his aspect of one of the gods of the dead, seldom has a place of his own in a temple. He is portrayed here (11) as usual as a man with a jackal's mask. The shrine consists of a 12-columned hall. On the N wall is a niche with figures of Anubis, Nekhbet and Wadjet. Off the columned hall to the W is a long chamber, and opening off this a second room turning towards the N. E of the chapel is the *North Colonnade* of fluted columns of the type called proto-Doric. They are extremely graceful, and taper slightly towards the top giving a general air of lightness as well as blending well into the landscape behind them.

Since 1961 the area beyond this has been closed for excavations and restoration by the Polish-Egyptian Expedition.

A ramp decorated on each side with the emblems of Upper and Lower Egypt leads through the *Upper Colonnade* to the much smaller *Upper Terrace* (restored by Naville as a columned court, but Polish architects have suggested recently that it is a hypostyle hall). Here stood the great Coptic monastery that gave its name to the site, but all traces of it have been removed. The terrace has an Osiride portico, the square pillars being faced by standing statues of Hatshepsut, some of which have been restored to give the general effect. On the left about halfway along is a restoration text of Horemheb. The hall is entered through a Ptolemaic granite gateway. The columns on the left, originally round, were converted to square pillars by Tuthmosis III who replaced Hatshepsft's name with his own, while on the S side he also erased her name but replaced it with that of her husband Tuthmosis II. In the middle of the W wall is the *Sanctuary of Amun*, with niches on each side in which stood statues of the queen. A second granite door, less well-preserved and also Ptolemaic, leads into the *Sanctuary*. This is a long narrow rock-cut room, with recesses in the side walls. The paintings in this inner area are much blackened with smoke. They show Hatshepsut and members of her family such as her daughter making offerings to the gods. On the far W side the Ptolemies cut out a *Sanctuary to Imhotep and Amenhotpe* (A), two deified officials, the first Zozer's chief of works and the other a wise man of the 18 Dyn. At this time the temple was used as a place of healing as were so many of the Ptolemaic temples. To the S of the Hypostyle Hall there is a complex of rooms while to the N is the *North Court*. This is entered by a vestibule which had four columns (one destroyed). It is an open court running E–W with a large limestone altar in the centre reached by a series of steps. It was dedicated by Hatshepsut to Reʿ-Harakhte. The scenes of the queen in this court have been largely erased and partly replaced by Tuthmosis II's name.

N of the causeway and just beyond the outer wall of the first terrace is the first *Tomb of Senenmut* (No. 353). The astronomical scenes on the ceiling make it well worth visiting, but the approach is very steep and impossible for large groups. On the S side of the Temple of Hatshepsut is the **Temple of Tuthmosis III**, dedicated to himself and to Amun-United-with-Eternity (now under investigation by the Polish/Egyptian Expedition). The presence of the causeway serving this temple had been known for many years, but the building itself had been buried beneath rock-fall from the hills behind. It was erected in the last years of Tuthmosis's reign between 1460–1450 BC, and was called Djeser-Akhet. It is built partly of sandstone, partly of limestone and contains a great deal of interesting material. The *Hypostyle Hall* consists of proto-Doric columns with a processional way flanked by eight central columns. The blocks are well engraved and coloured, and include scenes from 'the Feast of the Valley'. The temple was decorated by many fine statues of Tuthmosis III (mainly broken). It seems to have been destroyed by a landslide towards the end of the 20 Dyn. and thus must have been in use for some 250 years. It was joined to a *Valley Temple* excavated by Weigall before 1914. (A stele from this temple is now in the BM.)

To the SW and also set directly against the rock face is the earliest of the three temples, the 11 Dyn. **Mortuary Temple of Nebhetepre Mentuhotpe**. It is not easily accessible and is best viewed from the Temple of Hatshepsut.

At the New Year in the tenth month of the Civil Year the boat of Amun was taken from Karnak on the East Bank to this temple, stopping at way stations for certain ceremonies. This festival became one of the principal Egyptian feasts and was known as 'The Feast of the Valley'. It gave its name to the month in which it was celebrated, and was carried over into the Coptic calendar. Originally excavated by the EES before 1914, the temple has recently been re-examined by the German Archaeological Institute.

The temple was called 'Glorious are the Seats of Neb-hetep-Reʿ', the name determined by a central pyramid. The first 11 Dyn. kings were buried in simple rock-cut tombs in the cliffs but Mentuhotpe set his temple on a platform above which there appears to have been a pyramid supported on columns. However, the exact form of this temple is still under discussion. The original structure was extended at least once, and under the extension are the tombs of six of his queens: Mayt, Ashayt, Zadeh, Kauit, Kemsit and Henenit, whose limestone sarcophagi are beautifully carved with scenes of everyday life and inscribed with some interesting Coffin Texts (now in the EM). At the rear of the temple is the rock-cut tomb; at this time the two elements were still considered as a single unit. In front of the temple a stone wall surrounds a large forecourt in the centre of which an entrance, the *Bāb al-Huṣān* (Gate of the Horseman), leads to the earlier subterranean tomb. From the front of the enclosure a wide causeway joined the temple to a canal and a T-shaped turning basin. There does not seem to have been a valley temple.

At the head of the first small valley, c 100m to the S, is the uninscribed *21 Dyn. Tomb* (N.320) where the cache of Royal mummies was found in 1891 by Émile Brugsch. They had been reburied by King Siamun (21 Dyn.) because of the depredations of the tomb robbers. The cache included the bodies of various 17–21 Dyn. kings including Kamose, Tao II, Tuthmosis III, Seti I, and Ramesses II and III.

The *Tombs of the Nobles* (see Shaykh ʿAbd al-Qurnah, below) continuing S of the causeway of Hatshepsut are subdivided among two fields. Northernmost is **al-ʿAsāsīf** in which, among the 35 tomb-chapels, the most interesting and accessible tomb, standing just N of the Metropolitan Museum of Art Expedition House, is the **Tomb-Chapel of Ibi**, sometimes called Aba (No. 36). He was Steward of the Divine Votrice at the time of Psamtik I. It is reached down a flight of steps and consists of four main rooms and a vestibule. This tomb-chapel is a direct copy of one at Deir al-Gabrāwī (Rtc 33).

In the vestibule the paintings are: (1) Offering bearers. (2) Statue niche with titles of Psamtik I and Nitocris the votrice. (3) Ibi with gazelle under chair. (4) Ibi adores Reʿ-Harakhte. (5) Psamtik I before Osiris and Horus.

To the left of the vestibule is the *Hall*, originally with four square pillars (destroyed).

(6) Hathor pillar with text. (7) Ibi inspects sandal makers, sculptors and metal workers. (8) Ibi sees musicians and dancers. (9) Ibi in kiosk. (10) Statue niche with titles of Psamtik I. (11) Hathor pillar with autobiographical text. (12) Souls of Pe and mummified Reʿ-Harakhte. (13) Offering bearers before deceased.

Opening off this is the main *Open Court* with six columns.

## TOMB-CHAPELS OF THE NOBLES

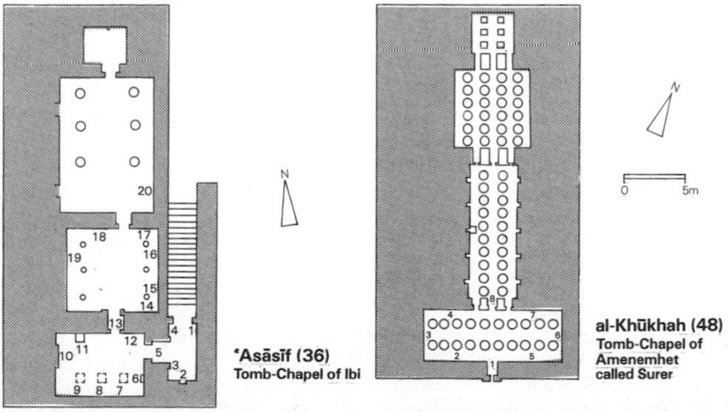
N
N
0
5m

**ʿAsāsīf (36)**
Tomb-Chapel of Ibi

**al-Khūkhah (48)**
Tomb-Chapel of Amenemhet called Surer

(14) Sons offer bouquets and tables of offerings. (15) Scenes of hunting and agriculture. (16) Funeral procession including tehnu. (17) Ibi and mother before a stele upon which is Anubis. (18) Ibi adores Osiris and a goddess. (19) Offering list.

Leading off this court by steps is a *Six-Columned Hall.*

(20) Isis and Nephthys followed by Anubis. (The lid of the sarcophagus is in Turin Museum.)

To the S is the area called **Khūkhah** with about 60 tomb-chapels. Just N of the main road is the **Tomb-Chapel of Amenemhet**, called Surer (No. 48), the king's steward (time of Amenhotep III). This is one of the most interesting of the tomb-chapels, as it was the first with a square hall with four pillars at the rear of the long axial hall. It is beautifully decorated with fresh clear paintings, but has been very much damaged (as is often the case of the tomb-chapels of king's stewards). If complete it would be one of the most splendid chapels. To make matters worse it is used as a store by the family who live next door.

(1) Amenhotep III before Amun-Reʿ, hymn to Reʿ. (2) Amenemhet adores Geb, Nut, Osiris and Isis (some of gods destroyed). (3) Amenhotep celebrating the harvest festival. (4) Amenemhet preceded by fan-bearer and followed by eight representations of himself with staves and bouquets offering to Amenhotep III. (5) Amenemhet with mother Mut-Tuy, royal concubine. (6) Double scene, Amenhotep III followed by ka. (7) Amenemhet before Amenhotep in kiosk with five registers of New Year Gifts.

## SHAYKH ʿABD AL-QURNAH

W of ʿAsāsīf and Khūkhah is the largest and most frequently visited section of the Tomb-Chapels of the Nobles. This is ***Shaykh ʿAbd al-Qurnah**, named after the village on the top of the hill. The most prominent feature is the *Mosque of Shaykh ʿAbd al-Qurnah* which has a cylindrical minaret (lit at night) and contains the tomb of the Shaykh.

Tomb-Chapels of the Nobles is strictly a misnomer as the nobles, officials and priests are buried not in the decorated chapels but in chambers cut in the rock at the foot of a shaft which descends either from the court in front of the chapel, or below it. After the chapels were abandoned they were often used for secondary burials at later periods.

There are six main groups of these chapels on the West Bank: Draʿ Abū-ʾl-Nagaʿ, ʿAsāsīf, al-Khukhah (see above), Shaykh ʿAbd al-Qurnah, Qurnat Muraʿī and Deir al-Madīnah (see below) containing over 400 tombs from the 6 Dyn. to Greco-Roman times, though the majority are New Kingdom. Many are at present inaccessible. The earliest group of chapels are those of ʿAsāsīf, mainly 11–12 Dyns (not accessible at present). Most usually visited are those at Shaykh ʿAbd al-Qurnah (18–20 Dyns) and those at Deir al-Madīnah (usually called the Workmen's Tombs) which belong to the artisans who constructed the great tombs (mainly 19–20 Dyns). The typical tomb-chapel seems to consist of two parts, a rock-cut chapel and an underground tomb-chamber. The chapel appears to reproduce the same elements found in the New Kingdom house, namely (a) a rock-cut court at the rear of which is a centre door opening into (b) a transverse hall, corresponding to the broad hall or reception area of the private house, running from which is (c) a corridor, cut deep into the native rock, at the far end of which is (d) a niche for statues or sometimes a small chapel or shrine, where the offerings were made and the funerary rite performed. At each end of the first broad hall is a stele, one with biographical details, the other a false door. Deir al-Madīnah chapels become irregularly shaped with a chapel in the form of a small pyramid at the top and steps down to a small burial chamber. Since the

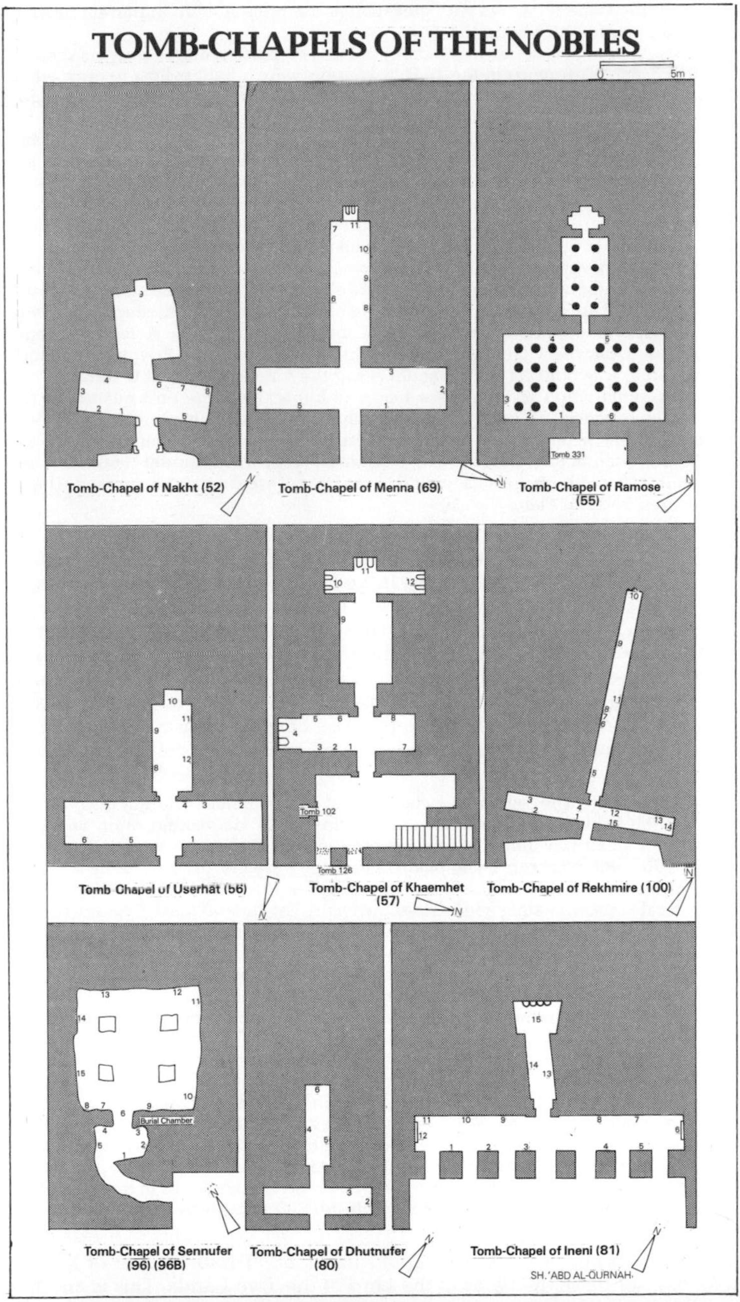
TOMB-CHAPELS OF THE NOBLES
0
5m
Tomb-Chapel of Nakht (52)
Tomb-Chapel of Menna (69)
Tomb 331
Tomb-Chapel of Ramose (55)
Tomb Chapel of Userhat (56)
Tomb 102
Tomb 126
Tomb-Chapel of Khaemhet (57)
Tomb-Chapel of Rekhmire (100)
Burial Chamber
Tomb-Chapel of Sennufer (96) (96B)
Tomb-Chapel of Dhutnufer (80)
Tomb-Chapel of Ineni (81)
SH. 'ABD AL-QURNAH
N

quality of the stone improves with elevation of the hill the more important officials are usually buried higher up the slope.

The majority of the scenes were simply painted on plaster, more rarely carved and painted. The backgrounds in the 18 Dyn. chapels were a light yellow to grey, while in the 19–20 Dyns the background became more ocherous. The scenes are arranged in a specific order: daily life in the broad hall, religious and funerary in the cross corridor. The walls of the shrine show funerary rites and lists of offerings, and sometimes the gods of the necropolis. The ceilings in the 18 Dyn. chapels are covered with bright patterns representing mats or hangings. Moving into the 19–20 Dyns the scenes on the walls change from everyday life to scenes of the Afterworld. The tombs at Deir al-Madīnah are often decorated like the royal tombs with sections from the Books of the Dead, or the Book of the Gates. Gods of the Dead also became more frequently represented in the late tombs. These tomb-chapels were robbed long ago and most of them have served as dwellings for the inhabitants of the village of Shaykh ʿAbd al-Qurnah; they are often damaged by smoke or neglect. They were not enclosed or provided with guardians until the early 20C. A model village, Qurnah al-Gadid (New Qurnah), designed by the distinguished Egyptian architect, Hasan Fathi, was built for the inhabitants but the villagers refused to move.

It is essential when visiting these tombs to know the name and number of the destination required, as many of the nobles have the same name and it is very easy to arrive at the wrong place. If time is short the tomb-chapels usually visited are Nakht (52), Menna (69), Ramose (55), Retehmire (100) and Sennufer (96B). This site of about 250 tomb-chapels is divided into three areas: the Lower and Upper Enclosures, and the Plain.

On the W side is one of the most easily accessible tomb-chapels, reached after a short climb. (It cannot take large groups and broken glass protects part of the walls.) This is the **Tomb-Chapel of Nakht** (No. 52), royal astronomer, keeper of the king's vineyards and chief of the granaries (time of Tuthmosis IV). It is one of the smallest but most brightly coloured of the tomb-chapels. Nakht was buried with his wife Tawi in a chamber at the foot of a shaft in front of the chapel. They were middle-aged and buried with cheap wooden furniture. The chapel consists of an undecorated ante-chamber, a transverse room and an interior undecorated room.

(1) Nakht and his wife, who was a chantress of Amun, before offering (incomplete, some of the baskets of grapes are only outlined). (2) Harvesting grain and flax; Nakht in a small pavilion counting his produce. (3) Stele with what is known of Nakht's life, with offerings being made to it, at the base the goddess of the West. (4) Funeral banquet. Nakht is shown but an enemy has destroyed the upper part of his body. A cat is shown eating a fish under the chair. The funeral feast show the friends of the deceased enjoying their food and drink and being entertained by a blind harpist, a girl harper and dancing girls. (5–6) Two scenes of Nakht and his wife before offering tables. In the upper register an enemy has destroyed their eyes, but has forgotten to do so in the lower picture. (7) Nakht hunting in the marshes, by the 18 Dyn. a mythical rather than an actual scene. Again an enemy has destroyed Nakht's eyes and cut his throwing sticks. He is supported in his reed boat by his wife and son. (8) Vintage scene, grapes are plucked from an arbour and then trodden out by men up to their knees in the juice. Above the wine jars are waiting to be filled. Below birds are caught in a clap-net and are then cleaned and placed in jars or hung to dry in shelters. The chapel is surrounded by a kherker frieze, and the ceiling represents different coloured woven mats. The inner room is undecorated, but the niche on the far side (9) originally contained a statue of Nakht holding a stele with a hymn to Reʿ upon it. In 1915 this was shipped to the United States in the White Star steamship 'Arabic' which was torpedoed off the S of Ireland by the Germans.

In the SE corner of the Upper Enclosure is the **Tomb-Chapel of Menna** (No. 69), scribe of the fields of the Lord of the Two Lands. This is another cruciform chapel. The paintings are in good condition but an enemy of Menna has destroyed his eyes in the paintings and cut through his throwing stick. Decoration on the ceiling is brightly coloured and represents matting.

(1) Menna and wife before offerings. (2) Stele. (3) Funerary rites and feast. (4) Menna and wife offer to Osiris. (5) Agricultural scenes with two quarrelling girls and one girl removing a thorn from the foot of another, Menna before offerings (damaged). (6) Funerary scenes. (7) Judgement scenes (the painting of the balance has been tampered with, by an enemy, so that Menna is not assured of a good future). (8) Funeral and the voyage to Abydos. (9) Fishing and fowling in the marshes (damaged). (10) Relations offering to the deceased, (11) Statue niche with Menna and wife (legs only).

In the SE corner of the *Lower Enclosure* is a group of three accessible tombs. The northernmost, lying in a seam of excellent limestone (unusual this low down the hill), is the **Tomb-Chapel of Ramose** (No. 55), vizier and governor of Thebes towards the end of the reign of Amenhotep III and the beginning of that of Akhenaten. Ramose seems to have had no children and the chapel was constructed for him by his brother Amenhotpe, chief of works at Memphis, which probably accounts for the excellent quality of the work. The family seems to have been Memphite and as the last date mentioned in the inscriptions is the 30th regnal year of Amenhotep III, Ramose probably died soon after this. Robert Mond cleared then restored the tomb for the University of Liverpool, the Metropolitan Museum of Art and the Dept of Antiquities. This chapel (which was never finished) has a square rock-cut court with a central doorway opening into a broad columned hall. This has 64 columns arranged in two groups with a processional way in the middle. The columns (heavily restored) are of papyrus bud form. The inner hall (undecorated) has eight columns with a central space to the shrine at the end. On the left of the broad hall and under the inner hall were shafts leading below to two burial chambers, but the body of Ramose was not found. The decoration is a blend of typical 18 Dyn. work and the al-ʿAmārnah style. The relief carving in this chapel is very fine and has been only sparsely painted. There is some evidence for the co-regency of Amenhotep III and IV and the chapel contains paintings of both kings, those of the latter unfinished.

(1) Reliefs of Ramose, in the roles of the vizier, and wife in front of offerings. (2) Amenhotpe and wife before offerings. (3) Funeral. (4) King Amenhotep III. (5) Amenhotep IV rewarding Ramose (unfinished). (6) Offerings.

Slightly to the S is the **Tomb-Chapel of Userhat** (No. 56), royal scribe and tutor (time of Amenhotep II). This is a small cruciform tomb.

(1) Userhat and his wife in front of a table of offerings. (2) Userhat offers to Amenhotep II (face damaged) fruit and flowers. (3) Bakery scene. (4) Bags of gold dust being brought, and counted; lower register, a barber cutting hair under a tree. (6) Agricultural scenes of harvest and cattle (some damaged). (7) The funeral feast (extensively damaged by early Coptic hermits). (8) Hunting in the desert with Userhat in his chariot. (9) Fowling, fishing and vintage scenes, statues of Userhat and his family. (11–12) Funerary scenes.

Adjacent to the S is the **Tomb-Chapel of Kha'emhet** (No. 57), of the end of the 18 Dyn. He was royal scribe and overseer of the granaries (time of Amenhotep III). There is some very fine low relief work in this chapel. Two transverse chambers are connected by a wide passage.

(1) Kha'emhet and offerings. (2) Renenet, snake-headed goddess of the harvest, seated in a shrine. (3) Theban harbour and boats. (4) Niche with statues of Kha'emhet and Imhotep. (5) Kha'emhet and Amenhotep III (damaged), and cattle. (6) Kha'emhet presents report to the king. (7) Offerings and agricultural scenes. (8) Amenhotep II on throne receiving Kha'emhet's worship, (9) Osiris (damaged), (10, 11 and 12) Niches each with two complete or part statues.

The next tombs to be visited are up a steep hill in the *Upper Enclosure*. The first, in the SW corner, is the **Tomb-Chapel of Rekhmire** (No. 100) who was vizier of Tuthmosis III and Amenhotep II. Rekhmire came from an administrative family, his great grandfather, grandfather and uncle had all been viziers and governors of Thebes although his father, Bakht, was a priest of Amun without high office.

The chapel is cruciform and very high. The paintings and inscriptions are important for the understanding of Egyptian foreign policies, taxation and the application of justice.

(1) Egyptian taxes. (2) Installation of Rekhmire as vizier. He receives his instructions from the king and is installed in his hall, dressed in his official garments, and seated upon a chair with a cushion and matting under his feet. (3) Five registers of the foreign tribute brought to Egypt. From the upper register they are: Punt, Crete and the Aegean Islands, Nubia, Syria, and Kush. These are very interesting both for the clothing worn by the different nationalities and the gifts typical of their area that they bring. Thus the Minoans (Cretans) bring beautiful vases; the Nubians, elephant tusks and gold; the Syrians, chariots and horses, a bear and an elephant. (4) The king and Rekhmire (damaged). (5–7) The workshops of Amun of which Rekhmire was in charge. These are represented somewhat like the store houses at the Ramesseum with mud-brick vaulted roofs. The seated Rekhmire is shown inspecting the workshops. There are scenes of stone-cutting, the sculpting and polishing of statues of the king, rope-making, smelting with men working the bellows with their feet. (8) The voyage to Abydos. (9) Funerary deities Anubis, Osiris and Hathor of the West. (10) Niches for statues of Rekhmire. (11) The Afterworld, with a lake and trees and the funerary feast. (12) Hunting and fowling scenes. (13) Vintage scene, with the winepress and grapes being trodden out. (14) Rekhmire's ancestors and their wives, and his sons. (15) Taxes and offerings.

Slightly to the W and up the hill is the **Tomb-Chapel of Sennufer** (No. 96B), mayor of Thebes, and overseer of the granaries and gardens of Amun (time of Amenhotep II). He was also probably chief vintner. The upper chapel is now used as a store and the lower chamber is reached by a flight of steps (no light—torch necessary). It is known locally as the *Tomb of the Vine* because of the paintings of these plants on the ceiling. There is an irregularly cut ante-chamber and the ceiling of the four-pillared chamber is also rough, giving a pleasant effect.

Sennufer is shown (1) with offerings; (2) with his daughter—damaged; (3–4) with his sister; (5) with his daughter. (6) Above the door, double figure of Anubis. In the chamber Sennufer is shown (7) with his wife Meryt entering the Afterworld; (8) seated with his wife; (9) purified by the semten priest; (10) offering to Anubis and Osiris; (11–12) as a statue and the voyage to Abydos; (13–14) before Osiris and Hathor. (15) Funeral furniture.

The next group of tombs is to the N towards the top of the slope. First is the **Tomb-Chapel of Dhutnufer** (No. 80), royal scribe and overseer of the treasury. It is a small cruciform chapel with the transverse hall wider than the axial.

(1) Dhutnufer offering on braziers. (2) Stele, (3) Offerings of bouquets, (4) Bringing Nubian gold. (5) Rites before mummy. (6) Dead man offers to Osiris.

Adjacent is the **Tomb-Chapel of Ineni** (No. 81), architect of Tuthmosis I and overseer of the granary of Amun. He was responsible for the construction of Tuthmosis I's tomb in the Valley of the Kings—'no-one seeing no-one hearing'. He also transported and erected the obelisks of Tuthmosis I at Karnak. This chapel, extending over several reigns from Amenhotep I to Tuthmosis III, is interesting more for the inscriptions than the paintings. In form the chapel has a long narrow transverse passage with six square pillars. Beyond this is an inner chamber with four statue niches on the back wall.

(1) Ineni hunting on foot. (2) House and garden. (3) Ineni and offering list. (4) Agricultural scenes. (5) Harvest. (6) Stele with autobiography. (7) Ineni and wife fowling and fishing. (8) Ineni seated, with dog under chair, and receives offerings. (9) Ineni inspects foreign tribute. (10) Produce of temple of Amun. (11) Weighing of treasure of Amun. (12) Stele with autobiography. (13) Ineni and wife with offerings. (14) Funeral procession. (15) Statues of Ineni and wife Ahotpe and 4 parents.

Due N on the path to the top of the hill (fine view of the cemetery and Nile Valley) is the **Tomb-Chapel of Horemheb** (No. 78), scribe of the recruits and royal scribe (Tuthmosis III to Amenhotep III). This is a cruciform chapel and most of the scenes are conventional, but a few are connected with Horemheb's military career.

(1) Stele, Horemheb adores Anubis and Osiris. (2) Tuthmosis IV and goddess in kiosk with recruits. (3) Stele. (4) Tuthmosis IV in kiosk receiving tribute. (5) Funeral procession. (6) Offering list and offerings. (7) Judgement scene with Thoth and Ma'at, cartouches of Tuthmosis III, IV and Amenhotep II and III. (8) Rites before mummies.

To the NW near the crest of the hill (a difficult climb) is the second **Tomb-Chapel of Senenmut** (No. 71), the chief steward of Queen Hatshepsut, who was responsible for the construction of her great mortuary temple at Deir al-Baḥrī (see above).

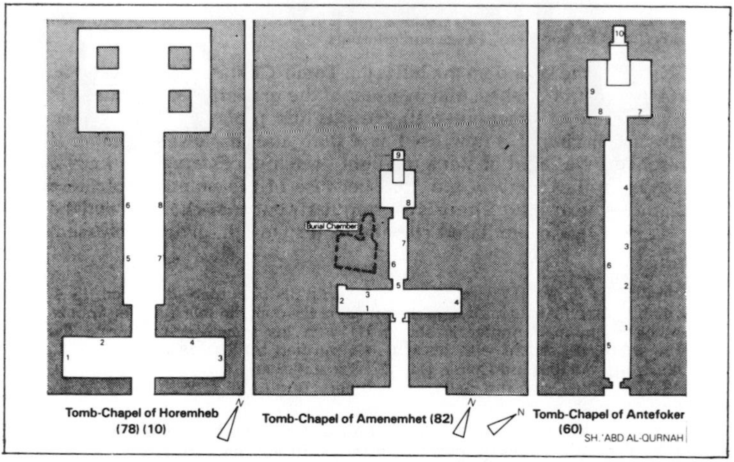
Burial Chamber
N
N
N
SH. 'ABD AL-QURNAH

Tomb-Chapel of Horemheb (78) (10) Tomb-Chapel of Amenemhet (82) Tomb-Chapel of Antefoker (60)

Down the hill from the tomb-chapel of Horemheb is the **Tomb-Chapel of Amenemhet** (No. 82), scribe and steward of the vizier (time of Tuthmosis III). It is also of cruciform type with a square chamber at the end.

(1) Relatives at banquet. (2) Deceased offers to ancestors. (3) Deceased before offerings. (4) Hunting in desert. (5) Passage to see sun-disk and funeral. (6) Procession to the Goddess of the West. (7) Dead man and wife with offerings. (8) Stele, funeral feast. (9) Niche with statues of Amenemhet and wife.

Due E is the **Tomb-Chapel of Antefoker** (No. 60), vizier and governor of Thebes (time of Senusert I), and also dedicated to his mother Sent. It is a long, narrow chapel with two chambers and a niche in the inner chamber. The paintings are on a poor straw plaster and of inferior quality.

(1) Agricultural scenes. (2) Antefoker fishing and fowling and (3) hunting. (4) Antefoker and wife inspect offerings. (5) Voyage to Abydos. (6) Funeral. (7) Harpists and offerings. (8) Offering bearers. (9) Antefoker and mother with offerings. (10) False door of Sent.

## THE RAMESSEUM

Beyond the Complex of Hatshepsut the road runs SW. E of the road are the sites of two destroyed temples, the *Temple of Tuthmosis III* and the smaller *Temple of Merneptah-Siptah*. W of the road is the Cemetery of Shaykh ʿAbd al-Qurnah (see above). At 800m, S of the *Ramesseum Resthouse* and E of a destroyed *Temple of Amenhotep II*, stands the ***Ramesseum**. In plan it is similar to a state temple. It is dedicated not only to Ramesses II but also to Amun-United-with-Eternity. To the Greeks this was the *Memnomium* or the *Tomb of Osymandyas*, their rendering of Usermaetre, one of the names of Ramesses II. Champollion called it the Ramesseum, a name it has retained.

*The Ramesseum seen in the early 19C by Napoleon's scholars for the* Description de l'Egypt. *The fallen colossus of Ramesses II can be seen in the courtyard*

It was constructed here because Seti I had already built a small shrine and the ground was therefore holy. It consists of the main temple, a palace to the S and a large number of mud-brick storerooms lying mainly to the N of the site, the whole complex being surrounded by a brick wall 260m by 170m. Although the building is nearly rectangular, its axis is distinctly oblique, and so every hall and court of the temple is slightly askew, more noticeable in plan than from the ground. The first two pylons have collapsed and the temple is entered from the level of the second court. They fell because of inadequate foundations, and because they were built on land annually inundated and therefore subject to change of level.

Against the NE wall is the small **Temple of Seti I**, rebuilt at the same time as the main temple, the original being the work of Seti I, with his foundation deposits. Built of limestone, it is approached by two parallel stairways leading to a columned portico fronting a columned hall. Two parallel square hypostyle halls follow, behind which are three chapels, apparently dedicated to different unknown deities, although it is probable that one was Amun.

Approaching the Main Temple, the stone *First Pylon*, 67m wide, has collapsed. On the inner face are scenes of the Battle of Kadesh. In the *First Court* in the centre of the colonnaded S wall is the entry to the *Palace*, in which Ramesses must have stayed during the principal feasts held on the West Bank. Similar in plan to the first of the two palaces at Madīnet Habu, it is slightly larger and of better workmanship. The *Audience Hall* possesses 16 columns as against 12 at Madīnet Habu.

To the W in front of the collapsed *Second Pylon* is the base of the black granite seated *Colossus of Ramesses II*, the head of which has fallen into the Second Court. Although now much worn, originally it must have been 17.3m high and weighed c 1000 tons. It was still upright when Diodorus Siculus visited the site in the 1C AD.

The *Second Court* is colonnaded and flanking the E and W walls are Osiride figures of Ramesses II. Fragments of two *granite colossi* lie in the courtyard. The upper section of the left-hand one is in BM, No. 19. It was on the arrival of this head in London that Sheeley wrote his sonnet 'Ozymandias':

I met a traveller from an antique land
Who said: 'Two vast and trunkless legs of stone
Stand in the desert ... Near them on the sand,
Half sunk, a shattered visage lies, whose frown,
And wrinkled lip, and sneer of cold command
Tell that its sculptor well those passions read
Which yet survive, stamped on these lifeless things,
The hand that mocked them, and the heart that fed.
And on the pedestal these words appear:
'My name is Ozymandias, King of Kings:
Look on my works ye mighty and despair'
Nothing beside remains. Round the decay
Of that colossal wreck, boundless and bare,
The lone and level sands stretch far away.

They once flanked the central stairway of the three that lead up to the *Hypostyle Hall* with 48 white sandstone columns, arranged in eight rows. In the upper register of the S side of the E wall is the famous scene of the storming of the city of Dapur, while on the base of the W wall are portrayed many of Ramesses' sons. A door in the centre of this wall leads to the *First Vestibule*, also called the Astronomical Room from the scenes on the ceiling. On the W wall are representations of the sacred boats of Amun, Mut and Khonsu. Beyond are *two small vestibules*, the second serving as the library, which each had eight columns. They are much ruined, as is the *Sanctuary* which lies behind to the W at the highest point of the temple. In the vaulted mud-brick *storerooms* found N and W of the

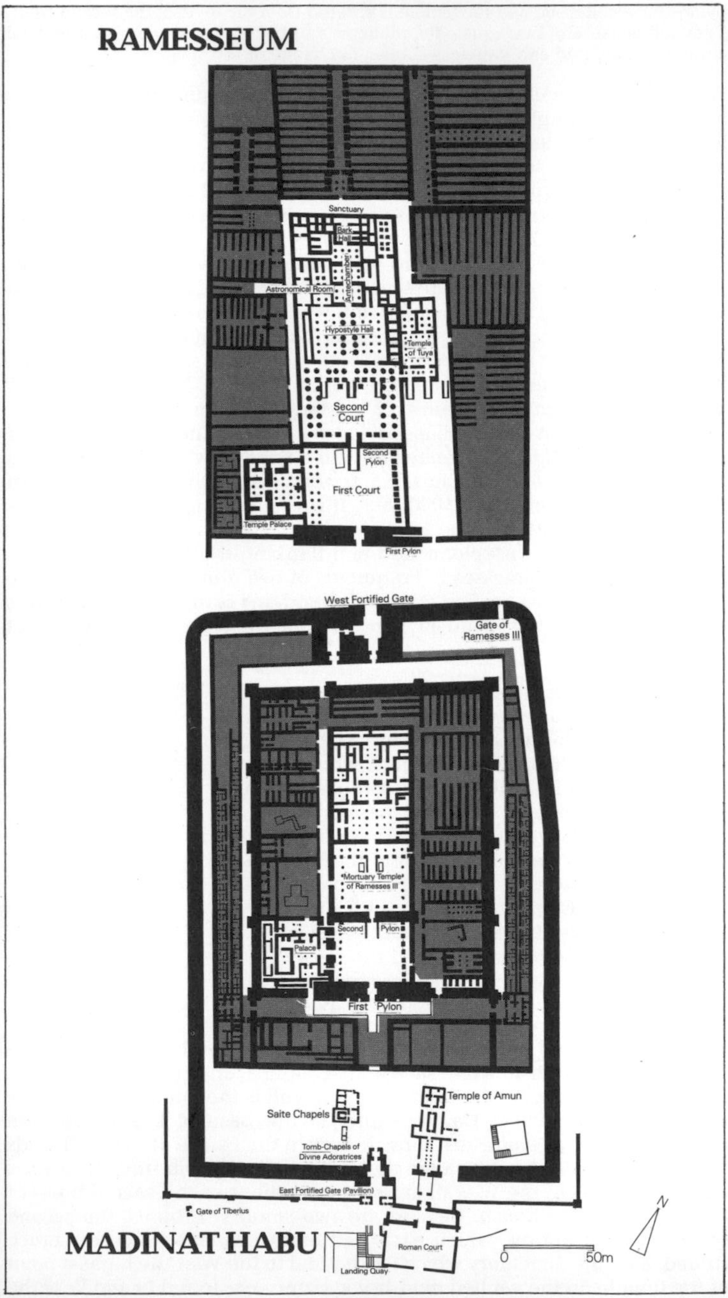
RAMESSEUM
Sanctuary
Bark Hall
Antechamber
Astronomical Room
Hypostyle Hall
Temple of Tuya
Second Court
Second Pylon
First Court
Temple Palace
First Pylon
West Fortified Gate
Gate of Ramesses III
Mortuary Temple of Ramesses III
Second Pylon
Palace
First Pylon
Temple of Amun
Saite Chapels
Tomb-Chapels of Divine Adoratrices
East Fortified Gate (Pavilion)
Gate of Tiberius
MADINAT HABU
Roman Court
Landing Quay
0
50m
N

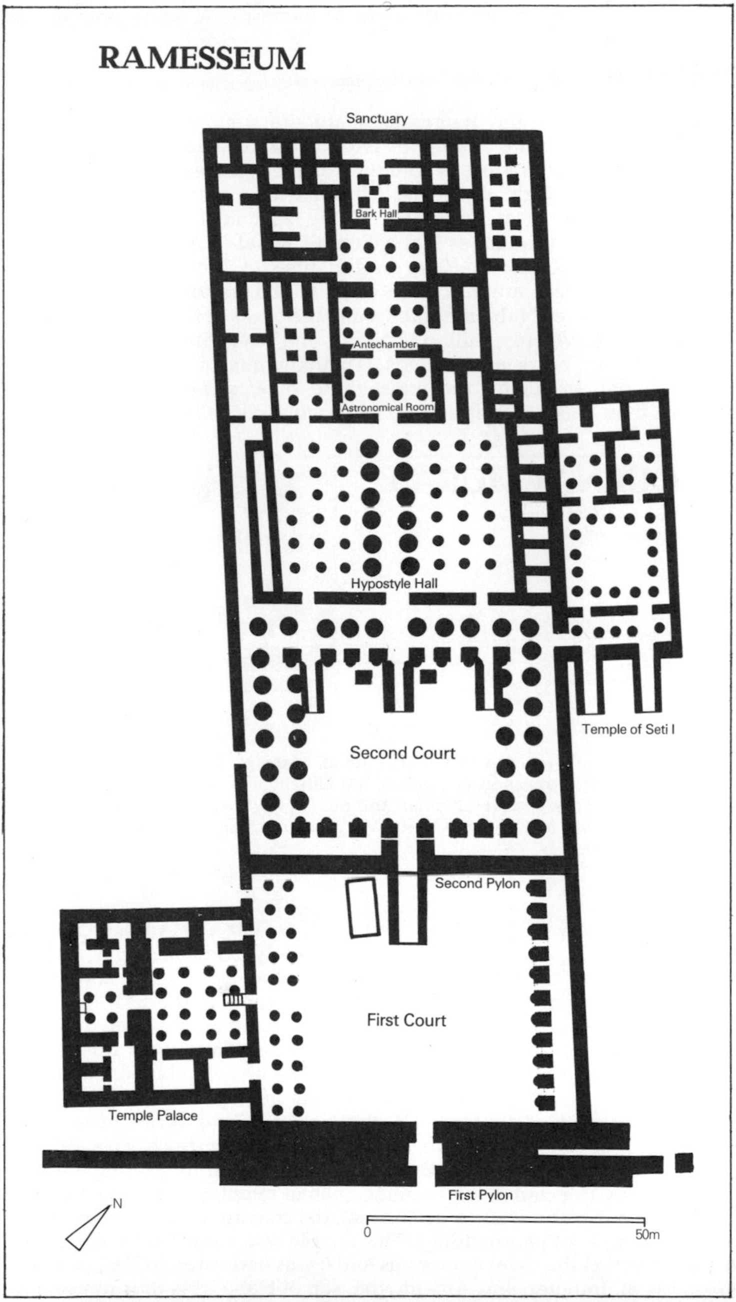
RAMESSEUM
Sanctuary
Bark Hall
Antechamber
Astronomical Room
Hypostyle Hall
Temple of Seti I
Second Court
Second Pylon
First Court
Temple Palace
First Pylon
N
0
50m

main building were many cartouches of Ramesses II, some now in the Berlin Museum.

## QURNAT MURAʻĪ.

Immediately SW of the Ramesseum are the sites of more destroyed temples. The first is the *Temple of Wazmose* and beside it are the much larger *Temple of Tuthmosis IV* and the *Temple of Tausert*. 250m W of the road is the **Cemetery of Qurnat Muraʻī** with more *Tomb-Chapels of Nobles*. Only the most accessible of the 20 tombs is worth visiting. Situated on the lower slopes is the **Tomb-Chapel of Amenhotep**, called **Huy** (No. 40), viceroy of Kush at the time of Tutankhamun (much damaged). The walls are thinly coated with mud plaster. Its main interest lies in the scenes of Nubian notables and the taxes of Kush. Scenes show Huy invested as viceroy, sailing to Nubia, and rows of taxes and presents, furniture, gold, bows and shields. Tutankhamun is shown in a light shelter under a canopy receiving these objects, and also receiving presents from Kush. The inner chamber with four pillars is very ruined.

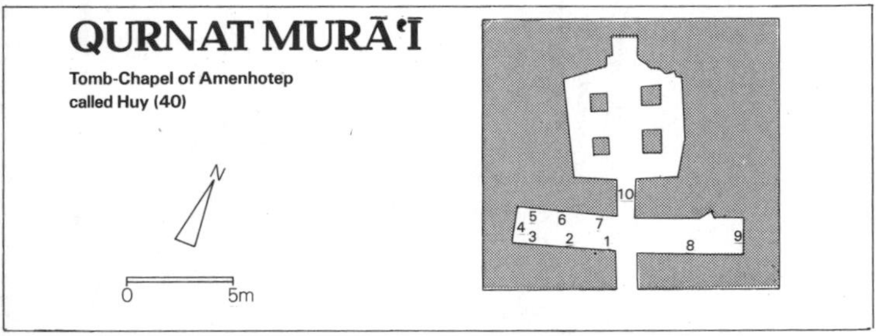
QURNAT MURĀʻĪ
Tomb-Chapel of Amenhotep
called Huy (40)
N
0
5m
10
4
5
3
6
2
7
1
8
9

Scenes on the walls are as follows: (1) Huy and family. (2) Huy inspects Nubian taxes. (3) Ships and transport of produce. (4) Offerings to Anubis. (5) Huy returns from Nubia. (6) Huy receives Nubian tribute. (7) Huy before Tutankhamun. (8) Appointment of Huy as viceroy of Kush. (9) Huy adores Osiris. (10) Hymn to Ptah at entry to inner room.

## DEIR AL-MADĪNAH

W of the cemetery (300m) is the site known as **Deir al-Madīnah** (Monastery of the Town), a name acquired during early Christian times when it was occupied by Coptic monks. The wide valley by which it is reached was decorated until the early 20C with stelae (now in the EM).

Originally the area was used by artisans working on the royal tombs in the Valley of the Kings, which was called the 'Place of Truth'. Three entities compose the site which catered for the life, worship and death of the workmen, the town, the temple and the necropolis. Westernmost is the small **Temple of Ptolemy IV**, the last of a long series of temples constructed on the same site, the earliest dating back probably to Amenhotep III of the 18 Dyn. Built of sandstone, and measuring 15m by 10m, it is tiny in comparison to other Theban temples. It stands within a mud-brick enclosure wall some 50m sq., the construction of which shows a good example of pan bedding. This temple was intended for the use of the workmen at the royal necropolis and it was dedicated to Hathor of the West, Ma'at, Imhotep and Amenhotpe, son of Hapu. It is thus unusual in having two deified men as its gods. Amenhotep I and Queen Ahmose-Nefertari, deified early 18 Dyn. rulers particularly connected with the necropolis workers, were also worshipped here.

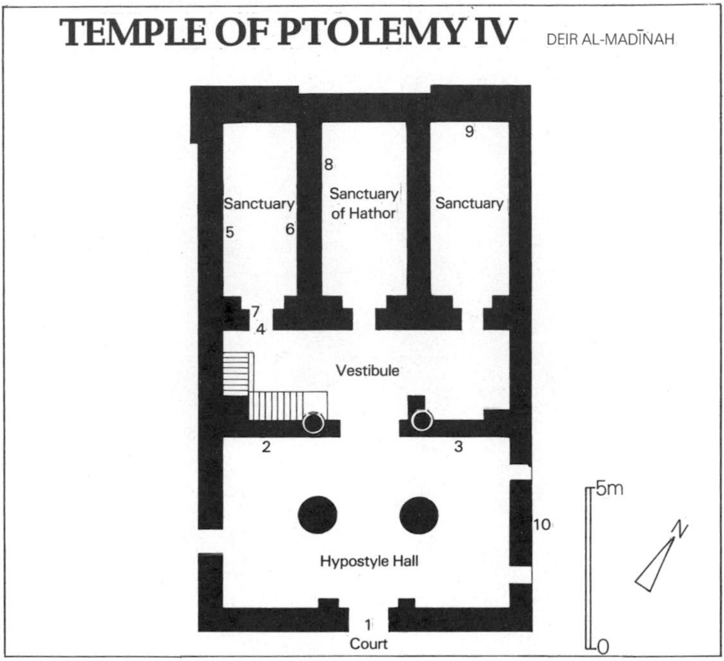
TEMPLE OF PTOLEMY IV
DEIR AL-MADĪNAH
9
8
Sanctuary
Sanctuary of Hathor
Sanctuary
5
6
7
4
Vestibule
2
3
5m
10
N
Hypostyle Hall
1
Court
0

The temple is very simple. On the outside are several Greek graffiti and a drawing of a camel. This is an indication of how far N the Blemmyes, a camel-riding Nubian tribe who left inscriptions at the Kalābsha Temple (Rte 39), penetrated. Inside there is first a two-columned hall with Hathor-headed capitals. On the screens separating this hall from the main structure are figures of Amenhotep and Imhotep. In the inner shrine Ptolemy appears, often accompanied by Arsinoe, his wife, sacrificing to the gods. There are three inner chapels and on the left wall of the left chapel is a judgement scene before the enthroned Osiris, rarely seen in temples, while above the lintel is a four-headed ram symbolising the four winds.

S of the temple is the most interesting site at Deir al-Madīnah, the **Workmen's Village**. It was excavated first by the Italian Mission before 1914 and later by the French Institute in Cairo between 1917–47.

There are 70 houses, of mud-brick on stone foundations, with stairs leading to an upper floor or roof. Most have three rooms and some have been decorated with simple wall paintings. The earliest village dates to the reign of Amenhotep III, but in the BM is a refoundation stele dating to Tuthmosis III. In time the workmen developed the cult of Amenhotep I and Queen Ahmose Nefertari, who were invoked especially for oracles. In fact stele and ostraca from the village show that Amenhotep was the patron god of the village. These ostraca also supply much information on life in the village. It is known, for example, that the men had a ten-day stint, and were divided into two gangs, each of which had two watches. Each gang had a foreman, a scribe, guardians of the tomb, doorkeepers, serfs and slaves. The slaves cleaned the houses, moving round on a weekly rota, while the serfs carried water, fruit, oil, vegetables and supplies to the village from Thebes. The workmen were all free men of the Land of Egypt as is testified by their wills and other documents. Many ostraca have trial drawings by the craftsmen, some of great beauty.

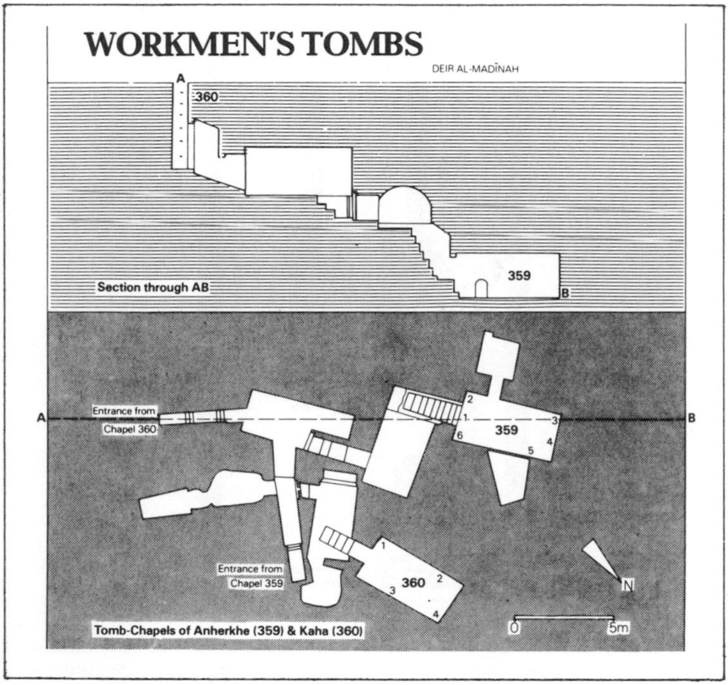
WORKMEN'S TOMBS
DEIR AL-MADĪNAH
A
360
359
Section through AB
B
Entrance from
Chapel 360
359
1
2
3
4
5
6
Entrance from
Chapel 359
360
1
2
3
4
N
0
5m
Tomb-Chapels of Anherkhe (359) & Kaha (360)

In the nearby hills surrounding the village, though mainly concentrated to the W, are the **Workmen's Tombs** built by the artisans for themselves. These are unlike those of the 18 Dyn. nobles. Many date to the 19–20 Dyns and the workmen were greatly influenced by their work on the royal tombs. Thus the decoration tends to have a dark orange background and to have more scenes of the Afterworld. Above the tomb a small chapel with a pyramidal roof was built, where offerings could be brought to the dead man. It is somewhat ironic that the pyramid which began as a symbol of the royal tomb came to be the mark of the workman's grave. Only a selection of the most important is given below.

One of the closest tombs to the temple is (NW) that of **Nefer'abet** (No. 5), a servant in the Place of Truth (Ramesside). A stair leads to a vaulted room, showing Nefer'abet worshipping the Goddess of the West. In the second room the deified Amenhotep I is shown worshipping Mertseger and Thoth purifies the dead man. There are no scenes of daily life. To the W is **Kha'a** (No. 8), chief of the Great Place of the time of Amenhotep II–III, a small chapel (the material from here is now in the Turin Museum). Just E is **Irinufer** (No. 290), a servant in the Place of Truth during the 20 Dyn. Although in a good state of preservation the paintings are of poor quality. To the SE is **Ipy** (No. 217), sculptor at the time of Ramesses II, unusual in this group in that there are more pictures of everyday life. The entrance wall of the chapel shows six registers of ploughing, reaping, flocks and herds, offering to the serpent goddess Renenutet, a vintage scene and fowling in the marshes (damaged). The rear wall is also very disfigured, but on the left the king is seen at the Window of Appearances and Ipy's house is shown in its garden, with fruit and flowers.

Closeby to the SE is **Peshedu** (No. 3), a servant in the Place of Truth during the Ramesside period. A steep entry stair leads to a vaulted corridor depicting on either side Anubis crouching on his shrine. Next is the burial chamber where Peshedu is shown praying under a palm tree by the side of a lake. On the walls are inscriptions from the Book of the Dead. The sarcophagus which stood against the rear wall was made not of a single block, but of limestone slabs.

Directly S up a slope is the *Resthouse of the Dept of Antiquities*, previously the expedition house of the IFAO, and beyond that **Nakht-Amun** (No. 335), sculptor and wb priest of Amenhotep I (Ramesside). The paintings are funerary scenes executed on a yellow ground in black and red. Some distance further S is **Khabekhnet** (No. 2), son of Sennedjem, of the time of Ramesses II, with a scene of mummified fish. E towards the Workmen's Village are the tombs of ***Amenennakht** (No. 218) and his sons ***Nefermaat** (No. 219) and ***Khaemteri** (220), all servants in the Place of Truth in Ramesside times. The chapels are built side by side and the three tombs communicate, one with another, underground. The shaft descends first to Amennakht's tomb where three doors lead to the burial chambers. The first room shows the dead man and his wife kneeling drinking from a basin under a palm. The other room shows Isis and Nephthys as kites, and Anubis before the mummy. Immediately S just above the workmen's village is the most frequently visited of the tombs, that of **Sennedjem** or Sennezem (No. 1), servant in the Place of Truth. In 1886 the tomb was cleared and the burial goods are now in the EM. A vaulted tomb-chamber is reached down a steep flight of steps. The tomb depicts Osiris, a cat killing a snake under the sacred tree, the Fields of Yaru, and Anubis engaged in embalming a mummy. The vaulted ceiling is divided into eight parts and shows Sennedjem opening the gates of the W to meet the gods of the Afterworld and the sky.

Adjacent to the S are three tombs belonging to members of the same family which run into each other. They are ***Anherkhe** (No. 359), chief workman; ***Kaha** (No. 360), foreman in the Place of Truth, and **Huy** (No. 361), great carpenter in the Place of Truth, the earliest and also the smallest. A section through these tomb-chapels gives an idea of their steepness and small size. In the tomb of Anherkhe the scenes are: (1) Anubis jackals. (2) Deceased and wife with offerings adore Osiris and Hathor of the West. (3) Deceased led by Anubis to Osiris. (4) Anubis tends mummy on a bier. On the vaulted ceiling the deceased and wife adore Thoth, Anubis, the sons of Horus, below is a text. In the tomb of Kaha they are: (1) Ahmose-Nefertari and Amenhotep I. (2) Deceased with staff leaves the tomb with his wife and son in a boat; negative confession, harpist with song and scenes in the Afterworld. (3) Deceased adores ba on a pylon, adores Ptah and offers to Osiris. (4) Deceased and sons before Ptah and Osiris. The tomb of Huy shows the Abydos pilgrimage and the funeral procession.

A track leads W to the Valley of the Queens (see below) and another returns S to the main road along the foothills past the monuments.

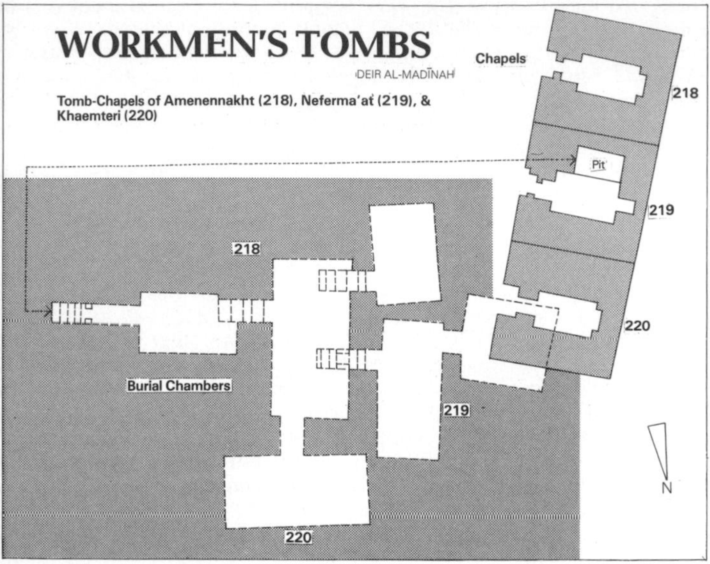
WORKMEN'S TOMBS
DEIR AL-MADĪNAH
Tomb-Chapels of Amenennakht (218), Neferma'at (219), & Khaemteri (220)
Chapels
218
Pit
219
220
218
Burial Chambers
219
220
N

## VALLEY OF THE QUEENS

Beyond Qurnat Muraʿī (500m) the road passes (W) the destroyed *Temple of Merneptah* and arrives at a crossroads. To the SW lies Madīnat Habū (see below). Take the road to the W to the **Valley of the Queens** (Ar. Bibān al-Ḥarim or Bibān al-Malikat: Gates of the Ladies or Gates of the Queens) which runs E to W. Toilets to the left of car park. Towards the middle of the 18 Dyn. this valley was used for the burial of several high officials. Most of the wives of the 18 Dyn. rulers were buried in the same tombs as their husbands and it was not until the 19 Dyn. that this area was used for the wives and children of the royal family. Called the 'Place of Beauty', it was utilised throughout this and the following dynasty but then gradually fell into disuse. The earliest royal tomb seems to be that of Queen Sit Reʾ, wife of Ramesses I, while the most notable is that of Queen Nefertari, wife of Ramesses II.

There are nearly 80 tombs in these shallow valleys but many of them are unnamed or uninscribed, or if inscribed the cartouches are often left blank. Unlike those in the Valley of the Kings, these are small tombs easily entered and with brightly coloured wall paintings. The plan usually consists of a small antechamber, long narrow corridor, several side chambers, many of which are undecorated, and at the end the tomb-chapel. Most of these tombs were cleared by the Italian Egyptologist Schiaparelli before World War I. Normally, unless there is a great deal of time, only three tombs are visited: those of Queen Tyti (No. 52), Prince Amun-hir-Khopshef (No. 55) and Prince Kha'emweset (No. 44).

The first tomb of note is on the N side some distance up the hill. This is the *Tomb of Queen Tent-Opet* (No. 74), wife of Ramesses IV (?). A little higher on the same side is the *Tomb of Queen Bant Anta* (No. 71), daughter of Ramesses II. Further W is the **Tomb of Queen Nefertari** (No. 66), wife of

Ramesses II. This is one of the most imposing tombs in the valley with workmanship varying from excellent to poor. In recent years it has suffered greatly from salt encrustation.

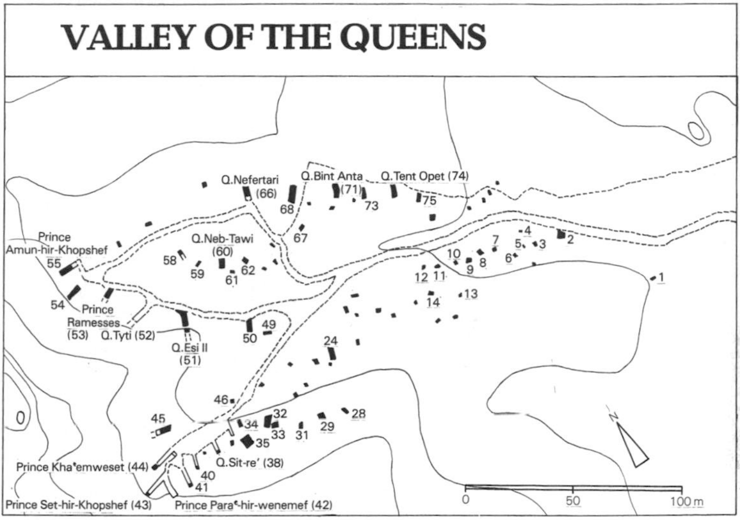
VALLEY OF THE QUEENS
Q.Nefertari (66)
Q.Bint Anta (71)
Q.Tent Opet (74)
Prince Amun-hir-Khopshef 55
Q.Neb-Tawi (60)
Prince Ramesses (53)
Q.Tyti (52)
Q.Esi II (51)
Prince Kha'emweset (44)
Q.Sit-re' (38)
Prince Set-hir-Khopshef (43)
Prince Para'-hir-wenemef (42)
0 50 100 m
N

Nefertari's origins are unknown. She was the principal consort of Ramesses II and already married to him when he ascended the throne in 1304 BC. Her pre-eminence over his other queens was shown by her accompanying Ramesses to Abydos to the royal audience at the appointment of the new high priest of Amun in year 1, by the appearance of her figure with his on the pylon of Luxor Temple carved in year 3, and by her sharing a temple at the Ramesseum with the Queen-mother, Tuya. Her greatest honour was in the temple at Abū Simbel (Rte 40) which she shared with the goddess Hathor. There she is depicted as often as her husband. This temple was dedicated in year 24 (1280 BC) but the fact that Ramesses II's eldest daughter, Meryetamun, carried out part of the ceremonies may indicate that Nefertari was either ill or dead. She is heard of no more after this.

A stairway leads down to the hall where the reliefs are largely on plaster overlying the base limestone. (1) Outer lintel, Nefertari's titles with the horizon disk between Isis and Nephthys. First Chamber (B). (2) Registers of the Book of the Gates. (5) Nefertari before Osiris. (6) Projection, Anubis and Neith. (7) Projection, Selket and Osiris. Inner side chamber (C), Nefertari makes offerings to the gods. (8) Above, Sons of Horus and Queen's titles. Corridor (D), Queen making offerings. (9) Nefertari making burnt offerings to Osiris and Atum. Burial Chamber (E), (10) W and N walls, Book of the Gates. (11) N and E walls, Nefertari adoring Book of the Gates. Pillars, Isis and Osiris symbols. (12) Cartouche between two uraei, Isis and Selket.

On the S side of the path is the *Tomb of Queen Neb-Tawi* (No. 60), mother of Ramesses II.

A side valley branches off to the SW (see below). Continue W along the main valley where the first important tomb on the S is the *Tomb-Chapel of Queen Esi II* (No. 51), mother of Ramesses VI.

Beyond, also to the S is the **Tomb of Queen Tyti** (No. 52). It is not established which of the Ramesside kings was the husband of this queen.

She is called royal daughter, royal wife and royal mother. The tomb consists of a long corridor leading to a square chapel on each side of which is a further smaller square chamber, that on the left being the burial chamber. The painting is unfortunately faded and rather damaged.

**TOMB-CHAPELS IN THE VALLEY OF THE QUEENS**

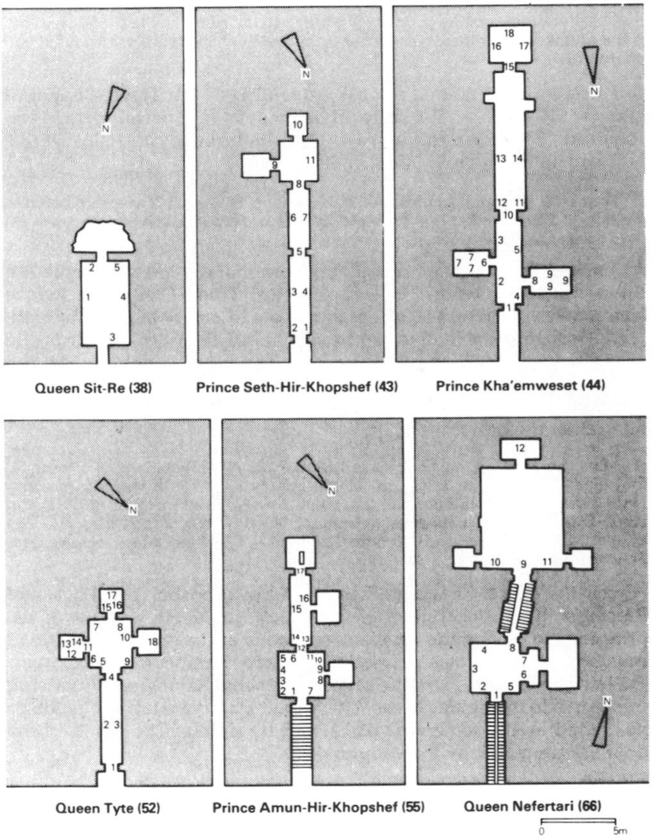
0
5m

Queen Sit-Re (38) Prince Seth-Hir-Khopshef (43) Prince Kha'emweset (44)

Queen Tyte (52) Prince Amun-Hir-Khopshef (55) Queen Nefertari (66)

(1) Name and titles of the queen. (2–3) Winged Ma'at kneeling, the queen before Thoth, Ptah and the four sons of Horus. (4) Winged Ma'at, Neith on left, Selket on right. (5) Jackal and lion guardians. (6) Two baboons and monkey with a bow. (7–10) Guardians of doorways including a curious naked squatting boy. (11) Anubis. (12–13) The four sons of Horus. (14) Osiris (damaged); (15–16) The queen. (17) Osiris with Nephthys, Thoth, Neith and Selket. (18) The queen and tree-goddess and Hathor as cow in the western mountains.

Where the path turns to the N is the *Tomb of Prince Ramesses* (No. 53), and at the westernmost point of the valley is the **Tomb of Prince**

**Amun-hir-Khopshef** (No. 55), son of Ramesses III, overseer of the horses and royal scribe. Steps lead down to the tomb which consists of a large square hall off which a corridor leads to the burial chamber, which is unfinished. Two side chambers are likewise incomplete. The colouring of the painting in the tomb is excellent and fresh. Accompanying the prince in the paintings is his father Ramesses III.

(1) Isis with Thoth keeping a record. (2) Ptah in a shrine. (3) Ptah Tatenen; two of the sons of Horus. (4) Duamutef and (5) Amset. (6–7) Isis and Nephthys. (8) Shu. The other two sons of Horus: (9) Qebenshef and (10) Hapi. (11) Hathor. (12) Isis. (13) Nephthys. (14) Inmutef. (15) Book of the Gates with the guardians holding knives. (16) Book of the Gates. (17) Above the lintel, winged uraei. Unpainted head and shoulders of the goddess Nephthys. In the centre of the burial chamber is the uninscribed anthropoid sarcophagus. Bones of a foetus were found in one corner.

The first tomb of note in the SW side valley is the **Tomb-Chapel of Queen Sit-Re** (No. 38), wife of Ramesses I. (Special permission required.) This is the earliest royal tomb in the valley and consists of a hall and an incomplete burial chamber.

(1) Four sons of Horus, Anubis, Ma'at, Nephthys, Neith. (2) The queen before a shrine. (3) Lion-headed god followed by Ma'at. (4) Kiosk containing gods. (5) Two boats and three gods.

At the westernmost end of the valley where it starts to rise steeply are three important tombs. The first is the **Tomb-Chapel of Prince Kha'emweset** (No. 44), son of Ramesses III and Sem priest of Ptah. Here two corridors lead to the square burial chamber with two side chapels opening off the first corridor. The tomb is narrow and the paintings protected by glass. Ramesses III is portrayed presenting his son to the deities of the Afterworld and is represented rather more often than the prince.

(1) Ma'at kneeling. (2–3) The prince before Ptah. (4–5) Ramesses III offering to Ptah-Sokar. (6) In the thickness Horus-Inmutef. (7) Neith, Selket, Isis and Nephthys. (8) Horus-Inmutef. (9) Isis, Nephthys, Neith and Selket. (10) Isis and Nephthys. (11–12) Kha'emweset as Inmutef. (13–14) Book of the Gates. (15) The king's titles. (16) The king offers to Thoth. (17) The king offers incense. (18) Seated Osiris.

Next is the **Tomb-Chapel of Prince Set-hir-khopshef** (No. 43), son of Ramesses III and charioteer of the Great Stable. He was one of the princes who died in the smallpox epidemic at the end of the reign of Ramesses III. Two corridors lead to a square chamber off which opens the burial chamber. Here the scenes also show Ramesses introducing the prince to the deities of the Afterworld. Unfortunately the painting has faded and is somewhat blackened by smoke. The lintels of the door are protected by the winged disk.

(1) The king and the prince before Geb, Ptah, Anubis, Re'-Harakhte, Isis and Nephthys. (2) The king and the prince before Osiris, Shu, Atum and (3) the four sons of Horus. (4) The king and the prince offering incense and libations. (5) Two figures of Osiris on throne, seated back to back.

S of the last is the tomb of another son of Ramesses III. This is the *Tomb-Chapel of Para'-hir-wenemef* (No. 42), charioteer of the Stable of the Great House. It consists of a corridor, square hall and side chapel.

The scenes in the corridor show Ramesses II and the prince offering to the gods, including Ptah, Mertserger, Geb and Osiris. In the hall the queen is shown with uraeus sceptre before Osiris, the king and the prince before Anubis, Nebnery (a lion-headed god) and Herema'at, a naked boy. By the doorway to the side chapel Horus is shown on the left and Anubis on the right, both on standards. The side chapel is undecorated.

## THE COLOSSI OF MEMNON

Turn down the road to the SE with a canal to the right. This road eventually leads back to the ferry. After 600m on the N stand the ***Colossi of Memnon** (Ar. al-Ṣanamān: the Two Idols). These two immense figures of Amenhotep III sat in front of the mortuary temple of the king.

The pylon, probably of mud-brick, has been washed away as for centuries this area was within the inundation zone. The main temple which stretched W behind the statues has been entirely destroyed, but it must have been a magnificent building. The stele on which Amenhotep recorded his work was removed by Merneptah (in the EM). On it the king claims that he built the temple of 'white sandstone, wrought with gold throughout, its floor covered in silver, its doors with electrum'. Unfortunately it was systematically robbed to build the temples of the later kings.

*The Colossi of Memnon, depicted in the* Description de l'Egypte

The colossi are made of sandstone, probably from the quarries at Gabal Silsilah. With their pedestals and crowns they were 21.3m high. Originally monolithic, they have been much damaged. In the earthquake of 27 BC part of the N colossus fell and was cracked. It became famous in the Roman period because it was said to sing. Theories attribute this to expansion of the stone when it was warmed by the sun in the morning and contraction in the evening, or to the wind reverberating through the cracks. Its restoration by the Roman emperor Septimius Severus (AD 193–211) corrected the fault, and it has been silent ever since. The Greeks regarded the statues as representing the Trojan hero Memnon, son of the goddess Eos, who was killed by Achilles.

During the Roman period the site became a popular resort and many prominent Romans and other travellers wrote verses and left epigrams upon the stone. The colossi are referred to by many classical authors including Strabo, Pausanius, Pliny and Juvenal. The statues show Amenhotep seated upon his throne on the sides of which the two Nile gods of Upper and Lower Egypt unite the Two Lands by tying together the lotus and the papyrus, symbolising the S and the N. Beside the legs of each of the statues there is a small figure of Queen Tiye, wife of Amenhotep III on the right, and on the left Queen Mutemua, his mother.

To the SW is the *House of the Dept of Antiquities*. After another 1.65km the road reaches the ferry for the return to **Luxor**.

## MADĪNAT HABU

500m beyond the crossroads the SE road terminates at **Madīnat Habu** (the Town of Habu). There is a cluster of buildings including the *Habu Hotel* (accom. basic and only for the hardy, but refreshments available for the casual visitor). Dominating the site is the **Mortuary Temple of Ramesses III** (fee), second only in size to the Great Temple at Karnak. It usually suffers by being the last monument visited but it is well worth a protracted morning tour. (See plan on p 588.)

The temple was built on a sacred site already occupied by a small temple raised by Hatshepsut and Tuthmosis III, which ironically remained in use long after the great temple had fallen into decay. The name of the area in ancient times was *Djamet* and during the Coptic period *Jeme* when it was a town of some size, extant until at least the 8C AD, of which the remains lie to the N and S of the temple.

The small **Temple of Hatshepsut and Tuthmosis III**, called Jeser Ast (Sacred Place) still stands to the SE of the main temple astride the two massive enclosure walls of Ramesses' temple, the outer of mud-brick, the inner of stone. The form of Amun worshipped here was from Hermopolis in Middle Egypt. Under the foundations are the remains of an earlier temple dating to the beginning of the 18 Dyn. or perhaps even to the Middle Kingdom. It was originally surrounded by a grove of acacia trees, which extended as far as the Colossi of Memnon, and which existed until the 18C. Built on a platform, it was a peripteral building, designed so that a view of the whole could be obtained from all sides. Around the *Sanctuary* for the sacred bark of Amun are several pillared halls, open on three sides. Screen walls connect the pillars as far as the main entry. At the rear are several cult rooms which would have been closed. The open aspect was immediately spoilt by the building of a high mud-brick girdle wall by Hatshepsut. That she ordered it is evidenced by the stamped bricks and foundation deposits. Hatshepsut's sanctuary was called the 'Holiest of Places'. Under the floor, now missing, a large granite statue of Tuthmosis III and Amun was found. It probably stood here but was mutilated and buried in the ʿAmārnah period. Inscriptions in this temple are extremely important. During the ʿAmārnah interlude the names of Amun were erased, to be restored by Horemheb and Seti I. Ramesses III removed the enclosure wall so that the temple could be incorporated within his larger complex.

During the 25 Dyn. the Great Royal Votress Amenordais, sister of King Shabaka,

**GREAT TEMPLE OF RAMESSES III**

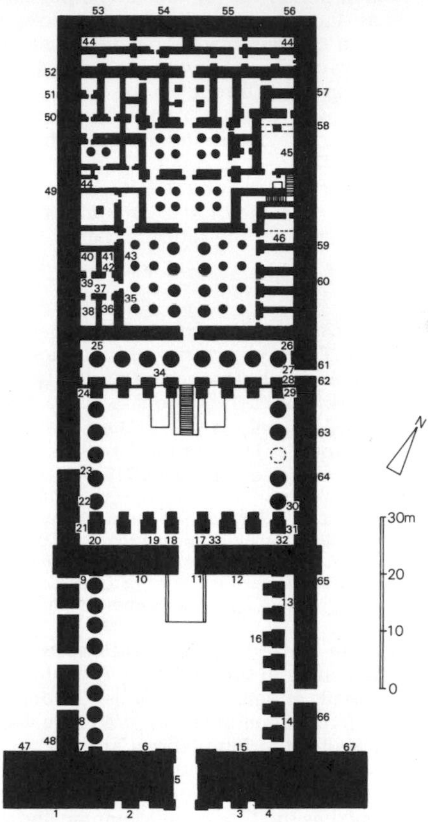
53
54
55
56
44
44
52
51
50
57
58
45
49
44
46
59
40
41
42
43
39
37
60
35
38
36
25
26
61
34
27
28
62
24
29
63
23
64
22
30
21
31
20
19
18
17
33
32
9
10
11
12
65
13
16
8
14
66
47
48
7
6
15
67
5
1
2
3
4
N
30m
20
10
0

**SAITE CHAPEL**

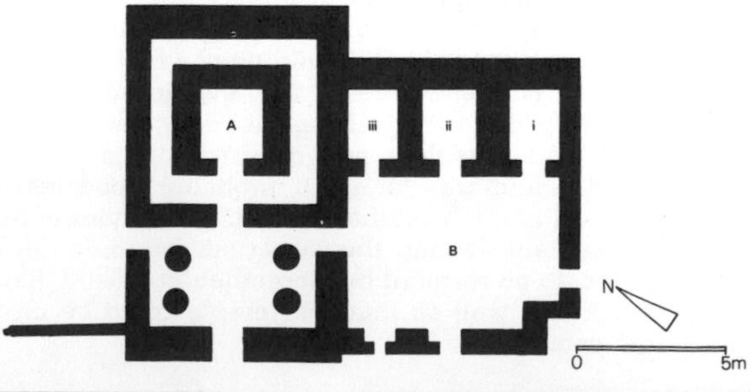
A
iii
ii
i
B
N
0
5m

undertook modifications to the interior. Because of the status of the building several high officials were interred here at this time. Further work was undertaken during the 26 Dyn. for Sabakon when the earliest pylon was erected in front of the temple, joined to the temple by an inappropriately long narrow hallway. At the same time the enclosure wall was rebuilt. After the Persian occupation the 30 Dyn. added to the structure, including the replacement of the mud-brick enclosure wall with one of stone. Nectanebo I had an open columned porch with screens and wooden beams supporting the roof built in front of the pylon, which served as a reception room for the sacred procession before it passed into the temple. In the Ptolemaic period further alterations were made and a large stone pylon was erected in front of the earlier one, with a portico. Antoninus Pius added the large forecourt (39.6m by

*Madīnat Habu. An engaged colossus of the king in the first court*

25.4m). The interior was used as a church during early Christian times and the walls still bear traces of Coptic wall paintings, including one of St. Menas.

Immediately W is the Eastern fortified pavilion called the *Syrian Gate*, a free-standing sandstone structure, originally 22m high. It is a crenellated ornamental tower in the form of an Asiatic fortress, similar to those often shown on Egyptian paintings. Scenes on the outside depict the usual struggle with the enemies of Egypt. There are three storeys, on the first of which it is assumed Ramesses had his private apartments, probably the abode of the harem, with scenes of women playing music and instruments and bringing flowers (now inaccessible).

In the recess on the S side of the passage Ramesses is shown offering a seated figure of the goddess Maʾat to Ptah and Sekhmet. The figure of Ptah was originally inset with faience. Messages addressed to this image by the ordinary people were passed on to the great god of the temple, Amun.

Inside the gateway is a very large *Forecourt*, almost 81m across, and just to the W is the *Saite Chapel of the Divine Votress of Amun*, also called the Chapel of Amenordais I, the daughter of Kashta, King of Kush and last king of the 25 Dyn., for whom it was originally built. It is entered through a small forecourt with four columns which leads to a sanctuary surrounded by a processional corridor. A door on the N of the forecourt leads into another court in front of the Chapels of Nitocris (Shepenwepet III, daughter of Psamtik I), Shepenwepet II (daughter of Piankhy) and Mehit-n-usekht (Queen of Psamtik I). These chapels became a place of pilgrimage where small votive figures, mainly of Osiris, were left.

At the NE angle of the forecourt is the *Sacred Lake*, a stone-lined basin 18m long. On the W and S sides stairs lead down into the lake which once possessed gates bearing the cartouches of Nectanebo II. Around the main temple are the remains of the mud-brick *store rooms* and *priests' houses*.

Directly NE is the ***Mortuary Temple of Ramesses III**, built in sandstone as a mortuary temple but also as a memorial to the king's Libyan and Asiatic wars. (See also plan on p 595.)

Ramesses III's admiration of his predecessor Ramesses II extended to his building; this temple is almost a direct copy of the latter's mortuary temple at the Ramesseum. It is dedicated to 'Amun-Lord-of-Eternity; His House of Millions of Years'. The temple was reached by a canal from the river ending in a T-shaped basin where the barks containing the sacred statues and boats could have been turned, but the whole course of the canal has not been traced.

On the exterior the S wall has the remains of the Great Calendar of Feasts of the Temple, one of the longest inscriptions in existence. The W wall shows the Nubian wars while the N wall is the Sea Battle where the king is shown with the standards before Amun. Also depicted is the Egyptian fleet and the overthrow of enemies including the Philistines and the Libyans.

A *Pylon* (65m long, 27m high), one of the best preserved in Egypt, fronts the temple. The N side has lost several courses, reducing its height to 19m. Reliefs on the E wall show Ramesses on the right of the gate in front of Amun and on the right in front of Ptah. He is also seen ceremonially slaying prisoners in front of other gods. The gateway in the pylon leads through into the *First Court* (48m by 34m), flanked on the W by eight columns and on the E by seven Osiride pillars, those at the N only with the king. On the inner face of the pylon the scenes represent the defeat of the Libyans in the 11th year of the reign. On the S wall the king is shown counting hands and driving his chariot while on the W wall he provides Amun with three lines of captives (including the Philistines with feathered headdresses). On the N wall Ramesses attacks an Asiatic city and offers Amun two strings of captives, Asiatics, Libyans and Philistines.

The king smiting captives before (1) Amun-Reʿ, (2) Ptah, (3) Reʿ-Harakhte and (4) Amun-Reʿ. (5) The king adores Ptah, Sokar and Osiris. (6) Text of Year 2, battle with the Libyans. (7) The king going to the Feast of the Valley. (8) The king in chariot, and five registers of the marching army. (9) Ramesses III. (10) The king leading six rows of prisoners to Amun and Mut; those in the third row are Philistines. (11) Text of Year 8. (12–13) Upper register, the king offers to various gods; lower register, battle scenes. (14) Texts usurped by Ramesses VI. (15) Osiride pillar with bound Philistine at base. (16) Baboons.

S of the first court is the *Palace*, built of mud-brick with stone used only for lintels and doorposts. It was rebuilt at least twice, at first consisting of a simple series of rooms, scarcely adequate for a protracted royal stay. However, late in the reign a new enclosure wall was built and the palace enlarged. As it now stands it contains three suites at the rear for the harem, the royal suite beside them. In front is the audience chamber, from which steps lead to the Window of Appearances opening into the First Court, where the king could show himself, and reward his favourites. This was part of the earlier palace, but was incorporated into the later building. This feature is portrayed in many of the New Kingdom reliefs, especially at al-ʿAmārnah, but this is the only complete one to have survived, although an earlier one was found in the Mortuary Temple of Tuthmosis IV on the West Bank at Thebes. The doors to the E and W of this window were used by the king during the Feast of Opet and Feast of the Valley.

The *Second Court*, entered by a ramp, has a gallery of eight engaged king's figures on the S side, five columns on the N and S sides and a double row of columns on the W side. This court appears smaller than the First Court but is actually larger. During the period of the Coptic occupation the *Church of Jeme* was situated here. Some of the standing figures of the king were cut away to fit it in and much damage was done to the decorations of the temple. Scenes on the walls are mainly religious in character; on the N wall the Feast of Min and on the S wall the Feast of Sokar. The W wall shows the king before divinities with his name being written by Thoth. This was fronted by a wooden balcony (destroyed).

(17–18) Architrave, the king before Delta goddesses and Amun. (19–24) Upper register, procession of Sokar. (20) Defeat of Temehu. (21–22) Counting of hands. (23–24) Lower register, text of Year 5. (25–26) Upper register, the king offering to divinities; lower register, princes and princesses. (27) Above door, the king kneeling on symbol of Upper and Lower Egypt. (28) The king before Seth who has been defaced and changed into Horus, the king with four bags before Nekhbet, goddess of Upper Egypt. (29–30) Lower register, Feast of Amun, above are representations of the Feast of Min with the god carried on a canopied structure. (31) The king purified by Seth and Horus of Edfu. (32–33) The king led by Wadjet and Nekhbet and the Souls of Pe and Nekhen before the Theban Triad. (34) The king before Nekhbet.

The W door leads into a *Hypostyle Hall* (much destroyed). At the base of the entry walls are 13 of the royal princesses with their names, and two of the princes and ten names. Above the door the king kneels on the symbols of Upper and Lower Egypt. In this upper gallery quite a lot of colour remains in the reliefs. Here there was a central aisle of eight large

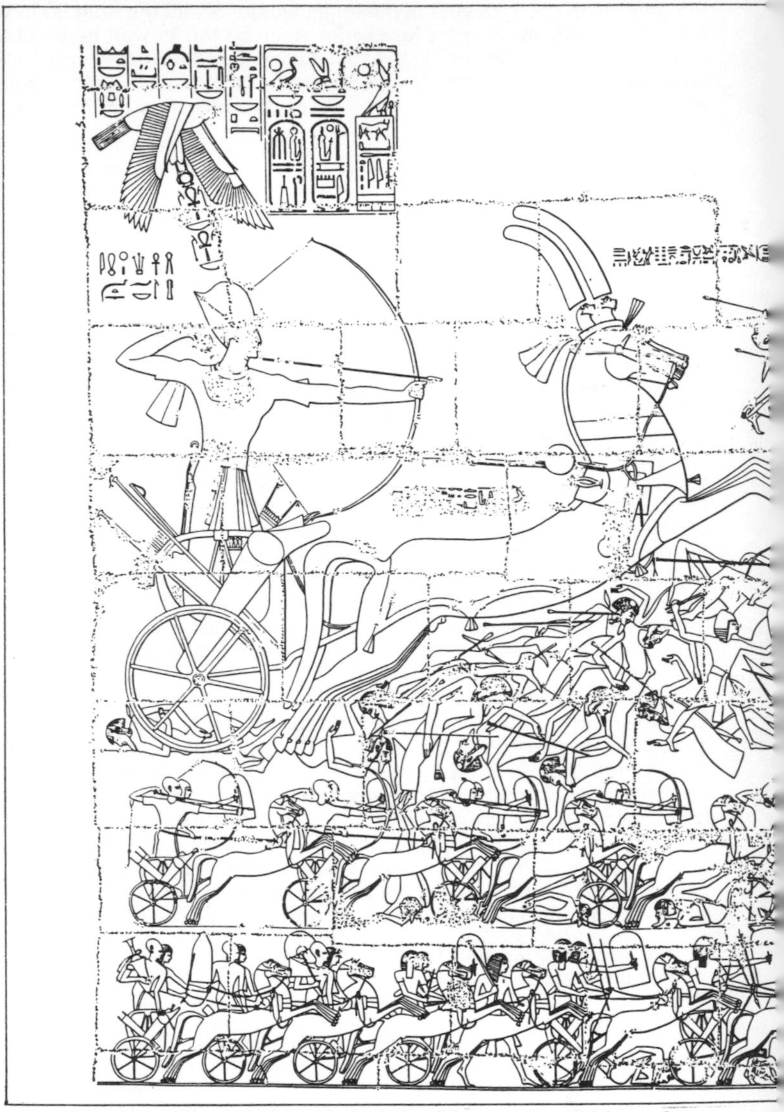

*Ramesses III campaigns against the Libyans: a relief from the wall of his mortuary temple (after Wrezenski). The Libyans are recognised by their long garments, sidelocks, beards and four-spoked chariots. Mercenaries fighting for the Egyptians are shown in the bottom register*

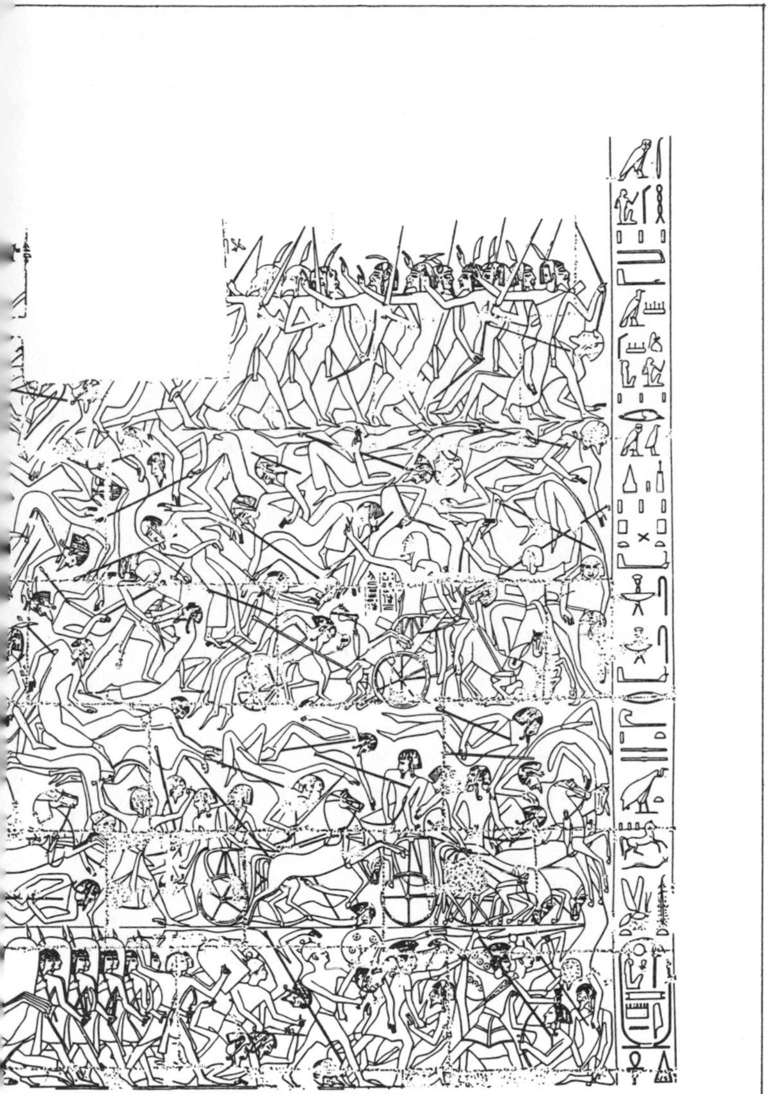

columns, presumably with clerestory windows, with a further eight columns on either side, deeply incised and filled with coloured faience decoration, fragments of which yet remain, although the columns are broken off short.

The only rooms that have survived more or less intact are the *Treasury* to the N and the rooms surrounding it. The scenes on the walls show the king offering gold and precious stones to Amun-Reʿ. In the adjoining rooms he presents coffers, pectorals and vases. On the opposite side in rooms 14 and 15 the animal sacrifices were made. The texts read: 'coming to make a pure sacrifice of oxen, cows, calves and beasts before Amun who has conferred royalty upon His Majesty'. Fat bulls are shown coming to be slaughtered, their heads decorated with plumes, and collars of lotus blossoms round their necks. After being purified by water, natron and incense the animals are killed and the flesh offered to Reʿ-Harakhte, Amun, Atum, Osiris and Isis. Wine is poured and offerings also made to Min, Amun, Mut and Khonsu. A long narrow chamber (9) opening directly off the hall was sacred to the deified Ramesses II, another example of Ramesses III's admiration of his predecessor. Here the king is depicted censing a sacred bark consecrated to Ramesses II-United-with-Eternity. Other rooms on the N side are sacred to Ptah-Sokar (16) and Ptah (18). The first room (19) on the right to the N of the hall is dedicated to the deified Ramesses III, who is shown seated on a throne followed by an unnamed queen receiving the homage of his children.

Behind the last hall is the *First Vestibule* (again badly damaged) and off the S side is a room (21) also sacred to the dead king where he is shown wearing Osiride symbols, the atef crown, crook and flail. On the N side is the *Chapel of Reʿ* (17). In the *Second Vestibule* are two groups of statues on each side of the central aisle. On the N side is a room (31) with niches for the Ennead worshipped in the temple, Amun, Mut, Khonsu, Ptah, Sekhmet, Nefertum, Reʿ-Harakhte, Min and Sokar. The *Sanctuary* has four square pillars (also damaged). There are further small rooms around and behind the sanctuary. It is possible that the extensive damage throughout was caused by the severe earthquake of 27 BC. Many of the fallen stones were used by the Copts to build their town.

(35) The king receives heb-sed from Amun and Khonsu. (36) The king with prisoners and treasure before the Theban Triad. (37) The king offers precious stones to Amun. (38) The king offers gold to Amun. (39) The king offers fortress, harp and statue to Amun. (40) The king presents caskets to Amun. (41) The king, with Thoth, presents treasure to Amun-Reʿ. (42) Three registers of vases and pectorals as offerings. (43) The king presents treasure to Amun. (44) Names of the gods of the districts of Egypt. (45) Upper register, the king and baboons adoring Isis and Nephthys. (46) Four registers showing the bringing of fat cattle, their purification, sacrifice and dismemberment, the king offers to Osiris, Atum, Amun, Isis.

The outer façades of the temple are highly decorated with scenes of the exploits of the king.

On the outer façade the scenes are: (47) The king hunting wild bulls and antelopes. (48–49) Calendar of religious feasts. (50) Text of Year 12. (51–52) Benefits conferred on Amun by the king. (53–54) Nubian war. (55–56) Libyan war. (57) The king charging Libyans. (58) The king addressing princes with captives and the counting of hands. (59) The king starts for the war. (60) Battle with the Philistines. (61) Lion hunt. (62–63) Naval battle. (64) The king with Philistine prisoners. (65) Amorite war. (66) Libyan war. (67) Storming Hittite fortresses.

Due S (212m) and facing SE stands the small and complete **Temple of Thoth**, locally called *Qaṣr al-ʿAgūz* (Palace of the Old Man). It was built by Ptolemy VII Euergetes II in sandstone and consists of a court, two small halls and a sanctuary. Although there is a painting of Thoth in his boat being censed by Ptolemy, there is little else of interest.

To the W (500m) is **Malqattah** and the **Palace of Amenhotep III**. It was probably sited on the edge of the desert so that Amenhotep could indulge his passion for hunting. The palace was excavated by the Metropolitan Museum of Art and later by Pennsylvania University. Store rooms of the palace yielded much information about the period. As it was built of brick, with stone used only for the door sills and column bases, little has survived and even the traces of the excellent plaster wall paintings have disappeared. Among the extensive gardens were several palace buildings, in one of which Amenhotep IV (later Akhenaten) lived during the early years of his reign. Also attached to the palace was a large lake and a canal to the river (see below).

S is **Birkat Habu**, the remains of a large lake excavated in front of his palace by Amenhotep III, and about 3km further S is **Deir al-Shalwit** with a **Temple of Isis**, Lady of the West. This is Roman, seemingly the work of Vespasian and Domitian. The temple, a square stone building, stands in an enclosure. Entry is through a court with an ambulatory around the sanctuary. To the left is a room with stairs to the roof. Antoninus Pius decorated the exterior of the sanctuary and Hadrian the interior.

# 37 Luxor to Edfū

Continuing S from Luxor, this route (total distance approx 110km) is again divided and there are important sites on either side of the Nile.

## A. East Bank

**Luxor**.—15km **Ṭūd**.—8km **al-Muʿallāh**.—28km **al-Deir**.—4km **al-Ḥillah**.—10km **al-Kilābiyyah**.—12km *al-Maḥāmīd* (for **al-Kāb**). 20km **al-Kalaḥ Sharq**.—14km road and bridge to **Edfū**.

Leaving Luxor to the SW, the H2 runs S parallel to the Nile (railway to the E), passing (5km) *al-Bayāḍiyyah* and (15km) **Ṭūd** where the river swings SW.

Here is the site of Ancient Egyptian *Djerty*, called in Gk *Tuphium*. Little remains of the Middle Kingdom and Ptolemaic *Temple of Montu*. In the NE corner of the temple area are remains of the *Church of Anbā Ibshay*, a local saint. The church was destroyed in late medieval times and now consists only of the columned apse and scattered carved stones. E of the town on a low mound on the edge of the desert is the *Deir Anbā Ibshay*; the older domed section contains many blocks from a temple of Tuthmosis III. The French have undertaken considerable excavations here and uncovered the Tud Treasure (now in the EM).

Continue S to (7km) **al-Muʿallāh** (perhaps ancient *Nefat*) with two First Intermediate Period rock-cut tombs of Ankhtifi and Sebekhotpe. Here the railway crosses to the W of the road.

At (28km) **al-Deir** a side road leaves the H2 SW to the Esna Barrage and bridge to Esna. The ancient walls of the monastery that gives al-Deir its name are still standing. Just S is the *Deir al-Rūmaniyyah* (Monastery of the Greeks).

Further S is (4km) **al-Ḥillah** (opposite Esna and called, logically, *Contra Latopolis* in Greek). 10km **al-Kilābiyyah**. The H2 continues into the province of Aswān, passing *Gabal Sharāwnah* to (12km) **al-Maḥāmīd**. Riverward is the site known now as **al-Kāb** (with Ticket Office and Rest Room).

In ancient times it was *Nekheb*, Domain of Nekhbet, the white vulture goddess, known here as 'Lady of the Valley'. She was adopted at a very early stage as the cult goddess of Upper Egypt, the counterpart of Wadjet of Lower Egypt. At first subordinate to Nekhen (Kom al-Ahmar on the E side of the river; see below) as a provincial town, it gradually assumed greater importance. In the New Kingdom it replaced the latter city as capital of the 3rd Nome of Upper Egypt, though this function later passed to Latopolis (Esna). In Ptolemaic times the fact that Nekhbet assisted at the births of gods and kings led the Greeks to equate her with Eileithiyia, goddess of women in labour, and the city was renamed *Eileithyiaspolis*. Evidence has been found of very early habitation in the area reaching back to c 6000 BC.

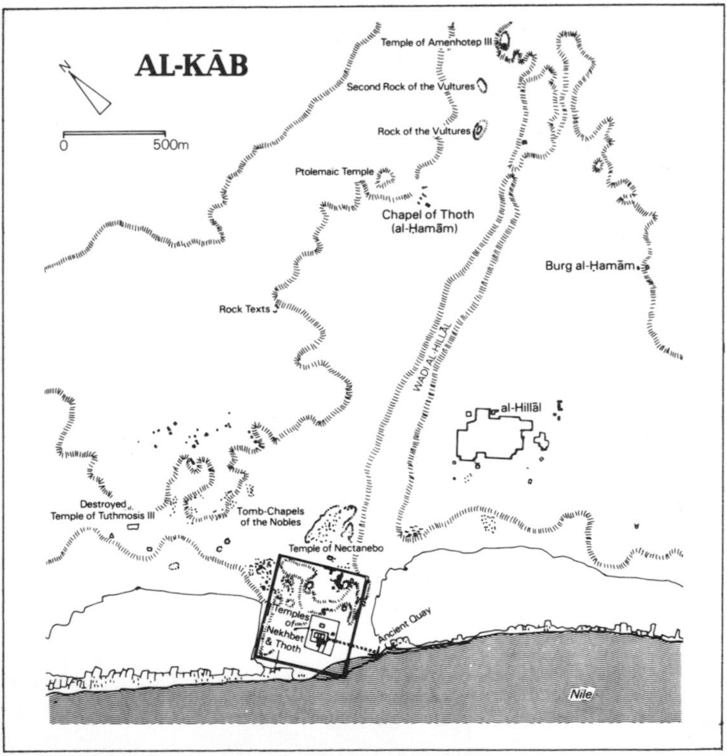
AL-KĀB
N
0
500m
Temple of Amenhotep III
Second Rock of the Vultures
Rock of the Vultures
Ptolemaic Temple
Chapel of Thoth
(al-Ḥamām)
Burg al-Ḥamām
Rock Texts
WADI AL-HILLĀL
al-Hillāl
Destroyed
Temple of Tuthmosis III
Tomb-Chapels
of the Nobles
Temple of Nectanebo
Temples
of
Nekhbet
& Thoth
Ancient Quay
Nile

The most noticeable remains are the vast *mud-brick walls* that enclosed the ancient town of Nekheb. On the riverward side to the SW these walls have been partially washed away but otherwise are in a remarkable state of preservation. They measure 566m by 548m and are 11.3m thick. In the

SW of this enclosure are two concentric enclosures, the innermost containing the devastated remains of two conjoined temples. These were destroyed and rebuilt many times—the Belgian expedition which excavated the site estimated that this had occurred at least ten times—which gives some indication of the importance of the site as a national shrine. The main structure is the *Temple of Nekhbet* built by Amenhotep II and subsequently enlarged by Ramesses II, who built a pylon 15m wide. To the SW is the *Temple of Thoth* raised by Tuthmosis III and rebuilt in the 26 Dyn. They were built of fine white sandstone but only the footings and the bases of the columns remain, still showing, however, a considerable amount of colour. Under the Temple of Nekhbet is a series of crypts, some of which have always been exposed while others are below floor level. Scenes here include a dance of baboons to the rituals of Mut performed at Karnak. One scene depicts Amun-Reʿ and Nekhbet associated in a coronation.

To the S of the main temples lie the foundations of several smaller chapels and other buildings while to the N are the remains of one mud-brick wall of a large *Coptic monastery*. A *sacred lake* lies to the SE between the walls of the two inner enclosures and under the SE wall of the main enclosure are the foundations of an earlier *fort*. It was originally thought that most of the main enclosure had been unoccupied but recent excavations have uncovered the foundations of a series of Ptolemaic and Roman domestic buildings between the inner enclosures and the E gate.

Close to the outer SW wall on the riverbank are the remains of the ancient *Quay* and adjacent to the NE (1km) a small 30 Dyn. *Temple of Nectanebo* of which only the footings remain.

To the N of the Great Enclosure wall (500m) are the *Tomb-Chapels of the Nobles*, cut into the S slope of the hills. These are the tombs of the worthies of Nekheb and date mainly to the early 18 Dyn. There are ten numbered tombs, all barrel-vaulted and some with a room opening off the main chamber to the E. Only a few are worth visiting. Tickets can be obtained from a kiosk at the foot of the hill (WC available). Access has been facilitated by the building of steps. The tombs are described here from E to W.

The first tomb, *Tentis* (TC1), sistrum-player of Nekhbet, is late New Kingdom, the façade with the name and titles. Next is *Ahmose* (TC2), called Pennekhbet, overseer of the Seal, chief king's son of Nekheb and royal herald. His tenure covered the reigns from Amosis to Hatshepsut. The inscriptions are interesting mainly for their historical content, as they give an account of the rise of the 18 Dyn. and of the wars against the Hyksos. Unfortunately this tomb has been badly damaged and the statues at the far end of the tomb are unrecognisable. The biographical texts are in the thickness of the entry passage.

(1–2) Titles of Ahmose. (3) Foreign campaigns. (4) Biographical texts.

Nearby is *Paheri* (TC3), Mayor of Nekheb and prince of the city. Outside the tomb entry is a flat space with Paheri kneeling before a hymn to Nekhbet. The tomb-chapel is long and narrow with the scenes arranged in a narrow register in low relief. Three undecorated side chambers open off the E wall. In a niche at the far end are statues of Paheri and his wife Henuterneheh and mother. On each side are scenes of offerings being made to him. On the E wall Paheri and wife are shown before a table of offerings accompanied by funerary prayers wishing Paheri egress and exit at will from the Afterworld. The rest of the scenes on this wall are concerned with a great feast prepared by Paheri's son, the guests entertained by a female harper and a pipe player. On the W wall are the funerary scenes with the sarcophagus dragged on a sledge by men and oxen. In the next register the funeral furniture is carried along. In the lower register Paheri is shown before Osiris. On the same wall further in are Paheri and wife enjoying the fruits of their estate while seated under a kiosk. There are scenes of vineyards and wine pressing similar to those in the tombs on the West Bank at Thebes (Rte 36). Offering bearers are shown bringing gifts. The dead man's son Amenmosi is shown before his father and mother with an offering list, and makes offerings to the statues with the rest of the family below. The colours are bright and the scenes animated.

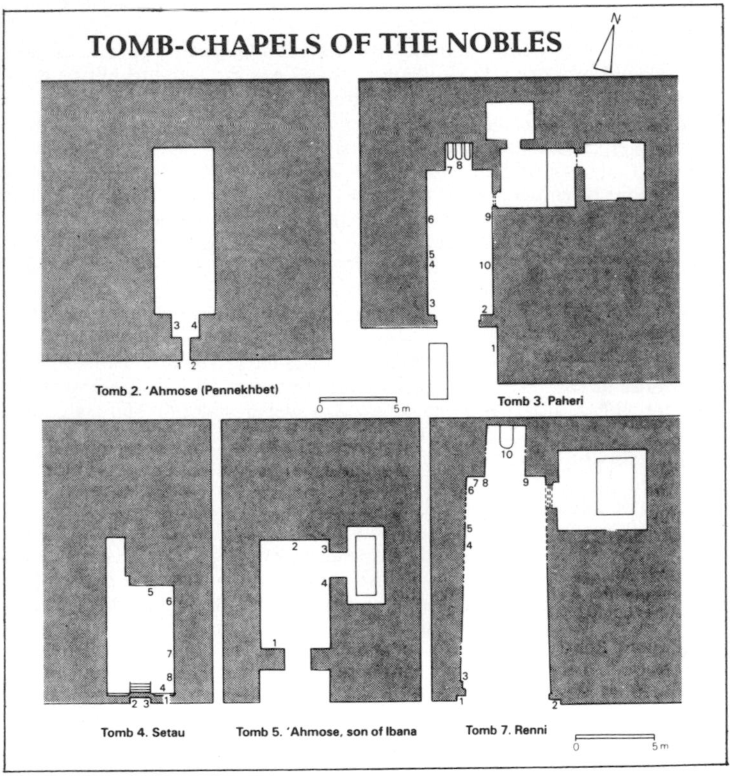
TOMB-CHAPELS OF THE NOBLES
N
Tomb 2. 'Ahmose (Pennekhbet)
Tomb 3. Paheri
Tomb 4. Setau
Tomb 5. 'Ahmose, son of Ibana
Tomb 7. Renni
0 5m

(1) Paheri kneeling with hymn to Nekhbet. (2) Destroyed scene showing a boat. (3–4) Agricultural scenes. (5–6) Offering bearers. (7) Son with offering text. (8) Statues of Paheri, his wife and mother. (9) Banquet scene.

After passing an uninscribed tomb-chapel that of *Setau* (TC4), first prophet of Nekhbet, is reached. This is later than the others and belongs to the period of Ramesses III. Outside the door to this tomb is a stele with the boat of Reʿ-Harakhte. The chapel is entered by four steps. On the W wall are four sacred boats. Sections of the pictures in this tomb have been ruined by later doorways in the wall. The defaced picture of Ramesses III is dated to year 29 of his reign.

(1) Stele with Setau adoring Reʿ-Harakhte and Khephera. (2–3) Offerings to Reʿ-Harakhte and Atum. (4) Offering scenes. (5) Text of Reʿ. (6–7) Funeral banquet. (8) Offerings.

Passing an unnumbered and uninscribed tomb the next reached is that of *Ahmose* (TC5), chief of sailors, son of Ebana of the early 18 Dyn. It is useful for the account it gives of wars against the Hyksos. This tomb was never finished and the lines showing where the painting was to have been placed are still outlined in red. It was constructed for the deceased by his grandson Paheri, who is shown on the back wall with his relatives offering to the deceased. The E wall has the biographical account, and the entrance to the side room shows the dedication text of Paheri to his grandfather. There is a large figure of Ahmose shown on the wall before the account of his life.

(1) Grandson Paheri and biographical text of Ahmose. (2) Paheri offers to deceased with other relatives. (3–4) Dedication text of Paheri.

To the W are *two unfinished tombs*, the second that of Amenmosi, a baker, before the tomb of *Reneni* (TC7), prince and overseer of prophets in the time of Amenhotep I. The E wall of the main chamber shows a chariot, harvest scenes, a banquet before his grandfather Sobek-hotep and wife Idy, with his daughters below in another register. The female offering bearers are followed by funeral scenes, including the purification, and Opening of the Mouth ceremonies. Among the animals kept are pigs, unusual in Ancient Egypt, as they were not very popular, but were connected somehow with the goddess Nekhbet. The niches show Reneni kneeling before the cartouches of Amenhotep I, or seated before texts.

(1–2) Biographical texts. (3–4) Top register, agricultural scenes. (5–6) Banqueting scenes. (7) Offering bearers. (8–9) Deceased before cartouches of Amenhotep I. (10) Statue of Renni.

Beyond Reneni is a *New Kingdom tomb* (TC8). The name of the owner has been destroyed although his wife Ahneferu still has her name on the lintel. Of similar date is *Bebi* (also TC8), administrator of the royal table. It is a somewhat smaller tomb with no side chamber and a small niche where the deceased is seen with a pile of offerings and his relatives. This is followed by a rock-cut stele but the name of the owner is lost.

The cliff here has fallen away and some of the chapels have been destroyed. Proceeding to the W the chapels become earlier in date. After passing two unnumbered and very badly damaged chapels the 12 Dyn. *Tomb-Chapel of Senusert* (unnumbered) is reached. This is another long narrow room, with scenes of offerings being brought and the deceased and wife at table. Beyond lies *Resonb* (TC9), administrator of the royal table, probably 13 Dyn. The next is difficult of access; it belonged to *Sebnakht* (TC10), overseer of prophets at the time of Sobek-hotep, 13 Dyn. It is a long narrow room with a finely decorated ceiling. The inscriptions on the lintel have his life and remains of an offering text. In the first room are depicted stone-workers and bakers, craftsmen and agricultural scenes, the funeral procession with boats, hunting in the desert and fowling in the marshes. Ptah and Osiris are shown, and at the entrance to the inner room the dead man is shown seated on each side of the lintel with offering texts. This is the last of the tomb-chapels of any interest. Another Temple of Tuthmosis III once stood c 2km NW beyond the tombs but it has been totally destroyed.

The Wādī Hillāl runs to the NE from the Town Enclosure. There are several interesting temples in the area, but the track is almost non-existent and it is necessary to take a guard from al-Kāb. On the NW side of the wādī after 2km are drawings of a predynastic boat and some Old Kingdom graffiti. On the same side of the valley (750m) are two small chapels, the first reached by 42 steps, the rock-cut *Ptolemaic Temple* also dedicated to Nekhbet. It is the work of Ptolemies VII, X and XI, although its core is an earlier tomb-chapel. A vestibule with the remains of floral capitals and screen walls still standing leads to a court, to the E of which is a *rock-stele of Ramesses II* before Reʿ-Harakhte and Nekhbet. The innermost part of the temple was originally an 18 Dyn. tomb-chapel but the later scenes show Ptolemy VII and Cleopatra III before various divinities, the king's titles and the king purified by Horus and Thoth. The ceiling is decorated with paintings of vultures. Slightly to the SE stands the small square stone *Chapel of Thoth*, locally called al-Ḥammām (the Bath) erected by Setau, viceroy of Kush, on the order of Ramesses II. Representations of Setau are found on each side of the entrance.

Further to the NE, deeper into the valley (500m), stands the isolated *Rock of the Vultures*, so called because the birds used to nest here. It is covered with rock-drawings, some of which are Predynastic, including boats and animals; others are Old Kingdom (6 Dyn.) and Middle Kingdom. Beyond the rock to the NE (200m) is the second rock which also contains rock carvings.

At the head of the valley, on the SE face (200m), is the *Temple of Amenhotep III* dedicated to Nekhbet, with Hathor-head columns. There are also later 19 Dyn. inscriptions including that of Prince Khaemwaset on the façade, dated to the 41st year of Ramesses II. Also on the SE side of the valley, but only 3.75km from the Enclosure, is another isolated rock called the *Burg al-Hamām* (Tower of the Pigeon) with 6 Dyn. inscriptions of the time of Pepi II, including his cartouche.

Continue S passing (20km) **al-Kalaḥ Sharq**. 14km further a branch road leads W for the bridge over the Nile to **Edfū** (see below).

A road leads E across the desert to *Marsā ʿAlam* (see Rte 49).

## B. West Bank

**al-Qurnah**.—10km road to **Armant**.—5km **Dimuqrāt**.—18km **al-Gabalayn**.—10km **ʿAsfūn al-Maṭāʿnah**—10km **Esna**.—28km **al-Baṣaliyyah al-Wusta**.—3km **al-Baṣaliyyah al-Qiblī** (for **Kom al-Aḥmar**).—21km **Edfū**.

S of al-Qurnah the H53 follows the river; at 10km a road runs E to **Armant**, Ancient Egyptian *Iuny*, Gk *Hermonthis*, Coptic *Ermont*, capital of the Fourth Upper Egyptian nome until the rise of Thebes. During the Coptic period it was the seat of a bishopric. It is now a very important sugar-producing area with a large factory. Ancient remains have been found in the area to the NE of the town but of the Temple of Montu and

Rat-tawy, nothing remains except the bases of the *Pylons of Tuthmosis III*. Directly in front of this is the enclosure of the *Church of the Virgin*, but of this, once renowned as one of the largest and most beautiful churches in Egypt, only the red granite columns are extant. The Coptic town was excavated in 1935–37 but revealed only poorly-built dwellings. Cleopatra VII and Ptolemy XV Caesarion also built a temple here but all trace of this has disappeared. The most important remains in the area are N of the town; the **Buccheum** (Necropolis of the Bucchis Bulls) and *Baqariyyih* (Necropolis of the Mothers of the Bucchis Bulls), the earliest burials in which dated to the reign of Nectanebo II.

S the H53 passes to the E of (5km) **Dimuqrāt**. To the E on the edge of the desert is the *Deir Mārī Girgis* (Monastery of St. George). Key with guardian in Dimuqrāt. It is a fine building with 21 domes and it is very unusual in having six haykals dedicated to (N to S) SS. Pachomius and Mecurius, the Virgin, SS. George, Paul of Thebes and Michael. To the NW is the Baptistry.

The next town is (18km) **al-Gabalayn**, Ancient Egyptian *Per Hathor*, Gk *Aphroditopolis* or *Pathyris*. It was excavated early this century by Turin University. Although there are some First Intermediate Period tombs nothing remains of the Temple of Hathor that stood here from the 2 Dyn. to the Roman period.

The H53 passes through (10km) **ʿAsfūn al-Maṭāʿnah** with (7km W) the *Deir al-Fakharani* (Monastery of the Potter, i.e. St. Matthew).

Key with Coptic priest in Esna. This is enclosed in high walls, the cemetery in front with 14–15C headstones. Originally founded by Matthew, a fisherman of Bishnay who retired to the desert here in the early 8C, it was destroyed in the 10C and rebuilt. Fine 11–13C wall-paintings of Jesus, the twelve apostles and other saints and angels.

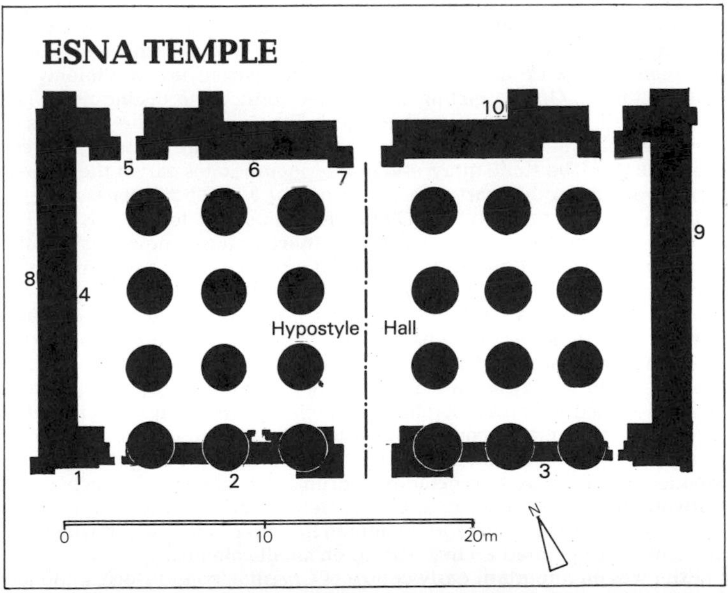
ESNA TEMPLE
10
5
6
7
9
8
4
Hypostyle
Hall
1
2
3
0
10
20m
N

The H53 runs through to (10km) **Esna** (Isnā), one of the smaller cities of Upper Egypt and chief town of the district in the province of Qena.

There is a barrage built in 1906 of sandstone from the Silsilah quarries. Within recent times it was extremely important as the Nile terminal for the Sudan caravan routes passing Derr and Kurkur Oasis, but this trade has declined since the 1890s. Now it is mainly a town of merchants and a centre of the weaving trade. The ancient name was *Ta-Sna*. It was a centre for the worship of the Lates, the Nile perch (*Lates niloticus*), and thus during the Ptolemaic period it was called *Latopolis*. Although doubtless of ancient lineage, its early history is lost and it is first mentioned in the Annals of Tuthmosis III for the taxes paid here. There would almost certainly have been a temple here at that date; Champollion referred to a cartouche of Tuthmosis III in the part of the temple now blocked.

Although there were originally three temples in the town, one of which was destroyed during the civil wars at the beginning of the 19C, the present **Temple of Esna** is Ptolemaic-Roman. It lies in the centre of the town in a depression—due to the rise in the level of the ground. It has never been completely excavated but was partly cleared by Mariette in the 19C. The temple, orientated E–W, was originally dedicated to Khnum and Khonsu as a form of Shu—worshipped here as a great creator god, his female associates were Neith of Sais, Tefnut and Menhyt, a local form of Sekhmet. The cleared part as it now stands is the covered Hypostyle Hall of the temple measuring 32.8m by 16.4m. On the outside are cartouches of Claudius (1), Titus and Vespasian (2–3) and Antoninus Pius (4). The last emperor mentioned is Decius (5) (killed AD 249). On the 24 columns in the hall are inscribed extremely interesting and important texts for the festivals of Esna and particularly of Khnum, and liturgies of the temple's main events. The left wall shows Septimus Severeus, Caracalla and Geta before the gods (7). Since Khnum and Neith were regarded as creator gods accounts of the creation of the world by the latter are given. Knowledge of this material is the result of painstaking work by French epigraphists in recent years. On the earlier W wall, which formed a common wall with the inner temple, are cartouches of Ptolemy VI Philometor (6). On the ceiling is a zodiac (difficult to distinguish). The outside walls show Titus, Domitian and Trajan smiting the enemies of Egypt before the gods (8–9). On the back wall are texts of Marcus Aurelius (10). The stone quay, still in use, incorporates part of the ancient structure and also has cartouches of Emperor Marcus Aurelius.

In the centre of the town, the *Gāmiʿ al-ʿAmrī* is an Ottoman mosque, but at the NW corner stands the **Fāṭimid Minaret**, all that now exists of the mosque built in 1081 by the high Fāṭimid official Abū Manṣūr Sārtakīn, a governor of Upper Egypt (died 1101 at Askalon). This building shows many characteristics confined to Upper Egypt during the period, and several other minarets of tombs (e.g. at Luxor, Qūṣ and Aswān) belong to the same local tradition. The whole is built of brick, the upper part being plastered and whitewashed. A square-sectioned base, with square and pointed-arched windows, displays the technique of the brickwork, set at intervals with bands of contrasting colour. A tapering cylindrical second tier supports a wooden balcony almost two-thirds of the height, resting on wooden brackets. A low octagonal drum, the corners of which curve outward, below the summit, and with trefoil arched windows (plastered over), is the base for a hexagonal domed lantern in each side of which are windows with pointed arches resting on small columns.

Esna was an important early centre of Christianity and Decius, the last emperor mentioned in the temple texts, forced Christians on pain of death to sacrifice to the Roman gods. Those who refused are commemorated in the next monument as the 3600 martyrs. 6km to the SW lies the **Deir Manayus wa Shuhadā** (Monastery of the Martyrs), surrounded by a high wall (keys from Church of the Virgin in Esna). It was founded by Ammonius, a bishop of Esna, in the early 4C. Inside are two churches, the modern *Church of the Virgin* (dedicated c 1931) and the 10–11C *Church of the Martyrs*. This, one of the finest churches in Upper Egypt, is composed of two chapels. In the E part are three haykals dedicated (N–S) to St. George, the Virgin and the Holy Martyrs of Esna, the last with fine wall-paintings. Other wall-paintings are dated 502 AM (AD 786). In the NW corner are a further two haykals. To the N of this monastery are the ruins of the *Deir Abū Ishāq* (Monastery of St. Isaac).

Beyond Esna the H53 passes *ʿAḍāymah, al-Sabāʿiyyah, al-Baṣaliyyah al-Baḥrī* and (28km) **al-Baṣaliyyah al-Wustā**, to the S of which is the site of the small **Pyramid of al-Kullah**, cleared by the Belgian expedition which excavated al-Kāb on the East Bank. While no positive conclusion could be reached, the construction suggests a 3 Dyn. date. It is a layer pyramid consisting now of a nucleus and three tiers of 12 courses of small local limestone masonry and, as in the construction of the early pyramids, the courses incline inwards. The base is 18.6m sq. There has been a lot of destruction during the last century and a half since the pyramid was described by Wilkinson, when it had 26 courses to a height of 10.6m; it is now only 4m high. It is peculiar in that the corners rather than the sides are orientated to the cardinal points, probably due to the course of the river. The mortar used is mud mixed with straw but no casing stones have been found. The entry has not been located. A second pyramid is said to have been found nearby.

The next town is (3km) **al-Baṣalliyah al-Qiblī**; along the foothills of the SW is the site of **Kom al-Aḥmar** (*Kawm al-Aḥmar*; Red Mound), the name derived from the quantities of red pottery which abundantly covered the mound lying in the centre of the main site.

It is infrequently visited by tourists as there is little to see. Archaeologically it is extremely important as this was the site of *Nekhen*, the capital of Upper Egypt prior to the unification of the country c 3100 BC. During the Ptolemaic period it was called *Hierakonpolis* (City of the Hawk). Up to the New Kingdom Nekhen remained the capital of the 3rd Upper Egyptian nome after which it was replaced by Nekheb on the East Bank of the Nile. The area had been occupied much earlier as the predynastic settlements and cemeteries found along the base of hills testify. The site is on the edge of the cultivated area and includes the rock face and wādī running to the SW. Quibell excavated the temple site between 1896–98 and the area has recently been re-examined.

A maze of small mounds and pits covers the area and the most imposing structure is the *'Fort'* (500m down the wādī) with massive walls still standing to a height of c 10m and 5m thick, built of mud-brick. Of uncertain purpose and probably early Dynastic in date, it is similar to the Shunāt al-Zibīb at Abydos (Rte 35), and here too the interior is full of mounds of debris and sherds. Closeby to the SW are some *Middle Kingdom Tombs* (formerly thought to be Old Kingdom) which include that of Haremkhauef, chief prophet of Horus of Nekhen. A further 1.5km down the wādī are about ten rock-cut *New Kingdom Tombs*, the best dating to the reign of Tuthmosis III. Some were usurped in later Ramesside times, others have fallen in.

Lying on the edge of the cultivation to the NE of the Fort is the *Town Enclosure*, also constructed of mud-brick, with the *Temple Precincts* occupying the SE corner. Here Quibell uncovered some very fine Early Dynastic and Old Kingdom objects that had been buried together. The cache included the Narmer Palette, the Scorpion Macehead, the copper statues of Pepi I and his son Meryenre, and a golden hawk's head (now in the EM and the Ashmoleum Museum, Oxford).

In the *Prehistoric Tombs* to the SE of the main site were found some of the earliest Egyptian wall-paintings; particularly fine were those in *Decorated Tomb 100*. On mud-plaster, the scenes depicted hunting, ships, animals and men (all now in EM).

Continuing S the H53 passes (11km) **al-Kalaḥ Gharb** and terminates at (10km) **Edfū** (Ar. Idfū), a fairly large town built over the mound of an ancient city. It is the chief town of the district in the Province of Aswan.

*Hotel*, Edfou East (2*), near station. Mainline railway station on East Bank. Bus station for local buses. The town can be reached from the station either by walking or hantur. Steamers dock on the West Bank.

The ancient city which stood here was *Djeba*, where Horus the Elder was worshipped, later called *Apollinopolis Magna* (to distinguish it from A. Parva, i.e. Qūṣ) by the Greeks who equated the solar aspects of Horus with those of Apollo. In myth it was here that Horus pierced Seth during their contention. Horus as worshipped here had the epithets the Bhtd, and the Winged Disk, and probably originated in Sambekedet in the Delta, but by the late period had become identified in many ways with the Younger Horus, son of Osiris and Isis. His consort was Hathor of Dendarah and their annual ritual marriage was one of the most important celebrations of the city. The winged disk associated with Edfū also stands as an emblem of United Egypt and was traditionally set up over temple doors in commemoration of the victory of Horus over Seth after their country-wide battles.

Mounds covering the ancient city spread over an area of c 2km but are consistently being whittled away by the sabbakhin. There are Old Kingdom and First Intermediate Period tombs and evidence of remains from later periods but the largest monument is the ***Temple of Horus**, to the W of the town. Ancient precincts spread to the E and S. This is the most complete of all Egyptian temples and is the final Ptolemaic rebuilding in sandstone of a religious foundation which stretches back to early dynastic times. Examination of the paving of the forecourt has revealed reused sandstone blocks from an earlier temple.

Until the 1860s debris covered the temple, except for the pylons, and a large number of dwellings covered the roof. Much damage had been done to the interior by the inhabitants of the town, who had defaced many of the figures and cut holes in the walls. Mariette cleared the main temple and considerable restoration work was undertaken by Maspero, when iron girders were implanted to shore up the roof of the interior. However, it was not until 1903 that the mammisi and enclosure wall were fully cleared.

Texts on the walls give an account of the original foundations of the temple and are doubtless copied from much earlier wall texts. This site was considered to be that of one of the mounds that rose from the Waters of Nun where the falcon first perched on a slip of reed. To defend him against his enemy the snake two weapons appeared—the mace, called the 'Great White' and the spear—both of which figure prominently in the Edfū ritual. The main building was begun on 23 August 237 BC (under Ptolemy III Euergetes I) and took 25 years to complete. The reliefs and inscriptions took another five years. A revolt in Upper Egypt halted the construction and the door and fittings were not set in position until 3 February 176 BC. The plating and the inscriptions had to be completed and the opening ceremony took place on 10 September 105 BC. Even so, work continued on the reliefs in the Small Hypostyle Hall for another two years.

*Festivals at Edfū.* The principal liturgical events of the year consisted of five main feasts. Two have already been mentioned: the New Year Festival common to all the temples of Egypt, embodying the 'Union with the Disk', and the 'Play of the Divine Birth' celebrated in and around the mammisi. In addition there was the miracle play of Horus, sometimes called the Festival of Victory, showing his struggle with, and final vanquishing of, Seth. This was portrayed on the inside of the outer corridor of the temple on the W side. Part of this took place annually on the sacred lake where Seth was defeated as either a hippopotamus or a crocodile. One of the main feasts was the annual journey of Hathor to Edfū from Dendarah and her sacred marriage to

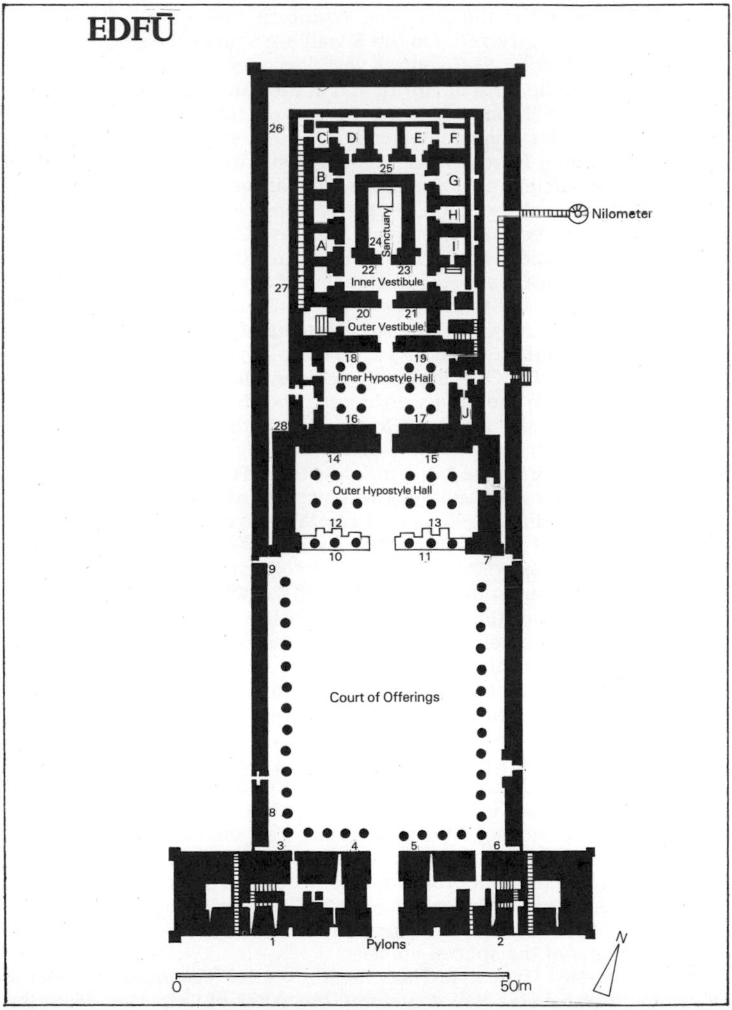
EDFŪ
26
C
D
E
F
25
B
G
Nilometer
H
A
24
Sanctuary
I
22
23
Inner Vestibule
27
20
21
Outer Vestibule
18
19
Inner Hypostyle Hall
16
17
J
28
14
15
Outer Hypostyle Hall
12
13
10
11
7
9
Court of Offerings
8
3
4
5
6
1
Pylons
2
N
0
50m

Horus. This journey took about two weeks and was celebrated with great joy not only at Edfū, but also at the other sacred spots that the procession visited upon the way. The journey was by river and many other deities joined the procession. It also proceeded to various places in the neighbourhood of Edfū. Because the reigning king was regarded as Horus, the Festival of the Coronation which stood for the symbolic renewal of royal power also took place annually at Edfū, in the Temple of the Falcon, now largely destroyed, which stood in front of the main pylon. It was followed by a crowning ceremony in the main forecourt of the temple. The scenes representing this are shown on the back of the pylon.

The temple area is entered through a gate to the N at the rear of the building, and the wall of the main building is followed to the courtyard in front of the temple. To the S is the *Mammisi of Horus*, aligned E–W, the work of Ptolemies VII and XIII. The exterior is much damaged but the interior shrine has survived. On the S wall are some reliefs which retain their original colouring. Here once a year was performed the miracle play that represented the birth of Horus, and at the same time the birth of the divine heir to the throne of Egypt. Scenes on the walls represent the divine birth (better shown at Dendārah), the seven Hathors, Hathor suckling the young Horus or else shaking a sistrum. To the E and W the remains of the ancient enclosure wall can still be seen.

The orientation of the main temple is from N–S. The two decorated *Pylons* are engraved with scenes of Ptolemy XIII smiting his enemies before Horus the Elder (1–2). The recesses in the pylons were intended for flagstaffs which always stood before late Egyptian temples. E of these pylons are the bases of two pylons of the earlier temple of Ramesses III, aligned E–W. In front of the gate stand hawks of Horus. Inside the door, which must originally have been wood plated with bronze, is the forecourt, the *Court of Offerings* with a colonnade of 32 columns covered with reliefs showing the king worshipping the deities of the temple.

Steps lead from the forecourt to the top of the pylons with, after a somewhat exhausting ascent, a fine view of the temple and town (recently these stairs have been inaccessible). The forecourt gives onto the *Hypostyle Hall* with another two hawks flanking the door, the roof supported by 18 with various types of capitals, once brightly coloured, but only traces of paint now remain. The six screen walls dividing the hall from the forecourt show Ptolemy IX making offerings to Hator and Horus. To the E of the main entry is a small chamber which contained a *small library* (13), scrolls of the temple ritual and the lists of principal feasts. This was not the main temple library as there are only two niches for rolls, and they may have contained only those to do with the daily service. An inscription over the door states that this was the library of Horus, and that the rolls were in the charge of the chief ritual priest. W of the door is a small room, the *Chamber of Consecration* or Vestry (12), where the ritual vases were kept. Many of the rooms are lit by vertical slits in the roofing blocks, providing a diffused light for the interior of the temple. As at Esna the columns contained shortened versions of the main festivals, offerings and observances carried out in the temple. The smaller *Inner Hypostyle Hall*, called the Festival Hall, lying behind, has two additional entries, one to the W and one to the E, from which entered the dry and wet offerings which formed part of the daily service. This hall has rather slender columns. Off this were small chambers in which the sacred amulets were kept, and many of the special utensils.

Behind the two Hypostyle Halls lies the *Outer Vestibule* or Court of Offerings, a transverse hall containing the Altar of Offerings. Here the daily offerings were made, and it must have been crowded with altars, offering tables, fruit, flowers, joints of meat, wine and milk. Stairs lead to the roof, where originally as at Dendārah there must have been a 'Chapel of the Disk' for the revitalising of the statues in the Union with the Disk ceremony, but this has been removed at some time. Scenes on the stairs still recall the priestly procession carrying images of the gods wending its way to the roof. The stairway to the E was for the ascending procession, that to the W for the descent. On the E side is the *Inner Vestibule*. Beyond is the *New Year Chapel* with a figure of Nut upon the ceiling. The *Sanctuary*, as is the case with other late temples, is almost a separate building within the main structure. The scenes on the walls decorated by Ptolemy IV Philopater show offerings to the two gods of the temple, Horus and Hathor, in their sacred boats, and various scenes of the ritual opening of the shrine and the offerings made. At the rear of the sanctuary, predating the main temple building, stands a small granite shrine or *Naos of Nectanebo*. In front of it is a grey granite pedestal intended as a support for the sacred boat of Horus, given as a votive offering by a private individual to Horus.

A corridor extends round the Sanctuary, off which open *ten rooms* concerned with the cult, some normally served as store rooms, but others are associated with deities, scenes above the doors indicating the purpose. From the W, the first is the room of Horus, protector of Osiris (H). The next is that of the sun god Reʿ (G) then the chamber of Hathor (F), from which leads the Khonsu room (E). The room directly behind the sanctuary was that of Horus the Harpooner. The next three rooms are connected with the worship of Osiris (B–D). Nearly all the temples have chapels of this kind. Also on the W side is the Room of the Throne of the Gods, and the Linen (A) and Silver rooms.

(3–4) Hathor's voyage to Edfū. (5) Ptolemy offering to Horus and Hathor. (6–7) The king before Horus, Hathor and Ihy. (8–9) Ptolemy X before the Edfū Triad. (10) Ptolemy VIII offers to Horus and Hathor. (11) Ptolemy XI offers a boat to Horus. (12) Vestry. (13) Library. (14) Deification ceremonies. (15) Foundation of the temple ceremonies. (16) Offering to the divinities of the temple. (17) Ptolemy before Inmutef. (18) Ptolemy IV offers to Amun and Mut. (19) Ptolemy offers four calves to Horus. (20) Offering scenes. (21) The king and Mnervis bulls before Horus. (22) Morning hymn to Horus. (23) Texts to Horus. (24) Liturgical texts and offering scenes. (25) Offering scenes, sacrifice of oryx, offering of ointment and driving four calves. (26–27) Mystery play of Horus.

On the E wall of the corridor surrounding the temple are the remains of the *Well*.

7km W of the town on the side of a small hill and surrounded by a rough brick enclosure lies the *Deir Anbā Bakhūm* (Monastery of St. Pachomius; key with Coptic priest at Edfū). The four haykals are dedicated to (N–W) St. Pachomius, the Virgin, SS. Michael and John the Baptist.

# 38 Edfū to Aswān

This route (total distance approx. 106km) continues S to Aswān. Although there is a passable road on the West Bank (see below), the sites on that side of the Nile are best visited by ferry from the main East Bank itinerary. There are no bridges.

## A. East Bank

**Edfū**.—(*Kanayis* 55km.)—27km **Silwah Baḥri**.—20km **al-Nāṣir**.—1km **Kagūg** (for **Gabal Silsilah**).—18km **Kom Ombo**.—40km **Aswān**.

Beyond the bridge to Edfū the H2 runs S and slightly inland.

A road runs E into the desert to *Bīr ʿAbbād* (30km) and *Kanayis* (25km).

The H2 bypasses *al-Radīsah*, returning to the riverbank after 17km. The next village is (10km) **Silwah Baḥri**, 7km beyond which a road branches off inland to the E for the village of *al-Nāṣir* (18km).

On the H2 lies (1km) **Kagūg**, just SW of which is the site of **Gabal Silsilah** (Mountain of the Chain), 61.2km downstream from Aswān. Although the actual mountain is on the East Bank (see below), the site extends on the West Bank for c 2km. At one time the river ran through rapids here and goods had to be porteraged round, but the obstructions have long since disappeared from the riverbed.

The quarries were mainly in use in the New Kingdom and because the stone quarried here was used for religious buildings the area also was regarded as being 'Gods' Land'. Most of the quarries are between 15–21m in height and cut with great precision. Extensive quarries on the East Bank provided stone used at Karnak, Luxor, the West Bank at Thebes and later Ptolemaic temples. The best stone was probably worked out by Roman times, but some quarries are still in use. Some of the sandstone was used for constructing the Nile Barrages. At the N end are some ruined mud-brick buildings and part of a temple built by Ramesses II, all that is left of the town of *Khenet*. Although the river area was generally avoided in the Middle Kingdom by travellers, many graffiti of this period have been found here.

On the East Bank there is no proper quay; the river has recently become very shallow, and steamers have to tie up at the N end of the site. Many of the earlier shrines have been cut away by later workings. The two main excavations have their entry guarded by iron gates, and one is entered through a narrow passage cut in the rock. The walls of the quarries have many Greek and Demotic inscriptions left by the quarrymen and the remains of the causeway down which the stones were dragged can still be seen. At some distance from the river are several unfinished sandstone sphinxes and a shattered naos inscribed with the name of Amenhotep III. Akhenaten also had stone quarried here for his temples at Karnak, and the names of Seti I and Psamtik II have been found. Because of the dangers of river navigation it was mainly the water gods who were worshipped here, Hapi, Sobek, Heqet and Amun-Reʿ and his trinity; as well as Ptah and the gods of Memphis.

The standard West Bank Silsilah shrine consists of a chamber entered through a door decorated with the name and titles of the king under whom the official who built the shrine served, followed by the htp-di-nsw (the offering inscription). Some of them contain statues either finished or unfinished (mostly badly damaged) belonging to the reigns of Hatshepsut, Tuthmosis III, Amenhotep II, Ramesses II and Ramesses III.

The general description of the shrines and their scenes is based on one of the earliest, that of Menkh (No. 21) dating to the time of Tuthmosis I. The principal elements are: scenes of presentation and feasting enjoyed by the shrine-owner and his wife, sometimes including his parents; some of the feasting is funerary, some show earthly enjoyment. Offerings to the gods, and to the owner of the shrine, the door with name and titles of the king, surmounted by a winged disk. Most of the shrines are so ruined that hardly any traces of decoration survive.

The principal shrines on the East Bank extend about 1km from the Speos of Horemheb in the N to the Nile stelae in the S. Here there are 32 shrines (11 uninscribed), the most distant 680.30m S of the Speos of Horemheb. Access to some is difficult, as they are right on the edge of the river, but others are easily visited. The best way of examining these chapels is to alight from the boat at the 19 Dyn. *Shrine of Merneptah* (about 20 minutes' walk S of the Speos of Horemheb). On the N wall are three registers of the king offering to Osiris, Isis and Ramesses II to Seth, Nephthys, Horus and Sobek, Rat-tawi, Hathor and another goddess, while Hapi offers before the king's cartouches. On the S wall the king offers incense and pours libations to Atum, Montu, Amenhotep I, Ounuris, Tefnut and Geb; while Queen Nefert-Iset is shown with a sistrum before the hippopotamus goddess, Thoth and Nut.

Between this and the next shrine is a *Stele of Merneptah* where the king is shown followed by a prince, the name destroyed but probably Seti-Merneptah, while the vizier Panhasc offers a figure of Ma'at to Amun-Reʿ. Next to this is the *Rock Shrine of Ramesses II*, the N wall showing the king writing his own name before Amun-Reʿ and Thoth, and kneeling before a tree in front of Reʿ and Ptah, while in another register he is shown making an offering of incense to Osiris, Isis, Rat-tawi, Sobek and Hathor; at the base of the scene are two figures of the Nile god Hapi. (These shrines are described in some guidebooks as the Southern Monuments.)

Proceed N along a well-defined track near the river to a *Stele of Ramesses III* cut in the king's sixth year, set at right-angles to the river and showing the king before Amun-Reʿ and Hapi. Nearby is a small figure of an official of Seti I called Horemheb. Next is the *Shrine of Amenenhet* (No. 25), prince and high-priest of Amun-Reʿ under Amenhotep II. On the N wall Amenenhet is shown with his wife Mimi before offerings made by their son Amenemwaskhet, also a priest of Amun. This is the best-preserved of the Silsilah shrines. The colours are bright and the hieroglyphs are painted in blue. It looks E across the Nile. After this point the path narrows and runs close to the water's edge. *Shrine No. 24* is uninscribed and cut high in the hillside. It also faces E and appears never to have been finished.

The *Shrine of Min-Nakhte* (No. 23) lies 64.4m N and dates to the reign of Hatshepsut and Tuthmosis III. Min-Nakhte was a prince, royal scribe, chief of the weavers of Amun, and overseer of the Granaries of Upper and Lower Egypt, son of Sendjehuty and Sennu. He was buried on the West Bank at Thebes in Tomb-Chapel No. 87. On the W wall Min-Nakhte is shown seated before an offering table surmounted by conventional offerings, while under the table is the usual offering formula in units, a thousand of bread, a thousand jars of beer, a thousand oxen, and a thousand of birds. The E wall shows offerings in four registers including the seven ritual oils. Three badly damaged statues at the rear of the shrine represent Min-Nakhte in the middle, Sendjehuty, his father, on the left (inscription erased) and Sennu, his mother, on the right.

Sethe has suggested that this is the same man as the owner of shrine No. 12, also called Min-Nakhte and bearing some of the same titles, but this equation is far from certain and if correct, it is the only case of one man having two shrines at Silsilah. The style of the inscriptions is not very similar.

Close to this to the N is *Shrine No. 22*, its owner unknown. It is situated high on the cliff and dates to the reign of Hatshepsut and Tuthmosis III. Of the N and S walls only the upper parts remain, with the rear wall taken up by four statues, two men and two women seated on a bench, all broken off at the shoulders when the floor of the shrine sheared off. High up the cliff and partially damaged by a landslide is the *Shrine of Menkh* (No. 21), a court official and steward of the queen (unnamed) at the time of Tuthmosis I. One scene fills most of the N wall, and shows offerings made to Menkh and his wife Rau. To the right of the offering table the decoration is divided into registers: the top one contains the shorter list of offerings, including water, bread, meat, wine, beer and spent drink. The inner room, very much damaged, contained two statues of a man and a woman seated on a bench, probably Menkh and his wife Rau. No other records of this man have been traced elsewhere. Close to the water-level c 4m N is *Shrine No. 20*, roughly contemporary with the last. It is considerably damaged and the front part was lost when the cliff front fell away at some time. The walls and floor are cracked. There is a small statue recess in the back, 1.20m deep. The two statues are now waist-deep in dried Nile mud. The plan is almost exactly similar to that of Shrine No. 21. The *Shrine of a treasurer of Amenhotep II* (No. 18) is unfinished and difficult of access; it now stands as a single square chamber without a statue niche.

At the top of the cliff is an elaborate structure (badly damaged), the *Shrine of Woser* (User or Usiamum) (No. 17), vizier under Tuthmosis III. He was the uncle of Rekhmire and had two tombs on the West Bank at Thebes, Nos 61 and 131. The interior is the usual single chamber with a statue niche at one end. It has been damaged by Aten worshippers who have hacked out the name of Amun. Not only are the servants of the vizier listed but also many of his relatives, including his five sons and seven daughters. The *Shrine of Senemut* (or Sennenemut) (No. 16), the architect and steward of Queen Hatshepsut, seems to have been begun before she was ruling as an independent queen. The façade is a framed doorway set in a recess, above which is an uninscribed recess. The lintel has the winged disk of Horus the Behdetite while the right-hand N door-jamb holds a htp-di-nsw formula in two columns. The N wall shows Senemut making offerings to eight gods in two registers including Amun-Reʿ, Nun, Sobek, Atum, Khnum, Satet, Anuket, and the elder Horus. S of the recess is a panel showing the queen embraced by Sobek, but she has been almost entirely obliterated.

Situated near the top of the cliff 3m N of the last is one of the finest shrines here, the *Shrine of Hepusoneb* (No. 15), first prophet of Amun, and overseer of the prophets of Amun; he seems to have been a noble holding considerable property both in Upper and Lower Egypt. His tomb is on the West Bank at Thebes (No. 67). Of the time of Hatshepsut, the shrine is set in a shallow niche but the lintel is much damaged. It has the usual table of offerings and offering formula. On the W side is a niche with a very defaced statue of Hepusoneb.

Hewn into the top of the cliff some 3.15m N of No. 15, of the same period but slightly later, is the *Shrine of Nehasy* (No. 14), an official of Hatshepsut and Tuthmosis III about whom little is known unless he was, as postulated by Sethe, the leader of Hatshepsut's Punt expedition. The lintel is decorated with a winged disk of Horus, and the names of the rulers. On the right, deeply incised, is 'Life to the good goddess Ma'kare, beloved of Amun-Reʿ, Lord of the Thrones of the Two Lands' (the words 'Amun-Reʿ' have been mutilated). On the left is the inscription 'Life to the good god Mankheperre, beloved of Nun, father of the gods'. On the right is the htp-di-nsw formula to Amun-Reʿ. The interior of the shrine has been extensively robbed.

At this point the cliff falls abruptly to the river. Near the top is the *Shrine of Sennuferi* (or Sennufer) (No. 18), a well-known official of the time of Hatshepsut, whose name is also found at Sarabīṭ al-Khādim in Sinai and who has a statue in the British Museum. His tomb is No. 99 on the West Bank at Thebes. The doorway is framed and set in a shallow recess, the lintels with the winged disk of Horus the Behdetite. The texts were written under Hatshepsut but later changed to the name of Tuthmosis, with the feminine endings plastered over, but the plaster has fallen off revealing the original carving. Originally the left-hand side of the door read 'Life to the daughter of Reʿ. Hatshepsut, may she live eternally united with Amun' but this was replaced by 'Life to the son of Reʿ, Tuthmosis ruler-of-truth, beloved of Reʿ Hatakhte'. The N wall has been damaged by having a door cut through to the adjoining *Shrine of Min-Nakhte* (No. 12) which was prepared for the inspector of granaries at the time of Tuthmosis III. It consists of a single rectangular room 3.3m deep, with the usual statue niche on the rear wall. The roof of the shrine is only partly preserved and the N wall has been partly quarried away, leaving a scene of Min-Nakhte and his wife or mother seated before an offering table.

Nearly 27m N is the *Shrine of Senynufe and his wife Hatshepsut* (No. 11), the names pointing to an 18 Dyn. date. It consists of two rooms, an outer narrow passage and an inner broader one with a row of five statues on the back wall. The top has been quarried away at some time. Another man is also mentioned, Userhat, viceroy of Kush, but what connection, if any, there is between the two is uncertain. There are two vertical lines of hieroglyphs painted yellow on each side of the statues. It was never finished as the dividers were marked out in red but never carved. There follow *three uninscribed Shrines* (Nos 8, 9 and 10), while 25.5m N of No. 8 is *Shrine No. 7*, dated to the reigns of Hatshepsut and Tuthmosis III, but the name of the owner has not been preserved. Cut in the base of the cliff c 4m above the water level is the *Shrine of Ahmose* (No. 6), of the time of Hatshepsut and Tuthmosis III. He seems to have been a priest of Amun and high priest of Nekhbet; attempts have been made to identify him with Ahmose Pennekhbet (buried at al-Kāb) but without success, as they do not appear to have held the same titles. The work was never finished, only half the ceiling being completed. The design on the completed S part consists of spirals of brown and white with blue and green centres. The scenes on the walls are all painted, the only incised work being on the lintels. In addition to Ahmose, User and his wife Aberui are mentioned, probably his parents. The rear wall niche holds a single male statue, probably of Ahmose.

The *Shrine of Min* (No. 5), an official at the time of Tuthmosis III, is 12m N. The ceiling is flat and rough, with some traces of red lines, the E wall has gone almost entirely and near the entry the signs have only been outlined in black ink; they were never carved. Min is described as treasurer of the king of Lower Egypt and judge. The unfinished state of this shrine enables the various stages of decoration to be easily examined. The S wall is undecorated save for a Coptic graffito.

**GABAL SILSILAH TWO SHRINES**

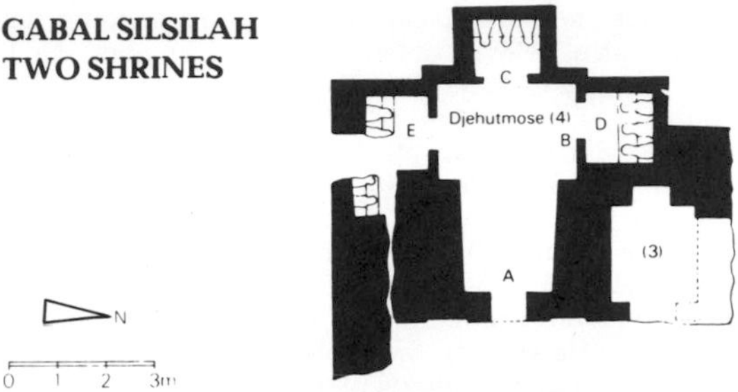
C
E
Djehutmose (4)
B
D
(3)
A
N
0
1
2
3m

The *Shrine of Djehutmose* (No. 4), who lived at the end of the 18 Dyn., is also unfinished. If completed it would have been unusually elaborate for the site. It consists of two rooms, both quite small. The door is flanked by two stelae incised in the sandstone face of the frontage, each crowned with a cavetto-like cornice cut in the rock. The left-hand stele shows a man in shallow sunk relief, his hands raised in adoration. The clothing worn is of the late 18 Dyn. and the name is given as Djetutmose, scribe of the treasury. The right-hand stele must originally have held another standing figure, but facing away from the door; unfortunately it has been almost entirely destroyed by the cutting of a large round depression. There are two chambers in the shrine and three statue niches, each with the remains of three statues. The ceiling of Room A is slightly vaulted and decorated in an unfinished quadruple spiral, in yellow, blue and red. The ceiling in room B is painted in two patterns, in lozenges and ovals and a semblance of a Maltese cross. The statue recess (E) has been split by movement of the sandstone cliff which has slipped towards the Nile. The figures in the niches are (C) figures of a man flanked by two women; (D) a woman and two men, and (E) two men and one woman. There are no texts in the niches.

Shrines Nos 1 and 2, near the top of the cliff, and No. 3, at the base, are unfinished, badly damaged and of uncertain date.

After a short slope the **Speos of Horemheb** is reached. This is locked and arrangements must be made with the Dept of Antiquities at Aswān so that one of the guardians will be present. The chapel was unfinished and many later inscriptions have been added. On the centre entry are the name and titles of Horemheb, who is said to be beloved of Amun-Reʿ. The roof is vaulted and the walls are marked by many beam holes made by squatters living here. Both roof and walls are marked by smoke traces. The Horemheb reliefs are only found either side of the entry and at the S end on the back wall, where the king is shown as a boy suckled by Tausert between Amun-Reʿ and Khnum.

(1) Ramesses III offers to Amun, Mut, Khonsu and Sobek. (2) Niche, Prince Kha'aemwaset as semtem priest, year 30 of Ramesses II. (3–4) Lintel and jambs of Horemheb. (5) Above niche, Pairi, overseer of the treasury, time of Ramesses III. (6) Ramesses III offers Ma'at to Onuris-Shu. (7–8) Ramesses II followed by Vizier

## SPEOS OF HOREMHEB

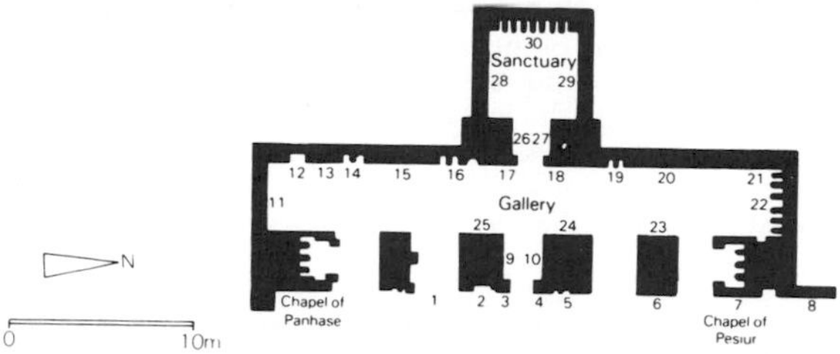
30
Sanctuary
28
29
26
27
12 13 14
15
16
17
18
19
20
21
22
11
Gallery
25
24
23
9 10
N
Chapel of Panhase
1
2 3
4 5
6
7
8
Chapel of Pesiur
0
10m

Neferronpet offers Ma'at to Ptah and Sobek. (9–10) Ramesses III offers bouquets to Ptah and Sekhmet and food to Sobek and Hathor; hieratic text above. (11) Horemheb suckled by Tawsert. (1N2) Horemheb before Amun. (13) Horemheb carried by soldiers. (14) The vizier Huy. (15) Siptah, Chancellor Bay and Merneptah. (16) Statue of Ramesses II. (17) Stele of Ramesses II and Prince Kha'aemwaset. (18) Stele of Ramesses II and Prince Kha'aemwaset. (19) Statue of Kha'aemwaset (destroyed). (20) Prince Kha'aemwaset before offerings. (21) Ramesses II offers to Ma'at. (22) Six statues of Panhase, Ma'at, Amunnakhte. songstress of Hathor, Ptah and Reʿ, (23) Siptah offers Ma'at to Amun and Ptah. (24–25) Horemheb offers to the gods. (26–27) Horemheb offers to Reʿ-Harakte, Amun and Mut. (28) Three registers of 12 seated divinities. (29) Two registers of 12 standing divinities. (30) Statues of seated divinities, Sobek, Tawsert, Mut, Amun-Reʿ, Khonsu, Horemheb and Thoth.

If the crossing is made by ferry (prior arrangement necessary) the tour of the site should start from here. About 2km SE of the site is the village of *Fāris*. Many of the people dispossessed by the flooding of Nubia following the construction of the Aswān High Dam have been resettled in the surrounding area.

The next major town is (18km) **Kom Ombo** (Ar. *Kawm Umbū*; the Mound of Umbū), an important centre for the sugar trade. It stands beside the river and has a mainline station and coach station for local buses and buses to Luxor and Aswān.

The ancient site of the city of *Nebet*, later called by the Greeks *Ombos* (to be distinguished from Tukh to the N near Dendārah, which also had both these names) is 4km SW of the modern town. Several very early cemeteries found in the neighbourhood attest the early settlement of the area. For a period the town was the capital of the Ombite nome as it was on the route from the gold mines of the Eastern Desert and the caravan trail to Nubia. It probably enjoyed its greatest prosperity during the Ptolemaic period when African elephants were trained for the Ptolemaic army here. Where the river bends to the W is a series of sandbanks which must, in ancient times, have been a favoured basking place for crocodiles and it is therefore not surprising that the town is associated with Sobek the crocodile god, later in association with Horus the Elder.

Although the principle gods of Kom Ombo are Sobek-Reʿ and Horus and their consorts, many other gods and goddesses were worshipped in the temple including Amun, Khnum, Ptah, and various other forms of both Horus and Hathor. The district in which Ombos was situated was known as 'the Great Seat' or 'the Great Throne', derived from the seat on which the goddess Tefnut sat when she visited the area, while Reʿ was upon his campaign. The site in myth was associated with Reʿ's fight for supremacy against Seth, in which struggle he was aided by Horus the Elder. Thus the two Horuses are amalgamated; as the Elder he helps his father Reʿ against

Seth for the possession of Egypt, as the Younger, he is Horus the 'Avenger of his father', fighting the same enemy to avenge Osiris.

Now that the Nubian temples have been inundated the present ***Temple of Sobek and Horus** is one of the most picturesque as seen from the river, and it is unusual, but not unique, in being dedicated to two deities. As at many other sites, it is only the last of a long series of shrines built on the same place. It is built of Silsilah sandstone and was completed under Ptolemy V although additions were made later. The infantry, cavalry and other troops stationed in the Ombite Nome erected the temple for the king.

Kom Ombo was one of those temples to which pilgrims came to be healed. They fasted, spent the night in the temple precinct and were treated by the priests of Horus, 'the good doctor'. There is evidence of their presence in the many graffiti scribbled on the pavement of the outer corridor. They wrote their names in Greek, they drew their feet pointing towards the shrines, even in the first hypostyle hall. They played games with stones, and the boards on which they threw are carefully drawn out. They also drew ships, trees and other objects to while away the long hours of the night.

Amelia Edwards, when she visited the temple in 1874, described it as 'a magnificent torso' and this is really what it is. The front of the temple, including the pylon, slipped into the river but was partly shored up by the Dept of Antiquities in 1893. The temple as it now stands, surrounded by the remains of a mud-brick enclosure wall, consists of a damaged pylon, a mammis and chapel of Hathor, a courtyard, inner and outer hypostyle hall, three vestibules, two sanctuaries and a series of small rooms grouped round these, and two ambulatory corridors. In the crypts were crocodile burials (many specimens are usually to be seen in the Hathor chapel). Also there is a little passage in the thickness of the walls which gave priests access to a chamber above the sanctuaries.

The E half of the temple was dedicated to Sobek-Reʿ, his wife (a form of Hathor) and his son, the young moon god Khonsu-Hor. The W side of the temple was dedicated to Horus the Elder (Haroeris), his wife Hathor (called Ta-Sent-Nefer, Good Sister) and his son, the young Horus (called Pa-Heb-Tawy, Lord of the Two Lands). This was not the only temple dedicated to two deities; there was a Middle Kingdom temple in the Fayyūm of the reigns of Amenemhat III and IV dedicated also to Sobek and Horus, and at the other Ombos, further to the N, both Horus the Elder and Seth were worshipped.

The complex is best entered from the NE, walking to the riverward side to the SW. In front of the temple to the W lies the *Mammisi of Ptolemy VII*; it is largely destroyed, the W half having fallen into the river. Steps lead up to a terrace, once a small court, where there used to be four Hathor-headed columns (recorded by Napoleon's scholars). Extant remains consist of a vestibule and two ante-chambers. There is only one notable scene, that of Ptolemy IX upright in his boat accompanied by two gods navigating through a forest of papyrus. Birds fly among the plants and on the left the scene is surveyed by Min-Amun-Reʿ holding lettuces. The hippopotamus goddess with other deities is shown on the border of this scene.

Against the mud-brick outer wall SW of the main temple stands the uncompleted stone *Chapel of Hathor* which was raised, as far as can be seen from a note on the lintel, by a certain Petronia and her children in the

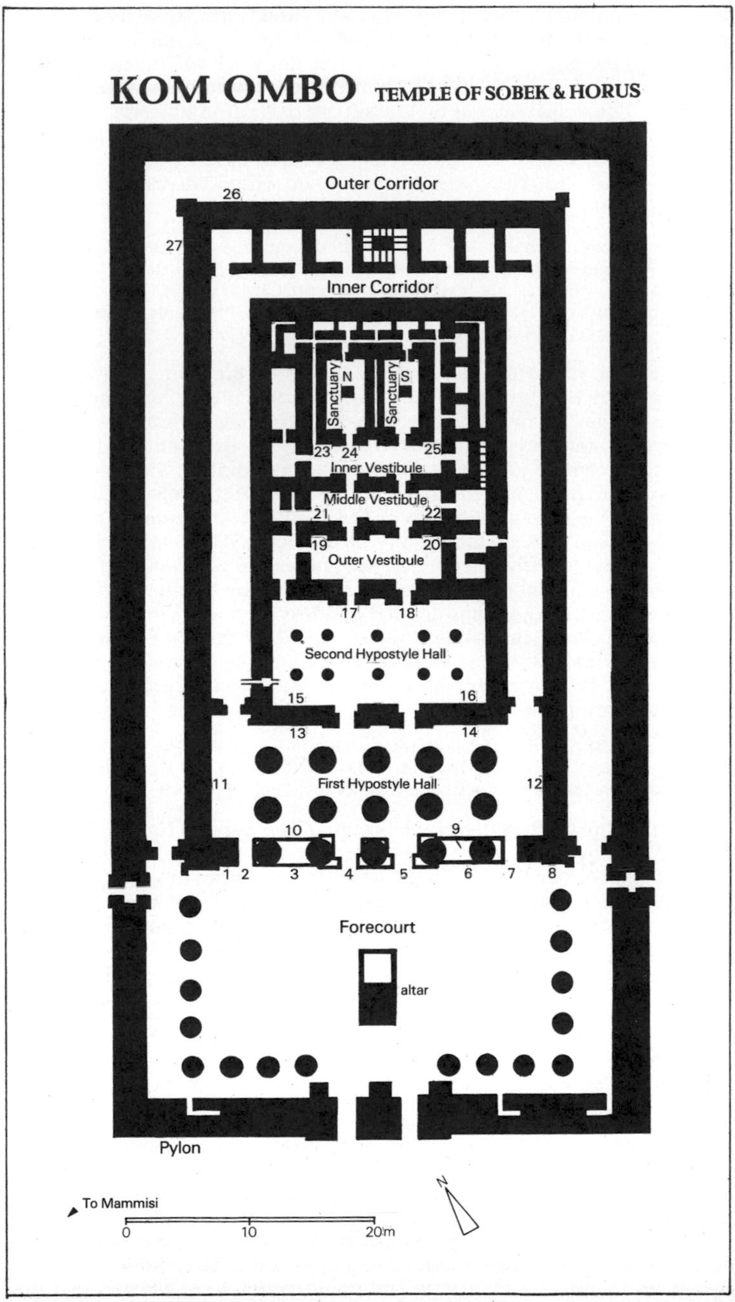
KOM OMBO TEMPLE OF SOBEK & HORUS
Outer Corridor
26
27
Inner Corridor
Sanctuary N
Sanctuary S
23 24 25
Inner Vestibule
Middle Vestibule
21 22
19 20
Outer Vestibule
17 18
Second Hypostyle Hall
15 16
13 14
11
First Hypostyle Hall
12
10 9
1 2 3 4 5 6 7 8
Forecourt
altar
Pylon
To Mammisi
0 10 20m
N

reign of Domitian (AD 81). It has two rooms and is now used as a store for mummified crocodiles found at the site.

Entering the *Forecourt*, the decoration is the work of Emperor Tiberius (AD 14). Only the bases of the columns remain, but there is still quite a lot of colour. The eight columns on the left are dedicated to Horus the Elder, those on the right to Sobek-Reʿ. In the centre is a massive altar flanked by two granite basins set in the paving. The NE side of the court is the temple façade, with a double entry under two winged disks and uraei and four half screen walls topped with uraei.

(1) Lower register, Ptolemy XIII with standards and texts. (2) Building texts. (3) Ptolemy XIII purified by Thoth and Horus before Sobek. (4) Texts of Ptolemy XIII and Cleopatra VI. (5) Texts of Ptolemy XIII and Cleopatra VI. (6) Ptolemy XIII purified by Thoth and Horus. (7) Lintels and door jambs, Nile gods binding the two lands. (8) Ptolemy XIII leaves palace, purified by the gods.

Adjoining the entry in the *First Hypostyle Hall* are scenes showing the king's baptism by Horus and Thoth who pour water over him, and a scene of the king going from his palace to the temple. He is wearing a long robe, leaning on a staff and preceded by a small figure, the inmuter priest, who offers him incense and the standards of seven divinities. The columns are composite and graceful, some of the finest late work. While the five on the façade have the base decorated with the southern lily, there are two in the body of the hall with northern papyrus emblems. The quality of the wall painting is particularly fine; one scene shows the coronation of the king before Horus and Sobek, and the goddesses of the South and the North. Nut is also shown, and a lion-headed goddess, perhaps a form of Menyhit or Isis Repet. On the inner side of the small door to the SW the king is seen in the presence of the four winds, represented as animals, a bull (?), a four-headed lion, a falcon and a four-headed snake. The ceiling is decorated with flying vultures.

(9) Ptolemy XIII crowned by Nekhbet and Wadjet. (10) Ptolemy XIII before Isis, Reʿet, lion-headed, and Horus the Elder. (11–12) The king and Nile gods and field goddesses. (13–14) Ptolemy VIII with texts of hymns to Nile gods.

Continuing the dual nature of the building, the *Second Hypostyle Hall* is entered also by two doors. On the shafts of the ten columns in this hall Ptolemy VII Eurgetes II is shown sacrificing to different gods. On the N wall Horus the Elder is shown giving the hps (a kind of curved weapon representing the sword of victory) to Ptolemy, behind whom is his wife Cleopatra II and his sister Cleopatra III. On the W wall between the two doors is a list of festivals and deities worshipped in the temple. In this hall would have waited the portable wooden shrine carrying the two gods' statues.

(15–16) Processions with Ptolemy VI Philometor and Upper and Lower Nile gods and field goddesses. (17–18) King offers Ma'at to Triads of Sobek and Horus.

The *Outer Vestibule*, decorated as are the next two vestibules to the order of Ptolemy VI, shows scenes of the foundation of the temple, Sheshat the goddess of writing laying out the temple with a measuring cord. There is also a scene of the king purifying a model of the temple. These foundation scenes had to be repeated, so that the temple would remain in a state of ritual purity. Offerings were brought to this hall, and the position of the table is marked by lines drawn on the pavement. The *Middle Vestibule* served as the Hall of Offerings and only priests were allowed into this area. Off this on both sides were ruined rooms which must have served, as in other temples like Dendārah and Edfū, as storerooms for the temple linen, silver and perfumes, and as laboratories and a library. On the S side is seen the lion-headed goddess presiding over the offerings while on the W wall is the temple calendar. To the S is a stair leading to the roof where there was the now-destroyed Chapel of the Disk, as at Dendārah, Edfū and Esna. The spiral stairway which used to be on the S side has been destroyed. On the N wall of the *Inner Vestibule* the two doors are the entries to the sanctuaries of Horus and Sobek, and show a double scene in each of which the king is presented by deities with a notched palm branch, from which a heb-sed (jubilee) sign is suspended, representing the years of his life. This is given by Khonsu wearing a blue crescent round a red disk, followed by Horus in blue representing the air and Sobek in green representing water. On the N side of this vestibule was the Chapel of the New Year (totally destroyed) with fragments of the ceiling with elongated figures of the goddess Nut lying to the E. To the E is the door into the *Chapel of Purification* in which the robing took place before the New Year Festival.

(19) Measuring the temple. (20) Offerings and libation before Sobek. (21) Ptolemy VI offers food to Horus the Elder. (22) Description of temple and address to Sobek-Reʿ. (23) The king before Horus. (24) Extensively destroyed scenes. (25) Offering scenes. (26) Medical instruments. (27) The king consecrates the temple. (28) Calendar.

Although little remains of the *Dual Sanctuaries*, the work of Ptolemy XIII, they seem to have been much smaller than those at Dendārah and Edfū and unlike these, but as in the sanctuary erected by Philip Arrhidaeus at Karnak, there was in each case a door in the rear wall. The chapels round the sanctuaries have been destroyed down to ground level. Neither of the sanctuaries seems to have contained a stone naos but instead each possesses a grey diorite altar on which the portable shrine stood. Under the sanctuaries are triple undecorated crypts and others, recently cleared, lie on either side. At the E end of the sanctuaries are a series of small *unfinished chapels* containing some interesting reliefs. On the NE outer face of the *Outer Corridor* are representations of a set of medical instruments dating to the 2C AD, similar to the Roman instruments to be seen in many museums. There is also a representation of the mummified Sobek on a cart and two hymns; one to Horus the 'Good Doctor', the other to Sobek-Reʿ. On the pavement of this corridor there are many graffiti left by pilgrims and patients waiting during their nightly vigils—drawings of ships, names in Greek and outlines of feet.

Situated to the NW of the main temple is an *Hydraulic Installation* consisting of a large circular well with a stairway, a cistern and a rectangular basin, all of which were probably connected in some way with the ministrations to Sobek. Close to the old entrance to the temple are the remains of a destroyed *Coptic Church*.

Continuing S, the H2 passes (5km) *Darāw* to reach (35km) **Aswān**.

## B. West Bank

Beyond Edfū the road has only recently been completed. The major villages and sites are (N to S): (40km) **Silsilah**, *Fāris*, **Binbān** and (58km) **Kūbaniyyah**, with the *Monastery of Matias*, excavated in 1910–11 by H. Junker but now mostly sanded-up. Mounds covered with potsherds and two walls are all that remain visible. The road continues to (13km) Aswān.

# 39 Aswān

**Aswān**, a town on the Northern border of Nubia, was once one of the most important cities in Egypt. It lay on the trade route between Egypt and the Southern territories along which ivory, gold, slaves and exotic animals passed into Egypt. It has recently regained prime status with the development of iron foundries and aluminum mining in the area and the construction of the High Dam. At present the area is under military control. The aspect of the town is pleasant with a wide corniche and several markets.

The original town was strategically situated on Elephantine Island. It was called *Abu* (Elephant), Gk *Syene* and Coptic *Sawan*. There seems to have been a settlement here from the earliest dynastic times and during the more settled periods a town probably grew up on the East Bank. Just upstream was the end of the First Cataract which started near Philae, but with the construction of the first Aswān Dam this ceased to exist. At this point the river runs between sandstone cliffs and is beset with granite islands.

**Airport**. 16km SW on West Bank beyond the High Dam.

**Railway Station**. Maydān al-Mahaṭṭah in town centre. Trains for Nile Valley and to the S.

**Bus Station**. For local buses and long-distance buses to Luxor.

**Boats**. Ferries to West Bank and Elephantine Island. Private arrangements should be made to visit other islands or sites.

**Hotels**. Shʿ. Ramsīs. *New Cataract*, (5*); *Cataract* (4*); *Kalabsha* (4*); *Nile City*, (2*); *Haby*, (2*); *Grand Hotel*. (2*); Shʿ. al-Kurnish (Corniche). *Philae Hotel* (2*); *Abu Simbel* (2*); Elephantine Island. *Oberoi Aswan* (5*). Amun Island. *Amun* (4*). **Youth Hostel** on Shʿ. Abṭāl al-Taḥrīr.

**Post Office**, Information bureau, travel agents, and bank, all on the Shʿ. al-Kurnish.

**History**. Although there was a settlement on Elephantine Island before the early dynastic period, after the Unification of Egypt it assumed much greater importance. It was the southernmost city in the First Nome of Upper Egypt. This was a control post for the trade with Nubia and it was also a starting point for the many expeditions to the S. The principal gods of the area were Khnum and his two consorts Satet and Anuket. Hapy the Nile god was supposed to live in a cave under one of the islands and another was considered the burial place of Osiris. Aswān was one of the last areas affected by Christianity and the cult of Isis lingered on at Philae until the 5C. However, with the final extinction of the ancient religion it became a Christian stronghold from which monks made missions into Nubia. After the Muslim conquest it was again the last area to be subdued and, with constant replenishment from the Christian Nobatae of Nubia, it remained a constant source of trouble. It was not until late Fāṭimid times that these were subdued and under Ṣalāḥ al-Dīn extinguished. The inhabitants of Aswān are mainly Nubians who have their own local customs and language, although Arabic is universally spoken also.

The main tourist area is confined to the 3km of roads along the riverbank—the SH'. AL-KURNISH (Corniche) and the ABṬĀL AL-TAḤRĪR (also called Sh'. Ramsīs). Most of the hotels are found along this stretch of road, as are shops, agencies and offices. Behind this, most of the city is modern but there are interesting local markets. Sites to be visited in the area include the ancient Muslim Cemetery and the Northern and Southern granite quarries, the islands in the river which contain several important sites, and on the West Bank the Tombs of the Nobles and the Monastery of St. Simeon. Upstream is the old Aswān dam and the Island of Agilqiyyaḥ (New Philae) and further S are the High Dam and New Kalābshah. Aswān is also the departure point for the sites on Lake Nasser, including Abū Simbel.

In the SE of the town is the suburb of *al-Qataniyyah*. It is bisected by the road to the High Dam. To the N and S, covering an area of c 1sq. km, lies the **Ancient Muslim Cemetery**, containing several hundred tombs built between the 8 and 12C with the majority being Ṭūlūnid (9C). Built of mud-brick, with baked brick often used for the arches and domes, they show an unbroken sequence from the simple open enclosure to complex domed cubes.

*Fatimid tombs in the Muslim cemetery at Aswan*

Many of these tombs had the original marble inscriptions attached to them giving the name of the deceased and the date. However, in 1887 some of these were detached in an unprecedented downpour. Tragically these, along with the majority which were still attached to the tombs, were collected and sent to Cairo without any record being kept of their original locations (they are now in the Mosque of Farag, Cairo, Rte 8), the whole unfortunate episode being innocently started by Wallis Budge.

# ASWAN

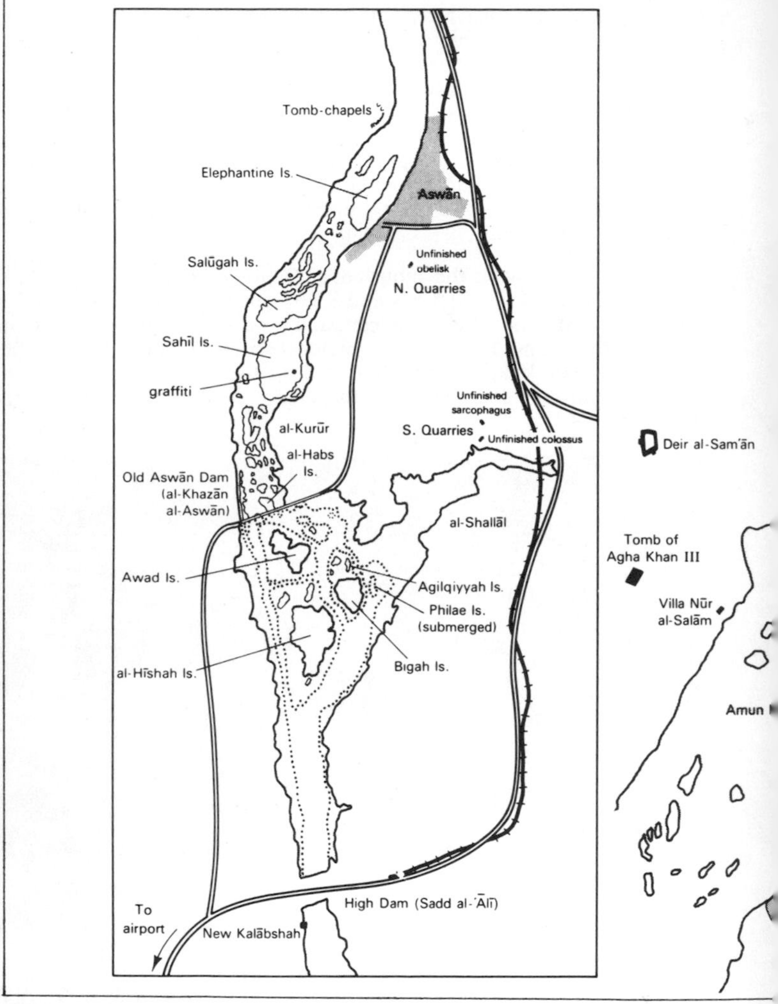
Tomb-chapels
Elephantine Is.
Aswān
Unfinished obelisk
N. Quarries
Salūgah Is.
Sahīl Is.
graffiti
Unfinished sarcophagus
al-Kurūr
S. Quarries
Unfinished colossus
Deir al-Sam'ān
al-Habs Is.
Old Aswān Dam (al-Khazān al-Aswān)
al-Shallāl
Tomb of Agha Khan III
Awad Is.
Agilqiyyah Is.
Villa Nūr al-Salām
Philae Is. (submerged)
al-Hīshah Is.
Bigah Is.
Amun
To airport
High Dam (Sadd al-'Ālī)
New Kalābshah

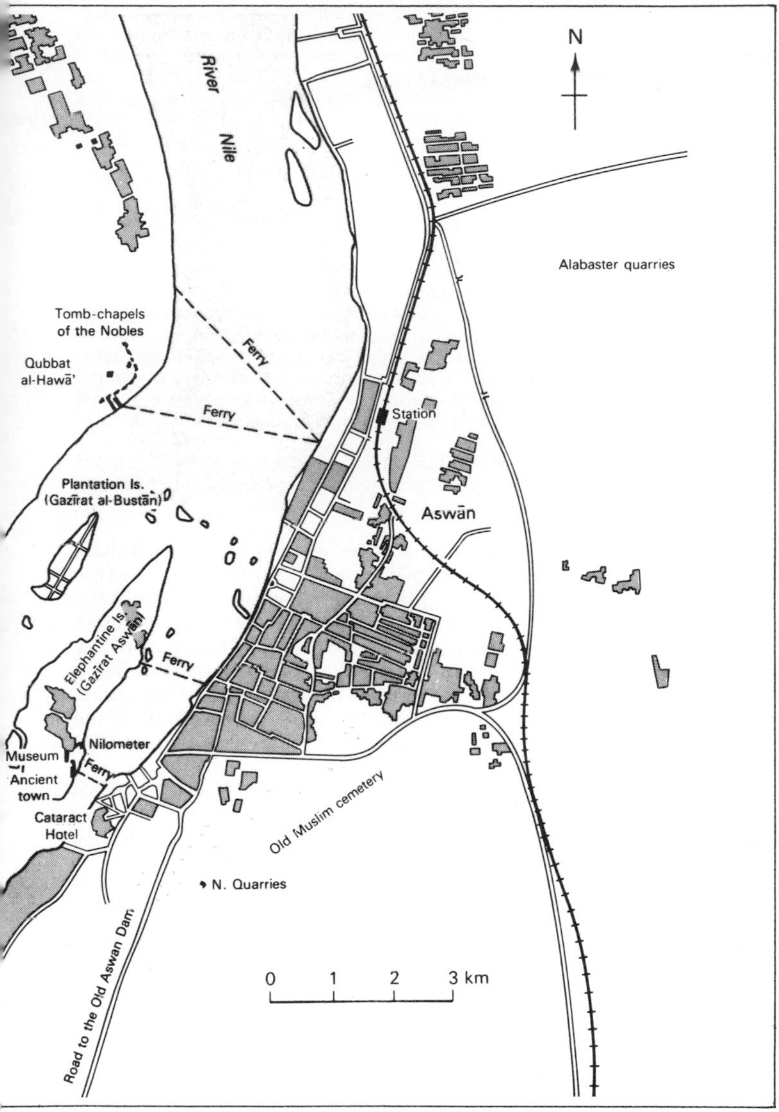
N
River
Nile
Alabaster quarries
Tomb-chapels
of the Nobles
Qubbat
al-Hawā'
Ferry
Ferry
Station
Plantation Is.
(Gazīrat al-Bustān)
Aswān
Elephantine Is.
(Gazīrat Aswān)
Ferry
Nilometer
Museum
Ancient
town
Ferry
Cataract
Hotel
Old Muslim cemetery
N. Quarries
Road to the Old Aswan Dam
0 1 2 3 km

The earliest tombs are small rectangular walled enclosures, the most primitive of which have plain walls. The later type have panelled walls with decorative openings through which the grave can be seen. These small enclosures were sometimes filled with earth and were a continuation of the Coptic tradition of tomb construction. The next stage is a low brick vault, occasionally covered with earth or with a brick block superstructure. The domed cube which appears in the 11C also has a well-demonstrated evolution. First is the canopy type open on all four sides. This is followed by tombs in which the qiblah wall is filled in and a miḥrāb placed in the wall so formed. Next all the walls are filled in and a door is left in the NW wall. Another form of tomb superseded the domed-cube in which the base was rectangular with a dome over the centre flanked by two tunnel-vaults. The sub-types of this are similar to those of the domed-cube with the earliest open on all sides, then with one wall closed and finally with only one door in the NW wall. This last type usually has a small forecourt in front of the entrance.

Several devices were used to set the dome over the base. The most primitive is a stone lintel set over the corners to create an octagon. Pendentives are also used as are half-conical or semi-domed squinches. Some of the last reach exaggerated proportions, giving an unusual exterior profile. The superstructure of the drums have outcorbelled corners which give a characteristic horned appearance to these tombs. This is uniquely a Southern Egyptian technique, probably a development of a NW African feature.

It is very difficult to be precise about dates of individual tombs, since although a certain type cannot be earlier than a specific date, tombs of primitive type would continue to have been built along with the more advanced forms.

The most important building remaining in the cemetery is the **Mashhad**, of an unknown person, built on the top of the hill. It has similarities to the Mashhad of al-Guyishi in Cairo (Rte 14). Certain modifications suggest a slightly later date of c 1105. In construction it is within the metropolitan canon and shows none of the S Egyptian techniques. The drum of the dome is raised on squinches with three niches and the miḥrāb has a pointed arched hood. In front of the miḥrāb is the remnant of a fine tomb. Close to this stood the Qubbat al-Sabʿa wa Sabʿūn Awliyan (Tomb of the 77 Governors), an 11C nine-domed mosque. It was destroyed in 1901 during the construction of a reservoir.

To the E of the station, in a hollow near the road to the Northern Quarries, is a small incomplete **Ptolemaic Temple** (fee), built by Ptolemy III Euergetes I and Ptolemy IV Philopator and dedicated to Isis.

It is entered through a doorway with the usual cavetto cornice, where scenes show Ptolemy III offering to Amun, Min-Amun, Mut and Khonsu. On the lintel he is seen accompanied by his wife Berenice before the gods. Two pillars support the main hall and beyond are three shrines with the centre chapel dedicated to the gods of the cataract. This temple is now used as a store by the Dept of Antiquities. This was converted into a church in the 6C. 95m to the S the Swiss Institute have discovered another sanctury built by Tiberius, Many decorated blocks from here have been used in the Byzantine Walls of Cyene which had towers at regular intervals.

Past the cemetery the road meets the railway and turns S through the desert towards the High Dam.

## The Islands

**Elephantine Island** (Ar. Gazīrat al-Aswān) lies in midstream opposite the modern town of Aswān. It is 2km long and 500m at its widest. There are two villages on the island which are independent of the mainland city. Two ferries serve the island, one from just N of the Cataract Hotel to the S end of the island, the other from the Philae Hotel to the N end. Museum and resthouse near the Temple of Khnum. (Fee for visiting island and museum.)

On this island was the ancient city of **Abu**, Gk *Elephantine*, the circular site of which is at the S end of the island. It is at present under investigation by a West German archaeological expedition. Prehistoric remains attest to the length of occupation of the island as do predynastic rock-carvings. The island was considered to be the home of Hapy, the Nile god, although the provincial god of the region was the ram-headed Khnum, Lord of the Cataract. Later there was a Jewish settlement here and many Aramaic papyri have been found.

Traces of ancient quay walls can be seen on the E side of the island, near where the S ferry docks. Just N of this is the **Nilometer**, discovered in 1822 and reused in the 1870s. It had been constructed during the Roman period on the site of an earlier one. The walls and steps are of sandstone and it was originally roofed with granite. The marble slabs denote its use in the 19C.

The ancient town extends over c 1.8sq. km. To the NW is the city gate, and in the centre the temple of Khnum. In Old Kingdom times the temple accounted for about two-thirds of the town area but by the Middle Kingdom the town had doubled in size, spreading to the NW. Outside the massive granite walls an outer city arose, the buildings of which, mainly domestic in character, show a wide variety in size and importance. For example some houses in the SW temple area had well-built walls with columned interiors and were decorated with wall panels. Some high officials who had houses here are known from their tomb-chapels in the rock face on the West Bank. The temples of Khnum and Satet are both Old Kingdom foundations.

W of the Nilometer, aligned to the shorter axis of the town, is the much ruined **Temple of Khnum**. Nectanebo II (30 Dyn.) was responsible for most of the building, but it was added to by Alexander II. Much of the material is reused and some of the blocks are 18–19 Dyn. Here Khnum and his two consorts Satet and Anuket—fertility goddesses and aspects of the Nile flood—were worshipped. The gateway shows Alexander II worshipping Khnum. At the NE of the site is the Greco-Roman **Necropolis of the Sacred Rams** discovered by M. Clermont-Ganneau in 1906–07. The rams were mummified and buried in stone sarcophagi, many still visible (mummies in the museum). The **Museum** was built in 1912 to house material rescued before the building of the first Aswān Dam. It contains many prehistoric pieces, pottery, flints, palettes and necklaces. The arrangement is chronological with small objects of the Middle and New Kingdom. In the corridor are several statues from the Sanctury of Neq'ib, including the Governor of the South, Amnei and a son of Serenput whose tomb is on the W bank. In the basement are Ptolemaic mummies of priests and a mummy of a Khnum ram coated with gold-leaf. In the garden are statues of Middle Kingdom local nomarchs. Recent work by the German Institute has revealed a fortress of the 1–2 Dyn, trapezoidal in form measuring 70 x 55m.

There is evidence for other temples at this site, one of Ptolemy VII to the N and a *Shrine of Heka-ib*, a 6 Dyn. governor of Abu who was later deified. Two larger buildings, a Temple of Amenhotep III (N of the present site) and a Temple of Tuthmosis III (in the centre of the island), were both described by the French expedition in 1800, but were totally destroyed in the civil conflicts shortly after.

To the N is the **Temple of Satet**, a New Kingdom building, but the cult niche on which it is based goes back to the 1 Dyn. It is known that Pepi II (6 Dyn.) had a naos here. Later, the early shrine was extended into a mudbrick temple with inscriptions and reliefs of Antef and Mentuhotep (11 Dyn.).

To the E excavation shows that the 1st Dyn fortress was preceeded by houses dating to Naqada II, the last stage of the pre-Dynastic period, prior to 3100 BC.

N of Elephantine Island, and usually visited just after, is **Gazīrat al-Bustān** (Plantation Island; fee; café). It contains fine specimen shrubs and trees, many of them from tropical Africa planted by the sirdar Lord Kitchener when this island was presented to him after his successful campaign in the Sudan.

About 4km upstream lies the **Seheil Island** (Ar. Gazīrat Sahayl), about 3–4 hrs by sailing boat. (Landing on the E side of the island.) It was sacred to the deities of the cataract and at least two temples to Anuket were situated here, the last being Ptolemaic. A notable collection of over 250 **rock inscriptions** can still be seen carved on the cliff to the E of the modern village. They are situated either side of a cleft and were placed there by the officials before they went to Nubia, or on their return in commemoration of some important act. They are all numbered and are mainly of the 18–19 Dyns. Several refer to a canal built in the area, during the reign of Senusert III, to by-pass the cataract. It was called 'Beautiful are the Ways of Senusert III'. Its exact location has never been established but another inscription of Senusert at the S of the island suggests that it might have passed S and W of the island. The canal remained in use until at least the mid-18 Dyn. as there are instructions from kings of this period about keeping it cleared.

Some of the most important historical inscriptions are Nos *72* Hor Viceroy of Nubia; *76* Viceroy Huy (Ramesses II); *78* King Neferhotep, 13 Dyn.; *79* Senusert III; Aahmes II, 26 Dyn; *81* known as the *Famine Stele*. Although it was written in Ptolemaic times this last tells of the seven-year famine in Egypt during the reign of King Zozer. To ameliorate the famine Zozer gave benefactions to the Temple of Khnum at Elephantine and restored the temple buildings. It also gives the Horus name of Zozer and thus enables him to be identified with certainty as the builder of the Step Pyramid. It was discovered by C.E. Wilbur, an American Egyptologist, in 1889. *101* Viceroy of Nubia; *117* Paser, high priest of Khnum, Satet and Anuket; *137* 33rd year of Ramesses II; *145* cartouches of Amenhotep III erected by Vizier Ramose; *198* Amenhotep Viceroy of Nubia; *199* Ramesses III and gods; *213* cartouche of Amenhotep II; *278* Tuthmosis III worshipping Khnum and his Triad.

## West Bank

The usual crossing method is by felucca. The town ferry to the West Bank is situated in front of the Ministry of Tourism offices on the Corniche. From the quay on the West Bank a rough track leads S to the rock-cut **Tomb-Chapels of the Nobles**. These are the burial places of the governors and priests who controlled the commercial traffic with Nubia. There is quite a hard climb to reach them, especially from the S where the sand is loose and slippery.

The sandstone is of inferior quality and the tombs containing poorly-executed carvings are interesting mainly for the historical information that three of them, Sabni, Harkhuf and Pepi-Nakht, provide. First discovered by Gen. Sir Francis Grenfell in 1885–86, others were exposed by the British Museum, L. Habashi and a

German expedition. The tombs are in three groups. Those of the Old and Middle Kingdom are highest up the slope and cut into the best rock. Below are an intermediate band of tombs of various periods, and a Roman group just above the water-line. Not all the tomb chapels are numbered, and only some are worth a visit.

Starting from the S, the first tomb-chapel to be visited is that of **Mehu** (No. 25) of the time of Pepi II (6 Dyn.). There are 18 roughly worked columns and on the rear wall a false door inside a recess. The inferior quality reliefs show the dead man making offerings, and sacrificing animals. Adjoining is the tomb of his son **Sabni** (No. 26), governor of the South. On the rear wall of this tomb is a scene of hunting in the marshes (most unlikely in this area). When Mehu was killed Sabni went to collect his body and brought it back. After several uninscribed tombs is No. 28, probably of a son of Sirenput (see below). Beyond several more unimportant ones is one of the finest of the tombs, **Sirenput II** (No. 31), governor of the South, Commander of the Troops (time of Amenemhat II, 12 Dyn.) and son of Satet-hotep. It consists of a narrow hall followed by a square six-pillared hall, a recessed corridor with Osiride statues of the dead man. At the end of the corridor is a small hall with columns with Sirenput portrayed on each. The tomb was never finished and the guidelines of the scenes are still visible. The reliefs at the rear of the inner hall are of better quality than elsewhere in this tomb.

Next is the unimportant tomb of **Aku** (No. 32). Further on is that of **Khuy** (unnumbered and usually sanded up) with a pillared hall with four columns. This man seems to have led several expeditions into Nubia. In the (unnumbered) tomb of **Ma**, his wife Ankh-sen and son Khunes of the 6 Dyn., the roof has collapsed. The next tomb is that of **Harkhuf** (unnumbered), governor of the South and caravan leader (time of Pepi II). He went into Yam (part of Nubia) on several expeditions, returning with incense, ebony, grain, leopardskins and throwing sticks. His greatest achievement was on his fourth voyage when he brought back a 'dancing dwarf ... from the land of spirits'. For this act he was rewarded by the king and allowed to place an account of the adventure in his tomb. It is not particularly imposing, consisting only of a small pillared hall and a sloping passage leading to the burial chamber.

The tomb-chapel that follows is that of **Pepi-nakht** (No. 35) who was caravan leader and scribe of the pyramid 'Neferkare remains alive' (time of Pepi II). His tomb is also quite small. On each side of the door are inscriptions which tell of the deceased being sent by Pepi to subdue the natives of Nubia and Asia. He also brought back the body of Ennkhet, another caravan leader who had been killed while building a ship to take part in the Punt trade. The final tomb-chapel which needs to be seen is that of **Sirenput I** (No. 36), governor of the South, overseer of the priests of Khnum and Satet, and hereditary prince. He was also grandfather of Sirenput II (time of Senusert I). This has a columned court originally roofed with a fine façade. Sirenput is shown each side of the door with his staff of office. On the back wall is a large figure of Sirenput followed by his sandal bearer. The hall of the tomb has four square pillars, and a long passage leading to a small chamber with two pillars and a small statue recess. His wife and mother both appear to be called Set-then. The scenes in the chapel are of the usual kind; hunting, fishing, offering bearers, and sacrificed cattle. Many of the sculptures have been badly damaged.

There is a later tomb belonging to the New Kingdom, that of

**Ka-kemkew**, high priest of Khnum and the Triad of Elephantine. This was found by Lady Cecil and Howard Carter in 1902. It had not been finished. It has a colonnaded court. There are some interesting funeral pictures showing a funerary boat, the mummy and the mourning family.

From here there is a climb to the top of the hill and the *Qubbat al-Hawā°* (Dome of the Wind), the tomb of Sīdī ʿAlī. 4km SW stands the *Monastery of St. Simeon* (see below)

On the West Bank opposite the S tip of Elephantine Island is the **Nūr al-Salām**, the villa of the former Agha Khan III. The Begum Agha Khan, his widow, now spends several weeks here each year. On the hill behind the palace stands the **Tomb of the Agha Khan**. It was built for the third Agha Khan (1877–1957) in solid marble at a cost of £150,000.

The Agha Khan is leader of the Shīʿī sect of Ismāʿīlī Muslims, centred on India but with large communities in E Africa and other parts of the world. The origins of this sect are within the same framework as those of the Fāṭimids and it is fitting that the form of the tomb is based upon a Fāṭimid prototype, the Mashhad al-Guyushī in Cairo (Rte 14).

Agha Khan III succeeded his father in 1885. He was educated in Europe and spent much of his life there. In 1906 he headed the All-India Muslim League in support of British Rule in India. His wealth was legendary and he was weighed in diamonds on his diamond jubilee in 1945. His son ʿAlī predeceased him and he was succeeded by his grandson Karīm in 1957.

About 1km N along the Wadī Qurqur is the **Monastery of St. Simeon** (Deir Anba Samaʿān), a high-walled compound on two levels. Although the present building is 10C it is a rebuilding of a 7C foundation. It was destroyed by Ṣalāḥ al-Dīn in 1173 as a possible refuge for the Christian Nubians who were still making forays into S Egypt.

The 7C foundation was dedicated to Anba Hadra, a saint of Aswān, who lived in the latter half of the 5C. Although married, he preserved his chastity and became a student of St. Baiman. He retired to the desert in emulation of the life of St. Anthony. Eventually he was consecrated bishop of Aswān.

Although much ruined the monastery retains many features intact. The surrounding wall is over 6m high; the base of stone, the rest of mud-brick. It measures c 100m by 90m. Entry is from the E through a door in a small tower. This leads into the *Lower Enclosure*. Near this gate is the *Church* consisting of a nave, aisles, choir and sacristy. Part of the roof, originally covered with domes, has collapsed. In the altar recess is a well-preserved painting of Christ Pantocrator flanked by angels. Below the church is a cave-chapel with painted ceiling and walls, showing various saints. To the N are steps to the *Upper Enclosure*, at the N end of which is the two-storeyed residence. In the second storey is a *large hall* with cells lining the sides. There are mud-brick bench-beds and six small wall cupboards for the inmates in each cell. At the NW angle is the *Refectory*. This building was apparently in the process of being whitewashed when Ṣalāḥ al-Dīn's forces arrived. Below this building are several rock-hewn cells. To the S are the stables, kitchen and wine press. The church is still used for occasional services.

**Northern Quarries and Old Aswān Dam**

The road to the first Aswān dam leaves S from the SW area of the town. To the E (750m) are the **Northern Granite Quarries** (fee), one of the sites in the district where the red granite was cut from the 1 Dyn. onwards and transported throughout Egypt. The most impressive object here is an unfinished obelisk, 41.75m long, which if completed would have weighed 1168 English tons. Although not inscribed, it is probably 18 or 19 Dyn.

During the cutting a flaw was discovered in the stone and the length was reduced to 32.1m and its weight to 507 tons. The obelisk was cleared by Rex Engelbach, inspector of the Dept of Antiquities in 1922. The black paint outlining the work to be done was still clearly visible when he started work at the obelisk. He also found small round holes on the top surface of the obelisk filled with grains of black gunpowder, probably the remains of an attempt to split the granite by the Ottomans. When found it was covered with burnt bricks and reeds and Engelbach considered that these were fired on the stone so that the burnt surface of the granite could then easily be pounded. Many dolorite pounders that the workers had used were also found, weighing 4 to 6.8kg. In an experiment Engelbach removed 5mm of rock from a strip 0.5m wide in one hour. The method used to detach the obelisk was to undercut from both sides with large wedge-shaped cuts or wet wooden wedges. Flat surfaces were obtained by using boning rods. Engelbach proposed that after it was undercut it was packed with wooden blocks and ropes were passed round it. The pull required to move it would be half the weight of the obelisk, i.e. 585 tons. The obelisk could be turned with levers 6.4m long. It is not known how long it would have taken to cut and shift this obelisk, but there is evidence that Hatshepsut had two obelisks cut, moved and erected at Karnak in seven and a half months. (For the Southern Quarries see below.)

The road continues S to (4.5km) the old **Aswān Dam**, begun by the British in 1898 and opened in December 1902. Originally it was 30.5m high and 27m thick at the base. However it soon needed adjustment and between 1907–12 another 5m was added to the height. Further work was carried out between 1929–32 and the final result was 42m high with a length of 2441m and a capacity of 5400 million cubic metres. It was built on the same principle as the river barrages further N, with a sandstone and granite structure resting on a cement base set on the bedrock. The flow of water was controlled by 180 sluices worked by a travelling crane. Provision was also made for generation of hydro-electricity and there is a navigation canal. Although this did much to control the seasonal height of water, it was not completely successful and in 1962 President Nasser announced the construction of a dam which would give total control of the Nile. The result was the Aswān High Dam (see below).

On the East Bank is the **Aswān Reservoir Colony**. From here boats may be hired for the island of Agilqiyyah (see below). The road crosses the dam to the West Bank and turns S to join (c 7km) the road from the High Dam to the temples of New Kalābshah and the airport.

## Agilqiyyah Island (Philae)

The island of ***Agilqiyyah**, onto which the structures from the submerged island of Philae have been transferred, has been reshaped to resemble the conformation of Philae as closely as possible. With the building of the first Aswān Dam Philae was submerged for part of the year, and with the equalisation of the water flow produced by the High Dam it would have been permanently below water. Thus it was decided to move all the buildings and reconstruct them on this neighbouring island. This was a massive project taking over ten years. A great coffer dam was erected around Philae and the temples were dismantled and transferred. They were finally opened on their new site in 1980. The earliest remains on the original island were of Taharqa (25 Dyn.) but the foundations have been removed to the Southern Quarry area.

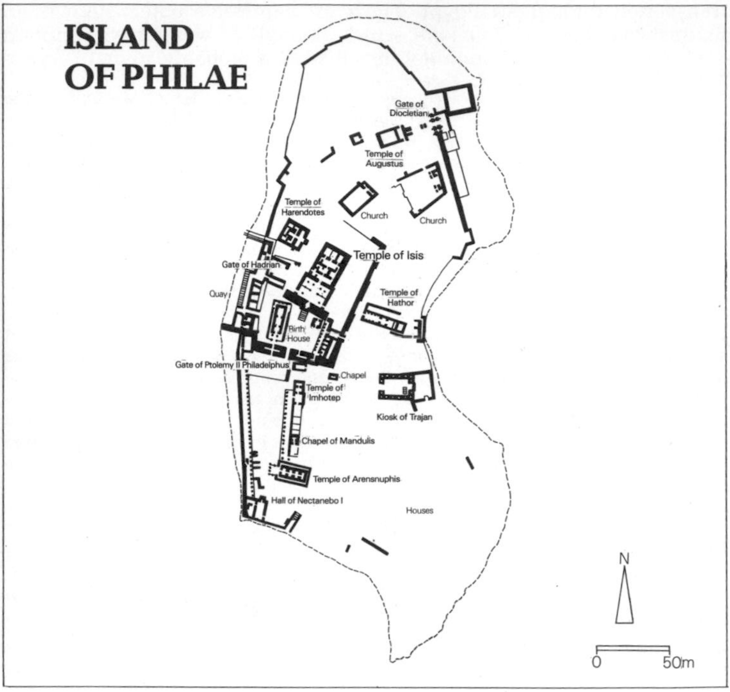
ISLAND
OF PHILAE
Gate of Diocletian
Temple of Augustus
Temple of Harendotes
Church
Church
Temple of Isis
Gate of Hadrian
Quay
Temple of Hathor
Birth House
Gate of Ptolemy II Philadelphus
Chapel
Temple of Imhotep
Kiosk of Trajan
Chapel of Mandulis
Temple of Arensnuphis
Hall of Nectanebo I
Houses
N
0
50m

Philae, which lay next to Bigah, the island of Osiris, was dedicated to Isis, and the largest and most important among the complex of temples and chapels is the **Temple of Isis** which occupies about one quarter of the island.

At the SE end of the island is a *Kiosk of Nectanebo I* (30 Dyn.), beyond which is a long court bounded by two Roman colonnades, the *West Colonnade* and the *First East Colonnade*. At the S end of the latter is a small *Temple of Arensnuphis* (a Nubian deity), Ptolemaic and Roman in date, while halfway up is a *Chapel of Mandulis* (i.e. Marul, another Nubian deity) which is Roman. At the N end stands the *Temple of Imhotep*, the deified architect of Zozer, here worshipped as a healing god. It was built by Ptolemy V Epiphanes. The colonnade court ends in front of the First Pylon of Ptolemy XIII Neos Dionysius. Two obelisks from here are now in Kingston Lacey, Dorset. On the E side is a Gate of Ptolemy II Philadelphus but the main entry is through the *Gate of Nectanebo II* (30 Dyn.). This leads into a large forecourt. On the W is the *Mammisi* built by Ptolemy VII Euergetes II and added to in Roman times. The opposite side of the court is occupied by the *Second East Colonnade* which is late Ptolemaic. This court leads to the *Second Pylon* built by Ptolemy XIII Neos Dionysius although the gateway is of Ptolemy VII Euergetes II.

(1–2) Above lintel, winged vultures and cartouches of Ptolemy Euergetes II. (3) Granite stele of year 24 of Ptolemy Philometer VII, text. (4) Upper register, the king

*The forecourt of the Temple of Isis, Philae*

offers to the gods, Horus and Isis, Geb, Nut and Horus the Elder; base, procession of the king followed by offering bearers, Osiris, Isis and Horus. (5–6) Grooves for flagstaffs. (7) The king offers to Osiris, Isis and the young Horus.

Beyond the gate is the *Hypostyle Hall* with ten columns, mainly the work of Ptolemy VII Euergetes II.

(8–9) Ptolemy and Cleopatra II offer vases to Khnum-Reʿ and Hathor. (10) Upper register, the king offers libations to Khephera, and Neb(t)hotep, incense to Khnum and Satet, and grape juice to Horus and Hathor. (11) The king offers incense and libations to Osiris and Isis, wine to Horus and Nephthys. (12) The king offers wine to Atum and meat to Geb and Nut, four calves are offered to Osiris and victims to Isis, Sekhmet, and Horus the Elder. (13) The king offers green and white linen to Reʿ-Harakhte and Nut. (14–15) The king followed by Wadjet receives life from Tefnut, and runs with an oar.

N of the hypostyle hall is a chamber with a small room to the W, from which stairs lead to the roof. This is followed by three chambers.

(16–17) Isis seated before standards, the king offers myrrh and wine. (18) The king offers flowers to Isis. (19) The king offers collar to Isis, Osiris and Nephthys, and pectorals to Osiris, Isis and Hathor. (20) The king offers libations before a heap of offerings. (21–22) Double scene on outer lintel, the king offers wine to Osiris and Isis, menat to Hathor and bread to Isis. (23) The king before Isis. (24) Doorway to stairs. (25–26) Double scene, the king offers sistrum on left and wine on right to Isis and Harpocrates; on W jamb the king offers leaves to Min, a basket to Sekhmet and wine to Osiris. Behind is the sacred bull and seven cows.

The central room leads into a *transverse room* from which three rooms lead to the N.

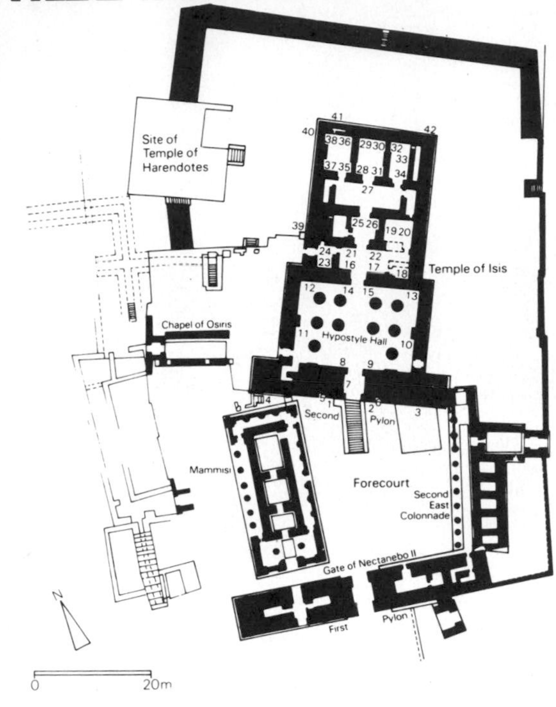
Site of Temple of Harendotes
Temple of Isis
Chapel of Osiris
Hypostyle Hall
Second Pylon
Mammisi
Forecourt
Second East Colonnade
Gate of Nectanebo II
First Pylon
N
0
20m

**PHILAE** TEMPLE OF ISIS

(27) The king offers wine, necklaces and eye paint to Osiris, Isis, Hathor and Nephthys. (28–29) The king in three scenes offers cloth to Isis and Nut, box to Osiris and Isis suckling boy, and image of Ma'at to Isis and Nephthys. He also offers linen to Osiris and a winged Isis. (30–31) Top register, three scenes, the king before Isis and Nephthys, adores Amun-Reʿ and Mut, offers to Isis and Tefnut, including collar.

Round the base of the *Sanctuary* are fertility gods of the country.

(32) Ptolemy II offers incense to Satet and ointment to Isis. (33) The king offers cloth and wine to Isis and Sekhmet. (34) The king before ram-headed Sheshmu (usually shown in lion form). (35–36) The king offers menat to Isis, incense to Nekhbet and wine to Nephthys. (37–38) The king offers mirror to Anuket, basket to Wadjet and wine to Isis.

The outside of the temple was decorated by Augustus.

(39–40) Augustus followed by fertility gods and goddesses before Osiris, Isis and the young Horus. (41–42) Augustus offers Ma'at to Amun-Reʿ and Mut and makes libation to Isis and Nephthys, offers vase to Khnum and Hathor.

The most important of the other chapels around the main complex is the unfinished *Chapel of Hathor* on the E side of the island. Built by Ptolemy VI Philometer and added to by Augustus, it has an interesting scene of musicians including the god Bes playing a harp. Just S of this is the *Kiosk of Trajan* with a charming façade on the river bank.

*The Kiosk of Trajan*

The larger island to the S is **Bīgah**. This was held to have been the burial place of Osiris and was for a long time a cult-centre.

**Southern Quarries and High Dam**

4.5km further on the W side of the road in a valley are the **Southern Granite Quarries**. First visible remains are two unfinished Ptolemaic sarcophagi, which have never been hollowed out. Nearby is stele cut in the rock face. It shows a man worshipping the cartouches of Amenhotep III. To the S is a large *unfinished statue*, and a large block probably intended for a naos. Further up the hill is an unfinished and uninscribed *Osiride colossus* about 6m long.

Beyond this the road divides. The W fork runs into **Shallāl**, a small town on the lake between the two dams. But continuing S the road reaches (12km) **al-Sadd al-ʿĀlī** (the High Dam) which was begun on 9 January 1960 and opened on 15 January 1971.

Although the first Aswān dam (see above) had done much to alleviate dependence on the annual inundation of the Nile, it had not proved entirely successful. In 1952 President Nasser announced his proposal for a larger dam, several kilometres upstream, to deal with the problem once and for all. Having met with refusals to cooperate on the part of the western nations Nasser turned to the Russians. The result was the present structure which, unlike the earlier ones, is a rock-fill dam. It is 3600m long, of which 530m stretches between the two banks. The height above the river bed is 111m and the base is 980m wide. The top, which is 40m wide, contains a dual carriageway. There is also a hydro-electric plant with six turbines capable of producing 2.1 million kilowatts. Lake Nasser, which has built up behind the dam, is 500km long, thus stretching into the Sudan, and averages 10km wide. The dam has provided perennial irrigation throughout Egypt, it produces more electricity than can at present be used and has enabled large tracts of land to be opened up for cultivation. There is also an immense fish population in the lake which is commercially exploited. On the debit side, the sediment which was brought down annually by the river now remains and settles in the lake, salinity has increased in the rest of the country and salts can be seen encrusting the edge of the lake. The large expanse of water has also provided refuge for the snail host of Bilharzia and the malaria-carrying mosquito. However these problems are not insurmountable and are being tackled by the Egyptian government. A change, the results of which—good or bad—have yet to be seen, is the difference in the weather produced by the large expanse of Lake Nasser. Rain is much more frequent in S Egypt than before. One tragic consequence of the raising of the waters of Lake Nasser was the loss of many of the Nubian monuments, Ancient and Christian. Although the Egyptian government aided by UNESCO and many countries worked with great speed to resite them, many of the buildings have disappeared and will probably never be seen again.

Crossing the High Dam, the road turns S again to (750m) **New Kalābshah**, the site of three re-erected temples saved from the waters. The temples are on an island (fee and special permit required) reached by motor-boat. They are just a handful of the southern temples and forts that would have been below the new level of the lake. Others have gone to countries co-operating in the massive UNESCO rescue operations and a few have been abandoned and are now under water.

Most impressive is the well-preserved **Temple of Kalābshah**, moved from its original site in 1970 by a team of West German engineers. The original site of this temple was Kalābshah (ancient Talmis), about 50km S of Aswān. Here the river once wound between cliffs, the Bāb al-Kalābshah, with granite rocks breaking up the surface of the water, making navigation difficult. Talmis was certainly settled by the 18 Dyn. as Amenhotep II is shown in the outer vestibule of the temple. There was also a statue of Tuthmosis III lying in front of the temple early in this century, but its present whereabouts is unknown. The temple is built of sandstone blocks and is dedicated to Marul (Gk Mandulis), a Nubian fertility god who is also associated with sun worship. For some reason Wadjet, the goddess of Lower Egypt, is also closely associated with this temple and is represented throughout in the paintings. This temple, a reconstruction by one of the Ptolemies on an 18 Dyn. foundation, was added to by the Romans, perhaps Augustus, but it was never finished. Like Edfū and Dendārah, it was a healing temple.

An imposing causeway (30.5m) leads to the front of the temple and the *Pylon*. This is set slightly askew to the axis of the temple and has 25 steps leading up to the temple platform. The pylon is well-preserved although it has lost its upper portions, including the cornice. It is undecorated except around the entrance.

(1–2) Outer doorway, the king offers milk to Mandulis and to Osiris and Isis, the king offers Ma'at to Mandulis and Wadjet. (3–4) The emperor before Mandulis and Augustus before Horus.

The entry leads to a *colonnaded court*, originally with a total of 14 columns on the S, N and E sides. Some of the colour remains on the inner paintings.

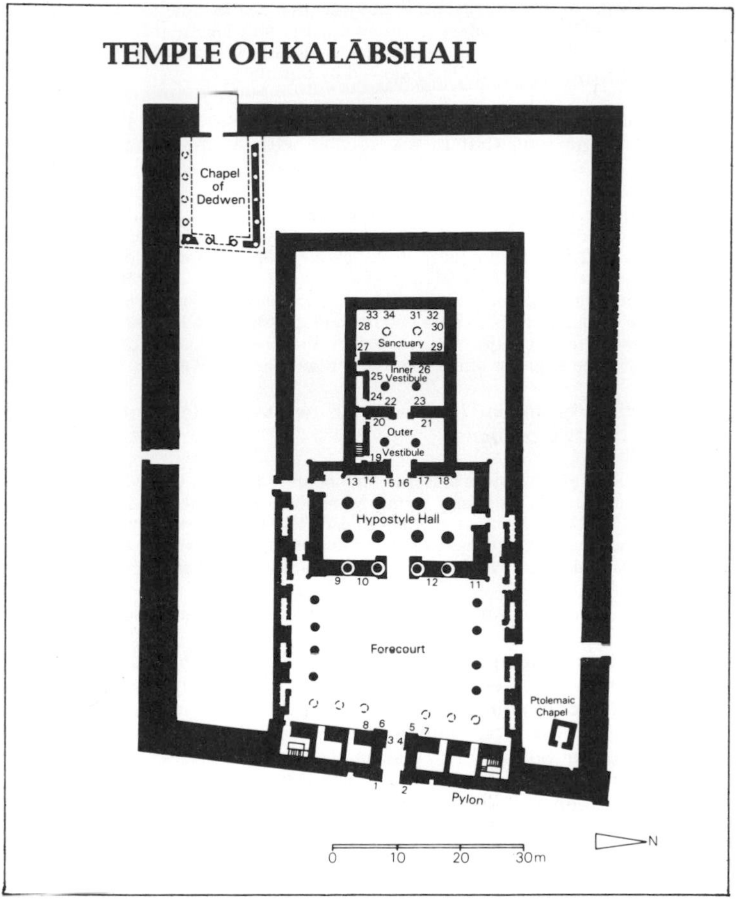
TEMPLE OF KALĀBSHAH
Chapel of Dedwen
33 34 31 32
28 30
27 Sanctuary 29
Inner Vestibule
25 26
24 22 23
20 21
Outer Vestibule
19
13 14 15 16 17 18
Hypostyle Hall
9 10 12 11
Forecourt
Ptolemaic Chapel
8 6 5 7
3 4
1 2
Pylon
0 10 20 30m
N

(5–6) Lintel, double scene, the emperor followed by fertility gods and field goddesses offers to Mandulis and Isis. The king with two genii behind him, adores Osiris and Horus, the king offers to Isis and Osiris and Isis gives life to Mandulis. The king offers to Mandulis and Horus (right). (7–8) Graffiti and hawks. (9) The emperor before Mandulis as a child and Isis. (10) The king purified by Thoth and Horus. (11) Inscription in inferior Greek of Silko, Christian king of the Nobati of Nubia who descended as far as ancient Kalabsha in a successful raid on the Blemmyes. Close to this is a picture of a man (perhaps Silko) in Roman dress, on a horse, receiving a wreath from the winged Victory. Next is an inscribed decree of Aurelius Besarion, governor of Ombos and Elephantine (c AD 248), ordering the expulsion of pigs from the precincts of this temple. (12) A Meroitic inscription of Kharahedeye, King of the Blemmyes.

The *Hypostyle Hall* has eight columns in two transverse rows of four. Some of the paintings are unfinished.

(13–14) The king offers crowns to Horus of Edfu and Mandulis, Ptolemy offers field to Isis, Mandulis and Horus, Khnum faces Reʿ-Harakhte, and Amenhotep II offers wine to Min-Reʿ and Mandulis. (This suggests that the foundation is in fact New Kingdom.) (15–16) Trajan offers to Mandulis, Isis and Osiris. (17–18) King (cartouches blank) kills an enemy before Horus, Shu and Tefnut. Offers incense to Mandulis and Wadjet. Processions followed by fertility gods.

Beyond this are *two vestibules*, each with two columns. To the S of each are stairs to the roof, that in the second with a small chapel perhaps dedicated to Osiris.

(19) Top register, the king offers wine to Osiris, Isis and a field to Isis and Mandulis. (20) Top and second registers, the king consecrates victims before Isis and offers wine to Osiris. (21) The king holds up sky before Ptah, Sekhmet and Mandulis (?), offers wine and lettuces to Min, Isis and Mandulis. (22–23) The king offers incense to Mandulis and Wadjet (left), the king offers milk to Osiris-Onnuphris and Isis (right). (24–25) The emperor offers incense and libation to Osiris, Isis, Horus, Mandulis and Wadjet. Lower register, the emperor offers incense to lion-headed Tutu, and Imhotep. (26) The emperor offers incense to Mandulis and Wadjet.

The *Sanctuary* is similar in size to the two vestibules and, like them, originally had two columns.

(27–28) The king offers crowns to Horus, Hathor and Mandulis. (29–30) The emperor offers vase to Khnum, Satis and young Mandulis and image to Mut, Horus and Amun-Reʿ. (31–32) The emperor offers lotuses to Mandulis and Wadjet, cloth to Mandulis and goddess, and incense to Isis and Horus. (33–34) The emperor offers lotuses to Isis and young Horus and milk to Mandulis and Wadjet.

Around the temple is an ambulatory. Lion-headed water spouts project from the wall.

Surrounding the temple is a thick temenos wall which also encloses to the SW a small rock-cut *Chapel of Dedwen* with an open columned forecourt. The only painting is of the king offering wine and incense to Dedwen, probably a local Nubian deity. Suggestions that this served as a mammisi are not borne out by the paintings. In the NE corner is a small Chapel, probably predating the present main temple. Although unfinished it seems to be the work of the Ptolemies V and X. Reliefs show the king offering to the Triad of Elephantine.

The second building re-erected here is the **Kiosk of Qirtasī**. This charming kiosk was originally at Qirtasī, 40km S of Aswān. There seemed to be no remains earlier than the Ptolemaic period at this site. It was connected with extensive quarries which were once worked there. Here there was a shrine and ex votos inscriptions in Greek of the priests presiding over the transport of the cut stone. They were addressed to Isis and two local Nubian gods, Srupkithis and Pursepmunis, who seems to have been a form of Osiris. Close to this shrine and now under water was a stone-built fortress with walls over 6m high. Inside this was a Temple of Isis, but this disappeared in the 19C.

The kiosk consists of a single chamber, rather like that at Philae. There are four upright columns with well-cut floral capitals. The screen walls connecting the capitals are preserved on the E, N and W sides, but that on the S side has been destroyed. Entry is from the N, flanked by two Hathor-headed columns. On the W there is another small door. Before it was moved the roof had fallen except for a single cross beam. On one column there is a relief of the king before Isis and Horus, otherwise the temple is undecorated. It dates therefore to the Ptolemaic or Roman periods.

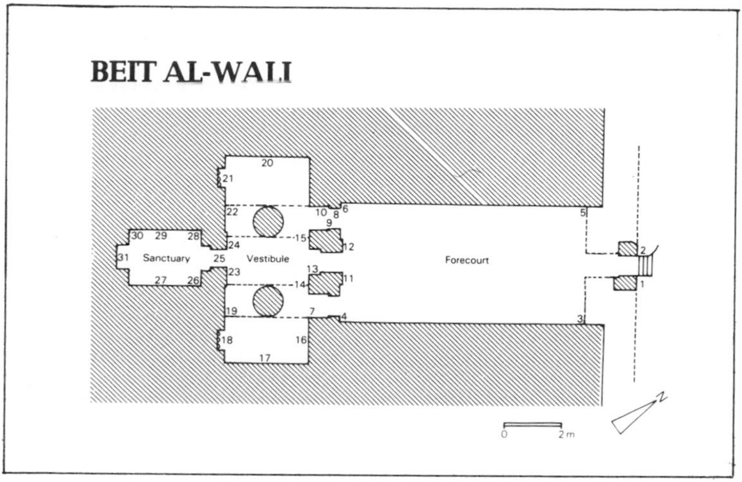
BEIT AL-WALI
Sanctuary
Vestibule
Forecourt
0
2 m
N

Behind the temple of Kalābshah is the third reconstructed temple, the **Temple of Bayt al-Wālī**. It is the earliest of the three and the most interesting. This was situated slightly NW of Kalābshah and was partly rock-cut. The modern Arabic name means House of the Governor. Messuy, viceroy of Kush, had this temple constructed for Ramesses II. Originally the temple was joined to the river by a long causeway but this has not been reconstructed, as it was lost with the building of the old Aswān Dam.

The temple consists of a mud-brick gate leading into an outer court, from which three doors open into the rock-cut interior. The vestibule has two fluted columns, with the titles of the king, and two statue niches. Beyond this is the sanctuary, also with a statue niche against the back wall.

(1–2) Ramesses performs purification ceremony. (3–4) Ramesses and sons in chariots charge Nubians, and receives tribute including leopards, giraffes, bulls, ostriches, ivory and gold and prisoners. (5–6) The king trampling on Asiatics, attacks fortress, charges Asiatics and Libyans in chariot, an attack on a Syrian fort, receiving Syrian spoils. (7) The king recounts his conquests to Amun-Reʿ. (8) The king kneels with water before Khnum (destroyed). (9–10) Royal titles. (11–12) The king running with hap and oar before Amun-Reʿ, receives life from Khnum, and Mut. (13) Messuy, viceroy of Kush, kneeling to Seti I. (14–15) The king embraced by Horus of Miʾam and receives life from Atum. (16) The king smites Nubia, Libya and Syria before Amun-Reʿ. (17) The king followed by Hathor offers incense and libations to Horus of Buhen and Isis as scorpion goddess. (18) Niche, three statues of the king between Horus of Baki and Isis with titles. (19) The king offers Maʾat to Amun-Reʿ. (20) The king followed by Anuket offers wine. (21) Niche, three statues, the king between Khnum and Anuket, with titles. (22) The king offers wine to Amun-Reʿ. (23–24) Double scene, the king before Amun-Reʿ, offers Maʾat, wine and bread to Amun-Reʿ, Sokar, Horus of Baki. (25) The king embraced by Satet. (26) The king suckled by Isis. (27) The king offers libations and wine to Horus of Baki and Amun-Reʿ. (27) The king suckled by Anuket. (29) The king taken by Satet and Khnum, the king offers to Amun-Reʿ. (30) Ptah. (31) Niche with three statues (destroyed).

Beyond New Kalābshah the road runs SW into the desert to (10km) **Aswān Airport**.

# 40 North Nubia and Lake Nasser

The vast distances on this route (more than 300km) can only practically be covered by boat or plane although road now skirts the E shore of Lake Nasser. The route leads S of Aswān to the southern border of Egypt and into the Sudan.

Since the creation of Lake Nasser the Nile Valley is flooded well S of the Sudanese border. The only way to traverse this stretch of water is by boat. Regular twice-weekly sailings are made by steamship to connect with the Sudanese railway at Wādī Ḥalfā. There is a hydrofoil service to Abū Simbel. Boats can (with difficulty) be hired to visit any particular site, but it should be remembered that it is a distance of several hundred kms and takes days rather than hours. A road along the East Bank to Wadī Halfā was completed in April 1985.

Nubia is a general term for the region from S of Aswān to S of Khartoum. Throughout history Egypt has exerted an influence on N Nubia to a greater or lesser degree. In ancient times gold, incense, wood, soldiers, police and slaves were the valuable products of the region and therefore the Egyptians made a continual effort to control it—with varied success. The modern name of Nubia derives from the Ancient Egyptian word for gold, 'nub', i.e. the land of gold. In the New Kingdom it was called Kush and placed in the charge of a viceroy, the third most important official in Egypt.

In the Old Kingdom trade, mining and military expeditions were undertaken to Nubia on a rather casual basis and it was not until the powerful kings of the Middle Kingdom that a methodical military campaign was waged. To support their presence Senusert III built a series of forts along the river as far S as the Second Cataract, which also served as trading posts with the tribal Nubians. The New Kingdom extended Egyptian control upstream to the Fourth Cataract in modern Sudan. Many rock-cut temples were excavated, especially in the reign of Ramesses II (19 Dyn.). As the strength of the Egyptian state declined its control of Nubia dwindled, but it left behind an indigenous highly Egyptianised culture centred on the city of Napata, below the Fourth Cataract. By the mid-8C these people, under King Piankhi, were so powerful that they were able to invade Egypt, oust the Libyan 22 Dyn. and contain the Egyptian princes in the Delta provinces. Installing themselves as the 25 Dyn., they ruled for nearly 100 years. Taharqa, however, interfered in the politics of Western Asia and his successor Tanutamun had to face the might of the Assyrian Empire under Ashurbanipal. In 656 BC the Assyrians invaded Egypt, sacked Thebes and Tanutamun retreated before them to Napata. For a thousand years henceforth they confined themselves to Nubia, where they controlled a vast territory. With local variations they continued the Egyptian tradition, even burying their kings in pyramidal tombs. Later the capital moved S to Meroe but the religious centre remained at Napata.

Retaining its power, the Napatan Empire made a treaty with Ptolemaic Egypt and N Nubia was ruled as a condominium—the Dodekas-choinus (12 Leagues)—and the Ptolemies built extensively in the area. Equality was anathema to the early Romans and they aggressively pushed back the southern borders of Egypt to Hiero-sykaminos (Maḥaraqah). In the late 3C internal crises within the Roman Empire caused Diocletian to abandon the area completely. A powerful Hamitic camel-riding nomadic tribe, the Blemmyes (perhaps the modern Beja) established themselves in the mid 4C along the foothills of the E mountains and moved W until they effectively formed a wedge between the Napatan Empire and Egypt N of Aswān. They continued to harry the frontiers of both Roman Egypt and Nubia until the late 5C. This cessation of trade between the two areas isolated and weakened the Napatans until in AD 350 Ezana, the Negus of Abyssinia, conquered Meroe and brought the empire to an end.

From the remnants of the Napatan Empire three kingdoms arose. The N region from Aswān to Ṣāyy, just above the Third Cataract, was *Nobatia* with its capital at

Bajrash (Faras). S of this to beyond the Fifth Cataract was *Makuria*, with its capital at Dongola. Extending beyond this to the swamps of the S lay *Alodia*, whose capital was Suba. In the mid 6C Silko, King of Nobatia, drove the Blemmyes back to the E hills and even invaded Southern Egypt. The magnificent tombs of this dynasty were discovered at Qustul and Ballanah, still showing Ancient Egyptian traditions except for the mass execution of servants and animals, a grotesque ceremony abandoned by the Egyptians after the 1 Dyn. Probably because of the pressure exerted by the aggressive Persian occupation in the 7C, the kingdoms of Nobatia and Makuria merged with the power residing at Dongola.

Although Christians had drifted into Nubia during the early centuries of the Christian era, from the mid 6C missionaries were sent directly from Constantinople in an effort to convert the Nubians, and for a time the kingdom wavered between allegiance to the Orthodox or Coptic churches. This influence was discontinued by the Persian invasion and subsequent Arab conquest and the field was left to the Copts. By the mid 7C the area was firmly within the Monophysite sphere, maintaining strong links with the patriarchate of Alexandria.

The Arabs called Nobatia *al-Maris* (from the Coptic for 'south') and from shortly after the conquest Arab tribes and individual merchants filtered into Nubia while other Arabs came across the Red Sea. A great number of Muslims of the Judhaym tribe were displaced from their lands in the Nile Delta by Ṣalāḥ al-Dīn in the 12C and were forced to move S into Nubia. Many of these men married into Nubian families and this produced a strange result. As the laws of inheritance in Nubia were

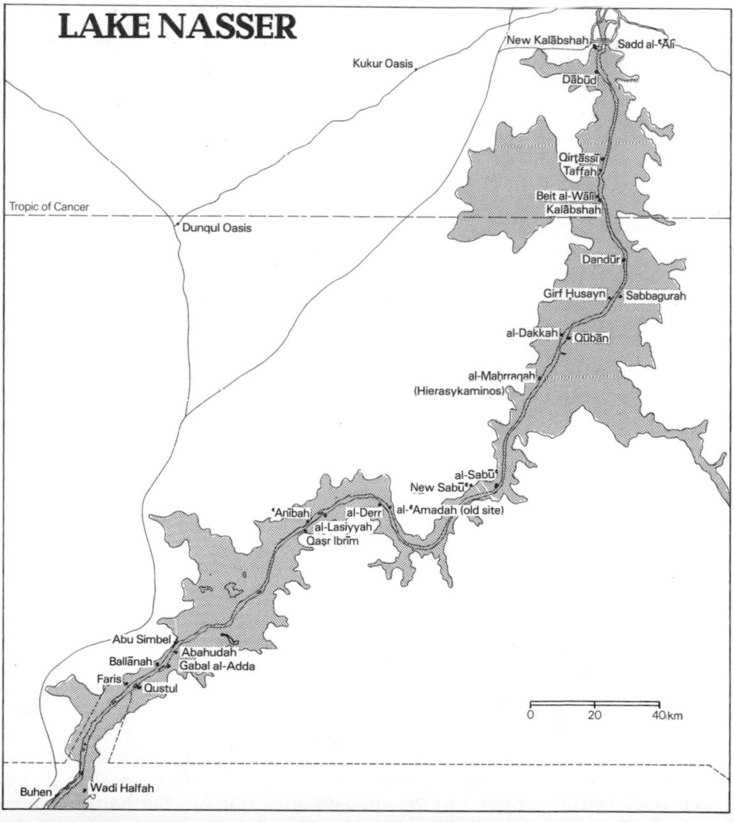
LAKE NASSER
New Kalābshah
Sadd al-ʿĀlī
Kukur Oasis
Dābūd
Qirṭāssī
Taffah
Beit al-Wālī
Kalābshah
Tropic of Cancer
Dunqul Oasis
Dandūr
Girf Ḥusayn
Sabbagurah
al-Dakkah
Qūbān
al-Maḥrraqah
(Hierasykaminos)
al-Sabū
New Sabū
ʿAnībah
al-Derr
al-ʿAmadah (old site)
al-Lasiyyah
Qaṣr Ibrīm
Abu Simbel
Abahudah
Ballānah
Gabal al-Adda
Faris
Qustul
0
20
40km
Buhen
Wadi Halfah

through the matrilinear line, the Muslims gradually acquired control of the estates and by marrying into the royal house ended up by inheriting the monarchy. By the late 13C al-Maris was totally Muslim and was absorbed into the Egyptian area of influence. Makuria retained its independence for a further hundred years.

During the Ottoman period the area remained a place of refuge for discontented factions within the beylicate of Egypt. In 1821, during the reign of Muḥammad ʿAlī, his son Ismāʿīl led an expedition into the Sudan and effectively subdued the country. It was annexed as a personal possession of the pasha and exploited as a source of slaves and soldiers.

Thrice before the building of the High Dam the monuments of Nubia had been threatened, the first time with the building of the old Aswān Dam in 1902 and subsequently each time it was raised (1912 and 1932). Each time a survey of the monuments had been undertaken and the sites recorded and mapped. When the High Dam was proposed, however, it became clear that the valley was going to be permanently flooded. Action was needed immediately. After an approach by Egypt and Sudan, UNESCO launched an appeal for what was to be perhaps the biggest archaeological rescue operation to date. Over 40 countries were involved, giving either money or practical help. Each national team undertook responsibility for specific tasks and all the sites, cemeteries, tombs, temples, forts and churches were to be fully surveyed and photographed. Some of the temples were dismantled and presented to the participating countries, others were moved with prodigious ingenuity to new sites along Lake Nasser. The work was virtually complete by the time that the water of Lake Nasser rose and the major monuments were saved. Nonetheless the unique fortresses and many fascinating minor sites have been sacrificed and now lie at the bottom of the lake. The people who inhabited the banks of the Nile were given new villages in the areas opened up to cultivation by new canals, particularly around Kom Ombo.

In this section, apart from the new sites on the banks of Lake Nasser, the former positions of the sites are given as distances S from the High Dam.

The first site on the West Bank (10km) was **Dābūd** with a 3C BC *Temple of Isis*. It was built by the Meroitic king Adikhalimani to the god Amun, but the patron deity was changed by the later Ptolemies who added further decoration. Likewise the Roman emperors Augustus and Tiberius contributed to the inscriptions. The temple was presented to the Spanish government and is now in Madrid. Also on the West Bank (23km) was **Qirṭāsī** which had a small Roman *Temple of Hathor*; this has been transferred to Aswān near the High Dam. A further 6km S lay **Taffah**, once the site of two Roman temples; the *Northern Temple* was uninscribed and is now in the Rijksmuseum Leiden, in Holland. The *Southern Temple* disappeared before the end of the 19C.

At (9km) **Kalābshah**, ancient *Talmis*, there were two monuments, both now transferred to Aswān, the *Temple of Mandulis, Osiris and Isis* built by Augustus and the rock-cut *Temple of Amun-Reʿ* built by Ramesses III at Beit al-Walī. 7km further the route crosses the *Tropic of Cancer* at 23°30′ N.

At (15km) **Dandūr** the *Temple of Peteese and Pihar* which stood here was raised by Augustus. The identity of these two men, the sons of Quper, is unknown as is the reason for their deification. At the rear of the temple the rock-sanctuary may date to the 26 Dyn. It was dismantled in 1963 and presented to the Metropolitan Museum, New York.

14km **Girf Ḥusayn** was the site of a rock-cut *Temple of Ramesses II* built by Setau, viceroy of Kush. Dedicated to Ptah, Ramesses, Ptah-tanen and Hathor, the decoration was as good as that at Abū Simbel, with colossi before the entrance. The whole complex was left and is now submerged. There were also important carvings of animals and ships on rocks just S of the temple. On the opposite East Bank at **Sabbagūrah** was a 14C walled *Christian town*, this also has been submerged. 22km further on the West Bank was **al-Dakkah**, called in ancient times *Pr-selket* and in Gk *Pselchis*. The Meriotic and Ptolemaic *Temple* which stood here has been transferred to Sabūʿ al-Gadīd. Opposite on the East Bank stood **Qūbān**, ancient *Baki, Gk Contra Pselchis*. Centred around a 12 Dyn. fort, this was an important commercial centre in the New Kingdom, all now submerged. From here a route to the gold-mines of Wadī Alagi began. On the East Bank (14km) the town of **al-Maharraqah** (Gk *Hierasykaminos*), marked the S frontiers of Egypt in the Ptolemaic and early Roman period. There was also an unfinished *Temple of Serapis*.

37km The site of **Wadī al-Sabūʿ** (Valley of the lionesses), named for the avenue of sphinxes which led to the temple of Ramesses II which has been moved 4km W to Sabūʿ al-Gadīd. The other bulding here, a *Temple of Horus* built by Amenhotep III, is still on the bed of the lake. After being damaged under Akhenaton, it was repaired by Ramesses II and rededicated to Amun.

At **al-Sabūʿ al-Gadīd** the partly rock-cut **Temple of Ramesses II** was moved from Sabūʿ. It was raised by Setau, viceroy of Kush, and dedicated to Amun-Reʿ, Reʿ-Harakhte and Ramesses himself. The avenue of sphinxes once led from the river to the pylon fronted by statues of Ramesses. Around the court were free-standing figures of Ramesses, damaged when the temple was turned into a church. Beyond is the Hypostyle Hall which leads to the rock-cut Sanctuary. The figures of Amun, Reʿ-Harakhte and Ramesses II were chiselled out during the Christian era and a wall painting of St. Peter was substituted. Thus it now appears that the side paintings of Ramesses II offer their lotuses rather incongruously to the saint. The other monument here moved from al-Dakhah is the **Temple of King Argamani and Ptolemy IV Philopator**. Later Ptolemies added to the inscriptions as did the emperors Augustus and Tiberius.

At **ʿAmadah** (50km) the temple has been moved 2.5km from its original site near Kuruskū. Adjacent to it was a large boulder with 12 Dyn. inscription, while to the N were Nubian cemeteries and an 18 Dyn. garrison town. The sandstone **Temple of Amun-Reʿ and Reʿ-Harakhte** was built by Tuthmosis III and Amenhotep II and the Pillared Court was added by Tuthmosis IV. Restoration was undertaken later in the 18 Dyn. On the left-hand thickness of the entrance is a statue of Merneptah, year 4, which describes his victorious campaigns against the Libyans, while in the Sanctuary is a stele of Amenhotep II, year 3, which similarly details his victory over the Asiatics. The French engineers who were responsible for moving the temple wheeled part of it weighing 900 tons as a single entity to the new site.

Also re-erected here is the **Temple of Reʿ-Harakhte**, built for Ramesses II at al-Derr. This rock-cut building is reminiscent of the temple at Abu Simbel, although without the colossi. It was dedicated to Reʿ-Harakhte, Ramesses II, Amun-Reʿ and Ptah. The paintings are notable for their excellent colour and preservation. It was later converted into a church. From the site of ʿAnībah is the rock-cut **Tomb of Penniut**, deputy of Wawat under Ramesses VI.

4km upstream on the East Bank stood **al-Derr** from which the rock-cut temple was removed to ʿAmādah. Also on the East Bank at al-Lasiyyah was a rock-cut *Temple of Horus of Miʾam and Satis* built by Tuthmosis III and restored by Ramesses II who rededicated it to Amun, Horus and himself. It was presented to Italy and is now in the Museo Egizo, Turin.

On the West Bank (10km) **ʿAnībah**, in ancient times Miʾam, was the administrative centre of Wawat (N Nubia). The town surrounded a 12 Dyn. *Fort* and the *Temple of Horus of Miʾam* was also of the 12 Dyn., reconstructed in the 18 Dyn. Several cemeteries surrounded the site and a tomb from one of them was transferred to ʿAmādah. The other monuments were left and are now submerged.

4km upstream on the East Bank is the island of **Qaṣr Ibrīm** (Gk Primis) which before the creation of the lake was a high bluff overlooking the valley. This was a strategic site since ancient times and was often the scene of conflict as various factions fought for possession. Robert Legh, MP, was probably the first European to visit the site, in 1812. The *Fort* is doubtless of ancient origin, probably Middle Kingdom, although the earliest remains were a Stele of Amenhotep I. There are the remains of a *Temple of Taharqa*. After the death of Cleopatra in 28 BC the Nubians attacked S Egypt and occupied the fortress, but the Romans under Gaius Petronius, the governor, retaliated vigorously, drove the Nubians out and pushed back the S frontiers of Egypt. In 1173 the brother of Ṣalāḥ al-Dīn, Tūrān-shāh, subdued Nubia and installed fellow Kurds in the fortress. After the destruction of Faris by the Muslims in the late 12C the seat of the bishopric moved to Qaṣr Ibrīm and the graves of several bishops have been excavated. The stone *Church* still has three walls standing. During the late 15C a southern tribe, the Fung, moved into Nubia and became the most powerful influence in the region. Although they were Muslims and their capital was in the far S at Sinnar, they occupied Qaṣr Ibrīm. In the early 16C the Ottoman conqueror of Egypt, Salīm, sent a force of Bosnians which reoccupied Qaṣr Ibrīm and were forgotten. Their descendants were to inhabit the pinnacle for 300 years. The church was converted into a mosque. Only when the recalcitrant bays fled S before Muḥammad ʿAlī in the early 19C were they displaced. The expedition of Ismāʿil Pasha, son of Muḥammad ʿAlī, ousted the bays during his campaign for control of the Sudan in 1821. Qaṣr Ibrīm has been investigated intermittently for the last 20 years by the EES which has unearthed a vast amount of Christian Nubian material.

## Abū Simbel

Below Qaṣr Ibrīm the next important site is (52km) **Abū Simbel** (Ar. Abū Sunbul), a corruption of the ancient name *Ipsambul.*

*Hotel*, Nefertari (2*). *Airport*, daily flight from Aswān. *Hydrofoil*, 5-hour journey from Aswān.

The area is very desolate and seems to have been so since the earliest times. Nonetheless it was visited in the prehistoric period as inscriptions and carvings in the surrounding rocks testify. Much later Ramesses II had two great temples cut into the rock on the site of an earlier shrine.

Southernmost is the massive ***Temple of Ramesses II**, dedicated to Reʿ-Harakhte, Amun and the deified Ramesses II. It was built by the king before his 34th regnal year on the site of a shrine to a local form of Horus. The location in the Hill of Libations was chosen with great precision so that twice a year (22 February and 22 October) the first rays of the rising sun illuminated the innermost wall of the sanctuary and the seated statues of the four gods there.

The rock-cut temple was discovered by Burckhardt in 1813 almost completely sanded up and Belzoni cleared it in 1817. When the rising waters of Lake Nasser threatened this temple, it was decided to move it to a new location. In 1964 a team of West German, Italian, French and Swedish engineers under the auspices of UNESCO began the work. A coffer dam was erected and the whole temple dismantled. It was re-erected inside a concrete shell 210m further inland and 65m higher. By the time the temple was reopened on 22 September 1968 the operation had cost $40 million.

## TEMPLE OF RAMESSES II

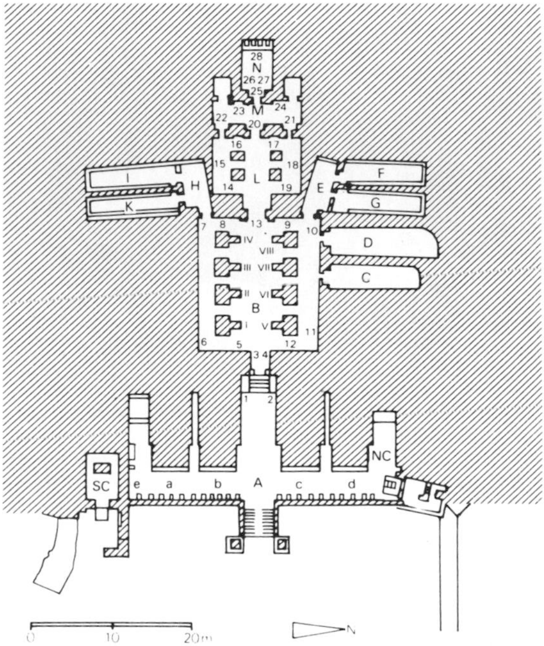
28
N
26 27
25
23 M 24
22 20 21
16 17
15 18
I
H
L
14 19
E
F
G
K
7 8 13 9 10
IV VIII
D
III VII
C
II VI
B
I V 11
6 5 12
3 4
1 2
NC
SC
e a b A c d
0 10 20m
N

The façade, 35m wide and 30m high, beyond a *Terrace* (A), is dominated by four *Seated Colossi* (20m high) of Ramesses II. Each wears the double crown and nemes headcloth and is accompanied by three smaller figures of his wives, daughters and sons, standing beside his legs. From left to right they are (a) Princess Nebtawi, Bant Anta and another unnamed, perhaps, Esenofre; (b) which is headless (upper section lying in front of the temple), Queen-mother Muttuy, Queen Nefertari and Prince Amunhirkhopshef; there is also a Greek inscription giving an account of an expedition by mercenaries to Abū Simbel in the reign of Psamtik II (26 Dyn.); (c) two figures of Queen Nefertari and one of Prince Ramessesu; (d) Queen-mother Muttuy, Queen Nefertari and Princess Merytamun. On the sides of the thrones of the colossi flanking the entry are figures of Nile gods entwining the plants representing Upper and Lower Egypt and below are the Nine Bows, enemies of Egypt, shown as bound Asiatics and

Nubians. In a niche above the entrance stands the figure of Reʿ-Harakhte (in rebus form). Along the summit of the façade is a row of baboons.

*Façade of the rock-cut Temple of Ramesses II*

At the S end of the terrace is the *Hittite Marriage Stele* (e) recording the marriage of Ramesses II to Princess Ma'at-Her-Neferure, daughter of the Hittite king Hattusilus II. Just beyond each end of the terrace is a small chapel. The *N Chapel* (NC), facing the rising sun, consists of an open court and an altar; the rock-cut *S Chapel* (SC) is larger.

(1–2) Double scene, Ramesses preceded by standards runs with hap and oar to Amun-Reʿ and Mut, gives vases to Reʿ-Harakhte and Wert-Hekau. (3–4) Inner Door, the king before Reʿ-Harakhte and Sekhmet and before Amun-Reʿ and Nut, he offers cloth to Amun-Reʿ and bouquets to Reʿ-Harakhte.

A door bearing Ramesses II's cartouches leads into a large rock-cut *Hall* (B) (16.4m by 17.6m). Supporting the roof are eight massive square pillars, in two rows of four. Each of these is fronted by a 9m figure of the king in Nubian Osiride form, wearing a short kilt. Those on the N side are wearing the double crown and those on the S the white crown of Upper Egypt. Between pillars III and IV is a stele of Ramesses II's 34th regnal year recording the erecting of a temple of Ptah at Memphis.

Scenes on the pillars are: (I) The king offers incense to deified self, Queen Nefertari offers incense to Hathor of Abeshek, the king offers flowers to Min and incense to Isis. (II) The king offers Ma'at to Amun-Reʿ and incense and libations to Ptah, bread to Sobek-Reʿ and flowers to Amun-Reʿ. (III) The king stands before Isis and receives heb-sed from Hathor, Princess Bant Anta offers sistrum and flowers to Anuket. (IV) The king offers wine to Reʿ-Harakhte and stands before Amun-Reʿ, offers wine to 'the noble of Hermopolis' and libation and incense to Osiris. (V) The king offers ointment to Menhit and Ma'at to Shu. (VI) The king offers wine to Horus of Baki (a local Nubian deity) and flowers to Mut. (VII) E face, the king offers flowers to Thoth.

N face, the king offers bread to Amun-Reʿ and flowers to Horus of Ha (local Nubian deity). W face, the king offers bread to Anubis and incense and a libation to Khnum. (VIII) E face, the king offers Maʾat to Amun-Reʿ and flowers to Reʿ-Harakhte.

The ceiling of the central aisle is decorated with vultures with outstretched wings, that of the side aisles with stars. On the walls the scenes are lively and well-carved and painted.

(5) The king followed by ka accompanied by eight sons kills Nubian and Hittite prisoners before Amun-Reʿ. (6–7) Upper register, offering scenes; lower register, Nubian and Syrian wars, the king attacks a Syrian fort. (8) The king presents two rows of Nubian prisoners to Amun-Reʿ and (9) two rows of Syrian prioners to Reʿ-Harakhte. (10–11) Battle of Kadesh in four registers; upper register, advance of Ptah Division, the king in chariot; middle register, town of Kadesh, the king in chariot; lower register, chariot fight, reception of spies; below, camp and chariot, arrival of recruits with reinforcements. (12) The king followed by ka kills prisoners before Reʿ-Harakhte; accompanied by nine daughters. Beneath the reliefs is a short inscription saying that they were made by the sculptor Mery-Amun Piyay son of Khanufer.

Off this hall open a number of *side chambers*, which must have been used as store-rooms for the temple linen, plate and clothing. Unlike the later temple the functions of the rooms are not stated. On the N side of the hall are two side chambers. In the first (C) the W wall is decorated with reliefs showing the king before the gods. The second room (D) has all its walls decorated with similar scenes. These include Hathor, Isis, Reʿ-Harakhte, Amun-Reʿ, Ptah, Khonsu and Maʾat.

Two side chambers open off the NW corner through a vestibule (E), embellished with offering scenes with the king offering to Thoth, Amun-Reʿ, the Theban Triad, Atum, Montu, Isis and Reʿ. The rooms (F) and (G) show the king before Maʾat, Wepwawet, Amun-Reʿ, Khnum, Ptah, Thoth and Montu. Four calves are driven before Khnum; cloth, wine, linen, ointment and vases are offered to the other deities. From the SW corner opens another vestibule (H) leading to two more side chambers (I and K). Here again the paintings are mainly concerned with religious subjects.

(13) Lintel, the king runs with hap and oar before Amun-Reʿ and Mut; left jamb, offers lettuces to Min; right jamb, offers wine to Ptah; in the thickness, texts of year I.

At the entrance to the *Second Hall* (L), 10.9m by 7.0m, two sandstone sphinxes originally stood; just beyond was found a headless seated sandstone statue of Pesiur II, viceroy of Kush (all now in BM). This room has four square columns and is also decorated with religious and offering scenes.

(14) The king offers flowers to Amun-Reʿ and Mut with a deified Ramesses II placed between them at later date. (15) The king and Queen Nefertari offer to boat of Amun-Reʿ. (16) The king in front of Amun-Reʿ. (17) The king receives heb-sed from Reʿ-Harakhte. (18) The king and queen before boat of deified Ramesses II. (19) The king offers lettuces to Amun-Min and Isis.

The *Vestibule* (M) must have been mainly for offerings as wine, fruit and flowers are shown on the walls.

(20) The king before deified self. (21) The king receives life from Amun-Reʿ and deified self. (22) The king offers wine to Horus. (23) The king offers incense to Amun-Reʿ. (24) The king offers flowers to Ptah in kiosk. (25) The king on either side.

Three doors open off the rear wall of the vestibule. The two side chapels are undecorated but the *Sanctuary* (N) has paintings and statues of the patron gods, and in the centre an altar of Ramesses II.

(26) The king before boat of Amun-Reʿ and anointing Amun-Min. (27) The king before boat of deified self and before his deified self. (28) Niche with four statues (left to right), Ptah, Amun-Reʿ, deified Ramesses II, and Reʿ-Harakhte.

About 120m N lies the **Temple of Queen Nefertari**, also dedicated to Hathor of Abshek. It is also mainly rock-cut and, although much smaller, it is nonetheless imposing. An inscription to the N of the temple indicates that the builder was 'The Viceroy of Kush, Ani of Heracleopolis'. The façade is 28.3m long and 12.2m high. On either side of the door, separated by buttresses, are *three standing colossi* (11.5m high), two of Ramesses II and in the centre Queen Nefertari (a–f). Each is accompanied by two smaller figures of their children. From the left the figure of Ramesses has the princes Meryatum and Meryreʿ, Nefertari has the princesses Merytamun and Hentawi and the second figure of Ramesses has the princes Amunhirkhopshef and Rahrirwemenef. Those on the right-hand side reverse the sequence.

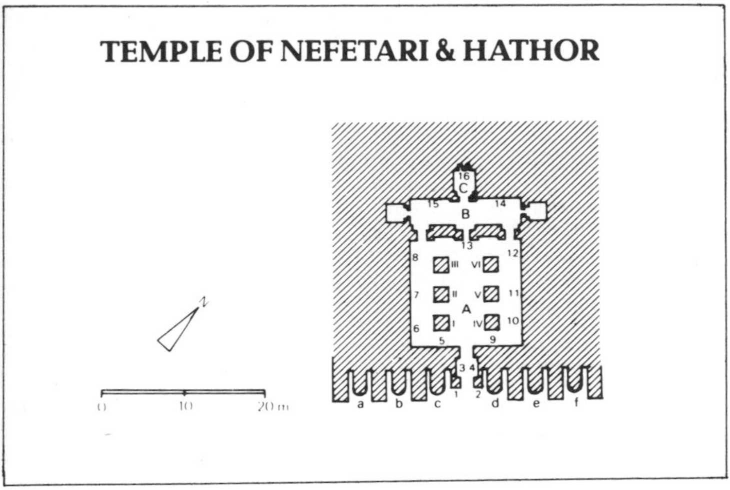
TEMPLE OF NEFETARI & HATHOR
16
C
15
14
B
13
12
8
III
VI
7
II
V
11
A
6
I
IV
10
5
9
3
4
1
2
a
b
c
d
e
f
0
10
20 m

On either side of the door (1–2) is a double scene of the king offering wine to Reʿ-Harakhte; on the jamb (3–4) are cartouches and building inscriptions of the king and queen.

A passage leads into a square *Hall* (A) with six square Hathor-headed and sistra pillars decorated with the king and queen making offerings to various gods of the area. The ceiling is decorated with a dedicatory inscription of Ramesses II to the queen.

(5) Ramesses accompanied by the queen kills a Nubian before Amun-Reʿ. (6) Ramesses before Hathor of Abshek. (7) Ramesses crowned by Horus and Set. (8) Nefertari before Anuket. (9) Ramesses accompanied by queen kills a Libyan before Reʿ-Harakhte. (10) Ramesses offers to Ptah in a kiosk. (11) Nefertari before Hathor. (12) The king offering wine to Reʿ-Harakhte. A doorway with the titles of the king has (13) Ramesses entering.

The doorway leads into the transverse *Vestibule* (B) (14) Ramesses offers wine to Reʿ-Harakhte and the queen offers flowers to Khnum, Satet and Anuket. (15) Ramesses offers flowers to the Horuses of Myan, Baki and Buhen, and wine to Amun-Reʿ. Above the doorway are the queen's cartouches protected by vultures. In the *Sanctuary* (C) there is a niche in the rear wall, supported by sistra, with a statue (16) of Hathor as a cow protecting Ramesses II.

Opposite Abū Simbel there were two ancient sites from which the monuments have been removed and re-erected here. From Abahūdah is the rock-cut **Temple of Amun-Reʿ and Thoth** built by Horemheb, and from Gabal al-Shams is the **Stele and rock-cut Chapel of Paser**, viceroy of Kush (18 Dyn.).

15km S of Abū Simbel lay **Ballānah** (on the West Bank) and **Qusṭul** (on the East) which were the sites of the impressive tumuli burials of the Nobatian kings of the 4–6C AD, whose capital Faras lay some distance to the S. They were discovered and excavated by W.B. Emery and L.P. Kirwan between 1931–39. The mounds covered built chambers in which the kings had been buried, crowned and in full regalia, along with their murdered queens, servants, all of whom seem to have been strangled and clubbed, horses, camels and dogs, and worldly wealth. Apart from these mass executions these burials showed the persistence of Egyptian practices long after they had disappeared in Egypt proper. The objects buried with them included weapons, lamps, bowls and jars and jewellery, the decoration of which displayed an amalgam of Ancient Egyptian and Byzantine motifs. Some ancient objects had been reused and in other cases, particularly the bronze lamps, they seem to have been imports from Byzantium. The material is now on display in the EM.

The borders of Sudan lie 7km upstream. On the West Bank (3km) lay **Faras** which was *Bajrash*, the capital of Nobatia between the 4–6C AD, and later *Pachoras*, the seat of the Metropolitan bishop. Among the ancient churches and monastries the largest building was the *Cathedral*, built in mud and stone and completed in 707 in the tenure of the fifth bishop, Paulus. It was planned and excavated by a Polish team in the 1960s, and contained many layers of superb wall paintings as each bishop contributed his portrait. Several other wall paintings depicted scenes from the Old or New Testaments, of which the most magnificent were a 9C scene of the Burning Fiery Furnace and a 10C Nativity. All these were removed with great care and are now in museums at Khartoum and Warsaw. The mid-12C was its greatest period of prosperity and it was destroyed during a battle with the Muslims. The bishopric subsequently moved to Qasr Ibrim.

45km S on the West Bank is the ancient site of *Buhen*. Opposite on the East Bank is **Wādī Ḥalfā** (train to Khartoum).

# III THE DELTA

## 41 The Desert Route to Alexandria

This, the first of the Delta routes, is comparatively straightforward. It runs directly between Cairo and Alexandria (total distance approx. 210km) with diversions to two important sites.

**Cairo.**—7km **Abū Ruwāsh.**—86km track to the **Wādī al-Natrūn.**—91km *al-ʿAmīriyyah.*—26km **Alexandria.**

Just before reaching the pyramids at Giza (Rte 23) the H11 leaves the Shʿ. al-Ahrām NW. 7km **Abū Ruwāsh** is a small village with (2km W) the **Pyramid Complex of Redjedef**, situated on the escarpment commanding a magnificent view, though at present it is inaccessible.

This king, the third of the 4 Dyn., resited his pyramid (because of some dynastic struggle of which nothing is known) to the N of the Giza necropolis in an area which had been used as a cemetery since the 1 Dyn. Lepsius records the existence of another pyramid here built of mud-brick; of this no trace remains. The earliest investigations of the site were undertaken by Perring and Vyse (1839) and their account shows that considerably more of the pyramid's superstructure was standing then. In the 1880s it was used as a quarry for buildings in Cairo—hundreds of camel-loads of stone were removed daily—and the extreme destruction of the pyramid is due to this rather than to the king's inability to finish his monument. Much more work needs to be done at this site.

E of the village is the *Wādī Qarūn* (2km), W of which lies the *Valley Temple*, unexcavated but indicated by blocks of limestone and chippings. The *causeway* leads SW for more than 1.5km and seems to have ended near the NW corner of the pyramid enclosure wall but unfortunately nothing is known of its structure.

At 76km the H6 leaves to the E (to al-Khaṭaṭbah; 28km) and at 10km a sign-post indicates a track to Deir Abū Maqar, the southernmost of the Monasteries of the Wādī al-Natrūn, but the main track to the valley is at 13km, leaving to the SW

**Wādī al-Naṭrūn** (Valley of Natron), 75km NW of Cairo, is a long natural depression c 6m below sea level, running SE–NW for 50km, though at no point is it more than 8km wide. Along the basin is a series of saline lakes and the ground is heavily impregnated with chlorides, carbonates and sulphates. A range of shallow hills surrounds the valley reaching their highest c 170m to the SW. For long an extremely isolated area, it has recently been developed. Many of the lakes have been drained and the area has proved amenable to the production of certain crops. Several small villages lie along the NE shores of the lakes. It has for the past 1700 years been a Christian area and, although the fortunes of the community have waxed and waned, four great monasteries are still here.

**Geology**. The surrounding hills, composed of late Miocene–Pliocene fluvial and lacustrine sands and clays, have yielded a number of important fossils.

**History**. This has been a sacred area since pharaonic times. The use of natron in purification ceremonies was universal in Ancient Egypt and to obtain it frequent visits were made to the valley which automatically became the gods' ground. Incorporated in Christian buildings are stones, columns and lintels which must have come from adjacent temples, though nothing is left of these save scattered remains at Qarat al-Dahr. The valley appears in the Ancient Egyptian folk tale of 'The Eloquent Peasant' who transported his goods via the area. The valley, known to the Copts as *Shihet*, was during Christian times called *Scetis*. Christianity arrived in the area with St. Macarius the Great (died 390) who in c 330 retreated here. His sanctity drew many other men of like mind and a loose community of anchorites was formed, each living in a cell in the hills. A more organised system gradually evolved with churches for the hermits to visit on the sabbath and feast days. To save and protect the community and visiting pilgrims hospices and keeps were built, with amenities for the religious who provided the labour. Thus a flourishing monastic system was created and with the Islamic conquest its isolation increased its importance. Depredations by the Beduin and Berbers necessitated the building of fortified enclosures with central keeps and interior churches but relationships with the Muslim rulers were generally excellent. In the 14C the two waves of plague that swept through the Middle East and Europe decimated the population of Wādī al-Natrūn and it never recovered.

Today there remain four thriving monasteries of varying degrees of accessibility. Architecturally the buildings and churches are Late Antique with unique local characteristics. Most of the extant buildings were raised after the destruction wrought by the Beduin in the 9C. All show a similarity of design, a high fortified wall surrounding several churches, living quarters and a qasr (keep), on the upper storey of which is the Church of the Angel Michael who is considered by Copts to be the guardian saint of the Delta.

The track from the H11 leads to **Bīr Hooker**, (c 3km), a small village surrounding the modern nitrate workings. It was created by the founder of the Salt and Soda Company in the wādī. There is a small *Rest House* where visitors can eat or stay, and a *Youth Hostel*. (The track continues across the wādī and into the desert to join the Cairo–Baḥriyyah road (65km)). Permission to visit the monasteries should be obtained from the Coptic Patriarchate, Cairo, or through the Egyptian Tourist Office or a travel agent. Transport can be hired at the rest house at Bīr Hooker.

**Deir Abū Maqār** (the Monastery of St. Macarius), the southernmost of the monasteries, can be reached either directly from the H6 (8km) or SE from Bīr Hooker by the road running NE of the lakes (c 15km).

This has always been the most important Christian foundation in the wādī and probably in Egypt. It has supplied many patriarchs for the Coptic church and for many centuries the patriarch used to visit it even if he had not been chosen from any of its members. It was traditionally founded by St. Macarius the Great (300–390), a camel driver who, after visiting St. Anthony as a young man, retired to the wādī, away from all the other anchorite communities for solitude. The monastery was sacked three times in the 5C by the Berbers but in the 6C it became important as the residence of the Coptic patriarch exiled by the Melkites from Alexandria. In the 7C another Berber attack destroyed the church and a new one was erected in 650, after which the monks increased to one thousand. After another sacking in 866 the patriarch Shanudah (859–81) rebuilt the church and refortified the walls and from this period much of the present building dates.

The three-storey *Qasr* is entered by a narrow drawbridge at first storey level. On the ground floor are store-rooms, mills and a well. On the first floor is the *Chapel of al-ʿAdhrā'* (the Virgin) with three haykals, the screen of which is probably 13C. The second floor contains three churches. To the N is the *Church of the Angel Michael*, with beautiful haykal screen. On the S wall are paintings by Takla al-Habashi (1517) of the Warrior Saints, members of the family of Basiledes of Antioch who suffered under Diocletian. The nave contains nine columns with Doric and Corinthian capitals. The *Church of SS. Anthony, Paul and Pachomius* has a wall-painting of the patron saints. Southernmost is the *Church al-Sawwāḥ* (of the Travellers) with paintings of SS. Samuel, John, Onuphris, Abraham, George, Apollo, Apip, Misayil and Pidjumi.

Little of the former glory of the *Great Church of St. Macarius* remains. This was the church where the Chrism, the unguent by tradition made from the oil used to embalm Christ, was kept.

The Copts believe that after the Resurrection of Jesus the disciples made up the first chrism, some of which was brought to the monastery. The ceremony of renewal was held with great solemnity at this church.

There are two haykals; to the N that of St. John the Baptist and to the NW that of St. Benjamin, Coptic patriarch of Alexandria (630–63) at the time of the Muslim conquest and sole patriarch after the Melkite Cyril had fled. He restored many of the ruined monasteries and made important additions to Coptic church law. These two sections of the church are very old, c 830; perhaps the lower sections are of the original fabric of 655. Many patriarchs are buried here as well as several saints including St. Macarius and St. John the Short. Much of the church, including the choir and the shrines, was restored in 1930 though some beautiful 11C paintings of the burial, anointing and embalming of Christ remain. The small *Church of St. Ishkhirūn of Killin*, dating probably to the 14C, has three haykals but only two altars and is used as a storage area. The 18C *Church of the Forty-Nine Martyrs* (al-Shuyūkh) is now used only for services during fasts and for the Feast of the Nativity.

The two central monasteries which lie close to each other are much more accessible from Bīr Hooker (7km to the SE). Easternmost is the **Deir al-Anbā Bishay** (Monastery of St. Pschoi, a disciple of St. Macarius). After the depredations of the Berbers it was restored several times and further work was required in 1096 after termite damage. There are five churches within the confines of the monastery, the main one being the *Church of St. Bishay* which is probably 9C, though the last restoration was in 1957. There are three haykals but the church is only used during the summer months. In the cemetery are the remains of SS. Bishay, Paul of Ṭammuh and Ephraim the Syrian. To the S is the *Church of St. Iskhirūn* while to the SE is the *Church of Al-ʿAdhrā*, used during the winter months. The *Church of St. George* is not used. The 12C *Qasr* is entered at first storey level by a drawbridge and on the second storey is the *Church of the Angel Michael* with 18C icons of the twelve apostles.

The **Deir al-Suryān** (Monastery of the Syrians) lies 500m to the NW. Women are not allowed in this monastery, the monks of which are particularly attentive to their offices. The monastery was founded in the 6C as a result of the Giainite dispute which, by throwing doubt on the Incarnation, lowered the status of the Virgin. The orthodox left the Deir Anbā Bishay and built the present monastery, calling it the Theokratos (Mother of God) Monastery of Anbā Bishay. With the demise of the dispute the monastery was abandoned and bought by some Syrian merchants for Syrian monks.

The *Church of al-ʿAdhrā*ʾ is the principal church, built c 980. The cell traditionally ascribed to St. Pschoi is off the N aisle. At the W end in the semi-dome is a 10C wall-painting of the Ascension. Seven rows of fine 10C ivory panels line the haykal door; the centre panels depict Christ and the Virgin, other panels show Egyptian and Syrian patriarchs and floral or geometrical motifs. In the semi-domes of the choir are paintings of the Annunciation, Nativity and Dormitian of the Virgin. This church is used during the summer months. In the NE section of the enclosure is the *Church of Sitt Maryam* (Lady Mary), sometimes called the Cave Church. It possesses three haykals and in the nave a marble lakane tank (for washing the feet at church ceremonies). The relics of St. John Kame (the Black, died 675), abbot of *Deir Abū Maqār*, are retained in this church. It is used in the winter months. To the N is the *Church of the Forty Martyrs of Ṣebaste* where Christodolous Abūna of Ethiopia is buried. The *Church of SS. Hinnis and Marutha* lies to the W. It is probably 15C and is named after the man who purchased the monastery for the Syrians. In the second storey of the three-storey *Qasr* is the *Church of St. Michael*. The tamarind tree growing in the grounds is traditionally connected with St. Ephraim, patriarch (977–81), who established an excellent relationship with the Fāṭimid rulers, Khalif al-ʿAzīz even occasionally staying at the monastery. There are a library and a museum within the complex, and also a printing press. A large farm is attached to the monastery.

*Deir al-Barāmus, Wādī al-Nāṭrūn*

Northernmost of the monasteries is the **Deir al-Barāmus** (Monastery of the Romans) c 14km from Bīr Hooker. It is probably the earliest settlement in the wādī. The rather confused tradition of its foundation involves two Roman princes who retreated to the area under persecution in the late 4C. Like other monasteries in the area it suffered many attacks and was finally fortified by the patriarch Shanudah in the 9C.

Within the enclosure are five churches. The oldest is the *Church of al-ʿAdhrāʾ* (the Virgin) which is surrounded by the main complex and possesses three haykals of various architectural periods, the earliest perhaps 9C (at present being restored. In cleaning the walls they have found even earlier wall paintings). In the feretory are the relics of SS. Moses the Black and Theodosius. To the W is the *Church of Anbā Tadrus* (Theodore the Commander), no longer used. Also to the W is the disused *Chapel of Mari Girgis* (St. George), while the 19C *Church of St. John the Baptist* is to the NE. The *Qasr*, part of which may date to the 7C, is a primitive three-storey building. On the second storey is the *Church of the Angel Michael* with dome-covered haykal. The University of Leiden and the IFAO have completed restoration of the paintings in this monastery which seem to date to the second half of the 12C.

From the road to the Wādī al-Natrūn the H11 continues NW. A road (the H7) leaves to the NE at 51km (to Abu ʿl-Matāmir al-Baḥarī; 26km).

Taking this NE road it leads after 20km to **Jyanaklīs** (famous for its grapes). To the E (20km) S of the Nubarīyyah Canal stretches the extensive site of **Kellia** where early Christian Antonian hermitages spread over an area of 25km. It was founded c 325 by Abba Amoun from the Wādī-Natrūn in an attempt to find an even more isolated retreat. The dwellings are quite distinctive consisting of several rooms surrounded by a low wall.

40km further the H11 reaches *al-ʿAmiriyyah*. Beyond the mainline railway a secondary road turns NE and then N for al-Maks. The main road continues NW across Lake Maryūṭ and E along the coast to (26km) central **Alexandria**.

# 42 Alexandria

**Alexandria** (*al-Iskandariyyah*) is the largest port and second largest and most populous city in Egypt. It is situated on the N coast at the NW extremity of the Delta, c 175km NW of Cairo at 31.13° N; 29.55° E. Two deep-water harbours make it one of the most important ports of the Mediterranean and it is the centre of the Egyptian fishing and cotton industries. It constitutes a province consisting of several districts. The population of three million has recently been greatly augmented by an influx of refugees from NE Egypt and Sinai. The foundations of the city rest on a great limestone ridge that fronts the sea; behind it is Lake Maryūṭ, now much reduced through canalisation and dyking. The Maḥmūdiyyah Canal runs along the S edge of the city.

Founded by Alexander the Great in 332 BC, it remained the capital city for nearly a thousand years. Few cities in the world can vie with its glorious past but the majority certainly have more to show. Virtually nothing remains of the marble palaces and temples for which the city was renowned in antiquity and even the sites are only approximately known. The Hellenic past has been completely submerged and today the city's aspect is entirely modern. The seafront with its railings and open-ended squares is reminiscent of a British resort and, although many of the buildings away from the front retain an Egyptian integrity, it is not coincidental that many of the European communities chose Alexandria for their residences. The British paid great attention to Alexandria and much of it shows the impress of British town planning, as do the dock and basin areas.

With its higher rainfall (166mm per annum) it is a much more humid city than Cairo and it has many parks and gardens. Temps: January average 15° C. (min. 8.8° C.), July average 25.5° C. (max. 30.1° C.).

**Hotels**. Since Alexandria is a holiday city there are a great many hotels. Only a small selection is given below.

*Alexandria to Abū Qir*. Mazariṭah: *Philip*, 236 Shʿ. 26 Yulyū (1*); Camp Caesar: *Makkah*, 88 Ṭarīq al-Gaysh (3*); Ibrāhīmiyyah: *Darwīsh*, 47 Ṭarīq al-Gaysh (1*); Cleopatra: *Nobel* 152 Ṭarīq al-Gaysh; *Cleopatra*, 172 Ṭarīq al-Gaysh (2*) Mustafa Pasha: *San Giovanni*; 205 Ṭarīq al-Gaysh (3*); Sīdī Gābar:*Latourelle*, 214 Ṭarīq al-Gaysh (4*); *Beau Rivage* 334 Ṭarīq al-Gaysh (4*); *Ciro*, 405 Ṭarīq al-Gaysh (2*); *Admiral*, 23 Shʿ. Amīn Fikrī (2*); *Capri*, 23 Mīnā al-Shargiyyah (1*); *Hyde Park*, 12 Shʿ. Amīn Fikrī (1*); *al-Naṣr*, 25 Shʿ. al-Ghurfah al-Tugāriyyah (1*); Sīdī Bishr: *Ramada Renaissance*, 544 Shʿ al-Gaysh (5*); *Villa Nana*, 558 Ṭarīq al-Gaysh (2*); *Golden Beach*, 585 Ṭarīq al-Gaysh; al-Muntazah: *Muntazah Sheraton* (5*); *Palastine*, grounds of al-Muntazah Palace (5*); *Salamlik*, grounds of al-Muntazah Palace (4*); *Mamoura Palace* (4*).

*Central Alexandria. Cecil*, 16 Maydān Saʿd Zaghlūl (4*); *Metropole*, 52 Shʿ. Saʿd Zaghlūl (3*); *Burg al-Thagha*, Shʿ. Safiyyah Zaghlūl (2*); *Piccadilly* 11 Shʿ. Nābī Danyāl (1*). *Isis Hotel* 34 Shʿ. Iyzīs.

**Airport**. 5km SE of Maydān Taḥrīr via H2 (the Delta road to Cairo), built on land reclaimed from Lake Maryūṭ. It is used for internal flights only.

**Railway Stations**. The sole mainline station in Alexandria, Mahaṭṭat Miṣr, occupies the S end of the Maydān al-Gumhuriyyah (Republic Square). There is a direct service to Cairo via Sīdī Gābir–Damanhūr–Ṭantā and Banhā. Single-track lines to the W for Abū Sīr–Sīdī ʿAbd al-Raḥmān–al-ʿAlamayn, Marsā Matrūḥ and Sallūm; to the E Abū Qīr–Idkū–Rashīd. Both these tracks have local and direct trains, the former stopping at all intermediate stations. *Maritime Station*, serving the port, is situated in al-Qabbarī. This line joins the mainline to Cairo just S of Alexandria.

**Restaurants** abound in Alexandria, the particular speciality being, of course, seafood. In the more expensive restaurants you can choose your fish from salt-water basins. All the large hotels have restaurants, but among others are the *Union*, 1 Shʿ. al-Bursah al-Qadimah; *al-Ikhlāṣ al-Sharq*, 49 Shʿ. Safiyyah Zaghlūl; *Ramses*, 25 Shʿ. al-Ghurfah al-Tugāriyyah; *Muṣṭafā Darwīsh*, 90 Ṭarīq al-Gaysh; *Pam-pam*, 33 Shʿ. Safiyyah Zaghlūl.

**Clubs**. There are also a great many of these in Alexandria and, as in Cairo, they range from the traditional to the modern.

**Cafés**. A great feature, there are many and with past experience of European tastes they provide all manner of pastries and cakes, with afternoon tea a speciality. Another international institution is **Pastroudis**, 39 Ṭarīq al-Ḥurriyyah, its art nouveau decor unchanged since the turn of the century.

**Post Offices**. Postal Services. Main office in Maydān Saʿd Zaghlūl and local offices throughout the city. Telephone and Telegram services are provided.

**Information Bureaux**: Ministry of Tourism offices in Maydān Saʿd Zaghlūl; and in the Port precinct.

**Travel Agents**. Many throughout the city. *American Express*, 26 Shʿ. al-Hurriyyah; *Eastmar*, 16 Shʿ. Ṣalāḥ Sālim; *Miṣr Travel*, 33 Shʿ. Ṣalāḥ Sālim; *Thomas Cook*, 15 Maydān Saʿd Zaghlūl; *Menatours*, 24 Maydān Saʿd Zaghlūl.

**Shipping Offices**. *Adriatica*, 33 Shʿ. Ṣalāḥ Sālim; *Alexandria Shipping and Navigation Co.*, 557 Ṭarīq al-Hurriyyah; *Hellenic Mediterranean Lines Co.*, 63 Shʿ. Nābī Danyāl; *Memphis Shipping Agency*, 17 Shʿ. Sizustris; *Thebes Shipping Agency*, 3 Shʿ. Igliz Dabbana.

**Airline Offices**. *British Airways*, 15 Maydān Saʿd Zaghlūl; *Air France*, 22 Shʿ. Salāh Sālim; *Egypt Air*, 19 Maydān Saʿd Zaghlūl; *Lufthansa*, 6 Maydan Saʿd Zaghlūl; *TWA*. Ṭarīq Gamal Abd al-Nassar; *Sudan Airways*, 6 Shʿ. Talaʿt Harb.

**Transport**. *City and Suburban buses*. From *Maydān al-Raml* 1—al-Qabbārī—*al-Maks*. 3—*al-Nuzhah*. 8—*Rā's al-Tin*. 9—Mahaṭṭat Miṣr—*Kawn al-Shawqāfah*. 11—al-Qabbārī—al-Maks—*ʿAgamī*. 15—Ikingi Maryut. From *Maydān al-Tahrīr*. 10—Zoo—*Airport*. 20—Corniche—*Muntāzah*. 28—*Abū Qīr*. Trams. *Tirām al-Madīnah* (town trams) al-Nuzhah—al-Maks. 3 Maydān al-Tahrīr—al-Wardyān. 4 Muharram Bak—Rā's al-Tīn. 5 al-Nuzhah—Fort Qā'it Bay. 6 al-Gumruk—Muharram Bak 7 al-Nuzhah—al-Wardyan. *Tirām al-Raml* (al-Raml trams, Metro) single and double-decker trams 1—al-Raml—Bakūs—al-Naṣr (Sīdī Bishr). 2—al-Raml-Glymnobūlū—al-Naṣr (Sīdī Bishr).

**Consulates**. *UK*, 3 Shʿ. Mina; *France*, 2 Shʿ. Urabi; *USA*, 15 Shʿ. al-Gabarti.

**Learned Institutes**. *Hellenic Society of Ptolemaic Egypt*, 20 Ṭarīq al-Hurriyyah; *Soc. Archaelogie d'Alexandrie*, 6 Shʿ. Maḥmūd Mukhtar; *Deutsche Kulturinstitut*, 10 Shʿ. Batlūmiyyah. *Alex. Inst. of Oceanography and Fisheries*, Qāytbāy; *Textile Development Centre*, al-Sayūf.

**Cinemas**. Throughout the central city, some specialising in European or American films.

**Sport**. Golf, racing, swimming, tennis, etc. can be enjoyed at *Samūhah Sports Club* and the *Alexandria Sporting Club* for a small fee. Other clubs are the *Yacht Club* and the *Automobile Club*.

**History**. In the 4C BC the most westerly branch of the Nile was the Canopic, now dry. It debouched on the SW side of Abū Qīr Bay. To the W for about 20km fronting the sea ran a great limestone ridge, landward of which lay the huge brackish Lake Mareotis (Mallāḥat Maryūt) set in a large marsh. At the mouth of the Canopic branch stood the city of Canopus (see Abū Qīr) from which it took its name, the main port of the Western Delta. About halfway along the ridge to the W and opposite a large island, Pharos, stood Rhakotis, a small town and cult centre of Osiris, founded about 1300 BC. W was Taposiris, also dedicated to the worship of Osiris. The island of Pharos was the exposed tip of an outer ridge, which ran for some distance parallel to the first and then curved round to the S to meet it at a spur (al-Silsilah) E of Rhakotis. Between the two ridges, past the reefs created by the outer ridge, the water was very deep, but the area in ancient times remained undeveloped.

In 332 BC the 25-year old Alexander the Great arrived in Egypt. Born in Macedonia, the son of King Philip, he continued his father's campaigns against the Greeks and by 335 BC the Greek cities were vassals of his expanding empire. He next turned his attention to the Persian Empire and by 332 he had wrested Syria from their control, thus cutting Persian access to Egypt, which consequently also fell to him. He entered Egypt and travelled to Memphis where he was received in triumph. In his youth he had had a dream which told of his divinity as the son of the god Amun and he therefore wished to visit this god's temple at the oasis of Sīwah. He ascended the Nile by ship and on the way stopped at Rhakotis. Very impressed by the site, with its obvious advantages, its great harbour and strategic position, controlling both Egypt and the Mediterranean, Alexander ordered his architects Dinocrates and Sostratus to build a city there. After visiting Sīwah, his divinity confirmed by the oracle, he left immediately for Asia to continue his attack on the Persian Empire. In each of the areas he won he left one of his comrades as satrap; in Egypt this was Ptolemy Soter. Alexander reached the River Indus in 326 BC and by 323 he was back in Babylon, planning the conquest of the Western Mediterranean seaboards, but in June of the same year he died of a fever. Ptolemy diverted his body to Egypt and he was buried in Alexandria.

The city built for Alexander was the first to be built in Egypt to a Greek plan. It completely crossed the limestone ridge and was surrounded by a fortified wall. It was quartered by two great roads: the Canopic Way ran from the W at the Gate of the Moon to the E, the Gate of the Sun. Crossing this at a right-angle was the Street of the Soma, from the lake at the S to the seafront to the N. Leading off these was a gridwork of streets, dividing the whole city into rectangular blocks. A causeway, seven stades long and therefore called the Heptastadion, linked the city with the Island of Pharos, thus creating two immense harbours, on the E the Great Harbour (the main anchorage), and on the W the Eunostos (Safe Return).

Alexander was buried with elaborate ceremony in the Soma at the junction of the two main roads and the city was completed under the direction of Ptolemy Soter. The palace enclosure was built on al-Silsilah spur. Besides the palace with its own harbour, it contained the administrative buildings. It was conjoined to the S by the Museion, a complex of schools, laboratories, observatories and the Great Library, built in emulation of the one in Athens. The librarian was appointed by the King and for life, the first being Zenodotus in 284 BC. According to Kallimachus, this library contained 490,000 scrolls. However, it soon outshone its prototype, and was controlled directly from the palace. At the SW of the city, and with its own library (with 42,800 scrolls), stood the Temple of Serapis, whose cult was introduced into Egypt by Ptolemy I. Among the other public buildings were the theatre and various gymnasia, covered markets and baths. Along the coast in both directions stretched a series of lighthouses controlled by the Great Lighthouse, towering about 120m at the E tip of Pharos Island, by which name it was to become renowned as one of the Wonders of the World. In all probability, although planned by Ptolemy I Soter, it was constructed for his son Ptolemy II Philadelphus. During the Ptolemaic period these buildings were augmented and replaced, but the palace and museum remained the most important area. Alexandria in the last centuries BC and the first centuries of the Christian era was not to be replaced as the capital of Egypt; indeed, with its control of the Mediterranean, it remained the obvious base for the interests of Rome and Byzantium when it was the seat of the Prefect.

The greatest contributions to learning during the Ptolemaic period from the museum were in the fields of science and medicine; little interest was taken in philosophy. Euclid (c 300 BC) was among the founders of the mathematical school and other scholars included Apollonius of Perya (fl. 260 BC), Hypicles and Theon (AD 360). Geography and astronomy had two great exponents—Eratosthenes (fl. 235 BC), who calculated the diameter of the sphere of the Earth to within 50km and suggested that the Earth revolved around the Sun, and Claudius Ptolemy (fl. AD 127–141). Although his reputation has suffered several setbacks recently, he was the creator of a world vision previously unknown and his map of the known world served for centuries. The calendar was also stabilised by the scholars at the museum, by the insertion of the Leap Year, a device which so impressed Julius Caesar that he incorporated it in his own reform when creating the Julian Calendar.

Under the Ptolemies the Jews also had a large colony in Alexandria and assimilated so well that they became largely Greek-speaking. The Septuagint was translated c 130 BC, and under the influence of the Stoic and Epicurean schools of philosophy several books of apocrypha were produced, the most important of which was the 'Wisdom of Solomon'.

From the earliest days of the millenium Alexandria was the centre of the dispersion of Christianity in Egypt. It was the seat of the senior bishop and synonymous with Egypt during the early history of the church.

Parallel to the early conversions to Christianity an interest in philosophy grew among the scholars at the museum. Christian philosophy was given great impetus by the foundation of the Catechitical School in the mid 2C. Ammonius Saccus founded the neo-Platonic School of Alexandria. Notable pupils were Longinus, Plotinus and the last great exponent, Theon (fl. c 360).

When the Arabs finally entered Alexandria as conquerers in 642 it was still a magnificent city. It was the gleaming white marble that attracted the Arabs, not the architectural style, but they did little to restore the buildings which gradually decayed or were deliberately robbed of their stone. Very often the new inhabitants of the city built their own habitations on top of the classical buildings. The Arabs did, however, restore and fortify the city with great walls but they seem to have enclosed only about half the area of the original Greek city. The Pharos was still standing and used for its original purpose. Of the two harbours, the Eastern, more difficult to navigate and easier to supervise, was used for non-Muslim ships while the Muslim traders used the Western Harbour. Four gates led from the new enclosure, the Bāb al-Rashid to the E, the Bāb al-Sidrah to the S, the Bāb al-Baḥr leading to the Heptastadian, and the Bāb al-Akhdār in the N wall. In the W part of the city were the royal palaces and workshops including the Dar al-Ṭirāz, the silk-weaving factory for which Egypt was to become renowned throughout the Islamic and Christian spheres in the following centuries. Water for the city was supplied by the canal, completed before the Arab invasion, from the Bolbitine branch of the Nile.

For some time the city was administered as a separate province from the rest of Egypt but with the first hint of independence in the 9C during the reign of Ibn Ṭūlūn it was included within the body of Egypt.

The population of Alexandria fluctuated but it remained the second most important city in Egypt after Cairo and for part of the year was the seat of the governor of the country. In the 11C the Coptic patriarch was forced to transfer his seat from Alexandria to Cairo. With its essentially maritime connections the city always had a large foreign community and special areas were reserved for their use. They enjoyed the same protection as the native merchants. During Mamlūk times it

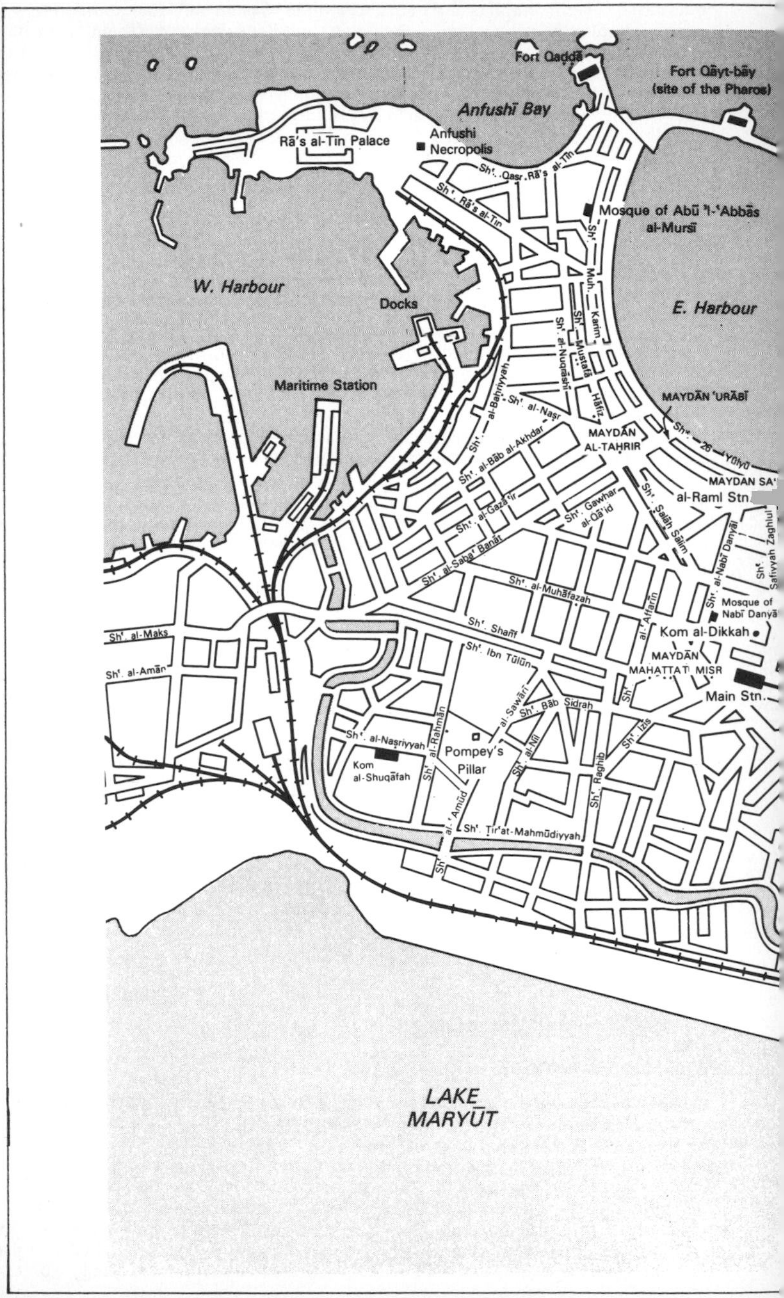
Fort Qaḍḍā
Fort Qāyt-bāy
(site of the Pharos)
Anfushī Bay
Rā's al-Tīn Palace
Anfushi
Necropolis
Sh'. Qasr Rā's al-Tīn
Sh'. Rā's al-Tīn
Mosque of Abū 'l-'Abbās
al-Mursī
W. Harbour
Docks
E. Harbour
Maritime Station
Sh'. Muh. Karim
Sh'. Mustafā
Sh'. al-Nuqrāshī
Hāfiz
MAYDĀN 'URĀBĪ
Sh'. al-Bahriyyah
Sh'. al-Nasr
MAYDĀN
AL-TAHRIR
Sh'. 26 Yūlyū
Sh'. al-Bāb al-Akhdar
MAYDĀN SA'
al-Raml Stn.
Sh'. al-Gazā'ir
Sh'. Gawhar
al-Qā'id
Sh'. Salāh Sālim
Sh'. al-Saba' Banāt
Sh'. al-Nabī Danyāl
Sh'. Safiyyah Zaghlul
Sh'. al-Muhāfazah
Sh'. Affarīn
Mosque of
Nabī Danyāl
Kom al-Dikkah
Sh'. al-Maks
Sh'. Sharīf
Sh'. al-Amān
Sh'. Ibn Tūlūn
MAYDĀN
MAHATTAT MISR
Main Stn.
Sh'. al-Sawārī
Sh'. Bāb Sidrah
Sh'. Izis
Sh'. al-Nasriyyah
Sh'. al-Rahmān
Pompey's
Pillar
Kom
al-Shuqāfah
Sh'. al-Nīl
Sh'. Raghib
Sh'. al-'Amūd
Sh'. Tir'at-Mahmūdiyyah
LAKE
MARYŪT

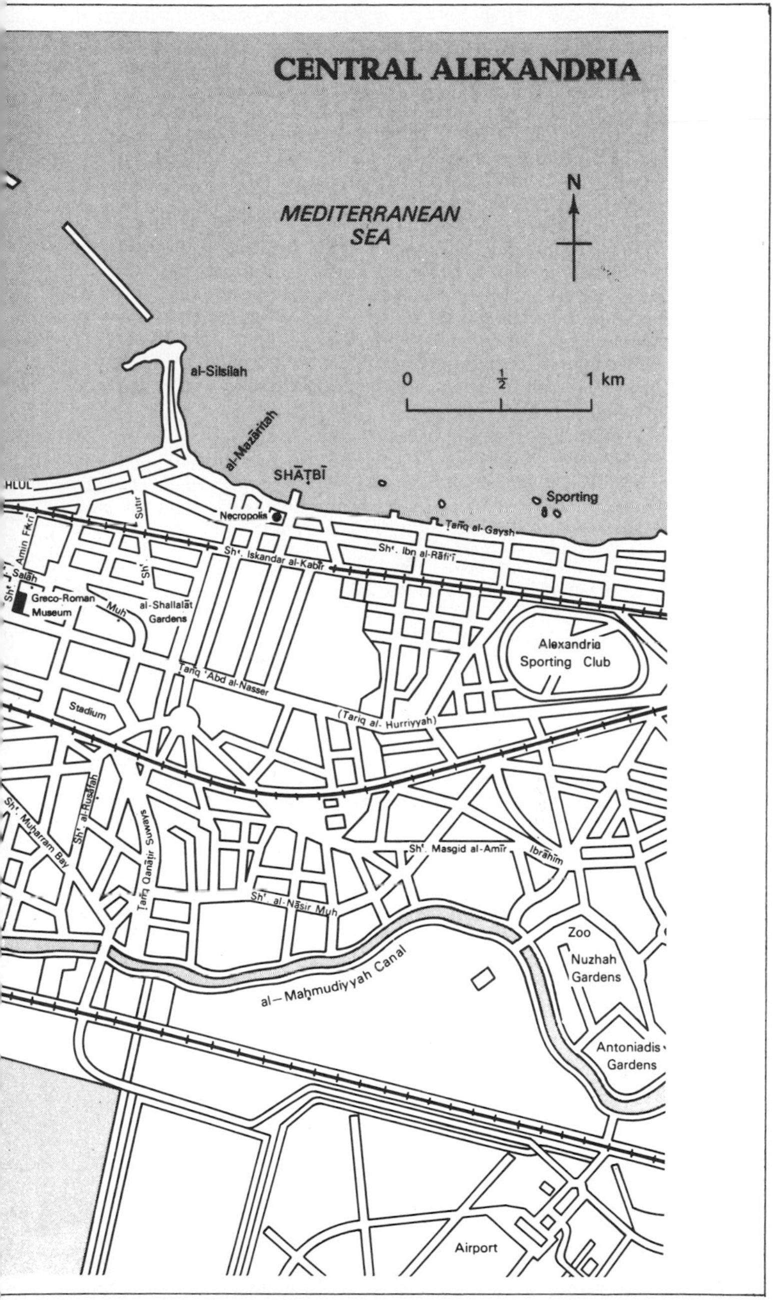
CENTRAL ALEXANDRIA
MEDITERRANEAN SEA
N
0
½
1 km
al-Silsilah
al-Mazāritah
SHĀṬBĪ
Sporting
Necropolis
Ṭarīq al-Gaysh
Shᶜ. Iskandar al-Kabīr
Shᶜ. Ibn al-Rāfiᶜī
Sutir
Amin Fikri
Salāh
Greco-Roman Museum
Muh
al-Shallalāt Gardens
Alexandria Sporting Club
Ṭarīq ᶜAbd al-Nasser
Stadium
(Tariq al- Hurriyyah)
Shᶜ. al-Rusāfah
Shᶜ. Muharram Bay
Ṭarīq Qanātir Suways
Shᶜ. Masgid al-Amīr
Ibrāhīm
Shᶜ. al-Nāsir Muh
Zoo
Nuzhah Gardens
al-Maḥmudiyyah Canal
Antoniadis Gardens
Airport

was, like Qūṣ, a place of exile for important political prisoners—deposed Sulṭans and recalcitrant amīrs. Despite its economic importance, little money was spent on building. Few great mosques, madrasahs or tomb complexes were built, most of the construction being of khans and wikālahs for merchants, since it was the Mediterranean outlet for the mechandise of India and the East. However during the Ottoman period it suffered a catastrophic decline, with the loss of eastern trade routes to other empires.

Muḥammad ʿAlī realised the importance of maritime domination and began to build an immense fleet. Alexandria was an ideal base for this fleet and he revitalised the city by cutting the Maḥmūdiyyah Canal, using in part the bed of the original Ptolemaic canal. The effect was immediate and Alexandria began to prosper once more. Within a few years it was a thriving port and the principal base of Egyptian military and civil shipping. Docks and basins were constructed in the W Harbour, a programme which was greatly accelerated during the British occupation. The British also built embankments around the E Harbour and a vast promenade along the seafront. Population increased at a great rate 15,000 in 1789, and with a population of 100,000 by the mid 19C, Alexandria had once more become the second city of Egypt.

By the time the British arrived in large numbers in the 1890s (pop c 200,000) Alexandria was already the summer seat of government, which moved *en masse* from Cairo. The city attracted not only Egyptians but also merchants and artisans from all around the Eastern Mediterranean coast, and large foreign communities were founded. Its more moderate climate endeared it to the British who built many homes in the suburbs. There emerged a cosmopolitan population of middle-class Europeans and wealthy Egyptians and Turks. In this strange world, caricatured in Lawrence Durrell's 'Alexandria Quartet', there was precious little to attract the ordinary Egyptian. However, this community did inspire a series of European authors and poets, including Cavafy, with his elegies to long-dead youths; E.M. Forster's fascinating histories of the city, and, during World War II, some fine work from military personnel stationed in Alexandria.

Since the Egyptian Revolution (1952) the city has undergone radical change with a massive population increase and many new buildings. Despite this Alexandria has an irresistible charm and an open, bouyant atmosphere which encourages long visits.

Under the auspices of the University of Alexandria an attempt is being made to inaugurate a centre of learning in Alexandria emulating the Great Library. The project is supported by the Egyptian Government, UNESCO, the UN Development Programme and several Middle Eastern presidents and rulers. A site has been designated at the NE of the city in the Ptolemaic royal quarter where the Museum was situated. A Norwegian firm won the competition for the design of the building of which the foundation stone was laid in June 1990 with estimated completion by July 1995. In addition to the library of 200,000 volumes it is to include a conference centre, audio-visual and electronic data facilities including a computerised catalogue with access to foreign data bases.

# North-West Alexandria

### NW of Maydān al-Taḥrīr to Anfushi Bay

The area covered here comprises the peninsula formed by the silting up of the *Heptastadion* (seven stades–1 stade c 184m) which left the mainland just W of this point and led to the island of Pharos. At the E end stood the great Pharos lighthouse. The island is now irrevocably joined to the mainland and forms the two horns of the promontory from Rāʾs al-Tīn in the W to Fort Qāyt-bāy in the E (3.5km). The coast of the *W Harbour* is taken up completely with docks and basins but the coast of the *E Harbour* is a beautiful semi-circular sweep of 6.4km followed exactly by the wide road, Shʿ. 26 Yūlyū.

There are several mosques, all Ottoman, in the area. In the SW on the corner of Shʿ. Gazayr is the **Mosque of Sh. Ibrahīm**, much reconstructed. The next road to the NW is the Shʿ. Bāb al-Akhdār with, on its W side, the **Mosque of Abū ʾl-ʿAlī al-Ginaynah**, reputed to be the oldest foundation in the city, but there is little to support this claim. An inscription inside records 677 AH (AD 1278) in figures but the present building has an Ottoman aspect. Of interest is the model of a boat over the minbar.

Running directly NW from Maydan al-Taḥrīr is the SHʿ. AL-MAYDĀN. To the E is the **Mosque of Sh. Ibrāhīm al-Shurbajī**, dated 1757. Similar in plan to the great Tarbanā Mosque (see below), it is flanked by an arcade outside and the rear opens into an arcaded court. A trefoil arch over the entrance has panels of tiles with a niche in the centre. Much restored inside, there are many panels of tiles and polished aggregate pillars. The miḥrāb is flanked by helically groved pillars and panels of tiles and decorated with mirror Kufic inscription.

Leading from the N corner of the Maydān al-Taḥrīr is Shʿ. al-Shahīd and to the E is **al-Tarbanā Mosque**, built by Hajjī Ibrāhīm Tarbanā in 1685, and heavily restored. The façade, in the distinctive Delta style of bricks and wooden beams set in courses, is extensively plastered-over. Above the door is the shahādah in Kufic script. Steps lead up to the entrance, above which are two great antique columns with Corinthian capitals which support the minaret. The doorway has a trefoil arch and tiled dado. Arcades of eight ancient columns support the painted ceiling and there is a tiled miḥrāb.

*The Memorial to the Unknown Soldier*

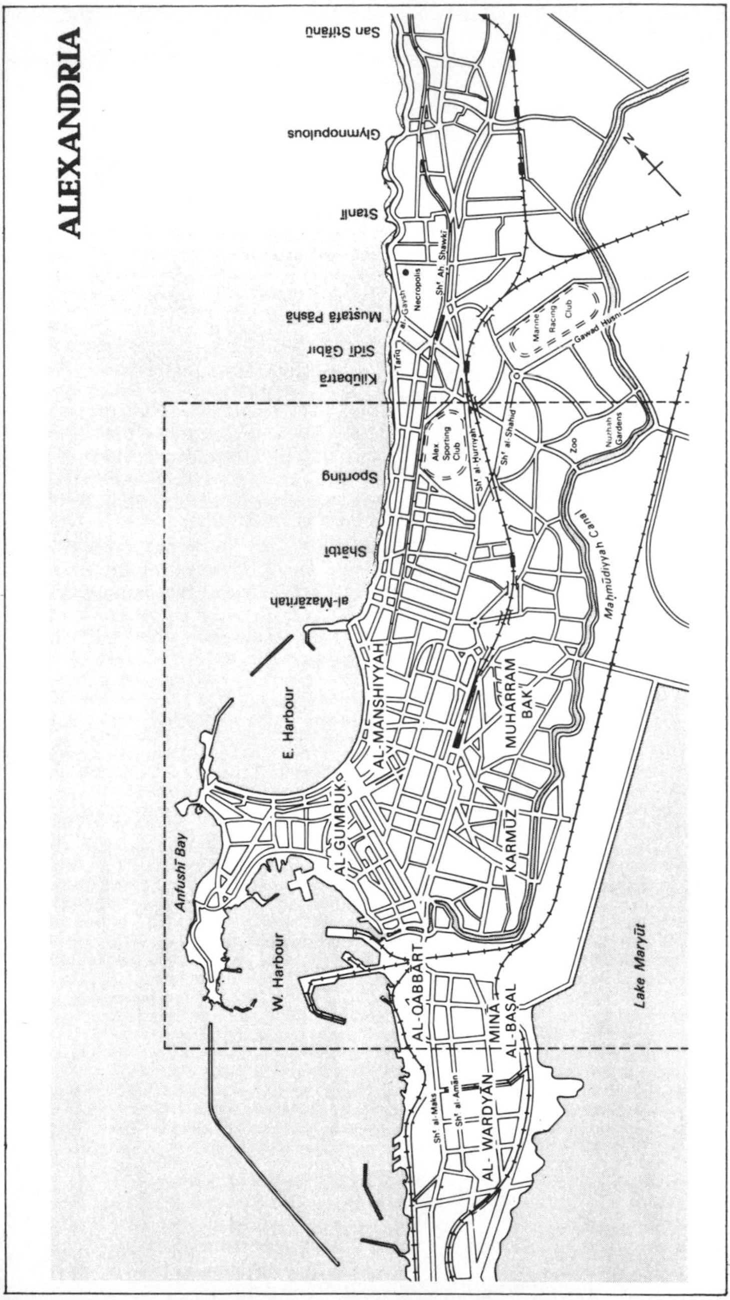
ALEXANDRIA
San Stifānū
Glymnopoulos
Stānlī
Muṣṭafā Pāshā
Sīdī Gābir
Kilūbatrā
Sporting
Shāṭbī
al-Mazāriṭah
E. Harbour
W. Harbour
Anfūshī Bay
AL-MANSHIYYAH
AL-GUMRUK
AL-QABBĀRĪ
MĪNĀ AL-BAṢAL
AL-WARDYĀN
MUḤARRAM BAK
KARMŪZ
Lake Maryūṭ
Maḥmūdiyyah Canal
Zoo
Nuzhah Gardens
Alex. Sporting Club
Marine Racing Club
Gawad Husni
Necropolis
Ṭarīq al-Gaysh
Shʿ Ah. Shawki
Shʿ al-Ḥurriyah
Shʿ al-Shahid
Shʿ al-Maks
Shʿ al-Amān
N

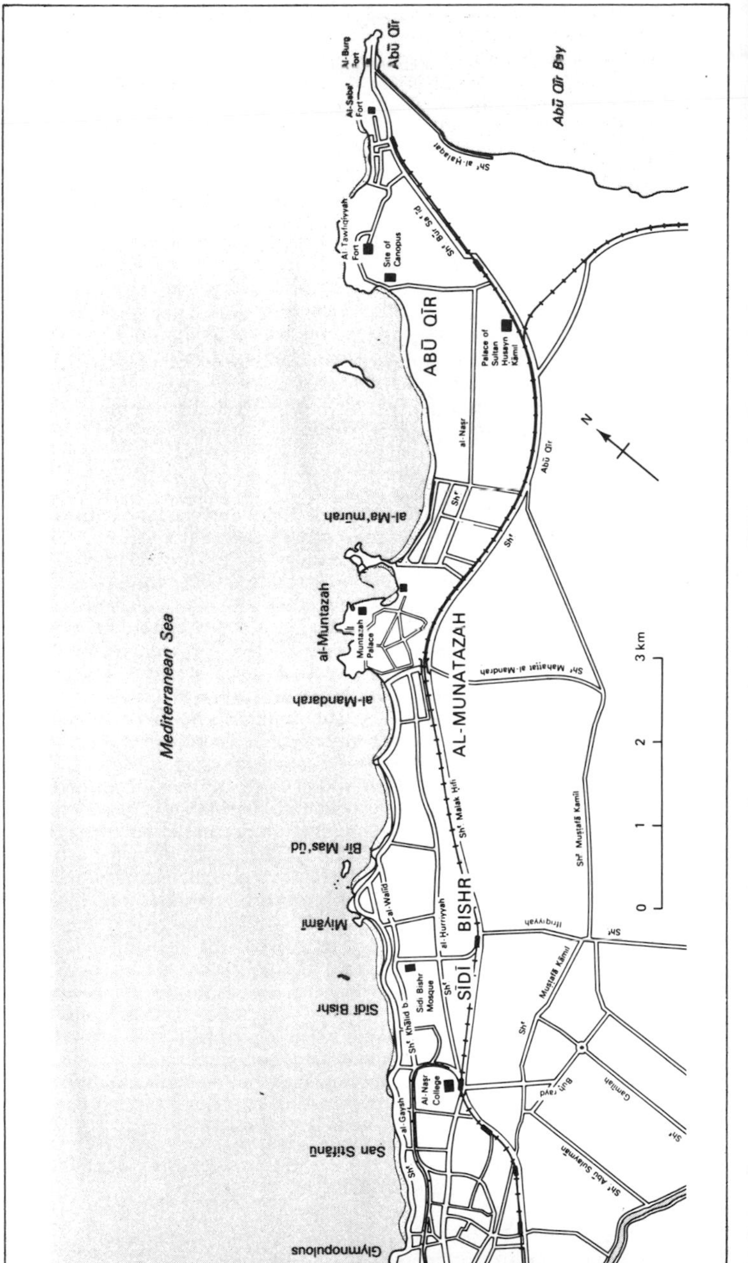
Mediterranean Sea
Abū Qīr
Al-Burg Fort
Al-Saba' Fort
Al Tawfiqiyyah Fort
Site of Canopus
Abū Qīr Bay
Sh' al-Halaqat
Sh' Būr Sa'īd
ABŪ QĪR
Palace of Sultan Husayn Kāmil
al-Nasr
Abū Qīr
N
al-Ma'mūrah
Sh'
al-Muntazah
Muntazah Palace
AL-MUNATAZAH
Sh' Mahattat al-Mandarah
al-Mandarah
0
1
2
3 km
Sh' Malak Hifi
Sh' Mustafā Kāmil
Bīr Mas'ūd
Miyāmī
al-Walīd
al-Hurriyyah
SĪDĪ BISHR
Ifriqiyyah
Sidī Bishr Mosque
Sidī Bishr
Sh' Khālid b.
Al-Nasr College
al-Gaysh
San Stifānū
Sh' Abū Sulaymān
Glymnopulous

Just to the N on the Shʿ 26 Yūlyū is **al-Gundī al-Maghūl**, the Memorial to the Unknown Soldier, in white marble with bronze decoration.

Follow the Shʿ 26 Yūlyū N. After 750m to the W stands the Maydān Abū ʾl-ʿAbbās. At the W end of this is the elegant **Mosque of Abū ʾl-ʿAbbās al-Mursī**, the present building of 1943 standing on the site of a much earlier ribāṭ and tomb.

Andalusian in origin, Aḥmad Abū ʾl-ʿAbbās al-Mursī (1219–87) came to Alexandria and joined the Shadhilī brotherhood under its founder Abū ʾl-Ḥasan al-Shadhilī. He became the shaykh of the brotherhood, attracting many learned people and the first ribāṭ was built for him here. In 1775 a rich Maghrabī merchant, observing the ramshackle condition of the mosque and tomb, had it renovated. The whole complex was completely demolished in 1943 and replaced by the present building.

This is one of the most pleasing and certainly one of the most unusual of all modern mosques, even though executed in artificial stone, to an octagonal plan. The minaret to the S rises in three stages to 73m while ornate domes cover the tombs. Inside, eight monolithic Italian granite columns support an arcade of elongated arches above which is a lantern, while against the walls are a further eight pillars. In alternate corners are the tombs of Abū ʾlʿ-Abbās and three other venerated shaykhs. Immediately in front of the mosque stands the *Mosque of Sidi Būsīrī*.

Continuing to the end of the corniche, a narrow peninsula reaches into the sea to the E. On the corner are the *Hydrobiological Museum* (open 09.00–14.00; small fee) and the *Marine Life Institute* (admission as above), an aquarium with specimens of fish and marine life found in Egyptian waters. To the E of this, now occupied by **Sultan Qāyt-bāy's Fort**, is the site of the **Pharos**.

It was this immense lighthouse, considered one of the Wonders of the World, that, in the words of E.M. Forster, '...beaconed to the imagination, not only to ships at sea and long after its light was extinguished memories of it glowed in the minds of men'. Probably visualised by Alexander the Great, it was built to the order of Ptolemy II c 279 BC by Sostratus, an Asiatic Greek. It stood c 120m high in a colonnaded court and consisted of four tiers. A square-sectioned, many-windowed base, c 60m high, contained c 300 rooms housing the attendants, a double spiral ascent and a hydraulic machine for raising the fuel to the roof. This was topped by a great cornice, at each corner of which was a huge statue of a triton. An inscription running just under the cornice read: 'Sostratus of Knidus, son of Dexiphanes, to the Saviour Gods for mariners'. The gods referred to are Castor and Pollux but also implied is the deified Ptolemy and his wife Berenice. The next tier (30m) was octagonal, containing only the spiral ascent topped by another cornice. A cylindrical section supported the lantern which held the fire which was probably magnified by a reflecting device; the light could be seen for 56km. A 7m tall statue of Poseidon crowned the whole edifice. It was still largely intact at the Muslim conquest in 641, but the lantern fell in c 700 and the building was restored by Ibn Tulun in 900. The great earthquake of 1100 dislodged the octagonal tier after which the base was buttressed and a mosque was built on top. During the next serious earthquake of 1307 the ancient structure crumbled and fell. For nearly two centuries the stones lay where they had fallen but in 1479, with the Ottomans on the N coast of the Mediterranean, Sulṭan Qāyt-bāy visited Alexandria and decided to build a fort on the peninsula, one of a series he built along the coast. The enclosure walls do not follow those of the Pharos but are realigned to the qiblah as there is a mosque in the keep.

A causeway leads into the irregular five-sided enclosure (c 110m by 100m) with three half-round towers on the SW and SE walls. The original entrance at the S corner is also flanked by two half-round towers, with interior rooms. Within the fabric of the walls to the NW of the gateway are antique granite and marble columns. Little of interest lies inside the courtyard (now occupied by the Egyptian Navy) except for the castle situated at the N corner. Half-round towers straddle each corner with overhanging *machicoulis* and half-round crenellations. The keep houses a *Naval Museum* (09.00–15.00, Friday closed 11.30–13.30; small fee) but the central feature is the mosque of typical metropolitan cruciform construction, not in the usual Delta style. At the entrance are five great monolithic pillars of red Aswān granite. This covered madrasah with remains of good stucco decoration has the floor of the ṣaḥn and raised līwāns lined with marble. On the second storey is a series of vaulted rooms.

A wide road, Shʿ. Ṣalāḥ Salīm, runs 1km W, following the sweep of Anfūshī Bay. At the E end on a small promontory is the late 19C *al-Qaḍḍā Fort*. The original was destroyed during the British bombardment of Alexandria in 1882. Offshore c 1km are some shallow reefs and exposed rocks, perhaps the remains of an ancient harbour, the haunt of local youths who fish for sea urchins. Boats may be hired for a pleasant days swimming from the sandbanks. At the W end the *Rā's al-Tīn* (Cape of Figs) is occupied by gardens, military installations and the **Rā's al-Tīn Palace**, built between 1834–54 by Muḥ. ʿAlī Pasha, later restored by Ismāʿīl Pasha and almost completely rebuilt by King Fū'ād. From the late 19C it was the summer seat of government, the Muntazah Palace (see below) being the royal summer palace. At present it is the headquarters of the Admiralty and cannot be visited but it contains many rooms furnished in the hybrid European-Turkish taste of the Egyptian royal family, and includes the Throne Room, the Gothic Hall and the Marble Hall. It was in this building in June 1952 that King Fārūq signed his abdication, after which he descended to his yacht and left for Italy. The main gate is quite impressive with inscriptions from the Qur'ān, surmounted by the Egyptian crown.

Set in a small enclosure immediately E of the palace, at the start of the SHʿ. RĀ'S AL-TĪN which runs E, are the **Anfushī Tombs**. This necropolis, cut in the limestone, dates from 250 BC, with Roman additions. As well as smaller tomb niches cut in the surface rock there are two groups of deeper tombs with a common entrance. Steps lead down into a large square hall off which open the tomb-chambers, decorated with stucco painted to resemble marble and tiles. Stairs descending into the right-hand complex are decorated with friezes depicting Horus, Osiris, Isis and Anubis. They lead into two chambers, each with a vestibule. The chamber to the right is undecorated except for some Greek graffiti including drawings of ships. Imitiation marble and alabaster lines the left-hand vestibule and above are a chequered pattern and mythological scenes, the ceiling with a geometrical design. Sphinxes flank the entrance of the tomb-chamber and above is a carved winged sun-disk. Inside, the decoration is similar to the vestibule and there is a shrine on the rear wall. In the left-hand complex the vestibule to the right-hand tomb has low benches and in the chamber is a very large red granite sarcophagus. The tomb to the left is similar to the others, but includes additional Roman sarcophagi.

From this point the SHʿ. AL-BAḤRIYYAH runs along the coast of the W Harbour to the mouth of the Maḥmūdiyyah Canal. Halfway along the SHʿ. AL-NAṢR leads E to Maydān al-Taḥrīr.

# Southern Alexandria

*Pompey's Pillar and the ruins of the Serapeum*

From the S corner of Maydān al-Taḥrīr the SHʿ. GAWHAR AL-QĀʾID leads into SHʿ. SĪDĪ ABŪ ʾL-DARDĪR and after crossing Shʿ. al-Amīr Abū ʿl-Munʿim and Shʿ. al-Khidiw al-Awal reaches SHʿ. AL-ʿAMŪD AL-SĀWARĪ. To the W is the site of the city of *Rhakotis*, the Ptolemaic *Temple of Serapis* and **Pompey's Pillar** (Ar. al-ʿAmūd al-Sawārī: Column of the Horseman), raised in AD 300 in honour of Diocletian who saved the city from famine prior to his massive Christian persecutions. It received its popular name from medieval travellers under the mistaken impression that it marked the site of the temple where Pompey's head was venerated. The Arabic name probably derives from the fact that the pillar still may have supported the equestrian statue of Diocletian when the Arabs invaded in the 7C and for some time after. It is set on a pedestal 8m sq., on the E face of which is a green granite inscription in Greek honouring Arsinöe, wife of Ptolemy II. On the W side is a recessed figure of Seti I. The column of red granite is 22m high and is crowned by an immense Corinthian capital. It may be one of the columns of the Temple of Serapis. To the SW are two great red *granite Ptolemaic Sphinxes* found in the area and an 8m statue of *Isis Pharia* found in 1961 in the sea near Qāyt-bāy's Fort. There is also an 18 Dyn. black granite sphinx (headless) and statues of Rameses II and Psamtik I. 40m W are the remains of the *Temple of Serapis*, long tunnels in the rock with crypts leading to niches and some marble pillars, probably all that remains of the Serapeum Library, second only to that at the Museion. Along with the temples, it was destroyed and the innumerable scrolls dispersed during the Christian anti-pagan riots in 391. To the N are the scattered remains of the *Temple of Isis*. Here also stood the

**KOM AL-SHUQĀFAH**

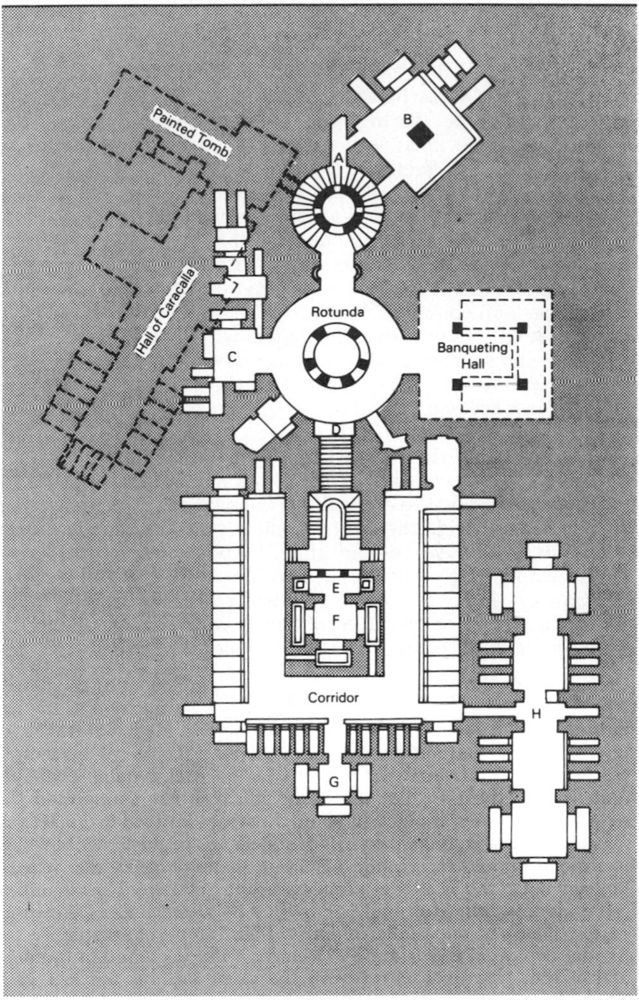
Painted Tomb
A
B
Rotunda
Hall of Caracalla
C
Banqueting Hall
D
E
F
Corridor
G
H

annexe to the Great Library of the Museion. It survived much longer, but finally succumbed to the depredations of the monks of St. Cyril who razed it to the ground in 411.

To the SW along the SH'. NAṢRIYYAH is the **Kom al-Shawqāfah** (Mound of Shards), a 2C AD burial site. Inside the enclosure are four porphyry sarcophagi and numerous architectural remains lie scattered over the area, but there has been a great deal of quarrying at the site. The main tomb lies to the NE. It consists of a complex of subterranean burial-chambers executed in a very unhappy marriage of Egyptian and classical Greek canons. Discovered in 1900, when a donkey fell into one of the tombs, they were originally private tombs later enlarged to serve the whole community. The mound received its name from the thousands of sherds found at the site, the remains of the dishes used by mourning relatives at funeral and anniversary feasts. Entrance is via a circular *Stairwell* (A) leading at the bottom into a passage, on either side of which is a shell-hooded niche. To the left is a later *Burial-Chamber* (B). The passage leads into a rotunda with a central dome resting on eight pillars. To the left lies the *Banqueting Hall* where relatives visiting the tombs would dine. Four pillars support the roof and stone couches rest against three of the walls. To the right is a *small room* (C) surrounded by burial niches. A breach in the wall leads to several large chambers; the *Hall of Caracalla* when opened contained skeletons of men and horses, while to the right is the *Painted Tomb* with paintings on stucco of various Egyptian funerary deities and sphinxes.

From the rotunda a *stairway* (D) roofed with a stone shell ornament leads down to the second level, dividing halfway down (around another stairway to the third level; flooded and inaccessible). At the bottom is a *Vestibule* (E) with roof supported on two pillars with Late Egyptian foliate capitals and two square piers with papyrus capitals. Above is a frieze of falcons and a winged disk. In each of the niches on the right and left walls of the vestibule is a statue, a man and a woman, both in Egyptian dress. On the far wall guarding the entrance to the next chamber are carved two bearded serpents wearing the pschent, encircling pinecones and caducei; above each is a medusa-headed shield. Above the door, the cornice contains a winged sun disk flanked by uraei. Immediately inside the *Burial Chamber* (F) to left and right are engaged statues in Roman military costume, that on the right of Sobek with a cloak and on the left Anubis with shield and sword. The chamber contains three rock-cut niches with false sarcophagi decorated with masks, ox-skulls and festoons. The walls of the niches are bas-reliefs of offering scenes with various deities, Anubis, Thoth, etc., portrayed in Greco-Egyptian style. Around this central chamber on three sides is a burial corridor lined with 91 niches each fitted to hold three bodies, many with the name and age of the deceased written in red paint. Beyond is a *small chamber* (G) containing three burial niches and to the left a passage leads to a series of *four rooms* (H), each with several niches for bodies.

Also on the site is a *Hypogeum* discovered in 1952 at 'Cleopatra's Beach' and reconstructed here. It contains nearly 40 wall-paintings. There are various other sarcophagi and sculptures found in the area.

THE PHAROS

*Reconstruction of the Pharos (after Thiersch). An indication of the size of the Pharos can be gained from the promenade below Maydān al-Taḥrīr, following the rather complicated instructions below. Face Fort Qāyt-bāy (1.5km away on the other side of the harbour) and, holding the Blue Guide at arm's length, align the base of the drawing with the waterline of the fort*

# South-East Alexandria

The MAYDĀN AL-TAḤRĪR (Liberation Sq) was formerly Maydān Muḥ. ʿAlī and later Maydān ʿUrābī. The central bus station and central Post Office are at the E end. A fine statue of Muḥ. ʿAlī Pasha by Jaquemart stands in the centre.

From the E end the SHʿ. SAʿD ZAGHLŪL leads to the Mahaṭat Raml (*Metro*: all stations to Kulliyat Naṣr, Sīdī Bishr) and on to Maydān Saʿd Zaghlūl.

Leaving the SE corner the Shʿ. Ṣalāḥ Sālim runs to join the main road, the ṬARĪQ AL-ḤURRIYYAH (formerly Shʿ. Fūʾād I) which follows the old Canopic Way (running as far as al-Muntazah).

Just to the E at the junction with Shʿ. Masgid al-ʿAṭṭarīn is **al-ʿAṭṭarīn Mosque**, on the site of the *Church of St. Theonas* where St. Athanasius was rector and, after the Muslim conquest, of the huge *Mosque of a Thousand Columns*. However, the wedge-shaped mosque is modern, with the three-tiered minaret at the apex and a dome covering the tomb of Saʿīd Muḥammad, a companion of Abū ʾl-ʿAbbās al-Mursī. A large sarcophagus was found inside. At first thought to be that of Alexander the Great, it was subsequently found to be that of King Nectanebo I (now in BM).

Turn S down the SHʿ. NABĪ DANYĀL. To the E is the **Masgid al-Nābī Danyāl**, popularly believed to be the tomb of the prophet Daniel but in fact that of Muḥ. Danyāl al-Maridī (died 1407), a venerated Shafiʿī shaykh who dwelt nearby and taught in the mosque. Excavations beneath the mosque have revealed an early 10–12C Muslim cemetery. This was probably the site of the Soma, the magnificent temple erected over the *Tomb of Alexander the Great*, at the main crossroads of the ancient city. The present building is 19C. The door in the NW wall leads into an arcaded courtyard. Inside the mosque, seven arcades parallel to the qiblah support the wooden roof. On the E wall is the domed tomb of Sh. Muḥ. Danyāl and also Sh. al-Ḥākim Luqmān, another venerated man. Behind the mosque stood (until 1984) the **Ḥawsh al-Malik**, with large Turkish tombs of the khedival family in carved and painted marble. They were removed because of civic development. The bodies have been taken to Cairo and reinterred in the Qubbat Umm Waldah Pasha (Rte 8).

E of the mosque is the **Kom al-Dikkah** (Hill of Rubble), thought to be ancient site of the *Paneion*, but recently the discovery of a **Roman Theatre** (probably 2C AD) has increased its importance. It is small and semicircular with 12 tiers of marble seats behind which are remains of a double-columned colonnade, while the stage has remains of square piers and mosaic wings. **Roman baths** have also been uncovered and restored and there is a small **Annexe of the Greco-Roman Museum**.

At the S end of Shʿ. Nabī Danyāl is the Maydān al-Gumhurriyyah with,

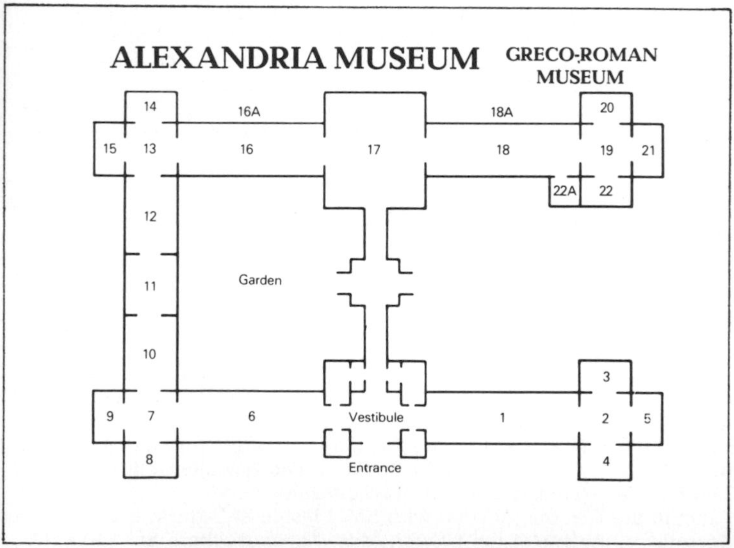
ALEXANDRIA MUSEUM
GRECO-ROMAN MUSEUM
14
16A
18A
20
15
13
16
17
18
19
21
22A
22
12
Garden
11
10
3
9
7
6
Vestibule
1
2
5
8
Entrance
4

at the E end, the **Mahaṭṭat Miṣr**, the mainline station (lines to Cairo, Rashīd, Sallūm).

Return to the Ṭarīq al-Ḥurriyyah. NW lies the **Greco-Roman Museum**. The museum was built in 1895 to house the Greco-Roman collections begun four years earlier. Most of the material in its 22 rooms comes from the Delta and Middle Egypt. To tour the museum chronologically turn right after entering through the vestibule.

Rooms 1–5: coins and later Christian material. Room 6: Ptolemaic and Roman inscriptions. Centre, a fine statue of the Apis Bull, diorite, found in fragments near Pompey's Pillar. It was apparently originally set up in the reign of Hadrian (AD 117–138) and buried during the sack of the Serapeum in 391.

Room 7: Pharonic period. Centre, a large statue of Ramesses II, red granite. Flanking this are two headless sphinxes originally made for Amenenhat IV but usurped by Ramesses II. In the space between the rooms is a small Hathor column from an Alexandrine shrine. Room 8: mainly mummies. Room 9: objects from Theadelphia (Baṭn Ihrīt), mainly from the Temple of Pnepheros, a crocodile god. They include a portable shrine for carrying the god, and a wooden door. There is also a statue of the goddess Sekhmet. Room 10: various objects, including a gigantic head of Ptolemy IV from Abū Qīr, amulets, vases and glass.

Room 11: Egyptian and Ptolemaic objects from Athribis in the Delta (Tell Atrīb) where Horus was worshipped. There is a statue of him as a warrior god. Votive objects to Isis and Serapis (Fayyūm). Room 12: Ptolemaic and Roman portrait busts and statues. Bust of Serapis found near Pompey's Pillar. Head of the emperor Hadrian, bronze, and an excellent head of Julius Caesar (No. 22902). Room 13: Ptolemaic and Roman sculpture. Centre, a colossal statue of a Roman Emperor, a head, reputedly of Cleopatra VII (No. 21992) and small objects and model altars from excavations around Alexandria. Room 14: the most important object in the room is the damaged Medusa mosaic from Gabbari.

Room 15: Tomb paintings, of which the most interesting is one depicting rural life. Room 16: Ptolemaic and Roman sculpture. A gigantic eagle found on the island of Thasos when it was part of the Ottoman Empire. A headless figure of the Nile god holding a cornucopia, white marble. Statues of priests of Isis, and a large figure of Serapis. Room 16A: the finest objects in the museum with the smaller objects round the sides and the larger sculpture in the middle. Large funerary stele; bust of Alexander (No. 3402); head of Serapis (No. 3519); head of Arsinöe II (No. 3262), and a torso of Aphrodite. Room 17: centre, statue of a Roman Emperor, probably Diocletian, porphyry (an extremely large object to be made in this material), Alexandria. Several marble sarcophagi decorated with wreaths; heads of minor Hellenistic deities; mosaic showing country life; sarcophagus carved with Ariadne on Naxos (mythological scenes are unusual in Alexandrian funerary monuments). Room 18: pottery and glass.

Room 19: stone and pottery vessels, including cinerary urns. Room 20: funerary urns and mortuary wreaths. Room 21: Funerary urns, skulls, and a fine collection of stamped Greek amphora handles. These were marked with their places of origin and enable a great deal to be discovered about the importation of island wines to Egypt in the Ptolemaic period.

Room 22: material from the excavations at Canopus (Abū Qīr) undertaken by Prince ʿUmar Ṭūsūn. Mainly mosaic fragments. Room 22A: the Treasury, containing material in silver and bronze. Two groups of foundation deposits from the Serapeum situated near Pompey's Pillar. They consist of dedication tablets in gold, silver and bronze (time of Ptolemy III; Nos 8357–66 and 9431–40). An ornamental silver-gilt goblet decorated with mythological scenes, 1 or 2C AD, al-Ashmunayn (Hermopolis).

The Garden is full of antiquities which have overflowed the museum rooms. In one corner are two reconstructed tombs, and a fine statue of King Ahmose II (26 Dyn.). On the N side is a reconstruction of a pylon and the chapel of the god Pnepheros from Theadelphia (Baṭn Ihrīt) in the Fayyūm.

Room G: statues from an Isis sanctuary, including Isis with her foot on a crocodile (No. 25783), white marble, Rā's al-Sudā. Two figures of Osiris, Canopus (Nos 25786 and 27587); the young Horus (No. 25784); a dedication to Isis for saving the donor in a chariot race.

Room 1–5: Coptic period; mainly early Christian saints. Rooms 4 and 5 contain Coptic textiles.

Continuing E, the Ṭarīq al-Ḥurriyyah passes to N and S between public gardens on the approximate site of the *Gate of the Sun*, the E entrance to the ancient city. To N and S are the **Shallalat Gardens**; those to the N contain remains of the *Arab city walls*. A series of long lakes is all that remains of the lower end of the *Farkhah Canal* which used to run between the Maḥmūdiyyah Canal and the sea but now terminates at the railway line. A little further on to the N is the impressive building of the *Faculty of Engineering* of Alexandria University. The next main turning to the S is the SHʿ. AL-SHAHĪD GAWAD ḤUSNI leading S to the H1, the main Delta route to Cairo (see below). To the N of Ṭarīq al-Ḥurriyyah is the *Alexandria Sporting Club*, just prior to **Mahaṭṭat Sīdī Gābir**. From here the avenue continues through to al-Muntazah.

Down the Shʿ. al-Shahīd Gawad Ḥusni, after crossing the main railway line the SHʿ. ZĀKĪ RAGAB leads into the Maydān Ismāʿīl Sirrī where the SE road leads to a series of gardens. To the NW are the **Alexandria Zoological Gardens**, opened in 1907 and comprising 26 acres. The zoo contains 200 spp. of animals and has a good breeding record. To the S are the **Nuzhah Gardens**, equally large and originally planted for Isma'īl Pasha with specimen trees. The **Antoniaidis Gardens** further S are a little larger and have more ancient tombs. This area was an ancient suburb of Alexandria and the home of the poet Kallimachus (fl. 264 BC).

From the Maydān Ismāʿīl Sirrī, the road rejoins Shʿ. al-Shahīd Gawad Ḥusnī, passing the *Marine Racing Club* and crossing the Maḥmūdiyyah Canal to join the H1.

## North-East Coast (al-Silsilah to Abū Qīr)

From al-Silsilah to the E to (18km) Abū Qīr stretches a coastline of beautiful bays and beaches. From W to E these are Shatbī, Kamp Shizār, Ibrāhīmiyyah, Sporting Club, Kilyubātrā, Sīdī Gābir, Muṣṭafā Pasha, Bulakly (Istanly Bāy, Karbān Bāy), Glymnobulu, San Stifanū, al-Raml, Sīdī Bishr, Bīr Masʿūd, Miyāmī, Mandarah, Muntazah and Maʾmurah, from which point the shore stretches unbroken to Abū Qīr.

A parallel road, the ṬARĪQ AL-GAYSH (Army Avenue), runs the whole length, turning inland at al-Muntazah, following the railway line to Abū Qīr, lined by hotels, restaurants, shops and villas. Slightly inland the Raml tramway follows the coast closely as far as Sīdī Bishr and a little further inland the mainline railway runs right to Rashīd with a branch line to Abū Qīr.

**Al-Silsilah**, marking the E end of the E Harbour, is a promontory extended by an artificial quay built over some exposed rocks. During Muslim medieval times a beacon stood on its furthest point and it takes its present name, 'The Chain', from the fact that a mechanism holding a chain (used to close the harbour) was suspended from this point. It is now a naval military establishment and entry is forbidden. Immediately in front of the entrance a modern statue commemorates the Egyptians who died in recent campaigns against Israel. This and the area to the S is the site of the *Royal Palace* enclosure and the *Royal Harbour* of the ancient Ptolemaic city. To the right of al-Silsilah, now beneath the sea, is the site of the first *Cathedral of St. Mark* where Arius was deacon.

Moving E, close to (500m) **Mahaṭṭat Shātbī** is another *Necropolis*, perhaps the oldest in the city, dating from Ptolemaic to Roman times and similar in construction to those at Anfushī.

1.5km **Camp Shizār** is the site of *Eleusis Maritimus* and to the S the *Alexandria Sporting Club*. The district of **Muṣṭafā Pasha** was the site of Augustus Ceasar's town of *Nikopolis* with a large Roman barracks built to celebrate his Egyptian victory. Meant to rival Alexandria it was however soon abandoned. The British also chose to site their main barracks here and during the construction of a football pitch another **Necropolis** was uncovered near the hill of Abū l'-Nawātir. Similar in construction to the Anfushī tombs, although they lack the Egyptian element in the decoration, they are still unlike any tombs in Greece. There are four tomb complexes of which No. 3 is the most complete and interesting. From **al-Raml** the tramway terminates near *Kulliyat al-Naṣr*, formerly *Victoria College*. This institution was run as an English public school open to all races and creeds in Egypt and later the Sudan.

Further E (6km) is **Sīdī Bishr**. At the junction of the Ṭarīq al-Gaysh with SHʿ. MASGID SĪDĪ BISHR is the *Mosque of Sīdī Bishr*, a modern building, built in 1939 by the Wizarāt al-Awqaf on the site of a much earlier tomb and later 19C restoration.

This is traditionally supposed to be the tomb of a companion of the Prophet, three of whom with the name Bishr came to Egypt. However, when the building was examined in the 19C the tabūt gave the name Bishr b. Ḥusayn Gawharī. This man, probably Maghrabī, came from a family of scholars, settled in Alexandria and attracted a large following through his piety and wisdom (died 1134).

The building is a forecourt mosque, the outer court with rīwāqs on three sides, the SE side with a doorway leading into the pillared interior. To the W of the miḥrāb is the tomb of Sīdī Bishr, a domed cube, the oldest part and all that remains of the 19C building.

A little further to the E on the point stands the *Automobile Club*, below which are the **Spouting Rocks of Bīr Masʿūd** where the sea has undercut the limestone and sends clouds of spume through holes in the rocks. Many of these holes were modified in Ptolemaic times and it has been suggested that machines or automata were placed over and powered by them. The largest are now enclosed as people would try the extremely dangerous practice of jumping into them.

Continuing along the coast, after passing through (4km) **al-Mandarah** the walled enclosure of the **Muntazah Palace** is reached. This complex, built by ʿAbbās II as his summer residence and restored by King Fūʾād I, is set in 350 acres of parkland around a small harbour. The gardens are very beautiful, planted with specimen trees, the stands of maritime pines (*Pinus maritima*) being especially fine. The main *Palace*, built by ʿAbbās II, is in a hybrid Turkish-Florentine style with the central tower a copy of that of the Palazzo Vecchio in Florence. Used as a hospital during World War I, it has now been converted into an hotel and the Salamlik has become a casino. Nearby, in a grove of trees, rises the high Muntuzah Lighthouse. On the W shore of the harbour stands the *Palestine Hotel*. On the E side of the harbour a promontory juts into the sea with a Turkish kiosk. This was the site of *Taprosiris Parva*, remains of which lie haphazardly. (The gardens and beach are open 07.00–late evening; fee.) To the E of the palace is *al-Ma'murah*, a pleasure resort with expensive apartments and chalets.

The road turns inland. After 5km directly N on the coast is the site of the city of **Canopus**. Built on a limestone outcrop, it was the capital of the Menelaite Nome and the most important Delta city and port prior to the building of Alexandria.

It was traditionally founded by Canopus, pilot of Menelaeus on his return from Troy. He died of snake-bite, was deified and set among the stars (Alpha Carinae; called Suhayl in Arabic). The star shines in the constellation of Argo (the ship), rising in the winter skies of Egypt and second only to Sirius in brightness. But in fact the site shows evidence of much earlier occupation. The city flourished due to its propinquity to the mouth of the Canopic branch of the Nile (now dry) but with the rise of Alexandria it dwindled into a cult and pleasure town although a canal connecting the Nile with Alexandria passing close to the town helped it retain some of its importance. Among the more famous buildings was the Temple of Serapis built by Ptolemy I Soter. Long after the official recognition of Christianity as the state religion, this city was an outpost of the Ancient Egyptian religion until finally extinguished by the Patriarch Cyril I who in the early 5C erected the Church of SS. Cyrus and John.

Little is to be seen at the site save an area of mounds of rubble. It would appear to have suffered most destruction in recent times at the hands of the British military authorities during World War I. Several statues of Ramesses II found at the site are now in the Greco-Roman Museum. To the E of the site is the pentagonal *Tawfīqiyyah Fort* built in the 19C. The remains of the *Temple of Serapis* lie to the W marked by some exposed sandstone and granite columns. Here in 237 BC the Decree of Canopus was proclaimed by Ptolemy III in an attempt to rationalise the calendar. On the coast are the remains of two sets of *Ptolemaic and Roman baths*, the *Upper Baths* lined with pink mortar and, to the E, connected directly to the sea by sluices, the *Lower Baths*. Further E again are some Ptolemaic rock tanks.

2km **Abū Qīr**, a small fishing town, stands on a promontory called by the Greeks *Zephyrion* (from the West wind). It takes its modern name from the now-destroyed Church of SS. Cyrus and John (Anbā Kyr).

*Hotel*: Abū Qīr al-Siyāhī; 30 Sh'. Gawhar al-Qā'id (T). *Restaurants*: several specialising in seafood.

E of the site of Canopus are two more forts; *Ṭābiyyat al-Saba'*, also pentagonal, and on the very point the 15C *Burg Abū Qīr*, built by Sulṭan Qāyt-bāy. This is on the site of a *Temple of Aphrodite* erected in 270 BC by Ptolemy II for his deified wife Arsinoe. To sea from this point in Abū Qīr Bay lies Nelson's Island.

From here in 1798 Admiral Brueys strung his fleet in line of battle defending Napoleon's land forces. The British fleet, commanded by Nelson, arrived in pursuit on the evening of 1 August. By concentrating his fleet at two points, the head of the French line and the flagship 'Orient' at the centre, Nelson achieved superior fire-power. The 'Orient', captained by Casabianca, caught fire at 9.45 p.m. and blew up, killing Brueys. By midnight the battle was effectively over, with most of the French ships sunk or crippled. The incident inspired Mrs F. Hemans (1793–1835) to commemorate the son of Casabianca in her poem beginning 'The boy stood on the burning deck...'. The disaster effectively ended Napoleon's vision of an eastern French empire.

S of Abū Qīr on the coast of the bay stands *al-Raml Fort*, on the site of ancient *Menouthis*. 1km S is a well-preserved Ptolemaic and Roman bath complex called erroneously *Cleopatra's Bath*. Further along the bay (4km) is the site of *Herakleum* and the mouth of the Canopic branch of the Nile which finally silted up in the 9C AD.

## West of Alexandria (Al-Maks to Abū Ṣīr)

Leave Alexandria at al-Qabbārī on the SHᶜ. AL-MAKS (H55) with the Mediterranean coast to the N and Lake Maryūt to the S. 1.5km **Al-Maks** is an important industrial suburb. At (85km) **al-Dikhaylah** the coast turns N to a cape.

A road leads N to al-ᶜAgamī (1.5km) with the holiday village of *Hannoville*. **Hotels**. *Hannoville* (3*); *Agami Palace* (2*); *Costa Blanca Minas* (T). At the point of the cape is *al-ᶜAyanah Fort*, where Napoleon landed on 2 July 1798, while off the coast are several islands; the largest is *Gazīrat al-Marābiṭ* with the tomb of a shaykh.

At (5km) **Azbat ᶜAlī Awād** a road leaves to the S to join the H11, the desert route to Cairo down which is the village of **al-ᶜAmiriyyah** (10km).

On the H55 the next town is (18 km) **Sīdī Kirīr**. At 10km are the ruins of *Plinthine* with a Ptolemaic necropolis, though the site is probably much older.

The next village on the H55 is (2km) **Abū Ṣīr** with S of the road the ruins of *Taposiris Magna* from which the modern name is derived, probably an ancient site though most of the remains are Ptolemaic. It is marked by the remains of a ancient *lighthouse* standing on a knoll and visible from a great distance. Like the Pharos, though much smaller, it consists of three tiers, a square-sectioned base, an octagonal second layer and a cylindrical top which has fallen. It is the only lighthouse now existing of a series

*Abū Ṣīr pylons of the temple*

that stretched along the coast of Egypt, all erected by Ptolemy II. Around lie *tomb shafts* and to the W (500m) the much ruined *Temple of Osiris* standing on the crest of the limestone ridge. The E pylons and great courtyard (N wall in good condition) are discernible but the temple has disappeared except for remnants of a colonnaded court and façade. In the E part of the enclosure is a *6C monastery and church*.

At the base of the ridge near the road are springs that must once have formed sizeable pools and could have supported a large community.

The road continues around the sweep of the Arabs Gulf to Shāṭā' al-ʿAlamayn (Rte 49).

Just N of al-ʿAmiriyyah on the H11 a road leaves to the SW, running parallel to the H55 on the coast, N of the mainline railway and S of Lake Maryūt. 4km **Ikingī Maryūṭ** (*Hotel*: Desert Home, 3*), **al-Hawāriyyah** and (17km) **Bahīg**.

From Bahīg a track leads SE to **Abū Minā** (10km), an extremely important Christian site. The town grew up around the tomb of the greatly revered Menas.

The son of Euoxius, governor of Pentapolis (W of Alexandria), Menas became a soldier and in turn assumed his father's post of governor. He was ordered to assist in Diocletian's persecutions of the Christians, but finding this distasteful he retired to the desert where he had a vision of crowned martyrs. After a public affirmation of the Christian faith he was martyred in Phrygia. His body was carried back to Egypt and buried (11 November).

A small oratory was built during the reign of Emperor Constantine (306–37) and the patriarch Athanasius had a church built in the mid 4C, at which so many miracles were performed that the emperor Arcadius (395–408) ordered the building of a large basilica. In the late 5C the emperor Zeno (474–91) visited the site and built a palace and town for the religious and pilgrims. Although it is difficult to estimate the numbers of religious attached to the church they must have numbered hundreds. Thousands of pilgrims visited the site to be healed by the sacred waters and flasks embossed with a relief of the saint are widely distributed, having been found throughout the Middle East and even in medieval sites in Europe. In the 7C the Melkites briefly controlled the shrine but after litigation to the Arab governor it was returned to the Copts. During the building of the great mosque in Samarra the khalif al-Mu'tasim had the coloured marble stripped from the church and in the late 9C the Bedouin ravaged the town. Though still standing in the 12C it was in ruins and no longer a place of pilgrimage. The first excavations at the site were undertaken by the Germans in 1905 and lasted two years, during which the Shrine of St. Menas was found. In 1951 further excavation undertaken by the Coptic Museum concentrated on the Pilgrim's Town.

The early limestone **Church of Abū Mīnā** has three apses and a crypt. Surrounding the church is the *Basilica of Arcadius* (384–412) with two arcades and a single apse, with a high altar and two side chapels. To the S is the *Atrium* and to the W the *Baptistry* with walls still standing to 12–14m and with a fount in the central courtyard. N of the basilica are the *Hospice* and *Great Bath complex*, with hot and cold cisterns and also a *small chapel*. Surrounding the whole are the remains of the *Pilgrim's Town*.

The new *Coptic Monastery of Abū Mīnā* was founded in 1959 and in 1962 the relics of St. Menas were transferred from Cairo at the instigation of the patriarch.

The road continues past (5km) **Burg al-ʿArab**, a small 'model town' designed and executed by W.E. Jennings-Bramley in the early 20C (road N to join the H55); (13km) **al-Hammām** and on to (44km) *Shataʿ al-ʾAlamayn*.

The route W is continued in Rte 49.

# 43 Southern Delta

Due N of Cairo, this route is divided into three itineraries, each of which leads into the main Delta routes, 44, 45 and 46.

## A. Central Area

Leave Cairo by Shubrā Miṣr (Rte 18) and cross the Ismaʿīliyyah Canal into the province of Qalyūbiyyah at Shubrā al-Khaymah. After passing an army post and then a police checkpoint, the H1 (agricultural road to Alexandria) leaves greater Cairo and runs due N. To the W at (12km) **Qalyūb** is the road to al-Qanātir al-Khayriyyah (see below) and to the E the road to the H3 (see below). N of Qalyūb the H1 passes (12km) **Qahā**, renowned as its name appears on tins of Egyptian agricultural produce exported throughout the world. The company was formed between the wars and nationalised after the revolution. Branches have now spread throughout Egypt. The fields belonging to the company stretch on both sides of the road but the processing plant is on the E.

Continuing N, the road passes (9km) **Tūkh** and after 12km reaches **Banhā**, the chief town of the province of Qalyūbiyyah. It is one of the most important cities in the Delta as it is the focus for all the arterial roads running S from Lower Egypt into Cairo and the Nile Valley. Known in ancient times as *Per Neha*, which became *Banahu* in Coptic, it was famed for its groves of sycamore fig trees. To the NW is **Tell Atrīb** marking the remains of the Ancient Egyptian city of *Hut-hery-ib*, Gk *Athribis*, capital of the 10th nome of Lower Egypt and associated with the worship of the black bull.

Excavations were undertaken in 1939 by Liverpool University and between 1961–64 by a Polish expedition. Despite extensive damage by the sabakhin, remains of 18, 19, 25 and 26 Dyn. temples were uncovered. Under the Romans it was an important town. As with many Delta cities it displayed an orderly plan with two intersecting main roads. In 1924 a cache of 26–30 Dyn. silver ingots and jewellery was discovered (now in EM). Among tombs discovered in the N Section was that of Queen Takhut (wife of Psamtik II). There is also an extensive Greco-Roman cemetery.

In the course of the 1980s the Polish Expedition uncovered a Ptolemaic quarter extending from *Kom Sīdī Yūsuf*. In addition to well preserved houses they revealed an industrial area with kilns which produced painted pottery. Main occupation was from 3C BC reaching its height during the reign of Ptolemy VI as attested by the well-preserved coins.

The H1 continues NE to *Ṭanṭā* (Rte 46).

From the H1 just beyond Qalyūb a road leads to the W to **al-Qanātir al-Khayriyyah** (8km) on the E side, c 1km N of the point at which the Nile divides into two great

*Qanātir al-Khayriyyah, the barrage of Muḥammad ʿAlī*

branches; the Faraʿ Dumyāṭ (Damietta Branch) to the E and the Faraʿ Rashīd (Rosetta Branch) to the W. The area, with its parks planted with specimen trees, is extremely pleasant and it is very popular during public holidays. Cycles can be hired.

Schemes to control the flow of water throughout the Delta were first tackled by Muḥammad ʿAlī in 1833. His architect was the great French hydroengineer Mougel Bey who decided to construct a barrage across each of the branches of the Nile to feed three large canals which would supply the Delta. Due to a series of misfortunes he was unable to complete the scheme, his barrages were virtually useless and the problem was then considered insurmountable. Thus things remained until 1883 when Sir Colin Scott-Montcrieff who had worked on a much vaster canal system in N India was persuaded to resurrect the scheme. He tackled the problem on a country-wide basis, dividing Egypt into five circles of irrigation, three in the Delta and two in the Valley (incidentally echoing the division of the country by the Ancient Egyptians). He decided to reconstruct the barrages from the foundations and by using the innovation of electric light for illumination at night he had completed the Rosetta Barrage by 1889 and the Damietta Barrage by 1891. His scheme had also involved extensive recanalisation throughout the Delta and the effect was immediate with a phenomenal increase in crop production, principally cotton. As a final act of magnanimity before leaving Egypt in 1892 he located the aged and impoverished Mougel Bey to display to him the feasibility of his original concept and insisted on his being provided with a state pension. The Damietta Branch Barrage is 521m long with 71 arches, each containing a sluice, while the Rosetta Branch Barrage is 438m long with 61 sluices; both have locks for boats. Along the top of each is a wide road and there are fortified battlements. On the down-river side rails and machinery operate the cone-shaped sluice-gates. The barrages are c 1km apart, the area between filled with parks and gardens. At the E end of the Rosetta Branch Barrage is the *Istarahah al-Qanātir*, the palace built for the engineers who constructed the barrages. It is now an official residence of the president. The 'Yakht al-Mahrūsa' is usually moored at the quay of the palace. Originally belonging to King Faruq, it is now the state barge. Mougel Bey's original barrages can be seen 100m upstream.

Part of the original scheme, three huge canals leave Qanātir. Fed by the barrages, to the W is the *Rayyah al-Biḥayrah*, to the E the *Rayyah al-Tawfiqī* and from the centre the *Rayyah al-Manūfiyyah*.

The H4 runs N from al-Qanātir to *Shaṭānūf*, crosses an isolated ancient arm of the Nile to *al-Bāgūr* and to (43km) **Shibīn al-Kawm** (principal city of the province of Manūfiyyah). From al-Bāgūr the H25 runs W through *Sirs al-Layānah* to **Minūf** (10km).

## B. Western Area

The H19 leaves Imbābah (Rte 22) and beyond (7km) **Kom al-Ahmar** a road to the W leads to **Ausim** (Ar. *Awsīm*) (3km), site of the ancient city of *Khem*, Gk *Letopolis*, capital of the 2nd nome of Lower Egypt. Here Khenty-Irty, a form of Horus, was worshipped. The Temple of Horus has been completely destroyed but seems to have been 26–30 Dyn. in date. Various blocks of Nectanebo I were found here (in EM). Literary texts indicate that it was occupied from at least Old Kingdom times.

Beyond this the H19 divides (to the E is Qanātir; see above). Turn to the W and follow the road for 8km and then N for 23km. To the E of the road on the bank of the Nile is **Merimde Banī Salāmah**, a prehistoric site. At (8km) *al-Khaṭāṭbah* the H9 terminates and is met by the H6 which runs SW to the H11, the Desert road to Alexandria (Rte 41). Follow the track on the W side of the Rayyah al-Bihayrah and the Cairo–Alexandria railway N to (9km) **Kom Abū Billo** (Ar. *Billaw*), site of the town of *Tarrana*, Gk *Terenuthis*, which name in turn is connected with the scorpion goddess, Renenutet (Gk Termuthis), in one aspect a deity of grain and the harvest. The *Temple of Hathor* built by the first two Ptolemies was discovered by Griffith in 1887–88; the town was, however, occupied from a much earlier period and burials in the cemetery date from the Old Kingdom to the Byzantine Period.

## C. Eastern Area

At Shubrā al-Khaymah the Shʿ. Būr Saʿīd crosses the Ismāʿīliyyah Canal where it meets the Shʿ. al-Muʿāhadah from the W. Beyond this point it becomes the H3 and runs NE to the W of the Ismāʿīliyyah Canal, passing *Bahtīm* and (5km) **Musṭurud** with the *Church of the Virgin* on a site said to have been visited by the Holy Family on their flight into Egypt. An immense mūlid, one of the largest Christian celebrations in the Delta, is held between 7–22 August to celebrate the Assumption of the Virgin.

Past Musṭurud the H3 passes (5km) **Siryaqūs** and (7km) **Abū Zaʿbal** where a road runs NW (to Shibīn al-Qanātir) to the N of which (4km) is the site of **Tell al-Yahūdiyyah** (Mound of the Jews), ancient *Naytahut*, Gk *Leontopolis* (one of two Delta cities of this name), situated within the 13th nome of Lower Egypt, that of Heliopolis.

Investigated by Naville and Petrie, it contains a large enclosure referred to as the '*Hyksos camps*', a vast structure over 500m long with a sloping glacis and plastered revetment, the only similar structure in Egypt being at Heliopolis. It has been likened to Hyksos fortifications found in Palestine and Syria. Inside were the remains of several temples, one of Ramesses II, another of Ramesses III. Outside the NE wall is evidence of a town and the temple built by Onias, an exiled Jewish priest at the time of Ptolemy VI Philometor (180–145 BC). This town was occupied until AD

71 when the temple was closed by Vespasian. There are cemeteries of the 12, 18, 19, 22–26 Dyns as well as a Jewish one on the edge of the desert.

From Maṭāriyyah (Rte 19), just beyond the limits of Greater Cairo, the Shʿ. Qiṭār al-Mārg becomes the H15 and passes (3km) **al-Mārg**. To the E is the **Birkat al-Ḥagg** (Lake of the Pilgrimage—now dry), once the assembly point for the immense caravan that set off from Cairo to Mecca. It passes (8km) **al-Khānkah**. Here stands the isolated **Mosque of Sultan Barsbāy**, the last of his three mosques; each built in a different style. This mosque (completed 1427) is of the enclosure type and was constructed for the benefit of pilgrims. It has been restored by the CPAM. The exterior is rather plain, the wall set with full-length recesses containing windows. Against the NE wall is an extension containing the main entrance with a high flat stalactite arch, to the left of which rises the minaret. The first storey has a square section with a medial window in each side and above the balcony is the second cylindrical storey with intertwined ribbing; the third storey is in the form of a pavilion. Right of the entrance is the completely reconstructed sabīl-kuttāb. In the NW façade is a secondary entrance. Inside, the NW riwāq has one arcade, the SW and NE riwāqs two arcades and the qiblah riwāq three arcades covered by a carved and painted wooden roof. Along the walls is a marble dado while the mihrab is also of marble and the minbar of wooden panels inlaid with ivory.

Beyond al-Khānkah the H15 runs into (5km) *Abū Zaʿbal* and joins the H3.

After Abū Zaʿbal the H3 passes **al-Zawāmil** and (20km) **Ghītah** and arrives at (4km) **Bilbays**, the chief city of the district in the province of Sharqiyyah. Here the Dept of Antiquities found a destroyed Temple of Nectanebo II. Just to the NW is the *Tell al-Shaghāmah* where a 19 Dyn. town and fort were located by Petrie.

# 44 Central Delta

Beyond Banhā (Rte 43A) the H1 passes (17km) **Qawaysnā**. At (4km) **Birkat al-Sabaʿ** a road leaves to the NE, running through **Hūrayn** to (20km) **Ziftā** on the W bank of the Damietta branch of the Nile. The H9 crosses the city W from *Ṭanṭā* (Rte 46), crossing the Nile to *Mīt Ghamr* and on to al-Zaqāzīq (Rte 45). Continuing N from Ziftā the H8 passes (14km) **Sunbat** and after 14km passes **Abū Ṣīr Banā**. 1km to the E on a bluff overlooking the river is the site of ancient *Busiris*.

Few remains mark the birthplace of Osiris except part of a 26 Dyn. basalt statue and a limestone fragment with the name of Sheshonq of the 22 Dyn. (now in the EM). A block from here with the cartouches of Darius I is in the BM. The site has fragments of a monumental gateway belonging to the same king. The original chief deity worshipped here was Andjety in the shape of a mummiform man. His cult was, however, usurped by that of Osiris who assumed his form and attributes.—2km W are the remains of the late cemetery.

Beyond this the H8 runs into (7km) **Sammanūd** W of which (near the hospital) is the site of ancient *Tjeboutjes*, Gk *Sebennytos*.

This was the capital of the 12th nome of Lower Egypt and birthplace of the chronicler Manetho. Remains of a large mound mark the Temple of Onuris-Shu, the chief deity, rebuilt by Nectanebo II. There are many red and black granite blocks scattered about and a black granite naos (now in the EM) is said to have come from here. It would appear that there was also a Middle Kingdom temple here as blocks of Amenemhat I have been found, but its exact location is uncertain.

To the E a road crosses to the E bank and Agā while to the W is al-Mahallah al-Kubrā. The H8 follows the river NE. At (9.5km) **Bahbayt al-Ḥagar**, W of the road is the site of ancient *Pr-Hebeit* principal centre of the worship of Isis, Gk *Isisospolis*, Roman *Iseum*, but the modern name reflects the most ancient.

There is a temple enclosure, two sides of which are clearly visible. However, the granite Temple of Isis was deliberately razed to a confused heap. It was begun by Nectanebo II and completed by Ptolemy II Philadelphus and Ptolemy III Eurgetes. Some of the carving on the granite blocks is of high quality and there are several good Hathor capitals.

Beyond this the H8 reaches (17km) **Talkhā** and passes **Baṭrah** to (25km) **Shirbīn**. S a bridge leads to *Manṣūrah* on the E bank but the H7 leads W to (12km) **Bilqās**. From here a road leads N and after 3km a track leads E to **Deir Sitt Damyānah** (Monastery of St. Damianah) which contains the tomb of the patroness. This is one of the most important Christian foundations in Egypt. Until the Revolution it was within the diocese of the Metropolitan of Jerusalem but inhabited by monks from St. Anthony's Monastery (Rte 50). Two courts surround the monastery; there are four churches to the N while the hospice and living quarters are to the W.

Damianah, who lived in the 3C, was the daughter of Marcus, governor of the Delta under Diocletian. She refused to marry and had her father build her a palace into which she retired with 40 other virgins to live in celibacy. After lapsing several times, her father finally refused to worship the Roman gods as demanded by Diocletian and he was executed. Damianah offered her life in lieu of that of her companions but they were all executed. Her mūlid is an immense affair (5–20 May) attended by pilgrims from all over Egypt. The tomb was built, according to tradition (as with many other Egyptian foundations), by St. Helena. At the beginning of the 6C a church was built on the site by Anba Yuhanna II.

At the SW of the enclosure is the long and narrow *First Church of St. Damianah*, with the interior divided into three sections: the Angel's Choir, the Saint's Choir and the Martyr's Choir. At the E end is the prayer niche. The *Second Church of St. Damianah* was built in the 19C; the haykal is dated 1845. In the W part of the church steps lead up to the Tomb of Sitt Damianah surrounded by a wooden screen, through which oval windows overlook the grave. In the outer court is the *Third Church of St. Damianah*, built in 1932 by Anba Butrus, bishop of Manṣūrah. On the first floor of the inner court is the *Church of the Virgin*, built in 1879.

Continuing NE on the H8, at 15km a road leaves to the NW to (20km) **Gamaṣah**, a village on the N coast. (From Cairo by train to Manṣūrah or Shirbīn and then bus, or direct coach from Cairo.) In contrast to many others, this is a quiet but charming resort with many kms of beach. (*Hotels.* Palm Hotel and Casino. Chalet and bungalow accommodation. 40 Government villas; several motels. Refreshments at the Palm Hotel, a great beach house.) Beyond the junction the H8 runs past **Kafr Saʿd** and (19km) **Kafr al-Baṭīkh**, 7km beyond which is a road running NE to (10km) **Rās al-Bārr**, another beautiful and quiet resort between the Mediterranean and the mouth of the Damietta branch of the Nile. (From Cairo by train to Damietta and then bus; directly from Cairo by coach. *Hotels.*

Mainly of the cabin type. Marine Fuad al-Malek; Marine Fuad al-Nil; At Home; Al-Shatt; Al-Magarbel; Beau Sejour, all 1*.) The H8 continues, crossing the Nile into Damietta (Rte 45)

From *Sammanūd* a road leads due W to (7km) **al-Mahallah al-Kubrā**, one of the main cities of the Delta (*Hotel*, Omar al-Khayyam, Sh'. 23 Yūlyū.) Beyond, at 13km the H23 takes off to the N, passing **Matbūl** (13km) and **Dukhmays** (5km) and at 12km crossing the trans-Delta H7. Still travelling N, it passes **al-Ḥāmūl** and continues across reclaimed land to **Balṭīm** on Lake Burullus, a very isolated and quiet resort. (From Cairo by train or long distance coach. *Hotel*. Baltim Hotel, or reed chalets.) **Al-Shaykh Mubarak** 4km to the N on the Mediterranean is the northernmost point of Egypt; just to the W at **al-Burg** is the mouth of the extinct Sebennitic branch of the Nile.

Leaving *al-Mahallah al-Kubrā* to the SW, the H22 runs directly to *Ṭanṭā*, while 8km E a road leads N to (30km) **Biyalā** on the H7 W of *Bilqās*.

Due N from *Ṭanṭā* (Rte 46) the H4 passes (27km) **Quṭūr** on the H26 (NW to *Dasūq*, SE to the H23), crossing which it runs on to (20km) **Sakhā**, the site of ancient *Xois*.

The remains are insignificant; a stele of Augustus and some Ptolemaic blocks (now in the EM) were found here.

3km beyond Sakhā the H4 reaches **Kafr al-Shaykh**, a large town and administrative centre of the province. From here the H28 runs N to **Sīdī Sālim** (28km). Crossing Kafr al-Shaykh from E to W is the H7. Beyond the town it turns NW and circles around to (25km) **al-'Agūzayn**. From here a road leaves to the N to the village of **Ibtū** (5km) to the N of which, on the edge of the marshes, is **Tell al-Fara'īn** (Mound of the Pharaohs), site of *Pr Wadjet*, Gk *Buto*, from which the village takes its name.

In fact it was a dual city—Dep dedicated to the worship of Wadjet (Gk Buto), cobra goddess of Lower Egypt, and Pe dedicated to the heron Djibut who was later replaced by Horus. The site, identified by Petrie, extends over three-quarters of a square kilometre, but has been much despoiled by the sabakhīn. It consists of two large city mounds and a temple enclosure with the mud-brick walls standing to a height of 15m. Of this *Temple of Wadjet* only the limestone paving and the base of the walls remain. The tops of the mounds yielded only Roman and Ptolemaic remains and in the temple the earliest level reached was Saite. Beyond broken lintels and a few remains of Ramesses II there is little evidence of the earlier structures which lie below the water level. During the Roman period, after the destruction of the temple the site seems to have been largely industrial and vast quantities of pottery were manufactured here.

Past al'Agūzayn to the W the H7 runs into **Dasūq** (8km) on the E bank of the Rosetta branch of the Nile, an agricultural town. It is distinguished since it contains the tomb of an eminent sufi shaykh. In the centre of the town is the **Mosque and Tomb of Sayyid Ibrāhīm Dasūqī**, a large but undistinguished modern building.

Ibrāhīm b. 'Abd al-Majd Dasūqī (c 1246–88) was born in Egypt into a sufi family. He studied under Aḥmad al-Badawī and reached such a high state of knowledge that he was encouraged to found his own brotherhood, known as the Dasūqiyyah or Burhaniyyah. His mūlid, second only in size to that of Aḥmad al-Badawī at Ṭanṭā is held directly after that of al-Badawī.

Crossing the Nile, the H7 continues SW to Damanhūr (Rte 45).

Following the East Bank of the Nile the H21 leaves Dasūq to the NW and runs through; **Fuwah** and (38km) **Muṭubis** with a road across the barrage to the West Bank, (4km) **Birinbāl** and into (27km) **Burg Mighayzil** at the mouth of the Rosetta branch of the Nile, opposite Rosetta.

# 45 Eastern Delta

The H6 leaves Banhā (Rte 43A) to the NE, passing **Shiblangah** and (18km) **Minyā al-Qamḥ** to (18km) **Zaqāzīq**, capital of Sharqiyyah province. Railway and bus stations. To the N (5km) is the small village of *Ḥūriyyat Rizānah*, birthplace of Aḥmad ʿUrabī (1839–1911), the great Egyptian military leader. As well as his *house* there is a *Zaqāzīq Museum* (open 07.00–13.00) with dioramas of ʿUrabī's life and a large annexe with material from excavations at Tell Bastah and Ṣān al-Ḥagar.

The H9 runs E to Ismāʿīliyyah but the H10 runs S to Bilbays. After 3km on the E side of the road is **Tell Basta**, site of the city of *Pr Bastet* (House of Bastet, the cat goddess), Gk *Bubastis* (W.C. available). The site covers a considerable area and it was the capital of the 18th nome of Lower Egypt.

The granite *Temple of Bastet*, excavated by Naville in 1887–89, is very ruined. Its main feature is the Festival Hall of Osorkon II and the structure seems to have been located on an island in the sacred lake. The foundation of the temple goes back to the 6 Dyn. To the N are the 6 Dyn. *Ka temples* of Pepy I and Teti and there are also 12 Dyn. *Chapels of Amenemhat III* and an 18 Dyn. *Chapel of Amenhotep III*. Extensive *animal burial places*, particularly cats associated with Bastet, have been found. A *small temple* is thought to be that of Mihos, son of Bastet. Apparently several important officials of the 19–20 Dyns came from this city and recently the tombs of two Viceroys of Kush (called Heri) have been found, as well as one of the vizier Ituti. Osorkon III seems to have built a temple to Atum here. Also recently unearthed was the 12 Dyn. *palace* of a local prince, with two rows of six column bases and some statues.

The H9 leaves Zaqāzīq by the SE and after 10km reaches **al-Ṣawah** and **Ṣafṭ al-Ḥinnah** to the S of the road, site of *Pr-Sopdu* (Gk. Phakusa), the early capital of the 20th nome of Lower Egypt, the domain of Sopd, the Falcon God of Lower Egypt and guardian of the Desert Ways.

The mound was partly excavated in 1885 by Naville, who found unbaked mud-brick walls of a temple enclosure. Also discovered were inscribed blocks of Ramesses II and a naos of Nectanebo I dedicated to Sopd.

Beyond Saft al-Ḥinnah the H9 passes (11km) Abū Ḥammād where it meets the H13 from Abū Kabīr to the N. At the W end of the *Wadī Ṭumaylāt*, the ancient route to Sinai, it meets the Ismāʿiliyyah Canal and at (2km) **al-ʿAbbasah al-Sharqiyyah** joins the H3 from Bilbays to the S. The H3 running E along the Wadī Ṭumaylāt passes (7km) **Tell al-Kabīr**, where Aḥmad ʿUrabī was finally defeated by British troops under Sir Garnet Wolseley in September 1882, (14km) **Qaṣṣaṣīn** and at 27km (S of the road) **Tell al-Maskhūṭa**, identified as the ancient town of *Pithom* of the Exodus. It was excavated in 1883 by Naville, who found a large mud-brick enclosure surrounding a temple structure, Pr Atum or the House of Atum, from which the town would have taken its name. Found here was a quartzite naos containing a sphinx of Ramesses II (now at Ismāʿiliyyah). S of here a red granite stele of Darius I was discovered (now in the EM).

It was occupied during the Second Intermediate Period (1750–1570 BC) and abandoned in the early New Kingdom not to be resettled until the reign of Nectanebo II (360–343 BC) when it was used during the recutting of the canal linking the Red Sea with the Mediterranean. Lack of relevant pottery indicates it was not occupied during the Ramesside period.

In 1978 an expedition from the University of Toronto and the American School of Oriental Research excavated this site. At the E extremity a cemetery of the 2C was exposed; it consisted of built brick chambers containing single and multiple burials with children's bodies buried in amphorae. Although robbed, a considerable amount of material had been overlooked. In the central part of the tell 5C BC Persian Period levels were unearthed which included a fine limestone building. Beneath this level there seems to be a Hyksos level with material from Middle Bronze II of Syro/Palestinian type.

The road continues E to (11km) Ismaʿiliyyah (Rte 47).

To the NE from Zaqāzīq runs the H6. At (12km) *Hiyhā* a track leads N to **Kafr Nigm** and the site of *Pharbaethos*. Here material of Ramesses II and later was excavated (now in various museums, including Hildesheim).

Continuing NE, the H6 runs into (11km) **Abū Kabīr**. Here the H13 runs S to Abū Ḥammād. N it passes through **al-Sinbillāwayn** (28km) where it is crossed by the H10 (S to Zaqāzīq, N to Manṣūrah) and on to Agā (see below). From *Abū Kabīr* the H6 continues E to (14km) **Faqūs**, just N of which lay ancient *Phakusa*. From here the H14 runs NE. There are several sites potentially of great historical significance, all N of the road. At **al-Khatāʿnah** (6km) the first site is **Tell al-Qirqatah** which has remains of the 12 Dyn., a granite gate of a chapel of Amenemhat I and Senusert III. E is **Tell al-Dabaʿ**, an extensive site currently under excavation by an Austrian mission. This was important in the Second Intermediate Period and may have been the site of the Hyksos capital of *Avaris*. Apparently abandoned during the 18 Dyn. it was reoccupied during the 19 Dyn. when a large temple was built which seems to have been dedicated to the god Seth.

The NE part of the tell was occupied during late Hyksos times whereas the central areas were inhabited earlier, in the 12–13 Dyns. The NE houses were of simple plan consisting of a single room with a large ante chamber. Excavation of the bodies in the cemetery suggest that the men were of foreign origin while the women were local Egyptians. No traces of the burning of Avaris were found.

Just to the N is **ʿAzbat Rushdī al-Saghīrah** with remains of a Middle Kingdom town and a temple apparently built by Amenemhat I. At **Qantīr** (9km) is a site excavated in the 1920s, though there is little now to see, since when it has been one of the contenders for the site of the vast *Pr Ramsses*, the Delta capital of Ramesses II. Quantities of 19–20 Dyn. glazed tiles bearing floral designs, animals and fish were found here (now in the EM). To the N is **Tell Abū ʾl-Shafiʿa** with the remains of a temple probably of the 19 Dyn.; the base of a colossus of Ramesses II has also been found.

Beyond Qantīr the next village on the H14 is **al-Ḥusayniyyah** (18km), just past which is the site of **Tell Faraʿūn** (Mound of the Pharaoh), Ancient Egyptian *Imet*, and later *Nabasha*, capital of the 19th nome of Lower Egypt. The mounds of debris covering the site were partly cleared by Petrie in 1886. He found the remains of a *Temple of Wadjet*, goddess of Lower Egypt, which was entered through a pylon. Also discovered were

Middle Kingdom and 19 Dyn. inscriptions and traces of a Ptolemaic town (fragments in the EM and Ashmolean Museum).

From *al-Ḥusayniyyah* the H32 runs N to the large site of **Ṣān al-Ḥagar** (88km), ancient *Djane*, later *Tanis*; although it was inhabited by the Hyksos, it is uncertain if it was the site of their capital *Avaris*. (WC near the French Mission Resthouse.)

This important town mound has been investigated over a number of years. Material from here was removed in 1825 by Drovetti. Between 1860–80 Mariette worked here for the government and in 1886 Petrie for the EEF. The French under Montet excavated here between 1927–55, since when it has remained in the French concession.

Its history dates from the Old Kingdom and remains of the 4–6 Dyns have been recovered. In the Middle Kingdom it was an important town and royal statues of the 12–13 Dyns have been found, some usurped by the Hyksos ruler Apopi. Visible remains are of a large Ramesside *Temple of Amun*, entered through a monumental gateway leading to a forecourt. On the S are the remains of the 21–22 Dyn. *Royal Necropolis* (closed to the public) discovered by Montet in 1939–40 (objects in the EM).

Excavations on the S side of the mound cleared the first pylon of a Temple of Amun. In the SE angle a foundations deposit was discovered consisting of three plaques, one bronze, one silver and one lapis-lazuli bearing the name of Osorkon II (874–850 BC), To the S the perimiter wall of the town was buttressed at regular intervals.

Beyond Faqūs the H6 continues NE to (20km) **al-Ṣāliḥiyyah**, founded in the 13C by Sulṭan al-Ṣāliḥ Ayyūb to assist pilgrims on the journey to Mecca. Here the road swings S and then E to join the H44 (28km) some distance N of *Ismāʿīliyyah*.

From Zaqāzīq the H10 leaves to the NW turning due N at (7km) **al-Qanāyat**. At 16km it is crossed by the H28 (from Mīt Ghamr in the N, E to al-Ibrāhīmiyyah) and at (15km) *Sinbillawayn* by the H13 (W. from Agā, E from Abū Kabīr). Beyond *Sinbillawayn* (15km) is the village of **al-Baqliyyah**, to the S of which are three low mounds marking the site of ancient *Baʾh*, Gk *Hermopolis Parva*, capital of the 15th nome of Lower Egypt.

The northernmost is the *Tell al-Naqūs* (Mound of the Bell) which probably indicates the town and the temple dedicated to the god Thoth. An inverted capital lying among the ruins gives the mound its name. Found here was a 26 Dyn. naos dedicated by Apries to Thoth (now in the EM). Another mound, the *Tell al-Zereiki* (Ziraykī), probably contains the ibis cemetery.

Beyond, the H28 continues to Manṣūrah.

Also leaving Zaqāzīq to the NW is the H9. To the N of the road (25km) is **Tell al-Muqdam**, extensive site of the second *Leontopolis*, chief town of the 11th nome of Lower Egypt during the Ptolemaic period.

It may have been the capital of the 23 Dyn. kings and was probably their burial place. At the E end of the site are ruins of a *Temple of Mihos*, the lion god, with many of the blocks reused. Stelae, statues and figures of lions have been found on the site. There must have been a New Kingdom temple here as 18–20 Dyn. statues and stelae have been recovered. The only royal tomb found was that of Queen Kamama, mother of Osorkon IV, to the W of the main mound. It is possible that the other tombs of the same dynasty have been destroyed.

The H9 runs through to **Mīt Ghamr** (see below).

Leaving Banhā to the NE and following the E bank of the Damietta branch of the Nile is the H5. It passes **Kafr Shukr** and **Ṣahragt al-Kubrā** and reaches (53km) **Mīt Ghamr**. Here the H9 crosses the Nile to Ziftā on the W bank and on to Ṭanṭā; to the E it runs to Zaqāzīq, while the H28 goes E to the H10. Continuing N, the H5 runs through (7km) **Bishlā**. At 7km, to the W of the road on the Nile bank is **Mīt Damsīs** and the *Church of St. George* where a very large mūlid is held (2–28 August) The ancient church was traditionally founded by St. Helena, while the New Church was built in the 1880s and has a hospice for pilgrims.

From here the H6 continues N to (15km) **Agā** where the H13 crosses the Nile (W to Sammanūd and E to Sinbillawayn) and reaches (13km) **al-Manṣūrah**. The dual minarets of the town's central mosque can be seen from a great distance. This is the capital city of Daqahliyyah province. Railway station (Maydān al-Maḥaṭṭah) and bus station for local and national buses.

Unlike most Egyptian cities, al-Manṣūrah is of comparatively recent foundation. It began as a camp built by Sulṭan al-Kāmil during the Siege of Damietta in 1220. During the invasion of the Sixth Crusade it was a crucial target and battle raged around it. After the Mamlūk triumph King Louis IX was imprisoned here. Since then it has grown into perhaps the most important city in the Delta and it is the centre of the raw cotton trade. An elegant city with tree-lined avenues beside the Nile, it has a university and several higher institutes. One of the particular local delicacies is buffalo-milk ice-cream.

Beside the Muwafī Mosque is the Ḥārat Muwafī and the Bayt Luqmān. This is the house of Qadī Ibrāhīm ibn Luqmān, a minister of Sulṭan al-Ṣāliḥ Ayyūb, in which Louis IX was imprisoned between 7 April–7 May 1250, although little of the medieval fabric is evident. It was opened by President Nasser in 1960 and contains furniture of some age.

From al-Manṣūrah the H10 runs SE. At 3km the H12 leads off to the E. Taking this road, after 6km a track leads S and then E for 12km to the site of two ancient cities. Just N of the road is **Tell Timai** (Timay), ancient *Anpet Djedet*, Gk *Thmuis*, much disturbed by the sabakhīn and the only visible remains are of Ptolemaic and Roman houses. It gradually eclipsed Mendes as the capital of the 16th nome of Lower Egypt. About 700m to the N is **Tell al-Rubʿa**, ancient *Pr Banab Djedet*, Gk *Mendes*, a large site covering four-fifths of a square kilometre.

Originally the chief deity of Mendes was Hat-mayhet, the fish goddess, but she was gradually overshadowed by Banedjedet, the sacred ram, whose worship was established here by the 2 Dyn. They became two members of the Mendesian Triad along with their son Harpocrates (the young Horus). It was also a place of worship for the Osirian Triad. The kings of the 29 Dyn. are said to have originated here and perhaps used it briefly as their capital. The first systematic excavation here was in 1860 for Mariette and further work was undertaken in 1869 and 1871 by A. Danois and E. Brugsch who discovered gold and silver objects (now in the EM). Naville spent a fruitless season here in 1892 looking for Hyksos monuments, and the site is still under excavation by an American team. Visible remains include an enclosure wall with a cemetery of coffins of the sacred rams in the NW, a 26 Dyn. red granite naos dedicated by Amasis, and some mud-brick houses and mastabas, some of the Old Kingdom. Little else is to be seen.

On the West Bank of the Nile opposite *Manṣūrah* is *Talkhā* (Rte 44). E, the H12 passes **Barq al-ʿIzz**, **Ṭanāh**, **al-Nassīmiyyah** and (22km) **Mīt Fāris** where it turns N into *Dikirnis*.

Beyond the junction with the H12, the H10 continues SE to *al-Baqliyyah* and *Sinbillawayn* (Rte 43).

From NE of *al-Manṣūrah* a road runs through **Sallamūn al-Qumāsh** (6km) and **Dikirnis** (13km). Joining the H7 NE, it passes **Birimbāl** (10km) **al-Gamāliyyah** (32km) **al-Manzalah** (7km) and **al-Maṭariyyah** (13km) on Lake Manzalah which it crosses on a causeway to **Port Said** (Bur Saʿīd, 32km, Rte 47) at the N end of the Suez Canal.

NW from Dikirnis a road runs to the bank of the Nile (15km) opposite *Shirbīn*. Here it joins the H5 and follows the riverbank NE through (42km) **Faraskūr** and on to (15km) **Damietta**.

The city of **Dumyāṭ** (Damietta) is on the E bank of the Damietta branch of the Nile. Its importance is such that it has the status of a province. It is a large port with thriving industries principal among which is that of furniture making. (Railway and bus stations.)

Although Damietta is the NE coastal counterpart of Rosetta on the NW, it has suffered much less as there is no city as large as Alexandria nearby. Its ancient history is obscure but it was probably always an important site dealing with the trade between Egypt and the eastern Mediterranean coast and Cyprus, the W tip of which lies due N. After the Muslim invasions its importance increased and when Egypt achieved independence and extended its influence into Palestine it became a vital link. During the Crusades, however, it proved to be a point of weakness. Several times it was occupied by the Christians in 1167–68 and 1218–21 but it was repossessed by Sultan al-Kāmil. It was captured again by the forces of the Sixth Crusade under Louis IX and from here the Crusaders advanced into the Delta. Louis was checked at al-Manṣūrah and finally captured. In 1250 the ascendant mamlūks razed the city and the river was made impassable. A new settlement was soon founded to the S and persisted through the Mamlūk and Ottoman periods. Here the last Ottoman pasha, Muḥammad Khusraw, surrendered to the bays just before the rise of Muḥammad ʿAlī.

Damietta, like Rosetta, has several areas where Ottoman buildings are excellently preserved.

# 46 The Western Delta

Leaving Banhā to the NW and crossing a bridge over the Damietta branch of the Nile, the H1 passes (15km) **Minshat Sabrī** with the H16 W to Shibīn al-Kawm, and (15km) *Birkat al-Sabaʿ* and on to (27km) **Ṭanṭā**. Although this is the capital of al-Gharbiyyah province and one of the principal cities of the Delta, it retains a thoroughly rural atmosphere. (Railway station and bus station for local and long-distance coaches.) The *Museum* contains material from the Delta and is the Delta headquarters of the Dept of Antiquities. It also has a university and several higher institutes. *Hotel.* Arafa, 3*. Shʿ. al-Sikkah al-Gadīdah.

The Coptic name of the town was Tantatho, derived from the ancient name. Apart from its strategic position, its fame rests on the tomb of Aḥmad al-Badawī, a 13C sufi. His major mūlid directly following the cotton harvest is the most important of these celebrations in the Delta, drawing up to two million visitors.

In the centre of the city is the Maydān al-Aḥmadi. Dominating the SE side of the square is the **Mosque and Tomb of Sayyid Aḥmad al-Badawī**.

Descended from an Arab family who had re-emigrated to Arabia from Fez, Aḥmad al-Badawī (1199–1276) travelled to Baṭa'ih in Iraq to receive instruction from the shaykhs of the Rifa'iyyah brotherhood. He was sent as their representative in Egypt and settled in Ṭanṭā in 1234. Subsequently he received permission to found his own brotherhood, the Badawiyyah (or Aḥmadiyyah), which flourished and, with related brotherhoods, still flourishes throughout the Middle East. After his death his successor, Ṣalāḥ 'Abd al-'Āl, built the tomb and mosque in Ṭanṭā. However, that building was demolished in the mid 19C and the present building was raised by the Pasha 'Abbās I and Khedive Isma'īl.

The mosque is large, the arcade on the main façade and the attached minaret were added in 1979. A large dome covers the tomb and the minaret on the SE wall is part of the 19C building. In the NW façade are two entrances separated by a large window overlooking the tomb. Immediately inside is a large room containing the *Tomb of Aḥmad al-Badawī* and other shaykhs of the brotherhood. The interior, with its parallel arcades, is entirely modern.

From Ṭanṭā the H23 runs NE to *al-Mahallah al-Kubrā*; the H9 E to *Ziftā*; the H4 S to *Shibīn al-Kawm* and N to *Kafr al-Shaykh*. The H1 leaves Ṭanṭā to the W, passing (4km) **Mahallat Marhūm**. From here the H43 goes NW to (32km) **Basyūn**. To the NW beside the Rosetta branch of the Nile and perched on a mound is **Ṣā al-Ḥagar**, Ancient Egyptian *Zau*, Gk *Sais*, capital of the 5th nome of Lower Egypt and capital of the kings of the 26 Dyn.

The activities of the sabakhin have left a gaping hole filled with stagnant water where the main monuments were located. This was the city of Neith, the archer goddess of the Delta, one of the great deities of Egypt, and it was an important site from the earliest times. As with most Delta sites, there is little to see. Up to the last century the plan of a vast temple enclosure was visible but this has disappeared. A considerable number of statues, stelae and inscribed blocks have been recovered from the mound but much of the history of the site is still obscure.

Beyond Mahallat Marhūm the H1 continues W to (26km) **Kafr al-Zayyāt** where it crosses the Rosetta branch of the Nile and turns NW, running parallel to and S of al-Khandaq al-Gharbī Canal to (27km) **Ityāy al-Barūd**. Just S of the road a track leads SW to **al-Niqrāsh**, with a mound marking the site of ancient *Naukratis* in the 5th nome of Lower Egypt, discovered by Petrie. It was settled by the Greeks as a trading colony in the 7C BC. It contained many Greek temples and an Egyptian temple dedicated to Amun and Thoth, but the stone of which they were built has been removed by the farmers.

Directly S from the H1 a road leads due S to **al-Ṭūd** (12km) beside which is **Kom al-Ḥiṣn** (Mound of the Fort), the large mound covering the ancient site of *Imu*, capital of the 3rd nome of Lower Egypt from the New Kingdom onwards. The most noticeable feature is a large rectangular enclosure of the *Temple of Sekhmet-Hathor*, identified by Middle and New Kingdom royal statues (now in the EM). Founded by Senusert I, it was symmetrical with pillared pronaos and the bark chapel flanked by three rows of rooms with three sanctuaries at the rear. Connected with the site are extensive cemeteries, the most important tomb in which is the Middle Kingdom stone-built painted *Tomb of Khesuwer*, inspector of the prophets of Hathor. There is also a necropolis of the Second Intermediate Period.

After *Ityāy al-Barūd* the next town is (36km) **Damanhūr**, the principal city of Baḥayrah province.

It is the site of the ancient city of *Tmn-Hor*, one of the towns dedicated to Horus. Objects from here, including several Hyksos heads, a granite statue base of Psamtik II and a black granite naos dedicated by Nectanebo I to Neith, are all in the EM.

To the NE runs the H7, crossing the Rosetta branch of the Nile to Dasūq and on to *Kafr al-Shaykh* (Rte 44), and the H17 N to **al-Maḥmūdiyyah** (25km) and from whence as the H20 it follows the W bank of the Rosetta branch of the Nile, passing through **Dayrūṭ** (7km) and **Idfīnā** (10km), another famous village as it is the other agricultural station chosen by Egypt as a trademark for tinned agricultural produce (see Qahā, Rte 43). Here there is also a barrage carrying a road to the E bank and the town of **Muṭubis** (Rte 44). Beyond *Idfīnā* (10km) the H20 joins the H18 from Alexandria and turns N to **Rosetta** (5km).

From *Damanhūr* the H7 (which completely crosses the Delta) runs NE crossing the Rosetta branch of the Nile to *Dasūq* and on to *Kafr al-Shaykh* (Rte 44); the H17 leaves due N to join the Rosetta branch of the Nile beside which it runs through *Idfīnā* into Rosetta (see above). NE the H1 continues to (39km) **Kafr al-Dawwār** and on to (26km) **Alexandria**.

**Rashid** (*Rosetta*) stands on the W bank of the Rosetta (ancient Bolbitine) branch of the Nile and is now a small maritime town. (Railway and bus stations.)

Little is known of its early history although it was obviously inhabited from ancient times. During the height of the power of Alexandria it remained a small station for the ships that passed down the Bolbitine branch of the Nile. In the 9C navigation of the Canopic branch became increasingly difficult and Rosetta rose in importance. However, it was not until after the Ottoman conquest in the 16C, with the decline of Alexandria, that the town became the principal port of the N coast. From this time until the 19C it retained its importance, serving the trade between Egypt, Turkey and the Peloponese. For 300 years it outshone Alexandria and had a many-times larger population. Many wikālahs and merchants' houses were constructed, while the river front was strongly fortified.

In 1799 during the French occupation of Egypt evidence of the city's earlier history was discovered by Lieutenant Bouchard. Finds included the Rosetta Stone, a record of gratitude from the chief Egyptian priests to Ptolemy V Epiphanes in 196 BC, written in three scripts—hieroglyphic and demotic Egyptian and Greek. It later passed to the British and was instrumental in Champollion's decipherment of the hieroglyphic script.

When Muḥammad ʿAlī constructed the Maḥmūdiyyah Canal between the Nile and Alexandria, revitalising the second capital, Rosetta was eclipsed. Within a few years it was little more than a small town dependent in the main on fishing and rural industry.

There are several areas in which the old buildings have been preserved and the town has many well-preserved examples of Ottoman architecture, built in the characteristic brick, which is often used to form decorative patterns on the façades.

N of the town (7km) the main road leads to the restored late 15C **Fort of Qāytbāy**. In the bath house the site of the Rosetta Stone, which was used as a paving slab, is indicated. This site is celebrated in Egypt since in 1807 it withstood two attacks by the British under General Frazer and witnesses their defeat, retreat to Alexandria and final expulsion from Egypt. From the ramparts there are fine views across the estuary.

# 47 The Canal Cities

There are several ways across the Delta to the Canal cities, but this route (approx. 265km) runs due E from Cairo to the southernmost city, Suez, and then N along the W bank of the Canal through Ismāʿīliyyah to Port Saʿīd.

The main road to Suez leaves Cairo at Heliopolis (Rte 20) and runs E across the desert. At 12km a road leaves to the N (to the Cairo–Ismāʿīliyyah road and Cairo airport). To the N at 34km stands the *Dār al-Baydā* (White Mansion), a ruined palace of ʿAbbās I Pasha. To the S a road leads to the al-Maʿādi–Red Sea road, and another at 23km also joins this.

Passing S of the Gabal ʿIwaybid, at 21km a road leaves NE to the H44 (see below). 4km beyond is **al-ʿAgrūd** where the Cairo–Suez railway from the NW runs parallel to the road for the remaining 23km into **Suez**, the southernmost town on the **Suez Canal**.

Since the European powers first took an interest in Egypt at the beginning of the 19C the building of a canal linking the Mediterranean and Red Seas had been a constant preoccupation. It seemed an impossible task as, by a strange miscalculation, it was considered that the water level of the Red Sea was lower than that of the Mediterranean. The French did consider a canal which used a series of locks but the project was abandoned. Later British reports corrected the mistake but the British government considered the project impracticable. An enthusiastic French vice-consul in Egypt, Ferdinand de Lesseps, promulgated the scheme throughout the 1830s and '40s but the British remained dubious. When Saʿīd Pasha, an old friend of de Lesseps, succeeded in 1854 he supported the plan and in the same year the articles of the Suez Canal Company were signed, with de Lesseps as director. Britain still opposed the scheme and by devious manipulation of the Ottoman administration in Istanbul attempted to halt progress even after work started in 1859. Gladstone, however, bowed to the inevitable and supported the project.

Ismāʿīl became pasha in 1863 and thereafter, with his active encouragement, work progressed to completion in 1869. Many thousands died during the canal's construction. European advisers had insisted that slave labour should not be used but there were many accidents. The opening ceremony was lavish and many European dignitaries attended, including Empress Eugenie of France. In a final attempt at sabotage the British encouraged the Ottoman sultan to act on the fact that the company had not been ratified, but, with the intervention of Napoleon III the rights of the company were approved.

During his rule Ismāʿīl ran up enormous bills and was heavily in debt to European finance houses. In 1875 he was forced to sell his canal shares—176,602 out of the company's total of 400,000. Despite his earlier contempt for the scheme, Disraeli acted quickly and purchased them for the British government for £4 million. Thus the British acquired 44 per cent of the shares. The canal quickly became a vital link in the British route to India and was soon grossing sums far in excess of its original potential. Little of this revenue was ploughed back into Egypt.

After the revolution of 1952 the British wished to keep a military base in the Suez Canal Zone but were refused by Nasser. In 1954 the British accepted this and agreed merely to maintain a presence of technicians serving the British companies on the canal. By April 1956 all British troops had left Egyptian soil. The subsequent unfortunate episode in which Britain, France and Israel tried to reinvade the Canal Zone is well-known and led to a long period of estrangement between Britain and Egypt. During the Egypt–Israel conflicts of 1967 and 1973 the canal suffered greatly and many ships were sunk in the channel. Following removal of the obstructions the canal soon reached its former levels of traffic. The first part of a two-phase development was completed in 1980 greatly increasing the width and depth of the

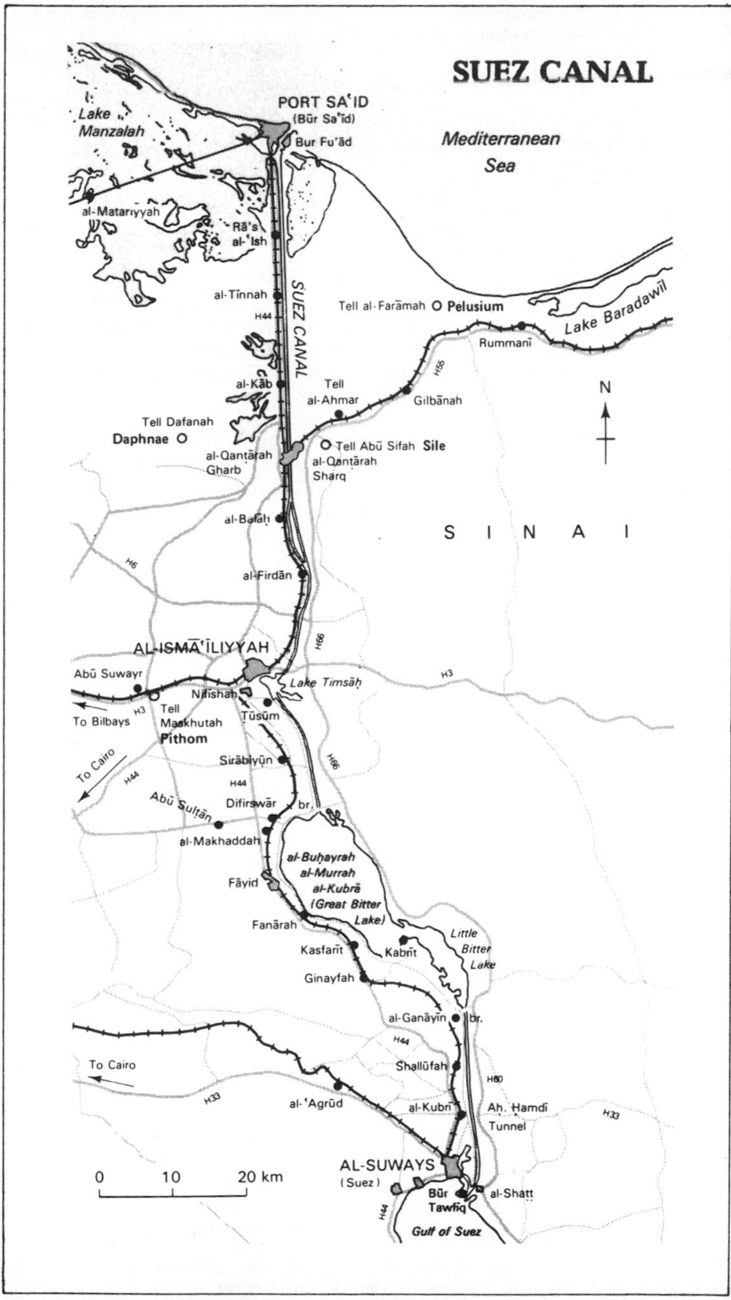
SUEZ CANAL
PORT SA'ID
(Būr Sa'īd)
Bur Fu'ād
Mediterranean
Sea
Lake
Manzalah
al-Matarıyyah
Rā's
al-'Ish
al-Tīnnah
H44
SUEZ CANAL
Tell al-Farāmah
Pelusium
Lake Baradawīl
Rummanī
H55
al-Kāb
Tell
al-Ahmar
Gilbānah
N
Tell Dafanah
Daphnae
al-Qanṭārah
Gharb
Tell Abū Sifah
Sile
al-Qanṭārah
Sharq
al-Balāḥ
S I N A I
H6
al-Firdān
H66
AL-ISMĀ'ĪLIYYAH
Abū Suwayr
Nifishah
Lake Timsāḥ
H3
To Bilbays
Tell
Maskhutah
Pithom
Tūsūm
Sirābiyūn
To Cairo
H44
Abū Sulṭān
Difirswār
br.
al-Makhaddah
al-Buḥayrah
al-Murrah
al-Kubrā
(Great Bitter
Lake)
Fāyid
Fanārah
Kasfarīt
Kabrīt
Little
Bitter
Lake
Ginayfah
al-Ganāyīn
br.
To Cairo
Shallūfah
H60
H33
al-'Agrūd
al-Kubrī
Ah. Hamdī
Tunnel
H33
0
10
20 km
AL-SUWAYS
(Suez)
Būr
Tawfīq
al-Shatt
H44
Gulf of Suez

canal. Although the second phase would accommodate the largest tankers the new Suez-Mediterranean pipeline could well render this redundant.

The canal is 160.3km long and single-carriage except for two passing places at al-Ballaḥ and the Bitter Lakes. There are three convoy bands, one N and two S.

Suez (*al-Suways*) is an ancient site. In the Ptolemaic period it was *Klysma*, and during medieval times *Qulzum*. It has provincial status.

*Station* and *bus station*. *Ferry* to Bur Tawfīq.

**Hotels**. *Beau Rivage*, 32 Shʿ. Zaghlūl; *White House*, 322 Shʿ. al-Gaysh.

*Ministry of Tourism and Tourist Police*: Shʿ. al-Shuhādah.

Three-quarters of the town was razed during the first Egypt–Israel conflict but much has been rebuilt. It is now a thriving industrial centre producing petrochemicals, cement and fertilisers. On a promontory to the S lies **Port Tawfiq** (*Būr Tawfīq*), a recent settlement which houses the officials of Suez and provides services for the port. (Hotels: *Summer Palace* and *Red Sea*.)

The H44 runs N from Suez along the coast of the Gulf of Suez (Rte 50) and continues inland of the Suez Canal, W of the railway and the Sweetwater Canal. A lesser road follows the canal bank more closely. The first village on the H44 is (7km) **al-Kubrī**. 4km further a road leaves E to the *Aḥmad Ḥamdī Tunnel* (Nafaq al-Shahīd Aḥmad Hamdī) which goes under the canal to the E bank and Sinai. Built by French and Swedish engineers, it is 1.4km long. The H44 continues N past (8km) *Ginayfah, Kasfarīt*, and (15km) **Fāyid**. It then runs due N for 30km before reaching al-Ismāʿīliyyah.

The subsidiary road leaves Suez and runs next to the bank of the canal. It also passes *al-Kubrī* and the Aḥmad Ḥamdī Tunnel but then continues to *Shallūfah* (6km) and *al-Ganayīn* (4km), just N of which is a bridge to the E bank. Here the canal enters the *Little Bitter Lake* and, at **Kabarīt** (10km), the *Great Bitter Lake*. The road follows the shore to the N end and at *Difirswār*, (33km) there is another bridge. (To the W is Abū Sulṭān.) Just beyond **al-ʿAqidah** (5km) a small road leads W to **Sirabiyūn** and 10km to the N the road passes *Ṭūsūn* and *Nifīshah* (5km) before entering al-Ismāʿīliyyah (2km) on the shore of Lake Timsāḥ.

**Al-Ismāʿīliyyah**, created in 1861 as the depot of the canal builders and named after the Khedive Ismāʿīl, is the most populous city on the Suez Canal and has the status of a province. Situated at the E end of the Wādī Ṭumaylāt, with the creation of the Ismāʿīlyyah Canal its importance grew.

*Station* and *Bus Station*.

**Hotels**. *ETAP Ismailia*, Firsan Island (4*); *Nefertari*, 41 Shʿ. Sulṭān Husayn (2*).

*Museum* with exhibits from excavation in the area including the stele of Darius describing his conquest of Egypt and the digging of the canal linking the Nile to the Red Sea.

The two roads continue N. At 10km the H44 crosses the H6 and runs on to (18km) the town of **al-Qantārah al-Gharbiyyah**. 15km NW is *Tell Dafanah* (ancient Daphanae), a late 7C BC town. Remains of a fortress (450m x 200m) have been found, destroyed by Cambyses in the Persian invasion of 525 BC. Beyond Qantārah the H6 continues due N through (10km) *al-Kāb, al-Tīnnah, Raʾs al-ʿIsh* and (34km) Port Saʿīd.

The lesser road passes through *al-Firdan* (12km) and *al-Ballaḥ* (10km) into **al-Qantārah al-Gharbiyyah** and E of the railway line to Port Saʿīd.

**Port Saʿīd** (*Būr Saʿīd*), at the entrance to the Suez Canal, is now a free port with seven customs gates. Visitors from inland should show passports at the gate and, if staying, they should inform the Passport Office (Shʿ. 23 Yūlyū) within 48 hours. If visitors from ships wish to visit the rest of Egypt they should possess a passport, landing card and a pass issued by the Passport Office; individuals should be prepared to change some money into local currency.

**Hotels**. *ETAP*, Shʿ. al-Kurnīsh (4*); *Holiday*, Shʿ. al-Gumhuriyyah (3*); *Abu Simbel*, 15 Shʿ. al-Gumhuriyyah (2*); *Riviera*, 30 Shʿ. al-Burg (2*); *Vendome*, 37 Shʿ. al-Gumhuriyyah (2*); *Grand Hotel*, Shʿ. Ṣalāḥ Sālim.

*Station* and *Bus Station*.

*Ministry of Tourism information* and *Tourist Police*: Shʿ. Filastin.

*Post Office*: Shʿ. al-Gumhuriyyah. *Telephone and Telegraph Office*: Shʿ. Filastin.

This city, now with the status of a province, was founded in 1859 with the start of the Suez Canal excavations, and named in honour of the viceroy Saʿīd Pasha. In the 1860s the French sculptor Bartholdi floated an idea for a 75m bronze statue (which would also have doubled as a lighthouse) called 'Egypt Carrying Light into Asia' to be set at the harbour entrance. However, he could not raise the capital and after several years in limbo the idea was revived and finally realised in the Statue of Liberty, which so beautifully graces the mouth of the Hudson River, New York.

Port Saʿīd is a very important maritime city but suffered greatly in the Egyptian–Israeli conflicts, although much of the damage has been repaired. One of its most famous buildings, known to many sea travellers, is the *Suez Canal Building*, on the Shʿ. Filastin. Its gleaming white two-storey colonnade is crowned with three brilliant green domes. Other places of interest are the *Military Museum* (Shʿ. 23 Yūlyū) and the Maydān al-Shuhadā with a re-erected *obelisk*. On the E side of the Suez Canal is the modern town of **Port Fuad** (*Būr Fūʾād*), see below.

The H66 runs parallel to the E bank of the canal and continues round the coast of the Sinai Peninsula (Rte 51) but to the N it passes through a series of station settlements. Several roads go E across Northern Sinai with the H3 leaving opposite al-Ismāʿīliyyah (80km). The only town of any size is **al-Qantārah al-Sharqiyyah** (32km). 4km to the SE lies *Tell Abū Sīfah*, probably site of Mesen and Tharu capital of the 14th Nome of Lower Egypt. Later called Sile it was another fortress town doubtless destroyed like Daphnae during the Persian invasion of Cambyses. Further N the H66 runs into **Port Fuad** (*Būr Fūʾād*), a town founded in 1925 as a suburb of Port Saʿīd.

# 48 The Oases (al-Wāḥāt)

This route consists of two widely separated itineraries in the Western Desert. The first is very long and involves a trip from Cairo in a half circle across the desert, rejoining the Nile Valley far to the S. The second takes off from Marsāh Matrūḥ (Rte 49) and goes E across the desert to Sīwah. The two westernmost oases are usually approached from Asyūṭ.

Spread across the Western Desert is a series of large depressions, some of which, fed by artesian wells, support agricultural communities. Five of these are major oases, and the three southernmost (al-Farāfrah, al-Dakhlah and al-Khārgah) make up the *New Valley Province* (Muhafazat al-Wādī al-Gadīd), while al-Bahrīyyah and Siwah are in the Province of Matruḥ. The four inner oases are connected by a trans-desert road that leaves Cairo through Giza. It passes S through al-Baḥriyyah, al-Farāfrah, al-Dākhlah and al-Khārgah. From here it turns NE and returns to the Nile Valley at Asyūṭ, a total of 1069km. This vast tract follows a natural depression which since 1958 has been under agricultural reclamation by the Egyptian Public Organisation for Desert Reclamation and is called the *New Valley*. Areas added to the original concept are the Qaṭṭārah Depression and Sīwah Oasis in the NW and the area surrounding Kurkur Oasis in the S. Complex surveys have been undertaken and the project is now well advanced. Power stations, factories, packing plants and housing complexes have been built. When complete it will increase the agricultural land of Egypt by many thousand square kilometres.

The early history of the oases is obscure. During late prehistoric times they were places of refuge for bands of hunters during the desiccation of the Sahara. The inner oases were brought under Egyptian control by Tuthmosis III (18 Dyn.) and lists of the products are depicted on the walls of 18 Dyn. tombs of the nobles of Thebes. Goods shown include wine jars, rolls of cloth and woven baskets in the shape of beehives, of a type still made in the oases. They were administered from Diospolis Parva (Hiw). During Mamlūk times each oasis was administered by tenant governors who were responsible directly to the sultan. This was probably a continuation of Ptolemaic and Roman practice. The isolation of the oases has always left them open to attack, in ancient times by the Libyans and later by the Nubians, Berbers and Bedouin.

Although a visit to the oases is a fascinating experience it should be borne in mind that accommodation is sparse or non-existent. Although the road is reasonable, if using a car enough petrol and water should be taken to cover any emergency. Otherwise the only method of travel is by coach.

## A. The Inner Oases

**Baḥriyyah Oases**. The road to Baḥriyyah leaves the H22 (to Fayyūm) 4.5km beyond the Pyramids Village (Rte 23). It runs due W for 12km and then turns SW to join the track of the Egyptian Iron and Steel Co. railway, running along a valley to the N of the Gabal Qaṭrānī with the railway to the S. Continuing through the desert, it runs for 316km past *Gabal Ghurābī* to the N into **al-Baḥriyyah Oases** (al-Wāḥāt al-Baḥriyyah, the Northern Oases) and the capital (18km) **Bawiṭī**.

The Precambrian granite basement is here about 2000m below the surface and is overlain by several strata, the most important being the sedimentary sandstones. These consist of layers of sand and gravel interspersed with clays and they contain the subterranean waters from which the springs issue. The uppermost layers are the Tertiary marine calcerous deposits. In the Cretaceous sandstones of this oasis fossils of the immense carnivorous dinosaur Spinosaurus were uncovered. The vertebrae were elongated into long spines, presumably as a form of thermo-regulator. Little is known of the oasis before the New Kingdom when it appears on the Kamose Stele (17 Dyn.) as Zeszes. By the 25 Dyn. there were two main towns in the area, one in the Bawiṭī al-Qaṣr area, the other to the E around Mandishah. The population became Christians at a fairly early date. The oasis fell to the Muslims soon after the conquest and in the 10C it was an independent Berber amirate. In the 11C the Fāṭimids reincorporated it within the frontiers of Egypt and appointed a governor.

The oasis covers an area of about 2000 sq. km, although up to the beginning of the New Valley project the area was decreasing due to dehydration of about a sixth of the natural springs. It is almost rainless. The main crop is dates, although rice, maize, wheat, olives and fruit, apricots and grapes are also important. The area to the N is rich in iron ore and foundries have been established.

From Bawiṭī a road leads NW across the desert through minor oases to Sīwah Oasis; another goes E to al-Bahnāsah (Rte 30).

The main area of population and the administrative centre is **Bawiṭī** (Resthouse 35km N; limited accommodation). In the town is a 26 Dyn. *Tomb-chapel* of one of the governors. The hill to the SW of the town is known as **Qarat al-Farārgī** (Ridge of the Chicken Merchant). It contains subterranean galleries of bird burials, including ibises and hawks, dating from 26 Dyn. to Roman times. It has been partly cleared and consists of a central gallery with several side branches and was obviously associated

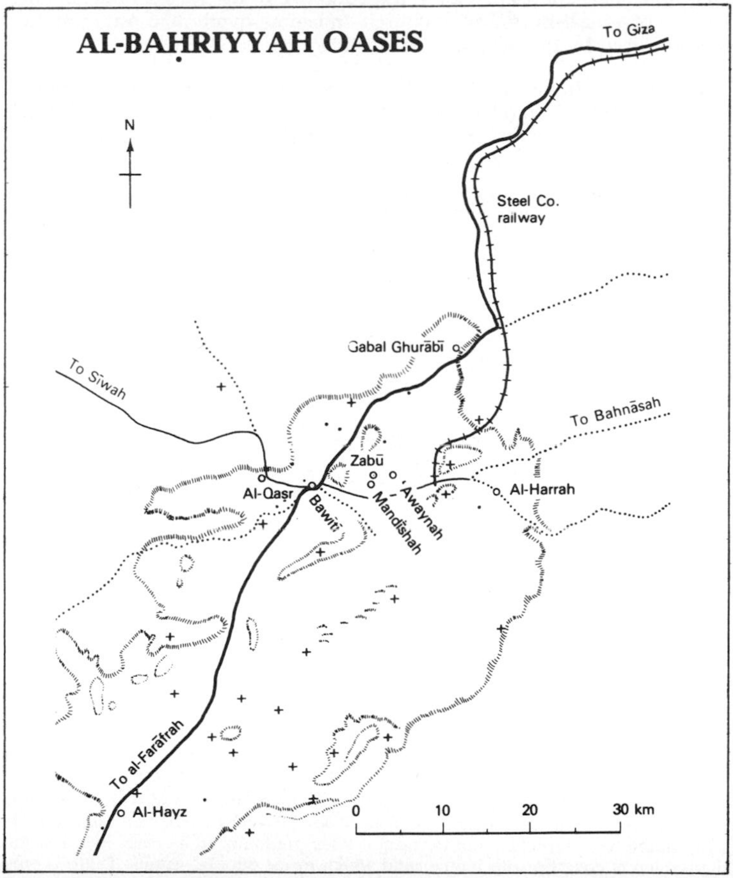
AL-BAḤRIYYAH OASES
To Giza
N
Steel Co.
railway
Gabal Ghurābī
To Sīwah
To Bahnāsah
Zabū
Al-Qaṣr
Bawiṭī
Mandīshah
'Awaynah
Al-Harrah
To al-Farāfrah
Al-Ḥayz
0
10
20
30 km

with the worship of the gods Thoth and Horus. Thus it is similar to the avian galleries at Ṣaqqārah and Tūnah al-Gabal. The main gallery shows evidence of a fire. Belief by the local inhabitants that the bones were those of hens gave rise to the modern name. In the cliffs are rock-cut *Tombs of the Governors*, also of the 26 Dyn.

Adjoining Bawiṭī to the W is **al-Qaṣr**, another population centre. SW of this is **Qaṣr al-Magisbah**, with a *Temple of Alexander the Great* surrounded by a girdle wall. Cleared in 1938–39 and 1942, it consists of two chambers. Alexander is shown on the walls before Amun-Reʿ and other gods. Inside the girdle wall are stores and priests' houses. Nearby is the site of a *Roman village*.

6km E of Bawiṭī is **Mandishah**, the other ancient centre, and just N is **al-Zabū**, with a large rock covered with ancient Libyan graffiti. 14.5km E at *al-Ḥārrah* are some late rock-cut tombs.

Leaving al-Baḥriyyah from Bawiṭī, to the SW on the main road is (42km) *ʿAyn al-Hayz*. This is really a separate oasis and may be the fourth oasis mentioned in the ancient texts at the Temple of Edfū. At Qaṣr Masʿudah is the site of a mud-brick *Fort*, a church and some dwellings. Although this was deserted by the 5C it is well worth a visit.

The road continues SW past several isolated springs and impressive formations of wind-eroded sandstone. After 128km it passes S of *ʿAyn al-Shigī* into the **Oasis of Farāfrah** (al-Wāḥat al-Farāfrah; small resthouse).

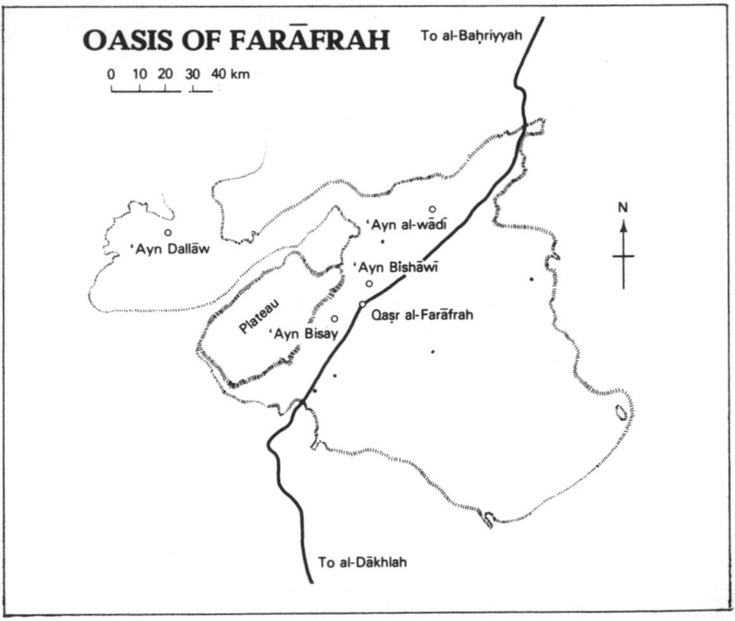
OASIS OF FARĀFRAH
0 10 20 30 40 km
To al-Baḥriyyah
ʿAyn al-wādī
ʿAyn Dallāw
ʿAyn Bishāwī
Plateau
Qaṣr al-Farāfrah
ʿAyn Bisay
N
To al-Dākhlah

This is the smallest of the major oases although the depression in which it is set is one of the largest in the Western Desert (c 200km NW–SE by 90km). To the NW it is surrounded by steep cliffs and to the S it rises gradually to a scarp. Much of the depression is covered with blown sand which forms parallel dunes. There is only one town. In ancient times it was known as *Ta-iht* (Land of the Cow) and is mentioned in Old Kingdom texts. It also appears in the inscriptions of Ramesses II and Merneptah (19 Dyn.) at Thebes; during the period of the latter it was occupied by Libyans. In the Ptolemaic texts at Edfū it is mentioned as the third of the seven oases in the Western Desert. Despite these pharaonic references, no ancient sites have so far been found here.

10km beyond ʿAyn al-Shigī is the small town of **Qaṣr al-Farāfrah**, the only town in the oasis. Nearby there is an ancient cemetery, but the tombs are undecorated and now covered with sand. At *ʿAyn Bishāwī*, 5km to the N, are some unfinished tombs and further N still at *ʿAyn al-Wādī* (20km) are the remains of an extensive field system. The houses were built of rough stone blocks and much Roman pottery and many amulets have been found. To the E the Wādī Abū Ḥinnis, with more Roman remains, one of which may be a villa, leads to *ʿAyn Dallaf* (100km). Here there is evidence of an early Christian town.

SW of Qaṣr al-Farāfrah is **ʿAyn Bisāy** (5km). This is the most important site with rock-cut, but uninscribed tombs, a brick building and a small limestone chapel.

Leaving al-Farāfrah to the SW, the road passes E of (35km) *ʿAyn Khalīfah*, ascends the scarp and at (35km) *Bīr Abū Munqār* it turns SE.

Beyond Abū Munqār the road runs 160km into **al-Dākhlah Oases** (al-Wāḥāt al-Dākhlah; the Outer Oases), usually approached from the E, and **al-Qaṣr al-Dākhlah**, the chief town. This is a sizeable town by oasis standards. The main *Mosque* is an Ayyūbid foundation rebuilt by the mamlūks. Only the base of the minaret is original. To the N of the town a track leads to the *Bāb al-Gasmund*, a pass in the hills, and on NW to al-Farāfrah Oases.

Al-Dākhlah and al-Khārgah being much closer to the Nile Valley, control by the central authority was much greater and these oases contained thriving communities. This is reflected in the number of monuments in both areas.

Just SW of al-Qaṣr is the village of *al-Amhādah* (1km), with *Tombs of the First Intermediate period*. Continuing SW, at *Qarat al-Mizawaqah* (Hill of Decoration; c 4km) there is a *Roman Cemetery*. Most significant of the monuments is the *Tomb of Petosiris* and his wife, dated AD 54–84. Some of the tombs contain interesting wall paintings. *Deir al-Hagar* (2km further) has a sandstone *Roman Temple*. It seems to have been dedicated to Amun, Mut and Khonsu, the Triad of Thebes. Surrounded by a brick enclosure wall, the temple consists of a two-columned court and a hypostyle hall with four columns, a vestibule and a sanctuary. Each of the columns in the hypostyle hall has inscriptions of the emperor Titus, while those of Domitian are found at the entrance to the sanctuary, and of Vespasian and Nero actually in the sanctuary.

From al-Qaṣr the main road passes E but at 5km turns due S. Passing several small villages, it reaches (27km) **Mūṭ**, the other main centre of population. However, there are only ruins now to be seen in the area. The road turns E again directly, passing through (10km) *al-Maʿṣārah* to the S and (1km) *Ismant* to the N. The next sizeable village is (30km) **Balāṭ**, an area well supplied with water and with 6 Dyn. mastabas. 3.5km E is *ʿAzbat Bashindī* and the site of a **Temple of Mūṭ**. It was exposed by the wind in 1951 but has since been sanded-up. The foundation dated to the 12 Dyn. and was restored by Ramesses IX. There is also an elaborately decorated Roman **Tomb of Kitnes** of the 1C BC. Other tombs in the area

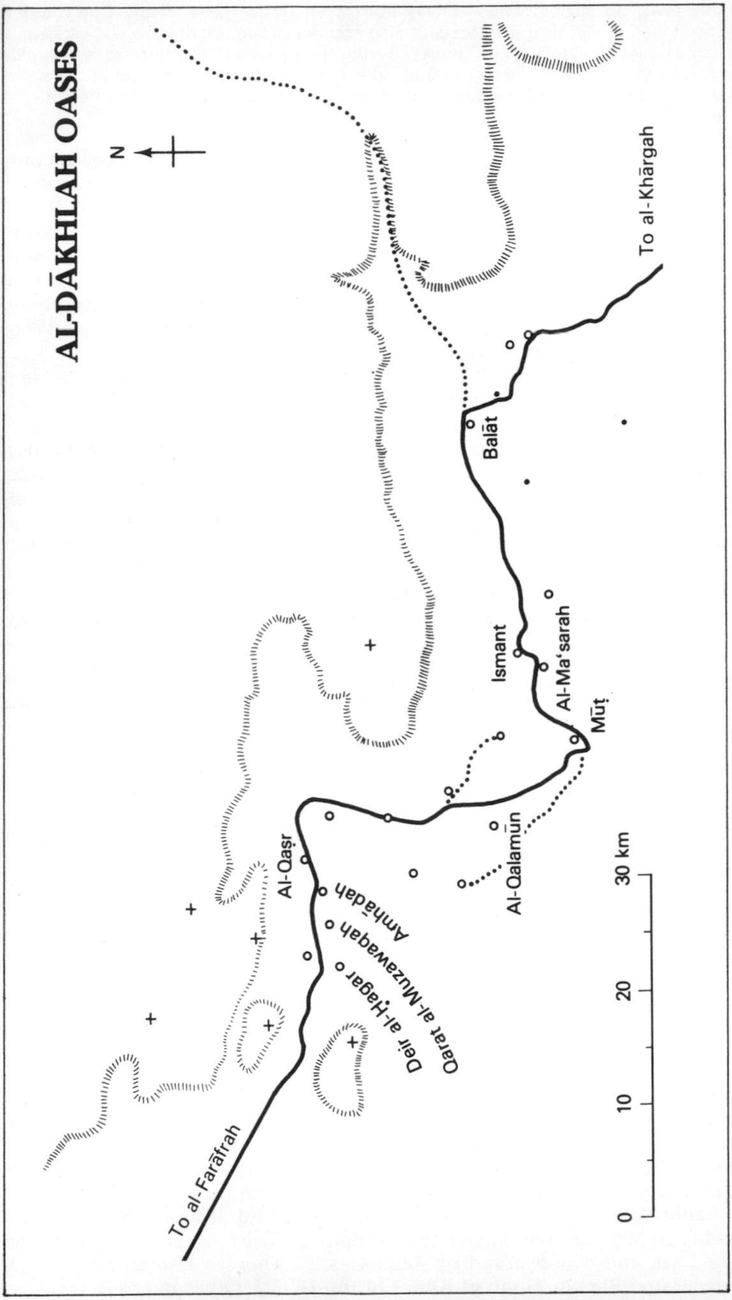
AL-DĀKHLAH OASES
N
To al-Khārgah
Balāṭ
Ismant
Al-Ma‘sarah
Mūṭ
Al-Qalamūn
Al-Qaṣr
Amhādah
Qarat al-Muzawaqah
Deir al-Hagar
To al-Farāfrah
0
10
20
30 km

date from the 6C BC to the Roman period. From Balāṭ the Darb al-Ṭawīl (the long track) leaves NE to the Nile Valley just N of Asyūṭ.

The main road turns SE and runs in a great sweep across the desert. At 95km due N into the desert lies **ʿAyn Amūr** (46km) which must once have been a thriving trade station. There are the remains of a Roman settlement and a temple. It can also be reached from the al-Khārgah Oases.

Continuing E, after 65km the road enters the **Oases of al-Khārgah** (al-Wāḥāt al-Khārgah; the Inner Oases). Here the road divides, the N branch running to the Nile Valley (see below) and the S branch further into the oases. The S route reaches (3km) **al-Khārgah**, the main town. *Al-Khārgah Oasis Hotel* on the edge of the town. *Museum* (fee) containing objects found at the oases of al-Khārgah and al-Dākhlah. Main exhibits are the 6 Dyn. stelae from Balāṭ, a figure of Horus and a painted sphinx from Deir al-Ḥagar, 12C Islamic pottery.

The depression of al-Khārgah is long and narrow, about 160km N to S and 25km wide. It is bounded to the E by a steep escarpment which presents some difficulty of access.

During Palaeolithic times the water table was considerably higher than it is now and the area was a major population centre of hunters of the Western Desert. It became in later times the junction of the caravan routes crossing the Sahara along which slaves and ivory were brought from the S. The granite basement rock is very close to the surface here and the wells and springs are therefore shallow. Although this makes for easier access, it also makes them vulnerable to dehydration. Before the present New Valley scheme a considerable number of springs were drying up but now new bores have been made and pumps installed.

The area was called *Kenem* by the Ancient Egyptians, and was fully under their control by the 18 Dyn. During the 26 Dyn. it experienced a period of great prosperity when the Temple of Amun was founded at Hibis, although the present building dates to the First Persian occupation (525–404 BC). During Ptolemaic and Roman times it also prospered and was used as a place of exile for political prisoners. Herodotus mentions it (III: 26) as the 'Land of Spirits' or 'Land of the Blessed'. The army of Cambyses visited al-Khārgah before the fatal Persian expedition to Sīwah. Metalled roads led from al-Khārgah to the Nile Valley to Lycopolis (Asyūṭ), Diospolis Parva (Hiw), Hermonthis (Armant) and Latopolis (Esna). The road to the Sudan was called the Darb al-Arbaʿīn (Forty-day track) from the length of time it took to traverse.

Slightly to the N of the town of al-Khārgah, on the W side of the road to Asyūṭ lies **Hibis**, the ancient town site built at the base of the *Gabal al-Ṭayr* which rises to the N (height 312m). It was a fairly large town, the remains of which cover an area of about 1sq. km. In the centre was a large lake. Unfortunately the town site has not been investigated but the central **Temple of Amun** has been well documented and reconstructed. It is at present (1992) enclosed in scaffolding for removal to a more stable area.

The foundation is probably Saite (26 Dyn.), but it was rebuilt in 510–490 BC in the reign of Darius I during the First Persian Occupation. It stood on the W shore of the lake and the foundations, resting on clay, have subsided somewhat. The first additions were made in 390–78 BC, when the building had already subsided slightly. In an attempt to correct this wooden clamps were inserted and the W end was buttressed. Although the walls subsequently cracked, the building remained standing. Work continued on the temple until Ptolemaic times. In 1832 it was visited by Hoskins, Hay and Catherwood and parts of the roof, the door, lintels and architraves were still in position. Shortly after, a factory was opened by Ayme, a Frenchman, nearby and the temple was used as a quarry. Many of the inscribed stones are found in the structure of the houses of the village. Baraize, however, reconstructed the building for the Dept of Antiquities (with considerable effort).

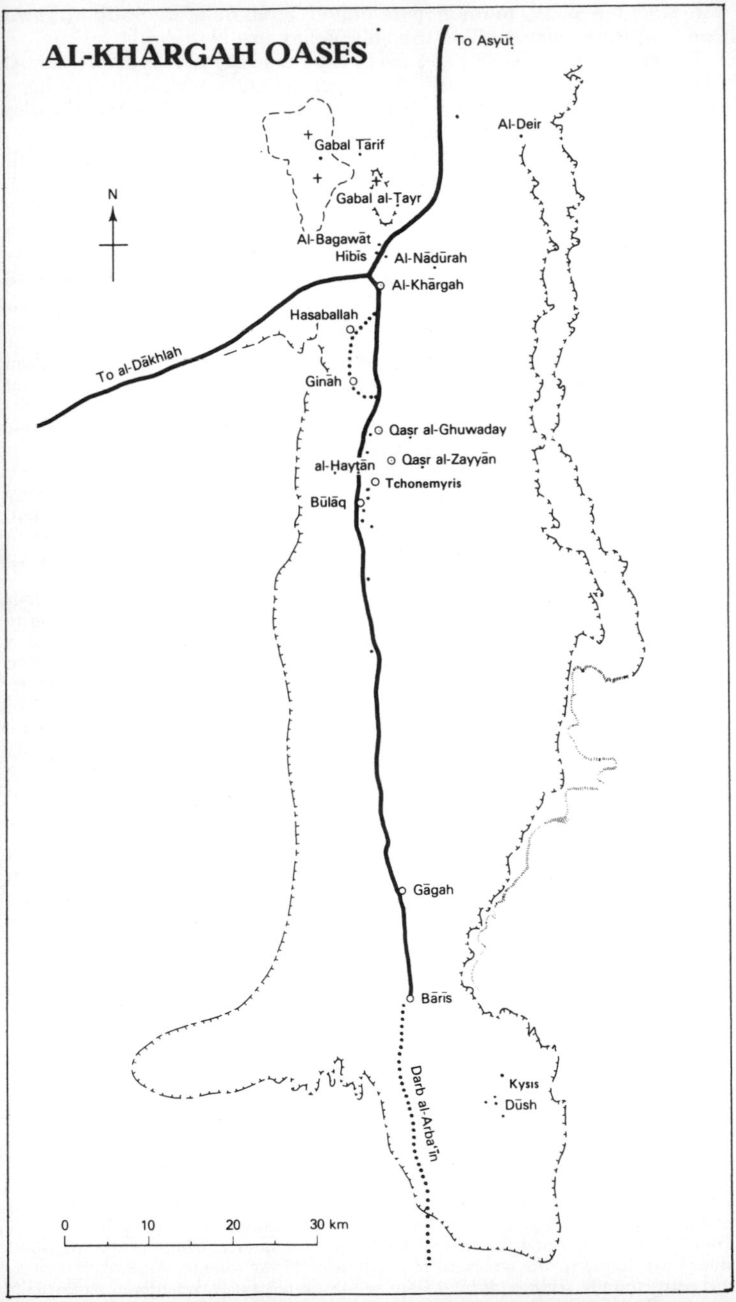
AL-KHĀRGAH OASES
To Asyūṭ
Al-Deir
Gabal Ṭarif
Gabal al-Ṭayr
N
Al-Bagawāt
Hibis
Al-Nādūrah
Al-Khārgah
Hasaballah
To al-Dākhlah
Ginah
Qaṣr al-Ghuwaday
al-Ḥayṭān
Qaṣr al-Zayyān
Tchonemyris
Būlāq
Gāgah
Bāris
Darb al-Arba'īn
Kysis
Dūsh
0
10
20
30 km

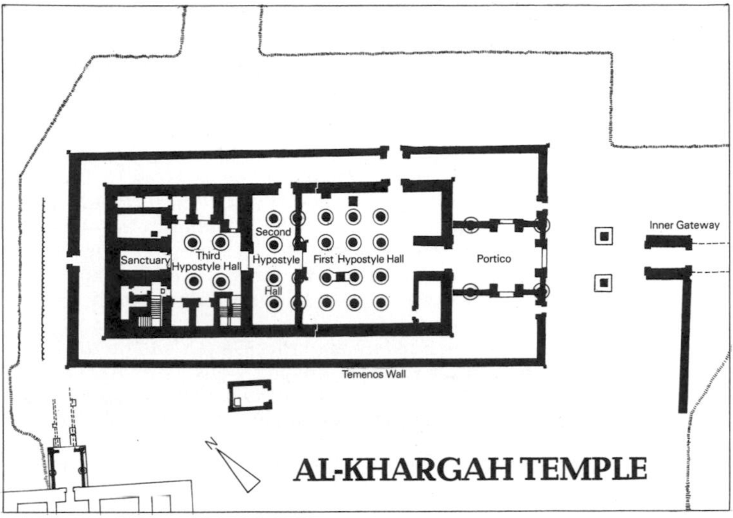
Inner Gateway
Second
Sanctuary
Third
Hypostyle Hall
Hypostyle
First Hypostyle Hall
Portico
Hall
Temenos Wall
N
AL-KHARGAH TEMPLE

From the quay and the Roman Outer Gate an avenue of sphinxes lead to the *Inner Gateway* of Darius beyond which are the bases of two obelisks. Surrounding the temple is a sandstone wall with a cavetto cornice erected by Ptolemy II, inside which is the *Portico* of Nectanebo I and II. This must once have supported a wooden roof as beam holes have been found. It contains inscriptions and cartouches of the Nectanebos. The *First Hypostyle Hall* (probably 29 Dyn.) has 16 columns in four rows of four. To give strength to the outer wall the floor was built of sandstone blocks two courses thick. Narrow slits in the roof slabs light the interior of the temple. The *Second Hypostyle* Hall, with four transverse columns, served as the portico of the building of Darius, which was finished about 490. A *Third Hypostyle Hall* also has four columns, but in groups of two. Around this hall is a series of small chambers and at the far end the *Sanctuary*. On the left of the third hypostyle hall stairs lead to the roof where there seems to have been a *Chapel of Osiris* consisting of a vestibule and a narrow chapel.

In the 4 or 5C, perhaps during the exile of St. Athanasius to the oasis in the mid 4C, a *Church* was erected against the N wall of the portico. It was destroyed along with the community, probably during the Nubian raid of 450 during which Nestorius, the exiled Patriarch of Constantinople, was captured (he was later released).

1km SE is **al-Nāḍūrah**. At the top of a small hill stands a small sandstone *Roman Temple* built by Antoninus Pius in AD 138. It is surrounded by a sandstone wall. Due N of Hibis is the Christian **Necropolis of al-Baqawāt** (1km). This covers several hundred square metres and contains hundreds of baked-brick tombs. Most of them are of the 4–5C and show various styles, often with small chapels above the tombs. Some of them have elaborate façades of blind arcading, others have domes, but of greater interest are the well-preserved wall paintings. These are mainly of biblical scenes with fewer from the New Testament; there are also portraits of the Virgin and St. Paul. In the necropolis is the ruin of a Basilica of similar age. Further N, the *Gabal al-Tayr* contains some rock-inscriptions from the 26 Dyn. to Ptolemaic times. NE of Hibis, on the E side of the road to Asyūṭ, is **al-Deir** (21km) with a *Roman Necropolis*.

The road runs due S from al-Khārgah town, passing several sizeable villages. 17km **Qaṣr al-Ghuwaydah** has remains of a 26 Dyn. Ptolemaic *Temple of the Theban Triad*, Amun, Mut and Khonsu. Work by the EAO has uncovered an ancient cistern. **Qaṣr al-Zayyān**, 3km further S, is the site of the ancient town of *Tchonemyris*. All that remains of the site is the Ptolemaic *Temple* which was restored by Antoninus Pius. Many Ptolemaic coins have been discovered in recent excavations by the EAO.—A further 3km and the road runs through **Būlāq**, another of the major towns of the oases.

Beyond, the road runs due S to (46km) **Azbat Gāgah** and on to (12km) **Baris**, the most populous town in this S group of wells. From here a track leads SE to **Qasr Dush** (14km), site of ancient *Kysis*. The only remaining evidence is a Roman *Temple of Serapis and Isis*, erected by Trajan.

The N road runs from al-Khārgah through the N section of the oasis and crosses the desert to (228km) the Nile Valley, 12km N of Asyūt (Rte 32).

## B. Sīwah Oasis

Permission to visit Sīwah can be obtained from the Government Offices in Marsā Maṭrūh.

From Marsā Maṭrūḥ (Rte 45) a metalled road leads SW to Sīwah Oasis. Its road runs across the desert through (57km) **Abar al-Kanayis**, (68km) **Bīr Fu'ād** and (61km) **Bīr al-Nisf** (last station for petrol before the oasis). Beyond it continues for 136km into **Sīwah Oasis** (Wāḥat Sīwah) and its chief town **Sīwah** (with resthouse, *Arūs al-Wāhah*).

The depression containing the oasis has its main axis running E to W; it is c 82km long with the greatest width of c 28km at the W end. There are several large lakes and many lesser bodies of standing water. Almost at the centre of the oasis is the town of Sīwah. This oasis has always been renowned for its dates and these are still the principal product of the area.

Although the eastern oases were controlled by the Ancient Egyptians, it is unknown whether Sīwah was also included. Even its early name is uncertain, it may have been *Tha* or *Thay*. There are no very early remains and it is not until the 26 Dyn. when it was called Sekhet-imit (Place of the Palm-Trees) that definite proof of Egyptian occupation is found. At this time the Temple of Amun was built, perhaps over an earlier foundation. In the Greek period Sīwah was known as *Ammoniun*. The oracle at this site was known throughout the classical world and widely consulted. During the First Persian Occupation Cambyses sent a large expedition to destroy the temple and oracle. It left the oases of al-Khārgah, but never reached Sīwah, presumably destroyed in a sandstorm. The fame of the oracle was crowned with the visit of Alexander the Great in 331 BC when his divinity as the son of Amun was confirmed. The subsequent history of the oasis is obscure and although the temple was closed on the orders of Emperor Justinian in the mid 6C the worship of Amun may have lingered here until the coming of Islām, which date itself is uncertain although definitely before the 11C.

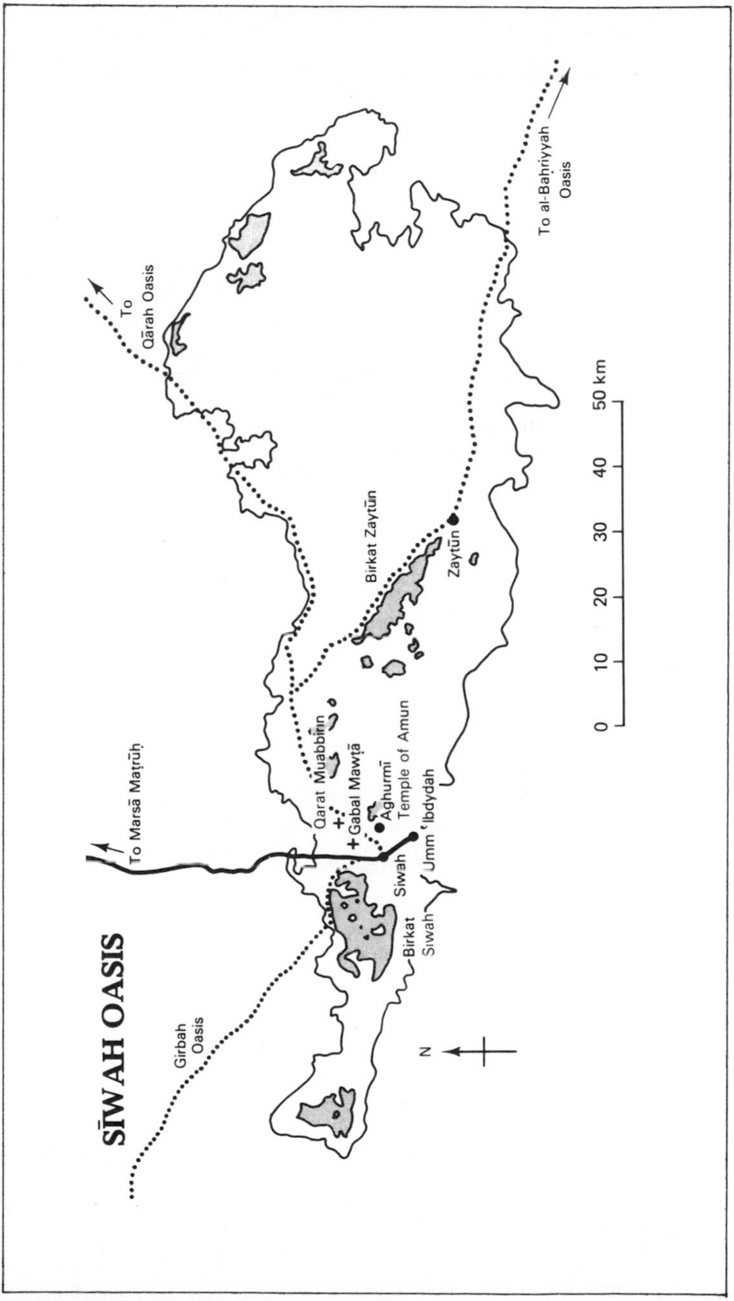
SĪWAH OASIS
To Marsā Maṭrūḥ
To Qārah Oasis
To al-Baḥriyyah Oasis
Girbah Oasis
Birkat Siwah
Siwah
Umm ʿIbdydah
Temple of Amun
Aghurmī
Gabal Mawtā
Qarat Muabbirīn
Birkat Zaytūn
Zaytūn
N
0 10 20 30 40 50 km

During medieval times Sīwah was known as *Santariyyah*. It was on the N caravan route from NW Africa to Mecca and a stopping place for pilgrims. However, it was also vulnerable to the attacks of Berbers and Bedouin. From the 18C several European travellers passed through the oasis and it was finally incorporated in the modern Egyptian state by Ḥasan al-Shamshirgī who subdued it for Muḥammad ʿAlī in 1820. Muḥammad al-Sanūssī, the Libyan sufi, stayed at the oasis for several months in the 1830s and the Samusīyyah brotherhood remained influential until the early 20C.

The original main town was Aghurmī but the inhabitants moved about 1km W in the early 13C and built fortified houses on a rocky spur. A specific history of the oasis gives details of the development since the late 17C and chronicles the constant feuds between the Eastern and Western inhabitants. Since the decline of the predatory desert tribes in the course of the last century most of the inhabitants have built homes at the base of the hill. Most are Berbers with a strong admixture of Sudanese. Their language is Zenati Berber but under the modern Egyptian education programme most of the inhabitants now also speak Arabic.

At **Aghurmī**, 1km E of Sīwah, stands the **Temple of Amun**, or Temple of the Oracle. It is comparatively well preserved, but needs consolidating. Ahmad Fakhry cleared it in 1970–71. Built in the reign of King Amasis (26 Dyn.), with subsequent additions, it consists of two courts in front of a sanctuary. The plain façade stands about 8m high. Only the sanctuary is inscribed and various deities are named, including Amun, Amun-Reʿ, Mut, Khonsu, a ram-headed god, probably Harsaphis, and a goddess with a double crown. In 1988 a geological survey of the site was carried out by the University of Cairo and the Nancy School of Mines, with a view to its preservation. To the SW at **Umm al-ʿIbaydah** is a second *Temple of Amun*, built by Nectanebo II (30 Dyn.); little is left in position. Around the site are scattered blocks of stone, some inscribed and retaining a trace of colouring. Although it was nearly intact at the beginning of the 19C and fully recorded, much of it was destroyed in 1811. The final destruction

*Sīwah Oasis, the old town of Aghurmi*

came in 1897 when one of the local governors blew it up to obtain blocks of stone for a stairway in his house. Surrounded by two precinct walls, it was square in plan. An unusual feature was the text of the Opening of the Mouth ceremony on the walls. Nearby is the most beautiful spring in the oasis, the *ʿAyn al-Qubbah*.

About 15km N of Sīwah rises the **Gabal al-Mawtā** (Mount of the Dead). This is a low ridge with tombs on the slopes and terraces at the foot. They have not been systematically excavated but generally the tombs consist of one or more chambers, sometimes with columns. The ground is littered with fragments of mummies, shrouds and sherds; many objects from here have found their way into dealers' shops in Alexandria. The tombs date from the 26 Dyn. to Ptolemaic and Roman periods and some of them were reused. Most important are the *Tomb of Niper-pathot*, prophet of Osiris, probably 26 Dyn. and the largest in the cemetery; the *Tomb of the Crocodile*, late Ptolemaic or early Roman, and the unfinished *Tomb of Mesu Isis* (she was the wife of the owner; his name cannot be deciphered). It was intact when discovered and probably dates to the 4–2C BC. Best preserved is the *Tomb of Si-amun*, who was without titles and was probably a merchant. Dating from the 3C, it was robbed in Roman times and the painting was mutilated by later additions. A courtyard on the N opens on the long narrow tomb. Scenes show Si-amun before the false door, with his son in a Greek garment, Osiris in his shrine (defaced) and the mummy of Si-amun in a shrine on a wheeled cart. Alternating falcons and vultures symbolise Upper and Lower Egypt, with stars and rosettes. The paintings were never completed and the squares painted by the ancient draughtsman are still visible around the figure of Si-amun who as though to emphasise his Greek origins retains his hair and beard.

From the town of Sīwah a track, Masrab al-Akhwān, leads NW around the N shore of Birkat Sīwah to the small **Ghirbah Oasis** (24km). To the NE another track, Masrab al-Khalīdah, runs across a gravel plain to **Qarā Oasis** (119km) which takes its name from the small inhabited village. A further track leads S along the S edge of the oasis, past Birkat Zaytūn and through the village of **Zaytūn** (29km). It continues across the desert, at 48km turning further to the S, and runs into the small **al-ʿArig Oasis** (19km), where it divides. The N track leads through **Sitrah Oasis** (58km) to al-Baḥriyyah Oasis (see above) while the S track passes through **al-Baḥrayn Oasis** (31km) to al-Fārafrah Oasis (see above).

# 49 The North-West Coast

Running W from Alexandria for c 500km, the coastal road runs all the way to the Libyan border. It passes several resorts with names associated with the crucial desert battles of World War II.

**Abū Ṣīr**.—56km **al-ʿAlamayn**.—32km **Sīdī ʿAbd al-Rahmān**.—155km **Marsā Maṭrūḥ**.—28km *al-ʿAgībah*.—130km **Sīdī Barrāni**.—80km **Sallūm**.

The H56 runs W along Egypt's northern coast from Abū Ṣīr, skirting the immense Khalīg al-ʿArab (Arab Gulf) although the view is obscured by mounds of sand. After some way it runs to the summit of the dunes, following their rise and fall. Passing many small villages, at 116km the road reaches **al-ʿAlamayn**. (Small resthouse.)

A lesser road runs parallel to the H56, N of it and slightly inland. Several roads give access to the H56. Beyond *Burg al-ʿArab* the minor road reaches *al-Ḥammām* (22km) and after another 37km joins the main road.

**Al-ʿAlamayn** (*el-Alamein*) marks the nearest approach of the German forces to the Nile Valley during World War II. Here was fought the crucial battle that turned the tide of the war in North Africa in the Allies' favour.

Below is appended a resumé of the major moves in the North Africa campaign fought between September 1940 and March 1943. It gives no indication of the tens of thousands of lives lost on both sides.

**1938**. *26 October*: Italy declares Libya to be an integral part of Italy.

**1939**. *3 September*: Britain declares war on Germany.

**1940**. *10 August*: Italy declares war on the Allies, invades Egypt. *3 September*: Italians reach Sidī Barrāni. *9 December*: British under Field Marshall Wavell attack Italians. *15 December*: Italians retreat over Libyan border.

**1941**. *3 January*: Italians surrender Bardiyyah, British take Kassala. *30 January*: British occupy Benghazi. *31 March*: German counter-attack under Field Marshall Rommel begins. *7 April*: British evacuate Benghazi. *20 April*: Germans take Bardiyyah and attack Tobruk. *1 July*: Field Marshall Auchinleck replaces Wavell in Middle East Command. *18 November*: British renew offensive against Axis powers in Libya. *11 December*: Axis powers declare war on USA. *19 December*: German retreat, British regain Benghazi and occupy Cyrenaica.

**1942**. *9 January*: British reoccupy Bardiyyah. *April*: Rommel receives reinforcements, bombards Malta. *2 June*: British withdraw to Gazalah-Bīr Hākim line. *10 June*: Free French surrender Bīr Hākim to Germans. *13 June*: Great Battle, British lose 230 tanks. *19 June*: British withdraw to Sallum-Sidī ʿUmar line. *21 June*: Germans take Tobruk. *25 June*: British withdraw to Marsā Matrūḥ. *28 June*: British withdraw to al-ʿAlamayn. *19 August*: Field Marshall Alexander replaces Auchinleck in Middle East Command, General Montgomery given command of 8th Army. *31 August*: British hold ʿAlam Halfā against German offensive. *23 October*: Battle of al-ʿAlamayn begins. *4 November*: Allied Army under General Eisenhower lands in Algeria. *10 November*: German Army expelled from Egypt. *13 November*: 8th Army retakes Tobruk.

**1943**. *23 January*: 8th Army retakes Tripoli. *10 February*: 8th Army reaches borders of Tunisia. *6 April*: 8th Army reaches Allied Army. *12 May*: German Army surrenders in N Africa. *8 September*: Italy granted an armistice by Allies.

At the beach, S of the lagoon, a Polish Expedition has found an ancient site extending over 1km. It consists of many stone built structures, including houses, shops and public buildings, a basilica, store rooms, a church with three naves and a gigantic rock-cut cistern. W of the site the *Necropolis* contains tombs dating from 2C BC–3C AD. The 2C BC tombs are rock-cut covered with limestone slabs or more elaborate superstructures such as small step pyramids or statues of lions, Horus or the deceased. Although usually consisting of single interments, larger tombs contained loculi with multiple burials.

6km to the W is the **Allied War Cemetery** containing the bodies of men of the Allied armies who fell. There are some 7500 graves marked with crosses and stones surrounded by beautiful bushes and trees. Around the walls are the names of thousands of the missing.

400m W the *al-ʿAlamayn Museum* contains examples of World War II weaponry, charts of troop movements and models of war leaders planning the campaign.

After another 11km stands the first cenotaph of the Axis powers the *German War Memorial* consisting of an octagon with an obelisk and 4km to the W the *Italian War Memorial* is a square enclosure with a central column.

11km W is **Sīdī ʿAbd al-Rahmān**, which also figured prominently in World War II. It is now a flourishing town being developed as a key port. (*Hotel*: (May to October) Alamein (4*).)

Continuing W, the H56 runs through several small villages to (161km) **Marsā Maṭrūḥ**, capital of the immense Wādī al-Gadīd Province that encompasses the northern half of the Western Desert. It occupies the site of the Ptolemaic city of *Paraetonium*. It is a port and resort city surrounded by beautiful beaches.

**Hotels**: *Beau Site*, Shʿ. al-Shatak (3*): *Arus al-Bahr*, Kurnish (2*); *Marine Fouad*, Rommel House (2*); *Reem*, Kurnich (2*); *Riviera*, on the suq (1*). *Youth Hostel*.

Offshore is *Rommel's Island*. SE a road leads to the oasis of Sīwah (Rte 48). 10km E is *Zāwiyat Umm al-Rukhām* with remains of a temple fort of Ramesses II built by Nebreʾ, head bowman and overseer of foreign lands.

More excellent beaches lie to the W. At (7km) *Cleopatra's Bath* the shore is surrounded by rocky cliffs. 3km further is *al-Nasr City Beach* with (10km W) *al-Abyaḍ Beach*. *Al-ʿAgībah*, 8km further, is again set within a cove.

A deserted stretch of road leads 130km due W along the coast to the town of **Sīdī Barrānī**, another site made famous during the North African campaign. The road finally leads 80km to the town of **Sallūm** and the Libyan border.

# 50 The Red Sea Coast

A road now runs the full length of the Red Sea Coast from Suez at the southern end of the Suez Canal (Rte 47) to Egypt's border with the Sudan (approx. 1250km).

S of Suez the H44 runs along the Gulf of Suez. At 15km it passes **Rāʿs Adabiyyah**, being developed as an important port. 38km further is the resort of **ʿAyn Sukhnah** (*Hotel*: Red Sea, 4*). Continuing S, the H44 passes (30km) *Rāʾs Abū Darag* and (32km) **Zaʿfarānah**. From here a road runs W to the Nile Valley at Burumbul (and Cairo).

30km down this road a track leads S along the wādī. 15km along the track, in the foothills of the *Gabal Gallālah al-Qibliyyah*, is the **Monastery of St. Anthony** (*Deir Anbā Antūnyus* or *Deir Qaddīs Antwān*). It was founded in the mid 4C by disciples of one of the earliest and most influential hermits, St. Anthony (251–356). Accommodation (with permission from the Coptic Patriarchate in Cairo) in guestrooms, but no food is provided.

The monastery is enclosed within a fortified wall 10–12m high. Around the inside of the wall is a catwalk for the whole 2km length. The monastery is almost self-contained, with churches, chapels, flour mills and ovens, a large garden and a permanent spring.

St. Anthony (dc. 356), a founder of Egyptian monasticism, was a formative influence on Coptic Christianity. His parents died when he was 18 and providing for his sister he sold his possessions and gave the proceeds to the needy. In 285 he settled in the desert to the E of the Nile (modern Deir al-Maymun) but soon moved to the nearby hills to live. Many came to hear him preach or to be healed, but their attention distressed him and he retreated into the mountains of this area. Here too he was followed and finally he was forced to seek refuge in a cave whilst his followers formed a community at the foot of the mountain. At his death the location of his grave was kept secret at his request.

Two hundred years later, St. John the Short sought refuge at the monastery and died here. Melkite monks occupied the monastery in the 7C but in the 8–9C it suffered the depredation of Bedouin tribes. In the late 8C Coptic monks stole the body of St. John the Short and took it to the Wādī al-Naṭrūn. The monastery was razed by Nāṣir al-Dawlah in the 11C but in the 12C it had been restored and was inhabited by Coptic monks. Several Ethiopan bishops were elected from among them. European pilgrims visited the monastery from the 13C onwards and it was represented at the Council of Florence (1438–45).

The community's servants revolted in the late 15C, massacred the monks and despoiled the buildings. Syrian monks were sent from the Wādī al-Naṭrūn to restore the monastery in the mid 16C and for some time after it was inhabited by a mixed community of Coptic, Syrian and Ethiopian monks. Its importance was such that during the 17–19C many patriarchs were chosen from among the monks. From the 18C the number of European visitors increased and the monastery was frequently mentioned in travel memoirs.

Inside the enclosure the two-storey habitations of the monks and several churches line the many small lanes. At the end of a lane running N–S is the oldest church, the **Church of St. Anthony**, parts of which date to the 12–13C (or even earlier) as is shown by some of the wall-paintings and Gothic graffiti. The church consists of a narthex and side chapel, a nave, an antechamber to the haykal, the haykal and two side chapels. The choir is vaulted while the rest of the roof is covered with domes similar to those in the Fāṭimid Necropolis at Aswān (Rte 39). Entrance is via the N wall into the centre of the nave. The wall-paintings are in several styles; those on the S wall were painted in 1232–33 (though only one is dated) by the sons of Ghālib. Others are almost certainly older but difficult to date precisely. It has proved extremely difficult to identify some of the saints depicted and several remain anonymous.

*Narthex and small chapel.* Flanking the door are paintings of two monks while on the wall to the left are four mounted saints, the second is perhaps St. George. Along the back wall are SS. Theodorus, Menas, Victor and Claude. Another mounted saint is depicted at the entrance to the small chapel, the jambs of which are painted with two angels. Around the walls of the apse Jesus is seen with the Virgin and St. John the Baptist while in the door angels adore the cross. On the remaining wall of the narthex paintings show two monks blessed by Jesus, St. Thuon and St. Arsophonius.

*Apse.* On the left-hand wall paintings depict a bishop, Anba Moses, two monks blessed by Jesus, an angel and a monk, two monks and an anonymous saint. On the right-hand wall are four monks, SS. Bishoy, Samuel, Paul the Simple (a disciple of St. Anthony), Isaac, and two monks, the last possibly St. Anthony.

*Antechamber.* In the jambs are archangels, Michael (left) and Gabriel (right). Inside to the left are three female saints, King Nebuchadrezzar and St. George. On the right are prophets, Abraham, Isaac and Jacob and St. Mercurius (the only dated painting—1232–33).

*Haykal and side chapels.* In the chapel on the left is a painting of St. Mark. In the right-hand chapel are SS. Theophilus, Peter of Alexandria, an anonymous saint, Dioscorus, Anasthasius of Alexandria and the patriarch Severus of Antioch. In front of the haykal Jesus is seen with two female saints and the three myrrh-bearing women, Mary Magdalene, Mary, mother of Jesus, and Salome. Above the haykal are paintings of Daniel, David, Moses, Isaiah, Elias, Jeremy, Abraham and Melkisdek, the Sacrifice of Abraham, and Christ enthroned. The dome shows Christ Pantocrator while in the semi-dome of the apse are angels at the cross. Smoke damage on the S wall dates from the servants' revolt in the 15C.

To the E is the *Church of the Apostles*, with three haykals. The 12-domed **Church of St. Mark**, with a Latin cross above the entrance, dates from 1766. It is the only church in the complex containing relics. Against the N wall is a chest containing relics of St. Mark the Evangelist. In the *Refectory* building is the **Church of the Virgin** and the *Library* with a fine collection of more than 2500 MSS and printed books. The *Keep* contains the *Chapel of St. Michael* (the whole structure is unsafe). Two further churches in the complex are the *Old Church of St. Paul*, built by Kirillus IV in the mid 19C, and the *New Church of St. Paul*, begun by Tawilus in 1930 but not completed.

2km NE and above the monastery is the *Cave of St. Paul the Simple*, a disciple of St. Anthony. 100m further up the mountain is the **Cave of St. Anthony**. It consists of a terrace, tunnel, cave and balcony. There are medieval graffiti on the walls. The terrace commands a magnificent view of the hills and valley. In the surrounding area are several other hermits' caves.

The H44 continues S from Zaʿfarānah. At 26km a track leads SW. Follow this for 10km S and 3km SW. It leads into the eastern foothills of the Gabal Gallalah and the **Monastery of St. Paul** (*Deir Anbā Būlā*), built around the cave of St. Paul. It is similar in layout to the Monastery of St. Anthony and consists of a high-walled enclosure containing habitations and chapels. There are guestrooms but women are not allowed to stay overnight in the monastery; a guesthouse has been built outside the walls for them.

St. Paul the Theban (228–348) was born in Alexandria. At the age of 16 he fled from the persections of Decius and retired to the Eastern Desert. Here he was visited by St. Anthony to whom he presented a tunic of palm leaves. He is the earliest hermit of whom we have knowledge. Founded shortly after his death, this monastery has always been dominated by that of St. Anthony whose fortunes it followed closely.

The **Church of St. Paul** contains the *Cave* of the saint in the sanctuary. Here the relics of St. Paul are preserved. While the wall paintings are in better condition, they are more restored and inferior in quality to those in the Monastery of St. Anthony. The central haykal is dedicated to St. Anthony, the S haykal to St. Paul, and the N haykal to the Twenty-four Elders of the Apocalypse. Among the numerous saints at the W end of the S wall are four archangels, Raphael, Suriel, Zaqiel and Sathiel, and the angel of the burning fiery furnace with Shadrach, Meshach and Abednego. Adjacent is the late 18C *Church of St. Mercurius*, with a fine haykal screen. The *Church of the Virgin* is on the third floor of the Keep, but it is unsafe.

The **Church of St. Michael** is the largest, with two sanctuaries. That to the N is dedicated to St. Michael and that to the S to St. John the Baptist. The screen of the latter contains a strange gilded ikon of St. John's head on a dish, painted by Ibrāhīm al-Nasīkh and dated 1760. There are several other hermits' caves in the surrounding hills.

Continuing S, the H44 passes (27km) **Rawahmī, Rā's Gharīb, Ra's**

**Shuqayr** and at 114km a road leaves to the SE to *Zaytiyyah* (15km). Off the coast to the S is a series of islands in the Straits of Gūbāl.

At 3km at Abū Sha'ār the Roman fortress of *Myos Hormos* has been investigated by the University of Delaware who found a triumphal arch over the W gate and two monumental Latin inscriptions in the name of the Emperor Galerius.

20km **Gamshah** is opposite the tip of Sinai and from this point the H44 skirts the Red Sea. 65km S the road reaches **al-Ghardaqah** (also known as *Hurghadah*) which is being developed as holiday resort. This is the capital of Baḥr al-Aḥmar (Red Sea) Province.

*Airport* 6km to the W.

**Hotels**: *Hurghadah Sheraton* (4*), at Abū Munkar, 5km S; *Magawish Village*, a luxury chalet complex (4*), 11km S.

Further S on the H44 is (60km) **Būr Safāgah** with a road W to Qēnā (Rte 34). Beyond (85km) lies **al-Qūṣayr** which until the 10C was the most important Muslim port on the Red Sea.

It was superseded by ʿAydhab (modern Ḥalayib) to the S and later by Qulzum (Suez) to the N. It served the cities of Qūṣ and Qift in the Nile Valley and from here pilgrims set out for, and returned from, the journey to Mecca. Here also the merchant ships from the Arab Gulf and Indian Ocean unloaded their rich cargoes. After a period of decline it was revived by the Ottomans but in the 19C the opening of the Suez Canal proved disastrous and the old port fell into disuse.

To the S the coast is rather desolate. At 107km is **Marsā ʿAlam** (with a road W across the desert to Maḥāmīd; Rte 37).

**The following journey should not be undertaken without the assistance of a guide**. 10km along the road to Maḥāmīd a desert track leads SW. Following this the road turns SE after 15km. 20km further on it crosses a track running E–W and continues another 23km to **Bīr Shādihli** with the **Tomb of Sayyid al-Shādhilī**.

Abū 'l-Ḥasan al-Shādhilī was born in NW Africa in 1196. His early life is obscure but after receiving instruction from Sidī Madyan he travelled to Egypt to study under Rifāʿī shaykhs. Returning to Tunisia, he was given permission to start his own tarīqah but in the process he offended many of the ʿulama and returned once again to Egypt. He collected a very large following through his knowledge, piety and charity. He travelled on the ḥajj every year and died here on his return from Mecca in 1258. He was one of the most influential of sufi shaykhs and many brotherhoods include him in their chains of authority.

The present buildings are modern. King Fārūq, during a visit to the area in 1947, ordered the restoration of the Tomb of al-Shādhilī and the construction of the adjacent **Mosque**. Despite its isolation, the mūlid of al-Shādhilī on 9 Dhū l-Ḥijjah is attended by up to 200,000 people.

The track continues S for 10km and then turns left and runs E 35km to join the H44 N of Rā's Banās.

After another 150km the H44 passes *Rā's Banas* and turns slightly inland to **Baranīs**, site of the ancient city of *Berenice*.

This was a trading-post founded by Ptolemy II Philadelphus and named in honour of his mother. Goods off-loaded here were taken across the desert to Koptos (Qift) and Edfū. It was abandoned in the 5C AD and rediscovered by Belzoni in the autumn of 1818. Lying in a natural depression, the site covers more than 2sq. km. Among the ruins of ancient dwellings is the *Temple of Serapis*, built by Tiberius with additions by later emperors. It consists of an outer court with an inner hall flanked by two chambers. That to the left has stairs to the roof. The sanctuary is also flanked by two chambers.

75km S is **Bīr Shalatayn** on the border of the administrative area of Egypt, the land to the S being administered by the Sudan. After a further 150km the road reaches **Ḥalayib**, the old port of *ʿAydhab* which was the most important port on the Red Sea during medieval times. 25km further is **Rā's Hadarbah** and the political border of Egypt and the Sudan.

# 51 Sinai

Sinai is covered in two sections. In the north the roads described all lead E across the plain (approx. 200km). The southern itinerary skirts the whole peninsula, a total of approx. 500km with diversions to the important sites in the interior.

## A. North Sinai

Travelling in Sinai is a captivating experience: the brilliant turquoise sea in stark contrast to the mountains glowing in pastel colours or striped with black and yellow. But despite the recent vast improvement in the state of the roads it can still be an extremely hazardous place. Never travel by car without a plentiful supply of water and an extra can of petrol. The wind which can blow unremittingly hot during the day can turn bitterly cold at night—it is better to be over than underdressed. Also not all the military software from the last campaigns has been cleared and visitors are discouraged from wandering off the roads. (See also Topographical Introduction p 14.)

Although the area may appear deserted there are as many as 40,000 Bedouin from a dozen tribes, some with venerable lineages inhabiting Sinai. Most numerous are the Suwārkash, numbering about 12,000 living around al-ʿArīsh in the extreme NE. The Tarābīn from the E coast claiming descent from al-Ḥusayn (d 680) are representatives of a tribe dominating S Palestine, while the Ḥawaytāt found mainly in NW Arabia also have a branch in W Sinai. The Qarāshah from the SW trace their ancestry to the Quraysh, the tribe of the Prophet Muḥammad, and around al-Ṭūr and Mt. Sinai the small tribe of al-Jabālyyah are the descendents of Byzantine and Egyptian guards from St. Catherine's Monastery who converted to Islam. Other tribes are the Awlad Saʿid (SW), ʿAlayqāt (W coast), Mazīnah (S regions) and Tiyahā (E and central areas).

There are four main routes across the N plains of Sinai. Northernmost is the H55, the coastal road. This route to Palestine was known in ancient times as the 'Way of Horus'. It leaves **al-Qantārah al-Sharqiyyah** (usually called *Qantārah Sharq*, Rte 47) and runs NE. After 6km the H66 leaves to the S (following the Suez Canal), and on the N is (4km) **Tell al-Aḥmar** and (9km) **Gilbānah**. Just N of the road at 7km is an ancient site which is almost certainly that of **Migdol** (Gk *Magdolos* or *Stratopeda*).

The centre of the site is occupied by the foundations of a massive *Fort*, 200m sq. The walls of sun-baked brick were 15.2m thick, built with a cellular construction to relieve the immense weight. Massive buttresses support three sides except for the E wall which contained the entrance, facing an ancient canal. Inside the walls are the remains of numerous buildings. Probably founded in the late 7C BC, the town shows occupation by immigrant Eastern Greeks, Phoenicians and Jews. The topmost layers of the site are totally burnt, evidence of the complete destruction of the town during the invasion of Cambyses in 525 BC. The town was reconstructed to the SE by the Persians (see below). 500m E is the *Cemetery* containing urn cremations which, if Greek, are the earliest examples in Egypt.

2km SE (to the S of the road) is *Tell al-Hayr*, site of the second city of Migdol, built during the Persian occupation in the early 5C BC. It was much larger than the earlier city, covering nearly half a square kilometre, and continued in use until the early Islamic period. It was abandoned with the silting up of the Pelusiac branch of the Nile.

A Roman fortress has recently been excavated by an Egyptian-French expedition and investigations made of the adjacent town.

8km further, N of the road is **Tell Faramā**, site of ancient *Pelusium* at the mouth of the extinct Pelusiac branch of the Nile; capital of the Roman Province of Augustamnica. This was one of the frontier towns founded in the late 6C or early 5C BC. In late Classical times it was famous for its

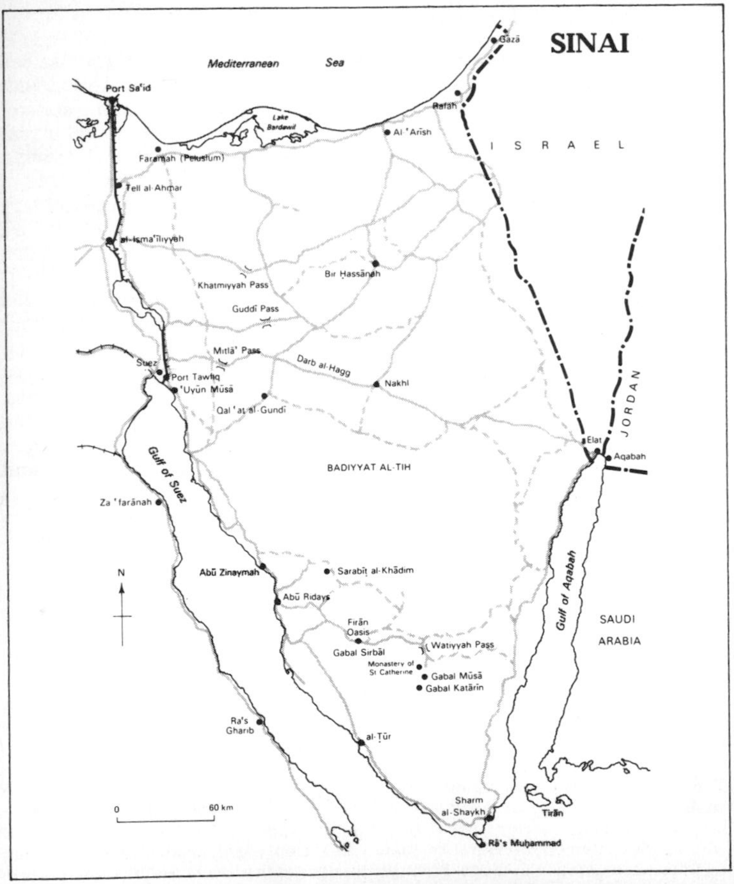
SINAI
Mediterranean Sea
Gazā
Rafah
Port Sa'id
Lake Bardawil
Al 'Arīsh
ISRAEL
Faramah (Pelusium)
Tell al-Ahmar
al-Isma'īliyyah
Bir Hassānah
Khatmiyyah Pass
Guddī Pass
Mitlā' Pass
Darb al-Hagg
Suez
Port Tawfīq
'Uyūn Mūsā
Nakhl
Qal'at al-Gundī
JORDAN
Elat
Aqabah
BADIYYAT AL-TIH
Gulf of Suez
Za'farānah
N
Abū Zinaymah
Sarabīt al-Khādim
Abū Ridays
Gulf of Aqabah
SAUDI ARABIA
Firān Oasis
Gabal Sirbāl
Watiyyah Pass
Monastery of St Catherine
Gabal Mūsā
Gabal Katārīn
Ra's Gharib
al-Tūr
0
60 km
Sharm al-Shaykh
Tirān
Rā's Muhammad

Tomb of Galen (129–199) the Pergamonese physician, doctor to Emp. Marcus Aurelius and three of his successors. During recent investigations by the EAO pedestals of Roman statues were found. From here ʿAmr ibn al-ʿĀṣ consolidated his forces and launched his successful invasion of Egypt in AD 640. With the silting up of the river in the early 8C AD the city was abandoned. To the S a road runs to the H3.

Continuing E, the next village is (6km) **Rummānī** and then (20km) **Bīr al-ʿAfayn** and (4km) **Bīr al-ʿAbd**. Just beyond a road leaves S via **Gabal Maghārah** to the H3. N of the H55 lies the *Sabkhat al-Bardawīl*, a great marshy lagoon, separated from the sea by a massive limestone ridge. This may be the Red sea over which the Israelites, led by Moses, passed in the Exodus from Egypt. The H55 passes **Misfaq**, **Bīr al-Mazār**, and (60km) **Bīr Masāʾid** and runs into (11km) **al-ʿArīsh**. This, the site of ancient *Rhinokoluria*, is the largest town in the peninsula, capital of the province of N Sinai and a popular holiday resort.

Hotels: *Oberoi El-Arish* (4*); *Sinai Beach* (3*).

From al-ʿArīsh a road leads S via **Bīr Lahfān** to **Abū Awaygilah** on the H3. E of al-ʿArīsh the H55 continues through **Al-Kharrūbah, Diklah** and (39km) **Sadut**. Beyond this (7km) is the present border of Israel which divides the town of **Rafaḥ** E of which lie **Khān Yūnis** and the **Gaza Strip**, occupied since the 1963 war.

The second route, H3, leaves the E bank opposite **al-Ismāʿīliyyah**. Beyond the H66 it runs slightly SE, crossing at 27km a road (N to the H55: S to the H33). At 45km it enters the **Khatmiyyah Pass** and on to (8km) **Bīr al-Gifgāfah** where it is crossed by another road (N to S). Continuing E, the road passes (26km) **Bīr Rawḍ Sālim**, beyond which several roads lead off: at 19km to the N, at 17km to the S, and at 5km another road to the N (to al-ʿArīsh, see above). The next village is (40km) **Abū Awaygilah**, with a road N to al-ʿArīsh, and at 36km the H3 reaches the border of Israel, beyond which is the town of **Gezl-ʾiot**.

The third route takes off N of the tunnel under the Suez Canal. After 24km it crosses a road (N to the H3; S to the H33) and beyond runs past (13km) **Bīr Gaddī** and into (11km) the **Gaddī Pass**. At 17km it reaches another road (NE to the H3) and turns S to (12km) **Bīr al-Thamūdah**. It then turns NE to (67km) **Bīr Ḥasanah**, E for 36km, and finally NE to (43km) **al-Qusaymah**. From here the road turns NW (to the H3) but a track leads NE to the Israeli border.

A fourth route, the H33, leaves the H66 opposite the Aḥmad Ḥamdi Tunnel from **al-Kubrī** and crosses Sinai much further S. It follows the ancient *Darb al-Ḥajj* (Pilgrimage Road) along which the great procession from Egypt travelled to Arabia. At 32km it enters the **Mitlā Pass**, beyond which (32km) a road crosses NE (to Bīr al-Thamūdah) to SE (to Raʾs al-Sudr on the coast).

Taking the SE route at 21km to the N of the road the *Raʾs al-Gundī* (ht 153m) is visible as an isolated conical spur of the Gabal Raḥā. At the summit stands the **Qalʿat al-Gundī** (Fortress of the Soldier) built in 1187 by Ṣalāḥ al-Dīn.

In 1185 Reynald de Chataillon, headstrong Crusader Lord of Karak, transported a fleet overland to Eylah and campaigned in the Red Sea. Although his fleet was soon destroyed it stimulated a flurry of Muslim activity in S Palestine and Sinai. It was during this period that Ṣalāḥ al-Dīn built this fortress probably under the direction of his brother al-ʿAdil who visited the site himself some fifteen years later when he was sultan. It must also have performed the added function of protecting travellers on the Darb al-Ḥajj from marauding tribes.

Access is from the N side where a steep track leads up the hill to a dry stone wall behind which is a moat. The main structure, in plan, is a distorted pentangle 140 x 100m with a 60m extension to the NE, in which is set the original entrance. Limestone walls 2m thick stand to about half their original height with round or square towers at the angles. There is much fallen masonry inside the enclosure but several structures are apparent. At the NE end is a small *underground hall* while around the inner walls of the fortress are the collapsed remains of c 40 *living rooms*. Three structures stand in a row to the W. First a small rectangular *mosque*, besides which is a plaster lined *water cistern* and last another better preserved *mosque* (20 x 10m) above another cistern. Stucco decoration remains above the mihrab and an inscription over the door records al-ʿAdil's visit. In the SW corner is the base of a minaret. In the NW corner of the fortress is a large *vaulted underground chamber* (20 x 20m). The S part of the enclosure contains the delapidated remains of other large buildings.

The H33 then runs SE for 58km to **al-Nakhl** and continues to (61km) **al-Thamad**. Here it turns briefly NE and then SE again. Beyond this the road reaches (75km) the Israeli border, inside which is the port of **Elat**.

# B. South Sinai

Beyond the H33 the H66 continues S along the E bank of the Suez Canal and passes (13km) **al-Shaṭṭ**.

Running S, the H66 reaches (12km) **ʿUyūn Mūsā** (Springs of Moses), a small oasis with, as the name suggests, several springs.

Traditions abound regarding this site, all concerning Chapter 15 of the Book of Exodus. It is proposed that the Israelites halted here after crossing the Red Sea and Moses is supposed to have thrown a tree into the largest spring, Marah, thus sweetening it. Here also the prophetess Miriam, sister of Aaron, danced with the women.

Recent investigation has uncovered Roman and Islamic remains in the neighbourhood, consisting of four furnaces for making coins and an Islamic bath.

Continuing S on the coast of the Gulf of Suez, the H66 passes (27km) **Sidr** and the first of the oilfields of Sinai. At (10km) **Rāʾs al-Sidr** the road swings inland and runs SE. It passes E of **Gabal Ḥammām Faraʿūn** (Mountain of Pharaoh's Bath). This is a natural blunted pyramid (height 494m); and at the N end (opposite a large cave in which the heat can be felt), are a number of hot springs and streams running into the sea. These are used locally as a cure for rheumatism, but great care should be taken as some of them are close to boiling point. Beyond this the H66 passes the track to Sarabīt al-Khādim (see below) to the E and turns to the coast into (7km) **Abū Zunaymah**, a small town. (Resthouse (no food). Petrol stations.) From here manganese, mined in Sinai, is transported and it was, in ancient times, the major port serving the copper and turquoise mines. It is possible to visit Sarabīṭ al-Khādim from here.

The track E of the H66 (N of Abū Zunaymah) runs along the **Wādī Humur**. It turns S (21km) and then E again at 4km and at 7km a further track leads due S to **Sarābīṭ al-Khādim** (5km). It can also be reached from the S, (see below). This site was discovered by Carl Neibuhr in 1762 but was not excavated until 1906. The deity worshipped here was Hathor and the rock-cut sanctuary, which dates from the 12

Dyn., was dedicated to her. Sopdu, the god of the Eastern Desert, was also worshipped here. The temple is a long narrow building consisting of many courts with numerous stelae inscribed by Middle and New Kingdom kings and officials. Hatshepsut and Tuthmosis III were the principal New Kingdom benefactors, at which time the shrine to Sopdu was built next to that of Hathor. It seems to have been abandoned in the reign of Ramesses VII. A rough stone wall demarks the sacred domain and cuts the valley off from the nearby mining area. Evidence of extensive mining in ancient times can be seen in the surrounding wādīs, with rock inscriptions from the 3 Dyn. onwards. 5km W at Rūd al-ʿAyr a Middle Kingdom rock inscription has been found.

S from Abū Zunaymah the H66 continues to (25km) *Abū Rudīs*. The S route to Sarabīt al-Khādim runs E along Wādī Sidrī. At 25km is the **Wādī Marāghah** with ancient turquoise mines. Unfortunately, many of the workings and commemorative stelae were destroyed by British mining ventures in 1901. Beyond is the **Wādī Mukhattab** (Valley of Inscriptions) where the road runs N to Sarabīṭ al-Khādim.

Beyond Abū Rudīs the H66 stays on the coast. At 20km it swings inland and a small road continues along the coast. Beyond this junction (12km) a track to the E leads to Fīrān and ultimately to Mount Sinai and St. Catherine's Monastery. The track follows the Wādī Fīrān in a semi-circle and at 36km runs into the **Oasis of Fīrān**, the largest oasis in the peninsula, with a sedentary population of several hundred.

During early biblical times this valley may have been inhabited by the Amalakites. Therefore it was here that the battle between them and the Israelites took place. By the 4C AD it was a Christian stronghold (*Pharan*) and the seat of a bishopric. In the surrounding mountains there was a large population of hermits. At the Council of Chalcedon in 451 it was created an archbishopric subject to the Patriarch of Jerusalem. Thus, prior to the rise of the community at Gabal Mūsā, this was the spiritual centre of Sinai and the object of pilgrimages from throughout the Middle East. During the 7C the inhabitants became Monophysites and then Monothelites. Increasing attacks by nomadic tribes caused many of the people to retreat further into Sinai and join the community at Gabal Mūsā. In the late 7C after the Muslim conquest the site was finally abandoned. The remains of the basilica can still be seen and scattered around the area are many capitals, pillars and other masonry from the ancient town. The German Institute at Cairo has finished investigating the main church and begun excavation of that in the village. This has proved to be a basilica of similar 5C date. There is a large plantation belonging to the Monastery of St. Catherine. This was established in 1898 and is watered by a large cistern. The *Convent of St. Heloise* was built in 1970 by two monks using material from an older monastery.

On the Acropolis a temple has been found dating to the 5C BC. Work has also been undertaken on the houses situated on the slopes of the Acropolis.

N of the oasis is *Gabal Tahūnah* (height 230m), the track to the summit lined with ruined chapels and sanctuaries. At the top is a ruined church with evidence of an apse and tiled floor. Further N is the *Gabal al-Banāt* (1510m) with a ruined *Chapel of the Virgin* on the summit. S of the oasis is another mountain, *Gabal Sirbāl* (2070m). The climb to the summit is difficult and the cliffs on the way contain many hermits' caves.

The Wādī Tarāfah leaves Fīrān Oasis to the E and at 6km enters the Wādī al-Shaykh. After 30km at the *Tomb of Sh. Muḥsin* it turns due S into the *Watiyyah Pass*. On the E side (6km) is the *Tomb of Nabī Ṣāliḥ* and just S a track leads E to the H66 on the E coast. 12km S it enters the *Plain of Raha*, where the Israelites were supposed to have rested. On the E side is a mound, on the top of which is the *Chapel of Aaron* (Hārūn) where the golden calf was supposedly fashioned. Running SE is Wādī al-Deir; 1km further is the **Monastery of Saint Catherine** (*Deir Sant Kātārīn*). It is set slightly above the floor of the valley and the level of flash floods and is enclosed within massive granite walls. (Airstrip to the E of the monastery, resthouse within the enclosure. Fees for entry, residence and visits to various chapels and peaks in the area.) Coaches have to park at the foot of the track to the Monastery leaving an uphill walk of about a kilometre.

Entry to some of the collections, library, museum etc. need special permission from the Archbishop in Cairo.

Hotels: *Al-Salam* (2*); *Sainte Catherine*.

3km from the monastery a small complex, *Magawish Village Hogara*, has been built. Designed by the Egyptian architect Ali Azam, it was opened in 1985. The stone chalets emulate Beduin tents with the dining area on top of a small hill.

The valley first rose to prominence in the 4C when it was inhabited by hermits from throughout the Byzantine Empire who sought refuge in the wilderness near Mount Sinai. Such was its reputation that in 337 the empress Helena, mother of Constantine, ordered the building of a sanctuary around the site of the Burning Bush, and may even have visited the site on her journey to the Holy Land. Although the community was occasionally attacked by nomadic tribes it attracted an increasing number of pilgrims. Because of its vulnerability the emperor Justinian built the fortified enclosure and Church of the Virgin in 537. About 562 he ordered the construction of the Basilica of the Transfiguration and provided 200 soldiers, 100 Slavs and 100 Egyptians, to guard and serve the community. It is highly unlikely that the present Muslim servants at the monastery are descendants of those Byzantine soldiers as has often been suggested. Throughout its history the community remained in touch with the See of Constantinople although few of the theological arguments affected it. After the Muslim conquest its relationships with the new rulers remained good. In the mid 9C it was created an independent bishopric and Constantius, the first bishop, attended the Fourth Council of Constantinople in 869. A century later the monastery was sacked and the inhabitants fled, but the discovery of the relics of St. Catherine renewed vitality and by the 11C it was flourishing once more. Monks toured Europe visiting the courts and collecting alms. At the end of the 11C it was made an archbishopric suffragan to the Latin Archbishop of Peha.

With the establishment of the Crusader Kingdoms on the eastern seaboard of the Mediterranean the number of European pilgrims increased greatly and special facilities were provided for them. Relationships with all Christian communities remained excellent and several popes confirmed the status of the monastery. From the mid 14C community of about 400 monks the numbers declined and by 1479 it was abandoned. This pattern of rise and decline persisted throughout the 16C and 17C and the monastery was often deserted. But in the 18C it gradually grew in strength. In 1782 the monastery gained full autonomy within the Greek Orthodox Church. Napoleon, during the French Occupation, had his engineers make repairs to the fabric of the monastery and Muḥammad ʿAlī undertook further works and provided revenues from the customs levies of Cairo. In 1872 the first archbishop since 1760 was installed. Although recent conflicts in Sinai put a temporary halt to visitors, modern transport has made the monastery much more accessible.

Throughout its history the monastery has received benefactions from the greatest Christian princes, beginning with Pope Gregory the Great (590–604) who sent furniture for a hostel. Of all the royal patrons the Russian tsars, who considered themselves natural successors to the Byzantine emperors, were the most generous. Many of their gifts can still be seen in the monastery. A survey of the monastery was undertaken in the 1970s by an expedition from the Universities of Michigan and Princeton, and Alexandria.

The stone walls of the off-square enclosure (75m by 80m) rest on the massive foundations of the 6C wall. To the NW is the monastery orchard and charnel house. Until recently entry into the enclosure was by basket and pulley into an elevated doorway still visible on the NW wall but the

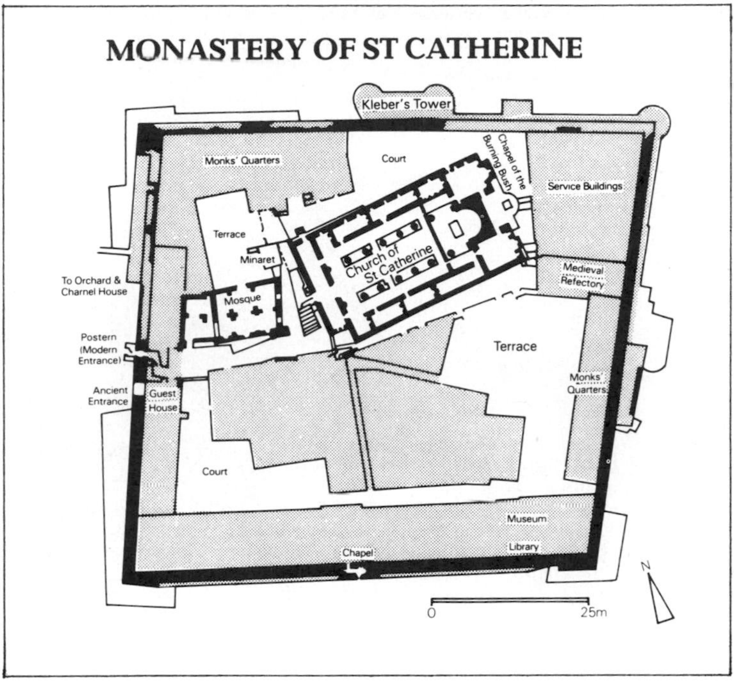
MONASTERY OF ST CATHERINE
Kleber's Tower
Monks' Quarters
Court
Chapel of the Burning Bush
Service Buildings
Terrace
Minaret
Church of St Catherine
Medieval Refectory
To Orchard & Charnel House
Mosque
Postern (Modern Entrance)
Terrace
Ancient Entrance
Guest House
Monks' Quarters
Court
Museum
Library
Chapel
0
25m
N

*Postern* of the original gateway has been opened up in the SE wall. The massive lintel of the main gateway can be seen to the right of the postern. Past a 19C copper-bound door the entry leads into a small court. On the right is the *Resthouse*. Various buildings fill the compound—monks' residence, kitchens, chapels and a mosque—but dominating the complex is the **Church of St. Catherine** which incorporates the *Chapel of the Burning Bush*. It is a basilica (40m by 20m), constructed of massive granite blocks. Above the side aisles the central nave rises as a clerestory, set with rectangular windows. At the E the roof of the apse projects at a lower level. Above is a double round-arched window with an oculus. Flanking the walls of the apse are two domes which cover terminal chapels. Lead covers the gable of the roof as it probably did when originally built. At the NW corner is the three tiered *Bell-tower* presented by the Russian Church in 1871. This last feature and the narthex (see below) apart, the church is almost completely unmodified since it was built c 552 by Justinian in memory of his wife Theodora (died 548). The architect was Stephen of Aila and the foundation inscriptions still exist on the beams of the roof. Originally it was dedicated to the Transfiguration of Christ and only after the discovery of St. Catherine's body in the 9C was it renamed.

The Transfiguration of Christ, in which he reveals his divine nature to the apostles Peter, James and John in the presence of Moses and Elias (Matthew, 17:2; Mark, 9:2), was always especially important for Eastern Christianity. St. Catherine, a patrician of Alexandria, criticised the emperor Maxentius and derided his adoration of idols. She was brought before a group of philosophers who attempted to persuade her of her error. However Catherine's arguments were so brilliant that they were confounded. In desperation Maxentius ordered her to be broken on the wheel, but when the execution was to be carried out the wheel shattered at her touch. She was finally executed by beheading and buried in Alexandria. Her remains were miraculously transported to the highest mountain in Sinai (Gabal Kātārīna) where they were discovered by monks in the 9C and reinterred within the monastery.

*The Monastery of St. Catherine*

Steps lead down to the entrance of the church as the level of the site of the Burning Bush was the lowest in the compound. A magnificent Fāṭimid *wooden door* (11C) with small carved panels of Jesus, apostles, saints and angels, gives access into the transverse *Narthex*, also added onto the basilica in the Fāṭimid period. The pilgrims would have entered by the left-hand door into the side aisles and proceeded N to the Chapel of the Burning Bush and back down the S aisle. Many graffito coats of arms left by medieval visitors can be seen on the walls of the narthex. A wooden portal contains the double folding doors into the body of the church. They are all original and magnificent examples of 6C Byzantine carving. Around the portal is a stylised vine; the panels of the doors contain carvings of plants, birds, fish and mammals.

The *nave* is unusually high because the floor is at the level of the Chapel of the Burning Bush. On each side of the nave six monolithic granite pillars with massive carved capitals support half-round arches and the upper walls of the clerestory. The floor, of coloured marbles in geometrical panels, is 18C and typical of those found throughout Egypt in mosques and churches. Each of the columns has a calendar ikon, depicting all the saints whose festivals fall within a particular month. A candle is lit in front of the relevant pillar to indicate which saint is being commemorated. Against the second pillar on the left is the wooden *anbon* (dated 1787) with spiral staircase and painted wooden panels. Beside the next pillar on the right is the canopied lectern which holds the ikon of the saint being venerated that day. On the opposite side of the nave next to the third pillar is the 18C *bishop's throne* which replaced the original (now in the apse).

Hanging from the ceiling are great chandeliers, made in the 18C in Nuremburg. The wooden trusses supporting the roof are original, and contain the foundation inscription of Emperor Justinian, but they were covered in the 18C by a flat wooden ceiling and only the *bracing beams* are visible. Although now painted red and gold, these are superbly carved with the Wonders of Creation, animals, plants and people, cherubs, rowing boats and Nile scenes. The 18C panels are painted in blue and gold with stars and the sun and moon. At the E end of the nave, in front of the ikonostasis, are three pairs of standing candlesticks dated 1701, 1716 and 1719. The *ikonostasis* presented by Cosmos of Crete, was painted by Jeremiah of Crete in 1612. Elaborately carved and gilded the central panels have individual paintings of Jesus, Mary, John the Baptist and the patron saint, St. Catherine. Above is another row of smaller ikons. The whole construction is crowned by a great crucifix flanked by two ikons. This was obviously not the original form and marble panels from the original low balustrade can be seen in other parts of the church.

Behind the ikonostasis are the *Sanctuary* and apse. On either side of the door is a magnificent silver chest inlaid with precious stones and a figure of St. Catherine in gold on the top. These were presented by the Russian royal family, that on the left by Peter Alexeivitch (later tsar), his step-brother Ivan and the regent Sophia Alexievia in 1688 and that on the right by Tsar Alexander II in 1860. The altar is original and consists of a marble table; it is covered by a 17C carved wooden canopy inlaid with ivory and mother-of-pearl. In the centre of the tribune is the original marble bishop's throne, removed from the nave. On the right side of the sanctuary is the *Tomb of St. Catherine*. This is an 18C structure with a marble canopy but it incorporates earlier work including a panel from the balustrade of the sanctuary. It contains the skull of the saint surmounted by a crown. On the left-hand plinth of the sanctuary is a 7C encaustic painting on the marble of the sacrifice of Abraham and on the right-hand plinth the sacrifice of Jephthath, a unique subject (see Judges, 11:30–40).

The semi-dome and arch of the *apse* contains the glory of the church, the superb 6C mosaic. Comparable to any in the Byzantine empire, the technique used here produces a more painterly and less graphic effect than others known from the period (e.g. at Ravenna) and includes subtleties of shade and light. It must have been executed by one of the artists from the Imperial School in Constantinople.

In the dome the Transfiguration of Christ is shown against a gold background. Christ is the central figure flanked by Moses and St. James (right) and Elias and St. John (left). St. Peter is shown kneeling below. Below and around the soffit of this scene is a series of 31 portraits of prophets, apostles and saints. At the end of the lower row to the right is the abbot Longinus and to the left the deacon John, both surrounded by the square nimbus of the living and obviously in post when the work was executed. The central medallion has a cross. On the left side of the arch is a medallion with the head of John the Baptist and on the right the Virgin. Above are two angels offering the orb and sceptre to the Paschal Lamb. In the right-hand corner Moses is shown receiving the tablets of the law and in the left removing his sandals before the Burning Bush. Although the coloured glass in the double window is late, the central column is covered with original mosaic.

Along the outside of each side aisle is a series of chapels. Although this is an unusual feature in a Byzantine church there is no doubt that it is part of the original plan. The ikons along the walls are taken down on the day that the saint depicted is venerated and placed in the central nave. In the N aisle the first is the *Chapel of St. Marisa*, a woman who spent her life in the monastery as a monk and whose sex was not discovered until after her death. Next is the *Chapel of SS. Constantine and Helena*, beyond which is the *Chapel of St. Antipas*. At the E end of the aisle is the *Chapel of St. James the Less*. This chapel is covered by a dome and in the apse is a late Byzantine painting, probably made by refugee monks after the fall of Constantinople in 1453. It shows the Virgin of the Burning Bush (symbolising the purity of fire and virginity) flanked by SS. James and John Chrysostom and SS. Basil and Moses. Christ is also shown presenting the Tablets of the Law and the Gospels. They are accurate copies of 12–13C originals. To the W is the entrance to the Sacristy and to the S the door to the Chapel of the Burning Bush (see below).

The first chapel in the S aisle is the *Chapel of SS. Cosimas and Damian*, the unmercenary physicians. Next to this is the *Chapel of St. Simeon Stylites*; beyond is the *Chapel of SS. Joachim and Anne*, parents of the Virgin. The last side chapel is the old *Treasury* and the terminal room is the *Chapel of the Holy Fathers*, the 40 martyrs of Ṭūr, also with domed roof. This leads from the E into the **Chapel of the Burning Bush**. Although this was the site of the first sanctuary in the area, it was not included in the original building of Justinian but probably stood in a court at the E end. During medieval times the area was enclosed and incorporated into the main church. Provincial Turkish tiles, probably 17C, cover the walls, in which (E side) is a small semi-domed recess. Below the altar a small silver plate marks the site of the Burning Bush where by tradition God appeared to Moses (Exodus, II:5). In the semi-dome of the recess is a simple mosaic of a cross within a circle.

To the W of the church stands the whitewashed **Mosque**; the minaret (10m high) is free-standing just to the N. The mosque, one of the original buildings of the complex, was a hospice for pilgrims. But in 1106 at the request of Amīr Anushtakin al-Amīrī it was converted into a mosque. The amīr provided the fine carved minbar and kursi, one of the earliest known, which contain excellent Kufic inscriptions. The EAO is continuing with a programme of restoration to this building.

There are several other chapels within the compound, many of them decorated by Fr Pachomius (died 1958) who was instrumental in preserving the monastery's unique collection of ikons and manuscripts.

SE of the church stands the *Refectory*. It is a long medieval building with a high vaulted roof of unknown function, although it may have been a hostel for pilgrims or yet another chapel. There is a chapel against the E wall. A painting of the Last Judgement fills the whole wall. It was executed in 1573 by a Cretan artist. Many of the wooden furnishings and fittings are covered with medieval graffiti inscriptions and coats-of-arms, mainly 15C. Other wall-paintings were contributed by Fr Pachomius.

To the SE a modern terrace of building covers the ancient wall. In the S corner is the **Library** containing a magnificent collection of manuscripts; about 2000 Greek, 700 Arabic, 300 Syriac, 100 Georgian and Armenian, 40 Slavonic and one Latin.

One of the greatest treasures is now in the collection of the British Library. This is the Codex Sinaiticus, a 4C Greek MS. It was obtained in 1859 by Konstantin van Tischendorf, taken to Russia and presented to Tsar Alexander II. In 1933 the Soviet government sold it to the British Museum for £100,000, some of which was raised by public contribution. In November 1971 there was a fire in St. George's Tower. During clearance afterwards eight more folios of the codex were discovered. The most important surviving MS is the Codex Syriacus, a 5C Syriac hagiographical text written over one of the earliest versions of the New Testament. Among the finest of the MSS is the Book of Job (Cod.Gr.3), 11C, beautifully illustrated. Liturgical Homilies of Gregory of Nazianzus (Cod. Gr. 339), the most lavish MS, executed at the Pantocratos Monastery in Constantinople. The Heavenly Ladder by St. John Climacus (Cod. Gr. 418), a description by the saint of the attainment of spiritual perfection, each stage being illustrated by a miniature. An Arabic version of the last work (Cod. Ar. 343). A Christian Topography by Cosmas Indicopleustes (Cod. Gr. 1186), an 11C attack on the Ptolemaic world system. There is also a collection of over 200 firmans (decrees) from sulṭans, khalīfs and other rulers confirming the protected status of the monastery.

Next to the Library is the **Museum** which contains the most precious ikons and objects presented to the monastery. The ikon collection of the monastery is extremely rich and unique in that it represents an unbroken accumulation since the 6C of 2000 paintings made in or for the monastery. Fr Pachomius, who decorated many of the chapels in the monastery, was responsible for gathering the ikons from their scattered locations and keeping them in the storerooms.

The earliest paintings are 6C and in the encaustic wax technique; three are superb: Christ Pantocrator, the Virgin flanked by SS. Theodore and George, and a life-size portrait of St. Peter. After the Muslim conquest the links with Constantinople were broken and the principal influences came from Palestine. Thus the ikonoclast movement (726–843) had little effect here. In the later 9C Byzantine influences were again felt in Sinai and issued in another great phase of ikon painting. From the 13C the influences of the Crusader states becomes apparent, mainly of the Italian School but the French and even the German and English schools are represented. Following the destruction of the Christian kingdoms Byzantium was again the major influence from the mid 13–mid 15C. Towards the end of the Byzantine Empire other centres produced schools of ikon painting, Crete, the Caucasus and Russia, which flowered fully after the fall of Constantinople. In addition to these sophisticated styles there are also Syriac or Arabic ikons and, of course, the ikons produced by the monks themselves. Gradually from the 18C the influences of Western art pervaded the local schools and eventually completely suppressed the ikon style.

Many of the treasured benefactions of the monastery have disappeared, but some of the more interesting objects are: an enamelled silver chalice presented by Charles VI of France (1411); a bronze Faṭīmid aquamanile in the shape of a pigeon; and a crystal cross from Venice.

In the SW wall is a tunnel-vaulted **Chapel**. It contains 6C paintings, the walls painted as imitation marble and the ceiling in panels enclosing birds and plants. At the E end is a niche with a cross painted on the shaft and a scallop in the semi-dome.

W of the compound lies the *Monastery Orchard*, containing fruit bushes and cypresses. In this garden stands the **Charnel House**. To the left of the door sits the cadaver of St. Stephen the Porter, a 6C monk, dressed in purple robes with his staff in his skeletal hand. This reflects his main function at the monastery as gatekeeper at the Plain of Cypresses (see below). On the right are the bones of the martyrs and archbishops exposed in open coffins. To the left in the ossuary are the bones of the monks in separate piles of skulls, limbs, and hands and feet. On the upper floor is the *Chapel of St. Tryphon*, dedicated in 1888. To the N is the small graveyard in which the monks are buried. As the last monk to die is buried the oldest corpse is exhumed and the bones placed in the ossuary.

There are several routes to the summit of **Gabal Mūsā** (*Mount Sinai* ht. 2285m), all of which need the assistance of a guide. It is a very exhausting climb particularly the last 200m with 700 rock cut steps. The usual route is the *Sikkit Sayyidnā Mūsā* (Path of our Lord Moses), which leaves the monastery to the S and starts to ascend. It soon reaches the *ʿAyn Mūsā* (Moses' Spring) and continues up the hill, to the *Easr Chapel of the Virgin*. Beyond this is the *Gate of St. Stephen the Porter*. Here he sat for many years issuing certificates to whose who had made confession at the monastery and wished to receive communion on the mountain. A second gate leads to a small plateau, the *Plain of Cypresses*, in the middle of which is a massive specimen tree. On the left is the *Chapel of Elias* and a small cell. A long flight of steps leads to the summit of the mountain. Here there is the *Chapel of the Holy Trinity* and the remains of the ancient *Basilica*. There is also a small *Mosque* used by the Muslims at the mūlid of Sh. Ṣāliḥ. On the return journey proceed from the Plain of Cypress to the NW. The first sanctuary passed is the *Chapel of St. John the Baptist*. Beyond are the *Chapel of St. Pantelemon* and the *Chapel of the Girdle of the Virgin* on the spur known as *Gabal Ṣafṣaf*.

To ascend the **Gabal Kātārīna** (ht. 2637m) follow the Wadī al-Deir NW. Beyond the mouth of the Wadī al-Shaykh and from the Plain of Raha turn SW into the Wadī Ligah. The wadī turns SE. On the E side is the ruined *West Chapel of the Virgin*, called al-Bustān, surrounded by a plantation. Just beyond is the *Chapel of the Unmercenary Physicians* and after about 30m the *Chapel of St. Onuphrius* and the *Monastery of the Forty Martyrs*. The Gabal Mūsā can be reached from here. An ascent of 2km to the SW leads to the summit of Gabal Kātārīna. On the top is a *Chapel of St. Catherine*, at the site where her transported body was found in the 9C. There are two other peaks in the same granite mass, the *Gabal Zabir* and *Gabal Abū Rumayl*.

From the point on the Wadī Ligah where it turns E to the Gabal Kātārīna the Wadī Laʿah runs NW. This leads to the *Deir al-Fuqarāʾ* (Monastery of the Poor) on the N side and beyond this on the S a carob tree and the *Cave of St. John Climacus* (525–600), the author of the Ladder to Paradise. He spent 40 years in this cave and was eventually elected head of the Monastery of St. Catherine.

S of the road to Fīrān the H66 continues inland and finally returns to (72km) the coast and the port of **al-Ṭūr**, capital of S Sinai province. This is the only part of the W coast free of coral, and it has a freshwater supply which has encouraged plantations of date-palms and acacia. It has been the principal port of Sinai since Ptolemaic times, when it was called *Raithou*. By the 4C there was a church here, followed by a monastery. The monks were slaughtered by nomadic tribes and are known as the Forty Martyrs of Ṭūr, or the Holy Fathers. The present *Church* is a dependency of the Monastery of St. Catherine. After the Muslim conquest it received the ships carrying pilgrims to Jiddah. With the eclipse of the Mamlūk empire it declined but in the 18C it was the principal quarantine station for the pilgrims returning from Mecca.

Beyond al-Ṭūr the road runs S slightly inland, following the curve of the coast. At 75km a second road leads due S to (18km) **Rāʾs Muḥammad** a promontory, the southernmost point of the peninsula (best visited with assistance from Sharm al-Shaykh, see below.

This is a most fascinating area, with a small mangrove forest, the most northerly in the world, which attracts a specific form of wildlife. The superb coral reefs are enhanced by the clarity of the water and are particularly dramatic where the coastal shelf abruptly descends in a sheer drop of many hundreds of metres to the sea bed.

Continue along H55 to (25km) **Sharm al-Shaykh** a village developed during the Israeli occupation, when it was called Ofira. Hotels *Marina Hotel; Marina Bungalow* (3*); *Sharm el-Sheikh City* (2*); *Marina* (1*) Youth Hostel and camping sites. This is now the main underwater centre in Sinai and diving holidays are provided from basic instruction to extensive underwater safaris. To the N (5km) is the dependent development of *al-Nuʿamah*.

From Sharm al-Shaykh the road turns N along the E coast and the Gulf of al-ʿAqabah (magnificent views over the Straits of Tiran, the islands and the coast of Saudi Arabia beyond) and runs inland over (71km) the **Sharīrah Pass** and reaches (27km) a road on the E into (8km) **Dahab**. A sprawling village now also being developed as a holiday and diving resort. Hotels: *Holiday Village* (3*). Skirting inland around the *Gabal Sukhn* at 25km a road to the W leads to St. Catherine's Monastery (85km), but the H55 continues N and reaches (40km) **Nuwaybaʿ**, a holiday village but expanding rapidly as it is the main port for the ferry to al-ʿAqabah (Jordan) at the head of the gulf. Hotel: *Nuweiba Village* (3*).

Continuing N along the coast the road runs below the *Gabal Ghazlān* and passes (67km) the small settlement at **Bir Murrāh** with 200m offshore the **Gazīrat Farāʾūn** (Pharoah's Island) known to the Crusaders and Western travellers as the Isle de Graye. It holds the remains of the only Crusader Castle built on Egyptian territory (best visited from Nuwaybaʿ).

Here in 1116 King Baldwin of Jerusalem built the fortress during the Crusaders brief control of the area of Eylah. It was always vulnerable as the approaches to Eylah were insecure and after the defeat of Reynald de Chataillon's rash expedition into the Red Sea in 1185 the area was retaken by the Muslims.

The island about 300m N–S by 150m has an elevation at either end and on the W side, opposite two stone jetties on the mainland, a small *harbour* (probably man-made) linked to the sea by a channel. Encircling the whole island is the vestige of a *Byzantine Wall* beset with 8–9 towers. Massive blocks form the outer and inner skins with the cavity filled with compacted rubble. Against the E side the foundation of living quarters are evident. On the S elevation is the remnant of the *Byzantine Fort* but the N hill holds the much more substantial remains of the *Crusader Castle*. The central complex c 40 x 20m is surrounded by the more extensive enclosure wall.

After 5km N the H55 passes **Bīr Ṭābah** to the W, held in dispute since the First World War, when it was included in Egyptian territory; the problem was settled in March 1989 when it was returned to Egypt. At 2km is the border with Israel beyond which the road continues to **Eylah**.

# CAIRO INDEX

All Muslim religious buildings are listed as mosques; the correct designation will be found in the text. (T) after an entry indicates an integral tomb, similarly houses and palaces. Sabils with associated Kuttabs will be found under the former heading with the indication (K). All commercial buildings are included under the heading of wikālah. Personalities will be found in the main index. dist. = qism i.e. official district.

# GENERAL INDEX

Only major or significant appearances of personalites, monuments and works of art are indexed. In addition to those used in the main text, the following abbreviations appear in the index: Am = amīr. arch = architect. dist = district. gov = governor. Khed = Khedive. K = King. N = noble. Pat = Patriarch. Pr/Prss = Prince/Princess. Q = Queen

# ATLAS SECTION

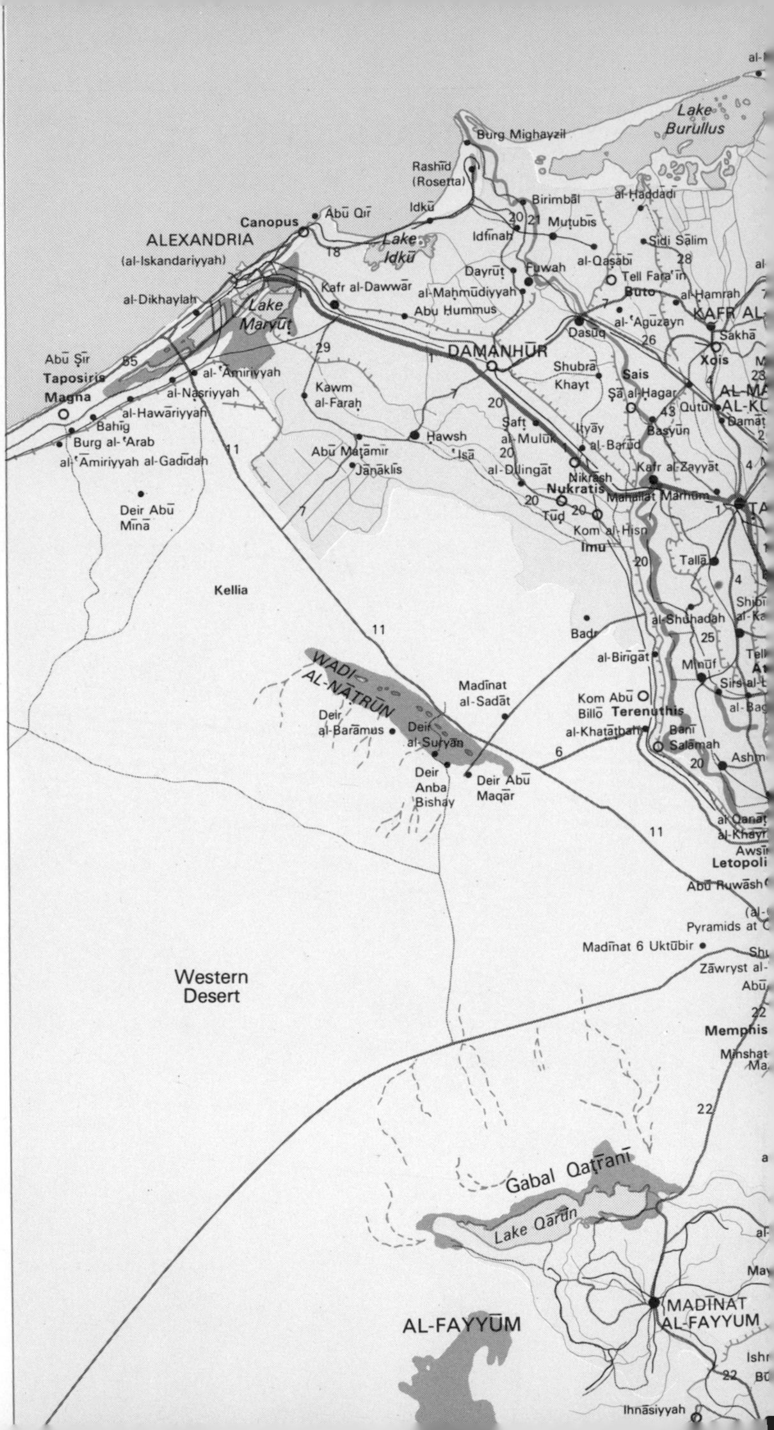

Lake Burullus
Burg Mighayzil
Rashīd (Rosetta)
Idkū
Birimbāl
al-Ḥaddādī
Abū Qīr
Canopus
ALEXANDRIA
(al-Iskandariyyah)
Lake Idkū
Idfīnah
Muṭubis
Sīdī Sālim
Dayrūṭ
Fuwah
al-Qaṣabī
Tell Fara'īn
Buto
Kafr al-Dawwār
al-Maḥmūdiyyah
al-Ḥamrah
KAFR AL-
al-Dikhaylah
Lake Maryūṭ
Abu Ḥummus
Dasūq
al-'Agūzayn
Sakhā
Xois
DAMANHŪR
Abū Ṣīr
Taposiris Magna
al-'Āmiriyyah
al-Naṣriyyah
al-Hawāriyyah
Bahīg
Burg al-'Arab
al-'Āmiriyyah al-Gadīdah
Kawm al-Farah
Shubrā Khayt
Sais
Ṣā al-Ḥagar
Quṭūr
Basyūn
Ḥawsh 'Īsā
Ṣafṭ al-Mulūk
Ityāy al-Bārūd
Abū Maṭāmir
Janāklīs
al-Dilingāt
Nikrāsh
Nukratis
Kafr al-Zayyāt
Maḥallat Marḥūm
Ṭūd
Kom al-Ḥisn
Imu
Deir Abū Mīnā
Ṭallā
Kellia
al-Shuhadah
Badr
al-Birigāt
Minūf
Wādī al-Naṭrūn
Madīnat al-Sadāt
Kom Abū Billo
Terenuthis
Deir al-Baramūs
Deir al-Suryān
al-Khaṭāṭbah
Banī Salāmah
Deir Anba Bishay
Deir Abū Maqār
Letopoli
Abū Ruwāsh
Pyramids at
Madīnat 6 Uktūbir
Western Desert
Memphis
Gabal Qaṭrānī
Lake Qārūn
MADĪNAT AL-FAYYŪM
AL-FAYYŪM
Ihnāsiyyah

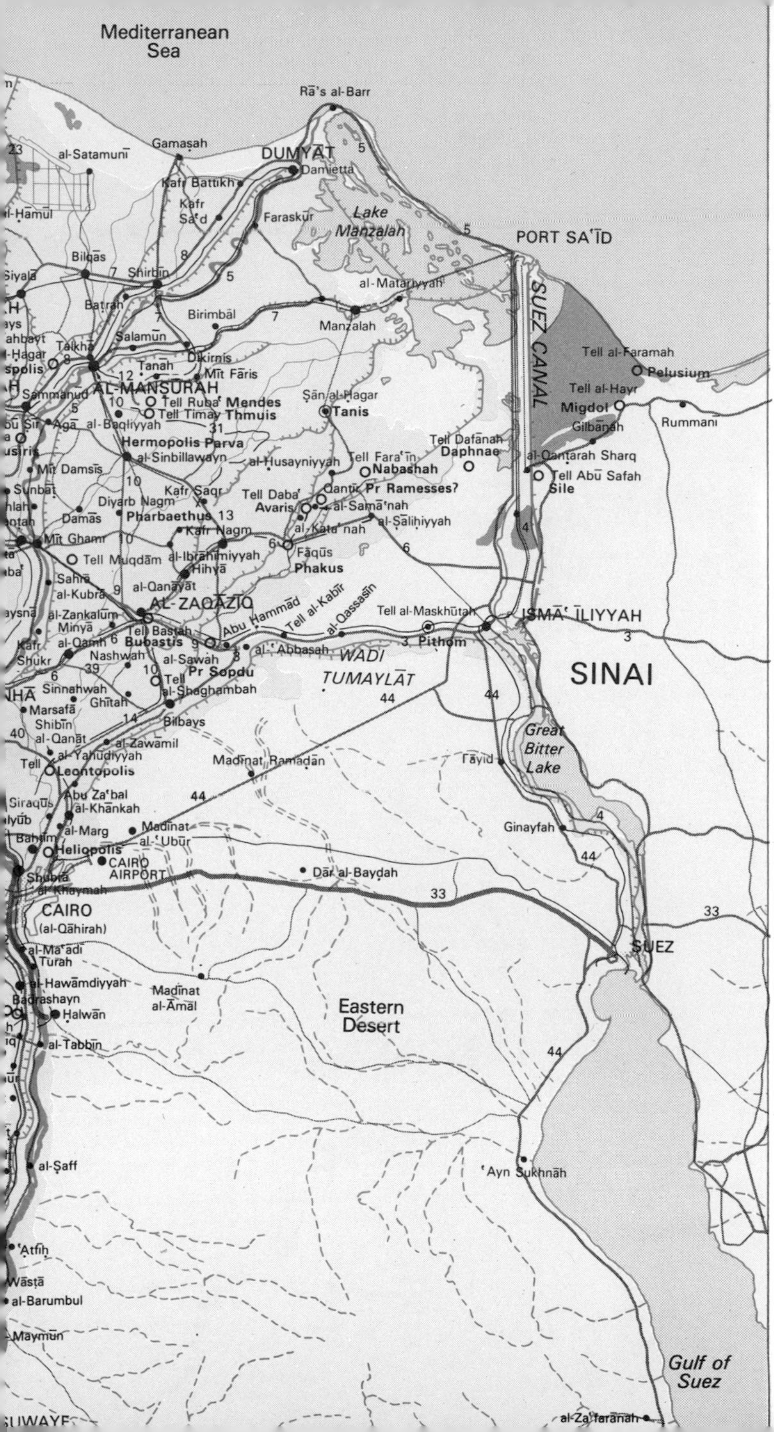
Mediterranean Sea
Ra's al-Barr
Gamasah
al-Satamuni
DUMYAT
Damietta
Kafr Battikh
Kafr Sa'd
Faraskur
Lake Manzalah
PORT SA'ID
Bilqas
Shirbin
Batrah
Birimbal
al-Matariyyah
Manzalah
SUEZ CANAL
Salamun
Talkha
Tanah
Dikirnis
Mit Faris
AL-MANSURAH
Sammanud
Tell al-Faramah
Pelusium
Tell al-Hayr
Migdol
Rummani
Gilbanah
San al-Hagar
Tanis
Tell Ruba' Mendes
Tell Timay Thmuis
Aga
al-Baqliyyah
Hermopolis Parva
al-Sinbillawayn
al-Husayniyyah
Tell Fara'in
Nabashah
Tell Dafanah
Daphnae
al-Qantarah Sharq
Tell Abu Safah
Sile
Mit Damsis
Sunbat
Kafr Saqr
Diyarb Nagm
Pharbaethus
Damas
Qantir
Pr Ramesses?
Tell Daba'
Avaris
al-Sama'nah
al-Kata'nah
al-Salihiyyah
Kafr Nagm
Mit Ghamr
Tell Muqdam
al-Ibrahimiyyah
Hihya
Faqus
Phakus
Sahra
al-Kubra
al-Qanayat
AL-ZAQAZIQ
Abu Hammad
Tell al-Kabir
al-Qassasin
Tell al-Maskhutah
ISMA'ILIYYAH
al-Zankalum
Minya
al-Qamh
Tell Basta
Bubastis
Pithom
Kafr Shukr
Nashwah
al-Sawah
al-'Abbasah
WADI TUMAYLAT
SINAI
Tell
Pr Sopdu
al-Shaghambah
Sinnahwah
Ghitah
Marsafa
Shibin
Bilbays
Great Bitter Lake
al-Qanat
al-Zawamil
al-Yahudiyyah
Madinat Ramadan
Fayid
Tell
Leontopolis
Siraqus
Abu Za'bal
al-Khankah
Ginayfah
al-Marg
Madinat
al-'Ubur
Bahtim
Heliopolis
CAIRO AIRPORT
Shubra
al-Khaymah
Dar al-Baydah
CAIRO
(al-Qahirah)
SUEZ
al-Ma'adi
Turah
al-Hawamdiyyah
Badrashayn
Halwan
Madinat al-Amal
Eastern Desert
al-Tabbin
al-Saff
'Ayn Sukhnah
'Atfih
Wasta
al-Barumbul
Maymun
Gulf of Suez
al-Za'faranah

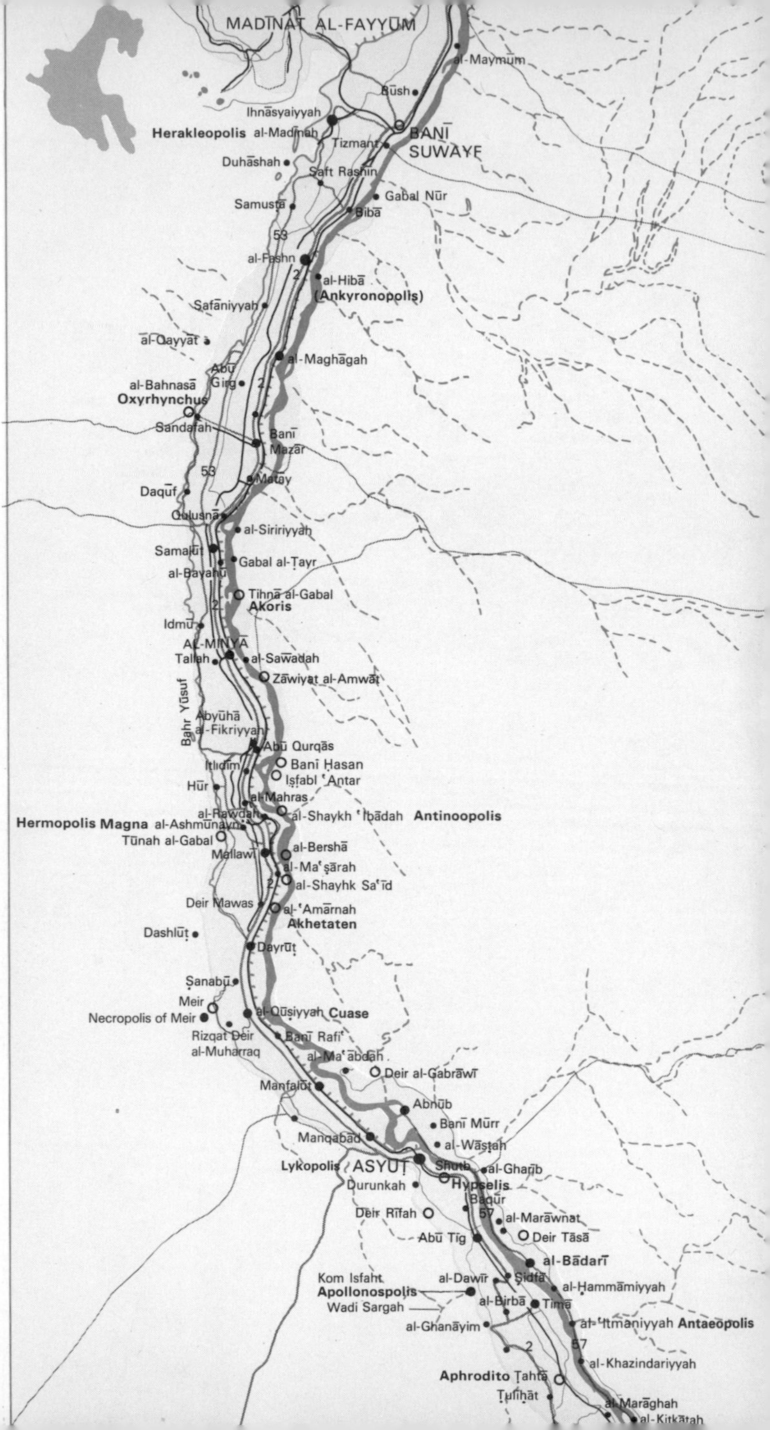
MADĪNAT AL-FAYYŪM
al-Maymūm
Bush
Ihnāsyaiyyah
Herakleopolis
al-Madīnah
Tizmant
BANĪ SUWAYF
Duhāshah
Saft Rashīn
Gabal Nūr
Samustā
Bibā
53
al-Fashn
2
al-Hibā
(Ankyronopolis)
Safāniyyah
al-Qayyāt
al-Maghāgah
Abū Girg
al-Bahnasā
Oxyrhynchus
Sandafah
Banī Mazār
53
Matay
Daqūf
Qulusnā
al-Siriiyyah
Samalūt
Gabal al-Ṭayr
al-Bayahū
Tihnā al-Gabal
Akoris
2
Idmū
AL-MINYA
Tallah
al-Sawādah
Zāwiyat al-Amwāt
Bahr Yūsuf
Abyūhā
al-Fikriyyah
Abū Qurqās
Itlīdim
Banī Ḥasan
Iṣfabl ʿAntar
Hūr
al-Mahras
al-Rawdah
al-Shaykh ʿIbādah
Antinoopolis
Hermopolis Magna
al-Ashmūnayn
Tūnah al-Gabal
Mallawī
al-Bershā
al-Maʿṣarah
2
al-Shayhk Saʿīd
Deir Mawas
al-ʿAmārnah
Akhetaten
Dashlūṭ
Dayrūṭ
Ṣanabū
Meir
Necropolis of Meir
al-Qūṣiyyah
Cuase
Rizqat Deir al-Muharraq
Banī Rafiʿ
al-Maʿabdah
Deir al-Gabrāwī
Manfalūṭ
Abnūb
Banī Murr
Manqabād
al-Wāsṭah
Lykopolis
ASYŪṬ
Shutb
al-Gharib
Durunkah
Hypselis
Baqūr
Deir Rīfah
57
al-Marāwnat
Abū Tīg
Deir Tāsā
al-Bādarī
Kom Isfaht
al-Dawīr
Ṣidfā
al-Ḥammāmiyyah
Apollonospolis
Wadi Sargah
al-Birbā
Tima
al-Ghanāyim
al-ʿItmāniyyah
Antaeopolis
2
57
al-Khazindariyyah
Aphrodito
Ṭahtā
Ṭulīḥāt
al-Marāghah
al-Kitkātah

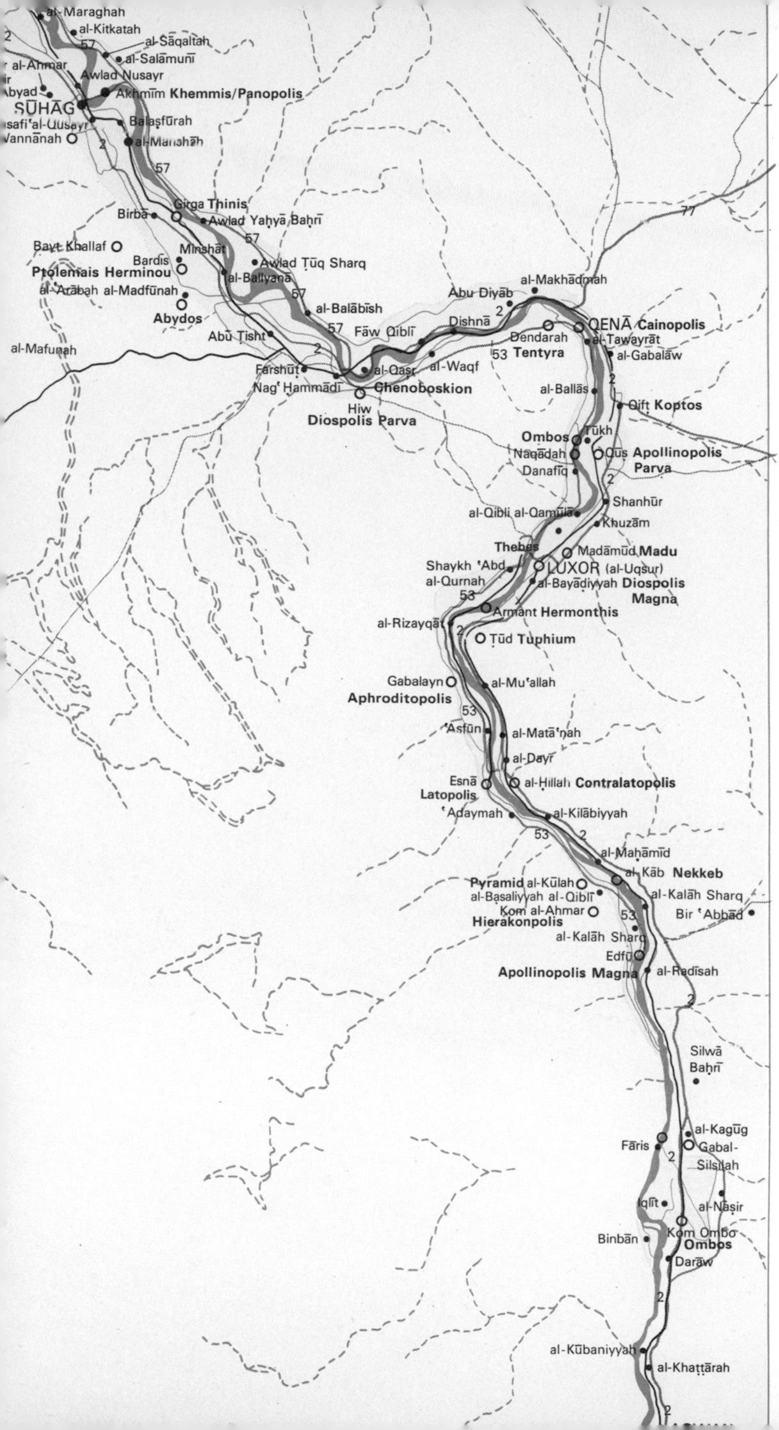
al-Maraghah
al-Kitkatah
57
al-Saqaltah
al-Salamuni
al-Ahmar
Awlad Nusayr
Abyad
Akhmim Khemmis/Panopolis
SUHAG
Balasfurah
al-Qusayr
Wannanah
2
al-Manshah
57
Girga Thinis
Birba
Awlad Yahya Bahri
57
Bayt Khallaf
Minshat
Bardis
Awlad Tuq Sharq
Ptolemais Herminou
al-Ballyana
al-'Arabah al-Madfunah
57
Abydos
al-Balabish
al-Makhadmah
Abu Diyab
2
57
Faw Qibli
Dishna
QENA Cainopolis
Abu Tisht
Dendarah
al-Tawayrat
al-Mafunah
2
53 Tentyra
al-Gabalaw
al-Waqf
Farshut
al-Qasr
Nag' Hammadi
Chenoboskion
al-Ballas
2
Hiw
Qift Koptos
Diospolis Parva
Ombos
Tukh
Naqadah
Qus Apollinopolis
Parva
Danafiq
2
Shanhur
al-Qibli al-Qamula
Khuzam
Thebes
Madamud Madu
Shaykh 'Abd
LUXOR (al-Uqsur)
al-Qurnah
al-Bayadiyyah Diospolis
53
Magna
Armant Hermonthis
al-Rizayqat
2
Tud Tuphium
Gabalayn
al-Mu'allah
Aphroditopolis
53
'Asfun
al-Mata'nah
al-Dayr
Esna
al-Hillah Contralatopolis
Latopolis
'Adaymah
al-Kilabiyyah
53
2
al-Mahamid
al-Kab Nekkeb
Pyramid al-Kulah
al-Basaliyyah al-Qibli
al-Kalah Sharq
Kom al-Ahmar
Bir 'Abbad
Hierakonpolis
53
al-Kalah Sharq
Edfu
Apollinopolis Magna
al-Radisah
2
Silwa
Bahri
al-Kagug
Faris
Gabal-
2
Silsilah
Iqlit
al-Nasir
Kom Ombo
Binban
Ombos
Daraw
2
al-Kubaniyyah
al-Khattarah
2
77